U0895385

中国版权年鉴 2019

CHINA COPYRIGHT YEARBOOK

中国版权年鉴编委会 编

中国人民大学出版社
· 北京 ·

2018年1月17日，中国音像著作权集体管理协会第二届理事会第五次会议在京召开，18家理事单位代表和个人出席本次会议并审议通过协会章程。（中国音像著作权集体管理协会供图）

2018年1月22日，中国国家新闻出版广电总局副局长、国家版权局专职副局长周慧琳（右一）在京会见新加坡知识产权局局长邓鸿森（左一）一行。双方就推进《视听表演北京条约》早日生效等共同关注的版权问题交换意见。（摄影/郁致原）

2018 年 2 月 26 日，由中国版权协会主办的北京国际网络版权监测研讨会召开，聚焦小网站跨国网络侵权盗版问题。国家版权局原专职副局长、中国版权协会理事长阎晓宏（前排中），国家版权局版权管理司司长于慈珂（前排右三）等出席会议。（中国版权协会供图）

2018 年 3 月 2 日，中宣部副部长、国家新闻出版广电总局（国家版权局）局长聂辰席在京主持召开推进使用正版软件工作部际联席会议第七次全体会议。（摄影 / 郁致原）

2018 年 3 月 19—23 日，江苏省版权局在扬州启动 2018 年江苏省第一期网络侵权盗版案件集中打击行动。（江苏省版权局供图）

2018 年 4 月 23 日，由国家版权局主办的 2018 年版权宣传周新闻发布会在京举行。中国国家版权局版权管理司司长于慈珂（主席台左四）、韩国著作权委员会委员长林元善（主席台左三）、日本内容产品海外流通促进机构常务理事永野行雄（主席台右四）等出席发布会。（摄影 / 郁致原）

2018年4月24日，国务院新闻办公室在京举行2017年中国知识产权发展状况新闻发布会。国家知识产权局局长申长雨（左二）、国家知识产权局商标局负责人崔守东（右二）、国家版权局新闻发言人于慈珂（右一）出席发布会。（摄影/郁致原）

2018年4月26日，国家版权局在京举办以“保护创作，推进运用”为主题的2018中国网络版权保护大会。来自相关政府部门、司法部门、权利人、版权产业界、学术界、法律实务界的代表，就网络版权创作、保护和运用开展广泛研讨。（摄影/郁致原）

2018年4月26日，河北省政府新闻办举办“河北省版权信息数据库平台上线”新闻发布会，河北省新闻出版广电局（版权局）党组书记、局长李晓明（右）介绍了河北省版权保护工作开展情况以及版权数据库平台建设相关情况。（摄影/李冬群）

2018年4月26日，由云南省版权局主办、云南财经大学承办的2018年云南省版权宣传周文艺演出在云南财经大学汇文礼堂举行。（云南省版权局供图）

2018年5月28日，由世界知识产权组织（WIPO）中国办事处、北京市新闻出版广电局（版权局）、北京市东城区政府主办的知识产权保护促进视听产业发展论坛在京举行。（摄影/窦新颖）

2018年6月1日，国家新闻出版署署长、国家版权局局长庄荣文，在京会见世界知识产权组织副总干事王彬颖一行。双方就进一步巩固和加强版权领域合作、推进《视听表演北京条约》早日生效等问题进行交流。（摄影/郁致原）

2018 年 6 月 19—20 日，由世界知识产权组织与中国国家版权局主办、上海市版权局承办的电影的经济及文化价值与版权保护高端论坛在上海举行。（摄影 / 郁致原）

2018 年 7 月 16 日，国家版权局、国家互联网信息办公室、工业和信息化部、公安部联合召开新闻通气会，通报启动打击网络侵权盗版“剑网 2018”专项行动有关情况。（摄影 / 郁致原）

2018 年 7 月 27 日，国家软件正版化工作督查组在甘肃召开督查情况反馈会，总结 7 月 15—27 日对甘肃省 40 家省级政府机关的软件正版化工作进行全覆盖督查的结果。（甘肃省版权局供图）

2018 年 10 月 19—21 日，由世界知识产权组织、中国国家版权局主办的 2018 国际版权论坛——21 世纪版权促进文化创意国际论坛在苏州举行。（摄影 / 郁致原）

2018 年 10 月 19—21 日，由国家版权局主办，江苏省版权局、苏州市人民政府承办的第七届中国国际版权博览会在苏州举行。（摄影 / 郁致原）

2018 年 10 月 19 日，在第七届中国国际版权博览会开幕式上，国家版权局和世界知识产权组织颁发了 2018 年“中国版权金奖”，包括作品奖、推广运用奖、保护奖和管理奖四个奖项。（摄影 / 郁致原）

2018年10月21日，由国家版权局主办、中国人民大学国家版权贸易基地和中国人民大学创意产业技术研究院承办的第十届全国大学生版权征文活动颁奖仪式在苏州举行。（摄影/郁致原）

2018年10月27—28日，以“亚太地区的版权许可及法律规范”为主题，由亚太版权协会、中国人民大学知识产权学院、新西兰维多利亚大学商学院主办的2018年亚太版权年会在京举行。（中国人民大学知识产权学院供图）

2018 年 11 月 27 日，由中国人民大学国家版权贸易基地主办的短视频作品创作与版权保护研讨会在京举行，与会者就短视频版权秩序、版权监测与技术保护路径等问题进行探讨。（中国人民大学国家版权贸易基地供图）

2018 年 12 月 17—19 日，由中国国家版权局与中欧知识产权合作项目 IP Key 主办的中欧数字环境下版权保护与许可研讨会在广州举行。（摄影 / 郁致原）

2018 年 12 月 20 日，由中国版权协会和腾讯研究院主办的第五届中国互联网新型版权问题研讨会在京举行。会上，由腾讯、百度、爱奇艺、搜狐、新浪、快手等公司共同发起和参与的中国网络版权产业联盟发布了《中国网络短视频版权自律公约》。（摄影 / 赖名芳）

2018 年 12 月 22 日，国际保护知识产权协会（AIPPI）中国分会版权热点论坛（2018 年度）在京举办。论坛发布 2018 年度中国版权行业十大热点案件以及《中国影视娱乐产业经典案例指引》，并就当下热点著作权问题展开主题研讨。（AIPPI 中国分会供图）

中国版权年鉴

2019

（总第十一卷）

中国版权年鉴编委会　编

中国人民大学出版社
·北京·

图书在版编目（CIP）数据

中国版权年鉴．2019/中国版权年鉴编委会编．--北京：中国人民大学出版社，2020.1
ISBN 978-7-300-27829-2

Ⅰ.①中… Ⅱ.①中… Ⅲ.①版权-中国-2019-年鉴 Ⅳ.①D923.41-54

中国版本图书馆 CIP 数据核字（2019）第 294215 号

中国版权年鉴 2019
（总第十一卷）
中国版权年鉴编委会　编
Zhongguo Banquan Nianjian 2019

出版发行　中国人民大学出版社
社　　址　北京中关村大街 31 号　　　**邮政编码**　100080
电　　话　010－62511242（总编室）　　010－62511770（质管部）
　　　　　　010－82501766（邮购部）　　010－62514148（门市部）
　　　　　　010－62515195（发行公司）　010－62515275（盗版举报）
网　　址　http：//www.crup.com.cn
经　　销　新华书店
印　　刷　涿州市星河印刷有限公司
规　　格　210 mm×297 mm　16 开本　　**版　　次**　2020 年 1 月第 1 版
印　　张　40.5 插页 54　　　　　　　**印　　次**　2020 年 1 月第 1 次印刷
字　　数　1 325 000　　　　　　　　**定　　价**　300.00 元
广告经营许可证　京海工商广字第 0086 号

《中国版权年鉴 2019》编纂委员会

《中国版权年鉴》特约编辑

（以姓氏笔画为序）

于晓红	辽宁省委宣传部版权管理处处长
马　达	内蒙古自治区党委宣传部版权管理处副主任科员
王　成	云南省委宣传部版权管理处主任科员
王　骞	上海市委宣传部版权管理处主任科员
王丹若	中国文字著作权协会办公室主任
王金根	海南省委宣传部版权处副处长
王新民	陕西省委宣传部二级巡视员
毛立华	最高人民法院知识产权审判庭三级高级法官
左图强	重庆市委宣传部二级巡视员
卢文俊	湖北省委宣传部版权管理处处长
史文霞	中国电影著作权协会秘书长
付成久	青海省委宣传部政策法规处副调研员
朱严政	中国音乐著作权协会信息宣传部主任
朱宝祺	中国摄影著作权协会副总干事
闫　石	黑龙江省委宣传部版权管理处副处长
孙　悦	中国版权协会秘书长
严庆荣	浙江省委宣传部版权处处长
杜宇震	吉林省委宣传部版权管理处副处长
李冬群	河北省委宣传部版权管理处副处长
何宏勇	江西省委宣传部版权管理处一级主任科员
余志军	四川省委宣传部版权管理处副处长
张文娟	中国版权保护中心党办主任
张宁学	宁夏回族自治区党委宣传部版权管理处调研员
张有立	中宣部版权管理局办公室主任
张荣涛	湖南省委宣传部版权管理处一级主任科员
张晓生	山东省委宣传部版权管理处处长
张新革	新疆维吾尔自治区党委宣传部版权管理处处长
张露娜	天津市委宣传部版权管理处调研员
易瑾媛	广东省委宣传部版权和印刷管理处二级主任科员
郑开辟	福建省委宣传部版权管理处三级调研员
赵　杰	中宣部版权管理局执法监管处处长
赵明明	广西壮族自治区党委宣传部版权管理处副调研员
赵晓鹏	北京市委宣传部版权管理处四级调研员
郝子谋	山西省委宣传部版权管理处四级调研员

《中国版权年鉴》编辑部

编纂说明

一、《中国版权年鉴》是由国家版权局组织编纂，中国人民大学出版社、中国人民大学国家版权贸易基地编辑出版，是我国唯一全面系统反映全国版权创造、运用、保护和管理基本概貌的大型专业性工具书。本年鉴于2009年创刊，逐年编纂，连续出版，每年一卷，2019年卷为第十一卷。

二、本卷年鉴主要汇辑2018年全国版权保护与版权相关产业发展的综合概况、动态信息、文献资料和统计数据，港澳台版权信息及国际版权动态。

三、本卷年鉴采用分类编辑法。根据2018年我国版权创造、运用、保护和管理的基本情况与主要特点，采用类目、分目和条目三个层次的结构，以文章、条目、条文和图表的形式表述。全书共设12个类目，分列41个分目或次分目。

四、本卷年鉴在延续前十卷编纂总体框架下，为实现年鉴的整体性和在有限篇幅里反映高度密集有效信息，对年鉴内容进行了必要的补充及调整，使之方便读者查阅。

1. 特载：刊登《关于加强知识产权审判领域改革创新若干问题的意见》和《2019年深入实施国家知识产权战略　加快建设知识产权强国推进计划》。

2. 版权工作概览：全面记录2018年我国各级版权行政管理部门、版权司法审判机构及版权管理与社会服务组织开展的版权工作概况。

3. 版权扫描：翔实记载2018年全国版权相关立法、司法、行政管理、宣传教育、交流研讨、社会管理与服务、国际交流与合作、产业发展等方面的动态信息及港澳台版权信息。

4. 版权相关产业与版权贸易：刊载《2017年中国版权产业的经济贡献》和《中国网络版权产业发展报告（2019）》，以及反映2018年我国新闻出版、数字出版、广播电视、电影、动漫、软件、网络游戏等版权相关产业基本状况与发展趋势的产业报告。

5. 典型案件选编：刊登2018年全国著作权司法保护典型案件、2018年度全国打击侵权盗版十大案件、2018年部分省（自治区、直辖市）著作权司法保护典型案件和行政执法典型案件。

6. 法律法规及规章文件：汇辑《中华人民共和国电子商务法》，以及《关于印发〈2017年推进使用正版软件工作总结〉和〈2018年推进使用正版软件工作计划〉的通知》等2018年国家版权局印发的版权相关工作文件。

7. 年度发布：刊登2018年中国网络版权保护年度报告、2018年“中国版权金奖”获奖名单、2018年度查处侵权盗版案件有功单位及个人、2018年中国版权十件大事、2018年（第十届）全国大学生版权征文获奖名单、2018 CPCC十大中国著作权人、2018年中国版权年会年度评选获奖名单。

8. 理论研究：集中反映2018年全国版权领域的理论研究成果。对2018年中国著作权法理论研究现状进行了梳理和回顾，并特别转载了反映版权界热点问题的9篇学术论文。同时对2018年出版的著作权相关图书进行了简要介绍。

9. 统计资料：收集2018年与版权登记、版权保护、版权管理和版权贸易有关的统计数据，以及新闻出版业、广播影视业和软件业的统计资料。

10. 名录：刊登版权行政管理部门、版权公共服务机构、版权协会、著作权集体管理组织、版权相关行业协会、版权代理公司、国家级版权交易机构及知识产权教学与研究机构最新的通信联络信息。

11. 国际版权动态：作为附录介绍 2018 年国外版权法律制度发展的最新动向，包括立法与行政、司法判例及业界动态。

12. 索引：采用内容分析和主题词检索的方式，按汉语拼音字母顺序编制本卷内容的主题索引。

五、本卷年鉴中所载内容无特别说明外，均按时间先后顺序排列；涉及各省（自治区、直辖市）的内容，均以全国行政区划为序。因组稿条件有限，本卷年鉴未包含香港、澳门特别行政区和台湾省的版权工作概况及相关统计数据。

六、本卷年鉴配备双重检索系统：书前刊有详细目录，书后备有内容索引。

七、本卷年鉴中统计资料由中国新闻出版研究院、工业和信息化部信息化和软件服务业司、国家广播电视总局发展研究中心等单位提供。

八、本卷年鉴在组稿和编辑过程中，得到了中央宣传部版权管理局、工业和信息化部信息化和软件服务业司、中国新闻出版研究院、国家广播电视总局发展研究中心、中国人民大学知识产权学院、地方版权局版权管理处及其他版权相关单位的大力支持和帮助，在此一并谨致谢意。

九、因为编辑部人员的水平和能力所限，本卷年鉴中定存有疏漏与错误之处，诚请版权界同人和广大读者给予批评、指正。

目　　录

特　　载

关于加强知识产权审判领域改革创新若干问题的意见　3
2019 年深入实施国家知识产权战略　加快建设知识产权强国推进计划　6

版权工作概览

2018 年全国版权工作　15
2018 年全国版权行政管理工作　中央宣传部版权管理局　15
2018 年全国版权司法保护工作　最高人民法院知识产权审判庭　19

2018 年地方版权工作　22
北京市　赵晓鹏　22
天津市　张　倩　25
河北省　李冬群　26
山西省　郝子谋　29
内蒙古自治区　马　达　31
辽宁省　田大鹏　32
吉林省　杜宇震　35
黑龙江省　闫　石　37
上海市　王　骞　38
江苏省　卢　寅　41
浙江省　严庆荣　44
安徽省　胡　子　46
福建省　郑开辟　48
江西省　阙米秋　50
山东省　蒋金坤　51
河南省　焦艳娜　54
湖北省　张　威　56
湖南省　宋　亮　58
广东省　易瑾媛　59
广西壮族自治区　赵明明　60
海南省　王金根　61
重庆市　张　锐　63
四川省　李晓曦　64
贵州省　徐　梅　65

云南省 王 成 67
西藏自治区 周祥祎 68
陕西省 王新民 71
甘肃省 夏 玲 71
青海省 付成久 73
宁夏回族自治区 张宁学 74
新疆维吾尔自治区 张新革 75
2018 年版权公共服务机构与社会服务组织工作 77
中国版权保护中心 张文娟 77
中国版权协会 连 熠 79
中国音乐著作权协会 张 群 83
中国音像著作权集体管理协会 苗熙梓 86
中国文字著作权协会 张洪波 88
中国摄影著作权协会 朱宝祺 92
中国电影著作权协会 史文霞 93

版权扫描

版权界动态 99
立 法 99
摄影界为《著作权法》修改稿献言献策 99
唱片公司为著作权法修法建言 99
《电子商务法》表决通过 着重强调知识产权保护 100

司 法 100
《关于加强知识产权审判领域改革创新若干问题的意见》印发 100
使用“葛优躺” 基金公司被判侵权 100
《芈月传》著作权引纠纷案 法院判决认为不构成侵权 101
“小咖秀”违法使用歌曲被判赔偿 101
《中国好声音（第三季）》信息网络传播权纠纷二审审结 101
小伙因非法获取课件被判拘役两个月 102
《雾都之恋》引纠纷 豆丁公司被判侵权 102
手游《花千骨》被判侵权 103
首例 VR 著作权案 被告判赔 46 万元 103
山西高院出台指导意见规范卡拉 OK 著作权纠纷赔偿标准 104
全国法院 2017 年审理版权案件大幅增长 104
北京高院发布《侵害著作权案件审理指南》 104
新中国成立以来最大盗版少儿图书案二审宣判 105
《九层妖塔》字体侵权 105
苏州市挂牌成立知识产权检察室 106
“上镜率最高”的《武夷之春》引发的著作权争夺 106
“中国喷泉著作权纠纷第一案”二审维持原判 107
杭州互联网法院首次确立区块链电子存证的法律审查方式 107
上海知识产权法院判令盗版软件侵权者赔偿 1 505 万元 108

北京电视台因擅自使用油画作品一审被判侵权 108
“混搭”销售教辅出版物书商因违法获刑 109
“面包新语”侵权案二审被判赔偿119万余元 109
“同人作品内地第一案”宣判 109
杭州法院宣判全国首例涉“小猪佩奇”著作权侵权纠纷判决案 110
今日头条为《一郭汇》维权获胜 110
赔1800万！网络点播公司因盗播热剧被重判 111
北京互联网著作权纠纷有了“全程在线”法院 112
剪辑影视作品发到短视频平台被判侵权 112
4篇新闻报道获赔10万元　给网络“新闻搬运工”敲响警钟 112
快手诉华多侵权一审获赔两万元 112
北京互联网法院首案开庭审理 113
一份许可合同引发多起版权诉讼 113
《一封家书》被改编　作者获单首作品高额赔偿 114
搜狐视频在一著作权许可使用合同纠纷案中胜诉 115
中国网络作家村正式上链杭州互联网法院司法区块链 116
文著协诉中国知网一审有果 116
VR非法提供作品　热波公司一审判赔35万元 117

行政管理 117
四川省版权局督导绵阳创建国家版权示范城市工作 117
河北省软件正版化工作考核组到衡水市督导考核 117
湖北省软件正版化工作督查小组到黄冈检查 118
山东省版权局召开版权工作座谈会 118
广东省工作组对茂名市版权工作进行考评 118
内蒙古开展2022年北京冬奥会会徽版权保护工作 118
安徽省版权局开展电影院线版权专项治理工作 119
推进使用正版软件工作部际联席会议第七次全体会议召开 119
陕西省版权局调研铜川版权公共服务工作 120
江苏省开展2018年第一期网络侵权盗版案件集中打击行动 120
福建省召开推进使用正版软件工作厅际联席会议第五次全体会议 120
北京市版权局组织召开网络盗版侵权案件推进协调会 121
江苏省版权局督查组对宿迁市侵权盗版案件查处情况进行督查 121
黄坤明出席国家广播电视总局、国家新闻出版署（国家版权局）和国家电影局揭牌仪式并召开座谈会 121
安徽省动员部署软件正版化工作 121
吉林省版权局：完善版权资产管理制度　提高版权保护能力 122
重庆市检察院和市文化委建立保护版权协作机制 122
云南省推进使用正版软件工作联席会议办公室召开2018年第一次联络员会议 122
湖北省召开使用正版软件工作领导小组成员单位联席会议 123
青海省直机关软件正版化工作会议召开 123
广西部署2018年全区自治区级机关使用正版软件工作 123
世界杯赛事节目纳入重点作品版权保护预警名单 123
河北廊坊：督导全国版权示范城市创建工作 124
全国版权执法监管工作会议在京召开 124

甘肃省级政府机关操作软件 97.98%为正版 125
国家版权局对网络转载等重点领域开展版权专项整治 125
北京市启动“剑网 2018”专项行动 126
广东启动“剑网 2018”专项行动重点监管《抖音》《快手》等短视频 APP 126
河北省：鼓励创作版权精品　满足人民精神文化需求 127
“剑网”专项行动启动　8 家沪上知名媒体签署自律公约 127
苏浙沪皖签署一体化合作协议　携手打造长三角出版高地 127
广东召开版权登记工作座谈会 128
国家版权局约谈“抖音”等 15 家短视频企业　严打侵权盗版 128
国家版权局约谈 13 家网络服务商　要求规范网络转载 128
国家版权局：短视频平台版权整改取得阶段性成效 129
《2018 年深入实施国家知识产权战略　加快建设知识产权强国推进计划》印发 129
国家版权局引导版权社会共治 130

宣传教育 130

湖北利用网络直播讲版权保护 130
2018 年国际版权贸易培训班在京举办 130
2018 年粤港两地中学生版权知识和版权保护交流活动在珠海举行 131
青岛市召开软件正版化工作培训会暨首批版权保护重点镇街培训会 131
武汉开展大学生版权辩论赛 132
2018 年全国知识产权宣传周活动启动 132
中日韩联合版权宣传活动启动 132
国新办举行 2017 年中国知识产权发展状况新闻发布会 133
广西壮族自治区版权局开展“版权四进”系列宣传活动 133
山东省举办“版权进校园”系列活动 134
“全省高校版权知识巡回宣讲”活动走进赣州高校 134
湖北省版权局举办 2018 年版权行政执法工作培训班 134
山东省“版权进乡村”行动在潍坊启动 134
内蒙古自治区版权局举办 2018 年区直机关单位软件正版化工作培训班 135
福建德化多部门联合推广版权保护 135
福建省局办 2018 年全省版权执法骨干培训班 135
“江西版权保护宣讲会”走进革命老区 135
北京市为区级国家机关进行软件正版化培训 135
《2017 年重庆区县知识产权发展状况报告》发布 136
天津市召开 2018 年政府机关使用正版软件工作培训会 136
江苏省医疗卫生机构软件正版化工作培训班在南京举行 136
内蒙古自治区国资委举办出资监管企业软件正版化业务培训 136
云南省版权行政执法骨干培训班举办 137
江苏省政府机关软件正版化培训班在常州举行 137
北京市举行市属国企软件正版化工作培训 137
全国首次青年版权征文大赛结果在上海揭晓 137
2018 年京沪知识产权诉讼报告发布 138
《中国知识产权指数报告》第十次发布 138
“文创西藏”以版权交易为核心　提升文旅创意设计水平 139
2018 年度中国版权行业十大热点案件公布 139

交流研讨 140
网络游戏产业法律问题研讨会举行 140
广东省版权局召开促进软件著作权创造、保护和运用专家座谈会 140
“数字时代下的著作权法修改”研讨会召开 141
北京国际网络版权监测研讨会召开 141
第九届首都互联网知识产权保护论坛聚焦视听作品知识产权保护 141
2018 中国知识产权保护高层论坛在京举办 142
2018 中国网络版权保护大会在京召开 142
苏州市召开图片版权保护座谈会 142
聚焦互联网与新媒体环境下体育赛事直播权利保护研讨会在京召开 143
“远集坊”：“童话大王”郑渊洁讲述创作维权 143
知识产权保护促进视听产业发展论坛在京举办 143
互联网内容平台的版权保护研讨会在京举行 143
游戏产业发展中的法律问题研讨会聚焦游戏版权保护 144
短视频版权与竞争问题研讨会举办 144
暨南大学发布基于区块链技术的版权链运行平台 145
2018 版权相关热点问题媒体研修班在京举办 146
2018 年内地与香港特区、澳门特区知识产权研讨会在敦煌召开 146
2018 中国文化 IP 发展高峰论坛在京成功召开 146
北京首届互联网影视著作权高峰论坛召开 147
首届中国剧本推优与版权保护论坛举办 147
第二届中国 IP 30 人论坛在京举行 148
中国国际漫博会聚焦版权交易和产业融合 149
短视频作品创作与版权保护研讨会在京举办 149
2018 中国版权年会在武汉召开 150
AIPPI 中国分会版权热点论坛举行 150

社会管理与服务 151
微博携手中国版权保护中心为原创内容开通版权认证 151
优秀原创动漫作品版权开发奖励计划启动 151
长春市首批版权示范园区（基地）揭牌 151
中国文联与首都版权产业联盟签约 152
国家版权局与中国版权协会、中国移动签署备忘录 152
河北省版权信息数据库平台正式上线 152
重庆首家区县级版权登记工作站启动 152
北方国家版权交易中心落户大连 153
河北版权登记时限从 30 个工作日变一周 153
第十三届中国文交会建立动漫版权交易平台 153
江苏知识产权仲裁调解中心成立 153
版权服务走进首届中国游戏节 153
中国音像著作权集体管理协会召开第七次会员大会 154
《国际影视版权授权协议范本》发布 154
江苏：国家版权贸易基地秘书处落户秦淮区 155
360 搜索上线原创图片版权认证平台 155
苏州推出“映光计划”应对原创音乐版权危机 155

少儿数字出版维权联盟成立 155
贵州省版权登记中心揭牌 155
浙江建立淘宝电子版权登记“快车道” 156
河北省版权保护中心在廊坊设立版权服务站 156
中国文化 IP 100 发展联盟在京成立 156
广深港高铁列车播放音乐获音著协许可 157
长春成立首批 4 家版权服务工作站 157
四川版权工作站正式揭牌 157
首个互联网企业版权资产管理应用示范成果花落京企 158
天合集团收费资格被音集协终止 158
音著协向进博会发放音乐著作权许可 158
中国版权保护中心与北京文投集团签约合作 159
百度等承诺落实版权监管主体责任 159
中版版权产业基金在沪发起筹备 159
中国财经媒体版权保护联盟成立 160
音集协版权收费将采取新模式 160
互联网企业发起短视频版权自律公约 160
横琴联手港澳打造大湾区知识产权保护新高地 160

国际交流与合作 161
周慧琳会见新加坡知识产权局局长邓鸿森一行 161
中日聚焦网络音乐版权保护应对方案 162
博洛尼亚童书展：中国达成 800 多项版权输出意向及协议 162
中国图书亮相突尼斯国际书展 162
中国九大原创节目登陆戛纳电视节 163
中国国际出版中心在伦敦正式成立 163
中墨正式建立版权双边合作框架 163
中国出版代表团亮相第 25 届匈牙利布达佩斯国际图书节 164
外研社“中国主题编辑部”落户匈牙利 164
中国图书亮相日内瓦国际书展 164
中国出版企业亮相伊朗书展 165
中国代表团参加都灵图书沙龙 165
北京新闻出版广播影视企业海外服务基地在伦敦挂牌 165
外研社·法国“中国主题编辑部”成立 165
北京出版代表团亮相 2018 美国书展 165
庄荣文在京会见世界知识产权组织副总干事王彬颖一行 166
中美法律专家纵论知识产权保护与创新 166
世界知识产权组织副总干事福尔班一行视察冠勇科技 167
“电影的经济及文化价值与版权保护高端论坛”在上海举行 167
中英版权圆桌会议聚焦数字环境下版权执法面临的问题及挑战 167
人民出版社与越南真理国家政治出版社签署版权合作协议 168
2017 年中国出版业版权输出同比增长 24.1% 168
第 25 届图博会达成中外版权贸易协议 5 678 项 168
习近平向 2018 年“一带一路”知识产权高级别会议致贺信 169
李克强会见世界知识产权组织总干事高锐 169

“中国图书展”首次亮相马尼拉国际书展 169
“中国图书展”亮相第20届科伦坡国际书展 169
“中国书架”亮相德语区最大连锁书店 170
中国主宾国活动在阿尔及尔国际书展掀起“中国热” 170
中欧数字环境下版权保护与许可研讨会在广州举行 170
中日网络影视作品著作权保护研讨会在京召开 170

产业发展 171
2017中国文化产业系列指数发布 171
《中国互联网络发展状况统计报告》解读内容产业发展 173
中超版权费大幅“缩水” 174
掌阅文学：精品化策略让40余位作者年收入过百万 174
腾讯音乐与网易云音乐就网络音乐版权事宜达成合作 174
网易云音乐和阿里音乐达成版权互授合作 174
小米音乐与太合音乐达成版权合作 175
网络文学为阅文创造41亿元年收入 175
粤港澳大湾区电影产业中心项目启动 175
小霸王公司宣布重新回归游戏机市场 175
辽宁出版集团与咪咕数媒开展战略合作 176
网易云音乐与索尼音乐达成深度合作 176
我国网络版权产值突破6 000亿元 176
中国版权产业占GDP比重达7.33% 177
《2018全球音乐产业报告》发布 177
磨铁动漫在杭打造“超级漫画家计划” 177
酷狗苏州音乐产业孵化基地落成 177
一批直播和短视频网站开展自查自纠 178
中影股份与甘肃文化机构开展战略合作 178
索尼收购百代音乐出版公司 178
腾讯设1亿元基金保护原创 178
方正电子与10家企业签订字体授权协议 179
腾讯内容开放平台对企鹅号版权保护系统整体升级 179
阅文集团举办IP生态大会 179
网络大电影市场正向院线电影看齐 180
阿里大鱼号合作法国希帕图片社　为创作者提供世界杯高清版权图片 181
腾讯音乐娱乐TMC为国产音乐与国际交流架起桥梁 181
上海发布《2017上海游戏出版产业数据调查报告》　多措并举保障游戏产业健康发展 181
苏宁与咪咕联合运营体育内容 182
爱奇艺收购天象互娱 183
百度首个基于区块链技术的原创图片服务平台“图腾”上线 183
PP体育与法甲联盟达成为期3年的新媒体独家版权合作 183
今日头条开展版权保护专项行动 184
中国国际数码互动娱乐展览会首办电竞大会 184
蜻蜓FM与纵横文学达成战略合作 184
北京成动漫游戏研发和出口中心 185

CNNIC：我国 74.1%的网民使用短视频应用 185
中图公司与三单位共推数字阅读人工智能应用 185
安徽出版集团文创产品走进“一带一路” 186
康佳与南方新媒体达成战略合作 186
2018 北京国际文创产品交易会开幕 186
有道乐读推出“万书计划” 187
抖音宣布加入 Apple Music 合作伙伴计划 187
方正发布新品赋能出版融合 187
咪咕联手微博布局体娱产业 187
京蒙发行集团共谋文化产业发展 187
浙江出版传媒股份有限公司成立 188
中央广播电视总台首个区域总部成立 188
全国首个省级电视 4K 超高清频道开播 188
巨人网络进军虚拟偶像市场　首位虚拟主播即将推出 189
阅文集团战略投资韩国网文企业文笔雅 189
第十三届北京文博会重点项目签约 68 亿元 190
《中影剧场》登陆美国城市电视台 191
2017 年全球版税收入达 96 亿欧元　中国市场潜力大 191
内蒙古出版集团携手联通共推“互联网＋出版” 192
字节跳动与 NBA 达成短视频版权合作 192
《2018 年中国网络视听发展研究报告》发布 192
趣头条：向“下沉市场”挖掘内容版权价值 193
2017 年北京版权产业增加值比上年上涨 9.2% 193
首届“国家音乐产业优秀项目奖励计划”入选项目公布 193
78 个原创动漫项目获扶持 193
新华网启动视频化战略 194

港澳台版权信息 195
粤澳保护知识产权合作协议在广州签署 195
澳门知识产权研究中心揭牌 195
粤港版权产业企业交流活动在香港举行 195
粤港知识产权与中小企业发展（佛山）研讨会在佛山举行 196
“澳门国际知识产权研讨会 2018”在澳门举办 196
第十四届海图会在台北举行 196
粤港保护知识产权合作专责小组第十七次会议在广州举行 197
广西书展在台北开幕 197
粤港澳大湾区知识产权法律联盟正式成立 198
“粤港澳大湾区知识产权合作及机遇”分论坛在香港举行 199
首届粤港澳大湾区知识产权拍卖成交额逾 600 万元 199
香港“知识产权贸易及管理的人力统计调查”公布主要结果 199

版权相关产业与版权贸易

2017 年中国版权产业的经济贡献　中国新闻出版研究院 203

中国网络版权产业发展报告（2019） 国家版权局网络版权产业研究基地 209
2018 年新闻出版产业分析报告 国家新闻出版署 227
2018—2019 年中国数字出版产业年度报告 中国数字出版产业年度报告课题组 251
2018 年中国广播电视产业发展报告 国家广播电视总局广播影视发展研究中心 267
2018 年中国电影产业发展报告 中国文联电影艺术中心 272
2018 年中国动漫产业发展报告 牛兴侦 288
2018 年中国软件产业发展概况 国家工业和信息化部信息化和软件服务业司 298
2018 年中国网络游戏产业发展报告 廖旭华 306

典型案件选编

2018 年全国著作权司法保护典型案件 319

2018 年度全国打击侵权盗版十大案件 331

2018 年地方著作权司法保护典型案件 334
北京市 334
河北省 335
黑龙江省 336
上海市 337
江苏省 338
浙江省 341
安徽省 343
福建省 344
河南省 346
湖北省 347
广东省 347
广西壮族自治区 348
海南省 348
陕西省 349

2018 年地方著作权行政执法案件 350
天津市 350
河北省 350
内蒙古自治区 352
辽宁省 352
吉林省 352
上海市 353
江苏省 358
安徽省 360
江西省 360
山东省 362
湖北省 364
湖南省 365

广东省 365
四川省 367
陕西省 368
青海省 370

法律法规及规章文件

中华人民共和国电子商务法 373
关于印发《2017 年推进使用正版软件工作总结》和《2018 年推进使用正版软件工作计划》的通知
（国版函〔2018〕4 号） 380
国家版权局关于奖励 2017 年度查处侵权盗版重大案件的决定
（国版函〔2018〕36 号） 384
国家版权局办公厅关于 2017 年全国著作权登记情况的通报
（国版办发〔2018〕3 号） 396
关于做好 2018 年全国知识产权宣传周版权宣传活动的通知
（国版办发〔2018〕4 号） 397
国家版权局等关于开展打击网络侵权盗版“剑网 2018”专项行动的通知
（国版发电〔2018〕1 号） 398

年度发布

2018 年中国网络版权保护年度报告 403
2018 年“中国版权金奖”获奖名单 410
2018 年度查处侵权盗版案件有功单位及个人 411
2018 年中国版权十件大事 422
2018 年（第十届）全国大学生版权征文获奖名单 424
2018 CPCC 十大中国著作权人 428
2018 年中国版权年会年度评选获奖名单 429

理论研究

2018 年中国著作权法研究综述 向　波　史若琪 433

2018 年版权热点问题研究 444
论版权法对滥用技术措施行为的规制 王　迁 444
中国著作权立法中的制度创新 熊　琦 453
著作权集体管理组织：市场功能、角色安排与定价问题 向　波 463
论著作权法对人工智能生成成果的保护
——作为邻接权的数据处理者权之证立 陶　乾 469
功能主义解释论视野下的“电影作品”
——兼评凤凰网案二审判决 万　勇 475
论著作权合理使用扩张适用的路径选择 刘宇晖 482

制度演进视角下我国广播权的范畴 刘银良 487
论网络环境下著作权侵权的刑事归责
——以网络服务提供者的刑事责任为中心 欧阳本祺 492
视频分享网站著作权间接侵权的过错认定 马一德 500

2018 年著作权相关图书简介 511

统计资料

2018 年中国版权统计资料 523
2018 年全国作品自愿登记情况统计（按作品类别） 523
2018 年全国版权合同登记情况统计 524
2018 年全国版权执法情况统计 525
2018 年全国版权引进地汇总表 525
2018 年全国版权输出地汇总表 526

2018 年中国新闻出版产业统计资料 527
2018 年全国各地区图书出版总量 527
2018 年全国各级报纸出版数量 528
2018 年全国各地区各类期刊出版的种数、印数、总印张、总金额（1） 530
2018 年全国各地区各类期刊出版的种数、印数、总印张、总金额（2） 532
2018 年全国各地区电子出版物出版品种、数量及发行数量（按载体形式分类） 534
2018 年全国各地区录音制品出版品种、数量及发行数量（按载体形式分类） 536
2018 年全国各地区录像制品出版品种、数量及发行数量（按载体形式分类） 538
2018 年全国新华书店系统、出版社自办发行单位出版物发行进、销、存情况 540
2018 年全国图书、期刊、报纸进出口情况 541
2018 年全国音像制品、电子出版物、数字出版物进出口情况 541

2018 年中国广播影视产业统计资料 542
2018 年全国广播电视发展主要指标一览表（一） 542
2018 年全国广播电视发展主要指标一览表（二） 544

2018 年中国软件产业统计资料 546
2018 年分省市软件和信息技术服务业业务收入表 546
2018 年全国软件和信息技术服务业主要经济指标表 547

名 录

版权行政管理部门 551
版权公共服务机构 553
版权协会 554
著作权集体管理组织 557
版权相关行业协会 558

版权代理公司 558
国家级版权交易机构 559
知识产权教学与研究机构 561

附录：国际版权动态

综　述 567

信息时代的著作权制度为市场发展保驾护航
——2018年国际著作权法制发展回顾 郭　禾　白志晖 567

2018年国际版权动态 573

立法与行政 573

欧盟理事会正式批准《马拉喀什条约》 573
日本大尺度修改《著作权法》 573
日本新法助力教育信息化改革：电子教材使用无须权利人许可 574
欧盟版权规则或将不再适用于脱欧后的英国 575
断开链接以保护漫画的著作权，政府的紧急对策涉嫌违宪而遭到反对 575
《广播组织保护条约》制定进行时 576
韩国扩大表演权范围 577
韩国《著作权法》修改中的争议：是否承认出版者的版式设计权 578
USMCA对著作权执法标准的新规定 579
欧洲议会批准通过颇具争议的《数字化单一市场版权指令》 580
美国《音乐现代化法案》深入改革音乐许可制度 580
美国颁布《马拉喀什条约实施法案》 581
澳大利亚议会通过《2018年版权法修正案》 583
西班牙议会通过新的《知识产权法》修正案 584
欧洲掀起《数字化单一市场版权指令》草案的反对浪潮 584

司法判例 585

H&M身陷街头涂鸦侵权争议 585
韩国：将未参与创作的人标注为作者需要承担刑事责任 586
“不爽猫”赢得454万元版权违约金 586
美国法院：深层链接不能规避版权侵权 587
因法院裁决　免费电子书网站“Project Gutenberg”不接受德国访问 588
甲骨文公司在与谷歌的版权之战中胜出 589
盗版网站“漫画村”运营者信息被公布 589
美国ABS娱乐公司诉CBS公司：以数字形式重录唱片不产生新的版权 590
欧盟法院新判决再解“向公众传播” 590
德国联邦最高法院提请欧洲法院裁定YouTube著作权纠纷 591
草裙舞的著作权获日本法院认可 592
欧洲法院裁定澄清非法文件共享的举证责任 592
Spotify与Wixen达成和解终结巨额诉讼 593
欧盟法院做出裁定：食物的气味不受著作权法保护 593

业界动态 594
日本卡通形象熊本熊版权新规正式实施 594
欧盟委员会发布打击在线非法内容的建议 595
CPTPP 协定里的知识产权条款仍具有积极意义 595
埃及为改善知识产权保护与执法创建数据取证试验室 596
国际作者和作曲者协会联合会：著作权“避风港”规则扰乱创作市场 596
日本：产品销售中使用公共领域作品可能侵犯作者人格利益 597
无协议脱欧将导致英国公民境外使用 Netflix 和 Spotify 账号受阻 597
日本提高海外电影的音乐版税 598
多名艺人要求特朗普停止在集会上使用自己的音乐作品 598
“骄傲男孩”的创始人因侵犯版权遭 YouTube 封杀 599
《美国经济中的版权产业：2018 年报告》发布 600

索　引

索引 601

Contents

Specials

Advices of Issues on Strengthening Reform and Innovation in Trials of Intellectual Property Cases 3
Deepening the Implementation of National Intellectual Property Strategy; Advancing the Initiative to Construct a Strong Country in Intellectual Property in 2019 6

Copyright Work Overview

National Copyright Work in 2018 15
National Copyright Administrative Work in 2018
Copyright Management Division, CPC Central Publicity Department 15
National Judicial Protection of Copyright in 2018
Intellectual Property Tribunal, Supreme People's Court of China 19

Regional Copyright Work in 2018 22
Beijing Municipality Zhao Xiaopeng 22
Tianjin Municipality Zhang Qian 25
Hebei Province Li Dongqun 26
Shanxi Province Hao Zimou 29
Inner Mongolia Autonomous Region Ma Da 31
Liaoning Province Tian Dapeng 32
Jilin Province Du Yuzhen 35
Heilongjiang Province Yan Shi 37
Shanghai Municipality Wang Qian 38
Jiangsu Province Lu Yin 41
Zhejiang Province Yan Qingrong 44
Anhui Province Hu Zi 46
Fujian Province Zheng Kaipi 48
Jiangxi Province Que Miqiu 50
Shandong Province Jiang Jinkun 51
Henan Province Jiao Yanna 54
Hubei Province Zhang Wei 56
Hunan Province Song Liang 58
Guangdong Province Yi Jinyuan 59

Guangxi Zhuang Autonomous Region Zhao Mingming 60
Hainan Province Wang Jingen 61
Chongqing Municipality Zhang Rui 63
Sichuan Province Li Xiaoxi 64
Guizhou Province Xu Mei 65
Yunnan Province Wang Cheng 67
Tibet Autonomous Region Zhou Xiangyi 68
Shaanxi Province Wang Xinmin 71
Gansu Province Xia Ling 71
Qinghai Province Fu Chengjiu 73
Ningxia Hui Autonomous Region Zhang Ningxue 74
Xinjiang Uygur Autonomous Region Zhang Xinge 75

Work of Public Copyright Service Institutions and Social Copyright Service Organizations in 2018 77
Copyright Protection Center of China Zhang Wenjuan 77
Copyright Society of China Lian Yi 79
Music Copyright Society of China Zhang Qun 83
China Audio-Video Copyright Association Miao Xizi 86
China Written Works Copyright Society Zhang Hongbo 88
Images Copyright Society of China Zhu Baoqi 92
China Film Copyright Association Shi Wenxia 93

Copyright Scanning

Copyright News 99
Legislation 99
Photography Circle Provided Comments and Insights for the Revision of the Copyright Law 99
Music Companies Provided Comments and Insights for the Revision of the Copyright Law 99
E-Commerce Law Approved, Emphasizing Intellectual Property Protection 100

Judicial Cases 100
Advices of Issues on Strengthening Reform and Innovation in Trials of Intellectual Property Cases Printed and Distributed 100
The Foundation Company Using "Ge-You-Styled Slumping" Ruled Infringement 100
Legend of Mi Yue Copyright Dispute Case Ruled Non-Infringement by the Court 101
Video-Filming APP "Xiaokaxiu" Sentenced to Compensation for Its Illegal Use of Songs 101
Trial of Second Instance of "The Voice of China" (Season Three) Information Network Transmission Rights Dispute Ended 101
Young Man Sentenced to a Two-Month Detention for Illegally Obtaining Courseware 102
Online Novel *Love in the City of Fog* Caused Disputes; Docin. com Ruled

Infringement 102
Cellphone Game *Hua Qiangu* Ruled Infringement 103
Defendant of First VR Copyright Case Sentenced to a Compensation of RMB 460,000 103
Supreme Court in Shanxi Province Issued Guidelines to Regulate Compensation Standard for Karaoke Copyright Disputes 104
Number of Copyright Cases Tried in Courts Nationwide in 2017 Increased 104
Supreme Court in Beijing Issued *Trial Guideline for Copyright Infringement Cases* 104
Trial of Second Instance of the Largest-Scaled Pirated Children's Book Case Since the Founding of the People's Republic of China Pronounced 105
Fonts of *Nine-Tier Demon Tower* Ruled Infringement 105
Suzhou Founded Intellectual Property Procuratorate Office 106
Disputes Led by the "Most-Photographed" *Spring of Wuyi* 106
Trial of Second Instance of "China's First Case of Fountain Copyright Disputes" Affirmed the Original Judgement 107
Hangzhou Internet Court Sets Legal Examing Standards for Blockchain E-Evidence for the First Time 107
Shanghai Intellectual Property Court Sentenced Pirated Software Infringing Subjects to a Compensation of RMB 15.05 Million 108
Beijing TV Ruled Infringement for Using Oil Paintings Without Asking for Proprietor's Permission in the First Instance 108
Book Sellers Sentenced for Illegally Selling Reference Books for Students 109
Trial of Second Instance of BreadTalk Infringement Ruled a Compensation of over RMB 1.19 Million 109
First Case of Fan Arts in Mainland China Ruled 109
Hangzhou Court Announced the Decision for China's First Peppa Pig Related Copyright Infringement Dispute 110
Toutiao Won in Right-Safeguarding Case for *Yiguohui* 110
A Compensation of RMB 18 Million! Internet Company Punished Harshly for Illegally Broadcasting Hit Drama 111
Internet Copyright Disputes in Beijing Won Assistance from "24-Hour Online" Court 112
An Act of Film-Editing TV Works and Uploading Them onto Short Video Platforms Ruled Infringement 112
Four News Reports Compensated RMB 100,000, Sounding Alarms for Online "News Porters" 112
Kuaishou Won the Lawsuit Against Huaduo for Infringement, Compensated RMB 20,000 112
First Case's Court Session in Beijing Internet Court Began 113
A License Agreement Led to Multiple Rights Lawsuits 113
A Family Letter Was Adapted; Authors Highly Compensated for Single Work 114
Sohu Won in a Copyright License Agreement Dispute Case 115
China Internet Writer Village Officially Initiated on Judicial Blockchain of Hangzhou Internet Court 116
China Written Works Copyright Society Sued China National Knowledge

Infrastructure; First Instance Adjudicated 116
VR Broadcast Works Illegally; Hotcast Ruled to Compensate RMB 350,000 in the First Instance 117

Administration 117
Sichuan Copyright Administration Guides National Copyright Model-City-Building Work in Mianyang 117
Hebei Software Legitimacy Work and Assessing Group Guided and Appraised in Hengshui 117
Hubei Software Legitimacy Work and Supervising Group Supervised in Huanggang 118
Shandong Copyright Administration Held Copyright Work Seminar 118
Guangdong Work Group Assessed Copyright Work in Maoming 118
Inner Mongolia Initiated Copyright Protection Work for 2022 Beijing Winter Olympic Emblem 118
Anhui Copyright Administration Carried Out Cinema Copyright Special Administration Work 119
The Seventh Plenary Session of Minitrial Joint Conference for Promoting Use of Licensed Software Held 119
Shaanxi Copyright Administration Surveyed Copyright Public Service Work in Tongchuan 120
Jiangsu Carried Out 2018 First Crackdown Action for Internet Infringement and Piracy Cases 120
Fujian Held the Fifth Plenary Session of Departmental Conference for Promoting Use of Licensed Software 120
Beijing Copyright Administration Organized and Held Promoting and Coordinating Meeting for Internet Piracy and Infringement Cases 121
Inspection Group of Jiangsu Copyright Administration Inspected the Investigation and Disposal of Infringement and Piracy Cases in Suqian 121
Huang Kunming Attended Lauching Ceremony of National Radio and Television Administration, State Administration of Press and Publication (National Copyright Administration of China) and China Film Administration, and Held Seminar 121
Anhui Mobilized and Deployed the Work in Using Licensed Software 121
Jilin Copyright Administration: Improving System of Copyright Asset Management and Advancing Copyright Protection Capability 122
Chongqing Procuratorate and Municipal Cultural Committee Built Copyright Protection Coordinating Mechanism 122
Yunnan Joint Conference Office of Promoting Use of Licensed Software Held 2018 First Liaison Officers Meeting 122
Hubei Held Leading Member Institute Joint Conference for Using Licensed Software 123
Working Conference for Promoting Use of Licensed Software in Provincial Organs of Qinghai Held 123
Guangxi Deployed 2018 Licensed-Software-Using Work in Region-Level Organs in the Whole Autonomous Region 123
World Cup Programs Included in Warning List as Key Copyright-Protecting

Subjects 123
Langfang, Hebei Province: Supervising National Copyright Model City Building Work 124
National Copyright Enforcement and Supervision Work Conference Held in Beijing 124
Licensed Software Accounts for 97.98% of the Software Used in Provincial Governmental Organs in Gansu 125
National Copyright Administration of China Carried Out Special Inspection Work Targeting on Key Realms like Network Reprinting 125
Beijing Carried Out "Sword Net 2018" Special Action 126
Guangdong Province Carried Out "Sword Net 2018" Special Action, Mainly Inspecting Short Video APPs like *Douyin* and *Kuaishou* 126
Hebei: Encouraging the Birth of High-Quality Copyrighted Work; Meeting People's Spiritual and Cultural Needs 127
"Sword Net" Special Action Carried Out; Eight Well-Known Media Based in Shanghai Signed Self-Disciplinary Convention 127
Jiangsu, Anhui, Shanghai and Zhejiang Signed All-in-One Cooperation Agreement, Joining Hands in Building Publication Highland in Yangtze River Delta 127
Guangdong Held Copyright Registering Work Seminar 128
National Copyright Administration of China Convened with 15 Short Video Enterprises Including "Douyin", Aiming to Crack Down Against Piracy Harshly 128
National Copyright Administration of China Convened with 13 Network Servers, Asking to Regulate Internet Reprinting 128
National Copyright Administration of China: Copyright Rectification of Short Video Platforms Achieved Phased Results 129
Deepening the Implementation of National Intellectual Property Strategy; Advancing the Initiative to Construct a Strong Country in Intellectual Property in 2018 Printed and Distributed 129
National Copyright Administration of China Guides Coordinated Copyright Management Throughout Society 130

Publicity and Education 130
Hubei Province Disseminated Copyright Protection Knowledge via Network Broadcasting 130
2018 International Copyright Trade Training Session Held in Beijing 130
2018 Guangdong and Hong Kong Middle School Students Copyright Knowledge and Protection Exchange Activity Held in Zhuhai 131
Qingdao Held Training Conference of Use of Licensed Software and Training for First Batch of Copyright Protection Key Counties and Streets 131
Wuhan Held College Students' Copyright-Themed Debates 132
2018 National Intellectual Property Publicity Week Launched 132
China-Japan-Korea Joint Copyright Publicity Activity Launched 132
State Council Information Office Held 2017 Press Conference on China Intellectual Property Development 133
Guangxi Copyright Administration Carried Out "Four Entrances of Copyright"

Serial Publicity Activities 133
Shandong Held "Copyright Into Campus" Serial Activities 134
"Provincial College and University Copyright Knowledge Tour Lectures" Came to Ganzhou 134
Hubei Copyright Administration Held 2018 Copyright Administration and Law Enforcement Training Session 134
Shandong "Copyright Goes into Villages" Action Launched in Weifang 134
Inner Mongolia Copyright Administration Held 2018 Regional Organs and Units Training Session in Using Licensed Software 135
Multiple Departments in Dehua, Fujian Jointly Promoted Copyright Protection 135
Fujian Held 2018 Provincial Copyright Enforcement Backbone Officials Training Session 135
"Jiangxi Copyright Protection Publicity Meeting" Held in Old Revolutionary Areas 135
Beijing Trained Region-Level National Organs on Use of Licensed Software 135
2017 Intellectual Property Development Report of Districts and Counties in Chongqing Issued 136
Tianjin Held 2018 Training Session for Governmental Organs' Use of Licensed Software 136
Training Session for Using Licensed Software in Medical and Health Care Institutions in Jiangsu Held in Nanjing 136
State-Owned Assets Supervision and Administration Commission of Inner Mongolia Held Business Training for Investing Inspection Enterprises' Use of Licensed Software 136
Yunnan Province Held Copyright Administration and Enforcement Training Session for Backbone Officials 137
Training Session on the Use of Licensed Software for Government Organs Held in Changzhou, Jiangsu Province 137
Beijing Held Training Session on the Use of Licensed Software for Municipal State-Owned Enterprises 137
Result of the First National Youth Composition Contest on Copyright Released in Shanghai 137
2018 Beijing-Shanghai Report of Claims on Intellectual Property Released 138
The 10th *China Intellectual Property Index Report* Released 138
"Cultural and Creative Tibet" Focused on Copyright Trade to Enhance Creativity and Designing Capability on Culture and Tourism 139
2018 Top 10 Hot Cases of China Copyright Industry Released 139

Exchanges and Discussion 140
Seminar on Legal Issues of Online Game Industry Held 140
Guangdong Copyright Administration Held Expert Seminar to Promote the Creation, Protection, and Operation of Software Copyright 140
Seminar on "Revision of Copyright Law in the Digital Era" Held 141
Beijing International Symposium on Online Copyright Monitoring and Protection Held 141
The Ninth Capital Internet Intellectual Property Protection Forum Focused on

the Intellectual Property Protection of Audio-Visual Work 141
2018 High-Level Forum on China IP Protection Held in Beijing 142
2018 National Conference on Internet Copyright Protection Held in Beijing 142
Seminar on Photo Copyright Protection Held in Suzhou 142
Seminar on Live Sports Event Copyright Protection Under Internet and New Media Circumstances Held in Beijing 143
"Yuanji Workshop": "King of Fairy Tales" Zheng Yuanjie Talked About Written Works' Rights Protection 143
Forum on Intellectual Property Protection's Positive Impacts on the Development of Audio-Video Industry Held in Beijing 143
Seminar on Copyright Protection of Internet Content Platforms Held in Beijing 143
Seminar on Legal Issues in Game Industry Development Focused on Game Copyright Protection 144
Seminar on Short Video Copyright and Competition Problems Held 144
Copyright Chain Operation Platform Based on Blockchain Released by Jinan University 145
Media Training Session on 2018 Copyright Related Hot Issues Held in Beijing 146
2018 Mainland China-Hong Kong S. A. R-Macau S. A. R Intellectual Property Seminar Held in Dunhuang 146
2018 China Cultural IP Development Summit Forum Successfully Held in Beijing 146
First Internet Film and TV Copyright Summit Forum Held in Beijing 147
First Distinguished Chinese Script Recommendation and Copyright Protection Forum Held 147
The Second China IP 30 Forum Held in Beijing 148
China International Animation Copyright Fair Focused on Copyright Trade and Industry Convergence 149
Seminar on Short Video Creation and Copyright Protection Held in Beijing 149
2018 China Copyright Annual Conference Held in Wuhan 150
AIPPI China Held the Copyright Hot Issues Forum 150

Social Management and Services 151
Weibo and China Copyright Protection Center Provided Copyright Authentication for Original Content 151
Copyright Development Awarding Plan for Outstanding Original Animation Works Initiated 151
First Batch of Copyright Demonstration Garden (Base) Unveiled in Changchun 151
China Federation of Literary and Art Circles Signed Agreement with Capital Copyright Industry Alliance 152
National Copyright Administration of China Signed Memorandum with Copyright Society of China and China Mobile 152
Hebei Copyright Information Database Platform Officially Launched 152
First District/County Level Copyright Registering Working Station in Chongqing Launched 152
Northern National Copyright Exchange Center Set in Dalian 153

Copyright Registration Duration Reduced from 30 Working Days to a Week in Hebei 153
The 13th China Yiwu Cultural Products Trade Fair Set Up Cartoon Copyright Trade Platform 153
Jiangsu Intellectual Property Intercession Center Founded 153
Copyright Service Entered the First China Game Festival 153
China Audio-Video Copyright Association Held the Seventh General Meeting 154
International Model Licensing Agreement for Film and Television Copyright Released 154
Jiangsu: Secretariat of National Copyright Trade Base Settled in Qinhuai District 155
WWW. SO. COM Launched Original Picture Copyright Authentication Platform 155
Yingguang Plan Launched in Suzhou to Cope with Original Music Copyright Crisis 155
Rights Protection League of Digital Publishing for Children Founded 155
Guizhou Copyright Registration Center Set Up 155
Zhejiang Established Green Channel for Taobao Digital Copyright Registration 156
Hebei Copyright Protection Center Established Copyright Service Station in Langfang 156
China Cultural IP 100 Development Alliance Founded in Beijing 156
Music Playing in High-Speed Trains of Guangzhou, Shenzhen and Hong Kong Permitted by Music Copyright Society of China 157
First Four Copyright Service Stations Founded in Changchun 157
Sichuan Copyright Station Formally Launched 157
A Beijing Enterprise Won the First Demonstration Award of Internet Enterprise Copyright Administration 158
China Audio-Video Copyright Association Stopped Excellent Union Group from Fee Charging 158
Music Copyright Society of China Licensed Music Copyright to China International Import Expo 158
China Copyright Protection Center Reached Agreement with Beijing Cultural Investment Development Group Co., Ltd. 159
Companies Including Baidu Committed to Undertake the Obligations of Copyright Supervision 159
China Copyright Industry Fund Raised in Shanghai 159
China Finance Media Copyright Protection Alliance Established 160
China Audio-Video Copyright Association to Adopt New Charging Pattern 160
Internet Enterprises Initiated Self-Disciplinary Copyright Convention on Short Videos 160
Hengqin, Hong Kong and Macau Jointly Strive to Reach New Heights of Intellectual Property in Greater Bay Area 160

International Exchange and Cooperation 161
Zhou Huilin Met the Delegation Led by Deng Hongsen, Director General of Intellectual Property Office of Singapore 161

China and Japan Focused on Online Music Copyright Protection Resolution 162
Copyrights of Over 800 Chinese Titles Licensed Abroad on Bologna Children's Book Fair 162
Chinese Books Appeared on Tunisia International Book Fair 162
Nine of Original Chinese TV Shows Broadcast in MIPTV 163
China International Publishing Center Officially Founded in London 163
China and Mexico Officially Reached Initial Copyright Bilateral Cooperation 163
Chinese Publishing Delegation Attended the 25th International Book Festival Budapest 164
"China Theme Editorial Branch" of Foreign Language Teaching and Research Press Settled in Hungary 164
China Books Appeared on Geneva Book and Press Festival 164
Chinese Publishing Houses Attended Tehran International Book Fair 165
Chinese Publishing Delegation Attended Turin Book Fair 165
Overseas Service Base of Beijing Enterprises of News, Publication, Broadcast, Film and Television Set Up in London 165
"China Theme Editorial Branch" of Foreign Language Teaching and Research Press Founded in France 165
Beijing Publishing Delegation Attended 2018 Book Expo America 165
Zhuang Rongwen Met the Delegation Led by Wang Binying, Deputy Director General of World Intellectual Property Organization in Beijing 166
Chinese and American Legal Experts Discussed Intellectual Property Protection and Innovation 166
World Intellectual Property Organization Delegation Led by Forbin Sylvie, Deputy Director General, Visited Firstbrave Group 167
"High-Level Forum on the Cultural and Economic Importance of Film and the Role of Copyright" Held in Shanghai 167
China-UK Copyright Roundtable Focusing on Issues and Challenges Facing Copyright Enforcement in the Digital Environment 167
People's Publishing House and Vietnam Truth National Political Press Signed Copyright Cooperation Agreement 168
Copyright Exported by China's Publishing Industry Grew by 24.1% Year-on-Year in 2017 168
A Total of 5,678 Sino-Foreign Copyright Trade Agreements Reached at the 25th Beijing International Book Fair 168
Xi Jinping Congratulates the 2018 High-Level Conference on Intellectual Property for Countries Along the Belt and Road 169
Li Keqiang Met World Intellectual Property Organization Delegation Led by Francis Gurry, Director General 169
"China Book Exhibition" Debuted on Manila International Book Fair 169
"China Book Exhibition" Opened on the 20th Colombo International Book Fair 169
"China Bookshelf" Introduced to the Largest German Bookstore Chain for the First Time 170
China as Guest of Honor Set off "China Fever" at Algiers International Book Fair 170
Sino-European Seminar on Copyright Protection and Licensing in the Digital

Environment Held in Guangzhou 170
Sino-Japanese Network Film and Television Works Copyright Protection Seminar Held in Beijing 170

Industry Development 171
China Cultural Industry Index 2017 Released 171
Statistical Report on Internet Development in China Interprets Development of Content Industry 173
Chinese Football Association Super League's Royalties Shrank Considerably 174
iReader: Quality Strategy Earned 40+ Authors More than a Million Dollars a Year 174
Tencent Music and NetEase Cloud Music Cooperated on Online Music Copyright Issues 174
NetEase Cloud Music and Ali Music Reached Mutual Copyright Licensing Cooperation Agreement 174
Xiaomi Music and Taihe Music Reached Copyright Cooperation Agreement 175
Online Literature Yielded RMB 4.1 Billion in Revenue for China Literature 175
Guangdong-Hong Kong-Macau Greater Bay Area Film Industry Center Project Launched 175
Xiaobawang Corporation Announced Re-Entry into the Game Console Market 175
Liaoning Publishing Group and Migu Digital Media Entered into Strategic Cooperation 176
NetEase Cloud Music Entered into In-Depth Cooperation with Sony Music 176
China's Online Copyright Output Value Exceeded RMB 600 Billion 176
China's Copyright Industry Accounted for 7.33% of GDP 177
IFPI Global Music Report 2018 Released 177
Motie Animation Launched "Super Cartoonist Project" in Hangzhou 177
Kugou Suzhou Music Industry Incubation Base Completed 177
Self-Examination and Correction Conducted in a Batch of Live and Short Video Websites 178
China Film Group Corporation Entered into Strategic Cooperation with Gansu Cultural Institutions 178
Sony Acquired EMI Music Publishing 178
Tencent Set Up 100-Million-Yuan Fund to Protect Original Works 178
Founder Electronics Signed Font Licensing Agreements with 10 Companies 179
Tencent Content Open Platform Comprehensively Upgraded Tencent Acount Copyright Protection System 179
China Literature Host IP Eco Conference 179
The Market of Movies Launched on Internet Platforms Aligning with Cinema Movies 180
Ali Dayu Account Cooperated with SIPA to Provide Creators with Copyrighted High-Definition Pictures of the World Cup 181
Tencent Music Entertainment TMC Acted as a Bridge Connecting Domestic Music to the World 181
Shanghai Released *Shanghai Game Publishing Industry Survey Report 2017*, Using Various Measures for Sound Development of the Game Industry 181

Suning and Migu Jointly Operated Sports Content 182
iQiyi Acquired Skymoons Inc. 183
Totem, Baidu's First Original Image Service Platform Based on Blockchain Technology Released 183
PP Sports and Ligue 1 Reached Three-Year Exclusive Copyright Partnership in New Media 183
Toutiao Launched a Special Copyright Protection Operation 184
ChinaJoy Held Its First Esports Conference 184
Dragonfly FM and Zongheng Reached Strategic Cooperation 184
Beijing Became the R&D and Export Center of Animations and Games 185
CNNIC: 74.1% of Internet Users in China Used Short Video Applications 185
CNPIEC and Three Other Institutions Jointly Promoted the Application of Artificial Intelligence in Digital Reading 185
Anhui Publishing Group's Cultural and Creative Products Introduced to Countries Along the Belt and Road 186
Konka Entered into Strategic Cooperation with South New Media 186
2018 Beijing International Cultural and Creative Products Expo Opened 186
Youdao Ledu Launched "Ten Thousand Books Project" 187
Douyin Announced Participation in Apple Music Partner Program 187
New Product Released by Founder Empowers Integrated Publishing 187
Migu Teamed Up with Weibo to Lay Out the Entertainment Industry 187
Distribution Groups of Beijing and Inner Mongolia Jointly Seeked Development of Cultural Industry 187
Zhejiang Publishing Media Co., Ltd. Established 188
CCTV's First Regional Headquarter Established 188
China's First Provincial TV 4K UHD Channel Launched 188
Giant Interactive Group Inc. Entered the Virtual Idol Market with Its First Virtual Anchor on the Way 189
China Literature Strategically Invested in South Korean Network Literature Company Munpia 189
Key Projects Amounting to RMB 6.8 Billion Signed at the 13th China Beijing International Cultural & Creative Industry Expo 190
"China Film Cinema" Hit CityTV in the US 191
Global Royalty Income in 2017 Reached EUR 9.6 Billion, with Chinese Market Showing Great Potential 191
Inner Mongolia Publishing Group Joined Hands with China Unicom to Promote "Internet + Publishing" 192
ByteDance Reached Copyright Cooperation Agreement with NBA in Short Video 192
2018 China Internet Audiovisual Development Research Report Released 192
Qutoutiao: Digging Content Copyright Value from "Sinking Markets" 193
Beijing's Copyright Industry Saw a 9.2% Increase in Added Value over the Previous Year in 2017 193
Projects Selected for the First "National Music Industry Excellent Project Award Scheme" Announced 193
A Total of 78 Original Animation Projects Won Sponsorship 193

Xinhuanet Launched Video Strategy 194

Copyright Information of Taiwan, Hong Kong S. A. R, and Macau S. A. R. 195
Guangdong-Macau Cooperation Agreement on Intellectual Property Rights Protection Signed in Guangzhou 195
Macau Intellectual Property Research Center Inaugurated 195
Guangdong-Hong Kong Copyright Industry Enterprises Exchange Held in Hong Kong 195
Guangdong-Hong Kong Intellectual Property and the Development of Small-Medium Enterprises Seminar Held in Foshan 196
Macau International Intellectual Property Symposium 2018 Held in Macau 196
The 14th Cross-Strait Book Fair Held in Taipei 196
The 17th Meeting of Guangdong and Hong Kong Intellectual Property Special Cooperative Team Held in Guangzhou 197
Guangxi Book Fair Opened in Taipei 197
Guangdong-Hong Kong-Macau Greater Bay Area Intellectual Property Legal Union Officially Founded 198
"Guangdong-Hong Kong-Macau Greater Bay Area Intellectual Property Cooperation and Opportunity" Sub-Forum Held in Hong Kong 199
Turnover on the First Guangdong-Hong Kong-Macao Greater Bay Area Intellectual Property Auction Exceeded RMB 6 Million 199
Hong Kong Released the Main Results of "Manpower Statistics Research on Intellectual Property Trade and Management" 199

Copyright-Related Industries and Copyright Trade

Economic Contribution of China's Copyright Industry in 2017
Chinese Academy of Press and Publication 203
2019 China Online Copyright Industry Development Report
National Copyright Administration of China Online Copyright Industry Research Base 209
2018 Press and Publication Industry Analysis Report
National Press and Publication Bureau 227
2018－2019 Annual Report on China's Digital Publishing Industry
China Digital Publishing Industry Annual Report Research Group 251
2018 China Radio and Television Industry Development Report
Radio, Film and Video Development and Research Center of National Radio and Television Administration 267
2018 Development Report on China's Film Industry
Film and Art Center of China Federation of Literary and Art Circles 272
2018 Development Report on China's Animation Industry Niu Xingzhen 288
2018 Development Survey of China's Software Industry
Department of Informatization and Software Services, Ministry of Industry and Information Technology 298
2018 Development Report on China's Internet Game Industry Liao Xuhua 306

Selected Compilation of Typical Cases

Typical Cases of National Copyright Judicial Protection in 2018 319

Top 10 Cases of Cracking Down Against Infringement and Piracy in 2018 331

Typical Cases of Local Copyright Judicial Protection in 2018 334
- Beijing Municipality 334
- Hebei Province 335
- Heilongjiang Province 336
- Shanghai Municipality 337
- Jiangsu Province 338
- Zhejiang Province 341
- Anhui Province 343
- Fujian Province 344
- Henan Province 346
- Hubei Province 347
- Guangdong Province 347
- Guangxi Zhuang Autonomous Region 348
- Hainan Province 348
- Shaanxi Province 349

Local Copyright Enforcement Cases in 2018 350
- Tianjin Municipality 350
- Hebei Province 350
- Inner Mongolia Autonomous Region 352
- Liaoning Province 352
- Jilin Province 352
- Shanghai Municipality 353
- Jiangsu Province 358
- Anhui Province 360
- Jiangxi Province 360
- Shandong Province 362
- Hubei Province 364
- Hunan Province 365
- Guangdong Province 365
- Sichuan Province 367
- Shaanxi Province 368
- Qinghai Province 370

Laws, Regulations and Regulatory Documents

E-Commerce Law of the People's Republic of China 373

Notice on Printing and Distributing *Report on Promoting the Work of Adopting Licensed Software in 2017* and *Plan of Promoting the Work of Adopting Licensed Software in 2018*
(Guo Ban Han [2018] No. 4) 380
Decision of National Copyright Administration of China on Rewarding Investigation of Major Cases of Infringement and Piracy in 2017
(Guo Ban Han [2018] No. 36) 384
Notice on the State of Copyright Registration in 2017 by General Office of National Copyright Administration of China
(Guo Ban Ban Fa [2018] No. 3) 396
Notice on Copyright Promotion Activities of National Intellectual Property Publicity Week in 2018
(Guo Ban Ban Fa [2018] No. 4) 397
Notice on Implementing "Sword Net 2018" Special Action to Crack Down on Network Infringement and Piracy by National Copyright Administration of China, etc.
(Guo Ban Fa Dian [2018] No. 1) 398

Annual Announcement

2018 Annual Report on China Internet Copyright Protection 403
2018 Winners of "The WIPO-NCAC Copyright Awards" 410
2018 Credited Institutions and Individuals in Investigating Infringement and Piracy Cases 411
2018 Top 10 Events of Copyright in China 422
2018 Winners of (the 10th) National College Students' Composition Contest on Copyright 424
2018 CPCC Top 10 Chinese Copyright Holders 428
2018 China Copyright Annual Conference's Awarding List 429

Theoretical Research

Review of 2018 China's Copyright Law Research Xiang Bo, Shi Ruoqi 433

2018 Research on Hot Issues of Copyright 444
On the Ruling of Copyright Law over the Misuse of Technological Measures Wang Qian 444
Institutional Innovation in China's Copyright Legislation Xiong Qi 453
Copyright Collective Management Organizations: Their Market Functions, Roles arrangement and the Pricing Issue Xiang Bo 463
On the Protection of AI-Generated Results by Copyright Law—The Justification of the Data Processor's Rights as Neighboring Rights Tao Qian 469
The "Cinematographic Work" Viewed from the Perspective of the Functionalistic Interpretive Theory—Also a Review of the Second-Instance Sentence on the IFENG. COM Case Wan Yong 475

On the Path Selection that Applies to the Expanded Fair Use of Copyright Liu Yuhui 482
The Category of Broadcasting Rights in China Viewed from the Perspective of Institutional Evolution Liu Yinliang 487
On the Imputation of Criminal Liability in Cases of Copyright Infringement in the Network Environment—Centering on the Criminal Liability of the On-Line Service Provider Ouyang Benqi 492
The Determination of Faults in Indirect Copyright Infringements by Video-Sharing Websites Ma Yide 500

Introduction of Copyright Books in 2018 511

Statistics

China Copyright Statistics in 2018 523
Statistics of Nationwide Voluntary Works Registration in 2018 (Categorized by Genre) 523
Statistics of Nationwide Copyright Contract Registration in 2018 524
Statistics of Nationwide Copyright Law Enforcement in 2018 525
Summary Table of Copyright Exporters to China in 2018 525
Summary Table of Copyright Importers from China in 2018 526

China Press and Publication Statistics in 2018 527
Total Numbers of Books Published in China in 2018 by Region 527
Numbers of Newspapers Published in China in 2018 by Administrative Level 528
Varieties, Print Runs, Numbers of Printed Sheets and Total Prices of Journals Published in China in 2018 by Region (1) 530
Varieties, Print Runs, Numbers of Printed Sheets and Total Prices of Journals Published in China in 2018 by Region (2) 532
Varieties, Quantities and Circulations of Electronic Publications Published in China in 2018 by Region (Categorized by Carrier) 534
Varieties, Quantities and Circulations of Audio Products Published in China in 2018 by Region (Categorized by Carrier) 536
Varieties, Quantities and Circulations of Video Products Published in China in 2018 by Region (Categorized by Carrier) 538
Nationwide Purchases, Sales and Stocks of Publications of the Xinhua Bookstore System and Publisher-Owned Distributors in 2018 540
Nationwide Import and Export of Books, Journals and Newspapers in 2018 541
Nationwide Import and Export of Audio-Video, Electronic and Digital Publications in 2018 541

China Broadcast, Film and Television Industry Statistics in 2018 542
Table of Major Indicators of National Broadcast, Film and Television Development in 2018 (1) 542
Table of Major Indicators of National Broadcast, Film and Television Development in 2018 (2) 544

China Software Industry Statistics in 2018 546

Table of Business Incomes of the Software and IT Service Industry by Province, Autonomous Region and Municipality in 2018 546

Table of Major Economic Indicators of the Software and IT Service Industry in 2018 547

Directory

Copyright Administrative Departments 551

Copyright Public Service Institutions 553

Copyright Associations 554

Copyright Collective Management Organizations 557

Copyright Related Trade Associations 558

Copyright Agencies 558

National-Level Copyright Exchange Institutions 559

Intellectual Property Teaching and Research Institutes 561

Appendix：International Copyright News

Overview 567

Copyright System in the Information Age Safeguards the Development of the Market—Review of the Development of International Copyright Laws in 2018 Guo He，Bai Zhihui 567

International Copyright News in 2018 573

Legislation and Administration 573

Council of the European Union Officially Approved the Marrakesh Treaty 573

The Copyright Law of Japan Substantially Revised 573

Japan's New Law Facilitates the Reform Towards Educational Informationalization：Permission of the Rights Holder Waived for the Use of Electronic Textbooks 574

Copyright Rules of the EU May Not Apply in Post-Brexit Britain 575

Protecting Comics from Copyright Infringement by Severing the Link，the Emergency Measure Taken by the Government Opposed for Suspected Breach of Constitution 575

The Formulation of the Protection of Broadcasts and Broadcasting Organizations Treaty Under Way 576

South Korea Expanded the Category of Performing Rights 577

Controversy in South Korea's Revision of the Copyright Law：Whether the Publisher's Rights in format Design Should Be Recognized 578

New Regulations of USMCA on the Standard of Copyright Law Enforcement 579

The European Parliament Passed the Controversial Directive on Copyright in the Digital Single Market 580

The Music Modernization Act of the US Deepens the Reform of Music Licensing System 580

The US Issued the Marrakesh Treaty Implementation Act 581

Copyright Amendment Bill 2018 Passed by the Parliament of Australia 583
The New Amendment to the Spanish Intellectual Property Law Passed by the Spanish Parliament 584
The Draft Directive on Copyright in the Digital Single Market Raised a Wave of Opposition in Europe 584

Judicial Cases 585
H&M Entangled in Controversy over Copyright Infringement of Graffiti 585
South Korea: Pinning Authorship on Anyone But the Authors Incurs Criminal Liability 586
Grumpy Cat Won RMB 4,540,000 in Copyright Infringement Lawsuit 586
Court in America: Deep-Linking Is Not Exempt from Copyright Infringement 587
Complying with the Court's Order, Free E-Book Website "Project Gutenberg" Blocked Access from Germany 588
Oracle Beat Google in the Copyright Case 589
Information of the Operator of Piracy Website Mangamura.org Made Public 589
The American Company ABS Entertainment Sued CBS: Digitally Remastering Sound Recording Does Not Qualify for Independent Copyright Protection 590
The New Ruling of the European Court of Justice Reinterpretes "Communication to the Public" 590
YouTube Copyright Conflict Referred to the European Court of Justice by Germany's Federal Court of Justice 591
Japan Court: Kumu Hula Can Be Copyrighted 592
Burden of Proof in Illegal File Sharing Clarified by Ruling of the European Court of Justice 592
Spotify and Wixen Settled the Multi-Billion Lawsuit 593
Taste Cannot Be Subject to Copyright, Ruled the European Court of Justice 593

Industry News 594
New Regulation on the Copyright in Kumamon the Japanese Mascot Officially in Effect 594
European Commission Issued Recommendations to Tackle Illegal Content Online 595
Copyright Provisions in CPTPP Remain Positively Significant 595
Egypt Launched Data Forensic Lab to Improve IPR Protection and Enforcement 596
CISAC: Copyright Safe Harbor Disrupts the Market of Artistic Creation 596
Japan: Using Public Domain Materials in the Sales of Products Risks Infringement on Personality Rights 597
No-Deal Brexit Could See Brits Face Spotify and Netflix Ban Abroad 598
Japan Demands Increased Music Royalties from Overseas Films 598
Musicians Barred Donald Trump from Playing Their Music at His Events 598
YouTube Bans Proud Boys Founder for Copyright Infringement 599
Copyright Industries in the US Economy: The 2018 Report Published 600

Index

Index 601

特载

TE ZAI

关于加强知识产权审判领域改革创新若干问题的意见

中共中央办公厅　国务院办公厅

知识产权保护是激励创新的基本手段，是创新原动力的基本保障，是国际竞争力的核心要素。人民法院知识产权审判工作，事关创新驱动发展战略实施，事关经济社会文化发展繁荣，事关国内国际两个大局，对于建设知识产权强国和世界科技强国具有重要意义。为深入贯彻实施创新驱动发展战略和国家知识产权战略，强化知识产权创造、保护、运用，破解制约知识产权审判发展的体制机制障碍，充分发挥知识产权审判激励和保护创新、促进科技进步和社会发展的职能作用，提出以下意见。

一、总体要求

（一）指导思想

全面贯彻落实党的十九大精神，以习近平新时代中国特色社会主义思想为指导，牢固树立"四个意识"，按照统筹推进"五位一体"总体布局和协调推进"四个全面"战略布局要求，紧紧围绕"努力让人民群众在每一个司法案件中感受到公平正义"目标，坚持司法为民、公正司法，不断深化知识产权审判领域改革，充分发挥知识产权司法保护主导作用，树立保护知识产权就是保护创新的理念，优化科技创新法治环境，推动实施创新驱动发展战略，为实现"两个一百年"奋斗目标和建设知识产权强国、世界科技强国提供有力司法保障。

（二）基本原则

——坚持高点定位。立足国家战略层面，紧紧围绕党和国家发展大局，积极适应国际形势新变化，加强事关知识产权审判长远发展的全局性、体制性、根本性问题的顶层设计，改革完善知识产权司法保护体制机制。

——坚持问题导向。紧扣人民群众司法需求，针对影响和制约知识产权审判发展的关键领域和薄弱环节，研究对策措施，着力破解难题、补齐短板，进一步提升知识产权司法保护水平。

——坚持改革创新。解放思想，实事求是，遵循审判规律，以创新的方法激励创新，以创新的方式保护创新，以改革的思维解决知识产权审判领域改革中面临的问题和困难，使改革创新成为知识产权审判持续健康发展的动力源泉。

——坚持开放发展。既立足我国国情，又尊重国际规则，借鉴国际上知识产权司法保护的成功经验，积极构建中国特色知识产权司法保护新模式，不断增强我国在知识产权国际治理规则中的引领力。

（三）改革目标

以完善知识产权诉讼制度为基础，以加强知识产权法院体系建设为重点，以加强知识产权审判队伍建设为保障，不断提高知识产权审判质量效率，加大知识产权司法保护力度，有效遏制侵犯知识产权行为，进一步提升知识产权领域司法公信力和国际影响力，加快推进知识产权审判体系和审判能力向现代化迈进。

二、完善知识产权诉讼制度

（一）建立符合知识产权案件特点的诉讼证据规则

根据知识产权无形性、时间性和地域性等特点，完善证据保全制度，发挥专家辅助人作用，适当加大人民法院依职权调查取证力度，建立激励当事人积极、主动提供证据的诉讼机制。通过多种方式充分发挥公证在知识产权案件中固定证据的作用。加强知识产权领域的诉讼诚信体系建设，探索建立证据披露、证据妨碍排除等规则，合理分配举证责任，适当减轻权利人举证负担，着力破解知识产权权利人“举证难”问题。

（二）建立体现知识产权价值的侵权损害赔偿制度

1. 坚持知识产权创造价值、权利人理应享有利益回报的价值导向。充分发挥社会组织、中介机构在知识产权价值评估中的作用，建立以尊重知识产权、鼓励创新运用为导向，以实现知识产权市场价值为指引，以补偿为主、惩罚为辅的侵权损害司法认定机制，着力破解知识产权侵权诉讼“赔偿低”问题。

2. 加大知识产权侵权违法行为惩治力度，降低维权成本。对于具有重复侵权、恶意侵权以及其他严重侵权情节的，依法加大赔偿力度，提高赔偿数额，由败诉方承担维权成本，让侵权者付出沉重代价，有效遏制和威慑侵犯知识产权行为。努力营造不敢侵权、不愿侵权的法律氛围，实现向知识产权严格保护的历史性转变。

（三）推进符合知识产权诉讼规律的裁判方式改革

进一步发挥知识产权司法保护的主导作用，依法加强对知识产权行政行为的司法审查，促进知识产权行政执法标准与司法裁判标准的统一。加强司法大数据的研究应用，完善知识产权案例指导制度，改进裁判方式，推进知识产权案件繁简分流，切实增强知识产权司法救济的便民性和时效性，着力破解知识产权案件审理“周期长”问题。

三、加强知识产权法院体系建设

（一）建立健全知识产权专门化审判体系

1. 按照《国家知识产权战略纲要》要求，从推动建成知识产权强国和世界科技强国的战略高度，认真总结知识产权审判基本规律和经验，加强现状分析和对国际趋势的研判，研究建立国家层面知识产权案件上诉审理机制，实现有关知识产权案件审理专门化、管辖集中化、程序集约化和人员专业化，从根本上解决知识产权裁判尺度不统一、诉讼程序复杂等制约科技创新的体制性难题。

2. 全面总结北京、上海、广州知识产权法院设立、运行、建设、发展的经验，提出可复制、可推广的意见，依照法定程序实施；进一步健全符合知识产权司法保护规律的专门化审判体系，有效满足科技创新对知识产权专门化审判的司法需求。

（二）探索跨地区知识产权案件异地审理机制

充分整合京津冀三地法院审判优势资源，探索北京知识产权法院集中管辖京津冀地区技术类知识产权案件，充分发挥知识产权专门化审判在推动京津冀创新驱动发展方面的独特作用，为京津冀形成协调创新共同体、实现经济转型和科学发展提供有力司法支持。

（三）完善知识产权法院人财物保障制度

1. 建立分类管理、定向培养、跟踪考核、适时调整相结合的知识产权法院法官员额动态调整机制。根据案件的受理数量、增长趋势、难易程度等，动态调整法官员额，化解人案矛盾，提升司法效率。

2. 根据知识产权法院隶属关系和工作实际，完善经费保障机制，明确知识产权法院购买社会服务的依据，促进知识产权法院财务工作规范化。

四、加强知识产权审判队伍建设

（一）加大知识产权审判人才培养选拔力度

1. 在保持知识产权审判队伍稳定的前提下，建立知识产权法院之间、知识产权专门审判机构之间、上下级法院之间形式多样的人员交流机制，有计划地选派综合素质高、专业能力强、有培养潜力的知识产权法官到有关党政机关等任职、挂职，可以从立法工作者、律师、法学专家中公开选拔知识产权法官，进一步激发知识产权审判队伍的积极性、主动性和创造性。

2. 增强培训的针对性和有效性，提高知识产权审判队伍的思想政治素质、职业素养和专业水平，加强对外交流与合作，努力造就一批政治坚定、顾全大局、精通法律、熟悉技术并具有国际视野的知识产权审判人才。

（二）加强技术调查官队伍建设

探索在编制内按照聘任等方式选任、管理技术调查官，细化选任条件、任职类型、职责范围、管理模式和培养机制，规范技术审查意见的采信机制，充分发挥技术调查官对有效查明技术事实、提高知识产权审判质量效率的积极作用，增强技术事实认定的中立性、客观性和科学性。

五、加强组织领导

（一）加强组织实施

有关地区和部门要高度重视人民法院知识产权审判工作，将其作为推进全面深化改革、全面依法治国和深入贯彻实施创新驱动发展战略、国家知识产权战略的重要内容，切实加强组织领导。要抓紧制定实施细则，明确责任部门，确定时间表、路线图，确保各项工作要求及时有效落实。

（二）强化工作保障

有关地区和部门要认真贯彻落实党中央关于充分发挥知识产权司法保护主导作用的要求，统筹调配人民法院现有司法资源和相关审判力量，在经费保障、物资装备等方面做好对人民法院知识产权审判工作的保障和支持，大力推进知识产权审判队伍正规化、专业化、职业化、国际化建设。

（三）完善相关法律规定

积极推进人民法院组织法、专利法、著作权法、有关诉讼法等相关法律的修订工作，研究制定符合知识产权审判规律的特别程序法，加强知识产权案件专门审判组织、诉讼管辖、证据规则、审理程序和裁判方式的法律化、制度化。

2019 年深入实施国家知识产权战略　加快建设知识产权强国推进计划

国务院知识产权战略实施工作部际联席会议办公室

一、深化知识产权领域改革

（一）推进知识产权管理体制机制改革

1. 推进全面创新改革试验区知识产权保护体制机制改革成果复制推广。（发展改革委、科技部、公安部、知识产权局负责）

2. 探索建立地理标志统一认定制度，优化地理标志登记注册和行政裁决程序。（知识产权局负责）

3. 整合专利、商标和地理标志政策、项目和平台，推动重大政策互联互通，统一服务窗口和办事流程，推动实现知识产权业务申请“一网通办”。（知识产权局负责）

4. 推进知识产权军民融合试点工作，在部分省市设置国防专利受理代办点，遴选一批机构从事国防专利代理业务，开展军民知识产权转化运用特色服务，建立国防知识产权军地协调保护中心。（中央军委装备发展部、知识产权局、国防科工局负责）

（二）改革完善知识产权重大政策

5. 出台知识产权强企建设工作方案，全面落实知识产权服务民营企业创新发展的若干措施。（知识产权局负责）

6. 研究出台中央企业知识产权工作指导意见。（国资委、知识产权局负责）

7. 推动制定知识产权（专利）密集型产业统计分类国家标准。（统计局、知识产权局负责）

8. 制定促进知识产权服务业发展的政策措施，培育一批品牌服务机构。继续扶持一批知识产权创业创新基地。（知识产权局负责）

9. 编制《创新过程知识产权管理》国家标准草案。（知识产权局负责）

10. 加强国家科技计划全流程的知识产权管理，研究推动科技创新知识产权工作发展新举措。（科技部负责）

11. 修订出台卫生健康领域科技计划知识产权管理办法。（卫生健康委负责）

12. 推动出台《关于加强新形势下国防知识产权工作的意见》。（中央军委装备发展部、财政部、国防科工局负责）

13. 按程序报批《国防专利定密解密工作规程》《军用计算机软件著作权登记工作暂行规则》，完成《国防专利行政执法办法》《国防专利代理管理办法》起草工作。（中央军委装备发展部、知识产权局、中央宣传部、国防科工局负责）

（三）深化知识产权“放管服”改革

14. 研究制定进一步深化知识产权领域“放管服”改革的指导意见。（知识产权局负责）

15. 落实研发费用税前加计扣除政策。（财政部、税务总局、科技部负责）

16. 推动知识产权认证体系建设。（市场监管总局、知识产权局负责）

17. 对专利商标代理机构实施“双随机、一公开”监管。（知识产权局、市场监管总局负责）

18. 依法对有关著作权集体管理组织和涉外著作权认证机构代表处加强监管。（中央宣传

部负责）

19. 开展地理标志产品专用标志审核批准改革试点。开通地理标志电子申请系统。推进地理标志产品保护示范区建设。（知识产权局负责）

二、加大知识产权保护力度

（一）完善法律法规规章

20. 配合做好《专利法修正案（草案）》审议工作，推进《专利法实施细则》修改，修订《专利审查指南》《专利代理管理办法》，制定《专利代理师资格考试办法》。（市场监管总局、知识产权局负责）

21. 推进《商标法》第四次修改，出台《关于规范商标申请注册行为的若干规定》《商标代理监管暂行办法》《商标电子申请和电子送达规定》，推进制定《官方标志备案保护办法》。（市场监管总局、知识产权局负责）

22. 配合做好《著作权法》修订工作。（中央宣传部、广电总局负责）

23. 推进有关不正当竞争行为配套规章的制修订工作。发布《关于知识产权领域的反垄断指南》。（市场监管总局负责）

24. 推进《人类遗传资源管理条例》立法进程，组织编制配套实施细则。（科技部、司法部按职责分别负责）

25. 修改完善《生物遗传资源获取与惠益分享管理条例（草案）》，推动立法进程。（生态环境部负责）

26. 推进《植物新品种保护条例》及其实施细则的修订。（农业农村部、林草局、知识产权局负责）

27. 推动《国防专利条例》修订工作。（中央军委装备发展部、国防科工局、知识产权局负责）

28. 推进《最高人民法院关于审理专利授权确权行政案件若干问题的规定（一）》《最高人民法院关于知识产权民事诉讼证据规则的若干规定》《最高人民法院关于技术调查官参与诉讼活动的若干规定》等司法解释的起草制定工作。（高法院负责）

（二）加强保护长效机制建设

29. 制定出台新时代强化知识产权保护政策文件。加强知识产权基础性法律制度和新领域新业态创新成果知识产权保护研究。（知识产权局牵头负责）

30. 推动知识产权保护体系建设，探索建立相应运行机制和工作平台，健全严保护、大保护、快保护、同保护工作体系。继续推进知识产权保护中心建设布局，开展建立国家知识产权保护中心的可行性研究。（知识产权局负责）

31. 深入推进“互联网＋”知识产权保护。鼓励电商平台为执法办案提供数据信息，发挥权利人企业在侵权调查和商品鉴别、鉴定中的作用。（知识产权局、市场监管总局、中央宣传部按职责分别负责）

32. 推动知识产权纠纷仲裁、调解工作开展，完善知识产权仲裁、调解工作规程。支持行业协会和业内专家开展知识产权纠纷化解工作，指导行业组织制定行业规范。支持律师事务所发展知识产权业务，加强知识产权领域律师调解工作。加强知识产权公证服务，遴选第二批知识产权公证服务示范机构。（知识产权局、司法部、市场监管总局、贸促会负责）

33. 加快推进知识产权诚信体系建设，严格实施《关于对知识产权（专利）领域严重失信主体开展联合惩戒的合作备忘录》，针对知识产权（专利）领域严重失信主体开展联合惩戒工作。规范互联网市场竞争秩序，建立健全企业主体信息库和企业违法不良记录数据库为核心的基础数据库。进一步优化国家企业信用信息公示系统。（发展改革委、人民银行、知识产权局、工业和信息化部、市场监管总局负责）

34. 推动有条件的版权园区、基地设立版权维权工作站，建立创新创业人才版权维权绿色

通道。（中央宣传部负责）

35. 持续推进全国知识产权保护社会满意度调查，探索开展中国企业海外知识产权保护满意度调查。（知识产权局、中央政法委负责）

36. 提高非物质文化遗产传承人的知识产权保护意识和能力，加强传统工艺相关资源的挖掘整理，支持各地开展非物质文化遗产知识产权保护研究。（文化和旅游部负责）

37. 进一步健全在新药创制等科技重大专项管理工作中的知识产权保护长效工作机制。（卫生健康委、科技部负责）

38. 完善软件正版化工作机制，推进党政机关督查全覆盖，加强企事业单位督查。完善国家版权监管平台，加强主动监管，加快“互联网＋”与版权监管的深度融合。扩大软件协议供货招标范围和软件联合采购范围，构建全国统一的正版软件采购网，推动软件正版化工作开展。（中央宣传部、国管局按职责分别负责）

39. 加快建设中医药传统知识保护数据库，发布保护名录，建立保护档案。推进中医药传统知识保护条例立法进程。开展古代经典名方产品知识产权保护研究。（中医药局负责）

40. 编制印发年度中国知识产权保护状况白皮书，发布专利、商标、版权等行政执法典型案例和专利复审、打击侵权盗版年度十大案件，加大知识产权保护成效宣传力度。（知识产权局、市场监管总局、中央宣传部按职责分别负责）

（三）强化知识产权行政保护

41. 组织开展针对商标、专利、地理标志等领域侵权假冒问题的专项执法行动，加强对重点区域、重点产品的整治。开展网络市场监管专项行动，继续开展反不正当竞争专项执法行动。加强重大案件的督查督办和跨部门跨区域的执法协作。推进打击侵权假冒行政执法与刑事司法衔接。指导推进电子商务、大型展会等领域专项整治。（市场监管总局、知识产权局负责）

42. 研究制定完善商标权、专利权侵权判断标准。制定出台《集成电路布图设计审查与执法指南》。实施《专利标识标注不规范案件办理指南（试行）》。开展商标专利执法检验、鉴定等相关标准及纠纷证据认定方法和标准研究工作。探索开展商标专利执法检验、鉴定地方试点工作。（知识产权局负责）

43. 开展打击网络侵权盗版“剑网 2019”专项行动。（中央宣传部、中央网信办、工业和信息化部、公安部负责）

44. 严厉打击侵犯知识产权犯罪，将涉外、民生和公共安全案件作为主攻方向，围绕重大恶性案件组织专案打击行动。（公安部负责）

45. 组织开展打击侵犯林业植物新品种权专项行动。（林草局负责）

46. 继续开展出口知识产权优势企业知识产权保护“龙腾”行动，继续加强外商投资企业知识产权保护工作。（海关总署负责）

47. 依法打击寄递企业违规收寄侵犯知识产权物品的行为。（邮政局负责）

（四）加强知识产权司法保护

48. 完善案件管辖、证据规则、审理方式、法律适用等知识产权诉讼制度，加强知识产权法院建设。（高法院负责）

49. 加强对重大敏感、涉民族品牌、涉外侵犯知识产权案件批捕、起诉工作指导，对严重侵犯科技创新和知识产权的犯罪案件予以挂牌督办。加强对知识产权领域新类型案件的研究和办案指导，发布 2018 年检察机关保护知识产权十大典型案例。针对知识产权犯罪案件中发现的薄弱环节、管理漏洞等，及时发出检察建议，开展个案预防和行业预防。在全国检察机关推行建立专门的知识产权犯罪案件办案组，培养一批专家型知识产权检察人才。（高检院负责）

三、促进知识产权创造运用

（一）提高知识产权审查质量和效率

50. 健全专利审查质量保障体系和业务指导体系，完善“双监督、双评价”质量管理，协

同运用优先审查、集中审查、专利审查高速路等多种审查模式。（知识产权局负责）

51. 开展“商标审查质量提升年”行动，完善商标审查质量管理，优化审查质量评价指标体系。全面深化商标注册便利化改革，上线图形商标智能检索系统，推进业务电子化，提高商标信息化基础支撑能力和信息安全水平。（知识产权局负责）

52. 修订《农业植物品种权申请审查指南》。初步建立我国植物新品种保护质量管理制度，重点开展测试机构考核评估和飞行检查。探索建立新技术辅助品种权审查机制。（农业农村部负责）

（二）强化知识产权创造质量导向

53. 严厉打击非正常专利申请和商标囤积、恶意注册行为，实施非正常申请筛查监管前置，依法依规予以处理。开展闲置商标摸排工作，探索制定规制措施。（知识产权局负责）

54. 研究制定推动知识产权高质量发展的年度工作指引，设置区域差异化的评价指标，分类引导地方知识产权事业发展。（知识产权局负责）

55. 分类制定以科技创新质量和贡献为导向的国家科学技术奖评审标准和评价指标体系，加大对重大科技创新成果的奖励力度。（科技部负责）

56. 完善中央企业专利评价体系，逐步引导企业专利工作重点由数量向质量转变。（国资委负责）

（三）加强知识产权综合运用

57. 统筹推进专利导航、知识产权区域布局和分析评议工作，大力推进国家知识产权试点示范园区建设。（知识产权局负责）

58. 做好各类知识产权运营平台建设布局，加快重点城市知识产权运营服务体系建设。研究制定促进知识产权质押融资业务良性发展的政策，完善知识产权质押融资风险补偿及分担机制，推动专利商标混合质押，建立知识产权质押融资统计制度。鼓励保险机构开发设计满足企业需求的专利保险产品。（知识产权局、财政部、人民银行、银保监会按职责分别负责）

59. 鼓励海南自由贸易试验区探索知识产权证券化，鼓励雄安新区开展知识产权证券化融资。（证监会、知识产权局负责）

60. 做好中国国际进口博览会知识产权相关工作，举办第十五届中国（无锡）国际设计博览会。（商务部、科技部、知识产权局、贸促会负责）

61. 鼓励信托公司综合运用股权、债权、投贷联动、产业基金、知识产权信托等方式开展知识产权投融资业务。鼓励融资担保公司开发适合知识产权的信用担保产品，加大对小微企业知识产权融资的支持力度。（银保监会、知识产权局负责）

62. 开展全国版权创新发展基地创建工作。开展中国版权产业经济贡献专题研究。（中央宣传部负责）

63. 实施地理标志运用促进工程，大力开展地理标志精准扶贫、商标品牌富农工作。（知识产权局负责）

64. 推进林业知识产权试点示范建设，组织实施林业知识产权转化运用项目。（林草局负责）

65. 加强制造业重点领域知识产权分析评估，编制发布2018年国防科技工业专利统计分析报告。（工业和信息化部、国防科工局按职责分别负责）

66. 推进实施中小企业知识产权战略推进工程。（知识产权局、工业和信息化部负责）

（四）促进知识产权转移转化

67. 做好企业、高校、科研组织、专利代理机构贯标工作。（知识产权局负责）

68. 继续实施国家科技成果转化引导基金，设立一批创业投资子基金。启动“科技成果转化贷款风险补偿试点”。（科技部、财政部负责）

69. 支持工业和信息化部部属高校、科研院所等加强技术转移专业机构建设，支持地方工业和信息化主管部门开展知识产权成果应用推广。（工业和信息化部负责）

70. 编制“军转民”“民参军”目录，组织第四届中国军民两用技术创新应用大赛。（工业和信息化部、财政部、国防科工局、中央军委装备发展部负责）

71. 研究国防科技成果转化政策措施，实施军工技术推广专项奖励性后补助，编制印发《国防科技工业知识产权转化目录（第五批）》。（国防科工局、知识产权局负责）

72. 开展农产品地理标志品牌价值评价工作。筹备第十七届中国国际农产品交易会农产品地理标志专展和推介会。（知识产权局、农业农村部负责）

73. 推进中科院所属单位贯标工作，培育一批示范单位。探索适合中科院的知识产权全过程管理模式。加强中科院知识产权运营管理中心建设。（中科院、知识产权局负责）

（五）完善知识产权信息服务

74. 整合基础数据，推动知识产权数据免费或低成本开放。推进开放共享的国家知识产权大数据中心和知识产权信息公共服务平台立项，研究制定全国知识产权信息公共服务体系建设方案。制定知识产权信息公共服务年度报告。（知识产权局负责）

75. 推进高校国家知识产权信息服务中心建设，完善知识产权信息公共服务网络，提升高校创新能力。（知识产权局、教育部负责）

76. 建立全国著作权登记信息查询公示系统，完善著作权登记数据统计、报送和公示制度，适时发布 2018 年全国著作权登记情况的通报。（中央宣传部负责）

77. 推进林业植物新品种网站平台升级，简化申请和受理程序，提高林业植物新品种申请效率。（林草局负责）

78. 完善国防知识产权信息平台及资源，完成国防专利网上查询、国防专利电子申请等应用系统开发和部署，实时向公众发布国防专利解密信息，运行完善国防科技工业领域知识产权信息系统，支撑国防科技工业知识产权信息报送、信息服务等工作。（中央军委装备发展部、国防科工局负责）

79. 加强中科院知识产权信息化服务平台建设，继续推行知识产权专员制度，逐步建立知识产权专员服务网络。（中科院负责）

80. 建设国外专利信息在线共享平台，提供科技公共服务产品。（中国科协负责）

四、深化知识产权国际交流合作

（一）提升知识产权国际合作水平

81. 积极参与世界知识产权组织、世界贸易组织等多边框架下的全球治理和规则制定，继续大力推广马德里商标国际注册体系和专利合作条约的运用，继续推动《外观设计法条约》外交大会尽早召开，做好加入外观设计国际注册海牙协定相关准备工作。推动《视听表演北京条约》早日生效，启动批准《马拉喀什条约》程序。积极参与并推动保护广播组织条约制定磋商进程。（知识产权局、商务部、外交部、中央宣传部、广电总局负责）

82. 积极推动二十国集团、金砖国家、亚太经合组织、共建“一带一路”国家知识产权合作。（商务部、知识产权局、外交部、中央宣传部按职责分别负责）

83. 在中欧知识产权合作项目项下加强与欧方合作，积极推进中欧地理标志协定谈判。积极推进区域全面经济伙伴关系协定、中日韩、中挪（威）、中摩（尔多瓦）等自贸区知识产权章节的谈判。（商务部、知识产权局、中央宣传部按职责分别负责）

84. 与世界知识产权组织签署技术创新支持中心合作文件，扩大技术创新支持中心建设试点。（知识产权局负责）

85. 落实“一带一路”知识产权高级别会议成果，推动沿线国家对我国专利审查结果认可和登记生效。（知识产权局负责）

86. 继续开展“中国政府知识产权奖学金”项目，支持“一带一路”沿线国家能力建设。（知识产权局、教育部负责）

87. 积极履行《生物多样性公约》《名古屋遗传资源议定书》，推进生物遗传资源获取与惠

益分享信息交换平台建设，加强生物遗传资源跨境转移和利用的追踪监测。（生态环境部、农业农村部、林草局、知识产权局负责）

88. 继续参与海牙国际私法会议《承认和执行外国民商事判决公约》涉及的知识产权谈判。（外交部、中央宣传部、高法院、知识产权局负责）

89. 深入推进多双边国际执法合作，积极参与世界海关组织、国际刑警组织、世界知识产权组织等有关国际组织的知识产权国际事务。（公安部、海关总署、知识产权局按职责分别负责）

（二）加强海外风险防控

90. 探索在重要国际展会上设立中国企业知识产权服务站。研究建立海外知识产权维权援助机制，推动建设国家层面的海外知识产权纠纷应对指导中心。建立海外知识产权问题及案件信息提交平台，推动形成海外知识产权维权援助服务网。推动成立中国企业知识产权海外维权联盟，设立维权互助基金。继续开展面向贸促机构和外向型企业的知识产权培训。（商务部、知识产权局、贸促会按职责分别负责）

91. 做好经贸领域的知识产权工作。充分利用现有多双边知识产权对话合作机制，加强知识产权合作交流，推动化解贸易摩擦。继续做好中美经贸磋商工作，推进知识产权相关议题的解决。加强对知识产权国际领域最新动态和重大知识产权案件的跟踪研判，完善知识产权风险预警反馈机制，发布重点产业知识产权信息和竞争动态，及时发布风险提示。（商务部、知识产权局、贸促会按职责分别负责）

92. 开展海外林业知识产权动态分析研究，针对容易遭到国外专利壁垒的重点林产品领域进行动态跟踪调查，提升知识产权预警能力。鼓励林业知识产权保护联盟加大海外关键生产技术、发展态势及维权援助机制研究。（林草局负责）

五、加强组织实施和保障

（一）加强知识产权战略谋划和实施

93. 做好知识产权强国战略纲要制定工作。推动地方完善知识产权战略实施统筹协调机制。（联席会议办公室、联席会议成员单位负责）

94. 深入推进《“十三五”国家知识产权保护和运用规划》实施。启动“十四五”知识产权规划编制工作前期研究。（知识产权局负责）

95. 巩固局省市联动、点线面结合的工作格局，加快推进知识产权强省、强市、强企建设。（知识产权局负责）

96. 制定实施工业和信息化领域知识产权年度推进计划。（工业和信息化部负责）

97. 组织实施加快建设知识产权强国林业年度推进计划。（林草局负责）

98. 编制中国知识产权发展状况评价报告。编制工业和通信业知识产权发展情况报告。（联席会议办公室、工业和信息化部按职责分别负责）

（二）夯实知识产权事业发展基础

99. 深入实施专业技术人才知识更新工程，加大对知识产权领域专业技术人才培养培训工作的支持力度。研究完善知识产权专业技术人员职称评价工作。（人力资源社会保障部、知识产权局负责）

100. 支持高水平高校设置知识产权相关专业，完善知识产权相关专业职业教育国家教学标准。推动高校修订知识产权专业人才培养方案。推出一批一流知识产权专业建设点和一批一流知识产权金课。（教育部负责）

101. 加大知识产权类人才引进培养支持力度。加大留学回国人员的知识产权保护力度，促进留学回国人员知识产权运用转化，支持和服务留学回国人员创新创业。（中央组织部、人力资源社会保障部、知识产权局按职责分别负责）

102. 在党政领导干部和中管企业领导班子考核中，注重知识产权相关工作成效。把知识

产权作为干部教育培训重要内容，继续指导有关部门加强干部知识产权培训工作。（中央组织部负责）

103. 协调推动中国特色知识产权新型国家智库建设。发挥好知识产权培训基地作用，引导社会开展更多知识产权培训工作。（知识产权局负责）

（三）大力倡导知识产权文化

104. 加强知识产权对外宣传，利用多双边场合积极宣传展示我国知识产权保护工作成效。继续组织好全国知识产权宣传周等大型活动，支持办好中国知识产权年会和中国国际商标品牌节。举办第十一届全国大学生版权征文活动暨大学生版权论坛。（知识产权局、中央宣传部负责）

105. 开展知识产权教育普及和普法，深化中小学知识产权教育试点示范工作，培育一批优秀师资，编写一批优秀教材，打造若干精品课程。（教育部、司法部、知识产权局负责）

106. 依托全国科技活动周、全国科普日等重点科普活动，推进知识产权科普工作。在各类知识竞赛中纳入知识产权相关内容。（科技部、中国科协负责）

上述各项任务分工中，由多个部门负责的，列第一位的部门为牵头部门，其他为参与部门。

版权工作概览

BAN QUAN GONG ZUO GAI LAN

2018年全国版权工作

2018 年全国版权行政管理工作

中央宣传部版权管理局

2018 年，国家版权局以习近平新时代中国特色社会主义思想和党的十九大精神为指导，深入贯彻落实全国宣传思想工作会议精神，坚持守正创新、稳中求进，推进各项版权工作全面提高。

一、不断加大打击侵权盗版力度

（一）加强工作部署，开展“剑网行动”

一是召开全国版权执法监管工作会议，传达中央领导同志重要批示精神，对打击侵权盗版工作进行部署。二是开展“剑网 2018”专项行动，自 2018 年 7 月开始，会同国家互联网信息办公室、工业和信息化部、公安部开展第 14 次打击网络侵权盗版专项行动，利用国家版权监管平台技术手段，运用分类监管、约谈整改、行政处罚、刑事打击等多种措施，集中整治网络转载、短视频、动漫等领域侵权盗版多发态势，重点规范网络直播、知识分享、有声读物等平台版权传播秩序，深入巩固网络影视、网络音乐、电子商务平台、应用商店、网络云存储空间等领域专项整治成果，维护清朗的网络空间秩序，营造良好的网络版权环境。在“剑网 2018”专项行动期间，各级版权执法监管部门删除侵权盗版链接 185 万条，收缴侵权盗版制品 123 万件，查处网络侵权案件 544 件，其中查办刑事案件 74 件、涉案金额 1.5 亿元，有效震慑了网络侵权盗版行为。

（二）狠抓案件查办，强化督查指导

一是加大案件查办力度。全国各级版权行政管理部门坚持党对版权工作的领导，紧紧抓住关系人民群众根本利益的突出版权问题，相继查处了一批涉案金额大、社会影响严重的大案要案。2018 年，各级版权执法监管部门共查办侵权盗版案件 2 500 余件，移送司法机关追究刑事责任 102 件，捣毁盗版窝点 203 个，收缴盗版制品 377 万件，案件信息公开 1 301 件。二是加大案件督办指导力度。会同全国“扫黄打非”办公室、公安部、最高人民检察院等部门联合挂牌督办了北京“10・17”销售盗版电子出版物案等 48 起侵权盗版大要案件。会同国家互联网信息办公室、工业和信息化部、公安部、最高人民检察院、全国“扫黄打非”办公室对江西、广东、天津等 10 省（市）打击侵权盗版专项行动开展情况和挂牌督办重点案件情况进行现场督查，有效解决地方案件查办瓶颈问题，强化版权、文化执法、“扫黄打非”、通信、网信、公安、检察等部门的工作合力与协同效应。及时对北京、黑龙江、湖北等地关于立案标准、案件管辖等的问题进行研究并回复，为多地案件办理提供协调、指导；与公检法等部门密切配合，及时解决案件查办过程中遇到的问题。

（三）紧盯重点领域，强化重点监管

一是规范网络音乐版权秩序。约谈华纳、索尼、环球三大国际唱片公司和国内大中型唱片公司，推动建立符合国际规则的网络音乐授权、合作模式；推动腾讯与网易达成音乐作品转授权合作，实现双方独家音乐作品 99%以上向对方开放转授权。二是开展网络转载专项整治。指导各地查处一批违法转载案件，依法取缔、关闭一批非法新闻网站（网站频道）及自媒体账号。集体约谈趣头条等 13 家网络服务商，要求有关互联网媒体和媒体平台完善内部版权管理，建立用户管理制度，加强对侵权行为的处置，主动做好执法协助工作。截至 2018 年 12 月，13 家网络服务商已签约的各类版权合作单位累计超过 4 300 余家。今日头条、趣头条、网易号等共对 124 436 个侵权自媒体账号进行封禁，对 19 882 个违规自媒体账号进行降级等处理；趣头条、百度百家号、网易号等共对 475 332 篇侵权内容进行删除或拦截；搜狐新闻、新浪看点、今日头条、百度百家号等建立了账号信用分制度或黑名单制度，网络转载版权秩序得到进一步规范。推动30多家主流财经媒体发起成立“中国财经媒体版权保护联盟”，共同抵制未经授权擅自转载新闻作品的行为，推动实现常态化监控和维权、市场化交易等。三是开展短视频专项整治。约谈抖音短视频、快手短视频、西瓜视频等15家企业，责令其进一步提高版权保护意识，切实加强内部版权制度建设，全面履行企业主体责任。经过整改，15家短视频平台共下架删除各类涉嫌侵权盗版短视频作品57万部，短视频版权保护环境取得显著改善。四是进一步规范电商平台版权秩序。及时回应权利人诉求，多次约谈拼多多等电商平台，要求其切实履行企业主体责任，建立完善版权相关制度；推动阿里巴巴集团与京版十五社反盗版联盟就图书版权保护计划签订合作协议，对重点图书线上盗版销售进行事前主动防控。推动拼多多平台与京版十五社反盗版联盟和少儿出版反盗版联盟就图书版权保护签订合作协议，共同保护权利人的合法权益。五是开展重点作品版权预警保护。公布七批72部重点作品版权保护预警名单，对春晚节目、世界杯赛事节目、《舌尖上的中国》（第三季）以及《红海行动》等院线优秀国产电影进行重点预警保护，要求相关网络服务商对重点作品采取预警保护措施。

（四）提升执法效能，完善激励机制

一是加大案件查办补贴力度。对2018年所有挂牌督办案件予以办案经费补贴，对部分2017年督办案件追加经费补贴，切实解决地方办案部门实际困难。二是对查处侵权盗版重大案件予以奖励，印发《国家版权局关于奖励2017年度查处侵权盗版重大案件的决定》，对2017年度在查处侵权盗版案件工作中做出突出贡献的212家有功单位、249名有功个人进行奖励。三是完善群众举报投诉快速反应机制，鼓励社会力量参与打击侵权盗版工作，广泛收集案源和案件线索，提高案件线索核实和案件查办效率。联合全国“扫黄打非”办公室对10名举报侵权盗版行为的有功个人进行了奖励。

二、持续推进软件正版化工作

（一）加强工作部署，科学工作指导

2018年3月，组织召开推进使用正版软件工作部际联席会议第七次全体会议，专题研究部署2018年工作任务。8月，对各地区软件正版化工作进展情况进行通报，对成效显著的地区提出表扬，对存在问题的地区点名批评，推动各地进一步提高思想认识、落实工作责任。同时，推广部际联席会议印发的《正版软件管理工作指南》，科学指导各级党政机关和企事业单位规范正版软件采购和使用管理工作，落实软件正版化工作相关政策要求，推进软件正版化工作规范化。

（二）创新工作模式，强化督促检查

充分发挥技术手段优势，利用国家版权监管平台和软件检查技术工具，大幅提高监管效率。通过政府购买服务方式，委托第三方专业机构参与督查，有效解决督查人员不足问题。2018年4—11月，组织11个督查组，对20家中央和国家机关、16个省（市）软件正版化工作进行督查，共督查单位374家，检查计算机5.04万台。其中对福建、重庆、四川、云南、甘肃、青海6个省（市）的省级政府机关软件正版化工作进行了全覆盖督查，对督查发现的典型经验和存在的问题进行了通报，推动政府机关和企事业单位进一步落实软件正版化工作主体责任。

（三）推动使用国产软件，开展相关试点工作

推进软件正版化与信息化、信息安全相结合，大力倡导使用国产软件，实现安全、发展两促进。在宁夏西吉县、湖北云梦县开展国产软件应用试点，推进使用国产操作系统软件取得预期效果。

（四）巩固工作成果，夯实工作基础

会同推进使用正版软件工作部际联席会议各成员单位，加强统筹协调、服务指导和督促检查，推进软件正版化工作取得新成效，有效夯实软件正版化工作基础。一是中央和省级机关软件正版率超过90%，突击安装正版软件比例同比大幅下降16.77%，党政机关软件正版化成果得到巩固。二是在巩固中央企业和大中型金融机构软件正版化工作基础上，推动省属国有企业总部基本实现软件正版化。三是党政机关和国有企业大范围使用国产软件，国产办公软件使用比例超过55%，促进了软件产业快速发展，进一步保障了国家信息安全。2018年，我国软件产业总值达到6.31万亿元，同比增长15.1%。

三、持续完善版权社会服务

（一）推进全国著作权登记工作

一是著作权登记继续保持快速增长势头。2018年，全国著作权登记总量突破345万件。其中，作品登记超过了235万件，软件著作权登记量突破了110万件，呈高速增长之势。二是建立著作权登记

信息统计和公示查询系统。要求各地登记机构使用国家版权监管平台报送作品登记信息，对作品重复登记情况进行全面核查通报。在国家版权局官方网站设立著作权登记信息统计和公示查询系统，将适时向社会公众公示作品登记主要信息。

（二）加强版权行政审批及监管工作

一是依法加强对著作权集体管理组织的监管。召开著作权集体管理组织工作会议，审核5家集体管理组织年检报告，指导中国音像著作权集体管理协会领导班子换届相关工作；督促指导、妥善协调解决集体管理组织与相关利益方之间的矛盾与纠纷。二是依法加强对涉外著作权认证机构、国际著作权组织在华常驻代表机构的监管，规范备案制度。召开涉外著作权认证机构在华代表处通气会，规范其在我国境内开展各项涉及版权的活动。依法对涉外著作权认证机构在华代表处年检报告进行审核；对美国电影协会北京代表处变更地址、商业软件联盟（美国）北京代表处的临时活动进行审核。三是加强行政监管制度建设。草拟《关于加强对著作权集体管理组织依法监管的通知（征求意见稿）》和《关于加强对境外著作权认证机构常驻中国代表机构管理的意见（征求意见稿）》，为依法加强对著作权集体管理组织、涉外著作权认证机构驻华代表处的监管提供制度保障。

四、着力促进版权产业发展

（一）举办第七届中国国际版权博览会

2018年10月，在苏州市举办第七届中国国际版权博览会。本届版博会举行了开闭幕式、“中国版权金奖”颁奖仪式、国际版权论坛等多项活动，40余个国家（地区）及世界知识产权组织等50余个国际版权行业组织、机构共计300余家单位参展，成为推动国际版权产业互动交流、促进中国版权产业发展的重要平台和中国版权“走出去”的重要窗口。

（二）评选颁发2018年“中国版权金奖”

为表彰在版权发展与保护方面做出突出贡献的个人和单位，建立长效版权激励机制，国家版权局申请设立的“中国版权金奖”于2016年获批纳入政府常设评比达标表彰活动序列。经过申报和评选，在第七届中国国际版权博览会上颁发了6个作品奖、5个保护奖、5个推广运用奖和4个管理奖共计20个“中国版权金奖”，有力促进了版权创作、保护、运用。

（三）规范全国版权示范创建工作

根据中央文件精神，对全国创建示范活动予以全面清理，按照要求对已开展的全国版权示范创建工作进行自查。完成《关于清理全国版权示范创建工作情况的自查报告》《创建示范活动清理情况汇总表》《拟保留或合并的创建示范活动基本信息表》，并分别报送有关部门，提出保留全国版权示范创建活动的工作建议。

（四）开展系列版权产业调研工作

开展中国版权产业对国民经济贡献的调研工作，发布2017年中国版权产业对国民经济贡献的调查报告，推动具备条件的地方开展相关调查。调查显示，2017年中国版权产业的行业增加值为60 810.92亿元人民币，占全国GDP的7.35%。发布2018年中国网络版权产业发展报告，完成“中国版权交易现状与发展趋势”等课题研究。系列调查研究成果为科学制定版权产业发展政策发挥了积极作用。

五、广泛开展版权宣传培训

（一）加强主题宣传

一是做好“4·26”知识产权宣传周主题宣传活动。围绕世界知识产权组织2018年度宣传主题，通过制作中日韩三国版权公益宣传片、出版版权宣传特刊、制作布设宣传海报等，充分利用全媒体宣传，全方位提升版权社会影响力。二是举办“2018中国网络版权保护大会”。大会发布《2017年中国网络版权保护年度报告》、“2017年度打击侵权盗版十大案件”等，围绕“保护创作，推进运用”主题进行深入研讨交流，有效提升网络版权执法监管影响，取得良好社会反响。三是举办第十届全国大学生版权征文活动。全国大学生版权征文活动自2008年至今已连续举办十届，成为“版权进校园”的名牌活动。本届征文活动共评审出优秀论文奖123个，优秀指导老师奖20个和优秀组织奖16个。四是发布相关年度报告、文献。编辑出版《中国版权年鉴2017》，评选发布“2017年中国版权十件大事”，发布《2017年中国网络版权保护年度报告》《中国版权年度报告（2017）》《2017年软件正版化工作汇编》等，从不同角度宣传版权工作，扩大版权工作影响。

（二）做好全媒体宣传

一是做好国家版权局中文网信息发布工作。2018年全年发布信息1 500余条，制作多个专区进行专题宣传，其中《软件正版化》专题获“2018·政府网站特色栏目”奖。二是扩大国家版权局微博影响。2018年底，微博账号粉丝达118.9万人，全年发布信息456条，同比增长210%。截至11月中旬，“版权执法监管”“版权宣传周”“软件正版化”

等微博话题阅读量均超百万。三是提高其他新媒体平台宣传作用。国家版权局微信公众号全年发布 63 期 77 条图文消息，粉丝增至 3.2 万人，同比增长 163%。国家版权局头条号全年发布信息 479 条，粉丝 107.8 万人，同比增长 191%。国家版权局百家号借助百度分发渠道，影响力不断扩大。

（三）加大版权对外宣传

一是利用国家版权局英文网站，通过线上、线下，文字、视频等不同方式有针对性地开展宣传，全年发布信息近百条，制作《4・26 版权宣传》《2018 版权国际交流》等专题。二是通过与周边国家合作，开展针对特定群体的版权宣传，与日韩共同设计、制作以知名动漫形象为主人公的宣传海报和视频，将“保护版权、繁荣创作”的理念植入民心。三是利用来访、出访、举办和参加国际会议等机会，主动做好版权对外宣传工作，发出权威声音，讲好中国版权制度建设与版权保护的故事，争取国际舆论的支持，营造我国版权涉外工作良好局面。

（四）做好版权培训工作

一是开展版权执法培训。分别在成都、西安、长春举办 3 期全国版权执法监管工作培训班，对 31 个省（自治区、直辖市）556 名版权执法监管工作人员进行培训，实现全国所有地市级版权执法监管部门全覆盖培训，有力提升基层版权执法监管工作水平。二是举办 5 期软件正版化工作培训班，累计培训相关工作人员 1 176 名。三是举办“版权媒体热点问题研修班”，对《人民日报》、新华社等 50 多家中央主流媒体新闻记者进行培训。通过对不同对象分类培训，不断提高版权从业人员工作能力。

六、大力拓展版权国际交流合作

（一）加强国际版权多边话语体系建设

一是继续巩固和加强与世界知识产权组织等国际组织的良好合作关系，积极参加相关委员会会议，参与重要国际版权条约磋商，合作举办“2018 国际版权论坛”等会议，推广版权优秀案例示范点，开展国际版权人才培训。二是采用多种方式推动《视听表演北京条约》早日生效，经过不懈努力，批准或加入的国家增加到 23 个，再有 7 个国家批准、加入，条约即可生效。三是参加由商务部牵头的世界贸易组织第七次对华贸易政策审议和我对其他成员贸易政策审议工作，参加亚太经合组织知识产权专题会议，参加外交部牵头的海牙国际私法会议“判决项目”会议，积极应对有关版权事务。

（二）加强版权双边、区域交流合作与应对水平

巩固中欧、中英、中日、中韩版权交流合作关系，与墨西哥正式建立版权双边合作框架，与欧盟、英国、日本、韩国进行政府间版权工作会谈并举办研讨会；配合商务部完成中国与欧亚经济联盟经贸合作协议签署相关工作，推进《区域全面经济伙伴关系》、中日韩、中国与巴拿马、中挪自贸协定等自贸区谈判进程，配合商务部、文化部等开展中欧、中日等工作组谈判，应对美国 301 调查和中美贸易摩擦，争取有利于我国发展的版权国际环境。推动《海峡两岸知识产权保护合作协议》的具体落实，执行香港海关与国家版权局“打击网络盗版合作互助安排”，推动两岸、内地与香港在版权领域的沟通合作。

（三）妥善处理其他涉外版权事务

一是积极配合首届中国国际进口博览会版权相关工作，及时提供会展所需版权信息，协调中国版权保护中心、上海市版权局进驻会展，配合做好版权服务，及时化解版权纠纷和争议，维护我国版权保护良好形象。二是妥善处理好全国“双打”办、我驻韩使馆转来的韩国公司版权纠纷事宜。三是妥善处理朝鲜驻华使馆关于处理侵权图片来函，迅速约谈主要网络服务商，要求其主动采取措施，全面清查、处理侵权图片。

（四）做好相关国际版权课题研究工作

有针对性地开展版权国际应对宏观策略研究、版权国际应对具体问题研究和图书馆、档案馆、教研机构的限制与例外，以及民间文艺的版权保护等版权国际热点问题调研工作，进一步提升我国国际版权应对能力。

2018 年全国版权司法保护工作

最高人民法院知识产权审判庭

一、2018 年度著作权案件审理情况及特点

2018 年以来，在各级党委和政府的高度重视下，在各级人大及其常委会的监督下，在社会各界的大力支持下，人民法院认真做好著作权审判工作，大力弘扬和捍卫社会主义核心价值观，坚守意识形态法律底线，著作权司法保护水平不断提高，为促进经济、文化和社会发展做出了积极的贡献。随着科技进步和新商业模式的出现，尤其是互联网的迅猛发展，著作权案件出现了一些新的变化。

（一）著作权纠纷案件数量持续增长

2016 年，地方各级人民法院共新收著作权民事一审案件 86 989 件，同比上升 30.44%，占当年全部知识产权民事一审案件的 63.72%；2017 年，地方各级人民法院共新收著作权民事一审案件 137 267 件，同比上升 57.80%，占当年全部知识产权民事一审案件的 68.28%；2018 年，全国法院共受理一审著作权民事案件 195 408 件，占全部一审知识产权民事案件的 68.95%，较 2017 年增长 42.36%，较 2016 年增长 124.64%。

2016 年，地方各级人民法院共新收著作权行政一审案件 37 件，新收侵犯著作权罪案件 195 件；2017 年，地方各级人民法院共新收著作权行政一审案件 17 件，新收侵犯著作权罪案件 169 件；2018 年，地方各级人民法院共新收著作权行政一审案件 17 件，新收侵犯著作权罪案件 156 件。可见，近年来新收著作权行政一审和刑事一审案件呈下降趋势，但由于绝对数不大，对著作权类案件总体增长趋势影响不大。

（二）涉网络著作权案件数量居高不下

2018 年，全国法院受理的一审涉网络著作权民事案件占全部一审著作权民事案件的 70%。而在网络产业发达的地区，这一比例更高。如北京地区的部分基层法院的案件比例高达 90%。北京基层法院（包括海淀、朝阳、东城、西城、丰台、石景山、互联网法院）自 2016 年到 2018 年，共受理一审涉网络著作权案件 49 130 件。北京互联网法院 2018 年 9 月 9 日至 12 月 31 日，正式立案互联网著作权侵权纠纷案件 2 187 件。杭州互联网法院自 2017 年 5 月至 2018 年 12 月共受理互联网著作权权属、侵权纠纷案件 6 437 件。随着 5G 技术的不断成熟并进入大规模商业应用，预计涉网络的著作权案件还将不断增多。

传统著作权侵权案件多存在侵权的有形载体，如盗版，存在盗版书、盗版光盘等有形物。这些有形载体在制作中均需必要的原材料以及运输等成本付出，证据较易获得且相对固定。围绕侵权复制品的制造、销售，在侵权行为人之间通常存在意思联络，或者存在合同等法律关系，在认定共同侵权时较易把握。随着网络的普及，信息网络传播行为更加隐蔽，侵权行为出现了碎片化、分散化和海量化的特点，行为人甚至是完全“隐形”的主体。

（三）系列化著作权案件不断增多

系列化著作权案件是指当事人、诉讼标的一致的多个著作权案件，如著作权集体管理组织或者通过许可使用合同获得专有权利的被许可人提起的大规模维权案件。卡拉 OK、视频网站、文学网站、聚合平台、直播平台等作为大量作品集散的平台，容易产生数量众多的系列化同质化案件。

（四）文化产业的发展催生新领域著作权案件

近年来，一些新领域的著作权案件不断涌现，是文化产业的繁荣发展催生而来，如网络游戏产业迅猛发展，带来许多涉网络游戏的著作权案件，而在短视频、网络直播等公众娱乐消费的热点领域，也不断出现著作权纠纷案件，并成为公众关注的热点。

（五）著作权与不正当竞争纠纷交叉的现象突出

近年来，出现一些当事人主张利益请求保护的新形态成果，而法律未予明确其权利属性，对此，理论与实务界对其是否属于著作权保护的客体存在争议，例如体育赛事直播，如何予以保护？当事人为了最大限度地保护自己的利益，往往在一个诉讼中同时主张著作权保护和不正当竞争保护，形成著作权与不正当竞争纠纷交叉的现象，产生法律适用

上的疑难问题。

2018 年，最高人民法院知识产权审判庭著作权纠纷反映出如下问题：

其一，最高人民法院受理的著作权案件数量占比较小。根据知识产权案件的管辖布局，著作权案件主要由中基层法院受理，且具有管辖权的法院地域分布较广、数量较多。如著作权案件数量最多的北京市、上海市、广东省等地，均设有多个可受理著作权案件的基层法院。此外，著作权案件通常标的不高、争议不大、系列案件较多，故和解撤诉的可能性也较高，这也在一定程度上反映了大多数著作权案件审判质效趋于稳定、裁判标准日趋统一的良好态势。

其二，最高人民法院始终高度关注著作权领域的基础性法律问题。近年来，随着经济社会生活的不断繁荣发展，著作权领域出现了一些因新技术模式、新商业模式的应用而产生的知识产权纠纷。在密切关注新类型知识产权案件的同时，最高人民法院对独创性认定、权利归属的认定、重复授权的判定等基础性法律问题的研究也给予高度重视，并着力通过个案裁判、审判业务指导等方式明晰裁判标准、统一裁判尺度，努力提高著作权案件的整体审理水平。

其三，涉著作权集体管理组织案件数量较多，部分法律问题亟待明确裁判标准。集体管理作为著作权法当中的一项具有特色的制度，近年来引发的著作权纠纷案件特别是系列案件的数量较多，尽快明确涉集体管理组织案件中所涉法律问题的裁判标准，是目前著作权司法审判中亟待解决的问题。最高人民法院在 2018 年继续通过个案审查、提审及调研论证等方式，积极探索涉集体管理组织案件的相关裁判标准，并待条件成熟时通过指导案例等方式进一步统一相关案件的裁判尺度。

其四，侵权责任的承担仍然是著作权案件的焦点问题之一。侵权责任的具体承担方式、赔偿数额的确定等问题，是近年来著作权案件当事人申请再审关注的主要问题。针对当事人诉讼请求计算方式日趋精细化的特点，最高人民法院积极探索在著作权案件中避免简单适用法定赔偿，并不断加强损害赔偿数额计算的精细化程度，切实保障权利人获得充分赔偿。

二、2018 年度著作权相关工作及活动

（一）密切关注新形势下知识产权司法保护热点问题，加强知识产权保护创新理论和司法政策研究

一是认真完成全国人大交办的工作任务。起草《最高人民法院关于研究落实全国人大常委会著作权法执法检查报告以及审议意见情况的报告》，围绕执法检查提出的问题，针对当前维权成本高、诉讼周期长、赔偿低、部分著作权案件裁判标准不统一、案多人少、著作权法修改等问题提出了改进措施。

二是通过制定司法政策，指导各级法院旗帜鲜明保护“红色经典”。制定并发布《最高人民法院关于加强“红色经典”和英雄烈士合法权益司法保护弘扬社会主义核心价值观的通知》，起草《最高人民法院办公厅关于修订著作权法时纳入“加强红色经典司法保护弘扬社会主义核心价值观”相关内容的函》《关于加强红色经典知识产权司法保护有关情况的报告》，严格依法保护红色经典传承和英雄烈士合法权益，倡导讲品位、讲格调、讲责任，教育和引导社会公众尤其是广大青少年自觉抵制“低俗、庸俗、媚俗”，抵制历史虚无主义，规范传播行为，维护社会公共利益。

三是开展著作权与外观设计专利权权利冲突调研。在北京和昆明举办了两次研讨会，起草了外观设计和著作权冲突调研报告，就著作权与外观设计专利权之间的竞合与权利冲突问题，凝练出具有操作价值的审判指导意见。

（二）积极参与知识产权相关法律修订工作，贡献知识产权司法保护新经验

一是积极参与著作权法的修订工作。结合审判实际，及时组织专项研究和论证，认真总结审判实践中形成的司法政策和经验，有针对性地提出修法建议。2018 年 1 月在北京召开全国部分法院著作权法修订座谈会。会议围绕著作权法修订草案送审稿修改稿中作品的分类、著作权的权利内容、权利的限制、著作权合同、集体管理、相关权的规定、法律责任以及与国际公约和其他法律的协调等问题进行了广泛和深入的讨论。在充分论证的基础上向司法部提交了《最高人民法院关于著作权法的修改意见》，受到高度评价。

二是出台各类规范性文件。北京高院于 2018 年 4 月 20 日发布《北京市高级人民法院侵害著作权案件审理指南》，明确提出著作权审判中应当坚持“加大保护、鼓励创作、促进传播、平衡利益”的基本审理原则，总结侵害著作权案件的审理思路，对北京互联网法院审理网络著作权案件以及北京法院著作权审判工作具有积极的指导意义，对首都文化产业的发展和创新发挥了推动作用。

（三）全力促进社会主义文化和科学事业发展繁荣

一是明确法律适用标准，加强对著作权人和相关权利人的保护。通过准确划定著作权保护范围和保护强度，合理界定著作权的权属判断标准，明确网络环境下先授权后使用的原则，妥善处理涉著作权集体管理和大规模系列化维权纠纷，全面维护权利人的利益。

二是依法采取综合手段，加大对侵害著作权行为的惩治力度。在著作权刑事保护上严格执行罚金刑，在民事保护上不断加大损害赔偿力度，增加惩罚性赔偿，积极适用知识产权临时措施。如在琼瑶诉于正著作权侵权纠纷中，人民法院在证据明显可以证明损失大于50万元法定赔偿上限的情况下，酌定赔偿500万元，最大限度地保护和鼓励原创。

三是推出典型案例，推动版权文化事业和产业的发展。人民法院在处理电影作品、动漫作品、计算机软件、网络游戏作品等与文化创意产业有关纠纷中，充分了解行业发展情况，顺应产业发展规律，营造有利于文化艺术产业繁荣发展的法治环境。

四是保护中国传统文化，贡献著作权司法保护的中国智慧。人民法院坚持传承与创新、保护和利用并重的原则，积极适用著作权法保护民间文学艺术和非物质文化遗产。乌苏里船歌侵权纠纷案的圆满解决，充分展现了人民法院在民间文学艺术保护方面的智慧和创造性。

（四）不断完善著作权多元纠纷解决机制

近年来，著作权收案数量总体上逐年上升，为及时定分止争，人民法院不断加大著作权纠纷调解工作力度，努力化解矛盾纠纷。此外，不断创新调解制度，引入外部力量，发挥行业协会、人民陪审员、专家咨询、集体管理组织在解决著作权纠纷中的作用。大力加强基层人民法院建设，设立派出法庭、巡回法庭，为高效便利解决著作权纠纷提供司法保障。

2018年地方版权工作

北　京　市

2018年，北京市版权局以习近平新时代中国特色社会主义思想为指引，认真贯彻落实市委市政府的相关工作要求，紧密围绕文化中心建设的新要求、新部署，积极推进著作权普法宣传活动，大力开展软件正版化工作，重点提升版权监测评估水平，全方位推进版权保护工作，取得了显著成效。北京地区作品自愿登记919 543项，比2017年增长13.58%，软件著作权登记量163 215项。

一、形式多样，多方参与，着力抓好版权普法宣传活动

（一）资源共享，务实合作，探索建立社会化维权服务新格局

4月25日，首都版权产业联盟与中国文联举行签约仪式，正式就共同开展文艺工作者版权保护服务建立合作关系。中国文联团结凝聚了大批优秀文艺创作者，首都版权产业联盟是政府支持设立的公益性权益保护组织，双方的合作是探索建立社会化维权服务新格局，实现资源共享、优势互补，为优秀作品的有序传播提供更加专业的维权服务。通过首都版权产业联盟与中国文联权保部的密切合作，积极探索保护版权、打击侵权盗版的有效途径，切实维护艺术家们的创作热情、良好声誉和经济效益，为艺术创作的创新、运用和保护贡献来自版权工作者的一分力量。

（二）加强交流，深化合作，助力《视听表演北京条约》早日生效

值《视听表演北京条约》（以下简称条约）缔结六周年之际，为推动条约早日生效，5月28日下午，世界知识产权组织中国办事处、北京市版权局、北京市东城区政府联合主办了“知识产权保护促进视听产业发展论坛”。WIPO副总干事王彬颖出席论坛。

欧盟驻华代表团公使衔参赞马君泽，华东政法大学教授王迁，著名影视导演、演员蒋雯丽，国际作者和作曲者协会联合会亚太区总裁吴铭枢，就“表演者对影视产业发展的关键作用”议题发表主题演讲，深入交流了提高表演者权益保护水平对促进全人类文化事业繁荣发展的积极意义和深远影响。蒋雯丽代表广大一线表演者发出呼吁，希望更多的国家批准和加入条约，以促成条约早日生效。世界知识产权组织中国办事处顾问吕国良、王晔，英国驻华使馆知识产权专员杜涛，搜狐公司总法律顾问庞小妹，美国电影协会亚太区副总裁冯伟，围绕“知识产权保护助力影视产业国际合作”议题发表主题演讲，从产业发展的角度，探讨了影视产业的版权保护与执法、事后防范与事后维权、遭遇国际纠纷的应对策略等若干焦点问题。

论坛气氛热烈，参会代表情绪高涨，纷纷表示嘉宾们的精彩演讲从各个角度深入浅出地讲授了知识产权保护对影视产业发展的重要作用，让人受益匪浅。同时，希望条约早日生效，从而更好地推进国际版权合作和世界各国文化产业健康发展。

（三）形式多样，内容丰富，全方位推进版权宣传

（1）为营造重视版权的良好社会氛围，全方位打造版权公益广告宣传。在“4·26”世界知识产权日、软件正版化推广使用和“6·26”《视听表演北京条约》签署纪念日期间，通过在地铁、公交站、楼宇等投放广告的方式大力宣传版权保护理念，收效良好。

（2）主办2018第二届中国“网络文学+”大会平行主题论坛——“网络文学版权保护论坛”。论坛邀请了网络文学产业领域权利人，相关产业界、学术界、法律实务界代表同与会者进行深入交流。知名作家月关，华东政法大学知识产权学院教授、博士生导师丛立先，北京知识产权法院冯刚，阅文集团高级副总裁张蓉，阿里文学副总裁、总编辑周运以及掌阅科技联合创始人、副总裁王良等在论坛上就网络文学版权相关热点问题发表看法并分享了经验。不少参会的网络文学产业界、权利人代表在接受采访时表示，在网络文学大会期间，举办这样一场高水平的版权保护论坛，对于增强业界对网络文学版权保护工作的关注、提升全社会版权保护意识、

促进网络文学产业健康发展，具有很好的促进作用。

(3) 积极参加第七届中国国际版权博览会、第十六届北京国际图书节、第十三届中国北京国际文化创意产业博览会，通过展出北京市近年来优秀版权项目，宣传北京市版权保护成果。参加“2018 国际版权论坛”，就版权对创新和发展的作用和意义，以及进一步提高版权创造、运用、保护和管理水平与其他省市深入交流探讨。

二、加强协作，攻坚克难，稳步推进软件正版化工作

(一) 软件正版化工作取得的成效

2018 年，推进使用正版软件工作联席会议各成员单位各司其职、密切协作，坚持制度与技术并重，加强政策指导和督促检查，进一步巩固扩大了软件正版化工作成果，正版化率达到 95%，国产办公软件的覆盖率达到 66%。

(1) 党政机关软件正版化工作不断规范。各级机关认真贯彻落实国家版权局及市使用正版软件工作联席会议相关文件精神，不断健全软件正版化工作机制，加强制度建设，规范软件采购，建立软件台账，严格使用管理，应用技术手段，软件正版化工作朝着规范化、常态化、制度化和信息化不断推进，为迎接推进使用正版软件工作部际联席会议的全覆盖检查做好了充足准备。

(2) 企事业单位软件正版化工作全面铺开。市属国企软件正版化工作常态化不断推进，医疗卫生系统按照三年工作计划有序推进，市属国企、医疗卫生系统发挥后发优势，按照国家版权局使用正版软件工作指南健全工作制度，运用技术手段提高工作效率，软件正版化工作成效明显。

(3) 软件版权保护环境持续改善。市使用正版软件工作联席会议加强软件采购源头管理，积极推进使用正版软件，促进了软件版权保护环境持续改善，为软件产业发展提供了良好的市场环境。目前，北京市的软件产业呈现出健康发展的良好态势，具有北京特色的软件正版化工作模式正在形成。

(二) 主要措施

(1) 创新宣传培训。利用户外宣传、内部宣传、版博会宣传三种途径进行软件正版化宣传。着眼于提高培训的针对性和实效性，有条不紊地进行分类分级分层培训（分为国家机关、市属国企、医疗卫生系统等三类，市、区、乡镇等三级，新入职人员与老同志、管理人员与使用人员等多层），同时把课堂讲解与实地答疑、思想教育与业务培训相结合，使培训内容能够内化于心、外化于行。

(2) 严格检查考核。把完善考核流程作为确保检查考核公平的生命线，把细化考核标准作为提高检查考核科学性的坐标系，把严格评定结果作为推动软件正版化工作的指挥棒，积极探索符合实际、高效便捷的检查考核新模式。

(3) 强化结果运用。狠抓问责制度建设，把软件正版化考核结果与评先评优、打击侵犯知识产权和制售假冒伪劣商品工作绩效考核、信息化建设、平安北京建设紧密结合起来，提高各单位开展软件正版化工作的积极性、主动性。

(三) 工作亮点

(1) 健全规章制度。根据 2017 年推进使用正版软件工作联席会议督查组对北京市进行督查反馈的制度建设不完善等情况，北京市以国家版权局《正版软件工作管理指南》为标准，加强国家机关、市属国企、医疗卫生系统软件正版化制度建设，建立软件正版化工作长效机制。

(2) 应用技术手段。北京市目前软件正版化工作范围涵盖 118 个市级机关、16 个区、51 家国企总部的三级以上企业 1 300 余家，以及 22 家市属医院、17 家市卫生计生委直属单位和区卫生计生系统相关单位，数量多，工作量大，每年软件正版化检查耗费大量人力，检查时间也相对滞后。为了节省人力投入，加快工作进度，按时完成全年软件正版化工作目标，版权局在培训时对国家版权局软件正版化检查工具进行重点讲解，并在年底检查中对检查工具进行应用，大大节省人力成本，加快检查时间，推动软件正版化检查工作按时完成。

(3) 动用外部力量。年底软件正版化检查单位数量多、时间周期长、组长人手有限，2018 年市版权局发函要求联席会议各成员单位及市卫生计生委、市医管局等行业主管部门一起参与检查，大大加快了检查进度，有效保证了软件正版化检查如期完成。

三、提升监测水平，聚焦大案要案，切实加强版权保护工作力度

(一) 启动“剑网 2018”专项行动，展现首都版权保护新气象

2018 年 7 月 27 日，按照国家版权局工作要求，北京市版权局正式启动北京市“剑网 2018”专项行动。本次行动以网络转载、短视频、动漫、影视等领域为治理重点，细化了各阶段的工作任务和任务清单，综合协调市文化市场行政执法总队、市公安局、市通信管理局和市网信办，保证治理措施配套到位，形成了协同工作、齐抓共管的工作格局。

北京市版权局以网络主动巡查为主，结合权利

人投诉举报，对“717电影网”等数十家网站进行了全方位跟踪监测，并对涉嫌盗版的10 519部作品进行了权利认证，对涉嫌侵权的网站IP地址、服务器地址和侵权播放链接进行了摸底排查。经与公安部门沟通协调后，将初步达到刑事立案标准的案件线索正式移送市公安局海淀分局。北京市版权局将继续全力推进本案件的侦办工作，并将继续加大网络盗版惩治力度，持续盗版惩治的高压态势。

（二）积极引导规范，构建版权保护共同治理新格局

（1）集中约谈短视频平台。聚焦短视频热点领域，防患版权问题突发态势，约谈首都地区十五家短视频平台企业，要求各短视频平台企业应当以“剑网行动”为契机，努力提升短视频领域版权环境，积极构建健康有序的产业发展模式，形成合法合理的行业自律规范和共识，促进短视频健康有序发展。

（2）走访调研重点企业。分别针对影视、短视频、网络云盘、应用商店等重点领域，对优酷、快手、百度、搜狗等互联网企业开展了走访调研工作，强调各互联网企业应当做好以下几方面工作：一是要牢固树立版权保护经营理念，继续履行主动审查义务，利用自身影响力形成行业示范效应，促进企业切实履行版权监管主体责任；二是要提高作品资源的版权利用水平，充分利用海量用户资源，深度挖掘自身版权潜力，提升平台作品质量和效益，形成更高层次的发展；三是要提升版权宣传教育力度，充分利用平台优势，宣传教育用户树立版权保护意识，在弘扬主旋律、正能量基础上探索建立更加积极有效的版权机制，切实保护权利人的合法权益。

（3）加大版权保护培训力度。为提高艺术作品版权保护水平和艺术从业者作品登记积极性，北京市版权局在怀柔红螺寺和通州宋庄组织了艺术版权专项培训。北京版权保护中心从作品自愿登记的受理、审查、审定等环节进行了讲解，对著作权法相关概念进行了解释答疑，并对作品自愿登记申请注意事项进行了说明介绍。

（三）推进共识协力创新，推动首都版权保护行业自律新局面

（1）推进《信息网络传播权保护指导意见》修改工作。北京市版权局于2011年出台的《信息网络传播权保护指导意见》，从当时版权保护的实际情况出发，着重解决“避风港”规则实施过程中遇到的问题，通过规范信息存储空间、搜索链接经营行为和贯彻落实“通知—删除”规定等举措完善信息网络传播权版权保护工作。2018年对该意见进行了修订，结合近几年出现的新问题和新情况，主要参考了立法、司法、执法等部门的相关文件和材料，并对相关互联网企业进行了调研走访，了解了最新的网络技术和信息传输方式。目前该意见修订稿草案全文共22条，已完成初稿。

（2）推进《关于规范应用市场版权秩序共同声明》签署工作。为落实《关于规范软件应用市场版权秩序的通知》工作要求，在借鉴以往工作经验的基础上，经过多次专家论证以及两轮权利人意见征询，完成了《关于规范软件应用市场版权秩序的共同声明》的初稿，下一步将继续持续推进该共同声明工作，积极争取实现软件应用市场版权保护的行业共识。

（四）科学部署主动监测，形成网络版权监测新态势

按照监测工作相关要求，完成对20家门户网站视频节目、文字作品、音乐作品、影视作品和综艺节目的经常性监测。以侵权链接下线比例和数量为依据，对重点网站主要在线作品的类别、数量、内容版权和传播情况进行了经常性监测评估。

根据专项监测工作要求，选取2017年12月1日至2018年1月31日时间段对今日头条进行了专项跟踪监测。监测梳理信息9 100万件，除广告、事实性报道、商品服务信息以外，对8 000万件信息进行了著作权作品的认定，并最终完成《今日头条版权状况监测评估报告》。

对2018春节联欢晚会和平昌冬奥会网络版权进行了监测工作，向170余家企事业单位发布了《关于进一步加强2018年春晚和冬奥会互联网版权监管责任的通知》，实现了直播阶段的全网监测，维护了互联网版权秩序。

（五）固本培元开拓进取，获得首都版权调解事业新突破

2018年，北京版权调解中心共受理权利人申请调解的各类著作权调解案件323起（其中行政调解案件52起），涉及争议金额27 500余万元，经调解化解纠纷达成和解的案件100起，为权利人挽回经济损失累计793万余元；接受朝阳法院委托案件2 171起，调解成功达成和解的159起；自10月份开始接受北京互联网法院委托案件505起。受理案件类型多样化，涵盖计算机软件使用、美术作品使用、音乐作品改编、影视作品信息网络传播权、传统出版物等各个版权领域。

（赵晓鹏）

天　津　市

2018年，天津市版权局以习近平新时代中国特色社会主义思想和党的十九大精神为指导，按照国家版权局的工作要求及市委、市政府有关部署，突出责任意识和担当精神，将突出版权保护、加快产业发展、巩固软件正版化成果作为重点工作，在净化网络版权环境、保护权利人的合法权益、推进软件正版化长效机制建设、积极开展版权宣传等方面取得了显著成绩。

一、开展专项行动，严厉打击侵权行为

2018年7—12月，天津市版权局、网信办、通信局、公安局、文化市场行政执法总队成立专项行动协调小组，联合开展了打击网络侵权盗版“剑网2018”专项行动。

（一）部署推进，行动迅速

在制定下发行动方案后，8月3日，天津市版权局会同市文化市场行政执法总队组织全市各区版权局以及相关单位负责同志召开专项行动动员部署会，在天津市多层次、广领域、全方位启动专项行动；8月21日，市版权局等五部门联合组织召开市重点网站负责人版权保护工作培训会，并组成联合检查组对辖区内网站开展了3次检查；11月16日，天津市版权局等五部门联合组织召开专项行动总结分析会，为后续工作总结经验、打好基础。

（二）协同配合，全面开展

在专项行动中，各成员单位以网站、应用程序、自媒体、新闻聚合类平台为重点，开展网络转载、短视频、动漫等重点领域专项整治。通过强化运用约谈、预警等工作手段，加大对网络侵权盗版案件的行政处罚工作力度，督促互联网企业落实主体责任。

专项行动期间，天津市承办国家版权局等4部门联合督办案件4件，其中天津百练教育科技集团有限公司销售盗版培训教材案入选2018年度全国打击侵权盗版十大案件。

二、扎实推进软件正版化工作，不断巩固成果

为进一步推动天津市软件正版化工作的开展，按照天津市政府印发的《天津市2018年推进使用正版软件工作计划》，天津市版权局会同市推进使用正版软件工作联席会议各成员单位强化制度保障、落实长效机制，以优化考核方式为切入点，组织推进软件正版化工作的开展。2018年，天津市共组织软件正版化培训31次，参训人数约1 500人次。同时按照国务院关于《政府机关使用正版软件管理办法》和国家版权局有关要求，加强对市区两级机关的工作督查，2018年，共组织市区两级管理部门对全市70家党政机关开展了工作督察。

2018年9月，国家推进使用软件正版化第三督查组对天津市软件正版化工作进行督查，检查了1 778台计算机，其中，操作系统正版率96.57%，办公软件正版率99.16%。督查组对天津市党政机关使用正版软件工作给予了充分肯定和高度评价。

三、加大版权保护力度，做好日常版权保护工作

2018年，按照国家版权局要求，在局政务网公布共7批重点影视作品预警名单，同时将预警名单通知市重点监管网站并提出要求。加大网络版权监管力度，在日常工作中，天津市版权局指派专人对市重点监管网站进行点击浏览，查找有无涉及预警名单内容，要求其提供授权证明或断开链接、删除相关内容，净化网络版权空间。2018年上半年，针对2022年北京冬奥会会徽及冬残奥会会徽版权专项保护工作，天津市版权局与市文化市场行政执法总队成立联合检查组，开展了版权保护联合检查，同时公布举报电话、查找网上侵权线索，深入旅游景区、印刷复制单位、农贸市场等区域开展专项检查，打击侵权盗版行为，出色完成第一阶段工作。

四、制定政策，推动版权质押贷款工作开展

为落实《中共天津市委　天津市人民政府营造企业家创业发展良好环境的规定》精神，2018年4月，天津市版权局联合市金融局、人民银行天津分行、天津银监局制定了《天津市版权质押贷款实施指导意见》，为做好政策宣传、推动工作，天津市版权局会同市金融局等4家单位联合组织了版权质押贷款宣传推介会，并就质押贷款工作进行有益的尝试。

为进一步推动《天津市版权质押贷款实施指导意见》的实施，引导具有版权资源的企业通过加强版权资产管理，利用优质版权资源开展版权融资，2018年天津市版权局开展了优秀版权单位推荐工作，全市各区及相关单位通过组织动员，初审上报28家参评企业。天津市版权局经组织相关专家评审后，共向市金融机构推荐优秀版权企业20家。

五、做好社会服务，促进版权产业发展

天津市积极推动版权贸易的开展。2018年天津市版权贸易品种数447种。版权贸易总数比2017年增加84种，增长23.14%；版权引进242种，比2016年增加16种，增长7.08%。新蕾出版社（天

津）有限公司立项的《博物馆里的中国·藏在指尖的艺术》入选 2018 年“经典中国国际出版工程”资助出版项目。天津人民出版社立项的《京剧知识词典》、天津人民出版社与五洲传播出版社立项的《中国特色社会主义为什么行》入选 2018 年丝路书香工程重点翻译资助项目。

六、加大著作权宣传，提高全社会维权守法意识

提升全社会版权意识，是做好版权保护工作的前提。天津市版权局将版权宣传工作与开展版权管理、版权服务工作相结合。在开展管理与服务工作的同时，向著作权人、相关企业进行法规宣传、著作权宣讲，使社会公众逐步树立了“尊重知识、尊重创新”的意识。每年以“4·26”知识产权宣传周和“12·4”全国法制宣传日为平台，联合举办大型宣传咨询活动，召开著作权保护工作研讨会，深入园区、社区、企业张贴发放公益广告和材料，利用报刊、互联网等媒体进行宣传，形成了著作权法宣传教育的常态机制；在 2018 书香天津·春季书展期间，集中进行版权宣传，书展现场设立了咨询服务区，对著作权法进行宣传，受到了群众的好评。

（张　倩）

河 北 省

2018 年，在省委、省政府的正确领导下，河北省各级版权行政和执法部门按照国家版权局的各项要求，不断提高版权服务水平，积极推进版权示范创建工作，进一步巩固政府机关和企事业单位软件正版化工作成果，严厉打击各领域侵权盗版行为，强化版权宣传培训，取得了显著成绩。

一、加大版权示范推进工作，优化版权登记环境，促进版权产业发展

一是积极开展版权示范调研工作。2018 年 4 月，省版权局巡视员董毅带队对福建省德化县、广东省东莞市、江苏省张家港市和昆山市的版权示范创建工作进行了调研。调研组先后参观了陶瓷、玻璃、软件、动漫、纺织和文创等版权企业，与相关单位负责人进行了座谈，就版权保护、创新和经营等具体问题进行了交流。5 月中旬，省版权局再次组织调研组赴山东省青岛市即墨区考察学习版权示范创建工作经验。两次调研结束后，调研组撰写了调研报告，提出了推动全省版权示范创建工作的五点建议。此外，省版权局还先后对河北钢铁集团、河北建投集团、石家庄信息工程职业学院、石家庄百年巧匠文化传播有限公司、河北工业设计创新中心等单位开展调研，精心培育百年巧匠等 6 家企业作为省级示范单位和示范园区（基地）创建培育对象。

二是扎实推进版权示范城市创建。7 月 5 日，廊坊市召开创建全国版权示范城市工作推进会暨廊坊市政府部门使用正版软件工作会议，就创建全国版权示范城市工作进行再动员、再部署。省版权局副局长部世泽出席会议，廊坊市委常委、宣传部部长、统战部部长王曦做动员讲话，副市长张春燕主持会议。会议宣读了《廊坊市创建全国版权示范城市任务分解方案》《廊坊市创建全国版权示范城市督导工作方案》。

三是优化版权登记环境。4 月 26 日，河北省版权保护中心上线了“河北省版权信息数据库平台”，充分利用技术手段，优化版权登记环境。平台上线后，权利人可通过登录网站进行注册，对文字、音乐、美术、摄影等多类作品进行在线登记、自主管理，确定版权归属，登记时限也由过去的 30 个工作日缩短到 7 个工作日。此外，该平台还提供了多项增值服务，如提供版权登记、版权信息等大数据统计及分析；建立创新作品之家，由著作权人对自己的作品自主选择展示和管理；提供多种权利的电子合同模板，著作权人对感兴趣的他人作品可以发起邀约，签订许可和转让合同，进行合同备案，促进作品价值转换等。据统计，平台上线后共注册账户 1 556 个，登记作品 9 782 件，平台登记作品数量占全年所有登记数量 11 871 件的 82.4%。

四是拓展版权服务体系。9 月 19 日和 12 月 13 日，省版权局、省版权保护中心分别在廊坊和唐山设立版权服务站，通过调动当地热情，授予地区管理权限，加快推动河北省版权服务平台在服务著作权人、服务版权产业、加强版权管理方面发挥作用。据统计，2018 年廊坊服务站登记量达到 4 832 件，约占全省登记总量的 40.7%，真正激活了服务站的潜在价值。

五是积极为会员单位服务。7 月，省版权协会按照中国版权协会通知要求，组织推荐了 8 家会员单位参选 2018 年度中国版权最具影响力企业、新锐企业。12 月 1 日，在第十一届中国版权协会年会上，河北教育出版社有限责任公司荣获“2018 年度中国版权最具影响力企业”称号；河北乐聪科技网络有限公司与河北精英动漫文化传播股份有限公司荣获“2018 年度中国版权新锐企业”称号。

二、进一步巩固各级政府机关和企事业单位软件正版化工作成果

一是开展考核评议和督导检查工作。1 月，省版权局组织了 11 个考核组，分别对全省 11 个设区市及其所辖 1 个“回头看”县级政府、定州和辛集市政府，以及 97 家省直单位 2017 年度软件正版化工作进行了考评。考核组按照事前的业务培训要求，依据《河北省政府机关使用正版软件工作考核办法（试行）》，先后查阅了被考核地区和单位的软件正版化有关资料，听取了汇报，利用正版软件检查工具上机检查了计算机安装软件情况，并对各地、各单位的实际情况进行了打分。考核工作结束后，省版权局印发了《关于政府机关软件正版化考核评议工作的情况通报》。6 月中旬至 8 月上旬，省版权局组织人员，对全省 9 个设区市和 17 个县级政府的 49 个市县机关、10 家国有企业、6 家金融机构、1 家私营企业进行了督导检查。督查组查阅了各单位相关材料，利用正版软件检查工具检查了 2 118 台计算机的软件安装情况，对存在的问题进行了现场指导，并提出了整改要求。督查结束后制发了《关于做好软件正版化整改提升工作的通知》。各市（含定州、辛集市）版权局也相继组织开展了督导检查活动，促进了本地软件正版化。

二是强化各阶段工作部署。3 月 12 日，省版权局对国家版权局下发的《关于对北京市、河北省等 10 省（区、市）软件正版化工作督查情况的通报》进行了转发，要求各地各单位，特别是通报中存在问题的单位要认真分析原因，对照问题，举一反三，全面开展一次自查工作，防止出现盗版软件反弹现象和督查前突击安装软件现象。4 月中旬，根据国家版权局相关要求，省版权局制发了《河北省 2018 年推进使用正版软件工作实施方案》，该方案针对省直单位进一步强调了计算机软硬件采购源头管理工作，要求各单位在新购计算机时，除了选择好预装的操作系统，同时将办公软件一并计划、预算和采购；针对各设区市政府，要求其再选定 1/3 数量的县级政府作为 2018 年重点督导对象，持续开展“回头看”活动，确保已列入活动的县级政府全部达到“办公软件正版全覆盖，操作系统所用即所买”的总体目标。

三是加大企业软件正版化推进力度。5 月，省版权局召集河北广播电视台、河北广电网络集团、长城新媒体集团等三家广电企业，部署和推进 2018 年软件正版化工作；10 月底，再次带领河北出版传媒集团、河北日报报业集团、河北新华书店集团参加国家版权局组织的业务培训，指导各单位安装使用正版软件管理工具。5 月，省国资委印发《省国资委 2018 年推进监管企业使用正版软件工作实施方案》，加快推进省国资委监管企业和委属事业单位软件正版化工作进程。河北银监局、河北证监局、河北保监局分别印发了软件正版化工作实施方案，督促金融行业企业（机构）开展了软件正版化自查、整改、提升等工作，明确工作措施和完成时限。

四是创新性开展工作。石家庄市继完成市本级政府机关办公软件年度场地授权续费、督促 13 个县级政府完成政府机关和事业单位（不含学校和医院）3～5 年办公软件场地授权外，12 月，再次为包括教育、医疗在内的 621 个事业单位的 44 997 台计算机购置办公软件，实现了所有事业单位的办公软件全覆盖。邯郸、辛集市也完成了市本级政府机关和事业单位（不含学校和医院）3 年的办公软件全覆盖工作。衡水市部分市县集中采购国产操作系统和国产办公软件，实现了国产操作系统的部分替代，满足了机关单位的日常办公需要。石家庄和衡水两地的经验受到了国家版权局的充分肯定。

三、采取有力措施，严厉打击各类侵权盗版行为

一是召开版权工作会议。7 月 31 日，省版权局在石家庄市召开河北省版权工作会议。会议传达了全国版权执法监管工作会议的主要精神，部署了河北省“剑网 2018”专项行动的具体工作，通报了全省版权工作的进展情况，局党组书记、局长李晓明出席会议并做重要讲话。会议强调：各级版权部门要提高认识，奋发作为，努力做好新时代版权工作；要突出重点，精准打击，维护版权市场秩序；要明确指标，强化手段，下大力查办大案要案。会上，保定、石家庄和廊坊市分别就版权执法、软件正版化和版权示范创建工作做典型发言，省版权局相关人员就版权执法和软件正版化工作进行了业务培训。各市（含定州、辛集市）版权局有关领导、文化市场执法大队和软件正版化工作方面的负责人共计 40 余人参加会议。

二是组织开展“剑网 2018”专项行动。8 月，根据国家版权局等四部门要求，省版权局会同省互联网信息办公室、省通信管理局、省公安厅等部门联合印发了《河北省版权局等关于开展打击网络侵权盗版“剑网 2018”专项行动的通知》。专项行动以打击网络侵权为目标，以查办网络案件为重点，集中整治网络转载、短视频、动漫等领域侵权盗版多发态势，重点规范网络直播、知识分享、有声读物等平台版权传播秩序，创新执法监管方式和手段，加强部门间协同行动，采取约谈整改、行政处罚和刑事打击等多种措施，依法治理网络空间，严厉打击网络侵权盗版违法活动，积极营造良好的网络版权环境，取得了良好效果。专项行动期间，全省主动监管网站 3 000 多家次，处理涉嫌侵权盗版违规网站 22 个，注销违规网站备案 13 个，取消违规网站接入 15 个，列入黑名单管理 18 个，停止域名解析 4 个，先后查处了国家挂牌督办的张某某销售盗版光盘案、王某某网上销售盗版图书案、韩国 MBC 影视作品被侵犯著作权案等网络侵权盗版大案要案。

三是开展出版物市场版权执法工作。全省各级“扫黄打非”和版权执法部门在元旦春节、全国“两会”、春秋开学季、暑期等重要时间节点，先后开展了环京 4 市等重点地区出版物市场专项整治、京冀毗邻地区联合督导检查、中小学校园周边文化市场专项检查、旅游旺季重点地区文化市场清理整治等系列行动，重点打击侵权盗版十九大辅导读物等重大题材出版物、畅销图书、少儿类图书、资格考试辅导丛书、教材教辅等违法违规行为，重点整治利用网站、微店销售侵权盗版出版物等非法活动。全省共检查印刷企业 2 万家次、出版物经营单位 8 000 余家次、打字复印单位 800 余家次，收缴各类非法出版物总数 52 万多件。

四是加大版权案件的查处力度。先后查处了石家庄张某某销售盗版光盘案、河北大德图书文化有限公司侵犯著作权案、石家庄中徽文化传播有限公司侵犯著作权案、河北鼎达创意文化有限公司侵犯著作权案、保定市清苑区霍某某销售侵权复制品案、保定市满城区乐播私人影院侵犯著作权案、保定市满城区乐喵影咖侵犯著作权案、邯郸科技信息工程学校私自盗印教辅图书案、衡水市舒心书店销售盗版教材案等侵权盗版案件，震慑了犯罪分子。

四、加强版权宣传、教育和培训等工作，提高公众的版权意识

一是重视版权保护宣传周宣传活动。4 月 20—26 日，河北省开展了形式多样的版权保护宣传周活动。其一是《河北日报》《河北青年报》等省级新闻媒体大篇幅登载了国家版权局制作的以“版权保护，让创作更自信”和“版权运用，让生活更精彩”为主题的宣传海报。长城网在对宣传海报进行转载刊发的同时，对国家版权局和日本、韩国共同制作的版权宣传片进行宣传推广。其二是公布版权典型案件。对全省 2017 年度具有代表性的 10 起侵权盗版案件在《河北日报》、长城新媒体、《河北青年报》等新闻媒体进行宣传报道。其三是召开版权信息数据库平台上线新闻发布会。多家媒体给予了跟踪报道。

二是注重日常宣传。充分利用《中国版权年鉴》《河北新闻出版广播影视年鉴》《软件正版化在中国》等出版物的地位及影响，积极总结全省版权保护经验，通过文字、图片等形式，全面展示版权保护成果，不断扩大对外宣传。

三是强化软件正版化工作培训。自 2 月份开始，邯郸、唐山、邢台、廊坊等 7 个设区市版权局、9 家省直单位分别组织了本级政府机关和所辖县级政府、所属事业单位及有关企业开展软件正版化培训，省版权局派员现场进行了专业授课。7 月 17 日，石家庄市召开了“软件正版化业务培训会议”，会议部署了下半年软件正版化工作，并就如何高标准完成全年工作任务等内容进行了认真培训。市直各部门相关责任人、各县（市、区）主要领导近 400 人参加了会议。9 月 6 日，省版权局培训中心召开“全省软件正版化工作业务培训班”，对各市局相关人员以及省重点期刊、省直主要报社和出版社的相关人员进行了软件正版化业务培训。张家口、沧州、定州、辛集等市也都分别自行组织了培训班。

四是加强对外交流。10 月 19—21 日，第七届中国国际版权博览会在江苏省苏州市举办，省版权局组织全省 23 家企事业单位的 236 件作品参展，内容包括图书、影视、游戏和动漫作品，以及雕刻、绘画、陶瓷、剪纸等传统工艺品。展会期间，国家版权局版权管理司司长于慈珂带队参观了河北省展区，观摩了吴桥方士英石影雕作品的创作过程，并与制作者进行了现场交流互动。闭幕式上，经版博会组委会认真评定，河北省版权局、石家庄市版权局、廊坊市版权局分别荣获“金慧奖”优秀组织奖。河北出版传媒集团、河北影视集团、河北乐聪网络科技股份有限公司、河北百年巧匠文化传播股份有限公司和吴桥方士英石影雕艺术有限公司分别荣获“金慧奖”优秀企业奖。

五是宣传查案有功单位和个人。11 月 20 日，国家版权局下发《关于奖励 2017 年度查处侵权盗版重大案件的决定》，对在 2017 年度查处侵权盗版案件工作中做出突出贡献的有功单位及有功个人给予奖励。河北省推荐的 18 家单位及 7 名个人全部获奖，其中河北省石家庄“8·12”销售盗版光盘案专案组获得有功单位一等奖，河北省版权局版权管理处、河北省通信管理局网络安全管理处、河北省石家庄市栾城区文化行政执法队、河北省衡水市文化市场行政执法大队和河北省邯郸市文化市场行政执法大队分获有功单位三等奖；河北廊坊“5·19”制售图书案专案组获得有功个人一等奖，河北省版权局版权管理处李振忠获得有功个人二等奖，河北保定周某某侵犯著作权案专案组、河北保定龙潭宾馆侵犯著作权案专案组分获有功个人三等奖。

（李冬群）

山　西　省

2018年，山西省版权局坚持全面从严执法、突出加强保护、注重版权服务和助推转型综改的工作目标，致力于创新版权管理方式、加大版权监管力度、提高公众版权意识，扎实开展打击侵权盗版和软件正版化等重点工作，努力实现由管理执法为主向“放、管、服、效”并重的良性转变。山西省版权局被评为全国打击侵权盗版有功单位二等奖，版权管理处杨志云处长作为获奖单位代表到中南海领奖并受到了汪洋常委的亲自接见。主要情况如下：

一、科学管理，突出重点，加强版权行政执法监管工作

版权管理与执法工作是全省打击侵犯知识产权和制售假冒伪劣商品工作的重中之重。山西省版权局将打击侵权盗版作为全年工作的重要任务，提高工作标准，加大打击力度，坚决保持对侵权盗版不法分子和违法行为的高压态势。切实发挥局“双打”领导小组办公室的职能作用，对全省版权领域“双打”工作进行部署，要求加强版权监管源头治理，开展大检查、大整顿、大治理工作，突出重点领域、重点环节、重点位置、重点对象的整顿工作，保持对生产、销售侵权盗版制品违法行为的高压打击态势。明确了打击侵权盗版工作的基本要求，要求狠打快打、聚焦重点、追根溯源、强力查办，确保各项行动落到实处，全面净化全省出版物市场。全省立案查办各类侵权盗版案件53起。认真组织开展全省版权执法人员培训，加强版权执法队伍建设，提高版权执法队伍素质。

二、重拳出击，聚焦难点，严厉打击网络侵权盗版违法行为

山西省版权局牵头，与省公安厅、省通信管理局、省互联网信息办公室于2018年7月起，在全省范围内联合开展了第14次打击网络侵权盗版专项治理“剑网行动”。以网络侵权多发领域为重点目标，以查办网络侵权盗版案件为重要抓手，集中整治网络转载、短视频、动漫等领域侵权盗版多发态势，重点规范网络直播、知识分享、有声读物等平台版权传播秩序，深入巩固网络影视、网络音乐、电子商务平台、应用商店、网络云存储空间等领域专项整治成果。积极开展重点网站主动监管工作，对传播文学、影视、音乐、新闻、游戏等作品的重点网站进行全面清理整顿，并将有关重点监管对象依法纳入版权监测范围。全省共主动监管网站100余家。部分市组织互联网企业开展自查自纠，全面清理整顿，约谈网站负责人，认真查找、及时整改侵权盗版问题。

处置国家版权局移转的涉嫌侵犯网上著作权案件线索5起。经认真核定，其中3起，山西省无管辖权；其余2起，山西版权局组织精干力量，开展调查取证和案件查办工作。一是“××电影网”涉嫌侵权案。该网站无网站备案信息。案件移转函中所提供的IP地址位置在湖南省衡阳市电信。该网站使用了云加速技术，实际IP地址暂无法查清。该网站上传了包含热播热映影视作品在内的海量影视作品，并有手机端APP程序，百度权重为7，非法获利可能巨大，影响极为恶劣。目前正在进一步处理。二是“××高清网”涉嫌侵犯著作权案件。已经对该网站进行了深入调查，网站备案信息中显示的地址在山西省阳泉市。目前，已经对网站相关信息以及涉案部分影视作品进行了勘验取证，并购买了相关商品作为证据。目前正在组织对该案相关涉案作品证据进一步进行固定，完善案件相关证据链条。

此外，山西省还办结了涉及网络侵权盗版的案件2起，分别是“朔州那些事儿”微信平台案和歪歪视频案。以上2个网站不但侵犯著作权，同时也含有淫秽色情等相关信息，所以由文化市场行政综合执法部门依据《信息网络传播权保护条例》和网络传播等相关条例，分别给予了3万元和1万元罚款的行政处罚。另外，运城市还处置了涉嫌非法转载新闻作品的网站2家。

三、牢筑根基，增强意识，加大版权宣传教育力度

社会公众的版权法制意识是版权管理工作的根本基础。以“倡导创新文化，尊重知识产权”主题，于4月20—26日组织全省各级版权管理部门开展版权宣传“七进”活动。一是版权宣传进媒体活动。组织各级版权管理部门运用广播、电视、公交移动电视等媒体，通过刊登公益广告、专栏专题宣传、播放宣传视频、播报宣传活动等方式进行广泛宣传。

二是版权宣传进机关活动。设计制作版权宣传漫画给100余个省级政府机关以及部分市级机关，要求在宣传栏、电梯口张贴并组织学习《政府机关使用正版软件管理办法》等相关文件。三是版权宣传进企业活动。深入版权密集型单位进行宣传，引导员工学习知识产权知识、树立创新理念。四是版权宣传进校园活动。太原市版权局深入校园，集中宣传著作权法律法规知识。五是版权宣传进社区活动。大同市通过群众喜闻乐见的形式，举办版权宣传进社区晋剧专场演出，深受社区群众欢迎。演出现场还设立了“侵权盗版举报点”，并讲解识别盗版图书常识。六是版权街头集中宣传活动。阳泉市举行了“知识产权宣传周”版权宣传活动启动仪式。大同市开展保护版权签名活动，宣传普及版权知识。太原、晋中、晋城、吕梁等市纷纷在城市广场、图书馆门前、主要街区以摆放宣传展板、发放宣传资料、现场解答问题等多种方式宣传法律知识。七是版权宣传进移动终端活动。如太原市利用移动在线服务向全市市民发送智能短信60万余条版权宣传主题短信，广泛开展版权知识宣传普及，力争扩大宣传活动的覆盖面、增强宣传活动的时效性，有力提升宣传效果。

四、落实责任，逐步推进，落实软件正版化工作长效机制

（一）认真安排部署

充分履行山西省版权局在省推进正版软件工作领导小组中的牵头职责，下发了《山西省2018年推进使用正版软件工作计划》，要求重点做好落实软件资产管理制度、规范计算机软硬件采购流程、探索实施软件集中采购工作、推广正版软件管理工作指南、开展政府机关软件正版化工作督促检查、加快推进企业软件正版化、做好预装正版操作系统软件监管等方面的工作。

（二）全面落实责任

为充分明确工作责任，对省直各单位软件正版化工作责任人信息数据库进行核实清理，督促各市建立健全软件正版化工作机构，确保各项工作精准对接、工作责任有效落实。

（三）开展自查整改

组织省级政府机关和各市推进使用正版软件领导小组对各级政府机关正版软件的购买、安装、使用、管理情况进行全面自查，要求进一步完善工作协调、经费保障、软件采购、日常监督、资产管理、审计考核和年度报告等工作制度，全面加强使用正版软件工作长效机制建设，开展年度使用正版软件工作总结统计工作。

（四）加强专项整改

要求省经信委等6个省直机关和汾酒集团等4个省属国企按照国务院推进使用正版软件工作部际联席会议的有关要求，对照督查中发现的问题，着重做好主要领导责任落实、软件安装使用维护、软件管理机制建设和正版化工作责任追究等方面的工作，彻底解决软件正版化工作中存在的问题。举一反三，逐项整改，确保各项措施落地生效。

（五）分批稳步推进

加快推进全省省属国有企业和银行业金融系统使用正版软件检查整改工作，要求各有关单位与信息化工作相结合，对使用正版软件工作情况进行严格自查，摸清使用正版软件工作底数，发现问题及时整改，建立健全推进使用正版软件工作长效机制。

（六）组织业务培训

山西省版权局组织全省省级政府机关使用正版软件工作责任人和具体负责人，开展了以软件正版化工作的新形势新任务、常用软件专业知识为主要内容的软件正版化工作培训。

五、转变思路，服务大局，加强版权公共服务体系建设

（一）建立版权工作机构

为服务全省转型综改发展大局，充分发挥版权要素在推动经济结构调整升级中的重大作用，山西省率先在省转型综改示范区和部分版权密集型单位共12家建设全流程管理的版权专业工作机构，目前山西出版传媒集团、山西传媒学院、山西日报社等单位机构已成立并初步投入运营。

（二）探索知识产权质押融资办法

认真落实省委省政府关于全省转型综改试验区建设的相关工作要求，认真研究知识产权质押融资工作，寻找突破办法。与国家版权局和兄弟省市积极沟通，对国家版权局和部分省市版权质押融资工作相关情况进行了持续跟踪，与省科技厅等畅通联系渠道，与省金控集团就版权质押融资工作开展了良好对接，力求推动工作进展。

（三）帮助解决版权实务难题

加强对图书、报刊采编人员的版权法律知识培训，提高其在版权工作新形势下使用、管理、保护版权资源的能力，2018年共有近千人参加了培训。为相关单位提供网络侵权纠纷、版权资源使用等方面的版权法律咨询服务，帮助解决其在经营活动中遇到的实际问题，努力在版权专业方面为相关单位做好参谋和助手。

（四）做好版权登记工作

努力发挥作品版权登记工作和版权贸易合同备案在厘清版权权属、化解版权纠纷、提供权利证据、避免版权侵权等方面的重要作用，积极扩大工作的覆盖面和社会影响。完成作品版权登记 300 余件，完成版权贸易合同备案 53 件。

（郝子谋）

内蒙古自治区

一、社会公共服务方面

一是建立全自治区首个版权服务工作站。4 月 21 日上午，在 2018 年全国知识产权宣传周内蒙古地区活动启动仪式上，内蒙古自治区版权局向内蒙古知识产权服务中心颁授了“内蒙古自治区版权服务工作站”牌匾和“著作权登记委托书”，内蒙古自治区首家版权服务工作站正式授牌成立。版权服务工作站是经自治区版权局批准，依托重点行业或重点单位建立，配合版权行政管理部门在指定区域开展版权服务工作的非营利机构。受自治区版权局委托，负责宣传贯彻著作权法律法规，帮助有关企事业单位建立版权管理与保护制度，配合版权行政管理部门和执法部门进行版权调查和统计工作，在指定区域开展版权相关服务，免费承担一般作品登记提交的申请、初审（包括电子版）及咨询等工作。二是推动版权公共服务向基层发展。制定印发了《内蒙古自治区版权局关于进一步加强作品著作权登记工作的通知》，鼓励支持各盟市开展作品登记业务，并通过设立“版权服务工作站”等方式对本地区的一般作品进行免费登记。积极探索为重点地区、行业、企业及团体提供便捷高效的作品登记服务方式，鼓励支持在有条件的旗（县区）、单位和园区设立版权服务工作点，开展以作品登记为核心的基础性版权公共服务。截至年底，全自治区 12 个盟市都已申请设立版权服务工作站。三是版权登记增量迅速。2018 年内蒙古自治区著作权登记总量达到 617 件，相比 2017 年的 299 件，同比增长 106%。从分布地区看，登记量最多的是呼和浩特市 323 件，约占登记总量的 52%；第二是呼伦贝尔市 109 件，约占登记总量的 18%；第三是包头市 33 件，约占登记总量的 5%。从作品类型看，登记量最多的是美术作品 354 件，约占登记总量的 57%；第二是类似电影方法创作的作品 111 件，约占登记总量的 18%；第三是文字作品 59 件，约占登记总量的 10%。四是扶持版权产业发展。10 月 19—21 日，第七届中国国际版权博览会在苏州国际博览中心举办。内蒙古自治区首次以参展省份的身份参展。本届版博会参展工作由版权局组织，来自全区各级版权管理部门、相关企业及版权服务机构 50 余人、394 件作品参加本届版博会。搭建了由现代元素与蒙元文化相结合，以蒙古包、绿草地等极具蒙古风情的自然风光和人文元素为背景的民族特色展区，运用模型和实物、视频、网络等多种模式，全方位展示了内蒙古自治区特色文化和优秀的版权成果。在 21 日下午进行的闭幕式中，内蒙古自治区版权局和两家行业企业分获优秀组织奖和优秀单位奖。

二、版权执法方面

一是开展“剑网”专项行动。连续 13 年会同网信、公安、通信管理等部门开展“剑网”专项行动，制定印发“剑网 2018”专项行动实施方案和宣传方案，共办理案件 5 起，共处罚金 6 万元整。二是开展打击侵权假冒工作。全区各级版权执法部门会同“扫黄打非”、文化、公安、工商、知识产权等相关部门持续开展打击侵犯知识产权和制售假冒伪劣商品行动，2018 年共查处各类侵权案件 56 起，处没罚金 21.14 万元，有力净化了内蒙古自治区市场秩序，营造了良好的版权产业发展环境。

三、软件正版化方面

一是推进考核工作。2018 年上半年，版权局积极协调自治区政法委、考核办等相关部门，修订了软件正版化考核平时和年终三级指标，并报送自治区依法治区目标考核组（政法委列入）年度实绩考核指标体系。连续四年将软件正版化工作纳入厅局、盟市领导班子考核指标体系。从 6 月底开始，组织开展本年度软件正版化日常督查工作。自治区直属机关方面：由自治区推进使用正版软件工作联席会议各成员单位带队，组成 18 个督查组同时进行。盟市方面：采取自治区版权局督查与盟市互查相结合的方式，共对 12 个盟市近 30 个旗县的软件正版化工作进行督查。本次督查共涉及区直机关单位 62 家、盟市级机关单位 70 余家、旗县级单位 123 家，查看文件 2 700 余份，实地查看计算机近 13 000 台。二是完善工作机制。1 月份，组织完成 2017 年度软件正版化考核任务。上半年，围绕软件正版化工作，先后完成并报送了《内蒙古自治区推进使用正版软件工作联席会议关于报送 2017 年软件正版化工作总结的报告》、《内蒙古自治区 2018 年软件正版化工作计划（代拟稿）》、《关于开展区直机关单位软件正版化工作督查的通知》（内版权联字［2018］3 号）、

《关于印发内蒙古自治区2018年推进使用正版软件工作计划的通知》（内版权联字〔2018〕4号）等文件，对软件正版化工作进行了一系列安排部署。5月16日，组织召开自治区推进使用正版软件工作联席会议2018年第一次会议，会议通报了自治区2017年度软件正版化工作督查考核情况，总结了2017年内蒙古自治区推进使用正版软件工作，安排部署了2018年重点工作任务及日常督查考核工作，要求按照国家全覆盖督查工作督查要求，开展全区范围内的日常工作督查。进一步明确了持续巩固政府机关软件正版化工作成果、加强侵权盗版执法监管、自上而下开展好宣传和培训、全面推进企事业单位软件正版化、做好软件正版化日常督查工作等五方面重点工作内容。

四、版权宣传培训工作方面

一是利用重要时间节点，开展版权宣传。4月初，按照国家版权局《关于做好2018年全国知识产权宣传周版权宣传活动的通知》精神，内蒙古自治区版权局印发《开展2018年知识产权宣传周版权宣传活动的实施方案》和《内蒙古自治区版权局关于做好知识产权宣传周版权宣传活动的通知》，对全区宣传活动进行具体安排部署，同时在《广播电视宣传提示》开设2期“版权宣传专刊”，刊发版权宣传内容，指导动员自治区主要媒体开展各种形式的版权宣传。

二是开展集中销毁侵权盗版及非法出版物活动。宣传周期间，全区组织开展了侵权盗版及非法出版物集中销毁活动。各盟市（含满洲里、二连浩特市）文化市场综合执法队及各界代表共计1万余人先后参加活动。在活动中，全区共销毁各类侵权盗版和非法出版物39.4万件，其中盗版书刊19.6万件、盗版音像电子出版物6.3万件。

三是发挥主流媒体的作用。利用各级政府和相关部门门户网站等宣传平台，充分发挥主流媒体的舆论引导作用，做好重大执法行动的跟踪报道，邀请媒体参加重要活动，适时召开新闻发布会，组织开展在线访谈，发布打击侵权工作进展情况，保持宣传报道工作的常态化。

四是发挥网络新媒体作用。利用微博、微信、移动客户端等新媒体平台，创新工作手段，丰富宣传载体，扩大宣传覆盖面，增强宣传效果。充分发挥“内蒙古自治区新闻出版局”微信公众号作用，及时更新充实地方站内容，动态反映工作进展，提升版权工作整体影响力。

五是加强户外、楼宇LED屏、公交车版权宣传。利用国家版权局提供的宣传素材，制作了2集版权宣传公益视频广告，确定了专门的版权宣传语，在全区公交车尾广告屏上进行循环播放。印制版权宣传海报和易拉宝，在各盟市写字楼各显著位置摆放。

六是开展宣传培训，加强版权人才队伍建设。5月29日，为进一步传达贯彻国家和自治区推进正版软件工作联席会议精神，内蒙古自治区对推进使用正版软件工作联席会议成员单位和各被督查单位进行相关内容和技术培训，自治区直属机关各委、办、厅、局90家单位共计141名有关人员参加了培训。7月31日—8月2日，在鄂尔多斯市举办2018年全区版权工作培训班，共涉及软件正版化、版权执法和公共服务等三方面内容，来自全区各盟市版权行政管理、版权执法相关人员共300余人次参加培训。

（马　达）

辽　宁　省

2018年，辽宁版权工作以习近平新时代中国特色社会主义思想和党的十九大精神为指引，全面贯彻落实创新型国家建设战略及版权工作“十三五”规划，积极发挥省政府使用正版软件工作领导小组办公室、省打击网络侵权盗版专项工作领导小组办公室、省打击侵权假冒工作领导小组主要成员单位职能，重点工作有新亮点，常规工作有新举措。

一、以“剑网2018”为主抓手，保持打击侵权盗版高压态势

（一）组织开展“剑网2018”专项行动

根据国家版权局等四部委的统一部署，辽宁省版权局、省互联网信息办公室、省通信管理局和省公安厅结合辽宁省工作实际，共同研究制定了《辽宁省打击网络侵权盗版“剑网2018”专项行动实施方案》，自8月至11月在全省范围内组织开展第十四次打击网络侵权盗版“剑网2018”专项行动，并组织召开了全省打击网络侵权盗版“剑网2018”专项行动工作部署会。

省版权局负责专项行动的牵头工作，组织开展专项行动的宣传报道，及时发布专项行动有关情况，督促落实各阶段重点任务，开展网上侵权盗版信息梳理、收集，汇总案件线索，组织查处侵权盗版案件，及时移送涉嫌犯罪案件，协调通信管理部门配合案件查办工作，并及时关闭侵权网站。

专项行动期间，全省将加强宣传造势、网络监管、查办案件三个重要任务贯穿始终。各地认真落实国家和全省的工作部署和打击网络侵权盗版“剑网2018”专项行动实施方案的要求，以网络、应用程序、自媒体、新闻聚合类平台、网络游戏、手机游戏等为日常巡视检查范围，并结合本地实际情况，把整治的重点放在网络侵权多发领域，尤其加大对未经授权复制、表演、通过网络传播他人影视、音乐、摄影、文字等作品侵权行为的整治力度。

一是积极发挥部门协同机制，组织协调网信、通信管理、公安部门，利用网络监测手段和技术，对在省内注册的短视频平台、动漫网站、新闻网站、视听网站、电子商务平台、应用商店等进行监管和巡查。市区两级文化执法部门确立了网络文化市场巡查制度，要求巡查人员在网络巡查时截屏记录，做好网络巡查台账，确保工作落实到岗，责任落实到人。

二是组织开展短视频专项整治。各市执法人员重点对“抖音”“快手”“火山”“美拍”“西瓜”等热门直播短视频平台进行远程勘验。

三是开展网络游戏出版专项整治行动。沈阳、大连、鞍山等较大地市对现有运营的网络游戏运营单位、网络游戏宣传推广单位、网络游戏虚拟货币交易服务企业进行了全面巡查，巡查重点包括是否存在侵权和打法律擦边球行为。

9月中旬至11月上旬，省版权局联合省通信管理局赴各市对“剑网行动”推进情况进行督查，对5个市的11家重点网站进行了现场检查，对各网站负责人就年度“剑网行动”重点任务、要求，以及相关版权法律、法规进行了宣讲，并就规范使用作品进行了面对面的交流。

专项行动期间，全省共查处案件22起，行政罚款3.5万元，关闭侵权网站14个。

（二）全力开展国家版权局等部委挂牌督办案件具体督导工作，并积极查办督办省内重大案件

省版权局先后于9月和12月两次赴大连市，对国家版权局、公安部等五部委挂牌督办的大连“8·29”宋长发等团伙制售侵权盗版图书案进行调研督导，积极协调指导案件查办工作，并协调国家版权局予以查办案件补贴10万元。目前，该案已进入法院审理阶段，择期将予以宣判。

此外，省版权局、省“扫黄打非”办积极指导和督办沈阳市和平公安分局立案侦办“4·25”网络批销盗版医疗美容类图书案件、王某某销售盗版教材案件、陈某擘等侵犯著作权案件等重大案件。2018年12月，为深入推动案件查办工作，省版权局及时将沈阳市公安局侦办的陈某擘等侵犯著作权案件向国家版权局申请予以挂牌督办。

（三）加强版权保护预警工作

根据国家版权局统一部署，2018年，及时部署和督导各市及省内主要网站，落实国家版权局包括中央电视台2018年春节联欢晚会在内的10批次重点作品版权保护预警工作。

（四）组织开展北京2022年冬奥会会徽和冬残奥会会徽版权专项保护工作

1—7月，按照国家版权局工作要求，组织全省开展北京2022年冬奥会会徽和冬残奥会会徽版权专项保护工作，重点工作包括宣传普及北京冬奥会版权保护相关法律知识、制定应急预案、健全施行应急机制、加强日常监管和市场巡查。

（五）指导和督促全省各市做好打击侵权盗版案件日常工作

开放举报电话，畅通举报途径。据统计，2018年，全省共查办侵犯著作权案件52件（其中网络侵权盗版案件22件），全省捣毁侵权盗版窝点56个。

（六）组织开展版权执法培训

12月6—7日，省“扫黄打非”办、省版权局举办2018年全省“扫黄打非”业务培训班，来自省内各市县基层的“扫黄打非”、版权管理与执法人员，各市公安、通信管理部门负责同志等共80人参加了培训。邀请了版权执法、“扫黄打非”、公安等部门的业务骨干和专家授课。

2017年度全国查处侵权盗版案件有功单位、有功个人名单公布，辽宁省共有1家单位获评有功单位二等奖，5家单位获评有功单位三等奖；4人获评有功个人二等奖，1人获评有功个人三等奖。

二、全面巩固政府机关和企业软件正版化工作成果

2018年，在国务院推进使用正版软件工作部际联席会议正确指导下，全省继续推进各级政府机关和企业使用正版软件工作，以推进使用国产软件促进民族产业发展、巩固成果、扩大软件正版化工作覆盖面为工作重点，强化落实主体责任，完善长效机制，加大调研和督查力度，使软件正版化工作进一步规范化、常态化、制度化。

（一）巩固和深化政府机关软件正版化工作成果

2018年，辽宁省政府机关软件正版化工作重点是巩固省级政府机关2017年正版化全覆盖工作成果，以国务院在辽检查提出的整改意见为首要工作指引，按照国务院《政府机关使用正版软件管理办法》和国务院联席会议《正版软件管理工作指南》

要求，推动落实采购经费、完善相关制度、开展深化自查整改，深化全省各级政府机关软件正版化工作。

（1）召开省政府使用正版软件工作领导小组成员单位联络员会议，重点工作专门会商。来自省直22家单位的联络员参加了会议，全面总结了2018年推进政府机关和企业软件正版化工作情况，讨论通过了《辽宁省2018年推进使用正版软件工作安排》，并与省国资委负责同志就全面推进国有企业软件正版化工作进行了专门会商。

（2）组织召开省市政府机关软件正版化业务培训，强调国产化优先。为贯彻落实国务院办公厅《政府机关使用正版软件管理办法》精神，根据《辽宁省2018年推进使用正版软件工作实施方案》的安排，省版权局组织召开了两期省直机关软件正版化业务培训会议，省直98家单位的相关负责人参会。省版权局负责人重点强调了优先使用国产办公软件和操作系统的工作要求。

（3）全面推进省直机关软件正版化考核评议。2017年5月，省政府使用正版软件工作领导小组制定出台了《辽宁省政府机关使用正版软件工作考核办法（试行）》，将软件正版化工作考核纳入省政府对省直机关及各市县政府“双打”考核重要内容。这些措施和制度性安排，有效地推动了长效机制的建立，进一步提升了考核工作的力度和效果。

（4）开展市县级政府机关软件正版化督导检查，强调主体责任。根据《辽宁省2018年推进使用正版软件工作实施方案》，以推动政府机关落实软件正版化工作主体责任，建立健全软件正版化工作长效机制、国产化软件优先为重点，省政府使用正版软件工作领导小组派出检查组，于2018年5月下旬至11月下旬对各市县级政府机关软件正版化工作进行了年度例行督查和调研。

（5）开展政府机关软件正版化管理情况审计工作。省审计厅结合预算执行、经济责任等审计项目对省直部门正版软件采购、资金使用和资产管理情况实施审计。

省审计厅在抓好省本级审计的同时，对全省各级审计机关开展软件正版化审计工作提出明确要求。省审计厅成立了14个派出处，会同各市、县级审计机关软件正版化工作纳入年度审计计划中去统筹，做出具体的安排部署，集中力量，组织实施。各市审计局普遍将正版化审计工作纳入政策跟踪审计中，作为重点内容进行了审计。

审计结果表明，全省软件正版化工作取得了良好成效，实现了工作机制健全、责任分工明确、软件采购规范、安装使用到位、软件台账齐全、资产管理有序。

（6）及时调整更新责任人数据库，着力加强对基层的业务指导。2018年以来，根据政府机关新一轮机构改革情况，及时调整和更新了80家省直机关的辽宁省政府机关软件正版化工作责任人数据库。为进一步加强对各个政府机关的业务指导、畅通信息报送渠道、密切各单位的沟通交流，省版权局统一建立了省政府机关软件正版化业务交流QQ群、专用工作邮箱以及专用微信工作群。截至目前，各省直单位责任人信息情况仍在更新阶段。

（二）扎实有序推进企业软件正版化工作

根据《辽宁省2018年推进使用正版软件工作实施方案》的部署，以省属国有企业和新闻出版行业企业为重点，有计划、分层次推进企业软件正版化工作。

（1）持续推进全省国有企业软件正版化工作。为落实部际联席会议的年度工作要求，省版权局联合省国资委通过开展培训、入企调研、督查指导等方式积极开展推进工作。各省属国有企业对推进软件正版化工作有了明确认识，基本进入使用正版软件工作制度化阶段。省版权局、省国资委实地指导企业如何选择、测试相关产品的兼容性、适用性，尤其强调了国有企业集中采购、优先使用国产化办公软件的两项要求。据统计，年内省属国有企业采购约530套WPS 2016办公软件，各市属国有企业采购（升级）约410套办公软件。

（2）全面巩固全省新闻出版广电行业软件正版化工作。在2015年底全面完成了全省新闻出版行业企业软件正版化工作后，省版权局重点工作着力在巩固全省行业企业正版化成果上。年内，通过培训、督查、调研等方式开展行业企业工作，推进全省新闻出版行业企业软件正版化常态化管理。

（3）以宣传培训为抓手，持续推进企业软件正版化工作。年内，省版权局联合辽宁银保监局、省工商联等成员单位先后举办了三期企业软件正版化培训班，省内勘察设计、机械制造、商业服务、金融保险等重点行业的72家企业100余名主管领导和信息化部门负责人参加了培训，讲解使用盗版软件的法律风险、信息安全风险，以及辽宁省年度工作部署。沈阳、大连等部分地区按照省里总体部署开展宣传培训工作，推进企业使用正版软件。通过各单位自查整改上报采购数据以及省版权局组织的抽检验收，共有103家企业实现了通用软件正版化工作任务。

（三）进一步完善版权公共服务体系建设，提升版权管理服务能力

（1）根据国家新闻出版广电总局工作要求，梳理统计省内出版单位版权引进和输出情况，严格按要求上报2017年度版权贸易统计相关报表。

（2）版权示范实地调研。根据《辽宁省版权示范城市、示范单位、示范园区（基地）管理办法》，省版权局对省直及沈阳、营口、盘锦等市推荐的单位、园区等进行实地考察调研。

（3）召开中国（辽宁）自由贸易试验区营口片区座谈会。5月初，组织营口市版权局、自贸区市场监管局（知识产权局）以及片区多家企业代表参加会议。省版权局领导就如何加强版权创造、运用、保护和管理，以版权促进产业发展为自贸区和各企业提出了针对性指导建议。

（4）著作权登记量显著提升。2018年共办理作品自愿登记10 221件，较2017年同期增长13%；办理著作权合同备案登记6件；审核出版境外图书著作权合同登记409件。

（四）组织开展2018年版权保护宣传周系列活动

（1）4月19日，田铁林副局长代表省版权局出席省政府举办的2017年辽宁省知识产权发展与保护状况新闻发布会，权威发布2017年度辽宁省版权工作情况，并就推进版权公共服务等相关工作回答了记者提问。

（2）4月20日上午，省版权局参加2018年辽宁省暨沈阳市知识产权宣传周启动仪式。

（3）4月23日，在第七届全民读书节开幕式主会场的公共活动区域设立版权宣传与咨询服务台，以宣教展示、定点咨询、发放资料等形式开展版权主题宣传活动，受到中国医科大学师生以及参展商的广泛关注和好评。

（4）组织全省广播电视媒体播放公益宣传片。在“4·26”世界知识产权日集中宣传期间，在全省各级广播电视台集中播放版权保护公益系列宣传片。据统计，自4月初至5月中旬，在全省20家市县广播电视台的30多个频道、频率，累计播放2 000余次。

（5）在“5·18”国际博物馆日，省版权局应邀参加了沈阳市文广局在沈阳宣和艺术馆举办的“5·18”国际博物馆日启动活动。省版权局负责同志从版权法律常识、版权助力文创产业发展、国家和省的版权相关政策等方面为与会各界代表做版权主题发言。并在活动现场为沈阳故宫博物院、沈阳宣和艺术馆等单位以及几位知名文创大师颁发作品自愿登记证书。

（五）组织辽宁展团参加第25届北京国际图书博览会

为充分利用好北京图博会这一国际平台，持续强化辽宁省图书海外市场影响力，省版权局组织和指导辽宁展团精心准备、积极参展。省内15家出版单位组成辽宁展团参展，举办了8场国际推广活动，共计达成各种合作意向162项，其中引进意向89项，输出意向73项；现场签约44项，其中引进签约24项，输出签约20项。

（田大鹏）

吉林省

2018年，吉林省各级版权管理部门坚持以习近平新时代中国特色社会主义思想为指导，深入贯彻党的十九大和十九届二中、三中全会精神，认真落实国家版权局和省委、省政府的工作部署，围绕中心工作，采取切实有效的工作举措，重点针对执法监管、版权宣传、版权社会化服务等内容开展相关工作，各项工作取得明显成效，确保全年工作任务圆满完成。

一、加强组织协调，版权执法监管成效显著

（一）组织各类专项执法活动，开展重点领域的集中治理

在2018年元旦和春节期间，以打击侵权盗版和净化网络市场环境为主要任务，吉林省版权局印发文件通知，组织全省各级版权管理部门及文化综合执法部门开展了元旦、春节期间的集中治理，维护版权市场秩序，营造良好节日氛围。7月至11月，吉林省版权局联合省通信管理局、省网信办、省公安厅共同组织开展了打击网络侵权盗版“剑网2018”专项行动，全省各级版权执法机关结合实际，以网络侵权多发领域为重点目标，以加强案件查办为主要手段，通过集中治理和规范引导，巩固网络转载、网络文学、网络视频、网络音乐、电子商务平台及网络广告联盟等领域的专项整治成果，维护良好的网络版权秩序，通过版权保护促进舆论环境净化，为全省经济社会发展营造良好的营商环境。省版权局继续开展对私人影院网络传播盗版电影行为的集中整治，开展定期巡查，查处典型案件，对3家私人影院侵权播放电影作品的违法行为做出行政处罚，有效地规范了私人点播影院系统的版权秩序。本年度全省共立案涉网侵权案件12件，做出行

政处罚 7 件，行政调解 2 件，关闭电脑服务器 3 台，约谈网站负责人 30 余次，行政罚款金额总计 11 万元。协调“扫黄打非”工作部门开展了“秋风 2018”专项行动，有力打击复制发行盗版出版物的违法行为。继续组织开展对省内印刷复制企业进行集中执法检查，规范印刷复制行为和市场秩序。

（二）强化对全省版权执法监管工作的统一领导，加大案件查处力度

省版权局严格落实版权执法工作月报制度，及时调度各市县版权执法工作进展情况，组织全省各级版权执法机关开展案件查办工作，强化对各市县级版权执法机关的指导，及时处理上级部门移转的案件，通过督办、转办等方式对各地查办案件工作进行督促检查。进一步完善落实版权执法案件信息公开制度，组织各级版权执法机关利用各类途径对本年度的行政处罚案件进行及时公开，加强社会监督，提高版权执法监管工作质量，全年共查处各类版权侵权案件 38 件，罚款总额超过 33 万元。吉林省的版权执法工作受到上级部门的充分肯定，省版权局版权管理处相关负责同志还受邀在全国性的版权执法培训班上对版权侵权案件查办情况做经验交流讲座。版权管理处及处内执法人员连续第三年获得国家版权局查处侵权盗版案件有功集体、有功个人一等奖，全省各级版权执法机关和执法人员获得奖励数量居全国前列。

二、落实工作责任，持续推进软件正版化工作

（一）制定工作方案，安排部署全省软件正版化工作

为加强对全省使用正版软件工作的统一领导，落实相关职能部门工作责任，省推进使用正版软件工作领导小组办公室（省版权局）协调领导小组各成员单位，完善工作机制及各项制度，充分发挥领导小组的统一领导作用，形成整体工作合力。年初，省版权局牵头组织领导小组各成员单位的软件正版化工作联络员召开了 2018 年度软件正版化专题工作会议，共同研究新形势下做好软件正版化工作的具体工作举措，确定本年度重点工作任务，并对省版权局拟定的软件正版化年度工作计划征求意见。制定印发了《吉林省 2018 年推进使用正版软件工作计划》，部署本年度全省软件正版化工作，指导各级政府开展软件正版化工作。省内各市县级政府成立的软件正版化工作领导机构按照省推进使用正版软件工作领导小组的统一部署和具体工作要求，结合本地实际情况，研究制定本地区软件正版化工作实施方案，明确各成员单位的责任分工和工作任务，有针对性地组织开展软件正版化工作。

（二）加强督促检查，完善软件正版化长效工作机制

为巩固省级政府机关软件正版化工作成果，省版权局在上半年开展了省级政府机关软件正版化检查“回头看”，了解各有关部门对本单位存在问题的整改落实情况，提出指导意见和整改要求，定期调度进展完成情况，持续推动相关问题的整改。为进一步推进市县级政府机关软件正版化工作，省版权局于下半年组织检查组分别对四平市、吉林市进行软件正版化现场工作督查。此外，省版权局及时了解各市县级政府软件正版化牵头业务部门的工作开展情况，督促有关业务部门落实软件正版化工作主体责任，加强对本级党政机关单位软件正版化工作自查整改落实情况的检查和指导，积极推进全省各级政府机关建立软件正版化工作长效机制。

（三）落实整改采购要求，确保机关单位正版软件全覆盖

督促、指导各省级党政机关单位及各市县级政府软件正版化工作牵头业务部门，按照上级有关部门督查反馈意见，结合本单位开展的自查，统计正版软件实际需求，做好新增正版软件采购和软件升级工作，持续推进各级党政机关单位正版软件全覆盖。省政府办公厅、省公安厅、省人民法院等省级机关单位根据本单位新增软件需要和系统升级要求，采购了正版操作系统和通用办公软件。吉林市政府、四平市政府及四平梨树县政府分别进行了通用办公软件统一采购，实现同级党政机关单位通用办公软件正版化授权全覆盖。2018 年，全省各级党政机关单位共采购正版操作系统 7 422 套，采购金额 997 万元；采购通用办公软件 8 188 套，采购金额 484 万元，其中国产办公软件 5 931 套，采购软件的国产率达 72%，全省正版软件国产化程度不断提高。

（四）加强检查指导，平衡推进企业软件正版化

按照年初确定的软件正版化工作计划，继续有重点地推进国有企业软件正版化。省版权局与省国资委共同组织召开省国资委监管企业软件正版化工作专题会议，对参会企业开展软件正版化工作进行业务指导，并提出工作要求，统一安排下一步整改工作。上半年，省版权局与省国资委组织联合检查组对省内 16 家省国资委监管企业的软件正版化整改落实情况进行现场工作检查，并向企业负责人反馈检查中发现的问题，同时就现场检查结果向各有关企业印发正式通报，提出明确整改要求和完成时限，

有效地推进了省属国有企业软件正版化整改工作。为确保有关企业正版软件采购工作顺利进行，降低采购成本，省版权局与省国资委协调组织有关国有企业与软件供应商召开软件采购洽谈会，为企业搭建软件采购谈判平台。

三、精心组织谋划，做好版权宣传培训工作

按照国家版权局统一安排部署，继续加强版权集中宣传工作，创新版权实践载体，积极策划“4・26”世界知识产权日版权宣传周集中宣传系列活动，及时安排部署全省各地的集中宣传工作。宣传周期间，组织开展的集中宣传报道，产生广泛社会影响。省版权局在动漫集团和吉林动画学院开展作品集中登记和版权知识宣讲活动；通过各类媒体公布2017年度打击侵权盗版十大案件；协调省电台、省电视台、网络电视台就第十八个世界知识产权日采写专题新闻报道，宣传吉林省版权保护工作及版权创意产业发展成就；组织拍摄制作的版权公益宣传片《孕育》在省内各级电视台、省内各中心城市各影院、国内各相关网站、手机移动端APP上集中播放，营造了良好的社会舆论氛围。宣传周期间，全省各级版权管理部门组织参与的各类街头、社区宣传活动超过50次，发放各类宣传品超过2万册，极大地提高了本次集中宣传活动的公众参与度。

除在重要时间节点开展集中宣传外，加强在日常工作中的宣传普法和专题培训活动，提高社会公众的版权意识。创新和强化软件正版化宣传手段，不断扩大软件正版化社会工作影响和工作范围。本年度，省版权局分别在吉林市、四平市、延边朝鲜族自治州举办3期政府机关软件正版化工作培训，与省国资委共同举办企业软件正版化工作培训1期，通过培训提高相关工作负责人的认识和工作水平，持续推动软件正版化工作。进一步加大版权执法培训力度，组织全省各级版权执法骨干人员开展专题执法培训和业务研讨，配合国家版权局举办全国第三期版权执法骨干培训班，全面提升基层版权执法人员的综合业务素质。同时，全省各级版权管理部门充分利用“4・26”世界知识产权日、“3・15”消费者权益日等重要节点对著作权法及相关知识进行重点宣传，提高社会公众的认识，为版权保护工作营造良好的社会舆论环境。

四、拓展服务手段，助推版权创意产业发展

根据总局改革办印发的《新闻出版广播影视企业版权资产管理工作指引（试行）》，结合吉林实际，制定印发了《加强新闻出版广播影视企业版权资产管理工作的实施意见》，指导新闻出版广播影视行业内的相关企事业单位建立版权管理制度，形成良性版权创造、保护和运用机制。为强化版权社会化服务，支持和指导版权示范基地（园区）、单位的创建工作，上半年启动开展了版权示范单位、版权示范园区（基地）的申报评选活动。指导长春市版权局在长春市版权保护协会、长春市图书馆等四家单位设立版权服务工作站，完善版权公共服务体系。成功组织吉林省相关单位参加第七届中国国际版权博览会，除了传统出版单位之外，吉林动漫集团、通化松花石、东丰农民画、辽源袜业的相关企业也第一次参加此类展会，不仅拓展了视野，同时宣传推介吉林省特色创意文化产业。继续完善改进版权作品自愿登记工作，为相关版权企业及著作权人提供多层次的法律服务，全年登记数量超过2 100件，同比增长超过100%。

（杜宇震）

黑龙江省

一、软件正版化工作

制定方案：制定《黑龙江省2018年推进使用正版软件工作实施方案》，并以省政府名义报国务院，将方案有关精神下发各市（地）人民政府，对软件正版化工作进行了总体部署。

组织培训：组织通用软件厂商，举办了15期软件正版化培训班，对省、市、县三级党政机关负责软件正版化工作同志及技术人员进行全覆盖培训。7月，组织各地版权局主管局长、业务人员进行软件正版化工作培训。

组织督促检查：下发《关于开展2018年度全省政府机关软件正版化自查自纠工作的通知》，明确自查形式、自查内容，要求省直各部门、各市（地）、县（市、区）政府落实自查工作，并根据自查情况开展考核评议工作。

规范计算机软件采购流程：召开两次推进使用正版软件工作联席联络员会议，严格贯彻落实预装正版操作系统软件的规定，严格审核需要购置的办公软件购置计划，从源头上防止盗版软件流入各级政府机关。

二、版权执法工作

（一）打击网络侵权盗版“剑网行动”

（1）制定工作方案。联合省网信办、省通信管理局、省公安厅制定《关于开展打击网络侵权盗版“剑网2018”专项行动的通知》，明确了任务、责任和工作重点。

（2）落实工作举措。一是紧紧抓住监管重点，变被动查办侵权投诉案件为主动监管网站，对省内有影响力的26家主要互联网媒体定期监控。二是组织各地根据本地区的网络分布情况，制定工作方案。三是加大宣传力度，利用报刊、政府机关官网大力宣传打击网络侵权、维护网络版权秩序的有关政策，公布投诉举报方式，发动权利人和群众维权投诉。

（3）案件挂牌督办。指导大庆市办结国家版权局、全国“扫黄打非”办公室、公安部、最高人民检察院联合督办的大庆市华兴书店销售侵权复制品案。目前，嫌疑人已被逮捕，大庆萨尔图区人民检察院提起公诉，法院正在审理中。

（二）打击侵犯知识产权和制售假冒伪劣商品专项行动

2018年，黑龙江省各级版权行政管理部门加强对出版物市场的监管执法，打击各类侵权盗版行为。“双打”行动期间和节假日，开展市场巡查，加强日常监管。共查缴侵权盗版出版物7 751件，对8起自媒体、出版物市场、软件等侵权盗版案件予以行政处罚。

三、宣传工作

加大政府宣传工作。联合省政府新闻办公室、省知识产权局、省工商局、省法院召开黑龙江省知识产权保护状况新闻发布会。

强化媒体宣传。发挥主流媒体宣传作用，在黑龙江卫视频道、东北网和省版权局机关官方网站上滚动播放宣传字幕。

开展集中宣传工作。4月22日，联合省“扫黄打非”办公室、哈尔滨市版权局等部门在哈尔滨中央大街中央商城门前设立版权保护宣传展板、现场开展版权法律法规咨询宣传活动，并发放宣传材料、海报2 000余份。

深入高校宣传。知识产权宣传周期间深入哈尔滨华德学院、黑龙江大学、东北林业大学、哈尔滨理工大学、哈尔滨师范大学开展普法讲座、现场咨询、张贴海报、发放版权宣传手册等活动。

四、组织北京国际图书博览会参展工作

印发《关于做好第二十五届北京国际图书博览会的通知》，组织全省13家图书出版单位参加第二十五届北京国际图书博览会。派专人赴北京，完成布展、参展、撤展工作任务，为企业版权贸易提供平台。展会期间，共展出出版物近900种，展示了黑龙江新闻出版业的最新成果。

五、调解各种版权纠纷

调解各类著作权侵权纠纷9起，当事双方对调解结果满意；组织相关人员鉴定出版物1 100余种20 000余册，其中侵权盗版出版物500余册。

（闫　石）

上　海　市

2018年，上海市版权局深入学习贯彻党的十九大精神，积极落实国家版权局、市委市政府对版权管理工作的各项要求，紧紧围绕上海建设全球卓越城市的发展目标，努力将版权工作置于创新驱动发展、营造国际一流营商环境的工作大局之中。

一、加强服务能力建设，完善版权公共服务体系

（一）推进作品自愿登记工作

2018年以来，重点从深挖资源、丰富登记类别、提高登记作品质量等方面入手。在保证作品登记数量稳步上升的前提下，严把登记作品质量关，完善作品登记数据报送、统计和发布工作。截至2018年10月底，共完成作品登记216 183件，同比增长11.37%。2018年实现了杂技艺术作品登记“零”的突破，进一步丰富了登记类别。在积极推进登记日常工作的同时，与浦东新区知识产权局建立完善工作合作机制，共同推进版权登记工作。协调落实保障作品版权登记保护应用平台的部分运营费用，保障平台有序运行。

（二）加强版权工作站联动

继续加强与15家版权服务工作站的联动，指导开展形式多样的版权公共活动。如长宁区版权服务工作站开展的“海上文博·上海创意设计大赛”，以上海博物馆提供的“10大国宝级馆藏文物”为设计元素，将文博艺术授权与童装设计、孕婴童产品设计相结合，在提升自身版权公共服务能力的同时，也推动了版权产业发展。组织开展2017年度版权服务优秀项目评选工作，树典型、立标杆，指导各工作站互相学习，带动各工作站不断提升工作能力。

（三）推动自贸区版权服务中心筹建

为了全面深化自贸区改革、深入推进国家知识产权战略，支持浦东在自贸区内建设自贸区版权服务中心。作为国家级功能平台，自贸区版权服务中心主要为自贸区内的权利人和创新主体开展作品快速登记、版权管理监测、维权保护、人才培育等服务。目前，已完成项目立项、工作团队组建，并多次向国家版权局汇报推进进展情况，争取国家层面支持，寻求政策上有所突破，先行先试，为自贸区提供有广度更有深度的版权公共服务支撑。

二、加强激励引导，持续推动版权产业发展

（一）开展版权示范培优

评出第六批11家上海版权示范单位和1家版权示范园区（基地）。培育、支持有条件的单位和园区（基地）申报“中国最具影响力版权企业”。组织召开工作交流会，引导示范单位进一步将版权融入具体经营管理之中。积极组织本市相关单位申报“中国版权金奖”，最终上海市公安局治安总队获“中国版权金奖”保护奖，上海歌舞团的舞蹈作品《朱鹮》获“中国版权金奖”作品奖。

（二）落实专项资金扶持申报工作

按时完成2018年度新闻出版专项资金（版权）的评审工作。积极发动版权企业申报新闻出版专项资金，共有12家单位，提交申报项目25个，计划总投资1 587.76万元，共申请资助776.06万元。经过初核、初评、定评等环节，最终评出6家单位的8个项目为本年度扶持项目，扶持资金共计385万元。同时，按照局里要求，顺利完成2016年度新闻出版专项资金（版权）的审计、结项和绩效评价工作。

（三）实施版权“走出去”项目

组织全市四十余家出版单位和民营文化工作室积极申报本年度版权“走出去”扶持项目，完成2017版权“走出去”扶持项目评审工作。2017年，共有14家单位申报48个项目，经初审和专家评审，最终评出30个优秀项目，资助金额共计115万元。

三、加强长效机制建设，巩固扩大软件正版化工作成果

（一）组织开展市级机关软件正版化全覆盖检查工作

为切实巩固本市政府机关软件正版化工作成果，按照国务院办公厅印发的《政府机关使用正版软件管理办法》和《上海市政府机关使用正版软件考核办法》的要求，深入推进本市政府机关软件正版化工作长效管理，市使用正版软件工作领导小组办公室组织部分成员单位及上海市数字认证中心有限公司组成督查组，对全市市级政府机关进行全覆盖督查，重点督查制度建设、责任落实、源头监管、日常管理等情况，并对被督查单位进行考核评议，根据督查和评议情况，要求被督察单位在规定期限内做好整改工作，对整改工作进展缓慢、落实不到位的单位，加大督查力度。

（二）不断建立健全软件正版化工作机制

贯彻落实国务院办公厅印发的《政府机关使用正版软件管理办法》等相关政策措施，按照市使用正版软件工作领导小组编制的《上海市政府机关使用正版软件考核办法》，完善软件正版化工作责任、软件资产管理等制度，建立软件正版化工作责任人数据库，明确各级政府机关软件正版化工作责任部门和责任人。通过国家版权监管平台，及时向国家推进使用正版软件工作部际联席会议办公室报送计划、责任人数据库、软件使用情况统计表、软件正版化工作总结等工作材料。

（三）接受中央督查组督导检查上海软件正版化工作

9月，中央督察组来沪对本市软件正版化工作进行了为期一周的督查，共抽查6家市级机关、4家上海国资企业，现场检查3 188台计算机软件安装情况。督查前，按照督查要求，部署被检单位做好自查迎检准备；督查中，全程陪同，做好解释、沟通、协调工作；督查后，协调相关单位专题研究部署整改落实方案。在督查结果反馈会上，督察组对上海软件正版化工作给予了高度肯定。

四、加强对重点作品、重点领域版权专项整治，做好版权主动监管与执法协调指导工作

（一）开展“剑网2018”专项行动

召开“剑网2018”专项行动动员部署会议，明确重点开展整治网络转载、短视频以及动漫作品等三项任务，提出了加大查处力度、强化主动监管、加强举报投诉、强化主体责任、加强宣传教育、加强信息沟通等六点工作要求。会同成员单位，继续通过版权案件协助取证、联合会商等制度，切实加大大要案查处力度。如高达模型侵犯万代株式会社著作权案件，已列为“剑网行动”重点挂牌督办案件。自2018年开展“剑网行动”以来，共立案查处网络侵权盗版刑事案件6件，依法刑事拘留1人，逮捕3人，取保候审9人，移送起诉3人。

（二）加强网络版权主动监管

按照中央有关开展“剑网2018”专项行动的要求，建立了涵盖所有重点领域的网络版权主动监管体系，涉及本市重点网站或相关互联网企业达69家，创历年主动监管重点网站数量之最。利用互联网版权监测平台，围绕重点作品进行主动监测，定期发布互联网版权侵权状况分析与对策报告。针对俄罗斯世界杯、亚运会、进博会等重大活动，进行重点监测。根据平台监测情况，向市文化执法总队移送9起重大网络侵权盗版线索，其中2起案件还涉及非法传播淫秽色情视频。

（三）推进网络版权自律工作

围绕“剑网 2018”专项行动重点任务，联合市网信办，积极引导澎湃新闻、东方网、趣头条等 8 家沪上知名网络媒体，共同发起成立“上海网络媒体行业媒体自律联盟”。目前，上海互联网版权自律公约成员单位数量已扩充至 30 家。根据“剑网行动”实施方案，组织本市重点网站开展自查自纠工作。截至目前，已有 27 家重点网站提交了自查自纠及整改报告。积极帮助出版社、出版工作室等传统行业单位进行网络维权，成功调处其与包括拼多多等在内的国内重点电商平台之间的版权纠纷。

五、加强调查研究，科学指导版权工作的开展

（一）开展版权产业统计分析工作

继续与市统计局、上海海关、国家外汇管理局上海市分局加强对接，完成上海版权产业数据收集工作。指导上海知识产权研究所，对数据进行科学、严谨的统计、分析，并最终形成《上海版权产业统计报告（2016）》《上海版权产业分析报告（2016）》，对指导本市版权工作开展有积极作用。2016 年，上海版权产业的产业增加值为 3 153.75 亿元人民币，比上一年增加 179.88 亿元人民币，占当年上海 GDP 比重为 11.19%。

（二）完成版权贸易统计工作

统计数据显示，2018 年上海共引进图书版权 1 683 种，录音制品 85 种，录像制品 49 种，电子出版物 199 种，电影 15 种，电视节目 72 种。共输出图书版权 372 种，电子出版物 49 种，电视节目 927 种。版权贸易数量较以前整体有了较大增长，并呈现出贸易逆差进一步缩小、图书版权输出增长迅速、数字出版领域的版权贸易异常活跃等三大特点。

（三）开展版权“大调研”

根据市版权大调研领导小组的工作要求，版权处积极开展相关调研工作。共调研了 30 家企业、16 家社会组织、7 家行政机关、1 家社会团体和 1 家事业单位，涉及新闻出版、影视、互联网、计算机软件、游戏等多个行业。根据调研情况共梳理出问题 43 个，已解决 16 个，同时形成 6 项工作措施。通过调研，更加深入地了解版权产业发展现状和存在问题，为进一步理清工作思路、提升工作水平打下了良好基础。

六、加强版权宣传培训，积极营造良好版权保护氛围

（一）做好版权重点宣传

以“4·26”知识产权宣传周为重要平台，以重大版权事件、版权活动为契机，充分发挥版权局门户网站及官方微信等主导作用，利用各种场合、媒体，不断创新宣传方式，做好版权重点工作的宣传，营造良好版权舆论氛围。如 4 月开展 2017 年度上海版权保护十大典型案件专家评选及发布活动，编印《上海 2016 年度十大版权典型案例》宣传手册，通过以案说法，增强全社会版权保护意识。7 月，与华东政法大学联合主办了短视频版权与竞争问题研讨会，邀请了国内版权领域知名学者、官员以及上海重点互联网企业代表，围绕短视频版权保护主题进行深入探讨。

（二）树立正面典型，积极扩大版权保护社会影响力

为进一步调动版权相关执法部门查处侵权盗版案件的积极性和主动性，充分发挥查处侵权盗版案件先进典型的引导、示范作用，完成 2017 年度全国查处侵权盗版案件有功单位及有功个人组织推荐及颁奖工作。本年度上海共有 14 家单位和 20 名个人获国家版权局表彰。另外，卿某侵犯著作权案被国家版权局评为 2017 年度全国十大版权典型案件。

（三）强化版权教育培训

4 月，召开“上海市软件正版化工作会议”，围绕软件正版化相关法律法规政策解读，国家软件正版化工作平台操作，正版软件台账日常管理、合法使用、有序流转等内容开展了重点培训和辅导，取得了良好的成效。为帮助企业有效维权与举报投诉，组织召开座谈会，广泛深入听取企业的维权需求与面临的问题，共同商讨有效打击网络侵权盗版事宜。

七、做好版权行政审批职能及其他工作，提高依法行政水平

（一）行政确认事项有序进行

截至 11 月 2 日，共完成各类行政审批工作 1 202 件，其中，境外图书出版合同登记 1 082 件，复制境外音像制品著作权授权合同登记 52 件，出版和复制境外电子出版物、计算机软件、电子媒体非卖品著作权授权合同登记 68 件。同时，根据市政府相关规定，积极配合版权局法规处做好“一网通办”工作。

（二）认真开展投诉咨询工作

为更好地维护权利人合法权益，全年共受理电话咨询近千次，从版权保护、产业发展等角度为企业提供指导，为权利人答疑解惑。处理侵权信访件 10 余件，为权利人维权提供法律帮助。

八、加强交流与合作，不断提升版权影响力

（一）承办“电影的经济及文化价值与版权保护高端论坛”

根据国家版权局的工作要求，在上海国际电影节期间，承办了由国家版权局和世界知识产权组织联合主办的“电影的经济及文化价值与版权保护高端论坛”。来自WIPO、欧盟及其相关国家的代表和我国政府、高校、产业界代表共百余人参加了会议并就相关问题展开了积极的讨论。

（二）组团参加第七届中国国际版权博览会

按照国家版权局和第七届中国国际版权博览会组委会的统一要求，以“版权与科技、版权与文化、版权与生活”为主题，组织了7家上海优秀版权企业参展，搭建了具有上海特色的展台，充分展示了上海版权产业在各个领域取得的成果，获得与会领导和观众的广泛关注。上海市版权局获评优秀组织奖，自贸区国际文化投资发展有限公司等4家参展企业获评优秀企业奖。

（三）全力保障首届中国进口博览会

会同本市相关部门共同商讨制定了《知识产权保护与商事纠纷处理服务中心工作流程》《关于加强中国国际进口博览会版权保护的工作方案》等规章，制作版权宣传资料，主动向各国参展商宣传我国版权保护制度、作品登记制度等内容。建立重点市场联合巡查、联合会商等制度，开展每日定期巡馆、信息通报等工作，设立进博会版权保护热线。进博会期间，共接到16起咨询、2起投诉，均成功予以解答与处理。同时积极配合国内各大媒体，进行进博会版权专题宣传，树立了良好的版权保护国际形象。

（王　骞）

江　苏　省

2018年，江苏省版权局深入贯彻落实党的十九大会议精神，按照国家和江苏省委、省政府对版权工作的总体要求，围绕中心，服务大局，认真落实年度工作安排，各项重要工作稳步推进，省版权局版权管理处被国家版权局评选为2017年度全国查处侵权盗版案件有功单位一等奖，成功承办第七届中国国际版权博览会，软件正版化工作通过国务院推进使用正版软件工作部际联席会议督查组督查。

一、系统谋划布局版权工作

2018年3月15日，召开江苏省版权工作座谈会，各市局分管局长、协会和部分版权示范单位代表参加了会议，省版权局局长焦建俊从“坚持质量取胜，着力强化版权创造；坚持全面从严，着力强化版权保护；坚持价值导向，着力强化版权转化运用；坚持常态长效，着力推进软件正版化；坚持点面结合，着力强化版权宣传教育”五个方面明确了下一步工作重点。

二、积极推动版权产业发展

（一）成功承办第七届中国国际版权博览会

由国家版权局主办，江苏省新闻出版广电局（版权局）、苏州市人民政府承办的第七届中国国际版权博览会，于10月19—21日在江苏苏州成功举办。本届版博会展示面积达26 000平方米，设有国际展区、国内展区、版权产业展区、江苏展区和版权项目路演五大展区，参展单位和机构300余家，包括国家版权局、各省市自治区版权局、全国版权示范城市以及全国知名版权企业、版权相关协会等，世界知识产权组织、国际唱片业协会、美国电影协会等多个国际组织和主宾国韩国参展，重点展示展销图书音像、影视音乐、动漫游戏、计算机软件、工艺美术等优秀版权作品，充分展示近年来国内外版权产业发展的成果。开幕式上，中宣部副部长梁言顺做书面致辞，中国国家版权局和世界知识产权组织举办了“中国版权金奖”颁奖仪式，苏州市版权局、江苏国泰新点软件有限公司分获“中国版权金奖”管理奖和推广运用奖。中国国家版权局与世界知识产权组织互换协议文本，国家版权局版权管理司与江苏省版权局、苏州市人民政府签署了三方合作框架协议。博览会期间还举办了21世纪版权促进文化创意国际论坛、第十届全国大学生版权征文颁奖仪式暨江苏省大学生版权论坛、全国版权示范城市联盟年会、太湖知识产权论坛、国际纪录片版权高峰论坛、版权与文化新经济峰会等10余项主题活动。世界知识产权组织副总干事王彬颖、韩国文化体育观光部著作权局局长文荣皓、中国国家版权局版权管理司司长于慈珂、江苏省新闻出版广电局（版权局）局长缪志红、苏州市人民政府市长李亚平，以及国际版权机构高级别官员、海内外版权政府部门官员、版权相关单位和产业界代表等中外嘉宾共同出席展会。

（二）扎实推进江苏省国家版权贸易基地筹建

会同江苏省版权协会分别与南京市建邺区、秦淮区、玄武区接洽并实地考察，通过可行性认证，贸易基地秘书处落地南京市，正式对外开展工作。投资开发江苏版权服务平台，成立紫金山版权律师联盟，充分运用科技手段增强专业取证能力。新增省级版权贸易基地3家，全年累计实现版权交易19.8亿元，同比增长85%。以第七届中国国际版权博览会为契机，积极组织江苏省版权贸易基地联盟成员单位参展，搭建江苏国家版权贸易基地展馆，在版博会精彩亮相。国家版权局版权管理司司长于慈珂、世界知识产权组织副总干事王彬颖莅临展位，对江苏版权贸易工作给予充分肯定，并鼓励贸易基地成员单位继续大胆尝试，创造江苏经验。

（三）促进优秀版权贸易输出

组织参加北京国际图书博览会，江苏展区与海外著名出版集团和版权代理机构共进行了160余场版权贸易洽谈活动，共实现非华语国家版权输出100项，凤凰集团荣获组委会颁发的“优秀版权贸易输出奖”。本届组委会在展场醒目位置专设“中国出版‘走出去’成果展区”，江苏70余种原创精品图书和外向型图书入选。

（四）推进全省版权示范创建

按照“版权示范创建全覆盖”的工作要求，积极推动、指导全省版权示范创建工作，并以版权示范创建工作为抓手，积极推进各地在作品登记、软件正版化、版权执法、产业促进等领域的工作，先后命名了江苏如意通动漫产业股份有限公司、苏州功夫家族动漫有限公司等19家企业为省版权示范单位，财智科技园等2家园区为省版权示范园区（基地），命名了国信集团等6家国有企业为省版权示范单位（软件正版化）。

（五）开展江苏省版权产业经济贡献率调查

发布《2016年江苏省版权产业经济贡献率调查报告》，从产业增加值、从业人数、从业人员平均薪酬等三个方面分析了江苏省版权产业对国民经济的贡献。2016年，江苏省版权产业的增加值为6 508.06亿元，占当年江苏省GDP（76 086.17亿元）的8.55%。其中，核心版权产业的增加值为3 874.58亿元，占当年江苏省GDP的5.09%。从业人数479.43万人，占江苏省各行业从业人数的10.08%。从业人员的平均薪酬为7.29万元/年，比江苏省当年全社会从业人员的平均薪酬高出0.13万元/年。

（六）发挥省版权研究中心和版权培训基地作用

与南京理工大学、苏州大学联合建立的省版权研究中心、版权培训基地效能逐步得到体现，省版权研究中心承担扬州毛绒玩具、东海水晶、工作站标准体系等3个研究课题并通过了专家评审，省版权培训基地完成全省版权执法和作品登记等培训任务，为全省版权理论研究和人才培养进一步夯实了基础。

三、抓实软件正版化工作

（一）顺利通过国务院督查

国务院推进使用正版软件工作部际联席会议对江苏省部分省级机关和省属企业使用正版软件工作进行督促检查，省版权工作领导小组办公室充分发挥工作机制优势，加强统筹协调，多措并举做好迎检工作。一是落实责任。省版权工作领导小组办公室就做好迎检工作两次发文，要求各省级机关和省属企业完善软件正版化工作考核和责任制度，对本单位软件使用情况进行全面自查，摸清底数，并做好查漏补缺工作，确保顺利通过检查。二是组织培训。省版权局于7月在常州举办了全省政府机关使用正版软件工作培训班，对迎检工作做出具体部署。三是强化指导。建立省级机关和省属企业正版化工作QQ群，在线为各机关和各省属企业软件正版化工作责任人提供工作咨询，对有需要的机关主动上门进行业务指导。通过迎检整改工作，各省级机关和省属企业使用正版软件工作意识得到了普遍提高，软件使用情况进一步得到规范，长效机制建设基本到位，10家省级机关和省属企业顺利通过国务院督查，省公安厅、人社厅、国信集团等单位受到表扬。

（二）基本完成省属企业软件正版化工作

省版权局、省国资委年初印发省属企业软件正版化实施方案并召开部署会，要求各省属企业在2018年6月底前全面完成省属企业总部及二级、三级企业软件正版化。指导省属企业积极与软件厂商进行谈判，创新性地提出“场地授权、购买服务”的模式，大大降低企业采购成本，受到企业一致好评，同时对进展缓慢的企业进行催办、督办，21家省属企业已有19家完成整改，剩余2家正在完成采购程序，省属企业基本完成软件正版化工作，提前一年半时间完成预定目标。

（三）启动全省医疗卫生机构软件正版化工作

2017年12月江苏省版权工作领导小组办公室、省卫生和计划生育委员会、省版权局联合发文，启动了全省医疗卫生机构软件正版化推进工作，要求全省各级医疗卫生机构在2018年底前基本完成计算机操作系统、办公软件、杀毒软件的正版化，并建立和完善软件正版化长效机制。省版权工作领导小组办公室、省卫健委和省版权局协同工作，2018年5月下发了实施方案，推荐各地医疗卫生机构采取集中采购方式，通过数量优势争取价格优势，尽量降低正版软件采购成本。2018年6月在南京举办了全省医疗卫生机构软件正版化工作培训会，对加快推动全省医疗卫生机构软件正版化工作做出了具体部署。

四、加大版权执法力度

（一）执法工作成效明显

2018年，全省侵权盗版案件共立案170起：刑事案件25起，行政处罚95起，行政调解50起。其中国家五部门挂牌督办1起，国家四部门挂牌督办2起，国家版权局挂牌督办2起，省版权局挂牌督办案件13起。在国家版权局查处侵权盗版案件有功单位和个人的评选中，江苏省获奖数量居全国前列，其中省局版权管理处被评选为有功集体一等奖，徐州“3·11”制售盗版图书案被列为2017年度全国打击侵权盗版十大案件。

（二）深入开展专项行动

与省委网信办、省公安厅、省通管局联合制定打击网络侵权盗版“剑网2018”专项行动工作方案，深入全省各设区市进行专项检查，指导各地组织网络巡查，主动出击，查办一批大案要案，切实规范了网络传播秩序。行动历时5个月，关闭网站19个，移送相关部门4起，关闭微信公众号5个，行政处罚12起，共没收违法所得10.98万元，罚款31.9万元。组织评选江苏省2017年度打击侵权盗版十大案件，较好发挥了查办典型案例的示范引导作用。

（三）扎实组织执法培训

省版权局组织一线版权执法人员参加了国家版权局在陕西西安和吉林长春举办的版权行政执法监管培训。根据近年来版权执法监管工作的新形势和新要求，加强同周边省市版权执法部门协作，组织参加在浙江金华举办的2018年江浙版权执法监管工作交流会。举办全省版权执法骨干培训班，邀请专家学者前来授课，安排一线执法骨干分享典型案件办案经验，取得较好的效果。

五、提升公共服务水平

（一）加强人才队伍建设

为应对日益增长的作品登记量，确保完成全年登记30万件的重点工作任务，面向社会公开招聘3名工作人员，并对全省新进作品登记工作人员进行岗前培训。举办全省作品登记培训班，进一步提升全省作品登记工作能力。委托南京理工大学知识产权学院完成基层版权工作站标准制定，委托江苏省版权协会开展版权工作站质量核验工作，从基础建设、登记数量、登记质量等多个维度考核，提升版权工作站服务质量。

（二）稳步提升作品登记质量

通过加大工作力度、创新工作举措，全年完成作品登记302 175件。开展优秀版权作品申报认定工作，激励著作权人创作更多优秀作品，共评定优秀版权作品77件。加大作品登记宣传力度，通过“4·26”世界知识产权日系列宣传活动和举办各类座谈会、研讨会等活动，全面宣传作品登记工作，扩大社会知晓度。严控低质量作品登记，开展“作品登记质量年”活动，着力提升文字作品登记质量。

（三）改进作品登记平台

一是优化云服务平台功能。随着作品著作权登记系统的使用率越来越高，平台操作记录达到180万条，现有平台的承载能力即将到达饱和状态，为保障完成2018年登记任务，对作品著作权登记平台现有云服务设备进行升级扩容，从技术上提升登记速度和效率。二是完善作品登记功能。平台上线3年至今已完成登记量73.8万余件，为解决工作中出现的新问题，组织技术力量对登记平台进行功能优化，提升用户体验，保障作品登记工作顺利开展。同时，完成历史纸质档案的数字化工作，历史数据成功入库。

六、创新版权宣传方式

（一）贴近产业积极开展版权进园区活动

全省各地版权部门以“保护创作，推进运用”为主题，积极开展版权宣传进园区活动，深入到水晶、家纺、刺绣、壁纸、玩具等版权密集型产业基地、专业市场集中开展版权宣传活动。省版权局在连云港东海水晶小镇、扬州五亭龙玩具市场、泰州高港壁纸基地开展“4·26”世界知识产权日版权宣传活动，南京、无锡、苏州、南通、昆山等地版权部门分别举办版权宣传进校园、进园区、进社区和进企业等活动，成立版权服务平台或版权保护联盟，举办版权知识讲座，向社会各界群众发放宣传手册，普及版权保护知识，努力营造打击侵权盗版、保护知识产权的良好氛围。

（二）形式多样全方位开展版权社会宣传

制作“保护正版，为原创者点赞”宣传片，在全省电视台、电台、影院、网络、地铁和公交移动电视、户外大屏等平台播放，江苏新闻广播和江苏交通广播两个频道滚动播出自制的版权公益广告，版权保护公益海报也亮相于江苏有线电视1 000多万用户的开机画面，南京四条地铁线路的35个重要站点、幸福蓝海院线170余家影院以及遍布全省各地的公共阅报栏、公交站点、学校、书店、写字楼等公共场所。《新华日报》、江苏电视台、江苏新闻广播、中江网等媒体对全省“4·26”世界知识产权日版权宣传活动进行了专题报道，“江苏版权”、“书香江苏”及“江苏版权保护中心”等微信公众号对全省各地的宣传活动内容进行了实时推送，取得良好成效。

（三）突出重点展示江苏版权工作成就

在“4·26”世界知识产权日前命名了一批省版权示范单位和示范园区，与省经信委启动了2018年度全省优秀版权作品评选，评选出了2017年度全省打击侵权盗版十大案件，公布了江苏省版权产业经济贡献率调查结果，并将相关内容制成展板在全省各地版权宣传活动中展出。在第七届中国国际版权博览会期间，有30多家中央媒体、省级和地方媒体参与宣传，集中报道江苏版权取得的成效，进一步提升了全社会的版权认知度。

（卢　寅）

浙　江　省

2018年浙江省版权工作在浙江省委、省政府领导下，认真组织开展打击侵犯知识产权和制售假冒伪劣商品专项行动，进一步推进政府机关党群系统软件正版化工作，举办以“保护创作，推进运用”为主题的版权系列宣传活动，努力提升版权服务水平，促进版权产业和版权事业的繁荣发展。主要工作如下：

一、版权保护方面

（1）做好2017年度打击侵犯知识产权和制售假冒伪劣商品绩效考核的有关工作。起草上报了《关于2017年浙江省打击侵权盗版专项治理“剑网行动”工作情况的自评报告》《关于2017年浙江省政府机关软件正版化工作情况的自评报告》。

（2）制定并印发了《2018年浙江省版权行政执法工作方案》。工作方案明确要求各地要落实执法责任、严格执法程序、加大执法力度，同时重申了案件查处信息报送、信息公开的有关规定。

（3）做好浙江省2017年度全国查处侵权盗版案件有功单位和有功个人推荐工作。全省共有10家单位、6名个人分获有功单位及有功个人二、三等奖，其中，浙江省版权局版权处荣获有功单位二等奖。

（4）组织开展“剑网2018”专项行动。根据国家四部门《关于开展打击网络侵权盗版“剑网2018”专项行动的通知》要求，浙江省版权局和浙江省互联网信息办公室、浙江省通信管理局、浙江省公安厅及时印发了《浙江省打击网络侵权盗版“剑网2018”专项行动实施方案》，2018年7月28日在金华市对全省各市县“剑网2018”专项行动进行了专门部署，2018年“剑网行动”重点任务一是开展网络转载版权专项整治，二是开展短视频版权专项整治，三是开展重点领域版权专项整治。

2018年主要采取大力查办案件、强化主体责任、加强社会共治等工作措施，进一步引导传统媒体与商业网站开展版权合作，完善网络转载版权许可付费机制，积极运用电信运营商、版权检测机构的技术优势，提高对网络侵权盗版信息的发现、研判、处置效率。截至2018年10月底，全省共立案查处侵权盗版案件36起，罚款29万元。

（5）举办了版权执法监管工作培训班。2018年7月23—25日在金华举办了版权执法监管培训班，这是第三次采用和江苏合办的模式，来自两省版权执法人员180余人参加了培训。培训班既有专家教授的授课，也有两省一线版权执法人员办案的经验介绍，很有针对性。培训班上江浙两省的版权执法人员还就各自执法困难和成功经验进行了交流，为今后共同探讨版权执法重点、促进信息共享、执法联动、跨区域执法打下了良好的基础。

（6）认真做好浙江省人大代表建议答复工作。2018年浙江省人大代表周骏提出的杭127号关于《加快修改完善著作权领域立法，着力保护浙江互联网企业合法权益》建议，浙江省版权局作为答复承办单位，主动与提出建议的人大代表联系，多次听取意见建议，并就浙江省互联网发展现状、浙江省在著作权法规制定和打击网络侵权盗版方面的主要做法及取得的成效、下一步浙江省版权局重点加以改进和完善的三项工作等给予书面答复。周骏代表对浙江省版权局的答复给予书面反馈，对办理态度、办理结果表示满意。

（7）做好全国政协社会和法制委员会赴浙江开展网络知识产权的法律保护专题调研相关工作。2018年9月4—7日，全国政协社会和法制委员会赴浙江开展网络知识产权的法律保护专题调研，浙江省版权局就贯彻实施著作权法律法规，促进著作权的创造、运用、保护和管理，加强版权行政执法机构和队伍建设，特别是网络环境下版权保护工作中存在的主要问题以及完善网络环境下版权保护工作的意见建议等进行了认真梳理，浙江省版权局单烈副局长做了题为《浙江省版权保护工作情况汇报》的报告。在听取各单位专题汇报后，调研组表示，浙江在网络环境下贯彻实施著作权法方面做了大量工作，取得了显著成效，并且创造性地开展区域版权保护工作，为其他地方开展网络环境下版权保护工作提供了示范，为著作权法贯彻实施总结出可复制的成功经验。

二、推进使用软件正版化工作方面

（1）印发了《2018年浙江省推进使用正版软件工作计划》。2018年的工作重点是全面推进软件正版化工作规范化、常态化、制度化和信息化建设，进一步完善长效机制、加大督查力度、加强信息融合、强化技术手段、巩固扩大软件正版化工作成果，推动软件正版化工作再上新台阶。一是完善长效机制，持续推进软件使用规范管理；二是密切协调配合，持续推进企事业单位软件正版化工作；三是强化督促检查，严格主体责任落实；四是夯实正版化基础，推进软件正版化与信息化融合；五是加强市场监管，维护软件市场公平竞争秩序；六是开展宣传培训，积极营造良好氛围。

（2）做好浙江省省级预算单位集中采购办公软件专项经费结算工作。

（3）召开了浙江省省市县三级软件正版化工作培训会。2018年8月28日，召开了省市县三级政府机关软件正版化工作培训会，全省83家省级单位、11个市90个县区的政府机关相关负责人共250人参加了培训，浙江省版权局单烈副局长在会上做了开班动员讲话，他要求参会人员进一步提高对推进软件正版化工作重要意义的认识，对下一步如何更好地做好软件正版化工作提出期望和要求。

在培训会上，浙江省财政厅有关部门负责同志就软件采购政策、软件资产管理等工作做了专门指导；浙江省审计厅有关部门负责同志就如何做好软件正版化审计工作给予详细说明；浙江省国资委负责信息化建设同志就如何推进国有企业软件正版化工作做了专题辅导，为下一步全面推进软件正版化工作打下了良好的基础。

（4）做好对部分市政府机关软件正版化实地检查工作。根据计划，2018年12月，组织联合检查组对宁波43家市政府机关软件正版化工作进行全覆盖检查，进一步推动软件正版化工作常态化、标准化、制度化，巩固软件正版化工作成果。

（5）做好政府机关软件正版化年度考核工作。根据浙江省软件正版化年度工作计划安排，2018年11月起对省级单位、设区市软件正版化工作进行年度考核，考核结果计入平安市县考核总分。

三、版权宣传方面

（1）在全省组织开展知识产权宣传周版权主题宣传活动。印发了《关于组织开展2018年知识产权宣传周版权宣传活动的通知》，明确活动主题为“保护创作，推进运用”，宣传重点是著作权法律法规，开展打击侵犯知识产权和制售假冒伪劣商品专项工作、“剑网”专项行动及软件正版化工作取得的成果。

（2）举办了浙江省第六届“知识产权杯”创意设计大赛活动。第六届“知识产权杯”创意设计大赛由浙江省版权局和温州市文化广电新闻出版局主办，温州大学瓯江学院、浙江省版权协会、温州市创意设计有限公司承办，前后历时4个多月，10所在温院校师生参与。大赛分专题命题设计、自由命题设计和多媒体设计三大类。命题设计是专门为企业需求而设立的。在征集的640余件参赛作品中，评出一、二、三等奖24件，优秀奖和入围奖150件。

2018年4月26日上午，浙江省第六届“知识产权杯”创意设计大赛颁奖典礼在温州大学瓯江学院举行，浙江省版权局党组副书记、副局长单烈和温州市副市长郑朝阳出席典礼。单烈表示，第六届“知识产权杯”创意设计大赛移师温州，目的是希望通过温州高校师生的创新精神、创新意识的引领和示范，促使尊重知识、尊重创新、尊重劳动之火在浙江10万平方公里大地上燃烧起来。大赛通过在校学生参与竞赛这样一种方式，为大家呈现了一个年轻多彩的交流平台；而与委托创作单位的合作，实现了作品创作与社会企业需求的有效对接，打通了从实践到运用的最后一公里，使大赛真正走向深入，体现出创新的实际价值和创意服务经济发展的理念。

（3）参与了长三角地区知识产权发展与保护状况新闻发布会。

四、版权服务方面

（1）设立了阿里巴巴版权服务工作站。2018年9月18日，浙江省版权局与阿里巴巴集团签约设立阿里巴巴版权服务工作站，在淘宝卖家市场为商家设立专门的版权登记服务模块。淘宝原创商家需要进行版权登记时，可直接在淘宝网提交电子版权登记材料，经过审核后，走上直达的浙江省版权局的“快车道”进行终审，终审通过后，商家将获得浙江省版权局颁发的版权登记证书，并按季在浙江省版权局网站公示。协议规定，阿里巴巴的线上版权登记初审须在7个工作日内完成，浙江版权服务中心的登记终审须在20个工作日内完成，与传统登记模式相比，极大地节省了商家的时间与精力。

（2）组织浙江省出版单位参加第二十五届北京国际图书博览会。2018年8月23—27日，第二十五届北京国际图书博览会在北京中国国际展览中心举办，浙江省14家图书出版社参加了博览会，参展出版物达 1 000 多种。

2018 年 8 月 24 日上午，中央政治局委员中宣部部长黄坤明视察了浙江展区，浙江省版权局副局长单烈汇报了浙江图书版权输出、“一带一路”出版项目等情况，黄坤明对浙江的出版和“走出去”工作给予充分肯定。北京市委常委、宣传部部长杜飞进等领导同志先后视察了浙江展区。

北京国际图书博览会已成为浙江省版权输出的一个重要平台，博览会期间，浙江省参展单位共达成 100 多项版权输出协议和意向。

（3）举办浙江版权贸易图书展。2018 年 9 月 22—30 日，由浙江省版权局和浙江省外宣办组织的浙江版权贸易图书展团对芬兰、瑞典两国出版界进行了交流访问。访问期间，代表团积极搭建海外文化交流平台，加深了与北欧国家同行的彼此了解和认同，为展示悠久的中华文明和宣传浙江人文历史、经济社会发展新貌做出了积极探索：一是充分展示了中国文化和浙江出版的优秀成果，浙江人民出版社、浙江教育出版社、浙江科技出版社、浙江大学出版社等都推出了各具特色的图书，瑞典出版界对反映中国传统文化和浙江特色鲜明的图书表示了浓厚的合作意向；二是成功举办了浙版图书海外“百柜工程——悦读浙江”活动，访问期间，在芬兰国际传媒时代集团、瑞典瑞京中文学校分别设立了专柜，使两国人民加深了对中国文化及浙江经济社会的了解；三是参与瑞典哥德堡国际书展版权贸易活动，现场感受了瑞典文明及民众对知识的渴求，同时也了解了海外出版界对中国文化图书的需求。

（4）组团参加第七届中国国际版权博览会。2018 年 10 月 18 日，第七届中国国际版权博览会在苏州市举行，浙江省版权局组织多家特色版权企业参展。版权博览会期间，国家版权局举行了“中国版权金奖”及“金慧奖”颁奖仪式，“中国版权金奖”是国家版权局与世界知识产权组织开展的合作项目，每两年评选一次，是中国版权领域内评选的唯一国际性奖项，也是国内版权领域的最高奖项。浙江省中国轻纺城花样版权登记管理保护办公室获“中国版权金奖”保护奖，浙江省版权局获优秀组织奖，杭州市版权保护管理中心、杭州奥罗拉实业有限公司、杭州玄机科技信息技术有限公司获“金慧奖”。

（5）召开了浙江省版权协会第二届四次会员代表大会。2018 年 9 月 18 日浙江省版权协会第二届四次会员代表大会在杭州召开，会上表彰了浙江教育出版社等 10 家先进会员单位，审议并通过了协会 2017 年工作总结和财务收支情况报告，表决通过了协会副会长、常务理事、理事及协会章程修改、办公用房购置等事项。

会上，浙江省版权局党组副书记、副局长，省版权协会会长单烈讲话。他指出，省版权协会各会员单位要结合省第十四次党代会提出的“六个浙江”中文化浙江的目标任务，按照推进“八八战略”再深化、改革开放再出发的要求以及新时代赋予版权工作的新任务，全面部署好版权协会的工作。他强调，版权工作要牢固树立“全局观、未来观、全球观和人才观”四大观念，进一步把握好版权工作中“社会化、专业化、国际化、数字化、市场化及意识形态化”六个特点，着力平衡好著作权人、传播者和社会公众三者的利益关系，从而不断优化和改善版权产业结构，不断加强版权工作信息化、数字化和网络化建设，探索版权产业融合发展的新路子，更好推动浙江省版权产业转型升级。

（6）作品自愿登记、著作权合同登记、备案等日常工作。2018 年登记一般作品 21 326 件，核准登记出版境外图书合同 591 件，办理涉外图书、音像制品、电子出版物制作合同登记 954 件，计算机软件著作权合同备案 212 件。

（严庆荣）

安 徽 省

2018 年，安徽省版权管理工作以习近平新时代中国特色社会主义思想和党的十九大精神为指导，坚持“五大发展理念”和“四个全面”战略布局，紧紧围绕全省中心工作，坚持依法管理、优质服务，较好地完成了既定工作任务，为知识产权强国建设提供了有力的版权支撑。

一、版权执法监管依法开展

（一）开展“剑网 2018”专项行动

根据国家版权局统一部署，结合本省实际，安徽省版权局与省公安厅、省互联网信息办公室、省通信管理局共同印发《安徽省开展打击网络侵权盗版“剑网 2018”专项行动实施方案》，明确工作目标、重点、措施和要求，从 7 月到 11 月开展安徽省打击网络侵权盗版“剑网 2018”专项行动。集中整治网络转载、短视频、动漫等领域侵权盗版多发态势，重点规范网络直播、知识分享、有声读物等平台版权传播秩序，深入巩固网络影视、网络音乐、电子商务平台、应用商店、网络云存储空间等领域专项整治成果，维护网络空间版权秩序。

（二）严厉查处侵权盗版违法行为

2018年，安徽省立案查处39起版权案件，其中国家版权局、全国“扫黄打非”办公室等多部门联合挂牌督办案件4起；刑事案件8起，办结1起；行政案件31起，全部办结；另外，责令停止侵权行为、主持调解、关闭网站或采取其他行政处理措施14起。涉案作品类型包括文字、影视、计算机软件等。案件查处工作涉及北京、山东、湖南、江苏、河南、广东等10余个省份。安徽省3个集体和18名个人获得国家版权局2017年度查处侵权盗版案件有功单位和有功个人表彰。

（三）加强版权执法培训

9月5—6日，安徽省版权局举办了安徽省版权执法监管工作培训班，邀请版权理论和执法实务界相关专家授课，各地版权执法一线骨干进行了版权执法经验交流，全省各级版权管理部门负责人和一线执法人员90余人参加。组织执法人员参加国家版权局在西安、长春举办的全国版权执法培训班。在全省文化市场综合行政执法人员资格认证培训班、“扫黄打非”工作培训班、全省编辑记者培训班等开展版权专题授课，讲授“著作权法基础理论和执法实务”“版权管理实务”“版权管理与实践”课目。

（四）巩固综合治理机制

安徽省版权局积极协调相关部门开展综合治理，加强同“扫黄打非”办、“双打”办、公安、检察院、法院等部门的工作协调，跨地区、跨部门综合执法协调机制进一步健全。积极发挥权利人、社会团体、广大群众的信息员作用，强化打击侵权盗版社会共治。加大对大案要案和典型案件的宣传力度，对具有恶劣情节的违法犯罪分子和不履行主体责任的互联网企业进行曝光。加强版权行政处理结果的运用，将严重恶意侵权行为列入黑名单管理，推动版权行业失信市场主体联合惩戒。

（五）做好案件信息公开和信息报送工作

安徽省版权局严格按照国家“双打”办和国家版权局《关于进一步加强版权行政处罚案件信息公开与信息报送工作的通知》要求，由专人每月按时向国家版权局和省“双打”办报送案件信息公开报表，并及时公开行政处罚案件信息。

二、软件正版化工作持续推进

（一）抓好政府机关软件正版化工作

2018年，安徽省加强督促检查，重点推进省直机关所属单位软件正版化工作，督促市级政府机关开展“回头看”自查自纠，进一步强化制度建设，不断提高工作水平。全省各级政府机关单位新增各类正版软件13 000多套，采购资金1 350多万元。

（1）规范软件日常管理和采购源头管理。一是根据国家版权局的要求，在全国率先推广和使用《正版软件管理工具软件》，制作3 000张管理工具软件光盘，分发到省、市政府机关单位，并对省直机关进行了技术培训。二是加强计算机生产企业预装正版软件监管力度。安徽省经济和信息化厅与省版权局组织开展了对合肥联宝、宝龙达和安徽酷米等企业预装正版操作系统督促检查，实时跟踪掌握企业生产销售和预装正版软件情况，从源头上杜绝盗版软件进入市场。三是加强对政府机关正版软件采购平台“徽采商城”的督促检查，对从平台上采购的软件正盗版情况进行梳理，核实软件采购合同的合法性和已经售出软件的版权属性。

（2）扎实开展省直机关软件正版化工作。一是明确责任。明确要求省直机关各单位建立健全责任制，对所属单位软件正版化工作负总责，明确责任部门和责任人，统一部署和推进所属单位软件正版化工作。二是督促推进。对省教育厅、省供销社等省直机关所属单位软件正版化工作开展了技术培训和督促检查，并要求省直机关确保所属单位按时完成使用正版软件工作。三是抓好问题整改落实。对9月份国家软件正版化工作督查组来皖检查中发现的问题进行情况通报，要求相关单位限期整改到位。加强跟踪督促检查，紧抓问题不放，确保整改到位。并强化服务指导，辅导、培训有关单位健全完善各项管理工作制度，协助相关单位验收把关，严防各类“变种”盗版软件流入机关单位。还对部分单位的整改情况开展复核验收，严格检查验收新购正版软件、采购合同和相关授权文件等，防止出现新的盗版软件。

（3）稳步推进市级政府机关单位软件正版化工作。对市级政府机关单位大力开展全覆盖督查和“回头看”自查自纠工作，对芜湖、安庆两市开展了市级政府机关软件正版化工作全覆盖检查。芜湖市政府采取多种措施推进政府机关软件正版化整改工作，开展业务培训、督促检查和自查自纠，推进了50多家市直机关单位进行了整改，新增各类正版软件2 900多套，采购金额147万元。安庆市政府将软件正版化工作任务分解落实，对78家市直机关单位使用软件情况开展全覆盖检查摸底，并聘请第三方技术人员进行复查核实，确保摸底统计数字真实可靠，摸清底数、找准问题、逐一整改。市政府安排专项资金150余万元，采购国产办公软件3 000余套，机关软件正版化率明显提升。

（二）加强企业软件正版化工作

2018年，安徽省重点推进省属企业及所属二级企业、新闻出版广电行业、诚信示范企业、村镇银行及民营企业软件正版化工作，全省共有80家各类企业完成了软件正版化整改工作，采购各类正版软件13 000多套，购置资金1 100多万元。一是确定重点。年初确定了28家省属企业及所属二级企业、5家新闻出版广电行业企业、50家第五批省诚信示范企业作为重点推进企业，并继续推进和完善58家村镇银行和30家民营企业软件正版化工作。二是加强培训。全省各级版权部门分别会同国资、商务、工商联、银监等行业部门对省属企业、诚信示范企业、民营企业、村镇银行等行业企业开展多轮次培训，解读软件正版化工作的意义，明确目标任务，厘清推进思路和方法，提高认识，增强企业推进工作的积极性和主动性。三是大力推进。安徽省版权局和省国资委、省商务厅利用培训班对省属企业、诚信示范企业集中开展督促检查，坚决杜绝企业使用侵权盗版软件。省工商联向各市工商联和所属协会下发《关于推进民营企业软件正版化工作的通知》。针对少数企业整改进度缓慢、推进不力的问题，版权部门下达整改通知书，要求限期整改。并在第五批省级诚信示范企业评选中对使用盗版软件的参评企业实行一票否决。

三、版权公共服务和理论研究水平不断提升

（一）开展作品著作权登记

安徽省版权局督促指导省版权交易中心开展作品著作权登记工作。为方便权利人办事，在作品版权密集地区设立多个作品登记服务点，并实现作品登记事项全程网上办理。2018年安徽省作品登记数量为20 225件，比2017年增长10 214件，同比增长102%。作品登记类型增长为16类，主要包括摄影作品、美术作品、文字作品及工程设计图、产品设计图等。

（二）推进版权示范创建

安徽省版权局梳理省内著作权重点企业，有针对性地培育帮助企业建立健全著作权保护工作制度，提高企业自觉守法及依法维权意识。2018年，全省共认定5家“版权示范单位”。截至2018年底，安徽省已创建“全国版权示范单位（基地）”8家、“全国软件正版化示范单位”1家，省级“版权示范单位”15家。

（三）推动版权贸易发展

安徽省版权局组织多家安徽省内知名企业参加第七届中国国际版权博览会。在“金慧奖”评选中，安徽省版权局荣获优秀组织奖；安徽少年儿童出版社和芜湖三只松鼠股份有限公司荣获优秀企业奖。2018年，安徽省版权输出共计452项。

（四）推进版权理论研究

安徽省版权局配合省政协完成全国政协在安徽关于“网络知识产权的法律保护”的专题调研工作，在调研座谈会上汇报了安徽省网络版权行政保护状况。配合省高级人民法院完成省委领导圈定课题“关于加强知识产权审判领域改革创新若干问题的意见”，形成综合调研论证报告。

四、版权宣传活动广泛开展

（一）开展知识产权宣传周版权宣传活动

安徽省围绕“4·26”世界知识产权日，开展知识产权宣传周版权宣传系列活动。省版权局转发关于做好2018年全国知识产权宣传周版权宣传活动的通知，在全省范围内广泛开展多种形式的版权宣传教育活动。发挥融媒体作用，综合运用传统媒体和新媒体开展宣传。安徽广播电视台、安徽广电移动电视有限公司及各地广播电视媒体通过播放版权公益视频广告、对宣传周开展情况进行跟踪报道等方式开展版权宣传，省版权局在政务门户网站和微信微博平台发布版权保护信息，各地版权管理部门利用政务门户网站、微博微信平台、手机短信等形式开展宣传。省版权局还开展版权宣传“进书店、进学校、进企业、进机关”的“四进”活动，走进安徽新华发行（集团）控股有限公司、安徽图书博物馆、24小时共享书店、安徽新闻出版职业技术学院、合肥市高新区软件园等及在局机关办公区开展版权宣传。宣传周期间，全省各级电视媒体播放版权公益广告2 200余次，时长近2 500分钟。

（二）举办知识产权博士论坛

安徽省版权局联合中国科大、省知识产权局、省版权保护协会等单位开展第十届“中国科大知识产权博士论坛”，在论坛上开展中国科大“墨子论坛”版权登记仪式、“版权、创新、发展”主题征文颁奖活动等，3家版权示范单位负责人就版权相关内容做了演讲，安徽广播电视台、中安在线等多家媒体进行了报道。

（胡　子）

福　建　省

2018年，福建省版权工作认真贯彻《深入实施国家知识产权战略行动计划（2014—2020年）》（国办发［2014］64号），积极实施版权发展战略，继续推进版权产业发展，努力提高版权监管水平，顺利完成年初确定的主要工作任务，多项工作进入全国前列，形成新的亮点，为“再上新台阶、建设新福建”做出应有贡献。

一、加强版权行政监管

（一）深入推进软件正版化工作

召开省推进使用正版软件工作厅际联席会议第五次全体会议，总结2017年工作，部署2018年工作。召开省直机关软件正版化工作培训会，指导各单位开展督查准备工作。完成国家使用正版软件工作部际联席会议办公室对福建省44家省级政府机关软件正版化的全覆盖督查，根据督查组反馈，福建省省级政府机关操作系统软件和办公软件的正版化率分别达到93.48%和93.17%，暂列全国第三。福建省正版化与信息化相结合的经验做法被国家版权局作为典型向全国推广。完善政府机关使用正版软件工作长效机制，强化软硬件采购源头管理，与省财政厅、审计厅联合制定《关于进一步加强计算机软硬件采购源头管理的通知》（闽版权［2018］7号），会同省财政厅、省公共资源交易中心规范政府采购网上超市软件供应类厂商的销售行为。

（二）着力打击侵权盗版行为

组织全省开展“剑网2018”专项行动。与省网信办、通管局、公安厅等四部门联合召开全省版权执法监管暨“剑网2018”专项行动工作会议，部署专项行动工作任务。以网络转载、短视频、动漫、影视、音乐、电子商务平台、应用商店、云存储空间等领域和网络直播、知识分享、有声读物等平台为重点监管对象，开展版权专项整治；将全省有影响力、规模较大的233家网站纳入主动监管对象范围，要求其中100家重点互联网企业、网站开展版权自查自纠，建立健全版权管理机制。开展北京2022年冬奥会会徽和冬残奥会会徽版权保护工作，制定专项保护应急预案。2018年，全省共查办各类侵权盗版案件74起，其中涉及网络侵权盗版的案件50起，占比67.57%；线下侵权盗版案件24起，占比32.43%。国家版权局、全国“扫黄打非”办、公安部挂牌督办的“7·13”系列游戏私服侵权案取得重大突破，相关涉案人员基本归案，案件已移交检察机关。全省10家单位和19名个人获评全国2017年度查处侵权盗版案件有功单位和有功个人。

二、加强版权公共服务

认真做好作品登记工作。新开发的“福建省作品自愿登记系统”投入运营，实现网上申报、在线审核、电子发证等全程无纸化运作，最大限度方便作品登记申请人，实现“一趟不用跑”。1—11月，全省共核准登记作品达到83 488件，已超过2017年全年登记数量（68 203件），同比增长44.3%。其中美术作品68 685件，占总登记量的82.3%；音乐作品8 423件，占总登记量的10.1%。登记量排名前三位的地市分别是泉州、福州、厦门。

三、促进版权产业发展

（一）开展版权示范创建

在2015年、2016年开展省级版权示范单位和示范园区（基地）评定工作基础上（已有42家企业被授予“福建省版权示范单位”称号，2家单位被授予“福建省版权示范园区”称号），继续开展第三批评定工作。目前相关工作正在实施中，共21家企业单位申报示范单位，1家企业申报示范园区（基地）。

（二）组织福建省原创动漫作品参评版权开发优秀项目

根据国家版权局通知要求，积极组织福建省原创动漫作品参加国家版权开发优秀项目评选，其中天翼爱动漫文化传媒有限公司获内容开发类银奖，厦门思倍旭公司和厦门漫际视界公司获内容开发类铜奖。

四、加强版权宣传培训

（一）开展版权宣传教育

在“4·26”世界知识产权日之际，按照国家版权局部署要求，组织开展知识产权宣传周版权宣传系列活动。全省各地统一开展以“护助少年儿童健康成长，拒绝有害出版物及信息”为主题的“绿书签2018”活动，共发放绿书签9万多份。协调全省电视台播出《申报版权保护版权用好版权》公益广告片，在全省126家影院播映版权知识公益宣传片，在福建电视台少儿频道播放版权知识系列动画片。在“5·18”海峡两岸经贸交易会上设立版权咨询服务台，为参展商和市民提供版权法律咨询等服务。

（二）组织参加征文比赛

根据国家版权局通知要求，组织福建省部分高校大学生参加征文比赛，其中集美大学陈慧《非人类摄制作品的法律保护》获得本科组二等奖。

（三）组织版权专业培训

组织省直相关单位、地市版权执法人员参加国家版权局软件正版化培训和行政执法培训，先后组织省直机关50人次开展软件正版化培训，市县版权行政执法骨干30人次开展业务培训，赴各地市开展版权业务授课10余人次。

（郑开辟）

江 西 省

2018年，以省级版权机构转隶中共江西省委宣传部为契机，各级版权部门深入学习贯彻习近平新时代中国特色社会主义思想和党的十九大精神，围绕中心，服务大局，大力加强版权执法监管，扎实推进软件正版化工作，不断优化版权服务和社会宣传，江西版权工作势头良好，影响力日益提升。

版权执法工作显成效。2018年，江西各级版权部门优化执法机制，创新方法手段，积极构筑联动联防体系，成效明显。一是推动版权执法规范化、常态化，工作成绩突出。2018年共办结版权案件90起，继续保持高位。版权执法多次获上级肯定和表扬，全省15家单位和23名个人获国家版权局查处侵权盗版案件有功单位和有功个人奖励，其中版权管理处和南昌市文化市场综合执法支队获有功单位一等奖。在7月召开的全国版权执法监管工作会议上，江西省版权局做经验交流。二是大力开展“剑网2018”专项行动，重点案件取得突破。以网络转载、短视频、动漫等领域专项治理为重点，全年共查办网络版权案件45起，6起网络刑事案件移交公安机关。其中，新余每日网络科技有限公司侵权案由国家五部门联合挂牌督办，已于11月正式判决；列入国家五部门督办的江西南昌“6·4”火课旗舰店侵犯著作权案，已于5月宣判；永新县“9·8”侵犯著作权案，涉案9人，判处2人实刑、5人缓刑并均处罚金，案件总罚金高达317万元，为近年来江西省以侵犯著作权罪判决刑期最长、罚金最高、个案判决人员最多的一起案件，有力地震慑了侵权盗版行为，案件的侦办和经验做法被《中国新闻出版广电报》等多家媒体报道。三是创新方法手段，深化联动联防。找准基层执法经验不足、技术手段落后、办案经费缺乏等薄弱环节，与网监、公安等相关部门开展技术合作，对互联网网站进行有效监管，发现并移转下发案件线索11条。以查处大案、典型案件为抓手，引导各地各版权执法部门积极联动，及时总结、交流经验，一年一度的版权执法监管工作培训成为惯例，有效提高执法水平。积极申请、及时协调下拨办案经费，充分调动各级版权执法部门的积极性、主动性，形成齐抓共管、主动作为、共同打击侵权盗版的良好局面。

软件正版化工作出实招。2018年，根据国务院工作部署，江西省认真贯彻落实国家推进使用正版软件工作部际联席会议精神，扎实推进软件正版化工作。一是拟制《2018年江西省推进使用正版软件工作实施方案》，主体责任进一步强化。拟制《实施方案》，并报送国家推进使用正版软件工作部际联席会议，同时下发至各设区市政府、省使用正版软件工作领导小组各成员单位。省委、省政府高度重视软件正版化工作，省使用正版软件工作领导小组办公室不定期召开专题会议、联席会议或以文件会签形式研究部署和推进全省软件正版化工作，各地各单位采取有效措施强化组织领导，落实第一责任人责任，软件正版化主体责任意识进一步强化，形成畅通有序的软件正版化工作机制。二是开展全覆盖核查，督查考核机制逐步完善。3月，对全省所有省直机关单位软件正版化工作开展了一对一的全覆盖核查。5月，结合书面佐证材料及上门核查结果，根据省政府办公厅《关于印发江西省推进使用正版软件工作督查考评办法（试行）的通知》要求，在全省通报了2017年软件正版化工作年度考评结果，对有问题的单位责令整改。7月，各设区市开展市直政府机关软件正版化督查工作，各市督查不少于20家的市直单位，在核查软件台账的同时，上机检查不少于10%。9月26—28日，抽查宜春、萍乡两地市直政府机关软件正版化督查工作的开展情况。9月上旬，对4家国有企业进行督查，推进国有企业全面落实软件正版化工作责任，软件正版化工作的全面督查考核机制已经形成。三是企事业单位软件正版化工作取得阶段性成果。截至2018年末，省级国有出资监管企业集团本部软件正版化任务基本完成。省工商联下发《关于印发〈江西省工商联2018年推进民营企业使用正版软件工作实施方案〉的通知》，规范指导民营企业推进正版软件工作。省使用正版软件工作领导小组办公室对新闻出版行业的企业软件正版化工作进行规范管理，在全面完成整改任务后，步入常态化和规范化管理的轨道，江西日报社在全国新闻出版企业软件正版化工作培训班上做经验交流发言。

首届版权输出奖评选表彰工作完成顺利。2018年，推动并牵头组织了首届版权输出奖评选及表彰工作，积极推动江西省新闻出版广播影视优秀作品走出国门。根据《关于表彰首届江西省版权输出奖获奖项目的决定》，对2014—2016年期间实现版权输出的优秀图书、报刊、广播影视（含动漫）类项目进行了表彰，共有15个优秀版权输出项目获首届江西省版权输出奖，《中国新闻出版广电报》、人民网、江西卫视、《江西日报》等多家媒体进行报道，产生广泛的社会影响。

版权示范工作有序推进。注重挖掘和培育一批自主创新和版权运用能力较强、示范作用发挥较好的版权企业提供版权服务，促进版权产业发展。2018年，共有8家单位申报了省级版权示范单位。在第十一届中国版权年会上，江西省出版集团公司党委书记、董事长赵东亮获得“中国版权事业卓越成就者”称号，这是江西省首次获得这一荣誉。二十一世纪出版集团有限公司、江西凯天动漫有限公司、景德镇陶邑文化发展有限公司等3家单位获“2018中国版权年度最具影响力企业”奖。

版权贸易活动积极开展。2018年，全省共引进图书版权406件，输出图书版权336件。在参展第二十五届北京国际图书博览会暨第十六届北京国际图书节期间，达成版权输出协议70余项，输出意向逾200项、引进意向20余项。4家出版社进入“中国图书海外馆藏影响力百强出版社”，2家出版社成功入选国家丝路书香工程“外国人写作中国计划”24家战略合作伙伴。景德镇市版权局及相关知名陶瓷企业参展第七届中国国际版权博览会，充分展示千年陶瓷文化的成果与运用，赢得广泛关注和认可。江西省版权局获“金慧奖”优秀组织奖，景德镇逸品天合陶瓷有限公司、名镇天下陶瓷文化创意公司获“金慧奖”优秀企业奖。

版权服务与社会宣传工作亮点纷呈。2018年，江西省作品登记量达到12 684件，同比增长22.85%。《并蒂雪莲》《红色基因》等一批喜迎十九大、纪念“三个90周年”的主题出版物，《丝游记》《东方的藏宝箱》等剧本，《共产党人》《家国情怀》等歌曲，《走进新时代》《绽放》等一批宣传贯彻十九大精神、庆祝改革开放40周年的作品，《名镇瓷毯》系列、南康春然系列家具、“样式雷三山五园长卷图系列”以及《美丽江西秀天下》《武宁好客气》《血染洪城》《湘赣边往事》《江西当代新诗编年纪事》等一批“讲好江西故事”的作品进行了版权登记。“4·26”世界知识产权日期间，整理发布2017年度江西省版权执法十大典型案例，以案释法，提高公众著作权法认知；组织制作网络音乐版权保护专题宣传片，在全省各网络、100多家影院累计播放宣传片5 348小时，受众50余万人次；联合省妇联、省文联、省出版集团，围绕“新时代·新女性·新创造——版权保护促进文艺创新”的主题，全省女作家向全社会发出《版权保护倡议书》。继续开展“高校版权知识巡回宣讲”活动，继续唱响“江西版权保护宣讲会”品牌，先后深入多家高校、市县局、企业单位开展宣讲活动。在中国（赣州）第五届家具产业博览会期间，设立“版权服务工作站”，现场为企业办理版权登记，解决版权难题。5月9日，中宣部《每日舆情汇报》“工作动态”栏目单条刊发《江西创新举措强化版权保护工作》，对江西版权保护工作予以肯定。

（阙米秋）

山 东 省

2018年，山东省版权管理部门高举习近平新时代中国特色社会主义思想伟大旗帜，深入学习贯彻党的十九大精神和习近平总书记视察山东重要讲话、重要指示、重要批示精神，以“版权强省”为目标，以“版权突破”为抓手，创新思路、强化措施，圆满完成了各项工作任务，展示了新时代版权工作新局面。先后荣膺“国家知识产权战略实施工作先进集体”、全国查处侵权盗版案件有功单位一等奖、“全省干事创业好团队”等荣誉称号。

一、加大版权执法力度，打击侵权盗版取得新成果

（一）案件查办督办工作有了新突破

“山东威海刘某等制售盗版光盘案”被国家版权局评为2017年度全国打击侵权盗版十大案件之一；山东滨州“11·22”涉嫌制售盗版图书案、山东济宁“10·19”王某某涉嫌侵犯影视作品著作权案被列入国家版权局、全国“扫黄打非”工作小组办公室、公安部和最高人民检察院四部门联合挂牌督办案件；山东青岛“8·1”涉嫌侵犯软件著作权案、山东菏泽“3·12”制售盗版图书案被列为国家版权局督办案件。这些案件查处充分体现了山东省打击侵权盗版工作成果，发挥了典型案件的示范引导作用。2018年山东省积极争取，获得国家版权局重大侵权盗版案件办案经费补贴共计46万元。

（二）积极做好推荐全国查处侵权盗版案件有功单位及个人工作

根据《国家版权局举报、查处侵权盗版行为奖励暂行办法》及实施细则要求，组织推荐山东省查处侵权盗版案件有功单位和个人。2018年11月20日，国家版权局正式公布查处侵权盗版案件有功单位及个人名单，山东省版权管理处等15家单位及省公安厅治安总队张继河等37名个人获奖，奖励金额65.1万元，获奖数量及奖励金额居全国前列。

（三）开展打击网络侵权盗版“剑网2018”专项行动

为进一步加强网络版权执法监管工作，打击网络侵权盗版，依法治理网络空间，维护清朗的网络空间秩序，营造良好的网络版权环境，山东省版权局、山东省互联网信息办公室、山东省通信管理局、山东省公安厅于 2018 年 7—11 月联合开展第 14 次打击网络侵权盗版专项治理“剑网行动”。“剑网 2018”专项行动以网络侵权多发领域为重点，严厉打击各类网站、移动客户端、自媒体等传播侵权盗版作品的行为，集中整治网络转载、短视频、动漫等领域侵权盗版多发态势，重点规范网络直播、知识分享、有声读物等平台版权传播秩序，深入巩固网络影视、网络音乐、电子商务平台、应用商店、网络存储空间等领域专项整治成果。“剑网行动”期间，全省共查处网络侵权盗版案件 27 起，其中已刑事移交的 4 起，关闭侵权网站 14 家，并列入黑名单管理，有效维护了全省网络版权环境。

（四）版权保护工作取得好成绩

2018 年 6 月 22 日，山东省版权局版权管理处荣获国务院知识产权战略实施工作部际联席会议表彰的“国家知识产权战略实施工作先进集体”荣誉称号，成为全国唯一受此表彰的版权管理部门。

二、常抓不懈，扎实推进软件正版化检查整改工作

（一）巩固党政机关软件正版化成果

一是完善体制机制，加强督导检查。2018 年 4 月 20 日，山东省版权局印发《关于在全省开展软件正版化检查工作的通知》（鲁版字［2018］7 号），计划 5—11 月对各市软件正版化工作开展情况进行督导检查。8 月 16—24 日、12 月 5—6 日，省版权局组成督查组赴临沂、济宁、菏泽、德州督查党政机关软件正版化工作，共检查 12 家市级政府机关、12 家区级政府机关，检查机器共计 240 台，同时召开软件正版化工作座谈会，积极推进党政机关软件正版化工作。5 月 21 日，省软件正版化工作联席会议印发了《2018 年山东省推进使用正版软件工作计划》（鲁版字［2018］5 号），对全省软件正版化工作进行了全面部署，将山东省软件正版化工作的制度建设、软件采购、软件使用、软件资产管理、监督检查、考评和责任追究等工作做出具体分工，提出明确要求。二是启动实施 2018 年度新购计算机配置国产办公软件场地授权服务。为进一步建立健全山东省党政机关软件正版化工作长效机制，科学合理解决省级预算单位新增计算机配置办公软件的问题，山东省投入资金 200 万元继续采用新购计算机国产办公软件场地授权服务模式，为部分省直预算单位 2018 年度新购计算机统一配装国产办公软件。2018 年，正版 WPS 办公软件总安装量为 13 770 台。

（二）扎实推进企业软件正版化工作

2018 年 8 月 10 日，会同省国资委在济南召开省属国有企业软件正版化工作推进会，传达学习国家推进使用正版软件工作部际联席会议办公室有关会议精神，总结国有企业软件正版化工作经验，安排部署下一步任务。会议指出，2017 年以来，各省属企业认真推进软件正版化工作，共有 28 家企业基本完成软件正版化检查整改任务。省属企业新增计算机采购正版办公软件 4 300 余套，采购金额 490 余万元，同比分别增长 8.3%和 8.5%。集团企业所属二、三级企业软件正版化工作正在积极推进。目前正在深入开展自查，分类汇总基础信息，系统梳理软件正版化完成情况和存在问题，进一步查缺补漏，巩固扩大国有企业软件正版化工作成果。

（三）顺利完成迎接国家督查组检查工作

2018 年 9 月，根据国家推进使用正版软件工作部际联席会议办公室《关于对部分地区软件正版化进行督促检查的通知》（国版函［2018］17 号）精神，省软件正版化联席会议办公室印发《关于做好迎接国家软件正版化工作督查组来山东省检查的紧急通知》（鲁版字［2018］16 号），要求省政府各部门、各直属机构，各省属企业要高度重视，并以此次国家督查为契机，认真搞好自查整改。在此基础上，重点到被检查单位进行督导检查，提前安装网络版检测工具，确保了国家督查工作的顺利进行。10 月中下旬，国家软件正版化工作督查组对山东省的 6 家省级政府机关和 4 家省属企业进行了督查，共抽查计算机 1 906 台，操作系统、办公软件、防病毒软件正版化率分别达到了 99.8%、94.3%和 100%。督查组认为，山东省软件正版化工作整体做得比较全面、扎实，成效显著，处于全国政府机关软件正版化工作前列。

（四）批复同意开发建设正版软件大数据服务平台项目

作为全省软件正版化工作基础信息库，项目建成后，将有利于对正版软件数据实时监测，为各级版权行政主管部门管理和决策提供参考和依据。正版软件大数据服务中心落户威海市，由威海市及威海南海新区负责具体实施。

三、强化服务，健全版权社会服务体系建设

（一）著作权作品登记体系进一步健全，登记数量进一步增长，作品质量不断提升

建立起以版权保护与服务平台为依托、以版权服务站为支点的全省著作权作品登记社会服务体系。

先后在全省建立了34家版权服务站，覆盖全省17市，直接受理著作权作品登记的初审和发证。2018年全省著作权作品登记达到84 500余份，比2017年同比增长0.93%，其中摄影作品41 236份，美术作品29 575份，文字作品7 774份，类似摄制电影方法创作的作品1 859份。

（二）成功举办“一带一路”国际版权贸易会，开拓版权“走出去”新路径

2018年5月29日—6月8日，由省版权局主办的“一带一路”国际版权贸易会，先后在匈牙利布达佩斯、罗马尼亚布加勒斯特、波兰华沙三地举办。省版权局组织25家省内优秀版权企业参展，副局长谢宁率队参加有关活动。

“一带一路”国际版权贸易会是同期举办的中国（山东）品牌产品中东欧展览会的重要组成部分，为山东省企业开拓中东欧版权市场搭建了良好平台。贸易会期间，山东省优秀版权企业代表团展出图书近千册、文化创意艺术品近百件、软件类产品20余种、动漫广告类作品10余种，并从图书出版、电子出版、文化创意产品开发、文化艺术交流等方面，向匈牙利、塞尔维亚、罗马尼亚、加纳等国家进行版权推介、项目交流，客户访问数量达2 000余人。据统计，展会期间现场成交额达40余万元，参展企业达成意向成交额400余万元。同时，山东省展团还举办了齐鲁文化贸易海外展示中心尼山书屋落地揭牌仪式、“中国民间孤本年画精粹”系列丛书（6种）匈牙利版新书发布会、《中外文学交流史　中国—中东欧卷》波兰语版翻译出版座谈会等一系列主题活动，全方位、多角度宣传展示山东省优质版权资源和版权贸易发展成果，促进版权交易合作。

（三）积极组织相关企业参加第七届中国国际版权博览会

由国家版权局主办的第七届中国国际版权博览会（以下简称版博会）于2018年10月19—21日在苏州举行。省版权局积极组织17家版权单位和机构参展，取得良好成效。山东展区阵容强大，涉及书籍出版、数字软件、文化创意、影视动漫等领域，同时，潍坊市以“版权进乡村”行动参展，即墨区作为国家级版权示范城市参展，引人注目。本届版博会，山东展区现场成交额达60余万元，参展企业分别与河北、北京、杭州、宁夏、陕西、文莱、马来西亚等多地版权企业达成合作意向金额1 000万元。

（四）做好涉外版权合同登记工作

加强图书出版、影视剧等涉外版权合同登记工作，开展图书选题合同登记备案工作。2018年，共办理引进图书版权合同315份，输出图书版权合同334份，与2017年同期相比均有增长。

四、加大版权宣传培训力度，扩大版权社会影响力

（一）实施“版权公益宣传工程”

2018年4月份，版权公益宣传片《“剑网”在行动》《尊重新闻版权》《正好，正版好》和版权微电影《嘿！别动》制作完成，并将样片发给省电视台、各市文化广电新闻出版局和文化市场行政执法局。省台和各市结合“4·26”世界知识产权宣传周活动，通过各种媒体形式进行宣传播放。其中，三部公益广告片分获全省广播电视公益广告评审一等奖和三等奖，版权微电影获国家广电总局2018年度“弘扬社会主义核心价值观　共筑中国梦”主题原创网络视听节目优秀奖。

2018年共组织全省版权部门开展版权宣传活动28次，举办版权培训班10个，印发版权宣传册（页）、宣传手账7 000余份，扩大了版权宣传的影响力，提高了公众的版权保护意识。

（二）举办2018年全省“版权进校园”活动暨版权宣传培训班

2018年5月15日，山东省版权局在济南举行2018年全省“版权进校园”活动启动仪式暨版权宣传培训班。各市文广新局、文化执法局有关负责同志，部分国家级版权示范单位代表、省级版权示范学校师生代表150人参加活动。同时举办了版权宣传培训班，团省委、潍坊市文广新局、青岛市即墨区文化市场执法局、山东世博华创动漫传媒有限公司等4个单位做典型交流发言，山东省版权局副局长谢宁出席并讲话。

（三）正式启动全省“版权进乡村”行动

2018年5月21日，山东省版权局在潍坊市举行2018年全省“版权进乡村”行动启动仪式暨版权执法培训班，各市、县（市、区）文化执法局有关负责同志、一线执法人员150多人参加活动及培训班。国家版权局版权管理司发来贺信，指出：山东省以深入贯彻习近平总书记参加十三届全国人大一次会议山东代表团审议时的重要讲话精神和党中央、国务院《关于实施乡村振兴战略的实施意见》为指针，以版权助力乡村振兴为切入点，在全国率先开展了“版权进乡村”行动，体现了高度的政治觉悟、强烈的大局意识以及勇于创新的责任担当，必将对强化农村版权创造、运用、保护和管理，对乡村振兴战略的实施起到积极推动作用。

在版权执法培训班上，潍坊市文化执法局做了版权工作经验介绍，青岛市、威海市文化执法局结合已经结案的大案要案，进行以案说法，着重培养一线执法人员办案能力。山东省版权局对下步版权执法工作进行重点部署。

“版权进乡村”行动开展以来，全省共组织活动 20 余次，发布宣传报道 12 篇，动员乡村版权创意产品登记 3 000 余份。“乡村处处有版权”“大山里面有版权”“农民同样需要正版”等普及宣传活动正在引向深入。

五、多措并举，推进版权产业发展

（一）编印出版《山东省版权产业经济贡献》一书

为全面掌握山东省版权产业的发展状况，充分发挥其在山东省经济转型升级发展中的作用，增强全省公众和政府部门对版权保护与版权产业发展的认识与支持，依据 2016 年和 2017 年两次“山东省版权产业的经济贡献”项目调研成果，完成《山东省版权产业经济贡献》编辑出版工作。

（二）拟定《山东省加快推进山东省版权产业发展指导意见》初稿

为深入实施创新驱动发展战略，激发版权产业创新、创造活力，以经济指数为坐标，为山东省版权产业可持续发展提供翔实的理论和数据支持，提出版权产业改革的新方向，依据两次版权经济贡献调研成果拟定《山东省加快推进山东省版权产业发展指导意见》初稿，目前正在进一步修改。

（三）批复设立山东大学版权教学科研基地及山东省版权研究中心

2018 年 2 月 24 日，山东省版权局批复在山东大学设立山东省版权教学科研基地。该基地将依托青岛市和即墨区国家级版权示范城市优质版权资源，以及山东大学丰厚的知识产权教学经验，推动实现产学研协调发展，逐步在全社会形成“尊重知识、尊重劳动、尊重创作、尊重版权”的良好氛围。6 月 25 日，在山东大学青岛校区举办挂牌仪式暨版权知识培训班，国家版权局版权管理司于慈珂司长出席会议并讲话，即墨区党政部门负责人以及山东大学法学院师生 200 多人参加会议。

2018 年 3 月 27 日，山东省版权局批复同意山东省区域文化产业研究院设立山东省版权研究中心。该中心依托现有研发队伍及智库平台，认真贯彻落实《国家知识产权战略纲要》，结合当前新旧动能转换，积极配合政府制定出台产业政策，为政府决策提供有效智力支持，不断促进山东省版权产业繁荣发展。

（四）进一步推动版权示范创建工作

为贯彻实施《国家知识产权战略纲要》《“十三五”国家知识产权保护和运用规划》，根据国家版权局工作部署，山东省着力培育一批在建立版权保护工作机制、注重版权产业发展、完成软件正版化检查整改工作任务等方面有典型示范作用的单位、园区（基地）。年初，山东省版权局印发《关于申报“版权示范单位”和“版权保护示范单位”的通知》，共收到申报版权示范材料 80 余份。2018 年 9 月 17 日，经各市、省直部门考察推荐，省版权局研究，印发《关于公布山东省“版权示范单位、园区（基地）”和“版权保护示范单位、园区（基地）”的通知》，山东世博华创动漫传媒有限公司等 24 家单位被评为“山东省版权示范单位、园区（基地）”，山东产权交易中心有限公司等 36 家单位被评为“山东省版权保护示范单位、园区（基地）”。

截至 2018 年底，山东省已成功创建全国版权示范城市 2 个，全国版权示范单位、园区（基地）25 家，省级版权示范单位、园区（基地）255 家。山东省示范争创工作在国家会议上交流，受到好评，《中国新闻出版广电报》全文发表经验介绍。

（蒋金坤）

河　南　省

2018 年，河南省版权局深入贯彻落实党的十九大精神，紧紧围绕省委、省政府中心工作，牢固树立政治意识、大局意识、核心意识、看齐意识，团结一致、不断创新、依法行政、积极作为，各项工作不断取得新的成绩。

一、版权社会服务工作情况

（一）普法宣传工作深入广泛

2018 年，河南省版权局加强版权普法宣传力度，扩大宣传范围，创新宣传方法。“4·26”世界知识产权日宣传周期间，在社区、学校采取多种形式宣讲国家政策、宣传典型案例，营造良好的版权舆论氛围，进一步提升公众的版权保护意识。同时组织 18 个省辖市、10 个省直管县开展版权宣传工作，做到了多层次、全覆盖对社会公众的版权普法宣传。

（二）作品登记和版权贸易合同审核工作重质提量

认真开展作品著作权自愿登记和法律咨询工作，严把作品质量关，缩短受理周期，提高服务质量。

2018 年，河南省共受理各类作品著作权登记 1 063 件和电话咨询 1 000 余人次，审核登记出版单位从国、境外引进版权贸易合同 163 件，为社会公众提供良好的公共服务。

（三）版权产业取得突破性发展

2018 年 10 月 19—21 日，河南省版权局首次组织了 19 家单位和机构，在苏州参加了第七届中国国际版权博览会，全方位展示了河南省特色文化和优秀的版权成果。此次版博会扩大了河南省文化产业影响力，在取得一定社会效益和经济效益的同时，也向国内外展示了河南省版权事业创新发展的新面貌，10 家参展单位与 20 家参展商达成了合作意向。国家版权局有关领导参观了河南展区并表示，河南初次亮相版博会，参展企业众多，展品类型丰富，展现了河南文化产业、版权产业健康发展的良好态势。在第七届中国国际版权博览会闭幕式暨“金慧奖”颁奖仪式上，河南展团共有 5 家单位获奖：河南省版权局荣获“金慧奖”优秀组织奖，河南日报报业集团、河南广播电视台、河南省版权交易中心和河南大学出版社获“金慧奖”优秀企业奖。

二、版权执法监管工作情况

（一）加强版权日常监管执法工作力度

2018 年，河南省版权局指导各省辖市、省直管县（市）版权行政部门的版权监管和执法工作，通过信息共享、上下联动、多方配合，强化对印刷复制源头企业、出版物仓储物流运输企业、出版物批发零售经营商家的监督和管理。2018 年，河南省查办侵权盗版案件 53 起，其中国家版权局移转涉嫌侵权案件线索 7 起，国家版权局挂牌督办案件 3 起；发现涉嫌网络侵权案件 4 起，删除、屏蔽各类有害信息 1.6 万条，关闭侵权网站 12 家，查扣盗版图书 160 万余册，涉案码洋 4 500 余万元。

2018 年，河南省共获得查处侵权盗版案件有功单位一等奖 3 项 8 个单位，二等奖 4 项 10 个单位；有功个人一等奖 6 项 19 人，二等奖 6 项 25 人，三等奖 9 项 25 人。获奖总额 49.3 万元。

（二）举办全省版权执法监管培训班

河南省版权局于 8 月 16—17 日在郑州召开了全省版权执法监管培训班，介绍了河南省版权工作取得的成绩，并对下一步工作做出部署，国家版权局有关领导出席培训班并做专题辅导报告。各省辖市、省直管县（市）文广新局分管版权工作的副局长和执法支队、执法大队的一线同志等 140 余人参加了培训。

（三）深入开展“剑网”专项行动

通过有关媒体进行宣传报道，公布举报电话、邮箱，发动权利人和群众举报投诉。每月对辖区内所有互联网网站、APP 等进行全面监测清查一次。

10 月 12 日，召开了河南省“剑网 2018”专项行动推进会。各省辖市、省直管县（市）和省内具有较大影响力的网站代表参加了会议。会议通报了“剑网 2018”专项行动主要工作任务和开展情况，并签订了《网络版权承诺书》。

10 月 30 日—11 月 1 日，国家“剑网 2018”专项行动及重点案件督查组对河南进行督查，先后对郑州市文广新局、大河网、猪八戒网进行了实地督查，听取了河南省“剑网 2018”专项行动及重点案件工作汇报。省检察院、焦作市等有关单位做了发言。督察组组长对河南省“剑网 2018”专项行动及重点案件查办情况给予了充分肯定，指出河南省版权局对打击侵权盗版工作非常重视，办案数量多、质量好，工作分工明确，省、市、县三级联动好，宣传教育有特色，取得成效显著。

（四）加大对大案要案的指导督办和查处力度

河南省版权局对南阳市内乡县奥斯卡影城涉嫌盗录热播电影案进行督办，指导南阳市文化市场综合执法支队立即采取行动，暂扣了该影院放映设备服务器主板。成功侦破了新乡张某某通过微信销售盗版图书案、焦作沁阳聚视网络科技有限公司开发的《今日影视》《韩剧大全》《影视大全纯净版》《芝麻影视大全》APP 涉嫌传播淫秽色情视频和盗版电影等一批大案要案。

三、全省政府机关、企事业单位软件正版化工作情况

（一）制定河南省 2018 年软件正版化工作计划

河南省推进使用正版软件工作联席会议办公室制定了《2018 年河南省推进使用正版软件工作计划》，经省政府同意，上报了推进使用正版软件工作部际联席会议办公室。

（二）召开省推进使用正版软件工作联席会议

5 月 17 日、9 月 6 日，分别召开了两次河南省推进使用正版软件工作联席会议成员单位会议，传达了推进使用正版软件工作部际联席会议第七次全体会议纪要和有关文件精神，介绍了河南省 2017 年软件正版化工作完成情况、存在的问题和 2018 年推进软件正版化重点工作。

（三）迎接国家督查组的督查

9 月 17—21 日，国家督查组对河南省软件正版化工作进行了为期 5 天的督查，先后对省政府办公厅、河南交通投资集团等 10 家单位进行了现场检查，查阅了相关资料，共检查 1 415 台计算机的软件安装情况。9 月 21 日，督查组在省政府召开了河南省软件正版化督查情况反馈会，认为河南省委、省政府高度重视软件正版化工作，作为河南省推进使用正版软件工作联席会议牵头单位，省新闻出版广电局（版权局）能够积极主动做好各项协调服务和指导工作，省联席会议各成员单位相互配合、密切协作、齐抓共管，推进软件正版化工作取得显著成效，一些新的做法、好的经验可以总结推广。

（四）开展政府机关、企业软件正版化督查和培训工作

2018 年，先后对 18 个省辖市、10 个直管县（市）和省直机关、省管国有企业开展了软件正版化督查工作，并召开了 300 余人参加的软件正版化工作培训班，对日常监督、考核与责任追究制度等 11 个方面的内容进行了培训，确保巩固扩大政府机关软件正版化工作成果和省管国有企业软件正版化工作的推进实施。

四、“双打”工作情况

2018 年，国家打击侵犯知识产权和制售假冒伪劣商品工作领导小组办公室对河南进行“双打”考核，考核内容中版权执法监管、软件正版化工作占 11 分，河南省版权局获得满分。

（焦艳娜）

湖　北　省

2018 年，湖北省版权局在省局党组的正确领导和分管领导的具体指导下，认真贯彻落实两级新闻出版广电工作会议精神，按照年初统一部署，有组织、有计划、有步骤地推进各项工作落实，取得初步成效。江岸区法院知识产权审判庭荣获国家版权局和世界知识产权组织合作项目“中国版权金奖”保护奖。湖北省版权局版权管理处被省“双打”工作领导小组评为 2017 年先进集体，被局党组评为 2017 年全局考核优胜单位。

一、积极迎考，执法管理出实绩

积极发挥“双打”量化考核的导向作用，明确任务目标，强化督办检查，突出案件查办，全年全省各级版权行政执法部门累计立案查处侵权盗版案件 54 件，其中行政处罚 40 件，移送公安机关 8 件，共涉及金额达 1 400 多万元。严密组织“剑网 2018”专项行动，重拳打击互联网领域各种侵权盗版行为。行动期间，各级版权相关执法单位先后巡查属地备案网站 7 000 多家，对发现的侵权线索及时依法处理。省局先后约谈了小明太极（湖北）国漫文化有限公司和斗鱼直播网站。组织对“91 资源网”“蓝光 VR”“星楚影院”等网络侵权案件线索进行了立案查处，有效遏制了日益猖獗的侵权盗版行为。其中，咸宁谢某某等制售盗版出版物案、襄阳刘某某等涉嫌侵犯著作权案、襄阳《绝地求生》游戏私服案等 3 起大案要案被国家版权局、公安部、“扫黄打非”办等四部门挂牌督办。湖北省恩施土家族苗族自治州查办的赵某某等人侵犯游戏私服著作权案被评为国家版权局 2017 年度全国打击侵权盗版十大案件之一；在国务院组织的“双打”绩效考核和国家版权局组织的“双打”部门考核中，湖北省版权行政执法管理和软件正版化工作等 2 项工作分别连续第 4 次、第 5 次获得满分成绩。在全国 2017 年度查处侵权盗版案件有功单位、有功个人评奖活动中，湖北省共有 23 个单位、15 名个人分别荣获有功单位和有功个人奖。其中，有功单位一等奖 6 个、二等奖 5 个、三等奖 6 个，有功个人一等奖 4 个、二等奖 1 个、三等奖 7 个，奖金总额 70.3 万元，综合排名全国第二位。

二、严密组织，软件正版化做实功

5 月下旬，组织召开了湖北省推进使用正版软件工作领导小组成员单位联席会议。省政府副秘书长刘仲初出席会议并讲话。传达了国务院推进使用正版软件工作部际联席会议第七次会议精神，通报了湖北省 2017 年推进软件正版化工作情况，审议通过了《2017 年全省软件正版化工作检查情况通报》《2018 年湖北省推进使用正版软件工作计划》《2018 年湖北省软件正版化督查实施方案》等相关文件，对 2018 年工作目标、任务和推进措施等进行了专题部署，为软件正版化工作的顺利推进奠定了坚实的基础。借鉴国务院的工作模式，积极推进市级政府机关软件正版化全覆盖督查。经省政府同意，省推进使用正版软件工作领导小组决定 2018 年在襄阳市、孝感市、十堰市、天门市等 4 个地市的 187 家市级政府机关进行软件正版化全覆盖督查。6 月 22 日，召开全覆盖督查专题动员大会暨软件正版化工作联络员培训班，安排部署督查任务。积极推进云梦县国产软件试用试点工作。省局先后三次赴云梦县调研指导，帮助县政府和软件开发公司及时解决试点中遇到的各种困难和问题，保障试点工作扎实推进。云梦县 51 家县级机关部门全部纳入试点范围，累计覆盖终端 377 台，其中单系统占实施总数比例为 75%，试点成果正在全力推广之中，并打算向上下游延伸。国家版权局国产软件试点项目组先

后两次进行现场调研，给予充分肯定，一致认为这是全国最成功的试点，并打算向全国推广。8月14日，推进使用正版软件部际联席会议办公室和国家版权局在孝感市云梦县召开国产软件应用试点总结会，检查验收此次国产软件应用试点推进项目，交流国产软件试点工作经验，畅想国产软件产业发展前景，现场参观云梦县机关国产软件使用情况，并授予云梦县“全国国产软件应用试点县”称号。深度操作系统软件——作为湖北省深之度科技有限公司创新开发出的一款完全拥有自主知识产权的操作系统软件，是在云梦县县级政府机关经过一年的试点应用推广，最终开发成功的。试点用户普遍反映，此款软件技术成熟、性能稳定、界面清晰、运行顺畅、使用便捷、安全可靠，达到国内领先水平，可以在全国推广应用。

三、注重创新，宣传教育出实招

省版权局积极发挥好行业主管部门的优势，创新宣传模式，突出重点时段，组织全媒体资源、各类社会力量、新兴平台进行宣传广告投放，取得了很好的宣传教育效果。“3·15”国际消费者权益日当天，由省版权局主办，省版权保护中心、华中国家版权交易中心有限公司和武汉斗鱼网络科技有限公司共同承办的主题为“拒绝侵权盗版　共享美好生活”的“3·15”国际消费者权益日版权专题宣传活动在斗鱼直播平台正式开播。活动采取嘉宾访谈+实地采访的形式，开设了省版权局和斗鱼官方两个直播间，省版权局版权管理处处长卢文俊、华中国家版权交易中心有限公司宋丕伟副总经理在官方直播间与广大网友就大家所关心的版权登记、法律维权、产业发展等问题进行互动交流。斗鱼官方直播间首次实地实景展现了版权行政执法管理活动的现场流程，现场执法人员介绍了侵权盗版的危害性和识别盗版侵权出版物的基本方法，斗鱼主播实地体验了版权登记流程和网上登记系统。活动吸引了大批网友关注，直播热度一度突破30多万人次，累计发送弹幕500余条。在“4·26”世界知识产权日版权宣传周期间，版权局联合省电影局积极组织各院线开展版权宣传活动，通过映前贴片广告播放版权宣传视频。宣传周期间，全省共投入银幕2 000多块，累计放映6万多场次，受到观影群众的一致好评。还组织华中国家版权交易中心联合武汉地铁集团在地铁广告终端插播版权知识专题宣传片，在武汉轨道交通二号线所有车厢的共2 579块显示终端进行全线覆盖式滚动播放，版权宣传周期间共计播放288 848次，覆盖人流量805万人次，取得了良好的社会效果。

四、夯实基础，业务培训求实效

建立完善总局轮训、省局培训、市州自训的三级教育培训体系，大力加强版权行政管理队伍建设，提升基层版权行政执法管理部门人员能力素质。连续6年举办版权行政执法管理工作人员培训班，采取理论讲解+案例剖析+座谈探析的形式，聚焦网络环境下的版权行政执法工作，5位来自版权行政执法、刑事执法和司法审判一线的基层代表分别围绕版权法律法规、互联网+大数据技术、案件证据采集与鉴定、“两法”衔接、著作权刑事案件审判等重点、难点、热点问题进行了专题授课，手把手教方法、点对点传经验，重点帮助基层版权行政执法人员解决在互联网环境下办什么案、怎么办案的问题，受到学员的普遍好评。6月份，举办了市级政府机关软件正版化工作全覆盖督查培训班，襄阳市、孝感市、十堰市、天门市等4个地市市级政府机关，以及市委、人大、政协等部门200多名软件正版化工作人员参训，对市级政府机关软件正版化全覆盖督查检查下一步工作进行了具体部署，重点介绍了全覆盖督查的主要内容、检查形式和方法，对软件正版化工作信息管理平台及其检测工具的具体应用问题进行了探索研究，并提供了解决方案。

五、加强指导，产业发展谋实惠

按照《湖北省创建版权示范城市、版权示范单位、版权示范园区实施办法》要求，认真组织开展版权示范创建活动，下发了2018年版权示范创建工作通知，完成了省级版权示范单位、版权示范园区的申报、资料收集整理，制定完善了验收考核评分细则，并对提交资料的申报单位、园区进行了初审。科学指导省版权保护中心完成了著作权登记系统二期升级维护项目，建立完善登记系统版权评级子系统评价指标模型并上线运行，为全省广大权利人提供规范、高效、便捷的版权公共服务。全年全省作品登记近3.09万件，办理出版外国图书合同登记和著作权合同备案登记438件，涉及美、英、德、法、日、俄等近20个国家和地区，合同金额达5 000余万元。坚持“走出去”与“请进来”相结合，组团参加国际版权博览会等对外交流活动，及时推广版权创新成果。10月中旬，省局组织18家省内优秀版权企业参展第七届中国国际版权博览会，展示湖北省近年来在版权事业、版权产业方面创造的优秀成果及取得的重大成就。湖北省版权局和武汉深之度科技有限软件公司、湖北商贸学院艺术与传媒学院城市创意礼物团体、武汉弘安梯创科技股份有限公司等4家单位分别获得“金慧奖”组织奖和优秀企业奖。积极指导华中国家版权交易中心举办第四届华中国际版权高峰论坛，齐聚业界精英，共商产业大计，将版权高峰论坛真正打造成湖北省版权行业的一块优质品牌，并逐步成为具有一定影响的版权盛会。积极指导华中国家版权交易中心有限公司创新经营模式、拓展业务范围、实现盈利增效，2018年全年交易中心平台实现交易额有望突破200万元。按照产业化、集约化、合作化、最大化的要求，积极指导交易中心在开展版权代理登记及增值服务等传统业务基础上，开发了全国首个点播影院版权发行平台，设立新型点播院线公司。积极争取设立湖北省影视引导基金，拟通过政府财政性资金投入、引导社会资本共计2.5亿元进入影视产业，推动影视产业跨越发展。

（张　威）

湖　南　省

2018年，湖南省版权局创新版权行政管理，做实版权基础服务，不断加大版权行政执法和监管力度，进一步推进软件正版化工作常态化、规范化，服务版权产业发展。

一、积极开展调研，创新工作思路

积极落实省委“抓重点、补短板、强弱项”大调研活动要求，细致谋划，聚焦版权行政管理和版权服务中的重点、难点，扎实开展调研活动。3月份赴浙江、上海等兄弟省市学习考察作品登记、版权交易、协会建设等方面先进经验，调研回来后立即对湖南省版权登记工作的流程和档案管理进行优化完善。针对省内文创企业版权资产运营水平不高的问题，与湘潭大学组成课题组，通过召开座谈会、走访企业和问卷调查等方式，撰写了题为《加强湖南省企业版权运营能力研究》的调研报告，从理论和实务两方面提出促进版权产业发展的措施。另外，湖南省版权局还承担了国家版权局制定起草《国家享有著作权作品管理办法》的调研工作，就《办法》的制定提出了可行性建议，受到国家版权局的肯定。

二、强化业务管理，强化版权服务

一直把版权服务作为一项基础性工作来抓，采取多项措施推进版权服务体系建设，努力提高作品登记等服务工作质量，加大版权服务工作对省内重点项目的支持力度。一是推动行业协会组织建设，指导湖南省版权保护协会完成换届。2018年5月，协调省民政厅等主管部门以及50余家主要会员单位，按照社团管理相关规定，召开协会换届大会，推选出了新一届的协会会长、副会长及秘书长等领导机构，指导其完成审计年检等工作，为协会正常运转奠定了良好基础。二是进一步强化对版权社会服务的管理，加大对省市两级版权登记受理点的业务考核和培训力度，制定了考核办法，要求其按季度定期制作登记信息报表，由湖南省版权局定期进行检查。截至12月中旬，全省共登记作品3 426件，完成引进外国图书合同备案410件，办结境外委托印刷著作权授权书备案30件。三是积极推介湖南省的优秀版权企业和作品，在国家版权局的指导下，组织马栏山视频文创产业园开展国家级的版权创新基地创建工作。推荐中南传媒、湖南广播电视台获评“中国版权最具影响力企业奖”。推介湖南电子音像社、金鹰卡通卫视等三家企业的7部优秀动漫作品入选在国家原创动漫作品版权开发优秀项目库，并获得扶持资金。指导中南传媒通过教材版权研发和文化“走出去”模式创新，承接中国援助南苏丹教育技术项目，在推进“一带一路”倡议、展示中华文化方面发挥了良好的示范作用。

三、加大执法力度，维护市场秩序

不断强化版权执法这一重要工作手段，加大版权纠纷调解力度，为版权产业发展创造良好市场环境。一是持续开展专项整治，先后就冬奥会版权保护、打击制售假冒伪劣和侵犯知识产权、打击网络侵权盗版开展专项整治，制定了方案，明确了任务。据统计，全省各级版权执法部门共出动1 560人次，巡查网站、摊点和市场2 965个，收缴或下线侵权盗版制品2.8万件，有效净化了市场。二是突出案件查办，始终将重大案件查处作为执法重中之重。全年各级版权执法部门共查处各类侵权盗版案件32件，其中查处了邵阳深度汽车影音网站侵犯音乐作品著作权案、长沙网盘影视网站侵犯影视作品著作权案等国家版权局交办的案件2起，以及国家版权局和全国“扫黄打非”办共同督办的重大案件3起。三是加强行政调解，妥善解决版权纠纷。调处潇湘电影集团与某作家版权纠纷、长沙电视台与某视频公司版权纠纷，化解矛盾，防范风险。对政府采购中未交付正版软件的供货商进行了约谈，要求合法合规经营并限期改正。因版权执法工作取得成效，全省版权10个执法单位和22名执法人员获评2017年度全国查处侵权盗版案件有功单位和有功个人，湖南省版权局版权管理处也因指导组织案件查处获评有功单位。

四、狠抓长效机制，推进软件正版化

把软件正版化工作常态化建设作为重点，强化部署，加大检查督促力度，确保各项管理措施有效落地，防止盗版软件使用反弹。一是做好统筹规划，落实监管职责。年初制定了《湖南省 2018 年推进使用正版软件工作计划》，明确了工作要求，印发给各市州政府和省直各单位。年中召开了全省推进软件正版化工作联席会议联络员会议，研究落实各职能部门的分工，协调推动工作进度。7 月份联合省国资委开展省属国有企业软件正版化座谈会，汇总各企业的正版软件需求，组织集中采购降低成本。协调省级审计部门继续将正版化工作纳入审计清单，对 2 家发现问题的省直单位进行通报并要求整改。二是加强技术保障，规范软件日常管理。通过服务外包方式，聘请技术公司帮助 46 家省直机关安装正版软件检查工具，在省监狱管理系统和长沙市直系统试点正版软件大数据管理系统，在日常管理中可以一键式清查未经授权的软件，提高自查清理的工作效率，各单位共清理卸载各类侵权盗版软件 2 370 余套。三是狠抓督促检查，实现检查全覆盖。6—9 月份，派出两个检查组对 46 家省本级单位的所有 6 673 台计算机使用软件情况进行实地开机检查，对检查发现的问题，当场向被检查单位反馈，要求立行立改。将检查结果报告省人民政府，并专门印发了工作通报，督促整改落实到位。

通过上述工作，2018 年以来，各地各单位进一步强化使用正版软件的意识，共投入经费 3 755 万元，采购正版软件 2.7 万套，正版软件使用比例显著提升。10 月，国家抽查组来湘检查正版化工作，对湖南省工作给予了充分肯定。

五、加强宣传培训，营造良好氛围

将版权社会宣传和版权企业宣传相结合，强化专业业务培训，努力营造良好的工作氛围。一是广泛开展社会宣传。在“4·26”世界知识产权宣传周期间，联合湖南省知识产权局发布了湖南知识产权保护白皮书，举办专题新闻发布会，介绍湖南版权执法和软件正版化工作的最新进展。设计制作了《著作权法》宣传海报、笔记本、文件袋和著作权法 U 盘，发放给各市州和主要版权企业。二是开展版权宣传进企业、进高校活动。组织省内高校师生积极参与第十届全国大学生版权征文活动，其中中南大学知识产权法专业多名学生分别获得此次征文活动的一、二等奖。指导长沙市举办了“文创企业版权保护运营交流会”，吸引百余家企业参加，交流分享版权资产运营的经验。三是加大行业队伍建设力度，积极开展专题培训。组织部分市州版权局参加了在北京举办的“2018 中国网络版权保护大会”。与湖南省文联组织“文艺作品著作权保护”研讨班，对 14 个市州文联的干部进行著作权法知识专题培训。联合国家版权局在广州举办省直单位软件正版化培训班，46 家省级政府机关以及 20 余家党委、人大、政协及群团组织的工作人员参加了培训。联合湖南省“扫黄打非”办对市县 200 余名基层版权执法人员进行网络版权案件查办技术培训，取得良好效果。

（宋　亮）

广　东　省

2018 年，广东省版权局以习近平新时代中国特色社会主义思想为指导，全面贯彻党的十九大和十九届二中、三中全会精神及习近平总书记视察广东重要讲话精神，以实施创新驱动发展战略、推动高质量发展为引领，深入推进版权的创造、保护和运用，创新工作理念和方法，版权工作取得新的突破。

一、版权执法监管取得新进展

以版权行政执法监管为手段，严厉打击侵权盗版违法行为，严格保护知识产权，激励创新创造，进一步优化法治化营商环境，推动经济高质量发展。一是长效机制进一步完善。建立了黑白名单制度、“广东省版权十大案件”评定公布制度等十余项制度，完善了广东省版权行政执法的制度体系。二是执法队伍业务水平进一步提升。组织了一期全省 2018 年度版权行政执法专题培训班，广东省版权执法一线队伍应对新形势新挑战的办案水平得到显著提升。三是版权执法专项行动成效显著。按照国家版权局等四部委要求，广东省版权局联合省通信管理局、公安厅、互联网信息办公室组织开展了“剑网 2018”专项行动，专项行动期间，广东省共查处网络侵权盗版案件 52 宗，已结案 41 宗，行政处罚 60.89 万元，移送司法机关 6 宗，调解结案 7 宗，关闭违规网站 42 个，收缴侵权盗版制品 8 976 件，删除侵权盗版链接 15 340 条，网络传播秩序明显好转。四是查办重大案件成绩突出。2018 年广东省各地级以上市版权行政管理部门共查处版权侵权案件 224 宗，行政罚款 79.05 万元。广东省版权局版权管理处荣获国家版权局 2017 年度查处侵权盗版案件有功单位一等奖，广州市文化市场综合执法总队等 17 个单位（个人）荣获 2017 年度查处侵权盗版案件有功单位（个人）称号，广州市文化市场综合执法总队、雅昌文化集团分别荣获国家版权局与世界知识产权组织颁发的“中国版权金奖”保护奖和推广应用奖。

二、软件正版化工作持续深入推进

强化突出重点、分类推进、以点带面，推进使用正版软件工作形势良好、进展顺利、成绩突出。一是党政机关软件正版化长效机制得到进一步强化。软硬件采购源头管理、日常使用管理、软件台账管理等制度得到贯彻落实。二是企事业单位软件正版化工作推进加速。医疗、教育等事业单位覆盖面逐步扩大；确定305家大型企业为2018年广东省软件正版化工作重点推进单位，比2017年增长91.8%。三是国有企业软件正版化成绩突出。省属国有企业一级单位已全面完成软件正版化，二、三级企业正全面推进中。

三、版权社会服务成效显著

突出版权工作的社会属性，紧紧围绕服务经济社会发展新常态，大力推进版权社会服务工作理念创新、内容创新、方法创新，版权社会服务体系进一步完善。一是版权社会服务组织建设得到进一步强化。版权协会等中介组织队伍进一步壮大，中介服务快速拓展。全省设立版权登记代办机构35家，实现了全省21个地市全覆盖。2018年全省共登记一般作品53 126件，位居全国前列；软件著作权登记近28万件，位居全国第一。二是展会版权工作再上新台阶。牵头广州、东莞市组织开展第七届中国国际版权博览会广东专题展览。广东省版权局和深圳市市场和质量监督管理委员会分别获得本届版博会“金慧奖”优秀组织奖，广州市朗声图书有限公司等四家企业获得“金慧奖”优秀企业奖。在广交会、文博会、漫博会等大型国际性展会上设立版权服务工作站，开展免费作品登记，强化版权保护，展会期间，版权纠纷实现“零投诉”，会展版权服务得到社会高度认可。三是版权宣传取得新成效。举办了“品时代经典，点版权风云”等多场大型版权宣传活动，版权保护宣传进社区、进企业、进校园“三进”工作进一步强化。四是版权产业发展步伐加快。据中国新闻出版研究院统计，2016年广东省版权产业增加值占全省GDP的8.61%，居全国前列。

四、粤港版权交流继续深化

借助粤港澳大湾区建设的重大机遇，深化粤港在跨境保护、版权贸易、交流研讨等领域的合作，携手香港共同探索版权合作新机制。与香港海关、香港知识产权署继续联手组织粤港两地中学生版权知识和版权保护互访交流活动和粤港版权产业企业交流活动，并邀请香港知识产权署组织香港版权产业界人士参加第十届漫博会版权保护促进交流论坛。为激励粤港企业版权的创造和运用，与香港知识产权署合作拍摄粤港澳大湾区版权品牌成功故事宣传片。

（易瑾媛）

广西壮族自治区

2018年，广西壮族自治区各级版权部门在国家版权局的指导下，在自治区党委、政府的领导下，认真履行职责，积极主动作为，抓好版权执法、软件正版化、版权服务社会等各项工作，从多个方面促进广西版权事业的发展。

一、狠抓版权执法，打击侵权盗版

广西版权局向全区印发了广西“剑网2018”专项行动方案，召开动员部署会，组织全区版权部门以“剑网2018”专项行动为抓手，以整治网络侵权盗版为重点，协同通信管理、公安、网信等部门，查处各类侵犯著作权的违法犯罪行为，提升知识产权保护水平。全区共查办各类侵权盗版案件156起，2018年当年办结125起，收缴各类侵权盗版制品50余万件，捣毁制售侵权盗版制品窝点6个，关闭网站7家，删除侵权链接165条。这些案件中33起是网络侵权盗版案件，数量较2017年增长37.5%。

在国家版权局2018年11月做出的表彰决定中，广西6家单位和5名个人被评为2017年度查处侵权盗版案件有功单位和有功个人，南宁市查办的皮皮小说网侵犯著作权案被评为全国年度十大版权案件之一。

二、大力推进软件正版化工作

广西版权局认真履行自治区推进使用正版软件工作领导小组办公室职责，牵头制定《2018年广西推进使用正版软件工作计划》，明确领导小组各成员单位在2018年工作中的任务分工，从健全工作机制、加强计算机软硬件采购管理、强化年度考核与督促检查、抓好宣传培训等方面着手，加强对全区软件正版化工作的部署。认真落实国家版权局关于扩大工作覆盖面的要求，制定《广西推进企事业单位使用正版软件工作规划》，以全区各事业单位、国有企业以及非国有重点行业上市企业、规模以上企业为重点，分三个阶段，力争到2023年底前实现全区企事业单位计算机软件的全面正版化。《规划》的出台，开启了广西推进企事业单位软件正版化工作的新阶段。

广西版权局重视宣传培训，2018年先后组织自治区级机关单位、自治区级国有企业、各地市进行了三期软件正版化工作培训。全区各市版权部门也举办了多次培训，提升了全区相关人员的工作能力，营造了推进工作的良好氛围。据统计，全区 2018 年共举办软件正版化工作培训班 38 次，1 626 家单位、3 216 人次参加培训。

在 2018 年的工作中，广西版权局充分利用督查考核手段，促使全区各单位落实工作主体责任，促进工作的巩固和提高。先后对 321 家区直、中直驻邕机关单位，市县机关单位以及自治区级国有企业进行了软件正版化工作督查考核，现场检查计算机 6 500 余台。

三、版权服务社会工作成效明显

广西版权部门积极开展版权宣传，做好版权服务社会工作，通过多种途径提升全社会版权保护意识，促进版权产业发展。

广西版权局于 2018 年 4 月开展全区首次版权保护优秀单位评选活动，评选出广西日报社、接力出版社有限公司、广西民族大学、广西经济管理干部学院、南宁峰值文化传播有限公司、齐迹智慧金融孵化基地、广西英腾教育科技股份有限公司、桂林力港网络科技股份有限公司、广西临届数字科技有限公司、桂林坤鹤文化传播有限公司等 10 家全区版权保护优秀单位。组织全区 11 家单位、16 个版权项目参加“中国版权金奖”“2018 年度中国版权新锐企业”评选，南宁峰值文化传播有限公司荣获中国版权协会授予的“2018 年度中国版权新锐企业”称号。这些评选活动很好地发挥了版权工作优秀单位的示范作用，促进了全社会版权保护意识的提升。

广西版权局在 2018 年“4 · 26”全国知识产权宣传周期间举办了广西版权工作新闻发布会，向区内外媒体介绍广西 2017 年度版权工作情况，公布全区十大版权保护典型案例、全区十家版权保护优秀单位，还制作了三集动漫宣传短片，在广西电视台以及各市电视台滚动播出。全区各市版权部门紧紧围绕宣传主题，创新方式方法，利用多种媒介进行了全方位、立体化、多样态的宣传，积极推动版权进机关、进校园、进社区、进基层，取得了良好的宣传效果。

广西版权局积极提升版权服务社会能力，认真做好作品登记、涉外版权合同备案工作，促进版权产业发展。2018 年全区作品登记量同比增幅超 100%，获得国家版权局通报表扬。全区图书出版社共输出图书版权 503 种，引进图书版权 368 种，是广西近年来难得的输出图书品种数量超过引进数量的年份。

（赵明明）

海 南 省

2018 年，海南省版权工作以习近平新时代中国特色社会主义思想为指导，深入贯彻落实党的十九大和十九届二中、三中全会精神，认真组织实施《著作权法》及著作权相关法律法规，严厉打击侵权盗版保护创新，积极开展版权宣传营造版权保护氛围，大力鼓励版权创作推动创新发展，为海南省创新发展助力。

一、扎实推进软件正版化工作

（一）取得的工作成效

（1）政府机关软件正版化进一步巩固。截至 2018 年底，海南省各级政府机关持有操作系统软件授权 5.16 万套、办公软件授权 6.16 万套、杀毒软件授权 5.16 万套，实现了正版软件全覆盖。在此基础上，继续抓好源头监管，查缺补漏，并组织问题单位落实整改。

（2）金融机构软件正版化取得新的突破。截至 2018 年底，实现海南财务、农垦财务等 2 家财务公司以及三亚惠民等 9 家村镇银行通用软件正版化，海口联合农商行等 7 家机构通用软件正版率继续保持 100%；完成金元证券、万和证券、金元期货、华融期货等 4 家海南本地证券期货机构和 90 家证券期货分支机构在核心业务系统软件和通用软件方面的正版化。全省企业采购操作系统软件投入 244.21 万元、办公软件投入 219.39 万元、杀毒软件投入 109.69 万元，升级及维护操作系统软件投入 1 020.55 万元、办公软件投入 84.97 万元、杀毒软件投入 33.43 万元。

（3）行业单位软件正版化正式启动。启动省属文化、旅游、勘察设计行业国有企事业单位软件正版化工作。9 月份印发通知，自 2018 年 9 月至 2021 年 6 月开展省属文化、旅游、勘察设计行业国有企事业单位软件正版化工作，将 40 家企事业单位纳入范围。12 月，举办培训班，解析国家政策，明确工作任务，提出工作要求。

（二）采取的工作措施

（1）持续开展督查和考核，完善长效机制。自 2015 年省政府办公厅出台《海南省政府机关使用正版软件工作考核实施细则》以来，按照《细则》对全省政府机关开展督查和考核，有效巩固了政府机关软件正版化成果，防止盗版现象反弹。2018 年，厅际联席会议组织全省政府机关软件正版化工作督查 317 家次，检查计算机 2 000 台次；完成对 89 家省直机关和 19 个市县的软件正版化工作考核，检查计算机 2 245 台次；检查验收开展软件正版化的企业 10 余家次。除督查和考核外，通过加强业务培训和软件资产台账管理，实现软件正版化长效管理。全年组织举办正版化工作培训班 3 次，培训 300 多人次。同时，各市县、各单位根据人员调整和计算机软硬件变化情况，及时完善软件资产台账，做到实时更新。

（2）加强正版配置，规范预装管理。2018 年，省版权局组织完成市县政府机关办公软件采购工作，由省财政出资 180 万元，为全省 27 个市县（区）政府机关和参公事业单位提供金山办公软件场地授权，彻底解决市县政府机关办公软件问题。此外，组织实施《海南省政府机关办公软件采购管理规定》《海南省政府机关计算机硬件采购管理规定》，督促各级政府机关严格落实“新购计算机须预装正版操作系统软件”规定，推动各市县、各单位就新购办公计算机是否预装正版操作系统、采购单价是否超标等内容向版权部门备案。

（3）坚持问题导向，抓好落实整改。针对 2017 年部际联席会议对海南省政府机关和国有企业使用正版软件工作督查中发现的问题以及省里对有关行业企业软件正版化工作验收情况，省版权局发出近 20 份整改通知，督促省交通厅等 4 家省直机关和海南华盈投资控股有限公司等 8 家企业限期完成问题整改。同时，就部分省直机关和市县单位授权底数不清、手续不全的问题，省版权局、省工业和信息化厅研究解决办法，由各级版权部门根据各单位软件申请文件和该单位电脑数量和已有软件情况，进行核实配发，并复函确认配发数量作为凭证。

二、严厉打击侵权盗版行为

（一）开展“剑网 2018”专项行动

2018 年 7 月 20 日，省版权局、通信管理局、公安厅、网信办召开工作会议，启动海南省打击网络侵权盗版“剑网 2018”专项行动。7 月 26 日，海南省在《海南日报》、南海网等海南省主要媒体发布专项行动消息，公布侵权盗版举报电话，鼓励权利人以及社会各界积极提供案件线索。8 月 22 日，海南省下发《关于开展打击网络侵权盗版“剑网 2018”专项行动自查自纠的通知》（琼权函［2018］13 号），要求省内主要互联网企业做好网络侵权盗版自查自纠工作。组织查处依美艾尔交友网（域名：http://www.ymeae.com）涉嫌侵权案件，下达责令改正通知书，责令改正通过信息网络擅自向公众提供他人作品、表演、录音录像制品的行为。

（二）开展出版物市场清理整顿

按照文化部、国家新闻出版署和全国“扫黄打非”办公室的部署，加强复制印刷、新闻出版、歌舞娱乐、互联网等市场的监管力度，开展各类专项整治行动，对全省出版物市场进行明察暗访，进一步规范了市场经营秩序。组织开展“秋风 2018”专项行动，共出动检查人员 7 163 人次，收缴非法出版物 56 834 本（张），检查书店、音像店、报刊亭（社）、印刷复制企业、文具店、流动摊贩、网站媒体等各类出版物单位 13 424 家次，取缔店档摊点 165 个（家），未发现非法网络报刊及非法网站。组织开展印刷复制发行暨内部资料性出版物专项督查，于全国“两会”、“博鳌亚洲论坛 2018 年年会”、“国庆节”等重要时段，组成督查组对海口、三亚等市县进行印刷监管随机集中督查，实现对重点市县全覆盖，随机抽查 147 家印刷企业，对万乘印务有限公司等 21 家违规企业给予行政处罚。组织网上书店清理整治，共查出非法经营书店 25 家，已发现违规信息 3 条。

（三）开展侵权盗版及非法出版物集中销毁活动

9 月 26 日，海南省“扫黄打非”领导小组办公室在省图书馆广场前举行 2018 年海南省侵权盗版及非法出版物集中销毁活动，此次活动共销毁侵权盗版及非法出版物 27 万多件。

三、大力开展版权保护知识宣传

按照国家版权局和海南省知识产权联席会议的通知要求，组织开展形式多样的首届海南省知识产权宣传月版权宣传活动。参加在海口市京华城举行的宣传月启动仪式，现场发放《著作权法》知识小册子近百份，接受群众咨询答问近 70 人次。组织参加知识产权联合执法活动，对海口市内部分大型超市图书、音像制品专柜进行执法检查。连续一个月通过有线电视开机广告和网站弹窗投放著作权公益广告，提升公众著作权保护意识。组织省市两级文化市场行政执法人员和歌舞娱乐场所从业人员，旁听省高级人民法院公开审理 76 件涉卡拉 OK 营业厅著作权纠纷系列案，有助于执法人员对著作权案件处罚尺度和适用法律的把握和理解，对从业人员起到较好的教育作用。各市县版权行政管理部门通过展板、海报、条幅、宣传栏、小册子、绿书签等形式，开展版权法律法规宣传、案例分析、举行版权现场执法、版权作品展示等丰富多彩的版权宣传活动，取得显著成效。

四、积极做好版权社会服务工作

2018 年，海南省共登记各类作品 169 件，审核备案涉外图书版权贸易合同168个，引进图书版权122种、输出图书版权3种。

（王金根）

重庆市

2018年，重庆市版权局深入学习贯彻习近平总书记关于知识产权保护的系列重要决策和指示，奋力、扎实、创新地开展了一些工作，取得了一定成效。市版权局版权处连续4年荣获国家版权局表彰的打击侵权盗版案件有功集体，汤裕洁获国务院部际联席会议表彰的“国家知识产权战略实施先进个人”称号。国务院督查组对重庆市47个市级政府机关软件正版化单位开展为期2周全覆盖检查中，总体情况良好，操作系统软件和办公软件的正版率居全国前列。

一、版权工作提升政治站位

在版权工作各个方面全面履行意识形态责任制，牢牢掌握意识形态工作领导权，出台《重庆市版权局作品登记审核通则》，从总则、审核要素、审核制度、审核原则、审核标准、审核程序、附则等7个方面对作品登记审核工作进行细化，撰写综合调研报告上报国家版权局和市委宣传部理论处。

二、软件正版化直击问题关键

2017年以来，原重庆市文化委主任办公会在4次主任办公会上专题研究软件正版化工作，以上率下，身体力行。

落实专项工作经费。于2017年11月—2018年10月，开展了市、区（县）两级机关、企业的一轮检查（含60个市级机关、3个区县的全覆盖检查及10个区县的抽查）和二轮复查，现场累计检查计算机24 000台次，重点督查各单位软件正版化第一责任人落实情况、长效机制建设情况、相关材料报送情况和软件安装使用情况。通过重庆市正版软件资产管理及日常监督平台向各级机关发送整改信息5 000余条，累计完成28万余字的点对点督查通报，以查督改、以查督建的工作机制运行良好。

全面落实《关于进一步加强计算机软硬件采购源头管理的通知》（渝版权〔2017〕19号），从经费、采购、资产、安全等各环节加强源头管理，在全市各级各部门强调落实严格遵循价格标准、合理制定采购计划、定期公布正版软件各项技术服务要求和供应商目录、加强资产管理、使用兼容性较好和自主可控的国产软件、提高业务系统对国产软件的兼容性等关键环节，推动重庆市软件正版化整体工作水平再上新台阶。

用好重庆市正版软件资产管理及日常监管系统，全年录入计算机信息14万余台，通过平台发送工作通知、督查通报、整改信息近万条。建立QQ工作群，强化软件正版化工作交流，指导各级各部门、企事业单位对本单位计算机、商业软件、OEM软件、免费软件等基础数据的录入，加强动态监管和日常维护，提升全市软件正版化工作数据的精准性，提高重庆市软件正版化工作信息化水平。

大力推动国产软件试点成效初显。重庆市加大督查力度、国产软件应用推广、正版软件资产管理平台等“三合一”联动工作机制；在智博会倡导组成“国产操作系统和办公软件联合参展团”，中国工程院院士倪光南亲临会场指导，评价此次尝试“对于其他地方也是很好的引导，提供了可资借鉴的样板”；创新产品、服务、价格跟踪央采平台等“三个跟踪”机制，推动国产操作系统进入政府采购协议供货平台等系列举措。《中国新闻出版广电报》3次专门报道。

三、版权公共服务注重提质增效

全年作品登记86 337件，同比增长14.2%。据抽样统计，已登记作品中有近一半是版权交易后或具有版权交易目的而申请确权的，交易成果金额约3.4亿元，通过作品登记解决版权纠纷14起，为权利人挽回经济损失850余万元。

与猪八戒网共同推进“酷版权开放平台”项目，引入可信时间戳、电子签章、智能识别等技术，实现“数字证书＋纸质证书”双证发放模式，重点解决因传统纸质作品登记导致的登记效率不高、确权维权烦琐、传播交易不畅等问题，实现对数字作品的全方位综合版权服务，2018年累计发放双证9 366件。

在全市区县试点建设版权登记工作站，引导各区县结合本地具体情况和发展特色，重点围绕具有市场前景、产业价值、文旅融合等紧密度高的版权资源和创作者，自愿向市版权局申报建设工作站，目前，渝中区依托“U创空间”等平台载体已验收授牌。

四、版权“走出去”，坚持开放引领

联合市商务委先后组织70余家文创企业参加东京动漫展、伦敦书展、法兰克福书展、科隆游戏展、美国E3游戏展、博洛尼亚国际童书展等展会。引进版权作品1 500余项，输出版权作品300余项，建成两江新区中日创意产业园，举办中韩（重庆）版权洽谈会。中英合作出版中国海外文物丛书，渝版

幼儿图书远销欧洲市场，重庆出版集团向越南输出图书版权 80 多项。

五、版权新兴领域探索协同战略

正视新问题、思考新办法，在重点企业中探索创新维权新模式，形成《规范网络版权秩序　促进媒体融合发展》综合报告。与重庆日报报业集团一道认真贯彻落实中央关于传统媒体和新兴媒体融合发展战略，并在“新闻生产及运营监管”平台的 6 大业务子系统中专设“版权保护”板块，自 2016 年 10 月运营以来，累计确权 350 余万条原创新闻作品（其中图片 160 余万张），确认网络侵权转载行为 13.16 万次，取证 8.46 万次，约谈 17 家涉嫌侵权单位，与百度签订 400 万元版权应用合同，与 10 余家报业单位商谈版权合作，多次受到中宣部、国家版权局领导肯定。

为中国（重庆）“长江杯”国际工业设计大奖赛，“重庆市网络剧、微电影等原创网络视听节目阶梯评比活动”，“逐梦他乡重庆人”摄影大展，第三届世界最美童画国际巡展暨“一带一路”城市小代表互访系列活动等重大活动开辟版权服务绿色通道，为 400 余件视频作品、800 余件摄影作品、557 件美术作品提供现场版权服务。

拓展版权服务范围，组织专家为 30 余家动漫企业开展版权创作、应用、保护和管理专题讲座；指导重庆演艺集团艺术营销、法务审计及五个下属部门防范版权法律风险；为全市服装行业、建筑勘察设计行业、非遗传承人及行业强化版权保护意识，提升创新能力和品牌价值进行专题培训或辅导。

六、版权社会共治，着眼长远发展

2018 年“4·26”宣传周活动期间，中外人士驻足观看；猪八戒网“酷版权开放平台”上线启动，并现场展示了创客设计开发的版画、背包、手机壳、伞具、丝巾、书签等琳琅满目的版权衍生品；渝中区版权登记工作站暨“U 创空间”版权产业成果展分会场特色鲜明，反响良好。据统计，重庆卫视、人民网、凤凰网、华龙网等网媒，日、晚、晨、商报等纸媒原创报道宣传周活动共 23 次。

举办版权作品登记、执法监管、软件正版化培训 16 期，参训单位覆盖各区县文化委、文化系统直属企事业单位、行业重点企业、版权中介机构、各区县党政群团机关 600 余家，累计参训人员 1 300 余人次，邀请两江知识产权法庭、市公安局打假总队、国产操作系统和办公软件企业、知名摄影家等各方力量设置精品课程 8 门，在全市社会各方面各领域全面普及版权意识和版权知识，版权工作的覆盖面不断扩大。

市检察院、市文化委签署保护版权协作机制。标志着在市文化委与市工商局、市公安局相继签署战略合作协议的基础上，涵盖行政、公安、检察、法院，集监管、执法、公诉、裁判等各项职能为一体的“重庆版权保护工作体系”日臻完善。

协同地方法院开展版权案件公开庭审进园区、进企业、进社区活动，敲响企业和个人版权保护警钟。

（张　锐）

四　川　省

2018 年，四川省版权局紧紧围绕版权创造、运用、保护、管理和服务，全面实施版权战略，强化宣传教育培训，深入推进作品登记制度改革，依法开展版权执法监管，持续推进软件正版化工作，大力推动版权社会服务体系建设，有效促进版权产业发展，取得了一定的成效。

一、版权宣传培训工作

按照国家版权局宣传工作要求，转发国家版权局办公厅《关于做好 2018 年全国知识产权宣传周版权宣传活动的通知》（国版发［2018］4 号），对全省宣传活动进行全面部署，开展知识产权宣传周版权宣传系列活动，主要包括：一是召集成都、自贡等 8 市版权局及示范园区、单位等 40 余人，以“保护创作、推进运用，促进作品成果转换”为主题，就版权社会服务工作座谈，把版权工作与促进产业发展相结合、把版权与促进服务体系建设相结合、把版权与促进服务体系相结合。二是联合相关部门，举行 2018 年四川省知识产权保护新闻发布会，发布《2017 年四川省知识产权保护现状》（白皮书）、《2017 年四川省知识产权保护典型案例》、《2017 年度四川省打击侵权盗版典型案例》。三是积极组织参与省知识产权领导小组组织的系列宣传活动，参加在北京召开的“2018 中国网络版权保护大会”，举办以“倡导创新文化　版权保驾护航”为主题的版权宣传周活动启动仪式。指导省版权协会与四川广播电视台旅游生活频率，在《970 说法》广播节目中开展版权以案说法宣传活动。四是组织开展版权行政执法及“剑网 2018”工作专项培训，全省 21 个市（州）的版权局分管领导、执法支队负责人、执法骨干共 100 余人，开展全省“剑网 2018”网络执法培训，邀请国家版权局版权司执法处、省网信办、省公安厅网安总队、省通信管理局网管处等单位领导和专家现场授课，讲授网络侵权盗版案件查办技巧，分享典型案例，指导开展跨部门联合执法方式方法，培训收到了良好的效果。

二、版权执法监管工作

在国家版权局2017年度查处侵权盗版案件有功集体和个人评选中，四川省相关单位获得12项集体、个人奖励，奖励经费达20万元。四川省版权局深入开展“剑网2018”专项行动，组织执法人员向国家版权局移交四川省7项案件线索，对1件投诉案件进行查处，特别是对涉嫌侵权的相关网站逐一远程勘验，确保证据完整；协调省通信管理局对涉嫌侵权网站备案信息进行核查；联系国家工信部、国家企业信用信息公示系统等监管平台，核验涉嫌侵权网站经营主体、所在地址、负责人信息，按照属地管理原则将案件移送所在地版权行政执法部门查处。重点跟踪巡查四川少年儿童出版社畅销的儿童读物《米小圈》在网上遭遇侵权盗版的情况，主动联系陕西省版权局配合，使四川少年儿童出版社获得侵权赔偿25万元，维护了版权所有者的合法权益。加强跨地区协作，协助青海省版权局，对藏文图书《普贤上师言教》进行版权鉴定，组织清理网上盗版图书，净化网络环境。

三、软件正版化工作

为贯彻落实国家推进使用正版软件工作部际联席会议年度工作部署，做好迎接国家全覆盖督查，制定《2018年四川省正版化工作计划》，印发《关于开展软件正版化工作自查的通知》，组织开展省级部门和市州正版化工作培训，开展软件正版化自查工作。9月下旬，组织4个联合督查组，对16个省级单位软件正版化工作进行抽查。针对国家督查组对四川省的全覆盖督查反馈意见，按照省委常委、省委宣传部部长甘霖，省政府副省长杨兴平做出的重要批示，要求省级有关部门（单位）务必站在国家信息安全的高度，重视软件正版化工作，存在问题要限时整改到位的要求，集中组织开展问题整改“回头看”，各受检单位对存在的问题及时纠正，强化责任落实，充实调整领导机构、建立健全工作制度，及时开展自查整改，完善承诺书，规范制定台账档案，巩固四川省软件正版化工作成果。

四、版权社会服务工作

为进一步做大四川版权，印发《关于进一步加强和改进作品登记工作促进成果转化的意见》，推动作品登记，促进成果转化，不断完善全省作品版权登记服务体系，全省21个市（州）、183个县（市）区全部建立了版权登记服务工作机构，健全专兼职作品登记工作队伍，设立作品登记专项工作经费。成都市在22个县（市）区全部设立56个版权工作站，自贡、攀枝花、泸州、德阳、绵阳、乐山、眉山等地相继在版权示范园区（基地）与版权示范单位设立作品版权登记工作站。同时，指导省版权事务中心在新华文轩、四川画报社设立省版权工作站。截至11月底，全省作品登记总量17万件（2017年同期129 126件，同比增长31.75%），推动版权作品成果转化取得新的进展，据不完全统计，截至12月底，全省版权交易金额达1亿元。其中，成都蓝顶艺术中心、画家村原创作品版权交易达3 000万元，成都盒中闪电、泼克文化传媒动漫卡通版权交易达1 000万元，自贡海天文化彩灯作品版权交易达1 000万元，凉山文化广播影视传媒集团与第三方签署投资《彝海结盟》合作协议金额达1 000万元。依托全省版权综合服务平台，实现了作品资源共享和优秀版权资源聚合，推动作品后续版权孵化运营交易，初步打通作品创作和成果转化通道。组织开展出版单位版权贸易工作，2018年四川省开展版权贸易工作1 036项（引进图书774项、输出图书254项、引进游戏8项），贸易总量突破1 000项大关，对开展版权贸易输出成绩突出的出版单位给予100万元补助。完成省版权协会换届并召开全体会员大会，推举产生新一届理事会及工作机构，进一步完善版权社会服务体系。

（李晓曦）

贵 州 省

2018年，贵州省版权局工作重点是提升版权服务水平和加强版权行政执法，持续巩固政府机关软件正版化工作成果。各项工作完成情况良好。

一、适应创新发展要求，提升版权社会服务水平

近年来，贵州省版权登记数量猛增，作品载体从传统纸质到数字化等呈多样化发展，作品形式也发生了巨大变化，现有版权登记工作机制已经远远不能适应与版权相关联的产业发展的需要。贵州省版权局与贵州广电传媒集团共同组建贵州省版权登记中心，8月30日，贵州省版权登记平台上线，实行“网上提交、线上审核”，极大地便捷了作品登记申请渠道。同时，登记平台建立了版权登记数字化体系，推出基于区块链技术的版权数字存证平台，固定了专门的登记机构，增加了专职平台工作人员。这些措施，极大地提高了贵州省作品登记数字化、信息化水平。2018 年，贵州省作品登记数量大幅上升，达到 1 200 余件。

二、重视版权执法，抓好案件查办，开展了系列专项行动

把“剑网 2018”专项行动作为版权行政执法工作的重要内容，高度重视专项行动的开展，省版权局联合省通信管理局、省公安厅、省互联网信息办公室四部门制定下发了《贵州省关于开展打击网络侵权盗版“剑网 2018”专项行动的通知》（黔新广发［2018］3 号），对全省专项行动工作进行了部署，明确了工作目标、重点任务、主要措施、职责分工和工作要求，为加强专项行动的组织领导，贵州省版权、网信、通信管理和公安等四部门成立省打击网络侵权盗版“剑网 2018”专项行动领导小组，领导小组办公室设在省版权局，统一部署和协调工作任务。四部门建立了联动机制，分别明确了机构和人员负责“剑网行动”工作的开展，协调解决专项行动中可能出现的重大问题。同时，各地成立了相应的专项行动领导小组，协调指导本地区工作的开展。版权局与其他三部门工作联系紧密，沟通渠道顺畅，能在最短的时间内处理专项行动中的情况。

虽然贵州省不是网络侵权案件高发的地区，但是打击网络侵权工作丝毫不能放松。根据贵州省实际情况，省版权局把强化版权保护宣传作为“剑网”专项行动工作重点，充分发挥舆论引导和监督作用。行动启动时，贵州省人民政府网站登载了《贵州省启动打击网络侵权盗版“剑网 2018”专项行动》信息，版权局网站也及时登载了“剑网”专项行动相关信息，营造了良好的舆论氛围。省内各级版权、网信、通信管理、公安部门充分发挥各自专业优势，坚持日常检查和重点检查相结合，积极开展网络侵权重点领域网上巡查。省版权局利用贵州省 CCDI“版权云”监测功能等新技术手段，对在贵州省注册备案的新闻网站、视听网站、出版网站、微博、微信等媒介进行了监管和巡查。省版权局还公布了网络侵权盗版举报投诉电话，对举报或转办案源，都进行了认真查实查办。

贵州省版权局深入贯彻执行《著作权法》及相关法律法规，重点抓好版权行政执法，于 2018 年 8 月 30 日在贵阳市组织了全省 9 个市、州和 5 个直管县版权局分管副局长、新闻出版版权科科长和执法支队负责人共 50 人参加版权行政执法培训，由国家版权局派员讲课。贵州省地处经济文化较落后的西部地区，版权案件数量较少，全年著作权行政处罚案件仅 4 件，和 2017 年零案件相比有所增长。

三、巩固政府机关软件正版化工作成果，推进企业软件正版化工作

有计划、有步骤地推进软件正版化工作。2018 年初，省政府调整了省推进使用正版软件工作领导小组组长，由副省长王世杰担任领导小组组长。省版权局制定了《贵州省 2018 年推进使用正版软件工作计划》，经省政府同意上报推进使用正版软件工作部际联席会议。《计划》对全省政府和企业软件正版化工作进行了安排和部署，要求全省各级政府和省直部门制定本级政府、部门软件正版化工作计划。根据工作计划的安排，3 月 29 日，省领导小组办公室组织召开了领导小组会议，部署全省全年软件正版化工作；严格正版化日常工作程序，落实正版化工作年度报告制度；按照工作计划和要求，指导、督促市（州）、县（区）政府机关对软件正版化工作进行常态化管理；健全软件正版化责任人数据库，及时更新和补充省、市（州）各级政府机关软件正版化责任部门及负责人的相关信息；进一步明确市（州）、县（区）各级政府机关软件正版化工作责任部门和责任人，确保推进工作落到实处。

国务院软件正版化部际联席会议督查组于 9 月 17—21 日对贵州省推进使用软件正版化工作进行了督查。督查组抽查了省政府办公厅等 6 家省级政府机关和盘江集团等 4 家省国资委监管企业总部共计 614 台计算机。省推进使用正版化领导小组办公室以督促检查为契机，要求省直机关各单位对本部门软件正版化工作进行一次全面自查，同时抓好受检单位整改工作的落实。此次督查，对推进各级政府机关和省属国有企业加强制度建设，建立长效机制，进一步落实软件正版化政策措施，健全督查考核和责任追究制度，层层落实责任起到积极作用。

继续有序推进企业软件正版化。省版权局联合省国资委发出了《关于推进使用正版软件工作的通知》（黔国资通办［2018］197 号），部署推进企业软件正版化工作。要求各单位做好整体规划，明确目标；组织开展企业软件正版化工作宣传培训和建立软件资产管理普及工作，建立健全使用正版软件工作长效机制。目前省属国有企业在已基本实现软件正版化的基础上巩固成果，建立了使用正版软件工作长效机制，开展使用正版软件工作体系建设和软件资产管理等相关工作，通过软件正版化工作提高了企业的信息化管理水平。

（徐　梅）

云　南　省

2018年，云南省版权工作深入贯彻落实党的十九大精神，以习近平新时代中国特色社会主义思想为指导，坚持依法行政、打建结合、统筹协作、社会共治，结合云南实际落实国家创新驱动发展战略，服务全省经济社会发展。在版权创作、运用、保护、管理和服务等方面积极作为，全面完成年度各项工作任务，在主要领域取得新突破、新进展。

一、版权宣传培训工作不断加强

一是整合网络资源，依托云南天之悦文化传播有限公司推出“云南版权”微信公众号，持续开展版权法规、知识线上宣传，全年共计发布宣传推文57期124篇。二是突出“保护创作，推进运用”年度主题开展宣传。4月20—26日，知识产权日版权宣传周活动期间，全省各地组织了形式多样、丰富多彩的主题宣传活动，共向公众发放各类版权宣传品10万多份，现场参与群众近8万人；昆明主会场由省版权局在云南财经大学组织开展版权宣传进校园系列活动，举办在昆高校学生作品创作征集比赛和主题文艺演出等系列活动。全年国家版权局网站刊载云南版权工作信息8篇。

培训工作突出针对性、实用性和可操作性，相继举办全省省级党政机关、全省边境州（市）县（区）两级政府机关、省属国有企业、省属教育系统事业单位软件正版化工作培训班，突出政策辅导及《正版软件工作管理指南》应用，全年共培训500多人。此外，为有效提高基层人员的业务能力，举办全省版权行政执法骨干工作培训班，州（市）县（区）两级版权行政执法人员70余人参加。

二、版权执法监管力度不断加大

发挥版权侵权查处机制，强化事中事后监管，落实行政执法与刑事司法衔接制度，重点突出大案要案查处和重点行业专项治理，加大侵权行为惩治力度，营造和维护了合法有序的版权环境。组织协调全省版权行政执法队伍查办版权案件，全年共检查经营单位4.24万家次，立案调查238件，办结196件，警告410家，吊销许可证3家，罚款100.36万元，没收违法所得1.01万元、音像制品5.97万张（盘）、非法书刊3.33万册，是近几年来查办版权案件最多的一年。坚持日常监管与专项行动相结合，2018年下半年，重点开展网络版权执法工作。省版权局联合省网信办、通信管理局、公安厅、文化和旅游厅等部门在全省范围内开展第十四次打击网络侵权盗版专项治理“剑网2018”专项行动，将网络作为履行版权监管职责重要阵地，不断净化网络版权环境。通过强化分类管理，加强重点领域监测监管，及时发现和查处侵权盗版行为，共查办重点版权案件19件，结案18件，做出行政处罚16件，其中网络案件14件，移送司法机关1件，有效打击和震慑了网络侵权盗版行为，相关工作成果得到国家督查组肯定。

此外，全年完成音像制品版权鉴定57份。11月，原省新闻出版广电局版权管理处、原昭通市新闻出版广电局荣获国家版权局2017年度查处侵权盗版案件有功单位三等奖，永善县文化市场综合执法大队张信荣获2017年度查处侵权盗版案件有功个人三等奖。

三、使用正版软件工作不断推进

认真落实国家推进使用正版软件工作部际联席会议、国家版权局和省政府部署要求，推进云南省政府机关、省属国有企业、省事业单位软件正版化工作。一是履行省推进使用正版软件工作联席会议办公室职责，召开两次联络员会议，制定全年工作计划，明确年度重点任务和职责分工，研究部署阶段性重点任务。二是云南省连续6年以全省场地授权方式集中采购国产办公软件的做法，得到国家部际联席会议办公室充分肯定并推为全国典型。三是持续推进政府机关、企事业单位软件正版化工作制度化、规范化、常态化和信息化，建立完善长效机制。巩固各级党政机关软件正版化工作成果，按计划推进19家省属国有企业集团公司及所属二、三级企业实现软件正版化，启动省属教育系统事业单位软件正版化工作。四是接受国家版权局“全覆盖”检查。10月8—17日，国家部际联席会议办公室软件正版化工作督查组对云南省41家省级政府机关软件正版化工作进行全覆盖检查。在国家督查组到来前，组织4个小组对被检单位进行为期两周的督导检查，共检查计算机10 000多台，查看台账资料1 000多份。国家督查结束后，根据省政府阮成发省长批示和李玛琳副省长指示，针对存在的5个方面问题认真督导各单位进行整改，已于年底前基本整改到位，结果上报国家版权局。

四、版权社会服务水平不断提高

以作品自愿登记和涉外著作权合同登记为重点的著作权登记工作逐步规范化、标准化，全年共办理作品登记322件、涉外著作权合同登记245件，受理作品登记咨询2 600多人次。工作中坚持服务宗旨，使用本处行政包干经费为全省权利人免费邮寄作品登记证书，全年共计支出 2 890 元。

五、版权工作调研能力不断提升

按照“大调研”部署积极开展版权工作调研。围绕持续推进全省软件正版化工作这一重点任务，聚焦建立完善全省软件正版化工作长效机制这一关键开展调研并形成调研报告；针对云南省版权行政执法工作现状，就进一步理顺全省版权执法体制机制、提高版权执法效能开展调研并形成书面报告上报省政府。

（王　成）

西藏自治区

2018 年，西藏自治区版权局紧紧围绕自治区党委、政府中心工作，认真贯彻落实国家版权局的总体安排部署和局党组布置的各项工作任务，以《自治区版权局 2018 年工作要点》《2018 年度全区推进软件正版化工作计划》为抓手，积极有序推进各项工作。

一、2018 年主要工作

（一）积极开展“双打”工作

（1）制定工作计划。根据《2018 年度全国打击侵犯知识产权和制售假冒伪劣商品工作要点的通知（征求意见稿）》等文件精神，结合西藏自治区新闻出版广电工作实际，安排部署全区新闻出版广电系统“双打”行动工作，并研究制定了工作计划，明确了全区新闻出版广电系统“双打”行动的工作目标和任务。

（2）大力开展专项行动。一是认真贯彻落实 2018 年全区“扫黄打非”工作部署会精神，特别是区党委常委、宣传部部长、区“扫黄打非”工作领导小组组长边巴扎西重要讲话精神，进一步加强西藏自治区 3 月敏感期“扫黄打非”工作和新闻出版广播影视领域的“双打”工作。积极组织自治区“扫黄打非”领导小组成员单位，于 2018 年 3 月 5 日起在全区范围内开展了第一阶段“扫黄打非”净化专项行动及净化专项行动督导检查工作。此次净化专项行动督导检查，由各成员单位厅级领导带队组成 7 个督查组，分别深入全区 7 个地市，覆盖 65 个县、61 个乡镇，检查 94 家歌舞娱乐场所、90 多家互联网服务场所、62 家出版经营场所、113 家印刷企业、30 多个县级新华书店，共收缴违禁出版物 53 件、侵权盗版出版物 5 件，删除侵权盗版歌曲 22 首，现场整改 221 家，限期整改 30 家，停业整顿 6 家。通过督导检查，确保了全区文化市场、网络空间、新闻出版广播影视领域、娱乐场所、舆论环境规范有序、更加清朗，净化专项行动督查成效明显，为全国“两会”的顺利召开创造了良好的舆论氛围，确保了西藏自治区 3 月敏感期意识形态安全。二是积极开展“扫黄打非·秋风 2018”专项行动，根据全国“扫黄打非”工作领导小组办公室《关于开展“扫黄打非·秋风 2018”专项行动的通知》要求，结合西藏自治区实际制定下发《西藏自治区“秋风 2018”专项行动工作方案》，全面启动以打击非法报刊、假媒体、假记者站、假记者和侵权盗版行为为重点工作内容的“秋风 2018”专项行动，坚决封堵反动出版物入藏关口，强化出版物市场监管，清查网络有害信息，组织开展了年度侵权盗版及非法出版物集中销毁活动。三是主动做好“剑网 2018”专项行动。根据国家版权局、国家互联网信息办公室、工业和信息化部、公安部《关于开展打击网络侵权盗版“剑网 2018”专项行动的通知》精神，西藏自治区结合工作实际，紧紧围绕专项行动重点任务，坚决打击网络侵权盗版，依法治理网络空间，净化网络版权环境，优化网络版权生态，积极有效地组织开展了“剑网 2018”专项行动，营造良好网络环境。截至 2018 年 11 月，全区共关闭网站 21 家，删除侵权盗版链接 31 条，收缴侵权盗版制品 1 111 件，受理处置网民举报信息 2 万余条。

（3）积极协助开展“双打”督查。根据自治区“双打”办《西藏自治区打击侵权盗版和制售假冒伪劣商品重点工作督导检查工作方案》的通知要求，结合版权的工作实际，深入林芝、昌都两个市的 11 个县区直部门进行了专项督导检查，并形成专项报告报自治区“双打”办公室。

（4）做好其他工作。多次参加侵犯知识产权和制售假冒伪劣商品工作领导小组工作会议，积极汇报“双打”各项工作开展情况，协助自治区“双打”办公室推进新闻出版广电系统“双打”各项工作，完成 2018 年工作总结。

（二）推进版权公共服务

（1）安排部署 2018 年版权工作。根据 2018 年全区宣传部长会议精神和新闻出版广播影视电视电话会议精神，版权管理处结合版权工作实际，制定了《自治区版权局 2018 年工作要点》，并下发至各地（市）版权局，要求做好贯彻落实。

（2）推动版权示范城市建设。根据《自治区版权局 2018 年工作要点》要求，推进西藏自治区版权示范单位建设，贯彻落实国家版权局《全国版权示范城市、示范单位和示范园区（基地）管理办法》

精神，结合西藏自治区实际，制定《西藏自治区版权示范单位管理暂行办法》，在版权工作相对集中的部门征求意见和建议。

(3) 推进著作权作品自愿登记工作。按照自治区版权局领导的批示要求，进一步完善细化《关于尽快开展著作权作品自愿登记工作的方案》，印制了《作品自愿登记证书》和《著作权作品自愿登记宣传手册》，刻制了西藏自治区版权局作品自愿登记专用章。于2018年7月25日下午，召集局系统内著作权工作相对集中的6个单位，就作品自愿登记工作进行了安排部署。一是召开动员会议。按照自治区版权局《著作权作品登记工作方案》的相关要求，于7月25日下午召开了以局系统内作品相对集中的著作权单位为主的原西藏人民广播电台、原西藏电视台、西藏人民出版社、西藏音像出版社、西藏自治区报刊出版中心以及西藏自治区文联相关部门负责人动员会，安排部署试点启动西藏自治区的著作权作品自愿登记工作，并要求各相关单位于8月25日前上报需要登记的作品。二是开展岗前培训。动员会上，结合工作实际，就著作权作品自愿登记工作的申报流程提交相关材料、作品申请表、作品说明书、权利保证书等的填写进行了解读培训，为下一步开展工作打下了坚实的基础。三是制定发证方案。根据自治区版权局主要领导的要求，制定了《著作权作品自愿登记证书发放仪式方案》。四是多次沟通催促。在协调沟通中，版权管理处多次询问相关单位，解释有关要求之后，于8月30日下午、9月4日上午分别向各参会相关单位要求提交需要登记的作品。西藏人民出版社明确答复出版单位不涉及此项工作；原西藏人民广播电台、原西藏电视台、西藏自治区报刊出版中心回复在推进，但是尚未申报；西藏自治区文联明确答复相关协会著作权人不准备申报；西藏音像出版社已经按要求在开展申报工作，并提交了申报材料。五是及时进行汇报。根据工作进展情况，形成了《关于发放首批作品登记证书的情况汇报》，上报局主要领导。

(4) 做好“中国版权金奖”推荐工作。按照国家版权局的文件要求，认真组织开展“中国版权金奖”推荐工作。经过筛选评估和局领导同意，向国家版权局推荐了四部作品参加“中国版权金奖”评选，为下一步参加第七届中国国际版权博览会打下了坚实的基础。

(5) 推进版权执法。根据青海省版权局提供的案件线索，积极协助青海省版权局开展对西藏人民出版社出版的《蓝琉璃》藏文图书的版权盗版案件查办工作。

(6) 落实平台建设。落实国家版权局监管平台建设，实现网络监管对接，发挥版权监督平台作用，运用技术手段，对侵权盗版进行监控取证。

(三) 深化软件正版化

(1) 制定工作计划。根据国家版权局的安排部署和自治区政府领导批示要求，结合西藏的工作实际，制定了《2018年度全区推进软件正版化工作计划》《西藏自治区推进企事业单位使用正版软件工作规划（2018—2021年）的通知》，以完善长效机制、推进责任落实、严抓日常工作、加强市场监管、做好宣传培训为主基调，以从严从实为基本遵循，深入持续地推进软件正版化工作。

(2) 召开联席会议。根据自治区推进使用正版软件工作厅际联席会议制度要求，于4月13日召开了自治区推进使用正版软件工作厅际联席会议，自治区版权局党组成员、副局长刘俐参加会议并做安排。会议传达学习了国家推进使用正版软件工作部际联席会议第六次全体会议的精神，总结了西藏自治区2017年软件正版化的工作情况，通报了2017年软件正版化工作督查情况，讨论通过了2018年软件正版化工作计划。

(3) 完善软件正版化数据库。以充实和健全西藏自治区政府机关软件正版化数据库建设为抓手，完善职责分工，进一步建立和完善了西藏自治区各地（市）级软件正版化责任人数据库，积极督促和指导县级建立和完善软件正版化责任人数据库。在反复核对无误的基础上，及时在版权监管平台上上报西藏自治区软件正版化工作计划、责任人数据等信息材料。

(4) 安排部署软件正版化工作。根据联席会议精神，按照《自治区版权局2018年工作要点》要求，在报请自治区人民政府同意后，下发了《2018年度全区推进使用正版软件工作计划》，安排部署2018年软件正版化工作，内容涉及：以健全长效机制为抓手，规范软件使用管理；以强化源头监管为抓手，规范计算机软硬件采购；以创新手段为抓手，巩固扩大企业软件正版化成果；以强化督促检查为抓手，推进落实主体责任；以软件正版化与信息化同步推进为抓手，保障信息安全；以做好软件采购指导服务为抓手，做好信息报送工作等。2018年，全区累计检查机关103个，其中，自治区级机关3个，3个地（市）县级机关100个；检查计算机603台；累计投入资金200.62万元，新更换非许可软件1 502套，其中，WPS办公软件734套，Windows

操作系统 768 套。

（5）推进企业软件正版化工作。按照国家部际联席会要求，结合西藏的实际，持续深入地开展西藏自治区的企事业单位软件正版化工作，制定下发《西藏自治区推进企事业单位使用正版软件工作规划（2018—2021 年）》，指导开展西藏自治区的企事业软件正版化工作，内容主要涉及：建立工作体系，落实工作责任；加强经费保障，做好采购指导；规范资产管理，建立长效机制；开展督促检查，强化工作考核；做好宣传培训，营造良好氛围等。目的在于全面推进西藏自治区各级政府、政府机关所属企事业单位软件正版化工作（政府机关所属企事业单位软件正版化工作，参照政府机关推进使用正版软件工作相关制度执行）。全区国资委监管企业，按照《关于推进自治区国有企业办公软件正版化工作的实施方案》（藏正联发〔2015〕2 号）文件精神，以“先易后难、分步推进”为原则，分阶段推进西藏自治区国有企业使用正版软件工作。自治区工商联按照《关于推进民营企业办公软件正版化实施方案》（藏联发〔2015〕70 号）文件精神，分步推进西藏自治区民营企业使用正版软件工作。

（6）推进自治区（版权）局部门软件正版化工作。结合有关工作会议精神，积极协助局办公室共同推进新闻出版广电系统开展软件正版化工作，对区新闻出版广电局机关和局系统计算机正版软件需求进行统计、招标等工作，并积极参与软件安装等各个环节，在此基础上推进软件正版化资产管理制度等长效机制建设。在原有已经采购安装正版软件的基础上，自治区版权部门于 2018 年又累计投入资金 47 万余元，采购正版 Windows 操作系统和 WPS 办公软件各 150 套，实现了版权部门正版软件全覆盖。

（7）组织开展培训工作。认真组织自治区推进使用正版软件工作厅际联席成员单位开展软件正版化工作培训，使各成员单位进一步明确职责分工，了解软件正版化工作意义，提高和掌握正版软件基本知识。一是在日喀则市开展了一期全区版权基础知识培训班（软件正版化基础知识培训班），二是协助林芝市开展了一期版权基础知识培训班，三是赴那曲地区组织参加软件正版化基础知识培训班，四是组织西藏自治区厅际联席会议部分成员单位参加国家版权局在内蒙古召开的国家部际联席会议软件正版化培训班。截至目前，西藏自治区累计投入资金 10 余万元，举办培训班 4 期，发放培训宣传资料 1 000 余份，协调专家授课 20 余节，自治区、市、区（县）三级政府机关参训人员达 500 余人。

（8）制作软件正版化宣传资料。为进一步巩固西藏自治区的软件正版化工作成果，指导和推进西藏自治区软件正版化工作，结合工作实际，收集汇总近年来下发的软件正版化相关文件制度进行汇编，制定《印制西藏自治区软件正版化工作文件选编的方案》，在此基础上经过多方请示汇报，在局主要领导同意后，投入资金 14 万余元，印发《西藏自治区软件正版化工作文件选编》12 000 册，发放给自治区、各市（地）、县各级各部门，实现了发放全覆盖。同时，西藏自治区还结合法制宣传节点，充分利用宣传优势，多措并举，推进西藏自治区版权宣传工作，通过开展日常版权宣传，提高全社会的版权保护意识。

（9）积极开展督促检查。根据国务院办公厅《2018 年全国打击侵犯知识产权和制售假冒伪劣商品工作要点的通知》精神，开展 2018 年度打击侵犯知识产权和制售假冒伪劣商品违法犯罪活动各项工作。同时，按照中共中央办公室印发的《关于统筹规划督查检查考核工作的通知》要求，积极主动协助自治区“双打”办公室和“扫黄打非”办公室，组成联合督导组，先后深入林芝、昌都、那曲的 20 余县市，行程 10 000 余公里，开展软件正版化督导检查工作。

（10）探索整体场地授权。根据自治区政府主要领导在《关于国家推进使用正版软件工作部际联席会议第五督查组对西藏自治区软件正版化工作督查情况的报告》上的批示精神，及 2018 年 4 月份召开的自治区推进使用正版软件工作厅际联席会议讨论通过的探索国产办公软件在西藏自治区新的授权方式要求，制定《西藏自治区政府机关金山办公软件整体场地授权推广实施方案》，征求了自治区政府办公厅、财政厅、市场监督管理局、经信厅、网信办等推进使用正版软件工作厅际联席会议成员单位的意见建议，并于 11 月 29 日上午召开西藏自治区推进使用正版软件工作厅际联席会议专题会议，研究讨论《西藏自治区政府机关金山办公软件整体场地授权推广实施方案》。以上工作正在有序推进。

（四）做好版权宣传工作

（1）开展世界知识产权日宣传。为迎接第 18 个“4·26”世界知识产权日，做好 2018 年全国知识产权宣传周活动，根据国家版权局的安排部署，结合西藏自治区的版权工作实际，版权管理处紧紧围绕 2018 年全国知识产权宣传周主题，安排部署宣传工作。一是除从国家版权局官方网站下载了以“保护创作，推进运用”为主题的宣传海报外，西藏自治区还自主设计了具有西藏民族特色的主题宣传海报，并以藏汉两种文字形式印刷各类宣传海报 12 000 张，分别发放给各市（地）版权主管部门和相关单位，要求配合做好相关宣传活动；二是为西藏电视台等本地区平面媒体、网络媒体等媒体资源提供宣传报道的素材，如在西藏卫视播放宣传周公益宣传短片，做到与国家版权局上下联动、形成合力，扩大版权宣传的社会影响力；三是采取丰富多彩的宣传方式，开展知识产权宣传进校园、进社区、进电影院、进书店等版权宣传活动。

（2）做好版权日常宣传。紧扣法制宣传节点，充分利用自身宣传优势，多措并举，推进西藏自治区版权宣传工作，通过开展日常版权宣传，提高全社会的版权保护意识。

（周祥祎）

陕 西 省

一、稳步推进软件正版化工作

一是制定印发了《陕西省 2018 年推进使用正版软件工作实施方案》，明确了目标任务，夯实了工作责任。二是加强日常检查，进行有效监督。积极配合国家推进使用正版软件工作部际联席会议督查组对全省软件正版化工作进行实地督查。三是加强人员培训，先后举办了省属国有企业和省级机关软件正版化工作培训班。四是充分发挥软件正版化先进典型的示范引领作用，对在 2017 年推进软件正版化工作中成绩突出的 5 家单位授予“2017 年陕西省版权示范单位”称号，并予以通报表彰。

二、有效开展版权宣传教育

一是举办了以“保护创作，推进运用”为主题的世界知识产权日系列宣传教育活动。二是组织省内各广播电视台、视听网站、电影院、互联网出版机构网站播发版权公益宣传广告。三是通过省政府新闻办“2018 年陕西省知识产权保护状况”新闻发布会，重点介绍全省版权工作的主要成绩。四是联合陕西广播电视台《陕西新闻联播》和《今日点击》两档栏目对全省版权保护情况进行了集中采访报道。五是组织侵权盗版及非法出版物集中公开销毁活动，展示全省打击侵权盗版、严格著作权保护的坚强决心。六是制作版权专题宣传片，集中展示全省版权保护、运用、管理、服务工作成效。七是组织省司法厅、省律协联合举办律师界版权保护座谈会。

三、着力推动版权产业发展

一是深入开展版权调研工作，采取调查问卷、座谈、实地调查等方式，撰写完成了《陕西省新闻作品版权保护调研报告》，同时组织编写出版了《2015 年陕西省版权产业的经济贡献》。二是有针对性辅导培育相关版权企业开展工作，取得良好成绩。10 月 19 日，在苏州国际博览中心举行的 2018 年“中国版权金奖”颁奖典礼上，西安电视剧版权交易中心有限公司荣获“中国版权金奖”管理奖，这是陕西省版权企业首次荣获该奖项。陕西人民出版社有限公司、陕西文化产业（影视）投资有限公司荣获“2018 年度中国版权最具影响力企业”，陕西广电影视文化产业发展有限公司荣获“2018 年度中国版权新锐企业”。三是组织出版单位参加第二十五届北京国际图书博览会，向国外输出图书版权达成意向 11 种、签约 15 种，同时引进海外图书版权达成意向 53 种、签约 10 种。

四、不断完善版权社会化服务管理

一是积极探索并启动“陕西省版权公共服务工作站”试点工作，先后为铜川市文广新局、西安电视剧版权交易中心、陕西动漫产业平台管理中心等三个版权公共服务工作站授牌。二是大力开展作品登记工作，累计登记作品 8 000 件，比上年增长了 62.6%。同时完成版权合同备案 241 件。三是深入开展作品登记和版权知识宣传“下基层、进校园”活动，受到广大师生的热烈欢迎，现场受理登记作品 500 余件。

五、依法组织指导版权行政执法

一是积极开展“双打”和“剑网”行动，与陕西省通信管理局、陕西省公安厅、陕西省互联网信息办公室联合印发了《陕西省打击网络侵权盗版“剑网 2018”专项行动工作方案》，进行周密的安排部署。二是严厉打击侵权盗版违法行为，指导榆林市成功办理了两起计算机软件侵权案。指导西安市查处了西安市未央区纳兰书店通过拼多多平台销售盗版图书案、马翔 08 影院网站侵犯电影著作权案、西安市碑林区花钥叔点播影咖侵犯电影著作权案等多起案件，有效净化了版权市场环境。经国家版权局评选，全省共荣获 2017 年度全国查处侵权盗版案件有功单位三等奖 3 项，有功个人三等奖 4 项，取得了较好成绩。

（王新民）

甘 肃 省

2018 年，甘肃省版权管理工作以国家版权局 2018 年重点工作部署为指导，以持续推进软件正版化工作和加强版权执法、抓好案件查办、开展系列专项活动为重点，同时做好日常行政管理并兼顾版权法律服务，以此带动全省版权行政管理工作的全面进步。

一、软件正版化工作推进

按照甘肃省软件正版化确定的“两巩固，两推进”的工作思路，省使用正版软件工作领导小组积极采取有效措施，巩固党政机关软件正版化工作成效，持续推进企事业单位软件正版化工作开展。

（一）工作成效

通过多举措推动协调，甘肃省软件正版化工作取得可喜成绩。2018 年，国家软件正版化工作督查组对甘肃省省级政府机关软件正版化工作进行了全覆盖检查，督查组检查认为，“甘肃省委、省政府高度重视软件正版化工作，在省委、省政府的领导下，省推进使用正版软件工作领导小组牵头单位省版权主管部门积极主动做好各项协调服务和指导工作，省领导小组各成员单位相互配合、密切协作、齐抓共管，推进软件正版化工作取得显著成效。省级政府机关操作系统软件和办公软件的正版率分别达到 97.98％和 96.08％”。

（二）工作措施

（1）加快工作节奏，持续有效巩固。继续加快工作节奏，强化督促检查，以检查促整改。新年伊始，甘肃省版权局即对河西五市党政机关的软件正版化工作进行了抽查，对各被检查单位存在的问题进行了工作指导，并提出了整改要求。各市州积极配合，甘肃省党政机关软件正版化工作得到进一步巩固。

（2）严格检查考核，强化管理手段。结合 2017 年底对全省 81 家党政机关软件正版化工作的全覆盖检查汇总情况，对省级党政机关软件正版化工作检查情况进行了通报。通报对正版率不足 100％的单位提出了整改要求，对 6 家工作推进落实没有成效的单位提出了批评，通过与其领导电话沟通进行了整改督促。督促整改取得显著成效。

（3）领导重视履职责，多重督促抓落实。以迎接国家软件正版化工作检查组对甘肃省省级政府机关软件正版化工作开展的全覆盖检查为契机，采取多种措施，积极推进甘肃省政府机关软件正版工作的常态化建设。积极组织由 81 家省级党政机关分管领导等参加的工作培训会；甘肃省版权局主管领导亲自与问题突出单位多次进行电话沟通，进行工作督办；主管领导亲自带队，对 40 家省级政府机关进行实地督导检查；针对复查中出现的盗版反弹问题，召集相关单位主管领导工作座谈会；核拨 20 万元资金编印《软件正版化工作手册》，用以指导工作有效开展；建立专门的软件正版化工作 QQ 群，传达政策、交流工作。

（4）企业推进明责任，分级考核加追责。以软件正版化工作领导小组办公室名义与省政府国资委联合召集省国资监管企业相关负责人软件正版化工作推进会议，明确建立领导小组考核主管单位、主管单位考核企业、企业考核员工的三级考核追责制度；软件正版化工作领导小组办公室（省版权局）与省政府国资委组成联合督查组，对国资监管企业集团及二级企业软件正版化长效机制、计算机正版软件安装使用两方面情况进行全面检查。

（5）事业单位建计划，积极部署促推进。按照推进使用正版软件工作部际联席会议《2017 年推进使用正版软件工作计划》及省政府、局领导批示要求，制定并以省政府办公厅名义下发了《2018 年甘肃省推进使用正版软件工作计划》，制定并以领导小组办公室（省版权局）名义下发了《甘肃省推进企事业单位使用正版软件工作计划》。两个计划分别对 2018 年软件正版化重点工作和甘肃省党政机关所属企事业单位软件正版化工作进行了全面部署。

二、强化版权执法，开展专项行动

（一）组织开展“剑网 2018”专项行动

积极联合公安、网信、通信等部门联合下发“剑网 2018”专项行动通知，制定工作方案，成立由省版权局专职副局长任组长、相关单位负责人为成员的“剑网 2018”专项行动工作领导小组，以网络侵权多发领域为重点目标，以查办案件为重要抓手，在全省范围开展了为期半年的打击网络侵权盗版的“剑网”专项行动。各市州按照省里安排，积极组织开展专项行动，及时与相关部门沟通协作，加强对主要网站的监管，持续保持对侵权网站的高压态势。

（二）组织协调“双打”专项行动

按照全国打击侵犯知识产权和制售假冒伪劣商品工作电视电话会议精神，围绕甘肃省版权局承担的打击著作权侵权的软件正版化、“剑网”专项行动、出版物市场监管等工作，积极协调审计、国资等厅局，协调局反非、“扫黄打非”、印刷发行等处室依法开展了一系列打击侵权盗版专项行动，并配合国家“双打”考核组完成了对甘肃省著作权保护的“双打”考核各项工作。

（三）积极查办著作权侵权案件

国家版权局移转给甘肃省通渭县司法局的通渭

文渊书店涉嫌侵犯北京某出版社著作权一案，由甘肃省市县三级版权管理部门组成联合检查组，第一时间赴案发地调查取证。经查证，所诉案情基本属实，此案已于年初结案，由通渭县文化广播影视局对被诉方通渭文渊书店做出没收非法所得、罚款、销毁经销盗版图书的行政处罚决定。国家版权局移转的网络侵权盗播案，省版权局联合省公安厅、网信办、通信管理局，按照职责权限，分工负责，积极调查，并将调查结果及时向国家版权局进行了反馈。

三、版权法律服务水平稳步提高

（一）法律服务水平稳步提高

为了提高甘肃省作品创作、运用、保护和管理水平，积极以作品登记为抓手、行政执法为支撑，通过压缩登记时限、提供免费登记、实施电子存档、联系使用渠道、强化监管保护等手段鼓励甘肃省作者积极创作作品。与此同时，甘肃省版权局注意强化诸如版权纠纷调解、咨询，涉外合同审核，合同签订指导等工作，积极为权利人服务、为版权产业单位服务。

（二）扎实开展“4·26”知识产权宣传周系列活动

向各市州及有关单位下发了《关于做好2018年全省知识产权宣传周版权宣传活动的通知》，对全省知识产权宣传周版权宣传活动进行了安排部署。全省各地也按照省局部署，组织了多种形式的宣传活动。

（夏　玲）

青　海　省

2018年，青海省版权局按照国家版权局的工作部署和要求，在省委、省政府的领导下，把握重点，认真谋划，精心实施，较好地完成了各项工作任务。

一、积极开展打击网络侵权盗版“剑网2018”专项行动

根据国家版权局、国家互联网信息办公室、工业和信息化部、公安部联合印发的《关于开展打击网络侵权盗版“剑网2018”专项行动的通知》要求，结合实际，青海省版权局制定下发了《青海省开展打击网络侵权盗版“剑网2018”专项行动实施方案》，对全省开展“剑网行动”做出了安排和部署，明确要求各市（州）紧密围绕工作重点积极组织开展网络转载版权专项整治、短视频版权专项整治、重点领域版权专项整治，查办网络侵权盗版案件。

二、开展集中销毁侵权盗版及非法出版物活动

4月23日上午，青海省版权局会同省“扫黄打非”领导小组、西宁市“扫黄打非”领导小组在西宁举行青海省2018年侵权盗版及非法出版物集中销毁活动。会后，西宁市“扫黄打非”部门将现场5.1万件非法出版物运往销毁地点进行了集中销毁。据统计，全省销毁侵权盗版及其他各类非法出版物共计8.5万件。

三、全面推进软件正版化工作

根据国家版权局《关于印发〈2018年推进使用正版软件工作计划〉的通知》要求，制定印发了《青海省2018年推进使用正版软件工作实施方案》《青海省推进企事业单位使用正版软件工作规划（2018—2022年）》《关于推进省直机关所属事业单位使用正版软件工作的通知》，为进一步巩固扩大省、市（州）、县级政府机关软件正版化工作成果，建立健全政府机关软件正版化长效机制，全面推进青海省软件正版化工作规范化、常态化、制度化和信息化提出了明确要求，及时调整了青海省推进软件正版化工作领导小组成员。2018年3月份举办了全省政府机关软件正版化工作培训班，对各市（州）、省级70家党政机关软件正版化工作责任人，就软件正版化工作相关政策措施、正版软件管理工作制度和台账、软件正版化工作检查和信息报送等进行了系统培训。4月份开展了对70家省直机关软件正版化工作的复查，复查情况向省政府主管领导进行了专报，并印发了整改督办通知。5月份组织召开了省直机关软件正版化工作会议，就切实做好国务院督查的各项准备工作做了动员部署，提出了具体要求。8月份配合国务院督查组圆满完成对青海省42家政府机关软件正版化工作的督查任务，并对69家省直机关正版软件采购工作进行审核把关。

四、加强宣传，提升公众版权意识

4月23日，省版权局、省“扫黄打非”领导小组办公室联合在西宁新宁广场进行集中宣传咨询活动。现场悬挂横幅3条、展出展板12块、散发海报等宣传资料1 000余份，集中展示宣传了青海省开展打击侵犯知识产权和制售假冒伪劣商品专项行动、推进全省政府机关软件正版化、版权保护工作取得的成果。另外，在厅属各单位及公共场所张贴版权宣传海报200余张，积极营造了以“尊重知识、崇尚创新、诚信守法”为核心的知识产权文化建设氛围，增强了公众的版权保护意识，同时，充分利用网络媒体进行广泛宣传。其间，在青海民族文化网和公众微信号“大美青海多元文化”等网络平台全面跟踪报道了各项活动，起到了良好的宣传效果。

五、积极开展执法培训工作

为切实提高行政执法人员法律素质和水平，举办了全省文化新闻出版系统依法行政（版权执法）培训班、全省软件正版化工作培训班和省直机关软件正版化工作会议，同时，组织20余人次参加了由国家版权局举办的版权执法和软件正版化工作培训。应省旅发委、省交通运输厅、省农牧厅、三江源国家公园管理局、西宁市文广局、玉树州文体局的邀请，省版权局分别进行了软件正版化工作培训。2018年，全省共计800余人次参加了执法培训，有效提升了行政执法人员的执法能力和水平。

六、积极开展盗版出版物认定工作

根据省“扫黄打非”办公室、西宁市大通县科技文化和旅游体育局的申请，对《颂词汇编》《现观论集》《四部医典注释（上）》《查理九世·深海里的哭声》《查理九世·潜伏的外星侵略者》《查理九世·神秘的亚库拉部落》《口语交际与写作技巧点拨》等10 107册图书进行了鉴定，并出具了认定书。

七、认真开展版权服务工作

全年共接待来人（来电）版权咨询400余人次，进行著作权作品登记75件。

（付成久）

宁夏回族自治区

2018年，宁夏回族自治区版权局紧紧围绕版权局中心任务，发挥岗位职能，加强版权监管保护力度，拓展版权宣传教育范围，推进打击侵权盗版和软件正版化工作，扎实开展版权公共服务，版权市场环境得到有效改善，版权管理和服务能力明显提高，版权工作的社会影响得到增强。

一、版权执法监管力度不断加大

2018年，自治区版权局认真履行版权执法监管职责，协调指导全区版权执法机关开展版权侵权案件查处和执法监管工作，2个单位和5名个人获得全国查处侵权盗版案件有功单位及有功个人称号，受到国家版权局表彰。一是加大打击侵权盗版查处力度。全年查办5起侵权盗版案件，行政处罚4.39万元，其中宁夏银川周某某等涉嫌侵犯网络游戏著作权案被国家五部门列为全国挂牌督办案件。二是“剑网2018”专项行动成效明显。2018年，自治区版权局与自治区网信办、通信管理局、公安厅等部门联合开展了“剑网2018”专项行动，对9名《快手》主播进行约谈，并提出严肃批评；对《快手》违规账号进行了处置，封停账号13个，其中永久封停账号7个，直播功能封停6个；禁言账号21个，其中封禁30天账号9个，封禁15天账号9个，封禁7天账号3个。移送公安部门7名《快手》主播，移交市场监管部门1名《快手》主播，刑事拘留违法《快手》主播1名，行政拘留违规《快手》主播1名。三是加强宣传，强化舆论引导。充分利用网站、微博、微信等渠道宣传有关法律法规和“剑网2018”专项行动，向社会公开了2017年8起典型侵权案件，如公布了宁夏银川周某某等涉嫌侵犯网络游戏著作权案，用实例以案说法，取得了良好的社会效果。四是举办了全区执法监管培训班。进一步加强了全区版权行政执法监管能力，提高了网络执法水平，参训人员60人。

二、软件正版化工作稳步推进

2018年，认真贯彻落实《政府机关使用正版软件管理办法》，进一步巩固和提升了软件正版化工作成果。一是软件正版化工作取得了新的进展。在深化市、县（区）党政机关软件正版化工作整改的基础上，着力加强计算机软硬件采购源头管理工作，出台了相关政策措施。全区党政机关新采购正版操作系统15 283套，其中国产操作系统700套；采购正版办公软件15 216套，其中国产办公软件14 421套，进口办公软件795套；采购国产杀毒软件660套。采购总金额3 515.4万元。二是党政机关软件正版化不断规范。继续以“三查一推进”为抓手，对3个市、10个县（区）的60家党政机关软件正版化工作进行了督查，检查计算机325台。推动了软件正版化工作主体责任的落实。截至11月底，各市、县（区）基本完成了使用正版软件工作。三是国产软件应用试点单位取得新进展。在上年完成盐池县国产软件应用试点工作的基础上，进一步总结经验，圆满完成了西吉县国产软件应用试点工作任务。7月份，国家推进使用正版软件工作部际联席会议办公室对试点工作进行了验收，并在全国国产软件应用试点工作总结会上，对西吉县试点工作给予了高度评价和充分肯定，向西吉县颁发了全国国产软件应用试点县牌匾。西吉县向全国介绍了国产软件试点工作的经验。四是积极推进企事业单位软件正版化工作。按照“先易后难，逐步推进”的原则，积极推进区属事业单位、部门事业单位软件正版化工作。2018年，共推进40家区属事业单位、部门所属事业单位实现软件正版化。8月，自治区版权局与自治区非公有制经济服务局联合举办了民营企业软件正版化工作培训班，引导民营企业加快推进使用正版软件工作，70余家企业参加了培训。五是持续推进教育医疗系统软件正版化工作。联合自治区教育厅对自治区8家高等院校使用正版软件情况进行了检查，为银川市第二中学等学校免费赠送国产一铭操作系统80套，进行国产操作系统使用试点，收到了良好的效果。

三、版权社会服务水平不断强化

一是突出调研抓落实。通过实地调研、数据分析等多种方式，对自治区作品登记情况进行了调研，并形成了调研报告，为更好地做好版权工作掌握第一手材料。二是强化版权公共服务体系建设。规范作品登记、涉外著作权合同登记工作，作品登记数量持续增长，达到502件；涉外著作权合同登记44件，比2017年增长100%。三是着力提高社会版权法律意识。组织全区版权管理部门集中开展了“4·26”版权宣传周、“12·6”法制宣传日系列活动，全年共印制宣传海报1 000套3 000张，分发全区各市、县、区及中心城镇，在全区各机关、街道、社区、书店等地进行张贴，通过电视台、新媒体多角度、多渠道开展知识产权的宣传报道，在全区各播出机构分别播放了版权公益宣传片，扩大了版权宣传，取得了良好的效果，提高了社会各界的版权意识。

（张宁学）

新疆维吾尔自治区

一、软件正版化工作

2018年，新疆维吾尔自治区版权工作以习近平新时代中国特色社会主义思想为指导，紧紧围绕社会稳定和长治久安总目标，加强制度建设，强化督促检查，完善长效机制，推进软件正版化工作，党政机关软件正版化不断规范。自治区党政机关认真贯彻落实国务院办公厅印发的《政府机关使用正版软件管理办法》、国家版权局印发的《正版软件管理工作指南》等相关政策措施，不断健全软件正版化工作机制，加强制度建设，规范软件采购，建立软件台账，严格使用管理。各级党政机关基本建立了软件正版化工作责任制度，明确了责任部门和责任人；企事业单位软件正版化全面铺开。基本完成自治区国资委直管13家企业总部的软件正版化，推进所属二级企业及事业单位软件正版化工作取得积极进展，加大督导检查力度。自治区软件正版化领导小组办公室先后对13家自治区级事业单位进行了全覆盖检查；对自治区厅局级事业单位进行抽查，共检查了91家1 010台计算机的通用软件（操作系统、办公软件、杀毒软件）安装使用情况，并对检查情况进行了反馈，提出整改时限，加大版权执法工作力度。

二、版权执法工作

全区版权部门通过主动监管查出立案的侵权盗版案件34件，办结的29件，捣毁窝点3个，案件信息公开11件，总罚款金额15.6万元；其中图书侵权盗版案件12件，音像制品侵权盗版案件8件，其他侵权盗版案件14件。受理了必能宝公司、欧特克公司、奥多比公司等3家软件公司的软件侵权投诉，向18家建筑设计企业发出《关于妥善应对侵权风险开展软件正版化工作的函》，督促这些单位及时完成软件正版化工作。指导地州开展版权执法，对石河子市执法支队办理的3件侵权盗版案件中出现的问题，予以复函指导。向石河子市执法支队移交并协商解决1件软件侵权投诉案件。组织全国查处侵权盗版案件有功单位和有功个人评选推荐工作，6个集体和9名个人获有功单位三等奖和有功个人三等奖。根据国家四部委“剑网2018”专项行动通知要求，自治区版权局、网信办、通信管理局、公安厅联合制定下发《关于在全区开展打击网络侵权盗版“剑网2018”专项行动的通知》，以网络侵权多发领域为重点，严厉打击网络转载、影视剧、短视频、动漫等领域侵权盗版行为，着力规范网络直播、知识分享、有声读物等平台版权传播秩序，进一步巩固网络影视、网络音乐、电子商务平台、应用商店、网络云存储空间等领域专项整治成果，以查处大案要案为重要抓手，通过集中整治和引导规范，有效运用分类监管、约谈整改、行政处罚、刑事打击等多种措施，有效整治互联网领域侵权盗版行为，开展版权宣传培训工作。

三、版权宣传工作

做好“4·26”知识产权宣传周版权宣传活动，通过电台、电视台等媒体开展广泛的宣传。委托文化传媒公司制作了30秒的动漫版权公益宣传片，在宣传周期间每天在新疆维吾尔自治区电视台循环播放4～6次，累计达385次192分钟；新疆维吾尔自治区人民广播电台根据自治区版权局提供的版权宣传标语制作了版权保护公益广告，同时在汉、维、哈、蒙、柯五种语言频率每天早中晚滚动播出，累计达432条次；在新疆维吾尔自治区少数民族公共文化网络出版平台每日推送版权宣传短片；自制5 000个新疆维吾尔自治区版权保护宣传鼠标垫免费向各地州广大市民发放。选送 3 起著作权侵权典型案件，其中 2 起入选自治区 2017 年度十大侵犯知识产权典型案例，在“4·26”知识产权宣传周新闻发布会上发布。发挥各地州市版权部门的优势在宣传周期间开展了各具特色的宣传活动，加强版权宣传培训工作。

四、版权社会服务工作

积极筹措资金 36 万元支持地州举办培训班。全年各地州共举办软件正版化工作培训班 16 期，培训人数约 2 500 人。举办了一期自治区级软件正版化工作培训班，邀请国家版权局版权专家授课，自治区党政机关、人民团体、事业单位以及各地州（市）行署（人民政府）办公室、软件正版化工作领导小组办公室和自治区国资委直接监管企业及下属二级企业派人参加了培训班，参会逾 300 人。加强执法人员培训。针对地州人员少的维稳任务实际，在全区软件正版化工作培训期间，组织各地州执法人员进行座谈，针对执法工作中遇到的困难进行指导，特别是对案件的上报做了进一步规范要求。组织各地州文化市场稽查支队参加国家版权局举办的版权执法监管培训班，有 10 个地州派人参加了培训；做好版权社会服务工作，热心服务群众，截至 11 月 15 日，共办理作品登记 1 100 件，引进版权 14 件，全年接待咨询群众 1 000 多人次。

（张新革）

2018年版权公共服务机构与社会服务组织工作

中国版权保护中心

2018年，中国版权保护中心（以下简称中心）在中宣部和国家出版主管部门党组的领导下，以习近平新时代中国特色社会主义思想和党的十九大精神为指导，认真学习贯彻全国宣传思想工作会议精神，不断增强“四个意识”，守正创新，充分发挥国家版权公共服务机构职责，紧紧围绕打造数字化、网络化环境下我国规模最大、功能最强、最值得信赖的国家版权公共服务机构的战略目标，在新的发展起点上，持续提升版权服务理念，再造科学管理机制，进一步夯实以版权登记为核心的各项基础工作，区域版权服务体系构建成效显著，版权公共服务覆盖面进一步扩大，以DCI体系为核心的数字版权公共服务体系实现更加广泛深化的示范应用，综合服务能力稳步增强，版权确权、授权、维权、研究咨询、宣传推广五大服务平台整合效能进一步显现。

一、持续夯实核心业务基础，不断扩大版权公共服务覆盖面，完善线上线下互动的版权服务网络，以DCI体系为核心的数字版权公共服务体系实现更加广泛深化的示范应用

（一）以高度的政治责任感，扎实抓好核心业务基础建设，全力保障登记工作高效运转，登记量不断再创新高

中心始终将版权登记作为公共服务职能的核心业务，持续完善细化登记工作流程、岗位设置、业务管理和操作规范，启动和实施著作权登记业务平台（三期）工程，致力于从根本上再次大幅提升版权登记信息化支撑能力，有效应对连年迅猛增长的登记量，全面提升中心著作权登记管理水平和服务能力。

截至2018年12月31日，中心共完成计算机软件著作权登记1 104 839件，登记量首次突破百万，再创历史新高，同时办理软件登记事项变更或补充登记28 583件；完成作品著作权登记216 035件/系列，同时办理著作权合同备案2 377件，变更登记1 053件；完成数字作品版权登记110 583件；完成出版境外音像制品合同登记1 891件；完成著作权质权登记197件，涉及主债务金额32.09亿元。此外，办理软件登记档案查询73 527件，司法机关查调档193件，法院查封软件746件，办理其他作品著作权登记档案查询5 746件。

按照国家版权局要求，继续扎实规范做好全国作品登记信息统计工作。截至2018年12月31日，全国作品登记信息数据库管理平台共审核通过并公告2018年1—12月作品登记信息2 460 666件，登记量较大的地区及机构分别是：北京919 543件、中国版权保护中心356 433件（其中作品登记244 150件、DCI 112 283件）、江苏299 856件、上海261 642件、四川169 133件、福建96 285件。

在首届中国国际进口博览会期间，中心应国家版权局和中国国际进口博览局要求，派员作为服务中心版权组成员入驻展馆，负责版权登记相关咨询、宣传等工作，获得与会人员和组织方的一致好评。

（二）不断优化区域版权服务窗口体系建设，区域版权综合服务能力进一步增强

持续完善现有北京天桥、雍和版权登记大厅和成都、上海、深圳的西南、华东、粤港澳版权登记大厅的运营，直接开通软件和其他作品著作权登记受理发证窗口，在武汉新建运营了华中版权登记大厅。目前，各版权登记大厅运行良好。同时，大力推进广州和厦门版权登记大厅的建设运营工作，不断扩大版权服务网络覆盖面，让更多地区的登记申请者享受到方便、优质的版权登记“一站式”窗口服务，把中心五大服务平台功能辐射延伸到各区域，为当地文化创意产业发展提供更加便捷、高效的综合性版权服务。

（三）以DCI体系为核心的数字版权公共服务体系的探索创新和示范应用进一步深化拓展，DCI体系建设应用工程的立项筹备工作积极推进

继续把DCI体系建设和应用推广放在核心战略位置，“十二五”期间，DCI体系在模式创新、技术集成、标准研发、平台搭建、示范应用等方面取得阶段性工作成果。“十三五”以来，在以DCI体系为核心的数字版权公共服务体系被写入国务院发布的《“十三五”国家信息化规划》、数字版权唯一标识符（DCI）体系建设工程等有关内容被写入《新闻出版广播影视“十三五”发展规划》的基础上，紧紧围绕将DCI体系建构成为与互联网产业共生、共治、

共享的互联网版权基础设施的定位，加紧推进 DCI 体系建设工程申请国家重大工程立项工作。

围绕“确权、授权、维权”不断拓展服务领域，加紧推进 DCI 体系示范应用不断取得新成果，获得产业领域的广泛认可和高度关注。一是继续创新和拓展在部分示范应用互联网平台的 DCI 体系嵌入式版权服务。在微博上开展基于区块链的社交媒体 DCI 体系应用；在京东上以商品 AR/VR 内容的 DCI 应用为切入点，逐步展开全面的 DCI 体系应用；在法院司法数据服务平台等重要领域开展了 DCI 示范应用。二是努力探索第三方版权费结算模式创新。CACC 数字阅读版权分发与费用结算服务平台开展合作运营，与微博联合探索基于区块链的付费内容第三方跨平台分发与结算，推进各领域版权分发与费用结算。三是进一步做好网络版权监测和快速维权工作。在前期申报“数字内容版权监测与维权管理智慧云平台”项目入库原总局改革发展项目库后，继续开展网络监测维权服务。全年共处理侵权链接 100 370 条，删除链接数 92 866 条，删除率为 92.52%；快速维权业务共处理侵权链接 73 163 条；已删除链接数 59 397 条，删除率为 81.18%。监测维权效果获得客户好评。

（四）持续做好版权鉴定等版权法律服务工作

接受公检法、版权行政管理部门、著作权人的委托，完成版权鉴定 99 件，其中美术作品鉴定 53 件、文字作品鉴定 16 件、网络游戏及计算机软件鉴定 24 件、视频类鉴定 5 件、电影剧本鉴定 1 件。参与开展“剑网行动”，为“剑网 2018”专项行动典型案件出具的鉴定报告被央视新闻报道，引起多家媒体转载，中心法律部获评 2017 年度查处侵权盗版案件有功单位。同时，积极探索版权网络调解新模式，在《中国版权服务》APP 开通版权线上调解平台。

（五）顺利完成中国 ISRC 中心运营等各项工作

继续做好中国 ISRC（中国标准录音制品编码）中心的日常工作，规范化拓展 ISRC 登记者申请范围，持续提升 ISRC 标准在产业的覆盖面和影响力。截至 12 月 31 日，全年共完成 ISRC 申请受理 48 875 件，其中录音制品 41 488 件、音乐录像制品 7 387 件，完成编码发放 47 732 件。

落实《国家新闻出版署关于征集原创动漫作品版权开发优秀项目的通知》要求，在国家新闻出版署指导和中央文化产业发展专项资金支持下，受托开展优秀原创动漫作品版权开发奖励计划，认真做好申报材料的整理和组织评审等工作，共有 25 个地区的 200 多家单位申报了 313 个优秀动漫作品版权开发项目，最终 78 个项目入选，奖励计划共向获奖单位拨付奖励资金 488.5 万元。

持续深化与北京市西城区人民政府的合作，积极推进国家数字版权产业基地建设，天桥演艺区专项工作小组为园区发展继续提供专业的版权服务支持，积极参与北京天桥演艺联盟的日常运营。

二、构建版权全媒体整合传播平台成效更加显著，高端版权咨询服务产业应用不断拓展，全流程综合版权服务体系持续完善，版权服务促进产业融合创新和发展的作用进一步显现

（一）践行“互联网＋”“全媒体＋”的工作思路，版权全媒体整合传播平台聚合力和影响力进一步扩大

以“中国版权服务”平台品牌的影响力为核心，以《中国版权》杂志社两刊，中心微信公众号、微平台、官网、头条号，杂志社官网、官微等新媒体传播力的聚合为拓展，推动构建全媒体整合传播平台和版权社会生态圈，不断完善中心与著作权人和业界交流互动的综合平台，成功举办“尊重原创·融合创新”2018 CPCC 中国版权服务年会、CPCC 十大中国著作权人年度评选活动、2018（首届）版权强国闵行论坛等活动，组织举办了全国版权经纪人专业培训班、全国版权登记及代理实务培训班、数字出版与版权管理培训班等 6 期培训班，不断研究摸索新媒体传播规律，运营好“中国版权服务”微信公众平台，2018 年底总订户数超过 22 万人，是版权服务领域第一大微信号。通过各类线上线下传播活动，整合中心各项版权服务产品，聚合版权业界各类人才和资源，展示版权服务创新成果、引领发展方向，实现版权服务供给侧核心资源、高端人才与社会需求的有效连接，发挥好版权行业主流宣传阵地的公信力、引导力、影响力、传播力。

（二）以版权资产管理为核心的版权咨询服务取得实质突破，持续开展版权服务基础理论研究，进一步巩固专业优势

2018 年初，总局改革办印发了《新闻出版广播影视企业版权资产管理工作指引（试行）》，在业界引起强烈反响，中心组织专业团队在天津、上海、武汉开展了《指引》政策解读培训。基本完成版权资产管理工具软件开发主体工作和《版权资产管理体系要求》作为行业标准的制定。在开展出版社版权资产管理试点工作的基础上，针对不同主体需求特点提供差异化的精准服务，进一步将咨询服务对象拓展到动漫、游戏、视频、广告和综合性传媒公司等领域，行业标准指引、政策推动、咨询服务配

套、信息化工具辅助、系统平台集成的版权资产管理工作模式逐步完善，为文化企业实现版权资产科学管理、精细运营提供引领性指引和全套解决方案，为版权相关行业规范发展，防控知识产权风险提供基础支撑。同时带动区域版权产业研究、版权资产评价与版权金融等高端专业咨询服务的研究和实践。

有序开展软件登记信息分析咨询服务，完成了2017年度全国软件登记信息分析工作。根据定制委托，完成了深圳、北京、武汉和上海浦东新区各地方区域的定制软件登记信息分析工作，完成了2017年度深圳南山区软件登记资助情况报告，完成了深圳、苏州、成都、广州、长沙、东莞6个城市和浦东新区的软件登记月报或季报，给相关产业发展决策部门提供参考依据。

完成了《版权公共服务对区域经济发展的促进机制与路径——以粤港澳登记大厅为例》《著作权登记服务的公共服务性质》等课题研究项目。完成了北京市科委“互联网图片课题”项目《数字图片资源侵权传播及受众分类数据分析报告》。翻译出版了《版权产业经济贡献调研指南（2015年修订版）》，该指南是世界知识产权组织在2003版基础上最新编制出版的指导版权产业经济贡献调研活动的重要文献。通过以上举措，不断夯实筑牢中心版权相关理论支持基础和领先信息优势。

（三）以全方位、全流程综合版权服务为支撑，以版权服务对接文化金融为切入点，深入产业链提供专业服务，促进相关产业融合创新和发展

不断加强业务资源、服务项目和营销工作的整合协调以及工作流程的衔接，与版权产业价值链紧密融合的全流程、全方位版权服务体系逐步成熟完善。与北京市文化投资发展集团签订战略合作协议，在版权资产管理、版权+金融方面开展合作，通过其融资租赁平台、“投贷奖”平台、文创板平台提供有针对性的服务，为文投集团下的文投租赁提供专项版权服务，为我国首只知识产权证券化产品12月在深交所成功获批提供版权方面的专业支撑。进一步发挥“影视版权产业联盟”平台的作用，深度挖掘客户需求，有侧重地设计版权服务方案，整体输出中心的版权服务。聚焦影视领域整合版权确权、授权、维权三阶段版权服务内容，推出了集剧本挖掘、孵化、新技术应用、网络视频授权分销、反盗版维权监测、版权资产管理以及基于版权的影视质押融资等服务于一体的集成化版权服务产品，截至目前协助企业共完成电视剧版权质押贷款8 500万元，孵化电视剧本7部。与中国传媒大学等机构合作举办首届中国软IP大会，这是我国首次举办覆盖IP全产业各个相关领域的产学研协作的大会。指导举办首届中国剧本推优与版权保护论坛，促进电视剧创作拍摄融资、主创专业人才融合等多方合作，18部电影、电视剧、网剧剧本与影视制作公司达成签约拍摄意向。

（四）指导和支持下属企业适应发展需要进行战略转型和业务创新，更好地发挥对中心版权服务体系的业务支撑作用

大力支持中华版权代理总公司在新的战略布局下开展版权服务工作，总公司在做好传统的版权代理、国际版权贸易和版权登记代理业务的基础上，不断拓展和完善战略布局，以高端版权服务技术支撑和业务拓展为重点构建更加多元化的业务发展体系，与中心形成更加顺畅的业务互动关系，设立北京华代版信科技有限公司作为专门的技术公司，为互联网环境下的专业版权服务提供了技术支撑服务团队和实体。积极服务文化“走出去”战略，总公司在英国设立的子公司正式开展运营，持续在世界各地书展上举办“China Day”版权贸易主题活动，取得经济效益和社会效益双丰收。以“一带一路”沿线国家为重点，对外版权贸易和交流成绩显著，以出版版权贸易为例，共引进与输出图书约400种，输出图书中包括少儿类、科普类和文学类。

《中国版权》杂志社有限公司注重策划宣传的导向性和权威性，充分发挥版权前沿理论研究和产业实践指导的作用，完成了杂志改版和日常出刊工作，得到业界和读者的广泛好评。初步完成并不断深化杂志社运营的全媒体、数字化传播转型，创办中国版权共享课堂线下公益讲座系列活动，在广州、上海、北京等地举办7期知名法官公益讲座，线下覆盖学员1 000余人，受到业界普遍关注。与人民网合作，推出原创短视频访谈节目《知产热点名家看》，探索融媒体发展实践方式。成功举办了新时代版权强国青年征文大赛，为国家版权事业发现、汇聚人才。

（张文娟）

中国版权协会

2018年，中国版权协会（以下简称协会）深入学习贯彻习近平新时代中国特色社会主义思想和党的十九大精神，结合协会工作实际，秉承服务会员、服务版权事业的宗旨，坚持正确导向，不断改进、创新工作内容与方法，围绕国家版权工作大局，努

力提高服务能力。协会团结了全国版权学术界、产业界的广大代表，充分发挥联系政府和产业界的桥梁纽带作用，在行业服务、行业自律、行业交流、行业维权等方面开展了大量工作。

一、加强组织建设、党风廉政建设、规章制度建设

协会根据国家有关社团管理规定，以及中央巡视组和出版主管部门人事、党务、纪检等部门的有关管理要求，采取多项措施加强协会组织建设，促进协会健康有序发展。协会现有会员单位 453 家，其中常务理事单位 152 家，理事单位 301 家，会员单位涵盖版权相关党政机关、行业协会，版权学术组织，出版企业，互联网、软件企业，影视传媒企业，版权服务、实业企业等多个领域。

针对中央巡视组和出版主管部门关于整顿检查局属社团的工作部署，协会领导高度重视，专门召开理事长会议研究贯彻落实措施，认真梳理存在的问题，积极开展自查自纠，切实做到立行立改，加强完善管理制度。认真贯彻执行中央八项规定精神，严格遵守党政机关干部（含离退休干部）兼职取酬的规定，现党政机关和事业单位在协会兼职的有关领导均未在协会取酬。

加强党建工作，发挥党组织政治核心作用。协会积极开展支部各项建设，坚持开展“两学一做”学习教育活动，在夯实组织建设基础上，严格落实出版主管部门人事、党务、纪检等工作要求，认真开展学习党的十九大会议精神相关活动，明确党组织在协会中的功能定位，发挥党组织在协会的政治核心作用，充分发挥党员先锋模范带头作用，深入开展各类党建活动，不断提高全体党员党性修养，促进党建工作和协会业务工作的深度融合，坚持正确的政治方向，积极发展党员，支部工作展现出生机活力，取得健康平稳的发展。

根据出版主管部门工作要求，协会修订完善了《财务管理制度》《合同管理制度》《工资及劳务报酬管理制度》《报销管理制度》《差旅费管理制度》《内部审计管理规定》《行政管理制度》《文件管理制度》等各项制度，重新制定《内部控制制度》，细化了管理办法。在制度落实方面，严格按照社会组织分类标准和具体办法开展业务，明确内部分工，落实相关工作责任人，并编制了《中国版权协会管理制度汇编》，加强日常和财务管理，明确了各项制度要求，确保协会工作有序开展。

按照《中国版权协会章程》规定，会员代表大会每五年举行一次，第五届理事会于 2018 年 1 月已届满。协会于 2018 年 9 月已向主管单位呈文，申请召开第六次全国会员代表大会，选举产生新一届理事会，完成换届工作。

根据工作需要，按照协会章程，协会于 11 月召开理事长会议，通过了关于增补、调整常务理事、理事的决议，并增补协会副秘书长。

2018 年，协会整体经营情况良好，不断提升服务水平，得到广大会员单位的认可与支持，95%以上的会员单位按时缴纳了 2018 年会费。

二、围绕版权中心工作，积极开展培训、研讨等相关工作

2018 年，协会继续秉承服务会员、服务版权事业的宗旨，努力提高服务会员单位的能力，着力为会员及版权产业服务。

培训工作是协会为会员单位提供的一项重要服务内容，协会每年举办一至两期面向会员的免费培训班，邀请立法、司法、行政、教学等单位的领导和专家，以及版权产业界的领军人物，围绕版权产业的热点、难点问题，结合版权工作的实际情况，为会员单位组织培训和讲座。2018 年 9 月，协会在山东枣庄举办版权实务培训班，中国版权协会理事长阎晓宏、华东政法大学教授王迁、全国审判业务专家林子英、中信出版集团副总编辑孔彦、腾讯研究院版权研究中心秘书长田小军等著名专家学者担任授课老师，就新时代版权发展基本趋势、版权典型案件、企业知识产权保护及版权保护前沿问题等对会员进行专题培训，共有 93 家会员单位的 136 人参加。

中国版权协会定期组织全国版权协会联席会议，加强与各省、市版权协会的沟通。2018 年 7 月，协会组织部分省、市版权协会在西安举办“全国部分省市版权协会联席会议”。会上讨论了协会的工作规划及各省、市协会相关工作事项，会议极大地增强了协会间的相互了解，促进了协会间的交流与合作。

在国家版权局的指导下，协会每年定期举办中国版权年会，已连续举办十届。在改革开放四十周年、《国家知识产权战略纲要》实施十周年之际，协会于 2018 年 12 月 1 日在武汉东湖宾馆举办第十一届中国版权年会。年会以“新时代助力文化发展”为主题，举办首届“远集坊”论坛，十二届全国人大教科文卫委员会主任委员柳斌杰、著名历史学家阎崇年、中国出版集团公司总裁谭跃、湖北省文联主席熊召政、当当网创始人李国庆、金山办公软件 CEO 葛珂、雅昌文化（集团）有限公司董事长万捷、百度副总裁梁志祥等重量级嘉宾致辞或演讲。本届年会，中国版权协会邀请社会各界卓越人士会聚一堂，包括年会特邀嘉宾，中国版权协会会员单位负责人，部分版权协会负责人，获奖代表，版权产业界、教学科研、法律事务、新闻媒体代表等。年会中颁发由协会评选的各奖项，柳斌杰、阎崇年获得“中国版权事业终生成就者”称号，白京兆、毕飞宇、江波、刘恒、刘昕、王斌、王亚民、张良成、赵东亮等九位获得“中国版权事业卓越成就者”称号，湖南广播电视台、江苏凤凰出版传媒股份有限公司、上海阅文信息技术有限公司等44家单位获得“中国版权最具影响力企业”奖，陕西广电影视文化产业发展有限公司、中国中医药出版社、恐龙园文化旅游集团股份有限公司等27家单位获得中国版权新锐企业奖。中国版权年度评选相关奖项是为在版权事业发展过程中取得突出成绩、做出突出贡献的个人和企业设立的，旨在弘扬版权从业人员和企业的开拓创新精神、艰苦奋斗历程和成功经验，推动我国版权事业的进步和发展。

2018年11月8日，首届中国国际进口博览会打击侵权假冒论坛在上海举办。协会协办的该届论坛以“合作　创新　共创”为主题，系统宣介中国打击侵权假冒工作成效，交流借鉴国际经验，提升侵权假冒社会共治和全球协同治理水平。国家市场监督管理总局副局长甘霖、中国外商投资企业协会会长陈德铭、中国版权协会理事长阎晓宏、世界知识产权组织中国办事处主任陈宏兵等嘉宾致辞或演讲。

由中国版权协会、中国文化产业发展集团共同主办的首届中国文化IP及创新设计展于2018年9月在全国农业展览馆举办。该展是国内首个基于“文化IP”的交流平台，阎崇年、王亚民、吴文辉、陈刚、张凌云、张云帆、陈彦、肖玢等嘉宾分别在展会首日的“2018中国文化IP发展高峰论坛——优秀内容创作　赋能运营传播”做了主题演讲。

协会举办了“2018中国首届嗨未来儿童有声阅读计划”发布会，通过听书的方式让2～12岁儿童爱上听书，收获知识。该计划旨在为中国少年儿童持续不断输出精品知识性儿童有声内容，让正版的好内容陪伴孩子度过七彩童年。

三、积极协助国家版权局推进各项版权工作

受国家版权局委托，协会在推进政府机关软件正版化工作方面主要做了如下工作：一是组织培训，协会在2018年分别在鄂尔多斯、成都、广州、北京承办了四期软件正版化培训班，来自全国31个省（区、市）的政府办公厅、工信厅、财政厅、发改委、版权局等部门的千余名公职人员参加了培训。二是承担政府机关软件正版化全覆盖督查的技术服务工作，根据国家版权局关于开展政府机关软件正版化督促检查的工作安排，协会在国家版权局的指导下，对福建、甘肃、青海、云南、重庆、四川等六省（市）的254家省级政府机关的33 446台计算机正版软件使用情况进行了检查，并根据实地检查结果，向国家版权局提交了该六省（市）使用正版软件检查工作报告和有关检查数据资料。

受国家版权局委托，协会承担编写《中国版权年度报告（2017）》的任务，并承办了“2017年中国版权十件大事”评选活动。《中国版权年度报告（2017）》汇总了2017年版权行业相关信息，如法律法规、工作概况、统计资料、典型案例、奖项评选、版权相关图书等。“2017年中国版权十件大事”评选活动由协会面向社会征集备选材料，组织专家进行评选，并在各大媒体上对评选结果进行宣传，扩大版权工作影响，提升全社会版权意识。

四、开展国际及台湾、香港等地区版权交流

协会与台湾著作权保护协会形成了互访机制，并已在北京、西安、银川等地成功举办了九届海峡两岸版权保护研讨会。2018年，协会本着积极推动海峡两岸版权交流的目的，应台湾著作权保护协会邀请，经批准，由中国版权协会理事长阎晓宏带队，赴台参加2018海峡两岸版权交流活动。活动期间，代表团拜会了台湾著作权保护协会，举行主题为“新媒体应用下两岸著作权”的研讨会。代表团还拜访了当地著作权保护组织，与台湾著作权权利人交流会谈，并参观了当地文创园区。台湾地区作为大陆版权贸易重要输出地，此行通过交流进一步增进海峡两岸版权保护的沟通与了解，推动建立有关协调机制，携手促进海峡两岸版权保护的发展，推动两岸版权贸易乃至思想文化交流，为两岸经济社会发展服务。

围绕小网站跨国网络侵权盗版问题展开研讨和经验分享，加强国际交流合作、联手打击跨国侵权，协会于2018年2月主办北京国际网络版权监测研讨会。中国版权协会理事长阎晓宏、国家版权局版权管理司司长于慈珂、时任商务部条约法律司司长陈福利出席会议并讲话，中国版权协会版权监测中心副主任、冠勇科技董事长吴冠勇进行了主题发言。来自WIPO中国办事处、美国电影协会、日本国士馆大学、日本内容产品海外流通促进机构、韩国著作权委员会等国际知名行业协会、著作权集体管理组织、国内各大网站及版权相关单位的40余人出席了会议。

香港海关助理关长黎流栢一行四人于2018年3

月拜访协会，双方就内地和香港的版权现状进行了深入交流，并参观了中国版权协会版权检测中心。

2018 年 4 月，中日韩联合版权宣传活动正式启动。中国版权协会是该活动的中方执行单位。活动推介了《中日韩版权保护宣传片》，三个国家的知名动漫形象“孙悟空”“柯南”“啵乐乐”，携手为版权保护代言。此举旨在将“保护版权、繁荣创作”的理念植入人心，进一步加强互联网领域版权保护，提升公众特别是青少年群体的版权保护意识。

日本内容产品海外流通促进机构（CODA）专务理事后藤健郎一行三人于 2018 年 6 月访问协会，CODA 希望可以与协会进行全方位合作，包括两个协会组织间的交流，两国版权保护的宣传及如何促进两国版权产业发展，并实现中日两国权利人和内容产品的互访交流。

韩国 GMCP 音乐公司 CEO 金美罗一行于 2018 年 8 月访问协会，双方就跨国音乐版权保护问题进行了深入的探讨和交流。

五、二级委员会工作情况

根据会员的实际需求，协会下设三个具有活力、面向社会和市场的二级委员会：版权监测中心、艺术品版权工作委员会、软件工作委员会。

版权监测中心启动版权监测服务，监测保护作品覆盖院线电影、电视剧、综艺、体育赛事、音乐、有声书、新闻资讯、网络文学、漫画等多个领域。其中包括《红海行动》《唐人街探案 2》《李茶的姑妈》《我不是药神》《无双》《复仇者联盟 3：无限战争》等院线热映的国产和进口优秀影片。2018 年 1—11 月，版权监测中心累计监测社区论坛、视频平台、音频平台、搜索引擎、网盘、影视移动应用、新闻资讯网站、网络文学平台、中小网站等各类互联网平台超过 10 万个，监测保护作品近 50 万个，向各类平台发布版权预警函超过 2.6 万封，监测盗版侵权链接近 680 万条，发送下线函超过 50 万封，下线盗版侵权链接近 400 万条，持续为国内外视频、音频、图片、文字等各领域作品版权方保驾护航。

艺术品版权工作委员会提供的中国艺术品鉴证备案服务是通过高新技术和行业资源推出的为艺术品建立“身份证”信息的服务，鉴证备案面向全球征集艺术家的艺术品，至今已有近 4 000 位知名艺术家加入鉴证备案行列，6 000 余位收藏家送检艺术作品，10 万余幅作品进入鉴证备案数据库，全面保障了艺术家权益。艺委会与雅昌艺术网于 2018 年共同组织发起举办了鉴证备案当代书画拍卖专场，参拍作品由艺术品版权委员会进行版权备案，雅昌进行技术备案保证作品真实性、唯一性，拍卖全程由中国版权协会艺术品版权工作委员会（以下简称艺委会）对其监督，该种专场拍卖模式为净化艺术品交易市场、保障艺术家及艺术品爱好者的合法权益提供了新思维、新模式。2018 年度鉴证备案拍卖专场已组织四场，有效保护了艺术家及收藏者的合法权益。艺委会在 2018 年举办多起大型版权活动，具体包括：艺术品版权保护高峰论坛、艺术设计 IP 授权产业峰会等；在艺委会提倡发起下，成立了青年设计师联盟，联盟旨在通过聚合优质设计机构和青年设计师，搭建多元化、多品类、国际化的设计交流及创作运营平台，以具有国际视野的设计标准和观念来影响艺术设计发展的方向，推动文化和经济创意产业的发展。艺委会成立的专家顾问委员会，截至 2018 年 8 月 31 日，聘请了 42 位国内知名艺术家和艺术机构领导作为专家顾问。同时，艺委会为会员提供全方面的版权维权服务，与多家知识产权机构达成了版权维权合作，跨地区多维度地为我国艺术品版权构筑版权保护和贸易服务平台。

软件工作委员会旨在充分发挥行业组织在维护会员权益，促进产业发展，协助推进使用正版软件等工作方面的协调和组织保障作用。在推进使用正版软件工作部际联席会议办公室的指导下，软件工作委员会（以下简称软工委）于 2018 年 6 月在国家版权局举办了推进自主基础软件创新发展研讨会，围绕进一步加强软件版权保护，探讨在新形势下如何推动国内基础软件产业发展。中国版权协会理事长阎晓宏，工业和信息化部信息化和软件服务业司司长谢少锋，国家版权局版权管理司司长于慈珂、副司长段玉萍，国务院机关事务管理局政府采购中心副主任赵绪选，中国工程院院士倪光南，金山办公软件 CEO 葛珂出席会议并发言。2018 年 11 月，软工委在北京故宫博物院举办了“中国传统文化与数字化科技融合创新研讨会”，会上发布了《新时代中文版式应用》倡议书，通过文化与技术相融合，实现传统文化赋能现代科技，现代科技助推传统文化。故宫博物院院长单霁翔、中国版权协会理事长阎晓宏、国家版权局版权管理司司长于慈珂、工业和信息化部信息化和软件服务业司司长谢少锋、时任故宫博物院副院长冯乃恩、故宫研究院古文献研究所所长王素、原国家新闻出版广电总局数字出版司副司长冯宏声、金山办公软件 CEO 葛珂、清华大学美术学院教授赵健等出席研讨会并发言。

六、举办“远集坊”讲座

秉承坚持正确导向、倡导平等交流、碰撞思想火花、汇集八方智慧的主旨，邀请社会各界卓越人士阐述有益于祖国繁荣发展、社会和谐进步的真知灼见，运用传统媒体与新媒体进行广泛传播，惠及更多的读者，努力为经济、社会、文化发展提供智力支持与服务，中国版权协会和国家版权创新基地在2017年共同创立了一个文化交流平台，取名“远集坊”。

“远集坊”自2017年9月29日首期开讲，至2018年10月7日，一年零八天里共举办了17期，阎崇年、王文章、雷军、柳斌杰、谭跃、王亚民、沈鹏、黄强、朱永新、郝林海、郑渊洁、黄书元、郑欣淼、刘珺、罗振宇、王秦丰、吴为山等17位主讲嘉宾为“远集坊”带来了高瞻远瞩、别开生面的精彩演讲，200余位特邀嘉宾光临“远集坊”并与主讲嘉宾积极互动、发表了他们的真知灼见。

协会对17期“远集坊”进行了回顾与总结，并在征求了各位主讲嘉宾的同意后，携手中信出版社，出版了《远集坊：名家论中华文脉与创新精神》一书。书中收录了“远集坊”全部17讲，从书中可以看到各位主讲嘉宾从不同的角度阐述了他们深入研究问题的观点与心得。书中同时收录了各位主讲嘉宾在“远集坊”的演讲视频，使阅读与视听能够融为一体。

（连　熠）

中国音乐著作权协会

一、会员发展

2018年中国音乐著作权协会（以下简称音著协）新发展会员数为506人（家），其中词作者169人、曲作者305人、继承人25人、其他1人、出版公司6家。截至2018年底，会员总数达9 413人（家）（见图1、图2）。

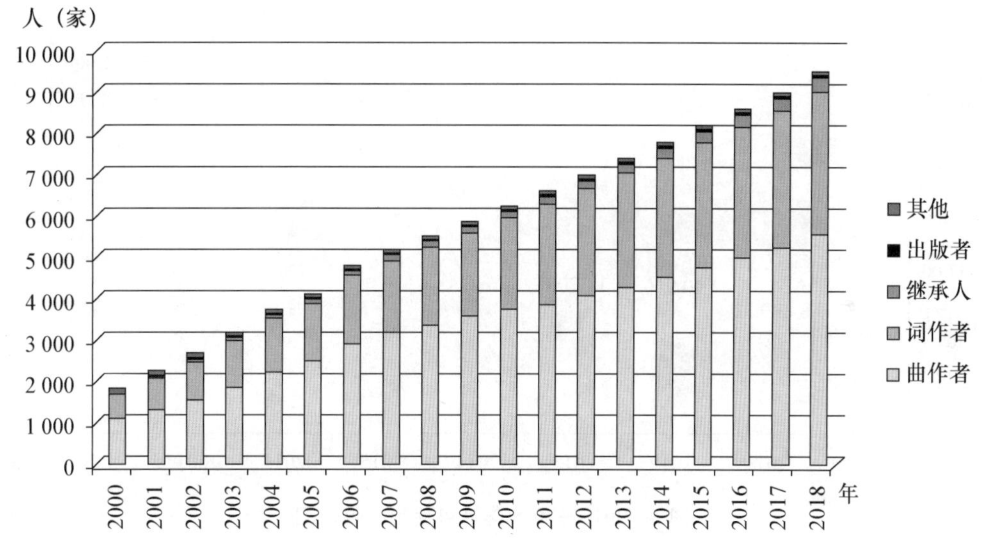

图1　历年会员数统计

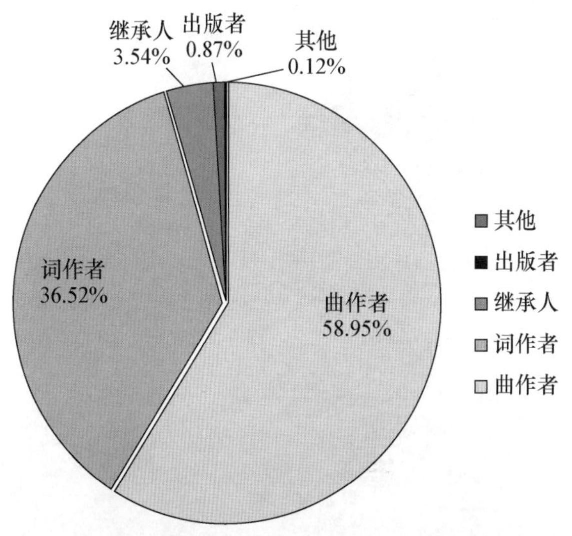

图2　2018年音著协会员类别占比图

在新发展的会员中，较有影响力的个人会员有：张天宇、王啸冰、李春、胡帅、郝雷、唐恬、崔凯、吴丹、杨臣刚、胡臻、高阳、刘一澜、黄铂、雷立、那仁朝格、方柏深、李瑜哲等。较有影响力的公司会员有：酷亚音乐（深圳）有限公司、北京梦织音传媒有限公司等。

二、音乐作品资料管理

作为中国大陆地区唯一的音乐作品著作权集体管理组织，音著协通过全球最大的中文音乐作品版权信息系统DIVA（Documentation Innovation Visionary Art）对海量的音乐作品进行管理。DIVA可凭借其强大而完善的数据库处理会员信息、作品资料及版税分配等工作内容。当会员加入音著协时，音著协会在DIVA系统中为每一名新会员建立一个专属的权利人识别编码，其中包含会员的姓名、身份证号码、住址、入会身份（词曲作者、继承人或其他著作权人）等个人信息，以及该会员公开发表的音乐作品名称和该音乐作品的详细权利信息，包括音乐的词曲作者、权益人、权利归属和权利比例等内容，这些都是附着在一首音乐作品上的重要法律信息。2009 年 2 月 1 日，音著协成为 ISWC（国际标准音乐作品编码）在中国大陆的唯一代理机构，负责 ISWC 编码在中国大陆地区的登记、发放和管理等工作。在数字音乐和网络环境下，ISWC 编码是一首音乐作品在世界范围内被有效给予辨识、版权保护的“身份证”号码。

截至 2018 年底，DIVA 数据库作品总数为 943 万余首。音著协登记作品数达 42.6 万余首，其中原创作品约 33.5 万首、影视作品约 7.6 万首、改编作品 8 000 余首、填词 5 000 余首，申请 ISWC 作品约 14.3 万首。

自 2013 年启动电子登记以来，共登记音乐作品 2.8 万余首。电子登记形式大大提高了新作品的登记效率，有效地增进了会员作品信息的更新与收集。

由于音著协是中国大陆地区唯一的音乐作品著作权集体组织，提供的版权归属证明具有重要的参考价值，因此自 2017 年起，音著协开始接受执法部门的委托，完成对侵权音乐作品版权信息的鉴定工作。2018 年，音著协帮助无锡市版权局、张家港市“扫黄打非”工作小组办公室、北京市文化市场行政执法总队、沧州市文化市场行政执法大队等单位提供相关音乐作品版权信息 6 500 余首，为司法机关最终认定非法经营等侵权行为提供了有效帮助。

三、音乐作品许可使用工作

2018 年，音著协许可使用费总收益突破 3 亿元人民币，达到 3.17 亿元（含海外收益人民币约 824 万元），创历年收入新高，较 2017 年增长 46.2%（见图 3、图 4）。

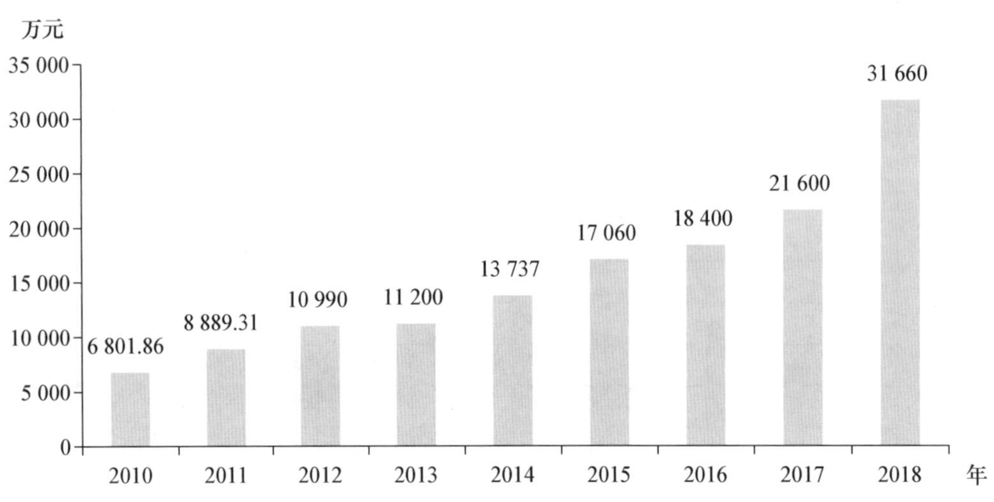

图 3　2010—2018 年许可使用费收入图

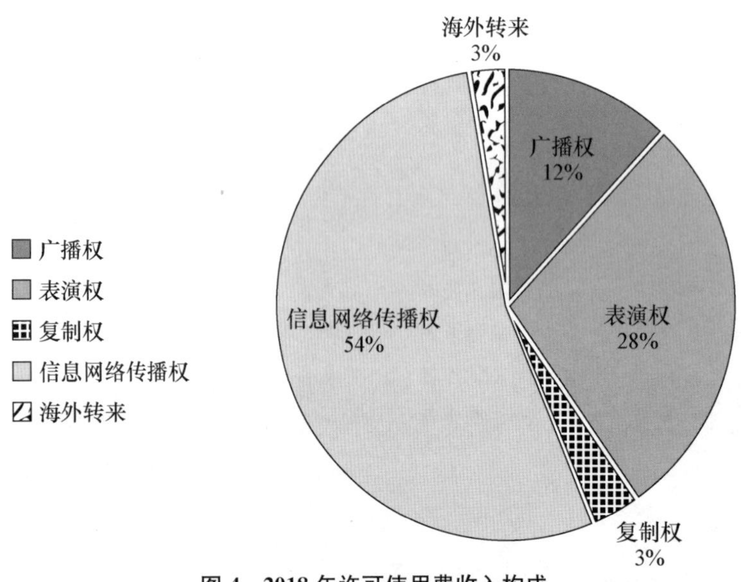

图 4　2018 年许可使用费收入构成

（一）表演权许可工作

2018年，音著协收取表演权许可使用费金额约人民币8 975万元，较2017年增长19.7%。

（1）现场表演方面。演出市场著作权许可收费平稳增长，且更加规范，许可收费金额约600万元，较前一年增长29%。

（2）背景音乐方面。以主题公园等为新增许可收费重点，继续按照“公证—诉讼—宣传”的思路开展工作，但是由于存在音乐服务公司的恶意竞争，且公开场所多改为播放海外音乐而导致公证取证难度越来越大、诉讼判赔金额仍然普遍偏低、媒体宣传还不够到位等困难，2018年许可收费金额与2017年相比基本持平。

（二）广播权许可工作

2018年，音著协收取广播权许可使用费金额约3 750万元，由于受到多家电视台组织机构改革影响，整体许可收费金额较2017年略有下降，但是实际许可覆盖面较2017年有所扩大。

广播权许可工作主要有三项内容：

（1）经过多轮谈判，音著协分别与中国广播电影电视社会组织联合会下的电视版权委员会、广播版权委员会制定了2016—2020年度许可使用费标准增长方案，这是自2010年广播电视组织向音著协缴纳音乐广播权许可使用费以来，双方首次就收费标准的提升问题达成一致。

（2）全力推进对侵权广播电视组织的诉讼。

（3）强化对广电行业的服务，增加行业间互动。

截至2018年底，已与音著协达成许可收费签约的电视台有48家、广播电台有66家，共计114家。较2017年增加了5家，其中电视台1家（银川广播电视台），广播电台4家（银川广播电视台、承德广播电视台、哈密人民广播电台、西藏人民广播电台）。

2018年，音著协继续推行“以诉促谈”的许可工作理念，发出律师函2封、催告函636封，提起诉讼6起，涉及广西广播电视台、成都广播电视台、厦门广播电视台、吉林广播电视台、济南广播电视台、南昌广播电视台等。

（三）复制权许可工作

2018年，音著协收取复制权许可使用费金额约1 100万元。

音乐类图书的著作权许可收费金额达到339万元，较2017年增长190余万元。在教科书法定许可方面，2018年5月音著协与辽海出版社签约，至此全国范围内九家出版涉音乐类教材的图书出版单位全部与音著协签署了音乐著作权许可合作协议。

影视、广告类音乐著作权许可方面，2018年许可收费总额约人民币450万元，较2017年增长了约170万元，主要影视音乐许可作品有《红海行动》《一出好戏》《永远的战友》《李茶的姑妈》《天衣无缝》《天气预爆》等。

（四）信息网络传播权许可工作

2018年，音著协收取信息网络传播权许可使用费金额约1.69亿元，较2017年增长金额约1亿元，增幅约133%。

由于此前的许可授权协议到期，音著协与腾讯公司根据腾讯音乐的市场规模、音乐使用情况等因素，重新签订了音乐著作权许可使用协议，许可使用费实现大幅增长。至此，音著协通过“数字音乐主渠道合作模式”，与包括腾讯、网易、阿里、酷狗、酷我、Apple Music、荔枝FM、陌陌、今日头条、爱奇艺、花椒直播等在内的众多数字音乐服务提供商、APP应用等主要网络音乐平台均达成了音乐许可合作协议。

针对网络侵权行为，在提起民事诉讼之外，音著协也采取向行政机关、运营平台投诉的维权方式。2018年音著协先后两次向国家版权局投诉9个网络平台：六间房、一直播、蜻蜓FM、好唱、快手、音悦台、9158、美拍、斗鱼。合计投诉侵权歌曲共计95首。在Apple Store进行维权投诉的APP约110家，与侵权使用者和Apple Store往来的邮件约1 250封，下架APP约40个。在安卓平台商店投诉维权的APP共10家，与侵权使用者和安卓平台商店往来的邮件约150封，下架APP 1个。

音乐平台之外的其他网络许可所涉使用方式包括H5页面、直播或短视频、网络宣传片、网络节目、网络翻唱、网络剧等等。

四、音乐作品许可使用费分配

2018年音著协共进行11次分配，涉及许可收入金额约1.7亿元，扣除增值税后约为1.6亿元，管理费比例约占17%（见表1）。

表1　2018音乐作品许可使用费分配明细

期数	分配号	扣税后许可金额（万元）	参与分配金额（万元）
2018年第一期	M172（2017下半年复制权使用费）	462	384
	P161（2016年现场表演许可使用费）	404	323

续表

期数	分配号	扣税后许可金额（万元）	参与分配金额（万元）
2018 年第二期	B161（2016 年互联网使用费 A）	1 792	1 566
	K161（2016 年卡拉 OK 许可使用费）	2 969	2 375
	2016 年机械表演许可使用费分配	1 231	994
	P162（2016 年背景音乐许可使用费）	1 314	1 062
2018 年第三期	M181（2018 上半年复制权使用费）	465	390
	P163（2016 年广播权许可使用费 A）	1 886	1 509
	B163（2016 年互联网使用费 B）	2 744	2 374
2018 年第四期	P164（2016 年广播权许可使用费 B）	1 990	1 654
	O171（2017 年海外协会转来使用费）	714	678

注：四舍五入至万位。

五、音乐作品诉讼维权工作

2018 年，音著协共办理民事诉讼案件 116 件。通过诉讼方式获得判赔、调解及和解金计 1.125 亿元，待执行款 32 万余元，诉讼花费总支出为 45 万余元。

重点案例：谭咏麟《银河岁月》40 载巡演金华站侵权案，蔡琴《琴暖羊城》经典金曲演唱会侵权案，黄丽玲声呐 SONAR 世界巡回演唱会广州站侵权案，协会诉上海欢乐谷背景音乐侵权案、无锡苏宁易购（聚丰园店）侵权案、南京中央商场（新街口店）侵权案、四川永辉超市（银泰城店）侵权案、江苏凤凰少年儿童出版社有限公司侵权案、珠海广播电视台侵权案、广州市广播电视台侵权案、济南广播电视台侵权案、苏州市广播电视总台侵权案、中国电信爱音乐侵权案、中国移动咪咕音乐侵权案、武汉斗鱼网络科技有限公司侵权案、小米音乐侵权案、北京快手科技有限公司侵权案。

六、信息宣传工作

2018 年，音著协继续通过网站、微信公众号、《理事工作简报》、《会讯》、《年报》等形式，向会员、使用者、政府、社会公众通报具体工作，主动做到公开、透明。

在常规工作之外，音著协就许可、维权等各方面工作中的重点内容，通过内外部平面、网络等媒体进行报道，扩大影响。包括：协会诉短视频平台“小咖秀”侵权案、协会诉珠海广播电视台侵权案、协会诉无锡苏宁易购（聚丰园店）侵权案、协会诉上海欢乐谷背景音乐侵权案、协会诉中国电信爱音乐侵权案、协会诉武汉斗鱼网络科技有限公司侵权案，广深港高铁获得协会著作权许可、协会为上海进博会使用音乐保驾护航等。

2018 年 3 月 15 日，音著协与日本远藤实歌谣音乐振兴财团在北京共同举办了“中日著作权研讨会”，促进了两国著作权保护方面的交流。

七、国际事务

2018 年，音著协与土耳其音乐著作权协会（MSG）、哈萨克斯坦音乐著作权协会（KazAK）、乌克兰音乐著作权协会（UACRR）签订了相互代表协议。至此，音著协已与 70 余家音乐著作权集体管理组织建立了相互代表关系。

（张　群）

中国音像著作权集体管理协会

2018 年是中国音像著作权集体管理协会（以下简称音集协）成立十周年。在这一年里，音集协面临解决历史遗留问题和应对来自各方挑战的艰巨任务，开启了力除积弊、创新未来的历史征程，在音集协发展史上 2018 年是具有转折意义的重要之年。在国家版权局、中央和国家机关工委的关怀和指导下，在理事会和广大会员坚定不移的支持下，音集协不断加强自身建设，勇于接受挑战，积极应对，开拓进取，敢于担当，深化服务，努力奉献，全年完成收取著作权使用费 1.91 亿元。同时，音集协锐意开拓创新收费模式，探索建立大数据收费系统、改革完善分配规则，努力促进著作权集体管理事业健康发展。

一、加强协会自身建设

（一）健全机构设置，调整领导班子，严格按章程规范议事规则和决策程序

音集协由代理总干事周亚平负责全面领导秘书处日常工作，重大事项提交理事会审议，涉及会员利益的重大事项必须经过会员大会审议，音集协内部的民主决策程序更加透明、健康；同时，监事会对会员大会负责，监事会成员列席理事会会议并对议事程序、决策事项进行监督。党支部发挥政治核心作用。音集协在议事规则、决策程序和运行机制上初步建立了公开透明、民主决策、监督制约的制度。

（二）完善协会各项管理制度

按照理事会的要求，2018年音集协实行预算管理，严格音集协的各项财务管理制度。完成了对前任总干事、法定代表人邹建华的离任审计；接受了民政部的年度报表审计，审计重点为2017年财务收支情况和报表编制等的合法合规性，经审计，会计师事务所出具了标准无保留意见审计报告。按照财政部和民政部的有关要求，结合音集协实际情况，制定了《中国音像著作权集体管理协会资产管理暂行办法》。为适应工作需要，音集协进一步加强人事制度管理，完善员工招聘、离职、转正晋升和辞退制度。音集协为发挥团队精神、增强凝聚力，对新员工进行了工作培训，对全体员工进行了团队建设培训活动。

（三）加强党建工作，确保正确的政治方向

音集协在中央和国家机关工委的领导下，以习近平新时代中国特色社会主义思想为指导，以开展“不忘初心，牢记使命”主题教育为重点，扎实开展好基层党建工作。音集协党支部组织学习《中国共产党章程》《中国共产党纪律处分条例》，传达贯彻中央和国家机关工委相关文件精神，促使党员坚定信念，强化“四个意识”，在政治上与党中央保持高度一致，自觉执行党和国家的各项方针政策。党支部通过组织全体党员和入党积极分子赴西柏坡红色教育基地开展“不忘初心，牢记使命，重温入党誓词”及参观历史博物馆“改革开放四十周年成果展”主题党日活动，加强党的组织建设，发挥党员的先进模范作用、党组织的政治核心作用。

二、坚决维护会员利益，解除与天合公司的合作关系，启动大数据著作权管理系统的改革发展

由于历史原因，音集协成立十年来一直委托天合集团及分公司开展卡拉OK收费工作，天合公司在收费过程中存在诸多违约行为，音集协于2018年11月5日发布公告解除天合集团和下属子公司代表音集协收取卡拉OK著作权费的资格，开启了清除历史积弊，在自己组建收费队伍的同时创新收费模式的全面转折，积极推进大数据著作权管理系统，实现卡拉OK曲库的正版化和信息化管理，创新卡拉OK著作权费收费模式，做到信息透明、精准收费、精准分配，彻底解决传统人工方式在收费与分配上的痛点。

三、深化会员服务，积极发展会员

截至2018年底，音集协新发展会员34家，增幅创历史新高，会员数达到了201家，包括360个著作权权利人。为了完善会员信息，加强管理，为今后大数据系统提供作品确权和标识的基础，2018年下半年开始，音集协对会员信息进行了重新采集，补充了歌曲别名、表演者别名、首次发表时间、时长、ISRC等重要项目，改变了以往会员信息资料不完整的状况，为将来大数据系统的作品确权及建立曲库、更精确地进行数据比对和分配、补充或申请ISRC码以及进行版权登记、维权等工作打下了基础。

四、积极开展许可业务，为会员实现收益

除卡拉OK歌厅的许可业务外，音集协还直接开展了卡拉OK移动包房（迷你KTV）许可业务、智能电视/智能机顶盒许可、VOD合作内容领域业务，为会员开拓了台湾地区市场，创造了收益。为避免过渡期人工收费可能带来的不规范行为，音集协于2018年下半年开始筹备启动电子合同与开票协同系统项目，现电子合同系统已经完成开发并进入试运行阶段。电子合同与开票协同系统将能很好地解决许可联络员监督、合同管理、发票开具、数据统计等工作，有利于加强对联络处的管理，统一市场规则。

五、妥善处理涉诉案件，努力解决小权利人商业诉讼及非法集体管理乱象，确保协会良性运行的健康外部环境

2018年音集协在全国28个省、区、市（除河北、宁夏、西藏及港澳台）均有与天合合作期间遗留下来的由天合子公司及其合作律所参与的维权活动，这些案件本质上都是为了促进收费，所以均按照程序正常推进。已判决执行完毕的案件全部以音集协胜诉为结果，其余大量案件还在审理和执行当中。

2018年，由于小权利人商业诉讼和非法集体管理活动持续，造成使用者享有集体管理的一站式服务降低交易成本的福利丧失，其成本被放大，甚至变得无法交易。同时权利人的收益受损，集体管理成本增加、边际效益递减，危害正常的著作权集体管理活动。音集协通过积极与法院沟通，希望通过司法实践遏制商业诉讼和非法集体管理，促进集体管理组织的健康发展。在河南省、山西省、黑龙江省的法院判决中取得了积极的效果，但在广东、湖北、浙江等地的法院判决中尚需要大量的工作。

关于《著作权法》的修法进程，音集协也在持续关注。除通过向立法部门提交书面意见，在新闻媒体组织百家会员联名发表呼吁书的方式，积极要求修改《著作权法》，增加录音制作者的广播权和表演权之外，音集协的主要负责人在参加各种会议时也为录音制作者增加两权持续发声，为作品权利人争取更多的合法权益。

六、积极完善分配机制

2018年音集协根据理事会通过的分配细则，以第三方专业调查公司出具的点播报告为基础，向会员分配 2017 年度卡拉 OK 著作权使用费 3 667 万元、VOD 商著作权使用费 644 万元。此次分配完成了从部分划档分配到完全按照市场调查的点播数据进行分配的过渡，分配完后有一些会员认为数据的代表性不够充分，其客观性和准确性不足。鉴于上述情况的存在，秘书处认为在大数据系统尚未落地之前，依靠部分 VOD 设备商提供的数据做出完全按照数据分配的方案精准度尚存在一定的抽样误差，建议 2018 年的分配以数据为主、划档为辅两相结合的方式进行，弥补抽样误差，这样可以综合平衡各方的利益，争取在无法让每个会员都完全满意的情况下做到让大家基本满意的结果。另外，对待分配年度之后加入协会的会员，按照理事会通过的分配方案，从非会员预留中进行补偿。对使用部分会员的作品进行维权诉讼所产生的赔偿，也向相应的会员单位进行了分配，本批次诉讼赔偿金分配 963 万元，涉及诉讼案件 924 起，共 34 家会员单位参与分配。

七、加强协会对外交流与宣传

为了更好地宣传集体管理的理念和大政方针，把音集协的意图快速地推进到卡拉 OK 市场，提高协会知名度及行业影响力，音集协新增设了宣传部，建立了微信公众号、微信订阅号、微博号、头条号等，配合并改版了协会的官方网站，及时更新内容，让卡拉 OK 市场及时了解音集协的大政方针，扩大音集协对社会的宣传。针对社会各界对音集协删除非会员歌曲公告、解除天合合作公告提出的种种质疑，及时通过协会的自媒体网络发声，澄清事实，消除负面影响。

为扩大音集协的社会影响，积极参加音乐产业社会活动，积极开展国际交流。2018 年上半年音集协参加由韩国音乐著作权委员会（KCC）主办的第六届中韩音乐著作权合作交流会；派员赴尼泊尔首都加德满都参加了由世界知识产权组织组织的区域性集体管理组织的培训，参加国际唱片业协会（IFPI）亚太区理事会，介绍音集协情况，加强与国际姊妹协会的合作。2018 年 11 月，周亚平代理总干事代表音集协参加中欧数字环境下版权保护与许可研讨会和第六届中国国际音乐产业大会，会上以“技术驱动，提升著作权集体管理水平”为题，与参会各方分享了音集协的大数据著作权管理系统的理念，让社会各界了解音集协未来的目标和集体管理组织对音乐产业健康发展所能起到的重要作用。其后，音集协代理总干事周亚平在全国政协就“网络环境下知识产权保护”专题调研的圆桌会议及其后的两次音乐产业大会上，均就弱势的中小权利人群体无法与掌握着互联网音乐定价权的巨头企业平等议价的现实提出异议。呼吁广大中小权利人加入音集协，将作品的信息网络传播权交给集体管理组织“集中行使”，从而形成规模化的运营能力，与拥有雄厚实力的平台平等地对话，从而抑制平台巨头利用自身优势侵占权利人利益的现象发生，为权利人谋取最大的交易红利和作品的传播价值。

（苗熙梓）

中国文字著作权协会

2018 年，中国文字著作权协会（以下简称文著协）在国家版权局、中央和国家机关工委的领导下，扎实开展党建工作，通过专业的版权服务，了解市场需求，积极主动推广会员作品，通过诉讼和调解等方式，有效维护会员合法权利，脚踏实地履行报刊转载和教科书“法定许可”稿酬收转的法定职能，稳步推进版权代理工作，创造性地将作品汇编权和戏剧表演权纳入集体管理范畴，取得显著成效，同时继续探索新时代的版权集体管理授权业务，执行中俄、中白政府间“文学作品互译出版项目”，加强国际交流和国际版权贸易，做了大量卓有成效的具体工作。

一、收转分配工作

文著协是向著作权人转付报刊转载和教科书等“法定许可”使用文字作品著作权使用费的法定机构，因此，“法定许可”稿酬收取和分配工作是文著协的法定职责，必须作为文著协工作的重中之重来抓。文著协采取主动查找作者、主动核实作者信息和转载信息、主动发放转载稿酬的“三主动”方法，向作者转付报刊转载和教科书选文稿酬，确保把每一笔稿酬发放到真正的权利人手中。文著协制定了严格的稿酬转付流程，给作者的每一笔稿酬都有作品使用明细单。保证每个月进行一次较大范围稿酬转付工作，同时，随时处理个别作者的申领稿酬。文著协确立的“三主动”方法获得广大作者好评。

2018 年，文著协全年共收取著作权使用费 1 047 万元，为文字作品著作权人收取的著作权使用费首次突破 1 000 万元，比 2017 年翻一番。其中：

报刊转载和教科书法定许可著作权使用费：181 万元；

汇编权使用费：403 万元；

信息网络传播权使用费：146 万元；

维权所得：101 万元；

版权代理著作权使用费：216 万元。

（一）具体分配情况

2018 年全年文著协共向会员和其他权利人分配

稿酬45次，总计571万元，涉及文字作品数千篇次，惠及作者、译者千余人次，图书300多种。其中：

报刊、教科书法定许可稿酬分配共计135万元，涉及文章2 048篇，惠及作者534人次；

汇编作品和版权代理稿酬分配共计335万元，涉及文章数千篇次，惠及作者、译者千余人次，图书200多种；

版权纠纷调处追讨稿酬分配共计101万元。

由于很多出版机构都在2018年12月份交纳著作权使用费，故大部分使用费的分配转付工作将在2019年第一、二季度进行。

（二）为老会员上门送稿酬

在2018年“4·26”世界知识产权宣传周期间，文著协先后拜访了著名作家毕淑敏、散文家梁衡、翻译界泰斗许渊冲和著名作家萧乾遗孀文洁若、刘绍棠遗孀曾彩美、陈敬容之女沙灵娜、建筑学家梁思成遗孀林洙、艾青遗孀高瑛、陈伯吹继承人陈佳洱、茅盾继承人沈韦宁、梁实秋女儿梁文茜等多位著作权人及其权利继承人，为他们送去稿费和样书，认真听取了他们对协会工作的建议、意见，热心解答他们的每一个提问，了解他们遇到的版权问题。这是文著协第十年开展为会员上门送稿酬活动，得到会员的好评。

2018年6月，陈建功会长和张洪波总干事还专门走访了冰心女儿吴青教授，就困扰她的很多版权问题提出专业意见和建议。

（三）发放样书

2018年文著协给权利人发放样书共计754册。

（四）提供稿酬清单

在日常的著作权使用费分配转付工作中，文著协都向权利人提供纸质版或电子版稿酬明细单，主动为会员和权利人进行稿费分配情况的核对工作，让权利人对自己获得的合法权益做到心中有数。

二、会员发展工作

会员是文著协立足业界之根本。文著协自成立以来，通过坚持不懈地为广大权利人办实事、办好事，维护他们的合法权益，在社会上产生了良好反响。2018年，新增会员656人，协会会员总数已达9 917人。

由于文著协定期发放稿费，许多权利人纷纷主动填写入会申请表要求入会，许多老会员陆续寄来新的作品备案，要求续签合同。

在2018年转付稿酬过程中，文著协通过主动查找，新增了数百位权利人信息，并通过对权利人信息库中相关信息的不断审核与补充，更新了多位权利人信息，增强了与会员联系和稿酬分配的成功率与准确率。

三、“法定许可”业务的开展

文著协根据法定职能和权利人反映，主动调查教科书出版机构和文摘类报刊社转载会员作品的付酬情况，为会员收取文摘类报刊和教科书出版社交纳的转载和选文稿费是国家法律赋予文著协的法定职能。经过文著协的不懈努力，2018年，文著协与20多家报刊社和教科书出版单位签订“法定许可”稿酬转付协议，包括上海教育出版社、中国青年出版总社、中国科学技术出版社、外语教学与研究出版社、江苏凤凰教育出版社、江苏凤凰报刊出版传媒公司、《青年文摘》杂志社、《格言》杂志社、《全国优秀作文选》杂志社、福建海峡文艺出版社、广西南方国土资源杂志社、《幼儿教育》杂志社、《演讲与口才》杂志社、广西《三月三》杂志社、《新疆党员之友》杂志社、三联书店（香港）有限公司等教科书和报刊出版机构。

其中，文著协与上海教育出版社往来联络达3年之久，2018年底双方终于签订了教科书“法定许可”稿酬转付协议。自2019年起，该社将其出版18年的九年义务教育教科书《语文》使用的文字作品稿酬依法交由文著协转付，涉及作品近千篇，惠及作者数百人。文著协正是这样一步一个脚印踏踏实实地践行“让权利人利益最大化”的宗旨。

在“法定许可”稿酬收转业务方面，无论是从合作的报刊社、出版社数量来看，还是从收取的著作权使用费数额，以及转付分配的著作权使用费金额来看，文著协都是法定许可业务开展最好的著作权集体管理组织。

四、版权集体管理业务

（一）信息网络传播权

2018年，文著协继续与北京世纪卓越信息技术有限公司（亚马逊中国）等机构合作，通过数字新媒体平台推广会员作品；同时与部分微信公众号开展合作，收取版权使用费，为会员创造更多的收益；为中宣部“学习强国”学习平台传播使用文字作品提供专业的著作权服务和稿酬转付业务。

（二）戏剧公开表演权

2018年，文著协为国内院团引进的俄罗斯著名话剧《办公室的故事》和《青春禁忌游戏》（原名为《亲爱的叶莲娜·谢尔盖耶夫娜》）继续在国内上演，观众反响热烈。

（三）汇编权

汇编作品是很多出版单位的重要产品线。多年来，文著协根据市场需求，通过授权推广会员作品，主动查找作者、译者，与很多会员和权利人建立了稳固的关系。文著协通过集体谈判、“一揽子”授权，将很多会员从烦琐的单篇文章授权业务中解脱出来，节省了会员的时间和精力，同时提高了会员的收益，解决了出版单位的后顾之忧。经过多年的实践，将作者汇编权纳入集体管理，是文著协版权集体管理工作的一大“创举”，得到会员和出版单位的认可和好评。

2018 年，文著协利用长期积累的会员和作者信息，与人民教育出版社、人民卫生出版社、人民邮电出版社、北京师范大学出版社、接力出版社、中国少年儿童新闻出版总社、长江少年儿童出版社、安徽少年儿童出版社、辽宁少年儿童出版社、河北少年儿童出版社、西南师范大学出版社、上海交通大学出版社、上海教育出版社、上海外语教育出版社、教育科学出版社、长江文艺出版社、春风文艺出版社、明天出版社、天天出版社、江苏凤凰美术出版社、吉林美术出版社、山东画报出版社、法律出版社、华语教学出版社、北教小雨文化传媒（北京）有限公司、北京韬奋书局有限责任公司、北京学而思教育科技有限公司、北京华樾教育科技有限公司、北京翰墨怡香图书发行有限责任公司、北京煊坤博文图书股份有限公司、北京创世卓越文化有限公司、北京天域北斗图书有限公司、北京奇妙之光文化传媒有限公司、网易（杭州）网络有限公司、上海盛尚文化传播有限公司、凤凰含章文化传媒（天津）有限公司、江苏亲近母语文化教育有限公司、重庆五洲世纪文化传媒有限公司、湖北知音动漫有限公司、武汉乐趣无限文化传播有限公司、广州开心教育科技股份有限公司、长沙潇岳文化传播有限责任公司、黑龙江天淘文化有限公司、陕西言鼎文化传播有限公司等逾百家出版社和民营出版策划机构签订了汇编作品授权协议 212 份，较 2017 年有较大幅度的增长，解决了数千篇次文字作品的汇编授权，涉及图书 200 余种，惠及作者译者千余人次，稿酬 400 余万元。

五、版权代理工作

（一）国内图书代理授权

由于文著协拥有陈伯吹、曹靖华等众多名家作品独家版权，教育部“全日制九年制义务教育语文新课程标准”将很多名家作品列为中小学生课外必读读物，为此，出版界对名家名作需求旺盛。2018 年，文著协为国内多家出版社、民营出版策划机构解决近百种单本图书的授权。

（二）海外版权代理

2018 年，文著协为英国、日本、新加坡、香港地区等的多家出版公司解决华文教材和教辅图书上使用华文作家作品的版权授权和稿酬转付问题。为接力出版社等出版机构引进俄罗斯著名儿童文学作家德米特里·利哈诺夫《幼小的心灵》等图书版权。

2018 年底，文著协与俄罗斯、乌克兰、亚美尼亚等的出版机构达成麦家、刘震云、阿来、盛可以、薛涛等作家的版权输出协议，合同正在陆续签署中。

（三）其他领域版权代理

2018 年，文著协为贵州茅台酒集团、华为公司解决了企业微信公众号、广告片中使用文字作品的版权授权问题，产生良好社会反响。

六、继续执行“中俄现代与经典作品互译出版项目”

（一）项目成果

2013 年，国家新闻出版总署批准文著协为“中俄经典与现代文学作品互译出版项目”的中方承办单位。通过文著协和中俄双方各出版机构以及双方翻译家的努力工作，“中俄经典与现代文学作品互译出版项目”结出丰硕的成果。截至 2018 年底，中方已出版“俄罗斯文库”中的文学作品共计 53 种，俄方已出版“中国文库”中的文学作品共计 35 种，总计 88 种，顺利完成项目的 88%。这是中国对外开展的最成功的互译出版项目。

（二）项目宣传

2018 年 8 月底，在第二十五届北京国际图书博览会期间，文著协和俄罗斯翻译学院在俄罗斯代表团展台共同举办“中俄经典与现代文学作品互译出版项目”圆桌会议，吸引了众多读者和中俄两国新闻媒体的关注。

俄罗斯出版与大众传媒署代表、俄方项目主任、青年汉学家、“品读中国”奖获得者玛莉娅·谢缅纽克，俄罗斯著名儿童文学作家尤里·涅奇波连柯，俄罗斯童书插画家叶夫根尼·波德科尔津，格奥尔基·古帕罗夫出版社社长格奥尔基·古帕罗夫，文著协总干事张洪波，中国社科院外文所译审、《外国文学动态研究》主编苏玲，参与互译项目的中国国际广播出版社、黑龙江少儿出版社、中国人民大学出版社、华东师范大学出版社、群众出版社等单位的领导和项目负责人，以及部分译者代表和媒体朋友参加了这一活动。

发布会上，中俄双方新译出版的图书精彩亮相，

“中国文库”中莫言的《红高粱》、贾平凹的《秦腔》、钱锺书的《围城》、杨绛的《干校六记》、茅盾的《子夜——茅盾作品集》、古华的《芙蓉镇》、张洁的《沉重的翅膀》、方方的《风景》、刘震云的《一句顶一万句》、黄蓓佳的《我要做个好孩子》等大家名作的俄文版悉数登场，“俄罗斯文库”中的《1962》、《再塑博斯》、《舌人》、《请叫我先知》、《一切皆可挽回》、《阳光闪耀》、《一个欧洲人的悖论》、《步履维艰》、《知识分子们的那些荒唐事》以及《俄罗斯当代戏剧集》（5卷）等作品的中文版也精彩亮相，引起了与会者的强烈关注。

《俄罗斯当代戏剧集》（5卷）是自20世纪80年代以来，中国第一次如此大规模翻译出版俄罗斯当代戏剧作品。

七、积极维护权利人的合法权益

（一）日常维权

2018年，文著协继续为维护广大权利人的合法权益而努力工作，成功调解会员梅洁、常福生等多位会员与相关出版机构的版权纠纷，追讨出版单位拖欠会员稿酬，为会员挽回经济损失100余万元，受到会员的肯定与好评。

（二）首个网络维权诉讼一审胜诉

2016年，多位会员投诉《中国学术期刊（光盘版）》电子杂志社有限公司和同方知网（北京）技术有限公司经营的中国知网未经许可，擅自上载传播大量作品，要求文著协出面依法维护会员合法权益。

文著协根据法庭建议，与对方进行长达一年半的交涉谈判，但到2018年6月，对方推翻所有谈判成果和原来达成的共识。鉴于对方出尔反尔，文著协向北京市海淀法院提出了尽快恢复诉讼程序的申请，恳请审判长及合议庭恢复诉讼程序，尽快予以判决，维护法律的公平正义。

2018年12月19日，北京市海淀法院对该案件做出一审判决：(1) 被告立即停止涉案作品的下载服务；(2) 赔偿原告文著协经济损失1万元；(3) 赔偿合理开支1万元。案件受理费1 300元由二被告共同负担。至此，该案件的一审以文著协胜诉告终。

该案的一审判决结果对于互联网环境下完善文字作品的合法传播与交易模式、保障著作权人在著作权交易中经济利益的实现具有非常积极的意义。此案一审胜诉在社会上引起较大反响。

（三）对侵权平台进行行政投诉

经过调查取证，2018年底，文著协针对部分会员的投诉将中国知网、重庆维普、超星、中国人民大学书报资料中心等知识分享平台侵犯会员权益的情况向国家版权局进行了举报，要求依法查处，维护法律的权威，维护社会公平正义和会员的合法权益。

八、版权公共服务与版权研讨

（一）为中宣部“学习强国”学习平台提供专业的著作权服务

2018年6月，中宣部开始建设“学习强国”学习平台。在文著协的建议下，从2018年6月，中宣部从文著协与其他兄弟协会抽调专人直接参与“学习强国”学习平台涉及作品版权问题的梳理和解决工作。这是党中央、国务院高度重视版权工作、认真落实《著作权法》、积极维护权利人合法权益、有效推进依法治国的重大举措，同时也大大提高了著作权集体管理组织的社会地位，宣传了著作权集体管理组织服务党和国家建设的社会职能。

（二）版权专业研讨

2018年，文著协参加中国传媒大学、北京外国语大学、北京第二外国语大学、北京印刷学院、浙江工商大学等多所高校的文化贸易、文化“走出去”的课题立项、评审、研讨活动。

多次参加与自身业务发展紧密相关的版权宣传研讨活动，包括“剑网2018”专项行动通气会、“剑网2018”调研座谈会、2018中国网络版权保护大会、全国版权监管工作会议、第九次网络信息法制圆桌会议暨“数字时代下的著作权法修改”研讨会、中国社科院著作权法修订座谈会、互联网内容平台的版权保护研讨会、区块链专题研讨会、第七届中国国际版权博览会、第五届北京国际服务贸易交易会、2018年第五届强国知识产权论坛、2018年著作权集体管理组织工作会议、中欧数字环境下版权保护与许可研讨会、中英版权研讨会、亚太版权协会年会、法国图书影视视频会议、全国博物馆版权交易研讨会、北京地区报刊社长总编培训会、浙江省新闻出版影视业“走出去”工作经验交流及培训会、中国网络文学版权保护大会、AIPPI中国分会版权热点论坛、2018海上丝绸之路文学发展国际论坛、知识经济时代知识产权国际战略研讨会、2018俄罗斯文学国际翻译家大会、中国文学国际翻译大会、中外文学翻译出版高研班、出版融合高研班等。通过参加这些活动，并在会上做专题发言，文著协积极宣传了自己的职能、宗旨和服务理念，扩大了在社会上的影响，同时有机会虚心学习国内外同行的先进经验，进一步普及版权法律知识。

九、国际交往

（一）参加俄罗斯举办的数字经济时代知识产权战略国际论坛

2018 年 4 月，应俄罗斯著作权协会和欧亚权利人协会联合会的邀请，文著协派员参加了数字经济时代知识产权战略国际论坛并发表演讲。

（二）参加俄罗斯远东媒体高峰论坛和第一届俄罗斯文学太平洋国际论坛

2018 年 6 月，应俄语世界基金会远东分会邀请，文著协派员参加俄罗斯远东媒体高峰论坛和第一届俄罗斯文学太平洋国际论坛，并发表演讲。

（三）参加莫斯科国际书展和俄罗斯文学国际翻译家大会

2018 年 9 月，应俄罗斯出版与大众传媒署的邀请，文著协派员参加了第四届俄罗斯文学国际翻译家大会和莫斯科国际书展，在莫斯科书展上举办中俄互译出版项目新书发布会、新书成果展，接受媒体采访，展示中国文化的魅力，展示文著协的工作成果，吸引了众多参展商和观众，获得了良好的宣传效果。

（四）参加土库曼斯坦阿什哈巴德国际书展

应土库曼斯坦国家出版局邀请，文著协派员参加了阿什哈巴德国际书展。土库曼斯坦副议长、副总理和当地有关政要，中国驻土库曼斯坦大使孙炜东专门视察了中国展台。文著协代表团应邀参加了中国驻土库曼斯坦大使馆举办的国庆招待会，向驻土库曼斯坦大使馆赠送中俄互译出版项目新书和有关出版社的新书。

（五）接待俄罗斯青年代表团

2018 年 11 月，文著协接待了来自俄语世界基金会组织远东分会组织的访华青年代表团一行七人，双方就我国“一带一路”政策、中俄互译出版项目情况等进行了友好深入的交流。

（六）参加国际复制权组织联合会亚太委年会

2018 年 5 月，文著协派员参加了在香港举办的国际复制权组织联合会（IFRRO）亚太委年会，并在会上做了年度工作报告，同时与前来参会的有关国家和地区的版权集体管理组织代表进行了深入交流，进一步增进了相互了解。

（七）参加 2018 海上丝绸之路国际文学发展论坛

2018 年 11 月，应广东省作家协会邀请，张洪波总干事参加 2018 海上丝绸之路国际文学发展论坛并做专题发言，同时，协助邀请罗马尼亚、越南、印度等国版权集体管理协会领导、出版商代表和著名汉学家参会。

十、对外宣传

（一）微信公众号

本着与时俱进、低碳环保的原则，文著协自 2017 年起不再印刷邮寄纸质版《通讯》，取而代之的是通过微信公众号、官网、微博、博客定期推送文章，介绍文著协工作动态，以及有关版权新闻。2018 年通过微信公众号共推送文章 57 篇，截至 2018 年底，关注文著协微信公众号的总人数为 2 507 人，阅读数量最多的两篇文章分别是《文著协提起首个网络维权诉讼一审胜诉》（1 802 人阅读）和《知产实务的现状与未来》（1 005 人阅读）。

文著协依法制定了《微信公众号转载文章图片版权规则》，要求公众号在转载他人文章前，每一篇都提前征求作者许可，并支付转载稿费，每千字 100 元。这一做法得到很多媒体的积极评价和作者好评。

微信公众号的推出在很大程度上起到宣传和扩大协会影响、普及版权法律知识的社会效果。

（二）在线版权沙龙

随着文著协业务范围的扩大和业务量的增多，文著协在业内的影响力也逐年增强。作为我国唯一的文字著作权集体管理组织，文著协经常会接到各使用单位、平台提出的关于著作权保护、稿酬转付等方面的各种问题。针对这一情况，文著协决定组织“出版编辑版权沙龙”，通过网络召集各出版机构的编辑人员，针对在出版编辑实务中遇到的各种版权问题共同研讨。

2018 年共策划组织线上沙龙九期，参加人员已达 3 000 多人次。沙龙研讨的问题不断深化，在出版领域的影响逐步增加，在宣传文著协法定职能和业务、彰显文著协的专业能力方面起到了非常积极的作用。《中国新闻出版广电报》《中国知识产权报》《文艺报》等多次进行专题报道，多篇公众号文章被其他公众号转载。

（张洪波）

中国摄影著作权协会

2018 年是中国摄影著作权协会（以下简称摄著协）与行政机关脱钩后的第一年。摄著协按照中共中央办公厅、国务院办公厅印发的《行业协会商会与行政机关脱钩总体方案》中“促进行业协会商会成为依法设立、自主办会、服务为本、治理规范、行为自律的社会组织……充分发挥行业协会商会在经济发展新常态中的独特优势和应有作用”的精神，

激发协会内在活力和发展动力，在国家版权局的领导下，大胆探索积极开拓，在发展会员、推动教科书依法转付摄影作品使用费、积极配合和参与国家修改《著作权法》、继续推进与国际组织开展版权保护合作等方面均取得了显著成绩。

一、创新工作机制，加大为会员服务的力度和手段

近年来，摄著协秉承积极发展会员，做好服务会员就是做好摄影版权保护工作的理念，积极努力拓展会员队伍，真正使之成为在全国具有广泛代表性的集体管理组织。

几年来，摄著协把发展会员的工作触角延伸到全国300多个地市级城市，建立了包括这些城市在内加30个各类全国性摄影协会的首席代表工作机制，在基层建立如此庞大的发展会员队伍力量，在全国摄影界唯摄著协一家。摄著协以这种方式和激励机制统领和带动多层面的力量大力发展会员，使得协会近年来每年平均发展会员人数在3 000人以上。截至2018年底，摄著协会员总数已达到1.8万人，成为中国五家集体管理组织会员最多的协会。

二、推动教科书依法向权利人支付作品使用费

摄著协大力发展会员，为会员争取越来越多的权利，为做好集体管理收费业务打下坚实基础。2018年摄著协执行教科书法定许可法律规定，克服困难努力与教科书出版社沟通联络，积极推动教科书使用摄影作品收费工作。一年来，摄著协与人民教育出版社、北京师范大学出版社和上海教育出版社等单位进行沟通，积极促进收费业务工作开展。2018年摄著协对教科书法定许可使用摄影作品收费数额实现历史性突破。

三、为了保护会员的权利，重拳打击网络侵权

2018年7月，摄著协会员武强的一组19幅摄影作品《中原饭场》，在没有获得摄著协授权的情况下，被几家在全国具有重要影响力的媒体公众号转发，导致近百家各类微信公众号连续转发。这一案例说明微信公众号侵权使用摄影作品现象依然严重，为此，摄著协迅速行动积极为会员依法维权，快速把首发侵权的几家媒体诉上法庭。由于摄著协所管理的会员作品权属明确、证据清晰，加之相关法院高效审理快速结案，使得侵权者依法一一向摄著协进行赔偿。这一案例是摄著协成立以来，为会员单次维权作品数量众多、上诉媒体数量众多、获得赔偿数额最高的典型案例，亦是摄著协为了保护会员的权利，重拳打击网络侵权的典型案例。

四、继续推进与国际组织开展版权保护合作

开展国际版权保护合作，是做好集体管理工作的重要内容。在国家版权局的大力支持下，2017年摄著协在纽约与美国、英国、法国、西班牙、瑞典、日本和澳大利亚版权保护组织签订了版权保护协议。按照协议约定先由这7个国家为中国摄影家进行版权保护，在上述国家的互联网、公共传播领域（包括有线、无线电视和卫星传播）、展览、广告、出版（书籍、报纸、期刊）、租赁和租借、任何类型的复制以及私人复制等多个领域为中国摄影家保护版权，这使摄著协版权保护开启国际合作迈出了重要一步。2018年6月，摄著协又与比利时SABAM签订版权保护相互代表协议，进一步扩大国际合作。目前摄著协正在积极为2019年加入国际作者和作曲者协会联合会（CISAC）做准备，摄著协今后可以获得国际组织的业务指导、技术资源支持和人员培训等，为摄著协集体管理工作向国际化方向发展而努力。

五、积极参与配合国家有关部门修改《著作权法》

2018年初，国务院法制办向摄著协致函，通过摄著协征求摄影权利人对《著作权法（修订草案送审稿修改稿）》的意见。1月3日，摄著协联合中国摄影家协会召开了摄影界修法征求意见座谈会，就修改稿征求广大摄影家的意见。来自各全国性摄影团体、机构和不同层面的摄影家以及老一辈摄影家的继承人出席了这次座谈会。会后，摄著协把摄影家的意见进行归纳整理，形成了《摄影界关于对〈著作权法〉（修订草案送审稿修改稿）的意见和建议》提交国务院法制办。

（朱宝祺）

中国电影著作权协会

2018年，中国电影著作权协会（以下简称影著协）在国家版权局的指导下，在会员单位的支持下，不断深入学习党的十九大精神，以习近平新时代中国特色社会主义思想为指导，围绕电影著作权保护和管理等重点任务，开展了系列工作。

一、完成脱钩工作

2018年1月10日，根据北京市外办的要求，影著协上报关于举办国际会议预报表。国家机构改革后，影著协按照要求，向中宣部填报行业组织以及涉企收费等相关信息。根据《著作权集体管理条例》的规定，协会继续接受国家版权局的管理，报送协会业务情况，接受监督。2018年2月8日，协会与其他四家著作权集体管理组织共同参加了由国家版权局版权管理司召开的 2018 年著作权集体管理组织工作会议。按照原国家新闻出版广电总局脱钩方案的要求，影著协于 2018 年 3 月 14 日，到民政部将社团法人登记证书更换为没有主管部门的新证书并按版权局版权管理司要求进行备案。同时，影著协党建、人事、机构、财务、外事等相关工作无缝转接到相关管理部门。

二、宣传与交流工作

（一）参与立法、司法和行政管理机关相关活动、提供咨询并协助执法

（1）2018 年 1 月，影著协接到国务院法制办关于修改《著作权法》（修订草案送审稿修改稿）的定向征求意见函。经认真研究阅读，并结合会员单位长期以来反馈的意见建议，协会回函就相关条款的修改提出意见。

（2）2018 年 7 月，影著协参加了国家版权局在京召开的全国版权执法监管工作会议。这次会议是深化党和国家机构改革，中宣部统一管理新闻出版、版权工作之后召开的第一次全国性的版权工作会议。通过会议，影著协工作人员深入学习贯彻习近平新时代中国特色社会主义思想和党的十九大精神，领会中央领导同志的重要批示，了解当前版权执法监管工作面临的新任务新要求，以及“剑网 2018”专项行动等版权执法监管重点工作的部署，认真听取了中宣部副部长、国家新闻出版署署长、国家版权局局长庄荣文在会议上的讲话。会议结束后，协会参会人员还与相关地方执法人员就电影作品的版权保护问题进一步交流。

（3）2018 年 1 月和 7 月，影著协分别参加国家版权局、国家互联网信息办公室、工业和信息化部、公安部在京联合召开的“剑网 2017”专项行动成果通气会和“剑网 2018”专项行动通气会。协会向会员单位宣传有关行动成果和计划，鼓励大家积极参与，主动维护自身权益。

（4）2018 年 4 月和 6 月，影著协理事长应邀出席国家版权局主办的“2018 中国网络版权保护大会”和国家版权局与世界知识产权组织共同主办的“电影的经济及文化价值与版权保护高端论坛”，并分别做主题发言。6 月，协会还应邀参加了国家版权局和英国知识产权局共同主办的中英版权圆桌会议。

（5）2018 年 1 月，影著协收到黑龙江省版权局发来的《关于协助认定出版物著作权的函》并随即展开工作。根据其提供的电影作品信息，整理出涉及影著协会员单位出品的电影作品，并向该局复函说明鉴定情况。

（6）就伊犁州税务稽查部门、内蒙古版权局等部门关于影视版权认证方面的来电，提供咨询。

（二）加强与权利人、使用者及相关机构的交流与调研

（1）2018 年 6 月和 10 月，影著协分别在第二十一届上海国际电影节的国际电影市场和第七届中国国际版权博览会设立展位。参展期间，影著协通过宣传片、展板和宣传手册相结合的形式，向国内外嘉宾全面展示了影著协成立近十年来在开展电影著作权集体管理工作、维护会员权益和促进产业发展方面所做的工作。参展人员还与与会的领导、嘉宾和专业人士，进行了深入的探讨和交流，对进一步完善和发展影著协的工作具有重要意义。

电影节期间，影著协通过向来展位参观的人员发放问卷的形式，完成了一个小范围的调研。从调研数据来看，大家对电影版权的重视程度显著提高，只是对电影版权的相关了解还有待提高。相关数据为协会开展工作指明了方向。

版权博览会期间，影著协因优秀的展示和宣传工作，获颁“金慧奖”优秀组织奖。

（2）影著协还通过参加由中国版权协会召开的网络监测会议、国家行政学院举办的“霍尔果斯影视文化行业协会授牌仪式暨影视文化产业项目推介会”等活动，加强与各界的交流。

四、版权管理相关工作

（一）相关调研

随着版权意识的提高，出版社、商场、轮船、休闲度假区等使用者纷纷电话咨询电影作品大规模使用方式的版权许可问题。鉴于此，协会申请承接了国家版权局的调研项目“传统影院外放映电影作品的版权问题”。希望通过实地调研以及研讨会等方式，探寻适合的解决方案。

（二）“学习强国”学习平台项目

2018 年 5 月，国家版权局版权管理司副司长汤兆志带队五家著作权集体管理组织相关负责人参加了中宣部宣传舆情研究中心（以下简称中心）召开的“学习强国”学习平台版权保护工作会议。2018 年 6 月，应中心要求，影著协抽调一名骨干人员到中心版权组工作，负责学习平台视频内容的版权管理工作。经过对平台已有视频内容及其获取版权许可的情况的梳理，影著协发现平台绝大部分的视频内容存在版权风险。结合中心对平台的规划以及上线期限等因素，经过与影著协法律顾问等法律专家的研讨，影著协于 2018 年 7 月向中心提交了平台视

频内容版权管理方案。方案被中心采纳。随后，协会按照此方案，开始具体的版权核实、签约等工作。截至2018年底，已经为平台近千部作品排除版权风险，为平台正式上线提供支持。

（三）致敬改革开放40周年纪录片项目

2018年11月，影著协收到国家版权局传达的中宣部新闻局来函，要求影著协协助解决纪录片《我们一起走过——致敬改革开放40周年》中采用的电影画面的相关使用权。影著协对函件提及的任务十分重视，于收函当日确定专责此项工作的联络员，并向函件中的联系人了解情况。鉴于纪录片即将公映，时间紧迫，且内容涉及电影作品17部，其中《霹雳舞》《泰坦尼克号》《追捕》《狐狸的故事》《望乡》等5部影片涉及境外制片方，影著协随即回函说明相关情况。随后，影著协会开始与国内制片方以及广播权和信息网络传播权的继受方核实版权。同时，跟权利方和纪录片制片方协商授权事宜。截至2018年12月底，已完成9部影片的授权工作。

（史文霞）

张家港市版权局

张家港市版权局以“全国版权示范城市”为新的起点，围绕创意港城、版权兴业主线，真抓实干、主动作为，全市版权各项工作继续保持领先水平。

版权示范创建成效明显。3家单位获评“江苏省版权示范单位”，2家单位被确定为2018年度苏州市版权工作示范单位推进指导性计划项目。版权创造量质同步提升。2018年全市成功登记一般作品25 667件，4件作品荣获江苏省优秀版权奖，1件作品荣获苏州市优秀版权奖，15件作品入选第七届张家港优秀版权作品。版权管理工作再铸辉煌。江苏国泰新点软件有限公司荣获“中国版权金奖”推广运用奖。张家港幸运金属工艺品有限公司荣获“2018年度中国版权新锐企业”。张家港市版权局连续六年获评“全国查处侵权盗版案件有功单位”，查处的张家港“4•28”侵犯著作权案被国家版权局列为挂牌督办案件，并获评“2018年度江苏省打击侵权盗版十大案件办案单位”；查处的“一本读小说网”侵犯著作权案被江苏省版权局列为挂牌督办案件。

1. 在第七届中国国际版权博览会上，江苏国泰新点软件有限公司荣获“中国版权金奖”推广运用奖
2. 张家港市版权局获评“2018年度江苏省打击侵权盗版十大案件办案单位”
3. 在第十一届中国版权年会上，张家港幸运金属工艺品有限公司荣获“2018年度中国版权新锐企业”奖

2019年6月11日，中宣部版权管理局副局长赵秀玲听取廊坊市创建全国版权示范城市工作汇报，河北省委宣传部副巡视员吴忠华，廊坊市委书记冯韶慧，市委副书记、副市长胡晓军参加

廊坊市版权局

近年来，在国家版权局、河北省版权局关心指导下，廊坊市建立起完善的版权管理工作体系，为提升城市自主创新能力，更好地为经济建设服务提供了有力保障。

一、落实专项资金，健全版权工作队伍

一是从2017年开始，廊坊市财政每年都安排版权工作专项资金，用于版权宣传、教育、培训、作品登记及软件正版化等项工作。二是从2018年起，采取购买服务方式成立廊坊市版权服务站并由河北省版权局、河北省版权保护中心授牌，接受廊坊市新闻出版局工作安排、指导，全力开展版权作品登记、著作权法律知识宣传、版权咨询等项工作。三是2018年以来，共在全市设立23个版权服务工作站，完善版权工作社会化服务队伍。2018年全市登记作品数量占河北省登记总量的40%，位居全省首位。

二、加强制度设计，培育壮大版权产业

一是在廊坊电视台、电台开设“版权产业巡礼”“版权知识点”专栏，集中展示廊坊通过创建全国版权示范城市，引领培育版权产业发展的情况。二是印制折页、手册、鼠标垫、文件夹等宣传品，积极开展版权知识宣传活动；利用廊坊日报社3 000名小记者，将版权知识带进学校、带进社区、带进机关；利用公交车广告、手机短信推送版权保护知识宣传语。三是2018年以来，累计组织版权登记培训班6次、版权知识讲座16期、作品征集比赛2次，通过主动服务、宣讲政策，引导帮助企业和个人自主创新并主动申报版权登记。

三、强化宣传引导，提升版权认知水平

近年来，廊坊市委、市政府相继出台《关于加强知识产权保护和运用工作的实施意见》等文件，全力打造知识产权强市。在版权产业发展方面，依托《只有红楼梦》戏剧幻城、大厂影视小镇等重点项目，推动以影视产业为龙头的文化创意产业集群发展；发挥廊坊一二O六印刷厂、纸辉家（廊坊）包装科技有限公司等的引领作用，引导全市包装印刷企业在文创产品开发、包装设计等方面登记版权、利用版权，促进企业转型升级；推动乐聪版权文化科技产业园项目，打造以版权输出、版权授权衍生配套为特色的版权文化科技产业园；围绕景泰蓝等传统工艺，挖掘和培育具有市场潜力和文化特色的工艺美术品牌；以茗卡通等为引领，发展漫画动画游戏原创，带动文创衍生品生产，促进互联网+、动漫游戏、文化科技融合为一体的高新技术企业发展。

2018年7月5日，廊坊市召开创建全国版权示范城市工作推进会

2019年3月14日，廊坊市委常委、宣传部部长、统战部部长奚献军（站立者右三）到河北乐聪网络科技股份有限公司调研版权工作

2019年5月14日，廊坊市委副书记、副市长胡晓军（主席台左二）主持召开全市使用正版软件推进会议

2019年6月11日，中宣部版权管理局副局长赵秀玲（右一）考察廊坊市一二O六印刷厂艺术品复制车间，市委副书记、副市长胡晓军（右二）陪同

中国人民大学国家版权贸易基地

中国人民大学国家版权贸易基地于2007年8月由国家版权局批复建设，2007年10月正式挂牌成立，为我国第一家国家版权贸易基地。基地定位于国家级版权产业要素市场与版权资产管理综合服务平台，在中关村拥有6.7万平方米的写字楼用于版权相关企业集聚及创新型版权企业孵化培育，先后探索开展了版权交易服务、版权资产评估、版权争议调解、版权理论研究、版权管理咨询、版权行业交流、版权企业集聚、《中国版权年鉴》编纂等服务版权产业发展的业务。

国家版权贸易基地
NATIONAL COPYRIGHT TRADE CENTER
国家版权局 制发
2007年8月6日

中国人民大学 国家版权贸易基地
版权评估中心

中关村
版权争议调解中心
Zhongguancun Copyright Dispute Mediation Centre

特色服务项目

版权资产评估

基地建有版权评估中心，与北京银行、中国银行、中国农业银行和中国进出口银行、上海文化产权交易所、深圳文化产权交易所等机构建立合作关系，围绕版权质押融资提供专业的版权资产评估服务。累计评估作品23部，评估价值超过7亿元，帮助企业实现融资近3亿元。

版权管理咨询

基地先后受文化和旅游部、国家文物局和国家版权局委托，研究起草了《艺术表演团体知识产权工作指南》《博物馆馆藏资源著作权、商标权和品牌授权操作指引》《出版企业版权管理指南》，为企业开展版权相关管理提供指引，并开展咨询服务。

版权行业交流

基地持续举办版权人沙龙、互联网文化沙龙、版权相关研讨会和高峰论坛等活动，促进行业交流与合作。截至2019年11月，已持续举办版权人沙龙38期、互联网文化沙龙6期、版权相关研讨会10期，每期都围绕当前行业热点问题展开深入探讨，促进学界、企业界和政府主管部门之间的深度交流。

全国大学生版权征文活动

基地于2019年承办第十一届全国大学生版权征文活动，并在成都举行颁奖仪式。此次颁奖仪式首次增设学术演讲和交流环节，旨在充分展现在校大学生版权理论研究水平和创新活力，打造全国性人才培养高端平台和大学生学术交流平台。

图片注释

1. 2012年1月6日，时任国家版权局副局长阎晓宏（左）与时任中国人民大学党委常务副书记牛维麟（右）为基地版权评估中心揭牌
2. 自2008年6月始，基地已持续举办38期版权人沙龙、6期互联网文化沙龙和10期版权相关研讨会
3. 2013年12月，基地举办第一期文化产业版权运营与管理高级研修班，国家版权局版权管理司司长于慈珂（前排左七）为学员授课
4. 2019年12月4日，第十一届全国大学生版权征文活动颁奖仪式在成都举办。图为中宣部版权管理局局长于慈珂（右一）为特等奖获奖代表颁奖

合力共治、开创花样版权保护“柯桥模式”

——中国轻纺城花样版权保护纪略

以中国轻纺城为龙头的轻纺产业群是绍兴市柯桥区主要的支柱产业。从1988年的一条“布街”起步，中国轻纺城至今已发展成为全球较大的纺织产品集散中心。目前，市场集群面积372万平方米，营业用房2.5万余间，经营品种5万余种，经营户2.9万多户，市场内有1 100余家国（境）外常驻代表机构，常驻境外专业采购商5 500多人，市场日客流量10万人次，销售网络遍布世界187个国家和地区。

作为轻纺产业的重要组成部分，面料花样是具有核心地位的知识产权。纺织品花样版权登记保护工作是保护纺织品花样设计者合法权益的有力手段，也是增强柯桥区纺织品核心竞争力、促进轻纺城市场长期繁荣稳定的重要举措。柯桥区在创新服务的同时，也在不断加强保护力度，提高市场经营户和企业加强纺织品开发创新的积极性，营造尊重知识产权、保护知识产权的良好氛围。2008年，中国轻纺城花样版权登记管理保护办公室（以下简称“花样办”）应市场发展需要正式诞生。

一、政府重视，政策支持，开创版权保护新局面

2008年，柯桥区政府专门建立由柯桥区委宣传部、区府办、区市场监管局、区文广局、区法院、区检察院等15个部门组成的加强中国轻纺城知识产权保护联席会议机制，由政府分管领导作为联席会议召集人，并在中国轻纺城市场监管分局设立花样办。政府还下发了《关于加强中国轻纺城知识产权保护工作的几点意见》《中国轻纺城纺织品花样版权登记管理保护办法》等文件，制定出台奖励政策，每年对市场前20位花样版权登记大户实施资金奖励。2017年，柯桥区委、区政府又出台了《关于进一步加强中国轻纺城花样版权登记保护工作的几点意见》，重新成立了中国轻纺城花样版权登记保护联席会议制度，联席会议办公室设在区市场监管局。随着纺织产业和创意产业的不断发展，纺织品花样更新换代日益加快，对纺织品花样版权登

记保护工作提出了更高的要求，花样办每年都会结合花样版权登记保护，开展形式多样的宣传活动，如围绕“4•26”世界知识产权日、春秋国际纺织品博览会等做集中宣传，邀请专家讲课普及版权保护知识等。

二、创新服务，规范管理，完善版权保护新机制

2009年1月，浙江省版权主管部门正式委托授权花样办受理中国轻纺城市场内纺织品经营者花样版权登记申请，对花样版权登记申请进行初审，代发省版权局作品登记证。柯桥区市场监管局专门划出超百平方米办公室区域，落实12名工作人员受理版权登记。2015年前后，在创意园等地新设5个受理点方便企业登记，并建立了重点经营户联系制度。2017年，柯桥区市场监管局又招收10名工作人员充实到花样办，并争取到了省版权局授权的审理及直接打印发证，提高了版权登记速度。

三、部门联动，齐抓共管，确立版权保护新模式

市场监管部门创造性地将《著作权法》和《反不正当竞争法》相关条文优势互补结合运用，通过认定市场知名商品，将花样作为其特有包装装潢的保护思路，开展综合行政保护，开创了市场监管部门参与花样版权保护的先河。2009年，由花样办在浙江省版权主管部门的协调支持下，柯桥牵头联络江苏南通、山东潍坊、广东佛山三地纺织品集散中心签订《四地纺织品市场版权保护与合作协议》。2017年又组建了由市场监管部门、文广部门、公安部门组成的联合执法机构，市场监管部门负责进行花样侵权行为的现场笔录，文广部门负责证据先行保存登记，扣押涉案物品，公安部门负责现场治安维护，各部门各司其职又相互配合，形成合力，增强执法威力。2017年，柯桥区市场监管局还联合区人民法院出台了《促进中国轻纺城花样版权保护实施办法》；在花样办设立中国轻纺城市场巡回法庭，靠前审理轻纺城市场花样版权侵权纠纷案件；设立中国轻纺城市场巡回调集室，就地引调轻纺城市场的花样版权纠纷。建立行政和司法联合执法、协同保护的工作机制，推行简易维权模式：权利人持有版权证投诉至花样办，花样办移送至柯桥区人民法院快速立案，由花样办和法院联合去侵权门市部处理花型投诉。

截至2019年7月底，花样办已受理花样版权登记申请48 213件，核发作品登记证36 258本，调解争议纠纷2 522件，行政查办案件66件，司法立案2 392件，办结2 346件，全面建立了行政保护、司法保护、仲裁保护、自律保护“四位一体”保护体系，筑起了市场花样版权保护的“防护墙”。2017年4月，全国人大

4

5

6

著作权法执法调研组对柯桥区的花样版权保护模式给予了充分肯定，认为柯桥区的做法形式新颖，并且在保护版权、鼓励创新、推动市场发展方面成果明显，全国独树一帜。2018年6月，世界知识产权组织（WIPO）副总干事西尔维•福尔班女士考察轻纺城花样保护工作，对柯桥的纺织品花样版权保护工作给予了充分肯定。2011年、2013年，花样办先后被国家版权主管部门、国家知识产权战略实施工作部际联席会议办公室授予国内专业市场“全国版权示范单位”和“国家知识产权战略实施工作先进单位”称号。中国轻纺城市场也于2012年被国家版权主管部门授予“全国版权示范基地” 称号。2018年，在国家版权主管部门与世界知识产权组织（WIPO）合作开展的2018年“中国版权金奖”奖项评选中，花样办获得了“保护奖”。2019年4月，花样办协助完成浙江省第七届“知识产权杯”创意设计大赛颁奖典礼，本次大赛历时4个月，共有11所在绍高校2 300余名大学生参与，收到各类参赛作品1 700余件，创历届赛事纪录新高。与浙江工业大学之江学院合作开发的中国轻纺城花样版权数据中心库及花型图案比对系统通过柯桥区政府部门的论证及立项，目前已开发完成并投入试运用，并争取省版权部门认可把全省其他地区的纺织品备案登记花样数据归并至柯桥区新开发的数据中心库，建成浙江省统一的数据中心库，扩容后的轻纺城花样版权数据中心库有近10万个花样版权数据。这是系统开发后的创造性应用，历史性地使全省纺织品花样备案登记借助中心数据库能够进行省辖范围比对，意义重大。

7

8

图片注释

1. 浙江省政府主要领导调研中国轻纺城花样版权登记受理点
2. 全国人大著作权法执法调研组调研花样办
3. 西尔维·福尔班女士和国家版权主管部门领导到花样办考察
4. 柯桥区政府领导调研中国轻坊城花样办
5. 花样办荣获“中国版权金奖”保护奖
6. 浙江省第七届“知识产权杯”创意设计大赛合影
7. 现场纠纷调解
8. 花样办工作人员检查布匹生产企业的仓库
9. 行政司法联合维权
10. 中国轻纺城知识产权巡回审判庭正式揭牌

9

10

中国南通家纺城版权事务服务有限公司

中国南通家纺城版权事务服务有限公司成立于1997年3月8日，20多年来，在各级版权管理部门的大力指导下，共登记美术作品56 805件，工作得到了国家、省、市、区各级领导的充分肯定。2005年，被国家版权主管部门授予“全国版权保护示范单位”称号。2008年4月，成立了专业市场的知识产权巡回审判庭。2008年10月，被世界知识产权组织（WIPO)授予“版权创意金奖”。2009年3月，举行了“世界知识产权组织版权保护优秀案例示范点项目专家会议暨合作签约仪式”。2010年7月9日上午，中国国家版权主管部门和世界知识产权组织共同在北京发布《加强版权保护对中国南通家纺产业发展的影响调研报告》。2010年7月，中央宣传主管部门组织新华社、《人民日报》等9大国内主流媒体集中报道南通家纺城版权保护经验，南通家纺城版权事务服务有限公司被中国版权协会评为“中国版权最具影响力企业”。2013年度、2017年度分别荣获国家版权主管部门颁发的“查处侵权盗版案件有功单位三等奖”。2018年荣获国家知识产权主管部门颁发的“知识产权保护规范化市场”。2018年度荣获江苏省“打击侵权盗版十大办案单位”。

1. 张謇杯·2018中国国际家用纺织产品设计大赛颁奖盛典暨第十一届中国(川姜）家纺画稿交易会开幕式
2. 2019年3月，中央宣传主管部门版权管理主管部门负责人段玉萍视察南通家纺城版权事务服务有限公司版权登记工作
3. 2019年7月2日，中央宣传主管部门国家版权管理部门领导赵秀玲视察南通家纺城版权事务有限公司版权登记、调解工作
4. 2017年度荣获国家版权主管部门颁发的“查处侵权盗版案件有功单位三等奖”
5. 2008年10月，世界知识产权组织授予南通家纺城版权事务服务有限公司“版权创意金奖”
6. 2005年，南通家纺城版权事务服务有限公司被国家版权主管部门授予“全国版权保护示范单位”称号

2018年4月11日，《习近平谈治国理政》第二卷多语种图书首发式在英国伦敦隆重举行。英国约克公爵安德鲁王子（左四），中国中宣部副部长、国务院新闻办公室主任蒋建国（右四）等一同为新书揭幕

中国外文出版发行事业局

中国外文出版发行事业局，又称中国国际出版集团（China International Publishing Group，CIPG），是承担党和国家书、刊、网络对外宣传任务的新闻出版机构，是中国历史悠久、规模宏大的综合性专业对外传播机构。

中国外文局下辖7家出版社、5家杂志社以及中国网、中国国际图书贸易集团公司、当代中国与世界研究院、融媒体中心、翻译资格考评中心等20余家单位，在美国、加拿大、英国、德国、法国等14个国家和地区设有26家驻外机构，形成了涵盖互联网和多媒体业务、书刊出版发行、对外翻译、海外舆情与智库研究、国际交流、教育培训及社会事业等领域的事业格局和覆盖世界主要国家、地区的对外传播格局。每年以40余种文字出版5 000余种图书，以14个文种编辑34本多语种期刊，书刊发行到世界180多个国家和地区，网络受众遍及世界各地。

"中国版权金奖"颁奖仪式

西安电视剧版权交易中心

西安电视剧版权交易中心（以下简称"西安版权"）是2010年8月经国家广电主管部门批准设立的专业影视版权交易机构，由陕文投集团联合上市公司、民营资本共同发起设立。2014年8月，被国家版权主管部门评为"全国版权示范单位"。2018年，获国家版权主管部门和世界知识产权组织联合颁发的"中国版权金奖"管理奖。自2011年以来，先后五次荣获陕西省委宣传主管部门颁发的"全省宣传思想文化工作创新奖"。西安版权坚持"版权社会化服务+版权市场化运营"的基本理念，以"版权+金融""版权+科技"为核心，从影视版权服务领域切入，同时涉及图文版权、动漫游戏版权、非遗文创版权等领域。西安版权积极打造版权价值发现、版权价值呈现、版权价值兑现平台，在影视大数据版权评估、影视众创空间综合服务领域取得了显著成绩。

地址：陕西省西安市曲江新区雁塔南路300-9号陕西文化大厦　电话：029-89131653
公司官网：http://www.ctvtc.cn/

"影视+大数据"探索　西部国家版权交易中心揭牌　第十届全国电视制片业十佳颁奖礼

版权扫描

BAN QUAN SAO MIAO

版权界动态

◆立　法

【摄影界为《著作权法》修改稿献言献策】 2018年1月3日，中国摄影家协会与中国摄影著作权协会联合举行座谈会，就《著作权法（修订草案送审稿修改稿）》（以下简称修改稿）倾听摄影家的意愿和心声、征求摄影家意见，意在向国家有关部门反映摄影家的诉求，力争使修改后的《著作权法》能够准确反映和切实保障广大摄影家应有的权益。

座谈会上，来自各摄影团体、机构，不同层面的摄影家以及老一辈摄影家的继承人，对修改稿畅所欲言、各抒己见，大家普遍认为，修改稿中所界定的摄影作品原件被高度重视，这标志着在国家法律中已经为摄影创作的客观表达下了一项全新且十分明确的定义，这也是摄影界几年来经过不懈努力为广大摄影家争取到的一项新权利，是全国摄影人共同努力得到的回报。

此外，与会人员还提出了很多修改意见：（1）修改稿对职务摄影作品的新规定，或将会使这部分作品的权利归属产生新的复杂关系，对这些作品的版权保护及作品的使用和传播带来新的问题，不利于平衡各方的利益关系；（2）修改稿延长了摄影作品保护期后，或把那些在摄影史上具有重要地位的一大批老摄影家的经典作品排除在外；（3）鉴于中国已经成为国际最大的艺术品交易市场，摄影作品在其中已经形成旺盛的活力和良好的发展势头，修改稿可增加对视觉艺术作品进行追续权保护；（4）鉴于国家对其他法定许可使用各类作品已经做了较详细的制度规范，修改稿可对电视台使用摄影作品向摄影家付酬做出具体和明确的规定。

中国文联党组成员、副主席李前光在谈及此次座谈会时表示，《著作权法》是涉及摄影家权益的重要法律文件，和文艺家的关系非常密切，中国摄影家协会与中国摄影著作权协会是文艺界的人民团体，作为党和政府联系摄影工作者的桥梁纽带，抓住机遇，努力反映广大摄影家的权益诉求，也必定进一步增强两协会在行业的凝聚力。中摄协此次召开的座谈会，是文联各文艺家协会中第一个组织行业专家学者征求意见的会议，与会代表来自各个方面，希望大家能够对法律修改提出中肯的意见，中摄协也理应代表广大摄影家发出声音，为依法治国和行业自律，推动摄影繁荣发展做出我们应有的贡献。

（资料来源：中国知识产权资讯网，
作者：刘蓓蓓）

【唱片公司为著作权法修法建言】 2018年3月27日，太合音乐集团、北京鸟人艺术、正大音乐、竹书文化、二十一东方艺术、华谊音乐、看见音乐等十余家唱片公司齐聚一堂，呼吁国家立法部门平衡各方利益，赋予录音制作者广播权的获酬权，即广播电台、电视台播放录音制品时应向录音制作者支付报酬。

自2006年开始，国内唱片公司就积极呼吁，录音制品是录音制作者投入巨资，组织编曲、演奏、演唱及录音混音的创造性劳动成果，录音制作者应享有广播权和公开表演权。2011年中国启动《著作权法》第三次修订后，这一问题引发广泛讨论。2012年12月28日，国家版权局提交国务院法制办的《中华人民共和国著作权法（修订草案送审稿）》，其中赋予了录音制作者广播权和公开表演获酬权。几易其稿后，2017年底，国务院法制办就《著作权法（修订草案送审稿修改稿）》小范围内定向征求意见，其中的第四十五条中赋予了录音制作者广播权的获酬权，但未赋予录音制作者公开表演权。

对此，鸟人艺术总经理周亚平认为，广播权和公开表演权应当是录音制作者应有的权利，目前录音制作者权项严重缺失，导致投入和收益严重倒挂，立法机关要考虑立法的公平性，才能促进产业的持续健康发展。太合音乐副总裁刘鑫认为，录音制作者享有什么权利，对于内容的创作具有导向作用。由于录音制作者目前回报主要来自信息网络传播权，近年来市场充斥了大量格调不高的网络歌曲。因为录音制作不享有广播权和公开表演权，导致适合在广播电台、电视台播放的弘扬社会主旋律的音乐以及适合在酒店、商场播放的具有艺术格调的音乐无法得到市场回报，进而导致投资和制作日渐衰微。唱片公司认为，赋予录音制作者广播权和公开表演权，能给产业正确的市场引导，鼓励音乐精品创作。

据了解，早在1961年通过的《保护表演者、录音制品制作者与广播组织公约》和1996年通过的《世界知识产权组织表演和录音制品条约》均确认了录音制作者的公开表演权和广播权。目前，世界上已有147个国家和地区通过立法赋予了录音制作者对其录音制品的广播权和公开表演权。

在中国现行《著作权法》下，录音制作者仅享有复制权、发行权、出租权和信息网络传播权，这意味着广电组织以及机场、饭店、酒吧等商家在利用录音制品提高其收视率、收听率和吸引客户并增加营业收入时，却不需向录音制品的制作者支付任何费用。业内人士认为，这既与市场经济公平原则相背离，也与民法公平原则相背离，对录音制作者严重不公。此外，录音制作者获得广播权和公开表演权不仅会极大地促进中国录音制品原创内容的创作、出版和传播，也可以让广播组织获得更多、更优质的节目源并从中获益。

（资料来源：中国知识产权资讯网，作者：刘仁，原标题为：《唱片公司再次为著作权法修法建言：录音制作者应享有广播权和公开表演权》）

【《电子商务法》表决通过　着重强调知识产权保护】 2018年8月31日，第十三届全国人大常委会第五次会议表决通过了《电子商务法》，其中着重强调知识产权保护，细化了知识产权权利人“通知—删除”的权利和平台“删除—公示”的义务。

《电子商务法》第四十二条规定，知识产权权利人认为其知识产权受到侵害的，有权通知电子商务平台经营者采取删除、屏蔽、断开链接、终止交易和服务等必要措施。通知应当包括构成侵权的初步证据。电子商务平台经营者接到通知后，应当及时采取必要措施，并将该通知转送平台内经营者；未及时采取必要措施的，对损害的扩大部分与平台内经营者承担连带责任。因通知错误造成平台内经营者损害的，依法承担民事责任。恶意发出错误通知，造成平台内经营者损失的，加倍承担赔偿责任。

法律人士表示，假货一直是电商平台的“原罪”，以往，电商平台会以“避风港”规则回避自己应尽的审查责任，直接或间接助长假货销售者气焰。《电子商务法》以鼓励创新和竞争为主，同时兼顾规范和管理的需要，对打击假货和防止恶意投诉方面将发挥积极作用，这为电子商务未来的发展奠定了基础。

（资料来源：《中国知识产权报》，作者：王康）

◆司　法

【《关于加强知识产权审判领域改革创新若干问题的意见》印发】 2018年2月26日，中共中央办公厅、国务院办公厅印发了《关于加强知识产权审判领域改革创新若干问题的意见》（以下简称《意见》）并发出通知，要求各地区各部门结合实际认真贯彻落实。

《意见》提出，加强知识产权审判领域改革创新，要以完善知识产权诉讼制度为基础，以加强知识产权法院体系建设为重点，以加强知识产权审判队伍建设为保障，不断提高知识产权审判质量效率，加大知识产权司法保护力度，有效遏制侵犯知识产权行为，进一步提升知识产权领域司法公信力和国际影响力，加快推进知识产权审判体系和审判能力向现代化迈进。

《意见》还就完善知识产权诉讼制度、加强知识产权法院体系建设、加强知识产权审判队伍建设、加强组织领导等方面的工作提出了具体要求。

（资料来源：央视网，原标题为：《中办、国办印发〈关于加强知识产权审判领域改革创新若干问题的意见〉》）

【使用“葛优躺”　基金公司被判侵权】 北京市海淀区人民法院审结了葛优与泰信基金管理有限公司肖像权纠纷，事由是泰信基金管理有限公司在其微信公众号上发布的推文，使用了“葛优躺”表情包，法院判其公开道歉，并向葛优赔偿9 500元。

葛优在饰演电视剧《我爱我家》中的“二混子”季春生时，应剧情需要以放松的姿势躺在沙发上的剧照，在2016年盛夏成为红极一时的“表情包”。泰信基金也跟了风，在其微信公众号上发布了一篇题为《假如葛大爷也炒股……》的配图文章，文中使用了多张剧照，并配上“跌，还在跌刹不住了”“我要补仓，别拦我”“这只股没买是我人生遗憾”等证券市场相关用语。

用表情包不是错，错在带有商业性质。法院认为，泰信基金为展示公司形象，向用户推送各类信息，属于公司经营行为，而在经营过程中使用了葛优的肖像，构成侵犯肖像权，应承担相应侵权责任。

（资料来源：《国际金融报》，作者：何思，原标题为：《使用“葛优躺”某基金公司被判侵权 表情包还能用吗？》）

【《芈月传》著作权引纠纷案　法院判决认为不构成侵权】 因认为《芈月传》小说抄袭《芈月传》电视剧剧本，东阳市乐视花儿影视文化有限公司以侵犯著作权为由将《芈月传》小说作者蒋胜男、《芈月传》小说出版商浙江文艺出版社和销售商北京中关村图书大厦诉至法院。北京市海淀区人民法院审结了此案，判决驳回了原告东阳市乐视花儿影视文化有限公司的全部诉讼请求。

法院经审理后认为，《中华人民共和国著作权法》第十一条规定，著作权属于作者，创作作品的公民是作者，由法人或者其他组织主持，代表法人或者其他组织意志创作，并由法人或者其他组织承担责任的作品，法人或者其他组织视为作者。如无相反证明，在作品上署名的公民、法人或者其他组织为作者。《最高人民法院关于审理著作权民事纠纷案件适用法律若干问题的解释》第七条规定："当事人提供的涉及著作权的底稿、原件、合法出版物、著作权登记证书、认证机构出具的证明、取得权利的合同等，可以作为证据。"根据上述规定，蒋胜男系《芈月传》小说的作者、花儿影视公司系《芈月传》剧本的著作权人。从双方合作的意思表示来看，《芈月传》小说的著作权归属与《芈月传》小说是否在《芈月传》剧本完成之前就已经完成无关，双方以合同的形式将《芈月传》小说的著作权（除改编成部分作品的权利外）均保留给作者蒋胜男。而《芈月传》剧本应为《芈月传》小说的改编作品。蒋胜男接受花儿影视公司的委托创作剧本，在剧本创作的过程中引入某些公司的意见对剧本进行修改，属于正常的剧本创作行为。在《芈月传》小说已经完成的情况下，再对其某些情节进行修改也合乎常理，不能因此而认定《芈月传》小说改编或抄袭了《芈月传》剧本内容。花儿影视公司在此后的电视剧播出和公开场合以自认的方式对此予以认可，故花儿影视公司关于蒋胜男创作的《芈月传》小说侵犯了《芈月传》剧本的改编权的主张，法院不予支持。在蒋胜男不构成侵权的情况下，浙江文艺出版社的出版发行行为及中关村图书大厦的销售行为亦属于合法行为，不构成对花儿影视公司享有的著作权的侵犯。故法院做出如上判决。

（资料来源：中国新闻出版广电网，作者：刘佳欣）

【"小咖秀"违法使用歌曲被判赔偿】 北京市朝阳区人民法院就中国音乐著作权协会（以下简称音著协）诉炫一下（北京）科技有限公司（以下简称一下科技）开发经营的短视频类产品"小咖秀"侵犯其享有著作权的音乐作品一案做出一审判决：判决一下科技败诉，并要求一下科技赔偿涉案歌曲的经济损失及原告合理开支。

尽管一下科技公司发展迅速，其用户规模和产品口碑都达到了很高的水准，但却在经营的最基本环节——版权问题上，没有很好地进行解决。音著协自 2017 年起即不断与一下科技进行沟通，希望对方重视其平台上大量侵权使用音乐作品的行为，妥善协商解决著作权问题。但一下科技并没有积极回应，始终以推诿拖延的态度应对。最终，音著协无奈只得将对方告上法庭。

音著协表示，在接下来的工作中，将重点关注该领域的侵权现象，加强维权力度。同时，广大经营视频类平台的网络公司也应将著作权视为自己经营活动的基础，对著作权人的付出和创作给予应有的尊重，避免侵权事件的发生，净化网络环境，维护中国互联网发展的健康形象。

（资料来源：《中国新闻出版广电报》，作者：殷协，
原标题为：《"小咖秀"违法使用歌曲被诉
短视频平台侵权播放音乐被判赔偿》）

【《中国好声音（第三季）》信息网络传播权纠纷二审审结】 北京知识产权法院审结深圳市腾讯计算机系统有限公司诉暴风集团股份有限公司侵害《中国好声音（第三季）》信息网络传播权纠纷系列案件。北京知识产权法院在该判决中认为，在确定侵权损害赔偿数额时，要善于运用根据具体证据酌定实际损失或侵权所得的裁量性赔偿方法。权利人提供了用以证明其实际损失或者侵权人违法所得的部分证据，足以认定计算赔偿所需的部分数据的，应当尽量选择运用酌定赔偿方法确定损害赔偿数额。

腾讯公司诉称：腾讯公司依法拥有由上海灿星文化传播有限公司制作的大型励志专业音乐评论节目《中国好声音（第三季）》独家信息网络传播权。经查证，暴风公司在未取得节目信息网络传播权的情况下，在其经营的网站上播放该节目第 1～6 期。暴风公司明知该节目的信息网络传播权由腾讯公司独家所有，却仍在其经营的网站上播放，严重侵害腾讯公司的合法权益。据此，请求依法判决暴风公司赔偿腾讯公司经济损失及诉讼合理支出 200 万元，包括经济损失 199 万元，诉讼合理支出 1 万元。

一审法院经审理认为，足以确信腾讯公司因暴风公司涉案行为所遭受的经济损失明显超出《著作权法》法定赔偿数额的上限 50 万元，为弥补权利人的经济损失、惩戒恶意侵权行为，酌定每案赔偿数

额为 100 万元，合理支出为 1 万元，6 案共计 606 万元。一审判决后，暴风公司以一审判决的赔偿数额没有事实和法律依据，对于经济损失的认定明显过高且极不公平合理为由提起上诉。

北京知识产权法院审理认为，侵害著作权损害赔偿的目的既包括弥补权利人的损失，也包括制止侵权人再次侵权，还包括有效遏制未来潜在侵权行为的普遍发生。在确定损害赔偿数额时，应当根据案件的具体情况，既考虑个案中权利人的实际损失、侵权人的违法所得，也考虑同一侵权人类似侵权行为被起诉的概率，综合确定损害赔偿的数额。

在确定侵权损害赔偿数额时，要善于运用根据具体证据酌定实际损失或侵权所得的裁量性赔偿方法，引导当事人对于损害赔偿问题积极举证，进一步提高损害赔偿计算的合理性。权利人提供了用以证明其实际损失或者侵权人违法所得的部分证据，足以认定计算赔偿所需的部分数据的，应当尽量选择运用酌定赔偿方法确定损害赔偿数额。

综上所述，北京知识产权法院认为，一审法院综合各项因素，确认腾讯公司因暴风公司涉案行为所遭受的经济损失明显超出《著作权法》法定赔偿额的上限的认定正确，据此酌情确定的赔偿数额 100 万元并无不当，从而维持了一审判决确定的赔偿数额。

（资料来源：《中国新闻出版广电报》，作者：张倩，原标题为：《〈中国好声音（第三季）〉信息网络传播权纠纷二审审结，维持一审判决》）

【小伙因非法获取课件被判拘役两个月】 本来是出于学习目的，但因正版培训课程需要付费且只能在线观看，小伙（陈某）便在网上寻购了一款破解器，解密下载了一批相关课件视频，随后又因急需资金而将自己下载的课件挂在淘宝上销售，前后非法获利共计 7 000 元左右。江苏苏州高新区（虎丘区）人民法院依法做出判决，被告人陈某犯非法获取计算机信息系统数据罪，判处拘役 2 个月，缓刑 3 个月，并处罚金 1 000 元。

2016 年 5 月，一家给培训机构和企业提供在线培训的网络科技公司接举报发现，淘宝上有网店出售其网站上的电子课程。原先用户注册付费后，也只能在线观看培训视频，不能下载。而淘宝上非法出售的电子课程，是有人利用破解器实现了对加密视频的解密播放。据该公司相关人员介绍，平台上有 300 余个视频都遭到非法下载，给公司造成不小的经济损失。经警方跟踪分析，确认一大批非法课件的源头是同一个人，并很快锁定了其 IP 地址和注册用户名。

法院经审理查明，陈某 1986 年出生，大学文化。2016 年 4 月，因为想创业，他在网上搜寻相关培训视频，发现有一个课程内容很好，但收看相关课件要收费。后来他以百余元的价格网购了一款专门针对该课件的免费下载器，然后从上述公司官网上下载视频。“最初下载是为了自己学习使用，到了 5 月时，我想创业急需资金，就将下载的视频挂在淘宝上销售。”陈某在庭审时自愿认罪，并表示自己就是因为法律意识淡薄，才导致一步步走向犯罪。

法院认为，被告人违反国家规定，非法获取计算机信息系统中存储的数据，情节严重，其行为已构成非法获取计算机信息系统数据罪，应当依法判处 3 年以下有期徒刑或者拘役，并处罚金。鉴于被告人如实供述所犯罪行，认罪态度较好，当庭自愿认罪，可以从轻处罚。又鉴于其主动退回违法所得，遂综合各种因素做出以上判决。

（资料来源：《中国新闻出版广电报》，作者：艾家静）

【《雾都之恋》引纠纷　豆丁公司被判侵权】 豆丁世纪（北京）网络技术有限公司未经许可，在其经营的豆丁网及豆丁书房 APP（安卓端、iOS 端）中提供上传由龚某（笔名：红豆豆）创作的文学作品《雾都之恋》（以下简称涉案作品），龚某认为豆丁公司的行为侵犯了其对涉案作品享有的信息网络传播权、获得报酬权等著作权权利，遂诉至法院。北京市海淀区法院审结了此案，法院判决豆丁公司赔偿龚某经济损失及合理开支共计 37 150 元。

原告龚某诉称，其创作完成并发表文学作品《雾都之恋》。豆丁公司未经许可，且未支付报酬，在其经营的豆丁网及豆丁书房 APP（安卓端、iOS 端）中提供了涉案作品，该行为侵犯了龚某对涉案作品享有的信息网络传播权、获得报酬权等著作权权利。

被告豆丁公司辩称，其经营的豆丁网仅为用户提供信息存储空间服务，在网站首页已经公开了豆丁公司的名称、联系人及网络地址，亦未对涉案作品进行主动归类或整理。豆丁公司并未接到龚某的侵权通知，无法知道用户上传的作品属于侵权作品，主观上不存在过错，且在接到法院诉状后立即删除涉案作品，尽到了合理注意义务，豆丁公司也未提供教唆帮助行为，依法不应承担赔偿责任。另外，豆丁公司认为豆丁书房 APP 的安卓端和 iOS 端均与豆丁网的PC端同步，上传用户不需要另行上传作品，属于一次上传行为，下载用户也仅需一次付费，即使存在侵权行为，也只需承担一次赔偿责任。

法院经审理后认为，网络服务提供者从网络用户提供的作品、表演、录音录像制品中直接获得经济利益的，人民法院应当认定其对该网络用户侵害信息网络传播权的行为负有较高的注意义务。豆丁公司经营的豆丁网向用户提供上传作品的信息存储空间，与上传用户共同分享收益，且对豆丁网站上每一份文档浏览、下载、购买、收益等情况都有详细具体的针对性统计，豆丁公司有能力获得上传用户的真实信息，也有途径对用户上传的文档是否侵权进行审查。在此情况下，豆丁公司一方面消极对待自己应履行的审查义务，放任豆丁网、豆丁书房APP上侵权行为的发生；另一方面，积极从侵权行为中获益，存在明显的主观过错。在缺乏证据证明上传用户取得了龚某许可的情况下，豆丁公司通过豆丁网、豆丁书房APP（安卓端及iOS端）传播涉案作品，使公众可以在个人选定的时间和地点获得涉案作品，豆丁公司对该行为提供了帮助，侵害了龚某享有的信息网络传播权，应依法承担侵权责任。同时，豆丁公司未经许可在不同的端口提供作品，其传播途径、传播范围、损害后果均不相同，故豆丁公司应当根据不同的端口分别承担相应的赔偿责任。故做出如上判决。

（资料来源：海淀法院网，原标题为：《文学作品〈雾都之恋〉引发信息网络传播权纠纷》）

【手游《花千骨》被判侵权】 经过近三年时间，手游《花千骨》被指侵权《太极熊猫》一案终于有了结果——苏州市中级人民法院一审判定，天象互动开发、爱奇艺运营的手游《花千骨》侵权蜗牛数字开发的《太极熊猫》，判决天象互动与爱奇艺赔偿蜗牛数字经济损失3 000万元。对此，蜗牛数字于4月11日召开《太极熊猫》维权情况通报会，进一步对案件进行说明。

据蜗牛数字方面透露，当时公司接到玩家举报，经工作人员比对发现，手游《花千骨》有大量疑似抄袭《太极熊猫》的内容。随后，蜗牛数字向苏州市中级人民法院提起诉讼，并于2015年8月5日正式立案。2018年3月30日，苏州市中级人民法院一审认为，“《花千骨》游戏在游戏玩法规则的特定呈现方式及其选择、安排、组合上整体利用了《太极熊猫》的基本表达，并在此基础上进行美术、音乐、动画、文字等一定内容的再创作，侵害了著作权人享有的改编权”。然而，在该案的立案初期，蜗牛数字的维权并不被业内普遍看好，曾有业内人士称，由于两款游戏在用户、IP等方面存在差异，以内容、玩法相似起诉，实现胜诉的难度不小。

蜗牛数字方面表示，当时公司在对比两款游戏时发现，在手游《花千骨》向中国国家版权局登记的计算机软件著作权登记证书登记文档中，功能模块结构图、功能流程图、功能详细设计等，均系对《太极熊猫》中武神系统的结构分析，且均使用了《太极熊猫》游戏截图。此案终审后，公司将会把维权所得用于中小游戏企业知识产权保护，由公司牵头，联合各中小游戏企业、律师事务所、知识产权服务机构共同组建知识产权保护联盟，下设版权维护基金和专利维护基金。

（资料来源：北京商报网，作者：卢扬　郑蕊，原标题为：《三年纠纷落定　手游〈花千骨〉被判侵权》）

【首例VR著作权案　被告判赔46万元】 北京全景客信息技术有限公司称，同创蓝天投资管理（北京）有限公司未经许可使用VR全景摄影作品，侵犯著作权，诉至法院。2018年4月18日，海淀法院开庭审理这起首例VR作品著作权案并当庭宣判：被告赔偿原告经济损失462 000元及合理开支32 500元。

全景客公司诉称，该公司是一家专业从事移动互联网和虚拟现实技术的研发公司，拥有专业的三维全景拍摄技术，创作完成了《故宫》《中国古动物馆》两部VR全景摄影作品，其中，作品《故宫》已由北京市版权局进行了版权登记。被告未经许可，擅自在其主办的网站上传了《故宫》《中国古动物馆》两部作品中的76幅VR全景摄影作品，侵害了原告享有的信息网络权。全景客公司要求被告赔偿462 000元及合理开支32 500元。

同创蓝天公司则辩称，原告主张的权利存在瑕疵，对于部分作品的权利无法得到有效证明：76幅作品中，仅有43幅作品进行了著作权登记。并且，涉案全景作品全部由用户免费注册和发布，公司已在用户协议中对遵守著作权法等规定进行了必要的提示。另外，公司未对涉案作品进行任何编辑、整理和推荐，也未从涉案作品中获得经济利益，在收到起诉材料后立即对涉案内容进行了强制关闭，因此，应适用“避风港”规则，不应承担赔偿责任。被告还提出，原告索赔数额过高。

法院经审理认为，原告方提供的涉及著作权的底稿、原件、合法出版物、著作权登记证书、认证机构出具的证明等材料，可以作为认定权利的证据。另外，经查证被告方网页，网页前端并未显示涉案作品的上传者信息，且被告的法律声明中声称网站上的所有内容均由其享有权利，因此，被告应当就本案侵权行为承担相应的法律责任。

关于赔偿损失的具体数额，因双方未提交原告实际损失或被告违法所得的证据，法院综合考虑相关因素，酌情判定赔偿数额。首先，涉案作品均为全景摄影作品，具有一定的拍摄和创作难度；其次，被告将涉案作品直接展示在其网站上用于商业案例宣传；最后，涉案作品的在线浏览量较大，受关注度较高。据此，法院支持了原告方的诉讼请求。

宣判后，被告公司代理人表示保留上诉权利。

（资料来源：《北京日报》，作者：高健）

【山西高院出台指导意见规范卡拉 OK 著作权纠纷赔偿标准】 2018 年 4 月 19 日，山西省高级人民法院召开新闻发布会，下发《山西省高级人民法院关于审理卡拉 OK 著作权纠纷案件的指导意见》，要求各中级人民法院在审理卡拉 OK 著作权纠纷案件中，参照中国音像著作权集体管理协会（以下简称音集协）公告的收费标准确定侵权赔偿额。

据音集协相关负责人介绍，近年来各地法院受理了大量卡拉 OK 歌厅侵犯著作权的案件，法院判赔标准不一，亦对集体管理组织许可收费工作造成困扰。山西高院在综合考虑国家版权局公告的使用费收费标准、卡拉 OK 场所包房数量、应缴费经营时间等因素，对集体管理组织起诉卡拉 OK 歌厅侵权案件，统一判赔标准，确定此类案件侵权赔偿额为每间包房每天 5～6 元。

山西高院意见明确了惩罚性赔偿标准。对无正当理由拒不缴纳著作权使用费且拒绝协商的场所，赔偿标准可达每间包房每天 12 元。

该负责人说，近期出现了一种情况，个别没有加入音集协的著作权人为了维权，在卡拉 OK 领域大规模、有组织地开展商业诉讼，索要天价赔偿款，给卡拉 OK 场所带来巨大经济压力，严重扰乱了著作权许可市场秩序。

针对此种情况，山西高院意见确定，要将卡拉 OK 场所是否同音集协签订许可合同作为考量因素，综合确定侵权赔偿数额。对于已与音集协签订著作权许可合同的，经法院审理，认为场所应承担赔偿责任的，侵权赔偿额参照音集协收取的著作权使用费确定。对于未与音集协签订著作权许可合同的，法院应综合考虑被诉场所应缴纳的著作权使用费情况、未参加音集协的原因等情节，确定赔偿数额。

（资料来源：法制网，作者：张红兵，原标题为：《山西高法发布卡拉 OK 著作权纠纷指导意见》）

【全国法院 2017 年审理版权案件大幅增长】 2017 年，全国法院新收知识产权民事一审案件增幅达到 47.24%。2018 年 4 月 19 日上午，最高人民法院通报了 2017 年中国法院知识产权司法保护的整体情况。当天，“全国法院知识产权宣传周”活动正式启动。

据最高人民法院相关负责人介绍，2017 年，全国法院审理的各类知识产权案件特别是著作权案件大幅增长。其中，涉著作权、商标和专利案件同比上升分别为 57.80%、39.58%、29.56%。从案件分布来看，北京、上海、江苏、浙江、广东五省市法院收案数量占全国法院案件总数的 70.65%。

知识产权案件呈现的一个特点是，新类型案件不断涌现，案件审理难度不断增大。从各地法院报送的案例来看，因抄袭他人网络游戏、网络商业模式运用、体育赛事直播等新型产业发展而引发的著作权纠纷或者不正当竞争纠纷越来越多，提出了很多亟待解决的问题。

2017 年，人民法院也在不断提高知识产权司法救济的及时性、便利性和有效性。如“新华字典”商标侵权及不正当竞争纠纷案涉及未注册驰名商标保护，此案裁判确立了对“新华字典”这类兼具产品和品牌混合属性的商品名称是否具备商标显著特征的裁判标准。“茅盾手稿”著作权纠纷案涉及美术作品拍卖活动中著作权法、物权法、拍卖法三部法律交叉调整地带的相关主体权利义务关系问题，该案判决明确了不同主体权利的边界，体现了对物权人和著作权人合法权益平衡保护的司法精神。

（资料来源：《中国新闻出版广电报》，作者：张蕾）

【北京高院发布《侵害著作权案件审理指南》】 2018 年 4 月 20 日，北京市高级人民法院正式对外公布《北京市高级人民法院侵害著作权案件审理指南》（以下简称《指南》）。

《指南》全文分为 11 个部分，共计 160 条，涉及基本规定，权利客体，权利归属，侵权认定（包括著作人身权、著作财产权、邻接权），抗辩事由，法律责任，侵害信息网络传播权的认定，侵害影视作品著作权的认定，侵害计算机软件著作权的认定等 11 个方面的问题。

据北京市高级人民法院民三庭庭长助理潘伟介绍,《指南》的主要内容为:一是明确案件的审理原则,总结案件的审理思路,提出了“加大保护、鼓励创作、促进传播、平衡利益”的基本审理原则,并对侵害著作权案件程序问题审查、诉权行使方式及实体问题审理的规范思路进行总结;二是规范客体审查标准,统一署名的认定规则,《指南》明确提出了作品审查的四要件,针对著作权案件近年来的新情况予以回应,厘清了互联网技术发展下的署名认定规则;三是界定权利保护范围,提出类案的审理规则,对侵害著作人身权、著作财产权以及邻接权的认定做出具体规定,并确定了实践中常见的侵害著作权案件的审理思路;四是加大权利保护力度,探索惩罚性赔偿机制,细化了损害赔偿的适用方法和计算依据,回应了赔偿数额“举证难”的问题,并针对“恶意侵权”行为提出惩罚性赔偿的思路。

潘伟表示,本次《指南》的发布,是对北京市高级人民法院以往规范性文件的修改、补充、汇总与完善,系统研究了著作权法立法者的相关释义,总体上是对司法实践中亟待解决的、具有共通性的问题做出了结论性或指引性的规定。《指南》的发布将推动北京法院著作权审判实践,是全市著作权审判工作的新起点。北京市高级人民法院将以此为契机,推进著作权审判工作向更完备、更全面、更科学的方向不断发展。

(资料来源:北京法院网,作者:王元义)

【新中国成立以来最大盗版少儿图书案二审宣判】 2018年4月24日,被称为新中国成立以来破获盗版图书册数最多、少儿出版物码洋最大的案件二审宣判。

2016年6月,全国“扫黄打非”工作小组接匿名举报称,北京市通州区宋庄镇某村涉嫌存在存放盗版儿童图书的仓库。接报后,全国“扫黄打非”办将线索转至北京市文化执法总队、北京市公安局处理。随着侦查人员工作的深入,这起地下盗版图书的制售交易链逐渐浮出水面。

法院审理查明,2015—2016年间,被告人赵某伙同其父亲、堂弟,雇用工人一起从事盗版图书活动。赵某盗版的图书主要为市面上流行的儿童书籍,如接力出版社出版的法国儿童科普经典“第一次发现”系列丛书、二十一世纪出版社出版的法国童书“不一样的卡梅拉”系列等,涉及数十家出版社1 800余种图书。

据了解,赵某等人先将绘本样本交由私人扫描、排版,然后发至地下印厂进行印刷装订,最后将图书运往在村庄租赁的仓库。这些图书除少部分在网店零售外,绝大部分批发到朝阳区王四营图书市场。市场个体户进价1.6元左右,售价1.7元至4元不等。他们平时用QQ联系赵某,赵某送货上门,双方支付宝结账。在整个盗版交易链中,以赵某为首,其和上下游联系基本通过电话、QQ、微信,交易主要使用现金和支付宝,其家人负责协助经营。

2016年9月,执法机关在通州区和朝阳区一举查获8个存书仓库,现场起获涉案书籍360余万册。经鉴定,328万余册为非法出版物或侵权复制品。案发后,8名被告人相继到案。

一审法院审理认为,被告人赵某等人以营利为目的,未经著作权人许可,发行其文字作品,情节特别严重,以侵犯著作权罪判决被告人赵某有期徒刑六年六个月,并处罚金人民币150万元;其余被告人皆被判处有期徒刑四年至二年六个月不等刑罚,并处罚金。一审宣判后,被告人赵某等人不服,上诉至北京第三中级人民法院,二审经审理,裁定维持原判。

(资料来源:《法制日报》,作者:黄洁 张雪泓,原标题为:《新中国成立来最大盗版少儿图书案宣判》)

【《九层妖塔》字体侵权】 2015年9月,“陕西女婿”陆川执导的灾难探险片《九层妖塔》上映,20天取得了超过6亿元的票房,并斩获多项大奖。不过,这部电影惹的官司也不少,继著作权、插曲的侵权诉讼外,2018年5月,一起字体侵权案也一审宣判。电影制作方、发行方等四被告被判共同赔偿书法家向佳红14万元。

2013年12月,向佳红向广东省版权局申请了作品名称为“向佳红毛笔行书字体”的作品著作权登记,且已在此套字体库中明确署名此套字体仅供学习交流使用,商业使用需经其授权,同时留有其联系方式。电影《九层妖塔》上映后,向佳红发现在该电影出现的道具《鬼族史》图书、《华夏日报》报纸上使用了他的书法作品“鬼”“族”“史”“华”“夏”“日”“报”。他认为,影片的制作、发行、投资和传播方未经过他许可,也未署名,侵犯了他对上述书法作品享有的署名权、复制权。此后,他将梦想者电影(北京)公司、北京环球艺动影业有限公司、乐视影业(北京)有限公司、中国电影股份有限公司诉至法院,请求判四被告共同支付版权使用费50万元、精神抚慰金1万元并在报纸上公开赔礼道歉。

北京市朝阳区法院审理认为，书法的书写虽然受限于汉字本身笔画和结构上的固定搭配，但书写者仍借助具体的线条、点画等，在字形结构、偏旁部首比例、笔画长短、粗细选择、曲直设计等诸多方面进行调整和创造，融入自己的选择和判断，表现出独特的艺术美感，体现出书写者自己的个性，从而具有符合著作权法要求的独创性，成为著作权法保护的美术作品。本案中，向佳红主张权利的“鬼”“族”“史”“华”“夏”“日”“报”7个单字在断笔方式，布局结构，笔画粗细、曲直、长短以及繁简字组合等方面均体现出了独特的艺术美感，呈现出了不同于传统行书及其他常见字体的独创性表达，融入了书写者独特的智力判断和选择，属于著作权法规定的美术作品。

四被告在使用涉案书法作品时未以适当方式表明向佳红是该作品的作者，侵害了其署名权。同时，法院认为四被告使用涉案单字的行为不属于合理使用。法院一审判决四被告在判决生效之日起30日内履行在报纸上登载声明的义务，向原告公开赔礼道歉，共同赔偿向佳红14万元。

（资料来源：新浪娱乐，原标题为：《〈九层妖塔〉被指字体侵权　遭索赔51万》）

【苏州市挂牌成立知识产权检察室】 2018年6月8日，江苏省苏州市检察院知识产权检察室揭牌，实现对涉及知识产权领域的刑事立案活动的监督，形成司法保护合力，全面保护科技创新。

该检察室实现了民事、行政、刑事检察权合一，将批捕、起诉、监督职能融合，对苏州、无锡、常州、南通辖区内，由苏州市中级人民法院知识产权法庭管辖的相关案件开展检察监督。在监督方式上，从地域管辖和级别管辖上实现对知识产权诉讼的对等监督，并承担知识产权领域的公益诉讼和行政检察监督。监督范围包括专利，技术秘密，计算机软件，植物新品种，集成电路布图设计，驰名商标认定，垄断纠纷以及诉讼标的额为300万元以上商标、著作权、不正当竞争、技术合同纠纷的一审知识产权民事案件，对国务院部门或者县级以上地方人民政府所做的著作权、商标、专利、不正当竞争等行政行为提起诉讼的一审知识产权行政案件进行检察监督，支持、督促起诉和公益诉讼等。

（资料来源：《法制日报》，作者：丁国锋）

【“上镜率最高”的《武夷之春》引发的著作权争夺】 人民大会堂福建厅大型漆画作品《武夷之春》被称为央视“上镜率最高”的当代漆画，但是，针对《武夷之春》的署名权和著作权，却引发了一场著作权争夺战。

画家吴景希的母亲李女士将画家陈文灿告上法庭，由此引爆了这场著作权和署名权的争夺战。原告李女士起诉称，她的儿子吴景希生前与陈文灿等人共同制作1987年版《武夷之春》，陈列于北京人民大会堂福建厅。1994年，因福建厅重新装修，对画作尺寸提出新的要求，吴景希抱病赶回厦门参加研讨设计稿，在原画设计稿的基础上进行修改，制作出1994年版《武夷之春》，并代替原作陈列于人民大会堂福建厅。

李女士还说，吴景希去世后，陈文灿作为画作的合作者之一，在其画展、画册中故意未署上吴景希的姓名，并将吴景希创作的画作表述为其创作，误导美术界和公众，侵犯了吴景希的权益。

因此，李女士作为吴景希的继承人起诉至法院。原告的诉求包括，要求被告立即停止侵害吴景希对《武夷之春》作品的署名权、复制权、发行权、展览权，而且还应撤销著作权登记，并公开赔礼道歉，消除影响。

案件审理期间，因福州大学主张其享有讼争作品的著作权，一审法院通知其作为有独立请求权的第三人参加诉讼。

对于著作权，福州大学也提出了自己的观点：请求确认1987年版《武夷之春》、1994年版《武夷之春》的著作权归福州大学所有。福州大学认为，《武夷之春》作品是相关部门下达给工艺美校的任务，虽然吴景希、陈文灿等工艺美校教师参与创作涉案作品，但其行为是完成工作任务，因此两幅作品的著作权为工艺美校所有。因工艺美校已并入福州大学，所以作品著作权应归福州大学所有。

陈文灿也主张，讼争作品《武夷之春》为法人作品，著作权归属于福州大学。

中院二审认定，两幅《武夷之春》作品的署名权由吴景希、陈文灿等人享有，工艺美校享有除署名权之外的著作权，工艺美校并入福州大学作为内设教学机构之后，相应的著作权由福州大学承继。

另外，二审还认为，陈文灿仅系两幅《武夷之春》作品的创作者之一，但在有关部门组织的画展暨学术研讨会以及之后汇编的论文集中确实存在突出陈文灿作为作品的创作者，而忽略吴景希等参与创作人员贡献的情况，一定程度上可能使社会公众误以为《武夷之春》是陈文灿独立创作的作品。另外，陈文灿擅自将1994年版《武夷之春》著作权登记在其个人名下，侵犯了吴景希的署名权。

2018年6月15日，厦门中院做出终审判决，要求被告陈文灿应在中国美术家协会的报纸、网站上公开发布消除影响公告，明确《武夷之春》(1994年版）的创作、设计者包括吴景希，消除其将《武夷之春》(1994年版）作品著作权登记于个人名下所造成的影响。另外，被告陈文灿还要赔偿原告为制止侵权所支付的合理费用13 330元。

（资料来源：《海峡导报》，作者：陈捷）

【“中国喷泉著作权纠纷第一案”二审维持原判】 西湖音乐喷泉是不少去杭州的游客必选的夜游景点，但不久前，杭州西湖风景名胜区湖滨管理处（以下简称西湖管理处）却被一纸诉状告上法庭，原因是中科水景公司认为西湖音乐喷泉涉嫌剽窃了青岛世园会音乐喷泉的喷射效果。法院一审判决西湖管理处停止侵权，赔偿损失。西湖管理处不服上诉。北京知识产权法院对该案二审宣判，驳回上诉、维持原判。该案因涉及音乐喷泉喷射效果的呈现是否构成作品、属于何种法定作品类型的法律认定，被称为“中国喷泉著作权纠纷第一案”。

一审法院经审理后认为，音乐喷泉作品所要保护的对象是喷泉在特定音乐配合下形成的喷射表演效果。著作权法虽无音乐喷泉作品或音乐喷泉编曲作品的类别，但这种作品本身确实具有独创性，应受到著作权法的保护。

由于中科水景公司对涉案作品享有著作权，中科恒业公司、西湖管理处曾接触过中科水景公司的相关喷泉视频、资料，西湖音乐喷泉相关曲目的喷射效果又与涉案作品构成实质性相似，故认定中科恒业公司、西湖管理处侵犯中科水景公司对涉案作品享有的著作权，法院判令二者停止侵权，公开致歉，赔偿经济损失及合理支出共计9万元。

中科恒业公司、西湖管理处不服一审判决提起上诉。

北京知识产权法院认为，尽管不同于常见的绘画、书法、雕塑等美术作品静态的、持久固定的表达方式，但是，由于喷泉客体是由灯光、色彩、音乐、水型等多种要素共同构成的动态立体造型表达，其喷射效果呈现具有审美意义，构成美术作品。

中科水景公司实际创作了涉案作品，在委托合同未对著作权做出约定的情况下，其依法享有涉案作品的著作权。通过原告与被告音乐喷泉的视频对比，二者对音乐喷泉喷射效果的呈现已经构成了实质性相似。在此情形下，鉴于中科恒业公司和西湖管理处有接触涉案作品的合理可能性，可以排除二被告独立创作的可能。二被告未经许可喷放涉案作品且未署名著作权人，已经构成侵权行为。

此外，被告喷放涉案作品的行为系商业行为，目的在于吸引消费者，促进消费，不符合合理使用的法律规定，也不符合对室外艺术品的复制构成合理使用的情形。

最终，北京知识产权法院判决驳回上诉，维持原判。

（资料来源：《北京青年报》，作者：李铁柱）

【杭州互联网法院首次确立区块链电子存证的法律审查方式】 2018年6月28日，杭州互联网法院对一起侵害作品信息网络传播权纠纷案进行公开宣判，首次对采用区块链技术存证的电子数据的法律效力予以确认，并明确了区块链电子存证的审查判断方法。

本案中，原告杭州某公司为证明被告深圳某公司在其运营的网站中发表了原告享有著作权的相关作品，通过第三方存证平台，进行了侵权网页的自动抓取及侵权页面的源码识别，并将该两项内容和调用日志等的压缩包计算成Hash值上传至Factom区块链和比特币区块链中。该种以区块链技术作为电子数据存储、确保数据完整性的方式，是互联网技术与电子数据存证的新融合，给机构创新、维权模式创新提供了更多的可能性，体现电子证据发展新趋势。

杭州互联网法院认为，对于采用区块链等技术手段进行存证固定的电子数据，应秉承开放、中立的态度进行个案分析认定。既不能因为区块链等技术本身属于当前新型复杂技术手段而排斥或者提高其认定标准，也不能因该技术具有难以篡改、删除的特点而降低认定标准，应根据电子数据的相关法律规定综合判断其证据效力。

杭州互联网法院结合区块链技术用于数据存储的技术原理，以电子证据审查的法律标准为基础，对区块链电子存证的效力认定确立了如下审查方式：

（1）审查电子数据来源的真实性。包括第三方存证平台资质合规、产生电子数据的技术可靠、传递电子数据的路径可查。

（2）审查电子数据存储的可靠性。包括电子数据上传至公共区块链、各区块链存放内容相互印证、区块节点生成时间符合逻辑。

（3）审查电子数据内容的完整性。即电子数据Hash值能验算一致未被修改。

（4）审查电子证据与其他证据相互印证的关联度，从而对该种证据的法律效力及证明力予以确认。

具体到本案，该院认为通过可信度较高的自动抓取程序进行网页截图、源码识别，能够保证电子数据来源真实；采用符合相关标准的区块链技术对上述电子数据进行存证固定，确保了电子数据的可靠性；在确认 Hash 值验算一致且与其他证据能够相互印证的前提下，做出了该种电子数据可以作为本案侵权认定依据的判定。

（资料来源：杭州市互联网法院）

【上海知识产权法院判令盗版软件侵权者赔偿 1 505 万元】 2018 年 6 月 29 日，上海知识产权法院就一起侵害计算机软件著作权纠纷案做出一审判决，判令被告上海某科技股份有限公司立即停止侵害原告达索系统股份有限公司 CATIA V5 系列计算机软件著作权的行为，并赔偿原告经济损失及合理费用共计 1 505 万元。上海知产法院此举再次重拳严惩盗版软件恶意侵权者，切实维护了权利人的合法权益。

原告达索系统股份有限公司是 CATIA 系列计算机软件作品的著作权人。原告发现被告作为一家独立汽车工程技术公司，在各大人才招聘网站发布招聘熟练运用 CATIA 软件的专业技术人员信息，原告认为，有证据表明被告公司存在大量非法使用原告 CATIA 系列软件的行为，故诉至上海知产法院，并向法院申请诉前证据保全。

原告认为，被告在其公司场所内的电脑上商业使用原告享有著作权的 CATIA 系列计算机软件的行为，构成软件著作权侵权，请求法院判令被告立即停止侵害原告 CATIA 系列计算机软件著作权的行为，赔偿原告经济损失 1 500 万元和合理支出 11 万元。

被告则认为，抽查中没有 CATIA 系列软件工作日志以及工作日志不完整的计算机不应视为使用过该被控侵权软件，此外，被告使用涉案软件是作为教学目的，属于合理使用，因此，被告不存在著作权侵权行为。

上海知识产权法院审理后认为，首先，依据《中华人民共和国著作权法》第二条第二款规定、《计算机软件保护条例》第五条第三款规定和《伯尔尼保护文学和艺术作品公约》第五条之一规定，结合原告提交的软件登记证明书、公证书等证据，可以证明其系涉案软件的著作权人，根据相关国际条约的规定，原告对涉案软件依法享有的著作权应受到中国法律保护。

其次，根据证据保全现场勘验笔录、相关摄影摄像记录以及司鉴中心鉴定意见书，可以认定被告在其公司工作场所内的电脑上安装过 CATIA 系列软件。鉴定人在抽检的 18 台电脑中通过日志文件的修改日期可以推定被告在证据保全过程中删除过相关软件，鉴于被告毁灭证据的行为，法院对被控侵权事实做出不利于被告的推定，也即认定被告在电脑上安装的 CATIA 系列软件系原告在本案中主张著作权的软件。

本案中，被告无论是从经营范围、企业介绍还是招聘信息内容来看，均是专业从事汽车设计的商业公司，并非教育机构或公益机构，属于 CATIA 系列软件的商业用户，因此，被告使用软件的行为并非属于合理使用。

综上所述，被告未经原告许可，在其经营场所内的电脑上安装了原告主张著作权的涉案软件，侵害了原告对涉案软件享有的复制权，依法应当承担停止侵权、赔偿损失的民事责任。

（资料来源：中国知识产权网，作者：陈颖颖　胡宓，原标题为：《再次重拳出击，严惩软件盗版！上海知产法院判令侵权者赔偿 1 505 万元》）

【北京电视台因擅自使用油画作品一审被判侵权】 北京市海淀区人民法院（以下简称海淀法院）对原告王某某与被告北京电视台侵犯著作权纠纷一案做出一审判决，判令北京电视台停止侵权，赔礼道歉并赔偿经济损失 10 万元等。

王某某诉称，其创作了《马踏匈奴》《霍去病收复河西》《劲风》《战神》4 幅油画作品（以下简称涉案作品），并依法享有著作权。在北京电视台承制并享有著作权的纪录片《大西山》的第四集《烽烟》中，有两处画面未经许可使用了涉案作品，并进行了动态处理，侵犯了王某某享有的署名权、修改权、保护作品完整权、摄制权、信息网络传播权。

北京电视台则认为，《大西山》系其委托第三方公司制作的，根据相关合同约定，其已尽到合理注意义务；同时，《大西山》是公益性质的纪录片，为说明历史场景“安史之乱”而适当引用涉案作品属于合理使用，不构成侵权。

法院经审理认为，《大西山》未经王某某许可，使用了涉案作品，也未为其署名；将原用于表现汉代将军、战争的涉案作品用于展示唐代“安史之乱”的历史事件，实质性地改变了作者想要表达的内容及思想感情，亦可能导致公众产生对涉案作品的理解和认识的误差。《大西山》将涉案作品呈现动态效果，属于将静态的作品用于以摄制电影或者以类似摄制电影的方法创作作品，故认为《大西山》侵犯了王某某的署名权、保护作品完整权和摄制权。北京电视台在享有《大西山》著作权的同时亦应承担该片因侵权产生的法律责任，故北京电视台应就《大西山》侵犯王某某上述著作权的行为承担侵权责任。

（资料来源：《中国知识产权报》，作者：海凡，原标题为：《擅自使用油画作品，北京电视台一审被判侵权》）

【“混搭”销售教辅出版物书商因违法获刑】 安徽省宿州市萧县人民法院判决了一起跨省制售盗版教辅出版物侵犯著作权案。法院判决被告人梁某某犯侵犯著作权罪，判处有期徒刑3年，缓刑4年，并处罚金人民币9万元。该案为国家版权局挂牌督办案件，也是宿州市查办的第一起涉著作权刑事案件。

2017年12月1日，宿州市“扫黄打非”办公室接到全国“扫黄打非”办公室转交的群众举报线索，称宿州市萧县某中学涉嫌使用盗版图书。接报后，宿州市“扫黄打非”办公室立即协调相关部门进行查办。

经查，2017年8月底，山东省济宁市梁山县图书供货商梁某某向宿州市萧县某中学高三年级推销教辅用书，并提供了正版的样书和相关证件，但在实际向学校提供图书时，掺杂了大量盗版书。同年12月3日，专案组负责人根据萧县文广新局执法人员掌握的证据和案情，果断决定由萧县公安局对返回萧县的梁某某依法采取强制传唤措施。据梁某某交代，为了掩盖自己的犯罪事实，他于12月1日将涉案盗版图书全部替换成正版图书，并将涉案盗版出版物当作废品卖掉。了解情况后，办案人员迅速对被梁某某卖掉的涉案出版物进行追缴，几经周折，最终在江苏省徐州市一处收购废品的仓库中找到，共计追回完整涉案出版物3 700余本。随后，执法人员又前往梁山县对印制该批涉嫌非法出版物的企业进行现场查证，对该企业负责人张某依法办理了刑事拘留手续，目前正在网上追逃。

经查明，梁某某向萧县某中学销售盗版教辅图书，涉案出版物7 845册，涉案金额超过17.15万元。

（资料来源：《中国新闻出版广电报》，作者：陈涛）

【“面包新语”侵权案二审被判赔偿119万余元】 2018年7月5日，上海知识产权法院就“面包新语”月饼包装礼盒著作权侵权纠纷案做出终审判决，依法驳回涉诉双方的上诉，维持一审判决，即上海新语面包公司（以下简称新语公司）等需停止侵权，并赔偿上海锦恒包装制品有限公司（以下简称锦恒公司）经济损失等119.7万元。

2016年3月，锦恒公司为新语公司设计了5款月饼外盒，后因新语公司内部人员变动，双方未达成合作。随后，锦恒公司发现，新语公司销售的5款“面包新语”品牌月饼套装使用了其设计，于是，以新语公司等侵犯著作权为由，向上海市普陀区人民法院（以下简称普陀法院）分别提起5起诉讼。新语公司表示，锦恒公司的设计是基于其已有作品改编而成，缺乏独创性，因此，不构成侵权。

2017年9月28日，普陀法院就相关5起涉诉案件做出一审判决，判令新语公司等停止侵权，并赔偿锦恒公司经济损失等119.7万元。双方对此判决均表示不服，分别上诉至上海知识产权法院。

上海知识产权法院经审理后确定，5款月饼外盒上的图案均属于具有独创性的、受著作权法保护的美术作品，其著作权由锦恒公司享有，一审法院认定事实清楚，适用法律正确，应予维持，驳回原被告双方的诉讼请求。

（资料来源：《中国知识产权报》，作者：张彬彬，原标题为：《因为5款月饼外盒，“面包新语”被判赔偿119万余元!》）

【“同人作品内地第一案”宣判】 乔峰、令狐冲、黄蓉、王语嫣……这些金庸笔下耳熟能详的名字，也是作家江南《此间的少年》书中的“汴京同学”。金庸的一纸诉状，掀起“同人作品内地第一案”的波澜。

2018年8月16日上午，广州市天河区法院对该案一审宣判，判决杨治（笔名：江南）不构成侵犯著作权，但构成不正当竞争，赔偿查良镛（笔名：金庸）经济损失168万元及为制止侵权行为的合理开支20万元。查良镛、杨治均未出庭，各方诉讼代理人亦未当庭明确是否上诉。

查良镛诉称，杨治创作的《此间的少年》未经许可，照搬其作品中的经典人物，在不同环境下量身定做与金庸作品相似的情节，擅自篡改作品人物形象，严重侵害了其著作权。

同时，杨治通过盗用上述独创性元素吸引读者、谋取竞争优势，获利巨大，违背了诚实信用原则，严重妨害了金庸对原创作品的利用，构成不正当竞争。

查良镛请求法院判令杨治停止侵权、赔礼道歉、消除影响并赔偿经济损失500万元及合理开支20万元。联合出版公司、精典博维公司未尽审查职责，应承担连带责任。广州购书中心销售侵权图书，也应承担停止侵权的法律责任。

对此，杨治辩称，《此间的少年》与查良镛的武侠小说存在根本区别，也未使用查良镛作品中具有独创性的表达部分，不构成实质性相似，没有侵犯查良镛的著作权。其在《此间的少年》中对查良镛作品要素的使用属合理使用。

杨治辩称，其创作、出版和发行《此间的少年》，并未违背诚实信用原则和公认的商业道德，亦未对查良镛的合法权益造成实际损害，不构成不正当竞争行为。

天河法院判决，杨治、联合出版公司、精典博维公司应立即停止涉案不正当竞争行为，停止出版发行小说《此间的少年》并销毁库存书籍；杨治、联合出版公司、精典博维公司应在《中国新闻出版广电报》中缝以外的版面刊登声明，同时在新浪新闻首页显著位置连续七十二小时刊登声明，向查良镛公开赔礼道歉，并消除不正当竞争行为所造成的不良影响；杨治应赔偿查良镛经济损失人民币168万元，联合出版公司、精典博维公司就其中30万元承担连带责任；杨治应赔偿查良镛为制止侵权所支付的合理开支人民币20万元，联合出版公司、精典博维公司就其中3万元承担连带责任；驳回查良镛的其他诉讼请求。

（资料来源：《广州日报》，作者：魏丽娜，原标题为：《金庸一审获赔188万元》）

【杭州法院宣判全国首例涉“小猪佩奇”著作权侵权纠纷判决案】 2018年8月20日，杭州互联网法院对一起“小猪佩奇”的著作权侵权纠纷案进行网上公开宣判。

艾斯利贝克戴维斯有限公司（以下简称艾贝戴公司）、娱乐壹英国有限公司（以下简称娱乐壹公司）于2005年8月19日向美利坚合众国申请“Peppa Pig”（“小猪佩奇”）著作权登记并获得登记证书，后向中国国家版权局申请“Peppa Pig”“George Pig”“Daddy Pig”“Mommy Pig”（“佩奇”“乔治”“猪爸爸”“猪妈妈”）著作权登记并获得作品登记证书。并且，艾贝戴公司、娱乐壹公司生产、制作《小猪佩奇》动画片及其他衍生产品（包括但不限于配套书籍、小猪布偶、玩具、APP应用程序等），并在全球范围推广。

不久之后，艾贝戴公司、娱乐壹公司发现汕头市聚凡电子商务有限公司（以下简称聚凡公司）在其淘宝网“聚凡优品1”店铺中大量销售印制有涉案作品人物形象的“小猪佩奇厨房小天地”玩具，且显示生产商为被告汕头市嘉乐玩具实业有限公司（以下简称嘉乐公司）。

艾贝戴公司、娱乐壹公司认为，聚凡公司未经许可销售涉案被控侵权产品并展示相关图片，嘉乐公司未经许可生产、销售涉案被控侵权产品，均已严重侵害其所享有的美术作品著作权。浙江淘宝网络有限公司作为网络服务提供商，并未对商家上架的产品是否涉嫌侵权进行主动审查，应当承担停止侵权的法律责任。

杭州互联网法院认为“佩奇、乔治、猪爸爸、猪妈妈”以线条、色彩或者组合呈现出富有美感的人物形象和艺术效果，具有独创性，属于著作权法保护的美术作品。

据此，判令嘉乐公司、聚凡公司停止侵权行为并赔偿艾贝戴公司、娱乐壹公司经济损失及合理费用共计15万元。

（资料来源：杭州网，作者：许佳炜　王川，原标题为：《“社会人”打假啦！杭州法院宣判全国首例涉“小猪佩奇”著作权侵权纠纷判决案》）

【今日头条为《一郭汇》维权获胜】 因认为百度在线网络技术（北京）有限公司、北京百度网讯科技有限公司未经许可，擅自播放视频节目作品《一郭汇》，“今日头条”运营商北京字节跳动科技有限公司以侵害作品信息网络传播权为由分别将百度在线网络技术（北京）有限公司、北京百度网讯科技有限公司诉至法院。2018年8月，北京市海淀区人民法院审结了此案，法院判决二被告分别向北京字节跳动公司赔偿经济损失及合理支出共计1.25万元。

原告北京字节跳动公司诉称，其是视频节目作品《一郭汇》的著作权人，合法享有《一郭汇》作品的完整著作权。除西瓜视频外，原告未许可通过其他平台传播该节目。百度在线公司为《好看视频》APP（安卓端）的开发者，百度网讯公司为《好看视频》APP（iOS端）的开发者，同时百度网讯公司为《好看视频》的运营者。二被告共同向用户提供《好看视频》APP的下载、安装、运营和相关功能的更新、维护服务。原告发现，二被告在未经其许可的情况下将其拥有著作权的《一郭汇》节目内容以相同标题名称发布至《好看视频》APP，并为其用户提供该作品的在线播放及下载服务。二被告的行为严重侵害了原告对涉案作品享有的信息网络传播权，给原告造成巨大的损失。原告要求判令二被告分别停止侵权，赔礼道歉并赔偿经济损失及合理支出 8 万元。

被告百度在线公司和百度网讯公司共同辩称，认可原告对涉案视频的权属，《好看视频》APP 是以短视频为主，主要采用 UCG 模式，基本为用户上传。经二被告反复查找，因《好看视频》用户上传入口统一在百家号，后台信息量较大，现仍未查找到涉案视频的上传者信息，对此二被告愿意承担责任。二被告已删除涉案视频并做了删除公证。关于诉讼请求，因涉案视频已经删除，故判令停止侵权的请求已无必要；由于二被告并未侵犯原告的著作人身权，故二被告不应承担赔礼道歉、消除影响的侵权责任；关于涉案视频的性质，原告制作的涉案视频，仅是对郭德纲讲述、聊天过程及周边环境的简单连续摄像，每段视频的场景单一、内容简单、创作程度不高，与法律规定的电影作品和以类似摄制电影的方法创作的作品的创作高度不符，故涉案视频应属于著作权法中规定的录音录像制品。涉案视频在被告平台播放次数少，且涉案视频仅为时长 15 分钟的脱口秀节目，故原告的索赔数额过高，请法院酌情裁量。

法院经审理后认为，涉案视频长度较短且场景固定，但涉案视频节目主题明确，亦通过镜头切换、画面选择拍摄、后期剪辑等过程完成，其连续的画面反映出制片者的构思，表达了与主题相关的思想内容，具备较强的独创性，已经不同于机械方式录制的录像制品，故法院认定涉案视频为以类似摄制电影的方法创作的作品。结合涉案视频的署名情况及作品登记证书记载的情况、今日头条有限公司的《说明函》等，在被告认可原告对涉案作品权属的情况下，法院确认北京字节跳动公司作为涉案作品的著作权人有权提起本案诉讼。

法院经审理认为，二被告作为《好看视频》APP 两个端口的开发者，虽辩称涉案视频系网友上传但未能提交相应证据，故其应当对未经原告许可提供涉案视频的行为承担侵权责任。但由于北京字节跳动公司诉求的依据是被告侵害了其信息网络传播权，这属于财产权的范畴，故北京字节跳动公司主张二被告应刊登声明向其赔礼道歉、消除影响的诉讼请求缺少法律依据，法院无法予以支持。

（资料来源：海淀法院网，作者：海法，原标题为：《百度“好看视频”被判侵权今日头条〈一郭汇〉著作权》）

【赔 1800 万！网络点播公司因盗播热剧被重判】 2018 年 8 月，因北京优朋普乐科技有限公司（以下简称优朋普乐）未经著作权人及被授权方腾讯公司许可，擅自提供《锦绣未央》和《大唐荣耀》热播剧的网络点播服务，北京市西城区人民法院依法判决，优朋普乐侵害腾讯公司享有的信息网络传播权，两部剧分别赔偿 1 000 万元和 800 万元。

2016 年 11 月 1 日，电视剧《锦绣未央》在东方卫视、北京卫视晚间黄金档开播，腾讯视频被授权在网络端同步更新播出。自首播以来，无论在电视荧屏还是在互联网，《锦绣未央》都获得了很高的收视率和社会关注度，并且名列国家版权局《2017 年第一批重点作品版权保护预警名单》。有数据显示，至 2016 年 11 月 14 日，《锦绣未央》在腾讯视频的播放量达到 71.3 亿次。

腾讯公司获得网络播放权的另外一部大型古装剧《大唐荣耀》在 2017 年初播出后，收视率持续上升。至 2017 年 2 月 9 日，《大唐荣耀》在腾讯视频的播放量达到 7.5 亿次。

明知两部电视剧处于在卫视及腾讯视频网站热播的时期，优朋普乐却未经权利人和腾讯许可，“零成本”向其用户提供播放服务。不仅如此，在天津地区，用户通过天津联通 IPTV 机顶盒进入“天津 IPTV”主界面购买“V 聚好看”套餐，从“VIP 专区”进入“优朋 OTV 聚好看”，才可以观看《锦绣未央》《大唐荣耀》。拿着盗取的版权资源，赚取用户的付费，盗播者此举令人气愤。

优朋普乐在收到权利人发送的律师函之后，短暂下架了视频，但之后又上线播放。明知两部电视剧热度很高，优朋普乐却在首播之后很短的时间内，没有经过权利人和腾讯公司的授权，擅自在其运营的 IPTV“朋友影视”专区，向北京、天津、重庆、河北及四川等地的互联网电视用户提供《锦绣未央》《大唐荣耀》的点播服务，并采取与首播节目相同的每天更新的形式，直到将全部剧集播放完毕。

对于优朋普乐的恶意侵权行为，北京市西城区人民法院判决其立即停止侵权，停止在其运营的 IPTV“朋友影视”专区对电视剧《锦绣未央》《大唐荣耀》提供在线点播服务，并且在判决生效 10 日内分别赔偿腾讯经济损失 1 000 万元、800 万元。如未在判决指定的时间内履行给付金钱义务，优朋普乐要加倍支付迟延履行期间的债务利息。

（资料来源：《中国新闻出版广电报》，作者：隋明照）

【北京互联网著作权纠纷有了“全程在线”法院】 北京互联网法院2018年9月9日正式挂牌收案，集中管辖北京市辖区内应当由基层人民法院受理的第一审特定类型互联网案件，在审理方式上以“全程在线”为基本原则。

受理案件包括互联网著作权权属纠纷、互联网著作权侵权纠纷、互联网域名纠纷、互联网侵权责任纠纷、互联网购物合同纠纷、互联网服务合同纠纷等。

由北京互联网法院一审审结的涉互联网著作权权属纠纷和侵权纠纷知识产权类的案件，若当事人不服，可向北京知识产权法院提起上诉。

（资料来源：《中国新闻出版广电报》，作者：鞠焕宗）

【剪辑影视作品发到短视频平台被判侵权】 2018年9月，江苏省苏州市中级人民法院就搜狐视频（以下简称原告）诉北京字节跳动科技有限公司（以下简称被告）侵害著作权一案做出一审判决，判决认定原告胜诉，被告构成帮助侵权，应承担相应的法律责任。

一审法院认为，原告享有《屌丝男士》第一季至第四季网剧作品的著作权。被告在其经营的网站“今日头条”及移动客户端中，向公众提供《屌丝男士》短视频的在线点播服务。被告明知或应知网络服务对象利用其平台传播侵权短视频，却怠于采取必要措施、放任侵权行为发生，存在主观过错，侵害了原告所享有的信息网络传播权。

法院认为，被告的侵权行为具体表现为以下几点：首先，原告针对被告网站平台存在侵权视频的情况，曾先后多次发函通知下线，相关通知定位清晰，但是侵权视频密集，且在被告每次删除后，侵权视频仍反复出现、屡删不绝。其次，被告所主张的“结合算法、个性推荐”的做法也可证明其对涉案视频已进行了一定程度的审查，应知晓用户上传涉案视频存在侵权行为。再次，从技术能力角度而言，被告已开发版权保护平台，可识别相应视频与版权库“原片”是否高度相似，即被告有能力预防侵权，但其并未采取排查、删除侵权视频的合理措施。最后，被告作为专业、大型的短视频运营网站，在影视作品权利人一次次发送侵权链接通知后依然无法真正消除侵权视频反复出现的问题，在侵权情形如此明显的情况下，应负有较高程度的注意义务。因此，法院判定被告实施了帮助侵权行为，侵害了原告所享有的信息网络传播权。

（资料来源：《中国新闻出版广电报》，作者：孙磊，原标题为：《剪辑影视作品发到短视频平台，小心侵权！》）

【4篇新闻报道获赔10万元　给网络“新闻搬运工”敲响警钟】 2018年10月8日，《现代快报》起诉《今日头条》所属北京字节跳动科技有限公司的侵犯著作权纠纷案历时3年获终审判决，江苏省高级人民法院驳回上诉，字节跳动公司因未经授权转载《现代快报》4篇文章，须赔偿经济损失10万元，另赔偿《现代快报》为维权支出的合理费用1.01万元。

回顾案件，2015年6月5日—8月31日，《现代快报》分别刊登了由该报记者署名的6篇新闻。在没有获得《现代快报》授权的情况下，《今日头条》予以转载。同年9月，江苏现代快报传媒有限公司以侵害著作权为由，将北京字节跳动科技有限公司起诉至无锡市中级人民法院。

字节跳动公司认为，除《叶落归根，九旬老太恢复中国国籍》一文外，其余涉案文章均篇幅短小，仅以平铺直叙的方式载明事实经过，且刊登在新闻栏目里，故属于不受《著作权法》保护的“时事新闻”。字节跳动公司据此认为，现代快报公司与涉案记者对该文章不具有著作权。

无锡市中级人民法院一审认为，涉案文章属于《著作权法》意义上的作品，属于作者的独创性智力劳动，符合《著作权法》保护的时事新闻，且涉案记者均为现代快报公司聘用的记者，所创作的作品系完成工作任务的职务作品，著作权属于现代快报公司及其无锡分公司，因此字节跳动公司所诉无法律依据，不予采纳。

一审判决后，字节跳动公司不服判决结果，提出上诉。江苏省高级人民法院审理后认为，一审法院认定的事实均有相应证据证明，适用法律适当，应予维持。判决认定的事实均有相应证据证明，字节跳动公司在《今日头条》客户端提供涉案4篇文章构成侵权，其仅提供链接服务的辩解不能成立。综上所述，江苏省高级人民法院做出终审判决：驳回上诉，维持原判。

（资料来源：《中国新闻出版广电报》，作者：袁舒婕，原标题为：《4篇文章获赔10万元，〈现代快报〉胜诉——给网络“新闻搬运工”敲响警钟》）

【快手诉华多侵权一审获赔两万元】 2018年10

月 15 日，北京市海淀区人民法院（以下简称海淀法院）就北京快手科技有限公司（以下简称快手公司）起诉广州华多网络科技有限公司（以下简称华多公司）侵犯著作权纠纷两案做出一审判决，认定《PPAP》（时长 36 秒）和《这智商没谁了》（时长 18 秒）两条短视频（以下统称涉案视频）构成作品，华多公司侵犯了快手公司依法享有的信息网络传播权，分别判决华多公司赔偿快手公司经济损失各 1 万元及相应的合理开支。

快手公司系《快手》APP 的运营管理商，《快手》APP 用户分别在《快手》APP 上传、发布了涉案视频。经该用户授权，快手公司取得了涉案视频的独家信息网络传播权。快手公司认为，华多公司未经其许可，在其运营的《补刀》APP 中上传并发布了涉案视频，该行为侵犯了其著作权。华多公司否认侵权，提出涉案视频时长很短故不构成作品等抗辩理由。

海淀法院经审理后认为，两案的主要争议焦点之一在于涉案视频是否构成作品。首先，涉案视频集合了音乐、表演者的表演、特效制作、对话、场景等一个或多个内容，既非对表演的机械录制，也不属于创意、思维方法、技术方案等抽象范畴的内容，或基本素材或公有领域的信息。其次，虽涉案视频仅有数十秒甚至是十几秒，时长短的确可能限制作者的表达空间，但这并不等于表达形式非常有限而不算作思想范畴的产物；相反在这较短的时间内亦可以创作出体现一定主题，且结合文字、音乐、场景、特效等多种元素的内容表达。据此，涉案视频是作者思想和情感的表达，且其作为数字化的视频，客观上亦可被固定并以有形形式复制，故结合其制作方式，涉案视频应属于类似电影方法创作的作品，受著作权法保护。

（资料来源：《中国知识产权报》，作者：司笛）

【北京互联网法院首案开庭审理】 2018 年 10 月 30 日上午，北京互联网法院公开开庭审理该院挂牌成立后受理的第一起案件——《抖音》短视频诉《伙拍》小视频著作权权属、侵权纠纷一案。

该案原告北京微播视界科技有限公司诉称：《抖音》短视频平台上发布的《5·12，我想对你说》短视频，由创作者“黑脸 V”独立创作完成，应作为作品受到《著作权法》保护。原告对于涉案短视频享有独家排他的信息网络传播权等权利。被告百度在线网络技术（北京）有限公司、被告北京百度网讯科技有限公司未经原告许可，擅自将涉案短视频在其拥有并运营的《伙拍》小视频上传播并提供下载服务。原告认为二被告未经许可擅自传播的行为给原告造成了极大经济损失，故提起诉讼，请求法院判令二被告在百度网站首页及《伙拍》小视频客户端首页显著位置连续 24 小时刊登声明，消除影响；赔偿原告经济损失 100 万元、合理支出 5 万元；并承担诉讼费用。

二被告辩称：涉案短视频不具有独创性，不构成著作权法上的“作品”，不属于著作权法的保护范围。原告无法证明其为涉案短视频的作者或权利人，无权就涉案短视频提起诉讼。《伙拍》小视频提供的是信息存储空间服务，涉案短视频系该平台注册用户上传，二被告不对用户上传的内容进行任何编辑、整理和修改，不知道也没有合理理由应当知道注册用户的上传行为，二被告已经尽到合理注意义务。原告在诉前未按照《信息网络传播权保护条例》第 14 条的规定向被告进行有效投诉，原告主张的损失赔偿缺乏事实基础和法律依据。请求法院依法驳回原告全部诉请。

庭审中，合议庭结合当事人诉辩意见，对涉案短视频是否构成作品、当事人主体身份是否适格、被控侵权行为情节与性质、被告主张的免责事由是否成立等问题进行细致调查。双方当事人针对案件争议焦点进行充分辩论。时长约 150 分钟的庭审，驾驭得当、脉络清晰。

本次开庭采用在线审理模式，双方当事人无须亲自到法院，而是通过远程登录北京互联网法院电子诉讼平台的方式参加诉讼。庭审全程采用语音自动识别系统进行记录，法庭内未设有书记员席。整个庭审过程顺畅有序，信号传输无任何卡顿，涉案视频的播放、庭审笔录的自动生成以及远端的庭审笔录电子签名等技术，有效节约了当事人的诉讼成本，提升庭审效率，带给当事人良好的参诉体验。

（资料来源：中国知识产权资讯网，作者：祝文明）

【一份许可合同引发多起版权诉讼】 因一份著作权许可协议，广东原创动力文化传播有限公司（以下简称原创动力公司）与北京优朋普乐科技有限公司（以下简称优朋公司）多次对簿公堂。2018 年 10 月，广州知识产权法院就上诉人原创动力公司（一审被告）与被上诉人优朋公司（一审原告）之间的著作权许可使用合同纠纷案做出二审判决，认定优朋公司请求返还许可使用费 107 万元及利息的诉讼请求没有依据，不予支持，撤销广东省广州市越秀区人民法院（以下简称越秀法院）做出的一审判决。此前，也因这份合同，原创动力公司将优朋公司诉至北京市西城区人民法院（以下简称西城法院），经北京知识产权法院二审判决，原创动力公司获赔逾期付款违约金 4.65 万余元。

2012 年 8 月 25 日，优朋公司与原创动力公司签订《许可使用协议》，约定原创动力公司以专有独占性授权将动画片《喜羊羊与灰太狼》《羊羊运动会》等作品部分剧集的信息网络传播权授予优朋公司，许可使用期限为 3 年。协议签订后，优朋公司于 2012 年 9 月 28 日向原创动力公司支付版权费 252 万元，原创动力公司亦向优朋公司交付了授权书等相关授权文件。

然而，两公司在合同履行过程中产生了纠纷。在未收到优朋公司应支付的 108 万元剩余款项，且多次催款未果后，原创动力公司于 2014 年 4 月向其发送《〈许可使用协议〉解除通知书》。因双方仍未能就剩余款项问题达成一致意见，2015 年，原创动力公司将优朋公司起诉至西城法院。西城法院一审判决优朋公司向原创动力公司支付逾期付款违约金 4.65 万余元，并驳回原创动力公司的其他诉讼请求。原创动力公司不服，向北京知识产权法院提出上诉。北京知识产权法院经审理后，维持一审判决。

优朋公司收到上述二审判决书后向原创动力公司发出一份《〈许可使用协议〉返还授权费通知函》，要求原创动力公司返还多支付的许可使用费 105 万元等。因原创动力公司没有返还上述费用，优朋公司将其起诉至越秀法院。

越秀法院经审理后，对优朋公司主张按授权期限起至协议解除前按实际使用期限及天数据实结算的意见予以接纳，并根据协议实际履行期限，考虑到优朋公司已支付的 252 万元授权使用费等因素后，判决原创动力公司应将剩余许可使用费 107 万余元返还给优朋公司。

原创动力公司不服，向广州知识产权法院提起上诉。广州知识产权法院经审理认为，该案《许可使用协议》的解除是因优朋公司未依照约定按期支付剩余许可使用费所致，原创动力公司对此无过错。如果优朋公司请求返还许可使用费及利息的主张得到支持，意味着优朋公司可以凭借单方意志改变双方通过协商共同确定的权利义务关系，借以逃避本应承担的市场风险或减损原属原创动力公司的利益。这种结果有违双方订立合同的初衷，违背诚实信用原则，对原创动力公司是不公平的，也会损害交易安全，破坏市场秩序，据此判决驳回优朋公司全部诉讼请求，撤销越秀法院做出的一审判决。

广州知识产权法院对该案做出判决后，引起业界关注。该上诉案的一个焦点是：可否参照租赁合同对著作权许可合同已经履行部分的相应价款据实核算。对此，广州知识产权法院经审理认为，在租赁合同中，权利人对同一出租标的在同一时间段内只能有一份收益。在著作权许可合同中，对权利人来说，每一次授权都有可能对应一个具体的增量收益，即在授权合同履行中出现被许可人违约情况时，权利人的损失是净损失，不会因为后续的其他授权得到弥补。因此，参照租赁合同对合同已经履行部分的相应价款据实核算对著作权许可使用合同的权利人是不公平的。

对于此类纠纷，广州知识产权法院认为，商业活动往往充满各种变数，有时收益甚至剧烈波动，对商事主体来说，每一次交易既是机会又蕴含风险。著作权授权合同应是版权人与被授权人之间达成的平等、有偿合同，无论是自然版权人，还是法人公司，作为商事主体应当具有专业的判断能力和注意义务，在签约时应对市场交易环境、履约成本、收益进行充分估算和预期，并对履约后果及可能产生的各种风险在合同中进行详细约定，并自愿承担责任。

（资料来源：《中国知识产权报》，作者：姜旭）

【《一封家书》被改编　作者获单首作品高额赔偿】 因认为其创作的歌曲《一封家书》未经许可被使用，作者李春波将云南俊发房地产有限公司、北京搜狐互联网络信息服务有限公司诉至法院，要求二被告停止侵权行为，立即删除侵权信息，公开道歉并赔偿经济损失 200 万元。北京市海淀区人民法院审结了此案。法院判决云南俊发公司向李春波赔礼道歉、赔偿经济损失 30 万元及合理开支 6 700 元。此案是涉单首音乐作品著作权纠纷判赔数额较高的案件。

原告李春波诉称，云南俊发公司未经其同意，使用其创作的知名歌曲《一封家书》制作视频，并将该视频在该公司认证的账号中发布，用于宣传促进其楼盘销售，侵犯了李春波对歌曲《一封家书》词曲享有的署名权、修改权、保护作品完整权、改编权、信息网络传播权及摄制权；搜狐公司在其网站中擅自发布上述视频，对云南俊发公司业务进行推广，与云南俊发公司共同侵犯了李春波的信息网络传播权。二被告应承担连带侵权责任。

被告云南俊发公司辩称，涉案视频中的歌词均是书信常用语，而非李春波创作的专有词汇，涉案视频与歌曲《一封家书》创作的时代、背景、传达的情感等不同，曲谱也有所不同，故不构成侵权。

被告搜狐公司辩称，涉案视频是由用户上传，其仅是信息存储空间服务提供者，且不存在侵权的主观过错，亦不构成侵权。

法院经审理后认为，本案主要争议焦点为涉案视频中的歌曲是否构成对《一封家书》词曲的改编，以及如果侵权成立，判赔数额应如何确定。

第一，涉案视频的歌曲是否构成对歌曲《一封家书》的改编。本案中，对于歌词部分，涉案视频歌词与《一封家书》歌词均采用了家书的格式，将家书形式与歌词结合起来用作音乐表达，开头和结尾处部分歌词相同，且表达了同样的思乡情感；同时，涉案视频歌词中又加入了体现独创性表达的新的叙事内容，因此涉案视频歌词在原有歌曲独创性表达基础上，形成了新的表达，构成对原歌词的改编。对于曲谱部分，涉案视频曲谱与《一封家书》曲谱的起音、落音、骨干音以及旋律均基本相似，歌曲风格、旋律走向亦相似，但部分旋律也存在明显差异，并加入了说唱的形式，因此，涉案视频曲谱使用了原歌曲曲谱的基本内容，并对原歌曲的旋律做了创造性修改，却又没有使原有旋律消失，构成对《一封家书》曲谱的改编。同时，将《一封家书》与涉案视频歌曲进行整体对比，两者名称相同，且开头结尾歌词相同，曲谱主旋律亦相似，使人听到涉案视频歌曲时便会联想到歌曲《一封家书》。因此，涉案视频词曲构成对歌曲《一封家书》词曲的改编。

第二，关于经济损失赔偿数额的确定，法院综合考虑到，歌曲《一封家书》发表于1994年，多年来久被传唱，具有较高知名度和影响力；云南俊发公司在其公众号文案中借助歌曲《一封家书》的影响力进行宣传，主观恶意明显；涉案视频内容中对云南俊发公司及其关联公司经营的房地产项目进行商业宣传，涉案视频点击量高达9万余次，影响范围较大，依法酌情判定经济损失赔偿额为30万元。

（资料来源：《中国新闻出版广电报》，作者：张筠曼）

【搜狐视频在一著作权许可使用合同纠纷案中胜诉】 天津市高级人民法院就搜狐视频（以下简称原告）诉北京优朋普乐科技有限公司（以下简称被告）著作权许可使用合同纠纷一案做出终审判决，最终维持一审原判认定原告胜诉，被告根据著作权许可使用合同支付原告涉案影视剧许可使用费共计410万元。

涉案电视剧《解密》于2016年6月20日晚在湖南卫视金鹰独播剧场首轮播出，原告通过版权采购方式于原始权利方处取得独占性信息网络传播权、网络定时传播权以及单独进行法律维权行动的权利。2016年5月，原、被告双方邮件沟通并达成合意，被告向原告采购含《解密》电视剧的非独家权利，在双方沟通采购合同过程中，原告在合意的上线时间前交付被告涉案电视剧《解密》的介质、片花、海报、剧照等正片及宣传物料下载链接以及FTP地址。其后，被告找借口拖延合同签署时间并单方告知终止此次合作，不再签署任何合同，对被告已经上线使用的《解密》电视剧不再向原告支付任何款项，故原告将被告诉至天津市第二中级人民法院。

一审法院经审理认为，虽然原、被告之间没有合法有效的书面合同，但根据原、被告的实际行为，可以认定双方就影视剧《解密》的授权使用、价款达成了一致，被告也已接受并通过信息网络向公众提供了在线播放服务，因此被告应当向原告支付授权使用费，故判决被告支付原告电视剧《解密》授权使用费410万元。

被告不服一审判决故提起上诉。二审法院经审理认为，原告提供的微信聊天记录和电子邮件往来记录，均系电子数据证据，从形成的时间、内容的连续性等方面可以形成完整的证据链条，证明被告首先向原告表明了采购《解密》的意愿；并且原告在涉案电视剧《解密》上线前已向被告发送网络上线要求和下载《解密》介质的FTP地址以及海报、剧照、片花的下载地址，被告不仅没有对原告交付介质提出异议，而且积极与原告拟定合同条款并一直在线播放电视剧《解密》。综上所述，可以认定原告已经依约履行了及时交付介质的主要合同义务，依据合同法的相关规定，原、被告之间存在电视剧《解密》信息网络传播权的许可使用合同，双方权利义务内容应当以邮件沟通合同中授权条款为准。故二审法院判决维持一审原判，被告应向原告支付影视剧《解密》授权使用费共计410万元，原告终审胜诉。

从本案一、二审法院认定可以看出，合同关系并非仅在有签署或盖章的书面合同的情况下才可成立，也可能存在没有书面合同但构成事实上的合同关系的情形。同时，这一案例也警示我们，在商务合作过程中，要及时保存从前期合作沟通、协议签署过程及双方全部义务履行过程中各环节的相关证据，这样可以减少或避免一方假借合作的名义达到自身占领不当竞争优势或损害合作方利益的违背诚信原则的行为，从法律上也可以防止诚信一方的缔约过失。

（资料来源：《中国新闻出版广电报》，作者：孙磊）

【中国网络作家村正式上链杭州互联网法院司法区块链】 2018 年 12 月 6 日，杭州互联网法院召开区块链运行情况暨中国网络作家村上链启动仪式新闻发布会，中国网络作家村正式上链杭州互联网法院司法区块链。

中国网络作家村于 2017 年在杭州市滨江区正式落户，目前已经集聚了唐家三少、月关、管平潮、蝴蝶蓝、猫腻等诸多网络作家。

这些网络作家创造了许多传播快、受众广、影响力大的网络文学作品。然而随之而来的侵权行为也呈现出侵权成本低、侵权手段隐蔽、侵权主体难寻等特点，特别是网络侵权取证难问题，给网络作家维权造成很大困扰。

此次，中国网络作家村的作家们将通过数字版权行业链上链杭州互联网法院司法区块链，进一步推进中国网络作家村建设，加大知识产权保护力度。

“司法区块链尤其适用于数字版权保护。通过司法区块链，维权者可在线上完成从创作到维权所有内容全流程记录、全链路可信、全节点见证，有效解决了作者身份确定难、作品形成时间及内容固定难和侵权证据取证难等问题。”杭州互联网法院副院长王江桥说。目前，杭州互联网法院已立案的 88 件通过司法区块链维权案件均为网络著作权、邻接权侵权纠纷。

发布会现场，网络作家倾城日光薇娜登录司法区块链平台，成功进行确权操作，成为中国网络作家村上链后第一个“吃螃蟹”的作家。中国网络作家村完成上链后，将进一步激发原创作家的维权热情，持续净化和维护版权生态，优化网络文学的发展环境。

自杭州互联网法院于 2018 年 9 月上线司法区块链以来，截至 12 月 5 日，司法区块链平台已经接入多个节点，存证量突破 1 200 万条。司法区块链平台对行业链和司法链基础节点进行见证，但不直接参与确权、取证等业务。普通用户需通过数字版权、金融服务、电子合同等行业链接入，行业链已经制定了标准的接入规范与通信协议，确保司法链能够标准化和规范化运作。

（资料来源：中国新闻网，作者：胡哲斐）

【文著协诉中国知网一审有果】 2018 年 12 月 19 日，北京市海淀区人民法院审结了中国文字著作权协会（以下简称文著协）诉《中国学术期刊（光盘版）》电子杂志社有限公司（以下简称学术期刊公司）、同方知网（北京）技术有限公司（以下简称同方知网公司）侵犯著作权纠纷一案。法院经审理认定，二被告未经著作权人授权，在中国知网、《全球学术快报》手机客户端提供汪曾祺作品《受戒》的下载服务，侵犯了著作权人享有的信息网络传播权，应承担停止侵权、赔偿经济损失及合理开支的法律责任。

原告文著协诉称，中国当代著名作家汪曾祺系作品《受戒》的作者，其去世后，作品著作权由三名子女汪明、汪朗、汪朝共同继承。文著协作为著作权集体管理组织，经著作权人授权，可以对涉案作品的信息网络传播权等相关事宜进行维权诉讼。文著协发现，二被告未经授权，通过电子化复制，将《北京文学》《文学界》《芳草》《朔方》《雪莲》《阅读》《天涯》《可乐》《名作欣赏》九种期刊中刊载的作品《受戒》，在中国知网及《全球学术快报》手机客户端平台上向公众提供，并通过付费下载的方式，获取非法收益，侵犯了涉案作品著作权人的信息网络传播权。

被告学术期刊公司辩称，其通过中国知网发布的涉案作品处于 2000 年 12 月 21 日施行的《最高人民法院关于审理涉及计算机网络著作权纠纷案件适用法律若干问题的解释》（以下简称 2000 年司法解释）施行期内，属于该司法解释第三条规定的网络转载法定许可期间。虽然最高人民法院在 2006 年 12 月废止了关于网络转载法定许可的规定，但根据法不溯及既往的原则，该案应继续适用该条司法解释。

被告同方知网公司辩称，其仅为《全球学术快报》手机客户端提供技术支持，不参与中国知网网站和《全球学术快报》手机客户端的运营，不应承担侵权责任。

法院经审理后认为，中国知网收费提供涉案作品的行为不属于 2000 年司法解释第三条规定的网站转载、摘编行为，与著作权法在个人利益与社会公共利益之间进行平衡的基本原则相违背，对著作权人的经济利益产生直接冲突和影响，无法适用该条规定予以抗辩。学术期刊公司未经涉案作品权利人或文著协的许可，在其经营的中国知网中提供九本期刊中涉案作品的下载服务，使用户可以在其个人选定的时间和地点获得涉案作品，侵犯了涉案作品著作权人的信息网络传播权；二被告通过分工合作的方式，通过《全球学术快报》手机客户端共同向网络用户提供涉案作品的下载服务，亦侵犯了涉案作品著作权人享有的信息网络传播权，应承担共同侵权责任。最后，法院判令二被告立即停止侵权行为；学术期刊公司赔偿文著协经济损失1万元，同方知网公司对其中的2 000元承担连带赔偿责任；二被告连带赔偿文著协合理开支1万元。

（资料来源：中国知识产权资讯网，作者：张彬彬　张筠曼）

【VR非法提供作品　热波公司一审判赔35万元】 因认为对方未经合法授权，擅自利用《VR热播》软件iPad端通过信息网络非法向公众提供《妄想症》《四大名捕2》《火锅英雄》3部影视作品的在线播放服务，北京爱奇艺科技有限公司（以下简称爱奇艺公司）将热波（北京）网络科技有限责任公司（以下简称热波公司）以侵犯作品信息网络传播权为由诉至法院。北京市海淀区人民法院做出一审判决，依法判决被告向原告赔偿经济损失及合理费用共计35.56万元。

原告爱奇艺公司诉称，其经授权取得涉案影视作品《妄想症》《四大名捕2》《火锅英雄》的独占性信息网络传播权，被告热波公司未经原告合法授权，在其运营的应用软件《VR热播》iPad端，通过信息网络非法向公众提供涉案影视作品的在线播放，该行为侵害了其合法权益，故诉至法院，请求法院判令被告热波公司赔偿原告经济损失及合理开支。被告热波公司未到庭亦未提交书面答辩意见。

法院经审理认为，原告爱奇艺公司基于授权继受取得涉案3部作品的独占性信息网络传播权，且在授权期间内有权以自己的名义进行维权，他人未经许可不得使用涉案作品。被告热波公司在其经营的《VR热播》iPad端上向公众提供《妄想症》《四大名捕2》《火锅英雄》3部作品，使相关公众可以在其选定的时间和地点获得涉案作品，该行为未经原告许可，侵犯了原告享有的作品信息网络传播权，依法判决被告热波公司赔偿原告爱奇艺公司经济损失及合理支出共计35.56万元。

如今，VR技术应用在生活的方方面面，包括视频、娱乐、新闻、旅游、展览、运动等场景。在以VR形式呈现他人原创作品时，使用者应遵循“先授权后使用”的原则，获得有关作品著作权人的授权，然后再进行合法使用，否则可能招致侵权风险。正如本案审理法官呼吁，在保护知识产权的前提下，推广技术创新，让技术发展与知识产权保护并肩同行。

（资料来源：《中国知识产权报》，作者：侯伟）

◆ 行政管理

【四川省版权局督导绵阳创建国家版权示范城市工作】 2018年1月8—9日，四川省版权局赴绵阳开展创建国家版权示范城市督导工作。

督导组一行认真听取绵阳市创建全国版权示范城市前期工作情况汇报，详细了解市、县（市、区）执法机构开展版权执法工作进展，逐一查阅2012年以来新闻出版广播影视（版权）行政执法案件卷宗，开展版权执法工作业务培训，细致讲解相关法律适用范围和版权行政执法案件办理要求。其间，督导组还深入三台县实地调研版权监管执法情况，检查指导包装印刷企业作品版权登记、版权保护及产业发展工作。

督导组要求，要抓住国家版权局正式批复同意绵阳市创建“全国版权示范城市”的契机，认真对照创建工作指标体系，全面推进版权保护、版权执法、版权成果转化等各项工作，加强版权执法监管，积极查办大案要案，营造版权工作有利环境，力争高质量、高水平建成“全国版权示范城市”。

（资料来源：绵阳市文化广电新闻出版局）

【河北省软件正版化工作考核组到衡水市督导考核】 2018年1月22—23日，河北省软件正版化工作考核组一行到衡水市就2017年度软件正版化工作进行督导考核。衡水市副市长崔海霞出席汇报会。

考核组听取了衡水市2017年度软件正版化工作开展情况的汇报，并实地检查了市政府办公室、市发改委及冀州区政府办公室、区财政局使用正版软件工作情况，查阅了相关资料。考核组对衡水市2017年度软件正版化工作开展情况给予肯定，认为衡水市领导高度重视，措施得力，各部门履职尽责，推进使用正版软件工作成效显著。希望衡水市在今后工作中，要进一步提高思想认识，加大资金投入，加强源头采购，强化基层培训，加强督导检查，确保软件正版化工作的制度化、规范化、常态化。

崔海霞表示，将以此次考核为契机，坚决落实省考核组提出的意见和建议，进一步加强组织领导，强化工作措施，狠抓任务落实，切实做到认识再提高，推进再加力，责任再强化，确保优质高效地完成各项工作任务。

（资料来源：《衡水日报》，作者：李晨阔）

【湖北省软件正版化工作督查小组到黄冈检查】 2018年1月，湖北省政府软件正版化工作督查小组到黄冈检查软件正版化工作。检查组先后实地检查了黄冈市政府办公室、市文广局、科技局、审计局、国资委、统计局、扶贫办、旅游委等部门和单位软件正版化工作情况，听取工作汇报，并就加强软件正版化工作提出指导意见。

省督查组成员、省版权处调研员邹喜玲反馈了检查情况，检查组认为黄冈市委、市政府高度重视软件正版化工作，工作推进有力，活动资料齐全规范，各相关单位积极配合，指导市直和各县市区工作到位，但也存在个别单位领导重视不够、少数被检单位随便下载软件、软件正版化长效机制不完善等问题。督查组组长、省经信委副主任卜江戎在充分肯定黄冈市软件正版化工作成效的同时，提出四点要求。黄冈市软件正版化工作领导小组组长、市人民政府副市长陈家伟陪同督查，并就落实省督查组要求，加强全市软件正版化工作提出具体要求。

（资料来源：黄冈市文化新闻出版广电局）

【山东省版权局召开版权工作座谈会】 2018年1月，山东省新闻出版广电（版权）局召开版权工作座谈会，谋划2018年版权工作。副局长谢宁出席会议并讲话。部分版权交易中心负责同志、版权示范单位代表参加座谈。

谢宁强调，当前，版权产业成为新旧动能转换的重要因素，要积极整合不同领域的版权资源，加强各部门间协作，形成版权产业发展合力。要进一步创新传播手段，扩大宣传力度，特别是抓住青少年这个重点群体，制定符合青少年特点的版权宣传活动。要充分发挥好山东版权协会在全省版权工作中的重要作用，积极搭建高起点平台，努力打造具有山东特色的版权品牌。

会上，山东城市出版传媒集团、山东文化版权交易中心、山东世博文化传播有限公司、山东省区域文化产业研究院负责人做了交流发言。

（资料来源：山东省版权局）

【广东省工作组对茂名市版权工作进行考评】 2018年1月，广东省版权保护组织建设与执法工作考评组就茂名市2017年版权保护组织建设与执法工作进行考评。经全面考评后，对茂名市版权保护组织建设与执法工作给予充分肯定。

考评期间，省考评组根据省委政法委、省全面依法治省工作领导小组有关文件及省版权局《关于印发〈2017年度广东省版权保护组织建设与执法工作考评办法〉的通知》要求，逐一对照考评标准，从版权组织建设情况、版权行政执法监管情况、版权社会服务情况、软件正版化工作情况及版权创新加分情况等五个方面对茂名市版权工作台账和考评佐证材料逐项进行检查验收及评分。同时采取听取汇报、查阅计算机软件使用相关授权书、购买合同和上机实地检查等方式，先后对茂名市神马物流有限公司、国鑫融资担保有限公司、粮食储备公司等3家国有企业及市交通局、市科技局、市府办等3家政府机关的软件正版化工作情况进行了检查。

考评组充分肯定了茂名市2017年版权保护组织建设与执法工作，认为茂名市此次考评备检材料规范翔实，工作开展扎实有效。同时，考评组对市府办使用正版软件工作也给予了充分肯定，认为市政府已全面使用了正版软件，为茂名市推广使用正版软件工作带了好头，起了很好的示范引领作用。

（资料来源：茂名网，作者：谭筱　陈伟涛）

【内蒙古开展2022年北京冬奥会会徽版权保护工作】 2018年1月，内蒙古自治区采取五项具体措施快速启动北京冬奥会会徽版权保护工作：一是制定工作方案。要求各盟市版权行政管理部门制定开展北京冬奥会版权专项保护工作方案和应急预案，健全执法检查和快速处理机制。二是明确监管重点。要求各地全面梳理线下重点监管对象、监管市场、监管区域，线上重点监管网站、电子商务平台和移动互联网应用程序（APP）商店，明确具体监管名单，实现线上线下执法全覆盖。三是公开举报方式。要求设立电话、网站、邮箱、微信等多种举报方式，通过各类媒体广泛宣传，并对如实举报者给予奖励。四是强化日常监管。加强对辖区内大型集贸市场、商品集散地、图书批发市场、著名旅游景点、电子商务平台的日常监管，建立重点单位沟通联系名单，及时掌握涉案线索，跟踪督办重点案件。五是加强宣传培训。各级版权管理和执法部门通过广播、电视、报纸、网站、微信等媒体对保护冬奥会会徽版权进行宣传，将北京冬奥会版权保护内容纳入“4·26”知识产权宣传周宣传重点，在版权培训中开设相应课程。

（资料来源：内蒙古自治区版权局）

【安徽省版权局开展电影院线版权专项治理工作】 2018年2月，安徽省版权局积极开展打击电影院线侵权盗播专项治理工作，通过实地检查、约谈、法规宣传普及等方式对省内主要电影院线提出明确要求，各电影院线必须加强播放行为管理，规范播放秩序，严防偷拍盗录，确保著作权人的权益得到保护。

安徽省版权局联合合肥市文化市场执法支队召集了部分在肥电影院线主要负责人会议，了解各单位情况，强调：各电影院线要加强版权保护意识，防止偷录行为，依法及时有效维护自身合法权益；同时，要树立依法经营意识，坚决杜绝未经授权放映、私自偷拍盗录等著作权侵权违法行为。

安徽省版权局要求各电影院线一要积极做好相关法律法规宣传工作，利用灵活多样的形式强化职工和观众的版权保护意识，形成全社会共同关注版权的良好氛围。可采取映前广播提醒、映前播放版权保护公益广告、在院线显著位置设置加强版权保护、禁止偷拍盗录警示标识等方式进行宣传。二要加强风险防控，增加工作人员巡场频率。特别要加强重点作品和重要场次的巡场。三要完善内部监督机制，推进相关管理制度落实，严防“内外勾结”传播作品行为。

（资料来源：安徽省版权局）

【推进使用正版软件工作部际联席会议第七次全体会议召开】 2018年3月2日，中宣部副部长、时任国家新闻出版广电总局（国家版权局）局长聂辰席在京主持召开推进使用正版软件工作部际联席会议第七次全体会议。聂辰席强调，2018年是全面贯彻党的十九大精神的开局之年，是改革开放40周年，是决胜全面建成小康社会、实施“十三五”规划承上启下的关键一年，软件正版化工作面临着新形势新任务，迫切要求有新气象新作为，部际联席会议要以习近平新时代中国特色社会主义思想为指导，强化知识产权创造、保护和运用，努力开创新时代软件正版化工作新局面。

会议认为，2017年部际联席会议认真贯彻落实党的十九大精神和国务院的决策部署，各成员单位齐心协力、攻坚克难，按照推进落实主体责任、规范使用管理、保障信息安全的工作思路，加强统筹协调、服务指导和督促检查，推动各地区各部门补齐制度短板，完善长效机制，进一步巩固扩大了软件正版化工作成果。一是党政机关软件正版化不断规范。各级党政机关认真贯彻落实国务院办公厅印发的《政府机关使用正版软件管理办法》等相关政策措施，按照部际联席会议编制的《正版软件管理工作指南》，不断健全软件正版化工作机制，加强制度建设，规范软件采购，建立软件台账，严格使用管理。30个省（区、市）出台了党政机关软件正版化工作考核办法，并开展了软件正版化考评工作。二是企事业单位软件正版化全面铺开。在巩固中央企业和大中型金融机构软件正版化工作基础上，推进小型金融机构和地方企事业单位软件正版化工作取得积极进展。三是软件版权保护环境持续改善。部际联席会议加强软件市场监管，积极推进使用正版软件，促进了软件版权保护环境持续改善，为软件产业发展提供了良好的市场环境。据统计，2017年，部际联席会议共督查单位389家、检查计算机26 989台；各级党政机关共采购操作系统、办公和杀毒软件127.7万套，采购金额达6.12亿元；中央企业和金融机构共采购操作系统、办公和杀毒软件245.11万套，采购金额21.45亿元；软件著作权登记量达到74.54万件（同比增长82.79%），软件和信息技术服务业收入达到5.5万亿元（同比增长13.9%）。截至2017年底，全国累计推进37 667家企业实现软件正版化。

聂辰席指出，持续推进软件正版化，是学习贯彻习近平新时代中国特色社会主义思想和党的十九大精神的必然要求，是落实新发展理念、深化供给侧结构性改革的必然要求，是加快建设创新型国家的必然要求，对营造创新环境、增强经济创新力和竞争力、保障国家信息安全，都具有重要意义。为扎实做好2018年推进使用正版软件工作，聂辰席提出了五点要求：第一，进一步突出工作重点，努力巩固扩大成果。要紧紧抓住长效机制建设、源头监督管理、终端使用检查、督促考核评议、年度情况报告等关键环节，切实巩固软件正版化工作成果。要以党政机关、中央企业和大型金融机构中的先进典型为示范，分类别、分行业深入推进企事业单位软件正版化工作，不断扩大软件正版化工作覆盖面。第二，进一步创新方式方法，实现安全发展两促进。要坚持推进软件正版化与大力发展软件产业紧密结合，综合运用法律、行政和技术手段，改善软件版权保护环境，加强软件产品研发指导，提高软件产业供给体系质量，推动软件产业高质量发展，为深化供给侧结构性改革、提升国民经济运行质量做出更大贡献。要坚持正版化与信息化、信息安全紧密结合，以信息安全为抓手，同步推进正版化与信息化，保障国家重要信息系统和基础设施信息安全。

第三，进一步加强协调配合，不断增强工作合力。随着推进软件正版化工作不断深入，工作涉及面越来越广，协调难度越来越大，艰巨性、复杂性的特点日益凸显，更加需要发挥联席会议制度优势，集中各成员单位智慧和资源，共同解决问题、推进工作。第四，进一步强化督查考核，推进责任落实。督查考核是推动落实责任、推进工作最直接有效的手段，正版化工作尤其需要通过督查考核反复抓、抓反复，确保各项政策措施落地生效。要进一步完善常态化督查机制，推进党政机关督查全覆盖，加强企事业单位督查，突出加强事中、事后监管，并适时开展“回头看”，对督查发现问题的单位，敢于亮剑、揭短亮丑，抓好督查通报，追究相关人员责任，提升震慑力。要抓紧抓实软件正版化考核评议工作，充分发挥考核“指挥棒”作用，激励先进、鞭策落后。第五，进一步做好宣传引导，积极营造良好氛围。总体看，当前中国公众版权保护意识仍需不断提高，一些地区和部门对软件正版化的重视程度也还不够。需要把宣传引导放在重要位置，通过多种形式宣讲国家政策，宣传典型案例，推广先进经验，增强各方面做好工作的自觉性、主动性。

时任国家新闻出版广电总局副局长、国家版权局专职副局长周慧琳通报了 2017 年推进使用正版软件工作进展情况和 2018 年工作计划。时任国家工商总局副局长王江平、银监会副主席周亮、保监会副主席黄洪、国家知识产权局副局长贺化、时任国管局副局长陈建明、中直管理局副局长张宇航以及工信部、财政部、商务部、国务院国资委、国务院法制办、证监会、全国工商联、全国打击侵权假冒工作领导小组办公室等部门有关负责人，部际联席会议各成员单位联络员出席会议。会议审议通过了《2017 年推进使用正版软件工作总结》和《2018 年推进使用正版软件工作计划》。

（资料来源：中国新闻出版广电网，作者：赖名芳）

【陕西省版权局调研铜川版权公共服务工作】 2018 年 3 月 7 日，陕西省新闻出版广电局（版权局）党组成员、版权局专职副局长沙庆超一行 4 人赴铜川调研版权公共服务工作。铜川市文化广电局局长梁秀侠、耀州窑文化基地管理委员会主任何建平一同调研。

调研组一行来到耀州窑文化基地，先后参观了耀瓷小镇大师创意园、铜川市观唐陶瓷有限公司、铜川市耀州窑陶瓷发展有限公司和耀州窑博物馆，详细了解了耀瓷小镇的规划布局、园区建设以及耀州瓷的发展历史、文化传承和烧制技艺，肯定了耀瓷小镇文化、旅游、产业、社区四位一体的发展理念。

在随后召开的座谈会上，调研组一行结合耀瓷小镇的实际情况，向耀州窑文化基地及参会企业详细介绍了版权制度的相关内容，对企业产品被侵权情况进行了询问调查，认真听取各企业提出的产权问题并给予了政策性的解答。沙庆超指出，版权是文化产业发展的核心资源，具有为文化产业服务、让文化产业受益的现实意义，要提高版权保护意识、加大版权宣传力度，培育版权服务机构，并就版权服务工作站试点与耀州窑文化基地进行了初步协商。

（资料来源：铜川市文化广电局，作者：梁晓沛）

【江苏省开展 2018 年第一期网络侵权盗版案件集中打击行动】 2018 年 3 月 19—23 日，江苏省版权局在扬州举办 2018 年江苏省第一期网络侵权盗版案件集中打击行动。国家版权局版权管理司副司长段玉萍、江苏省新闻出版广电局副局长于国民在行动期间到现场指导，对集中行动办案模式予以肯定，要求以创新精神提高办案质量。

此次集中行动采取先期排查案件线索、集中开展远程勘验，分组进行落地查人的办法，集中时间、集中场地、集中办案。经过一周的紧张工作，集中行动已初见成效，执法队员办案能力明显提升。下一步，各地将根据省局统一部署分头行动，加大大案要案查办力度，依法打击各类侵权盗版行为。

各设区市、省管县（市）版权执法骨干参加行动，省通信管理局、省“扫黄打非”办以及常州、南通和扬州执法支队专家应邀到现场指导。

（资料来源：江苏省版权局）

【福建省召开推进使用正版软件工作厅际联席会议第五次全体会议】 2018 年 3 月 30 日，福建省推进使用正版软件工作厅际联席会议第五次全体会议在福州召开。会议由厅际联席会议牵头单位福建省版权局副局长肖贵新主持，厅际联席会议各成员单位相关部门负责人和联络员出席会议。

会上，福建省版权局通报了全省 2017 年推进使用正版软件工作情况和推进使用正版软件工作部际联席会议对福建省软件正版化工作督查情况。福建省国资委、银监局、保监局、工商联等成员单位分别通报了 2017 年所监管行业企业软件正版化工作开展情况。会议研究讨论并审议通过了《福建省 2018

年推进使用正版软件工作实施方案》。

肖贵新在会上强调，2018 年软件正版化工作的重点是进一步加强制度建设，强化督促检查，完善长效机制，坚持制度与技术并重，正版化与信息化同步推进，巩固扩大工作成果，开创新时代推进使用正版软件工作新局面。同时对做好全省 2018 年推进使用正版软件工作提出五点意见：一是要继续充分发挥联席会议作用，二是要不断完善长效工作机制，三是要进一步巩固和扩大工作成果，四是要持续加强督促检查，五是要广泛开展宣传培训。

（资料来源：福建省版权局）

【北京市版权局组织召开网络盗版侵权案件推进协调会】 2018 年 3 月，为有效推进网络版权治理工作，突破盗版侵权案件治理瓶颈问题，北京市版权局版权管理处组织召开网络盗版侵权案件推进协调会，北京市公安局海淀分局、首都版权产业联盟参会，权利人优酷、腾讯、爱奇艺派相关人员参加。

会上市公安局海淀分局相关负责同志从网络盗版侵权案件的立案调查、证据固定、法律适用和办案技巧等方面做了分析介绍。首都版权产业联盟监测中心对典型案件的技术特征、盈利模式和运营特点做了分析和演示，随后权利方代表对盗链、盗播等具有典型性的盗版侵权技术进行了详细讲解说明。会议指出当前网络侵权盗版环境日益复杂，盗版技术层出不穷，为有效推进版权案件办理，各部门应做好以下几方面工作：一是要建立部门协作联动机制，畅通监测、举报、治理等环节的信息共享渠道，实现网络侵权的综合治理；二是要紧跟新技术、新方法，提高案件办理的主动性和灵活性；三是要重视证据工作，提高监测的针对性、有效性和技术性；四是要发挥典型案例的震慑作用，通过办理有社会影响力的案件，树立版权保护意识，净化网络版权空间。

（资料来源：北京市版权局）

【江苏省版权局督查组对宿迁市侵权盗版案件查处情况进行督查】 2018 年 4 月 3 日，江苏省版权局督查组赴宿迁市，对两起侵权盗版案件查处情况进行督查。

在汇报会上，宿迁市公安局和市文化行政综合执法支队相关同志分别就“7·20”张某等人侵犯著作权案和某网站侵犯著作权案汇报了相关工作进展以及在查办过程中遇到的困难和问题。督查组对宿迁市案件查办工作采取的措施及取得的成绩给予了肯定，并对下一步工作提出了三点要求：一是进一步加大各部门之间的合作力度，凝聚工作合力，建立打击网络侵权盗版的长效机制。二是加大对上级交办案件线索追查和落实力度，及时跟进，确保案件办理的质量和成效。三是强化案件信息报送，及时向省局报送案件查办进度，加强信息沟通交流。

（资料来源：宿迁市文化广电新闻出版局，作者：闫维龙）

【黄坤明出席国家广播电视总局、国家新闻出版署（国家版权局）和国家电影局揭牌仪式并召开座谈会】 2018 年 4 月 16 日，中共中央政治局委员、中宣部部长黄坤明出席国家广播电视总局、国家新闻出版署（国家版权局）和国家电影局揭牌仪式并召开座谈会，强调要坚持以习近平新时代中国特色社会主义思想为指导，切实把思想和行动统一到党中央决策部署上来，用机构改革的新成效，激发宣传思想文化工作的新能量新作为。

黄坤明指出，党中央决定中宣部统一管理新闻出版和电影工作，组建国家广播电视总局，充分体现了以习近平同志为核心的党中央对宣传思想文化工作的高度重视，体现了加强党对新闻出版、广播电视和电影工作全面领导的必然要求，是推进宣传思想文化领域治理体系和治理能力现代化的重大举措，对于更好推动宣传文化事业繁荣发展、满足人民美好生活需要，更好服务党和国家工作大局，具有重大现实意义和深远历史意义。

黄坤明强调，要以这次机构改革为契机，紧紧围绕学习宣传贯彻习近平新时代中国特色社会主义思想和党的十九大精神这条主线，坚定文化自信，勇于改革创新，积极担当作为，始终坚持正确导向，坚持以人民为中心，坚持高质量发展，不断谱写新时代宣传思想文化工作的新篇章。

中宣部部务会成员、国家广播电视总局党组成员出席相关活动。

（资料来源：新华社）

【安徽省动员部署软件正版化工作】 2018 年 4 月 19 日，安徽省召开软件正版化工作联席会议全体会议，安徽省版权局副局长董荣出席会议，对 2018 年工作进行了动员部署并提出了要求。会议学习了推进使用正版软件工作部际联席会议第七次（2018 年）全体会议精神，总结了 2017 年全省软件正版化工作，安排了 2018 年的重点工作任务，重温了联席会议成员单位工作职责，听取了各成员单位 2017 年工作情况汇报和2018年工作打算，审议并通过了《安徽省2018年软件正版化工作实施方案》。联席会议12家成员单位悉数出席了会议。

会议部署了2018年的重点工作。一要着力强化工作责任落实，大力推进市、县级政府机关建立健全管理制度，积极开展“回头看”和查遗补漏。二要着力提升政府机关单位软件正版化工作水平，重点推进省级政府机关所属机构软件正版化工作。三要着力扩大企业使用正版软件覆盖面，重点推进和完善省属企业及所属二、三级企业，新闻出版广电企业，诚信示范企业，农村中小金融机构等企业的软件正版化工作。四要着力加强工作督促检查，采取有效措施，坚持依法推进；坚持服务督促并举，确保软件正版化工作取得实效。

（资料来源：安徽省版权局）

【吉林省版权局：完善版权资产管理制度　提高版权保护能力】 2018年4月19日，吉林省版权局制定印发了《关于加强新闻出版广播影视企事业单位版权资产管理工作的实施意见》(以下简称《实施意见》)，指导省内新闻出版广播影视行业各相关企事业单位，建立和完善版权资产管理制度，进一步提高相关企事业单位版权保护和运用的能力。

《实施意见》要求，各有关单位应建立或指定专门的工作机构作为版权资产管理部门，负责制定、执行本单位版权资产管理制度，开展版权资产的清查、管理及运用等业务，确定版权资产管理绩效目标，加强版权资产管理绩效评价，保证版权资产的保值、增值及有效利用。相关单位应保证给予版权资产管理机构必要的物质条件，配备专职工作人员，确保机构有效运行，切实发挥作用。

同时，要求各单位参照《新闻出版广播影视企业版权资产管理工作指引（试行)》，根据行业特点和自身实际情况，制定相应的版权资产管理制度，围绕本单位所拥有版权资产的形成、保护、使用、交易、流转等环节，建立完整的决策、计划、组织、领导、监控、评价的管理机制，规范版权资产管理行为，有效评价版权资产管理效能，为本单位发展提供内生动力。

此外，该《实施意见》还建议各有关单位加强与版权管理部门的沟通，做好版权作品自愿登记工作，通过版权作品登记开展本单位版权资产的清查工作，划清现有版权资产权利归属，对其核心、重要版权资产授权使用和流转交易等重大合同行为向版权行政管理部门进行备案，确保有关合同行为依法依规，防范版权资产交易的法律风险。

（资料来源：《中国新闻出版广电报》，作者：张席贵）

【重庆市检察院和市文化委建立保护版权协作机制】 2018年4月，重庆市人民检察院、市文化委正式建立保护版权协作机制。这标志着在市文化委与市工商局、市公安局相继签署战略合作协议的基础上，涵盖行政、公安、检察、法院，集监管、执法、公诉、审判等各项职能为一体的“重庆版权保护工作体系”日臻完善。

该项机制通过开展普法教育、推进协同作战、强化案件办理等举措，按照最高检、国务院“双打”办、国家版权局工作部署要求，致力于在全市范围内加大对各类侵权盗版行为的打击力度，联合开展针对非法传播音乐、影视、新闻、游戏、文学、软件等作品的重点网站和智能移动终端第三方应用程序（APP)，以及网络云存储空间、网络广告联盟、智能移动终端应用软件商店、网络销售平台等违法犯罪行为的综合整治行动。两部门将立足各自的职能分工与专业特长，突出查办大案要案，依法整治网络空间，净化网络版权环境，优化网络版权生态，为全社会的创新创造和经济社会发展保驾护航。

重庆市检察院党组成员、政治部主任钟勇，市文化委副主任、市版权局副局长王增恂分别代表双方在合作协议上签字，并分别发表了讲话。市高法院、市公安局有关部门同志出席签约仪式。

（资料来源：重庆市文化委）

【云南省推进使用正版软件工作联席会议办公室召开2018年第一次联络员会议】 2018年5月15日，云南省推进使用正版软件工作联席会议办公室召开2018年第一次联络员会议。云南省新闻出版广电局副局长、省推进使用正版软件工作联席会议办公室主任洪耀星主持会议并讲话。

会议传达学习了国家推进使用正版软件工作部际联席会议第七次全体会议精神；研究了云南省2018年软件正版化重点工作任务，对《云南省党政机关推进使用正版软件工作考核办法（试行)》进行了讨论；通过了关于举办2018年云南省边境州（市）县（区）级政府机关软件正版化工作培训班等相关事宜。

云南省工信委、商务厅、审计厅、国资委、工商局、法制办、工商联、知识产权局、银监局、证监局、保监局，省政府督查室，省机关事务管理局等成员单位代表参加了会议，省新闻出版广电局版权处全体人员列席会议。

（资料来源：云南省版权局）

【湖北省召开使用正版软件工作领导小组成员单位联席会议】 2018年5月29日，湖北省推进使用正版软件工作领导小组成员单位联席会议在武汉召开，省政府副秘书长刘仲初出席会议并讲话。会议传达贯彻国务院推进使用正版软件工作部际联席会议第七次会议精神，通报了湖北省2017年推进软件正版化工作情况，审议通过了《2017年全省软件正版化工作检查情况通报》《2018年湖北省推进使用正版软件工作计划》《2018年湖北省软件正版化督查实施方案》等相关文件，重点研究部署了2018年工作任务。

湖北省新闻出版广电局、省版权局专职副局长胡伟主持会议，省机关事务管理局副局长、党组成员戴峰，湖北证监局副局长、党委委员郑秀荣，省知识产权局副局长程浩，省经济和信息化委员会副巡视员聂晓勤，省商务厅二级巡视员卢大珍，省工商行政管理局二级巡视员瞿常琦，省工商联二级巡视员宋维，省政府采购中心副巡视员徐进，省政府国有企业第一监事会主席牟秉夔，及省法制办、省财政厅、湖北银监局、湖北保监局等成员单位负责人及联络员出席会议。

（资料来源：湖北省版权局）

【青海省直机关软件正版化工作会议召开】 2018年5月29日，青海省直机关软件正版化工作会议在西宁召开。会议肯定了所取得的成绩，深入分析了面临的问题和不足，明确了改进措施和要求。副省长、省推进软件正版化工作领导小组组长张黎出席会议并讲话。

会议强调，各部门各单位必须进一步强化问题意识，坚持问题导向，针对日常监管不到位、制度建设不完善、使用盗版或未授权软件等问题，建立问题清单和责任台账，制定整改方案，明确时间表、路线图和责任人。要强化主体责任，健全责任链条，拧紧责任螺丝，切实提高履责效能，确保如期整改到位。要高度重视，严肃对待，以不整改到位不松手的坚决态度，抓实抓细各个环节，把好源头关口，为国家全覆盖检查交出一份满意的答卷。

青海省政协办公厅、省直机关工委、省食品药品监管局、省总工会代表在会上做了交流发言。

（资料来源：《青海日报》，作者：李欣）

【广西部署2018年全区自治区级机关使用正版软件工作】 2018年6月7日，广西自治区级机关使用正版软件工作会议暨培训班在南宁举办。会议通报了广西2017年使用正版软件工作整体情况以及2017年度自治区级机关使用正版软件工作考核结果，强调要从促进知识产权保护、提高民族创新能力、维护国家安全的高度进一步增强推进软件正版化工作的责任感和紧迫感。

会议对推进2018年各中直、区直驻南宁机关单位使用正版软件工作进行部署。要求：一是加强组织领导，在工作中形成“统一领导、分级负责”的工作格局，把工作责任落实到位；二是加强常态化管理，落实工作长效机制，从落实主体责任、落实采购经费预算、采购安装正版软件、规范使用管理、保管工作台账等方面着手，建立完善各个环节的工作制度；三是加强源头管理与软硬件资产管理，按照《关于进一步加强全区机关单位计算机软硬件资产采购管理工作的通知》要求，把好采购关，规范计算机软硬件资产管理；四是加强督促检查和宣传培训，要结合国家督查组、自治区督查组的督查开展自我检查，有效整改发现的问题。同时积极开展宣传培训，提升推进软件正版化工作的能力。

（资料来源：广西壮族自治区版权局）

【世界杯赛事节目纳入重点作品版权保护预警名单】 2018年6月14日，国家版权局公布2018年度第五批重点作品版权保护预警名单，2018俄罗斯世界杯赛事节目入选。根据要求，相关网络服务商应对版权保护预警名单内的重点作品采取以下保护措施：直接提供内容的网络服务商未经许可不得提供版权保护预警名单内的作品；用户上传内容的网络服务商应禁止用户上传版权保护预警名单内的作品；提供搜索链接的网络服务商、电子商务平台及应用程序商店应加快处理预警名单内作品权利人关于删除侵权内容或断开侵权链接的通知。

而在此之前，国家广电总局也发出通知，称根据互联网电视管理的181号文，2018年俄罗斯世界杯比赛不允许在互联网电视平台上进行赛事的直播和延时播出，否则都属于违规，只能在赛事结束后提供比赛点播服务。6月5日，中央广播电视总台曾发布了2018俄罗斯世界杯相关节目版权声明，称根据国际足联授权，其拥有此届世界杯中国大陆地区独家全媒体转播权及分授权权利。未经书面授权，任何机构或个人不得在中国大陆地区通过电视、广播、互联网、移动通信网、IPTV、互联网电视、移动媒体电视、各类应用软件及其他任何音视频转播技术或平台以直播、延迟播出、点播、轮播、下载或剧场院线播放、公共场所播放等其他任何方式使用 2018 年世界杯比赛的音视频节目内容、广播电视信号或任何相关素材。根据与国际足联达成的协议，该台负有维护世界杯节目权益、打击盗版盗播行为的法律义务。为此，其将联合各方加大维权力度，依法采取包括法律手段在内的有效措施坚决打击任何侵犯世界杯节目版权的盗版盗播行为。

（资料来源：《中国知识产权报》，作者：侯伟）

【河北廊坊：督导全国版权示范城市创建工作】 2018 年 7 月 5 日，河北省廊坊市召开创建全国版权示范城市工作推进会暨廊坊市政府部门使用正版软件工作会议，就创建全国版权示范城市工作进行再动员、再部署。

2017 年 8 月，国家版权局正式批复同意廊坊市创建全国版权示范城市，廊坊成为河北省首个获得全国版权示范城市创建资格的城市，是继 2016 年廊坊市通过国家公共文化服务体系示范区验收后，打造的又一块国家级试点示范金字招牌。

廊坊市委常委、宣传部部长王曦在发言中提出，创建全国版权示范城市涉及面广、包容性强，各级各部门要突出重点，统筹兼顾，全面完成示范城市创建任务。要建立完善版权工作机制和工作体系；培育版权产业，打造版权品牌；创新体制机制，强化管理服务；加强宣传引导，营造良好氛围。要明确责任，精心组织，切实做到组织领导、资金投入、责任落实、督查考核和宣传引导“五到位”，确保示范城市各项创建工作落到实处、取得成效。

河北省版权局副局长郜世泽说，希望廊坊在创建全国版权示范城市工作中，进一步加强制度设计，强化组织建设，推动自主创新，履行管理职能，加强执法监督，建立长效机制，全域使用正版软件，决战决胜，确保以优异成绩完成创建任务。

为加快推进全国版权示范城市创建工作，廊坊市组建 11 个督导小组，围绕创建重点任务进行督导，加快推进全国版权示范城市创建工作。据悉，督导小组将本着实事求是的原则，重点围绕全国版权示范城市的 7 条标准开展督导，全面、准确、客观地反映创建工作的落实情况。

会上宣读了《廊坊市创建全国版权示范城市任务分解方案》、《廊坊市创建全国版权示范城市督导工作方案》和《关于对全市版权产业和版权产业园区进行调研的通知》。会后，河北省版权局相关负责人就使用正版软件进行授课。

（资料来源：《中国新闻出版广电报》，作者：赵新乐）

【全国版权执法监管工作会议在京召开】 2018 年 7 月 12 日，国家版权局在京召开全国版权执法监管工作会议。这次会议是深化党和国家机构改革，中宣部统一管理新闻出版、版权工作之后召开的第一次全国性的版权工作会议。会议深入学习贯彻习近平新时代中国特色社会主义思想和党的十九大精神，传达中央领导同志的重要批示，分析研判当前版权执法监管工作面临的新任务新要求，研究部署“剑网 2018”专项行动等版权执法监管重点工作，推动版权执法监管工作实现新发展。中宣部副部长、国家新闻出版署署长、国家版权局局长庄荣文出席会议并讲话。

会议强调，要以习近平新时代中国特色社会主义思想为指导，深刻把握新时代版权工作的新使命新方向，奋力开创版权工作新局面。充分发挥版权对推动社会主义文化繁荣兴盛的保障作用，不断强化版权创造、保护、运用，充分调动广大作者的创作热情，激发文化创新创造活力，让创新成果源源不断地涌现，努力满足人民群众对美好生活的新期待。充分发挥版权对创新驱动发展的激励作用，加大版权资源的转移转化力度，促进传统产业转型升级，推动经济高质量发展。充分发挥版权对扩大对外开放的助推作用，努力构建法治化、国际化、便利化营商环境，维护公平有序的竞争环境，向国际社会表明中国坚定不移扩大对外开放的决心。

会议指出，新时代版权执法监管工作要按照“严格保护、提升效能、分类监管、引导规范”的工作思路，深入推进版权执法监管工作专业化、社会化、国际化建设，实现新发展。一是要把严格保护作为当前版权工作的重中之重，进一步加大对侵权盗版的惩治力度，进一步提升案件质量与数量，把违法成本显著提上去，把法律威慑作用充分发挥出来。二是要充分发挥行政执法优势，积极主动履行版权监管职责，突出执法重点，加强信息化建设，不断提升版权执法效能。三是要实施版权分类监管，把握不同地区、不同行业、不同作品的特点和版权保护的不同需求，提高监管针对性和精准性，拓展版权保护覆盖面。要综合运用法律、行政和技术等手段，持续推进软件正版化，切实巩固好党政机关软件正版化工作成果。四是要积极引导规范，注重打建结合，推动社会共治，落实主体责任，构建版权保护共同治理新格局，努力营造尊重版权、崇尚创新、诚信守法的良好社会风尚。

会议对组织开展“剑网2018”专项行动提出五项工作要求。第一，抓好重点任务环节。针对目前行业反映多、问题比较严重的新闻转载、短视频、动漫、有声读物和知识分享等领域存在的侵权盗版问题，要突出工作重点，细化工作方案，明确责任措施。第二，抓好大要案件查办。要主动巡查，扩大案源，聚焦大案，依法依规加大行政处罚和刑事打击工作力度。第三，抓好夯实基层基础。要健全完善指导督办机制、奖励培训机制、执法协作机制、快速反应机制，探索建立版权信用评价机制。第四，抓好强化舆论宣传。持续推动社会公众版权意识的提高，加强著作权国际交流合作，利用多双边场合，积极发出中国声音。第五，抓好工作责任落实。发挥领导干部表率带头作用，加强统筹领导，加强督促检查和教育培训，营造良好工作氛围。

国家版权局版权管理司司长于慈珂主持会议。会议通报了“剑网2018”专项行动的具体部署。国家网信办、工信部、公安部有关部门负责同志就各部门开展“剑网”专项行动情况做了发言。北京、江西、江苏等地版权部门代表就开展版权执法监管工作做法经验做了大会交流。来自全国31个省（区、市）和中心城市版权局、文化市场行政执法总队，以及各著作权集体管理组织等的120余名代表出席会议。

（资料来源：国家版权局网站，作者：赖名芳）

【甘肃省级政府机关操作软件97.98%为正版】 2018年7月15—27日，国家软件正版化工作督查组对甘肃省40家省级政府机关软件正版化工作的制度建设和责任落实、软件日常使用管理、计算机软件安装等情况进行了检查。

从现场检查情况看，甘肃各省级政府机关基本成立了软件正版化工作机构，建立了计算机软硬件采购、正版软件管理、考核评议等软件正版化工作相关制度，软件日常管理维护情况比较规范。省级政府机关操作系统软件和办公软件的正版化率分别达到97.98%和96.08%。截至目前，在省级政府机关软件正版化检查中，甘肃的正版化率位居全国第二。

（资料来源：《中国新闻出版广电报》，作者：田野）

【国家版权局对网络转载等重点领域开展版权专项整治】 2018年7月16日，国家版权局、国家互联网信息办公室、工业和信息化部、公安部联合召开新闻通气会，通报启动打击网络侵权盗版“剑网2018”专项行动有关情况。

国家版权局版权管理司司长于慈珂介绍说，“剑网2018”将以网络侵权多发领域为重点目标，以查办案件为重要抓手，通过集中整治和引导规范，有效运用分类监管、约谈整改、行政处罚、刑事打击等多种措施，集中整治网络转载、短视频、动漫等领域侵权盗版多发态势，重点规范网络直播、知识分享、有声读物等平台版权传播秩序，深入巩固网络影视、网络音乐、电子商务平台、应用商店、网络云存储空间等领域专项整治成果，维护清朗的网络空间秩序，营造良好的网络版权环境。

此次专项行动自7月上旬开始，利用4个多月的时间开展三项重点整治：一是开展网络转载版权专项整治。针对目前网络媒体特别是微博、微信公众号、头条号等自媒体侵权现象，将重点打击未经许可转载新闻作品的侵权行为和未经许可摘编整合、歪曲篡改新闻作品的侵权行为，坚决整治自媒体通过“洗稿”方式抄袭剽窃、篡改删减原创作品的侵权行为，着力规范搜索引擎、浏览器、应用商店、微博、微信等涉及的网络转载行为。通过集中查处一批违法转载案件，依法取缔、关闭一批非法新闻网站、网站频道及微博账号、微信公众号、头条号、百家号等互联网用户公众账号来实现整治规范的目的。二是开展短视频版权专项整治。针对当前短视频领域存在的未经授权复制、表演、网络传播他人影视、音乐、摄影、文字等作品，以合理使用为名对他人作品删减改编并通过网络传播，短视频平台以用户上传为名、滥用“避风港”规则对他人作品进行侵权传播等版权问题，专项行动将把抖音短视频、快手短视频、西瓜视频、火山小视频、快视频、哔哩哔哩等热点短视频平台纳入重点监管，一方面重点打击短视频领域的各类侵权行为，另一方面引导短视频平台企业规范版权授权和传播规则，构建良性发展的商业模式。三是开展重点领域版权专项整治。具体包括三个重点领域：第一，动漫领域版权集中治理。将重点打击通过网站、应用程序、互联网用户公众账号、视频字幕组等非法传播盗版动漫作品的行为，以及未经授权使用他人动漫形象制作传播游戏、玩具、文具、服装等动漫衍生品的侵权行为。第二，网络直播、知识分享、有声读物平台版权集中治理。针对这些平台存在的未经授权大量使用音乐、文字、口述作品版权问题，将从规范新型商业模式健康发展的角度，着力整治相关平台未经授权使用他人作品的行为，主动加强监管，制定相关规则，积极加以引导，构建平台良好版权秩序。第三，巩固“剑网行动”治理成果。将进一步加强对网络影视、网络音乐、电子商务平台、应用商店、网络云存储空间等领域的版权监管，突出打击通过网络销售教材教辅、少儿出版物、音乐和影视移动存储介质以及使用聚合链接、设置境外服务器等手段的侵权行为。

于慈珂强调说，专项行动期间，各地版权执法部门将集中力量、快速查办各类网络侵权盗版案件，对人民群众意见强烈、社会危害大的侵权盗版网站，将从严查处并提请相关管理部门依法吊销电信业务经营许可证或注销 ICP 备案、停止提供网站接入服务等；对涉嫌构成犯罪的，将根据“两法衔接”机制及时移交公安机关立案查处。各互联网企业要严格落实主体责任，完善企业举报受理和快速处理机制，加强内部版权监控管理，实施侵权盗版信息巡查清理及记录留存，积极履行企业违法犯罪线索报告、配合调查义务和“通知—删除”等法定处置责任。专项行动鼓励社会各界向版权执法部门投诉举报，对经核实线索查处案件的举报人将予以奖励，同时将加大对大案要案和典型案件的宣传力度，坚决曝光不履行主体责任的互联网企业。

（资料来源：人民网，作者：张贺）

【北京市启动“剑网 2018”专项行动】 2018 年 7 月 27 日，北京市版权局、市网信办、市通信管理局、市公安局和市文化市场行政执法总队在京召开会议，正式启动北京市“剑网 2018”专项行动。北京市版权局副局长王野霏、国家版权局版权管理司执法监管处处长赵杰等出席会议并讲话，腾讯、百度、新浪、字节跳动等近百家互联网单位参会。

会议指出，2018 年“剑网行动”将开展三个方面的重点整治：一是开展网络转载版权专项整治，严厉打击微博、微信、头条号等自媒体和网络媒体未经许可转载、摘编整合、歪曲篡改和“洗稿”等违法侵权行为；二是开展短视频版权专项整治，在引导短视频平台企业构建良性发展商业模式下，规范整治平台盗版侵权行为；三是开展重点领域版权专项整治，集中治理动漫、网络直播、知识分享、有声读物等平台的盗版侵权行为，并继续对影视、音乐、电子商务平台、云存储等领域保持高压态势。

会议对此次“剑网行动”提出以下几方面要求：一是要严格落实重点任务，各“剑网行动”成员要建立信息共享、协作联动的工作机制，确保按要求完成重点工作任务；二是要严格落实主体责任，各互联网企业和个人要树立版权保护意识，严格履行各项法定义务，依法维护权利人合法权益；三是要广泛动员，层层发动，提高人民群众版权意识，鼓励权利人积极举报盗版投诉，向行政执法机关广泛提供线索来源；四是精准打击，形成震慑作用，以大要案为抓手，惩治盗版侵权，营造良好的从商和版权环境。

会议强调，此次“剑网行动”要按照“严格保护、提升效能、分类监管、引导规范”的工作思路，以监管保护为手段，引导规范互联网企业建立健康有序的版权机制，通过优质的正版资源供给让市民和公众有充分的获得感。希望各单位能够传达好、筹划好并落实好本次会议精神，继续提升首都的版权环境。北京市网信办、市公安局、市通信管理局和市文化市场行政执法总队对此次“剑网行动”也做了相关的要求和部署，并公布了投诉举报电话，鼓励权利人对盗版侵权行为进行举报投诉。

（资料来源：中国知识产权资讯网，作者：窦新颖）

【广东启动“剑网 2018”专项行动重点监管《抖音》《快手》等短视频 APP】 2018 年 7 月 31 日，广东省版权局、省通信管理局、省公安厅、省互联网信息办公室在广州联合召开广东省打击网络侵权盗版专项治理“剑网 2018”专项行动视频会议，正式启动广东省打击网络侵权盗版“剑网 2018”专项行动。抖音短视频、快手短视频、西瓜视频、火山小视频、快视频、美拍、秒拍、微视、梨视频、小影、56 视频、火萤、哔哩哔哩等短视频平台被列为本次行动重点监管对象。

会议明确，广东省“剑网 2018”专项行动将重点开展三项版权专项整治行动。一是开展网络转载版权专项整治，严厉打击未经授权转载新闻作品的侵权行为，严厉打击未经授权摘编整合、歪曲篡改新闻作品的侵权行为；坚决整治自媒体通过“洗稿”方式抄袭剽窃、篡改删减原创作品的侵权行为。二是开展短视频版权专项整治，严厉打击短视频平台和短视频作品上传者未经授权复制、表演、通过网络传播他人影视、音乐、摄影、文字等作品的侵权行为，坚决整治短视频作品上传者以合理使用为名对他人作品删减改编并通过网络传播的侵权行为，坚决整治短视频平台以用户上传为名滥用“避风港”规则的侵权行为。三是开展重点领域版权专项整治，严厉打击未经授权通过网站、应用程序、互联网用户公众账号、视频字幕组传播动漫的侵权行为，着力整治网络直播、知识分享、有声读物等平台未经授权复制、表演、通过网络传播他人文字、音乐、口述等作品的行为，进一步加强对网络影视、网络音乐、电子商务平台、应用商店、网络云存储空间等领域的版权监管。

（资料来源：《羊城晚报》，作者：黄宙辉　宁建芳）

【河北省：鼓励创作版权精品　满足人民精神文化需求】 2018 年 7 月 31 日，河北省版权局在石家庄市召开全省版权工作会议，会议传达了全国版权执法监管工作会议的主要精神，部署了河北省“剑网 2018”专项行动的具体工作安排，通报了全省版权工作的进展情况。

河北省版权局党组书记、局长李晓明建议，下一步的版权工作一方面要鼓励创新创造，努力提供优秀的文学艺术等版权作品，满足人民群众精神文化需求；另一方面，要加大版权保护力度，严厉打击侵权盗版违法犯罪活动，为“经济强省、美丽河北”建设营造良好版权环境。此外，还要强化版权运用，发挥版权作品作为生产要素和财富资源的作用，提升产业品质，促进经济发展、文化繁荣。

对于全国各地陆续开展起来的“剑网 2018”专项行动，河北省将从三个方面抓紧落实：一是开展网络转载版权专项整治，二是开展短视频版权专项整治，三是开展重点领域版权专项整治。会上，李晓明还特别提醒工作人员要明确指标，强化手段，大力查办大案要案；要强化案件信息上报和通报制度，主动巡查，扩大案源，创新工作方式方法。

保定市、石家庄市和廊坊市的代表还分别就版权执法、软件正版化和版权示范创建工作做典型发言，河北省版权局相关人员就版权执法和软件正版化工作进行了业务培训。

（资料来源：《中国新闻出版广电报》，作者：冀版）

【“剑网”专项行动启动　8 家沪上知名媒体签署自律公约】 2018 年 8 月 13 日，为打击各类网络侵权盗版行为，净化网络传播环境，上海“剑网 2018”专项行动工作会议在科学会堂举行，市公安局、市通信管理局、市互联网信息办公室、市版权局、市文化广播影视管理局、市文化市场行政执法总队等 6 家市网络版权综合治理领导小组成员单位相关负责人，与百视通、阅文集团、哔哩哔哩网、澎湃新闻、沪江网、蜻蜓 FM、拼多多等上海网络视听、网络媒体、网络文学、网络游戏、电商、动漫及出版等行业 73 家企业代表参加会议。

会议传达了国家版权局等四部门有关开展“剑网 2018”专项行动工作的精神与要求，对上海实施“剑网 2018”专项行动进行了动员部署。根据上海实施方案，明确了以大要案件查处为抓手，开展整治网络转载、短视频及动漫作品等三项重点任务，提出加大查处力度、强化主动监管、加强举报投诉、强化主体责任、加强宣传教育、加强信息沟通等六大工作要求，并全面启动“剑网 2018”上海实施方案。

上观新闻、文汇、新民、第一财经、澎湃新闻、看看新闻、东方网、趣头条等 8 家沪上知名媒体，在市版权局、市网信办的引导下，共同发起成立“上海网络媒体行业媒体自律联盟”，并签署自律公约，一致承诺“尊重他人版权，依法依规使用他人作品，自觉抵制各类与新闻作品相关的违法违规行为”，共同呼吁上海网络媒体和谐相处、相互督促、互助共进，共同营造良好的网络媒体版权秩序，促进网络媒体产业健康发展。

（资料来源：《解放日报》，作者：施晨露）

【苏浙沪皖签署一体化合作协议　携手打造长三角出版高地】 2018 年 8 月 15 日，由上海市新闻出版局倡议的长三角一体化出版发展战略合作协议签约仪式在上海书展举行。江苏、浙江、安徽、上海三省一市新闻出版（版权）部门负责人共同签署了《关于共同推动长三角区域出版和版权发展的框架协议》。

《框架协议》明确：长三角区域三省一市将在行业监管、产业发展、公共文化服务以及合作交流等方面深化合作，共促发展；建立长三角新闻出版（版权）局长联席会议机制，每年召开一次“长三角新闻出版高峰论坛”，由三省一市轮流举办等合作机制。

上海市委常委、宣传部部长周慧琳表示，长三角是中国出版业最为发达的地区之一，出版历史悠久、资源丰富、市场广阔，具有携手打造出版高地的历史基础和现实条件。希望三省一市以此次签约为契机，持续深化区域文化的交流交融，积极推动区域文化的协同发展，持续提升区域文化软实力，更好助力长三角成为全国转型发展的“主引擎”、创新发展的“主阵地”。

上海市新闻出版局局长徐炯介绍，为进一步推动长三角出版业更高质量的合作共赢，三省一市新闻出版（版权）部门达成了共识——以“聚焦高质量，聚力一体化”为引领，共同推动事业和产业发展，包括优化营商环境、规范市场秩序、加强版权保护、完善公共文化服务等。

安徽省新闻出版广电局局长陈烨表示，安徽省局将以本届上海书展合作为契机，全面实现发展战略上的等高对接、合作项目上的深度对接、机制保障上的无缝对接，真正落实一系列务实合作，培育一批优质品牌。

江苏省新闻出版广电局局长缪志红表示，江苏省局将认真贯彻落实框架协议内容，发挥自身优长，全力推动协议落地见效，力争每年都有标志性成果，为推进长三角新闻出版（版权）业更高质量一体化发展做出江苏贡献。

浙江省新闻出版广电局局长寿剑刚表示，此举有利于促进产业优势互补和政策互动，推动区域性一体化发展；有利于增强合作交流，形成区域品牌；有利于区域内信息共享，共同推动行业监管。

（资料来源：《中国新闻出版广电报》，作者：金鑫）

【广东召开版权登记工作座谈会】 2018 年 8 月 30 日，广东省新闻出版广电局政务服务中心在中山市组织召开“2018 年版权登记工作座谈会”。广东省 33 家版权登记代办机构代表等近 60 人参加会议。

会上，广东省局政务服务中心通报了 2018 年上半年全省版权登记基本情况、工作亮点和下一步工作计划，并就版权登记全流程网上办理推进过程中遇到的新问题、新情况组织了业务培训和交流讨论。

会议还邀请中山市版权局、广东省版权保护联合会、广州市版权保护中心、佛山市版权保护协会、深圳市精英知识产权运营服务有限公司、中山市游戏游艺行业协会等单位代表做经验交流发言，分享推进版权登记服务工作的好做法、好经验，并对 2017 年度作品著作权自愿登记优秀代办机构和工作人员进行了表彰。

（资料来源：《中国新闻出版广电报》，作者：粤文）

【国家版权局约谈“抖音”等 15 家短视频企业　严打侵权盗版】 2018 年 9 月 14 日，针对重点短视频平台企业自查自纠情况和存在的突出版权问题，国家版权局在京约谈了抖音短视频、快手短视频、西瓜视频、火山小视频、美拍、秒拍、微视、梨视频、小影、56 视频、火萤、快视频、哔哩哔哩、土豆、好看视频等 15 家重点短视频平台企业。

2018 年 7 月起，国家版权局、国家互联网信息办公室、工业和信息化部、公安部联合开展打击网络侵权盗版“剑网 2018”专项行动，以短视频版权专项整治为重点，强化对短视频企业的版权监管。国家版权局要求相关短视频平台企业进一步提高版权保护意识，切实加强版权制度建设，全面履行企业主体责任。一是加强内容版权管理，坚持先授权后传播的著作权法基本原则，规范内容版权管理使用制度，未经授权不得直接复制、表演、网络传播他人影视、音乐、摄影、文字等作品；二是加强维权管理，完善版权投诉处理机制，及时受理权利人的通知投诉，并快速移除相关侵权作品或断开相关侵权链接；三是加强侵权处置，采取有效措施防止用户未经许可违法上传、分享他人作品的行为，特别是以合理使用为名对他人作品删减改编并通过网络传播的行为；四是加强社会共治，对国家版权局发布的重点保护预警作品及权利人提交的热播热映作品，加强版权审核并及时处置。

下一阶段，国家版权局将重点打击短视频领域侵权盗版行为，引导短视频平台企业规范版权授权和传播规则，强化行业自律，推动相关权利人组织与短视频企业建立版权保护合作机制，推动短视频行业健康发展，为广大网民提供风清气正的网络版权环境。

（资料来源：新华社，作者：史竞男）

【国家版权局约谈 13 家网络服务商　要求规范网络转载】 2018 年 9 月 29 日，针对网络转载版权专项整治中发现的突出版权问题，国家版权局在京约谈了趣头条、淘新闻、今日头条、一点资讯、百度百家号、微信、东方头条、北京时间、网易新闻、搜狐新闻、新浪新闻、凤凰新闻、腾讯新闻等 13 家网络服务商，要求其进一步提高版权保护意识，切实加强版权制度建设，全面履行企业主体责任，规范网络转载版权秩序。

网络服务商直接转载传统媒体作品的，要进一步完善版权管理制度，坚持“先授权、后使用”的著作权法基本原则，未经授权不得直接转载他人作品；依法转载他人作品时，要主动标明作者姓名和作品来源，不歪曲篡改标题和作品原意；要积极与权利人及相关版权组织开展版权合作，完善授权许可机制，遏制网络侵权盗版。

网络服务商为用户转载他人作品提供平台的，要切实强化用户管理，在平台显著位置提示用户遵守著作权法，不违法转载他人作品；要采取有效措施防止用户未经许可违法转载他人作品、“洗稿”等侵权行为；不得鼓励用户或假借用户名义，滥用

"避风港"规则转载他人作品；对于多次侵权被投诉的用户，应当采取列入黑名单、暂停或者终止服务等惩治措施。要积极履行"通知—删除"法定义务，完善版权投诉通道；及时处理权利人的通知，快速移除相关侵权作品或断开相关侵权链接。要加强执法协作，对版权部门发布的重点保护预警作品，加强版权审核并及时处置，主动履行违法犯罪线索报告和配合调查义务。

下一阶段，各级版权执法部门将重点打击网络转载领域存在的各类侵权盗版行为，引导网络企业加强版权自律、规范版权管理，推动网络平台与权利人（组织）、版权相关联盟（协会）开展版权合作、探索符合网络使用需求和传播规律的转载授权模式，共同维护良好的版权秩序。

（资料来源：中国知识产权资讯网，作者：窦新颖）

【国家版权局：短视频平台版权整改取得阶段性成效】 2018年11月7日，《中国知识产权报》记者从国家版权局获悉，"剑网2018"专项行动中，针对短视频平台版权整改取得阶段性成效，按照国家版权局的整改要求，15家重点短视频平台企业认真开展自查，严格清理侵权盗版账号，严厉打击侵权盗版行为，截至目前共下架删除各类涉嫌侵权盗版短视频作品57万部。

9月14日，国家版权局按照打击网络侵权盗版"剑网2018"专项行动的部署安排，针对重点短视频平台企业存在的突出版权问题，约谈了抖音短视频、快手短视频、西瓜视频、火山小视频、美拍、秒拍、微视、梨视频、小影、56视频、火萤、快视频、哔哩哔哩、土豆、好看视频等15家企业，责令相关企业进一步提高版权保护意识，切实加强内部版权制度建设，全面履行企业主体责任。通过一个多月的整改，短视频版权保护环境取得显著改善。按照国家版权局的整改要求，15家重点短视频平台企业认真开展自查，严格清理侵权盗版账号，严厉打击侵权盗版行为。目前，15家短视频平台共下架删除各类涉嫌侵权盗版短视频作品57万部。其中，秒拍、土豆、美拍、哔哩哔哩、小影、56视频等平台企业清理下架数量较多；好看、微视、抖音、西瓜、快手、火山等平台企业严厉打击涉嫌侵权盗版的违规账号，采取永久封禁账号、短期封禁账号、停止分发、扣分禁言等措施予以清理。

各短视频平台企业通过建立7×24小时用户投诉举报处理通道、三审三查版权审核制度等，完善版权投诉处理机制，加强维权管理，及时受理权利人的通知投诉。火山、西瓜、快视频等平台针对封禁账号建立黑名单制度；好看、哔哩哔哩、美拍、快手、火山、微视等平台对照国家版权局发布的重点作品版权保护预警名单，积极开展清理自查，删除涉嫌侵权作品；抖音、西瓜、好看、秒拍、快视频等平台企业分别与中国音乐著作权协会以及相关新闻单位、唱片公司、影视公司等开展版权合作，加强内容版权管理。

国家版权局相关负责人表示，将进一步加强对短视频平台企业的版权监管，通过行政约谈、行政处罚、刑事打击等手段，有效整治短视频行业存在的侵权问题，规范短视频行业的健康发展，构建风清气正的网络版权环境。

（资料来源：中国知识产权资讯网，作者：窦新颖）

【《2018年深入实施国家知识产权战略　加快建设知识产权强国推进计划》印发】 2018年11月9日，经国务院知识产权战略实施工作部际联席会议第三次全体会议审议同意，《2018年深入实施国家知识产权战略　加快建设知识产权强国推进计划》（以下简称《推进计划》）正式印发。《推进计划》明确了6大重点任务，15个重点部分，共109项具体措施。

在深化知识产权领域改革方面，《推进计划》提出，推进知识产权管理体制机制改革，改革完善知识产权重大政策，深化知识产权"放管服"改革，包括做好重新组建国家知识产权局工作、探索建立国家层面知识产权案件上诉审理机制、落实研发费用税前加计扣除政策、推进知识产权领域军民融合改革试点等措施。

在强化知识产权创造方面，《推进计划》提出，加大高价值知识产权培育力度，提高知识产权审查质量和效率，包括深入实施专利质量提升工程、加快新兴领域和业态的专利审查制度建设、将商标注册审查周期从8个月压缩到6个月、建立全国作品登记信息公示查询系统等措施。

在强化知识产权保护方面，《推进计划》提出，完善法律法规规章，加强保护长效机制建设，开展重点领域专项治理，加强日常监管执法，包括推动在著作权法、专利法等法律中规定惩罚性赔偿制度，加快知识产权保护中心建设和布局，制定"互联网+"知识产权保护工作方案，依法惩治侵犯知识产权犯罪等措施。

在强化知识产权运用方面，《推进计划》提出，加强知识产权转移转化，强化知识产权信息利用，包括深入推进知识产权运营服务体系建设、推广专利权质押等知识产权融资模式、深入推进商标富农工作、制定实施知识产权服务促进产业转型升级三年行动计划等措施。

在深化知识产权国际交流合作方面，《推进计划》提出，提升知识产权对外合作水平，加强重点产业海外布局和风险防控，包括办好 2018 年“一带一路”知识产权高级别会议，与世界知识产权组织合作开展中国专利奖、中国版权金奖评选活动，引导企业加快商标品牌海外布局，搭建企业知识产权海外维权平台等措施。

在加强组织实施和保障方面，《推进计划》提出，加强政策制定和推进落实，加强人才培养和宣传引导，包括完成《国家知识产权战略纲要》实施十年评估工作、启动知识产权强国建设纲要研究制定工作、加快知识产权高层次人才引进力度、深入实施知识产权文化建设工程等措施。

（资料来源：《中国知识产权报》，作者：刘斌，原标题为：《百余项具体措施推进知识产权强国建设》）

【国家版权局引导版权社会共治】 2018 年 11 月 9 日，在国家版权局的支持推动下，主要电商平台与两大反盗版联盟积极开展版权合作，合力遏制通过电商平台销售盗版图书等侵权行为。

据国家版权局相关负责人介绍，在 2018 年 10 月举办的第七届中国国际版权博览会期间，阿里巴巴集团与京版十五社反盗版联盟就图书版权保护计划签订合作协议。在 11 月中国国际进口博览会期间，拼多多平台与京版十五社反盗版联盟和少儿出版反盗版联盟就图书版权保护签订合作协议。

这位负责人说，多年来，国家版权局深入推动社会共治，积极引导电商平台与权利人开展版权合作，以建立良性的版权保护合作机制，从源头遏制各类侵权盗版行为。今后将进一步加大网络版权保护工作力度，全力助推版权产业繁荣发展。一是不断加强打击网络侵权盗版工作，各地版权执法部门将持续加大对侵权盗版的行政处罚力度，做好与刑事司法的衔接工作，营造开放、规范、诚信、安全的网络交易环境；二是继续强化网络版权保护社会共治，充分发挥权利人组织的协调、统筹作用，进一步推动网络平台与权利人、版权相关联盟开展版权合作；三是大力推动网络企业全面履行主体责任。

（资料来源：《法制日报》，作者：张红兵）

◆ 宣传教育

【湖北利用网络直播讲版权保护】 2018 年 3 月 15 日，在湖北武汉斗鱼网络科技有限公司提供的房间号为 4518214 的直播间内，进行了一场形式新颖的版权宣传活动。这是湖北首次利用网络直播开展版权专题宣传活动。

当天，湖北省新闻出版广电局版权管理处处长卢文俊、华中国家版权交易中心有限公司副总经理宋丕伟走进网络直播间，通过现场问答的形式，向网友普及版权知识，引导广大消费者特别是新兴消费群体拒绝盗版、使用正版。广大网友就版权相关问题积极提问，如：遇到侵权盗版时，如何维护自身合法权益；著作权登记的作用及方法是什么；版权产业主要包含哪些内容……卢文俊与宋丕伟一一作答，并围绕版权保护和版权创造等主题进行知识普及。

除了室内访谈，湖北省版权保护中心工作人员还化身“网络主播”，跟随武汉市江岸区文化市场综合执法大队的执法人员来到华中图书交易中心，随机对市场经营户进行执法检查，说明侵权盗版的危害性，并从印刷质量、防伪标记、版权信息等方面教授网友识别盗版图书。在湖北省版权服务大厅，“主播”带领网友了解了网上登记系统和版权登记流程，吸引更多直播用户关注。

据斗鱼统计，此次活动共吸引 30 余万名网友参与，累计发送弹幕 500 余条，达到了良好的宣传效果。“作为近年发展最迅速、热度最持久的互联网产品，网络直播是非常具有感染力的传播途径。”卢文俊说。未来，湖北省将利用各种传播形式尤其是新型传播形式，全方位地进行版权宣传，提升全社会版权认知度。

（资料来源：《中国新闻出版广电报》，作者：汤广花　邓军）

【2018 年国际版权贸易培训班在京举办】 2018 年 3 月 20—23 日，2018 年国际版权贸易培训班在京举办。本期培训班聚焦中国当代主题图书“走出去”。

新闻出版广电部门有关负责人赵海云围绕“贯彻落实习近平新时代中国特色社会主义思想和党的十九大精神，推动出版‘走出去’高质量发展”这一主题，与学员们进行了交流。中国人民大学副校长贺耀敏分享了关于新时代中国主题图书“走出去”

的思考；中国人民大学国际关系学院教授王义桅从历史出发，阐释了出版“走出去”如何服务于构建人类命运共同体；杭州电子科技大学主题出版研究院院长韩建民分享的则是如何提升当代中国主题图书国家编辑能力；中国人民大学出版社社长李永强在介绍相关实践经验时说，2017 年 8 月，由中国人民大学出版社发起的“一带一路”学术出版联盟在纵深推进合作出版，聚合平台之力讲好中国故事方面发挥了重要作用。

中国图书进出口（集团）总公司数字发展中心李甲荣介绍，中图公司设计开发的易阅通数字平台，对接上游出版商的优质中文资源，面向国内机构用户群及海外阅读市场，全方位推动数字化出版内容的国内销售及“走出去”工作，为出版企业带来社会效益和经济效益。

究竟海外出版企业、海外读者对当代中国主题图书的内容需求是什么？这也是很多业界人士非常关心的话题，亚马逊数字内容高级经理高嘉麟、商务印书馆《汉语世界》杂志主编储丹丹对此进行了分享。此外，俄罗斯尚斯国际出版社总裁穆平介绍了当代中国主题图书海外营销推广的新做法、新举措，中国人民大学出版社国际出版中心主任刘叶华就“小切口、大主题”和如何做好今后几年重大主题出版“走出去”工作与学员进行了交流。

（资料来源：《中国新闻出版广电报》，作者：范燕莹）

【2018 年粤港两地中学生版权知识和版权保护交流活动在珠海举行】 2018 年 4 月 3—4 日，根据粤港保护知识产权合作专责小组第十六次会议商定的粤港知识产权合作计划，粤港中学生版权知识和版权保护交流活动在广东省珠海市举行。

3 日下午，香港代表团一行 21 人和珠海市三所中学的学生代表参加了粤港两地中学生版权知识与版权保护交流活动座谈会，广东省版权局专职副局长陈春怀出席了座谈会。座谈会上，香港海关助理监督石玉英和珠海市版权局副局长翟名分别介绍了香港和珠海版权保护的基本情况；香港的学生代表介绍了香港保障的知识产权类别，珠海的中学生从自身经历出发，谈了对于盗版危害性的认识；同学们围绕“拒绝盗版、从我做起”分享了各自的体会和做法，并就版权保护对促进创新和产业发展的作用等内容进行了深入的交流和探讨。

4 日上午，香港代表团参观了中国最早的互联网软件企业之一、国内领先的应用软件产品和服务供应商金山软件公司，了解了金山软件公司的发展壮大历程以及信息技术、知识产权和软件之间的紧密关系，学生们纷纷表示回香港后会下载个人版 WPS 试用。

广东省版权局、珠海市版权部门和教育部门的相关人员，以及珠海市师生代表共计 50 余人参加了此次活动。

广东省版权局与香港海关每年都会联合举办粤港中学生版权知识和版权保护交流活动，希望通过这项交流活动打造粤港版权交流的良好平台，使两地更多群众特别是年轻人参与到版权保护工作当中，促进两地版权产业的进一步蓬勃发展。

（资料来源：广东省版权局）

【青岛市召开软件正版化工作培训会暨首批版权保护重点镇街培训会】 为深入贯彻党的十九大精神，全面落实《版权工作“十三五”规划》和《青岛市深入实施知识产权战略行动计划（2015—2020 年）》有关要求，强化版权创造、保护、运用，进一步做好青岛市国有企业软件正版化工作，推进版权保护工作进基层，2018 年 4 月 12 日，青岛市文化市场行政执法局分别组织召开了 2018 年第一期全市国有企业软件正版化工作培训会暨全市首批版权保护重点镇街培训会。

培训会邀请了国家版权局版权管理司执法监管处调研员郑良斌为企业软件正版化工作进行专题辅导，青岛啤酒集团有限公司介绍了与一铭软件公司签订合作协议的有关经验做法和国产软件的使用情况，金山、中望等高水平国产软件企业进行了现场演示推介活动，全市 29 家市属国有企业负责人参加培训。据初步统计，截至 2017 年底，全市国有企业共购买各类正版软件 40 余万套，购买金额达 1.5 亿元，国产软件采购率达 70%以上。下一步，青岛市将加大督查力度，持续推进国有企业使用正版软件工作。

青岛市首批版权保护重点镇街培训会邀请了山东省版权局、青岛市版权保护协会有关负责同志分别进行版权服务基层专题辅导和版权作品登记、版权维权等业务专题培训。各区市文化执法部门、首批版权保护镇街负责同志 60 余人参加培训。下一步，青岛市文化市场行政执法局将以版权执法和版权服务“两手抓、两手都要硬”为工作思路，继续保持对侵权盗版的高压打击态势，深入推进版权保护重点镇街建设，推动版权强市建设。

（资料来源：青岛市文化市场行政执法局）

【武汉开展大学生版权辩论赛】 2018 年 4 月 20 日，在武汉教育电视台举行的第八届“法理争鸣”湖北高校法学专业辩论赛暨 2018 年武汉市大学生版权辩论赛决赛上，来自华中师范大学和武汉大学的学生们展开了激烈的辩论。最终武汉大学队摘得桂冠。

本次辩论赛也是武汉市“4·26”世界知识产权宣传周活动之一。比赛由武汉市文化局（版权局）、湖北高校法学辩论联盟主办。自 3 月 16 日启动以来，湖北 9 所重点高校通过初赛、复赛、半决赛和决赛的精彩角逐，为观众展现了一场场唇枪舌剑的听觉盛宴。

武汉市文化局（版权局）有关人士表示，举办版权辩论赛，旨在进一步做好世界知识产权宣传教育活动，在武汉高校广大师生中营造崇尚创新精神、尊重知识产权的浓厚氛围，提高全社会版权意识，让尊重和保护版权成为全社会的文化信念与自觉行动。

（资料来源：《中国新闻出版广电报》，作者：汤广花）

【2018 年全国知识产权宣传周活动启动】 2018 年 4 月 20 日，主题为“倡导创新文化　尊重知识产权”的 2018 年全国知识产权宣传周活动在京启动。国务院领导出席宣传周活动启动仪式并做重要讲话。

国家知识产权局、中宣部、最高人民法院、最高人民检察院、外交部、科技部、公安部、农业农村部、国务院国资委、国家林业和草原局等部门的领导出席了启动仪式。世界知识产权组织（WIPO）负责人以及埃及、印度尼西亚、摩洛哥等国家有关知识产权部门的负责人应邀参加了启动仪式。

在启动仪式上，全国知识产权宣传周活动组委会主任、国家知识产权局局长申长雨介绍了宣传周活动期间的主要安排。宣传周活动期间，全国知识产权宣传周活动组委会各成员单位将单独或者多部门联合开展多场重点活动，其中包括国家知识产权局和国家版权局将在国务院新闻办公室联合召开中国知识产权发展状况新闻发布会，最高人民法院将发布《中国法院知识产权司法保护状况（2017）》（白皮书），最高人民检察院将发布 2017 年度全国检察机关保护知识产权十大典型案例，司法部将在全国范围内组织开展知识产权法治宣传教育主题活动，农业农村部将分别组织召开中国—乌兹别克斯坦、中国—日本植物新品种保护交流与合作活动等。

WIPO 副总干事王彬颖宣读了 WIPO 总干事弗朗西斯·高锐发来的贺信。在贺信中，高锐对中国知识产权宣传周活动的启动表示祝贺。他表示，2017 年中国的 PCT 国际专利申请量居全球第二位，中国的商标注册量超过了 570 万件，中国的著作权登记总量达到 274 万件，这些数字充分体现了中国知识产权工作的不凡成就。2018 年的宣传周活动适逢中国改革开放 40 周年、中国知识产权战略实施 10 周年，具有重要意义。高锐总干事预祝本次宣传周活动圆满成功。

在启动仪式上，中国科学院院士、北京科技大学材料科学与工程学院教授葛昌纯代表两院院士宣读了倡议书《加快自主创新，提升竞争实力》。此份倡议书由近 20 名两院院士联合签名发起，他们向全社会倡议，加强知识产权创造、保护、运用，加快各领域自主创新，提高中国经济竞争力。

来自有关国家驻华使馆官员和知识产权专员、全国知识产权宣传周活动组委会成员单位有关负责人、国内外知名企业代表、行业协会代表、专家学者等 300 余人参加了宣传周活动启动仪式。

（资料来源：人民网）

【中日韩联合版权宣传活动启动】 2018 年 4 月 23 日，中日韩联合版权宣传活动在京启动。该活动由中国国家版权局、日本文化厅、韩国文化体育观光部联合开展，三国知名动漫形象“孙悟空”“柯南”“啵乐乐”携手为版权保护代言。

国家版权局有关负责人表示，改革开放 40 年来，中国版权事业取得了显著成就，党的十九大报告特别提出了“倡导创新文化，强化知识产权创造、保护、运用”。“版权”的概念从 40 年前的不为人知，到现在广为人知，是版权事业快速发展、人民群众文化生活丰富多彩的体现，也是政府高度重视、常抓不懈地提升公众版权意识的成果。

此次中日韩联合版权宣传活动通过采用中国动画片《大闹天宫》中的“孙悟空”、日本动画片《名侦探柯南》中的“柯南”和韩国动画片《小企鹅啵乐乐》中的“啵乐乐”三个国际熟知、深受公众喜爱的动漫形象，由中日韩三国共同设计、制作宣传海报和视频，以生动有趣、为大众喜闻乐见的形式，在各自国家向公众同期宣传推广。希望通过这一方式，将“保护版权、繁荣创作”的理念植入民心，进一步加强互联网领域版权保护，提升公众特别是青少年群体的版权保护意识。这是中日韩三国通过国际合作为加强版权宣传进行的创新实践。

（资料来源：新华社，作者：史竞男　周圆）

【国新办举行 2017 年中国知识产权发展状况新闻发布会】 2018 年 4 月 24 日，国务院新闻办公室在京举行新闻发布会，国家知识产权局和国家版权局共同发布了 2017 年中国知识产权发展状况。

2017 年中国知识产权发展状况呈现出五大特点：知识产权创造量质齐升、知识产权保护更加严格、知识产权运用效益明显提升、知识产权重点领域改革不断深化和知识产权对外合作交流深入开展。

在版权工作方面，国家版权局印发《版权工作“十三五”规划》，进一步做好“十三五”时期版权工作的顶层设计；印发《关于规范电子版作品登记证书的通知》，加强作品登记规范管理。2017 年中国著作权登记量快速增长，全年登记总量达 274.7 万件，同比增长 36.86%。其中，作品登记 200.1 万件，同比增长 25.15%；计算机软件著作权登记量达 74.53 万件，同比增长 382.79%。此外，全国共办理著作权质权登记 299 件，涉及主债务金额 29.74 亿元。印发《关于做好 2017 年推进使用正版软件有关工作的函》，推进各省（区、市）建立健全计算机软硬件采购制度和软件正版化考核评议制度，规范正版软件管理。推动版权示范创建工作深入开展，目前已评选出 35 家示范单位、5 个示范园区（基地）并予授牌。开展中国版权产业对国民经济贡献的调研工作，发布 2015 年和 2016 年中国版权产业对国民经济贡献的调查报告。

在版权行政执法方面，国家版权局不断加大执法力度，强化网络领域版权监管，打击各类侵权盗版行为。2017 年版权部门查处侵权盗版案件 3 100 余件，收缴盗版品 605 万件。国家版权局还联合国家网信办、工信部、公安部开展了“剑网 2017”专项行动，聚焦网络版权保护及电子商务平台和移动互联网应用程序（APP）的版权整治，各级版权执法监管部门巡查网站 63 万家（次），关闭侵权盗版网站 2 554 个，删除侵权盗版链接 71 万条，收缴侵权盗版制品 276 万件，立案调查网络侵权案件 543 件，会同公安部门查办刑事案件 57 件，涉案金额 1.07 亿元。此外，还狠抓大案要案督查督办，联合全国“扫黄打非”工作小组办公室、公安部、最高人民检察院组成 5 个督导检查组对北京等 10 省（市）开展案件专项督导检查，全年督办浙江嘉兴“3·11”案、河南尉氏“12·15”系列案等重大案件 23 起。在深入推进软件正版化工作方面，国家版权局组织重点督查，推进软件正版化长效机制建设。全年共检查单位 389 家、计算机 26 989 台，同比分别增长 35.54%、242.94%。

此外，国家版权局还推动淘宝网严格出版物证照审核，促使出版物证照审核拦截率提高到 58.7%；推动人民日报社等 10 家主要中央新闻单位和新媒体网站联合发起成立中国新闻媒体版权保护联盟，全国 132 家报纸、期刊、电台、电视台共同发布《关于加强新闻作品版权保护的声明》。

国家知识产权局局长申长雨，国家版权局新闻发言人、版权管理司司长于慈珂及国家知识产权局商标局负责人崔守东出席发布会并回答记者提问。

（资料来源：《中国新闻出版广电报》，作者：赖名芳）

【广西壮族自治区版权局开展“版权四进”系列宣传活动】 2018 年全国知识产权宣传周期间，广西壮族自治区版权局积极开展“版权四进”系列宣传活动，营造了加强版权保护的良好社会氛围。

一是版权进城市广场，开展板报宣传和法律咨询活动。组织全区开展侵权盗版及非法出版物集中销毁活动暨“绿书签行动”宣传活动，集中销毁侵权盗版非法图书、报刊、音像制品等 61 万件；各市在城市广场组织开展版权宣传活动，公开展示宣传板报 100 余块、宣传横幅 40 多条，设法律咨询点受理群众举报、咨询，接受群众关于版权登记、侵权盗版投诉等方面的问题咨询 6 400 余人次。

二是版权进中小学校，开展版权普法宣传进校园活动。通过观看文艺演出，设置宣传展架，发放宣传资料、宣传小物品等方式开展《著作权法》普法宣传，从小培养孩子们保护版权、抵制盗版的意识。其间，全区版权普法进校园活动已走进 100 所中小学校，参与师生上万人。

三是版权进社区，多种方式宣传版权保护。南宁版权局在社区公益放映的电影片头插播《抵制盗版出版物》等专题宣传片；北海版权局以“倡导创新文化，尊重知识产权”为主题在社区举办文艺演出，并邀请相关单位进行正版图书、软件的宣传。

四是版权进广播电视，利用新闻媒体广泛宣传。一方面，邀请《广西日报》、《光明日报》、广西记者站等 14 家区内外媒体参加 2018 年广西版权工作新闻发布会；另一方面，借助人气动漫形象“可可小爱”影响力，制作 3 部“可可小爱”系列版权保护主题动漫公益剧，并于 4 月 20—26 日在广西电台、广西电视台滚动播放。此外，充分利用传统媒体和新媒体平台，持续宣传打击侵权盗版工作的进展和成效。

（资料来源：广西壮族自治区新闻出版广电局）

【山东省举办“版权进校园”系列活动】 2018年5月15日，山东省版权局在济南召开全省“版权进校园”系列活动启动仪式暨版权宣传培训班。通过这一活动，强化版权创造、保护、运用，引导少年儿童的创新意识和版权保护意识。仪式上，学生代表宣读版权倡议书，号召全省中小学生行动起来，为普及版权贡献力量。济南出版有限责任公司、北京金山办公软件股份有限公司分别向版权示范学校捐赠正版图书与软件。

“版权进校园”系列活动是山东省版权局、山东省教育厅、共青团山东省委共同指导，各市文化广电新闻出版局、文化市场执法局，有关版权单位共同开展的版权校园普及活动，旨在提升版权宣传力度，正确引导少年儿童的创新意识和版权保护意识，推进版权普及教育，最大限度地发挥和调动有利因素，形成政府主导、媒体配合、社会公众广泛参与的版权宣传合力，在全社会树立“尊重知识、尊重劳动、尊重创作、尊重版权”的良好氛围。

在版权宣传培训班上，有关单位围绕版权宣传方面的经验做法进行交流发言。当前在国家政策的推动下，山东省的版权产业规模得到不断扩大，产业结构逐渐优化，盈利模式日趋成熟，发展环境日益改善，共创建国家级版权示范城市2个，国家级版权示范单位、园区（基地）25个，数量和质量都位居全国前列。版权产值连创新高，占国民生产总值的比例连年上升，呈现出健康持续发展的良好态势。

（资料来源：齐鲁壹点，作者：刘雅菲）

【“全省高校版权知识巡回宣讲”活动走进赣州高校】 2018年5月18日和19日，江西“全省高校版权知识巡回宣讲”活动来到赣州，在赣南师范大学和江西理工大学分别举办版权知识专场讲座，来自两校各院系近800名师生代表参加活动。

宣讲活动现场，秩序井然，气氛活跃。省版权保护中心的老师以丰富的案例、浅显的语言，给在场师生上了一堂生动的版权知识普及课。大家纷纷表示，通过聆听讲座受益匪浅，既增长了版权基本知识，又掌握了版权确权方法，更坚定了版权维权信心。大学生们表示，作为社会中最有活力和创造力的群体，作为“大众创业、万众创新”的生力军，在今后的学习生活中，将以这次宣讲为契机，不断提高认识，争做版权意识的引领者；做到知行合一，争做版权保护的践行者；积极投身宣传，争做版权保护的推动者。

两所高校大学生积极性都非常高，踊跃争当“版权服务志愿者”，踊跃进行版权登记。一批美术、摄影、文字作品成功进行版权登记，100余名大学生被聘为“版权服务志愿者”。活动现场举行了版权服务工作站授牌以及为版权服务志愿者、作品登记权利人颁证仪式。这两场活动也是江西省新闻出版广电局（版权局）、团省委联合主办的2018年“全省高校版权知识巡回宣讲”首次走进设区市。

（资料来源：江西省版权局）

【湖北省版权局举办2018年版权行政执法工作培训班】 2018年5月24—25日，湖北省2018年版权行政执法培训工作班在武汉举行，湖北省版权局副局长胡伟做开班动员讲话，各市、州及直管市、林区版权局对口科室负责人，各市州及部分县市版权行政执法人员共计80人参加培训。

此次培训采取理论讲解＋案例剖析＋座谈探析的形式，聚焦网络环境下的版权行政执法工作，围绕版权法律法规、互联网＋大数据技术、案件证据采集与鉴定、“两法”衔接、著作权刑事案件审判等重点、难点、热点问题进行了专题授课，重点帮助基层版权行政执法人员解决在互联网环境下办什么案、怎么办案的问题。

（资料来源：湖北省版权局）

【山东省“版权进乡村”行动在潍坊启动】 2018年5月28日，山东省“版权进乡村”行动启动仪式在潍坊市寒亭区杨家埠大观园举行。全省各地级市文化执法部门、潍坊市县两级文化执法部门执法业务骨干，版权保护示范镇村（园区）负责人，寒亭区各街道、杨家埠旅游开发区负责同志和版权保护带头人，部分小学生代表共计400余人参加了活动。

启动仪式上，山东省版权局相关同志对此次活动进行了动员部署：一是要增强开展“版权进乡村”行动的责任感和使命感；二是要充分发挥村镇创建主体作用，逐步建立版权保护助力乡村振兴战略的体制机制；三是要把选拔培养版权保护带头人、示范企业和园区、示范村镇作为工作重点，以点带面、全面推进，为助力乡村振兴做出积极贡献。

活动中，对获得“潍坊市民间艺术品版权保护工作站”“寒亭区版权重点保护对象”等荣誉的代表进行了颁奖授牌，组织参观了杨家埠村版权保护工作站、杨家埠民间艺术大观园年画、风筝展室和年画古版仓库等现场，同时开展了版权执法培训。

（资料来源：潍坊大众网，作者：范素娟　贾宾）

【内蒙古自治区版权局举办2018年区直机关单位软件正版化工作培训班】 2018年5月29日，内蒙古自治区版权局举办2018年区直机关单位软件正版化工作培训班。本次培训是为贯彻落实内蒙古自治区推进使用正版软件工作联席会议2018年第一次会议精神，旨在传达贯彻国家和自治区推进正版软件工作联席会议精神，为即将开展的全区软件正版化督查做好业务和技术准备工作。自治区直属机关各委、办、厅、局共计90家单位的141名有关人员参加了培训。

本次培训按照务实、高效、节俭的原则，分别从软件正版化工作的意义、督查内容、如何上机检查、准备哪些印证材料、常见问题解答等方面，详细讲解了软件正版化工作的具体内容、方法、指标、要求等，并进一步巩固了区直机关单位软件正版化工作成果，为下一步开展为期3个月的督查工作奠定了基础。

（资料来源：内蒙古自治区版权局）

【福建德化多部门联合推广版权保护】 2018年5月，福建省德化县文体新局联合德化县人民法院、科技局等部门组织开展版权保护宣传活动，积极主动营造版权保护的舆论氛围。

德化县通过组织开展知识产权知识竞赛，鼓励群众在微信上参与版权知识答题，普及版权法规；在德化县瓷都广场举行大型宣传活动，宣传版权等法律法规，进一步营造全县尊重版权的氛围。

德化县文体新局还将知识产权教育带进校园，在德化县第三实验小学开展侵权产品销毁活动，并将销毁过程在人民网、泉州网同步直播。

针对目前存在的版权“存证难、自证难、取证难”问题，德化县通过“政府购买服务、企业免费使用”的形式推出“互联网存证＋司法鉴定”知识产权电子数据存证云平台，通过存证云的推广，扭转企业在版权纠纷中存证难、自证难、取证难的现状。

（资料来源：《中国新闻出版广电报》，作者：张福财）

【福建省局办2018年全省版权执法骨干培训班】 2018年6月12—14日，福建省版权局举办2018年全省版权执法骨干培训班。省、市、县三级版权行政管理部门和重点市、县文化市场综合执法部门的业务骨干共30余人参加培训。

福建省版权局副局长肖贵新出席培训开班仪式并做动员讲话。他指出，此次培训的主要目的是提升基层执法人员在新形势下的版权执法能力，深入推进版权执法工作，逐步化解全省版权管理和执法工作中存在的发展不平衡、不充分的矛盾，营造良好的版权保护环境。他强调了三点意见：一要认清形势，明确版权执法工作的重要性；二要主动作为，纵深推进版权执法工作开展；三要加强学习，切实提高版权执法工作能力。

培训内容丰富，形式多样，聚焦新形势下版权执法工作，采取理论授课、案例解析、座谈交流相结合的形式，邀请了福州大学法学院教授刘宁、泉州市文化市场综合执法支队二大队大队长陈能贤、福建省通信管理局网络安全问题专家陈尚国等三人，分别围绕著作权法律法规、侵犯著作权类案件办理、互联网背景下行政管理与执法相关业务等内容进行专题授课，并组织参训学员对版权执法工作中遇到的典型案例和难点疑点问题进行了探讨交流。

（资料来源：福建省版权局）

【“江西版权保护宣讲会”走进革命老区】 2018年6月20日，“江西版权保护宣讲会”永新专场活动在江西永新县举行。

活动现场，江西省版权保护中心主任赖政兵以“版权保护与文化产业发展”为题，为与会人员阐述了版权和版权制度的基本含义、特点及其与文化产业的关系，分享了做好版权保护工作的体会，受到与会人员的欢迎。

这是“江西版权保护宣讲会”首次走进革命老区进行宣讲。艺术家们对省版权保护中心把宣讲会开到基层，把版权课堂搬到广大基层文化艺术工作者的面前，有效搭建起版权保护与文化艺术工作者之间桥梁的做法给予高度赞扬和充分肯定。

（资料来源：《中国新闻出版广电报》，作者：赣文）

【北京市为区级国家机关进行软件正版化培训】 2018年6月22日，北京市使用正版软件联席会议办公室举行了2018年北京市区级国家机关和区卫生计生系统软件正版化工作培训，各区软件正版化牵头单位、政府办、财政局、卫计委、国资委等单位的80余人参加了培训。

培训阐述了做好软件正版化工作的重要意义，

提出了 2018 年北京区级国家机关和区卫生计生系统软件正版化工作的新要求，解析了 2018 年度区级国家机关和区卫生计生系统软件正版化工作考核标准，重点介绍了国家版权局正版软件管理工作指南和软件正版化检查工具。北京市版权局有关负责人表示，区级国家机关和区卫生计生系统软件正版化工作培训的举办，为完成年度区级国家机关和区卫生计生系统软件正版化工作任务打下了坚实的基础。

（资料来源：《中国新闻出版广电报》，作者：王坤宁）

【《2017 年重庆区县知识产权发展状况报告》发布】 2018 年 6 月 27 日，由重庆市知识产权信息中心和重庆大学共同编制的《2017 年重庆区县知识产权发展状况报告》（以下简称《报告》）正式发布，2016 年，全市知识产权总体发展状况良好，知识产权综合发展指数为 62.70%，处于全国中上游水平。

《报告》根据知识产权综合指数将全市 38 个区县划分为四个梯队，从知识产权创造、运用、保护、管理、服务五个方面反映了全市 2016 年在知识产权发展方面的变化，客观展示了各区县的知识产权发展水平。

从知识产权综合发展指数看，38 个区县中属于第一梯队的有九龙坡区、渝北区、江北区、南岸区、北碚区、沙坪坝区，综合发展指数均高于 60%。九龙坡区综合发展指数为 86.32%，位列全市第一。

（资料来源：中国知识产权资讯网，作者：崔芳）

【天津市召开 2018 年政府机关使用正版软件工作培训会】 2018 年 6 月 28 日，天津市推进使用正版软件工作联席会议办公室组织召开 2018 年政府机关使用正版软件工作培训会，市软件正版化工作联席会议成员单位、市级机关和 16 个区政府软件正版化工作有关负责同志约 90 人参加了培训会。

会议强调，各单位要按照天津市政府机关使用正版软件工作考核实施方案要求，进一步建立健全使用正版软件工作责任制度，规范正版软件管理和计算机硬件采购制度，不断推进正版化工作，紧紧抓住长效机制建设、源头监督管理、督促考核评议等关键环节，切实巩固软件正版化工作成果，推进我市政府机关使用正版软件工作再上新水平。

培训会邀请中国云计算专家委员会专家，金山办公软件公司副总裁刘昌伟做了关于信息安全与软件正版化工作的专题讲座，从信息安全的角度就软件正版化工作的背景、意义、成效和软件知识产权保护态势及应对做了详细讲解，介绍了目前全国各地在软件正版化长效机制建设方面存在的问题及解决方案。市推进使用正版软件工作联席会议办公室对贯彻落实天津市 2018 年推进使用正版软件工作计划及政府机关软件正版化考评工作进行了部署落实和指导推动。

（资料来源：天津市版权局）

【江苏省医疗卫生机构软件正版化工作培训班在南京举行】 2018 年 6 月 29 日，江苏省卫生计生委、省版权局在南京举办了全省医疗卫生机构软件正版化工作培训班，省卫生计生委副主任兰青出席并讲话，省版权局版权处对软件正版化工作进行业务辅导。

兰青指出，做好软件正版化工作，是保护知识产权的需要，是加强网络和信息安全的需要，更是提高卫生与健康信息水平、提升行业形象的需要。各地各单位要采取有效措施，加强经费保障，加快推进工作，将软件正版化与信息化建设紧密结合，在信息安全和信息化项目建设、检查和验收等专项工作中，将软件正版化作为一项重要内容，做到同步要求与落实。

2017 年 12 月，江苏省版权工作领导小组办公室、省卫生计生委和省版权局联合发文，启动全省医疗卫生机构软件正版化推进工作，要求全省各级医疗卫生机构在 2018 年底前基本完成计算机操作系统、办公软件、杀毒软件的正版化。同时，建立协调机制，积极与相关软件厂商进行价格谈判，通过集中采购方式，为各级医疗卫生机构降低成本。

省卫生计生委直属机构、各市卫生计生委、版权局及相关医疗卫生机构代表参加了此次培训。

（资料来源：江苏省版权局）

【内蒙古自治区国资委举办出资监管企业软件正版化业务培训】 2018 年 7 月 3 日，内蒙古自治区国资委举办出资监管企业软件正版化业务培训，自治区国资委党委委员、副主任及永乾做了开训动员讲话。自治区版权局相关同志到场指导，并围绕正版软件工作法规政策进行了梳理解读和专题讲座。

此次培训是贯彻落实国家和自治区推进地方国有企业使用正版软件工作政策规定，全面推进自治区国资委出资监管企业软件正版化的有力举措。通过业务培训，引导出资监管企业提高思想认识，强化版权意识，形成任务共识，确保规划的目标任务如期实现。自治区国资委出资监管企业分管领导和部门负责同志共80余人参加了培训。

（资料来源：内蒙古自治区版权局）

【云南省版权行政执法骨干培训班举办】 2018年7月5日，2018年云南省版权行政执法骨干培训班在昆明举办，来自云南省、州（市）两级版权行政管理部门和文化市场综合执法部门的业务骨干共70余人参加培训。培训结合实际，注重将法理讲解与操作实务有机结合，邀请云南省内版权法律法规和执法方面的专家分别就著作权法律制度、著作权行政执法等方面的知识和操作实务进行了讲解。

（资料来源：《中国新闻出版广电报》，作者：滇闻）

【江苏省政府机关软件正版化培训班在常州举行】 2018年7月5—6日，江苏省政府机关软件正版化工作培训班在常州举行，来自各省级机关，各市政府办、版权、财政、经信、商务、机关事务管理等推进使用正版软件工作机制成员单位以及常州市各市级机关的软件正版化工作负责人共计230余人参加培训，江苏省新闻出版广电局（版权局）副局长于国民出席并讲话。

于国民强调，做好政府机关软件正版化工作，一是要防止出现松懈情绪，要充分认识软件正版化工作长期性；二是各部门要密切协调配合，形成推进软件正版化工作合力；三是要继续加强制度建设，完善软件正版化工作长效机制；四是要加强督促检查，促使推进软件正版化政策落地生效；五是要落实主体责任，推进政府机关软件正版化工作向纵深发展，进一步加强全省事业单位和国有企业的软件正版化工作；六是要积极做好宣传培训，营造软件正版化工作良好氛围。

常州市政府副秘书长黄建德在致辞中表示，将紧紧围绕高质量发展根本要求，对标先进、取长补短，解放思想、担当作为，着力推动常州版权工作在新时代有新提升，为加快建设引领型知识产权强省贡献力量。

培训邀请了省机关事务管理局资产管理处相关负责人就软件资产管理要务进行授课，省农业委员会、省委党校、省监狱管理局、昆山市文化广电新闻出版局（版权局）分别就开展政府机关软件正版化工作做了经验交流。

（资料来源：常州市文化广电新闻出版局）

【北京市举行市属国企软件正版化工作培训】 2018年7月6日，北京市使用正版软件工作联席会议办公室联合北京计算机软件登记中心举办了市属国企软件正版化工作培训暨北京地区软件登记专办员培训会，培训范围覆盖5家市属国有企业集团总部及其所属三级以上企业，培训人员100余人。

此次培训是为进一步推进北京市属国企软件正版化工作，加强对北京地区软件著作权登记和软件正版化工作指导，提高市属国企工作人员版权保护意识，进一步优化首都软件产业发展环境而举办的。培训重点就市属国企普遍关心的软件正版化检查考核评分标准、正版软件管理工作指南的应用、软件正版化检查工具的使用、软件著作权登记等内容进行了详细讲解。通过培训，提高了参训各单位工作人员版权保护意识和软件著作权登记能力，为市属国有企业圆满完成全年软件正版化工作目标打下了良好基础。

（资料来源：北京市版权局）

【全国首次青年版权征文大赛结果在上海揭晓】 2018年11月30日，由中国版权保护中心指导、《中国版权》杂志社主办、中华版权代理总公司协办的“新时代版权强国青年征文大赛”评审结果在上海揭晓，并在2018（首届）版权强国闵行论坛上举行了颁奖仪式。原国家新闻出版广电总局政策法制司司长王自强、中国版权保护中心副主任魏红为组织奖获奖代表颁奖；当当创始人、Crysto战略投资人李国庆，AIPPI中国分会版权委员会主席、北京韬安律师事务所首席合伙人王军为一等奖获奖代表颁奖。

这是中国首次在全国范围内开展青年版权征文大赛。征文大赛自2018年4月正式启动，历经7个月的宣传、征稿，经专家严格评审，最终产生一等奖15名、二等奖20名、三等奖30名、优秀奖30名、组织奖7家。上海广播电视台姚岚秋、上海市第二中级人民法院袁博、北京市知识产权局杨晋、爱奇艺法律部胡荟集、搜狐法律中心马晓明、北京市海淀区人民法院张璇、人民网法务部滕力、北京韬安律师事务所孙皓、华东政法大学阮开欣、中国人民大学刘洪灏、中南财经政法大学邵华、华东政法大学程章、清华大学许佳楠、同济大学罗媛瑗、北京大学初萌获一等奖。中国知识产权报社刘仁等20人获二等奖。杭州互联网法院张书青等30人获得三等奖。铸成律师事务所林娜等30人获得优秀奖。爱奇艺法律部、搜狐法律中心、华东政法大学、中南财经政法大学、华中师范大学、重庆理工大学、集美大学7家单位荣获组织奖。

本次大赛将征文对象定位为18～45岁的青年。大赛旨在全面展现新时代版权领域青年的专业精神和职业风采，让青春智慧激发创新活力，使青年人才成为版权强国的主力军，推动新时代创新发展，为国家版权事业发现、汇聚青年才俊。

（资料来源：人民网）

【2018年京沪知识产权诉讼报告发布】 2018年12月17日，由高文律师事务所组织编写的《北京知识产权诉讼报告2018》《上海知识产权诉讼报告2018》在京发布。

在侵犯著作权案件专题部分，研究人员分别采集了2015—2017年间北京、上海两地法院侵犯著作权案件判决书各300份，通过对判决书内容进行归纳提炼，得出了一系列结论。

观察发现，两地法院近年来新收一审知识产权民事案件量呈大幅增长趋势，其中以著作权案件占比最高，而在著作权案件中，侵犯作品信息网络传播权所占比例最大。研究采集的两地600件案例中，涉及信息网络传播权的案例多达303件，占比超过50%。报告认为，著作权纠纷的占比较高，说明中国尤其是京沪两地的文化创意产业、网络信息产业繁荣发展，但同时存在版权管理与保护的风险和漏洞。事实上，随着计算机网络的应用普及，网络著作权保护已成为全球范围内的热点和难点问题。

报告指出，移动互联网环境下，作品遭侵权呈现出侵权方式移动化、APP侵权成主流、恶意搜索侵权成主导等新特征。报告建议，保护移动互联网环境下的文学作品，由于侵权发现难、取证难、赔偿难等因素，需要构建以规范化建设为根本，以反盗版等新技术为手段，以联合执法为抓手，以司法保护为保障的综合一体化方式，以促进文化大繁荣大发展。对著作权的创造者、传播者和使用者而言，其在利用网络时应善意谨慎、诚信经营，避免侵权。

此外，研究者通过对两地的600件著作权纠纷案例深入分析，总结出四个特点。

一是原告所属地域以“北上广”为主。研究选取的判决书中列明原告所属地域的，原告来自北京的著作权案件多达313件，其次为上海的78件，再次是广东的54件，分别占比约52%、13%和9%，表明这3个省市的文化创意产业相对发达，著作权人较多。

二是原告一方聘请律师的比例较高。研究样本中，原告聘请律师的案件共有529件，而被告聘请律师的案件则有317件，且双方聘请律师的案件数量和比例近年来持续增长，当事人单枪匹马上法庭的情况越来越少。说明著作权侵权案例越来越具有细分领域和难度分级的特点，需要专业的法律服务支持。

三是诉争标的物以5类作品为主。在诉争标的物种类方面，摄影图片、歌曲（包括音像制品和KTV侵权）、文学作品、美术作品及影视作品和以类似摄制电影的方法创作的作品（包括电影、电视剧、动画片、综艺节目、纪录片、动漫等）占比80%以上。其他诉争标的物包括图形作品、录音录像作品、计算机软件、网页设计等。

四是原告胜诉比例高。600件案例中，原告胜诉的有569件，占比近95%，法院判决驳回原告诉讼请求的只有31件，占比约5%。法院判决的赔偿数额与原告索赔数额的比值即判赔比，以2015年、2016年和2017年3年逐年统计分析，上海市法院判赔比依次为9.6%、8%、20.9%，判赔比正在明显提升，说明法院对于权利人的保护力度在加强，使得侵权成本在提高，在引导著作权创造和传播方面开始发挥更大的正向作用。

上述数据表明，著作权纠纷民事诉讼中，原告胜诉率虽然很高，但单个案件的判赔额仍然较低，600个样本案例中，上海法院的判赔额为平均2.1万元，北京法院的判赔额为平均1.7万元。这一统计结论恰恰说明了社会舆论普遍呼声的重要性。加大司法判赔额和判赔比，充分发挥法律的规制效应，引导著作权创作方和传播方在良性秩序下保护和运用著作权，是社会各界的共同愿望。

（资料来源：《中国知识产权报》，作者：王少冗）

【《中国知识产权指数报告》第十次发布】 2018年12月17日，由高文律师事务所王正志律师主持编写的《中国知识产权指数报告2018》（以下简称《报告2018》）在京发布。报告显示，中国31个省、自治区和直辖市（不含港澳台）的知识产权综合实力排名中，北京、广东、江苏、上海、浙江、山东、安徽、天津、湖北、重庆位居前十位，其中北京已连续九年领跑全国。

《中国知识产权指数报告》自2009年首次问世，本次是第十次发布。课题组通过对全国各省份每年度的知识产权产出水平、知识产权流动水平、知识产权综合绩效、知识产权创造潜力等四个一级指标以及相应的上百个二级指标、三级指标数据进行搜集和权重处理，建立数学模型加以运算，用指数方式对各省份知识产权综合实力、发展特点及趋势等进行评价。其丰富翔实的数据积累和精确量化的表达方式，为研究区域知识产权与经济发展间的关系提供了充分的依据，为各界提供了观察、了解和研究中国各地区知识产权发展状况、发展质量、未来趋势的重要窗口及通道。

王正志律师介绍，多年以来，中国区域知识产权指数“东高西低”的特征明显，排名前十的省份基本集中在东部沿海地区，排名中游的省份多数处于中部腹地，排名后十位的省份则以西部边远地区居多，三者形成了阶梯状，知识产权指数区域分布的特点与其经济发展水平总体是相吻合的。

分析《报告 2018》，王正志说，从知识产权产出水平、流动水平、综合绩效和创造潜力四个一级指标排名来看，综合实力排名前三的京、粤、苏优势各有不同，北京强在产出和绩效，广东强在知识产权的应用和转化，而江苏强在知识产权潜力最大。与以往数据相比，排名前五的省份领先优势依然明显，其余各省份间的差距正在变小；中部地区开始呈现爆发势头，个别省份已经多年位居前列；西部地区也呈现后发趋势。

《报告 2018》特别针对当前知识产权发展的两个重要议题——移动互联网环境下的文学作品保护和科技成果转化新政落地的知识产权认知障碍进行了专题研究。《报告 2018》指出，移动互联网环境下，作品遭侵权呈现出侵权方式移动化、APP 侵权成主流、恶意搜索侵权成主导等新特征。《报告 2018》建议，保护移动互联网环境下的文学作品，由于侵权发现难、取证难、赔偿难等因素，需要构建以规范化建设为根本，以反盗版等新技术为手段，以联合执法为抓手，以司法保护为保障的综合一体化方式，以促进文化大繁荣大发展。

《报告 2018》同时认为，中国高校和科研机构整体上对知识产权认知度不够高，阻碍了科技创新转化。其成因除了通识教育和培训的不足，还有高校和外部产业间固有的“两极构造”：学术研究与外部市场目标关联弱、大学科研机构和产业间知识产权要素互动少、大学科研机构的技术转化体系缺乏市场和社会的协同塑造，而这样的两极构造与各种显性及隐性障碍交织仍会存续较长时间。因此《报告 2018》建议，应通过“通达民情，化育人心”的普及方式、体制内构建沟通交流途径和重视社会组织的力量来扭转。

（资料来源：中国知识产权资讯网，作者：王少冗）

【“文创西藏”以版权交易为核心　提升文旅创意设计水平】 2018 年 12 月 20 日，为提升西藏文旅创意设计水平，搭建行业交流协作平台，由西藏文化厅主办的“文创西藏”版权交易设计大赛启动。

“文创西藏”是西藏文化产业领域由政府打造的对外唯一备案品牌。本次大赛向全球的机构和个人发出邀请，征集品牌 logo 和优秀产品及设计，大赛旨在夯实“西藏特色文化产业贸易服务窗口”的项目和产品基础，以大赛为纽带，以版权交易为核心，汇聚区内外优质创意设计资源，提升西藏文旅创意设计水平，搭建行业交流协作平台。

凡入选本次版权交易设计大赛的产品，将纳入“文创西藏”品牌备案库，享受西藏自治区政府的品牌认证，获得全球范围内的“西藏特色文化产业之窗”线下实体店、“西藏宝贝”文化电商平台、“西藏特色文化产业之窗·航悦悠享”空中平台等官方授权展销平台的大力推介。

（资料来源：《中国新闻出版广电报》，作者：藏闻）

【2018 年度中国版权行业十大热点案件公布】 2018 年 12 月 22 日，在由国际保护知识产权协会（AIPPI）中国分会在京主办的 2018 年度 AIPPI 中国分会版权热点论坛上，AIPPI 中国分会版权专业委员会主席王军、《中国知识产权》杂志编辑部主任李雪联合发布了由部分知识产权法院法官、版权界专家学者评出的“2018 年度中国版权行业十大热点案件”。这十大热点案件包括：

（1）李子成与葛怀圣侵害著作权纠纷案，由最高人民法院裁判。案件亮点：认定点校行为构成著作权法意义的表达。

（2）北京瑞森新谱科技有限公司、魏茂林与 LISTEN，Inc. 确认不侵害著作权纠纷案，由北京市高级人民法院审理。案件亮点：确认不侵害著作权之诉中侵权警告的要义。

（3）东映动画株式会社等与北京有爱互娱科技有限公司改编权、信息网络传播权纠纷案，由北京市海淀区人民法院审理。案件亮点：确认《海贼王》元素“山寨”游戏侵权原动画片中的对应形象美术作品。

（4）北京快手科技有限公司与广州华多网络科技有限公司侵害著作权纠纷案，由北京市海淀区人民法院审理。案件亮点：认定短视频属于作品第一案。

（5）北京中科水景科技有限公司与北京中科恒业中自技术有限公司等侵犯著作权纠纷案，由北京知识产权法院审理。案件亮点：认定音乐喷泉效果属于美术作品第一案。

（6）北京华彩光影传媒文化有限责任公司与北京时光梦幻科技有限公司侵害著作权纠纷案，由北京市海淀区人民法院审理。案件亮点：涉及虚拟现实场景（VR 场景）中使用美术作品的行为定性问题。

（7）查良镛与杨治等著作权侵权及不正当竞争纠纷案，由广东省广州市天河区人民法院审理。案件亮点：同人作品第一案。

（8）苏州蜗牛数字科技股份有限公司与成都天象互动科技有限公司等侵害著作权纠纷案，由江苏省苏州市中级人民法院审理。案件亮点：游戏规则抄袭侵权第一案。

（9）北京焦点互动信息服务有限公司南京分公司与北京百度网讯科技有限公司侵害作品信息网络传播权纠纷案，由江苏省南京市中级人民法院审理。案件亮点：确认直接从网盘服务器删除侵权文件第一案。

（10）深圳市腾讯计算机系统有限公司与上海千杉网络技术发展有限公司侵害作品信息网络传播权纠纷案，由广东省深圳市中级人民法院审理。案件亮点：确认通过技术手段破坏他人技术措施的信息网络传播权侵权。

（资料来源：《中国新闻出版广电报》，作者：赖名芳）

◆ 交流研讨

【网络游戏产业法律问题研讨会举行】 2018 年 1 月 20 日，由清华大学法学院、中国知识产权法学研究会、中国民法学研究会主办，中央财经大学法学院知识产权研究中心协办的网络游戏产业法律问题研讨会在清华大学法学院举行。来自北京大学、中国人民大学、清华大学、中国政法大学等高校的学者，来自全国人大常委会法工委、最高人民法院、文化部、国家版权局、国家知识产权局、北京市高级人民法院及三大知识产权法院等单位的专家以及来自华多公司、腾讯公司等实务界的人士共两百人参加了本次研讨会。

研讨会开幕式由清华大学法学院党委副书记程啸教授主持。中国人民大学常务副校长王利明教授发表致辞。王利明指出，互联网时代网络游戏与直播已经成为一个内容丰富、市场价值巨大的产业，由此也引发民法、知识产权法等多方面的法律问题。当前中国未成年人上网人数已近 1.5 亿人，网络游戏对青少年身心健康的影响至关重要，凸显了青少年人格权保护的重要性，未来民法典人格权编应当对此做出回应。《中国法学》总编辑张新宝教授认为，如何使得网络游戏产业成为更好的产业，既能保护未成年人的网络权益，又能丰富我们的文化生活、保护个人信息，是需要认真探讨的问题。未来网络游戏产业界应当开发出更智慧化、更有文化涵养、更符合社会主义核心价值观的网络游戏产品，服务于不同的人群。中国知识产权法学研究会会长刘春田教授认为，互联网技术打开了人类思维创新的新闸门，也为知识产权法学的发展提供了新契机。知识产权本质上就是私权利，民法典应当将知识产权纳入其中。清华大学法学院院长申卫星教授指出，新的技术和产业发展给法治建设和法学研究带来了新的挑战，亟待理论界与实务界的深入合作与积极回应。中央财经大学法学院知识产权研究中心主任杜颖教授认为，网络游戏不仅涉及传统版权业和互联网产业之间的利益冲突问题，还涉及互联网产业内部不同链条和节点之间的利益冲突问题。

研讨会为期一天，分为四个单元，主题分别为“网络游戏直播产业的知识产权问题”“反不正当竞争法下的网络游戏竞争问题”“网络游戏中的虚拟财产保护问题”“网络游戏与民法典侵权责任编”。与会专家学者深入地探讨了网络游戏产业中网络游戏开发商与网络游戏直播商的利益与知识产权保护问题、网络游戏纠纷中如何适用反不正当竞争法问题、虚拟财产的民法保护以及网络游戏侵权行为问题等重要的议题。

（资料来源：《法制日报》，作者：李松　朱宁宁）

【广东省版权局召开促进软件著作权创造、保护和运用专家座谈会】 2018 年 1 月 30 日，广东省版权局召开促进软件著作权创造、保护和运用座谈会。广东省版权局专职副局长陈春怀主持座谈会并讲话。

座谈会上，来自版权理论界、产业界、法律界及版权行业协会的代表就现阶段影响和制约广东省软件著作权创造、保护和运用的突出问题和困难，如何制定出台促进软件著作权创造、保护和运用的政策措施等充分发表意见建议。大家认为，要充分利用新举措和新技术加强软件著作权保护，要优化软件企业吸引人才的环境，要通过完善税收政策减轻软件企业负担，要运用大数据理念构建版权云平台，要加强软件著作权审查管理，提高软件著作权登记质量。

陈春怀指出，各位专家从不同方面提供了很多宝贵的意见建议，省版权局将认真总结梳理，并抓好重点方向的调研论证，为广东省软件著作权相关法规政策的制定提供有益的借鉴。

广东省新闻出版广电局办公室、政策法规处、出版管理处、网络视听节目管理处、版权管理处等有关人员参加了座谈会。

（资料来源：广东省版权局）

【“数字时代下的著作权法修改”研讨会召开】 2018年1月30日，由中国法学会网络与信息法学研究会、中国社会科学院法学研究所主办的第九次网络与信息法治圆桌会议暨“数字时代下的著作权法修改”研讨会在北京召开。

网络与信息法治圆桌会议是由主办方双方共同发起的跨学科、跨领域、小型务实的政产学研媒多方参与的会议机制。会议不定期地就网络信息法治发展中的重大问题进行讨论，本次圆桌会议聚焦数字时代下的著作权法修订。中国社科院法学研究所知识产权研究室主任管育鹰研究员对著作权法修改过程中与网络有关的条款及争议问题进行详细介绍。她认为，网络环境下争议较大的问题有广播电台、电视台的信息网络传播权问题，网络环境下合理使用的相关问题，以及“避风港”规则、技术保护措施和权利管理信息相关问题等，这些都需要进一步加强理论研究，以回应社会实践需求。

（资料来源：《检察日报》，作者：仲创法）

【北京国际网络版权监测研讨会召开】 2018年2月26日下午，由中国版权协会主办的北京国际网络版权监测研讨会在京召开。

中国版权协会理事长阎晓宏在致辞中指出，经过多年的发展，中国大网站的守法意识相对比较强，版权保护成绩明显。但小网站的侵权盗版情况不容忽视，就小网站的侵权盗版和监测维权问题举行研讨，很有针对性和现实意义。

国家版权局版权管理司司长于慈珂认为国际网络版权监测维权是个非常重要的话题，他用三个主题词来阐释了他的观点。第一，协同。网络版权的保护手段很多，有技术手段、市场手段、法律手段等。当前应该把这些手段协同起来，使其发挥整体的效应。其中，技术手段是比较重要的一种手段。第二，协调。网络版权涉及许多环节和方面，如创作者、权利人，使用者、传播者、服务商等，要把这些环节和方面协调起来。目前协调得还不够，特别是服务商、运营商，要发挥更多的版权保护的主体责任，权利人组织、著作权集体管理组织也责无旁贷。第三，协作。如何解决网络传播的无国界和司法、行政执法的主权性有疆界之间的冲突？需要国与国之间进行更有效、更有力的合作、协作，来打击跨国网络侵权盗版。除了国家间的合作外，企业之间、协会之间、民间组织之间的合作也非常重要。于司长说，国家版权局将进一步发挥版权行政执法监管的特点和优势，对准新问题、新挑战出击，促进网络版权的创造、运用、保护和管理。

来自WIPO中国办事处、国际知名行业协会、著作权集体管理组织、国内各大网站及版权相关单位的40余人出席了会议。

（资料来源：《中国日报》，作者：罗望舒）

【第九届首都互联网知识产权保护论坛聚焦视听作品知识产权保护】 2018年4月20日，由北京市高级人民法院知识产权庭、中关村社会组织联合会、中国互联网协会网络版权工作委员会、中国广播电影电视社会组织联合会电视制片委员会联合主办的第九届首都互联网知识产权保护论坛在京召开。

论坛的主题为“视听作品知识产权保护”。在论坛上，中国互联网协会调解中心与北京市海淀区人民法院民五庭共同发布了《关于影视作品著作权案件署名问题调研报告》，49家从事互联网行业和影视制作行业的企业共同发布《规范视听作品署名　促进版权保护和流转倡议书》，期望能共同推动影视作品规范管理进程。

在论坛上，北京市高级人民法院介绍了2017年北京法院知识产权司法审判总体情况，并着重介绍了刚刚发布的《侵害著作权案件审理指南》。来自北京知识产权法院和各基层法院的知识产权法官从网络游戏著作权及不正当竞争保护、涉VR技术相关著作权问题的思考、涉网络知识产权案件多元纠纷解决机制的建设等角度进行了主题发言。

近年来影视产业发展迅速，但不相匹配的是影视产业运行尚不规范引发的各种问题，其中的突出问题是影视作品的署名不规范问题。故海淀法院民五庭课题组以2013—2017年共5年海淀法院审理的影视作品著作权纠纷案件为样本进行研究，形成《关于影视作品著作权案件署名问题调研报告》并发布。

49家互联网企业和影视制作公司联合发布《规范视听作品署名　促进版权保护和流转倡议书》，目的是为了规范视听作品署名管理，保护视听作品著作权人的合法权益，促进视听作品的版权交易。

（资料来源：《中国新闻出版广电报》，作者：邹韧）

【2018 中国知识产权保护高层论坛在京举办】 2018 年 4 月 20 日，以“强化知识产权保护　塑造良好营商环境”为主题的 2018 中国知识产权保护高层论坛在京举办。中国国家知识产权局局长申长雨，世界知识产权组织副总干事王彬颖，十三届全国政协文化文史和学习委员会副主任阎晓宏，中国国际贸易促进委员会副会长卢鹏起，欧洲专利局首席经济学家杨·伊夫·莫尼尔，埃及专利局局长阿代尔·埃韦达，印度尼西亚法律人权部知识产权总司总司长弗雷迪·哈里斯，摩洛哥工业和商业产权局局长阿迪勒·艾尔·马里奇等中外嘉宾出席论坛并做主旨发言。中国国家知识产权局副局长廖涛主持论坛。

为期两天的论坛聚焦新时代中国知识产权保护新理念、新思路、新举措，共设 1 个主论坛和 6 个专题论坛，涵盖互联网、企业“走出去”、医药、人工智能、大数据、反不正当竞争等领域知识产权保护前沿和热点话题。来自国际组织、国内外相关政府部门、有关国家驻华使馆、行业协会的代表，司法机关、知名企业、高校院所的近 70 位专家学者，就加强知识产权保护相关话题发表演讲，并与 1 200 余名参会者展开深入交流。

中国知识产权保护高层论坛由中国知识产权报社和世界知识产权组织中国办事处共同主办。

（资料来源：知识产权局网站，作者：王宇）

【2018 中国网络版权保护大会在京召开】 2018 年 4 月 26 日，国家版权局在京举办以“保护创作，推进运用”为主题的 2018 中国网络版权保护大会。

会上，国家版权局与全国“扫黄打非”办公室联合发布了“2017 年度全国打击侵权盗版十大案件”，中国信息通信研究院发布了《2017 年中国网络版权保护年度报告》。

世界知识产权组织（WIPO）副总干事王彬颖为大会发来贺信。她在贺信中说，18 年前 WIPO 的两个成员国提议设立世界知识产权日，中国就是其中的一个。今天，创新和知识产权保护已成为中国创意经济的重要驱动力。根据中国权威机构发布的数据，2016 年中国的 GDP 有 7.33％来自版权创意产业。2017 年中国网络版权产业的市场规模达 6 364.5 亿元，相较 2016 年增长 27.2％。

全国政协文化文史和学习委员会副主任、中国版权协会理事长阎晓宏在大会上致辞。他说，中国保护知识产权的决心是坚定的。对中国这样一个处于转型期的发展中国家而言，我们在知识产权保护方面投入了大量人力物力，成效也是显著的。同时，也要看到由于中国还处于转型期，市场经济还不完善，在推动知识产权的创新、使用、管理、保护和服务等方面依然存在不少问题。对于解决这些发展中的问题，特别是新技术带来的问题，他提出三点建议：一是以立法机关为主导，加快推动知识产权法律体系的修订完善；二是建议实施版权严保护，推动形成司法保护、政府监管、行业协调、企业自律的社会共治格局；三是鼓励支持更多优质、精品创作诞生。

国家版权局版权管理司司长于慈珂在大会上做了主旨演讲。他认为，倡导创新文化、着力保护创作、推动创造运用，是满足人民美好生活需要、推动解决社会主要矛盾的有效途径。目前，在网络领域，随着人工智能、云计算、大数据等新技术与网络聚合等商业模式的不断发展，网络直播、电子竞技等新型业态发展活跃，为版权工作带来了诸多挑战。今后，要综合运用多种手段，为版权创新、创作、创造提供更加强有力的服务和保障。

大会还汇聚了众多互联网界“大咖”。中国移动通信集团有限公司副总裁简勤以“版权新时代，构建新生态”为题，介绍了中国移动依靠强大的技术力量协助国家版权局打造晴朗有序的版权空间的实践经验。IDG 资本全球董事长熊晓鸽在演讲中提出“文化产业，版权先行”，他建议在版权保护方面要充分利用区块链技术。爱奇艺创始人、首席执行官龚宇在演讲中说，如果没有政府 13 年来持续打击网络侵权盗版，爱奇艺就不可能有今天的发展。北京知识产权法院副院长宋鱼水，腾讯集团副总裁、腾讯影业首席执行官程武，上影集团董事长任仲伦，金山办公软件首席执行官葛珂等在大会主论坛上就数字环境下版权相关问题发表看法并分享了经验。

当天下午，大会还举办了“新技术变革与网络版权创新”、“动漫与短视频网络版权保护及规范”和“新时代网络版权‘她动力’”3 个分论坛。

（资料来源：《中国新闻出版广电报》，作者：赖名芳）

【苏州市召开图片版权保护座谈会】 2018 年 5 月 3 日，苏州市版权协会召开图片版权保护座谈会。

苏州市版权局、市版权协会理事单位及特邀嘉宾 20 余人参加了座谈。

苏州市版权局通报了近期图片版权使用中的热点问题；市版权协会做了图片版权保护知识讲座，结合丰富案例深入浅出地分析了图片版权保护的作用和意义；相关从业企业做了图片版权使用规则及防侵权指南，详细介绍图片使用中的注意事项；与会代表相互交流了本单位在图片使用中遇到的版权问题及相关情况。

（资料来源：苏州市版权局）

【聚焦互联网与新媒体环境下体育赛事直播权利保护研讨会在京召开】 2018 年 5 月 5 日，由中国知识产权法学研究会主办的聚焦互联网与新媒体环境下体育赛事直播权利保护研讨会在京举行，来自法院、高校、企业等诸多部门的嘉宾针对体育赛事直播权利保护等话题进行了探讨。与会嘉宾建议，针对体育赛事节目涉及的知识产权纠纷，中国著作权法并非没有弹性解释和适用的空间，在多种法律保护路径并行的情况下，应当选择最有利于行业发展的保护路径。

研讨会上，中国版权协会版权监测中心发布的一组关于体育赛事直播领域盗播行为的数据引起与会人员关注。据中国版权协会版权监测中心副主任吴冠勇介绍，中国版权协会版权监测中心针对足球类、篮球类、乒乓球类、格斗搏击类、综合赛事等共计 546 场赛事，进行了不同场次、不同方式的监测。在直播方面，共监测到 4 633 个未授权播放链接；在点播方面，共监测到 62.31 万个侵权链接。在所有赛事的未授权直播流链接中，直播秀平台链接占比超过 50%。

（资料来源：《中国知识产权报》，作者：冯飞）

【“远集坊”：“童话大王”郑渊洁讲述创作维权】 2018 年 5 月 27 日，由中国版权协会主办的“远集坊”第十一期讲坛在京举行。著名儿童文学作家郑渊洁在讲坛上做了题为《作家最好的理财是维护版权》的主题演讲。

原国家新闻出版署署长于友先等 20 余位特邀嘉宾出席。全国政协文化文史和学习委员会副主任、中国版权协会理事长阎晓宏致辞。

郑渊洁是中国儿童文学界的一个传奇。他创办并独自撰写的《童话大王》月刊历经 33 年畅销不衰。他还是版权保护的积极倡导者和践行者，曾荣获世界知识产权组织（WIPO）授予的首届中国版权创意金奖，被国家新闻出版管理部门授予“反盗版形象大使”称号。

郑渊洁在演讲中还用生动的语言讲述了他创作和维权的故事。2010 年，他在通州某印厂被盗印者武力相逼，助理通过微博向@平安北京报案，“仅仅十几分钟，警察从天而降。我当时深深体会到国家对版权保护的力度太大了。从最初面对盗版叫天天不应，曾多次无奈声明罢笔，到后来通过主动维权，体会到政府为权利人撑腰，真切地感受到中国版权保护环境在不断好转”。

阎晓宏在致辞中表示，给儿童提供好的读物，是非常有价值有意义的事情，在“六一”儿童节即将到来之际，郑渊洁所述的创作和维权经历，将对中国儿童文学创作和版权维权产生积极的影响。

（资料来源：《中国新闻出版广电报》，作者：赖名芳）

【知识产权保护促进视听产业发展论坛在京举办】 2018 年 5 月 28 日，世界知识产权组织（WIPO）中国办事处、北京市新闻出版广电局、北京市东城区政府联合主办了知识产权保护促进视听产业发展论坛。WIPO 副总干事王彬颖出席论坛，国家版权局版权管理司司长于慈珂、WIPO 中国办事处主任陈宏兵、北京市东城区副区长葛俊凯、北京市新闻出版广电局副局长王野霏出席并致辞。欧盟代表团、美国驻华使馆、英国驻华使馆代表，国际唱片业协会等世界及国内主要著作权组织代表等共 150 余人参会。

会上，华东政法大学教授王迁等知名专家就“表演者对影视产业发展的关键作用”议题发表主题演讲，深入交流了提高表演者权益保护水平对促进全人类文化事业繁荣发展的积极意义和深远影响。著名影视导演、演员蒋雯丽代表广大一线表演者呼吁，希望更多的国家批准和加入《视听表演北京条约》，以促成其早日生效。英国驻华使馆知识产权专员杜涛、搜狐公司总法律顾问庞小妹等业界代表围绕“知识产权保护助力影视产业国际合作”议题发表主题演讲，从产业发展的角度探讨了影视产业的版权保护与执法、事后防范与事后维权、遭遇国际纠纷的应对策略等若干焦点问题。

（资料来源：中国知识产权资讯网，作者：窦新颖）

【互联网内容平台的版权保护研讨会在京举行】 2018 年 6 月 15 日，由中国版权协会主办、中国版权产业网承办的互联网内容平台的版权保护研讨会在北京举行。来自政府部门、法院及产业界的代表就当前环境下互联网内容平台版权保护与产业发展的热点和痛点问题进行探讨，其中快速发展的短视频产业的版权保护问题备受关注。

“今日头条”法务总监郃江丽介绍，在短视频发展过程中，维权成本较高、判赔的金额较低、证据收集难度较大、维权周期较长，是当前短视频版权法律保护遇到的难点。对此，短视频企业希望建立数字确权与取证平台，也希望通过区块链技术在版权保全证据方面进行突破性的技术创新，以提高证据保全效率，方便权利方更好地维权。此外，面对短视频版权争议，郃江丽建议诉讼之外补充多元化纠纷解决机制，完善非诉讼程序，以适应社会纠纷解决的现实需求。

华东政法大学知识产权学院教授丛立先分析了短视频的法律性质、权利主体以及平台责任。面对目前短视频大量侵权情况的存在，丛立先认为现有授权规则已难以适用大量短小作品的广泛传播。他建议，从授权规则上创新，将现有报刊转载的法定许可扩大到包括短视频、图片等在内的短小作品的使用和授权上。同时，他也呼吁我国著作权法在此次修改后能引入视听作品的概念，将所有短视频纳入视听作品范畴予以著作权法保护。

此外，来自人民教育出版社、阅文集团、深圳迅雷集团、腾讯音乐娱乐集团的相关负责人分别介绍了目前在教材、网络文学、数字音乐等领域的版权保护情况。来自版权管理部门、权利人组织、互联网平台、司法界的代表和专家学者等近百人参加了研讨会。

（资料来源：中国知识产权资讯网，作者：刘仁）

【游戏产业发展中的法律问题研讨会聚焦游戏版权保护】 2018 年 6 月 23 日，游戏产业发展中的法律问题研讨会在北京大学举行。此次研讨会吸引了众多在游戏产业知识产权领域具有丰富的实践和理论经验的法官、律师、学者等业界人士，以及主题征文优秀作者参会，共同对游戏作品版权如何保护等热点问题进行了探讨。

业界人士认为，网络游戏程序属于计算机软件，属于著作权法所规定的作品类型，网络游戏中的故事表述、玩法介绍、人物角色形象、工具装备、背景音乐、界面设计、地图路线等则需要单独考量其是否属于法定的作品类型来加以保护，而对整个网络游戏到底是否受保护则莫衷一是。

对此，中央民族大学法学院副教授熊文聪认为，这是一种典型的作品分割论，即把作品分割为若干元素（要素），而单独考虑这些元素（要素）的可版权性。他反对生硬地将作品切分为若干元素（要素），且单独考虑这些元素（要素）可版权性（是否具有独创性、是否属于法定的作品类型），进而从这些元素（要素）的不可版权性直接推出作品整体的不可版权性。他认为，应采用与“分割论”相对应的“整体论”，从整体上去考量、判断该智力成果是否具有可版权性，特别是是否具有独创性，这无疑是合理恰当的。

北京知识产权法院审判委员会委员冯刚法官也认为，网络游戏尽量以整体保护优先。虽然分要素保护具有作品类型明确无争议的优点，但也存在很多缺点，比如客体的复数性决定主体的复数性，不利于整体交易及整体维权；侵权判定标准的个别性与整体性存在差异；法律责任上存在差异等。不过，北京市海淀区人民法院知识产权庭杨德嘉庭长却认为，不应当单独设立游戏作品进行整体保护。除此之外，会议还就侵权赔偿、网络游戏的海外法律、游戏规则的保护等热点问题进行了探讨。

此次会议由中华全国律师协会知识产权专业委员会、北京市影视娱乐法学会、北京大学国际知识产权研究中心主办，北京韬安律师事务所协办。

（资料来源：中国知识产权资讯网，作者：侯伟）

【短视频版权与竞争问题研讨会举办】 2018 年 7 月 7 日，上海市版权局和华东政法大学联合举办短视频版权与竞争问题研讨会，来自产业界、司法界和理论界的相关人士进行了深入探讨。

腾讯研究院秘书长张钦坤介绍，2017 年我国网络版权产业市场规模达 6 364.5 亿元，且新业态形式不断涌现。其中，短视频成为行业黑马，异军突起，在很短的时间内用户规模突破 4.1 亿人，但随之而来的问题也开始显现。

“内容从哪里来？现在很多内容来自社会化媒体的贡献，包括各种各样的‘号’，比如企业号、头条号等社会化媒体，每天会贡献大量内容。这里有一个问题是，在社会化媒体中，‘搭便车’的情况特别多。”张钦坤说，这些内容供给者的版权保护问题值得关注。

爱奇艺诉讼维权总监胡荟集对此也深感无力。他表示，在平台输入一个关键词，随便一搜就会出现大量未经授权的与这个内容相关的碎片化短视频。

“比如，现在热播的《扶摇》，只要搜‘扶摇’，就有很多相关的短视频，让人根本不用再去相关平台看付费的内容，这会让购买了版权的人根本无法获得相应的合法收入。”

与会者还指出，短视频维权成本太高。遇到侵权情况后可以使用的手段非常少，虽然可以向平台投诉，但基本只能在平台内部处理；同时，整个举报流程很长、成本很高，这些都是短视频内容提供者或机构遇到的普遍问题。

与会专家也谈到了短视频版权存在的一些有争议的问题。比如，从《著作权法》的角度该怎样理解短视频的概念？侵权程度和视频长短有没有直接关系？如何区分短视频是不是合理使用？

华东政法大学教授丛立先认为，针对短视频的版权保护，首先要辨别清楚要保护的短视频是否能构成作品，因为《著作权法》保护的一定是作品，短视频只有构成作品，即具有独创性和可复制性，才能成为版权保护的对象。

针对目前有很多短视频是借鉴了别人的创意后再进行创作的现象，丛立先表示，“如果仅是借鉴别人的思想再创作，这是属于合理使用的借鉴再创作，著作权应该归作者所有。但是如果是拿别人的短视频演绎成新的作品，则必须获得原作者授权，只有征得原作者许可才能进行演绎，这与传统《著作权法》规定相同。另外，如果想把别人的短视频汇编成一个新的短视频，同样要征得原作者许可才能进行汇编”。

李琛认为，人们的偏好已经发生变化，现在是“短”更受欢迎。而短视频产业的兴起，使“短”里面包含的利益空间更大，这就会对曾经作为判定合理使用的考量因素产生影响。“我个人认为，至少还要综合考量一些因素。比如短视频制作的目的，很多制作都是为了吸引流量、广告、打赏，并不是出于单纯的自娱自乐的目的，还应该考虑整体的利用量、他人作品在短视频中的比例等因素。此外，短视频传播的独立许可市场也应该受到关注。”

短视频时长虽短，但版权保护不可短视。与会专家表示，目前产业界、司法界已经开始探索短视频版权的保护之道。

在李琛看来，对短视频的保护不能仅仅依靠法律途径，需要将市场、技术、法律等手段综合运用起来。李琛说：“我发现现在已经有短视频的交易平台了，比如说阿里鲸观、微博云剪、MF＋即视链，都是正面的，提供了一个合法买卖的渠道，这是非常重要的一个思路。”

此外，李琛认为，短视频发布平台首先应当对短视频内容进行形式审核，尽到基本的注意义务。李琛说，因为短视频的制作者大部分是个人，他建议平台编制一份用户上传指南，把可能涉及的版权问题都列出来，用户在上传视频前通过弹出的这份上传指南，可以先进行自查，这也可以成为平台履行合理注意义务的检验指标。

丛立先则认为，现行规定先授权后使用的规则，虽然是世界通行的规则，但在网络的发展背景下会产生很多现实问题，比如要面对普遍性违法、普遍性侵权这样无奈的现实。

“很多权利人都懒得去维权，例如一个短小的评论被各个平台转来转去，如果为了几十块钱去索赔，会耗时耗力，权利人都嫌麻烦。”丛立先提出了对短视频版权利用规则调整的思考，比如短小作品转载法定许可制度建立与推广的可能性、通过法定许可还是重新设定调整权利人的专有权范围等问题。

（资料来源：《中国新闻出版广电报》，作者：金鑫，原标题为：《短视频版权问题中的“迷思”有哪些保护对策？》）

【暨南大学发布基于区块链技术的版权链运行平台】 2018年7月21日，由暨南大学知识产权研究院和广东省知识产权研究会共同主办的基于区块链技术的版权链运行平台成果发布暨版权链司法认定的证据效力及相关问题的研讨会在暨南大学举行，会上正式发布了由暨南大学联合相关企业历时3年研发的基于区块链技术的版权链运行平台。据了解，该平台旨在构建完整的区块链版权授权与维权模型，意在解决基于区块链的去中心化版权登记和授权机制、基于区块链的数字产品非法转让追责模型、基于区块链的数字版权保护法律效应等问题，希望为数字版权在线上产权管理中提供法律服务与技术支持。目前，研发团队已就相关技术提交了15件发明专利申请，并对相关模式进行了著作权登记。

据暨南大学知识产权研究院院长徐瑄介绍，如今，网络侵权盗版比较常见，但权利人在维权诉讼时，普遍面临线上侵权主体难确定、取证难且证据有效判定难、侵权损害赔偿额认定难等多个问题。利用计算机区块链新技术，希望既能保护所有上线作品的权利人利益不受侵害，又便于权利人在线授权版权资源给社会各界合法使用。暨南大学知识产权和网络空间安全团队联合区块链技术企业经过3年研发，打造了基于区块链技术的版权链运行平台。

在发布会研讨环节，与会专家学者和法律人士对该平台前期研发的成果表示乐观，综合这两年区块链技术应用到版权保护领域的场景和已开发的功能，大家普遍认为该平台在功能开发与市场结合方面具有可行性并将对版权保护起到重大的保障作用。随着版权链平台运行机制的逐步成熟和不断完善，必将实现《著作权法》中版权保护的宗旨，并通过版权的有效保护，激励更多更好的作品诞生，支持文学艺术文化的繁荣。

（资料来源：中国知识产权资讯网，作者：姜旭）

【2018 版权相关热点问题媒体研修班在京举办】 2018 年 8 月 2—4 日，30 余家主流媒体的近 60 名编辑、记者共同在京参加了由国家版权局主办、中国新闻出版广电报社承办的 2018 版权相关热点问题媒体研修班。3 位业界专家对目前媒体以及社会最关注的版权相关热点问题进行了讲解并与编辑记者们进行了交流和研讨。

国家版权局版权管理司副司长汤兆志对一些比较抽象的版权概念进行了解读，并从宏观以及微观层面剖析了如何正确认识版权及版权制度的价值，对新闻出版单位该如何通过版权资产管理增加企业核心竞争力，以及版权工作面临的新形势、新问题、新挑战进行了全面分析。在答疑环节，汤兆志还对目前媒体最关注的部分新媒体、自媒体“洗稿”问题进行了分析，他认为简单的“洗稿”很好判定，但随着技术的发展出现了很多特殊的“洗稿”行为，虽然目前没有一个统一标准，但判断一个行为是否侵权，可以从著作权中的“接触＋实质性相似”原则进行考量，当判定实质性相似后，如果对方没有其他抗辩理由，法院可以认定其侵权行为成立。

清华大学法学院副院长崔国斌针对新技术给著作权法带来的挑战，如人工智能、大数据、区块链等在版权应用中的优势和欠缺等新问题，进行了梳理和讲解。浙江省高级人民法院知识产权庭副庭长王亦非则根据自己审理判决的几个典型案例，通过以案说法的形式，分析了其中涉及的版权问题。

（资料来源：《中国新闻出版广电报》，作者：邹韧）

【2018 年内地与香港特区、澳门特区知识产权研讨会在敦煌召开】 2018 年 9 月 13 日，2018 年内地与香港特区、澳门特区知识产权研讨会在甘肃省敦煌市召开，研讨会由国家知识产权局港澳台办公室、香港特区政府知识产权署、澳门特区政府经济局联合主办，甘肃省知识产权局承办。

国家知识产权局副局长甘绍宁表示，改革开放40 年来，内地知识产权事业蓬勃发展，在知识产权创造、保护、运用、服务和管理等方面取得了一系列令人瞩目的成就。多年来，内地与香港、澳门特区各界知识产权人士以研讨会为平台，交流工作经验、研究讨论热点重点知识产权话题，为推动知识产权事业和经济社会的繁荣发展做出了积极贡献。希望内地与香港、澳门特区知识产权界继续以研讨会为契机，在完善知识产权基础保障、开展深层次交流互动、严格知识产权保护等方面取得更多的务实合作成果。

甘肃省政府副秘书长贾宁介绍，甘肃作为“一带一路”建设的重要一环，将持续推进丝绸之路国际知识产权港建设，不断加强知识产权保护力度，营造良好的营商环境，引导集聚各类创新资源，打造全生命周期的知识产权产业发展链条，建设特色型知识产权强省，为促进甘肃省产业转型升级和绿色发展崛起提供支撑。

香港特区政府知识产权署署长梁家丽和澳门特区政府经济局副局长刘伟明共同表示，将持续推动和深化香港、澳门特区与内地知识产权领域的合作交流。香港、澳门特区将充分利用“一带一路”和粤港澳大湾区建设的发展机遇，结合自身优势，与内地各方一起共同推动创新发展。

研讨会以“知识产权：推动创新、增长与繁荣”为主题，在为期一天半的会期当中，来自内地、香港特区和澳门特区知识产权界共计 180 余名代表围绕加强知识产权保护、支撑创新发展，加强知识产权运用、实现知识产权价值，加强知识产权服务、支持企业“走出去”等议题进行深入交流与研讨。

（资料来源：《中国新闻出版广电报》，作者：田野）

【2018 中国文化 IP 发展高峰论坛在京成功召开】 2018 年 9 月 21 日，2018 中国文化 IP 发展高峰论坛在中国 IP 展开展首日成功举办。本次论坛以“优秀内容创作、赋能运营传播”为主题，邀请了诸多中国文化界学者、专家及知名企业家，围绕文化 IP 在博物馆文创、网络文学、共享设计、赛事节目以及软件办公等多个专题领域进行了研究成果和实践案例分享，共同探讨了何为文化 IP 最核心的竞争力，以及如何应用文化 IP 赋能新时代运营传播等话题。

论坛上，就如何更好地开发文化 IP，与会嘉宾普遍认为：要深挖中国传统文化精髓，将传统文化植根于内容创作中，对其进行与时俱进、符合现实主义价值观的创新性开发。

对此，著名历史学家阎崇年先生在演讲中开宗明义道，中国文化IP开发要把握住“大文化”、“出精品”和“产品化”这三个关键词。故宫博物院常务副院长王亚民介绍了《清明上河图3.0》《故宫日历》等精品文创开发案例。他表示，在文化IP具有高创意附加值的前提下，一定要将文化IP与产品信息和时尚文化相结合，要在推动文化IP创造性转化和创新性发展的过程中设计出具有时代使命感的作品。洛可可创新设计集团董事长贾伟作为文创设计机构代表，进一步强调了想象力和创造力对于打造文化IP的重要性，“因为每个文化IP带给我们的都是无限的想象和创意，关乎人设、世界观、甚至是内容”。贾伟也列举了猫王收音机、故宫猫、四季盖碗茶等设计赋能文化IP的案例，生动诠释了想象和创意的魅力。

对于中国文化IP产业未来发展趋势，中国文化产业发展集团总经理陈彦在论坛上做了概括性陈述。她认为，知识产权保护力度的提升正在为文化IP产业创造更好条件，文化IP运营的早期化、立体化、专业化程度也在逐步加深，文化IP主流市场与小众市场呈现出更明显的分化趋势，互联网平台在更加积极布局文化IP市场，新技术也将对文化IP行业产生重大影响。纵横文学CEO张云帆、咪咕文化科技有限公司总编辑王寒英等也在各自演讲中对上述观点表示认同，并进行了详细阐释。

此外，版权价值的挖掘服务、版权确权和维权服务、设计制作服务、授权交易服务以及供应链管理服务等作为文化IP产业生态链中的支撑层，也是此次论坛的主要议题。“支撑层够不够专业、精细，非常关键。”对此，阿里鱼资深总监胡丹青介绍道，阿里鱼正是主张利用其整体生态资源，为内容方提供数据服务、电商、线下分销和维权服务等全链路系统支持。北京中视瑞德文化传媒股份有限公司CEO马炬则具体分享了区块链技术在交易确权中的作用，对现场文化IP版权方有很大启发。

（资料来源：中国知识产权资讯网，作者：李杨芳）

【北京首届互联网影视著作权高峰论坛召开】

2018年10月11日，2018北京首届互联网影视著作权高峰论坛在京举办。

数据显示，超过一半的互联网百强企业在北京，北京网络普及率位列全国第一。与此同时，也有大量互联网著作权纠纷案件发生。在司法实践过程中，互联网影视著作权相关案件也不断升级，审理、判决的技术难度越来越大，如何通过互联网快速解决影视版权纠纷成为行业内关注的话题。

北京市新闻出版广电局副局长戴维在致辞中说，北京市新闻出版广电局与北京市高级人民法院、北京互联网法院等司法部门以及影视版权行业协会共同加强行业管理引导，完善法律保护体系，加快构建统一开放、安全透明、公平公正的影视版权交易生态环境。

“2017年，全国共受理著作权案件137 267件，同比上升58%。其中，北京共受理22 701件，占全国受理总数的16.5%，涉及网络著作权案件达15 000件。”北京互联网法院副院长姜颖以一组翔实的数据，阐释当下著作权侵权案件尤其是网络侵权案件节节攀升的态势。

北京互联网法院院长张雯说，从北京互联网法院成立以来收到的立案申请来看，互联网著作权、邻接权权属及侵权纠纷两类案件在申请立案的案件中数量最多，达到1 430件，占比达48%。

本次论坛还邀请了与互联网影视版权保护密切相关的企业人员。爱奇艺法务部总监胡荟集说，爱奇艺已建立版权审核机制、全端监控机制、司法救济机制。胡荟集表示，知识产权的保护需要长久不断的努力、不断的创新。“我们可以想象，互联网法院的设立与推广，会开启互联网影视著作权保护的新征程。”

阿里大文娱内容线法务总监李巍说，阿里通过区块链版权登记等举措，从版权产生到播出、播后的每个维度上运用技术手段进行全链路的保护，“技术的赋能，让版权保护多一些可能”。

论坛由北京市新闻出版广电局、北京市互联网信息办公室、北京市文学艺术界联合会、中国电视剧编剧委员会指导，北京互联网法院、北京影视版权文化艺术促进会、首都互联网协会共同主办，北京影视著作权专家鉴定委员会承办。

（资料来源：《中国新闻出版广电报》，作者：李婧璇　王坤宁）

【首届中国剧本推优与版权保护论坛举办】

2018年10月11日，首届中国剧本推优与版权保护论坛在2018年秋季北京电视节目交易会上成功举办。

论坛由中国电视艺术家协会、中国版权保护中心指导，中国电视艺术家协会编剧专业委员会、北京影视艺术学会、北京怀柔国家影视产业示范区管理办公室联合主办，北京小土科技有限公司承办。

结合量化评估，推优专家委员会从征集的众多剧本中推选出《片警大华》等 4 部入围优秀电视剧剧本，推选了《第一声春雷》等 6 部优秀电视剧剧本。推荐 122 部剧本参加中国电视艺术家协会“征集重点现实题材电视剧剧本”活动，推荐 5 名青年编剧创作的 8 部电视剧剧本参加中国视协 2018 年度青年编剧扶持计划项目资助活动。此外，论坛首次采取大数据与专业协会专家相结合的创新审评机制。

论坛上，就“剧本推优与版权保护”“加强数据力量、培育优秀剧本”“中国（怀柔）影视产业示范区产业扶持政策”等主题，中国电视艺术家协会编剧专业委员会主任、编剧王海平，中国版权保护中心副主任、版权专家魏红，北京怀柔国家影视产业示范区管理办公室、北京市怀柔区文化产业发展促进中心主任吕晓国，北京小土科技有限公司董事长、北京工商大学副教授祝金甫等分别做主题发言或政策解读。

论坛以专家高端对话的形式与参会代表进一步深入交流。编剧王海平，全国政协委员、中国电视剧导演协会会长郑晓龙，北京市广播影视作品审查中心主任智黎明，北京仲裁委员会秘书长林志炜等就剧本推优与版权保护等进行解读。专家高端对话由中国电视艺术家协会编剧专业委员会副秘书长曲士飞主持。

论坛组委会秘书长、中国电视艺术家协会编剧专业委员会常务副主任张连生告诉记者，要创新服务举措，促进人才培育，探索实施电视精品工程、打造电视剧精品力作的规律，使剧本创作贯穿融入社会主义核心价值观，促进电视节目制作业健康有序发展。

为了促进国台办 31 条惠台措施的落实，北京影视艺术学会与中华广播电视节目制作商业同业公会签订共同促进实施“海峡两岸题材的中国电视剧本精品工程”，两岸同胞携手用优秀电视剧讲好中国故事。中国电视艺术家协会、中国版权保护中心等发起并联合 224 家影视制作公司、239 名编剧会员代表、66 家版权律师所发出《中国电视剧版权保护倡议书》，倡导加强行业自律，自觉维护知识版权，遵守国家关于版权保护的政策法规，确保知识产权事业健康发展。中国（怀柔）影视产业示范区“中国视协编剧专业委员会剧本创作坊”举行了揭牌仪式。

（资料来源：人民网，作者：陈灿）

【第二届中国 IP 30 人论坛在京举行】 2018 年 10 月 28 日，由中国传媒大学、中国版权保护中心、中国广告协会联合主办的第二届中国 IP 30 人论坛在京举行，来自学界、业界的 30 余位嘉宾共同围绕“聚焦拐点下的 IP 新生态”主题展开讨论，探讨拐点下的中国 IP 身在何处，路在何方。

从 2012 年发展至今，IP 成为文化产业中炙手可热的名词。“IP 热”从文学、影视、音乐扩展到文旅、游戏和周边商品等多个领域，带来了围绕 IP 授权、开发、运营等一系列相互协作的海量业务。一些优质 IP 作品兼顾思想性与艺术性，产生较大的社会影响，同时也收获了较好的市场回报。与此同时，版权、财税、行业监管等问题也集中出现在大众视野。

论坛上，中国传媒大学校长廖祥忠强调了 IP 之于未来文化产业的重要性，表示青年人是不可忽视的力量。中国广告协会会长张国华提到，此次论坛的举办对更加科学理性地开发、运作 IP 有重要意义，中国广告协会作为行业组织将重点关注 IP 评估标准体系的建立。中国版权保护中心著作权登记部主任李明英说，互联网环境下应该强化规则意识、尊重意识、保护意识，重视知识产权的保护与运用，使其惠及企业、行业以及市场，促进 IP 快速发展。

华策影视董事长、总裁赵依芳认为，IP 内容的把控要回归它的思想价值、文学价值、艺术感染价值，要有温度和正能量。“午夜文库”IP 开发中心主任、香港和平图书总裁谢刚以悬疑推理题材作品举例说：“只有关注现实，作品才有生命力，才能进入主流的文学行业。”面对题材同质化的问题，企鹅影业 IP 储备及研发中心总监周宇、上海润金文化传播有限公司总裁吴林励均认为，解决此问题关键在于寻找新角度进行创作。而面对新兴的网生内容和年轻化的网生群体，知名制作人、导演、编剧白一骢提出，寻找到恰如其分的共鸣点十分重要。

2017—2018 年，IP 行业经历了从“狂热期”到“冷静期”的转变，并进入新的拐点。国家对知识产权的保护展现出前所未有的重视，整个行业对 IP 的认识也更加理性。面对政策收紧、投融资遇冷、过度明星化等外部环境，如何布局拐点后的 IP 新生态，实现 IP 在经济意义和文化意义上的有机统一，推动文化产业健康理性发展，成为 IP 行业共同关心的话题。

中国传媒大学 IP 跨界传播研究中心副主任郎劲松以“痛点、拐点、新起点”为题进行了发言。她总结了目前 IP 行业所遭遇的叠加痛点，以及拐点阶段出现的包括注意力、价值观以及新场域等多方面的格局再造。她认为：“我们应该以乐观的心态看待这次拐点，这是重构 IP 生态的一次契机，拐点后的

IP行业发展将进入一个新的时代。”她透露，中国传媒大学IP跨界传播研究中心的第一本年度发展报告即将于2018年底出版，希望能对IP行业的发展给出思考方向，以推动中国IP的健康发展、有序发展。

咪咕文化科技有限公司首席运营官颜忠伟认为，随着4K和5G技术时代的到来，未来将是“无处不屏”，他提出打造全场景沉浸生态，把线上线下，场景、服务和体验打通。启迪数字天下（北京）科技文化有限公司总裁王宣也表示，新的技术发展一定会为IP赋予新的生命力和新的产业链条。中农盛通有限公司董事长、国家农业科技园区联盟母基金创始发起人李茉溪通过特色小镇开发项目举例，关注将IP与产业相结合，对有地理标识意义或历史文化价值的IP进行包括投资、教育、旅游等全产业的开发。

中国传媒大学IP跨界传播研究中心主任王晓晖提出，IP其实就是内容，而影视化可以将内容与动力源结合，进而带起产业链发展。各个文化产业的参与者应该以改革开放的精神来面对今天的形势，真正勇敢往前迈。影视行业要充满信心，进一步把内容做精，敢于突破。“百姓需要有梦想、需要有共鸣，对于制作者包括平台而言，都需要大胆创新，同时对这个行业充满信心。在这个拐点上把握住，真正的春天离我们不远。”王晓晖说。

（资料来源：《中国文化报》，作者：马霞，原标题为：《中国IP：身在何处，路在何方》）

【中国国际漫博会聚焦版权交易和产业融合】 2018年11月15—18日，第十届中国国际影视动漫版权保护和贸易博览会（以下简称漫博会）在广东东莞开馆，本届漫博会以“新时代、新动漫”为主题，聚焦版权交易和产业融合。

第十届漫博会是历届漫博会中国际化程度最高的一届，第十届漫博会规划了美国好莱坞动漫展区、日本动漫展区、韩国动漫展区、欧洲和北美动漫展区及港澳台动漫展区。邀请了来自美国、加拿大、法国、日本、比利时等国家的动漫大师，包括好莱坞、迪士尼、漫威、派拉蒙、梦工厂等知名动漫、影视品牌企业的10位大师，如中美合拍大片《巨齿鲨》的制片人兰迪·格林伯格、《101斑点狗》的动画大师克里斯·亨德森等。

展会期间，举办多场对接会，包括多场“动漫+”IP对接会、港澳台IP专场对接会、韩国IP专场对接会、日本IP专场对接会、好莱坞IP专场对接会、腾讯视频动漫专场对接会、优酷视频动漫专场对接会等。参与此次展会的好莱坞展团，偕好莱坞、迪士尼等的共10位动漫大师带着好莱坞动漫作品及影视IP参与到展会活动中来交流对接。多位好莱坞大师甚至带来最新的作品，并在展会期间全球首发推广，寻求合作机会。

手代木史织、秋乃茉莉、真崎春望、立野真琴等日本知名漫画家也受邀参与到对接会活动中来。

（资料来源：中国新闻网，作者：李映民　李荻）

【短视频作品创作与版权保护研讨会在京举办】 2018年11月27日，由中国人民大学创意产业技术研究院、中国人民大学国家版权贸易基地联合主办，中国版权产业网承办的“短视频作品创作与版权保护研讨会”在中国人民大学举办。与会嘉宾围绕如何规范短视频版权秩序以及短视频版权监测与技术保护路径等主题进行了深入探讨。

国家版权局版权管理司副司长段玉萍表示，由于当前我国短视频行业出现爆发式增长，但版权问题突出，已影响短视频创作与传播秩序，不利于行业健康发展，因此“剑网2018”专项行动将短视频纳入重点治理领域。针对如何规范短视频版权秩序的问题，段玉萍指出，短视频制作者和传播者须严格遵守法律规定，在短视频内容创作和传播中不得侵犯他人权利；短视频平台应严格履行法定义务，在依法履行“通知—删除”义务的同时，对明知应知存在侵权问题的短视频内容，要主动采取措施，对反复上传、反复侵权的短视频内容提供者，要采取严格的措施。她建议在短视频平台显著位置做出版权保护声明，并提供“通知—删除”的联系方式。段玉萍要求，短视频相关企业要特别重视版权保护问题，遵守法律规定，并采取必要的技术措施保护版权，最终实现短视频行业的公平竞争和健康发展。

中国人民大学新闻学院宋建武教授从公众重要表达工具的角度对短视频的发展特点进行了分析，建议主流媒体建设自有的短视频平台，从内容供应商、内容生产商向平台运营商过渡。对外经济贸易大学法学院卢海君教授和中央民族大学法学院熊文聪副教授分别对短视频的著作权法律地位和侵权责任认定进行了法理分析。

中国版权协会秘书长孙悦建议政府主管部门继续加强对短视频版权保护的监管，引导社会力量开发完备的版权数据库和内容识别系统，增强事前的侵权防范；建议加强短视频版权保护问题的研究和讨论，注重借鉴国外先进经验。他表示，中国版权协会将在国家版权局的领导下继续加强协调，维护短视频发展的良好环境，促进短视频行业的高质量发展。

北京市文化市场行政执法总队五队队长刘立新介绍道，为治理短视频领域的版权侵权问题，北京市文化市场行政执法总队一方面增加了对短视频互联网方面的巡查、检查频次，约谈了相关短视频平台方和内容生产方，对其提出明确的版权要求；另一方面，按照著作权法的规定，严厉查处了数起短视频相关案件。北京市海淀区人民法院知识产权庭副庭长曹丽萍在分析当前短视频主要类型的基础上指出，在判断短视频是否构成作品时容易陷入误区，因此审理短视频侵权案件时，要具体案件具体分析。

来自字节跳动、东方明珠新媒体、梨视频、爱迪德等公司的代表从产业的角度，就版权保护的重要性及各自探索的版权保护模式进行了分享。字节跳动副总裁、总编辑张辅评重点介绍了字节跳动在版权保护方面的“双 24 投诉模式”，并首次公开了字节跳动自主研发的视频版权保护系统“灵石系统”。

（资料来源：中国知识产权资讯，作者：刘仁）

【2018 中国版权年会在武汉召开】 2018 年 12 月 1 日，由中国版权协会主办的第十一届中国版权年会在湖北武汉召开，以“新时代助力文化发展”为主题的首届“远集坊”论坛同时举办。第十二届全国人大教科文卫委员会主任委员、中国出版协会理事长柳斌杰，第十三届全国政协文化文史和学习委员会副主任、中国版权协会理事长阎晓宏，湖北省人大常委会副主任周洪宇出席并致辞。中国出版集团公司总裁谭跃等针对知识革命、区块链技术等问题进行了演讲。

柳斌杰在致辞中表示，2018 年是我国改革开放 40 周年，版权年会恰在此时召开具有特殊的重要意义。这次年会汇集了版权产业界、文化界、出版界诸多专家、学者和业界的精英，充分显示了版权协会在社会上的影响力，也让我们看到 40 年来中国版权工作的一个缩影。如今大家会谈到一个新的版权问题，即知识革命和版权重构。由于科学技术的发展，人类社会已经到了以数字文明为基础的智能化时代，一场知识革命正在发生，它将整体性地改变我们几千年来知识生产的模式和知识发展的逻辑。在知识革命的大势之下，版权事业也遇到了新技术、新业态、新形态和知识创新领域产生新问题的挑战，现在还没有一个国家能对这些问题做出新的论断，而这些问题也是各国法律和版权事业实践中的问题，尚未有新的理论，我们应该更早地去研究。但各国专家一致认为，在知识经济时代，知识成为人类重要的资源，版权保护要进一步加强，才能保证知识创新不断保持活力。

周洪宇在致辞中介绍，近年来，湖北省全面贯彻实施国家知识产权战略纲要和国家版权“十三五”规划，大力推进版权强省建设战略，不断完善版权服务管理体系，重点培育优秀版权企业，为优化版权行业管理创建了湖北标准，为推进版权产业发展打造了湖北品牌。下一步湖北省将抢抓历史机遇，把湖北版权工作提升到一个新水平。

与会代表认为，当前人工智能、区块链、5G 技术正加速实现应用产品落地，用户和版权内容的连接更加智能和高效，与此同时，技术的飞速进步也让网络侵权盗版变得更加方便和快捷，内容产业界要注意新知识生产中的整个知识产权问题，同时要在法律层面上积极跟进，特别是要关注目前数据储存管理、处理分析数据成果的运用，并将这两项纳入著作权保护范围。

在本届年会上，柳斌杰、历史学家阎崇年获得“中国版权事业终生成就者”称号。福建省版权协会理事长白京兆、作家毕飞宇、腾讯集团法务副总裁江波、著名编剧刘恒、咪咕文化董事长刘昕、中信出版集团董事长王斌、故宫博物院原常务副院长王亚民、湖北省版权局原局长张良成、江西省出版集团公司董事长赵东亮等 9 人获得“中国版权事业卓越成就者”称号。湖南广播电视台、江苏凤凰出版传媒股份有限公司、上海阅文信息技术有限公司等 44 家单位获得中国版权最具影响力企业奖。陕西广电影视文化产业发展有限公司、中国中医药出版社、恐龙园文化旅游集团股份有限公司等 27 家单位获得中国版权新锐企业奖。

（资料来源：《中国新闻出版广电报》，作者：赖名芳）

【AIPPI 中国分会版权热点论坛举行】 2018 年 12 月 22 日，由国际保护知识产权协会（AIPPI）主办的中国分会版权热点论坛（2018 年度）在京举办。来自司法界、版权领域的专家、学者以及版权企业代表 200 余人，共同对人工智能生成内容是否受版权保护等热点、难点问题进行研讨，并从理论和实践的维度进行了深入交流。

最高人民法院知识产权庭高级法官秦元明说，目前司法界对于人工智能生成内容的主体资格认定依然存在争议：一部分人认为法院无权通过判决认定人工智能具有权利主体资格；另一部分人认为法院有权通过判决认定人工智能生成的内容是否构成作品，或者裁定生成的内容是不是由人工智能创造的。

搜狐集团法律中心政策研究部主任研究员马晓明在论坛上说，人工智能需要根据大量的数据库才能生成内容，而使用这些数据库是否需要授权许可，目前我国版权界并没有一致的结论。中央民族大学副教授熊文聪在演讲中首先提出“人工智能能创作吗?”“人工智能会创作吗?”的问题。他还结合著作权的本质，从稀缺性、独创性以及供求关系的角度分析了独创性的认定门槛，提出人工智能创作物并不具有财产的稀缺性，因此不应该过度保护。

北京互联网法院副院长姜颖现场介绍了北京互联网法院2018年9月成立后的基本情况。

论坛还就音乐版权相关问题，探讨了我国著作权集体管理如何进一步规范、涉综艺节目歌曲翻唱如何解决相关版权问题、如何完善演唱会音乐版权授权模式、数字音乐产业链下的音乐版权交易如何公开透明和便捷畅通等热点问题。

（资料来源：《中国新闻出版广电报》，作者：赖名芳）

◆ 社会管理与服务

【微博携手中国版权保护中心为原创内容开通版权认证】 2018年3月19日，微博正式与中国版权保护中心、平壑科技达成合作，接入中国版权保护中心DCI（数字版权唯一标识符，Digital Copyright Identifier）体系，为平台原创内容开通版权认证。微博平台上的头条文章原创内容，将由中国版权保护中心提供基于DCI体系的数字作品版权登记。经过登记认证的微博原创内容，中国版权保护中心将为拥有其版权的用户提供盗版侵权监测及快速维权服务。

DCI体系是中国版权保护中心自主创新推出的数字版权公共服务新模式，通过为互联网上的数字作品分配永久的DCI码、DCI标，颁发数字版权登记证书，从而为版权相关方在数字网络环境下的版权确权、授权和维权等提供基础公共服务支撑。

微博认证的原创作者，需要主动发起版权认证，填写认证必需的信息，通过平壑科技提供企业级技术支撑平台服务，在中国版权保护中心DCI体系的支撑下快速完成登记确权。经过认证的作品可以在文章页面底部展示标识——版权所有者唯一认证码及电子版权证书。

除了为优质内容和创作者提供版权认证，微博后续还将为取得DCI体系版权认证的作品提供互联网环境下的盗版侵权监测及维权服务。经过认证的文章，DCI体系将可为其提供完全监测服务，一旦通过检测发现侵权，中国版权保护中心可依用户的需求和委托，通知侵权人或侵权内容所在平台下架文章。多次通知之后，侵权平台仍不处理，可通过DCI体系将侵权平台和侵权人列入黑名单重点监控。版权方还可以据数字作品版权登记证书及侵权监测结果等证据提起法律诉讼。

（资料来源：中国知识产权资讯网，作者：侯伟）

【优秀原创动漫作品版权开发奖励计划启动】 在2018年3月22日开幕的2018 CPCC中国版权服务年会上，由中国版权保护中心组织实施的优秀原创动漫作品版权开发奖励计划宣布启动。原国家新闻出版广电总局规划发展司司长朱伟峰、中国版权保护中心主任段桂鉴出席启动仪式并共同启动了该项计划。

中国版权保护中心副主任魏红介绍了优秀原创动漫作品版权开发奖励计划的相关内容。该计划是通过文化产业发展专项资金的支持集中奖励一批优秀原创动漫作品的版权开发成果，旨在提升原创动漫作品版权的社会影响力，鼓励优秀动漫作品在版权领域的发展，促进动漫版权的产业化进程。

优秀原创动漫作品版权开发奖励计划设3个大项、9个小项奖励项目，申报范围针对近三年来在境内外已出版、发行或播映的著作权完整的动画和漫画作品（包括网络动画和网络漫画作品）。项目评选从奖励原创动漫作品版权开发入手，重点奖励已经在原创动漫作品的品牌开发、市场开发与内容开发等方面取得一定社会和经济效益的动漫作品著作权人，包括在中国依法成立的从事原创动漫作品策划、编辑和出版的出版单位，从事原创动漫作品策划、制作和传播的法人单位以及个人等。申报主体可通过中国版权保护中心网站获取该项目申报的详细须知和具体材料。

（资料来源：人民网，作者：王小艳）

【长春市首批版权示范园区（基地）揭牌】 2018年4月19日，2018年长春市版权示范园区（基地）和版权示范单位揭牌仪式在吉林动漫游戏原创产业园举行。6 家市级产业园区和 10 家单位成为首批“版权示范园区（基地）”和“版权示范单位”。

为进一步强化版权社会化服务，扶持创新型版权企业，带动相关产业快速发展，长春市版权局 2018 年启动了版权示范园区（基地）和版权示范单位申报评选活动。经各县（市）区和企事业单位推荐、申报，市版权局考察审核，确定吉林动漫游戏原创产业园、吉林省广告产业园、吉林省东北亚文化创意科技园等 6 家产业园区为长春市版权示范园区（基地），吉林动画学院、长春联合图书城有限公司、长春新曦雨文化产业有限公司、吉林禹硕影视传媒股份有限公司等 10 家单位为长春市版权示范单位。

（资料来源：《长春日报》，作者：毕馨月）

【中国文联与首都版权产业联盟签约】 2018 年 4 月 25 日，中国文联权益保护部与首都版权产业联盟举行签约仪式，就共同开展文艺工作者版权保护服务建立合作关系。这是中国文联加强文艺维权社会化合作，利用社会资源为文艺工作者拓展维权平台、开辟维权渠道的一项重要举措。

此次签约活动也是中国文联权益保护部为迎接世界知识产权日所组织的“中国文联知识产权周”的重要活动之一。中国文联党组成员、副主席李前光表示，中国文联首次与社会权益保护组织正式签约建立维权合作关系，是一次维权工作的积极探索和有益创新。他希望合作双方始终坚持合作的公益性、普惠性、服务性，积极争取司法、行政、业界和社会各界的支持，不断完善社会化文艺版权服务机制并切实发挥其作用，更好地维护文艺工作者的版权等合法权益。

活动中，著名鼓曲表演艺术家杨菲表达了文艺工作者对双方合作的期待。著名作曲家李海鹰通过自身经历，介绍了版权产业联盟为艺术家提供的具体维权服务。法律专家为在场的艺术家及中国文联权保干部做了版权保护知识讲座。

（资料来源：《北京日报》，作者：路艳霞）

【国家版权局与中国版权协会、中国移动签署备忘录】 2018 年 4 月 26 日，国家版权局版权管理司与中国版权协会版权监测中心、中国移动咪咕文化科技有限公司签署《网络版权保护合作备忘录》，就共同打击网络侵权盗版、探索网络版权保护新模式达成共识，将围绕联合推进网络版权执法落地、推动社会参与网络版权保护及行业自律、探索网络版权保护创新模式三大方面展开合作。

国家版权局发布的《版权工作“十三五”规划》明确要求，要加大版权执法监管力度，突出网络领域版权监管，强化版权执法协作，建立完善长效机制，提升执法监管信息化水平。要完善打击网络侵权盗版的快速反应机制，健全与基础电信企业、互联网信息服务企业快速有效的“通知—删除”工作机制。要充分利用云计算、物联网、大数据、移动互联网等新一代信息技术，创新版权监管手段，提高执法有效性和精准度。

此次三方的合作是落实规划的又一成果。中国版权协会版权监测中心、中国移动咪咕文化科技有限公司将配合国家版权局版权管理司，着力扩大以“剑网行动”为代表的网络版权治理专项行动的覆盖面和影响力，探索版权执法监管新机制、构建网络版权保护新生态。

（资料来源：《中国新闻出版广电报》，作者：赖名芳）

【河北省版权信息数据库平台正式上线】 2018 年 4 月 26 日为世界知识产权日，河北省版权信息数据库平台同日正式上线，这对推动河北版权产业在内容、渠道、管理、服务等方面的发展具有里程碑式的重大意义。

河北省版权信息数据库平台从登记确权入手，为作品登记、许可转让、价值转化等各个环节采用多种新技术提供相应的保护措施，从而形成版权保护的链条，促进版权价值转化。著作权人可通过平台注册登录，对文字、音乐、美术、摄影、动漫、影视等各类文化创新作品进行在线登记、自主管理，确定版权归属。登记时限将从过去的 30 个工作日，缩短为一周以内。河北省版权信息数据库平台网址为 https://www.hebeibanquan.com.cn，著作权人可按流程在线登记，审核通过后会得到作品登记的电子证书，也可申请打印纸制证书。河北省出版物审读中心负责河北省的一般作品登记服务工作并对平台进行维护。目前，河北省采取作品登记免费政策，作品登记为属地管理，凡具有河北省常驻户口的个人、省内的法人单位与非法人单位均可申请作品免费登记。

（资料来源：《燕赵晚报》，作者：黄鎏）

【重庆首家区县级版权登记工作站启动】 2018 年 4 月 26 日，渝中区版权登记工作站在中山四路“U 创空间”产业园正式启动，这是重庆市文化委员会（版权局）授牌的重庆第一家区县级版权登记工作站。

渝中区版权登记工作站位于“U创空间”产业园，由重庆科莱姆企业孵化器有限公司负责日常运行管理。渝中区内的自然人或法人可向该工作站申请作品著作权免费登记，作品著作权登记的范围为自然人或者法人的原创、具有可复制性的作品，包含文字、口述、音乐、戏剧、曲艺、舞蹈、杂技、美术、建筑、摄影、电影、图形、模型等类型作品，可以是自主创作、合作创作、委托创作、职务作品和法人作品。

申请人只需提供身份证复印件和拟登记作品，填报《作品登记申请表》《作品自愿登记权利保证书》，版权登记工作人员再将信息录入重庆版权云端服务平台，市版权保护中心审核通过后，申请人就可在30个工作日内领取到作品著作权登记证书。

（资料来源：《重庆日报》，作者：汤艳娟）

【北方国家版权交易中心落户大连】 2018年4月26日，大连金普新区管委会与辽宁出版集团就北方国家版权交易中心、“盛文·北方新生活”大型文化商业综合体、金普文化传媒公司3个项目签署合作协议。

根据协议，3个项目注册资金总额为1.5亿元，双方将联合担负起优秀文化传承创新使命，深度激发融合发展动能，为经济文化共赢发展和社会和谐进步提供助力。

辽宁出版集团党委书记、董事长杨建军表示，版权是文化产业的源头，辽宁出版集团将引进借鉴国际先进的版权经营管理理念，打造面向东北亚的集版权交易、贸易、评估、孵化和金融服务于一体的国际版权商务港，与金普新区携手，助力金普新区、大连市乃至辽宁省的文化产业立足东北、走向世界。

（资料来源：《中国新闻出版广电报》，作者：王坤宁）

【河北版权登记时限从30个工作日变一周】 2018年4月26日，河北省版权信息数据库平台上线。平台上线后，登记时限从过去的30个工作日缩短为一周。

著作权人通过平台注册登录，对文字、音乐、美术、摄影、动漫、影视等各类文化创新作品进行在线登记、自主管理，确定版权归属，为今后维权提供法律依据，使著作权人的创新创作没有后顾之忧。版权信息数据库平台除了在线登记外，还为著作权人提供多项增值服务。一是提供版权登记、版权信息等大数据统计及分析，为著作权人的再创作提供方向和指导；二是著作权人可以通过平台建立自己的创新作品之家，对自己的创新作品自主选择展示和管理；三是平台提供多种权利的电子合同模板，著作权人对感兴趣的他人作品可以发起邀约，签订许可和转让合同，进行合同备案，促进作品价值转换。平台上线运行后，还将根据著作权人的需求，提供版权产品在线交易等多项服务。

（资料来源：《中国新闻出版广电报》，作者：冀菊）

【第十三届中国文交会建立动漫版权交易平台】 2018年4月27日，第十三届中国（义乌）文化产品交易会开幕，本届文交会首次举办大型漫展并同时举办首届保利动漫产业高峰论坛，为国内外动漫产业搭建动漫版权交易平台。

在27日上午的动漫高峰论坛上，保利文化集团成立了保利国家艺术品版权贸易基地，并同时建立动漫版权交易平台以促进动漫IP提供方（包括成熟知名IP与高校毕业生优秀创意）与动漫衍生品制造商进行广泛有效的交流，多元开发版权交易渠道，使版权产品真正实现潜在的经济价值，促成合作，促进品牌授权与版权交易。此次有印纪娱乐、华映星球等十一家动漫公司，北京电影学院、鲁迅美术学院等十二所高校签约动漫品牌交易平台，品牌授权额度为未来3年100亿元。

中国文交会动漫产业高峰论坛及动漫IP交易平台将推动国内动漫形象授权、品牌运营、版权交易等衍生产业发展，建立有效资源服务平台，让中国动漫品牌在全球市场占据一席之地。

（资料来源：中关村在线）

【江苏知识产权仲裁调解中心成立】 2018年4月27日，江苏（南京）知识产权仲裁调解中心和江苏省知识产权纠纷人民调解委员会在南京揭牌。

江苏（南京）知识产权仲裁调解中心实行理事会管理模式，由江苏省发明协会、省科学技术协会、省商标协会、省版权协会等11家理事单位组成，中心将根据当事人自愿原则，充分发挥调解与仲裁的各自优势，灵活高效地解决知识产权争议。

（资料来源：《法制日报》，作者：张维）

【版权服务走进首届中国游戏节】 2018年5月25—27日，2018首届中国游戏节在武汉国际会展中心隆重举行。本届游戏节汇集了 200 多位行业精英、140 余家游戏厂商的 170 余部游戏产品，其中包括 20 余部顶级国漫 IP，吸引了超过 2 万人次的游戏玩家、粉丝热情参与。

动漫游戏属于核心版权产业，其生存和发展高度依赖于版权制度保障。游戏节期间，湖北省版权保护中心和华中国家版权交易中心深入现场宣传普及版权法规知识，开展版权宣传、登记、交易、维权等社会服务，积极营造“尊重版权，崇尚创新，诚信守法”的良好氛围。在游戏节展览会上，中心还与主要参展企业围绕加强行业自律、保护自主创新、促进版权运用展开了探讨交流，并与阅文集团、卓讯互动、新快游戏等多家企业达成合作共识。

据了解，2019 年起中国游戏节将永久落户武汉光谷，这是湖北游戏及相关产业发展的重大机遇。省版权保护中心和华中国家版权交易中心将继续发挥专业职能与优势，以优质高效便捷的版权服务为湖北省包括动漫游戏在内的版权产业持续健康发展提供有力支持保障。

（资料来源：湖北省版权局）

【中国音像著作权集体管理协会召开第七次会员大会】 2018 年 5 月 30 日，中国音像著作权集体管理协会第七次会员大会在京召开，来自全国的 100 多家会员单位代表和个人会员出席了本次大会，国家版权局社会服务处处长宋萍萍应邀参加会议。大会由协会理事长周建潮主持。

大会审议通过了理事会提交的《2017 年度协会工作报告》、《2017 年度财务报告》、《协会章程》和《协会资产管理暂行办法》。

以上报告指出协会在面对复杂多变的卡拉 OK 市场环境下，积极应对、开拓发展、深化服务，目前市场收费规模达到了 1.93 亿元，其中卡拉 OK 收费达到了 1.76 亿元。在肯定成绩的同时，也正视存在的问题，对收费覆盖率不高、结算不及时、操作不规范等情况，提出了改进措施。

此次大会投票审议通过增补索尼音乐娱乐（上海）有限公司和北京竹书房文化传播有限责任公司为协会理事，大会同意邹建华辞去协会常务副理事长和总干事职务，投票增补周亚平为协会副理事长，同时，理事会决定周亚平代理协会总干事。根据本次会议审议通过的《协会章程》要求，协会应设立监事，此次大会，投票选举刘文和为协会监事长，崔婷琪、刘光涛为监事。

周建潮理事长在大会发言时指出，协会脱钩后要转变观念，建立科学、合理、有效的运行机制与监督机制；面对市场，挑战和机遇并存，希望广大会员团结一心，共同迎接音乐产业的美好前景。

（资料来源：中国音像著作权集体管理协会官方网站）

【《国际影视版权授权协议范本》发布】 2018 年 7 月 12 日上午，第三届中国互联网纠纷解决机制高峰论坛暨“一带一路”影视产业发展与保护论坛在北京国家会议中心召开。在论坛上首次发布《国际影视版权授权协议范本》（以下简称《协议范本》），为中国影视作品“走出去”提供了一个更易操作的授权协议范本。

《协议范本》由北京市高级人民法院指导，中国广播电影电视社会组织联合会电视制片委员会、中国互联网协会网络版权工作委员会组织起草。在制作过程中参考了大量国内影视制片人、互联网公司使用的合同版本，同时还结合了国际通行的影视版权交易条款，力求具有普适性。在初稿完成后又听取了最高人民法院和国家版权局的意见并加以完善，力求对国内的影视作品权利人起到一定的指导和示范作用。

《协议范本》从交易条款的授权作品、使用方式、授权格式、授权语言、转授权、限制和许可使用、授权费及支付方式等方面逐一进行了规范。北京天驰君泰律师事务所高级合伙人郭春飞介绍，《协议范本》以授权方角度制作，但考虑到合理性、公正性、双方可接受性，规定了各方权利和义务，杜绝“霸王条款”等显失公平的条款。同时增加了一些中国授权协议中的特色条款，包括维权条款及赔偿金的分配、违约条款的细化、赋予授权方解约权等。同时，她也强调，《协议范本》只是参考，不能照顾所有使用者的问题，好的协议应该“量身定做”，如费用支付条件、违约责任等，需要根据使用者需求调整。

《协议范本》由中国广播电影电视社会组织联合会电视制片委员会、中国互联网协会网络版权工作委员会、北京市高级人民法院知识产权庭、北京海淀区人民法院知识产权庭、北京天驰君泰律师事务所、怡光国际经济文化集团有限公司、慈文传媒股份有限公司、北京华录百纳影视股份有限公司、华谊兄弟传媒股份有限公司、北京锐风行艺术交流股份有限公司、浙江聚丽影视传媒文化有限公司、上海腾讯企鹅影视文化传播有限公司、阿里巴巴大文娱、北京新浪互联信息服务有限公司、北京搜狐互联网信息服务有限公司、国广星空视频科技（北京）

有限公司、北京瑞奥视科技有限公司、星光互动（北京）文化传播有限公司联合编写。

（资料来源：中国知识产权资讯网，作者：刘仁）

【江苏：国家版权贸易基地秘书处落户秦淮区】 2018年7月18日，江苏省版权局、南京市版权局和秦淮区人民政府联合举行了江苏国家版权贸易基地秘书处成立仪式。江苏国家版权贸易基地于2017年9月正式成立，其对活跃江苏版权交易市场、促进版权贸易顺利开展起到了一定作用。

随着秘书处的成立，江苏国家版权贸易基地将不断创新运营模式，并通过市场化运作聚合全省优质内容资源，为广大创作者和创作型企业服务。基地还将建立良性的版权保护和交易机制，实现版权保护的有效性和版权交易的便利化，持续改善版权市场环境，为文化产业高质量发展注入新活力新动能。

此外，江苏国家版权贸易基地秘书处落地秦淮区，将会提升秦淮区文化产业层次和规模，并推动该区文化产业发展和升级。秦淮区将借助版权力量，集聚头部内容企业，努力将秦淮区建成全国重要的文化创意核心区，实现文化产业领跑全国、走向世界的发展目标。

（资料来源：江苏省版权局）

【360搜索上线原创图片版权认证平台】 2018年7月30日，360搜索原创图片认证平台——图刻正式上线，标志着360搜索正式进军区块链领域。据悉，图刻将借助360区块链技术来维护原创权益、打击侵权行为，并依托360十大产品矩阵进行图片内容分发，以帮助创作者获取收益。

据悉，该平台具有区块链版权认证、品牌流量收益、全网版权保护三大核心功能，除了帮助创作者进行图片版权的确权、侵权监控之外，还能凭借360产品体系的庞大流量，为创作者获取价值收益。360区块链采用Lattice（格密码学）签名加密算法，在实现交易隐私保护的同时，通过人工智能模型调节链间交易及通信，可以提高链上交易处理效率。

同时，依托360安全技术，360区块链能实时感知链上安全态势，对异常交易及时预警，全面监控整个区块链网络。

（资料来源：《中国知识产权报》，作者：窦新颖）

【苏州推出“映光计划”应对原创音乐版权危机】 2018年8月15日，针对当下音乐作品面临被盗用、未经授权转载等版权危机，苏州在长三角地区率先推出“映光计划”，旨在打造以苏州为中心、辐射长三角地区的音乐版权保护新模式，为原创音乐保驾护航。

该项目以公证法律服务为核心，将传统公证服务搬上云端，线上对接苏州公证处“电子数据保管平台”，对音乐作品版权信息及时保管存证，为音乐作品版权的权属认定和被侵权事实固定提供有法定公信力的证据。同时，线下对接市知识产权综合法律服务中心，配套知识产权律师、司法鉴定、人民调解等专业团队，处理涉及版权侵权、权属纠纷等具体维权事宜，涵盖音乐作品版权的确权、用权和维权的全过程，集版权专业服务、公证保护、交易安全、权益服务于一体。

（资料来源：《法制日报》，作者：丁国锋）

【少儿数字出版维权联盟成立】 2018年8月22日，给孩子一片纯净的阅读天空——中国出版协会少儿数字出版维权联盟成立仪式在京举行。联盟旨在推动少儿数字出版市场健康良性发展，营造创作的净土，为孩子的阅读世界带来碧海蓝天。

少儿数字出版维权联盟由动画书阅读平台咿啦看书首倡，联合25家出版机构共同发起。维权联盟针对少儿数字出版面临的版权问题，通过实行搭建少儿数字出版物盗版举报平台、组建专业的法律维权律师团队、建立少儿数字出版物盗版信息共享机制等一系列举措，从法律法规建设、技术创新应用等多角度、深层次重拳打击侵权行为，维护少儿数字出版产业的健康发展。

咿啦看书创始人兼CEO任晖表示，非常高兴见到业内各方联合起来形成合力，共同打击肆意侵权行为。作为儿童数字阅读平台，咿啦看书自成立以来，深知原创内容生产的不易以及推动版权保护的紧迫性，咿啦看书尊重和保护每一部原创作品，并努力和更多的版权方达成合作，让全世界儿童享受到优质内容。

（资料来源：中国知识产权资讯网，作者：侯伟）

【贵州省版权登记中心揭牌】 2018年8月30日，贵州省版权登记中心在贵阳揭牌。该中心将版权工作与“大数据”战略相结合，提升版权社会服务水平，发挥版权社会服务在推动整个版权内容创新产业发展中的作用。揭牌仪式上，贵州省版权登记中心向贵州岩博酒业颁发了版权登记证书。

贵州省版权中心由贵州省新闻出版广电局（版权局）与贵州广电传媒集团共同组建，贵州广电传媒集团旗下 CCDI 版权云运营公司——中云文化大数据科技有限公司负责运营和管理。该中心充分运用了区块链技术，使数字版权登记更快捷、更高效、更安全。同时，在原有贵州省作品登记平台基础上，运用“无钥签名区块链技术”升级，还开发了数字版权认证登记平台，该项新运用作为优秀案例被国家工业和信息化部的信息中心载入了《2018 年中国区块链产业白皮书》。

（资料来源：《贵州日报》，作者：彭芳蓉）

【浙江建立淘宝电子版权登记“快车道”】 2018 年 9 月 18 日，浙江省版权局与阿里巴巴集团正式签约建立浙江阿里巴巴版权服务工作站，将在淘宝卖家服务市场上，为商家设立专门版权登记服务模块。

工作站建立后，淘宝原创商家需要进行版权登记时，可直接在淘宝网提交电子版权登记材料，经审核后，走上直达浙江省版权局的“快车道”进行终审。终审通过后，商家将获得省版权局颁发的版权登记证书，并按季度在省版权局网站公示。按照协议，阿里巴巴的线上版权登记初审将在 7 个工作日内完成；浙江版权服务中心的登记终审将在 20 个工作日内完成，极大节约了商家的时间与精力。

“对包括动漫形象、演艺娱乐、工艺美术、文化创意设计等在内的作品提供登记服务，着力宣传、推介、保护这些作品，为加快建成文化强省，大力发展与打造万亿级文化产业起到积极的推动作用，这是我们建立阿里巴巴版权服务工作站的初衷和应有之义。”签约现场，浙江省新闻出版广电局（版权局）党组副书记、副局长单烈表示。

“这是阿里巴巴通过技术推动解决社会问题，探索数字经济时代政企合作的新实践。”阿里巴巴集团副总裁孙军工表示，为了让知识产权保护变得简单，阿里巴巴已经创新推出了原创保护平台、首发创意保护机制等新举措。“数字化的版权登记，极大降低了淘宝原创商家保护知识产权的成本，这是阿里巴巴使用互联网技术，升级知识产权保护体系的又一探索。”

（资料来源：《中国新闻出版广电报》，作者：黄琳）

【河北省版权保护中心在廊坊设立版权服务站】 2018 年 9 月 19 日，河北省版权保护中心在廊坊市设立版权服务站。同日，廊坊市创建全国版权示范城市工作领导小组办公室也在全市设立了首批 18 个版权服务工作站，完善版权公共服务体系，提升版权公共服务能力，促进文化创意产业发展。据悉，服务站的设立将搭建完善的版权保护政策体系，为著作权人提供作品登记、版权评估、版权质押、版权交易等一系列服务。

河北省版权保护中心主任刘浏表示：“在廊坊设立版权服务站，正是为更好地服务广大著作权人，推动版权产业持续健康发展，以创新的发展理念完善版权保护制度、推动版权成果转化、提升版权管理水平、促进全省新型版权产业发展，在全社会营造良好的创新发展环境所做的一个有益探索。希望廊坊借助这个服务站，架起与著作权人沟通的桥梁，探索建立快速授权、快速确权、快速维权的工作机制，做好服务保障，让大家能够把更多的精力用于创新创作。”

（资料来源：《廊坊日报》）

【中国文化 IP 100 发展联盟在京成立】 2018 年 9 月 21 日，中国文化 IP 100 发展联盟在中国 IP 展现场正式成立，并协同中国版权协会、中国文化产业发展集团启动了中国文化 IP“金竹奖”。中国版权协会理事长阎晓宏、中国文化产业发展集团董事长孔繁新及联合发起方代表们，共同启动了中国文化 IP 100 发展联盟。

活动现场，中国版权协会秘书长孙悦介绍道，中国文化 IP 100 发展联盟由中国版权协会、中国文化产业发展集团联合中国各领域知名文化 IP 及相关方共同发起，联盟将以整合上下游资源、打通文化 IP 全球产业链、倡导健康生态为宗旨，建立长效交流与协作机制，高效对接资源与资本，打造一个“共享、共创、共赢”平台。此外，联盟将联合产业各方面成立智库，共享智慧成果与专业指导，服务企业高效运营与创新发展，介绍新技术，研究新业态、新标准，引领新趋势。

孙悦表示，人民日益增长的文化自信、文化内涵和消费需求，与文化供应的不丰富、不平衡，是文化产业新的矛盾。为助力文化 IP 成长发展，既需要搭建起优质的交流合作平台，也需要积极促进法律与政策环境的不断完善。此次发起联盟，意在邀请相关方群策群力，共享社会资源，共促中国文化 IP 健康发展。

据介绍，保利文创、中国工艺集团、上海交大海外教育学院、阅文集团、掌阅科技、纵横文学、中国移动咪咕公司、阿里鱼、金山软件、洛可可、瑞德传媒、汉仪字库、可米生活、枫声传媒等已成为联盟联合发起方。未来，联盟还将吸纳更多文化 IP 全产业链的优秀企业加入。

在中国文化 IP“金竹奖”启动环节，中国文化产业发展集团总经理陈彦对“金竹奖”的设立背景、维度和赛事计划进行了介绍：“金竹奖”将秉承“以联盟筑平台、以平台促对接、以对接带产业”的发展理念，从内容、营销、服务、商业价值、品牌影响力等五大横向维度，以及设计类、文学类、动漫类、视频类、生活类、文博类、教育类等七大纵向维度进行综合考量，立体化评价文化 IP 的价值，寻找文化 IP 发展的新动能。“金竹奖”奖杯也在启动仪式上首次亮相。

（资料来源：中国知识产权资讯网，作者：李杨芳）

【广深港高铁列车播放音乐获音著协许可】 2018 年 9 月 23 日，中国音乐著作权协会（以下简称音著协）与中国香港铁路有限公司（以下简称港铁公司）就广深港高铁列车上使用背景音乐所达成的著作权许可合作正式实施。这是音著协首次实现对整条线路的铁路客运列车内使用音乐发放著作权许可，也是自大力发展动车及高铁列车以来首次对高铁列车发放音乐使用授权。

音著协有关负责人介绍，早在 2018 年 6 月初，广深港高铁的所有方港铁公司就主动与音著协取得联系，希望通过音著协来解决广深港高铁列车上使用音乐的著作权许可事宜。在确认该条线路将途经中国香港的西九龙地界后，音著协第一时间与中国香港音乐著作权集体管理组织——香港作曲家及作词家协会（CASH）核实情况，在得到 CASH 明确答复，即“遵循《广深港高铁（一地两检）条例》及适用有关内地法律实施管辖的精神，港铁公司应直接向音著协取得许可申请”后，随即启动与港铁公司的谈判工作。依音著协有关铁路列车使用音乐的著作权许可收费标准，双方于 8 月底达成了协议，由港铁公司向音著协支付相应的著作权使用费，音著协向其发放音乐著作权许可。

“随着建设法治国家的进程不断深入，法治大环境持续改善，许多在公共场所提供音乐服务的行业都已经依法向著作权人缴纳了著作权使用费，包括飞机客舱、大型连锁酒店、零售业等均已与音著协建立了长期的著作权合作关系，而它们支付的著作权使用费也已通过音著协的分配工作转化为音乐作者再创造的动力源。”上述负责人表示，面对数字化发展，音著协早在 2002 年就引进先进的音乐版权管理技术，对音乐作品进行管理，为词曲作者等权利人发放费用，并积极发起维权诉讼，以切实保障会员的合法权益。

（资料来源：《中国知识产权报》，作者：侯伟）

【长春成立首批 4 家版权服务工作站】 2018 年 9 月 27 日，吉林省长春市文化广电新闻出版局（版权局）在长春市图书馆、长春市版权保护协会等 4 家单位设立了“长春市版权服务工作站”。

据介绍，长春市设立版权服务工作站，是完善版权公共服务体系，提升版权公共服务能力，促进文化创意产业发展，实施文化兴市战略，繁荣文化事业、发展文化产业，不断提升长春市文化软实力和城市影响力，加快打造东北亚现代文化名城的具体举措。

4 家版权服务工作站将开展版权法律法规及相关知识的宣传、培训，开展版权咨询、代办版权登记、纠纷调解、信息服务等社会服务，配合版权行政管理部门开展版权产业统计、调查研究和相关活动等。

此外，工作站还将积极促进版权创造运用，通过完善授权机制、搭建交易平台等方式，营造良好的版权生态环境，激励创新创造，促进版权成果转化。

（资料来源：《中国新闻出版广电报》，作者：张席贵）

【四川版权工作站正式揭牌】 2018 年 10 月 24 日下午，由四川省新闻出版广电局、四川省版权局主办的“四川省版权局·四川数字出版传媒有限公司版权工作站揭牌暨区块链知识产权资产联盟链版权认证、确权平台上线仪式”在西部智谷举行。

四川省新闻出版广电局副局长、四川省版权局副局长周青在致辞中表示，版权工作作为知识产权工作的重要组成部分，在鼓励和保护创新、创造，推进创新成果转化方面承担着重要职责和义务，四川省版权局研究后决定延伸版权工作链条，选择原创能力强、覆盖面广、自身版权保护体系成熟的专业单位建立版权工作站，打通版权工作“最后一公里”。

据了解，选择的专业单位是新华文轩四川数字出版传媒有限公司。该公司把区块链底层技术实际运用于知识产权领域并形成联盟链，这将开创区块链时代全新的知识产权服务模式，来助力四川版权工作。

当天，由四川数字出版传媒有限公司携手四川省大数据发展研究会、成都万象百汇科技有限公司、成都高新科技服务有限公司等单位发起成立的“区块链知识产权资产联盟链”一期工程“版权认证、确权平台”正式上线，平台上线后将无缝链接四川版权局版权登记、认证平台，具备不可伪造和不可篡改等特性的区块链技术运用于版权登记和保护中，是版权存证、保护最完善和有力的保证。首批拟入驻联盟链的节点包括西部智谷产业园区、四川数字出版产业基地、虚拟现实孵化发布产业基地、成都市高新区软件园、兴业证券股份、华夏幸福大厂影视小镇、重庆未来影视小镇、Hanhai Studio 洛杉矶文创园、中关村西部文创中心、中国西部音乐基地、四川省网络作家协会、香城国际文化艺术港。

值得一提的是，“四川数字出版传媒有限公司版权工作站”挂牌服务后，将通过区块链知识产权资产联盟链版权认证、确权平台为苍穹看书网络文学平台广大网络文学写作者提供免费、快捷的著作权登记通道，这是四川省第一个提供网络文学类著作权综合服务的互联网平台。

（资料来源：四川在线，作者：肖珊珊）

【首个互联网企业版权资产管理应用示范成果花落京企】 2018 年 10 月 25 日，全国首个互联网企业版权资产管理应用示范成果揭晓，曾推出过《山海异闻录》《凹凸世界》等多款原创游戏及动漫作品的北京盖娅互娱网络科技股份有限公司（以下简称盖娅互娱），成为首个版权资产管理应用示范单位，中国版权保护中心主任段桂鉴为盖娅互娱合伙人兼总裁安安颁发了示范单位牌证。

版权资产是新闻出版广播影视企业的核心资产，开展科学高效的版权资产管理工作，可以帮助企业通过版权资产管理运营获取稳定的竞争优势和盈利能力。2018 年 2 月，国家新闻出版广电总局改革办公室印发了《新闻出版广播影视企业版权资产管理工作指引（试行）》的通知，中国版权保护中心在这一文件的指导下，积极开展版权资产管理相关研究咨询及应用推广工作，取得了较大的成果。

2018 年 8 月，中心与盖娅互娱启动版权资产管理咨询专项工作，经过 2 个多月的共同努力，根据中心提出的版权资产管理改善方案，盖娅互娱进一步完善了版权资产管理制度，健全了版权资产管理组织机构及人员配置，增强了版权资产实务与价值相关的常规管理，建立了版权资产管理绩效评审及持续改进机制，取得了良好的效果。

经过认真严格的评选，中国版权保护中心认为盖娅互娱版权资产存量丰富，具备较强的游戏、动漫类版权资产研发、发行及运营能力，在国内外行业市场中均具较强的竞争实力，通过版权资产管理的改善提升，达到了版权资产管理应用的示范目标。

（资料来源：人民网，作者：吕骞　张欢欢）

【天合集团收费资格被音集协终止】 2018 年 11 月 5 日，中国音像著作权集体管理协会（以下简称音集协）发布公告，宣布解除与天合文化集团公司持续十年之久的合作关系，终止天合集团的代收费资格。这意味着音集协委托天合集团向卡拉 OK 场所收取版权费的模式被彻底废止。

音集协相关负责人称，此次强势发挥集体管理组织地位、坚决抵制市场不良行为的决定，旨在重振市场信心，构建公平高效卡拉 OK 版权新秩序。

公告明确指出，天合集团在收取卡拉 OK 著作权许可费业务中存在四类严重违规违约行为：一是拖延向音集协结算版权费，导致音集协无法向权利人及时分配版权费，最长近一年半时间未结算版权费；二是不按照合同约定使用音集协账户、开具音集协发票；三是收费信息不透明、逃避音集协监督；四是通过隐蔽方式变向分流版权费。

这名负责人说，这些行为导致了市场乱象，抹黑了音集协市场声誉，直接损害了权利人和使用者的利益。

这名负责人指出，音集协成立初期，委托天合集团收费确实快速推动了卡拉 OK 市场版权收费工作的起步，但这种收费模式暴露出成本高、监管困难等一系列不可避免的问题。

据记者了解，解除与天合集团的合约后，音集协将颠覆传统的“上门谈判＋维权诉讼”的卡拉 OK 收费手段，通过新技术搭建平台，依靠平台建立公开透明的授权收费及分配体系，压低收费成本，构建权利人、使用者、消费者和谐共赢的市场新秩序。

（资料来源：《法制日报》，作者：张红兵）

【音著协向进博会发放音乐著作权许可】 2018 年 11 月 5—10 日，首届中国国际进口博览会（以下简称进博会）在上海国家会展中心举办。为确保进博会期间音乐使用合乎法律要求，经与进博会组织方协商，中国音乐著作权协会（以下简称音著协）在进博会期间全程进驻进博会知识产权保护与商事纠纷处理中心，为进博会音乐著作权工作保驾护航。

据介绍，此次进博会期间，有超过 130 个国家和地区的 3 000 余家企业参展，其中世界 500 强企业有 200 余家参展，6 天时间里将进行 100 余场大型商务主题活动。在进博会举办期间，不仅组织方在展馆内会使用背景音乐，而且来自全球范围的参展者也会用到大量的国内外音乐作品。为此，进博会借鉴了2010年上海世博会著作权保护工作的成功经验，采取现场进驻方式，为国内外参展者提供音乐著作权法律咨询及授权许可服务。

作为中国唯一的音乐著作权集体管理组织，音著协也是国际作者和作曲者协会联合会（CISAC）成员，管理着全世界范围里300多万名音乐作者的1 400多万首音乐作品。继北京奥运会、上海世博会、广州亚运会、深圳大运会、南京青奥会之后，音著协进驻进博会，再一次成为大型国际性活动的音乐著作权服务单位。

“值得一提的是，此次进博会播放音乐获音著协许可，是进博会组织方主动联系音著协寻求授权的。”音著协有关负责人表示，随着中国法治大环境持续改善，越来越多的使用者尊重版权的意识提升，主动联系音著协获得权利授权。

（资料来源：《中国知识产权报》，作者：侯伟）

【中国版权保护中心与北京文投集团签约合作】 2018年11月12日，中国版权保护中心与北京市文化投资发展集团有限责任公司在京签订战略合作协议。

此次合作，双方将通过资源的共建共享，进一步将中国版权保护中心确权、授权、维权、研究咨询、宣传推广五大平台服务与北京文投集团业务相融合，构建文创产业共生、共治、共享的生态型服务平台。

除了为各类文化企业提供版权登记、版权相关专项培训、版权保护等基础服务外，双方将发挥各自优势，依托版权资产管理咨询、版权金融等创新服务，助力版权相关产业健康、快速、可持续发展。双方将共同探索一套集文化企业版权管理、评估、融资、流转于一体的有效机制，进一步创新文化企业无形资产融资租赁服务模式，助力文化企业发展。

当天，双方还签署了《北京市文创金融服务网络平台入驻协议》，以“版权＋金融”的创新业务模式，为全国文化企业投融资提供服务。

（资料来源：《中国新闻出版广电报》，
作者：赵新乐）

【百度等承诺落实版权监管主体责任】 2018年11月14—15日在京召开的“剑网2018”专项行动工作会议上，百度手机助手、豌豆荚、小米应用商店等10余家应用商店签署了《关于规范应用市场版权秩序的共同声明》。

各互联网企业在声明中表示，将积极配合权利人进行维权工作，与权利人建立良好的沟通桥梁，维护权利人的合法权益；愿协助版权行业主管部门共同规范软件应用市场版权秩序，抵制侵权盗版内容进入软件应用市场，维护软件应用市场网络版权保护环境。各互联网企业承诺认真贯彻国家版权局“剑网行动”的要求，配合、支持版权行政部门依法查处侵权盗版软件进入应用市场的第三方侵权行为；将建立健全投诉受理通道，及时受理权利人的通知，在接到投诉后及时响应；相关软件经营者24小时内未经反馈的，根据具体情况决定移除侵权APP。声明呼吁广大同行，向用户提示不得上传含有侵犯第三方合法权益内容的应用及权利人通知已经移除的作品和版权行政部门公布予以保护的作品。

各互联网企业代表在发言中表示，将积极开展自查自纠工作并落实平台版权监管的主体责任，推进垂直媒体和自媒体的规范经营和融合发展，积极深化与版权方的沟通合作，扩大主流媒体和社会主义核心价值观的影响力，加强行业自律。首都版权产业联盟作为版权保护工作的社会团体，将继续把推动企业自律管理、推动产业的健康发展作为重要的工作职责，协调指导各会员单位将本次签署的《共同声明》落到实处。

百度手机助手、豌豆荚、小米应用商店等10余家应用市场行业单位代表，新浪微博、快手、抖音等20余家重点网络企业和平台经营单位代表50余人参加了会议。

（资料来源：《中国新闻出版广电报》，
作者：李婧璇　王坤宁）

【中版版权产业基金在沪发起筹备】 2018年11月30日，在2018（首届）版权强国闵行论坛上，以中国版权保护中心版权服务体系为依托的国内首家版权产业基金——中版版权产业基金发起筹备。

中华版权代理总公司总经理贺传军、上海市莘庄工业区经济技术发展有限公司副总经理王阳阳、上海昇禾水润文化投资有限公司董事长瞿凡壹代表三家单位签署战略合作备忘录，标志着该基金进入筹备启动。中国版权保护中心主任段桂鉴，上海市闵行区委常委、副书记于勇，中国版权保护中心副主任魏红，上海市闵行区政府副区长吴斌，上海市莘庄工业区党工委书记李建华等参加了发起筹备仪式。

该基金将主要针对版权数据服务市场、内容打造与授权衍生市场、版权资产管理市场，面向文化创意产业、版权赋能相关领域产业转型、消费升级的创新创业型企业及优质项目、重点项目进行支持与投资。中版版权产业基金以中国版权保护中心版权服务体系为依托，将以产业投资、创业投资的方式支持版权产业链上下游的中小型企业、民营企业的创新发展，推动中国版权产业市场的繁荣新兴。

（资料来源：中国知识产权资讯网，作者：窦新颖）

【中国财经媒体版权保护联盟成立】 2018 年 12 月 15 日，在第三届中国产经媒体融合发展高峰论坛期间，由中国行业报协会召集，《传媒茶话会》与各主流财经媒体共同发起成立了中国财经媒体版权保护联盟。

该联盟旨在联合各财经媒体，共同抵制未经授权擅自转载新闻作品的行为，保护财经媒体版权。同时提高各财经媒体对其作品转载的议价能力，努力实现常态化监控和维权、市场化交易等，从而推动整个新闻版权市场的健康发展。

（资料来源：《人民日报》，作者：王珏）

【音集协版权收费将采取新模式】 2018 年 12 月 17—18 日，国家版权局和欧盟委员会“IP Key 中国”项目在广州联合举办了为期两天的中欧数字环境下版权保护与许可研讨会。中国音像著作权集体管理协会（以下简称音集协）副理事长兼代理总干事周亚平与参会各方分享了音集协的大数据著作权管理系统。

周亚平认为，音集协以往采取的以第三方人工谈判收取版权使用费的模式不仅成本高、效率低，更由于信息不透明、缺乏有效的监管、分配数据缺乏公信力等因素，使得版权方和使用者都不满意。长此以往，必将使著作权集体管理事业受到损害，卡拉 OK 市场也会陷入混乱无序的状态。为改变这一切，音集协将通过技术驱动建立大数据著作权管理系统，满足合理的收费和精准分配的需求，大幅度降低成本、提升效率，使著作权集体管理的各项要素能够实现。

周亚平指出，面对数以万计各自独立的卡拉 OK 经营实体店，只有通过设计共赢的商业模式，才能有效地调动产业各端的积极性。音集协也要充分发挥自身作为著作权集体管理组织的功能和作用，协同并整合行业资源，使大数据著作权管理系统能顺利且高效落地。

周亚平强调，著作权大数据系统带来的辐射性效益，在短期内即可见。它最重要的进步就是实现了对作品使用数据的精准和透明化，这是所有变革的基础和前提。同时，系统落地将普及卡拉 OK 场所联网，对实时更新并规范作品使用、提升唱片公司及著作权人版权收入、对产业各端提升效率、降低成本、创建新的商业模式和业务增长点都带来了巨大的想象空间。著作权集体管理组织将会更好地发挥权利人和使用者之间的桥梁作用，在满足著作权集体管理业务的同时促进行业良性竞争和繁荣。

通过这次中欧研讨会，首次亮相就引发关注的大数据著作权管理系统已经成为著作权领域的专家和卡拉 OK 行业所共同关注的新议题。若系统顺利落地，将会在实践中证明中国著作权集体管理制度设计的优越性，同时也会促使中国的著作权集体管理实践上升到新的水平。

（资料来源：《法制日报》，作者：张红兵）

【互联网企业发起短视频版权自律公约】 2018 年 12 月 20 日，在第五届中国互联网新型版权问题研讨会上，腾讯、百度、爱奇艺、搜狐、新浪、快手等公司共同发起中国网络版权产业联盟，并发布《中国网络短视频版权自律公约》。

该《自律公约》规定，联盟成员在短视频版权业务运营中，应该加强自律，严格遵守我国法律法规，尊重彼此知识产权，提倡正版，反对盗版。同时，应加强内容版权管理，大力鼓励支持内容原创，坚持先授权后传播的《著作权法》基本原则，规范内容版权管理使用制度，不滥用“避风港”规则。在加强维权管理方面，要完善版权投诉处理机制，认真履行法定的“通知—删除”义务，及时受理权利人的通知投诉，并快速移除相关侵权作品或断开相关侵权链接。此外，还应积极参与社会共治，对国家版权局发布的重点保护预警作品及权利人提交的热播、热映作品，应加强版权审核并及时处置。对涉嫌严重侵权的用户及时向版权执法部门进行举报，履行社会责任。

（资料来源：《中国新闻出版广电报》，作者：赖名芳）

【横琴联手港澳打造大湾区知识产权保护新高地】 2018 年 12 月 26 日，横琴国际知识产权保护联盟第三届成员大会在横琴长隆会展中心举行，大会新吸收了来自香港、澳门、北京、广州等地的 35 家社会团体、专业机构和企业为联盟成员，目前成员单位已达 101 家，其中香港机构 6 家、澳门机构 16

家。联盟成员单位代表、专家委员会成员等共140余人出席了会议。

横琴新区党委副书记李伟辉到会致辞时指出，联盟成立以来构建了区域性知识产权保护高地，联手港澳打造“一带一路”和“中国—拉美”知识产权保护新平台，为构筑粤港澳大湾区核心竞争力提供了助力。联盟理事长单位横琴新区工商局局长吴创伟做了2018年度联盟工作报告，并提出了2019年工作设想。百威投资（中国）有限公司、香港丝路智易通科技有限公司、澳门凯旋知识产权代理有限公司分别作为内地、香港、澳门成员单位代表做了发言。内地知识产权领域权威专家、广东太平洋联合律师事务所主任董宜东和横琴国际知识产权交易中心有限公司总经理季节分别做了自贸区知识产权发展与保护主旨演讲。

横琴新区国际知识产权保护联盟自2016年成立至今，取得了一系列成果。

一是在知识产权注册方面，设立了国家知识产权局商标局横琴商标受理窗口和广东省作品著作权自愿登记代办机构，截至2018年12月21日，商标受理窗口共受理商标注册业务3 493件，其中受理境外商标（含港澳台）279件；在版权方面，受理企业、个人等作品著作权登记共360余件。

二是在知识产权培育方面，出台《横琴新区促进知识产权工作暂行办法》《珠海市横琴新区工商行政管理局商标注册扶持申请工作规则》等配套措施，对注册商标和专利予以扶持。2016年以来横琴新区共扶持注册商标784件，其中，国际注册商标58件，港澳台注册商标21件；扶持发明专利70件、软件著作权超过1 000件、实用新型专利158件和贯标认证54个。累计扶持资金1 601.48万元。

三是在知识产权使用和交易方面，横琴国际知识产权交易中心有限公司上线首个金融创新知识产权运营交易国家平台，建立了线上知识产权质押融资业务模块，探索建立覆盖全国的知识产权质押融资市场化业务模式，积极利用自有资金开展知识产权质押融资业务，规模达到1 200万元。设立横琴商标质押登记窗口。截至2018年12月底，横琴商标受理窗口共受理商标质押业务8件，商标质押业务额达1.38亿元，其中单笔融资额最高达3 055万元。

四是在知识产权保护方面，与香港中小型企业联合会、澳门连锁加盟商会签订了《琴澳两地商标知识产权跨境保护与服务合作协议》，建立商标知识产权跨境保护与服务合作机制；与横琴法院签订《关于共建中国（广东）自由贸易试验区珠海横琴新区片区知识产权侵权惩罚机制合作备忘录》，在知识产权行政和司法保护衔接、构建知识产权行政和司法保护相互支撑、构建知识产权侵权惩罚机制、完善知识产权领域失信企业联合惩戒机制、拓展多元化的知识产权纠纷解决机制等五个方面开展合作。

五是在知识产权法制保障方面，设立了横琴知识产权巡回法庭，可以直接受理一般性知识产权诉讼；在商标侵权纠纷中引入知识产权商事调解，通过该机制快速处理商标权质押纠纷，落实“司法裁定、商标专用权转让、市场化变现”三层次的商标质押融资生态补偿；在商标权申请、登记、流转、纠纷预防与调解、侵权行为和事实保全等各个环节注重引入公证服务，发挥公证制度在商标权保护中的功能和优势。

（资料来源：中国新闻网，作者：邓媛雯　刘心宇）

◆ 国际交流与合作

【周慧琳会见新加坡知识产权局局长邓鸿森一行】 2018年1月22日，中国国家新闻出版广电总局副局长、中国国家版权局专职副局长周慧琳在京会见新加坡知识产权局局长邓鸿森一行。双方就推进《视听表演北京条约》早日生效、加强在世界知识产权组织（WIPO）框架下的沟通和交流、版权立法与制度等共同关注的版权问题交换了意见。

周慧琳对邓鸿森先生当选世界知识产权组织版权及相关权常设委员会（SCCR）主席后开展的一系列重要工作表示赞赏。他指出，中国正在迈向高质量的发展，未来还将不断强化知识产权的创造、保护、运用。中国国家版权局愿意继续积极、灵活地参与SCCR相关议题磋商，参与版权国际新规则制定。中新双方在版权领域保持着良好沟通，对话日益频繁。希望中新加强SCCR框架下的交流互动，进一步推动双方开展更加广泛务实的版权交流合作。

周慧琳强调，作为SCCR近年来的重要成果，《视听表演北京条约》的生效工作正在有序推进。中国已于2014年7月正式批准条约，目前该条约还需要11个国家批准或加入才能生效。中方愿与新方就此展开合作，也希望邓鸿森局长作为SCCR的主席，继续关注批约相关工作进展，推动条约早日生效，惠及更多表演者和公众。

周慧琳还介绍了中国《著作权法》第三次修订相关工作情况。他表示，网络侵权盗版不断出现新形式，给版权保护工作带来巨大挑战。版权法律和制度必须不断完善和发展，与技术进步相适应。中国政府高度重视新型侵权盗版行为的整治，持续开展相关调查研究工作，在《著作权法》修订时考虑新技术因素，积极营造良好网络版权生态。

邓鸿森表示，新加坡也正在修订本国的著作权法。在修订著作权法的同时，新加坡正认真研究加入《视听表演北京条约》。期待新加坡与中国未来不仅深入推进两国间版权合作，还为深化版权领域国际合作共同努力。

中国国家新闻出版广电总局（国家版权局）版权管理司司长于慈珂、副司长汤兆志等陪同会见。

（资料来源：国家版权局网站，作者：李明远）

【中日聚焦网络音乐版权保护应对方案】 2018年3月15日，由中国音乐著作权协会（以下简称音著协）与日本远藤实歌谣音乐振兴财团共同主办的2018年度“中日著作权研讨会”在北京诺富特和平宾馆召开。本次研讨会主要围绕“互联网音乐的现状与问题”展开，通过介绍中日两国互联网音乐的发展状况与数字音乐版权保护的具体实务，相互分享观点、交流经验，探讨数字时代下网络音乐版权保护的应对方案。来自版权行政管理部门、国际组织、中日著作权集体管理组织、司法机关、高校、研究机构、互联网公司、音乐出版公司、相关媒体的80余位专业人士参加了会议。

音著协总干事屈景明与远藤实歌谣音乐振兴财团代表、日本音乐著作权协会主席、著名歌曲《北国之春》的词作者井出博正先后为研讨会致辞。国家版权局版权管理司执法监管处相关负责人以“规范网络音乐版权秩序”为题进行演讲，介绍了中国互联网音乐发展的现状及国家版权局打击网络音乐侵权盗版的各项举措，并表示支持网络音乐平台与著作权集体管理组织合作解决网络使用音乐的著作权问题。日本国士馆大学知识产权研究生院客座教授上原伸一先生以“国际热议数字时代的版权问题”为题进行演讲，从国际法律规范和实务层面介绍了国际网络音乐版权保护的操作模式。

在讨论环节中，日本 RecoChoku 互联网音乐公司代表山崎浩司、日本音乐著作权协会常务理事世古和博、词曲著作权人代表井出博正、中国音乐著作权协会副总干事刘平、网易公司战略发展部总监朱继国等就中日双方在音乐创作者权益保护的需求、网络音乐市场模式、音乐著作权管理等内容分别做了介绍，并对与会嘉宾关注的问题给予了解答。

（资料来源：《中国新闻出版广电报》，作者：殷珠）

【博洛尼亚童书展：中国达成800多项版权输出意向及协议】 意大利当地时间2018年3月29日下午，伴随着第55届博洛尼亚国际儿童书展闭幕，中国主宾国活动圆满结束。经初步统计，活动期间，国内各出版单位现场共达成中国童书版权输出意向及协议800多项。

书展期间，由近百家单位的200多位出版人和曹文轩等近50位中国儿童文学作家、插画家、学者等组成的中国主宾国代表团与其他国家同行们进行了广泛贸易洽谈，并通过书展主宾国平台，充分展示了中国原创童书的实力和中国童书与国外童书出版界平等交流合作的能力。

在本次博洛尼亚国际儿童书展上，来自中国的插画家大放异彩。其中，已故漫画家张乐平先生的“三毛”系列作品荣获世界无字书大奖“特别荣誉奖”，插画家熊亮入围国际安徒生奖（插画家）五人短名单。此外，越来越多的中国青年插画师在世界舞台展露才华，逐渐走进国际视野。他们在中外插画师交流分享会、罗杰·米罗与中国插画师谈绘本创作等活动上与世界各国的插画大师对话交流，吸引了许多国际出版人的关注。活动结束后，美国皮博迪·埃塞克斯博物馆主动邀请其中几名中国青年插画师与其展览项目进行合作。

本次主宾国活动举办了多场实效性显著的专业交流活动。在中国童书市场发展趋势报告会上，国内童书出版人代表从创作、市场等不同角度，向100余位国外同业者介绍了中国童书市场的现状及发展趋势。中国少年儿童新闻出版总社社长李学谦在活动发言中提到，中国少儿出版更加关注质量和效益。中国图书进出口（集团）总公司总经理张纪臣介绍了中图公司为中国童书走向世界搭建的发行平台，特别是数字渠道。“曹文轩国际作品研讨会”作为另一场重要活动，则邀请了19位国际插画师、译者、国际安徒生奖评委及麦克米伦等中外童书出版人，通过分享围绕曹文轩作品开展合作的不同心得，反映出他们对中国原创童书高品质的新认识。

（资料来源：《中国新闻出版广电报》，作者：李明远）

【中国图书亮相突尼斯国际书展】 第34届突尼斯国际书展于2018年4月6日开幕，于4月15日结束，共吸引来自30多个国家和地区的700多家出版商参加。人民出版社、人民教育出版社、人民卫生出版社和中国教育图书进出口有限公司等多家中

国出版商组团参加。

在中国展台前，突尼斯商人礼萨·马哈古卜驻足浏览，并选购了多本图书。他告诉新华社记者，中国经济飞速发展令人印象深刻，他希望通过阅读相关书籍，进一步了解中国人的思维方式。

人民出版社社长黄书元说，这是中国出版商第二次参加突尼斯国际书展，他们为当地读者带来600多册图书，涵盖政治、文化、医疗、语言学习等类别。中国出版商参展的目的是让更多突尼斯读者了解中国、读懂中国，并期待与突尼斯出版商加强交流沟通，寻求更多合作机会。

（资料来源：《中国新闻出版广电报》，作者：马迪　刘锴）

【中国九大原创节目登陆戛纳电视节】 当地时间2018年4月7日下午，集结《国家宝藏》《朗读者》《经典咏流传》《天籁之战》《声临其境》《跨界歌王》《明日之子》《功夫少年》《好久不见》等九大中国原创节目模式亮相的中国原创节目模式推介会登陆法国戛纳电视节。这是中国电视人首次以“原创节目模式”的名义集体发声于戛纳电视节的主舞台。

本场推介活动由中国广播电影电视社会组织联合会电视版权委员会和上海广播电视台联合发起。9位来自中国的节目主创全程用英文向全球顶尖的行业大佬和模式买家们推介了中国原创节目模式。这九大中国原创节目既有最新在电视台、网络平台播出的爆款节目，也有制作公司还没有播出但是模式新颖完善的“纸模式”，分别来自中国中央电视台、东方卫视、湖南卫视、北京卫视、腾讯视频、恒顿传媒和千足传媒。

如由中央电视台和央视纪录国际传媒有限公司共同制作的《国家宝藏》，创新了国宝文物类文化节目的模式，在全球都有复制推广意义。董卿是中央电视台知名主持人，同时也是《朗读者》节目的制作人、主持人。她说，《朗读者》就是让特别的人读特别的文字，于是个人的生命体验和经典文字当中所包含的情感和哲理，就紧密地结合在了一起。

推介会现场，戛纳电视节电视节目板块负责人Garaude（葛厚德）女士表示，在过去的几年中，中国一直是一个至关重要的节目消费国，但现在中国也已成为一个优秀节目内容的全球供应商。

（资料来源：人民网，作者：曹玲娟）

【中国国际出版中心在伦敦正式成立】 2018年4月9日，由中国青年出版社和英国布卢姆斯伯利出版公司合作成立的中国国际出版中心在伦敦正式成立。

这是国内出版机构与海外同行合作，在欧洲创办的第一家中国主题图书出版中心，致力于推广中国文化，面向国际市场出版和销售。

中国青年出版社（英国）国际出版传媒公司总经理郭光在当天的启动仪式上说，中国国际出版中心正式运营后，计划每年从中国引进100种以上图书版权，与中国各出版社合作翻译出版，利用布卢姆斯伯利的全球出版和营销渠道，同时以纸质书和电子书、数据库的形式，把关于中国文化、艺术、政治、经济、科技、教育、旅游及生活的优秀作品以更快速度在更大范围内介绍给国际读者。

国际出版商协会前主席、英国布卢姆斯伯利出版公司执行董事理查德·查金说：“随着中国在国际社会影响力的提升，国际读者迫切希望对中国文化和社会发展有更多的了解，中国主题图书也越来越受到欢迎。”

英国出版商协会执行副总裁埃玛·豪斯肯定了中英出版交流近年来取得的成果，认为伦敦中国国际出版中心的成立对于促进中英文化界的合作和交流具有重大意义。

布卢姆斯伯利出版公司曾出版过“哈利·波特”系列小说等畅销书，并在数字出版领域走在世界前列。2017年与中国合作出版的《汤显祖——中国的莎士比亚》英文版也获得读者热烈欢迎。

2018年伦敦书展于4月10—12日举行。

（资料来源：新华网，作者：金晶）

【中墨正式建立版权双边合作框架】 墨西哥当地时间2018年4月12日，中国国家版权局与墨西哥文化部在墨西哥城签署版权合作谅解备忘录，这标志着中墨之间正式建立版权双边合作框架，开始展开常态化、机制化的版权交流与合作。这是中国国家版权局在全球范围内签署的第八个版权双边合作备忘录。

中国国家版权局版权管理司相关负责人介绍，中墨版权合作谅解备忘录的签署，是积极响应“一带一路”倡议，加强版权双边交流与合作的又一成果，对扩大中国版权的国际影响力，特别是加强与拉美国家的版权合作，将起到重要示范与推动作用。当日，中国国家版权局版权管理司司长于慈珂与墨西哥文化部下属的墨西哥国家版权局局长曼努埃尔·格拉·萨马罗分别代表双方在备忘录上签字。

根据该备忘录，中国国家版权局版权管理司与墨西哥国家版权局将加强合作，围绕版权热点问题开展研讨，交流版权立法、执法、保护、争议解决等方面的信息和做法。双方将根据需要制定并执行年度工作计划，在版权领域开展具体的合作交流活动，充分发挥该备忘录的作用。

（资料来源：《中国新闻出版广电报》，作者：赖名芳）

【中国出版代表团亮相第 25 届匈牙利布达佩斯国际图书节】 2018 年 4 月 19—22 日，第 25 届匈牙利布达佩斯国际图书节于布达佩斯千禧文化中心举办。在国家新闻出版署的组织领导下，由来自人民卫生出版社、清华大学出版社、江西人民出版社等 4 家国内出版单位组成的中国出版代表团亮相本届图书节。中国图书进出口（集团）总公司负责中国出版代表团参展组织服务工作。

本届图书节，中国展台面积 50 平方米，共选送参展图书近 200 种共 300 册，内容丰富、种类多样，分为主题图书、传统文化、中国文学、人文社科等专题，集中展示了一批反映中国改革开放以来在政治、经济、文化和社会等方面取得重大成就的精品图书，为匈牙利和中东欧地区民众了解当代中国发展现状、感知中华文化打开了重要窗口。

2008 年中国曾作为主宾国参加布达佩斯国际图书节，2016 年匈牙利作为中东欧 16 国主宾国之一参加了北京国际图书博览会，这对深化中匈出版文化交流与合作起到了促进作用。

当地时间 4 月 19 日 15 时，在中国展台中国出版代表团与第十届中华图书特殊贡献奖获奖者中匈友好协会会长宗博莉·克拉拉女士等三位匈牙利著名汉学家就中匈翻译出版进行了座谈交流。中国出版代表团通过版权洽谈、中国图书版权推介，以及与匈牙利出版商协会举办多种形式的出版交流活动，以进一步扩大中匈出版的交流与合作。

（资料来源：人民网，作者：于洋）

【外研社“中国主题编辑部”落户匈牙利】 2018 年 4 月 20 日，中国外语教学与研究出版社（以下简称外研社）与匈牙利科苏特出版集团共建“中国主题编辑部”签约仪式在第 25 届匈牙利布达佩斯国际图书节展场举行。

这是外研社在中东欧地区继保加利亚和波兰之后的第三个海外编辑部。编辑部依托中匈两大出版社的优质资源，相互推介和翻译优秀的文学、文化作品，为实现中匈两国文化的双向交流搭建桥梁。

中国驻匈牙利大使馆政务参赞刘波、外研社党总支书记兼副社长王芳、科苏特出版集团社长科奇什、匈牙利汉学家及出版业人士出席了签约仪式。

刘波致辞说，现在是中匈两国关系最好的时期，两国文化交流愈加深入，“中国主题编辑部”的成立既是两国文化交流的成果，又是一个良好开端，期盼编辑部首批图书早日与匈牙利读者见面。

王芳说，截至 2017 年，外研社已与全世界近 700 家出版机构建立合作关系，拥有 80 多个语种的出版能力，出版规模达 1.2 万余种，是中国最知名、规模最大的出版机构之一。她相信，随着匈牙利“中国主题编辑部”的成立，越来越多的外研社优秀作品将以本土化出版的形式与匈牙利读者见面。

科苏特出版集团是匈牙利规模最大的出版集团之一，已出版 50 多种中国主题图书，并把莫言等多位中国作家的作品介绍到匈牙利。科奇什表示，该集团愿与外研社一起将更多匈中两国的优秀作品介绍给对方。

（资料来源：《中国新闻出版广电报》，作者：杨永前）

【中国图书亮相日内瓦国际书展】 2018 年 4 月 25 日，一年一度的日内瓦国际图书展开幕，中国展台展出图书 500 余种，内容涉及传统文化、人文社科、中国文学、语言学习和儿童图书等，吸引了不少读者驻足。

此次中国出版代表团由中国社会科学出版社、人民东方出版传媒有限公司、商务印书馆有限公司等 8 家出版单位组成。据代表团团长赵剑英介绍，此次参展图书不仅有反映中国古老文化的题材，也有展示当今中国经济发展和社会进步的书籍，包括诠释中国梦，介绍中国道路、中国经验和承载社会主义核心价值观的优秀读物。

他说，参加国际图书展是实现中国出版业“走出去”的重要途径之一。参展期间，中国展团还计划组织作家交流、版权签约仪式、重点图书推介等多种活动，加强与当地出版机构的交流，探索建立国际合作的途径。

日内瓦国际图书展是瑞士重要书展活动之一，从 1987 年起每年举办一次，展品多元化是图书展的一大特色。

本届书展持续 5 天。据组织方估计，书展参观者有望达到 10 万人次。

（资料来源：新华网，作者：施建国）

【中国出版企业亮相伊朗书展】 2018年5月2日，第31届德黑兰国际书展在伊朗首都德黑兰阳光之城展览中心举办，中国多家知名出版企业参展。

本届书展为期11天，中国出版传媒股份有限公司、人民出版社、商务印书馆有限公司、新华联合发行有限公司等多家出版企业此次带来传统文化、人文社科、语言学习等多个领域的精品图书近200种共400余册，其中近一半参展图书为波斯文和英文图书。中国参展团此次还特别推出《中国走社会主义道路为什么成功》等一批反映中国改革开放以来在政治、经济、文化和社会等方面取得重大成就的主题图书。

负责中国参展团协调和布展工作的中国图书进出口（集团）总公司会展中心项目经理侯润天说，参加国际书展是实现中国出版“走出去”和加强国际出版交流合作的重要途径之一。本届书展期间，中方代表团与伊朗出版商协会举行座谈交流，就中伊互译出版合作深入交换意见。

（资料来源：新华社，作者：穆东　马骁）

【中国代表团参加都灵图书沙龙】 2018年5月10—14日，第31届意大利都灵国际图书沙龙在灵格托展览中心举办。受国家新闻出版署委托，中国图书进出口（集团）总公司承办组团参展工作。

继2017年首次参加都灵书展后，2018年中国出版代表团再次组团参加。本届中国出版代表团展示的中英文图书，包括主题图书、传统文化、中国文学、人文社科、少儿读物、语言学习等类别，展出精品图书近150种。其中，三联书店与意大利多家出版社洽谈《中华文明的核心价值》《御窑千年》等图书的版权输出项目，荣宝斋出版社拟与布雷拉美术学院洽谈设立“荣宝斋出版社阅读及国际艺术创作基地”，商务印书馆重点推广汉语学习类词典、系列丛书。

（资料来源：《人民日报》，作者：韩硕）

【北京新闻出版广播影视企业海外服务基地在伦敦挂牌】 英国当地时间2018年5月11日，在“2018北京优秀影视剧海外展播季·英国段”的开幕式上，由北京市新闻出版广电局支持的北京新闻出版广播影视企业海外服务基地正式成立，并率先挂牌英国普罗派乐卫视。

该基地旨在构建北京伦敦新闻出版广播影视交流的长效机制和版权交易的长期高效平台，促进北京新闻出版影视企业拓展海外市场、推进文化产品和服务出口，在建设版权数据库、建设版权交易平台、提供版权咨询服务、促进文化交流等方面进行建设。未来依托基地的影视版权资源，“打造常演常新的北京剧场”，推动北京影视作品更多更快地“走出去”，展现中华文明独特的价值与魅力，让全世界人民更好地认识中国，服务好弘扬中华优秀传统文化、文化“走出去”的大局。

基地在北京挂牌于西京文化传媒（北京）股份有限公司，该公司连续多年被评为“国家文化出口重点企业”。

（资料来源：《中国新闻出版广电报》，作者：王坤宁　李婧璇）

【外研社·法国“中国主题编辑部”成立】 2018年5月16日，中国外语教学与研究出版社和法国映象文库出版社在巴黎共同举办外研社·法国“中国主题编辑部”揭牌仪式。

该编辑部策划、翻译、出版包括中国传统文化经典和反映当代中国经济社会发展成就与面貌的优秀中国主题图书，出版板块分为经典中国、当代中国、博雅中国三部分。编辑部出版的第一部图书——清代孙温插画版《红楼梦》已在法国上市并受到读者欢迎。《中华思想文化术语》1～5辑、《中国文化读本》也即将在法国出版。编辑部还在法国和加拿大等地书店建设“中国书架”，展示中国主题图书。同时，编辑部还设计制作了多种形式的中国文化主题文创产品，在海外打造中国文化创意生态。

（资料来源：《中国新闻出版广电报》，作者：宗边）

【北京出版代表团亮相2018美国书展】 纽约当地时间2018年5月30日至6月1日，2018年美国书展（BookExpo America）在美国纽约贾维茨会展中心举行。书展上，由北京新闻出版广电局组织的北京出版代表团设立了北京出版联合展区。联合展区内专门设立数字出版区、冬奥主题区，并通过在展会上举办图书推介会、投放平面广告和展馆现场广告、分发宣传品等形式多角度推广北京出版图书，促成北京出版企业与国外展商的版权合作。

5月31日，北京出版代表团在北京出版联合展区现场举行了北京图书推介会暨北京联合出版有限责任公司与美国贝尔伦克雷出版社合作意向签约仪式。北京出版代表团团长、北京联合出版有限责任公司总经理张金龙，美国贝尔伦克雷出版社代表迈克·巴斯克斯以及受邀外国展商出席了活动。此次签约，北京联合出版有限责任公司与贝尔伦克雷出版社达成了版权出口五年战略合作关系。贝尔伦克雷出版社引进北京联合出版及其下辖的中国北京出版创意产业园区企业的版权30余种，在北美地区出版发行，并协助北京联合出版就以北京冬奥会为主题的图书在美国进行宣传推广。张金龙表示，贝尔伦克雷出版社有着丰富的推广经验，此次合作促进中国北京出版创意产业园区图书的海外推广和海外本土化出版，对北京出版企业与北美市场的结合起到了良好的示范作用。

（资料来源：中国知识产权资讯网，作者：窦新颖）

【庄荣文在京会见世界知识产权组织副总干事王彬颖一行】 2018年6月1日下午，国家新闻出版署署长、国家版权局局长庄荣文在京会见世界知识产权组织（WIPO）副总干事王彬颖一行。双方就进一步巩固和加强版权领域的合作，推进《视听表演北京条约》早日生效等进行了交流。

庄荣文对王彬颖副总干事一行的来访表示欢迎。他表示，自中国1980年6月3日加入WIPO以来，中国国家版权局与WIPO在国际版权事务中相互支持、真诚合作、加强交流，取得了良好的效果。特别是2012年6月，WIPO在北京召开保护音像表演外交会议，成功缔结《视听表演北京条约》，有效提升了中国在国际版权领域的话语权和影响力。2015年12月，双方在上海签署合作谅解备忘录，版权领域全面合作迈上新台阶。他对WIPO与中国共同开展版权产业经济贡献率专项调研，在中国颁发世界知识产权组织“中国版权金奖”，向全球推广南通纺织和福建德化陶瓷版权保护经验表示感谢。

庄荣文希望WIPO在培训版权专业人员、完善版权保护制度等方面继续与中国加强合作，并推动中国在国际版权事务中发挥更大作用。国家版权局愿意与WIPO通过联合举办国际版权论坛等活动，向世界介绍中国在版权创造、保护和运用等方面的做法和经验，并将继续积极参与国际版权事务，通过与WIPO成员国之间的充分交流，推动版权国际新规则的制定，推进《视听表演北京条约》尽快生效。

王彬颖首先代表WIPO总干事高锐先生，向庄荣文任中国国家版权局局长表示祝贺。她高度肯定中国近年来在版权领域所做出的努力，特别是在打击网络侵权盗版领域持续开展的“剑网”专项行动所取得的重大成果，认为中国国家版权局在推动版权产业发展方面做了许多务实、具体的工作，对于推动中国经济发展、提升国民版权意识起到了积极作用，创造了颇具中国特色的版权管理模式。WIPO愿与中国国家版权局继续加强交流合作，共同推进全球范围的版权创新和保护。

会谈中，双方还就在上海国际电影节期间合作举办以“电影的经济及文化价值与版权保护”为主题的国际会议、续签合作备忘录，以及举办第七届中国国际版权博览会、颁发“中国版权金奖”等事宜进行了商讨。

中宣部出版局局长郭义强、国家版权局版权管理司司长于慈珂以及WIPO中国办事处主任陈宏兵等陪同会见。

（资料来源：《中国新闻出版广电报》，作者：赖名芳）

【中美法律专家纵论知识产权保护与创新】 2018年6月9日，中美知识产权比较研究专题研讨会在北京举行，中美两国法律专家、企业高层围绕商业方法创新、商业法律保护、知识产权保护等话题展开深入探讨与交流。

阿里巴巴集团副总裁、阿里巴巴知识产权研究院负责人孙军工表示，中美两国高度重视知识产权、不断深化保护知识产权领域的合作，不仅有利于中美两个国家的发展，也有利于全球经济贸易的稳定和繁荣。

谈到中美知识产权保护制度的比较研究问题，孙军工提出，要从提升企业核心竞争力的角度加强商业方法创新的保护。他认为，商业方法创新是企业经营逻辑的系统再思考，是对技术创新、产品创新、管理创新等传统创新方式的包容和超越。

孙军工还倡议从维护中小企业和年轻人利益的角度，加大知识产权保护。他认为，随着电子商务迅猛发展，商界话语权从数百家跨国公司手中让步到中小企业手中。中小企业在全球贸易中大放异彩的条件和时机已经成熟，因此要加大中小企业知识产权保护力度。

此外，孙军工提出，要从全球化角度加强知识产权保护的国际合作。他认为，创新的全球化和经贸的全球化，要求知识产权保护必须走经商之路，构建平衡有效的知识产权国际规则，促进双方合作共赢，实现共同发展。

针对中国知识产权保护的发展，美国联邦上诉巡回法院前首席法官兰达尔·雷德认为，近年来，中国在知识产权保护方面做了很多努力，某些方面做得比美国还好。他希望中国也像美国一样建立联邦上诉法院，解决专利问题，对知识产权保护具有推动作用。

国家知识产权局知识产权发展研究中心韩秀成表示，中国有着极其广大的市场和利益，但是一个严重的问题是缺乏核心技术，尤其是没有掌握核心技术的知识产权。

韩秀成指出，从中央到地方都应该重视核心企业关键技术的培育，特别是拥有关键核心技术的知识产权。中国要以更加开放的心态和先进的理念看待知识产权制度，使其更加适应时代和高科技发展的需要。同时，中国也要高度重视新商业模式、新业态的保护和研究，特别是要高水平运用好知识产权的战略和策略。

韩秀成认为，未来世界的竞争，归根结底是知识产权的竞争，是高技术的竞争，创新是根本。而创新的基本保障应该是知识产权，知识产权是市场经济的产物，根本的任务是激励和保护创新成果。

（资料来源：中国新闻网，作者：于立霄）

【世界知识产权组织副总干事福尔班一行视察冠勇科技】 2018 年 6 月 18 日，世界知识产权组织（WIPO）副总干事西尔维·福尔班一行调研了第 21 届上海国际电影节市场并视察了冠勇科技，冠勇科技集团创始人兼 CEO 吴冠勇向福尔班一行汇报了 FB 版权大数据的建设情况。

冠勇科技成立于 2011 年，是一家数据驱动的版权贸易与保护平台，以版权金融贸易、版权监测保护及版权大数据等业务为核心，致力于推动全球更健康的内容生态环境，2016 年荣获“中国版权金奖”。旗下的全资子公司巨视影业已新媒体独家发行《你的名字。》《太空救援》等 50 多部院线电影，与美国、日本等 20 多个国家和地区的 80 多家影视公司建立了长期合作关系，每年引进约 300 部海外优质电影，包括约 2 000 集梦工厂动画系列等。此次电影节，巨视影业 24 部海外佳片入围了线下展映环节，其中来自法国的动画电影《白牙》成功入围上海国际电影节金爵奖最佳动画单元，《白牙》的导演、曾获得“奥斯卡最佳动画短片奖”的亚历山大·埃斯皮加雷斯也参加了 6 月 22 日的电影首映仪式，向中国的影迷们介绍这部优秀的动画作品。福尔班希望冠勇科技继续努力，打造全球领先的版权贸易与保护平台。

（资料来源：中国知识产权资讯网，作者：窦新颖）

【“电影的经济及文化价值与版权保护高端论坛”在上海举行】 2018 年 6 月 19—20 日，在第 21 届上海国际电影节框架下，“电影的经济及文化价值与版权保护高端论坛”成功举办。本次论坛由国家版权局与世界知识产权组织共同举办，论坛以第 21 届上海国际电影节为契机，聚焦版权保护和电影产业发展，从保护试听表演的重要性，促进影视产业和其他文创产业发展，为文化创意产业使用版权作品提供便利等方面进行深入探讨。与会者还交流了国家和国际层面通过完善版权制度、加强版权保护等促进电影产业实现经济价值和文化价值的成功经验，并呼吁各国尽快批准或加入《视听表演北京条约》。

本次论坛邀请了世界知识产权组织高层官员，“一带一路”沿线国家的版权主管部门或驻华使馆代表，国内相关部委、著作权涉外认证机构、集体管理组织代表，以及版权业界代表、权利人和专家学者代表 150 余人参加。

（资料来源：中央广电总台国际在线，作者：王澂时）

【中英版权圆桌会议聚焦数字环境下版权执法面临的问题及挑战】 2018 年 6 月 26 日下午，在中英版权政府间会谈结束后，由中国国家版权局和英国知识产权局共同主办的中英版权圆桌会议在京举行。中英双方围绕版权政策制定新动态、版权执法活动和成果新进展、数字环境下版权执法面临的问题及挑战这三个主题进行了研讨。这是自 2010 年签署《中英版权战略合作谅解备忘录》后，双方在备忘录的框架下进行的第四次高层互访和交流活动。

国家版权局版权管理司司长于慈珂在会上表示，目前全球正处于一个快速发展变化的新时代，不仅技术在寻求发展，而且文化、艺术等各方面都发生着新变化，所有这些都对版权和版权所依赖的环境提出了新问题和新挑战。权利人以及相关版权组织不仅要面对，国与国之间也要共同面对并予以解决，这就需要我们共同去研究和完善版权法律制度以及版权执法措施。多年来中国国家版权局和英国知识产权局一直保持着良好的合作关系，双方举办了形式多样的论坛、人才培训等交流活动。面对数字环境下的新问题、新挑战，中英双方不仅需要在版权制度基础上寻求新的观念突破和新的制度设计，还要有信心在数字环境下构建一个动态的版权利益平衡机制，以迎接版权新的美好时代。

英国知识产权局版权与行政执法司司长罗斯·林奇在会上高度肯定了中国政府近年来在打击侵权盗版方面取得的成绩，并介绍了欧盟在版权执法政策方面的最新动态。她说，近年来英国知识产权局与中国国家版权局开展的合作交流非常顺畅。在此基础上，英方相关版权机构和组织与中国部分省、市版权执法部门就部分侵权盗版案件进行了沟通与协调，同时还与阿里、腾讯、百度等互联网企业签署了合作协议。当前，数字技术的进步，既给内容产业创造了更大的市场，也给了侵权盗版分子乘机牟利的空间。应对网络版权执法新挑战，不可能靠一个国家的单打独斗，而需要各国交流、共享、互助。在欧盟制定、实施数字单一市场改革的过程中，包括在数字环境下权利的限制与例外，以及出版商新权利的设定、确认平台商的责任等方面，英国都发挥了引导牵头作用。中英两国虽远隔万里，但我们共同担负着保护知识产权的使命。在网络版权执法方面，中英需要更加深入地探寻新的法律制度，以规制来自强大互联网平台的技术挑战，同时支持权利人更有效地维权。

会上，中方向英方介绍了中国开展“剑网2017”专项行动取得的成果，以及启动的“剑网2018”的重点任务和初步考虑，把新闻转载、短视频、动漫及有声读物等相关作品纳入专项行动整治的重点领域。在华国际出版商版权保护联盟主席张玉国等介绍了英国出版商在中国市场上获得的三个“受益匪浅”和面临的四种挑战，以及所发现的网络版权新情况和新型案例。

国家版权局版权管理司副司长汤兆志主持会议。中国国家市场监督管理总局和英国驻华大使馆部分官员，来自著作权集体管理组织、相关行业协会、企业的30余名代表，共同分享了数字环境下中英版权执法的实践经验、具体案例，并探讨了在技术环境下，如何更好地进行版权制度建设、权利管理、国际合作等重要问题。

（资料来源：《中国新闻出版广电报》，作者：赖名芳）

【人民出版社与越南真理国家政治出版社签署版权合作协议】 2018年7月5日，人民出版社与越南真理国家政治出版社在越南首都河内签署中国改革开放与越南革新开放等相关图书版权合作协议，标志着中越两国权威出版机构合作继续深化。

在签约仪式现场，人民出版社社长黄书元与越南真理国家政治出版社社长范志成代表各自出版社在版权合作协议上签字。

2018年是中国改革开放40周年，也是越南革新开放32周年。此次，人民出版社授权越南真理国家政治出版社出版《中国改革为什么成功》和《中国对外开放40年》两书的越南文版，旨在向越南读者简要系统地介绍中国改革开放40年的历史与成就。越南真理国家政治出版社也向人民出版社授权出版《越南革新事业（1986—2016）理论问题与实践总结报告》和《越南共产党在法治国家构建中之领导工作创新》两书的中文版，这两本书是反映越南革新事业和法治建设的权威著作。

据悉，人民出版社与越南真理国家政治出版社自1993年即建立业务关系、开展互访交流，为两国人民友好交往架起了一座文化桥梁。2017年1月12日，两社签署《中国人民出版社与越南真理国家政治出版社2017—2021年合作协议》。本次签约活动是为落实两社合作协议迈出的具体一步。

（资料来源：新华网，作者：王迪　陶军）

【2017年中国出版业版权输出同比增长24.1%】 2018年8月8日，第25届北京国际图书博览会暨第16届北京国际图书节新闻发布会举行。据悉，2017年，全国出版业共输出版权13 816项，其中输出图书、音像制品、电子出版物等出版物版权12 651项；版权输出总量较上年增长24.1%，其中出版物版权输出增长29.0%。这从一个侧面反映出出版“走出去”步伐加快，出版单位越来越重视海外版权合作，并且将其纳入社会效益考核指标。

从数据来看，中国出版业版权输出呈现以下几个特点：一是版权输出主要集中在北京、上海、广东等地区，其中北京版权输出超过6 600项，占据了全国版权输出的近半壁江山。二是版权输出对象地区主要集中在美国、英国、德国、韩国等发达国家和地区。三是对越南、泰国、印度尼西亚、印度、尼泊尔、吉尔吉斯斯坦、阿联酋、黎巴嫩、埃及等“一带一路”沿线国家版权输出量增长较快，表现抢眼。

（资料来源：中国知识产权资讯网，作者：姜旭）

【第25届图博会达成中外版权贸易协议5 678项】 2018年8月26日，为期5天的第25届北京国际图书博览会（以下简称图博会）暨第16届北京国际图书节在京落下帷幕。据现场初步统计，本届图博会共达成中外版权贸易协议5 678项，同比增长7.9%。其中各类版权输出与合作出版意向和协议达成3 610项，同比增长11.28%；引进意向和协议达成2 068项，同比增长2.48%。引进输出比为1∶1.75。

本届图博会期间，共举办了1 000多场文化活动，吸引了30万人次进场参观，其中专业场达15万人次，同比增加近30%。为期5天的图书节期间，进馆读者超过20万人，共举办近百场各类文化活动、版权合作论坛等。

主题图书“走出去”成为本届图博会和图书节的一大亮点，多种形式的展示和发布活动，展示了国内出版机构推动主题图书数字阅读和版权输出的重要成果。为纪念改革开放40周年，本届图博会举办了改革开放40周年精品出版物展，重点展示改革开放以来中国出版业取得的成果。

（资料来源：《中国知识产权报》，作者：姜旭）

【习近平向2018年“一带一路”知识产权高级别会议致贺信】 2018年8月28日，2018年“一带一路”知识产权高级别会议在北京开幕，国家主席习近平向会议致贺信。

习近平指出，中国发扬丝路精神，提出共建“一带一路”倡议，得到有关国家和国际社会广泛认同和热情参与，取得了丰硕成果。我们愿同各方继续共同努力，本着共商共建共享原则，将“一带一路”建设成为和平之路、繁荣之路、开放之路、创新之路、文明之路，让丝路精神发扬光大。

习近平强调，知识产权制度对促进共建“一带一路”具有重要作用。中国坚定不移实行严格的知识产权保护，依法保护所有企业知识产权，营造良好营商环境和创新环境。希望与会各方加强对话，扩大合作，实现互利共赢，推动更加有效地保护和使用知识产权，共同建设创新之路，更好造福各国人民。

（资料来源：新华社）

【李克强会见世界知识产权组织总干事高锐】 2018年8月28日，国务院总理李克强在中南海紫光阁会见来华出席“一带一路”知识产权高级别会议的世界知识产权组织总干事高锐和与会代表。

李克强表示，产权保护是市场经济的基石，保护知识产权是实现创新发展的必然要求。在新一轮科技革命大背景下，在发展中国家经济转型升级过程中，创新日益成为世界各国引领发展的第一动力。保护知识产权，就是保护创新、保护创新人才的热情。

李克强指出，中国作为世界最大的发展中国家，经济正处在提质升级的关键阶段，将采取更为严格的知识产权保护制度，进一步完善相关法律法规。对于侵犯知识产权的行为，一经查实将严厉处罚。我们对内外资企业一视同仁、同等保护，决不允许强制技术转让，发现一起，将依法查处一起。这不仅是中国扩大开放、融入世界经济的需要，也是中国经济实现转型升级、向高质量发展的内在需求。

李克强强调，中国坚定维护多边主义。国家不论大小，都应在国际事务中寻求最大公约数。中方愿继续深化同世界知识产权组织的合作，将一如既往支持世界知识产权组织工作，共同推动构建开放包容、平衡有效的知识产权国际规则，为完善知识产权全球治理体系做出新的贡献。

高锐表示，中国的发展成就令人赞叹。过去40年，中国建立起高水平的知识产权保护制度，把知识产权作为创新和经济发展的驱动力，对中外企业一视同仁。祝贺中国在2018年全球创新指数报告中的排名位置显著提升，相信中国还将不断发展和进步。世界知识产权组织愿进一步深化同中国的合作，维护多边主义，共同应对挑战。

（资料来源：新华社）

【“中国图书展”首次亮相马尼拉国际书展】 2018年9月11日，第39届马尼拉国际书展上午在菲律宾马尼拉SMX会议中心开幕，由中国国家新闻出版署主办、中国教育图书进出口有限公司协办的“中国图书展”在展会上首次亮相，为当地读者和出版商展示了多种当代中国图书。

“中国图书展”共展出11个类别420余册精品图书，包括《习近平谈治国理政》第一卷和第二卷等主题类图书，满足菲律宾当地汉语学习者需求的国际汉语教材，以及反映中国人文社科、科学技术领域最新研究成果的图书。

由中国教育图书进出口有限公司、高等教育出版社、科学出版社等组成的中国出版代表团同菲律宾多家出版社展开版权贸易洽谈，寻求在出版领域进一步加强双边合作与交流。

一年一度的马尼拉国际书展创办于1980年，是菲律宾国内规模最大、持续时间最长的书展。据主办方统计，在为期5天的本届书展期间，有120多家图书出版商参展。

（资料来源：新华网，作者：郑昕　王羽）

【“中国图书展”亮相第20届科伦坡国际书展】 2018年9月21日，第20届科伦坡国际书展在斯里兰卡首都科伦坡的班达拉奈克国际会议大厦拉开帷幕。由中国国家新闻出版署主办、中国教育图书进出口有限公司协办的“中国图书展”在科伦坡国际书展上亮相。

“中国图书展”负责人介绍，为方便斯里兰卡民众更好地感知中国、了解中国、读懂中国，本次“中国图书展”共展出 9 个类别、500 余册精品图书，其中包括《习近平谈治国理政》等展现当代中国发展道路和中国价值观的主题类图书，针对斯里兰卡汉语学习者的僧伽罗语版国际汉语教材教辅类图书，以及反映中国人文社科、科学技术领域最新研究成果的优秀出版物等。

（资料来源：新华社，作者：朱瑞卿　唐璐）

【“中国书架”亮相德语区最大连锁书店】 2018 年 10 月 9 日，“中国书架”项目落户德语区最大连锁书店的签约仪式在德国法兰克福举行。

这一项目由中国图书进出口（集团）总公司（以下简称中图公司）与塔利亚连锁书店合作，落户德国柏林、汉堡、明斯特、曼海姆、德累斯顿以及奥地利维也纳这 6 座城市的 16 家塔利亚书店。首批书架计划于 2019 年 3 月正式推出。

塔利亚在德国、奥地利、瑞士拥有约 300 家连锁书店。此次进入德国和奥地利书店的“中国书架”展销约 100 种、1 000 余册德文版和英文版的中国图书，包括《习近平谈治国理政》第一卷和第二卷（德文版）、《世界是通的：“一带一路”的逻辑》（英文版）和科幻小说《三体》（德文版）等。

“中国书架”是由中国国家新闻出版署主办、中图公司负责实施的重要图书对外推广项目，通过在全球各地的大型书店集中展销反映当代中国政治、经济、文学、艺术等方面的图书，满足当地读者直接、客观、全面了解中国的需求。此前，“中国书架”已先后进入古巴、泰国和白俄罗斯等国家。

（资料来源：《中国新闻出版广电报》，作者：沈忠浩）

【中国主宾国活动在阿尔及尔国际书展掀起“中国热”】 2018 年 11 月 10 日，第 23 届阿尔及尔国际书展闭幕，中国首次作为主宾国参加了本届书展，参展的 2 500 多种精品图书受到当地民众欢迎。

书展期间，40 多家中国出版单位的 100 多名出版人以及莫言、阿来等 6 位中国优秀作家、学者组成的中国代表团与其他国家同行进行了积极交流与洽谈，展示了中国出版业的实力及合作能力。

“中国主题图书展区”展示了近年来出版的 2 500 多种精品图书，其中学习汉语的图书受到热捧，开展前 3 天就全部售罄；阿拉伯文、法文版图书、儿童读物以及具有中国特色的文创产品持续热销。内容丰富充实的中国主宾国展台是整个书展中人气最旺的区域。

中方还以主宾国身份举办了多场专业交流活动。来自中国的作家和学者在书展期间与阿方同行进行了对话；在中国—阿尔及利亚出版文化高峰论坛上，两国出版人围绕合作成果和未来机遇进行了对话；中阿作家、学者、翻译家及出版社代表为阿尔及利亚民众推介中国优秀图书；中阿出版机构就一批中国优秀图书达成版权输出协议，推动相关图书走进阿尔及利亚及其他阿拉伯国家。

（资料来源：新华社，作者：黄灵）

【中欧数字环境下版权保护与许可研讨会在广州举行】 2018 年 12 月 17—18 日，由中国国家版权局与欧盟委员会“IP Key 中国”项目联合主办的中欧数字环境下版权保护与许可研讨会在广州举行。如何有效地规范和提升版权管理，如何加强互联网版权执法等成为研讨会热议的话题。

中宣部版权管理局副局长、国家版权局版权管理司副司长汤兆志在会上表示，迈入 21 世纪的网络时代，版权问题已超越国界成为各国共同面对的挑战和机遇。经过多年的努力与实践，中国在构建版权法律制度体系、不断提高版权司法保护强度、加大版权行政执法监管力度、推动版权产业快速发展、进一步完善版权保护和社会服务体系、不断深入版权国际交流合作等方面取得了一定的进展，也积累了部分经验。据统计，中国网络版权产业持续保持着快速增长趋势，2017 年市场规模达 6 365 亿元，其中，用户付费规模为 3 184 亿元，占比规模 50%，这说明中国版权生态环境在不断优化，国民版权意识在不断提升。2018 年中国迎来改革开放 40 周年，中国坚定推进版权保护和发展的态度一直是明确和坚定的，中国版权制度发展的每个过程都体现着国际合作的成果，我们愿意交流、分享一切有益于版权制度发展的信息、经验和建议。

来自中欧版权管理机构、著作权集体管理组织以及互联网平台、高校的百余名嘉宾，围绕数字环境的版权保护法律框架与执法、管理、治理和许可进行了研讨。

（资料来源：《中国新闻出版广电报》，作者：赖名芳）

【中日网络影视作品著作权保护研讨会在京召开】 2018 年 12 月 18 日，由中国版权协会和日本内容产品海外流通促进机构（CODA）共同主办的中日网络影视作品著作权保护研讨会在北京召开。

研讨会聚焦网络影视作品，尤其是海外影视作品在网络传播中遇到的版权问题，旨在加强国际合作，共同保护影视作品的著作权。

中国高度重视版权保护，国家版权局等四部委连续14年开展的打击侵权盗版“剑网”专项行动，持续把网络影视作品作为保护重点。特别是近年来，中国国家版权局每年都发布数批重点作品版权保护预警名单，众多网络影视作品都在名单保护之列，网络影视版权保护环境得到极大改善。越来越多的民众加入了“支持正版、拒绝盗版”的行列。

在版权保护意识增强带动下，中国网络影视付费用户量和付费规模大幅增长。但同时，网络影视作品中的版权保护新问题不断涌现，特别是随着技术的发展和作品使用形式的增多，海外影视作品在网络传播中遇到的版权问题、国际版权治理与合作等问题亟须得到重视和解决。

研讨会上，CODA总裁后藤健郎介绍了日本目前网络影视作品存在的侵权问题，以及CODA在国际范围内保护网络影视作品著作权的做法和成果。日本电影振兴协会副理事长、日本映像产业交易博览会代首席执行官椎名保介绍了日中影视产业发展和交流的动向。据椎名保介绍，近年来，不仅日本电影输入中国，越来越多的中国电影也开始进入日本市场，电影作品的交易额逐年提升。

围绕会议主题，北京市石景山区人民法院知识产权庭庭长易珍春、咪咕公司法律共享中心维权总监贾洪香、爱奇艺法务经理朱媛、腾讯研究院版权研究中心高级研究员王金凤，分别以《影视作品的侵权现状及司法保护》《网络影视的传播现状及存在问题》《网络影视作品著作权保护》《海外影视作品版权的引进》为题进行了主题演讲。

来自日本影视著作权保护机构、国内各大视频网站、司法及版权相关单位的50余位代表出席了本次研讨会。

（资料来源：《中国新闻出版广电报》，作者：赵新乐）

◆ 产业发展

【2017中国文化产业系列指数发布】 2018年1月19日，由中国人民大学主办、中国人民大学文化科技园和文化产业研究院承办的2017中国文化产业系列指数发布会在北京举行。

发布会上，中国人民大学文化产业研究院战略委员会主任白连永发布了“中国省市文化产业发展指数（2017）”，中国人民大学文化产业研究院执行院长曾繁文发布了“中国文化消费指数（2017）”。“中国省市文化产业发展指数”本次为第8次发布，“中国文化消费指数”本次为第5次发布。两大指数通过对国家相关统计数据及市场调研数据的综合分析，客观反映了中国各省市文化产业发展和文化消费的总体情况、主要特点和未来趋势，对中央和地方政府制定文化产业政策、编制文化产业发展规划具有参考意义。

“中国省市文化产业发展指数（2017）”结果表明，从综合指数排名来看，全国各省市综合指数排名与上年相比有一定幅度的变动。北京凭借文化产业影响力和驱动力的优势，依旧处在第一的位置；上海凭借文化产业的社会影响、市场环境和公共环境的优势，排名第二；湖南通过加大文化资源投入和提升社会影响，排名第七；河北在经济影响和社会影响方面有一定提升，进入全国前十名。综合指数排名前十的省市中，除四川、湖南以外，其余省市都位于东部地区。从数值来看，全国省市文化产业发展指数的均值达到了74.10，比上年的73.71有一定增长，文化产业保持上升发展态势。从增速来看，2017年指数增速略高于2016年指数增速。

三个分指数方面，第一个分指数是生产力指数，排名跟上年相比整体上变化浮动较小，前十名的省市中，除了四川、湖北、河南外，其他均来自东部地区。从增速看，北京、江苏、湖南、湖北、浙江的得分增速分列生产力增长率前五名。

第二个分指数是影响力指数。从排名来看，跟上年相比整体上有一定的变化，东部地区文化产业经济影响和社会影响优势比较明显，前十名的省市中，有七个来自东部沿海发达地区。从增速看，江苏、湖南、山东、河北、北京分列影响力增长率前五名。

第三个分指数是驱动力指数。从排名来看，和上年相比有较多的省份上升幅度较大，比如黑龙江、山东、湖北、陕西、广西等。从增速看，黑龙江、海南、山东、重庆、云南分列增长率前五位。

从2010年到2017年指数的变化来看，中国文化产业发展指数平均值基本呈现正增长的态势。在经历了2010—2011年的高速增长、2012—2014年的稳步增长、2015—2016年的基本稳定之后，2017年文化产业发展指数又再次呈现增长态势。中国文化产业在巩固前一阶段的发展成果之后，继续稳步向前发展。

从区域指数排名的变化来看，2017 年东部省市依旧占据了前十名的大多数席位，但值得注意的是，中西部地区不断有新的省市进入综合指数前十名。2016 年江西、四川两省进入榜单前十名，2017 年四川、湖南两省进入前十名，这样交替进入榜单前十名的状况体现了中西部地区文化产业的快速发展以及未来的发展潜力。

从增长率来看，2017 年增长前十名的省市，东部地区有河北、山东、海南，中部地区有吉林、黑龙江、安徽、湖南、河南，西部地区有陕西、云南，前十名的省市在地理位置上分布比较均衡。这种情况表明：一是中西部地区各省市不断挖掘利用文化资源，激发文化产业发展潜力，促进文化产业发展；二是东部地区的文化产业仍有发展空间。

2010—2013 年变异系数呈现明显的下降趋势，说明中国文化产业发展日趋均衡，2014—2015 年小幅上升，2016 年又出现了下降，到 2017 年又有小幅上升。大体上来看，全国各个省份的文化产业都呈现均衡化发展趋势，但是目前还存在一定程度的不均衡问题。随着中西部地区文化产业持续发展，东部地区文化产业稳定升级，未来文化产业的发展会更加均衡。

“中国文化消费指数（2017）”表明，中国文化消费综合指数持续增长，由 2013 年的 73.7 增至 2017 年的 81.6，年平均增长率为 2.6%。一级指标中，文化消费环境和满意度指数呈稳步上升趋势。其中，文化消费环境指数上升速度最快，年平均增长率为 6.9%。说明这四年中国文化消费环境有了很大改善，文化产品种类不断丰富，质量逐步提升，消费渠道也越来越多样化、便捷化，为居民进行文化消费营造了良好的氛围。

从区域角度看，北京、上海、浙江、广东、天津、江苏、山东的文化消费综合指数连续五年位居全国前十，且这七个省市均位于东部地区。可见，东部地区文化消费整体情况要好于中西部地区。一级指标方面，文化消费意愿、能力、水平、满意度指数的全国前十名省份中，东部地区均占了一半以上。相比中西部地区，东部地区居民收入、消费水平相对较高，更加注重生活质量和精神享受。

从城乡角度看，相比 2016 年，城镇居民文化消费总体情况依然好于农村居民，但是差距明显缩小。具体到一级指标，城乡居民的文化消费环境和满意度指数均有所上升，其中文化消费满意度指数上升明显；农村居民五项分指数均缩小了和城镇居民的差距。

从性别角度看，2017 年男性文化消费综合指数首次超过女性，女性的文化消费综合指数比 2016 年略微降低。一级指标方面，男性除满意度指数外，各项一级指标均略高于女性。和 2016 年相比，女性的文化消费意愿和水平指数有一定程度的下降。

从年龄角度看，和往年一样，26～40 岁居民的文化消费综合指数高于其他年龄段。一级指标方面，18～25 岁居民的文化消费意愿和水平指数最高，表明这一年龄阶段的青年人对文化消费的需求最旺盛，实际发生的文化消费支出也最多，已经成为文化消费的主力军；26～40 岁居民的文化消费能力指数优势比较明显，这是因为这个年龄段群体正当年，收入情况比较好；66 岁以上居民文化消费环境与满意度指数高于其他年龄段。

从学历角度看，和 2016 年一样，不同学历人群的文化消费差异较为明显，其中，本科及以上尤其是研究生以上学历人群的文化消费综合指数相对较高，而且与其他学历人群差距进一步拉大，特别是文化消费意愿、能力和水平指数明显高于其他学历人群。

数据显示，2017 年十大文化产品/服务的消费情况如下：

在国内外文化产品/服务的消费选择上，国内的文化旅游、电影和游戏以及国外的动漫比较受消费者欢迎。和 2016 年相比，2017 年国产电影、动漫和游戏的受欢迎程度都有较大幅度的提升。

在“居民主要消费的文化产品/服务有哪些”这一问题的调查中可以发现，广播电视、电影、图书/报纸/期刊、网络文化活动、文化娱乐活动比较受欢迎。

在十大文化产品/服务的消费支出水平方面，文化娱乐活动、电影、文化旅游、网络文化活动、图书/报纸/期刊排在前五位。和 2016 年相比，2017 年图书/报纸/期刊的支出超过了工艺美术品和收藏品，排进了前五名。

结合居民的文化产品/服务消费意愿支出和实际支出，我们测算文化产品/服务的市场成长空间情况，排名由高到低的顺序依次是文化娱乐活动、电影、网络文化活动、文化旅游、图书/报纸/期刊。其中，2017 年，网络文化活动和文化旅游较 2016 年排名上升，而工艺美术品和收藏品排名则有所下降。

在文化消费补贴方式偏好方面，受访者更倾向于打折卡或一两百元的储值卡两种补贴方式，而返利补贴方式的受欢迎程度明显低于前两种补贴方式。

对于"如果消费者拿到补贴，希望将补贴花在哪儿"这个问题，大多数受访者选择了广播电视、图书/报纸/期刊、电影、文艺演出、文化娱乐活动这几类文化产品。和2016年相比，2017年广播电视和文化娱乐活动的排名有所上升。

（资料来源：中国知识产权资讯网，作者：冯飞）

【《中国互联网络发展状况统计报告》解读内容产业发展】 2018年1月31日，中国互联网络信息中心（CNNIC）在京发布第41次《中国互联网络发展状况统计报告》。截至2017年12月，我国网民规模达7.72亿人，普及率达到55.8%，超过全球平均水平（51.7%）4.1个百分点，超过亚洲平均水平（46.7%）9.1个百分点。尤为值得一提的是，包含网络音乐、网络游戏和网络视频在内的内容产业在2017年迎来全面发展。

报告显示，截至2017年12月，我国网络音乐用户规模达5.48亿人，较上年底增加4 496万人，占网民总数的71.0%。手机网络音乐用户规模达到5.12亿人，较上年底增加4 381万人，占手机网民总数的68.0%。

2017年，我国网络音乐行业格局基本确立，版权竞争和泛娱乐生态融合趋势得到延续，线上线下音乐产业联系更加密切。

从网络音乐行业自身发展来看，版权仍是未来各厂商的长期竞争重点。从网络音乐与其他新生业态的融合发展来看，音乐与社交、短视频的融合有望成为行业未来新的增长点。由于传统网络音乐行业的版权壁垒已经建立，创业者很难在该领域与大型网络音乐集团进行竞争，因此UGC音乐内容和新的展现形式成为行业创新的焦点。在国内，于2016年底上线的音乐短视频社区应用《抖音》在2017年用户规模快速增长，并在11月以10亿美元并购了北美同类产品Musical. ly。

截至2017年12月，我国网络游戏用户规模达到4.42亿人，占网民总数的57.2%，较上年增长2 457万人。手机网络游戏用户规模较上年底明显提升，达到4.07亿人，较上年底增长5 543万人，占手机网民总数的54.1%。

2017年国内网络游戏行业营收规模持续增长，用户游戏类型偏好的变化、精品游戏在海外市场的成功和行业规范化的提升是行业发展的三个主要特点。

从产品类型变化来看，得益于游戏直播的强大宣传能力，新兴的沙盒类射击游戏在2017年取代MOBA游戏成为最受用户喜爱的游戏类型。在PC端，其代表《绝地求生》销量达到2 700万份，成为史上最畅销的游戏；在手机端，应用商店11月下载量最大的前五款游戏中有四款为这类游戏。另外值得注意的是，微信在12月底推出"小游戏"功能，使其有望成为手机端H5游戏的新型入口，并为这类游戏未来的蓬勃发展带来新的机会。

从市场覆盖范围来看，以腾讯、网易、蓝港互动、心动网络为代表的中国游戏厂商在2017年"出海"热情高涨。虽然中国已经超越美国和日本成为全球最大的游戏市场，但国内市场竞争的激烈程度也在不断加剧，使得本土游戏厂商逐渐将下一步增长希望寄托于海外，并将自身优秀的产品经验和运营模式向其他国家输出。一些代表性国产自主研发精品游戏在本土市场获得成功后"试水"欧美和东南亚市场，并于年底获得多个国际性游戏奖项。

从行业监管情况来看，主管部门和游戏厂商在2017年共同致力于规范市场经营行为，在一定程度上降低了不良网络游戏内容可能对未成年用户身心健康造成的危害。2017年2月，腾讯在文化部指导下推出未成年人家长监控体系和健康游戏防沉迷系统，协助家长对未成年子女的游戏账号进行监护，并限制了低龄群体的游戏时长。2017年10月，国家新闻出版广电总局表示《绝地求生》同类游戏中的血腥暴力内容不利于青少年的健康成长，推动国内游戏厂商对于类似游戏内容进行改进，避免了可能产生的不良社会影响。

截至2017年12月，网络视频用户规模达5.79亿人，较上年底增加3 437万人，占网民总数的75.0%。手机网络视频用户规模达到5.49亿人，较上年底增加4 870万人，占手机网民总数的72.9%。

2017年网络视频行业保持良性发展，用户付费能力明显提升。调查数据显示，2017年国内网络视频用户付费比例达到42.9%，相比2016年增长了7.4个百分点，且用户满意度达到55.8%，预计未来仍将保持较高速的增长趋势。从行业自身发展来看，网络视频行业移动化、精品化、生态化进程在2017年得到持续推进。

网络视频移动化发展趋势相比2016年更加明显。从终端设备的使用情况来看，随着大屏手机的普及，手机与电脑、电视、平板电脑等设备收看视频的体验差距明显减小，同时由于手机在私人化、碎片化等方面存在明显优势，使得用户愈发倾向使用手机收看网络视频。从视频类应用的发展情况来看，以《快手》为代表的移动端短视频应用在 2017 年迅猛发展，并吸引了阿里、360、今日头条等大型厂商进入该领域进行布局。

网络视频内容正规化和精品化进程不断推进。在内容正规化方面，国家新闻出版广电总局宣布仅上半年就处理了 155 部违规的网络原创节目，并且未来将坚决杜绝问题节目以“未删节版”或者“删减内容花絮”的名义在网络上播出，以规范行业内容发展。在内容精品化方面，爱奇艺和优酷分别与 Netflix、索尼影视等海外版权方达成内容授权协议，通过引进海外正版视频资源提升自身内容竞争力。

网络视频行业的生态化程度进一步加深。在视频行业内部，搜狐、腾讯、完美、阿里、爱奇艺等厂商均陆续在 2017 年发布了视频内容创作计划或投资视频内容创作机构，通过布局视频内容制作上下游的全产业链，以独家原创内容吸引观众。在视频行业外部，网络视频企业还积极与文学、漫画、电影、游戏等相关内容行业进行联动，生态化平台的整体协同能力和商业价值正在逐步凸显。

（资料来源：中国知识产权资讯网，作者：姜旭）

【中超版权费大幅“缩水”】 2018 年 1 月，围绕中超联赛版权合同期问题，中超联赛有限责任公司与体奥动力体育传播有限公司达成协议，从原先的 5 年延长至 10 年，总价格从原先的 80 亿元增至 110 亿元。虽然合同期延长，但平均每年的版权费却从 16 亿元降至 11 亿元，可谓大幅“缩水”。根据新协议，体奥动力公司前 5 年每年支付 10 亿元，共支付给中超公司版权费用 50 亿元，后 5 年则一共要支付 60 亿元。

此次中超版权合同修改后，2018 赛季到 2020 赛季的版权成本，从 60 亿元下降到 30 亿元，体奥动力公司未来 3 年的运营压力将减少近半。有分析认为，由于年均版权费减少，中超公司可能损失了一些眼前利益，而实际上新协议才是中超长期稳定健康发展的保障。此次新协议的达成，体现了中国足协、中超公司、体奥动力公司之间的合作精神，兼顾了各方的利益，是共赢的结果。

还有专家表示，前两年中国足球市场无论是版权价格，还是球员的转会费，都近乎“天价”，一再突破人们的心理承受力。这种现象不可能一直持续，也与社会发展阶段和足球市场规律严重脱节。版权费的调整，是中国足球市场的一种理性回归。

（资料来源：《工人日报》，作者：刘兵）

【掌阅文学：精品化策略让 40 余位作者年收入过百万】 2018 年 2 月 1 日，掌阅文学在京举行新年媒体沟通会，就 2017 年网络文学发展成果进行总结，并对来年发展计划进行布局。得益于掌阅文学原创精品化策略的推动，2017 年，超过 40 位掌阅文学签约作者在平台的收入超过 100 万元。

（资料来源：中国知识产权资讯网，作者：姜旭）

【腾讯音乐与网易云音乐就网络音乐版权事宜达成合作】 2018 年 2 月 9 日，国家版权局官网宣布，腾讯音乐与网易云音乐就网络音乐版权合作事宜达成一致，相互授权音乐作品，达到各自独家音乐作品数量的 99%以上，并商定进行音乐版权长期合作，同时积极向其他网络音乐平台开放音乐作品授权。

（资料来源：《科技日报》，作者：翟冬冬）

【网易云音乐和阿里音乐达成版权互授合作】 2018 年 3 月 6 日，网易云音乐与阿里音乐共同对外宣布，双方达成音乐版权互相转授权的合作。至此，两大音乐平台的网络音乐版权结构得到进一步完善，用户的视听体验将更加丰富。2018 年春节前，腾讯音乐与网易云音乐在国家版权局的推动下达成版权互授合作，再加上 2017 年 9 月腾讯音乐、阿里音乐达成的版权转授权合作，可以说，至此，腾讯音乐、阿里音乐、网易云音乐这三大音乐平台的音乐版权已共通。

此次网易云音乐与阿里音乐合作，一方面，网易云音乐将天娱、爱贝克思（Avex）、丰华、华研国际等优质音乐版权转授给阿里音乐；另一方面，阿里音乐将滚石、SM、BMG 等优质音乐版权转授给网易云音乐。

随着此次网易云音乐与阿里音乐版权合作的达成，李宗盛、周华健、刘若英、梁静茹、任贤齐、Super Junior、少女时代、EXO、陈小春、彭佳慧等多位主流华语和韩流歌手的歌曲已在网易云音乐全新上线。同时，也意味着阿里音乐旗下虾米音乐除了可以继续使用田馥甄、林宥嘉、S. H. E 等华研国际艺人的歌曲版权外，其用户还可以畅听张惠妹、张雨生、华晨宇、陈翔、滨崎步、幸田来未等艺人的音乐。

此次网易云音乐和阿里音乐的携手合作，目的是希望共同探索音乐平台如何建立起更加良好有效的网络音乐版权授权、合作和运营模式，为广大用户更好地提供音乐作品和服务。

（资料来源：《中国新闻出版广电报》，作者：易云）

【小米音乐与太合音乐达成版权合作】 2018年3月14日，小米音乐宣告正式与太合音乐集团签署合作协议，达成了包括音乐版权、演出票务合作、粉丝运营等全方面合作。该协议的签署预示着小米与太合音乐集团达成战略合作伙伴关系，双方将共同为超过3亿人的小米手机用户提供优质的服务和丰富的内容。

签约太合音乐版权之后，小米手机用户可以通过《小米音乐》APP欣赏近百位国际巨星的音乐作品，包括薛之谦、林俊杰、张韶涵、品冠、许嵩、阿杜、戚薇、刘惜君、金莎、BY2、果味VC、M.I.C男团、徐佳莹、蔡健雅、杨乃文、李健、胡彦斌、谢天笑等歌手。至此，《小米音乐》已经拥有滚石唱片、太合音乐集团等30多家优质唱片公司的歌曲版权。

此次小米音乐与太合音乐集团的合作签署也再一次彰显了小米打造内容生态平台的决心，这也是继2017年小米音乐与华纳音乐、滚石唱片达成版权合作之后的又一重大部署。本次合作不仅能够给小米手机用户提供海量优质的音乐资源，也将为太合音乐集团旗下的众多艺人提供全新的发行渠道，最终实现多方共赢。

（资料来源：中国知识产权资讯网，作者：侯伟）

【网络文学为阅文创造41亿元年收入】 2018年3月19日，阅文集团公布了其上市后的首份年度财务报告，2017年阅文集团总收入达到41亿元，较上一年度的26亿元增长了57.7%，同期毛利由2016年的11亿元增长至2017年的21亿元，经营盈利则由2016年的3 330万元大幅增长至2017年的5.1亿余元。尤为值得一提的是，2017年阅文集团在线阅读收入达到34.2亿余元，版权运营业务收入超过3.66亿元，分别同比增长73.3%和48%。此外，财报还显示，除在线阅读和版权运营两大主营业务的高位增长外，阅文集团还在作品和作者培育、版权海外输出等多个领域实现突破，整合协同效应日益显现。

财报显示，2017年，阅文产品及自营渠道的在线阅读收入达到29.5亿余元，同比增长71.4%。之所以取得如此成绩，得益于阅文集团在丰富原创内容品类、提升用户体验以及拓宽分销渠道等方面所做的努力。为拓宽移动互联网的分销渠道，让优质内容多点触达更广泛的用户群体，阅文集团与OPPO、Vivo、华为等手机制造商合作，预装移动应用程序；继续与股东兼战略伙伴腾讯的合作，在手机QQ、QQ浏览器等多个平台上发布内容；还与百度、搜狗、京东、小米及快猫等第三方平台加强合作，把内容在网络上全面铺开。

为提升用户使用体验、保持用户阅读黏性，阅文集团还加强了技术创新和模式优化，将内容与渠道优势转化为可感知的用户体验升级。除上线作家问答、章节评论等互动新功能外，阅文集团还借力数据分析及人工智能技术，提升旗下产品功能与服务。

财报显示，2017年，阅文集团不仅售出了优质作品的改编权，还加大了对一些作品改编项目的参与程度。通过将文学内容改编成电视剧、网络剧、动画、网络游戏及电影等娱乐形态，有效地延长了文学作品的变现周期。

（资料来源：中国知识产权资讯网，作者：姜旭）

【粤港澳大湾区电影产业中心项目启动】 2018年3月27—28日，在广东佛山召开的2018广东电影年会暨粤港澳大湾区电影产业峰会上，广东省电影行业协会联合粤港澳大湾区11个城市的协会、企业共同筹组粤港澳大湾区电影产业联盟，签署了《粤港澳大湾区电影产业联盟共同宣言》，并启动了粤港澳大湾区电影产业中心项目。

此次峰会是在广东省新闻出版广电局指导和推动下，由广东省电影行业协会举办的，以“深度融合、创新发展”为主题。广东省局提出粤港澳大湾区电影产业的融合发展，在深度上，要从单个项目的合作转向电影全产业链的合作；在创新上，要在合作形式、机制、紧密程度等方面有所突破；在互鉴上，要优势互补、错位发展、互惠互利、共享成果。

围绕粤港澳大湾区电影产业的融合发展，会议邀请专家学者建言献策，其中制定立足粤港澳、面向东南亚的战略发展目标，聚集整合三地的创作、制片、发行等电影人才，探索电影衍生品尤其是电影主题乐园的发展思路，建立电影的音乐版权和网络版权的交易平台等成为与会者热议的话题。

第二批广东艺术电影放映联盟的10个成员单位也在会上亮相，该联盟自2017年成立以来，成员单位已发展到20个，为粤港澳大湾区出品的电影提供了一个良好的放映平台。

（资料来源：《中国新闻出版广电报》，
作者：魏晓薇）

【小霸王公司宣布重新回归游戏机市场】 2018年4月5日，小霸王公司发布版权公告，称决心正式重新回归游戏机市场，大力开发更加重视玩家体验的游戏主机与游戏平台，并将充分尊重知识产权尤其是游戏版权作为自己的企业战略。

小霸王公司强调，为稳步推进发展正版游戏、高端游戏机的战略规划，并配合计划中的小霸王品牌新一代主机和相关平台升级，公司正在计划着手停止并撤销对第三方生产商的游戏机生产授权，努力确保在未来避免出现装有未授权游戏的游戏机的销售。

这意味着，此前以“小霸王游戏机”名义销售的仿制游戏机产品，将从市面上消失。而“红白机”游戏等未授权游戏产品也将不复存在。

（资料来源：《北京商报》，作者：金朝力）

【辽宁出版集团与咪咕数媒开展战略合作】 2018 年 4 月 12 日，辽宁出版集团与咪咕数媒在浙江杭州签署战略合作协议，双方将围绕优质内容资源全面展开全媒联合开发、传播渠道互通等深度合作，在数字阅读、听书业务、纸质图书出版等领域开发出更多精准而优质的产品，并通过渠道融合、粉丝互动、大数据挖掘等模式开拓更大市场，充分实施优势互补、资源共享，打造跨界融合发展新模式。

根据协议，辽宁出版集团将全面开放图书、优质 IP、在线教育资源、产业链协同能力，与咪咕数媒的市场渠道、营销资源、品牌资源等进行融合联动，释放优势互补的乘数效应。双方将发挥各自拥有的国家级出版融合发展重点实验室的技术优势，围绕协同创新进行更深度的合作。

辽宁出版集团董事长兼党委书记杨建军在致辞中表示，辽宁出版集团一是要用最好的图书资源、最核心的内容资源，拥抱咪咕数媒的市场渠道、营销资源和公司品牌翅膀，扩大优秀出版内容的传播力；二是要围绕技术创新和内容创新，以大数据分析为基准，与咪咕联合打造精准的融合出版产品和平台型项目；三是既有线上联动，又有线下牵手，多维发力，不断巩固双方的战略伙伴关系。

咪咕数字传媒有限公司总经理张燕鹏表示，咪咕数媒愿和辽宁出版集团建立长期稳固的联合出版合作，积极致力于打造出版精品力作，以多媒体、多渠道、多形式扩大优秀出版物的社会影响力，积极致力于全民阅读活动的开展，开拓建立文化出版领域的创新性业务合作新天地。

（资料来源：《中国新闻出版广电报》，作者：王坤宁）

【网易云音乐与索尼音乐达成深度合作】 2018 年 4 月 20 日，网易云音乐与索尼音乐在京达成深度合作，双方将共同探索线下 live 业务合作。这也是网易云音乐“云豆现场”上线后，首次成规模、深度合作的音乐厂牌。

2013 年 4 月上线的网易云音乐凭借高质量的乐评氛围、海量的歌单内容、精准的个性化推荐等优势，成为广受年轻用户喜爱的音乐平台，而世界三大唱片公司之一的索尼音乐旗下拥有众多杰出音乐作品，此次达成深度合作，基于双方对线下 live 业务前景的一致看好。网易云音乐副总裁丁博表示，音乐不仅是纯粹的线上听觉享受，优秀的作品内容、舞台表演的张力以及现场观众的呼应，更能展现最真实、最全面的音乐。在接下来的一年中，双方将联合推出 10 场“云豆现场”，并在音乐作品宣发、海外市场拓展等方面展开深层次和多样化的合作，集中双方优势共同推进线下 live 市场的前进。

（资料来源：《中国新闻出版广电报》，作者：李淼）

【我国网络版权产值突破 6 000 亿元】 2018 年 4 月 23 日，国家版权局网络版权产业研究基地在京发布《中国网络版权产业发展报告（2018）》。报告显示，我国网络版权产业继续保持快速增长趋势，2017 年中国网络版权产业的市场规模为 6 365 亿元，较 2016 年增长 27.2%。

该报告依据世界知识产权组织关于版权产业的界定，将网络核心版权产业界定为依托版权保护，依赖于网络技术和应用，完全地从事创造、生产与制造、表演、传播与展出、发行与销售内容产品的产业。

报告指出，传统文化产业正在积极拥抱互联网，加快数字转型。如数字阅读平台培育了用户的在线阅读习惯，电子竞技的飞速发展盘活了赛事推广、票务、赛事经纪等线下版权业务，移动 K 歌模式正在向线下延伸等。

报告显示，2017 年，中国网络视频用户付费市场规模为 218 亿元，同比增长翻番，预计未来两年仍会保持超过 60%的高速增长；网络游戏市场规模达 2 355 亿元，同比增长 32%；网络音乐市场规模达 175 亿元，同比增长 22%；网络新闻资讯市场规模达 305 亿元，同比加速增长超过 40%，其中移动端新闻收入占比超过 75%，主要收入来源是原生信息流广告和头部品牌广告；数字阅读市场规模突破 100 亿元，同比增长 31.1%。

报告称，网络直播打赏模式异军突起，拉动了整体市场规模的增长。2017 年，中国网络直播用户规模达 4.2 亿人，产业市场规模近 400 亿元，成为仅次于游戏用户付费的产业。短视频产业也实现迅猛增长，用户规模突破 4.1 亿人，同比增长 115%。短视频市场用户流量与广告价值爆发，预计 2020 年短视频市场规模将超过 350 亿元。

（资料来源：新华社，作者：史竞男　周圆）

【中国版权产业占 GDP 比重达 7.33%】 2018 年 4 月 23 日，国家版权局举办的 2018 年版权宣传周新闻发布会透露，2016 年中国版权产业的行业增加值为 54 551.46 亿元人民币，同比增长 9.0%，占 GDP 比重为 7.33%。

中国新闻出版研究院副院长范军对 2016 年中国版权产业经济贡献调研结果进行了解读。2006—2016 年，中国版权产业行业增加值持续攀高，从 13 489.33 亿元人民币增长到 54 551.46 亿元人民币，占 GDP 的比重也从 6.39%提高至 7.33%，提高了 0.94 个百分点。从增速上看，中国版权产业行业增加值名义增长速度整体上高于 GDP 的增长速度。特别是版权产业中最具代表性的核心版权产业发展迅速，在版权产业中的比重显著提高，其行业增加值在全部版权产业中的比重从 2006 年的 48%提高至 2016 年的 62%，成为推动中国版权产业发展的主要力量，反映出中国版权产业创新能力和核心竞争力的增强。

此外，中国版权产业除了产业规模有所扩大，还在推动社会就业、促进外贸出口方面发挥了积极作用。2006—2016 年，中国版权产业的城镇单位就业人数从 762.92 万人增长至 1 672.45 万人，占全国城镇单位就业总人数的比重也从 6.52%增长到 9.35%；商品出口额也从 1 492.62 亿美元增长至 2 416.74 亿美元。

（资料来源：中国新闻出版广电网，作者：赖名芳）

【《2018 全球音乐产业报告》发布】 2018 年 4 月 24 日，国际唱片业协会（IFPI）在英国伦敦发布《2018 全球音乐产业报告》。报告数据显示，2017 年全球录制音乐行业总收入达 173 亿美元，比上年增长 8.1%。报告认为，由于中国政府加大版权监管力度，以及唱片公司、权利人的共同努力，中国在版权保护方面发生了重大转变。中国音乐市场生态环境的进一步优化，吸引了国际唱片公司投入巨资。

报告称，全球音乐市场已连续 3 年实现增长。其中，流媒体是收入增长的主要动力，其占全球录制音乐总收入的 38.4%。2017 年数字音乐收入首次占到全球音乐总收入的一半以上，达 54%。特别是中国音乐产业总收入同比增长 35.3%，流媒体音乐收入增长 26.5%。报告认为，中国对版权价值认识的提升和版权保护力度的加大，都促使音乐产业发生了重大转变。

报告还提到了腾讯公司与网易公司在音乐版权合作方面签署的协议，称这份协议加快了中国网络音乐产业向更具有市场竞争力的方向发展的步伐，因为腾讯公司在更早就已将音乐版权转授给阿里音乐、太合音乐、唱吧、苹果等公司。一些国际知名音乐人也同样看好中国市场。环球唱片公司市场拓展执行副总裁亚当·格兰尼特（Adam Granite）分析道："现在中国音乐市场的发展不仅引人注目，还机会很多，让人不可能不兴奋。"华纳音乐亚洲区总裁西蒙·罗布森（Simon Robson）表示，国际唱片公司很愿意在中国投入巨资，因为目前中国不仅是国际艺人的市场，更是音乐消费的地方。腾讯音乐娱乐集团副总裁吴伟林分析认为，目前中国音乐产业发展又快又好，得益于版权保护环境的极大改善、使用者对音乐价值认识的提升，特别是中国本土艺人推出了很多高质量的音乐作品。

（资料来源：《中国新闻出版广电报》，作者：赖名芳）

【磨铁动漫在杭打造"超级漫画家计划"】 2018 年 4 月 26 日，北京磨铁图书有限公司在浙江杭州举行发布会，宣布旗下磨铁（杭州）控股有限公司（以下简称磨铁动漫）正式成立，并重磅发布"超级漫画家计划"，为优秀漫画人才提供包括创作、后台服务、出版、流量、衍生及资金支持在内的全产业链服务。

磨铁动漫在杭州提供 3 000 平方米的办公空间，创立磨铁衡次元创作空间，宣布与有狐文化联合打造杭州漫画创作出版平台，并推出"超级漫画家计划"。有狐文化创始人、漫画家郭斯特在主题宣讲中表示，"超级漫画家计划"设置了 5 000 万元的扶持基金，在 5 年内达成出版 1 000 本书，推出 10 部以上动画、10 部以上影视，以及实现海外授权推广的目标，全方位服务漫画人才，助力动漫行业发展。

（资料来源：《中国新闻出版广电报》，作者：李婧璇）

【酷狗苏州音乐产业孵化基地落成】 2018 年 4 月 27 日，由国内互联网音乐服务商酷狗音乐打造的产业孵化基地，正式落户苏州姑苏·69 阁文化创意产业园。

这是酷狗继南宁、成都、重庆、长春后，线下布局的第五个音乐众创孵化平台。基地将集音乐训练、直播、创意孵化等服务于一体，为苏州热爱音乐的创业者们打造一站式创新培训服务，激发地方音乐人才产出。

酷狗音乐产业孵化基地落户苏州，旨在引入当地音乐人才，搭建更多优质音乐内容的输出平台。酷狗致力于原创音乐内容孵化，线下布局主流城市，打造优质健全的音乐孵化基地，为音乐人提供全方面包装；线上打通酷狗音乐、酷狗直播、5sing 原创音乐基地，为音乐人增加曝光机会。

（资料来源：《中国新闻出版广电报》，作者：佚名）

【一批直播和短视频网站开展自查自纠】 自国家新闻出版广电总局针对网络视频行业存在的突出问题进行深入整改以来，一批社会直播和短视频网站主动响应管理要求，开展自查自纠，进一步深度清理了网络空间的精神毒品、垃圾和糟粕，提升了责任意识，强化了管理措施。

微博、秒拍、好看视频、好兔视频、快视频、虎牙、斗鱼等短视频和直播网站以及腾讯视频、优酷、爱奇艺等综合性视频网站，纷纷响应管理要求，组建专项清查团队，集中对涉黄、格调低俗、宣扬暴力、恶搞经典、歪曲历史、非法剪辑拼接等问题节目进行清理，共计自查清理下线问题音视频节目 150 余万条，封禁违规账户 4 万余个，关闭直播间 4 512 个，封禁主播 2 083 个，拦截问题信息 1 350 多万条。

在主动清理问题节目的同时，各家网站均重视和加强了审核管理长效机制建设。有的网站新增完善了涉及恶搞经典、儿童邪典和相关有害敏感信息关键词库 8 800 余条，建立了有害视频样本库，提高了问题节目的排查能力，遏制了问题节目的再次传播。有的定期发布不良信息自查通告，公布下架节目名单和处罚账号，公开不良内容举报电话，鼓励社会监督。有的升级账号管理措施，将黑名单与身份证、手机号信息挂钩，并应用人脸识别技术进行用户认证。有的建立红色经典节目库对节目源进行保护。有的新建正能量内容池进行首屏优先推荐。有的制定增加了公序良俗审核标准和未成年人保护防控手段。

（资料来源：《中国新闻出版广电报》，作者：刘蓓蓓）

【中影股份与甘肃文化机构开展战略合作】 2018 年 5 月 8 日，中国电影股份有限公司、兰州电影制片厂有限责任公司、甘肃电视台文化影视频道在甘肃兰州签署战略合作协议。三方将通过推广实施“中影影视频道营销平台”项目，在影视剧多媒体的发行、出版、版权、广告、宣传等营销领域开展业务合作，积极为甘肃省各级电视台、网络媒体提供以电影节目为主的各类影视节目。

据中国电影股份有限公司中影营销有限公司总经理刘树森介绍，中影合作剧场在甘肃电视台文化影视频道的落地，有利于推进中影股份和甘肃电视台资源互联互通、共同打造战略平台，有利于发掘经济新增长极、保持行业的领先优势，有利于宣传中国电影，互利共赢。目前，中影合作剧场已经在全国 72 家电视台落地，其中包括 11 家省级频道和 9 家省会城市频道。

据介绍，通过在甘肃电视台文化影视频道周末晚间黄金时段开辟《中影剧场》栏目，大时段、大手笔播出国内外优质、经典的电影剧目，将为甘肃观众带来高端的视听享受。三方还将充分发挥各自优势，大力推广“中影影视频道营销平台”项目，提升战略协同层次和水平，为甘肃影视文化产业发展带来更多机遇。

（资料来源：《中国新闻出版广电报》，作者：田野）

【索尼收购百代音乐出版公司】 2018 年 5 月 22 日，索尼公司与穆巴达拉投资公司达成协议，将斥资 23 亿美元收购该公司旗下的百代音乐出版公司（EMI）60％的股权。业内人士分析，此次收购后，连同全资拥有的音乐出版公司在内，索尼公司总计拥有超过 230 万首音乐作品版权，将有望超过环球唱片，成为全球最大的音乐版权公司。

索尼公司总裁兼首席执行官吉田宪一郎表示，过去几年，在付费订阅的流媒体服务增长推动下，音乐产业已经复苏。在娱乐领域，索尼公司专注于打造强大的版权组合，将 EMI 纳入索尼家族，有助于保持索尼在音乐出版业的地位，对于公司的发展具有里程碑式的特殊意义。未来 3 年，索尼公司将在音乐、影视、网络游戏等重点领域加强直接面向消费者的服务和内容建设，提高内容的质量和数量。

（资料来源：《中国知识产权报》，作者：孙芳华）

【腾讯设 1 亿元基金保护原创】 2018 年 5 月 28 日，腾讯 IP 衍生品生态平台——“鹅漫 U 品”上线，并面向多个领域开展合作，猫眼、奥飞娱乐成为首批合作伙伴。同时，发起衍生品行业正版化及建立行业质检标准的倡议，并宣布设立行业原创项目基金1亿元，用以推动行业健康发展。会上，鹅漫U品也推出了独立的APP以及小程序。

经过一年的孵化，鹅漫U品已经成为一站式衍生品生态平台，拥有设计、开发、生产、仓配、商城、用户流量及客户服务等七大业务能力，拥有超过200个海内外核心IP正版授权。鹅漫U品将通过系列扶持计划和服务，为用户和市场提供更好的衍生品服务，推动行业良性转型，助力中国文化产业发展。

腾讯公司副总裁殷宇表示，在鹅漫U品中，创意者、周边制造商、用户之间将通过直接互动刺激更多作品的生产，鹅漫U品将通过IP周边成为粉丝和其喜爱的IP之间的连接器。

（资料来源：《中国新闻出版广电报》，作者：张明晓）

【方正电子与10家企业签订字体授权协议】 2018年5月29日，在第五届中国（北京）国际服务贸易交易会（以下简称京交会）上，北京北大方正电子有限公司举行了方正字体授权签约仪式，与正邦创意（北京）品牌科技股份有限公司等10家企业现场签约，推广中文字库正版使用。

此次签约仪式上，正邦创意（北京）品牌科技股份有限公司、北京盟享加信息技术有限公司、上海友拓公关顾问有限公司、北京世纪好未来教育科技有限公司、北京绿伞科技有限公司等分别与方正电子签署字库授权书。主办方希望通过此次签约来推进字库正版化，提升大众的知识产权保护意识，同时希望借助京交会平台推动中文字库国际化，向全世界展示和输出中国汉字文化。

（资料来源：《中国知识产权报》，作者：窦新颖）

【腾讯内容开放平台对企鹅号版权保护系统整体升级】 2018年6月7日，腾讯内容开放平台对企鹅号版权保护系统整体升级，为平台原创作者提供全流程维权服务。无论图文类原创作者，还是短视频原创作者，可以通过平台提供的“电子化授权”“24小时全网监测”“一键维权”服务，授权平台对盗版侵权行为进行维权。即日起，上述功能将对原创作者持续开放公测。

腾讯内容开放平台一直以来鼓励原创，保护原创。此次版权保护升级，真正解决了原创作者授权难、监测难、维权难的痛点，成为首个采用自媒体电子化授权—监测—维权为原创作者提供一站式维权服务的平台。

（资料来源：中国知识产权资讯网，作者：姜旭）

【阅文集团举办IP生态大会】 2018年6月18日，阅文集团在上海举办一年一度的阅文IP生态大会，这场以“合火”为主题的IP大会，吸引了包括万达、腾讯等在内的影漫游出版等新文创上下游领域的数百家厂商齐聚。会上，阅文集团重申了其IP核心战略“IP共营合伙人”制度，并展示了“合火”的深度、广度、精度上如何迎来升级，将“IP共营合伙人”制度推向“生态化”。

阅文集团由腾讯文学与原盛大文学于2015年3月整合而成。经过多年的积累和发展，如今的阅文集团已经是中国最大的数字阅读平台和文学IP培育平台。旗下包括QQ阅读、起点中文网等业界知名品牌，拥有1 000余万部作品储备，近700万名作者，覆盖200多种原创内容品类。

如何处理海量的IP？最初，阅文集团也像其他公司那样，做着“一锤子”买卖，即把IP销售出去，生意就算做完了。但很快阅文集团就意识到，在这种模式下IP的价值并没有得到最大限度的开发，尤其对那些有潜力的IP来说更是一种巨大的资源浪费。

2016年，阅文集团推出“IP共营合伙人”制度，将包括作家、版权方、影漫游等开发商、投资方等在内的产业链各端的不同合作方即合伙人纳入同一体系，围绕IP不同形态不同阶段的衍生开发协同合作，希望在这一模式的助推下，让IP开发真正成为全产业的共赢。

制度落地两年已初见成效。2017年阅文平台共对100余部作品进行了IP授权改编，合作伙伴超过200个。阅文集团以参投、出品、联合开发的形式参与了多部IP影视剧的开发，如《庆余年》《黄金瞳》《你和我的倾城时光》《国民老公》《将夜》《武动乾坤》《择天记》《斗破苍穹》等。

2017年经阅文集团改编作品累积全网观看量达880亿次，其中自制网文改编动漫的成绩尤为亮眼。《斗破苍穹》动画第一季全网播放量超15亿次，取得年度国产3D动画播放量第一。《全职高手》动画第一季全网播放量突破12亿次，取得年度国产2D动画播放量第一。2018年5月收官的《全职高手》动画特别篇播放量也轻松突破3亿次。

大会现场，阅文集团公布了覆盖多元品类的数十个IP项目：与京剧艺术“梅派”传承人梅玮共同发起“梨园计划”项目，试水运作中国传统文化IP；与知名影星刘德华旗下梦造者公司携手，开发潜力 IP“神藏”；与达达影业、可为互娱、万达影视、梦造者等合伙人联合开发“CMFU 学园”系列、“兵者为王”、“斗战狂潮”、“神藏”等。阅文集团朝着合伙人制度的 IP“生态化”开发目标再接再厉。

阅文集团高级副总裁罗立表示，未来，阅文集团将以开放、共生、共赢的理念继续优化“IP 共营合伙人”制度。在广度上，不仅要打通影视、动漫、游戏、周边、音乐等不同的内容形态，而且要打破文创产业边界，将 IP 运营至旅游、餐饮、快消品、主题公园等更多实体经济领域；在深度上，推出品质与口碑兼具的标杆性作品；在精度上，将依托对用户的大数据分析以及专业的内容运作团队，满足更多垂直用户的直接需要。

据介绍，阅文集团的“全职高手”IP 运营已迈出了探索性的一步，与麦当劳、美年达等品牌的成功合作，将这一 IP 的二次元人气引向了三次元消费。由人气偶像杨洋主演的电视剧版《全职高手》和动画大电影项目也已启动，将陆续和粉丝见面。

“对 IP 升级的推动，需要更加系统、长线的规划。系统，源自更全面的合作；长线，则源自更广泛的链接。”阅文集团联席首席执行官吴文辉在大会上如是说。网络文学正成为中国文创产业在世界舞台上的一张新名片，而要将这张名片转化为实实在在的商业价值，仍有赖于“IP 共营合伙人”制度的持续深耕。

（资料来源：《中国新闻出版广电报》，作者：金鑫）

【网络大电影市场正向院线电影看齐】 2018 年 6 月 20 日，中国电影出版社推出《2018 中国电影产业研究报告》（以下简称《报告》），就网络大电影 2017 年的表现做了详细分析。

《报告》显示，我国 2017 年上线的网络大电影共 1 973 部，在各大视频网站上创造点击量总计 79.46 亿次，较 2016 年的 209.84 亿次的点击量下降 62.13%，平均每部网络大电影的点击量为 402.74 万次，较 2016 年的 956.86 万次下降了 57.91%。《报告》认为，这一现象的主要原因是各大平台数据统计系统规范化、市场去泡沫化，虚假“刷量”的行为得到了遏制。

2017 年，哪几家视频平台处于领先地位？《报告》指出，爱奇艺 2017 年上映网络大电影数量为 1 311 部，取得了 45.3 亿次的播放量，占市场份额 57.01%，继续处于第一梯队。位列第二梯队的是腾讯视频和优酷土豆，搜狐和乐视则处于第三梯队。第二梯队和第三梯队所占的市场份额总计为 42.92%。

针对爱奇艺独占市场鳌头的情况，《报告》认为，主要是独播内容占据了绝对优势。由于独播的商业回报率远高于非独家影片，因此爱奇艺等平台多以独播作为差异化竞争的主要策略。比如，爱奇艺的 5 部独播影片《斗战胜佛》《陈翔六点半之废话少说》《超级大山炮之夺宝奇兵》《降龙大师》《星游记之风暴法米拉》，分别是 2017 年度播放量排名前十位中的第三、第四、第八、第九、第十，爱奇艺也因此被认为是最大赢家。

哪些观众喜欢观看网络大电影？对于这个问题，《报告》在参照院线电影占比后得出的结论是：男性喜欢看屏，女性喜欢走进影院。

《报告》列出以下数字：2017 年观看爱奇艺网络大电影的男性观众占 66%，虽然较 2016 年的 70%有所下降，但与中国网民中 52.4%为男性的比例相比，仍可认为网络大电影更受男性观众喜爱。同样，观看腾讯视频网络大电影的男性观众也不少，占比 72%。

相比男性观众，《报告》认为女性观众更喜欢走进电影院。《报告》指出，喜欢看网络大电影的女性占 37.64%、男性占 62.36%；喜欢看院线电影的女性占 58.6%、男性占 41.4%。

《报告》认为，网络大电影观众群体以年轻人为主，院线电影观众群体则年龄偏大。比如，2017 年爱奇艺的网络大电影观众构成比是：30 岁（含）以下占 81%，而腾讯视频这一年龄段的观众比例更高，达 84%。不过，2017 年 31 岁（含）以上的网络大电影观众和 2016 年相比有增多趋势。35～44 岁的网络大电影观众占 16%，而这一年龄段的院线电影观众为 10.4%。45 岁及以上的网络大电影观众占 3.5%，而这一年龄的院线电影观众为 2.5%。

值得关注的是，《报告》对观众的学历也进行了分析，比如，腾讯网络大电影观众学历构成比例是：小学占 7%，初中占 34%，高中占 18%，大专占 8%，本科及以上占 33%。

《报告》还借助艾漫数据指出，网络大电影观众所在城市占比前 20 位依次为：北京、上海、广州、深圳、成都、杭州、苏州、武汉、重庆、枣庄、天津、南京、西安、郑州、长沙、济南、青岛、温州、东莞、福州。

（资料来源：《中国新闻出版广电报》，作者：章红雨）

【阿里大鱼号合作法国希帕图片社　为创作者提供世界杯高清版权图片】 2018 年 6 月 26 日，阿里大文娱旗下内容创作服务平台大鱼号宣布与世界四大图片社之一——法国希帕图片社（SIPA）达成合作。世界杯期间，优质原创大鱼号创作者可以从编辑后台获取希帕图片社提供的正版高清世界杯图片素材。

作为 2018 年世界杯一手资讯首选平台，UC 已经从央视获得了世界杯相关短视频版权，能够第一时间把现场最新鲜的赛况、集锦和花絮送到用户面前。此次通过与希帕图片社的合作，大鱼号平台从生产侧赋能，让创作者们能够获取正版高质图片进行创作。同时，UC 将对大鱼号创作的高品质原创图文内容进行加权分发，以满足用户对世界杯精彩内容的多样需求。

希帕图片社每天为全球 80 个国家传送 8 000～10 000 张图片。世界杯期间，希帕图片社平均每日更新图片 1 000 多张，总计更新量 4 万张，包括球队情况时效图、赛事报道时效图、赛场内外花絮图以及围绕世界杯的世界各地周边图片等。体育赛事图片版权管理严格，与希帕图片社合作后，大鱼号解决了围绕世界杯这一顶级流量 IP 进行内容创作的“图荒”痛点。达成合作起的整个世界杯期间，大鱼号平台内原创优质体育账号可以在编辑后台看到世界杯素材入口，点击入口打开弹窗后，通过关键词搜索图片并插入正文，即可发布文章。

创作者内容能够从大鱼号一点接入、多点分发到优酷、UC、土豆、淘票票、虾米等多个用户入口。

此前，大鱼号与视觉中国集团达成战略合作。视觉中国集团向大鱼号平台开放正版图片等全部自有内容及获得合法授权的内容。阿里大鱼号为内容创作者提供丰富内容创作素材的支持。此次与希帕图片社合作，大鱼号在从内容层面赋能创作者的同时，继续推动世界杯的内容创作正版化。

（资料来源：央广网）

【腾讯音乐娱乐 TMC 为国产音乐与国际交流架起桥梁】 “得益于中国政府等有关部门持续打击侵权盗版、加大版权保护力度，中国的音乐产业持续发展，行业产值逐年提升。越来越多的国外音乐公司和从业者将目光放到中国市场。我们愿与中国音乐从业者一起把中国优质音乐作品带到全球各地，也愿意把全球音乐作品版权引进到中国市场。”2018 年 6 月 28 日，在 Tencent Music Connects（TMC）全球音乐产业峰会上，环球音乐集团高级副总裁乔恩·德沃金（Jon Dworkin）的演讲赢得场下阵阵掌声。在为期一天的峰会中，来自全球 20 多个国家和地区的音乐业界从业者，围绕“China is Now”主题，就全球范围内的音乐交流与合作、如何打造优质音乐作品、如何挖掘音乐版权价值等多个热点话题进行了探讨。

对于乔恩·德沃金的感受，腾讯音乐娱乐集团副总裁吴伟林表示深有感触：“我很自豪可以看到整个中国音乐产业在过去几年有非常良性的发展，这表现在多个方面，比如人们意识到版权保护的重要性，音乐平台的正版付费用户规模越来越大，社会公众为正版付费的意愿越来越高等。这既得益于国家的大力支持，也受益于业界伙伴的共同努力。在此背景下，越来越多的全球音乐合作伙伴，愿意同中国的音乐从业者合作，这既表明中国的音乐市场有无限的潜力，也表明国际合作伙伴对中国音乐版权保护的肯定。我们希望在全球先锋观点的碰撞中共同勾勒出关于音乐的美好未来，让世界听见蛰伏已久的大国声响。”

据悉，TMC 全球音乐产业峰会由中国演出行业协会、中国音乐著作权协会和中国音像与数字出版协会音乐产业促进工作委员会担任指导单位，中国唱片集团有限公司提供战略支持。“China is Now”主题聚焦中国音乐，充分发挥中国主场优势，TMC 也就此议题，以“中国正发生”“世界看中国”“中国正潮流”三大板块，与全球音乐领袖进行探讨。来自环球音乐、华纳音乐、索尼音乐、YG 娱乐、贝阁唱片、AEG、Live Nation、中国唱片集团、安谱 AI 音乐、谭旋音乐工作室、草台回声、战马时代、中国传媒大学等的海内外业界领袖畅所欲言，就音乐出版、文化“出海”、未来潮流等焦点话题带来前沿观点，打开中国音乐与世界交流之门。

据主办方相关负责人介绍，伴随中国音乐市场的崛起，TMC 所聚焦的“China is Now”话题其实正是全球关注的话题，在前沿的产业讨论与激烈的中西碰撞中，音乐文化所承载的衍生价值也将得到扩张，并影响至更多层面。而随着北京首站的圆满落幕，TMC 将陆续在新加坡、上海、成都和深圳 4 站开启，通过对不同议题的研究探讨，探索属于中国音乐产业的新时代。

（资料来源：中国知识产权资讯网，作者：姜旭）

【上海发布《2017 上海游戏出版产业数据调查报告》　多措并举保障游戏产业健康发展】 2018 年 7 月 10 日，2018 上海游戏精英峰会暨游戏出版产业报告发布会在沪举行，《2017 上海游戏出版产业数据调查报告》（以下简称《报告》）正式发布。《报告》显示，2017 年上海游戏出版产业仍维持较高的增长速度，上海近年来针对游戏产业所设立的相关政策与监管措施，成为推动上海游戏产业快速发展的主要原因。

《报告》显示，2017 年上海网络游戏销售收入约为 683.8 亿元，同比增长 21.1%，在目前销售收入基数较大的状况下依然能维持较高的增长速度。其中，自研产品、海外产品、移动游戏细分领域等多个方面表现突出。具体表现为：上海自主研发网络游戏销售收入约为 534.8 亿元，约占全国自主研发网络游戏销售收入的 38.3%；移动游戏销售收入约为 334.5 亿元，同比增长 69.1%。在海外产品引入上，2017 年上海共有 111 款进口游戏通过国家新闻出版广电总局审批，占全国游戏进口审查总数的 23.6%，海外引进游戏销售收入占比达到 21.8%，成为上海网络游戏销售收入的重要组成部分。尤其值得一提的是，2017 年上海网络游戏海外销售收入约为 13.457 亿美元，同比增长约 73.6%，达到历史最高点。

《报告》分析，2017 年上海出台《关于加快本市文化创意产业创新发展的若干意见》，明确强化文创产业发展决心，上海将建设全球动漫游戏原创中心，对游戏产业所设立的相关政策成为上海推动游戏产业快速发展的主要原因之一。2017 年上海新设立文创产业基金数百亿元，开通国产网络游戏属地管理“绿色通道”，出台《上海市文化市场黑名单管理办法（试行）》等数项监管措施，保障了上海游戏产业健康发展。此外，上海拥有 1 600 余家游戏企业，千余家游戏企业的聚集也带来了全球化发展契机及产业集群化效应。

（资料来源：《中国新闻出版广电报》，作者：金鑫）

【苏宁与咪咕联合运营体育内容】 2018 年 7 月 11 日，苏宁宣布与咪咕公司达成战略合作，双方将在赛事直播、内容制作、智能硬件、大数据应用、体育设施等多领域展开全产业链合作。并将联手打造咪咕- PP 体育联运平台，PP 体育的丰富赛事内容将在咪咕客户端等产品内呈现。

着眼未来，苏宁与咪咕共同启动了“451”计划。“4”是指 4K，依托苏宁的 4K 高清实验室和中国移动超高清视频实验室，中国移动咪咕作为中国超高清视频产业联盟的组长单位，将和苏宁一起通过视频内容与前沿科技的互相搭配，全面推进 4K 内容的生产和供给。“5”是指 5G，苏宁也将积极加入 5G 多媒体创新联盟（5MII），与咪咕一起结合 5G 特点开展多媒体技术创新和应用创新，致力于为广大用户带来全新的产品和服务体验。“1”是指双方希望通过这样的合作打造一个全新的体育生态。

这些都将为双方合作的体育赛事这样的 IP 内容运营带来更大空间，包括全场景呈现、线上与线下的互动等，也推动智能硬件和终端的全面升级，使得虚拟现实等技术广泛应用成为可能，为用户带来随时随地全沉浸的颠覆式体育娱乐体验。双方将立足 4K 标准、5G 技术进行广泛合作，形成内容、技术、场景的完整产学研用链条。

“咪咕作为运营商的新媒体板块，可以提供品质更高清、更稳定可靠的网络服务给用户；而苏宁体育是国内首个集齐英超、西甲、德甲、意甲、法甲等欧洲足球五大联赛版权的传媒平台，同时拥有欧冠、中国之队、中超、亚冠、WWE 等重量级体育赛事版权，并拥有庞大的体育内容生产团队；双方的联手水到渠成。”苏宁体育集团副总裁米昕透露，“我们希望未来双方能在 5G 领域共同制定行业标准，成为三网融合的经典案例。”

“众所周知，目前苏宁体育拥有几乎所有顶级足球赛事的版权，是国内极为专业的互联网足球平台。而世界杯开赛至今，通过咪咕视频观看世界杯赛事的用户，每天也都超过了 1 亿人次。‘451’计划，以咪咕与苏宁合作的顶级赛事内容为内容基础，以 4K+5G 进行超前的产业布局，利用 AI 和大数据技术为产业赋能，我们将开创一个全新的体育生态。”咪咕公司副总经理颜忠伟在谈到“451”计划启动时表示，“这将是一个懂科技、懂生活，也更懂用户的互联网体育新蓝图。对于用户来说，广大用户享受到的将是最前沿的观赛生活、最新鲜直观的体育资讯、最完善的球迷互动以及最全面的沉浸体验。”

据悉，苏宁和咪咕将打通旗下 PP 体育和咪咕视频两大视频平台，共同搭建咪咕视频- PP 体育联运平台，PP 体育拥有的版权赛事内容也将通过专属频道进入咪咕各客户端，以及中国移动 8 000 万魔百盒（IPTV/OTT）终端。同时双方将在赛事节目制作、4K 产品开发、运营商业务拓展以及广告销售等多方面进行合作。

此次苏宁携手咪咕，通过科技研发、文化影视和体育产业等多个领域的深度合作，利用联运平台的形式，不仅可以逐渐打通互联网和运营商网络，而且势必会推进 PP 体育专业的体育足球内容生态在运营商渠道的快速覆盖，促进咪咕视频在体育内容业态的强势扩张，并通过双方的优势资源形成覆盖广、影响大、热度高的体育 IP 资源地。世界杯热潮后，体育消费的大流量入口将花落谁家已不言而喻。

（资料来源：人民网，作者：牛闻文）

【爱奇艺收购天象互娱】 2018 年 7 月 18 日，爱奇艺正式宣布，该公司已经完成收购 Skymoons Inc. 和成都天象互动数字娱乐有限公司 100%的股权。

总部位于四川成都的天象互娱专注于手机游戏的研发及全球发行，已与多家知名国际知识产权巨头达成合作协议，涉及基于 IP 资源的手机游戏同步开发和推广。爱奇艺创始人、首席执行官龚宇表示，爱奇艺致力于为用户提供多元化的娱乐内容体验，并在商业上不断探索利用内容 IP 价值、追求多元化变现模式，此次将天象互娱收入囊中将进一步推动爱奇艺业务的深入发展。

（资料来源：《中国新闻出版广电报》，作者：李森）

【百度首个基于区块链技术的原创图片服务平台“图腾”上线】 2018 年 7 月 18 日，百度正式宣布推出基于区块链技术的原创图片服务平台“图腾”，也是该产品在 4 月公测后的正式上线。

据了解，百度图腾主要依托于区块链、人工智能以及大数据 3 种核心技术。基于区块链技术，百度图腾打造了一个版权存证系统，该系统可以为内容作品提供具有明确时间标记的“存在性证明”，而因为有诸多图片版权机构伙伴的加入，相关原创内容作品的授权流转信息同样会被记录。区块链技术还被应用在了百度图腾的一站式在线维权系统中，该系统会在发现侵权行为后，对该侵权行为进行在线取证并记录至区块链中。而借助于人工智能和大数据技术，百度图腾则打造了一个版权检测系统，该系统覆盖全网千亿规模的数据，识别的准确率超过 99%，可以全天候运行，万张图片最快 2 小时即可产出版权检测报告。

除了可以帮助图片原创作者更好地确权、维权之外，百度图腾还可以为他们提供多渠道的分发能力以及价值变现能力。通过百度搜索的平台影响力，百度图腾可以让原创图片获得更多的曝光机会，并由此带来更多的潜在交易机会。

在图片版权行业之外，百度图腾未来的应用场景还会得到更多的拓展，百度图腾产品负责人梁子表示，图腾始于图片，但不终于图片。未来，图腾将面向图片、文字、视频、音频等更多的原创内容领域开放，希望技术能够更好地服务更多的版权生态。在此次活动上，百度图腾就公布了首个技术能力输出的应用场景——熊掌号原创保护计划。基于百度图腾所提供的能力，熊掌号作者可以获得更加完善的版权保护功能，其原创版权被确权后，可以获得百度搜索的收录加速、原创标识以及优先展示等特权；同时，如果它的原创内容被侵权，也可以借助图腾提供的能力更方便地申请维权。

百度图腾已引入包括视觉中国、高品图像、景象、锐景创意、拍信、联合信任·时间戳、计易、快版权、比目鱼等生态合作伙伴，进一步扩大平台的影响力。

（资料来源：中国知识产权资讯网，作者：侯伟）

【PP 体育与法甲联盟达成为期 3 年的新媒体独家版权合作】 2018 年 7 月 28 日，苏宁集团旗下 PP 体育在南京博览中心举行了“超燃体育　过足球瘾——2018 PP 体育 818 发布会”。作为“苏宁 818 发烧节”的重要组成部分，在欧洲足球五大联赛即将开打之际，PP 体育与法甲联盟携手向全球宣布，双方达成 2018—2021 赛季、为期 3 年的新媒体独家版权合作。此外，PP 体育还推出了全面升级的会员权益和玩法，为用户带来更多选择。

根据 PP 体育和法甲联盟的合作协议，从 2018—2019 赛季开始，PP 体育将独家拥有法甲联赛、法国联赛杯、法国超级杯的新媒体独家直播和点播权益，还包含法甲系列节目《法甲 show》《法甲 highlights》。PP 体育将依托自身的足球基因，基于版权内容，围绕直播+点播观赛、互动、资讯、短视频、球迷社区、衍生周边，为用户提供更丰富立体的沉浸式服务。

此次合作达成之后，随后在深圳举办的法国超级杯赛事，PP 体育将享有现场 LED 屏展示“PP 体育”品牌的权益。不仅如此，随着合作的逐步深入，PP 体育还将与法甲联盟在衍生品和青少年训练营等方面展开合作，共同培育中国足球文化氛围。

PP 体育常务副总裁曾钢表示：“PP 体育牵手法甲对双方而言都具有历史性意义。PP 体育将基于专业化的版权运营和身后苏宁集团的强力支撑，持续提升法甲在中国市场的商业价值。法国足球有着辉煌的历史，法甲联赛潜力新星的涌现和高水平球员的引进，无疑将进一步提高法甲联赛的竞赛水平及观赏性。相信通过双方合作的达成，能够让更多中国的年轻人喜欢足球，进而推动中国足球以及整个足球产业的发展。”

法甲首席执行官迪迪埃·奎罗特（Didier Quillot）表示：“我们非常高兴能和苏宁这样的国际化集团在中国建立起重要合作关系。本次合作将最大限度地覆盖中国市场，并打牢法甲在中国的粉丝基础。我们相信，法甲在中国的竞争力与吸引力将会与日俱增。”

（资料来源：南都体育）

【今日头条开展版权保护专项行动】 2018 年 8 月 3 日，今日头条旗下头条号平台发布公告称，截至 2018 年 7 月，头条号平台已经通过自查、用户举报等方式，处罚了 2 475 个违规账号。

根据不同账号违规情节的严重程度，头条号平台对 2 173 个存在侵权行为的违规账号进行了扣分、禁言处罚，对 302 个多次侵权、违规情节恶劣的违规账号则予以永久封禁。

这是今日头条推进平台治理、净化网络空间的又一次专项行动。公告称，头条号平台积极响应国家版权局与国家网信办、工信部、公安部等关于“剑网 2018”专项行动号召，将持续不遗余力地打击侵权违规行为，保护版权方及原创作者权益，以建设健康有序的内容生态。

公告显示，此次受处罚账号主要因为有三类行为：一是未经许可转载、摘编整合或歪曲篡改新闻作品；二是通过“洗稿”方式抄袭剽窃、篡改删减原创作品；三是未经授权复制、表演、通过网络传播他人影视、音乐、摄影、文字等作品，或以合理使用为名对他人作品删减改编。为警醒广大自媒体作者，避免相应误区，公告还列举了详细案例。

目前，在版权保护、打击侵权方面，今日头条已经推出多项积极举措。这些举措尝试从技术角度切入，规模化、低成本地解决相关问题，形成防患未然、规则健全、治理有效的机制。

在数字版权方面，今日头条上线了国内首个视频版权保护系统“灵石”。该系统会对上传到平台的版权内容给予唯一的“内容指纹”文件，并将这个文件与其他上传的视频进行对比，视频版权方可以立即让侵权视频下架。头条号平台还与第三方机构合作，对原创文章进行权属、时间认证，并为作者提供原创内容版权登记电子证书，丰富原创证据。

在维权赔付方面，今日头条联合“维权骑士”“快版权”等第三方维权机构帮助创作者全网维权。针对头条号作者的原创文章，系统会进行全网范围的侵权监测，对于确认侵权的内容，机构将代作者与侵权方沟通删除赔偿，包括发起维权诉讼。

在侵权投诉方面，头条号平台设有官方投诉通道，24 小时受理投诉和举报，方便用户参与和社会监督。平台会根据投诉情况和相应证明材料，在第一时间核查处理。

此外，头条号平台设有侵权自媒体黑名单。若账号确认出现严重侵犯版权情况，将被平台立即封禁且永久拉黑，其身份信息无法再次注册新账号。

头条号平台表示，将继续切实履行企业主体责任，积极加强平台自律监管，共建清朗的网络空间。

（资料来源：中国经济网）

【中国国际数码互动娱乐展览会首办电竞大会】 2018 年 8 月 4 日，2018 全球电竞大会在上海浦东召开。2018 年是中国国际数码互动娱乐展览会（ChinaJoy）10 多年来首次举办全球电竞产业大会。

会上，上海电子竞技产业发展核心功能区落户浦东并正式揭牌。未来浦东将借势发力，把电竞产业作为区域功能规划产业发展和经济提升的重要引擎之一，着力发挥区域的综合优势，用产业链、价值链、资本链、服务链支撑电竞产业发展。

浦东新区区委常委、宣传部部长王宏舟介绍，上海电子竞技产业发展核心功能区具体体现在：打造包括资本、龙头企业、综合赛事展会在内的三大平台，打通人才培养、产业服务和政策环境三个链条。

Steam 平台是全球最大的综合性数字发行平台之一，平台游戏数量超过 2 万款。“上海有很多游戏研发企业，Steam 引入浦东以后，能帮助众多中小游戏研发商，将包括电竞游戏在内的精品打入海外市场，助推游戏产业‘走出去’。”上海市新闻出版局局长徐炯说。

2018 全球电竞大会由上海市新闻出版局、上海市浦东新区人民政府联合指导，上海汉威信恒展览有限公司主办。

（资料来源：《中国新闻出版广电报》，作者：全鑫）

【蜻蜓 FM 与纵横文学达成战略合作】 2018 年 8 月 9 日，蜻蜓 FM 与纵横文学在北京举行战略合作签约仪式，宣布双方达成文字及音频版权互授、联合打造文学 IP 等合作计划，将聚合双方平台优质资源，以多种手段助力有声精品内容的创作、传播和变现，携手开拓有声阅读市场新阵地。

此次与蜻蜓 FM 的战略合作中，纵横文学将为蜻蜓 FM 每年独家开放 1 000 本作品的优先选书权，作品由蜻蜓 FM 制作成有声书后，除了在蜻蜓 FM 播出，还将反哺给纵横文学旗下的《熊猫看书》APP，形成双向互动。

首年合作的 1 000 本作品中，还包括纵横文学计划进行影、游、听、读“四位一体”IP 开发的 5 部核心作品。纵横文学 CEO 张云帆介绍，随着有声阅读被市场逐渐认可，有声化作为纵横文学打造 IP 的试水动作，已成为优质文学作品走向全产业化的重要一步。在未来，会有越来越多根据 IP 改编的影视作品先以有声书、广播剧的形态登陆音频平台，网文作品在出版前也将优先做有声化尝试，以内容付费或广告的形式测试市场接受程度，再确定作品开发方案。

事实上，音书同步已经成为有声阅读产业的流行趋势，蜻蜓 FM COO 肖轶提到，蜻蜓 FM 已与博集新媒体等机构开展相关合作，合作书籍的有声版先于图书在蜻蜓 FM 上线，出版后再联合推广。这不仅能让用户同享听读体验，也便于平台和版权机构协同资源共同打造文学 IP，分享利益蛋糕。

（资料来源：中国知识产权资讯网，作者：侯伟）

【北京成动漫游戏研发和出口中心】 2018 年 8 月 12 日，由北京市文化局主办的第七届“动漫北京”主会场活动在北京国家会议中心落下帷幕。四天时间内，十万人次动漫迷享受了沉浸在二次元世界的喜悦，各类限量版、首发版和正版动漫游戏周边产品拉动现场文化消费超过 5 000 万元；产业界人士则通过推介会达成合作意向约 1 500 万元。北京已成为全国动漫游戏产业研发中心和出口中心，漫展的火爆只是产业发展的一个缩影。

北京市文化局相关负责人介绍，漫展规模的扩大建立在产业繁荣发展的基础上。2017 年，北京动漫游戏产业产值达 627 亿元，同比增长 20%；北京动漫游戏出口额约 116 亿元，同比增长 93%。截至 2017 年，北京共有 48 家动漫游戏企业在新三板挂牌。2018 年 5 月，北京有 5 个项目斩获文化和旅游部颁发的动漫领域最高奖——中国文化艺术政府奖第三届动漫奖，获奖数占奖项总数的 1/4。在动漫游戏领域，北京已成为全国的产业研发中心和出口中心。北京涌现出一批全国知名的动漫游戏企业和优秀产品，形成了包含创作、出版、运营、发行以及产品开发的全产业链，涵盖了从研发型到渠道型的全产业类型。

在此次展会期间，璀璨星空推介的《京剧猫》，是中国首部将京剧元素与动画相结合的国产原创动画 IP，目前全网点击率已超 20 亿次。该公司还带来了新作——中国首部古诗词类系列短片《中国唱诗班》。网络漫画平台“有妖气”是一个占据市场份额 56%，汇集了超过 2 万名漫画家和近 100 万读者的平台。该平台带来的原创作品《雏蜂 SOE》点击量已超过 13.6 亿次。有狐文化原创漫画《给我来个小和尚》实现全网阅读点击量 30 多亿次，实体漫画单行本首版发行 20 万册的佳绩。

第七届“动漫北京”除展览展示外，还组织了三场业内论坛、一场一对一推介，通过多种战略合作机制为产业搭起服务网，切准行业新增长点，给予产业及时支持。

（资料来源：《北京日报》，作者：李洋）

【CNNIC：我国 74.1%的网民使用短视频应用】 2018 年 8 月 20 日，中国互联网络信息中心（CNNIC）在北京发布第 42 次《中国互联网络发展状况统计报告》（以下简称《报告》）。

《报告》指出，2018 年上半年，网络娱乐市场需求强烈，相应政策出台以鼓励引导互联网娱乐业态健康发展。网络音乐原创作品得到扶持，网络文学用户阅读方式多样，网络游戏类型的多样化和游戏内容的精品化趋势明显。短视频应用迅速崛起，我国 74.1%的网民使用短视频应用，可以满足其碎片化的娱乐需求。

与此同时，网络文化娱乐内容进一步规范，网络音乐、文学版权环境逐渐完善，网络游戏中违法违规内容得到整治，视频行业构建起以内容为核心的生态体系，直播平台进入精细化运营阶段。

（资料来源：人民网，作者：孟哲）

【中图公司与三单位共推数字阅读人工智能应用】 2018 年 8 月 23 日，中国图书进出口（集团）总公司与中国联通、阅文集团、掌阅科技在京进行战略合作签约。中图公司与三家单位在移动资讯、数字阅读、中国出版内容“走出去”、人工智能等领域开展深入合作。第十三届全国政协文化文史和学习委员会副主任、中国版权协会理事长阎晓宏出席活动。

联通在线信息科技有限公司总经理马彦、阅文集团高级副总裁张蓉、掌阅科技创始人张凌云、中图公司总经理张纪臣先后致辞。

据介绍，本次战略合作打造新渠道、开拓新市场，共同推动中国数字内容全球推广。中图易阅通与联通沃阅读、阅文、掌阅共同推动内容、渠道、资源的全方位深度融合，利用易阅通平台、海外数字渠道、全球按需印刷网络、海外书展平台，推动中国优秀数字内容在海外主流渠道落地。

战略合作还共同打造国际合作出版拳头产品。通过充分发挥中图公司的翻译、作者和出版资源优势，深耕各家的优质内容，开展中国图书国际出版合作。同时，针对全球市场挖掘培育畅销品种，策划拳头产品，探索全版权 IP 运营，创新阅读服务模式，树立全新阅读品牌，推动全民阅读。

中图公司和 3 家合作单位还共同推动数字阅读领域的人工智能化应用。结合各方的软硬件优势，升级再造中国云数据中心，以技术、渠道、内容“三位一体”模式，开展智慧冬奥平台、智能阅读分发平台、智能“书联网”等项目。

（资料来源：《中国新闻出版广电报》，作者：李明远）

【安徽出版集团文创产品走进“一带一路”】 2018 年 8 月 23 日，安徽出版集团在京举办相识美好安徽暨美好安徽文旅文创走进“一带一路”启动仪式。

此次活动上，集团旗下安徽时代艺品文化投资有限责任公司展出了具有徽文化特色的文房、茶礼、艺术文创衍生品等六大系列的文创精品 600 余件。来自罗马尼亚、波兰、保加利亚、匈牙利、塞尔维亚等“一带一路”沿线国家负责文化旅游的驻华官员及出版商参加活动。

安徽出版集团董事长王民表示，安徽出版紧跟国家文化“走出去”“一带一路”合作愿景，在合作战略上，不断推动“走出去”从版权输出向多元合作转型升级，从产品和服务出口向文创文旅转型升级；在内容上，以“丝路书香出版工程”为抓手，在社会效益和经济效益相统一的基础上，构建“文化＋产品＋项目＋产业”的合作模式；在合作层级上，积极承担国家级和省级文化交流项目，探索打造安徽特色文化的出版、文旅文创国际品牌。

活动现场，大家还观看了《美好安徽》文化推介宣传片，欣赏了独具中华传统文化魅力的茶艺和书法表演。

（资料来源：《中国新闻出版广电报》，作者：刘蓓蓓）

【康佳与南方新媒体达成战略合作】 2018 年 8 月 23 日，康佳集团与南方新媒体进行了战略合作签约仪式，旗下品牌也正式签约战略合作，开启了彩电行业 OTT 运营的新篇章。在人工智能等技术飞速发展的当下，内容丰富度、独家版权内容等渐渐成为电视厂商之间竞争的“王牌”，并将最终决定整个 OTT TV 格局。

广东南方爱视娱乐科技有限公司作为南方新媒体的参股公司，成为康佳的合作首选。通过与爱视的深度合作，KKTV 由一家纯硬件公司向内容＋硬件＋运营的互联网运营公司转型，产品竞争力得以进一步提升。对于康佳、南方新媒体、KKTV 和广东爱视而言，这次合作开创了在互联网电视运营、内容、技术等层面的深度合作模式。

（资料来源：《北京商报》，作者：金朝力）

【2018 北京国际文创产品交易会开幕】 2018 年 8 月 24 日，2018 北京国际文创产品交易会（以下简称文交会）启动仪式在北京全国农业展览馆开幕。在 13 000 平方米的场馆内，数百家文创企业和机构汇聚一堂，数万件精美展品亮相文交会六大主题展区。2018 北京文交会作为全国文化创意产业的交易平台，在运行机制、活动规模、品牌打造、展商服务、交易模式等五大方面进行了全面提升，紧抓产品发布、产品传播和产品交易三大环节，力争打造全国规模最大文创产品交易大会。本届文交会立足文创产品交易，搭建综合服务平台，助力文创产业发展。

作为第六届北京惠民文化消费季的重点活动，本届文交会共有五大主题展区：传统文化创新区、台湾文创区、文博衍生区、原创设计区、生活美学区。将古典与现代结合，将艺术融入生活。300 多家展商将既有文化底蕴又有创新技艺的文创产品带到文交会，“新概念、新工艺、新技术、新设计、新产品、新业态”汇聚一堂，体现了北京文交会之美。

本次展会吸引了包括政府机构、博物馆、美术院校、文化基金组织、老字号等 60 多个团体、300 多家企业的积极参与，它们将这些文创产品以及背后所承载的历史文明重新在文交会散发光彩，回归到人们的视野，并更好地融入我们的生活中去。

本届文交会在现场特设 2018 北京文交会现场服务处，包含采购洽谈服务、版权服务、惠民文化消费券兑换服务、一点资讯直播间等功能区域，组委会媒体宣传、设计服务等机构已全程入驻，为参会群体提供更为完善的、精准的产业全链条解决方案。

文交会还优化升级了一整套买家精准采购营销服务，针对买家的采购需求与参展商的细分开展配对服务，精准提升文创产品的市场转化率。

（资料来源：人民网）

【有道乐读推出“万书计划”】 2018年8月24日，《有道乐读》APP在京发布乐读“万书计划”，呼吁共建正版优质的少儿阅读环境。

网易有道副总裁刘韧磊与浙江少年儿童出版社等5家出版社代表在发布会上签约，合作引入正版少儿图书版权。此次参与现场签约的有道乐读合作方包括浙江少年儿童出版社、上海译文出版社、法国知名儿童出版传媒机构巴亚出版集团与挚信环球传媒联合成立的儿童出版品牌“巴亚桥”、广西师范大学出版社集团“神秘岛”品牌和提倡科学思维深层次阅读的小多传媒。

（资料来源：《中国新闻出版广电报》，作者：李明远）

【抖音宣布加入Apple Music合作伙伴计划】 2018年8月31日，抖音宣布加入Apple Music合作伙伴计划，中国内地的用户可以在《抖音》APP内聆听Apple Music曲库内的完整歌曲。

加入该计划后，已订阅Apple Music会员方案的抖音用户可以在《抖音》APP内直接收听完整歌曲；未订阅Apple Music会员方案的抖音用户也可通过歌曲详情页中的“Apple Music即刻聆听”标签获取三个月免费试用，并在试用期间聆听完整歌曲。

类似的合作在抖音海外版*TikTok*上已经先行一步。2018年8月初，抖音海外版*TikTok*就已经在Apple Music上推出*TikTok Top Hits*、*Trending NOW*等11个品牌歌单，为用户带来*TikTok*音乐体验之旅。同时，用户也可以在*TikTok*上关注Apple Music，体验Apple Music的精彩音乐内容。

（资料来源：光明网）

【方正发布新品赋能出版融合】 2018年9月5日，方正飞翔V7.1新品发布会在京举办。方正飞翔V7.1提出了内容产品创意制作、多元发布整体解决方案。

发布会上，中国编辑学会会长郝振省表示，新闻出版领域的升级改造是为了高效率、高质量、高品质的服务与产品有效地传达给读者，方正飞翔正是为此发挥作用，赋能新闻出版行业实现传统出版与数字出版的融合。

中国新闻出版研究院副院长张立说，方正电子从排版、版式、流程到新媒体移动端交互，一路走来不忘初心。未来，希望方正电子深入参与国家知识服务平台建设，通过共建平台来推动数字出版转型。

原国家新闻出版广电总局信息中心有关负责人倡议，新闻出版单位在做好自己的同时，也要影响周边企业去使用正版软件，共同创造一个尊重知识产权的社会环境，支持企业去发展创新。

（资料来源：《中国新闻出版广电报》，作者：李子木）

【咪咕联手微博布局体娱产业】 2018年9月5日，咪咕与新浪微博共同举办了以“新视界、新平台、新融合”为主题的战略合作发布会。双方基于咪咕拥有的赛事、演艺等内容和新浪微博拥有的社交平台资源能力，开展体育赛事、演艺内容宣传推广、自有IP联合孵化等一系列合作。

在体育赛事方面，继在世界杯期间与新浪微博启动“MW”计划后，咪咕又开启了“451”计划，布局了包括中超、欧冠、亚冠、欧洲足球五大联赛在内的赛事内容。未来咪咕的赛事内容将通过新浪微博传递给更多用户，咪咕也将通过直播等多种方式合作推广新浪微博及新浪体育赛事。

在演艺IP方面，双方推进视频彩铃合作，共同打造视频彩铃的内容，方便用户通过微博使用视频彩铃。对于“咪咕汇”等成熟的演艺活动，双方制定了专项运营计划，实现演艺品牌升级。

（资料来源：《中国新闻出版广电报》，作者：李森）

【京蒙发行集团共谋文化产业发展】 2018年9月14日，北京发行集团和内蒙古新华发行集团在京签署《京蒙合作战略协议》。双方在图书配送、图书云平台、文创产业、实体书店创新合作、文化产业研究和干部交流等多领域达成了合作意向。

北京发行集团有关负责人表示，《京蒙合作战略协议》的签订是北京发行集团落实北京市委书记蔡奇关于京蒙合作“搭建多层次的民族交往交流交融平台，深化文化交流合作”指示精神的重要举措，进一步推动京蒙两地出版发行业协同发展进入新阶段。

据了解，签约当天，双方还在实体书店建设、物流配送合作和多元业务拓展3个合作领域成立了对接工作小组，先行推进相关业务合作进程。今后，两地发行集团将以协议签订为契机，深度整合和开发京蒙两地文化资源，促进两地文化产业繁荣和发展。

（资料来源：《中国新闻出版广电报》，作者：王坤宁）

【浙江出版传媒股份有限公司成立】 2018年9月18日，浙江出版传媒股份有限公司创立大会举行，选举产生了公司董事会、监事会和高管团队，并正式启动IPO（首次公开募股）相关申报工作。

当选的浙江出版传媒股份有限公司董事长鲍洪俊表示，股份制改造后，公司秉持“思想引领时代 知识服务用户”的价值观，以“聚焦高水平高质量发展，干在实处永无止境、走在前列要谋新篇、勇立潮头方显担当，把股份公司建设成为具有强大精品生产力、用户服务力和品牌影响力的新型出版传媒集团，核心竞争力和综合实力居全国前茅的行业领跑者”为发展目标，实施“对标赶超、精品出版、发行转型、数字融合、改革驱动、合作共享、投资运营、管理提升、人才引领、党建保障”十大战略，坚持以精品出版为核心，以数字融合为关键，以深化改革为动力，加快推进股份公司高水平、高质量发展，为文化浙江建设贡献力量。

（资料来源：《中国新闻出版广电报》，作者：黄琳）

【中央广播电视总台首个区域总部成立】 2018年10月8日，中央广播电视总台与上海市人民政府举行深化战略合作框架协议签约仪式。中央广播电视总台第一个区域总部和地方总站——长三角总部和上海总站同时在沪成立。中共中央政治局委员、上海市委书记李强，中宣部副部长、中央广播电视总台台长慎海雄等人出席活动。

慎海雄表示，9月26日，习近平总书记就中央电视台建台暨新中国电视事业诞生60周年发来贺信，高度肯定中央广播电视总台组建以来取得的成绩，对中央广播电视总台未来工作提出殷切希望。总台以总书记的贺信精神为动力，奋力打造具有强大引领力、传播力、影响力的国际一流新型主流媒体。上海是改革开放的排头兵和创新发展的先行者，总台与上海市的战略合作，有助于充分利用上海得天独厚的优势，不断提升引领力、传播力、影响力。总台将以长三角总部和上海总站为前沿阵地，为新时代上海的改革发展、加快建设“五个中心”、卓越的全球城市和具有影响力的社会主义现代化国际大都市做出贡献。

根据协议，双方将围绕重大文化项目、服务长三角、版权运营、超高清产业、体育产业、影视剧译制、影视技术等方面开展全方位深度合作。

（资料来源：人民网）

【全国首个省级电视4K超高清频道开播】 2018年10月16日，广东广播电视台4K超高清综艺频道开播活动在广东广播电视台举行。这意味着，广东广播电视台综艺频道成为全国首个省级电视4K超高清频道。

业内人士评价，开办4K超高清电视频道，是广东开展“新数字家庭”行动、推动4K电视网络应用与产业发展的重要举措，对深化广电媒体供给侧结构性改革，提高广电媒体引领力、传播力、影响力，具有积极的意义。

9月4日，国家广播电视总局批复同意广东广播电视台综艺频道调整为4K超高清方式播出（广电函［2018］225号）。批复明确广东综艺频道调整为采用4K技术播出后，频道呼号为“广东广播电视台综艺频道”，频道标识为“台标＋综艺”，屏幕右上角加透明的“4K”字样。

调整为4K超高清方式播出后，广东综艺频道将按照每天24小时版面，以4×6小时方式播出，即首播时长4小时，6次滚动播出。节目内容仍以综艺节目为主，同时配比播出影视剧、纪录片、综艺类趣味体育、综艺类生活等4K超高清节目。观众可拨打广东广电网络电话96956报装，或拨打广东IPTV电话10000、10086、10010报装，安装后即可收看广东广播电视台综艺频道播出的4K超高清电视节目。

广东广播电视台党委书记、台长蔡伏青介绍，为确保4K超高清频道如期开播，广东广播电视台组建了广东4K电视节目创作中心，通过自制、引进等方式储备了1 500小时全4K节目；与此同时，加速制作一批高质量4K节目，包括原创音乐节目《国乐大典》和原创纪录片《通海夷道——丝路上的岭南文化》、《老广的味道》（第四季）、《粤港澳大湾区》等。据悉，目前在制节目23个，时长共计215小时。

该频道还专门引进了一批4K纪录片，如BBC的自然纪录片《鸟瞰地球》《狂野非洲》等，还准备了精品影视剧、新奇时尚的动画片、以大型演唱会为代表的综艺节目，以及风靡互联网的互动体育赛事和不拘一格的专题节目等，为4K综艺频道开播增加节目储备。

与此同时，搭建广东广播电视台南方新媒体4K

云平台，充分发挥云端内容聚合管理生产功能，吸纳有线电视、IPTV 等平台的 4K 节目资源，为 4K 综艺频道开播做好了充分的节目准备。

4K 超高清频道无疑对播出技术提出了更高的要求。蔡伏青介绍，广东广播电视台为此加快技术建设，升级改造制作播出技术系统。目前，1 600 平方米的演播室和 600 平方米的演播室具备了自制 4K 节目的功能，规划中的虚拟系统、4K 电视转播车、4K 后期制作系统等也将陆续到位。与此同时，制定技术标准和技术规范，积极推进国家自主标准 AVS 2 编解码技术在 4K 超高清电视领域的应用，为 4K 综艺频道高质量播出提供了技术保障。

值得关注的是，广东广播电视台与 IPTV、有线电视、移动互联网等渠道合作，让 IPTV 和有线电视的 EPG（电子节目指南）成为创新应用的切入口。

“让频道平台化，链接 4K 上下游产业。”广东广播电视台综艺频道总监周繁表示，希望把频道打造成一个版权交易平台、话语平台以及产业链聚集平台。

（资料来源：《南方日报》，作者：毕嘉琪　肖文舸）

【巨人网络进军虚拟偶像市场　首位虚拟主播即将推出】 2018 年 10 月 23 日，巨人网络宣布，正式进军虚拟偶像（Virtual Idol）市场，推出首位虚拟主播 Menhera Chan（又称“Menhera 酱”）。公司预计每年为该项目投入上亿元资金，重点投入研发与内容生产环节。这是巨人在移动电竞之后重拳出击的又一核心领域，意味着该公司将布局二次元细分领域，打造超级虚拟偶像 IP 生态。

据悉，巨人网络已与日本 Joynet 株式会社达成合作，获得 Joynet 旗下现象级动漫作品 Menhera Chan 全部品类的全球独家代理授权。Menhera Chan 是巨人在该细分市场投入运营的第一个虚拟偶像。

巨人网络方面表示，二次元文化在年轻群体拥有广泛影响力，虚拟偶像作为二次元文化中的新兴形态，在中国尚处萌芽阶段，未来具有极大的市场潜力及价值。巨人在过去十余年发展中积累了深厚的 IP 开发、运营能力和丰富经验，已将《征途》《球球大作战》等培育为行业内知名的原创优质 IP。在虚拟偶像领域，巨人网络计划每年投入上亿元资金，从内容制作、游戏研发、商业演出、衍生品开发、授权合作等多方位打造虚拟偶像，深度挖掘虚拟偶像 IP 价值。

作为巨人旗下第一个虚拟偶像 IP，Menhera Chan 由日本 Joynet 株式会社于 2017 年制作出品，最初以动漫表情形态在日本即时通信应用 LINE 中上线，因可爱、萌态、个性化的形象而备受日本网友喜爱，成为日本现象级的虚拟偶像。2018 年，Menhera Chan 进入中国市场后，在国内二次元粉丝群体中迅速引爆，被喜欢她的粉丝们昵称为“Menhera 酱”。据悉，Menhera Chan 在国内已积累超过 5 000 万名目标用户。

版权方代表表示，对双方的合作充满期待，巨人网络在游戏研发运营、IP 衍生打造领域拥有丰富的经验和资源积累，此次合作推动 Menhera Chan 形象在中国本土的运营推广和 IP 生态开发，让更多用户看到、熟悉 Menhera Chan 的魅力，进一步扩大该 IP 在中国的影响力。

虚拟偶像产业在中国处于早期阶段，但在其发源地日本已是一个相对成熟的产业，且市场规模仍然在不断上升。2007 年，在日本诞生的初音未来是日本生命力最长、衍生价值最高的虚拟偶像 IP。资料显示，初音在 70 个国家运营，俘获全球超过 6 亿粉丝，代言过上百家品牌，身价接近人民币 10 亿元。

随着泛二次元用户规模日益庞大，“95 后”“00 后”群体逐渐主导中国网络流行文化。作为二次元领域的新兴热点，虚拟偶像在国内迎来风口，具有巨大的发展空间及潜力，有望复制日本虚拟偶像产业的成功模式，与之相关的 IP 衍生开发市场前景可期。

此次与 Joynet 株式会社达成合作，巨人网络整合自身的研发、运营及资源优势，全链路打造 Menhera Chan，深度挖掘该 IP 形象的价值和内容本土化空间。以 Menhera Chan 形象为基础、由巨人旗下小怪兽工作室研发的手游《表情包少女 Menhera》已在手游分享社区 TapTap 开放预约，预约量截至目前已突破 17 万人次。

未来，Menhera Chan 有望成为巨人网络旗下继《征途》《球球大作战》之后又一重磅 IP。

（资料来源：人民网）

【阅文集团战略投资韩国网文企业文笔雅】 2018 年 10 月 25 日，阅文集团正式完成对韩国原创网络文学平台株式会社文笔雅的投资，阅文集团持有该公司约 26%的股份。

作为韩国网络文学原创品牌先锋，文笔雅拥有和阅文集团相似的付费阅读商业模式。截至 2018 年 9 月，文笔雅拥有超过 70 万注册用户，作品数量约 3.5 万部，作者数量达 2.1 万人。

据介绍，阅文集团已与文笔雅共同启动“星创计划”，旨在结合中韩双方力量共同培养作家，打造潜力原创作品，发布具有权威性的原创作品榜单，获得广泛关注。未来，以文笔雅为立足点，中国优质内容将通过当地渠道输送至韩国，满足广大读者阅读需求；韩国网文更将借力于阅文提升在中国的知名度。

同时，此次战略投资还将从创作者源头锁定 IP 全球开发潜力。按计划，阅文与文笔雅将通过签约作者获得作品版权，为后续的内容衍生开发打下扎实基础。阅文将协同开拓包括漫画、影视、游戏在内的 IP 运营业务，推动企业以及全球产业链的向上发展。

（资料来源：《中国新闻出版广电报》，作者：金鑫）

【第十三届北京文博会重点项目签约 68 亿元】
2018 年 10 月 28 日，第十三届中国北京国际文化创意产业博览会（以下简称文博会）在京闭幕。历时 4 天的文博会围绕“引领文化产业高质量发展　助推全国文化中心建设”的主题，汇聚海内外优质文化产业资源，聚集中国文化创意产业融合、创新、发展的新成果，全面展示北京加快建设全国文化中心的新成就等。此届文博会以文化创意产业投融资、文化产品交易、产业合作为主要内容的 25 场项目推介交易签约活动，吸引了海内外 1.5 万位客商到会洽谈交易。据不完全统计，此届文博会文化创意产业重点项目签约仪式上共签署文化创意产业项目 39 个，金额 68.135 亿元。其中“文化＋金融＋科技＋创意”类项目签约金额大，占总金额的近 65％；“一带一路”等中外合作成绩凸显，合作项目金额占比 22％；传统文化类项目稳步提升，金额占比近 20％。

文化与各产业加速融合，促进了文化产业的大发展。在此届文博会上，一系列文化与科技、金融、旅游、体育融合发展的新业态、新产品、新技术、新平台纷纷亮相，显示中国文化产业融合发展水平全面提升，文化产业提质增效成果明显。新闻出版与广播电影电视展区展示了人工智能、虚拟现实技术、全息投影、3D 投影、大空间定位等技术的全方位应用。在 2018 中国数字创意与技术博览会上，全国首部 4D 城市 IP 电影《漫游朝阳》上映，3R 体验中心亮相。文化和旅游融合，创造了新业态。北京旅游馆以“让文化鲜活、让旅游生动”为主题，集中展示了北京文旅融合的成果。老字号浓缩北京味道，京城百工坊聚集非遗，北京礼物承载古都情意。

此届文博会集聚优秀传统文化产品，彰显传统文化的力量，展示中华文化创新发展。博物馆是传统文化的重镇。此届文博会上，全国几十家博物馆展示文创新品，让文物活起来。沈阳故宫博物院的八旗兵文具套装、宫廷萌娃钥匙扣等组成盛京礼物。在工艺美术展区，张同禄、李佩卿、刘永森等一批大师工作室联袂出展。省区市文化创意产业展区内，黄山徽派雕刻细腻传神；33 家中国台湾文创品牌生动演绎了传统的创新性转化；传统的螺丝刀变成精巧可爱的卡通造型；茶具、皮具，无一不体现各种创意巧思。

传统文化是创新的源泉。故宫卡通 IP 孵化、古建梦工厂古建文化创意产业基地、中华古建系列传统文化课程等项目，依托传统，再造传统；大型系列文化纪录片《匠心中国》项目，则以讲述中国传统文化的价值、推动文创品牌为旨归；北京印刷学院的传统壁画仿真复制技术，为传统文化传承发展注入新动能。

此届文博会全面展示了北京文化供给质量不断提升的新气象。大运河文化带、长城文化带、西山永定河文化带是北京建设全国文化中心的 3 个标志性文化品牌，此届文博会首次举办了 3 个文化带论坛，通过展览、论坛、纪录片、动漫短片等形式，对一年来在积极开展 3 个文化带建设方面所取得的成果进行了集中展示。把老旧厂房改造为文创产业园区，成为北京文化产业一道亮丽的风景线。北京海淀区中关村 768 创意产业园已经成为文化科技创新策源地、独角兽的孵化基地。朝阳区展示了 60 家从老旧厂房转型升级的文创产业特色园区，这些文创园区实现了 4 个转变。在东城区展区，一批优秀剧目上演，其中有保利演出公司的《故宫里的小不点》，央华时代的《犹太城》等。朝阳区以 1 个主会场＋N 个分会场的形式全面参与文博会活动，主会场推介百余个“高精尖”文化产业项目。海淀区展现海淀文化产业发展新动力、新形态，突出文化与科技融合、文化产业与城市新形态构建的特色。

此届文博会举办 40 多个分会场、7 场创意活动和一系列文化创意大赛，激励创新创业。2018 北京文化创意大赛优秀成果展、第 12 届“工美杯”北京工艺美术创新设计大赛、首都大学生创意集市、北京青少年文化创意节等的创新成果在文博会展出亮相，既培育人才激励创新，又加快成果的市场化推广。

此外，在京津冀文创产品开发成果展区，京津冀三地甄选具有代表性的文化企业和项目出展，内容包括传统文化、文化与科技融合的新产品等。北京画院展示一批画作，首都图书馆展示利用馆藏文献、馆舍建筑等元素制作的书画、复制古籍等传统文化创意产品。天津老字号焕发新生机，杨柳青年画、泥人张彩塑已经开发了年画瓷瓶、年画帆布包、收卷册页轴画、丝绸系列等传统美术衍生产品。天津博物馆以馆藏文物元素为基础，通过设计、授权开发的方式，衍生出多形式的文化创意产品300多种。天津邮政博物馆成功开发了一批津味文化特色的文创产品。文博会还搭建"一带一路"文化交流合作平台，促进"一带一路"沿线国家文化资源的深度开发。第四届北京塞隆国际文化艺术节聚焦"一带一路"文化艺术，在世界上最大的水泥筒仓群举办俄罗斯版画精品收藏展，30余件创作于20世纪的俄罗斯版画精品亮相。台湖国际图书分会场汇集60万种中外出版精品，英、美、法、德等国的48家出版集团、380余家国外出版社的外文原版图书就有5万余种。

（资料来源：中国知识产权资讯网，作者：窦新颖）

【《中影剧场》登陆美国城市电视台】 中国电影股份有限公司同美国鹰龙传媒有限公司合作，在美国城市电视台开设《中影剧场》。中国电影股份有限公司副总经理任月、美国鹰龙传媒有限公司董事长苏彦韬、中国驻洛杉矶总领事张平、美国制片协会国际委员会主席伊丽莎白·黛尔等于2018年11月1日共同为《中影剧场》开播揭牌。

中国电影股份有限公司首次将《中影剧场》推向国际市场，选择与在美国有30年媒体运营经验的鹰龙传媒旗下的美国城市广播电视台联手，在美国城市电视台开设《中影剧场》，每周六晚上黄金时段播出一部优秀的中国电影，通过优秀影视作品向美国民众展示中华文化和新时代的中国故事。中影股份通过美国城市电视台无线频道向美国民众定期播出更多优秀中国电影，通过好莱坞的国际舞台向世界讲好中国故事。鹰龙传媒旗下的美国城市电视台将首先在无线电视频道推出《中影剧场》，根据当地权威机构尼尔森评估的当地电视市场规模，预计初步覆盖超过5 654 260户，初步覆盖人口17 200 000人。

在中美建交40周年来临之际，中影股份在美国影视之都好莱坞与鹰龙传媒合作开设长期固定时段的《中影剧场》，把中国故事以国际语言向世界传播，其意义深远。合作双方表示将充分发挥各自优势，进一步提升融媒体的播出平台和提供多元化的播出内容，大力优化中影影视版权合作开发与中美影视内容联合制作，提升战略协同层次和水平，让更多的美国民众通过中国电影了解中华文化、理解中华文化、喜爱中华文化。

据了解，美国城市电视台《中影剧场》栏目的首批授权影片包括12部中影出品的新老经典，其中有2010年徐静蕾（代表作《绑架者》《亲密敌人》）导演并主演的人气都市职场爱情片《杜拉拉升职记》和2010年张杨（代表作《冈仁波齐》《洗澡》）导演的剧情爱情片《无人驾驶》以及2012年叶伟民（代表作《人在囧途》《百变星君》）导演的喜剧爱情片《亲家过年》。

（资料来源：人民网，作者：王如君）

【2017年全球版税收入达96亿欧元　中国市场潜力大】 2018年11月8日，国际作者与作曲者协会联合会（CISAC）在上海举行的中国国际进口博览会期间，发布了《全球版税报告2018》和中国市场的专题报告。CISAC总干事甘迪·奥龙（Gadi Oron）先生在发布会后接受了记者采访。他表示，中国市场具有进一步增长的巨大潜力，这将有利于创作者，有利于中国经济，有利于提升中国在全球创意产业的影响。

CISAC发布的《全球版税报告2018》显示，2017年音乐、视听、视觉艺术、戏剧和文学创作者的全球版税收入跃升至96亿欧元，较上年增长6.2%。主要受流媒体热潮的推动，加之消费者对网络视频的热衷，2017年来自数字渠道的版税猛增24%，首次突破10亿欧元大关，并在过去五年中实现了166%的增长。音乐版税增长6.0%，攀升至83亿欧元。

2017年是全球创作者版税收入连续第五年增长，也是所有门类的作品首次实现全部增长。电视和广播版税的稳健增长表明，飙升的数字收入目前并未取代传统渠道。在数字版税排名前20的国家中，有16个国家的广播版税同样也实现了增长。

报告指出，中国音乐著作权协会过去五年的收入翻了一番，达到了2017年的2.06亿元人民币，其中约有三分之一分配给了海外创作者。中国是世界上数字版税比例最高的国家之一，数字版税收入自2013年以来已经增长了五倍，甘迪·奥龙称，这些数字证明了中国的数字环境已成功转型为正版模式。

对于如何更好地保护中国版权市场良性发展，

甘迪·奥龙给出了几点建议：一是强化网络服务商的责任，以保护新的正版音乐市场及其中的投资者；二是引入“视觉艺术家追续权”，保护当地和世界各地的中国艺术家权益；三是承认电视、电影导演和编剧的作者权，使他们从其作品的二次使用中获得经济收益。

（资料来源：人民网，作者：龚霏菲）

【内蒙古出版集团携手联通共推“互联网＋出版”】 2018 年 11 月 15 日，内蒙古出版集团与中国联通内蒙古分公司在呼和浩特签订战略合作协议。

根据协议，内蒙古出版集团与中国联通内蒙古分公司正式建立战略合作关系，并在新闻出版信息化、联合办公系统开发应用、智慧党建及智能通信等 6 个领域展开合作。中国联通将开放大数据、云计算、物联网、移动互联网等核心技术资源，与内蒙古出版集团共建大数据中心，内蒙古出版集团整合数字出版、云教育、全媒体发布、电子商务、全民阅读等方面的资源，与联通公司展开数字化合作。双方各自发挥优势，共同促进“互联网＋出版”发展，共同构建“通信＋出版”的信息化、数字化新生态。

内蒙古出版集团及所属新技术公司经过近 10 年的努力，突破了蒙古文字信息化基础技术和核心技术，相继获得 33 项计算机软件著作权登记证书和 4 项软件产品登记证书，现已进入全方位应用、推广阶段。推动内容资源的数字化传播，从内容产品提供商转变为内容资源运营商是出版集团产业转型升级的着力点和主攻方向。这需要现代化的网络信息技术与手段加以支撑，而联通公司拥有技术、人才、资金和管理等优势，拥有覆盖全国、通达世界的现代通信网络。双方认为，内蒙古出版集团和联通公司互为信息化道路上的同行者和好伙伴。双方的合作具有重要战略意义。

（资料来源：《中国新闻出版广电报》，作者：内闻）

【字节跳动与 NBA 达成短视频版权合作】 2018 年 11 月 27 日，字节跳动公司与国际体育及媒体集团 NBA 共同宣布，双方达成长期全球合作伙伴关系，NBA 短视频内容可通过字节跳动公司旗下的移动平台，呈现给全球用户。

作为 NBA 中国官方的内容智能分发平台，《今日头条》、《抖音》以及《西瓜视频》已经为 NBA 及 30 支球队开通了官方账号。同时，全球的用户还可以通过《抖音》或 *TikTok*，使用 NBA 主题的贴纸和特效拍摄创意短视频。此外，NBA 也将与字节跳动公司的人工智能实验室合作，运用人工智能领域的创新技术，进一步升级球迷的视频观赏体验。NBA 还将与字节跳动公司共同开展 NBA 主题的在线活动，如挑战赛和定制表情活动，以鼓励球迷参与和互动，让更多人了解和喜爱篮球运动以及 NBA 赛事。

（资料来源：《中国知识产权报》，作者：窦新颖）

【《2018 年中国网络视听发展研究报告》发布】 2018 年 11 月 28 日，中国网络视听节目服务协会在四川成都发布《2018 年中国网络视听发展研究报告》。该《报告》显示，2018 年，网络视听市场用户需求日趋强烈，相应政策陆续出台引导了行业健康发展。

《报告》显示，截至 2018 年 6 月，中国网络视频用户规模为 6.09 亿人，占网民总数的 76.0％，较 2017 年底增加 3 014 万人，半年增长率 5.2％，比整体网民的增速高 1.4 个百分点；手机视频用户达 5.78 亿人，占手机网民的 73.4％，较 2017 年底增长 2 929 万人，半年增长率为 5.3％，亦高于手机网民整体增速（4.7％）；短视频用户规模达 5.94 亿人，占网民总数的 74.1％，其中 30 岁以下网民对短视频的使用率在 80％以上。

2018 年，预计整个视频内容行业的市场规模为 2 016.8 亿元，同比增长 39.1％。随着视频内容产业生态圈的形成，用户娱乐方式多样化，用户体验、活跃用户数量、用户使用时长等进一步提升，未来整体视频内容行业规模仍将保持高速增长。

《报告》数据显示，网络视频行业用户、内容、流量向腾讯视频、爱奇艺、优酷三大平台集中，头部平台与第二、第三梯队之间差距拉大。用户规模层面，2018 年上半年，通过腾讯视频、爱奇艺、优酷三大平台收看过网络视频节目的用户占整体网络视频用户的 89.6％，第二、第三梯队平台的用户使用率下降，市场格局进一步清晰。

《报告》相关数据显示，电视剧、新闻资讯、网络电影是网络视频用户最爱看的节目类型，经常收看的比例分别为 60.4％、57.8％和 56.1％；其次是综艺节目和院线电影，四成以上用户经常收看；再次是纪录片、动漫节目、体育节目，三成以上用户经常收看。

此外，影院热映新片、电视台热播剧成为用户付费的主要驱动因素。《报告》数据显示，分别有

44.7%、39.1%的用户愿意为影院热映新片、电视台热播剧付费。愿意为网络电影或微电影、综艺节目付费的用户比分别为32.1%、23.7%。另有16%～19%的用户愿意为网站自制剧、视频课程、体育节目付费。

（资料来源：《中国新闻出版广电报》，作者：李雪昆）

【趣头条：向“下沉市场”挖掘内容版权价值】 2018年11月29日，主攻“下沉市场”（指以三线及以下城市人群为主要目标用户群的市场）的内容平台趣头条在京举行内容生态大会，对未来6个月的内容布局进行规划，宣布在与近千名原创者签约的基础上，继续做好内容建设，探索内容变现新路径。

《趣头条》是一款内容资讯APP，于2016年6月上线，其旨在通过大数据算法和云计算等技术，为用户提供其感兴趣、有价值的个性化内容及服务。2018年9月14日，趣头条正式在纳斯达克上市，成为国内发展最快的内容平台之一。趣头条创始人谭思亮表示，平台自成立之初就与其他内容平台走差异化竞争道路，主攻“下沉市场”和“下沉用户”，经过两年半的发展，已经证明在“五环外”还存在一个内容产品的“快车道”。接下来，趣头条将加大内容建设和人才培养，在发展“快车道”上下慢功夫打磨内容精品。

（资料来源：《中国知识产权报》，作者：姜旭）

【2017年北京版权产业增加值比上年上涨9.2%】 2018年12月4日，由北京市新闻出版研究中心主编的北京版权蓝皮书《北京版权发展年度报告（2017～2018）》由社会科学文献出版社出版发行。《报告》显示，2017年北京市版权产业实现增加值3 908.8亿元，比上年增长9.2%，增速分别高出地区生产总值和第三产业增加值2.5个和1.9个百分点。

《报告》的分报告及专题报告通过对影视、音乐、软件等重点版权领域及区块链、短视频、人工智能等版权新问题的专题研究，梳理当前北京版权发展取得的重要突破和面临的挑战，并针对存在的问题提出建议。

《报告》显示，北京版权产业增加值在地区生产总值中的占比连年提升，由2013年的12.3%提高到2017年的14%，5年间提高了1.7个百分点。北京地区核心版权产业收入连续3年保持10%以上的高速增长，3年平均增速为14.2%。版权产业作为北京战略性支柱产业的地位更加突出，对首都经济增长的拉动作用更加显著，在疏解非首都功能、构建首都“高精尖”经济结构、落实“四个中心”城市战略定位中发挥的作用越来越重要。

（资料来源：《中国新闻出版广电报》，作者：王坤宁）

【首届“国家音乐产业优秀项目奖励计划”入选项目公布】 2018年12月19日，首届“国家音乐产业优秀项目奖励计划”入选项目在京正式发布。中央音乐学院的“交响乐《草原之歌》《鲁迅》的创作与推广”等35个项目入选。

“国家音乐产业优秀项目奖励计划”实施单位人民音乐出版社社长莫蕴慧代表“国家音乐产业优秀项目奖励计划”工作小组表示，“国家音乐产业优秀项目奖励计划”的主要目的，是通过对音乐产业链上下游具有代表性的优秀项目的征集和评选，总结和推广发展成果，鼓励优秀作品创作传播，推动产业创新发展。最终评选出的项目，既全面涉及音乐创作、出版复制、版权交易、演出培训以及音乐衍生产品等纵向产业链，又基本囊括音乐与广播影视、动漫游戏、网络设备、乐器生产等横向产业链；既体现了国有企事业单位、科研教育机构的实力和担当，也体现了民营市场主体的探索与创新。

项目评审专家代表、中国音乐家协会副主席张千一在致辞中说，此次音乐产业优秀项目的征集、“国家音乐产业优秀项目奖励计划”的实施，是首次从国家层面针对音乐产业实行的工程带动和项目引领。他希望通过国际交流与学习，脚踏实地地推进中国音乐产业发展。

（资料来源：《中国新闻出版广电报》，作者：孙海悦）

【78个原创动漫项目获扶持】 2018年12月20日，由国家新闻出版署指导、中央文化产业发展专项资金支持的“优秀原创动漫作品版权开发奖励计划”在京举行颁奖仪式。泡泡玛特、网元圣唐、北京紫媒等78个国产优秀原创动漫项目荣获“优秀原创动漫作品版权开发奖励计划”奖项，并获得中央文化产业发展专项资金支持。

2018年8月27日，国家新闻出版署下发了《国家新闻出版署关于征集原创动漫作品版权开发优秀项目的通知》，在全国范围内征集、遴选在内容开发、品牌经营、海外市场开拓等方面，对国产原创动漫作品版权开发具有代表性的优秀项目。

在国家新闻出版署指导和中央文化产业发展专项资金的支持下，中国版权保护中心受委托配套开展奖励计划，邀请来自动漫版权管理部门、动漫行业协会、版权公共服务机构、动漫教育研究机构、动漫企业等方面的专家针对国家新闻出版署征集推荐的 160 个优秀项目，最终评选出 78 个优秀项目。据了解，中国动漫作品的版权开发主要集中在授权许可与衍生品开发等方面，版权价值的开发推动中国原创动漫作品不断向前。

（资料来源：《中国文化报》，作者：马霞）

【新华网启动视频化战略】 2018 年 12 月 25 日，新华网在京召开发布会，正式启动视频化战略，将视频业务作为构建内容新生态的战略支点，全面推动新华网向视频化、移动化、知识化、智能化转型。

发布会上，新华网董事长、总裁田舒斌表示，未来两到三年，新华网将加大资金投入力度，用于视频化和移动化领域的优质内容生产、专业人才扩充、应用技术研发、先进设施建设、创意创新扶持、产业空间拓展等；同时将调整业务流程和组织架构，于 2019 年启动“百名高端视频专业人才招募计划”，吸引更多人才投身视频事业。

根据视频化战略，新华网将推出两大计划：一是推动规模化优质短视频自制生产体系的“源创计划”，按照“精品制胜”思路，以正能量融合短视频为特色构筑核心业务线；二是与众多伙伴联合发起“共鸣计划”，构建开放生态体系，成立跨行业的“视频战略联盟”，联手推动网络视频事业繁荣发展。

此外，新华网还将建成创意孵化、整合传播、技术驱动、人才支撑四大能力体系，用以支撑“源创计划”和“共鸣计划”。

（资料来源：《中国新闻出版广电报》，作者：余俊杰）

港澳台版权信息

【粤澳保护知识产权合作协议在广州签署】 2018 年 1 月 10 日下午，粤澳合作联席会议在广州召开，广东省委书记李希、省长马兴瑞，澳门特别行政区行政长官崔世安等出席了会议。会议上，广东省知识产权局局长马宪民与澳门特别行政区政府经济局局长戴建业共同签署了《粤澳保护知识产权合作协议（2017 年—2018 年）》，协议确定粤澳双方将在“深化粤澳知识产权合作机制、加强粤澳知识产权跨境保护合作”等 17 个领域开展深入合作，共同推动两地在知识产权领域建立更紧密的合作关系，增强两地自主创新能力、经济实力和国际竞争力，推动粤澳知识产权合作全面发展。

（资料来源：广东省知识产权局）

【澳门知识产权研究中心揭牌】 2018 年 4 月 16 日，教育部人文社会科学重点研究基地中南财经政法大学知识产权研究中心伙伴基地澳门知识产权研究中心和内地其他三所兄弟院校伙伴基地揭牌仪式在澳门科技大学演讲厅举行。教育部部长陈宝生、澳门特别行政区社会文化司司长谭俊荣、中央人民政府驻澳门特别行政区联络办公室副主任孙达、中南财经政法大学党委书记栾永玉及其他三所兄弟院校领导共同揭牌。中南财经政法大学学术委员会主任、知识产权研究中心名誉主任吴汉东教授，知识产权研究中心副主任彭学龙教授参加揭牌仪式并与澳门科技大学法学院进行友好交流。

教育部人文社会科学重点研究基地是中国人文社科领域的重大建设项目，对培养相关学科的优秀人才、提高学术水平、推动学科发展发挥了重要作用。2017 年，经教育部批准，澳门科技大学与复旦大学、中国海洋大学、中南财经政法大学、广州中医药大学等四所内地著名高校共建教育部人文社科重点研究基地伙伴基地。另外，中南财经政法大学知识产权研究中心与澳门科技大学共建澳门知识产权研究中心。两校将发挥知识产权法学科优势，进一步推动学科建设、人才培养及学术研究。

中南财经政法大学知识产权研究中心与澳门科技大学开展交流合作已有先例。2017 年，中南财经政法大学知识产权研究中心名誉主任吴汉东教授受邀开始在澳门科技大学法学院招收博士研究生。此次澳门知识产权研究中心揭牌是两校合作交流史上的大事。在揭牌仪式前，中南财经政法大学党委书记栾永玉，校学术委员会主任、知识产权研究中心名誉主任吴汉东教授，校社会科学研究院院长康均心教授，知识产权研究中心副主任彭学龙教授一行拜会了澳门科技大学校长刘良教授并参访了澳门科技大学法学院，就加强两校合作、共建伙伴基地深入交换意见。栾永玉书记表示，中南财经政法大学将全力支持澳门知识产权研究中心的建设与发展，并以此为契机，积极探索两校校级、院级和各学科全方位、分层次合作交流新模式，培养一流人才、推出高端成果，以回馈社会、报效国家。

在澳门回归祖国将近二十周年之际，在国家制定和实施粤港澳大湾区建设方略的大背景下，中南财经政法大学知识产权研究中心与澳门科技大学共建澳门知识产权研究中心有利于充分发挥两校学科优势，促进中南财经政法大学与澳门及境外的科研机构深度合作，对推动粤港澳大湾区建设做出重要贡献。

（资料来源：中南财经政法大学知识产权研究中心）

【粤港版权产业企业交流活动在香港举行】 2018 年 6 月 13—15 日，广东省版权局与香港特别行政区政府知识产权署共同组织了粤港版权产业企业交流活动，本次活动的目的是分享粤港版权产业创造、管理、保护和运用的经验，进一步推进粤港两地版权产业企业版权保护和版权贸易等方面的交流合作与协同发展。

广东省版权局专职副局长陈春怀带领版权管理处相关人员及获得 2016 年度“广东省版权兴业示范基地”的企业代表共 23 人参加了此次活动。交流团全体成员参加了“亚太经合组织工作坊——探讨创意产业知识产权授权的最佳实践方法”论坛，参观了香港海关百年光影展及电子科技罪行研究所，与香港海关代表就版权保护和版权业界合作进行了座谈交流，并到创新创意特色浓厚的 PMQ 元创方参观学习。该版权创意园由特区政府知识产权部门指导香港设计中心、香港理工大学和香港知专设计学院等单位联合创办，在活化具有历史价值建筑群的基础上，培育和推动本地的创意文化。此次交流活动搭建起粤港版权界交流的桥梁，将会进一步促进粤港澳大湾区版权产业的协同快速发展。

（资料来源：广东省版权局）

【粤港知识产权与中小企业发展（佛山）研讨会在佛山举行】 2018 年 6 月 21 日，粤港知识产权与中小企业发展（佛山）研讨会在佛山举行。佛山市委常委、常务副市长蔡家华，广东省知识产权局副局长谢红，香港特别行政区政府知识产权署副署长吴凯诗等出席并致辞。佛山市各区、镇（街）知识产权负责人，以及知识产权服务机构、重点企业代表等共 250 余人参加研讨会。

蔡家华围绕佛山与香港加强知识产权合作提出愿景：加强高等教育资源合作，共同推进知识产权专业课程开设；促进产业知识产权交流合作，引导香港各类科研技术、专利成果应用在佛山成功转化，共建知识产权运营平台；推进两地高端人才资源的交流合作，支持和鼓励香港知识产权人才团队利用佛山资源和商机创新创业。

谢红指出，佛山市政府高度重视知识产权工作，多项国家级知识产权平台落户佛山，下一阶段，粤港双方将与时俱进，开拓创新，进一步拓宽领域，深化合作，推动两地知识产权事业共同发展。

吴凯诗表示，香港特区政府一直重视中小企业发展，知识产权署不断优化知识产权保护制度，积极协助中小企业保护和运用知识产权，从而把握知识产权贸易带来的商机。

研讨会上，与会专家分别结合各自专业及工作经验，围绕“知识产权保护和运用——助力大湾区创新发展”这一主题展开研讨。研讨会由广东省知识产权局、佛山市人民政府、香港特别行政区政府知识产权署、香港贸易发展局主办，佛山市知识产权局承办，香港特别行政区政府驻粤经济贸易办事处等协办。研讨会的举办，为粤港知识产权以及中小企业发展交流搭建了良好平台。

（资料来源：广东省知识产权局，作者：邱文业）

【“澳门国际知识产权研讨会 2018”在澳门举办】 2018 年 8 月 6 日，由澳门贸易投资促进局、澳门商标协会主办，中美知识产权协会、澳门凯旋知识产权代理有限公司协办的“澳门国际知识产权研讨会 2018”（第二届）在澳门举办。

本次活动得到了横琴知识产权交易中心、知识产权界权威媒体知产力及 IPRdaily 的鼎力支持。

出席本次研讨会开幕式的嘉宾有：中央人民政府驻澳门特别行政区联络办公室法律部副部长王恒女士、法律处处长徐祥生先生，澳门贸易投资促进局投资者服务厅代高级经理陈家齐先生、企业拓展服务处代经理莫洁仪女士，世界知识产权组织中国办事处顾问吕国良先生、王晔先生，美国驻广州总领事馆知识产权顾问郑丹丹女士，澳门连锁加盟商会主席黄仁民先生，澳门知识产权保护协会会长萧颂铭先生，澳亚卫视副总裁吴斌女士，澳门青年创业孵化中心总监林子恩先生。

在研讨会上，世界知识产权组织中国办事处顾问吕国良先生发表了以“WIPO 替代性争议解决机制（ADR）”为主题的演讲。他表示，当前知识产权纠纷的解决机制呈现多元化趋势，纠纷解决机制在积极追求公正、效率、效益并举的价值目标，ADR 以其自身优势为依托而发展，必将成为知识产权争议解决机制选择的一大趋势。

澳门大学协同创新研究所代所长、创新中心主任及工商管理学院特聘教授颜至宏先生发表了以“科技创新与经济发展”为主题的演讲。他表示，在经济全球化和信息化迅猛发展的今天，城市创新能力将决定综合竞争力，就目前来说，澳门在全球仍是一个科技创新的洼地，因此，澳门大学正肩负使命，由教学型大学向教学研究型大学发展，未来目标是建设成一所教学、研究和创新创业相平衡的世界性高水平大学。

澳门商标协会会长、澳门凯旋知识产权代理有限公司总经理王爱民女士表示：与其他国家及地区相比，澳门知识产权的研究从保护、运营到成果转化等，皆相对薄弱；但他山之石可以攻玉，希望通过办国际知识产权研讨会，由来自世界各地的专家为澳门的知识产权发展献计献策，从而推动知识产权研究在本澳的发展。

本次论坛以“知识产权商业化”为主题，中间分为主题演讲、世界知识产权法律最新发展、粤港澳大湾区知识产权保护及运营等多个环节，进行分享、交流和探讨，现场十分热烈，共有来自中国、美国、加拿大以及澳大利亚等地的 100 余名专家、学者及知识产权实务界人士参加。

（资料来源：每日经济网，作者：唐新勇）

【第十四届海图会在台北举行】 2018 年 8 月 17—23 日，第十四届海峡两岸图书交易会（以下简称海图会）在台北主会场开展。海峡两岸约 300 家出版社、版权机构和图书馆参与了这场两岸图书交流嘉年华。

本届海图会台北主会场面积达 8 000 平方米，设立大陆图书展销区、台湾图书展销区、湖北主宾省展区等主题展区。参展单位中大陆占 180 余家、台湾占 120 余家，涵盖两岸相关图书、数字出版、期刊、动漫、图书馆等上下游产业机构，共有约 10 万种新书、精品书和畅销书参展。

除在台北设立主会场外，本届海图会在基隆市、台中市、南投县、嘉义县、屏东县等地设立了 5 个分会场，展场总面积达 11 200 平方米。

作为本届交易会的大陆执行机构，厦门外图集团有限公司总经理申显杨介绍说，海图会是两岸出版界共同发起的交流盛会，既是两岸出版产业最新成果的全面展示，也是两岸出版人汇聚一堂、共谋发展的大平台。本届海图会活动精彩多元，文化底蕴丰富，更加突出出版产业的交流实效。

本届书展的主宾省湖北省组织了 32 家出版发行机构，为台湾读者带来了 4 000 多册图书，还带来了武当拳、黄梅戏、楚菜展示等特色文化活动。湖北省版权保护协会常务理事胡伟说，希望通过海图会搭建起鄂台文化交流的友谊之桥，促进两地图书版权贸易合作，进一步弘扬优秀传统文化，推动出版繁荣发展。

1988 年，两岸出版交流启航。30 年过去了，第十四届海图会还将举办海峡两岸出版交流 30 周年成果图片展，举行优秀版权图书评选颁奖仪式。

台湾华品文创出版股份有限公司总编辑陈秋玲说，两岸出版发行交流不断深化，形成优势合力，市场前景可期。公司从北京中华书局引进的国学类图书在岛内销售得很好，有助于为台湾青少年打下良好的传统文化基础。国学是中华文化之本，应在基础教育中扎根。

海图会自 2005 年起在厦门和台北两地成功举办了 13 届，累计参展图书 800 余万册，实现图书销售采购 4.2 亿元人民币，达成版权贸易等业务合作项目 2 360 项。

（资料来源：新华网，作者：陈君　查文晔）

【粤港保护知识产权合作专责小组第十七次会议在广州举行】 2018 年 8 月 21 日，粤港保护知识产权合作专责小组（以下简称专责小组）第十七次会议在广州举行。专责小组同意进一步加强合作，巩固已有合作成果，继续推动知识产权贸易及高端服务业发展，促进区域科研成果创新发展，并围绕粤港澳大湾区和“一带一路”建设，推动粤港知识产权合作的进一步发展。

在会议上，双方代表分别总结过去一年两地完成的合作项目。在推进大湾区知识产权合作方面，专责小组透过举办多项活动，积极探索大湾区内的合作机遇，包括：有关仲裁与调解的交流活动；以“特色老店、老字号的品牌发展”为主题的座谈会；以“高端知识产权服务支持青年创业”为主题在广东自贸试验区横琴片区举行的交流活动，以及制作有关大湾区知识产权商品化的宣传短片等。

其他完成的合作项目包括：举办“粤港知识产权与中小企业发展研讨会”；邀请粤方成员机构及企业参加由香港特别行政区政府、香港贸易发展局及香港设计中心合办的“亚洲知识产权营商论坛”；就知识产权的保护和运用举办交流活动，以及举办以两地青少年为对象的宣传教育活动等。

2019 年的重点合作项目包括：继续推动粤港知识产权贸易发展，举办大湾区知识产权高端研讨活动；推动以仲裁或调解解决知识产权的争议；推动粤港澳三地的培训机构在培养知识产权人才方面的合作；继续制作宣传短片以推广大湾区知识产权商品化的机遇，以及推动知识产权信息共享。

在知识产权跨境保护合作方面，粤港执法部门透过情报交流、信息资源共享、联合行动、专案合作等协作机制打击跨境侵权行为。2019 年两地海关将继续重点打击输港或经香港输往“一带一路”沿线国家的侵权活动，并且粤港双方会根据形势变化，适时组织其他专项联合执法行动。

香港知识产权署署长梁家丽表示，专责小组在 2017 年完成了 29 项合作项目，成果令人振奋。2019 年的合作项目当中有多项关于大湾区的知识产权合作，期望粤港两地能更紧密合作，互补共赢，好好把握大湾区和“一带一路”建设所带来的前所未有的机遇，共同推动区域知识产权创新发展。

广东省知识产权局局长马宪民认为，自 2003 年专责小组建立以来，双方构建了畅通、高效的合作体系，粤港知识产权合作机制不断深化，粤港合作项目不断推进，为两地创新发展做出了积极贡献。

专责小组于 2003 年 8 月第六次粤港合作联席会议后成立，旨在加强粤港两地在保护知识产权不同范畴的交流和合作，包括推广和教育、培训、执法、调查研究及资讯发布。

（资料来源：香港知识产权署网站）

【广西书展在台北开幕】 2018 年 11 月 2 日，2018 广西书展在台北开幕，几十名桂台出版界代表出席。

自 2010 年开始，广西壮族自治区新闻出版广电局已连续 9 年在台湾举办广西书展系列活动，除举办书展外，还举办两地出版同人座谈会、版权贸易洽谈与签约、向台湾公益图书馆赠书等活动。

广西新闻出版广电局副局长吕洁表示，图书是人类文明进步的阶梯。弘扬瑰丽灿烂的中华文化，推动人类进步，推动中华文化走向世界，是出版人的追求，也有赖于两岸出版界的共同努力。自 2010 年以来，广西坚持来台开办书展、进行版权交流合作和赠书活动，一是希望满足台湾读者对大陆图书、广西图书的了解需求；二是希望打开一扇台湾民众了解大陆、了解广西的窗口，增进两岸同胞的彼此了解；三是便利桂台两地民众互相阅读对方的图书，增强两岸同胞对中华文化的认知、认同。

台湾两岸出版交流协会理事长沈荣裕表示，广西出版的图书在台北简体字书店销量很好，广西出版界坚持到金门、澎湖、花莲等地和学校送书，为两岸文化交流做出很大贡献，希望广西书展能坚持办下去。

台湾龙图腾文化有限公司专门从事简转繁书籍出版，总经理罗爱萍表示，该公司自 2012 年在台湾创办以来，已出版了 600 多种简转繁的优质图书，希望公司以后能将广西的图书在龙图腾的平台出版。

广西师范大学出版社有限公司总编室副主任沈红子表示，两岸图书界交流有语言文化等方面的天然优势，书展活动有利于两岸文化交流，希望两岸出版界多举办这样的交流活动。

两岸出版从业者当天还举行了版权贸易签约仪式。

9 年来，广西在台湾累计销售图书超过 5 万册，向台湾大学、高雄中山大学、金门大学、澎湖马公高中、马祖高中、花莲市立图书馆等近 30 家教育文化机构和乡镇图书馆赠送了价值近 200 万元的桂版优秀图书，使图书成为台湾读者、民众了解大陆、了解广西的重要窗口。

（资料来源：新华网，作者：吴济海　刘欢）

【粤港澳大湾区知识产权法律联盟正式成立】

2018 年 12 月 4 日，由澳门科技大学主办的粤港澳大湾区知识产权法律联盟成立仪式暨粤港澳大湾区知识产权法高峰论坛在珠海举行。中央人民政府驻澳门特别行政区联络办公室法律部副部长王恒，广东省知识产权保护中心主任马宪民，澳门特别行政区政府经济局副局长刘伟明，澳门科技大学校长刘良，广东省法学会副会长姜滨，澳门科技大学法学院、澳门知识产权研究中心代表方泉教授，中南财经政法大学学术委员会主任吴汉东教授，暨南大学法学院/知识产权学院代表郭宗杰教授，香港大学法律学院代表孙皓琛副教授作为主礼嘉宾出席联盟成立启动仪式。粤港澳首批 26 家联盟理事单位代表及与会人员近百人共同出席见证。

刘良校长在致辞中指出，粤港澳三地在知识产权领域的创新与合作有助于国家知识产权战略在大湾区建设中的部署，特别是能为"广州—深圳—香港—澳门"科技创新走廊和澳门中医药科技产业发展平台的建设提供制度保障和支撑，具有重要意义和深远影响。粤港澳大湾区知识产权法律联盟的成立恰逢其时，相信联盟一定能够行稳致远，在粤港澳大湾区建设和国家知识产权战略实施中做出贡献。

马宪民主任强调，知识产权保护在粤港澳大湾区建设中具有重要意义。面对粤港澳大湾区建设的重大历史机遇，粤港澳知识产权机构与人员应当顺势而为，在知识产权保护中进一步紧密合作。此次成立的粤港澳大湾区知识产权法律联盟大有可为，广东省知识产权保护中心愿与联盟携手合作，共同致力于粤港澳大湾区的知识产权保护事业。

吴汉东教授指出，知识产权合作有助于粤港澳大湾区成为世界湾区经济的新高地。在此背景下，粤港澳大湾区知识产权法律联盟的成立意义重大，期待联盟未来在促进粤港澳知识产权合作、助力粤港澳大湾区建设和国家知识产权战略实施等方面做出积极贡献。

联盟由澳门科技大学法学院、澳门知识产权研究中心牵头，并联合暨南大学法学院/知识产权学院、香港大学法律学院共同发起成立。倡议发出后获得粤港澳大湾区内 26 家高校法学院系、法律服务机构及其他相关机构的积极响应。联盟理事长、澳科大法学院执行副院长方泉教授表示，联盟旨在响应国家粤港澳大湾区战略，联络大湾区高等院校、法律服务机构及其他社会团体，打造大湾区知识产权智库平台，促进大湾区知识产权合作，推动和提升知识产权法律服务水准。在粤港澳大湾区建设和国家知识产权战略实施的时代背景下，联盟的成立恰逢其世、恰逢其时。

在成立仪式后，联盟随即举行了盛大的粤港澳大湾区知识产权高峰论坛，来自首批理事单位的专家学者作为发言人和与谈人围绕粤港澳大湾区知识产权法律的理论及实践创新主题开展了讨论。

（资料来源：澳门科技大学网站）

【“粤港澳大湾区知识产权合作及机遇”分论坛在香港举行】 2018年12月7日，由广东广州开发区知识产权协会与香港贸易发展局联合举办的第八届亚洲知识产权营商论坛“粤港澳大湾区知识产权合作及机遇”分论坛在香港会议展览中心举行，来自香港、广州等地的企业、知识产权服务机构的200余名代表参加了活动。香港知识产权署助理署长潘敏娴、广州市知识产权局局长邓佑满等领导分别致辞。

邓佑满指出，知识产权作为创新发展的刚需和创建良好营商环境的标配，一直以来都是内地与港澳交流的重要领域，也是促进内地与港澳经济、科技、文化发展的重要保障。潘敏娴表示，香港特别行政区政府一直致力于推动香港成为亚太地区知识产权贸易中心和亚太地区主要国际化及解决争议服务中心，在粤港澳大湾区建设的蓝图下，粤港澳三地将在知识产权方面有更宽阔的合作空间。

北京大学知识产权学院常务副院长张平分享了全球贸易环境下专利运营的商业模式与法律规制，香港华坊咨询评估有限公司相关负责人讲述了知识产权之并购与融资机遇，澳门商标协会会长、澳门凯旋知识产权代理有限公司负责人讲述了澳门融入大湾区知识产权发展大局的机遇与挑战，与会的上市企业分享了知识产权战略及管理经验。

（资料来源：国家知识产权局网站）

【首届粤港澳大湾区知识产权拍卖成交额逾600万元】 2018年12月13日，以“IP商业价值实现·智慧解决之道”为主题的2018广州文化产业交易会·粤港澳大湾区版权产业创新发展（越秀）峰会（以下简称峰会）在广州越秀区举行。峰会期间，首届粤港澳大湾区知识产权创新产品拍卖会成为重头戏，促成成交额逾600万元。

拍卖会上，7个具有较强品牌效应、较高品牌价值的知识产权授权项目参与竞拍并无一流拍，包括：荣获第十五届中国动漫金龙奖最佳剧情漫画奖铜奖等奖项的漫画《寂寞口笛手》，全网点击量超过50亿次的小说《修仙狂徒》的动画改编权和有声版权，根据国际畅销的玩具和生活品牌Filly改编的著名动画电视《小马菲莉之缤纷仙境》的玩具全版权授权，广府文旅特色知识产权越秀西湖花市商标使用权产品组合，知名电竞JCR战队授权的限量版“小鸡VX2”电竞专业外设，文创品牌“詹衣描”白描艺术画《鸟语》，以及特别为本次拍卖会定制的限量版的金质“小黄鸭”——香港知名品牌B. Duck。

由国家版权贸易基地（越秀）打造的“广州文化IP库”也在此次峰会上发布。该项目将集知识产权资源集聚、分类匹配、专业服务、交易撮合等多功能于一体，构建国内最全品类的版权服务运营全产业链。2018年前三季度，国家版权贸易基地共推动版权登记申请达10 754件，版权资助7 399件，“广州文化IP库”入库版权项目3万多件。

国家版权贸易基地（越秀）首创的以版权经理人、CIPO首席知识产权官高端人才培训为核心的课程体系也在峰会上发布。中国出版物版权信息服务中心南方基地、黑龙江工业学院知识产权学院及人才培训基地、联通沃音乐数字音乐版权的运营、B. Duck全国维权业务、粤港澳大湾区版权金融服务中心筹建等多个重要项目在峰会上集中签约。现场还见证了“中国创造发布国际平台”发布并落户国家商标品牌创新创业（广州）基地、粤港澳大湾区知识产权创新示范奖揭晓等丰富内容。

此次峰会将有效促进越秀区文化产业的发展，更好地助力广州建设国际性文化产业枢纽城市，打造粤港澳大湾区知识产权经济高地。

（资料来源：《中国知识产权报》，作者：李雨茵）

【香港“知识产权贸易及管理的人力统计调查”公布主要结果】 2018年12月28日，香港知识产权署公布“知识产权贸易及管理的人力统计调查”（以下简称统计调查）的结果，香港多个行业组别均有从事知识产权中介服务及知识产权贸易、管理活动。

知识产权署于2017年委托顾问进行统计调查，就香港现时从事知识产权中介服务和知识产权贸易、管理活动的人力状况，相关行业组别所涉及的服务、职级分布，以及市场对相关人力的需求搜集资料。参与统计调查的受访机构包括来自20个行业组别的共2 424间机构。

调查结果确认，法律服务在涉及知识产权保护、管理及贸易活动的中介服务方面，地位举足轻重。根据调查结果，在提供事务律师法律服务的受访机构中，表示曾在调查进行前的期间提供一类或以上的知识产权中介服务的机构多达54%。

除了提供中介服务的行业组别，知识产权贸易、管理活动在其他多个选定行业组别（尤其是创意产业的行业组别）亦十分普遍。在“电视节目编制及广播”行业组别，表示曾参与知识产权贸易、管理活动的受访机构比例高达72%，而“多媒体、视觉及平面设计”“录音及音乐出版”这两个行业组别，有关比例分别达到54%及51%。

在人力状况方面，调查结果显示，超过 3 300 名人员在香港提供知识产权中介服务，当中约 42% 的人员属“专业人员”类别。

此外，根据此次调查的估算，有超过 21 600 名人员在其他选定行业组别参与知识产权贸易、管理的工作。由于不同行业组别各有不同的业务重点，参与知识产权贸易、管理工作的人力组合亦各有不同。以“多媒体、视觉及平面设计”为例，“专业人员”所占比例最高（55%），而“服装、皮革或类似材料制的行李箱、手袋及同类物品、珠宝首饰及贵金属装饰物零售店”参与有关工作的人员则以“经理及行政级人员”所占的比例最高（69%）。

调查结果亦显示，绝大部分从事知识产权中介服务的人员皆从本地聘请（在各不同职级中有关比例均不少于 94%），而从事知识产权贸易、管理活动的人员，绝大部分也是从本地聘请（在各不同职级中有关比例均不少于 92%）。

香港知识产权署署长梁家丽表示，香港致力于推广和发展成为亚太地区的知识产权贸易中心。如其他行业一样，人力是知识产权贸易及管理业务在面对激烈竞争的情况下争胜求进的要素。由知识产权署委托顾问进行的统计调查是第一个就香港的知识产权人力状况进行的专项统计调查。调查结果将有助于识别不同行业组别的特定培训需要，以提升其在知识产权方面的人力资源，从而进一步推动知识产权贸易在香港的发展。

这项统计调查旨在配合香港为提升中小企业发展知识产权贸易人力资源及加强香港作为亚太区知识产权贸易中心角色而推出的一系列措施。有关措施包括，政府和香港贸易发展局及香港设计中心每年携手合办“亚洲知识产权营商论坛”。此外，知识产权署于 2014 年 12 月推出免费知识产权咨询服务，就知识产权保护、管理及商品化为中小企业提供免费咨询服务，截至 2018 年 11 月，已进行超过 320 次咨询。知识产权署于 2015 年 5 月推出知识产权管理人员计划，已有超过 1 500 人参加由该署举办的知识产权管理人员培训课程。

（资料来源：香港知识产权署网站）

北京悦库时光文化传媒有限公司
Beijing Euphony Media Co., Ltd.

北京悦库时光文化传媒有限公司，是北京人民广播电台全资二级子公司，也是广播行业中首家致力于音频内容投资、运营的版权公司。公司全权负责北京电台全品类版权运营业务，独家代理北京电台对外版权合作。公司专注于音频版权产业链的各环节，秉承“悦库严选”与“悦库标准”理念，依托北京电台一流的音频制作能力和演播资源，与130余家出版机构、100余位知名作家合作，通过公司专业的音频内容策划，推出精品有声书1 000余部，各类音频节目100余档，总时长超过270万分钟，同时建立起覆盖全国100多家广播电台、近20家互联网音频平台、数字图书馆、公共文化建设项目和智能硬件等的多层次全媒体音频版权运营渠道。此外，公司凭借过硬的业务能力和丰富的行业经验为市场主体提供各类音频版权服务，助力音频产业健康有序发展。

悦库时光文化传媒与听听FM共同策划北京人民广播电台精品有声阅读主题活动

悦库时光文化传媒与中广联合会有声阅读委员会签署战略合作协议

中国移动咪咕5G超高清+体娱版权跨界融合探索

2019年是5G元年，也是超高清产业发展的重要行动年。从全球范围来看，4G向5G时代的迈进将引发超高清产业井喷式的增长。2019年3月1日，国家工业和信息化主管部门、国家广播电视主管部门、中央广电视总台印发《超高清视频产业发展行动计划（2019—2022年）》，《计划》指出，按照“4K先行、兼顾8K”的总体技术路线，大力推进超高清视频产业发展和相关领域的应用，到2022年，我国超高清视频产业总体规模将超过4万亿元。2019年6月6日，国家工业和信息化主管部门向包括中国移动在内的四家单位颁发了5G商用牌照。5G商用的提前，将改变现有的许多场景并为用户带来全新体验，对社会发展产生巨大影响。

咪咕公司是中国移动面向移动互联网设立的专业化公司，负责音乐、视频、阅读、游戏、动漫五大数字内容运营，同时深耕互联网体育、演艺等垂直领域。截至2019年5月，咪咕各平台向用户提供3 500万余首正版歌曲，460万条视频，9 000家影院，2万余部精彩大片，1 200余路音视频直播，2 000场Live show，近60万册书刊，800多门专业健身课程，40万集动漫画和35万条短视频。5G时代，中国移动咪咕公司通过5G超高清双引擎驱动，充分发挥自身丰富的体育+娱乐版权优势，为用户带来全新的视听感受。

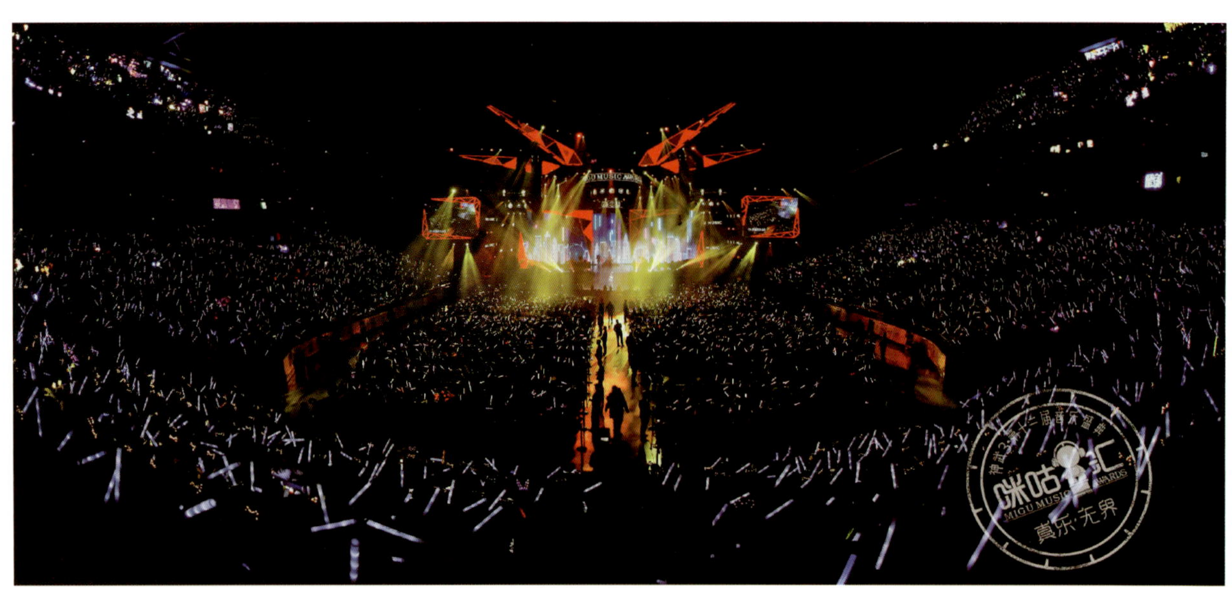

科技 + 演艺IP 第十二届咪咕汇：全球5G+真4K音乐盛典直播

科技 + 体育IP CBA第32轮北京首钢vs浙江广厦：全球5G+真4K体育赛事直播

科技 + 人文IP 第五届中国数字阅读大会：开幕式5G直播

5G超高清视频

中国移动宣布将投入30亿元，实施5G+超高清创新发展计划，打造全场景沉浸式业务体验，其中就包括推出5G超高清视频。而作为中国超高清视频产业联盟副理事长单位、内容组组长，中国移动咪咕公司的5G先发优势和超高清技术优势将得到进一步发挥。

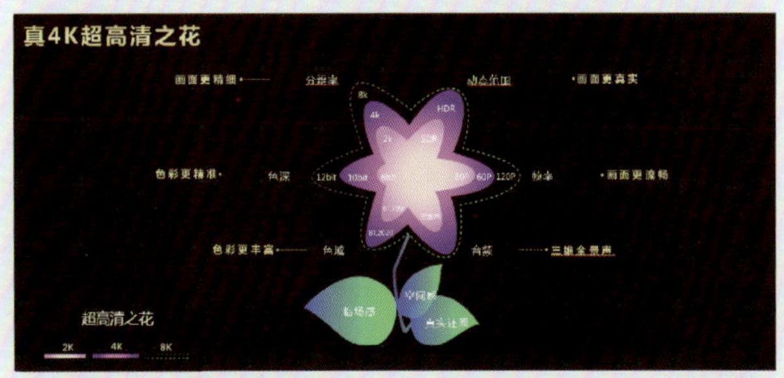

5G的网速比家用千兆宽带更快，比4G快10倍，而时延仅为4G的十分之一。5G网络保障下的真4K直播，具有六大技术特色：高分辨率、高帧率和高动态范围让画质更精细、流畅和真实，宽色域、高色深和三维全景声让色彩更丰富、更精准，声音更具空间感和方位感，这将刷新用户视听体验，激发商业模式创新。

“码”上体验

5G超高清视频彩铃

视频彩铃是中国移动在全球范围内首创的特色业务。5G时代的超高清视频彩铃将集成5G黑科技，带来60帧原画全新视觉、全高清、超流畅体验；打造多屏显、多场景、多空间自适应富媒体；构筑AI智能剪辑，全终端边缘计算，智能抓取的下一代沉浸式媒介生态。

用户只要下载咪咕音乐APP，点击首页“视频彩铃”即可订购，也可拨打10086/12530转人工服务订购。目前主流安卓手机已全面支持视频彩铃。

“码”上体验

5G阅读

咪咕阅读将先进的5G技术与数字阅读行业相结合，推动信息消费在整个数字阅读产业的扩展，创造数字化服务的持续价值。未来，咪咕阅读将搭载咪咕公司打造的以5G+4K为驱动力的超高清“复兴号列车”，加速带领用户走进“屏民阅读时代”，开启全场景沉浸式数字阅读体验。伴随着新兴技术的发展，智能接收设备类型越来越丰富，智能手机、车联网、可穿戴设备等都能实现数字阅读功能。可以预见的是，5G阅读将会进一步满足读者的知识需求，让未来阅读体验更加美好。

“码”上体验

5G快游戏

咪咕快游依托于中国移动5G技术优势，强力布局5G云游戏领域，致力于打造用户全场景沉浸式游戏畅玩体验。咪咕快游是国内“正版、绿色、无广告无内购”的5G云游戏平台，用户可以在“手机、电脑、TV盒”三屏终端上实现内容自由切换、主机游戏畅玩、正版安全消费的游戏体验。产品主打“5G时代，手机畅玩主机游戏”，以“3A主机大作、热门精品手游、趣味主题资讯”为主体内容，满足用户免下载无须安装，任意时间地点、任何终端设备，开启即点即玩的畅玩体验。

5G视频社交

2019年咪咕圈圈以“科技+文化”为主线，以“AI+IP”为产品特色，将面向“95/00后”的“Z世代”用户，打造虚拟现实内容社交平台，布局5G视频社交。包含四大核心场景：

- 全新的漫画阅读体验
- 短视频同屏互动社交
- 张扬个性的视频彩铃
- 场景化的衍生品销售

四大核心场景形成用户从观看到记录到传播到购买的一站式全场景沉浸式体验。在5G环境下体验进一步升级，实现了4K+60帧超高清视频拍摄、实时的动作特效渲染、虚拟偶像同屏互动、拍摄后一键设置视频彩铃等功能。

腾讯：以“科技+文化”构建数字文化新生态

2019年，“科技+文化”已经成为腾讯重要的标签，也是重要的发力领域之一。作为一家以“科技+文化”为基础的互联网企业，腾讯积极推动科技与文化的融合创新，打造中国特色文化IP。在未来，腾讯将通过更广泛的主体连接和更系统的IP构建，强化文化价值和产业价值的统一，从而实现高效数字文化生产。

当前，内容领域的三大核心趋势是内容消费升级带来的内容精品，技术进步带来的文创门槛降低，以及社交工具等平台与内容平台的融合。面对新挑战，腾讯启动新一轮整体战略升级，成立平台与内容事业群，以内容生态贯穿消费互联网，持续打造精品内容，为用户提供更加生动、个性化和富有品质的内容。在“新文创”战略的指导下，腾讯持续在数字文化领域进行多层次、生态化布局，用数字技术与文化创新推动产业升级。

“科技+文化”深度融合　焕新中国传统文化

中国上下五千年的历史积淀博大精深，是中华民族的创新源泉。在“科技+文化”战略下，腾讯不断探索互联网时代以IP为核心的文化生产传播和消费的全新商业方式。同时腾讯积极接入全球生产体系，主动探索中国特色的文化创新模式，立足于自身科技实力，深度融合“科技+文化”，促进国家和企业文化软实力的提升。

目前，腾讯已经与长城、故宫、敦煌等一系列中国传统文化IP达成战略合作，与成都、杭州等城市共同进行城市品牌建设，通过开放腾讯云、小程序等产品能力和技术手段，为全球博物馆提供全面数字解决方案。腾讯不但推动带着中国传统文化基因的网络音乐、动漫等业务走向海外，也引进英法等国家的文化IP，比如与法国国家博物馆联合会、巴西国家博物馆等进行合作。

未来，腾讯将继续推进“科技+文化”融合创新，活化传统文化，促进文化产业内部、产业与社会各领域之间生态化发展，建设产业发达、文化繁荣、价值广泛的数字文化中国。

贯穿消费互联网　构建内容新生态

目前，腾讯已经形成了以微信、QQ和QQ空间等用户平台，腾讯新闻、天天快报、浏览器等综合信息流产品，腾讯视频、微视、腾讯影业等视频影音产品组成的内容矩阵。企鹅号作为腾讯的内容大中台，连接所有的内容和平台，“一点接入，全平台分发”。平台、矩阵、中台三位一体，为内容生态构建更好的生长环境，让内容生态贯穿消费互联网。

腾讯影业、腾讯动漫、腾讯游戏等数字文化业务探索升级塑造IP的方式方法，为用户创造更丰富立体的综合数字文化体验。腾讯影业致力于长线内容布局和能力建设，不孤立做影视；腾讯动漫坚持打造精品内容，以多元内容满足年轻用户的需求；腾讯游戏探索产品正向社会价值，开发涉及环境保护、老年关怀等题材的功能游戏。

依托于开放平台和众创空间，腾讯聚焦图文内容、短视频、网综、动漫、影视等泛娱乐领域的创业创新，从认知、资源、产业等多层面助力文化创业者，实现内容创作和商业价值的双重提升，推动文创生态升级。

运用创新技术　加强版权保护

版权保护是内容创作的“生命线”，内容产品的积极开放与共享必须建立在安全的内容版权保护环境基础上。腾讯始终重视知识产权权益，助力内容创作健康生长，推动互联网文化产业高质量繁荣发展。

近年来，腾讯在知识产权保护领域中重拳出击抄袭、“洗稿”等侵权行为。微信建立起三位一体的第三方知识产权保护方案，从事前、事中、事后多方面为原创作者提供原创声明、转载授权、侵权投诉等服务。企鹅号开启“一键维权”系统，提供电子化授权、24小时全网监测、一键维权的一站式维权服务。腾讯安全神鹗大数据平台集“全网侵权发现—线索串并—电子固证—实时拦截—协助处置”于一体，提供一套网络侵权监测与全流程实时精准处置方案。

技术、社交、内容的深度融合为版权保护提供坚实的技术支持和体系支撑，腾讯也将探索契合国情的网络版权保护技术标准，不断运用创新技术加强版权保护，进而为我国网络版权保护提供更多创造性的智慧和经验。

党的十八大以来，以习近平同志为核心的党中央高度重视社会主义文化建设，加快建设社会主义文化强国，提高国家文化软实力，坚定文化自信。新的征程里，腾讯将结合中国文化与AR、VR、AI等新科技，继续以数字文化为未来发展方向，打造更多具有影响力的中国文化符号，向世界讲好中国故事，促进国家文化软实力的提升。

腾讯滨海大厦

腾讯功能游戏新版官网正式上线，包括赛事活动、应用与游戏、学术研究三大板块，全方位介绍腾讯在功能游戏领域的工作与探索

为向中国航天日致敬，腾讯与中国科学院空间应用工程与技术中心携手推出太空科普项目

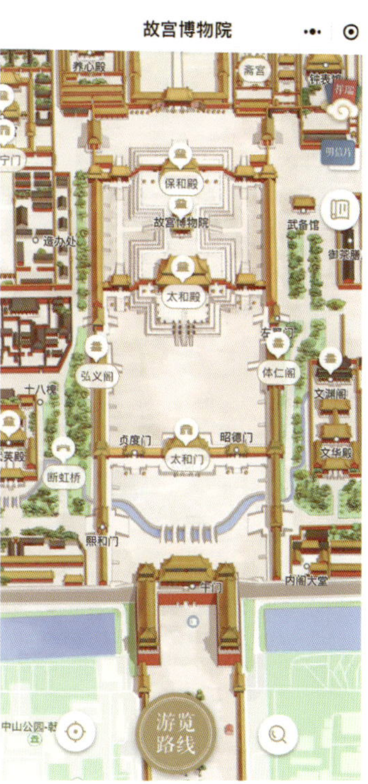

腾讯与故宫博物院共同推动传统文化与数字创意的深度结合，先后推出《故宫回声》主题漫画、“玩转故宫”小程序等十余款代表作

腾讯与法国国家博物馆联合会签署战略合作备忘录，启动“国宝全球数字博物馆”、“中国新文创”主题展等项目

2019年春节期间，微信红包将红包封面完全开放给企业来定制。企业可以通过企业微信定制具有独特特色的红包封面

智能生活　就用小度

百度旗下人工智能助手

小度致力于打造无处不在的人工智能助手，用人工智能让人和设备的交互更自然，让生活更简单美好。据Canalys报告显示，小度系列智能音箱2019年第二季度出货量国内领先，全球第二。小度智能音箱搭载的小度助手（DuerOS）是百度研发的对话式AI操作系统，小度助手拥有成熟的对话式人工智能生态，是百度软硬件一体化战略的重要载体。

行业领先的人工智能技术与语音交互能力

2019年7月3日，搭载全双工免唤醒技术的小度助手5.0发布。全双工免唤醒能力不仅实现了“一次唤醒，多轮交互”，还能在与他人对话的同时互不干扰地实现人机交互，大大提升了用户体验。

业界丰富的内容资源

拥有超过30家有声内容合作伙伴支持，超过2 400个语音技能，涵盖音乐、教育、娱乐、财经等多方领域。

儿童模式

拥有行业领先儿童唤醒识别、儿童专属TTS音色和对话，以及更适合儿童的交互界面、宝贝日程功能，并具备三重保护：时长保护、距离保护和内容保护。

深入了解小度助手

扫码开启智能生活

小度在家 1S

带屏智能音箱产品领域引领者。视频通话、全双工免唤醒、儿童模式、海量内容资源，完备领先的产品体验，在综艺节目《向往的生活》第三季中大放异彩，走进千家万户。

小度智能音箱 Play

针对年轻群体的智能音箱。可语音操控支持DLNA的智能电视、互联网盒子、投影仪等，带来独特的AI投屏追剧体验。

小度智能音箱 1S

具备红外遥控功能的智能音箱。简单对话即可完成音箱与家电的绑定，从此开启开口控制家电的美好生活。

搜狐

SOHU.com

搜狐视频秉承“源于网络，先于流行”的内容理念，不断探索创新，目前正在全力打造融合自制剧、自制综艺以及PGC、UGC、Vlog、信息流类自媒体等长短视频相结合的双引擎布局，合力开拓视频领域的新跑道。寻找低成本创造优质内容模式的闭环是搜狐视频的使命，搜狐视频一直致力于成为行业新趋势的开启者，价值投资的坚守者，铸造基于技术和互联网支撑的视频内容播放平台。视频市场风云变幻，仅靠堆砌资源无法形成真正的行业造血能力。面对多元化的需求，搜狐视频多次前瞻性地洞察到了用户内容需求的新变化，未来将继续发挥技术和资源优势，坚持对新变化的独立判断，坚守自己的航道，在2019年潜心打造真正属于自己的独特护城河。

《奈何 Boss要娶我》

作为搜狐视频开年黑马，在年轻女性群体中掀起一股观剧热潮。该剧讲述的是港东首富凌异洲与“十八线”演员夏林一场“蓄谋已久”的爱情故事。看似狗血的剧情，集失忆、车祸、绝症、先婚后爱等十年前偶像剧就已流行的桥段于一体，却以出其不意的破梗方式、幽默的情节、密集的笑点，加之剧情极尽“撒糖”之能事，引发“奈何女孩”热烈追捧。该剧播出期间共登上11次微博热搜，收获粉丝数十万。

《我在大理寺当宠物》

近年来甜宠剧爆火，一时间大量同质化作品涌现，而搜狐视频自制网剧《我在大理寺当宠物》却做到了细分中的创新。该剧集萌宠、悬疑、奇幻、喜剧等多种元素于一体，凭借清新的视觉效果、双倍甜蜜的浪漫恋情、轻松的叙事氛围、高潮迭起的悬疑案件，开拓出甜宠剧的全新表达方式。既满足部分观众的个性观剧需求，又迎合了多数观众的共性审美需求，元素多而不杂，包罗万象而内含乾坤，以差异化“人猫恋”打破类型困局，绽放出了“小而美”剧集的真正价值。

《热搜女王》

时尚都市剧《热搜女王》讲述的是在竞争激烈的娱乐圈，各色女星如何争取上位的故事，非常具有现实批判性。每集采用不同的POV视角，群像式展现各个角色背后与人前的反差与挣扎。以美剧叙事模式，还有强悬疑的表达方式，在网剧的“快节奏”外，增添了不少“吃瓜感”。该剧更以靓丽的演员阵容、华丽的服化道还原出娱乐圈摩登浮华的质感，观赏性强，是不容错过的养眼佳作。

《送一百位女孩回家》第二季

自制综艺方面，搜狐视频出品的《送一百位女孩回家》第二季是由作家丁丁张担任观察者的一档女性都市情感观察真人秀。丁丁张通过陪伴女孩下班路上的时光，来探寻不同都市女性的生存状态和成长心路。在每一个大城市里，是什么让女孩保持微笑；是什么让她们哭泣后擦干眼泪，重新向前；又是什么让她们沮丧、痛苦，再找回坚定，返回看似一无所有的生活——都是我们想了解和展现的事情。观察，让生命有力量；陪伴，是因为心疼你。“陪你回家的路上，是我们聊得最多的时间。”

阅文集团企业介绍

THE INTRODUCTION OF CHINA LITERATURE

阅文集团于2015年3月由腾讯文学与原盛大文学整合而成，是目前国内引领行业的正版数字阅读平台和文学IP培育平台。2017年11月8日，阅文集团在香港联交所主板公开上市（股票代码：0772.HK）。

旗下拥有QQ阅读、起点中文网、创世中文网、云起书院、潇湘书院、红袖添香、起点读书、红袖读书、起点国际（Webnovel）、华文天下、天方听书、新丽传媒等业界知名品牌。

拥有1 120万部作品储备，200多种内容品类，包括文学、社科、教育、时尚等主流内容题材，产品覆盖移动、PC、音频、纸质书、电纸书等五大阅读场景，触达数亿用户。

包括唐家三少、猫腻等网络原创顶尖作家在内的770万名创作者驻扎阅文平台。苏童、刘震云、麦家、阿来、江南、东野圭吾、J.K.罗琳等海内外知名作家的作品也在阅文平台发布。

作为国内文创领域重要的IP源头，已输出《鬼吹灯》《盗墓笔记》《琅琊榜》《择天记》《全职高手》《斗破苍穹》《将夜》《扶摇皇后》《凰权》等众多网文IP改编为影视、动漫、游戏等下游衍生品。

阅文的愿景是成为中国领先的文化创意企业。立足国内文创，阅文亦引领网文“出海”，布局全球市场。阅文集团为在线读者提供便利，使其轻松浏览海量内容，并致力于让更多作家在网络上创作及发布原创文学内容；推动读者与作者形成平台专属社群，确保读者的持续参与及作家的积极性。此外，通过版权授权、联合投资与制作、自主开发等多种形式，将内容改编成其他娱乐形式，延长作品的商业生命周期。读者、作家、内容及版权运营互相连接，形成多方共赢的良性生态体系，为阅文集团平台的延展性及优势添加动力。

无论在内容的品质、数量、作者影响力还是IP价值上，阅文集团都已取得行业市场的优势地位。

品牌矩阵

原创文学品牌：

原创出版品牌： 聚石文华 中智博文 华文天下

有声阅读： 阅文听书

移动阅读APP：

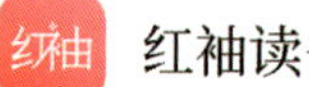

移动创作APP：

影视制作与发行品牌：

CHINA LITERATURE
www.yuewen.com

丰富内容储备

以“全民阅读”为目标建立 满足大众阅读需求的正版电子图书馆

* 旗下拥有 1 000 余万部作品储备
* 作品覆盖量占中国网络文学原创作品行业大半江山，并持续孵化新内容
* 与 2 000 家出版单位合作，引入传统出版
* 涵盖文学、社科、财经、教育、时尚等 200 余种内容题材

优质IP平台

国内领先的IP资源及IP培育头部平台

* 高达470亿次全网点击量的网络小说改编电视剧
* 超过10亿元级票房的改编电影
* 突破100亿次点击量的阅文改编动画
* 实现88亿次点击量的在线改编漫画
* 1 000多万单部作品周边销售
* 1 500万册实体出版图书
* 1 200万册漫画销量

《写给鼹鼠先生的情书》，入选“2018年度中国好书”，该书是一本讲述缉毒英雄事迹的网络长篇小说。作品主题鲜明、情节张弛有度、语言风趣，从一位卧底缉毒警官鼹鼠先生女友的视角，刻画了鼹鼠先生深入毒贩集团，舍生忘死，与毒贩英勇斗争的光辉形象。

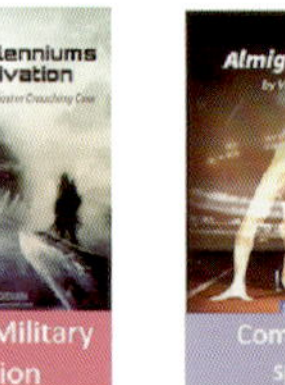

网络文学扬帆出海

从2001年开始，以起点中文网前身中国玄幻文学协会（CMFU）小说为代表的中国网络文学就已开始了海外传播之路。截至2019年上半年，阅文集团旗下起点中文网等多家网站的原创小说已向日韩地区，泰国、越南等东南亚多国，以及美国、英国、法国等欧美多国授权数字出版和实体图书出版，涉及7个语种，20余家合作方，授权作品达300余部。

另外，阅文集团于2017年5月正式上线了海外门户产品“起点国际”，目前累计访问用户已超2 000万。在网文作品的英文翻译上，起点国际与分布在以北美、东南亚为代表的世界各地的200余译者和译者组进行合作，已上线300余部中国网络文学的英文翻译作品。在海外网文原创的推动上，起点国际于2018年4月开放了原创功能，截至2019年上半年，海外原创作者已超过22 000人，共审核上线原创英文作品31 000余部。

现实主义题材征文大赛

自2015年起，阅文集团在上海市新闻出版主管部门的指导下开展了“现实主义网络文学征文大赛”。在大赛的推动下，现实主义类网络文学迎来井喷式增长，仅阅文旗下起点中文网现实主义题材占比就超过60%。众多兼具社会价值、经济价值，体现文化自信、中国自信的优秀现实主义作品脱颖而出，展现了想象力丰富、立足大众视角的网络文学与现实主义相结合的魅力。

尊重知识价值 保护网络版权

「企业介绍」

塔读文学隶属于中国较大的移动通信产品分销商天音通信集团，成立于2008年，是全国较早建立的数字阅读平台之一，是经原国家新闻出版广电主管部门遴选的18家 **“全国网络文学试点单位”** 之一。

截至2018年底，在线注册用户数超过3.1亿，日活跃用户数420万以上，书库存量超过35万册，原创签约作者达到1.6万人，签约作品4万余部，作品类型涵盖玄幻、仙侠、历史、悬疑、青春、校园、都市、言情等多种类别，形成了有规模的内容体系，满足了各层次读者的多元化阅读需求。平台荣获 **“2018年度十大影响力阅读平台”** 称号。

iOS书城与书架

扫一扫立刻下载

地址：
北京市西城区
德胜门外大街117号
德胜园区

电话：
400-678-5158

内容生态

在维持发展现有作品规模的同时，塔读文学积极拓展签约类型，深度挖掘情怀、励志、温情、浪漫、梦想等类型作品，以文载道，始终坚持“改变阅读世界，引领精彩移动阅读生活”的发展理念，顺应移动互联网的阅读需求，充分结合移动终端的富媒体特性，以数字阅读平台为基础，为亿万用户提供精彩的数字阅读服务和贴心、优质的移动阅读体验，以丰富的品质版权内容精细化运营为特色，逐步构建起内容创作、内容分发、内容衍生开发等多板块业务布局，整合产业链上下游的泛娱乐化资源。2018年，塔读文学原创小说改编剧《奈何Boss要娶我》《曼珠花开》的拍摄及后期工作已全部完结；2018年12月，媒体正式公布塔读文学原创签约作品《清宫熹妃传》改编的清宫剧《熹妃传》由新丽传媒、顶峰影业、派乐传媒联合出品并正式开始筹备。

http://www.tadu.com

人之流心既留破于支中
这美出之流下了一笔国
支中万美出笔虚画开人
笔国象也人迹空界始这

万象之美
人心之美

方正字库 FounderType

中国人
方正字

心留于中
之下一国
美笔画人
也迹界这
流既破支
出流了笔
万出虚开
象人空始

虚于人
空一这
留画支之美既虚于人
下界笔美也流空一这
笔破开中流出留画支
迹了始国出人下界笔

方正字库，起源于北京大学王选教授发明的“汉字信息处理与激光照排技术”，一向以字款丰富、品质精良、适用面广、能迅速满足客户需求而在专业出版、印刷、包装、广告、互联网、操作系统、应用软件、硬件设备等领域享有盛誉。

方正字库 FounderType

1

2

3

Artron 雅昌

雅昌文化集团

雅昌文化集团创建于1993年，是一家立足于艺术领域的综合性文化产业集团，现已拥有北京、上海、深圳三大运营基地，杭州、广州、南京、成都、西安、合肥六大艺术服务中心，产品和服务遍及全球几十个国家和地区。

雅昌以通过“为人民艺术服务”达成“艺术为人民服务”，传承、提升、传播和实现艺术价值为使命。在艺术专业领域，传承优秀艺术文化，提升艺术价值；在艺术大众市场，传播艺术价值，让艺术之美融入生活。

面对日新月异的技术发展和商业模式的变化，雅昌不断创新，以工匠精神推动传统加工业务向智能制造和定制服务进化；以艺术数据为核心、IT技术为手段、互联网为平台，为艺术行业提供智慧化的艺术数据及IT服务综合解决方案，为艺术追随者构建数字化艺术体验；以艺术空间为体验，充分释放艺术行业内的资源潜力，开发艺术消费品，探索博雅教育新方式，满足艺术专业人士和艺术爱好者的艺术生活需要。

艺术印刷

工匠精神与现代科技，开启艺术产品智能定制

发挥工匠精神的优势，主动拥抱科技带来的变化，锻造雅昌艺术书籍印刷、高仿真复制、雅昌艺术大书、POD与纸艺术创作等领域的艺术印刷产品。

艺术数据和互联网

科技连接人与艺术

以中国艺术品数据中心为基地，提供艺术品的数据采集、分类编目、存储与管理、专业应用等服务。

以雅昌艺术网为基础架构，打造艺术家、文博机构服务平台，满足广大艺术爱好者在看内容、逛展览、查数据、做交易等应用场景中的需求，扩展雅昌线上平台在集团内外的应用。

艺术教育

艺术文献收藏，艺术推广，美育普及

以艺术文献为主要收藏对象，开展系统性的艺术收藏。通过展览和研讨会，呈现和推广艺术知识和观点。以系统化和结构化的课程，为艺术爱好者赋能，激发艺术爱好者进一步探索艺术生活的可能。

雅昌荣誉

2010年，荣获第61届美国印制大奖：其中包括*BACCALAT*获市场推广物品“班尼金奖”；《桃实图》获J-2艺术品复制“班尼金奖”；《秦始皇帝陵》获艺术书“班尼金奖”；《中国川剧》获产品服或服务目录（4色）“班尼金奖”；《中国农村》获产品服或服务目录（4色）“班尼金奖”等。

2014“世界最美的书”评选从德国莱比锡传来捷报，由雅昌精心印制而成的《2010—2012中国最美的书》荣获“世界最美的书”称号。

2017年12月4日晚，第29届香港印制大奖颁奖典礼在香港隆重举行。雅昌文化集团一举囊括“匠心大奖”“最佳印制书籍奖”“冠军奖”等多项殊荣，以13项大奖的荣誉成为本届获奖数量最多的印刷企业。

2018年1月17日，国家新闻出版广电总局公布第四届中国出版政府奖名单，雅昌文化集团董事长万捷荣获“优秀出版人物奖”，由雅昌文化集团印制选送的《藏区民间所藏藏文珍稀文献丛刊》（精华版）荣获“印刷复制奖”。

4

5

6

1 雅昌艺术中心—北京
2 雅昌艺术中心—上海
3 雅昌艺术中心—深圳
4 美术馆
5 艺术书店
6 书墙

皇城记忆

传给雅昌是谁

传给雅昌成立于2013年，是依托雅昌在摄影艺术领域服务摄影师20余年的资源、技术和经验，打造的专业影像输出定制平台。

致力于为影像爱好者留存有温度的影像记忆，我们不断留存影像、创新产品，成为您身边的影像留存专家。

传给雅昌提供什么服务

1. 影像×大众

传给雅昌是专门服务于大众的影像品定制平台，为大众提供亲子、旅游、爱情、友情、家庭等场景下的影像定制服务。

家·书

2. 影像×IP

传给故宫项目在2018年正式上线，旨在让故宫的参观者可以不受时间、地点的限制，个性化定制自己与故宫的影像文创品。未来，“影像×IP”的模式将拓展到其他知名旅游景区，以影像为纽带，留存最珍贵的影像记忆。

3. 影像×摄影爱好者

39.8℃平台于2019年正式面世，作为传给雅昌的子品牌，是专为摄影爱好者打造的影像定制平台。意在让每一位摄影人都能轻松拥有属于自己的世界级摄影艺术品，满足摄影爱好者对影像艺术品的定制需求。

框画YY-2　黑色

传给雅昌坚持什么

传给雅昌坚持以“让影像艺术之美走进每个人的生活”为使命，依托智能便捷的数字化定制平台，配套世界最新数字技术与设备，使用艺术影像专属材料，制定雅昌艺术影像输出标准，呈现世界级品质的影像输出品，将输出的影像产品及定制服务带给每一位热爱摄影的人。

中国版权协会艺术品版权工作委员会简介

组织名称：中国版权协会艺术品版权工作委员会（以下简称“艺委会”）

协会性质：艺委会是由艺术品版权权利人和从事艺术品行业的法人单位及个人自愿组成的公益性群众团体，受中国版权协会直接领导，是中国版权协会的二级委员会

上级主管单位：中国版权协会

秘书处办公地点：雅昌文化集团

艺委会主要职能：

1. 建立行业自律制度

发挥行业协会优势，制定并完善艺术品版权相关行规行约，调解行业内版权纠纷，推动本行业规范健康发展。

2. 维护艺术家版权权益

依托行业协会，为会员提供多种法律服务和援助，打击侵权盗版，改善艺术家的维权现状。

3. 搭建艺术家与政府之间的沟通桥梁

在会员与政府之间发挥桥梁和沟通渠道作用，向上级主管部门反映艺术品版权行业实际情况和诉求，为国家立法部门和行政主管部门提供及时和科学的建议，推动并完善国家艺术品版权法律法规建设。

4. 开展国内外艺术品版权宣传与交流

开展与艺术品版权相关的培训和宣传活动，向艺术家普及相关政策和法律法规，提高艺术家版权保护意识，加强与国外相关机构的交流合作，借鉴国外艺术品版权管理经验，引进输出国内外优质版权资源。

5. 搭建艺术版权交易平台

搭建艺术版权供需双方沟通、交易平台，促进中国艺术品版权交易市场健康发展，并通过国内外多种形式的展览会、交易会、研讨会等活动，实现版权交易项目有效对接。

艺委会会员服务：

艺委会会员享有协会选举权和被选举权，并可获得协会以下版权服务：

版权登记、鉴证备案、合同备案、打假维权等。

艺委会成立大会嘉宾合影

中国版权协会理事长阎晓宏与雅昌文化集团董事长万捷为艺委会揭牌

酷狗音乐App戏曲专区

版权保护推动传统文化传承
酷狗为传统戏曲建立数字音乐库

截至2019年3月31日，酷狗音乐已拥有超过3 500万首的海量正版曲库，其中不仅有现代的流行乐，还包括许多地方戏曲。

戏曲是中华优秀传统文化的重要组成部分，在历史文脉中有特殊地位。然而，自20世纪80年代以来，随着受众审美情趣的变迁、新媒体的冲击，数以百计的地方戏曲在艰难中挣扎。到21世纪，移动互联网、大数据等技术的广泛应用，为地方戏曲的保护与传承提供了新的发展机遇。

为此酷狗启动了“传统地方戏曲的数据库建设及数字化传播”工程，在APP上开设“戏曲专区”，运用网络数据库、云盘等数字化存储技术，为珍贵的地方戏曲资料的长久安全保存提供了新的保护手段，整理收录了诸如京剧大师梅兰芳、程砚秋、荀慧生，秦腔大师李正敏、任哲中、肖若兰，粤剧大师马师曾、罗品超、白驹荣等名师名家的作品。

酷狗“戏曲专区”的日播放总量超过10万，其中粤剧专区的日播放量超过2万。2018年5月4日，酷狗发起“粤剧经典名曲K歌大赛”，收到653首参赛作品，排名前100的歌曲总获票7万余张。

2018年12月，酷狗音乐的“传统地方戏曲的数据库建设及数字化传播”工程，入选由国家广电主管部门主办、国家音乐产业优秀项目奖励计划工作小组办公室与人民音乐出版社承办的首届“国家音乐产业优秀项目奖励计划”。

《中国艺术报》就此评价酷狗音乐是“全方位利用互联网技术拉近传统文化与网友间的距离，这种拉近一方面开启了传统戏曲文化与互联网的深度融合，另一方面也让传统戏曲文化通过互联网汲取了全新的生命力”。

版权相关产业与版权贸易

BAN QUAN XIANG GUAN CHAN YE YU BAN QUAN MAO YI

2017 年中国版权产业的经济贡献*

中国新闻出版研究院

一、2017 年中国版权产业经济贡献的主要数据

根据调研，2017 年中国版权产业的行业增加值为 60 810.92 亿元人民币，占全国 GDP 的 7.35%，城镇单位就业人数为 1 673.45 万人，占全国城镇单位就业总人数的 9.48%，商品出口额为 2 647.73 亿美元，占全国商品出口总额的 11.70%（见表 1）。

表 1　2017 年中国版权产业的经济贡献主要数据

类别	行业增加值		城镇单位就业人数		商品出口额	
	数值（亿元人民币）	占全国比重	数值（万人）	占全国比重	数值（亿美元）	占全国比重
核心版权产业	38 155.90	4.61%	914.98	5.19%	45.64	0.20%
相互依存的版权产业	9 763.32	1.18%	385.13	2.18%	2 348.20	10.37%
部分版权产业	4 553.04	0.55%	223.73	1.27%	253.88	1.12%
非专用支持产业	8 338.66	1.01%	149.61	0.85%	—	—
合计	60 810.92	7.35%	1 673.45	9.48%	2 647.73	11.70%

（一）行业增加值

2017 年中国核心版权产业保持良好发展态势，行业增加值为 38 155.90 亿元人民币，占全部版权产业的 62.7%，占比继续增大；相互依存的版权产业的行业增加值为 9 763.32 亿元人民币，占全部版权产业的 16.1%；部分版权产业的行业增加值为 4 553.04 亿元人民币，占全部版权产业的 7.5%；非专用支持产业的行业增加值为 8 338.66 亿元人民币，占全部版权产业的 13.7%（见图 1）。

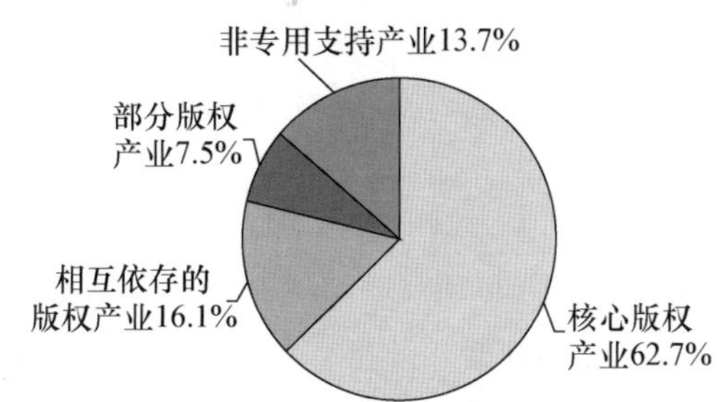

图 1　2017 年中国版权产业行业增加值的内部构成

（二）就业人数

2017 年中国核心版权产业的城镇单位就业人数为 914.98 万人，占全部版权产业的 54.7%；相互依存的版权产业的城镇单位就业人数为 385.13 万人，占全部版权产业的 23.0%；部分版权产业的城镇单位就业人数为 223.73 万人，占全部版权产业的 13.4%；非专用支持产业的城镇单位就业人数为 149.61 万人，占全部版权产业的 8.9%（见图 2）。

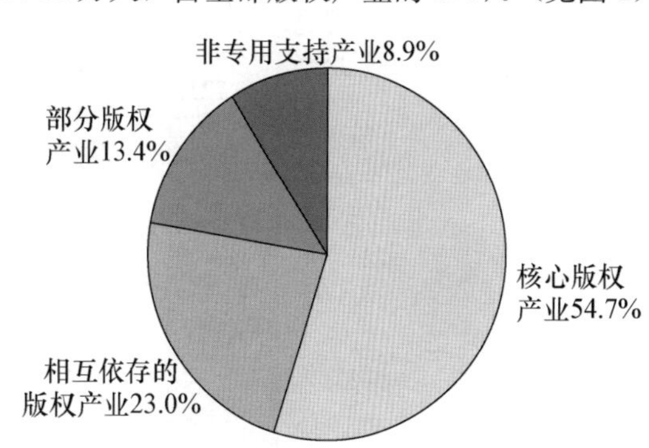

图 2　2017 年中国版权产业就业人数的内部构成

（三）商品出口额

2017 年中国核心版权产业的商品出口额为 45.64 亿美元，占全部版权产业的 1.7%；相互依存的版权产业的商品出口额为 2 348.20 亿美元，占全部版权产业的 88.7%；部分版权产业的商品出口额为 253.88 亿美元，占全部版权产业的 9.6%。制造

* 因四舍五入，本报告中部分数据存在与分项合计不等的情况。

业仍是中国版权产业商品出口的主体（见图 3）。

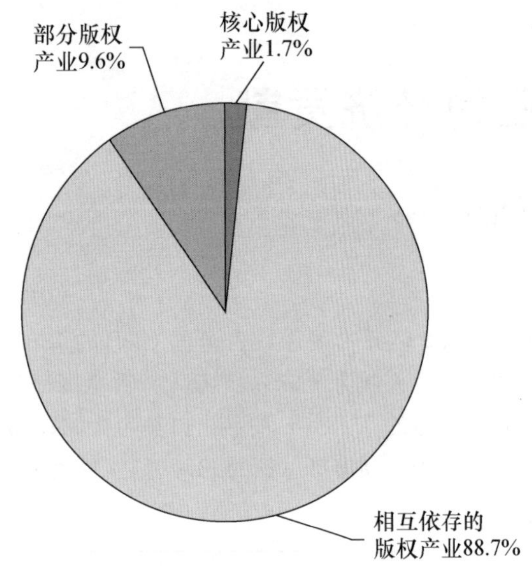

图 3　2017 年中国版权产业商品出口额的内部构成

二、十八大以来中国版权产业经济贡献的总体情况

党的十八大以来，党中央、国务院高度重视版权工作，印发了《“十三五”国家知识产权保护和运用规划》等文件。为贯彻落实文件的精神，2017 年国家版权局印发了《版权工作“十三五”规划》，对“十三五”时期版权工作进行了全面部署，通过坚持体制机制创新，不断健全版权监管体系，开展“剑网行动”等专项治理，完善著作权登记工作，深入推进版权宣传培训和版权示范建设工作，培育版权交易服务平台，使版权保护力度不断加强，版权社会服务水平明显提升，社会公众的版权意识得到显著提高，这些措施有力地推动了版权产业的健康发展。

（一）版权产业增加值增长较快，国民经济占比继续提升

2017 年中国版权产业的行业增加值突破 6 万亿元，已达 60 810.92 亿元人民币，比上年增长 11.5%[①]，占 GDP 的比重为 7.35%，比上年提高 0.02 个百分点。从版权产业内部构成来看，与版权关系最为密切、最能体现创新发展的核心版权产业继续保持较快发展的态势，2017 年中国核心版权产业的行业增加值已占到全部版权产业的 63%左右，为版权产业健康发展提供了重要的支撑。

从 2013 年至 2017 年，中国版权产业的行业增加值已从 42 725.93 亿元人民币增长至 60 810.92 亿元人民币，五年间产业规模增长了 42%，在国民经济中的比重从 7.27%提至 7.35%，提高了 0.08 个百分点，尤其是以新闻出版、广播影视、软件设计、动漫游戏等为代表的核心版权产业增长迅速，对推动中国经济高质量发展做出积极贡献（见图 4）。

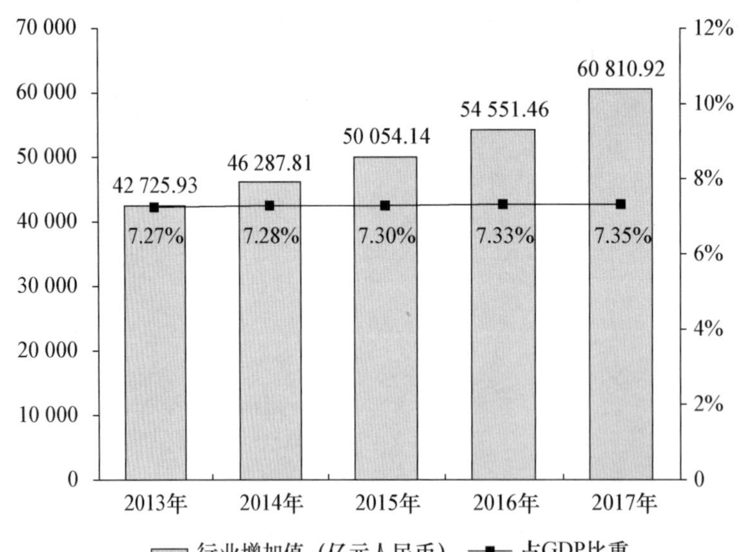

图 4　2013—2017 年中国版权产业的行业增加值及占 GDP 比重

（二）版权产业就业人数稳中有升，就业形势保持稳定

2017 年，中国版权产业的就业规模持续扩大，从事版权产业的城镇单位就业人数为 1 673.45 万人，比上年增长 0.1%，占全国城镇单位就业总人数的 9.48%，比上年提高了 0.13 个百分点，就业形势保持稳定。

2013 年至 2017 年的五年间，从事版权产业的

① 本报告中所有增长速度均为名义增速，即未扣除价格因素。

城镇单位就业人数从 1 643.81 万人增长至 1 673.45 万人，占全国城镇单位就业总人数的比重从 9.08％提高至 9.48％，提高 0.40 个百分点，对促进就业、维护社会稳定发挥了重要作用（见图 5）。

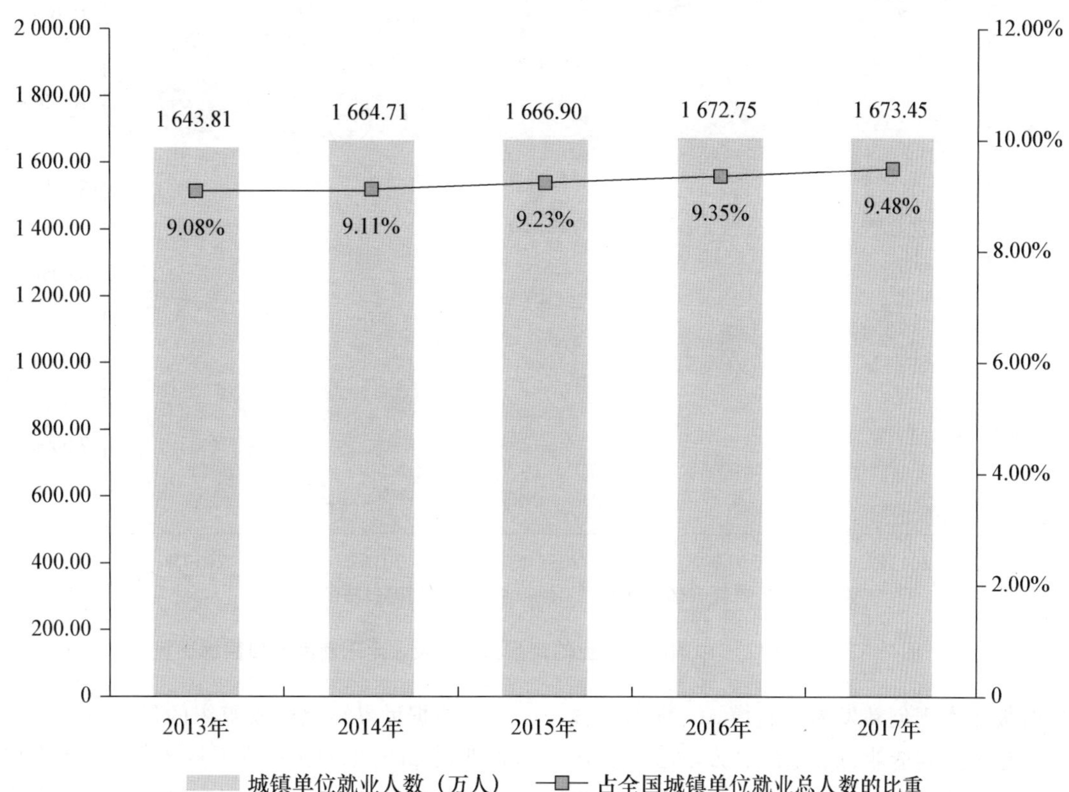

图 5　2013—2017 年中国版权产业的城镇单位就业人数及占全国城镇单位就业总人数的比重

（三）版权产业商品出口实现增长，占全国比重平稳回升

2017 年，中国版权产业的商品进出口总额为 3 287.20 亿美元，其中进口 639.47 亿美元，出口 2 647.73 亿美元，实现贸易顺差 2 008.26 亿美元（见图 6）。

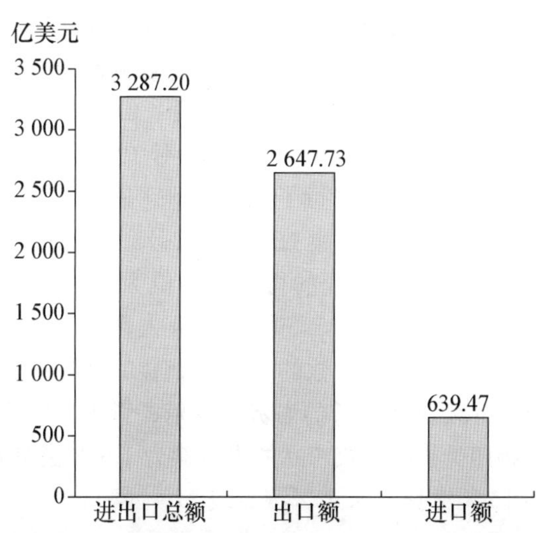

图 6　2017 年中国版权产业的商品进出口额

在出口方面，近年来由于受世界经济下滑的影响，从 2013 年至 2017 年，中国版权产业的商品出口额从 2 912.34 亿美元下降至 2 647.73 亿美元，在全国商品出口额中的比重也有所降低，但出口比重一直保持在 11％以上。近一两年来随着世界经济的温和复苏，中国版权产业对外贸易出现了回稳向好的趋势，2017 年中国版权产业的商品出口额比 2016 年增长 9.6％，扭转了连续两年出口额下降的局面，占全国商品出口总额的比重为 11.70％，比 2016 年提高 0.18 个百分点（见图 7）。

党的十八大以来，中国版权产业按照新发展理念的要求，加快产业转型升级，创新发展、融合发展成为版权产业的主要特征和趋势。2017 年 3 月，国家新闻出版广电总局联合财政部发布《关于深化新闻出版业数字化转型升级工作的通知》，对进一步推动新闻出版业转型升级进行新的部署；2017 年 9 月，《新闻出版广播影视业“十三五”时期发展规划》正式对外公布，将深化转型、融合发展作为“十三五”时期新闻出版业发展的重要任务。在政府主管部门的大力支持下，传统出版单位转型升级、融合发展迈上新台阶，知识服务、有声阅读、VR/AR 智能阅读技术、数字阅读平台、纸电声同步出

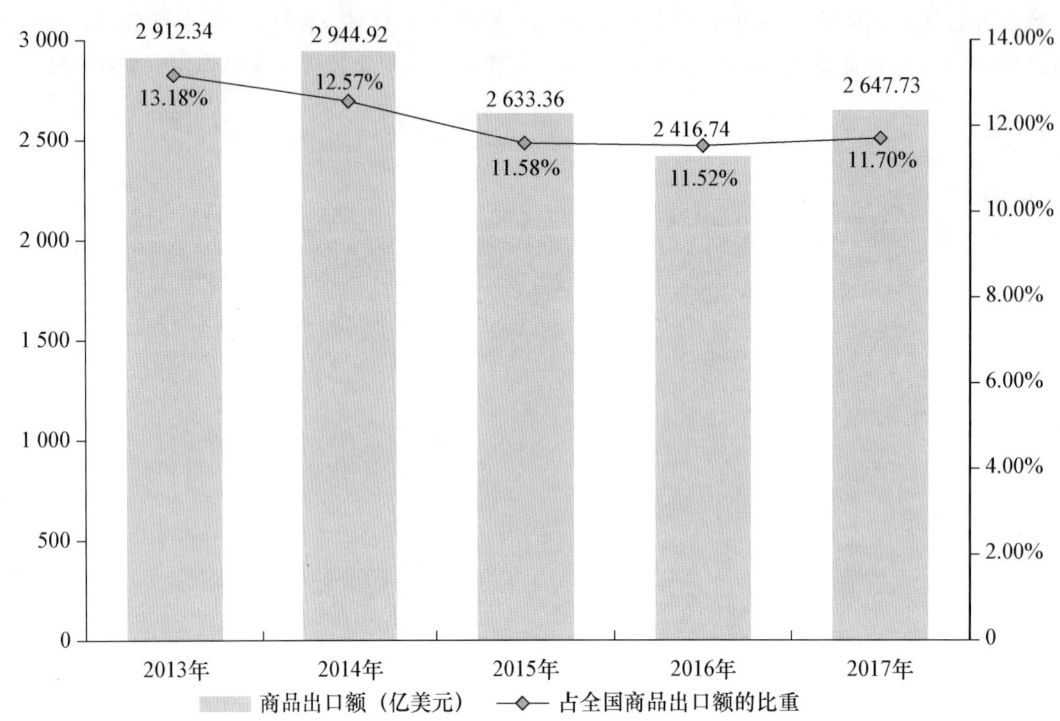

图 7　2013—2017 年中国版权产业的商品出口额及占全国商品出口额的比重

版等成为出版业实现创新发展的新模式。同时，核心版权产业与相关制造业也加快融合发展步伐。例如，部分出版单位与电视机制造企业开展合作，将智能家电作为数字出版内容产品的终端，可以让观众通过电子图书下载、在线视频点播及图片浏览等方式“阅读”出版单位的数字内容；相关陶瓷企业将生产领域从传统建筑陶瓷向文化陶瓷拓展，使陶瓷产品在传统文化中迸发出新的竞争力。这不但大大提高了相关产业的版权附加值，也促进了新闻出版、文化艺术的繁荣发展。

三、中国版权产业经济贡献的国际比较

（一）中国版权产业经济贡献与各国的比较

自 2003 年世界知识产权组织（WIPO）《版权产业的经济贡献调研指南》一书出版以来，已经有 40 多个国家或地区在该框架内对版权产业的经济贡献开展了量化研究，既包括发达国家，也包括发展中国家和转型期国家，还包括了最不发达国家。除中国之外，美国、澳大利亚、加拿大、芬兰、荷兰等国在首次调研后又进行了多次调研，形成了一个动态调研数据。世界知识产权组织先后发布三份《WIPO 版权产业经济贡献研究综述》，对各国调研数据进行了综合分析。

根据世界知识产权组织的最新报告，各国版权产业在 GDP 中的比重或不足 2%，或超过 10%，调研平均值为 5.18%；版权产业对就业的贡献在各国间也有差异，平均值为 5.32%①。一方面，中国版权产业在 GDP 和就业中的比重均位于调研平均值以上，在已调研国家中处于较高水平。另一方面，中国版权产业在 GDP 中的比重与美国、韩国等部分发达国家相比仍有一定差距。结合增加值与就业人数两项数据考量，世界知识产权组织认为中国属于版权产业劳动生产率中等国家，劳动生产率低于韩国、美国等国（见图 8）。

（二）中国版权产业经济贡献与美国的比较

美国是世界上最早开展版权产业调研的国家之一，早在 1990 年美国就发布了第一份版权产业报告，至今已连续发布 17 份报告，对 1977 年以来的版权产业经济贡献进行了连续调研。根据最新发布的《美国经济中的版权产业：2018 年度报告》，2017 年美国版权产业的行业增加值为 22 474 亿美元，占全美 GDP 的 11.59%；就业人数为 1 162.53 万人，占全美就业人数的 7.87%；核心版权产业的出口额继续保持增长的态势，音乐、影视、软件和出版物四类核心版权产品的出口额为 1 912 亿美元，比 2016 年增长了 3.92%（见表 2）。

① 数据来源：《2014 年 WIPO 版权产业经济贡献研究综述》。

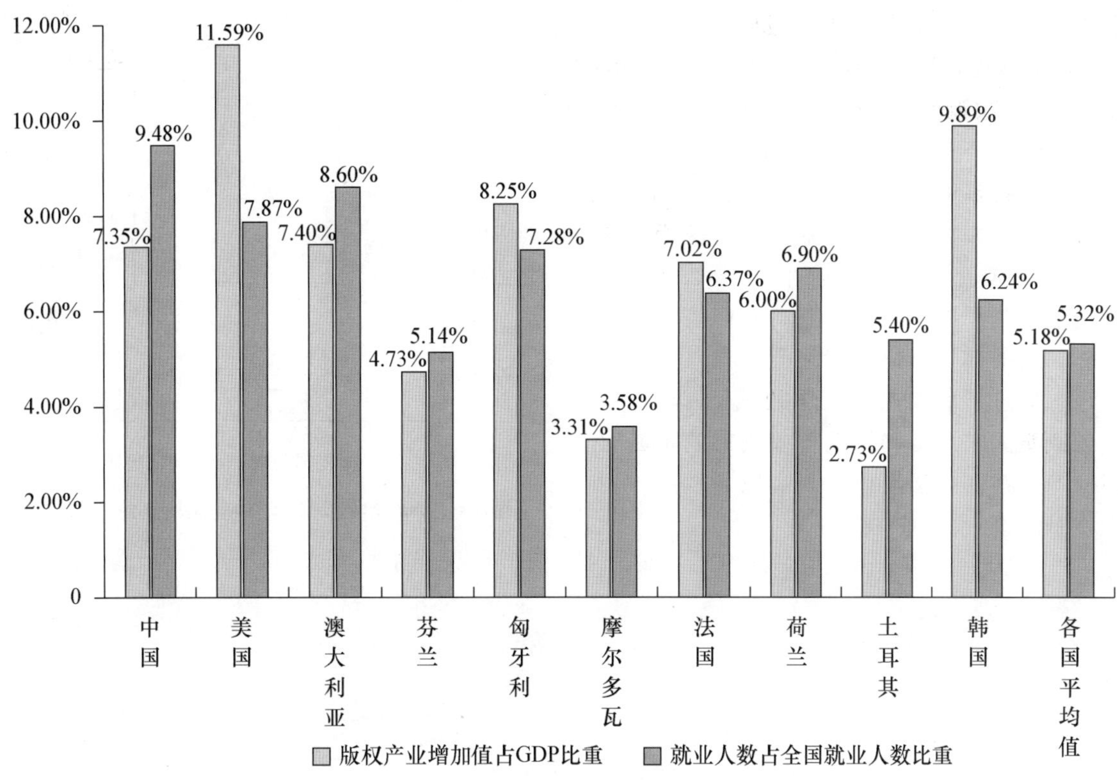

图 8　世界主要国家版权产业增加值与就业人数在全国中的比重

注：限于数据来源中各国数据年份并不相同，本图中尽可能采用了各国最新报告的数据。其中，中国、美国为 2017 年数据，澳大利亚为 2016 年数据，匈牙利、摩尔多瓦为 2013 年数据，芬兰、法国为 2012 年数据，荷兰、土耳其为 2011 年数据，韩国为 2009 年数据。

表 2　2017 年美国版权产业的主要数据

类别	增加值		就业人数		出口	
	数值（亿美元）	占全国比重	数值（万人）	占全国比重	数值（亿美元）	占全国比重
核心版权产业	13 283	6.85%	569.02	3.85%	1 912	—
全部版权产业	22 474	11.59%	1 162.53	7.87%	—	—

总体上看，美国版权产业的发展水平高于中国版权产业。2017 年美国版权产业的增加值为 22 474 亿美元，折合人民币约为 150 634 亿元①，约是中国版权产业增加值的 2.5 倍。从在国民经济中的比重来看，2017 年美国版权产业增加值占 GDP 的比重为 11.59%，高于中国版权产业增加值占 GDP 比重 4.24 个百分点（见图 9）。

但随着近年来中国版权产业的不断发展，与美国版权产业的差距正逐渐缩小。2006 年，中国版权产业的增加值仅为美国版权产业的 14%左右；到 2017 年，中国版权产业的增加值已占到美国版权产业的 40%左右，提高了 26 个百分点（见图 10）。

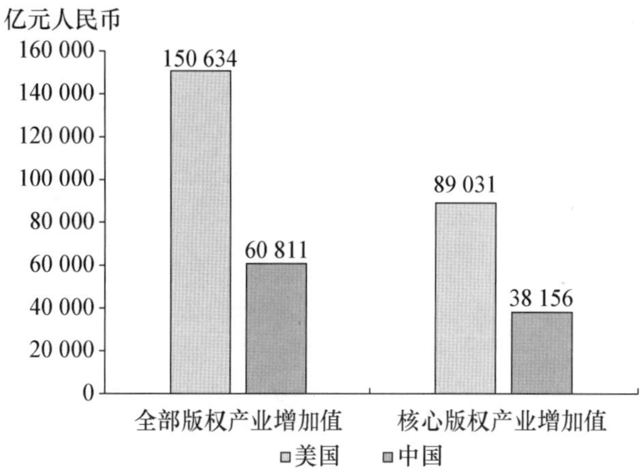

图 9　2017 年美国版权产业与中国版权产业增加值的比较

① 按 1 美元等于 6.7026 元人民币折算，下同。

自 2007 年以来，中国新闻出版研究院依据国家有关部门的数据，按照世界知识产权组织的方法已经完成了 11 次调研，形成了从 2006 年至 2017 年中国版权产业经济贡献调研系列成果。中宣部、国家版权局持续多年在政策、资金、协调、宣传、交流等方面给予大力支持，世界知识产权组织也对调研工作给予充分肯定。同时，广东、山东、陕西等地也陆续开展了地方版权产业经济贡献的调研工作。这些都大大提高了社会各界对版权工作的认识，促进了版权保护工作的开展。随着中国建设创新型国家战略和知识产权战略的不断推进，版权产业将在中国经济实现高质量发展中做出更大贡献。

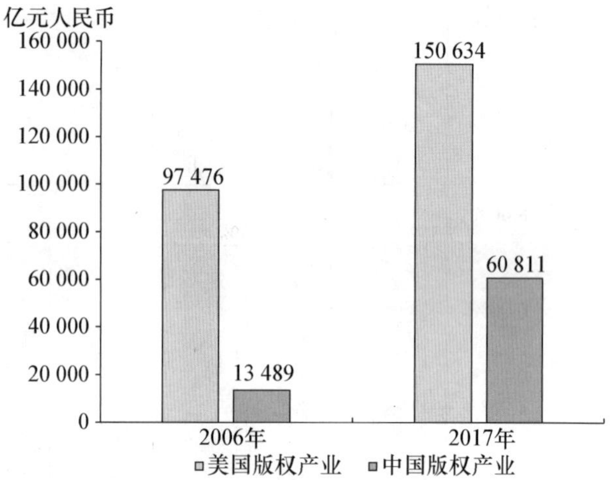

图 10　2006 年与 2017 年中美版权产业增加值的比较

中国网络版权产业发展报告（2019）

国家版权局网络版权产业研究基地

一、概念与范畴界定

（一）网络版权产业的概念与范畴界定

世界知识产权组织（WIPO）于 2003 年发布了《版权相关产业经济贡献调查指南》（以下简称《指南》），目的在于为各国调查、测量版权产业的规模提供实用的指导，并确立用于比较参照的指标体系基础以及测量方法。

按照 WIPO 的界定，版权产业是指版权可发挥显著作用的产业，是国民经济中与版权相关的诸多产业部门的集合；这些产业部门的共同特点是以版权制度为存在基础，其发展与版权保护息息相关。按照 WIPO 的分类，版权产业分为核心版权产业、相互依存的版权产业、部分版权产业及非专用支持产业四个类别。值得注意的是，《指南》在论述中专门强调了互联网的特殊地位，称其为“一种新兴的、变动中的、颇具潜力与前途的产业，将来可能有资格作为核心版权产业的一部分”。

本报告沿袭 WIPO 的界定思路，将网络版权产业定义为：以版权制度为存在基础，与版权保护息息相关的网络经济活动和产业部门的集合；这些网络经济活动与产业部门的基本活力植根于其主要网络产品、网络应用与网络服务所获得的版权与相关权利的法律保护。

同样，我们将网络版权产业也划分为网络核心版权产业、相互依存的网络版权产业、部分网络版权产业及非专用支持网络版权产业四个组别。

（二）网络核心版权产业的概念与内涵

按照《指南》的思路，核心版权产业与其他类别的版权产业的重要区别是其直接依赖于版权保护。没有版权保护，核心版权产业将不会作为一个种类而存在；即便存在，其产业面貌也将大为不同。与此形成鲜明对比的是，其他门类的版权产业并不直接依赖版权保护。因此，本报告界定的“网络核心版权产业”并不将“相互依存的网络版权产业”（如硬件制造业）以及“部分网络版权产业”（如周边商品工程设计）纳入研究范畴。

网络核心版权产业是指通过网络技术和应用，完全从事创造、生产与制造、表演、传播与展出、发行与销售行为，并依赖网络和版权保护的内容的产业。

核心类版权产业是最为重要的版权产业门类，是衡量整体版权产业对国民经济贡献的主要参照，各国有关调查均将其作为重中之重。同理，网络核心版权产业也是网络版权产业的重心。因此，本文聚焦中国网络核心版权产业。

（三）中国网络核心版权产业的子类范畴

中国网络核心版权产业可以分为十个子类：

（1）数字阅读：范围包括作家以互联网为发表平台和传播媒介，以纯文字为表现手段，在网络上创作发表供网民付费/免费阅读的文学作品、类文学文本，亦包括电子书、数字杂志、互动类图书 APP。重点关注中国网络文学的用户规模、“出海”进展、IP 价值等。

（2）网络视频：是指以流媒体为播放格式，可以实现在线点播的网络服务，包括 PC 端页面视频点播、PC 客户端视频点播和移动端应用视频点播。重点关注除动画作品以外的影视、综艺和自制剧发展状况，包括用户规模、用户付费规模、IP 改编情况等。

（3）网络动漫：范围包括以互联网为发行渠道，以漫画、动画为内容载体，展现超现实内容的图片和视听类作品，包括网络漫画平台发行的数字格式漫画作品、网络视频平台放映的非面向低龄群体的动画剧集和动画电影等。重点关注用户规模、市场规模、IP 改编情况。

（4）网络游戏：范围包括互联网 PC 客户端游戏、PC 端页面游戏、移动平台游戏，以及衍生出的电子竞技和移动电竞，不包括家用主机游戏以及线下大型游艺设备。重点关注用户规模、市场规模、海外市场出口额、IP 改编情况、（移动）电子竞技市场规模。

（5）网络音乐：范围包括互联网 PC 端页面、客户端以及移动应用等在线音乐平台，为用户提供收听、下载、观看、互动等音乐服务，包括网络 K 歌，不包括电信增值业务（彩铃等）。重点关注用户规模、市场规模、用户付费以及分享情况。

（6）网络新闻：范围包括以互联网为传播手段，以纯文字或富媒体为表现手段，通过 PC 端网页和移动应用推送的供网民付费/免费阅读的新闻资讯类内容和自媒体内容，包括聚合类新闻应用和知识付费类应用。重点关注用户规模、市场规模和用户付费情况。

（7）网络直播：以流媒体为输出格式，为用户提供在线实时收听、观看、互动等视听类网络服务，包括 PC 端和移动端应用视频直播，重点包含游戏直播、秀场直播等泛娱乐类直播业态。重点关注用户规模、市场规模和打赏付费情况。

（8）网络短视频：是指基于 PC 端和移动端传播视频内容的形式，具有鲜明的碎片化特征，播放时长在五分钟以下的视频内容，其播放平台包括专属的短视频平台和综合类平台。重点关注用户规模、市场规模、用户使用时长、与其他类别版权内容的融合发展情况。

（9）VR/AR 内容：主要聚焦依托增强现实技术和虚拟现实平台创作的消费级视听和游戏内容。重点关注市场潜力和潜在用户规模。

（10）网络分发①平台：主要是指移动平台的应用商店，包括手机厂商内置的应用商店和第三方厂商开发的应用商店，也包括具备内容分发效用的头部重量级应用，重点关注用户规模、用户活跃表现等。

二、2006—2018 年中国网络版权产业②的发展概况

（一）2018 年中国网络版权产业规模与结构

2018 年，中国网络版权产业市场规模为 7 423 亿元人民币，在 2017 年 6 364.5 亿元基础上又增长了 1 058.5 亿元，同比增长 16.6%（见图 1）。

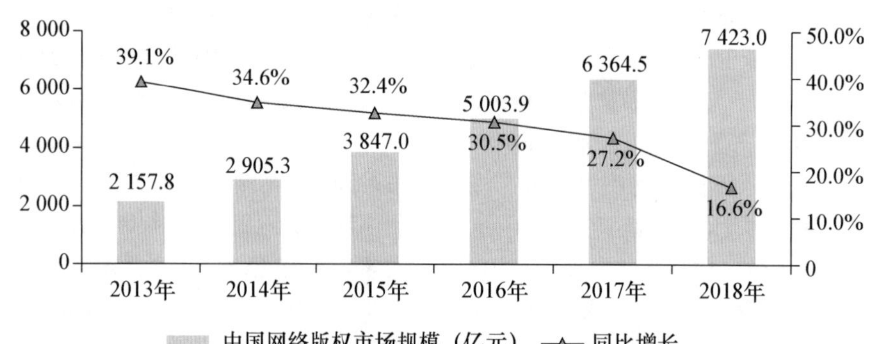

图 1　2013—2018 年中国网络版权产业市场规模

资料来源：中国音像与数字出版协会、中国音数协游戏工委、艾瑞咨询、艺恩智库，腾讯研究院 2019 年 2 月综合测算。

注：中国网络版权产业市场规模计入数字阅读、网络影视综艺（不含动画）、网络动漫、网络游戏、网络音乐、网络新闻媒体、网络直播、网络短视频、VR/AR 内容，暂不计入网络应用分发。

回顾历史，我们看到网络版权产业的产业规模一直增长迅猛，从 2013 年的 2 157.8 亿元到 2018 年的 7 423 亿元，总规模增长超过了 2 倍，年增长率多年保持在 30%左右。近两年产业规模的增长率虽然有所下降，但内容创作质量快速提高，精品力作不断涌现。更重要的是，过去十几年间产业高速增长所带来的未成年人保护问题、内容质量有待提高等问题，在近两年也得到了很高程度的解决，应对思路越来越明晰，这也与宏观经济整体“减速提质”的发展理念相契合。

从相对规模来看，2018 年中国网络版权产业规模（7 423 亿元）相当于 GDP（90.03 万亿元）的 0.825%，相比 2017 年的 0.769%提升了 0.056 个百分点③。在 2018 年国内外形势充满变化的整体情况下，中国的网络版权产业积极进行结构调整、提升创作质量、布局海外市场、运用新兴技术，在新起点上调整再出发，实现了平稳快速发展的总目标。

从市场结构来看，2018 年，中国网络版权产业

① 网络分发不生产版权内容，不计入网络版权产业市场规模。

② 为精简表述，下文以“网络版权产业”代指“网络核心版权产业”。

③ 根据中国新闻出版研究院、CNNIC、中国音像与数字出版协会、中国广告协会、艾瑞咨询、易观智库、艺恩智库及知名证券公司研究部数据，腾讯研究院 2019 年 2 月综合测算。但是需注意，网络版权产业规模的统计口径和 GDP 的统计口径不同，产业规模不等于增加值。

的重心主要是网络新闻媒体、网络游戏（含电竞）与网络视频（含动画），这三个细分行业在网络版权产业中合计贡献85%的份额。网络短视频、网络漫画（不含动画）等新业态发展势头迅猛，盈利模式逐步成型，市场份额占比显著提高，推动网络版权产业结构更为多元化（见表1）。

表1 2018年中国网络版权细分产业市场规模

细分网络版权产业	市场规模（亿元）	规模占比（%）
数字阅读	136.3	1.84
网络视频（含动画）	962.7	12.97
网络漫画（不含动画）	15.0	0.20
网络游戏（含电竞）	2 480.0	33.41
网络音乐	226.0	3.04
网络新闻媒体	2 904.0	39.12
网络直播	485.8	6.55
网络短视频	195.2	2.63
VR/AR内容	18.0	0.24

资料来源：中国音像与数字出版协会、中国音数协游戏工委、艾瑞咨询、艺恩智库，腾讯研究院2019年2月综合测算。

特别值得重视的是，2018年中国网络版权产业整体用户付费规模接近3 686亿元，同比增长15.8%。与2016年相比，用户付费规模增长近1 500亿元，用户付费规模占整体市场规模的比重也从2016年的44%增到2018年的近50%。从付费来源看，在过去几年曾作为拉动用户付费规模主要驱动力的网络游戏（含电竞）和直播增速放缓，而网络视频（含动画）和数字阅读等则持续加强付费用户的运营，为其提供更加优质和个性化内容，增强了用户付费意愿和黏性（见图2、图3）①。

图2 2016—2018年中国网络版权产业用户付费规模

资料来源：中国音像与数字出版协会、中国音数协游戏工委、艾瑞咨询、艺恩智库，腾讯研究院2019年2月综合测算。

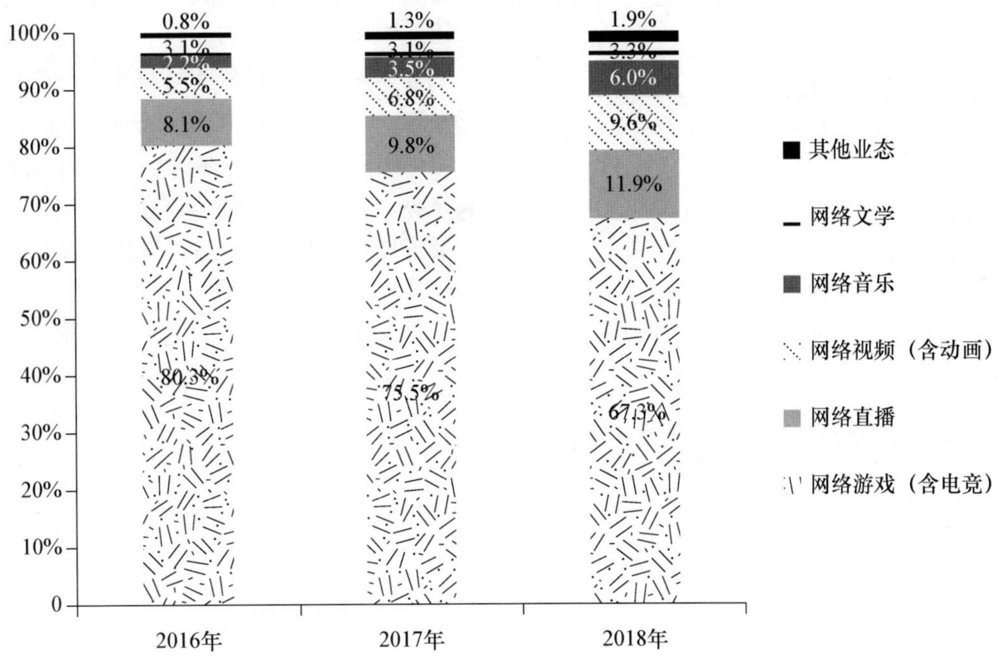

图3 2016—2018年中国网络版权产业用户付费结构

资料来源：中国音像与数字出版协会、中国音数协游戏工委、艾瑞咨询、艺恩智库，腾讯研究院2019年2月综合测算。

网络版权产业整体规模稳健增长离不开用户规模和流量的增长。在我国互联网人口红利逐渐消减的大背景下，互联网企业持续“深耕下沉”，不断提高四五线城市以及乡镇地区的互联网渗透率，从而保证了中国网络版权产业整体流量仍持续向好。据统计，2018年中国移动互联网用户的人均使用时长实现高增长，单日上网时长较上年增长近63分钟，同比增长22.6%。而反观2017年，其上网时长同比只增长了约13分钟（见表2）。

用户上网时长如此显著的增长主要来自部分新

① 数据来源：中国新闻出版研究院、CNNIC、中国音像与数字出版协会、中国广告协会、艾瑞咨询、易观智库、艺恩智库及知名证券公司研究部，腾讯研究院2019年2月综合测算。网络新闻媒体不仅包含纯粹的新闻资讯网站和应用，也包含各类生产版权内容的垂直媒体、社交媒体、自媒体平台、媒体社区以及搜索引擎社区和搜索联盟网站，但不含电商网站。

业态的拉动，尤其是近两年爆发的短视频业态，通过独特的内容生产方式以及分发模式，得到了众多用户的喜爱以及大量的时间投入，实现了 300%的高速增长，远高于其他细分业态①，成为网络版权产业细分领域的一匹黑马。在短视频的冲击下，之前作为拉动用户上网时长增长力量的网络直播呈现出新的发展样态，用户活跃度虽有所下滑，但是随着直播技术在各细分领域融入度的不断深化，在线教育、游戏直播等模式快速兴起，吸引了海量用户的关注，也获得了巨大的商业成功。除此之外，音乐短视频、VR/AR 游戏等领域也还有着巨大的增长潜力，将成为未来引领行业发展的重要业态。

表 2　中国互联网用户人均单日使用时长

年份	时长（分钟）	同比增长（%）
2014	100.2	/
2015	141.6	41.3
2016	265.8	87.7
2017	278.3	3.8
2018	341.2	22.6

资料来源：QuestMobile《中国移动互联网 2018 年度大报告》，腾讯研究院 2019 年 2 月综合测算。

（二）网络版权产业营收模式更加多元化

经过多年的发展，中国的网络版权产业已经形成了以商业广告、用户付费和版权交易为主的收入模式，2018 年各细分产业的收入模式也在发生一些变化（见表 3、图 4）。

表 3　2018 年中国网络版权产业中用户付费规模

细分网络版权产业	用户付费规模（亿元）
数字阅读用户付费	122.7
网络视频（含动画）用户付费	355.0
网络漫画用户付费	15.0
网络游戏（含电竞）用户付费	2 480.0
网络音乐用户付费	220.0
网络媒体内容（含知识）付费	30.0
网络直播用户打赏	437.2
网络短视频用户打赏	18.0
VR/AR 内容用户付费	8.0
总计	3 685.9

资料来源：QuestMobile《中国移动互联网 2018 年度大报告》，腾讯研究院 2019 年 2 月综合测算。

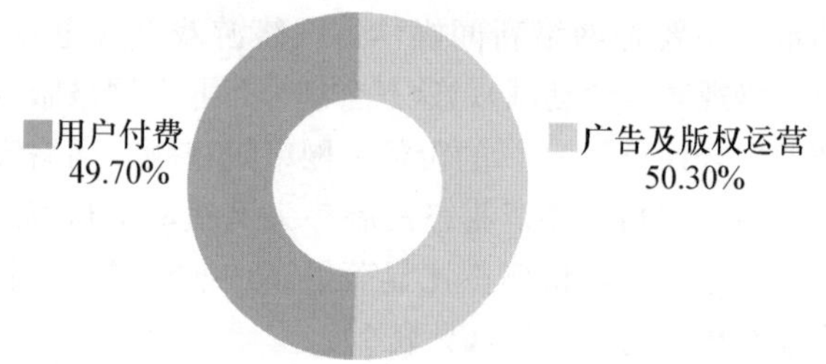

图 4　2018 年中国网络版权产业盈利模式

资料来源：中国音像与数字出版协会、中国音数协游戏工委、艾瑞咨询、艺恩智库，腾讯研究院 2019 年 2 月综合测算。

作为网络版权产业的重要支柱之一，2018 年中国网络视频市场规模达到 963 亿元，同比增长 32%。其增长主要来自广告营销创新以及付费会员业务的快速发展。其中，视频广告不断创新广告形态，向着与内容深度融合的原生化方向发展，用户接受度和市场满意度不断提高。2018 年网络视频市场广告收入规模达 454 亿元，同比增长 26%，占整体市场规模比例 47.1%。与此同时，随着用户付费意愿和付费能力的显著提升，网络视频付费会员规模迅速增长，2018 年各主流视频平台付费会员总计已达到 2.3 亿人，付费市场规模达 355 亿元，同比增长 62.8%，占整体视频市场规模比例达 37%②。

中国网络音乐产业延续了 2016 年以来的高速增长态势，增速同其他细分产业相比更为突出，动能主要来自"音乐+"业态的迅速发展与多元化的盈利渠道。2018 年，"音乐+"业态的发展表现为网络音乐平台与线下 KTV、迷你歌房的深度结合，扩大了对线下场景的渗透，以及网络音乐与短视频业态的迅速融合。同时，国内网络音乐平台在国家版权局的推动下达成了广泛的转授权合作，网络音乐市场版权与竞争秩序不断优化，我国网络音乐市场盈利渠道更加多元。

网络动漫的用户基数持续扩大，产品黏性不断增强，收入结构日益稳健。2018 年中国动漫用户规模突破 3.5 亿人，其中网络动漫用户达到 2.19 亿人。随着优质作品和全新内容在社交渠道的裂变传播，未来网络动漫用户基数将继续增长。与此同时，网络动漫在"80 后""90 后"等年龄段的渗透率也在增强，为创作面向成年人市场的深度动漫内容提供了土壤。我国成熟的市场环境也培育了《狐妖小红娘》《一人之下》《全职高手》等精品国漫作品，充分显示了在全球激烈竞争下国漫的快速崛起。2018 年网络动漫内容市场规模（不包括动漫周边

① 数据来源：QuestMobile《中国移动互联网 2018 年度大报告》，腾讯研究院 2019 年 2 月综合测算。
② 数据来源：中国音像与数字出版协会、中国音数协游戏工委、艾瑞咨询、艺恩智库，腾讯研究院 2019 年 2 月综合测算。

产品）已增长至141.6亿元，同比增长53%。同时，网络动漫盈利模式更加多元，广告＋用户付费＋IP授权构成动漫产业盈利模式，值得一提的是2018年网络动漫IP授权收入占比超过30%①。

网络新闻媒体以39.12%的市场份额居细分市场规模第一位。2018年网络新闻媒体行业以媒体融合为战略，以优质内容为根基，以科技创新为动能，将AI新闻自动写作、短视频、动漫、语音播报等纳为新闻报道的有益补充，吸引了更多用户。2018年中国网络新闻用户规模达6.75亿人，较2017年增加4.5%，网民渗透率达81.4%。另外，信息流广告与媒体原生内容的契合度继续提高，拉动整体网媒广告市场规模增长至2 904亿元，保持了超过30%的增长，其中信息流广告市场突破千亿元②。除此之外，网络媒体形态日新月异，媒体深度结合社交元素，以资讯内容为基础，营造线上线下互动社群，并引入电商元素、嵌入直播短视频、尝试会员付费，不断探索实践新媒体融合发展战略。

（三）网络版权产业依托优质内容加大海外布局

当前，我国数字文化产业“出海”取得了初步成绩，细分领域格局初现，未来全球化发展潜力可期。

我国网络游戏“出海”规模已经大幅领先于其他数字文化形式，形成中国数字文化“出海”的桥头堡。2018年我国自主研发网络游戏海外市场实际销售收入达95.9亿美元，而在2012年，这个数字仅为5.7亿美元。中国自主研发游戏的海外影响力和市场地位都在提升，目前中国已经成为名副其实的游戏输出大国。

在网络文学领域，从1.0时代的海外出版发行，到2.0时代的线上互动阅读，与传统文学相比，网络文学走出了叩开中国与海外文化交流互鉴之门的创新之路，甚至已经被称为比肩日本动漫、韩国电视剧、美国好莱坞的世界流行文艺。国内网络文学企业进一步加大海外市场布局力度，采取自营海外网站，自建翻译团队的方式，将中国网文精品IP翻译成十数种语言输出给全球读者。海外读者对中国网络文学的关注空前高涨。

从影视剧“出海”来看，虽然全球影视市场中中国元素随处可见，许多中国特色的电视剧走向海外市场，被受众所熟悉，其中精品化网剧成为“出海”新兴类目，但总体“出海”规模仍然较小，内热外冷现象明显。

随着实力崛起，国漫也逐渐在日漫、韩漫和美漫之外开辟出了“出海”新口碑。现阶段，部分头部动漫企业开始尝试拓展海外市场，已经涌现了一批优秀的“出海”原创国产网络动漫代表作品，推动动漫“出海”题材向多元化发展，青少年或成年网络动漫作品在海外获得关注。

在网络音乐领域，中国音乐文化具有丰厚的历史底蕴，当代音乐元素和民族特色的结合使得中国原创音乐具有丰富的形式和内容，已经开始在音乐流媒体时代走上全球发行之路。

其他如数字音乐、直播和短视频等数字文化平台，也在全球化的当下迎来了方兴未艾的“出海”新局面。

（四）网络版权产业新业态层出不穷

2018年，在网络游戏、网络动漫、网络文学等传统业态发展的同时，中国网络版权产业一些全新的产业形式快速发展壮大，其中最为典型的是网络短视频和网络直播。

网络短视频是2018年中国网络版权产业细分业态的“黑马”，其用户使用时长占比优势明显。根据QuestMobile的统计，短视频用户使用时长占移动互联网总时长比例已从2016年的1.2%迅猛增长到2018年的11.4%。该优势推动其市场规模突飞猛进至195亿元，用户规模也已增至6.48亿人。另外，随着网络短视频与其他网络版权业态的快速融合，以短视频为基础的业态共振效应越发显著。根据TrustDate的数据，因短视频具有碎片化属性且临场感强烈，79%的互联网用户会通过短视频获得新闻资讯，70%的用户会通过短视频观看音乐MV③。

随着电子竞技以及全民直播时代的到来，网络直播在2018年得到了进一步发展。根据CNNIC的统计，虽然中国网络直播用户规模在2018年出现下降态势，较2017年减少2 533万人，但在网络直播用户增势分化的过程中，游戏直播借助电竞列入亚运会表演项目的契机取得迅猛发展。中国选手屡获重量级电竞赛事冠军又为游戏直播带来创纪录的用户关注，游戏直播市场规模突破140亿元，同比增长62%④。同时，面对增速降低的挑战，网络直播与短视频开始进行交叉联动，短视频原创者纷纷入

① 数据来源：《中国网络版权产业发展报告（2018）》。
② 同①.
③ 数据来源：QuestMobile、TrustDate，腾讯研究院2019年2月综合测算。
④ 数据来源：CNNIC，腾讯研究院2019年2月综合测算。

驻直播平台，业态跨界带来主播和内容供给的扩充，探索产业未来发展方向。

（五）网络版权产业更加积极承担社会责任

2018 年，网络版权产业更加注重在内容创作中融入社会正能量的传播和优秀传统文化的弘扬。

第一，版权内容传播主流价值观。2018 年网络视听内容领域涌现出一大批以新时代中国风貌、五年建设成就、民众生活改进、绿色大美河山、地方特色文化为主题的网播内容，承载了新时代中国人的自信与骄傲，特别是直播、短视频等新形式的运用，吸引了大量年轻人的参与。

第二，发展功能游戏，完善游戏市场。2018 年，网络游戏行业继续积极探索转型升级，以更好实现游戏的社会价值。在此背景下，功能游戏①得到了游戏产业界的重视。功能游戏具有跨界性、多元性和场景化三大特征，在文化传承、前沿探索、理工科普、亲子互动等领域具有积极的促进作用，寓教于乐、传播正能量，有助于解决现实的社会问题。2018 年国内游戏厂商发布多款功能游戏，包括冒险类型打字游戏《纸境奇缘》、航空航天模拟游戏《坎巴拉太空计划》、癌症治疗相关模拟游戏《肿瘤医生》、节奏类游戏《尼山萨满》、教育类游戏《极客战记》等②。这些游戏作品，涉及传统文化、实操模拟和科学普及等，既可以满足游戏性的需求，又寓教于乐，得到社会各界的欢迎。

第三，网络版权产业重视利用前沿科技手段推动中华优秀传统文化创造性转化、创新性发展。产业界与故宫、敦煌景区等传统文化机构深入合作，运用新的科技手段挖掘传统文化魅力。数字技术天然的参与式特性使得普通大众以前所未有的机会接近和体会传统文化的魅力，为传统文化的传承提供了新的可能性。以敦煌为例，通过数字化技术，用户足不出户就可以感受敦煌的全貌；每个人都有机会通过重新编辑、组合敦煌的各种文化符号，参与到对敦煌文化的创新和传承中来。数字文化以技术连接和融合线上线下文化资源，让昔日被埋没的传统文化走入日常生活，也让年轻人喜闻乐见的新内容不断诞生。

（六）网络版权产业拉动产业升级，积极吸收就业

网络版权产业作为高新技术与版权内容融合发展的成果，不断催生新业态、新就业，已成为数字经济的重要组成部分和国民经济发展的新动能。

网络版权产业深刻改变着社会分工链、产业链、价值链、创新链，为全社会带来巨大活力，不断融入经济发展的新形态。在体育赛事领域，移动电竞的飞速发展，催生了一大批优质赛事的举办，相应地带动起赛事推广、票务、比赛场地、俱乐部建设、赛事经纪等线下版权业务。网游 IP 同名的网络综艺节目，直接带动了作为拍摄实景的线下特色小镇和主题公园的旅游热度，同时，节目中的 cosplay 也带动了演出服装生产。在音乐娱乐市场，移动 K 歌模式不仅满足了用户线上实时 K 歌的需求，还向线下延伸，在核心商业地段推出了同品牌同 IP 的线下移动 K 歌房，与线上内容实时同步，盘活传统 KTV 市场。

网络版权产业具有成为解决就业问题“蓄水池”的巨大潜力。网络版权产业在就业方面具有容量大、领域宽、门槛低、创新性高、方式灵活等特点，成为重要的就业部门。2018 年，与网络版权产业领域大量交叉融合的文化体育娱乐业新登记企业数量同比增长 52.7%，远高于 10.3%的平均水平，是当前创新创业的沃土。其中网络版权产业成为青年就业的优先选择。特别是网络游戏、电竞、网络直播作为新兴业态，凭借人才缺口较大、薪酬较高等因素，成为毕业生的优选职业理想。相关统计表明，包括网络游戏、视频直播、动漫等在内的网络版权产业在过去 3 年间，人才需求年均增幅达到 20.1%。其中，网络游戏对人才需求增长最快，达到 26%。2019 年初，人社部拟发布 15 个新兴职业，包括电子竞技运营师、电子竞技员。

三、2018 年中国网络版权细分产业发展现状和新亮点

（一）数字阅读产业：强化版权运营，发力海外输出

2018 年中国数字阅读市场更加成熟，用户在线阅读习惯基本养成。优质内容和优质作家培育成效显著，用户付费意愿增强，IP 变现模式多样化，市场空间不断增大。由于移动设备具有的便捷、碎片化等特征，移动阅读成为市场主流，移动端市场成为各大文学平台竞争瞄准的核心战场。

1. 数字阅读产业用户规模快速增长

网络文学作为数字阅读中最具代表性的部分，2018 年用户规模增长迅猛，达 4.32 亿人，较 2017

① 功能游戏是一个舶来词，英语原文是“Serious Game”，指那些以解决现实社会和行业问题为主要目的的游戏。

② 数据来源：伽马数据《2018 年功能游戏报告》。

年增加 5 427 万人，网民渗透率达 52.1%；其中手机网络文学用户规模达到 4.10 亿人，较 2017 年增加 6 666 万人，手机网民渗透率达 50.2%①，是所有细分产业中用户规模增长最多的（见图 5）。

网络文学用户快速增长的原因有三点：第一，网络文学优质内容创作和优秀作家培养方面成效显著，精品力作持续涌现；第二，优秀作品得到影视剧改编市场的追捧，优质改编的影视剧进一步扩大了原作的知名度，将一批视频用户反向带动为网文用户；第三，各平台推出免费阅读产品，吸引了一大批新读者。

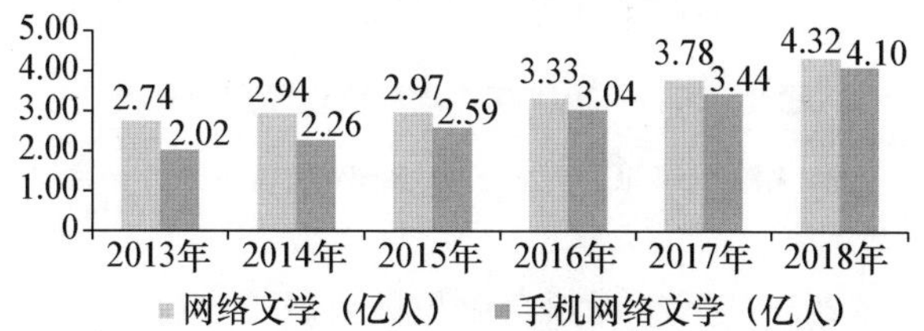

图 5　2013—2018 年中国网络文学用户规模

资料来源：CNNIC，腾讯研究院 2019 年 2 月综合测算。

2. 开拓付费阅读，强调版权运营，数字阅读市场规模持续攀升

2018 年中国数字阅读市场规模突破 100 亿元，增长至 136.3 亿元，同比增长 30%（见图 6）。其中网络文学市场规模达 90.5 亿元，电子书市场规模达 45.8 亿元。预计未来几年复合增长率仍将继续增长，市场规模继续扩大。在网络版权产业的生态体系中，文字作品的内容质量将被提到更重要的位置②。

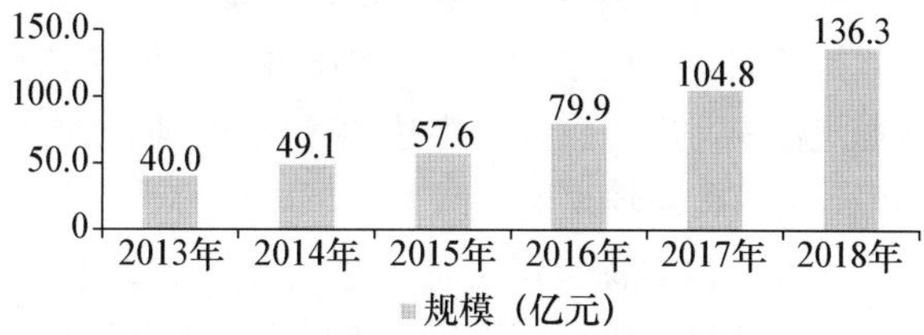

图 6　2013—2018 年中国数字阅读市场规模

资料来源：中国音像与数字出版协会、阅文集团、中金公司、中泰证券、艾瑞咨询、阅文集团，腾讯研究院 2019 年 2 月综合测算。

注：数字阅读市场规模包含网络文学市场规模和数字出版市场规模，除网络文学外，亦包括数字杂志、电子书、互动类图书 APP 等多元形式。

数字阅读市场规模的持续攀升主要得益于两个方面：一是用户付费的市场培育成效显著，营收增长强劲；二是网络文学 IP 加速改编为其他版权内容，版权运营的营收进入快速增长期。目前网络文学几乎成为各类版权内容的 IP 原点，为各类内容的剧本、脚本提供世界观、素材和架构支撑，绝大部分网络版权内容均依赖网络文学的哺育③。网络文学付费市场的培育也拉升了 IP 产业链的整体付费意愿。由于文字对视觉表达的限制，网络文学读者期待看到优质的改编作品，并愿意为优质的 IP 改编作品付费，尤其是影视、动漫、游戏等网络版权作品，这形成了 IP 运营的付费产业链。

3. 正能量作品不断涌现，IP 改编带动版权内容繁荣

2018 年，中国的网络文学以弘扬社会主流价值、讲述中国发展新篇章为创作主旋律，讴歌新中国成立 70 周年伟大历程的现实主义题材作品比例明显增多，作品整体更加契合时代召唤，体现时代风貌。以《大江东去》《复兴之路》等为代表的反映改革开放中国人发展的“爽文”成为创作新趋势。这体现出中国的网络文学逐渐探索出一种既满足当代中国人精神向往，又蕴含厚重气息和为民情怀，并体现以人民为中心之价值导向的全面展现民族精神、文化传统、现代生活的创作方式。

网络文学创作质量提高的同时，依靠优质作品改编的影视作品也逐渐增多。2018 年网络文学 IP 改编向着聚焦精品、长效运营方向继续深化发展，特别是网文 IP 改编的影视剧风靡全国。数据显示，137 部国产电视剧中 26 部改编自网络文学，228 部网络剧中 66 部改编自网络文学④。改编内容的增多和优质作品口碑票房双丰收，也反向带动了网络文学原著的知名度和商业价值提升。

4. 海外输出力度加大，成为撬动版权产业“出海”的杠杆

2018 年中国网络文学企业加大海外市场布局力度，采取自营海外网站、自建翻译团队的方式，将中国网文精品 IP 翻译成十数种语言输出给全球读者，海外读者对中国网络文学的关注空前高涨。

中国网络文学“出海”已经覆盖 40 多个“一带一路”沿线国家，上线英、法、日、韩、俄、印尼、阿拉伯等十几种语言版本，近 70 部中国网文作品外语版本的点击量超千万，累计吸引访问用户超过

① 数据来源：CNNIC，腾讯研究院 2019 年 2 月综合测算。
② 数据来源：中国音像与数字出版协会、阅文集团、中金公司、中泰证券、艾瑞咨询、阅文集团，腾讯研究院 2019 年 2 月综合测算。
③ 数据来源：易观智库，腾讯研究院 2019 年 2 月综合测算。
④ 数据来源：一鱼数据、中金公司，腾讯研究院 2019 年 2 月综合测算。

2 000 万人[①]。网络文学作为撬动整个中国网络版权产业“出海”扩展的杠杆，突围作用和战略价值越发明显，网络文学“出海”市场潜力依然十分巨大（见表 4）。

表 4　2018 年海外访问中国网络文学翻译作品基本情况

分类	数量
海外中国网络文学网站访客来源国家和地区	超 115 个
海外中国网络文学网站日活跃用户数（DAU）	超 50 万人
海外中国网络文学网站累计访问用户数	超 2 000 万人
海外中国网络文学网站日访问量（PV）	超 500 万次
翻译作品数量（含未经授权）	超 500 部
海外点击量超千万作品数	近 70 部

资料来源：中国音像与数字出版协会、《中国网络文学发展报告》、阅文集团，腾讯研究院 2019 年 2 月综合测算。

网络文学“出海”的迅速成长得益于网络文学企业不断孵化精品力作，积极探索“出海”有效模式，通过因地制宜地建立付费阅读模式，推动海外网文市场深入化及标准化发展。未来，更加体系化和专业化的海外输出将更加深入地推动海外市场规模化发展。“出海”内容题材将更加细分，满足差异化阅读需求。此外，中国网文“出海”的产业模式也将持续优化，深化建构正版市场，进一步壮大中国网文海外影响力。

（二）网络视频产业：精品内容与运营创新，保障广告收入与用户付费双增长

1. 网络视频产业概况

2018 年，中国网络视频产业抓住了版权保护和移动视频的发展机遇，增长迅猛，市场规模突破 962.7 亿元，同比增长 32.6%，正式迈向千亿级市场[②]。其中广告收入规模达 454 亿元，同比增长 26%，仍然是网络视频产业收入的主要构成部分。与此同时，网络视频付费会员规模迅速增长，截至年底主要视频平台付费会员已达到 2.3 亿人（见图 7）。

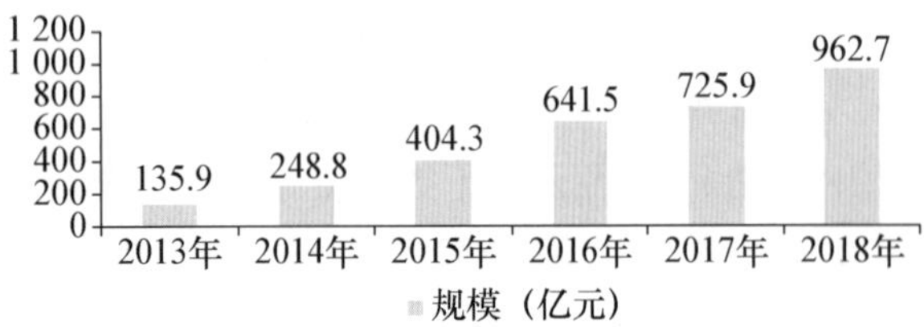

图 7　2013—2018 年中国网络视频市场规模

资料来源：艾瑞咨询《2018 年中国动漫行业报告》，腾讯研究院 2019 年 2 月综合测算。

市场规模增长的同时，用户数量也有所增加。2018 年中国网络视频用户规模达 6.12 亿人，较 2017 年增加 3 309 万人，网民渗透率达 73.9%；2018 年手机网络视频用户规模达到 5.90 亿人，较 2017 年增加 4 101 万人，手机网民渗透率达 72.2%（见图 8）。

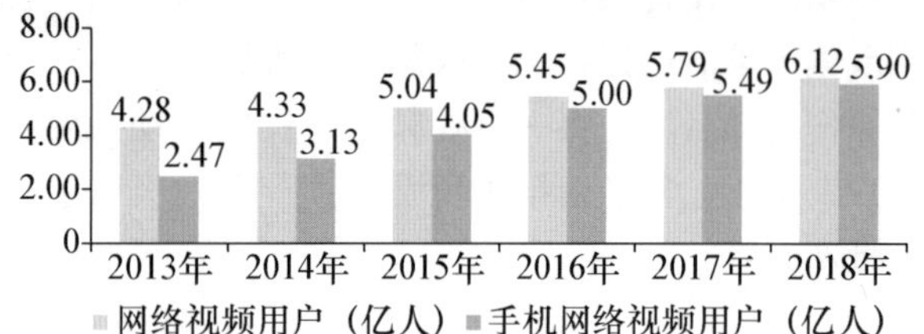

图 8　2013—2018 年中国网络视频用户规模

资料来源：CNNIC、奥维云网，腾讯研究院 2019 年 2 月综合测算。

2018 年网络视频产业积极拓展用户触达场景，视频厂商加大与各类屏幕和终端硬件的合作力度，拓展多场景下的用户触达与用户付费。同时继续狠抓影视综艺节目内容质量，提高用户黏性。2018 年 OTT（智能电视和网络机顶盒）普及率提升，激活量突破 2.1 亿台，同比增长 23%，渗透 51%的中国家庭，覆盖 5.76 亿人，内置网络视频应用对家庭客厅场景的渗透增强。

2. 网络视频广告形态创新，仍是视频收入主要来源

网络视频主要依托广告和付费观看盈利。2018 年，视频广告依然是最主要的盈利来源，广告展现形式持续向多元化方向发展。2018 年中国网络视频市场规模中，广告收入规模达 454 亿元，同比增长 26%，占整体市场规模比例 47.1%（见图 9）。视频广告向着与内容深度融合的原生化创新方向发展，将广告要素与创作要素进行有机融合，提高用户的可接受度和沉浸感。除了内容形式创新外，通过人工智能的数据分析，广告的精准投放度不断提高，广告转换效果显著增长。除广告外，网络视频企业也在开拓新思路，多元探索网络游戏联运、电子商务业务以及爆款 IP 的硬件和周边授权业务，但在短期内，广告收入仍会高于用户付费以及其他各形式收入。

① 数据来源：中国音像与数字出版协会、《中国网络文学发展报告》、阅文集团，腾讯研究院 2019 年 2 月综合测算。

② 中国网络广告服务市场规模指中国互联网企业的广告营收总和，包括 PC 端广告和移动端广告，包括且不限于品牌图形广告、搜索广告、电商广告、视频网络广告、富媒体广告、文字链广告、电子邮件广告等广告形式。与中国网络视频市场规模做加总统计时，需对视频网络广告规模进行去重。

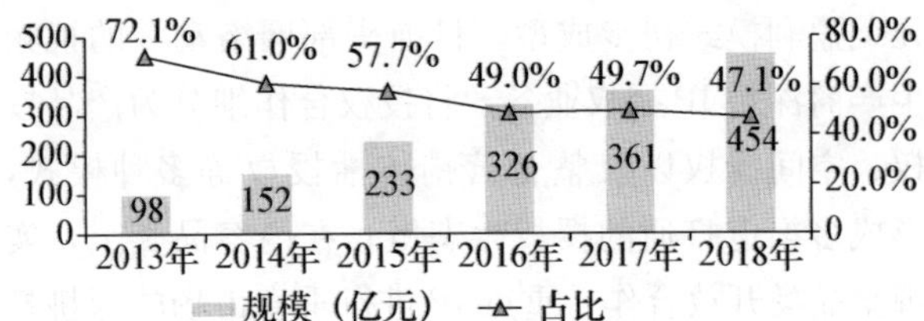

图 9　2013—2018 年中国网络视频广告市场规模

资料来源：艾瑞咨询、艺恩智库、易观智库，腾讯研究院 2019 年 2 月综合测算。

3. 会员精益化运营持续发力，优质内容是吸引流量的硬通货

随着网络视频版权保护的正外部效应不断提升，加之网络视频行业强力发展会员业务，网络视频付费会员的规模迅速提高，到 2018 年各平台付费会员未去重总计已达到 2.3 亿人。相比 2015 年的 2 200 万会员，四年间中国网络视频付费会员规模扩大近 10 倍（见图 10），随着网络视频与硬件厂商、电信运营商、其他版权企业对会员机制的联合运营，付费用户规模还会继续增长。而且视频平台的会员制度持续规范，会员的权益不断扩充，优质内容的增多提高了会员用户的黏性和忠诚度。

2018 年中国网络视频用户付费市场规模为 355 亿元，在网络视频整体收入结构中占比接近 37%。其中值得注意的是，用户付费市场规模同比增长 62.8%，高于会员数量同比增速 43.8%，这说明增长动力不仅来自付费用户基数的扩大[①]，网络影视综艺平台为付费会员提供的更多元和阶梯状的增值服务是其主要驱动力。会员权益体系的细化提高了会员优享的权重，拓展了付费购买的长尾场景，提高了会员人均消费水平。

图 10　2015—2018 年中国网络视频付费会员规模（未去重）

资料来源：艺恩智库《2018 年中国视频内容付费产业观察》，腾讯研究院 2019 年 2 月综合测算。

2018 年面向付费会员的网络影视综艺不断扩充，在上线的全部 3 134 部内容中，有 1 853 部内容属于付费会员专属，占比达到 59%；这 1 853 部中有 74%是电影、17%是剧集、5%是综艺节目[②]。更多现象级的网播剧和网络自制综艺出现，使用户的关注度和会员规模得到提升，越来越多的用户愿意为优秀的创作团队和高质量的作品持续消费。

4. 平台自制综艺节目亮眼，探索植入式营销和粉丝经济

2018 年，综艺节目的制作和播放继续向互联网端倾斜，大量优质作品出现，视频平台也开始借助综艺节目探索挖掘粉丝的商业价值。

2018 年，中国网络自制综艺蓬勃发展，节目数量达到 262 部，相比 2017 年大幅增长 52%，相比 2013 年扩大 6 倍有余，并涌现出《创造 101》《偶像练习生》等头部作品，播放量惊人[③]。视频平台借助自制综艺的流量优势，探索植入式营销，为制作方带来大额广告营收；同时亦在探索 IP 化运营，推出同名或同 IP 的会员专属视听内容，在广告营销之外，试水面向粉丝的用户付费模式。

（三）网络动漫产业：基数扩大黏性增强，内容付费初步普及

1. 网络动漫产业概况

在用户大众化和优质 IP 的双驱带动下，中国网络动漫内容市场规模 2018 年已增长至 141.6 亿元，同比增长 53%（见图 11）。中国广义网络动漫用户（即泛二次元用户）规模突破 3.5 亿人，其中网络动漫用户达到 2.19 亿人（见图 12）。伴随优质作品在“00 后”和“10 后”年轻群体中的口耳相传，未来几年用户规模将继续扩充，其中，核心用户对网络动漫用户规模拉动不容小觑，在目前 3.5 亿广义用户中，至少有 9 000 万核心高频高黏性用户，带动了其亲友、同学、同事和朋友圈人群的观看，助推网络动漫的影响力不断增强[④]。除了低龄群体外，网络动漫在“80 后”“90 后”等年龄段的渗透率也在增强，为创作面向成年人市场的深度动漫内容提供了土壤。

随着越来越多年轻用户群体走入社会，他们的内容消费能力不断提高，再加上中国本土动漫作品水平的不断提升，使得中国动漫市场规模连年扩大，市场规模和用户规模也不断扩大，广告＋用户

① 数据来源：艾瑞咨询《2018 年中国网络视频行业经营状况研究报告》。

② 数据来源：艺恩智库《2018 年中国视频内容付费产业观察》。

③ 数据来源：智研咨询《2018 年中国网络自制节目综合分析报告》。

④ 数据来源：艾瑞咨询《2018 年中国动漫行业报告》，腾讯研究院 2019 年 2 月综合测算；QuestMobile《中国移动互联网年度大报告》，腾讯研究院 2019 年 2 月综合测算。

付费+IP授权多元盈利模式基本形成，收入来源和收入结构趋于稳定。

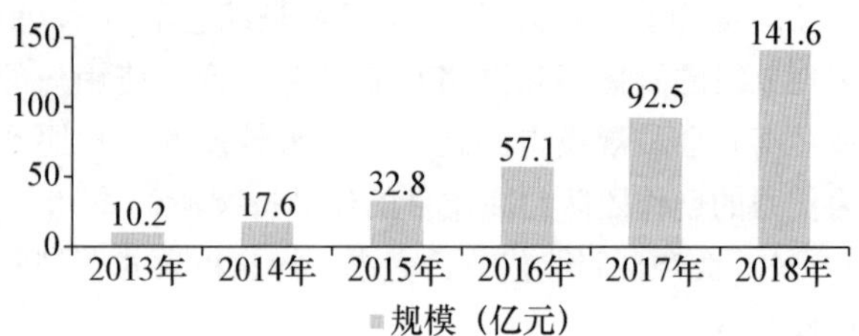

图 11　2013—2018 年中国网络动漫内容市场规模

资料来源：艾瑞咨询《2018 年中国动漫行业报告》，腾讯研究院 2019 年 2 月综合测算。

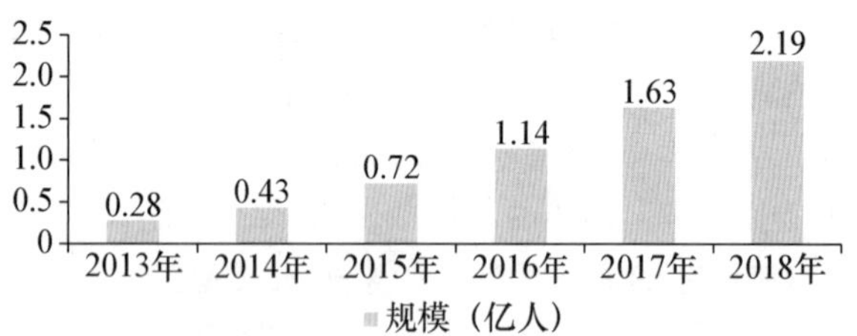

图 12　2013—2018 年中国网络动漫用户规模

资料来源：艾瑞咨询《2018 年中国动漫行业报告》，腾讯研究院 2019 年 2 月综合测算。

2. 优质作品带动明显，用户消费潜力释放

2018 年，伴随着网络漫画新品在漫画类 APP 上更新频率的加快，以及网络动画大电影作品数量的增长和正版新番长篇动画在视频网站的扩充，用户对网络动漫相关应用的使用次数和投入时间均显著增长，分别同比增长 55.4%和 23.5%①。

目前，“90 后”“00 后”已经成为网络漫画的主要消费群体，根据国家统计局和艾瑞咨询的调研数据，“90 后”和“00 后”人群规模达 2.8 亿多人，家庭月平均收入高达 10 676 元，其中文娱消费支出占总消费支出的 28.9%，平均每天在网络娱乐上花费时间超过 1.6 个小时，这群成长于相对优越的物质条件中的年轻人，更乐意进行文化娱乐服务消费②。这使得不论是自行观看动漫的“95 后”青少年群体或更高年龄段群体，还是陪伴子女观看动漫的家长群体，相比以往都具备更强的消费实力，必将带动市场规模的提升（见图 13)。

3. IP 运营不断成熟，多元模式保障产业可持续增长

一段时间内，我国网络动漫商业模式以广告和用户付费为主，2018 年以来，网络漫画开始发力 IP 运营，2018 年 IP 授权产生收入占比超过 30%。多元化盈利模式初步成型。目前头部网络动漫的视频生产商深耕 IP 授权业务，将授权合作细分为产品授权、空间授权以及整合营销传播授权等多种模式，形成多渠道打通的授权生态链；在内容品类上，实现全品类开放合作，重点 IP 进行垂直市场的深耕打造；在授权政策上，提供灵活的授权期限，预售金采用保底加分成的模式，多元化盈利模式初步成形。

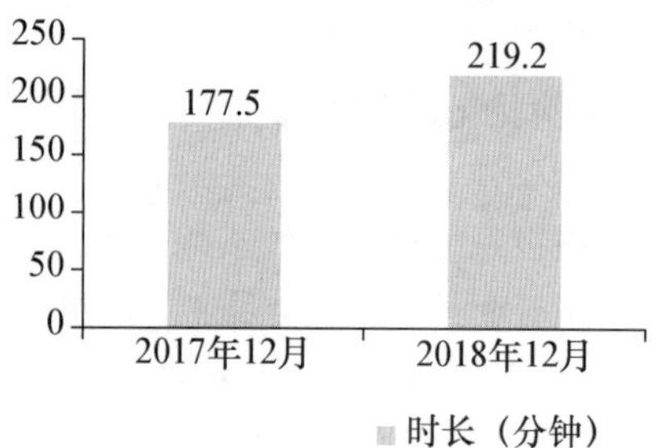

图 13　2017 年 12 月 vs 2018 年 12 月中国手机动漫用户人均月度投入时长

资料来源：QuestMobile《中国移动互联网 2018 年度大报告》，腾讯研究院 2019 年 2 月综合测算。

4. 正版付费意识与作品质量相互促进，形成产业发展良性循环

2018 年，网络动漫的平台化运营使得版权保护力度得到加强，创作者的创作环境持续改善，动漫作品质量不断提高，版权保护与内容生产相互促进，带动产业更好更快发展。网络动漫用户对正版内容的付费意愿提升，逐步接纳付费会员等模式，2018 年网络漫画用户付费规模达 15 亿元，同比增长 114%；网络动画用户付费规模达 30 亿元，同比增长 61%③。正版内容通过用户付费获得了较为稳定的现金流，有助于全新作品的再创作，同时有助于创作不以收视率为导向的精品内容，反过来进一步激发用户消费热情，助推动漫行业高质量增长。

（四）网络游戏产业：电竞游戏乘风而起，海外布局日趋紧要

1. 网络游戏产业概况

2018 年中国网络游戏市场规模达到 2 480 亿元，同比增长 5.3%。与此同时，中国网络游戏用户基数继续扩大。2018 年的用户规模达到 4.84 亿人，较 2017 年增加 4 224 万人，网民渗透率达 58.4%；其中手机网络游戏用户规模达到 4.59 亿人，较 2017 年增加 5 169 万人，手机网民渗透率达 56.2%（见图 14、图 15)。用户基数的扩大又反向促进了电

① 数据来源：QuestMobile《中国移动互联网 2018 年度大报告》，腾讯研究院 2019 年 2 月综合测算。

② 数据来源：艾瑞咨询《2018 年中国动漫行业研究报告》。

③ 数据来源：艾瑞咨询、三文娱、有妖气，腾讯研究院 2019 年 2 月综合测算。

竞赛事的发展，2018 年国内电竞赛事体系继续不断成形，联赛和俱乐部运营步入正轨，知名选手及团队不断涌现①。

图 14　2013—2018 年中国网络游戏市场规模

资料来源：中国音数协游戏工委、艾瑞咨询、易观智库，腾讯研究院 2019 年 2 月综合测算。

注：网络游戏市场规模包括 PC 端游、PC 页游、移动游戏市场规模总计，此处不含电竞生态和主机游戏市场规模。

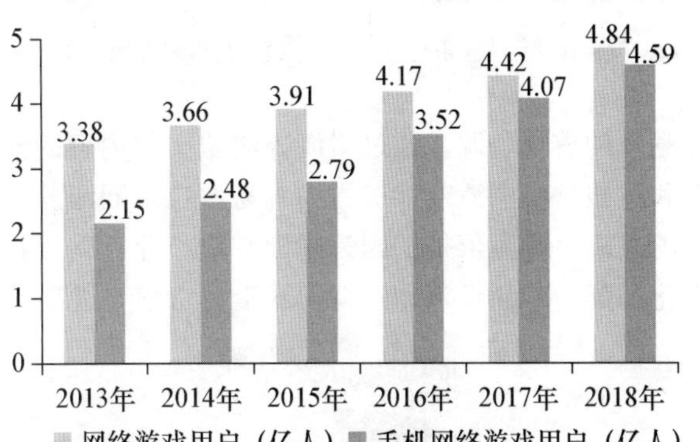

图 15　2013—2018 年中国网络游戏用户规模

资料来源：CNNIC，腾讯研究院 2019 年 2 月综合测算。

网络游戏市场规模和网游用户加速增长的动力主要来自两方面：一是头部作品带来的全民移动电竞风潮。在头部多人在线战术竞技游戏（MOBA）大作的带动下，2018 年移动电竞风靡全国，成功吸引了新玩家。尤其值得一提的是下半年新兴的沙盒类射击游戏成为最受用户关注的游戏类型，这对于移动游戏用户规模高速增长起到了显著的推动作用。移动游戏在整体网游市场所占比例不断提高，预计到 2020 年将接近 75%②。二是网游厂商在海外市场取得的突破。2018 年我国自主研发网络游戏的海外市场实际销售收入达 95.9 亿美元，而在 2012 年，这个数字仅为 5.7 亿美元。中国自主研发游戏的海外影响力和市场地位都在提升，目前中国已经成为名副其实的游戏输出大国。

2. 电子竞技用户基数扩大，移动电竞成为市场核心增长引擎

2018 年电子竞技持续发力，成为网络游戏行业最火的细分类型。其中，移动端电子竞技发展加快，成为电子竞技市场的重要组成部分。

电子竞技发展中一个历史性节点是 2018 年电子竞技被纳入雅加达亚运会表演项目，中国国家队勇夺两金一银，随后中国战队又夺取《英雄联盟》全球总冠军，这一夺冠热潮极大地助推了电竞普及，用户规模迅速发展到 4.28 亿人，同比增长 17.5%③。随着 2022 年杭州亚运会电竞被列入正式比赛项目，以及国内电竞赛事体系的成形，联赛和俱乐部运营步入正轨，知名选手及团队不断涌现，电竞关注度持续得到放大，形成了产业发展的正向循环。

2018 年中国电子竞技游戏市场实际销售收入达 834.4 亿元，同比增长 14.2%。其中传统的 PC 端游电竞游戏规模下滑到 371.8 亿元，移动电竞游戏规模猛增到 462.6 亿元，占整体市场比重大幅提升至 55.4%④。移动电竞游戏市场规模占比过半，标志着网游市场增长动力彻底移动化。和 PC 端游电竞游戏占整体 PC 端游的比例相比，移动电竞游戏占整体移动游戏的比例仍然较低，未来移动电竞市场增量空间依然可期（见图 16、图 17）。

图 16　2016—2018 年中国电竞游戏市场规模

资料来源：中国音数协游戏工委《2018 年中国游戏产业报告》，腾讯研究院 2019 年 2 月综合测算。

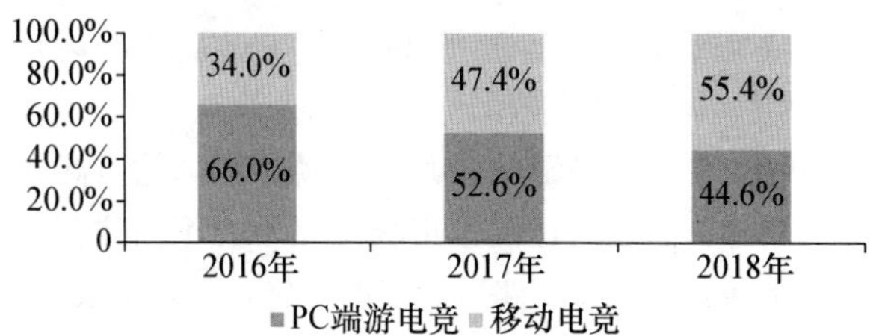

图 17　2016—2018 年中国电竞游戏市场结构

资料来源：中国音数协游戏工委《2018 年中国游戏产业报告》，腾讯研究院 2019 年 2 月综合测算。

3. 休闲游戏受到热捧，角色扮演和 MOBA 类贡献过半收入

2018 年，网络游戏类型分布特征显著，休闲类

① 数据来源：CNNIC，腾讯研究院 2019 年 2 月综合测算。

② 数据来源：中国音数协游戏工委、艾瑞咨询、易观智库，腾讯研究院 2018 年 2 月综合测算。

③ 数据来源：中商产业研究院整理的《2018 中国电子竞技市场产业报告》。

④ 数据来源：中国音数协游戏工委《2018 年中国游戏产业报告》，腾讯研究院 2019 年 2 月综合测算。

游戏渗透率明显更高，而角色扮演和多人在线战术竞技游戏（MOBA）占据网络游戏收入的半壁江山。以应用商店榜单反映出的用户付费情况为例，2018年角色扮演和MOBA类游戏贡献了超过58%的收入，其中角色扮演类游戏占比为34%，MOBA占比为24%①。

2018年移动游戏领域休闲游戏用户渗透率最高，超过70%。主要原因是这类游戏可以随时开始或结束，适宜碎片化的消费场景。角色扮演和MOBA则均超过60%（见图18）。

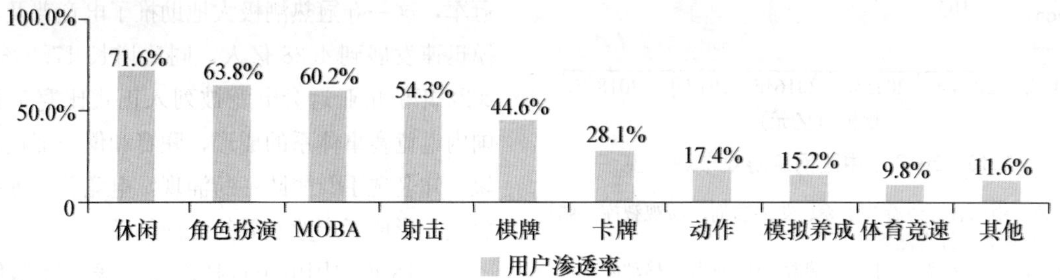

图18　2018年中国各类型移动游戏用户渗透率分布

资料来源：易观《2018年中国移动游戏市场发展白皮书》、艾瑞咨询《2017年中国互动娱乐行业年终盘点》，腾讯研究院2019年2月综合测算。

4. 网络游戏国际竞争力不断增强，游戏“出海”成重要收入来源

2018年，越来越多中国自主研发的网络游戏风靡海外，游戏已经成为中国文创产业出口创汇的重要力量。随着国内市场人口红利的见顶，全球市场的布局和深耕对中国游戏行业未来的持续繁荣有着重要的战略意义（见图19、图20）。

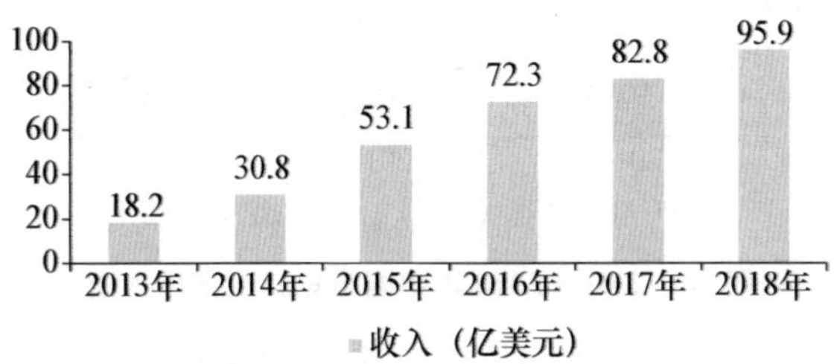

图19　中国自主研发网络游戏海外市场实际销售收入

资料来源：中国音数协游戏工委、TalkingData，腾讯研究院2019年2月综合测算。

中国网络游戏尤其是移动游戏，凭借高质量的头部作品在发达国家市场的竞争力不断增强。尤其是随着“一带一路”倡议的实施，中国游戏“出海”的路线与“一带一路”不谋而合，越来越多的游戏厂商开始将游戏“出海”提上日程。当前，网游企业在海外产品和渠道上双发力，一方面加强产品研发，产出符合海外用户审美需求的作品，另一方面与海外渠道商及手机厂商建立长期稳定的合作关系，并尝试收购或自营海外游戏平台。

在输出中国元素优秀作品的同时，中国游戏企业也尝试用自己的语言讲好全球故事，IP成为全球竞争的重要资源。通过对海外优质文化内容的改编和重塑，中国游戏能够更加容易地拉近同海外用户的距离，背后依托的则是中国游戏产业近些年在文化理解、产品设计和运营模式上的自信与进步。

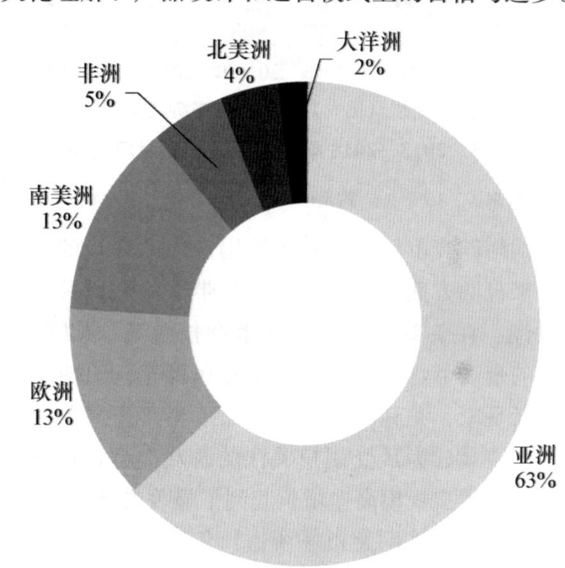

图20　2018年中国移动游戏海外用户分布

资料来源：中国音数协游戏工委、TalkingData，腾讯研究院2019年2月综合测算。

（五）网络音乐产业：全能平台扩展消费场景，付费价值共识初成

1. 网络音乐产业概况

在“音乐+”业态下，2018年网络音乐的市场规模与用户规模大幅提升。2018年中国网络音乐市场规模（不含电信音乐增值业务）已达到226亿元，同比增长29%，延续了2017年以来的高速增长态

① 数据来源：艾瑞《2017年中国互动娱乐行业年终盘点》，腾讯研究院2019年2月综合测算。

势。2018 年中国网络音乐用户规模达 5.76 亿人，较 2017 年增加 2 751 万人，网民渗透率达 69.5%；手机网络音乐用户规模达到 5.53 亿人，较 2017 年增加 4 123 万人，手机网民渗透率达 67.7%（见图 21、图 22）[①]。

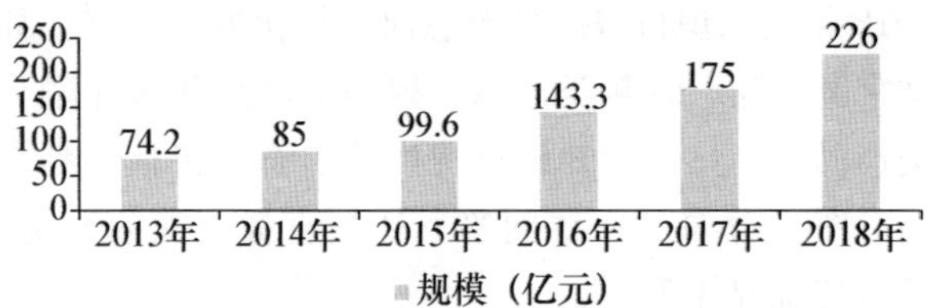

图 21 2013—2018 年中国网络音乐市场规模

资料来源：中国音像与数字出版协会音乐产业促进工作委员会《2019 年中国互联网发展全瞻》，腾讯研究院 2019 年 2 月综合测算。

注：网络音乐市场规模指 PC 端和移动端各类音乐服务产值，此处不含电信音乐增值业务收入；包含音乐 APP 端的直播收入，不再重复计入网络直播。

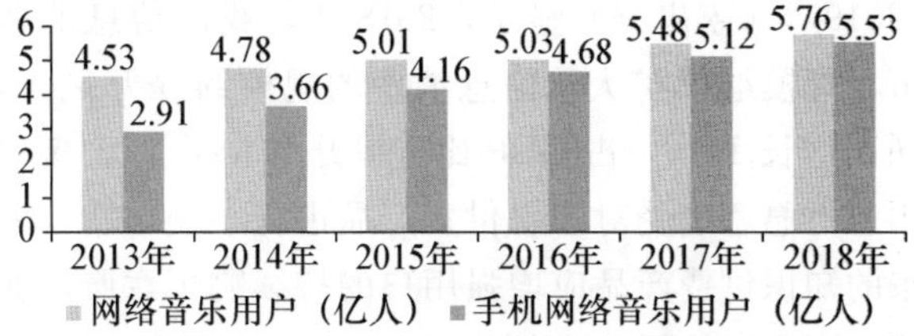

图 22 2013—2018 年中国网络音乐用户规模

资料来源：中国音像与数字出版协会音乐产业促进工作委员会《2019 年中国互联网发展全瞻》，腾讯研究院 2019 年 2 月综合测算。

网络音乐移动平台的规模迅速扩大，用户付费增长明显。2018 年，用户网络音乐付费习惯日趋成熟，付费类型主要是购买会员、专辑/单曲和音乐流量包，数据显示，19～30 岁的年轻群体在网络音乐方面的消费潜力比 30 岁以上的群体更突出[②]。用户对版权内容的价值认可持续提升，用户逐渐适应内容付费与原创打赏模式，用户付费规模扩大将推动中国网络音乐产业迈向重视内容原创的新时代。

2. 网络音乐与社交元素深度融合，“音乐＋社交”模式逐渐成熟

近年来，网络音乐在业态融合和场景渗透方面不断创新，“音乐＋”模式不断发展，为网络音乐注入了新的活力。2018 年，我国移动音乐平台的社交化趋势日益明显，逐渐发展出“音乐＋社交”模式。“音乐社交”的形式满足了用户的情感需要，吸引了大量新用户。截至 2018 年第一季度末，我国手机音乐客户端用户规模累计已经达到 5.33 亿人，庞大的用户市场成为移动音乐平台功能升级和服务转型的强大动力[③]。

移动音乐平台的社交化是媒介的社交属性决定的。结合两个平台的“社交化”实践来看，2018 年，移动音乐平台社交属性增强主要依靠评论、好友及分享等基础社交功能的设置。在此基础上，形成了“消费—互动—社交”和“社交—音乐社交”两种社交途径。另外，2018 年，“音乐＋”业态迅速普及，网络 K 歌的线上线下联动继续深化，音乐平台纳入直播打赏模式，音乐推广尝试社交元素，多元模式确保产业活力。

3. 政策保障音乐版权，行业步入健康发展轨道

2018 年，中国音乐市场实现了短时间内的高速增长。这一成果的取得一方面得益于政策对于音乐正版化的支持，另一方面得益于用户付费意识的形成。另外，在国家版权局积极协调推动下，腾讯音乐与网易云音乐就网络音乐版权合作事宜达成一致，相互授权音乐作品达到各自独家音乐作品数量的 99%以上。

一方面，网络音乐平台加大版权保护力度，扶持原创，用户付费意识初步成型，实际用户付费率不足 4%，但已有近六成用户表示愿意付费表达对作品价值的认可，用户付费市场潜力巨大。另一方面，年轻有消费实力的群体付费意愿更为突出，为网络音乐行业量质双双健康发展奠定了坚实的土壤。2018 年除音乐直播打赏外，纯网络音乐订阅用户付费规模近 45 亿元，同比增长近 50%[④]。

4. 网络音乐多场景渗透，转型一站式平台

随着后音乐产业的到来，新一轮的行业竞争已然拉开序幕。在线音乐平台之间的竞争已经扩散至更多元的战场，多渠道多场景消费模式的构建成为重点。从网络音乐用户的接触渠道看，2018 年消费平台主要集中在移动端音乐 APP 以及网络电台、网络 K 歌和音乐直播等，并包括线下商业网点的迷你 K 歌房，丰富的消费场景促使网络音乐企业向一站式平台转型。由于网络音乐具备碎片化和背景化双重消费特性，用户可在音乐陪伴下同时聚焦学习、工作、生活甚至是阅读和游戏等活动，这使得网络音乐的投入时长不易受到其他文娱活动的挤压，未来市场空间依然较大。

① 数据来源：CNNIC，腾讯研究院 2019 年 2 月综合测算。
② 数据来源：艾瑞咨询，腾讯研究院 2018 年 2 月综合测算。
③ 数据来源：艾媒报告《2018Q1 中国手机音乐客户端季度监测报告》。
④ 数据来源：中商产业研究院《2018—2023 年中国音乐产业市场前景及投资机会研究报告》。

（六）网络媒体产业：人工智能精准推送，融合发展多向探索

1. 网络新闻媒体产业概况

2018 年中国网络新闻用户规模达 6.75 亿人，较 2017 年增加 4.5%，网民渗透率达 81.4%；手机网络新闻用户规模达到 6.53 亿人，较 2017 年增加 5.4%，手机网民渗透率达 79.9%（见图 23）。2018 年网络新闻以优质内容为根基，以科技创新为动能，将 AI 新闻自动写作、短视频、动漫、语音播报等纳为新闻报道的有益补充，吸引了更多用户①。信息流广告与媒体原生内容的契合度继续提高，网络媒体广告市场规模持续增长，2018 年已达 2 904 亿元，同比增长仍高于 30%（见图 24）②。

7.00
6.00
5.00
4.00
3.00
2.00
1.00
0
4.91
3.67
5.19
4.15
5.64
4.82
6.14
5.71
6.47
6.20
6.75
6.53
2013年
2014年
2015年
2016年
2017年
2018年
网络新闻用户（亿人）
手机网络新闻用户（亿人）

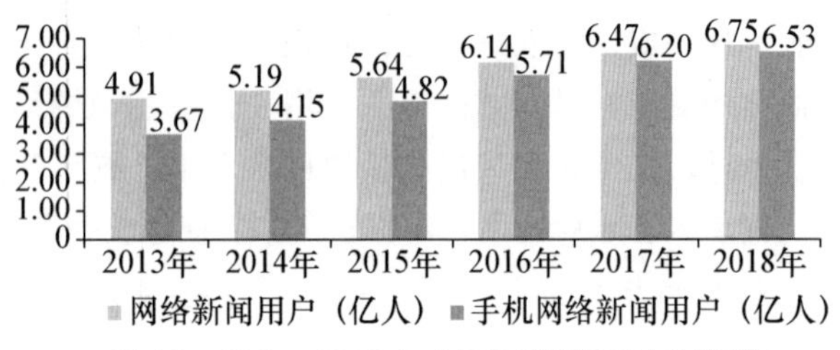

图 23　2013—2018 年中国网络新闻用户规模

资料来源：CNNIC，腾讯研究院 2019 年 2 月综合测算。

3 500
3 000
2 500
2 000
1 500
1 000
500
0
708
994
1 363
1 745
2 201
2 904
2013年
2014年
2015年
2016年
2017年
2018年
规模（亿元）

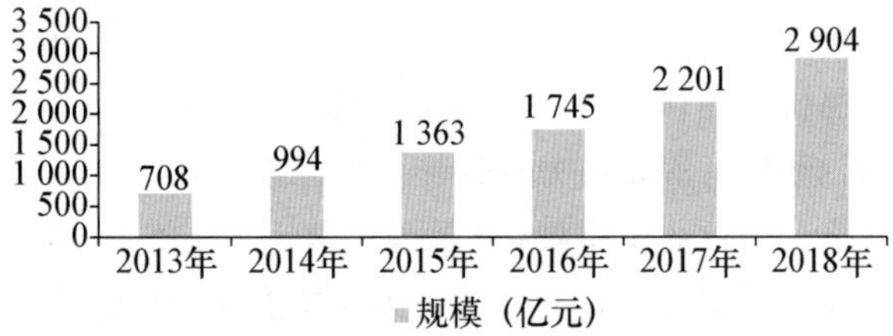

图 24　2013—2018 年中国网络媒体广告市场规模

资料来源：艾瑞咨询《2019 年中国互联网发展全瞻》，腾讯研究院 2019 年 2 月综合测算。

注：网络媒体不仅包含纯粹的新闻资讯网站和应用，也包含各类生产版权内容的垂直媒体、社交媒体、自媒体平台、媒体社区以及搜索引擎社区和搜索联盟网站，但不含电商网站。

网络媒体形态日新月异，社交、电商元素融入网络媒体。以资讯内容为基础，营造线上线下互动社群，并引入电商元素、嵌入直播短视频、尝试付费会员，不断探索实践新媒体融合发展路径。未来，移动端新闻收入占整体市场比例预计还将继续提升，原生广告与媒体内容融合嵌入，而商业模式也不只局限于广告，用户为优质媒体内容（知识）付费将成为常态③。

2. 知识付费产品发展迅猛

2018 年，网络媒体领域消费趋于多样化。艾瑞调查报告显示，用户常用原创平台阅读深度洞察类新闻，而在门户和聚合平台看新闻快讯。这使得 2018 年的知识付费产品形态向多样化方向发展，如文字类产品、音频类产品、视频类产品和媒介融合类产品等，具体的知识付费产品形态又包括音频录播、图文分享、在线问答、视频直播、视频录播、付费传统媒体等。

随着用户收入水平和知识水平的提高，以及移动支付便捷度的提升，用户对直接向优质媒体内容付费的意愿也在不断增强，催生出相当数量的连接用户和媒体内容的付费订阅平台，人们越来越愿意为高质量的知识产品付费。《中国新媒体发展报告（2019）》（蓝皮书）显示，2018 年，我国信息消费市场规模继续扩大，信息消费的规模约 5 万亿元，同比增长 11%，占 GDP 比重提升至 6%④。大多数用户更愿意接受对知识付费产品进行小额付费，未来的知识付费产品应增强用户的持续购买意愿，促进知识生产的可持续发展。

3. 算法推荐成为主要推送方式，信息流市场有所突破

2018 年，人工智能、大数据等新技术在网络新闻媒体领域的广泛应用使得推送更加智能化，个性化推荐成为信息推荐的主要方式，信息流市场规模扩大。2018 年以来，网络新闻媒体运用人工智能机器算法向用户推荐兴趣内容的方式成为各大主流应用的技术选择。网络聚合类新闻客户端，运用算法向用户推荐兴趣内容也已成为主流，与此对应的信息流广告在 2018 年突破千亿元大关，未来将占据中国网络广告市场规模的近半比例（见图 25）⑤。

基于个性化推送的信息流广告也日益成为媒体平台流量变现的主要模式，结合大数据进行精准投放，无论是品牌曝光还是获取效果都能更好地满足广告主和用户双方的需求。

2018 年网络资讯企业承担了更多的社会责任，在运用人工智能提升资讯分发效率的同时，增大了深度和正向内容的算法权重，并配合人工审核过滤

① 数据来源：CNNIC，腾讯研究院 2019 年 2 月综合测算。

② 数据来源：国家版权局网络版权产业研究基地《中国网络版权产业发展报告（2018）》。

③ 数据来源：艾瑞咨询《2019 年中国互联网发展全瞻》，腾讯研究院 2019 年 2 月综合测算。

④ 数据来源：《中国新媒体发展报告（2019）》（蓝皮书）。

⑤ 数据来源：QuestMobile、艾瑞咨询、易观，腾讯研究院 2019 年 2 月综合测算。信息流广告市场规模包括网络社交媒体、社交网络、新闻资讯、搜索引擎、浏览器、短视频等信息流广告收入规模。

低质内容，让网络环境更为清朗。

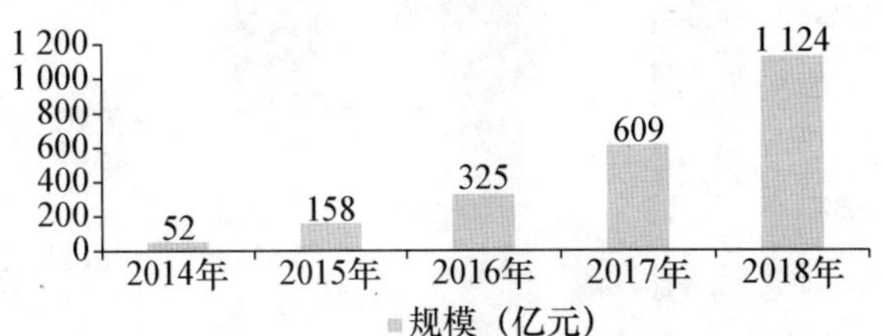

图 25　2014—2018 年中国信息流广告市场规模

资料来源：QuestMobile、艾瑞咨询、易观，腾讯研究院 2019 年 2 月综合测算。

注：信息流广告市场规模包括网络社交媒体、社交网络、新闻资讯、搜索引擎、浏览器、短视频等信息流广告收入规模。

4. 信息流广告盈利能力提高

2018 年，信息流广告的发展使得整个网络广告市场规模得到扩大，产业盈利能力提高。信息流广告精准度提高，市场份额扩大，拉动整体网络广告市场规模。网络媒体形态日新月异，媒体深度结合社交元素，以资讯内容为基础，营造线上线下互动社群，并引入电商元素、嵌入直播短视频、尝试付费会员，不断探索实践新媒体融合发展战略。

（七）网络直播产业：直短交叉扩充供给，深度内容优化体验

1. 网络直播产业概况

直播起源于秀场社区，自 2008 年上线后发展至今，在 PC 端拥有较为稳定的用户基础并向移动端发展。至 2018 年，中国网络直播用户规模达 3.97 亿人，较 2017 年减少 2 533 万人，网民渗透率达 47.9%；其中游戏直播用户规模达到 2.38 亿人，较 2017 年增加 1 391 万人，网民渗透率达 28.7%，游戏直播市场规模突破 140 亿元，同比增长 62%（见图 26、图 27）[①]。

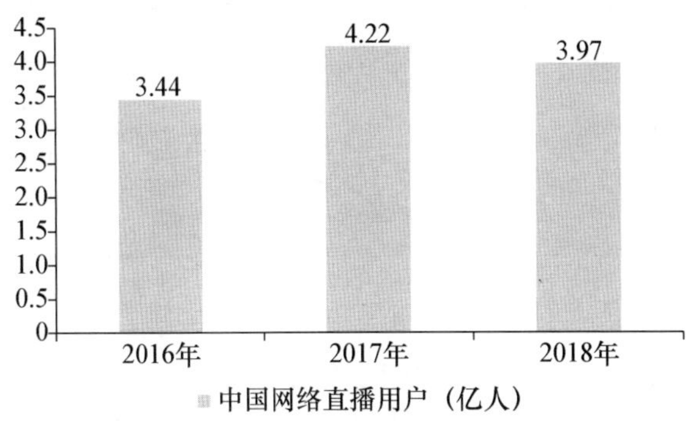

图 26　2016—2018 年中国网络直播用户规模

资料来源：CNNIC，腾讯研究院 2019 年 2 月综合测算。

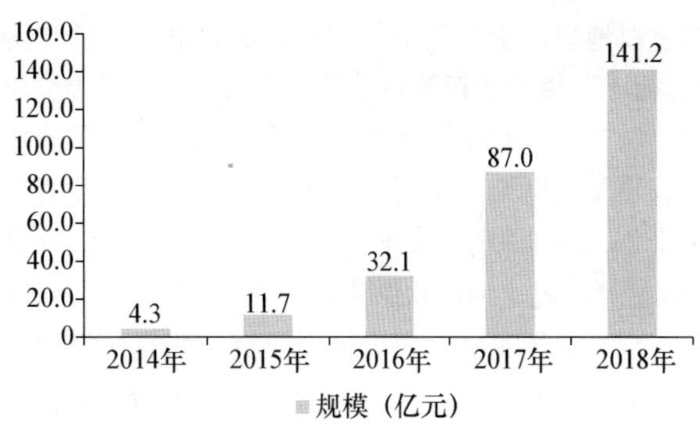

图 27　2014—2018 年中国游戏直播行业市场规模

资料来源：艾瑞咨询《2019 年中国互联网发展全瞻》，腾讯研究院 2019 年 2 月综合测算。

2018 年，中国网络直播市场规模近 486 亿元，同比增长 10%（见图 28），其中来自用户付费的营收规模占比将近 90%，产业拥有庞大的用户基础和完备的商业模式，呈现出明显的内容付费特征。未来在 5G 技术发展背景下，网络直播将更为重视头部内容的精品化，网络直播的内容质量有望进一步提升，网络直播市场规模将持续增长[②]。

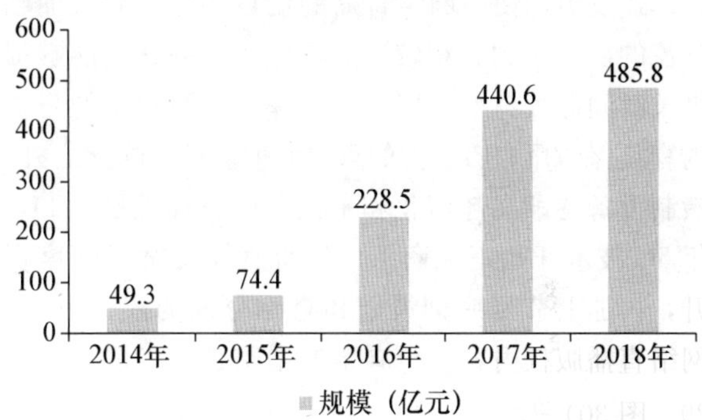

图 28　2014—2018 年中国网络（泛娱乐）直播市场规模

资料来源：艾瑞咨询《2019 年中国互联网发展全瞻》，腾讯研究院 2019 年 2 月综合测算。

网络直播市场规模迅速扩张，一是随着网络直播的参与主体、主播与客体、观众之间的高度双向互动，网红经济、粉丝经济都推动了网络直播的兴盛；二是互联网线上支付便捷性提高，用户打赏更加方便，反哺直播主体以及内容的更新。

2. 游戏直播借力电竞大举攀升，成为市场增长重要引擎

作为网络直播的重要组成部分，游戏直播在 2018 年抓住电竞产业发展的重要机遇，在行业内占

① 数据来源：CNNIC，腾讯研究院 2019 年 2 月综合测算。

② 数据来源：艾瑞咨询《2019 年中国互联网发展全瞻》，腾讯研究院 2019 年 2 月综合测算。

据重要地位，驱动整个行业的发展。电竞直播作为“直播＋”模式的新潮，市场潜力和发展空间十分可观。2018 年，电竞列入亚运会表演项目，中国选手屡获重量级电竞赛事冠军，在这一契机下电竞直播带来创纪录的用户关注，游戏直播市场规模突破 140 亿元，同比增长 62%①。

电子竞技赛事直播成为产业竞争焦点。根据直播分析公司 Conviva 的统计，在 OTT 平台上，2018 FIFA 世界杯上法国与阿根廷比赛的直播收看时长高达 55 亿小时。根据电竞分析公司 Newzoo 的数据，2018 年度全球四个最重要的电竞赛事的直播观看时长达 1.901 亿小时。可见电子竞技赛事直播将带来巨大的经济收益。未来中国电竞赛事机制将更为成熟，电竞赛事直播内容的版权保护将更加严格，围绕赛事直播的市场化运营潜力可期。

3. 深耕内容将成为网络直播发展重点

超清画质的精品内容一直是网络直播的价值根基，随着技术升级和用户需求多样化，这一方面的改进和提升正逐渐得到行业的重视。2018 年，短视频迅速发展，使得网络直播的用户和浏览时长面临分流的巨大压力。相较于短视频，网络直播能够提供长时间深度体验，因此，有深度、精致化的直播内容是保障用户吸引力的重要价值基础。除此之外，摄制设备逐渐向超清化和平民化的方向发展，2018 年 5G 技术开始正式商用也使得直播带宽大幅度提升，再加上节目原创策划和自制分发的能力升级，网络直播版权内容质量有望迎来跨越式发展（见图 29、图 30）②。

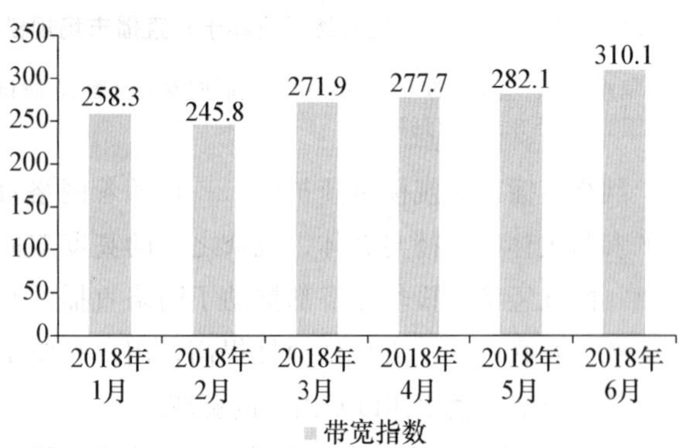

图 29　2018 年上半年中国游戏直播带宽指数增长

资料来源：网宿科技《2018 上半年中国网络直播行业景气指数及短视频报告》，腾讯研究院 2019 年 2 月综合测算。

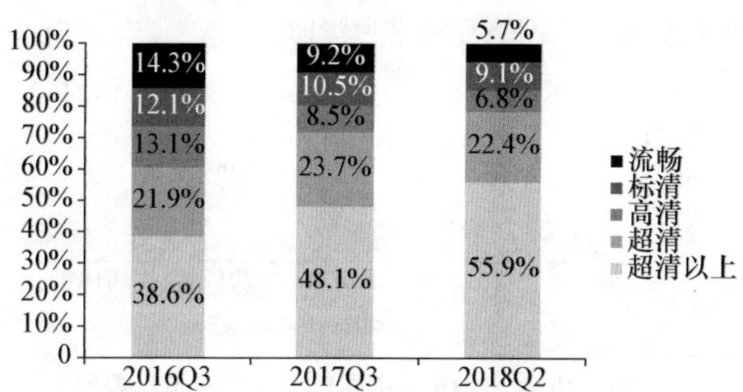

图 30　2016—2018 年中国游戏直播推流清晰度分布

资料来源：网宿科技《2018 上半年中国网络直播行业景气指数及短视频报告》，腾讯研究院 2019 年 2 月综合测算。

（八）网络短视频产业：吸引流量优势明显，业态融合消弭边界

1. 网络短视频产业概况

2018 年，中国短视频用户规模已突破 6.48 亿人，较 2017 年增加约 2.38 亿人，手机网民渗透率达 79.3%。2018 年，短视频的月度使用时长同比增长 170%，短视频使用时长占移动互联网总时长比例已从 2016 年 1.2% 连续高倍增长到 2018 年的 11.4%（见图 31、图 32）③。网络短视频具有体量轻便、形式新颖、社交属性突出、创作门槛低、观看场景便捷等特点，使全民用户碎片时间得到利用，提高了用户黏性。

图 31　2016—2018 年中国网络短视频用户规模

资料来源：CNNIC、QuestMobile，腾讯研究院 2019 年 2 月综合测算。

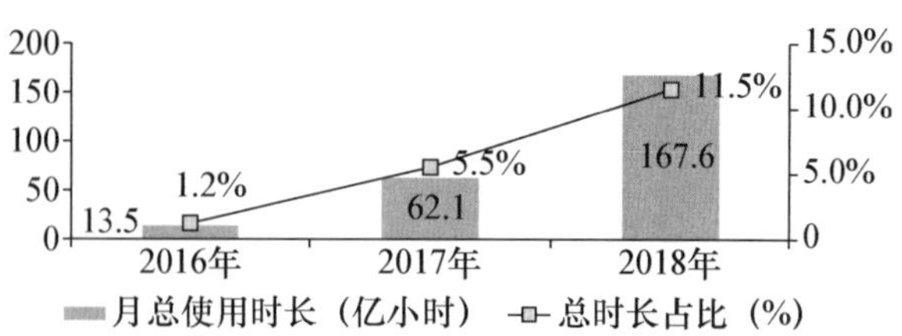

图 32　2016—2018 年中国短视频用户月总使用时长

资料来源：QuestMobile《中国移动互联网 2018 年度大报告》，腾讯研究院 2019 年 2 月综合测算。

① 数据来源：艾瑞咨询《2019 年中国互联网发展全瞻》，腾讯研究院 2019 年 2 月综合测算。

② 数据来源：网宿科技《2018 上半年中国网络直播行业景气指数及短视频报告》，腾讯研究院 2019 年 2 月综合测算。

③ 数据来源：CNNIC、QuestMobile，腾讯研究院 2019 年 2 月综合测算。

2018年短视频流量迅猛增长，吸引了广告商的青睐，市场规模突飞猛进至195.2亿元（见图33）。短视频契合移动互联网时代的碎片化内容消费习惯，与其他版权业态的融合取得了显著的叠加效应，将各细分版权产业的边界模糊化。由视听平台、资讯平台等单一平台向一体化一站式大平台发展，成为当下最大流量红利。

图33　2016—2018年中国短视频市场规模

资料来源：艾瑞咨询《2018年中国网红经济发展研究报告》，腾讯研究院2019年2月综合测算。

2. 移动端短视频发展迅猛，用户使用时长持续增长

在网络视频用户增速放缓、月度活跃用户及使用时长进入瓶颈的状况下，2018年网络短视频却一路逆势上涨，极大冲击和分流网络视频流量。2018年，短视频成为用户使用时长增长最为迅速的类别之一，也是流量增长最快的网络版权内容。短视频占网络版权内容的使用时长比例仅次于移动游戏，在网络视听类别中位列第一。

移动端时代为短视频消费的增长提供了技术支撑，2018年，移动端短视频持续发力，成为短视频消费的主要形式，用户对于短视频的使用频率呈现大幅度增长。根据CNNIC发布的第42次《中国互联网络发展状况统计报告》，截至2018年6月，各热门短视频应用的用户总体规模达到5.94亿人①。截至2018年11月，抖音的国内日活跃用户突破2亿人，月活跃用户突破4.5亿人；截至2018年12月，西瓜视频累计用户超过3亿人，用户日均观看时长80分钟，日均播放量超过40亿次；截至2018年10月，火山小视频日播放量超过60亿次；截至2018年11月，快手国内日活跃用户达1.5亿人，月活跃用户达3.2亿人②。

未来，短视频巨大的时长规模是盈利变现的基础，而去俗存精治理将为健康发展和持续盈利提供长期保障。

3. 流量变现商业价值，业态融合引发共振效应

流量的迅速增长使得短视频商业价值凸显，同时，多元化的盈利模式成为发展方向，短视频与其他业态的相互融合为其他领域注入了更多的活力。

2018年短视频流量迅猛增长，一方面，短视频平台积极清理低俗内容，实施正向精品策略，提升了短视频的营销价值，吸引了品牌商的青睐，市场规模突飞猛进至195.2亿元。同时，随着短视频平台对精品内容加大推荐算法权重，知识型短视频的兴起，优质的短视频版权内容吸引用户打赏，未来短视频商业模式有望摆脱单一的广告模式，趋向多元化。

另一方面，短视频与网络新闻、网络音乐等融合趋势加快。凭借其短小且临场感强烈的形式，短视频成为新闻资讯标配，79%的互联网用户通过短视频获取新闻资讯。而短视频与音乐MV体裁一致，迅速交融，70%的用户通过短视频观看MV③。短视频与其他版权业态的融合取得了显著的叠加效应，将各细分版权产业的边界模糊化，推动视听平台、资讯平台向一体化一站式大平台发展，未来或能重新定义网络版权产业构成。

4. 大众化、草根化成为短视频创作的主要特点

经历了民间的自我生长和发展，短视频自媒体逐渐脱颖而出，2018年短视频在内容创作上更加呈现草根化趋势。一方面，以自我为主，以日常生活为场景的短视频越发成为主流，呈现出主体多样、碎片化、粗加工的特点。多数短视频的视角选择是拍摄者的主观视角，呈现出的也是拍摄者的主观表达；生活场景是短视频最常见的选择背景，其所带有的真实感不会让观看者产生心理上的距离感，反而能够引起观看者的情感共鸣，即便一些短视频以创作表演为内容，但多数也置身于日常场景之中。另一方面，一些具有完整故事表达的短视频开始出现，记录生活、旅行等的Vlog出现。明星或公众人物也倾向于用生活化的视频进行表达，吸引观众。短视频的内容创作更加接地气，成为大众文化的重要组成部分。

四、中国网络版权产业未来展望

（一）网络版权企业将更好地承担提高中国文化软实力的责任

互联网等新兴技术的应用，为传统文化的传承

① 数据来源：CNNIC《第42次中国互联网络发展状况统计报告》，腾讯研究院2019年2月综合测算。

② 数据来源：今日头条、抖音、快手，腾讯研究院2019年2月综合测算。

③ 数据来源：TrustData《2018年短视频行业发展简析》，腾讯研究院2019年2月综合测算。

和创新创造了更为有利的条件。新兴科技为传统文化的内涵加入了现代审美，增强其传播力、影响力。视频、音乐、游戏等多种形式载体实现传统 IP 的创意性表达，使得传统文化资源能够与产业价值链紧密融合。互联网使得文化产品与普通民众之间的距离不断拉近，优质版权内容在互联网平台传播能够引起广泛的社会共鸣，传递社会核心价值，满足人民群众对美好精神生活的追求。网络版权企业作为精神文化产品的生产者，未来将不仅追求自身经济效益，更要注重社会效益。随着文化强国战略和网络强国战略的不断推进，未来，网络版权企业将更加注重创新性继承传统文化，弘扬时代主旋律，展现出企业的文化担当，在文化建设中发挥越来越重要的作用。

（二）用户版权意识将不断提高，版权保护制度不断完善，创作环境更加清朗

长期以来，我国网络版权主要的商业模式为“免费内容＋广告推广”。近年来，优质原创内容的生产和正规版权的运营将成为行业发展的主导模式。目前，我国的版权保护制度建设取得了一定的成效，版权意识也得到了一定的提高，行业内建立起了有效的自律机制，市场环境得到显著改善。

从需求端看，居民消费结构不断升级，文化娱乐消费不断增多，用户的付费意愿快速提升。不仅网络游戏和网络直播的用户付费意愿强劲，网络文学、网络音乐、网络视频、网络漫画、网络媒体的用户付费规模和人均付费值都将有显著增长，网络版权产业发展潜力巨大。

在创作环境改善的背景下，深耕内容创作，保护原创精神将是网络版权产业新时代的奋斗方向。培养并扶持内容创作人才，提供并维持清朗的创作环境，尊重和保护创作人才的劳动成果，将是版权产业未来发展的重要课题。

（三）全新技术和全新市场将助推网络版权产业融合发展

科技进步带来了全新的文化生产、传播与消费模式，“互联网＋”“文化＋”的大背景将产业间的界限逐渐模糊化，产业跨界融合的趋势日益明显。一方面，版权产业内部融合型产品层出不穷，例如游戏改编电影、网络文学改编游戏等。另一方面，IP 版权的打造也促进了与旅游业、制造业等传统产业的结合。未来，网络版权产业引领下的产业跨界融合将向着更加纵深化的方向发展。跨界融合也将促成一些新的产业生态，创意生成、生产制作、传播推广、衍生开发、版权交易和保护、投融资服务等环节都将被重构。

5G 技术将于 2020 年大规模商用，2019 年是关键的先期试验和技术储备年份，新型柔性屏移动端、VR 云计算均切实可见，4K 极高清影视将得益于传输速度而大幅普及，这些都将直接变革版权内容形式。AI 技术也将优化版权内容的传播分发效率，基于对用户偏好大数据的分析以及对社群活跃情况的判断，第一时间推送兴趣内容，并迅速将用户反馈呈现给创作者，革新用户与创作者的互动形态。未来，技术迭代的速度将超过以往任何一个时期，业态的不断创新和迭代升级将成为网络版权产业发展的常态，并为产业发展提供强大动力，赋予巨大的发展动能。

（四）海外布局持续发力，原创文化将得到全球认可

在很长一段时间内，我国的网络版权产业一直处在全球产业链的下游，影视、游戏等产业附加值相对较低。2018 年，我国的电影、网络文学等领域在出口方面取得了一定的成就，中国原创文化在“一带一路”周边国家得到广泛认可。但是，相较于欧美文化出口大国，我国的网络版权产业依然缺乏国际竞争力。在未来，通过国内企业联盟、国际合作开发等形式加速中国故事有效“出海”依然是网络版权产业发展的重要方向和课题。

中国网络版权产业具有强劲的内部动能和外部动能。中国优秀传统文化滋养下的网络版权产业具有强大的生命力和影响力。近几年，我国版权保护取得突破性进展，对侵权的查处力度日趋严格，盗版内容获取成本增加，最终用户的版权保护意识、付费意识显著增强，为网络版权产业的发展奠定了良好的政策和社会环境。中国良好的移动网络基础也是产业发展的重要优势，目前中国网络版权产业技术发展迅速，在技术探索方面有一定优势，为网络版权产业再度跨越奠定技术基础。未来五年，中国将凭借更为优质的内容作品向网络版权强国的目标进一步迈进。

2018 年新闻出版产业分析报告

国家新闻出版署

一、综　述

2018 年，新闻出版业以习近平新时代中国特色社会主义思想为指导，认真贯彻落实党中央关于新闻出版改革发展要求，坚持贯彻新发展理念，坚持守正创新，坚持以人民为中心，坚持把社会效益放在首位、社会效益和经济效益相统一，围绕推进行业高质量发展，不断深化供给侧结构性改革，持续挺拔主业、优化结构，着力融合创新、提质增效，实现了稳步发展。

新闻出版产业规模平稳增长。2018 年，全国出版、印刷和发行服务实现营业收入 18 687.5 亿元①，较 2017 年增长 3.1%；拥有资产总额 23 414.2 亿元，较 2017 年增长 5.6%；所有者权益（净资产）11 807.2 亿元，较 2017 年增长 4.4%（见图 1）。图书出版营业收入增长 6.6%，在新闻出版 8 个产业类别中增速第一。

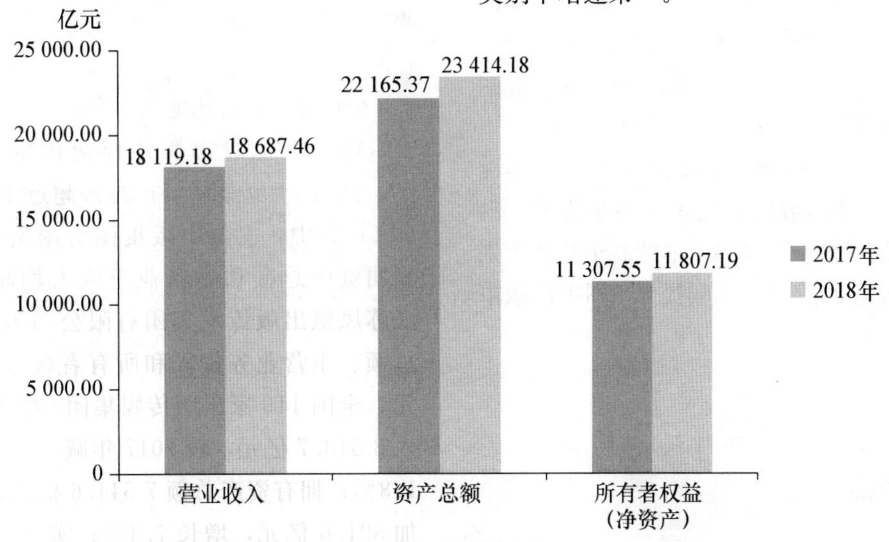

图 1　新闻出版产业营业收入、资产总额和所有者权益（净资产）增长情况

主题出版图书印数大幅提升。2018 年，全国出版马克思主义、列宁主义、毛泽东思想、中国特色社会主义理论体系类图书 2 497 万册（张），较 2017 年增加 1 370 万册（张），增长 1.2 倍，在 22 类图书中增速居首位。年度印数超过 100 万册的主题图书达 35 种，增长 1.1 倍，占年度印数 100 万册及以上一般图书②的 38.9%，提高 9.6 个百分点；其中 7 种主题图书进入印数前 10。《习近平新时代中国特色社会主义思想三十讲》年度印数超过 3 200 万册，《习近平谈治国理政》（第一卷、第二卷）超过 600 万册，《新时代面对面——理论热点面对面・2018》超过 980 万册；《红岩》、《红星照耀中国》、《红星照耀中国》（青少版）年度印数继续超过 100 万册，《共产党宣言》年度印数首次超过 100 万册。中宣部“2018 年主题出版重点出版物”图书单品种平均印数 27.8 万册，增长 3.1 倍，相当于书籍单品种平均印数的 18.6 倍。主题图书在弘扬主旋律、传播正能量、满足人民群众精神文化需求方面的积极作用进一步彰显。

① 另据中国新闻出版研究院数字出版研究所调查汇总数据，2018 年数字出版实现营业收入 8 412.3 亿元，较 2017 年增长 19.0%。因该数据非政府统计数据，故不纳入全国总量。

② 排除课本、中小学学习辅导材料等学生用书的书籍，通称“一般图书”。

主流报刊发行量不断扩大。《人民日报》平均期印数突破 350 万份，连续蝉联综合类报纸第一；《参考消息》《环球时报》等报纸平均期印数继续超过 100 万份，《参考消息》稳居综合类报纸第二；《光明日报》平均期印数首次超过 100 万份，进入综合类报纸平均期印数前十名；《经济日报》和《中国纪检监察报》分别首次跻身综合类报纸和专业类报纸平均期印数前十名。《求是》平均期印数继续增加，位居期刊第三位，《中国纪检监察》首次进入期刊平均期印数前十名。《时事报告》（大学生版）平均期印数超过 450 万册，继续名列期刊平均期印数第一。主流报刊舆论强势得到巩固，传播力、影响力进一步增强。

图书出版结构持续优化。2018 年，新版图书品种下降，总印数与单品种平均印数均有较大增加。全国出版新版图书 24.71 万种，较 2017 年降低 3.1%；总印数 25.2 亿册（张），增长 10.7%。重印图书品种与印数继续保持较快增长。全国出版重印图书 27.22 万种，较 2017 年增长 5.7%（见图 2）；总印数 57.7 亿册（张），增长 7.2%。90 种一般图书年度印数达到或超过 100 万册，增加 32 种；其中新版图书 48 种，增加 26 种，重印图书 42 种，增加 6 种。课本品种、总印数所占比重进一步降低。科学技术类书籍品种增速（5.3%）继续高于其他类别书籍，总印数增速（8.4%）大幅提升。图书出版单品种效益提升。

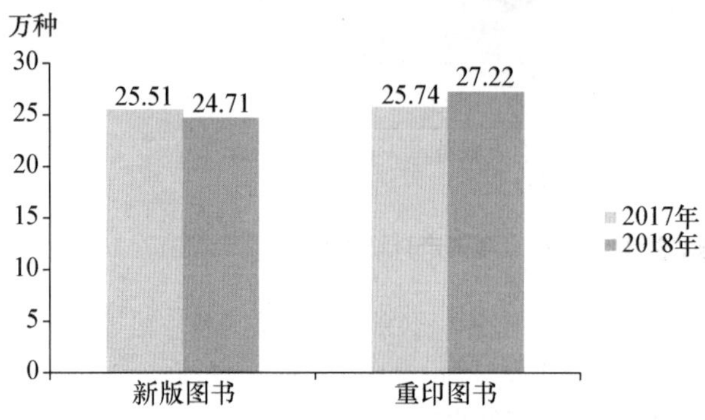

图 2　2017—2018 年新版与重印图书品种

原创图书出版进一步增温。2018 年，24 种原创文学、少儿图书年度印数超过 100 万册，较 2017 年增长 33.3%；其中新版图书 12 种。67 种原创少儿图书年度印数达到或超过 50 万册，增长 39.6%，占年度印数 50 万册及以上少儿图书品种的 73.6%，提高 13.6 个百分点。原创新版图书中，《梦回万里　卫黄保华》《时代大决战——贵州毕节精准扶贫纪实》《中国长岗坡》《山本》《苦难英雄任正非》《见识》《智能商业》《历史的温度 2》《四时之诗：蒙曼品最美唐诗》《听什么歌都像在唱自己》等一批作品年度印数均超过 10 万册，《你坏》《笑猫日记：又见小可怜》出版当年即突破百万册。原创重印图书中，《红岩》《平凡的世界》等优秀作品长销不衰；《米小圈上学记》《米小圈脑筋急转弯》等少儿读物后劲十足。

报刊出版降幅普遍收窄。报纸出版总印数较 2017 年降低 7.0%；总印张数降低 13.8%，收窄 1.3 个百分点；定价总金额降低 1.4%，收窄 0.9 个百分点。全国性报纸总印数近五年来首次回升，占比继续提高；综合类与专业类报纸总印数降幅保持稳定，读者对象类报纸降幅显著收窄 4.0 个百分点。期刊出版总印数降低 8.0%；总印张数降低 7.3%，收窄 2.8 个百分点；定价总金额降低 2.7%，收窄 1.0 个百分点。哲学社会科学类期刊印数降幅收窄 1.5 个百分点，占比继续提升。

资产百亿级出版传媒集团继续扩容。2018 年，共有 21 家集团资产总额超过 100 亿元，增加 3 家；其中，安徽出版集团有限责任公司等 3 家集团资产总额和主营业务收入均超过 100 亿元，江苏凤凰出版传媒集团有限公司等 6 家集团资产总额、主营业务收入和所有者权益均超过 100 亿元。全国 119 家出版传媒集团①共实现主营业务收入 3 513.7 亿元，较 2017 年减少 45.9 亿元，降低 1.3%；拥有资产总额 7 544.6 亿元，较 2017 年增加 521.6 亿元，增长 7.4%；实现利润总额 319.5 亿元，较 2017 年增加 14.1 亿元，增长 4.6%。其中，108 家图书出版、报刊出版和发行集团共实现主营业务收入占全国书报刊出版和出版物发行主营业务收入的 77.9%，拥有资产总额占全国出版发行全行业资产总额的 90.8%，利润总额占全国出版发行全行业利润总额的 70.7%。部分集团聚焦主业，降低风险性业务，缩减大宗贸易，发行集团整体收入近年来首次下滑。出版传媒集团收入利润率有所提高。

出版传媒上市公司主业经营突出。2018 年，37 家

① 截至 2018 年底，全国共有经国家出版管理部门或省级出版管理部门批准的出版传媒集团 126 家。其中，中国人力资源和社会保障出版集团有限公司、中国书法出版传媒有限公司、人民卫生出版集团、中国环境出版集团有限公司、人民法院出版集团、中国健康传媒集团有限公司和武汉出版集团有限公司 7 家集团尚不能提供有效的集团财务数据，故纳入 2018 年财务状况与经营成果统计的出版传媒集团为 119 家，其中图书出版集团、报刊出版集团和发行集团为 108 家。

在中国内地上市的出版传媒公司[①]实现营业收入共计1 501.4亿元，较2017年同口径增加57.4亿元，增长4.0%。新媒体公司和发行公司营业收入实现两位数增长，报业公司同口径收入止跌回升。出版公司、发行公司主业收入持续增长，出版公司编印发主业收入整体占比72.3%，提高3.0个百分点。各公司持续探索转型升级、融合发展之路，成效明显。

二、产业结构分析

2018年，新闻出版产业营业收入、资产总额和所有者权益继续增长，经济规模稳步提升。图书出版营业收入、利润总额增长提速，营收增速在8个产业类别中名列第一。期刊出版营业收入连续两年保持增长，报纸出版营业收入、利润总额再次下滑。印刷复制营业收入继续增长，利润总额减少。出版物发行营业收入、利润总额出现下滑。图书版权输出增加，版权贸易逆差有所减少。

（一）产业总体情况

1. 经济总量规模

2018年，全国出版、印刷和发行服务实现营业收入18 687.5亿元，较2017年增长3.1%；利润总额1 296.1亿元，降低3.6%；拥有资产总额23 414.2亿元，增长5.6%；所有者权益（净资产）11 807.2亿元，增长4.4%。产业结构如表1所示。

表1 新闻出版产业结构

单位：亿元，百分点

产业类别	营业收入			
	金额	增长速度（%）	所占比重（%）	比重变动
图书出版	937.30	6.56	5.02	0.17
期刊出版	199.41	1.46	1.07	−0.01
报纸出版	575.95	−0.40	3.08	−0.11
音像制品出版	30.10	6.14	0.16	0.00
电子出版物出版	15.20	1.67	0.08	0.00
印刷复制	13 727.56	4.34	73.46	0.85
出版物发行	3 116.28	−1.99	16.68	−0.87
出版物进出口	85.66	0.25	0.46	−0.01

2. 图书出版总量规模

2018年，全国共出版新版图书24.7万种，较2017年降低3.1%；重印图书27.2万种，增长5.7%；总印数100.1亿册（张），增长8.3%；总印张882.5亿印张，增长9.2%；定价总金额2 002.9亿元，增长15.7%。图书出版实现营业收入937.3亿元，增长6.6%；利润总额141.3亿元，增长2.8%（见表2）。

表2 图书出版总量规模

单位：万种，亿册（张），亿印张，亿元

总量指标	数值	较2017年增减（%）
新版品种	24.71	−3.14
重印品种	27.22	5.74
总印数	100.09	8.28
总印张	882.53	9.22
定价总金额	2 002.91	15.69
营业收入	937.30	6.56
利润总额	141.28	2.76

3. 期刊出版总量规模

2018年，全国共出版期刊10 139种，较2017年增长0.1%；总印数22.9亿册，降低8.0%；总印张126.8亿印张，降低7.3%；定价总金额217.9亿元，降低2.7%。期刊出版实现营业收入199.4亿元，增长1.5%；利润总额26.8亿元，降低2.0%（见表3）。

表3 期刊出版总量规模

单位：种，亿册，亿印张，亿元

总量指标	数值	较2017年增减（%）
品种	10 139	0.09
总印数	22.92	−8.03
总印张	126.75	−7.25
定价总金额	217.92	−2.67
营业收入	199.41	1.46
利润总额	26.81	−2.01

4. 报纸出版总量规模

2018年，全国共出版报纸1 871种，较2017年降低0.7%；总印数337.3亿份，降低7.0%；总印张927.9亿印张，降低13.8%；定价总金额393.5亿元，降低1.4%。报纸出版实现营业收入576.0亿元，降低0.4%；利润总额33.0亿元，降低12.2%（见表4）。

① 康得新复合材料集团股份有限公司因数据严重失实，不纳入分析范围；成都博瑞传播股份有限公司业务转型，亦不再被视为报业公司。因此参与分析的出版传媒上市公司现为37家，此处与2017年数据的比较系同口径比较。

表 4 报纸出版总量规模

单位：种，亿份，亿印张，亿元

总量指标	数值	较 2017 年增减（%）
品种	1 871	−0.69
总印数	337.26	−6.96
总印张	927.90	−13.78
定价总金额	393.45	−1.35
营业收入	575.95	−0.40
利润总额	32.96	−12.20

5. 音像制品出版总量规模

2018 年，全国共出版音像制品 11 063 种，较 2017 年降低 18.4%；出版数量 24 124.1 万盒（张），降低 5.7%。音像制品出版实现营业收入 30.1 亿元，增长 6.1%；利润总额 3.7 亿元，增长 3.9%（见表 5）。

表 5 音像制品出版总量规模

单位：种，万盒（张），亿元

总量指标	数值	较 2017 年增减（%）
品种	11 063	−18.37
出版数量	24 124.09	−5.74
营业收入	30.10	6.14
利润总额	3.73	3.90

6. 电子出版物出版总量规模

2018 年，全国共出版电子出版物 8 403 种，较 2017 年降低 9.1%；出版数量 25 884.2 万张，降低 8.0%。电子出版物出版实现营业收入 15.2 亿元，增长 1.7%；利润总额 2.8 亿元，增长 3.3%（见表 6）。

表 6 电子出版物出版总量规模

单位：种，万张，亿元

总量指标	数值	较 2017 年增减（%）
品种	8 403	−9.06
出版数量	25 884.21	−7.99
营业收入	15.20	1.67
利润总额	2.80	3.32

7. 印刷复制总量规模

2018 年，全国印刷复制（包括出版物印刷、包装装潢印刷、其他印刷品印刷、专项印刷、印刷物资供销和复制）实现营业收入 13 727.6 亿元，增长 4.3%；利润总额 835.2 亿元，降低 1.7%（见表 7）。

表 7 印刷复制总量规模

单位：亿元

总量指标	数值	较 2017 年增减（%）
营业收入	13 727.56	4.34
利润总额	835.23	−1.74

8. 出版物发行总量规模

2018 年，全国共有出版物发行网点 17.2 万处，较 2017 年增长 5.4%。出版物发行实现营业收入 3 116.3 亿元，降低 2.0%；利润总额 250.7 亿元，降低 11.5%（见表 8）。

表 8 出版物发行总量规模

单位：处，亿元

总量指标	数值	较 2017 年增减（%）
出版物发行网点数量	171 547	5.37
营业收入	3 116.28	−1.99
利润总额	250.74	−11.51

9. 出版物进出口总量规模

2018 年，全国累计出口图书、期刊、报纸、音像制品、电子出版物、数字出版物（不含游戏）1 701.4 万册（份、盒、张），较 2017 年降低 21.9%；出口金额 10 092.6 万美元，降低 6.3%［其中，全国出版物进出口经营单位累计出口 1 479.3 万册（份、盒、张），较 2017 年降低 21.0%；出口金额 5 935.2 万美元，降低 4.1%］（见表 9）。全国累计进口图书、期刊、报纸、音像制品、电子出版物、数字出版物（不含游戏）4 096.9 万册（份、盒、张）①，较 2017 年增长 25.3%；出口金额 74 222.1 万美元，增长 11.5%（见表 10）。进出口总额 84 314.7 万美元（其中，全国出版物进出口经营单位进出口总额 80 157.3 万美元，增长 10.2%）。出版物进出口经营单位实现营业收入 85.7 亿元，增长 0.3%；利润总额 2.5 亿元，增长 14.4%。

表 9 全国出版物出口情况

单位：万册（份、盒、张），万美元

类型	数量	金额
图书、期刊、报纸	1 696.10	7 194.80
其中：进出口经营单位	1 478.09	5 723.00
音像制品、电子出版物、数字出版物（不含游戏）	5.30	2 897.90
其中：进出口经营单位	1.24	212.20
合计	1 701.36	10 092.61
其中：进出口经营单位	1 479.33	5 935.20

① 因数字出版物目前只能统计金额，无法统计数量，故进出口数量中未包含数字出版物。

表 10　全国出版物进口情况

单位：万册（份、盒、张），万美元

类型	数量	金额
图书、期刊、报纸	4 088.02	36 202.2
音像制品、电子出版物、数字出版物（不含游戏）	8.84	38 019.9
合计	4 096.86	74 222.1

10. 版权贸易总量规模

2018 年，全国共输出版权 12 778 项，其中输出出版物版权 11 830 项，包括图书 10 873 项，音像制品 214 项，电子出版物 743 项；图书版权输出较 2017 年增长 1.9%。共引进版权 16 829 项，其中引进出版物版权 16 602 项，包括图书 16 071 项，音像制品 317 项，电子出版物 214 项；引进版权总量降低 7.1%，其中引进出版物版权降低 8.0%。版权贸易逆差有所减少。

（二）各产业类别总体经济规模综合评价

选取营业收入、增加值、总产出和利润总额等 4 项经济规模指标，采用主成分分析法对图书出版、期刊出版、报纸出版、音像制品出版、电子出版物出版、印刷复制、出版物发行和出版物进出口等 8 个新闻出版产业类别的总体经济规模进行综合评价，其排名结果与 2017 年相比保持不变（见表 11）。印刷复制、出版物发行和图书出版分居前 3 位，实现营业收入共计 17 781.1 亿元，较 2017 年增长 3.3%，占全行业营业收入的 95.2%，提高 0.2 个百分点。

表 11　各产业类别经济规模综合评价

综合排名	产业类别	综合评价得分	2017 年排名	排名变化
1	印刷复制	2.407 5	1	0
2	出版物发行	0.173 5	2	0
3	图书出版	−0.228 3	3	0
4	报纸出版	−0.374 9	4	0
5	期刊出版	−0.443 0	5	0
6	出版物进出口	−0.507 8	6	0
7	音像制品出版	−0.512 1	7	0
8	电子出版物出版	−0.514 8	8	0

说明：综合评价得分系选取营业收入、增加值、总产出和利润总额等 4 项指标，采用主成分分析法，通过 SPSS 直接计算所得，仅用来显示各产业类别的相对位置，负数并不代表负面评价。

（三）各产业类别增长情况

以各产业类别营业收入增长速度衡量，前 3 位降序依次为图书出版、音像制品出版和印刷复制。与 2017 年相比，图书出版、音像制品出版、期刊出版和报纸出版营收增速排名上升，电子出版物出版和出版物发行排名下降，印刷复制、出版物进出口排名保持不变（见表 12）。

表 12　各产业类别营业收入增长速度（%）

排名	产业类别	增长速度
1	图书出版	6.56
2	音像制品出版	6.14
3	印刷复制	4.34
4	电子出版物出版	1.67
5	期刊出版	1.46
6	出版物进出口	0.25
7	报纸出版	−0.4
8	出版物发行	−1.99

说明：各产业类别增长速度＝(该产业类别本年营业收入－该产业类别上年营业收入)÷该产业类别上年营业收入×100%。

三、产品结构分析

主题出版、主流报刊传播力影响力持续提升。在单品种年度印数和平均期印数排名前 10 位的图书、期刊、报纸中，主题图书、主流报刊占据多数；列入中宣部“2018 年主题出版重点出版物”的图书单品种平均印数大幅增长，继续高于全部图书平均水平；《习近平新时代中国特色社会主义思想三十讲》超过 3 200 万册，《习近平谈治国理政》（第一卷、第二卷）超过 600 万册，《新时代面对面——理论热点面对面·2018》超过 980 万册。马克思主义、列宁主义、毛泽东思想、中国特色社会主义理论体系类图书总印数较 2017 年增长 1.2 倍，《共产党宣言》年度印数首次超过 100 万册。《人民日报》平均期印数持续增长，突破 350 万份，继续稳居综合类报纸第一位；《光明日报》平均期印数突破 100 万份；《经济日报》和《中国纪检监察报》分别首次跻身综合类报纸和专业类报纸平均期印数前十位。《求是》平均期印数继续增加，保持期刊前三位；《中国纪检监察》进入期刊平均期印数排名前十位。

新版图书品种继续减少，印数大幅回升；重印图书品种与印数继续较快增长，在品种上继续超过新版图书。90 种一般图书年度印数达到或超过 100 万册，较 2017 年增加 32 种。其中，新版图书 48 种，增加 26 种；重印图书 42 种，增加 6 种；文学类图书 10 种，增加 3 种；少儿图书 28 种，增加 10 种；红色经典 4 种，增加 1 种。人文社科类书籍品种、总印数和单品种平均印数继续增加，品种和总印数所占比重继续提高；科学技术类书籍品种增速继续高于其他类别图书，总印数增速大幅提升；课本品种、总印数所占比重进一步降低。少儿图书总印数和单品种平均印数保持增长，但新版品种略有减少、印数增加，重印品种增加、印数减少。

报刊出版总印数、总印张与定价总金额继续降低，降幅整体收窄。哲学社会科学类期刊总印数降幅缩小，所占比重继续提高；文学艺术类期刊继续大幅下滑，比重持续降低；文化教育类期刊降幅明显加大。全国性报纸总印数首次回升，在全国报纸总印数中所占比重持续提高；省级报纸和地市级报纸降幅仍然较大，所占比重继续下降。综合类与专业类报纸降幅保持稳定，读者对象类报纸降幅明显缩小；专业类和读者对象类报纸比重有所提高。

（一）整体结构

2018 年，全国共出版图书、期刊、报纸、音像制品和电子出版物 465.3 亿册（份、盒、张），较 2017 年降低 4.1%。其中，出版图书 100.1 亿册（张），增长 8.3%，占全部数量的 21.5%；期刊 22.9 亿册，降低 8.0%，占 4.9%；报纸 337.3 亿份，降低 7.0%，占 72.5%；音像制品 2.4 亿盒（张），降低 5.7%，占 0.5%；电子出版物 2.6 亿张，降低 8.0%，占 0.6%（见表 13）。

表 13 出版物产品结构

单位：亿册（张、份、盒），百分点

出版物类型	总印数			
	数量	增长速度（%）	所占比重（%）	比重变动
图书	100.09	8.28	21.51	2.46
期刊	22.92	−8.03	4.93	−0.21
报纸	337.26	−6.96	72.49	−2.21
音像制品	2.41	−5.74	0.52	−0.01
电子出版物	2.59	−7.99	0.56	−0.02
合计	465.27	−4.11	100.00	0.00

说明：1. 数量指标书报刊采用总印数，音像制品和电子出版物采用出版数量。

2. 表中部分数据因四舍五入的原因，存在总计与分项合计不等的情况。

（二）图书结构

1. 新版与重印图书

2018 年，全国出版新版图书 24.7 万种，较 2017 年降低 3.1%；重印图书 27.2 万种，增长 5.7%。重印图书在品种上连续两年超过新版图书，且差值继续扩大。

全国出版新版图书 25.2 亿册（张），增长 10.7%，占图书总印数的 25.2%，提高 0.6 个百分点；重印图书 57.7 亿册（张），增长 7.2%，占 57.7%，减少 0.6 个百分点；租型图书 17.2 亿册（张），增长 8.6%，占 17.2%，与上年基本持平。重印图书总印数为新版图书的 2.3 倍（见图 3）。

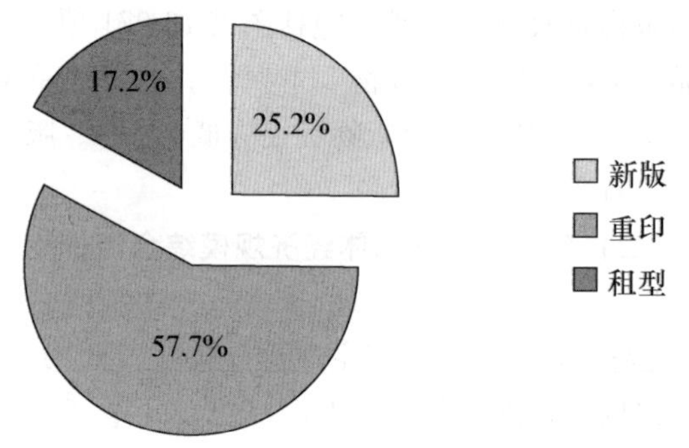

图 3 新版、重印与租型图书印数结构

2018 年，全国新版图书单品种平均印数 10 186 册（张），增加 1 272 册（张）；重印图书单品种平均印数 21 218 册（张），增加 286 册（张）。

2. 书籍与课本

图书主要包括书籍①、课本②和图片③ 3 类。

2018 年，全国出版新版书籍 22.6 万种，较 2017 年降低 2.3%，占新版图书品种的 91.4%，提高 0.8 个百分点；新版课本 2.1 万种，降低 11.4%，占 8.5%，降低 0.8 个百分点；新版图片 102 种，降低 35.0%，占 0.04%。重印书籍 21.0 万种，增长 8.1%，占重印图书品种的 77.2%，提高 1.7 个百分点；重印课本 6.2 万种，降低 1.6%，占 22.7%，降低 1.7 个百分点；重印图片 235 种，增长 91.1%，占 0.1%。

全国出版书籍 65.1 亿册（张），增长 9.0%，占

① 书籍系指使用标准书号或统一书号，但不属于课本和图片的出版物。

② 课本系指使用标准书号或统一书号的以下各类出版物：(1) 由国家教育行政部门和中央各部委、各地区审定、规划的，列入教材征订目录，供高等学校、电视大学、函授大学等高等教育机构，中等专业学校（包括中等师范学校）、技工学校使用的教材、教材习题解答集，以及对成人进行政治、业务、文化教育所使用的课本，包括广播电台、电视台举办或与其他单位合办的业余讲座使用的课本及其他业余教育课本；(2) 在国家教育行政部门每年春秋两季颁发的《全国普通中小学教学用书目录》和由各省（自治区、直辖市）教育行政部门审定、补充下达的《中小学教学用书目录》中所列的课本、教学挂图和随课本做教材用的习题解答集，以及由省（自治区、直辖市）以上教育行政机关统一规定为各级学校教员必须采用的"教学参考资料"及"教学大纲"（包括少数民族自治州出版社出版，由少数民族自治州教育行政机关规定的此类出版物）；(3) 专供扫盲使用的课本。具体包括大专及以上课本、中专技校课本、中小学课本、业余教育课本、扫盲课本和教学用书。

③ 图片系指单张或折页的美术画片，包括绘画的印制品和摄影的印制品，年画也归入图片。

图书总印数的 65.1%；课本 34.8 亿册（张），增长 6.9%，占 34.9%；图片 211 万册（张），降低 15.9%。

2018 年全国书籍单品种平均印数 14 917 册（张），增加 893 册（张）；课本单品种平均印数 42 012 册（张），增加 4 409 册（张）。

（1）书籍。

书籍按照内容划分为社科人文、科学技术和综合三大类。

2018 年，全国出版社科人文类书籍 36.3 万种，较 2017 年增长 2.0%，占书籍品种总数的 83.2%；科学技术类书籍 7.0 万种，增长 5.3%，占 15.9%；综合类书籍 0.4 万种，降低 2.6%，占 0.9%（见图 4、表 14）。

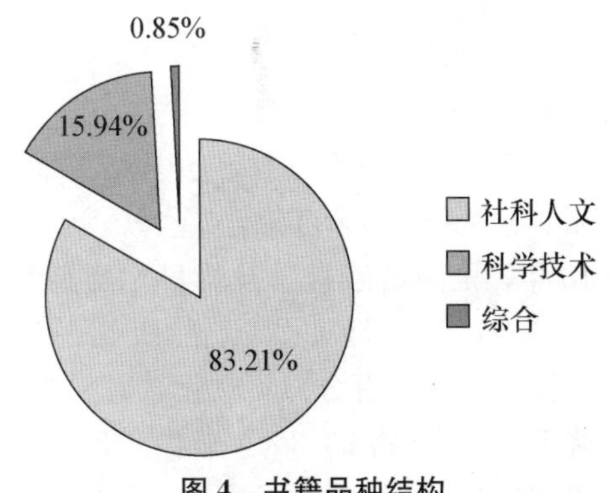

图 4　书籍品种结构

全国出版社科人文类书籍 61.9 亿册（张），增长 9.1%，占书籍总印数的 95.2%；科学技术类书籍 2.9 亿册（张），增长 8.4%，占 4.4%；综合类书籍 0.3 亿册（张），降低 7.1%，占 0.4%。

2018 年全国社科人文类书籍单品种平均印数 17 067 册（张），增加 1 109 册（张）；科学技术类书籍单品种平均印数 4 108 册（张），增加 122 册（张）；综合类书籍单品种平均印数 7 080 册（张），减少 300 册（张）。

（2）课本。

课本分为大专及以上课本、中专技校课本、中学课本、小学课本、业余教育课本、扫盲课本和教学用书 7 类。

2018 年，全国出版中学课本 5 715 种，较 2017 年降低 5.0%，占课本品种数的 6.9%；小学课本 5 058 种，降低 8.5%，占 6.2%。中小学课本合计 10 773 种，占课本品种数的 13.1%，占图书品种数的 2.1%，减少 0.1 个百分点。

全国出版中学课本 15.8 亿册（张），增长 4.3%，占课本总印数的 45.5%；小学课本 14.8 亿册（张），增长 11.4%，占 42.6%。中小学课本合计 30.6 亿册（张），占课本总印数的 88.1%，占图书总印数的 30.7%，减少 0.2 个百分点。

2018 年全国中学课本单品种平均印数 277 146 册（张），增加 24 739 册（张）；小学课本单品种平均印数 293 258 册（张），增加 52 542 册（张）。

表 14　书籍、课本与图片品种、印数结构

单位：万种，亿册（张），百分点

类型	品种				总印数			
	数量	增长速度（%）	所占比重（%）	比重变动	数量	增长速度（%）	所占比重（%）	比重变动
书籍	43.61	2.45	83.98	0.94	65.05	8.98	65.13	0.44
社科人文	36.29	2.00	69.89	0.47	61.94	9.09	62.02	0.48
科学技术	6.95	5.30	13.38	0.50	2.85	8.37	2.85	0.00
综合	0.37	−2.63	0.71	−0.03	0.26	−7.14	0.26	−0.04
课本	8.29	−4.31	15.96	−0.94	34.81	6.91	34.85	−0.43
中学	0.57	−4.99	1.10	−0.07	15.84	4.32	15.86	−0.59
小学	0.51	−8.54	0.98	−0.09	14.83	11.43	14.85	0.43
图片	0.03	20.36	0.06	0.00	0.02	−15.94	0.02	−0.01
合计	51.93	1.33	100.00	0.00	99.88	8.24	100.00	0.00

说明：1. 社科人文类书籍系指属于中国图书馆分类法马克思主义、列宁主义、毛泽东思想、邓小平理论，哲学、宗教，社会科学总论，政治、法律，军事，经济，文化、科学、教育、体育，语言、文字，文学，艺术，历史、地理 11 大类（A—K）的书籍；科学技术类书籍系指属于中国图书馆分类法自然科学总论，数理科学和化学，天文学、地球科学，生物科学，医药、卫生，农业科学，工业技术，交通运输，航空、航天，环境科学、安全科学 10 大类（N—X）的书籍；综合类书籍系指属于中国图书馆分类法综合性图书类（Z）的书籍。

2. 以上数据不包含国部标准及小件印品。

3. 主题出版重点图书

2018年，全国出版《习近平新时代中国特色社会主义思想三十讲》、《习近平谈治国理政》（第一卷、第二卷）、《新时代面对面——理论热点面对面·2018》、《党的十九大全面从严治党精神十二讲》、《马克思画传：马克思诞辰200周年纪念版》、《巨变：改革开放40年中国记忆》等入选中宣部"2018年主题出版重点出版物"的图书183种，涉及马克思主义、列宁主义、毛泽东思想、中国特色社会主义理论体系，哲学、宗教，社会科学总论，政治、法律，经济，文学，历史、地理，自然科学总论，交通运输等诸多类别；其中新版图书174种。

全国出版"2018年主题出版重点出版物"图书5 086.5万册，单品种平均印数277 948册，远高于全部书籍单品种平均印数。其中，《习近平新时代中国特色社会主义思想三十讲》年度印数超过3 200万册，《习近平谈治国理政》（第一卷、第二卷）超过600万册，《新时代面对面——理论热点面对面·2018》超过980万册。

4. 少儿图书

2018年，全国出版新版少儿图书2.3万种，较2017年略有减少；重印少儿图书2.1万种，增加1 798种，增长9.2%。

全国出版少儿图书8.9亿册（张），增加6 852万册（张），增长8.4%。其中，新版图书4.1亿册（张），增加7 922万册（张），增长23.8%；重印图书4.8亿册（张），减少1 070万册（张），降低2.2%。

2018年，全国少儿图书单品种平均印数20 105册（张），增加782册（张）。其中，新版图书18 055册（张），增加3 503册（张）；重印图书22 289册（张），减少2 589册（张）。

5. 年度印数百万册及以上书籍

《习近平新时代中国特色社会主义思想三十讲》、《习近平谈治国理政》（第一卷、第二卷）、《习近平扶贫论述摘编》、《中国共产党纪律处分条例》、《新时代面对面——理论热点面对面·2018》、《中华人民共和国宪法》等90种一般图书年度单品种累计印数达到或超过100万册。其中，主题图书35种，占年度印数100万册及以上一般图书的38.9%，提高9.6个百分点。《习近平新时代中国特色社会主义思想三十讲》超过3 200万册，《习近平谈治国理政》（第一卷、第二卷）超过600万册，《习近平扶贫论述摘编》（小字本）达到330万册，《新时代面对面——理论热点面对面·2018》超过980万册，《中华人民共和国宪法》各种版本总计近2 000万册，《中国共产党纪律处分条例》各种版本总计超过1 700万册。《红岩》《红星照耀中国》《平凡的世界》等10种文学类图书，《曹文轩纯美小说：草房子》《曹文轩纯美小说：青铜葵花》《动物小说大王沈石溪品藏书系：狼王梦》《笑猫日记：又见小可怜》《不一样的卡梅拉》《米小圈上学记》《米小圈脑筋急转弯》等28种少儿图书年度印数均达到或超过100万册，分别较2017年增加3种和10种。

在2018年单品种年度印数排名前10位的一般图书中，主题图书占7种。前10位图书总印数合计8 665.4万册，较2017年减少1 996.9万册，降低18.7%。《百年追梦　全面小康》《时刻听党话　永远跟党走》《科学学生活动手册》等中小学学生用书当年单品种累计印数均超过100万册，进入中小学学生用书印数前10位。

（三）期刊结构

1. 内容结构

期刊按照内容划分为哲学社会科学、文化教育、文学艺术、自然科学技术和综合5类。

2018年，全国出版哲学社会科学类期刊11.5亿册，较2017年降低4.2%，占期刊总印数的50.0%，提高2.0个百分点；文化教育类期刊5.3亿册，降低9.2%，占23.3%，减少0.3个百分点；文学艺术类期刊1.7亿册，降低20.7%，占7.2%，减少1.2个百分点；自然科学技术类期刊3.0亿册，降低10.6%，占13.0%，减少0.4个百分点；综合类期刊1.5亿册，降低10.4%，占6.5%，减少0.2个百分点。文学艺术类期刊印数继续大幅下滑，文化教育类期刊降幅加大，哲学社会科学类期刊所占比重继续提高（见图5）。

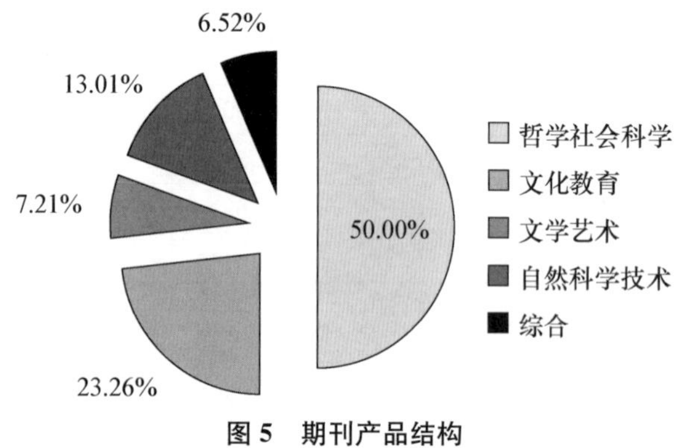

图5　期刊产品结构

2. 平均期印数百万册及以上期刊

2018年，共有《求是》、《中国纪检监察》、《时事报告》（大学生版）、《时事》（初中版）、《读者》等10种期刊平均期印数超过100万册，较2017年减少1种（《家庭医生》）。其中，《时事报告》（大学生版）平均期印数超过450万册。

与2017年相比，《中国纪检监察》进入前10，《家庭医生》退出前10；《中共中央办公厅通讯》《小学生时代》排名上升，《特别关注》排名下降；《时事》（《时事报告》中学生版）扩充为《时事》（初中版）和《时事》（高中版）两种，《时事》（初中版）排名第6；每种平均期印数185.8万册，增加4.7万册，增长2.6%（见表15）。

表15　2018年平均期印数排名前10位的期刊

排名	期刊名称	刊期	所在省份	2017年排名	排名变化
1	时事报告（大学生版）	半年刊	中央在京	1	0
2	读者	半月刊	甘肃	2	0
3	求是	半月刊	中央在京	3	0
4	中共中央办公厅通讯	月刊	中央在京	5	1
5	小学生时代	月刊	浙江	6	1
6	时事（初中版）	季刊	中央在京	—	—
7	青年文摘	半月刊	中央在京	7	0
8	半月谈	半月刊	中央在京	8	0
9	特别关注	月刊	湖北	4	−5
10	中国纪检监察	半月刊	中央在京	11	1

（四）报纸结构

1. 层级结构

报纸根据地域层级划分为全国性报纸、省级报纸、地市级报纸和县级报纸4类。

2018年，共出版全国性报纸78.3亿份，较2017年增长0.2%，占报纸总印数的23.2%，提高1.7个百分点；省级报纸152.0亿份，降低8.8%，占45.1%，减少0.9个百分点；地市级报纸105.9亿份，降低9.4%，占31.4%，减少0.8个百分点；县级报纸1.0亿份，增长28.7%，占0.3%，提高0.1个百分点。全国性报纸总印数近五年首次上升，在全国报纸总印数中所占比重持续提高；省级报纸和地市级报纸仍保持较大降幅，所占比重继续下降。

2. 内容结构

报纸根据内容划分为综合、专业、生活服务、读者对象和文摘5大类。

2018年，全国出版综合类报纸210.4亿份，较2017年降低8.2%，占报纸总印数的62.4%，减少0.8个百分点；专业类报纸100.0亿份，降低3.3%，占29.7%，提高1.1个百分点；生活服务类报纸8.0亿份，降低18.0%，占2.4%，减少0.3个百分点；读者对象类报纸15.5亿份，降低2.9%，占4.6%，提高0.2个百分点；文摘类报纸3.4亿份，降低22.2%，占1.0%，减少0.2个百分点。读者对象类报纸和专业类报纸降幅较小，所占比重提高；综合类、生活服务类和文摘类报纸所占比重继续下降，生活服务类和文摘类报纸降幅加大（见图6）。

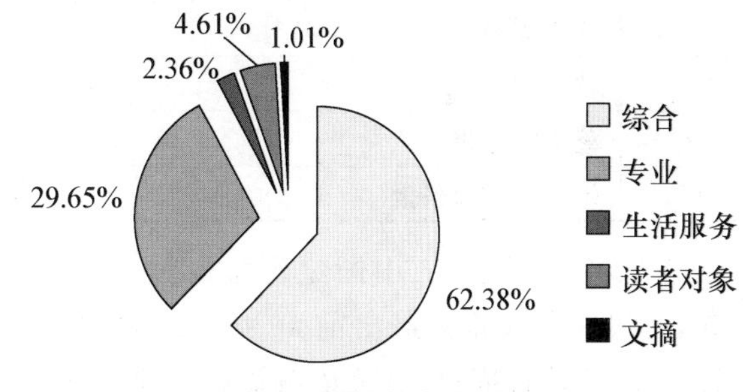

图6　报纸的内容结构

3. 平均期印数百万份及以上报纸

2018年，共有《人民日报》《参考消息》《环球时报》等22种报纸平均期印数达到或超过100万份，较2017年减少2种；其中综合类7种，减少2种［《扬子晚报》、《广州日报》（社区版）］；专业类报纸13种，其中教学辅导类11种，读者对象类报纸2种，均与上年持平。

2018年平均期印数排名前10位的综合类报纸见表16。

表16　2018年平均期印数排名前10位的综合类报纸

排名	报纸名称	刊期	所在省份	2017年排名	排名变化
1	人民日报	周七刊	中央在京	1	0
2	参考消息	周七刊	中央在京	2	0

续表

排名	报纸名称	刊期	所在省份	2017 年排名	排名变化
3	新华每日电讯	周七刊	中央在京	3	0
4	南方都市报	周七刊	广东	4	0
5	环球时报	周六刊	中央在京	7	2
6	半岛都市报	周七刊	山东	8	2
7	光明日报	周七刊	中央在京	15	8
8	南方日报	周七刊	广东	10	2
9	经济日报	周七刊	中央在京	13	4
10	都市快报	周七刊	浙江	6	−4

与 2017 年相比，《光明日报》《经济日报》跻身前 10 位，《广州日报》（社区版）、《扬子晚报》退出前 10 位；《环球时报》《半岛都市报》《南方日报》排名上升，《都市快报》排名下降；每种平均期印数 138.1 万份，减少 10.7 万份，降低 7.2%。

2018 年平均期印数排名前 10 位的专业类报纸见表 17。

表 17　2018 年平均期印数排名前 10 位的专业类报纸

排名	报纸名称	刊期	所在省份	2017 年排名	排名变化
1	英语周报	周一刊	山西	1	0
2	当代中学生报	周一刊	江西	2	0
3	学习方法报	周一刊	山西	3	0
4	中学生学习报	周一刊	河南	4	0
5	英语辅导报	周一刊	吉林	5	0
6	语文学习报	周一刊	吉林	6	0
7	学生周报	周一刊	福建	9	2
8	教育周报	周一刊	辽宁	7	−1
9	英语测试报	周一刊	吉林	8	−1
10	中国纪检监察报	周七刊	中央在京	11	1

与 2017 年相比，《中国纪检监察报》跻身前 10 位，《快乐老人报》退出前 10 位；《学生周报》排名上升，《教育周报》《英语测试报》排名下降；每种平均期印数 446.6 万份，增加 3.3 万份，增长 0.8%。

四、地区结构分析

东部地区保持规模优势，继续占据总体经济规模综合评价前 7 位；营业收入增长贡献排名前 10 位的地区中，东部地区占 6 席；增长贡献率超过 10% 的前 4 位地区，全部为东部地区。中西部地区继续保持较好增长态势，增长速度排名前 10 位地区中，中西部地区占 5 席，较 2017 年增加 1 席。

（一）总体经济规模综合评价

选取营业收入、增加值、总产出、资产总额、所有者权益（净资产）、利润总额和纳税总额等 7 项经济规模指标，采用主成分分析法对全国 31 个省（自治区、直辖市）及新疆生产建设兵团新闻出版业的总体经济规模进行综合评价。

广东、山东、北京①、江苏、浙江、上海、河北、四川、福建和安徽依次位居全国前 10 位（见表 18）。其中，前 7 位均属于东部地区。与 2017 年相比，前 10 位地区保持不变但名次有所改变；前 10 位中江苏、四川和福建排名上升，浙江和安徽排名下降。

前 10 位地区实现营业收入共计 14 085.3 亿元，占全部地区营业收入的 75.4%，较 2017 年减少 0.1 个百分点（见图 7）；拥有资产总额共计 16 799.2 亿元，占全部地区资产总额的 71.7%，减少 0.1 个百分点（见图 8）；实现利润总额共计 947.1 亿元，占全部地区利润总额的 73.1%，提高 2.7 个百分点（见图 9）。

① 包括中央在京新闻出版单位，后同。

表18　总体经济规模综合评价前10位的地区

综合排名	地区	综合评价得分	2017年排名	排名变化
1	广东	2.693 9	1	0
2	山东	2.020 3	2	0
3	北京	1.896 6	3	0
4	江苏	1.827 5	5	1
5	浙江	1.666 4	4	−1
6	上海	0.766 7	6	0
7	河北	0.426 2	7	0
8	四川	0.335 5	9	1
9	福建	0.285 2	10	1
10	安徽	0.282 6	8	−2

说明：1. 选取营业收入、增加值、总产出、资产总额、所有者权益（净资产）、利润总额和纳税总额等7项经济规模指标，采用主成分分析法，通过SPSS直接计算所得，仅用来显示各地区的相对位置。

2. 未包括数字出版、打字复印、邮政发行、版权贸易与代理、行业服务与其他新闻出版业务。

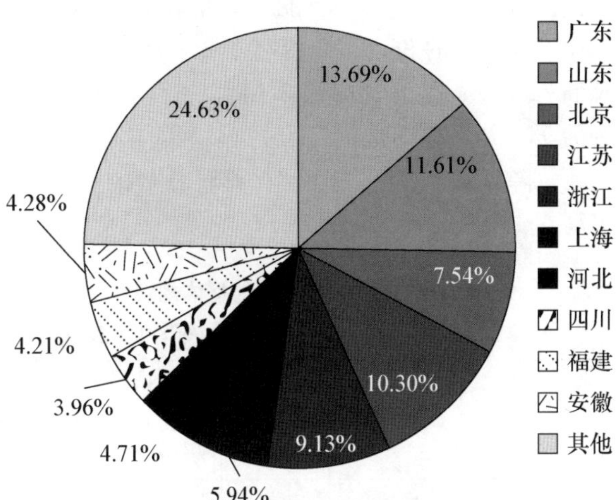

图7　营业收入的地区结构

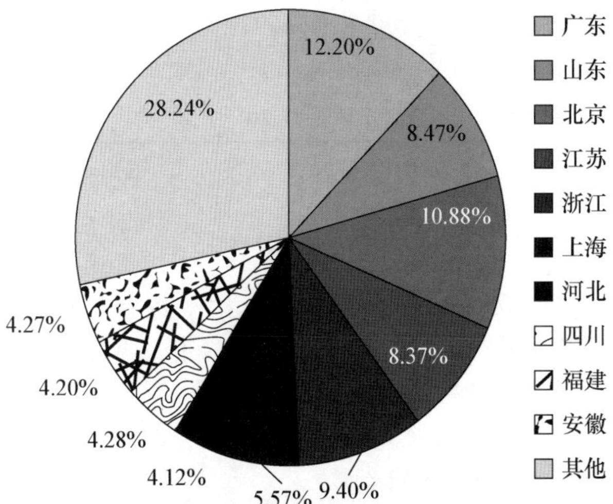

图8　资产总额的地区结构

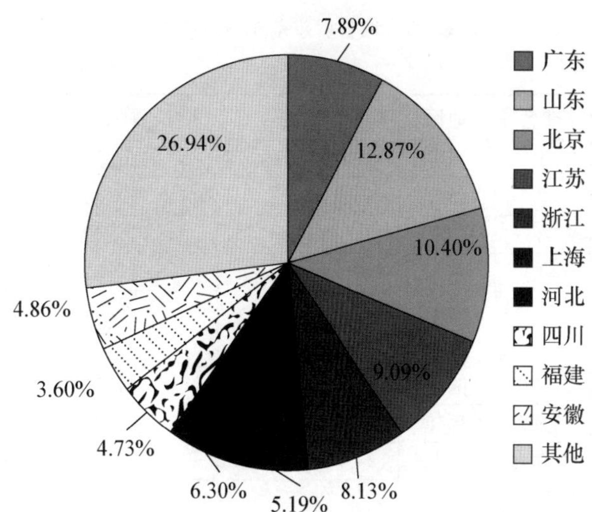

图9　利润总额的地区结构

（二）增长情况

1. 增长速度

以各地区新闻出版全行业营业收入同口径增长速度衡量，前10位降序依次为河南、云南、江苏、浙江、贵州、四川、北京、湖北、福建和天津。其中，东部地区5席，中部地区2席，西部地区3席（见表19）。

表19　增长速度前10位的地区（%）

排名	地区	增长速度
1	河南	10.20
2	云南	9.84
3	江苏	8.50
4	浙江	6.92
5	贵州	6.20
6	四川	4.82
7	北京	4.69
8	湖北	4.50
9	福建	4.45
10	天津	4.43

说明：地区增长速度=（该地区本年营业收入−该地区上年营业收入）÷该地区上年营业收入×100%。

2. 增长贡献

以各地区新闻出版全行业营业收入增长贡献率衡量其对全国新闻出版产业增长贡献，前10位降序依次为江苏、浙江、广东、北京、河南、山东、四川、福建、湖北和上海。其中，东部地区7席，中部地区2席，西部地区1席。江苏、浙江、广东和北京4省市的贡献率均超过10%（见表20）。

表 20 增长贡献前 10 位的地区

单位：亿元

排名	地区	增长额	增长贡献率（%）
1	江苏	150.83	26.54
2	浙江	110.49	19.44
3	广东	96.55	16.99
4	北京	63.15	11.11
5	河南	43.20	7.60
6	山东	37.62	6.62
7	四川	33.98	5.98
8	福建	33.59	5.91
9	湖北	30.92	5.44
10	上海	25.89	4.56

说明：各地区增长额＝该地区本年营业收入－该地区上年营业收入，各地区增长贡献率＝(该地区本年营业收入－该地区上年营业收入)÷(各地区本年营业收入合计－各地区上年营业收入合计)×100%。

与 2017 年相比，东部地区增加 1 席，中部地区减少 1 席，西部地区数量不变；贡献率超过 10%的省份减少 2 席。

五、单位数量及就业人员分析

新闻出版单位数量略有增加，企业法人单位数量基本稳定，在全行业营业收入、资产总额和利润总额中所占比重继续提高。在印刷复制企业中，民营企业各项指标所占比重均有所提高；在出版物发行企业中，国有企业营业收入所占比重继续降低，民营企业所占比重继续提高。

（一）单位数量与构成

2018 年，全国共有新闻出版单位 23.2 万家，较 2017 年增长 0.2%。其中，法人单位 14.4 万家，基本持平，占单位总数的 62.1%，减少 0.1 个百分点；非法人单位 0.9 万家，增长 0.9%，占 3.8%，基本持平；个体经营户 7.9 万家，增长 0.3%，占 34.2%，提高 0.1 个百分点（见表 21、图 10）。

表 21 新闻出版单位数量与构成

单位：家，百分点

类型	数量	增减百分比（%）	所占比重（%）	比重变动
法人单位	143 909	0.01	62.06	−0.08
其中：企业法人单位	141 295	0.05	—	—
非法人单位	8 702	0.92	3.75	0.03
个体经营户	79 271	0.31	34.19	0.06
合计	231 882	0.15	100.00	100.00

说明：未包括数字出版单位、打字复印单位、邮政发行单位、版权贸易与代理单位和行业服务与从事其他新闻出版业务的单位。

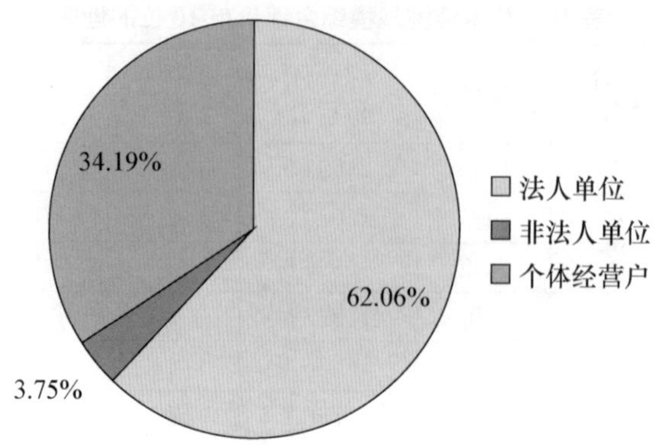

图 10 新闻出版单位类型构成

（二）企业法人情况

1. 整体规模

2018 年，全行业共有企业法人单位 14.1 万家，较 2017 年增长 0.1%，占全行业法人单位和非法人单位（不包括个体经营户）总数的 92.6%。企业法人单位营业收入 17 896.4 亿元，增长 3.1%，占全行业营业收入的 96.0%，提高 0.2 个百分点；资产总额 21 740.6 亿元，增长 5.5%，占全行业资产总额的 93.2%，提高 0.2 个百分点；利润总额 1 230.3 亿元，降低 3.7%，占全行业利润总额的 95.4%，提高 0.4 个百分点（见表 22）。

表 22 企业法人单位的整体规模

单位：家，亿元，百分点

指标	数额	增减百分比（%）	占全行业比重（%）	比重变动
单位数量	141 295	0.05	92.59	0.00
营业收入	17 896.36	3.10	95.95	0.15
资产总额	21 740.57	5.46	93.23	0.22
所有者权益	10 868.66	4.11	92.55	0.23
利润总额	1 230.34	−3.70	95.40	0.36

说明：同表 21。

2. 所有制结构

（1）数量结构。

在 141 295 家企业法人单位中，国有全资企业 13 789 家，较 2017 年降低 5.5%，占企业法人单位数量的 9.8%，减少 0.6 个百分点；民营企业 120 663 家，增长 1.2%，占 85.4%，提高 1.0 个百分点（见图 11、表 23）。

（2）印刷复制企业。

在印刷复制企业中，国有全资企业营业收入占行业营业收入的 3.8%，较 2017 年减少 0.2 个百分点；

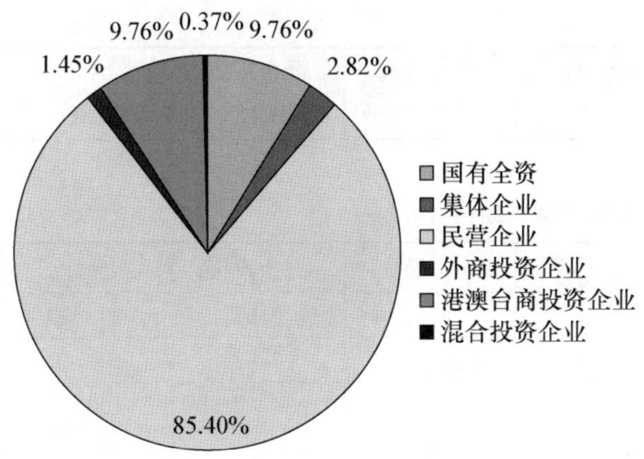

图 11　企业法人单位的所有制结构

表 23　企业法人单位的所有制结构

单位：家，百分点

类型	数量	增减百分比（%）	所占比重（%）	比重变动
国有全资企业	13 789	−5.52	9.76	−0.57
集体企业	3 983	−7.72	2.82	−0.24
民营企业	120 663	1.21	85.40	0.98
外商投资企业	2 051	−10.79	1.45	−0.18
港澳台商投资企业	281	4.46	0.20	0.01
混合投资企业	528	1.54	0.37	0.00
合计	141 295	0.05	100.00	0.00

说明：同表 21。

民营企业占 90.3%，提高 0.9 个百分点（见图 12）。国有全资企业资产总额占行业资产总额的 3.7%，减少 0.1 个百分点；民营企业占 90.2%，提高 0.8 个百分点。国有全资企业利润总额占行业利润总额的 2.7%，减少 0.1 个百分点；民营企业占 91.4%，提高 0.9 个百分点。

印刷复制企业法人单位的所有制结构及变动见表 24、表 25。

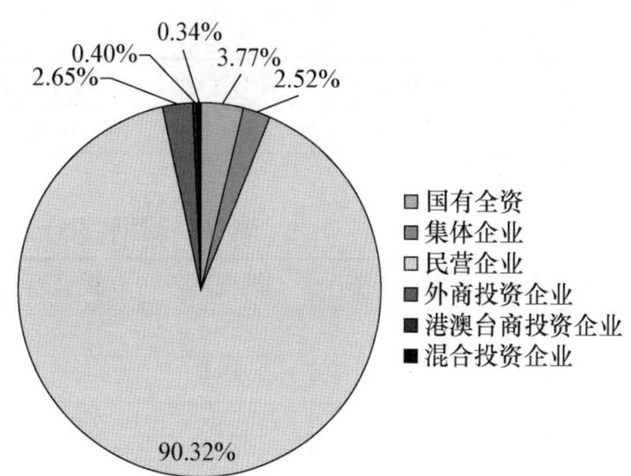

图 12　印刷复制企业法人单位营业收入的所有制结构

（3）出版物发行企业。

在出版物发行企业中，国有全资企业营业收入占行业营业收入的 24.2%，较 2017 年减少 3.6 个百分点；民营企业占 72.4%，提高 3.6 个百分点（见图 13）。国有全资企业资产总额占行业资产总额的 31.6%，提高 2.1 个百分点；民营企业占 65.4%，减少 1.9 个百分点。国有全资企业利润总额占行业利润总额 31.9%，提高 3.4 个百分点；民营企业占 65.0%，减少 3.6 个百分点。

出版物发行企业法人单位的所有制结构及变动见表 26、表 27。

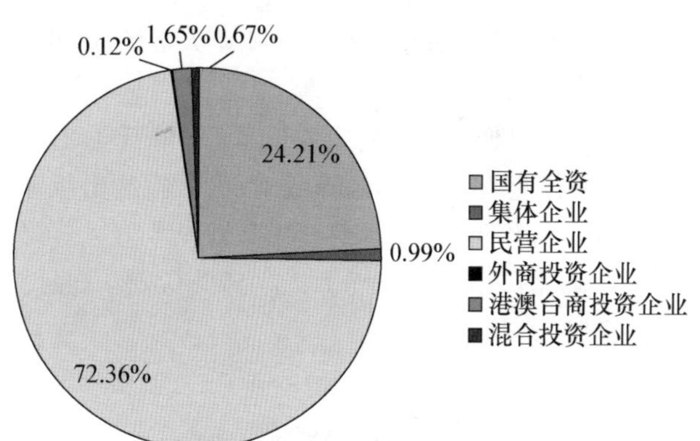

图 13　出版物发行企业法人单位营业收入的所有制结构

表 24　印刷复制企业法人单位的所有制结构（%）

主要指标	国有全资	集体企业	民营企业	港澳台商投资	外商投资	混合投资	合计
营业收入	3.77	2.52	90.32	0.40	2.65	0.34	100.00
资产总额	3.71	2.75	90.22	0.40	2.56	0.36	100.00
所有者权益	3.48	2.81	90.40	0.40	2.54	0.37	100.00
利润总额	2.66	2.71	91.35	0.39	2.57	0.32	100.00

说明：同表 21。

表 25　印刷复制企业法人单位的所有制结构变动

单位：百分点

主要指标	国有全资	集体企业	民营企业	港澳台商投资	外商投资	混合投资	合计
营业收入	−0.15	−0.21	0.89	0.02	−0.56	0.01	0.00
资产总额	−0.06	−0.24	0.82	0.02	−0.54	0.00	0.00
所有者权益	0.04	−0.27	0.74	0.02	−0.54	0.01	0.00

续表

主要指标	国有全资	集体企业	民营企业	港澳台商投资	外商投资	混合投资	合计
利润总额	−0.06	−0.26	0.87	0.02	−0.56	−0.01	0.00

说明：同表 21。

表 26　出版物发行企业法人单位的所有制结构（%）

主要指标	国有全资	集体企业	民营企业	港澳台商投资	外商投资	混合投资	合计
营业收入	24.21	0.99	72.36	0.12	1.65	0.67	100.00
资产总额	31.64	0.88	65.42	0.11	1.33	0.62	100.00
所有者权益	31.28	0.88	65.62	0.13	1.42	0.67	100.00
利润总额	31.86	1.03	64.97	0.10	1.39	0.65	100.00

说明：同表 21。

表 27　出版物发行企业法人单位的所有制结构变动

单位：百分点

主要指标	国有全资	集体企业	民营企业	港澳台商投资	外商投资	混合投资	合计
营业收入	−3.61	0.02	3.55	0.01	0.05	−0.02	0.00
资产总额	2.05	−0.07	−1.87	−0.01	−0.09	−0.01	0.00
所有者权益	2.27	−0.05	−2.14	−0.01	−0.07	0.00	0.00
利润总额	3.41	0.09	−3.59	0.00	0.04	0.05	0.00

说明：同表 21。

（三）就业人员状况

2018 年全国新闻出版业就业人数为 390.3 万人，较 2017 年降低 3.8%；其中男性 204.8 万人，女性 185.5 万人，分别占全行业就业人数的 52.5% 和 47.5%，男女比例基本平衡。

印刷复制业就业人数 297.6 万人，降低 4.2%；出版物发行业 56.3 万人，降低 1.3%；报纸出版业 19.3 万人，降低 6.1%；期刊出版业 9.5 万人，降低 5.5%；图书出版业 6.7 万人，降低 0.2%（见图 14、表 28）。

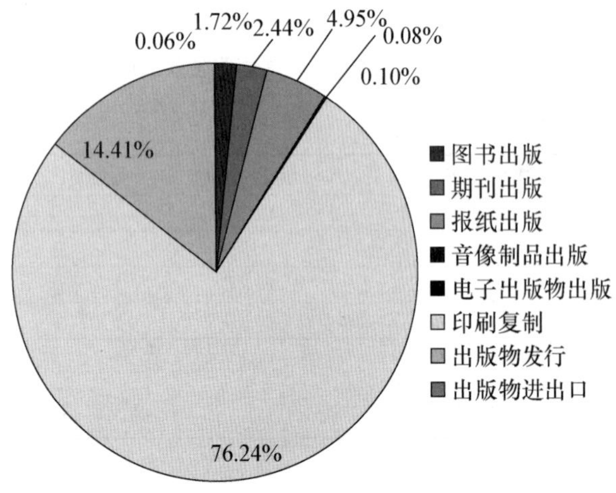

图 14　就业人员的产业类别构成

表 28　就业人数的产业类别构成

单位：万人，百分点

产业类别	人数	增减百分比（%）	比重（%）	比重变动
图书出版	6.72	−0.15	1.72	0.06
期刊出版	9.52	−5.46	2.44	−0.04
报纸出版	19.33	−6.12	4.95	−0.12
音像制品出版	0.40	−2.44	0.10	0.00
电子出版物出版	0.32	10.34	0.08	0.01
印刷复制	297.55	−4.20	76.24	−0.28
出版物发行	56.25	−1.26	14.41	0.37
出版物进出口	0.25	−3.85	0.06	0.00
合计	390.34	−3.84	100.00	0.00

说明：未包括数字出版、打字复印、邮政发行、版权贸易与代理、行业服务与其他新闻出版服务就业人数。

六、出版传媒集团分析

出版传媒集团资产规模进一步扩大，利润总额继续增长，行业占比继续提高。共有 21 家集团资产总额超过 100 亿元，较 2017 年增加 3 家；其中，6 家集团资产总额、主营业务收入和所有者权益均超过百亿元；3 家集团资产总额和主营业务收入均超过百亿元。图书出版集团收入稳定，资产和利润增长较快；报刊出版集团收入继续增长，利润受投资收益减少等因素影响继续降低；发行集团受缩减大宗贸易等因素影响，主营业务收入近年来首次下滑，资产规模和利润保持较快增长；印刷集团收入继续增长，资产规模显著增加，利润因营业外支出增加大幅下滑。

（一）总体情况

截至2018年底，全国共有经国家出版行政管理部门或省级出版行政管理部门批准的出版传媒集团126家①，其中图书出版集团40家、报刊出版集团47家、发行集团28家、印刷集团11家。

2018年，出版传媒集团资产规模进一步扩大，利润总额继续增长，受缩减大宗贸易等因素影响，主营业务收入近年来首次下滑。纳入统计的119家图书出版、报刊出版、发行和印刷集团②共实现主营业务收入3 513.7亿元，较2017年减少45.9亿元，降低1.3%；拥有资产总额7 544.6亿元，增加521.6亿元，增长7.4%；实现利润总额319.5亿元，增加14.1亿元，增长4.6%（见表29）。

表29　119家集团收入、资产与利润合计情况

单位：亿元

指标	金额	增长率（%）
主营业务收入	3 513.66	−1.29
资产总额	7 544.57	7.43
所有者权益	4 181.73	8.23
利润总额	319.51	4.61

其中，108家图书出版、报刊出版和发行集团共实现主营业务收入3 455.5亿元，较2017年减少48.4亿元，降低1.4%，占全国书报刊出版和出版物发行主营业务收入的77.9%，降低1.8个百分点；拥有资产总额7 400.7亿元，增加497.8亿元，增长7.2%，占全国出版发行全行业资产总额的90.8%，基本持平；实现利润总额319.3亿元，增加17.9亿元，增长5.9%，占全国出版发行全行业利润总额的70.7%，提高8.7个百分点。

（二）图书出版集团

1. 经济规模

2018年，图书出版集团资产规模、利润总额增长较快，收入稳中有增。33家图书出版集团③共实现主营业务收入1 990.7亿元，较2017年增加14.5亿元，增长0.7%；拥有资产总额3 929.8亿元，增加236.0亿元，增长6.4%；实现利润总额195.7亿元，增加16.8亿元，增长9.4%（见表30）。

表30　图书出版集团经济规模情况

单位：亿元

指标	金额	增长率（%）
主营业务收入	1 990.74	0.73
资产总额	3 929.81	6.39
所有者权益	2 378.93	8.88
利润总额	195.67	9.37

江苏凤凰出版传媒集团有限公司、江西省出版集团公司、湖南出版投资控股集团有限公司、浙江出版联合集团有限公司和中国出版集团公司等5家集团资产总额、主营业务收入和所有者权益均超过100亿元，组成“三百亿”集团阵营。安徽出版集团有限责任公司、湖北长江出版传媒集团有限公司和中原出版传媒投资控股集团有限公司等3家集团资产总额、主营业务收入均超过100亿元，组成“双百亿”阵营。另有中国教育出版传媒集团有限公司、山东出版集团有限公司、河北出版传媒集团有限责任公司、贵州出版集团有限公司和广东省出版集团有限公司等5家集团资产总额超过100亿元。

2. 总体经济规模排名

选取集团合并报表中的主营业务收入、资产总额、所有者权益和利润总额等4项经济规模指标，采用主成分分析法，对图书出版集团的总体经济规模进行综合评价。前10位降序依次为江苏凤凰出版传媒集团有限公司、江西省出版集团公司、中国教育出版传媒集团有限公司、湖南出版投资控股集团有限公司、山东出版集团有限公司、浙江出版联合集团有限公司、安徽出版集团有限责任公司、湖北长江出版传媒集团有限公司、中国出版集团公司和中原出版传媒投资控股集团有限公司。

与2017年相比，中原出版传媒投资控股集团有限公司跻身前10位，河北出版传媒集团有限责任公司退出前10位；前10位中中国教育出版传媒

① 新增江苏凤凰新华书店集团有限公司1家发行集团。2011年，江苏凤凰出版传媒集团有限公司为适应上市需要，调整企业组织架构，江苏凤凰新华书业股份有限公司不再是独立法人，此后江苏凤凰新华书业股份有限公司不再以集团身份报送财务状况与经营成果数据并且不参与发行集团综合评价。2017年9月，经江苏省委宣传部、省财政厅批复，江苏凤凰出版传媒集团有限公司再次调整发行组织结构，恢复设立具有独立法人的江苏凤凰新华书店集团有限公司，相关调整工作已于2017年内完成。应江苏省有关部门要求，现将江苏凤凰新华书店集团有限公司纳入发行集团财务状况与经营成果统计范围。

② 中国人力资源和社会保障出版集团有限公司、中国书法出版传媒有限公司、人民卫生出版集团、中国环境出版集团有限公司、人民法院出版集团、中国健康传媒集团有限公司和武汉出版集团有限公司7家集团尚不能提供有效的集团财务数据，故纳入2018年财务状况与经营成果统计的出版传媒集团为119家。其中，图书出版集团、报刊出版集团和发行集团为108家。

③ 2013年批准成立的中国人力资源和社会保障出版集团有限公司及中国书法出版传媒有限公司，2016年批准成立的人民卫生出版集团、中国环境出版集团有限公司、人民法院出版集团和中国健康传媒集团有限公司，以及武汉出版集团有限公司7家图书出版集团尚不能提供有效的集团财务数据，故纳入2018年财务状况与经营成果统计并参与综合评价的图书出版集团为33家。

集团有限公司和山东出版集团有限公司排名上升，湖南出版投资控股集团有限公司、浙江出版联合集团有限公司和安徽出版集团有限责任公司排名下降（见表 31）。

表 31　总体经济规模综合评价前 10 位的图书出版集团

综合排名	集团名称	综合评价得分	2017 年排名	排名变化
1	江苏凤凰出版传媒集团有限公司	3.593 3	1	0
2	江西省出版集团公司	1.606 9	2	0
3	中国教育出版传媒集团有限公司	1.361 2	4	1
4	湖南出版投资控股集团有限公司	1.248 5	3	−1
5	山东出版集团有限公司	1.006 8	7	2
6	浙江出版联合集团有限公司	0.971 2	5	−1
7	安徽出版集团有限责任公司	0.903 1	6	−1
8	湖北长江出版传媒集团有限公司	0.897 9	8	0
9	中国出版集团公司	0.728 2	9	0
10	中原出版传媒投资控股集团有限公司	0.534 6	11	1

说明：综合评价得分系选取主营业务收入、资产总额、所有者权益和利润总额等 4 项指标，采用主成分分析法，通过 SPSS 直接计算所得，仅用来显示各单位的相对位置，负数并不代表负面评价。

（三）报刊出版集团

1. 经济规模

2018 年，报刊出版集团资产规模基本保持稳定，收入有所增长，所有者权益与利润总额大幅下降。47 家报刊出版集团共实现主营业务收入 404.7 亿元，较 2017 年增加 13.1 亿元，增长 3.3%；拥有资产总额 1 674.5 亿元，增加 2.1 亿元，增长 0.1%；实现利润总额 21.1 亿元，减少 8.8 亿元，降低 29.4%（见表 32）。

表 32　报刊出版集团经济规模情况

单位：亿元

指标	金额	增长率（%）
主营业务收入	404.66	3.34
资产总额	1 674.50	0.12
所有者权益	885.67	−0.56
利润总额	21.13	−29.39

上海报业集团、浙江日报报业集团和成都传媒集团 3 家集团资产总额超过 100 亿元。

2. 总体经济规模排名

采取同样的评价方法，报刊出版集团总体经济规模的前 10 位依次为浙江日报报业集团、上海报业集团、成都传媒集团、湖北日报传媒集团、山东大众报业（集团）有限公司、河南日报报业集团有限公司、深圳报业集团、广州日报报业集团、南方报业传媒集团和江苏新华报业传媒集团有限公司。

与 2017 年相比，深圳报业集团和江苏新华报业传媒集团有限公司跻身前 10 位，陕西华商传媒集团有限责任公司和重庆日报报业集团退出前 10 位；前 10 位中浙江日报报业集团、湖北日报传媒集团、河南日报报业集团有限公司和南方报业传媒集团排名上升，上海报业集团和广州日报报业集团排名下降（见表 33）。

表 33　总体经济规模综合评价前 10 位的报刊出版集团

综合排名	集团名称	综合评价得分	2017 年排名	排名变化
1	浙江日报报业集团	3.551 3	2	1
2	上海报业集团	3.360 8	1	−1
3	成都传媒集团	1.521 0	3	0
4	湖北日报传媒集团	1.419 0	7	3
5	山东大众报业（集团）有限公司	1.166 9	5	0
6	河南日报报业集团有限公司	1.157 8	8	2
7	深圳报业集团	0.962 3	11	4
8	广州日报报业集团	0.940 8	6	−2
9	南方报业传媒集团	0.839 7	10	1
10	江苏新华报业传媒集团有限公司	0.761 2	12	2

说明：同表 31。

（四）发行集团

1. 经济规模

2018 年，发行集团资产规模与利润总额快速增长，收入受缩减大宗贸易等因素影响近年来首次下滑。28 家发行集团①实现主营业务收入 1 060.1 亿元，较 2017 年减少 76.0 亿元，降低 6.7%；拥有资

① 新增江苏凤凰新华书店集团有限公司 1 家。

产总额 1 796.4 亿元，增加 259.8 亿元，增长 16.9%；实现利润总额 102.5 亿元，增加 10.0 亿元，增长 10.8%（见表 34）。

表 34 发行集团经济规模情况

单位：亿元

指标	金额	增长率（%）
主营业务收入	1 060.08	−6.69
资产总额	1 796.42	16.91
所有者权益	834.52	15.17
利润总额	102.53	10.82

安徽新华发行（集团）控股有限公司资产总额、所有者权益和主营业务收入均超过 100 亿元。四川新华发行集团有限公司、江苏凤凰新华书店集团有限公司、上海新华发行集团有限公司和江西新华发行集团有限公司等 4 家资产总额超过 100 亿元，较 2017 年增加 2 家。

2. 总体经济规模排名

采用同样的评价方法，发行集团总体经济规模的前 10 位依次为安徽新华发行（集团）控股有限公司、四川新华发行集团有限公司、江苏凤凰新华书店集团有限公司、江西新华发行集团有限公司、山东新华书店集团有限公司、浙江省新华书店集团有限公司、湖南省新华书店有限责任公司、河南省新华书店发行集团有限公司、河北省新华书店有限责任公司和重庆新华书店集团公司。

与 2017 年相比，江苏凤凰新华书店集团有限公司跻身前 10 位，上海新华发行集团有限公司退出前 10 位；前 10 位中湖南省新华书店有限责任公司、河南省新华书店发行集团有限公司和河北省新华书店有限责任公司排名下降（见表 35）。

表 35 总体经济规模综合评价前 10 位的发行集团

综合排名	集团名称	综合评价得分	2017 年排名	排名变化
1	安徽新华发行（集团）控股有限公司	3.674 8	1	0
2	四川新华发行集团有限公司	1.861 2	2	0
3	江苏凤凰新华书店集团有限公司	0.933 1	—	—
4	江西新华发行集团有限公司	0.840 0	4	0
5	山东新华书店集团有限公司	0.793 4	5	0
6	浙江省新华书店集团有限公司	0.543 9	6	0
7	湖南省新华书店有限责任公司	0.458 0	3	−4
8	河南省新华书店发行集团有限公司	0.384 6	7	−1
9	河北省新华书店有限责任公司	0.300 2	8	−1
10	重庆新华书店集团公司	0.069 3	10	0

说明：同表 31。

（五）印刷集团

1. 经济规模

2018 年，受中国文化产业发展集团公司新增子公司及非经常性损益等因素影响，印刷集团资产规模显著壮大，利润总额大幅下滑。11 家印刷集团实现主营业务收入 58.2 亿元，较 2017 年增加 2.5 亿元，增长 4.6%；拥有资产总额 143.9 亿元，增加 23.7 亿元，增长 19.8%；实现利润总额 0.2 亿元，减少 3.9 亿元，降低 95.8%（见表 36）。

表 36 印刷集团经济规模情况

单位：亿元

指标	金额	增长率（%）
主营业务收入	58.18	4.57
资产总额	143.85	19.77
所有者权益	82.61	29.81
利润总额	0.17	−95.81

2. 总体经济规模排名

采用同样的评价方法，对 10 家印刷集团①总体经济规模进行综合评价，依次为中国文化产业发展集团有限公司、上海印刷（集团）有限公司、湖南天闻新华印务有限公司、浙江印刷集团有限公司、江西新华印刷集团有限公司、辽宁新闻印刷集团有限公司、广西正泰彩印包装有限责任公司、河南新华印刷集团有限公司、北京印刷集团有限责任公司和北京隆达印刷包装集团有限公司。

与 2017 年相比，湖南天闻新华印务有限公司和辽宁新闻印刷集团有限公司排名上升；浙江印刷集团有限公司和北京印刷集团有限责任公司排名下降（见表 37）。

① 黑龙江新华传媒集团有限公司长期处于停产状态，不进行综合评价，故参与综合评价的印刷集团为 10 家。

表 37　印刷集团总体经济规模综合评价

综合排名	集团名称	综合评价得分	2017 年排名	排名变化
1	中国文化产业发展集团有限公司	2.783 9	1	0
2	上海印刷（集团）有限公司	0.039 4	2	0
3	湖南天闻新华印务有限公司	－0.081 9	4	1
4	浙江印刷集团有限公司	－0.116 7	3	－1
5	江西新华印刷集团有限公司	－0.291 7	5	0
6	辽宁新闻印刷集团有限公司	－0.332 8	9	3
7	广西正泰彩印包装有限责任公司	－0.405 3	7	0
8	河南新华印刷集团有限公司	－0.428 3	8	0
9	北京印刷集团有限责任公司	－0.539 3	6	－3
10	北京隆达印刷包装集团有限公司	－0.627 5	10	0

说明：同表 31。

七、出版传媒上市公司分析

出版传媒上市公司营业收入同口径稳步增长，新媒体公司、发行公司整体营业收入实现两位数增长，报业公司收入同口径止跌回升。出版公司、印刷公司和新媒体公司主业收入增加，占比进一步提高。报业公司、新媒体公司和发行公司主要受计提减值准备影响，利润大幅下降。资本市场表现持续低迷，股市市值大幅缩水。各公司努力探索转型升级、融合发展之路，多方开拓新业务领域，取得新进展。

（一）总体情况

截至 2018 年 12 月 31 日，中国内地在中国内地和香港特别行政区上市的出版传媒公司共计 42 家。其中，出版公司 14 家，报业公司 5 家，发行公司 8 家，印刷公司 10 家，新媒体公司 5 家；在中国内地上市 38 家，在中国香港上市 4 家（见表 38）。

表 38　出版传媒上市公司的业务类型与上市地点

业务类型	中国内地	中国香港	合计
出版公司	13	1	14
报业公司	3	2	5
发行公司	7	1	8
印刷公司	10	0	10
新媒体公司	5	0	5
合计	38	4	42

说明：出版公司包括业务内容描述为出版、出版发行和期刊的上市公司。

与 2017 年相比，减少 1 家，即成都博瑞传播股份有限公司①。

（二）经济规模

1. 总体规模

出版传媒公司股市市值继续减少。以 2018 年 12 月 28 日收盘价计算，41 家在中国内地和香港上市的出版传媒公司②流通市值共计 2 149.0 亿元人民币，较 2017 年同期减少 672.7 亿元，降低 23.8%③。其中，在中国内地上市的 37 家出版传媒公司流通市值共计 2 124.8 亿元，减少 664.2 亿元，降低 23.8%；总市值共计 2 797.2 亿元，减少 1 220.5 亿元，降低 30.4%④。

2018 年，出版传媒公司收入有所增长，资产有所减少，利润大幅下降。在中国内地上市的 37 家出版传媒公司实现营业收入共计 1 501.4 亿元，较 2017 年增加 48.7 亿元，增长 3.4%；拥有资产总额共计 2 688.8 亿元，减少 36.9 亿元，降低 1.4%；实现利润总额共计 71.5 亿元，减少 123.1 亿元，降低 63.3%（见表 39）⑤。

流通市值、总市值、营业收入、资产总额的公

① 博瑞传播于 2017 年末完成传统报媒印刷、发行业务剥离，2018 年户外广告和学校业务收入占公司主营业务收入的 63.4%，故不再将其作为报刊上市公司加以分析。出版传媒上市公司减少 1 家。

② 2018 年 7 月 5 日，中国证监会宣布：因康得新涉及信息披露严重违法行为，已向涉案当事人送达行政处罚及市场禁入的事先通知书。据事先通知书认定，康得新在 2015 年 1 月至 2018 年 12 月，通过虚增营业收入和营业成本、研发费用和销售费用，虚增利润总额 119 亿元。鉴于其年报披露数据严重不实，本报告不再将康得新纳入分析，并与 2017 年进行数据比较时做同口径处理。因此，纳入分析的出版传媒上市公司现为 41 家，其中内地 37 家。

③ 如排除上市公司数量变动影响，则现有 41 家出版传媒上市公司 2018 年流通市值较 2017 年同口径减少 634.0 亿元，降低 22.8%。

④ 如排除上市公司数量变动影响，则现有 37 家内地出版传媒上市公司 2018 年流通市值较 2017 年同口径减少 625.6 亿元，降低 22.8%；总市值减少 1 162.9 亿元，降低 29.4%。

⑤ 如排除上市公司数量变动影响，则现有 37 家出版传媒上市公司实现营业收入较 2017 年同口径增加 57.4 亿元，增长 4.0%；拥有资产总额增加 5.4 亿元，增长 0.2%；实现利润总额减少 122.8 亿元，降低 63.2%。

司类型构成如图15～图18所示。

表39 出版传媒上市公司经济规模情况

单位：亿元

指标	金额	较2017年增减（%）
在香港上市公司流通市值	2 148.95	−23.84
其中：在中国内地上市公司流通市值	2 124.78	−23.82
在中国内地上市公司总市值	2 797.24	−30.38
在中国内地上市公司营业收入	1 501.38	3.35
在中国内地上市公司资产总额	2 688.80	−1.35
在中国内地上市公司利润总额	71.45	−63.28

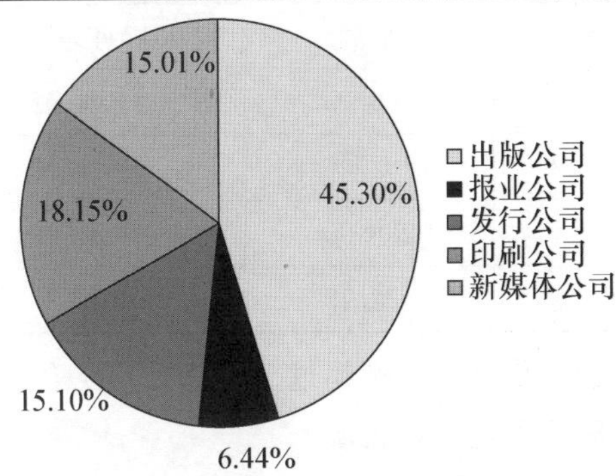

图15 境内外股市流通市值的公司类型结构

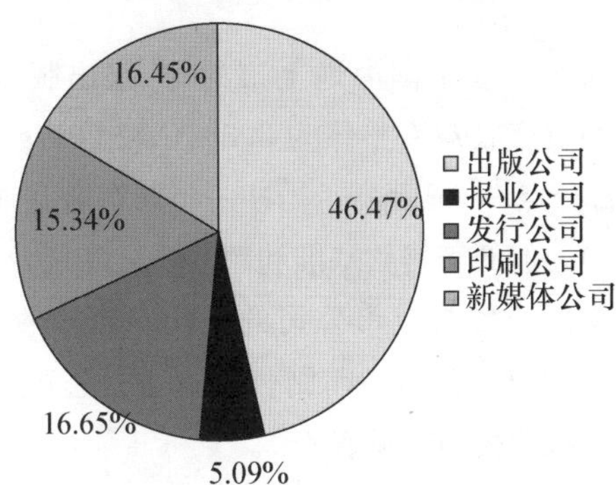

图16 股市总市值的公司类型结构

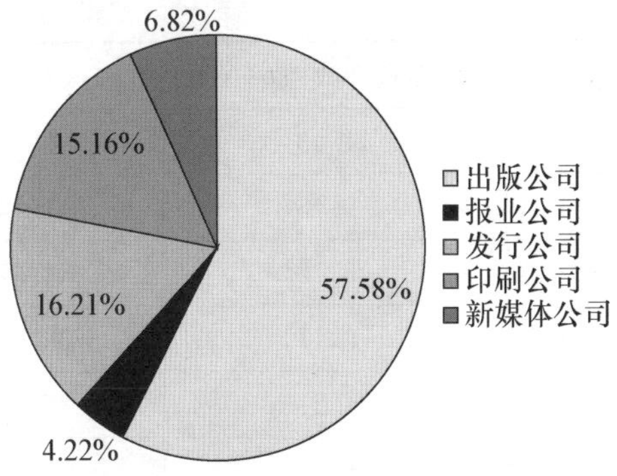

图17 营业收入的公司类型构成

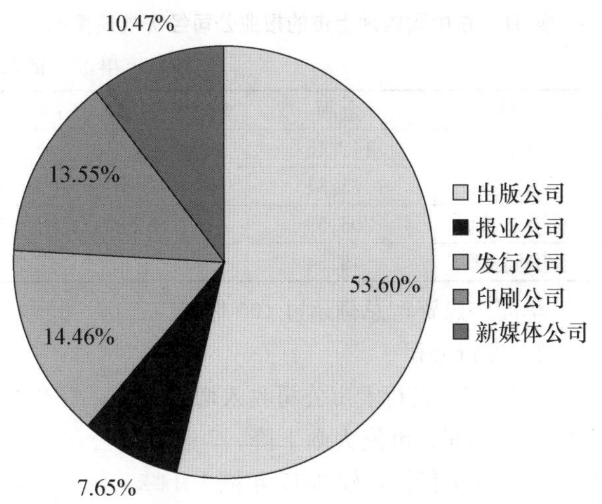

图18 资产总额的公司类型构成

2. 出版公司

2018年，收入稳中有增，资产和利润继续增长，总市值有所减少。13家出版公司总市值共计1 299.8亿元，较2017年减少360.1亿元，降低21.7%；实现营业收入共计864.5亿元，增加1.7亿元，增长0.2%；拥有资产总额共计1 441.2亿元，增加88.1亿元，增长6.5%；实现利润总额共计101.8亿元，增加5.5亿元，增长5.8%（见表40）。

表40 在中国内地上市的出版公司经济规模情况

单位：亿元

指标	金额	较2017年增减（%）
总市值	1 299.81	−21.69
营业收入	864.51	0.20
资产总额	1 441.20	6.51
利润总额	101.75	5.76

凤凰传媒、中文传媒和长江传媒等3家公司营业收入和资产总额均超过100亿元，另有中南传媒、山东出版、中原传媒和中国出版等4家公司资产总额超过100亿元，与2017年相比数量不变。

3. 报业公司

2018年，报业上市公司减少1家，各项经济指标继续全面下滑，收入降幅明显趋缓，利润亏损。3家报业公司总市值共计142.5亿元，较2017年减少233.8亿元，降低62.1%；实现营业收入共计63.3亿元，减少6.9亿元，降低9.8%；拥有资产总额共计205.6亿元，减少70.3亿元，降低25.5%；亏损46.5亿元，利润总额减少55.7亿元，降低609.7%（见表41）①。

① 如排除上市公司数量变动影响，则现有3家报业公司总市值较2017年同口径减少176.2亿元，降低55.3%；营业收入增加1.8亿元，增长3.0%；资产总额减少28.0亿元，降低12.0%；利润总额减少55.4亿元，降低627.6%。

表 41　在中国内地上市的报业公司经济规模情况

单位：亿元

指标	金额	较 2017 年增减（%）
总市值	142.45	−62.14
营业收入	63.31	−9.78
资产总额	205.59	−25.49
利润总额	−46.54	−609.74

华闻传媒资产总额超过 100 亿元。

4. 发行公司

2018 年，发行上市公司收入增长较快，资产有所增长，利润、市值大幅下降。7 家发行公司总市值共计 465.7 亿元，较 2017 年减少 142.7 亿元，降低 23.5%；实现营业收入共计 243.4 亿元，增加 22.9 亿元，增长 10.4%；拥有资产总额共计 388.7 亿元，增加 11.7 亿元，增长 3.1%；实现利润总额共计 16.1 亿元，减少 12.4 亿元，降低 43.4%（见表 42）。

表 42　在中国内地上市的发行公司经济规模情况

单位：亿元

指标	金额	较 2017 年增减（%）
总市值	465.71	−23.46
营业收入	243.42	10.40
资产总额	388.74	3.09
利润总额	16.13	−43.37

新华文轩、皖新传媒 2 家公司资产总额超过 100 亿元。

5. 印刷公司

2018 年，印刷上市公司资产、收入增加，利润、市值减少。9 家印刷公司[①]总市值共计 429.0 亿元，较 2017 年同口径减少 108.5 亿元，降低 20.2%；实现营业收入共计 227.7 亿元，增加 20.6 亿元，增长 9.9%；拥有资产总额共计 364.4 亿元，增加 6.2 亿元，增长 1.7%；实现利润总额共计 23.3 亿元，减少 0.2 亿元，降低 1.0%（见表 43）。

表 43　在中国内地上市的印刷公司经济规模情况

单位：亿元

指标	金额	较 2017 年增减（%）
总市值	429.03	−20.19
营业收入	227.68	9.93
资产总额	364.38	1.74
利润总额	23.29	−1.03

紫江企业资产总额超过 100 亿元。

6. 新媒体公司

2018 年，收入继续增长，利润出现亏损，资产、市值有所减少。5 家新媒体公司总市值共计 460.3 亿元，较 2017 年减少 375.4 亿元，降低 44.9%；实现营业收入共计 102.5 亿元，增加 10.3 亿元，增长 11.2%；拥有资产总额共计 288.9 亿元，减少 72.6 亿元，降低 20.1%；亏损 23.2 亿元，利润总额减少 60.4 亿元，降低 162.4%（见表 44）。

表 44　在中国内地上市的新媒体公司经济规模情况

单位：亿元

指标	金额	较 2017 年增减（%）
总市值	460.25	−44.92
营业收入	102.46	11.19
资产总额	288.90	−20.08
利润总额	−23.19	−162.35

浙数文化资产总额超过 100 亿元，昆仑万维资产总额降至不足 100 亿元。

（三）经济效益

1. 总体情况

2018 年，在中国内地上市的 37 家出版传媒公司平均净资产收益率整体为 3.5%，较 2017 年减少 7.4 个百分点[②]，显著高于当期一年期存缴基准利率（1.50%），但低于贷款基准利率（4.35%）。

各类出版传媒上市公司的平均净资产收益率，降序依次为出版公司、印刷公司、发行公司、新媒体公司和报业公司（见表 45）。

表 45　在中国内地上市的出版传媒公司平均净资产收益率

单位：百分点

公司类型	平均净资产收益率（%）	较 2017 年增减
出版公司	11.03	−0.38
印刷公司	9.16	−1.04
发行公司	5.15	−4.67
新媒体公司	−9.17	−23.09
报业公司	−34.21	−37.88
整体	3.46	−7.44

说明：平均净资产收益率＝净利润/[(期初所有者权益＋期末所有者权益)÷2]×100%。

① 不包括康得新，与 2017 年采取同口径比较。

② 如排除上市公司数量变动影响，则现有 37 家出版传媒公司整体平均净资产收益率较 2017 年同口径减少 7.3 个百分点。

平均净资产收益率前10位的出版传媒公司，降序依次为昆仑万维、东港股份、山东出版、新经典、城市传媒、掌阅科技、广弘控股、南方传媒、永新股份和中文传媒（见表46）。其中，出版公司4家、发行公司2家、印刷公司2家、新媒体公司2家。出版公司和发行公司各增加1家。

表46　在中国内地上市的平均净资产收益率前10位出版传媒公司（%）

排名	上市公司	股票简称	业务类型	股票类型	收益率
1	北京昆仑万维科技股份有限公司	昆仑万维	新媒体	深证A股	21.12
2	东港股份有限公司	东港股份	印刷	深证A股	16.38
3	山东出版传媒股份有限公司	山东出版	出版发行	上证A股	16.08
4	新经典文化股份有限公司	新经典	发行	上证A股	14.74
5	青岛城市传媒股份有限公司	城市传媒	出版发行	上证A股	14.24
6	掌阅科技股份有限公司	掌阅科技	新媒体	上证A股	12.93
7	广东广弘控股股份有限公司	广弘控股	发行	深证A股	12.69
8	南方出版传媒股份有限公司	南方传媒	出版	上证A股	12.67
9	黄山永新股份有限公司	永新股份	印刷	深证A股	12.57
10	中文天地出版传媒股份有限公司	中文传媒	出版发行	上证A股	12.56

2. 出版公司

出版公司平均净资产收益率11.0%，高出出版传媒上市公司整体水平7.6个百分点；较2017年减少0.4个百分点。

13家出版公司的平均净资产收益率，降序依次为山东出版、城市传媒、南方传媒、中文传媒、中国科传、长江传媒、凤凰传媒、中原传媒、中南传媒、中国出版、出版传媒、时代出版和读者传媒（见表47）。

表47　在中国内地上市的出版公司平均净资产收益率（%）

排名	上市公司	股票简称	股票类型	收益率
1	山东出版传媒股份有限公司	山东出版	上证A股	16.08
2	青岛城市传媒股份有限公司	城市传媒	上证A股	14.24
3	南方出版传媒股份有限公司	南方传媒	上证A股	12.67
4	中文天地出版传媒股份有限公司	中文传媒	上证A股	12.56
5	中国科技出版传媒股份有限公司	中国科传	上证A股	12.43
6	长江出版传媒股份有限公司	长江传媒	上证A股	11.56
7	江苏凤凰出版传媒股份有限公司	凤凰传媒	上证A股	10.27
8	中原大地传媒股份有限公司	中原传媒	深证A股	9.90
9	中南出版传媒集团股份有限公司	中南传媒	上证A股	9.76
10	中国出版传媒股份有限公司	中国出版	上证A股	9.01
11	北方联合出版传媒（集团）股份有限公司	出版传媒	上证A股	8.35
12	时代出版传媒股份有限公司	时代出版	上证A股	6.93
13	读者出版传媒股份有限公司	读者传媒	上证A股	2.31

3. 报业公司

报业公司平均净资产收益率－34.2%，低于出版传媒上市公司整体水平37.7个百分点；较2017年减少37.9个百分点①。

3家报业公司的平均净资产收益率，按降序依次为华媒控股、粤传媒和华闻传媒（见表48）。

表48　在中国内地上市的报业公司平均净资产收益率（%）

排名	上市公司	股票简称	股票类型	收益率
1	浙江华媒控股股份有限公司	华媒控股	深证A股	7.60
2	广东广州日报传媒股份有限公司	粤传媒	深证A股	1.28
3	华闻传媒投资集团股份有限公司	华闻传媒	深证A股	－63.23

① 如排除上市公司数量变动影响，则现有3家报业公司平均净资产收益率较2017年同口径减少38.6个百分点。

4. 发行公司

发行公司平均净资产收益率 5.2%，高出出版传媒上市公司整体水平 1.7 个百分点；较 2017 年减少 4.7 个百分点。

7 家发行公司的平均净资产收益率，按降序依次为新经典、广弘控股、新华文轩、皖新传媒、世纪天鸿、新华传媒和天舟文化（见表 49）。

表 49　在中国内地上市的发行公司平均净资产收益率（%）

排名	上市公司	股票简称	股票类型	收益率
1	新经典文化股份有限公司	新经典	上证 A 股	14.74
2	广东广弘控股股份有限公司	广弘控股	深证 A 股	12.69
3	新华文轩出版传媒股份有限公司	新华文轩	上证 A 股	11.33
4	安徽新华传媒股份有限公司	皖新传媒	上证 A 股	11.15
5	世纪天鸿教育科技股份有限公司	世纪天鸿	深证 A 股	7.32
6	上海新华传媒股份有限公司	新华传媒	上证 A 股	1.15
7	天舟文化股份有限公司	天舟文化	深圳创业板	−29.25

5. 印刷公司

印刷公司平均净资产收益率 9.2%，高出出版传媒上市公司整体水平 5.7 个百分点；较 2017 年同口径减少 1.0 个百分点。

9 家印刷公司的平均净资产收益率，降序依次为东港股份、永新股份、劲嘉股份、紫江企业、盛通股份、珠海中富、陕西金叶、鸿博股份和界龙实业（见表 50）。

表 50　在中国内地上市的印刷公司平均净资产收益率（%）

排名	上市公司	股票简称	股票类型	收益率
1	东港股份有限公司	东港股份	深证 A 股	16.38
2	黄山永新股份有限公司	永新股份	深证 A 股	12.57
3	深圳劲嘉彩印集团股份有限公司	劲嘉股份	深证 A 股	12.11
4	上海紫江企业集团股份有限公司	紫江企业	上证 A 股	9.84
5	北京盛通印刷股份有限公司	盛通股份	深证 A 股	8.07
6	珠海中富实业股份有限公司	珠海中富	深证 A 股	3.39
7	陕西金叶科教集团股份有限公司	陕西金叶	深证 A 股	1.69
8	鸿博印刷股份有限公司	鸿博股份	深证 A 股	0.81
9	上海界龙实业集团股份有限公司	界龙实业	上证 A 股	−2.16

6. 新媒体公司

新媒体公司平均净资产收益率−9.2%，低于出版传媒上市公司整体水平 12.6 个百分点；较 2017 年减少 23.1 个百分点。

5 家新媒体公司的平均净资产收益率，降序依次为昆仑万维、掌阅科技、浙数文化、掌趣科技和中文在线（见表 51）。

表 51　在中国内地上市的新媒体公司平均净资产收益率（%）

排名	上市公司	股票简称	股票类型	收益率
1	北京昆仑万维科技股份有限公司	昆仑万维	深证 A 股	21.12
2	掌阅科技股份有限公司	掌阅科技	上证 A 股	12.93
3	浙报数字文化集团股份有限公司	浙数文化	上证 A 股	6.61
4	北京掌趣科技股份有限公司	掌趣科技	深证 A 股	−45.09
5	中文在线数字出版集团股份有限公司	中文在线	深证 A 股	−62.07

（四）业务经营

1. 出版公司

主题出版成果丰硕，社会效益显著。各出版公司围绕庆祝改革开放 40 周年、纪念马克思诞辰 200 周年等主题，策划出版一批高质量的主题图书。中国出版推出《天开海岳》《国家相册》《春天的画卷》

《中国改革为什么能成功》《那些你一定知道的事》等图书，承担中宣部“中华先贤人物故事汇”“中华传奇人物故事汇”等重点出版项目；凤凰传媒立项主题读物精品 40 种，累计达 101 种，全年完成 48 种；中南传媒“强军新方略丛书”等 3 种出版物入选中宣部“2018 年主题重点出版物”；长江传媒推出《马克思主义大辞典》和《马克思主义在中国早期传播著作选集（1920—1927）》等重点图书；中原传媒策划出版了《中国共产党革命精神史读本》、“共和国大科学家故事丛书”等一批主题出版物。

收入与收益率基本稳定，利润有所增长。13 家出版公司整体收入水平略有提高。8 家公司营业收入增长，其中城市传媒、出版传媒、中原传媒、中国科传和中国出版等 5 家公司均实现两位数增长。另外 5 家公司营业收入有所减少，其中中文传媒减少 17.9 亿元，长江传媒减少 8.7 亿元。11 家公司利润增长，其中长江传媒增长 19.1%，增速最高；中文传媒收入虽有下降，但因出版、发行和贸易等板块毛利率提高，利润不降反增。出版公司整体平均净资产收益率与 2017 年基本持平，高出出版传媒公司整体水平。

出版业务收入稳中有升，编印发主业占比进一步提高。13 家出版公司出版业务整体增长 6.1%。11 家公司出版业务收入增长，其中出版传媒、城市传媒、长江传媒、山东出版、中原传媒、南方传媒和中国出版等 7 家公司实现两位数增长，出版传媒增长 25.2%，长江传媒和时代出版等公司虽然总收入减少，但出版业务逆势上扬。出版、发行、印刷业务收入整体增长 5.4%，12 家公司编印发主业增长，主业收入对公司业绩的支撑和影响愈发明显。13 家公司编印发主业收入占比整体为 72.3%，提高 3.0 个百分点；10 家公司占比均在 70%以上，其中城市传媒、凤凰传媒、中国科传和读者传媒等 4 家公司超过 90%；8 家公司编印发主业占比有所提高。

积极培育发展新业态，出版融合发展取得新进展。中国出版大数据内容知识挖掘与分析平台成功构建近 300 万个知识单元，商务工具书云平台推出近 20 种权威字典 APP，集聚用户 1 196 万人。中国科传完成“中科云教育平台”“爱一课移动端互动教学平台”“状元共享课堂”等多个数字教育云服务平台，“科学文库”包括 4 万余种电子书。凤凰传媒上线“凤凰易教”“凤凰享学”等网络产品，用户数达 100 多万人。读者传媒微信平台新增用户 110 万人，增长 32%，用户数达 460 万人。时代出版新业态业务营业收入增长 60.9%，毛利率提高 13.3 个百分点；中文传媒新业态业务毛利率 60.2%。

2. 报业公司

新兴业务拉动收入增长，投资损失造成巨额亏损。华闻传媒因数字内容服务和信息技术服务业务大幅增长，营业收入增加 3.6 亿元，带动报业公司整体营业收入增长 3.0%[①]。3 家公司利润均以超过 20%的降幅下滑，其中华闻传媒因确认投资损失，亏损近 50 亿元，导致报业公司整体亏损，整体平均净资产收益率也由正转负（−34.2%），同口径减少 38.6 个百分点。

力主传统主业挖潜，积极推进媒体融合发展。华媒控股大力推进“党员订党报”工作，报刊发行收入增加 7 890.4 万元，增长 41.6%；积极搭建“报网端屏楼”全媒体矩阵，旗下杭州新闻“两微一端”本地直接用户超 1 500 万人。华闻传媒策划“唐长安城建城 1 400 年”等活动，带来良好的社会效应和影响力。粤传媒以“产媒融合”为目标，积极探索媒体转型升级。报刊发行与广告业务在 3 家报业公司收入中所占比重均超过 60%，居于核心地位。

多方开拓业务范围，相关收入增长较快。华闻传媒收购深圳市麦游互动科技有限公司和车音智能科技有限公司，新增信息技术服务业务[②]，当年实现营业收入 7.3 亿元，毛利率 40.2%；以视频信息服务为核心的数字内容服务收入增加 2.1 亿元，增长 69.0%。华媒控股拓展泛文化产权交易板块，全年实现产权交易成交额 2.7 亿元，增速超 30%，教育类业务收入增加 4 865.7 万元，增长 22.9%。粤传媒推出“西关博雅”合作办学、“读者专享游”和“精英小记者”等项目。

3. 发行公司

营业收入保持较好增长，净利润大幅下滑。7 家发行公司营业收入整体增长 10.4%，其中天舟文化、皖新传媒和新华文轩等 3 家实现两位数增长，天舟文化增长 20.3%。4 家公司净利润增长，3 家公司净利润减少，其中天舟文化主要因商誉计提减值损失 12.9 亿元，导致净利润减少 890%，亏损 10.9 亿元，带动发行公司净利润整体降低 45.6%，

① 由于不再将博瑞传播作为报刊上市公司，报业公司数量减少 1 家，因此在与 2017 年比较时整体营业收入降低 9.8%。但如对现有 3 家公司进行同口径比较，营业收入实际反而增加 1.9 亿元。

② 主要为手机游戏和车载电子软硬件产品。

整体平均净资产收益率减少 4.7 个百分点。

发行出版主业普遍增长，经营模式转型、升级加速。7 家发行公司主业整体增长 6.9%。其中广弘控股增长 15.5%，增速最快，主业收入占比提高 3.2 个百分点。新华文轩形成以文轩网综合旗舰店为基础的销售网络。新华传媒与虹桥火车站合作开设“微书城”，塑造实体书店多元化的新形象。皖新传媒“阅+”共享书店在安徽、上海、北京等地开设 53 家。新经典旗下 Pageone 北京坊店正式运营，举办多种创意活动。

不断拓展新领域，其他业务发展较快。7 家发行公司其他业务收入整体增长 20.1%。新华文轩文化产业基金群实现基金管理规模约 15 亿元。皖新传媒供应链与物流服务业务实现营业收入 15.8 亿元，增长 1.6 倍。天舟文化游戏业务增长 37.2%。世纪天鸿教育信息化业务增长 59.0%。

4. 印刷公司

主业占比有所提高，经营业绩分化。9 家印刷公司[①]全部实现营业收入增长，整体增长 9.9%；各公司印刷包装主业占比均超过 60%，增长 10.3%。各公司经营业绩差异明显。其中盛通股份营业收入增长 31.4%，净利润增长 35.6%。劲嘉股份营业收入增长 14.6%，净利润增长 21.2%。永新股份营业收入增长 16.1%，净利润增长 9.1%。界龙实业、陕西金叶和珠海中富等 3 家公司虽收入有所增长，但利润巨幅下滑[②]，带动印刷公司整体净利润降低 2.1%。

推动“绿色化”发展，持续深化自主创新。紫江企业全年投入环保治理改造费用 2 951.2 万元，基本完成“一厂一方案”环保改造；获得国家授权专利 81 项。永新股份获得国家授权专利 32 项。鸿博股份在绿色印刷认证和环保投入方面持续投入。劲嘉股份累计获得授权专利 565 项。东港股份研发非税电子票据、票 e 送、区块链电子票证等产品。

5. 新媒体公司

全部 5 家新媒体公司营业收入和主业收入均实现增长，整体分别增长 11.2%和 14.7%。4 家公司营业收入实现两位数增长。其中掌阅科技阅读平台月活跃用户数量约 1.2 亿人，实现版权分发及衍生收入共 1.4 亿元，增长 2.7 倍。中文在线数字阅读收入和数字版权分销业务收入增长。昆仑万维巩固海外市场份额。

① 不含康得新，均为同口径比较。

② 界龙实业纸浆模塑包装产品和干压纸模产品项目尚处于产品开发、前期市场开拓与业务导入阶段，再加上房地产项目完工，而政府动迁房配套资金未按期到位，对借款利息等支出进行费用化处理，营业收入增长 2.1%，净利润减少 170%，由 2017 年盈利 2 890.8 万元转为亏损 2 010.6 万元。陕西金叶营业收入增长 26.1%，但因计提减值损失增加 1 669.1 万元，再加上管理费用增加，净利润减少 2 690.2 万元，降低 53.2%。珠海中富 2017 年下属公司获得土地收储补偿款 6 000 万元，2018 年无此项收入，再加上原材料与人力成本上升，营业收入增长 0.2%，净利润减少 7 070.0 万元，降低 77.8%。

2018—2019 年中国数字出版产业年度报告

中国数字出版产业年度报告课题组

2018 年，出版业转型融合持续深入，创新能力取得显著提升；网络文学保持良好发展态势，良性生态环境逐步构建；在国家教育信息化加快推进下，数字教育出版持续快速发展，并呈现垂直化、精品化发展态势；报刊转型全面加速，着力打造新媒体传播矩阵；知识付费经过近三年的发展，面临发展的分水岭，市场筛选机制逐渐形成；短视频风口持续强劲，成为媒体布局重点；互联网内容加强规范化管理，主体责任逐步明确；数字出版产业保障体系进一步完善，为融合发展提供有力支撑。数字出版产值突破 8 000 亿元，再创新高，持续提升对数字经济的助力支持。

一、数字出版产业规模分析

2018 年，我国数字出版产业持续保持快速发展势头，全年收入规模超过 8 000 亿元。其中，互联网广告、移动出版、在线教育、网络游戏依然处于收入榜前四位，互联网广告、移动出版、在线教育依然保持迅猛的发展势头。

（一）整体收入规模持续增长

2018 年国内数字出版产业整体收入规模为 8 330.78 亿元，比上年增长 17.8%。其中：互联网期刊收入达 21.38 亿元，电子书达 56 亿元，数字报纸（不含手机报）达 8.3 亿元，博客类应用达 115.3 亿元，在线音乐达 103.5 亿元，网络动漫达 180.8 亿元，移动出版（移动阅读、移动音乐、移动游戏等）达 2 007.4 亿元，网络游戏达 791.1 亿元，在线教育达 1 330 亿元，互联网广告达 3 717 亿元。收入比例情况如图 1 所示。

（二）传统书报刊数字化收入占比增幅下降态势依旧

图书、报纸、期刊一直是我国传统新闻出版单位的主营业务，其发展的质量直接决定着新闻出版业的发展水平与前景。近年来，传统出版单位在主管部门的引导和市场需求的推动下，转型升级、融合发展渐趋深入，着力布局新领域、开拓新业务。随着新业态、新产品的不断涌现，占比日益提升，传统书报刊数字化业务在数字出版领域的比重逐渐降低。

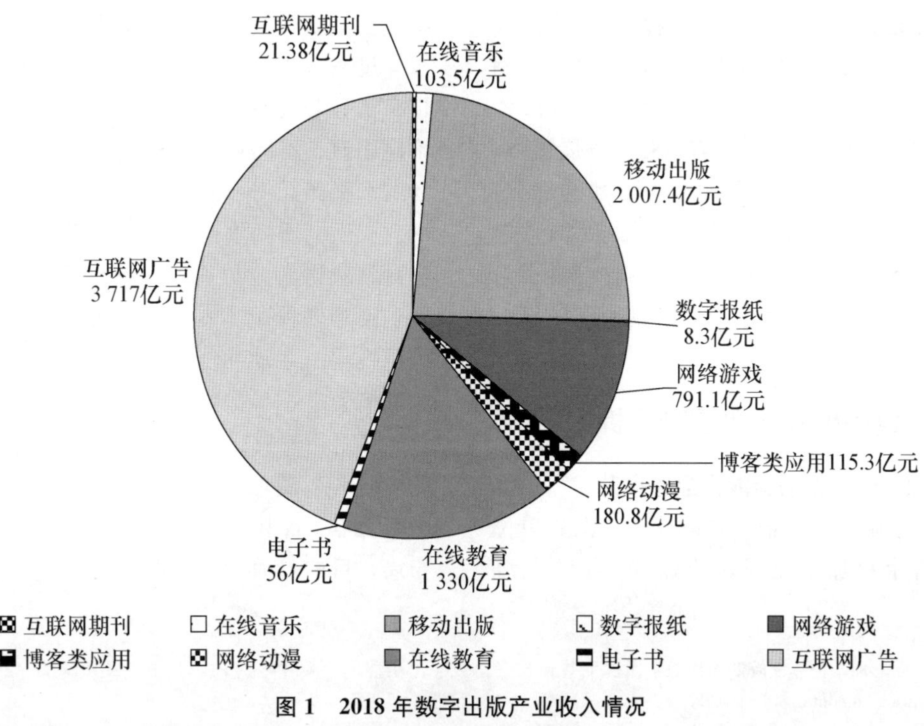

图 1　2018 年数字出版产业收入情况

2018 年互联网期刊、电子书、数字报纸的总收入为 85.68 亿元，相比 2017 年的 82.7 亿元，增长幅度为 3.6%，低于 2017 年 5.35%的增长幅度，在数字出版总收入中所占比例为 1.03%，相较于 2017 年的 1.17%和 2016 年的 1.54%来说，继续处于下降态势。这表明在全媒体发展已成为必然趋势的当下，出现了全程媒体、全系媒体、全员媒体、全效媒体，信息无处不在、无所不及、无人不用，舆论生态、媒体格局、传播方式正面临深刻变革。传统书报刊数字化业务的日渐式微，已是不可逆转的趋势。这也要求传统新闻出版单位积极适应信息化要求、强化互联网思维，要善于学习和应用互联网，利用互联网这个最大变量给新闻出版业的发展带来最大增量；要坚持导向为魂、移动为先、内容为王、创新为要，加大数字化转型升级的力度、加快推进融合发展进程，建立产业融合发展矩阵，打造融合产品，努力将融合发展的整体优势发挥出来；要以资源整合、内容品质提升、价值导向、技术研发与应用、人才培养等为着力点，进行生产要素整合、流程优化、平台再造，推动融合发展由相加阶段向相融阶段过渡；要做好新闻出版业供给侧结构性改革，协同推进，探索产业新形态、研发新产品、开展新服务，提升产品质量与服务水平，推动新闻出版业数字化转型升级不断深化、产业融合向纵深发展的新局面，增强传统书报刊企业在数字内容产业中的核心竞争力。

（三）新兴板块持续发力

2018 年，移动出版收入规模为 2 007.4 亿元，在线教育收入规模为 1 330 亿元，网络动漫收入规模为 180.8 亿元，三者占数字出版收入规模的比例为 42.23%，与 2017 年基本持平，表明移动出版依然是数字出版发展的主力军，具有较强的发展潜力。在线教育作为数字教育出版发展最为强劲的部分，市场格局已基本形成，资源趋向集中化，头部效应明显；网络动漫经过多年的探索与坚持，培育了大量付费用户，推动网络动漫的消费市场实现了良性发展。

二、数字出版产业态势分析

（一）出版单位转型创新能力显著提升

2018 年，出版业转型融合持续深入。出版单位对融合发展有了更加全面深入的思考，纷纷围绕“融合出版”进行规划布局，借助新技术、新形态和新媒介，在内容、产品、品牌、模式等方面持续探索，创新能力有了显著提升。如山东教育出版社以“内容为本、科技引领、一体化融合发展”为发展理念，以有声阅读、纸电纸网融合书、数字教育产品等领域为发展重点，全媒体融合产品矩阵初步形成。其中，《不一样的数学故事》运用 AR 增强现实技术开发了动画视频图书，并以该书为蓝本，开发了同名知识性动画片，目前就该动画片已与国内国外多家电视台达成了播出授权签约协议，在融合发展和品牌建设方面迈出了扎实的一步，实现了内容多元开发和版权的多维增值。中国出版集团旗下的东方出版中心提出“3+2”发展模式，将现代管理和资本运作相结合，紧紧围绕出版主业、产业园区、融合发展三条主线，向高质量发展持续迈进。此外，还有一些出版单位，发挥借力优势，与互联网企业加强合作，充分吸纳互联网企业的先进经营理念和运营模式，提升融合发展质量。如 2018 年贵州出版集团与京东达成全面战略合作协议，向“无界零售”领域发力，并携手共同推进贵州省全民阅读工作。值得一提的是，过去一年来，出版单位的创新意识有了显著提升，上海世纪出版集团、江苏凤凰出版传媒集团、浙江出版联合集团和安徽出版集团于 2018 年 12 月，按照习近平总书记提出的“支持长江三角洲区域一体化发展并上升为国家战略”的这一重要战略部署，签署战略合作协议，共同规划在上海张江科学城建设长三角数字出版协同创新中心，构建区域出版业融合发展协同创新体系，共同打造融合创新高质量发展的良好局面①。

过去一年来，出版单位在产品方面的创新能力也有了显著提升，以顺应媒体融合发展形势，满足不同用户、不同场景的阅读需求。如岳麓书社将该社的拳头产品——四大名著进行多元化开发，在为用户提供纸质图书的同时，还聘请专家对四大名著进行精彩讲解，再通过自研的小程序平台提供听、阅、读等多种版本，并搭配漫画、游戏、场景 VR 等可视化的互动功能。随着产品创新，出版单位的服务能力进一步提升，充分顺应全媒体融合发展趋势，满足用户移动化、碎片化、细分化、多场景化的内容获取需求。近年来，传统出版单位以音视频为着力点，深耕自身优势内容资源，开展知识服务布局，目前已涌现出多个知识服务品牌，《中读》

① 汪婷婷，于彩丽. 沪苏浙皖四家出版集团携手共建长三角数字出版协同创新中心［EB/OL］.［2019-07-12］. http://www.apgmart.com/frontarticle/detail/48-10199.

《中信书院》《小荷听书》《湛庐 FM》等产品都形成了自身的优势特色，并取得了较好的市场反响。《三联生活周刊》打造了《我们为什么爱宋朝》等多个爆款栏目。《中信书院》融知识服务和在线大学于一体，提供有声读物、音视频课程、电子书等三类内容，满足用户多元化内容消费需求。2018 年初，《中信书院》的用户总数已经超过 300 万人，该产品的全年知识服务总收入也已超过 7 000 万元①，推出的首档栏目《阅读时差》上线 20 天销售量就突破 1 万份。山东教育出版社推出的《小荷听书》，产品市场定位清晰，专注为青少年群体提供阅读服务，以微信公众号为内容发布端，提供包括“文学佳作”“唐诗宋词”“家庭教育”等 18 类内容，并组织多场线上线下活动，为青少年的阅读习惯养成做出了有益示范。区别于零散的、碎片化知识的兜售，传统出版单位开展知识服务的优势在于提供的知识体系架构更加完整、系统，同时还有严谨的内容审核机制和版权管理机制。此外，自媒体平台已成为出版单位内容和产品输出、提供知识服务、聚拢读者用户和提升产品影响力的重要平台载体，中国出版集团、黑龙江出版集团、新华文轩出版集团等出版单位的微信号都已收获了百万以上的用户关注。

出版融合重点实验室实施建设一年多以来，成果显著，为出版业融合发展的路径创新积累了有益经验。如国家出版融合发展（辽宁）重点实验室，在辽宁出版集团融合发展整体战略部署下，逐步明确了“融出版”“融资产”“融管理”“融团队”“融发行”的“五融”战略，目前该实验室重点围绕数据库、IP 运营和在线教育三大领域，着力打造融媒体内容制作中心、泛娱乐文创中心、鼎籍学堂大教育中心，融合创新能力逐步增强②。

（二）网络文学良性生态逐步构建

2018 年是中国网络文学发展的第 20 个年头，在中央政策强劲指引和主管部门有力引导下，网络文学保持着良好的发展态势，逐步迈进健康发展的良性轨道。据相关数据，截至 2018 年 12 月，我国网络文学用户规模达到 4.32 亿人，占网民总数的 52.1%。

在内容创作方面，习近平总书记提出的“举旗帜、聚民心、育新人、兴文化、展形象”的新时期宣传思想工作的使命任务，为网络文学发展提出了新的精神指引和总体要求。网络文学作品质量有了显著提升，主流化、精品化趋势日益明显，特别是现实主义题材持续蓬勃发展，成为网络文学发展的强劲动力。越来越多的作者在创作中主动靠近现实，贴近生活。而在幻想类题材中，也有越来越多的作品开始注重融入鲜明的中华传统文化特色标识，人文情怀日益凸显。在由国家新闻出版署和中国作家协会共同发布的“2018 年优秀网络文学原创作品”推荐名单中，现实题材作品占比进一步提升。多名以幻想架空类题材见长的网络作者开始聚焦现实，从事现实题材创作。由此可见，网络文学在保持着其强劲创新创造活力的同时，正逐渐向主流文学审美靠拢，实现从注重娱乐性向注重思想性、艺术性的有益转变。同时，各家网络文学网站平台纷纷着力增加现实题材储备，并结合改革开放 40 周年、新中国成立 70 周年等重大节日、重大事件、重要节点和重要社会热点进行作品征集，在主题出版中的表现日益突出。如点众科技打造了《北京背影》《花剑男神是女生》《冰上的华尔兹》《风华正茂》《甘霖》等多部现实题材作品。其中《北京背景》入围 2018 年第五届中国数字阅读大会“鹤鸣杯”2019 潜力 IP 价值榜 50 名榜单，《运河天地之策马春风堤上行》等四部以大运河文化为主题的作品入选北京影视出版创作基金重点奖励项目，另一部大运河主题作品《运河天地之运河武工队》入选 2018 年“北京市向读者推荐的优秀网络文学原创作品”名单。网络文学积极正向的发展态势，逐步得到主流文学的认同。2019 年世界读书日揭晓的 2018 年度“中国好书”，首次将网络文学纳入评选范畴，《写给鼹鼠先生的情书》等三部网络文学作品入选。

2018 年 9 月，第二届中国“网络文学+”大会在北京举办。大会以“网络正能量，文学新高峰”为主题，积极搭建网络文学及相关行业权威发布、行业交流、IP 交易、成果展示、互动体验、宣传推广等六大平台。第二届中国“网络文学+”大会以网络文学发展 20 年和改革开放 40 周年为契机，全面展示了网络文学顺应改革发展大潮取得的丰硕成果，展现了网络文学 20 年欣欣向荣的良好风貌，首次由主管部门组织指导、行业研究机构核心参与，行业协会发布了《2018 中国网络文学发展报告》，并评选出中国网络文学 20 年前行历程中的“二十件大事”、“二十部优质 IP 作品”和“二十个关键词”。

① 卢俊. 中信书院营收 7 000 万的秘密［EB/OL］.［2019-05-07］. http://www.cbbr.com.cn/article/119439.html.

② 来，晒晒各出版融合发展重点实验室成绩单，有你们家的吗?［EB/OL］.［2019-06-03］. http://www.sohu.com/a/252280705_267807.

相较于首届大会，第二届大会的权威性、功能性和影响力有了进一步提升，在抓导向、出精品、促融合等方面发挥了重要推进作用，已成为中国网络文学行业的重要平台和北京文化中心建设的一张亮丽名牌。除了中国“网络文学+”大会，网络文学周也自2018年起在杭州成功举办两届，这些活动不仅为网络文学从业者搭建了沟通交流的有益平台，也为IP产业链上下游合作建立了桥梁。

2017年12月，首个中国网络作家村在浙江杭州成立，旨在打造网络文学作家集群，为网络作家提供创作和沟通交流的平台。成立一年来，已有100多名作家签约入驻并注册了工作室。2018年6月，上海率先面向网络文学推出《上海市文学创作系列网络文学专业职称评审办法（试行）》，为网络文学人才选拔、评价、考核机制的建立健全做出了有益尝试。2018年7月底，江苏网络文学谷在江苏南京挂牌，将着力打造网络文学以及网络文学相关产业集群，构建以网络文学为源头，以IP版权转化为纽带，集网络文学、动漫、游戏、影视、图书出版、有声读物、演艺、文化周边等文、艺、娱于一体的IP全产业链生态[①]。2018年11月，江苏网络文学作家村和中国网络文学泛娱乐产业孵化基地在江苏省镇江市揭牌成立。江苏网络文学作家村将规划建设“网络文学众创空间”“网络作家培训基地”“中国网络文学IP形象展览馆”“国家级网络文学IP路演基地”等功能平台[②]，不仅通过提供各种服务为网络作家创作打造良好空间，为网络文学创作优秀人才培养提供有力支持，而且将着力推动优质网络文学IP的孵化、培育。

可以看到，网络文学已成为全国，特别是北京和长江三角洲地区文化建设的重要着力点，并呈现出集群化、生态化、差异化、特色化的发展态势。

（三）数字教育出版垂直化、精品化发展

2018年，伴随我国教育信息化加快推进，数字教育出版保持良好的发展势头，并呈现垂直化、精品化发展的态势。2018年4月，教育部颁布《教育信息化2.0行动计划》，标志着我国教育信息化步入新阶段。该计划提出要积极推进“互联网+教育”，将信息技术与教育教学深度融合，搭建“互联网+教育”大平台，推动从教育专用资源向教育大资源转变，构建网络化、智能化、个性化、终身化的教育体系，发展基于互联网的教育服务新模式，探索信息时代教育治理新模式。该计划的实施，为我国数字教育出版带来了新的发展机遇。

基础教育一直是数字教育最活跃、产品种类最丰富的领域。2018年，国家有关部门加大了对中小学教育教学类APP的管理力度。11月，教育部办公厅、国家市场监督管理总局办公厅和应急管理部办公厅三部门联合发布《关于健全校外培训机构专项治理整改若干工作机制的通知》，明确提出要做好面向中小学生的利用互联网技术在线实施培训教育活动机构的备案工作，加强对线上培训内容的监管。12月底，教育部印发《关于严禁有害APP进入中小学校园的通知》，要求建立学习类APP进校园备案审查和日常监管制度。此外，2018年被称为“最强减负年”，2018年底，为减少中小学生课程学习负担，教育部出台《中小学生减负措施》，明确提出合理使用电子产品的要求。规范学生使用电子产品，养成信息化环境下良好的学习和用眼卫生习惯，全面提升信息素养，严禁学生将手机带入课堂。相关政策的密集出台将对基础教育领域的数字教育产品市场带来一定影响，但在某种程度上将有效推动基础教育领域数字教育实现规范化、高质量发展。

当前，职场人群工作和生活压力不断加大，个人素养和专业能力的提升逐渐成为刚性需求，继续教育和职业培训两大领域数字教育呈现出良好的市场发展前景。同时，在知识付费等新模式影响下，在线学习的付费习惯已基本普遍养成。由于成年人学习需求呈现个性化、差异化特点，继续教育和职业培训的数字教育产品垂直化发展趋势明显，目前已涵盖语言学习、资格考试应试培训和咨询、学历教育、招聘求职、专业垂直领域的知识提升、心理健康辅导等多个层面，产品类型包括知识社群、学习类APP、在线课程等多样化形态。

2018年，随着教育出版转型升级、融合发展渐趋深入，数字教育出版发展模式日趋多元。各家出版单位纷纷基于自身资源优势，在“垂直化、精品化、品牌化”方面下功夫，探索“专、精、特、新”的发展路径，打造专业化、个性化的数字教育产品。人工智能技术在教育出版领域的应用日趋深入，研发智能化的数字教育产品成为各家出版单位的重要着力点。如外语教学与研究出版社在少儿教育、高等教育等多个领域，打造多款数字教育产品，形成

① 褚珺.“江苏网络文学谷”落户南京秦淮［EB/OL］.［2019-06-21］. http://www.njdaily.cn/2018/0730/1715246.shtml.

② 王艳.“江苏网络作家村”落户镇江　天下归元任“村长”［EB/OL］.［2019-08-06］. https://js.qq.com/a/20181119/005583.htm.

了鲜明的品牌特色。其中,“七色龙”是面向国际为K-6阶段的少年儿童打造的数字教育品牌,包括纸质图书、互动游戏APP、在线学习平台和猫头鹰阅读机器人等产品,实现了“传统出版+数字产品+文创产品”的多元融合。为响应国家“一带一路”倡议,外研社于2018年3月上线运营我国首个以外语学科特色为主的慕课平台UMOOCs。该平台聚合了国内外高校的教学资源,提供包括10个语种、11个课程方向、5个特色专题的在线课程①。UMOOCs是外研社打造的面向高等院校和学生外语学习品牌——“Unipus数字化教学共同校园”的核心产品之一,除了该平台外,Unipus品牌下还包括U校园智慧教学云平台、Utalk视听实训智慧学习平台、U讲堂数字课程平台、iTest大学外语测试与训练系统、iWrite英语写作教学与评阅系统、iSpeak爱口语APP、iLearning 2.0外语自主学习资源库、iResearch外语学术科研平台等多款数字教育产品,以满足多元化、个性化、交互化的外语教学需求,并结合品牌特色,组织Ucreate备课沙龙、“外研社·国才杯”Uchallenge大学生英语挑战赛等线下活动,实现矩阵化品牌建设和线上线下的有机融合。

(四)报刊转型全面加速

长期以来,相较于图书出版,报刊领域的转型融合进程则稍显迟缓。2018年,随着媒体融合迈向纵深,报刊转型迎来了全面加速,取得多项突破。过去一年来,多家报刊单位停止纸媒刊发,一时间引发了各界对报刊业前景的担忧。事实上,多家报刊在停止纸媒刊发的同时,积极转战新媒体,并借此焕发出新的活力。由此可见,纸媒停止发售并不意味着报刊业的衰败,反而是在媒体融合发展形势下转型升级的路径选择,也是抢占主流舆论的新阵地和新制高点的客观需要。

一方面,报刊媒体纷纷借助新兴媒体渠道,构建新媒体传播矩阵。人民日报社、新华社等中央主要新闻单位和各级党报的主流媒体都开设了媒体公众号,中央和地方各级政府也都开通了政务微博,在舆论格局中发挥“风向标”的作用。2018年6月,人民日报社全国移动新媒体聚合平台“人民号”正式上线,依托《人民日报》客户端,力求打造成为媒体、党政机关、各类机构、企业、优质自媒体和个人入驻的全新内容平台。北京日报报业集团、上海报业集团、广州日报报业集团和南方报业传媒集团等多家传媒集团均形成了“报+网+端+微”的多介质、多形态、立体化的融媒体矩阵。如广州日报报业集团设立了广州日报数据和数字化研究院,以数据挖掘、分析以及数字新闻传播和新型智库构建为主要业务,打造大数据分析与数字传播平台。上海报业集团则衍生出20个智媒体单元,包括智能硬件、智能融媒体中心、新闻内容可视化、新媒体内容标签系统、沉浸式新闻体验、虚拟主播与互动式新闻、舆情监测系统与新媒体传播力指数等。《新京报》在“报+网+端+微”的基础上,将新闻可视化作为发展方向,作为其媒体融合的重要一环,新媒体APP于2018年10月底正式上线,制定了移动传播优先、视频表达优先、用户体验优先的产品策略,并提出“使报社内容生产视频化程度达到50%,在APP首页甚至是推送(push)中,含视频表达方式的报道优先”的目标②。可以看到,报刊业在媒体融合的进程中,正在以大数据、人工智能等新一代技术为协助,运用可视化、移动化手段,着力提升舆论传播力、影响力。各报业集团基本建成了各家独特的融媒体矩阵,“报+网+端+微”已经成为固定配置。依托网站、客户端、微信、微博等发布平台,通过图文、短视频、直播、H5等多种形式,实现多层面、多形式、多渠道的传播构架,提供丰富、及时的信息内容。同时,顺应融媒体建设需要,过去一年来,多地报刊单位通过机构整合组建融媒体集团,实现优势资源和品牌的集约式发展,实现了报刊单位在内容、技术、人才等各方面资源的优化重构、有效聚集和一体化发展,以期产生“1+1>2”的叠加效应③。

此外,多家报业集团、报刊社积极发力跨界融合,或拓展新领域新业务,或借助互联网企业的技术优势,提升融合发展水平。如河南日报报业集团布局在线教育,建设基于高等教育的“河南省在线教育课程平台”,并在青少年培训和幼儿教育领域积

① 高校外语慕课平台UMOOCs培养复语及复合型人才[EB/OL].[2019-05-24]. http://edu.sina.com.cn/l/2019-03-25/doc-ihsxncvh5452613.shtml.

② 新京报将打造一款现象级App?听听社长宋甘澍怎么说[EB/OL].[2019-07-27]. https://baijiahao.baidu.com/s?id=1615931457529470396&wfr=spider&for=pc.

③ 辽宁报刊传媒集团(辽宁日报社)挂牌成立[EB/OL].[2019-06-18]. http://k.sina.com.cn/article_5822206027_15b07d04b02700afan.html.

极探索，不断丰富教育产品体系①。北京日报报业集团则在 2018 年 12 月与百度百家号达成战略协作，依托百度的人工智能技术和搜索引擎支持，优化北京日报客户端的产品服务和用户体验②。

（五）知识付费分水岭逐步显现

知识付费在经过近三年的市场历练后，展现出了独有的发展逻辑和轨迹。随着行业发展的日趋成熟，用户对自身知识的学习需求有更加明确的自我认识，因此对知识付费产品有了更加理性的选择。同时，随着行业马太效应的日益加剧，主播资源、版权资源和用户资源向头部平台加速集中，行业竞争格局和市场筛选机制初步形成，行业分水岭逐步显现。

2018 年，各家知识付费平台在功能、内容生产、运营模式上趋于成熟和多元化。整体产业角色与传统教育、传媒、传统出版优势互补、趋向纵深融合。知识付费内容方和平台方逐渐形成共生体系，产业发展呈“腰部形态”结构分布，头部格局占产业规模 35%、“腰部”玩家占据 25%、长尾参与者分享其余 40%的份额。其中头部内容平台方在用户基数、产品质量、版权保护、资本投入、技术支撑、人才培养等方面逐渐规范化并形成基本壁垒。

在服务用户需求方面，头部平台针对用户的需求层次提供了阶梯式产品矩阵，通过分层次的差异化服务来满足用户，因此用户向头部内容加速集中。在内容质量方面，一些头部平台建立了自己的内容把控体系，如《得到》出台了《得到品控手册》，对内容品质有严格把控，细致到文本括号中文字的处理，每一步策划流程的细节等。《知乎》的私家课，主讲人花费大量时间研究授课细节，与团队反复沟通选题和录制音频声音等细节。《喜马拉雅 FM》则成立专门服务于音频生产的公司，深度参与课程的定位、内容规划、体系设计等生产过程。一些具有特色的小而美垂直类平台，植根于更加细化的专业领域，提供特殊场景面向特定用户群体和消费场景，如面向儿童的《凯叔讲故事》、面向 IT 互联网的《极客时间》、面向法律领域的《简法》、面向股市的《股市汇》、面向金融行业的《小红圈》等。垂直类知识付费产品可以更加精准地帮助用户解决实际问题、满足高频次刚需，从而形成稳定高速的发展模式。

从知识付费平台的发展规模来看，用户数仍在持续增长，如头部领航者《喜马拉雅 FM》注册用户数量已达到 5.3 亿人，2018 年付费内容数量是上一年度的 4 倍，热门有声书播放量已突破 10 亿次，高频有声书用户日均收听时长超过 180 分钟。在 2018 年“喜马拉雅 123 狂欢节”中，参与用户达到 2 135 万人，总播放时长达 1.3 亿小时，销售额达到 4.35 亿元，超过上一届狂欢节 2.2 倍③。《得到》APP 在 2018 年付费用户达到 2 300 万人。《得到》在其 KOL 知识生产者主导下的 PGC 分享模式的基础上，于 2018 年 9 月推出了新的知识服务产品“得到大学”，通过线上线下结合的学习方式，为来自不同行业领域的学员，通过面对面的方式构建多元思维模型。

2018 年，知识付费内容覆盖了更为广泛的领域，涉及的种类和范围进一步丰富。一方面，知识付费产品逐渐成为深度学习的入口，注重向用户输出跨领域基础与技能，将理论与实践结合，覆盖领域广泛、应用性强；另一方面，以兴趣为主导的内容娱乐特征逐渐显现，寓教于乐、传播观点的付费产品越来越多。用户选择知识付费产品内容逐渐转化，从 2018 年“喜马拉雅 123 狂欢节”前 10 位的付费产品可以看出，《蒙曼品最美唐诗》《蔡康永的 201 堂情商课》等娱乐性和人文类的内容最受消费群体认可。用户对内容付费需求正在从消弭焦虑转向兴趣培养，内容范围从知识“轻学习”朝着多元化垂直化发展。此外，随着知识付费日趋成熟，产业化进程不断加快，行业分工趋于专业和细分，第三方支持机构逐渐成熟，在内容生产、跨平台品牌运营、技术服务、版权分销等方面都发展出了独特的路径。

（六）短视频风口持续成为媒体布局重点

短视频作为近两年互联网的风口领域，2018 年发展势头持续强劲，并在行业格局上发生较大改变。《快手》《秒拍》两大短视频平台与今日头条旗下《西瓜视频》三方分立的格局被打破，《抖音》迅速崛起，追平《快手》。与此同时，腾讯、阿里巴巴、

---

① 2018 传媒十大经营案例：新京报版权收入覆盖采编成本［EB/OL］.［2019-07-11］. http://www.guanmedia.com/news/detail_10854.html.

② 北京日报报业集团与百度达成战略合作协议［EB/OL］.［2019-06-17］. https://baijiahao.baidu.com/s?id=1619813644401851016&wfr=spider&for=pc.

③ 2018 喜马拉雅 123 狂欢节成交额 4.35 亿，创内容付费历史新高［EB/OL］.［2019-08-01］. https://finance.qq.com/a/20181205/014342.htm.

百度和新浪等大型互联网企业也向短视频市场集体发力，或基于自身优势，进行特色短视频平台搭建，并注重与自身优势业务相结合；或通过战略投资，将短视频作为数字内容生态布局中的一环；或扶持创作团队，提升内容优势。如阿里巴巴旗下《鹿刻》短视频，就是以"短视频＋电商"的模式，为阿里巴巴的电商业务提供支持。淘宝商家可以通过短视频达到更好的营销效果。百度旗下的《好看视频》则借助百度的人工智能优势，在技术上拥有先进的视频理解技术，能够更好地对视频进行自动分类和对原创视频进行保护。《好看视频》作为百度布局短视频生态的重要产品，上线不到一年日活跃用户数就已经突破 1 200 万人。同时，腾讯也在加快布局短视频市场，对快手进行了战略投资，并于 2018 年 11 月正式推出了原创短视频平台——Yoo 视频。今日头条旗下孵化了火山小视频、西瓜视频和抖音三家短视频平台，充分满足用户对短视频的多元需求。网易则着力培育优质短视频创作者，2018 年网易推出"万人万粉"计划，大力扶持中腰部短视频账号，给予其最大限度的流量支持，建立了"订阅＋垂直化推荐"机制。继 2017 年在网易号上线了 MCN 功能之后，网易于 2018 年初投入 10 亿元用于补贴短视频及 MCN，向 MCN 机构开放平台 50%的资源，全面助力 MCN 在流量、品牌等方面获得收益①。

过去一年来，传统媒体也纷纷涉足短视频，借助这一新兴领域，提升自身舆论传播能力。如深圳报业集团旗下《深圳晚报》在微视、头条号、大鱼号和人民号等近 10 个平台开设了短视频账号。浙江日报报业集团、四川日报报业集团等都纷纷在短视频平台布局。由此可见，短视频已成为当前媒体传播格局中的重要组成部分。

（七）互联网内容规范化管理进一步加强

当前，移动互联网已成为人们获取信息的重要渠道，也是意识形态传播的重要阵地，网络直播、短视频等新媒体形态不断涌现和快速发展，不断重塑着媒体生态格局，在舆论传播和价值观传递方面发挥的作用日益凸显。

互联网内容建设作为国家网络强国建设战略的重要组成部分，得到中央政府的高度重视。过去一年来，国家相关部门围绕新媒体形态，出台多项规范制度和实施多项重要举措。2018 年 8 月，全国"扫黄打非"工作小组办公室联合工业和信息化部等六部委，共同下发《关于加强网络直播服务管理工作的通知》，细化了网络直播服务提供者的主体责任，主要包括以下三个方面：一是进一步强化网络直播的许可和备案管理。涉及互联网新闻信息、网络表演、网络视听节目直播等业务的网络直播服务提供者需向有关部门申请取得相关资质许可，并前往属地公安机关履行备案手续。二是强化网络直播服务基础管理工作。特别提出要落实用户实名制度，加强网络主播管理，建立黑名单制度。三是加强直播内容的监管与审核，不得制作、复制、发布法律法规禁止的信息内容，建立内容全天候应急响应机制。2018 年 11 月，中央网信办联合公安部发布《具有舆论属性或社会动员能力的互联网信息服务安全评估规定》，对论坛、短视频、网络直播、公众账号、微博客、小程序等互联网信息服务活动予以规范，对适用的企业（尤其是大型的互联网企业）在审查、评估等各个方面应履行的义务提出更为详尽规范的要求，以维护国家及社会安全、扼制不良信息传播、构建正能量的社会舆论导向为出发点，要求互联网信息服务从业者进一步提高合规意识，着力改善现阶段网络存在的网络暴力、人肉搜索、以讹传讹等不良现象，以构建文明、安全、和谐、有序、健康的互联网绿色生态环境。此外，该规定对监管机关的相应职责也做出明确说明。2019 年初，中国网络视听节目服务协会发布《网络短视频平台管理规范》，要求网络短视频平台须持有信息网络传播视听节目许可证等相关资质，并实行节目内容先审后播制度，包括标题、简介、弹幕、评论等内容必须经过平台审核后方可播出。上传视频的注册账号，也须执行实名认证。此外，《规范》还提出强化短视频版权保护责任，不得未经授权剪辑、改编、上传视听作品。《网络短视频内容审核标准细则》也同时发布，针对短视频的标题、名称、评论、弹幕、表情包以及短视频内容中的语言、表演、字幕、背景提出了 21 类共计 100 条禁止内容条款。相关制度的陆续出台，推进互联网内容向法治化、规范化、制度化持续迈进，互联网内容规范体系逐步完善。与此同时，2018 年，相关监管部门对互联网内容的监管力度也进一步加强。10 月，国家网信办会同有关部门，对微博、微信公众号等自媒体公共账号开展专项整治活动，20 天内共依法清理近万个违规自媒体账号。在相关部门的有力监管下，各类新媒体

① 网易号发布"万人万粉"计划 赋能中腰部短视频创作者［EB/OL］.［2019-07-09］. http://tech.huanqiu.com/news/2018-04/11932270.html.

平台的自律意识也不断加强，注重内容审核，加强日常自查自纠，互联网内容建设的清朗生态环境逐步构建。

（八）保障体系进一步完善

2018 年，我国数字出版产业保障体系在诸多方面得以完善与丰富，尤其是在标准建设和版权保护方面取得了新的进展，成为产业发展的有力支撑。

标准化体系基本建立。以团体标准为“破局点”，加强工作力度，在标准撰写层面，依据 GB/T 20001—2015《标准编写规则》、GB/T 20002—2008《标准中特定内容的起草》，已形成若干团体标准草案，完成了若干团体标准组织化建设，标准工作体系化建设基本实现。标准工作机制不断创新。横向合作、学术交流不断加强，标准科研工作已形成合力，联合攻关得到进一步推进，集中力量研发标准化应用产品得到重视与关注，落地应用业已形成突破。行业标准工作基础得到进一步夯实。由中国新闻出版研究院组织建设的新闻出版标准化服务平台，有助于进一步提高行业科技能力和标准化工作水平，健全新闻出版标准化工作机制，有助于推动新闻出版标准的贯彻与实施，有望成为标准化走向行业实践的工作基础。标准工作思路发生较大转变。标准申报流程更为严谨、申报审批更为严格、标准的行业使用度和适用度得到进一步强调，从做多到做精、由数量到质量转型的效果进一步显现，这些变化提升了标准含金量，使标准化工作力量更集中，推动标准应用水平的提高，能够进一步发挥标准对行业的指引、规范和提升作用。标准培训工作持续发力，人才队伍已渐成体系。标准培训课程结构已实现全面覆盖，内容更趋于均衡合理，高水平师资团队业已形成，受训人员的年龄逐步降低，受训人数逐年增加，这将为数字出版产业标准化升级打下坚实基础。

数字版权保护是数字出版产业发展的基本保障。为了尽量避免作者权益受到损害、稳固企业发展基础与动力、平衡各方利益，构建和维护良好的网络传播秩序，多方力量进行了不懈的努力。《最高人民法院关于审查知识产权纠纷行为保全案件适用法律若干问题的规定》明确了知识产权案件中的“紧急情况”，确定了行为保全审查标准，加强了知识产权的保护，使权利人在符合条件的情况下可以考虑使用知识产权临时救济措施，进一步完善行为保全制度。《最高人民法院关于互联网法院审理案件若干问题的规定》明确了电子证据的规则，间接地为著作权权利人举证提供了便利，也降低了权利人维权成本。北京互联网法院联合 25 家互联网技术公司建成“一托九”的电子诉讼平台，实现了全部案件一体化的互联网诉讼模式。杭州互联网法院支持原告采用区块链作为存证方式并认定对应侵权事实，在全国首次明确区块链电子存证的审查判断方法。国家版权局、国家网信办、公安部、工信部等四部门联合启动的“剑网 2018”专项行动，重拳整治网络转载、短视频等领域，约谈 15 家短视频企业，删除各类涉嫌侵权盗版短视频作品 57 万部，删除侵权盗版链接 185 万条，收缴侵权盗版制品 123 万件，查处网络侵权盗版案件 544 件，会同公安部门查办案件 74 件，涉案金额 1.5 亿元。在“剑网行动”的多次重拳出击下，版权治理力度整体提升，自媒体版权环境有所好转，多家内容平台对侵权的治理机制不断完善，日益彰显数字版权行政保护的力度与重要性。阿里巴巴、拼多多等电商平台与京版十五社反盗版联盟签订的合作协议，由腾讯、百度等发起的中国网络版权产业联盟发布的《中国网络短视频版权自律公约》，中国网络视听节目服务协会发布的《网络短视频平台管理规范》和《网络短视频内容审核标准细则》，不仅增强了从源头遏制侵权盗版行为的可行性，也将促进视频行业有序发展，保证视频的内容质量。这也昭示着各方面力量积极加入到版权保护工作中来，不断推进着数字版权保护工作社会化进程。

三、数字出版产业问题与对策分析

过去一年来，国家改革发展持续深化，在媒体融合迈向纵深发展的趋势下，数字出版意识形态主阵地作用日益凸显，对数字出版提出了新的要求。数字出版需要承担起新时期新的使命任务，增强导向意识，持续内容深耕，向高质量发展奋勇前进；创新路径探索，推进融合发展出成果、出实效；深耕 IP 价值，推动内容多维增值；精准把握用户需求，优化市场供给；加强品牌建设，提升品牌效益；规范自媒体发展，构建清朗网络空间。

（一）围绕改革发展大局，推进产业高质量发展

2018 年，是改革开放持续全面深化的一年。2019 年，是新中国成立七十周年。站在新的历史起点，数字出版要借助改革开放的东风，自觉承担新时期赋予的使命任务，向高质量发展持续迈进。《关于加强和改进出版工作的意见》中对新形势加强出版工作提出了明确要求，明确指出要加强内容建设、深化改革创新，着力构建把社会效益放在首位、社会效益和经济效益相统一的出版体制机制，努力为人民群众提供更加丰富、更加优质的出版产品和服务。数字出版作为新闻出版业的新生力量和重要构成部分，虽然在各方面取得了长足进步，但与高质量发展尚存在不小的差距。有些传统出版单位对融合发展的认识还不到位，对数字出版的业务布局还停留在较浅层次；而有些新兴出版企业则仍然存在过于追求点击量、注重经济效益，从而忽视社会效益的现象。

在媒体融合迈向纵深发展趋势下，出版业要着眼于深化改革大局、媒体融合发展大势，进一步增强融合发展的使命感和紧迫感，充分认识我国从出版大国迈向出版强国过程中数字出版应承担的重要职责，坚定不移地走融合发展和高质量发展之路。加快推进数字出版产品的供给侧结构性改革，实现内容从高原到高峰的跨越转变，推动数字出版向高质量发展。以更高站位、更大格局、更宽视野、更强定力，提升文化自信，为加快建设网络强国、坚定文化自信贡献力量。

数字出版工作者要以习近平新时代中国特色社会主义思想为指引，深入学习贯彻习近平总书记重要讲话精神，增强“四个意识”、坚定“四个自信”、做到“两个维护”，注重价值导向引领和内容质量把关，自觉肩负起“举旗帜、聚民心、育新人、兴文化、展形象”的使命任务，坚定不移地把坚持正确导向作为数字出版工作的首位要求，牢牢占据舆论引导、思想引领、文化传承的传播制高点，在数字出版方面做大做强主流舆论。坚持弘扬社会主义核心价值观，弘扬主旋律，传递真善美，坚决抵制低俗、庸俗、媚俗，始终把提升内容质量作为发展的生命线，坚持以人民为中心的生产创作导向，以导向正确、主题鲜明、特色突出、健康向上、格调高尚的数字出版产品和服务丰富出版物产品市场，以内容优势巩固发展优势，以文化自信筑牢数字出版阵地，以精品力作不断增强人民群众的获得感、幸福感和安全感，满足人民对美好生活的新期待、新向往、新追求。

（二）努力创新发展路径，提升出版融合效能

融合出版是未来一段时间出版业发展的方向，也是出版业实现高质量发展的必要途径。经过多年探索，出版业转型升级基本完成，正处于传统出版与新兴出版从“相加”迈向“相融”的关键阶段。目前，在融合出版方面，还存在融合出版产品质量不高、融合程度不深的情况，特别是传统出版单位的思维固化，对新领域、新技术、新业态的感悟力、适应力偏弱，产品重功能、轻细节，影响用户体验；产品的运营能力不足，“重制造、轻运营”的现象较为普遍，导致融合出版影响力偏弱；同时，一些出版单位对于处理传统业务和新兴出版业务之间的关系仍然把握不准。

融合出版是出版业发展的必然趋势。出版单位在推进融合发展时必须坚定信念，增强融合发展的紧迫感和主动性，加深对融合发展的认识与理解。一是要把融合发展当作“一把手”工程进行全局式部署，集中资源力量深入推进。坚持传统出版业务与新兴出版业务一体化发展的工作思路，进行统筹部署、统一管理、合理布局，将融合出版理念落实到主题策划、资源整合、技术应用、产品设计、品牌建设、市场运营等各个环节和出版单位的各个部门，建立与融合出版相匹配、相适应的体制机制，有效破除传统出版与新兴出版的壁垒，建立传统出版和数字出版有机结合的融合产品矩阵。二是建立融合出版的短期目标和长期规划，为融合出版制定清晰的路线图和时间表，有计划、分步骤地推进融合发展逐步深入。不断拓宽融合发展思路，开展融合发展路径创新探索，加大力度、下足功夫找差距、学经验、补短板、强本领。三是面对新环境、新技术、新领域、新业态，要进一步加强前瞻思维和开拓精神，特别是要加强对云计算、大数据、人工智能、物联网、虚拟/增强现实等技术的跟踪研究，以技术应用创新引领内容呈现、产品形态和服务体验的创新升级。要加强对有声读物、知识付费、短视频等新领域的了解与把握，找到与自身优势相契合的融合发展路径。出版单位要敢于直面迎接全媒体趋势下传播格局的变化，顺应信息传播移动化、个性化、可视化的特点和需求，实现产品和服务的智能化、分众化、交互化。5G时代的来临，必将催生出版的新形态、新领域、新业态，为融合发展带来新的机遇与挑战，出版单位要抓住这难得的发展契机，在产业变革中找准自己的位置，进行5G环境下的出版流程改造、平台优化、资源整合、技术应用、产品设计和品牌运营，拓展技术应用和内容消费体验新场景，抢占5G环境下的竞争优势。四是借助社群营销等营销新模式，全面提升融合出版产品的营销能力、服务能力和盈利能力，让融合发展有成果的同时，也能真正实现有影响、有效益。五是借助资本力量，通过融资、上市寻求文化产业基金扶持等手段，持续增强融合发展动力，释放融合发展活力。

（三）深耕IP价值，推动内容多维增值

自2015年IP浪潮全面兴起，IP多元开发已成

为以网络文学为代表的源头内容向游戏、动漫、影视等文化形态的多元开发，从而提升内容价值的重要手段。然而，过去一年以来，“IP 失效”“IP 浪潮大势已去”的声音不绝于耳。这主要源于近两年多部由热门网络文学 IP 改编、由当红明星出演的影视作品播出后，没有获得预期中的口碑与市场双赢，反而反响平平，由此引发了整个文化文艺领域和资本市场对于 IP 的质疑。

事实上，IP 开发仍然是内容增值的重要手段。之所以会出现 IP 失效的现象，是由于随着 IP 市场的日趋成熟，无论是受众方还是资本方，对于 IP 的态度都更加理性，对 IP 品质的要求越来越高。过去粗放式的运营模式已不适用于当前产业发展的需求，需要对 IP 从源头进行审慎选择和精细打磨。“IP 失效”并不是 IP 的势能有所衰减，而是偏离价值的 IP 越来越难以获得市场认可。因此，与其一味强调或者弱化 IP 效应，不如着手构建 IP 生产、运作的良性机制和产业生态环境，推进优秀 IP 的孵化、培育、开发，使优秀的内容脱颖而出，真正充分发挥其潜在价值。当前，制定一套科学、合理、普遍适用的 IP 价值评价标准体系已成为行业的共同诉求，也是主管部门、研究机构、资本市场、相关企业等各方持续努力的一项重要工作。该标准体系需要以社会效益为先、兼顾社会效益和经济效益的统一，不能过分强调点击量、下载量等用户数据。

IP 开发是出版单位提升内容价值和品牌价值的重要手段，也是全媒体融合发展背景下，出版单位融合创新、多元发展的重要途径。传统出版单位应进一步强化 IP 思维，进行基于优势内容的 IP 多元开发，将自身的内容影响力转化为品牌影响力，将内容优势和品牌影响力延伸至其他文化领域，从而实现内容和品牌的多元增值。同时，出版单位要主动融入 IP 产业链中，提高参与度。从内容的选题策划环节开始，就要对 IP 的开发形式进行考虑，包括对市场、对受众的研究分析，找到 IP 作品最佳的呈现方式和运作方式，避免盲目开发造成的收效甚微或负面影响。同时，加强 IP 策划、IP 运营、版权代理、IP 资产管理等相关专业人才的培养与引进。

在主管部门层面，需要为建立 IP 良性运作机制和构建良性 IP 产业生态提供政策保障与支持。加快推进数字内容 IP 价值评估指标体系的研究制定和实践应用。集合上下游企业、科研学术机构、金融投资机构等 IP 产业链各环节的智慧力量，让评估体系既能突出导向引领又能反映市场需求，既能代表产业供给能力也能经得起资本市场和广大受众的检验。此外，加快推进数字内容资源库平台建设，建立优质 IP 资源库和项目库，能够促进 IP 产业链供需双方的有效对接。

（四）精准把握用户需求，增强市场供需适配度

媒体介质和产品形态随着技术的发展不断更新迭代，媒体格局和产业结构的重塑也催生了新的市场需求。与此同时，新的市场需求又在反向推动企业在产品形态和服务模式的创新，产业就在这个周而复始、不断循环的过程中持续运转、不断衍生发展。当前，信息传播渠道和传播方式的多元化，让用户在信息获取方式上有了更加多样化的选择。而用户的需求本身也不是单一的，可能随时在发生转变。不同时间、不同地域、不同场景，甚至不同的心情下，用户对内容和产品的需求可能都会有所差异。这就对企业在把握用户需求方面提出了更高要求。当前，数字出版产品与用户需求之间还存在一定的断层，包括内容的整合与呈现方式，尚不能做到与用户需求的完全匹配，导致产品的留存率低，用户忠诚度差。

面对激烈的市场竞争，在提升质量、巩固内容优势的同时，数字出版产品的着力点不仅是吸引用户，更重要的是用户的留存。数字出版企业，特别是传统出版单位需摆脱固化的生产经营思维，在把握用户需求上下功夫。一方面，做好市场调查和研究工作，兼顾大数据、智能算法分析和问卷调查等多种方式，对用户的需求目的、阅读情景状态、喜好偏好等方面精准把握，并做到实时追踪，实现产品与需求的精准匹配。另一方面，出版单位要学会换位思考，建议组织一支专业的用户需求研究团队，对产品进行测试体验，不断优化，切实做到尊重用户、理解用户，从用户的角度出发，把自己当成产品的使用者，设身处地地做好产品设计工作。在产品设计上更新理念，注重细节，做到内外兼修。此外，要注重用户反馈，积极借助新媒介，通过建立顺畅的企业、产品和用户之间的沟通渠道，把用户对产品的体验直接反馈给运营团队，及时进行产品优化。

（五）注重多维度、多渠道营销，不断提升品牌效益

数字出版离不开品牌建设。品牌是企业和其产品在用户心中的印记，不仅代表着企业和产品在用户心中的形象，同时也是一种价值观的传递；品牌是一种无形资产，反映了产品的认知度，有了认知才能形成凝聚力和影响力，才能打造竞争力。品牌建设包含了产品、标识、名称、企业文化、营销等各个层面。特别是在移动互联网时代，用户在产品选择上有了更大的空间。可以看到，当前很多数字出版产品在内容质量和功能方面都很出色，但却缺乏市场影响力，很大程度上正是由于品牌建设不足。出版单位要进一步提升对品牌经营的重视程度，把品牌纳入资产管理的范畴，通过品牌设计、品牌保护、品牌延伸、品牌升级，让品牌价值不断提升。

数字出版单位开展品牌建设要借助多维度、多渠道的多元化营销方式，不断强化品牌标识，持续提升品牌经营力度，提升品牌的影响力。具体而言，可以从以下几个方面予以着力：一是做好品牌策划。要有清晰的品牌定位，数字出版产品的品牌首先在名称上要做到朗朗上口，简单易记；品牌形象和品牌名称是品牌带给用户最直观的感觉，是决定用户对品牌第一印象的关键要素。因此在品牌形象设计方面要有较强的辨识度，应与企业和产品特色相契合，与目标用户的审美相契合。二是要注重品牌产品的体系化，在根据用户需求进行多元开发的同时，避免品牌的分散。三是要充分借助微博、微信等各类新媒体社群，结合线下沙龙、讲座等多种形式，打造线上、线下有机结合的品牌营销矩阵。四是开展跨界营销。出版单位可在新闻媒体、音乐、综艺、服饰、礼品、文化消费场所等其他领域寻找契合点，通过跨领域跨品类不同品牌的联合营销，让品牌可触达更广的用户，最大限度地提升品牌的覆盖面、增强品牌对目标受众的感染力。五是数字出版产品的品牌营销还可以与热点事件相结合，在强化品牌的同时，也彰显了一种态度和价值理念，从而增强用户对品牌的认同感。

（六）加快健全管理机制，加快推动自媒体自律发展

近年来，自媒体快速发展，成为信息传播和内容营销的重要渠道。在迅速发展的同时，自媒体也涌现了一些突出问题，主要集中在内容和版权保护两个层面。2018 年 11 月，中央电视台《焦点访谈》节目报道了“低俗色情”“标题党”“谣言”“黑公关”“花钱购买阅读量”等自媒体行业存在的一系列乱象，引发了广泛关注。构建自媒体良性发展秩序，已成为当前网络空间治理的迫切需求。某自媒体账号发布的《甘柴劣火》一文更是引发了针对自媒体大量存在抄袭侵权、“洗稿”盛行的广泛热议。所谓“洗稿”是指对原创稿件进行重新加工润色，再以原创稿件的名义进行发表，事实上在观点上并无实质创新。媒体发布的报道凝聚了写作者的心血，然而其传播效力远远不如自媒体，自媒体将稿件重新包装打造“爆款文”，获取了大量流量和不菲的经济收益。“洗稿”行为在自媒体领域并不罕见，然而，对于整合新闻稿件属于合理引用还是构成抄袭侵权，尚无明确定论，而在合理引用和“洗稿”之间也缺乏清晰的界定标准。2019 年的“剑网行动”，将未经授权转载主流媒体新闻作品的侵权行为作为打击重点，严厉查处自媒体通过“标题党”“洗稿”方式剽窃、篡改、删减主流媒体新闻作品等侵权行为，由此可见，基于自媒体的版权保护已经引起了主管部门的高度重视。

除了版权问题，自媒体存在的价值导向问题也尤为突出。标题党、散播谣言、内容格调低俗、内容违背社会主义核心价值观等问题屡见不鲜。有些自媒体为了吸引流量，罔顾社会道德，甚至已经建成灰色产业链。2018 年 5 月，知名自媒体平台“二更食堂”以舆论热点 21 岁女孩深夜乘网约车遇害事件为素材，撰写并发布文章《托你们的福，那个杀害空姐的司机，正躺在家数钱》，文章中多处用语失当、用词粗鄙，涉嫌消费受害者，造成了极为恶劣的社会影响，引发了网民的强烈声讨[①]。“二更食堂”负责人被有关部门依法约谈，随后其创始人宣布将永久停止更新。

自媒体作为网络内容建设的重要阵地，不应成为法外之地，不应成为抄袭、谣言、低俗内容的摇篮。一方面，需要行业加强行业规范制度和管理手段的进一步优化完善，强化自媒体的主体责任，建立完善的行业准入、奖惩机制，加强对违法违规行为的打击力度，健全自媒体版权保护机制，加快建立行业统一的规范标准；另一方面，自媒体从业者也应自觉肩负起社会责任，弘扬社会主义核心价值观，注重价值导向引领和内容把关，坚守底线，不触红线，共同构建自媒体发展良性生态。

四、数字出版产业趋势分析

2018 年，在习近平新时代中国特色社会主义思想的指引下，数字出版产业整体呈现出健康持续发展的面貌，向高质量发展持续迈进。数字出版内容精品化趋势日益明显，注重价值引领、深耕内容质量将成为内容建设的主旋律；媒体融合向纵深发展，

① 郭晶璇．自媒体价值观导向不可丢 受众辨识能力不可无［EB/OL］．［2019-04-02］．http://report.hebei.com.cn/system/2018/05/16/018810475.shtml.

县级融媒体中心建设加快推进，媒体多元发展格局逐步构建；人工智能在出版业应用场景逐步深化拓展，将在 IP 价值评估体系建设中发挥重要作用；5G 提前实现商用，将为出版融合创新提供更多可能性和想象空间；知识付费在质疑声中将迎来发展拐点；数字内容产业发展格局将得以重塑；跨品类跨场景融合加深，业态复合化趋势渐显；电子竞技蓬勃发展将成为产业融合新节点。具体到未来一年，我们有望看到数字出版产业呈现以下发展趋势。

（一）数字内容精品化趋势日益明显

随着产业环境的不断优化与国民消费升级，粗放式发展已经越来越不能满足产业发展和人们日益提高的精神文化需求。新时代的数字内容产业在不断创新升级、创造更多的经济价值的同时，也被赋予了更大的社会责任和更重要的历史使命。特别是在 IP 市场逐渐趋于理性，流量效应渐渐削弱的形势下，数字内容产业正在加快向精品化发展的步伐。无论是网络文学、网络游戏，还是知识付费、短视频等领域，都逐渐认识到深耕内容才是提升价值的根本。

可以看到，越来越多的数字内容产品在娱乐属性之外，融入了更多的文化内涵，更加注重思想性和艺术性。发生这样的改变，一方面源于相关政策制度体系的日益健全，相关管理部门加强对互联网内容在内容导向和意识形态方面的把控与引导，加强对违法违规内容的查处与打击。另一方面，受众对数字内容的关注点逐渐回归到内容质量本身。流量明星和大 IP 成就爆款的范式逐渐失效，反观之下《大江大河》《都挺好》等一批优秀现实主义题材作品成为年度现象级 IP；《我在故宫修文物》等一批包含人文情怀的节目走红于网络；在抖音短视频平台上，书画、传统工艺、戏曲等传统文化成为播放热点，其中《铡美案》梅葆玖选段的相关视频累计获得超过 500 万次点赞。种种现象表明，大众对精品数字内容有着强烈的诉求，数字内容的审美价值取向正在逐步去低俗化、去庸俗化，向传统主流文化逐渐靠拢。主管部门把关的趋于严格和人们审美趣味的提高，推动数字内容平台增强导向把关意识和精品生产意识，逐步完善内容审核机制，调整内容建设重点，增加思想导向正确、内容健康，正能量、接地气、有温度、有深度、有丰富思想文化内涵的内容储备。此外，继 2018 年 9 月爱奇艺关闭前台播放量后，另一知名视频平台优酷也于 2019 年 1 月宣布关闭了前台播放量显示，意味着网生内容正在逐渐摆脱唯点击率、唯播放量的不良风气。在网络文学领域，书写时代变迁、反映现实生活的作品日益增多。在仙侠等非写实题材作品中，也愈发注重融入中国传统文化元素。在网络游戏领域，功能性游戏或者称严肃游戏，正在成为网络游戏的重点发展方向。网络游戏在休闲娱乐之外，有了知识传递乃至价值观输出等多元功能。特别是游戏与教育之间有了紧密的结合，把知识点融入游戏之中。由此可见，在各个细分领域，数字内容精品化、精细化良性生态正在逐步构建。

（二）媒体融合迈向纵深发展

2019 年 1 月，习近平总书记在中共中央政治局第十二次集体学习时强调，推动媒体融合发展、建设全媒体成为我们面临的一项紧迫课题。媒体融合不仅仅是传统媒体和新兴媒体的简单相加，而且是传播的全方位覆盖、全天候延伸与多领域拓展。随着技术的不断进步，新媒体形态不断涌现，信息渠道日益多元，媒体多元发展格局逐步构建。突出表现在政务媒体、主流媒体紧跟移动互联网时代潮流，遵循移动优先原则，采用微博、微信、短视频等新兴媒体形态日益普遍。同时以今日头条为代表的基于算法的新媒体平台和以抖音为代表的短视频平台也加大了对政务媒体、主流媒体的引入。据了解，已有 7.8 万余家各级党政机关开通政务头条号。据抖音发布的数据报告显示，截至 2018 年底，5 724 个政务号和 1 334 个媒体号已入驻《抖音》，《抖音》逐渐成为政务媒体和主流媒体官方信息发布的重要手段。“两微一抖”（微博、微信、以抖音为代表的短视频平台账号）已成为媒体布局的新标配。主流媒体正在媒体融合大潮中实现自我迭代，采用短视频、网络直播、H5、VR 全景等新形式，丰富信息呈现方式，拓展传播渠道。2018 年 6 月，《人民日报》客户端推出聚合媒体平台“人民号”，截至 2019 年 8 月，已入驻媒体机构 7 000 家，不仅包括全国媒体、党政机关、各类机构，而且还有不少优质自媒体；新华社打造短视频在线加工平台，每天发起直播报道 300 余场；经济日报社也成立了短视频工作室，在抖音、快手等短视频平台上打造品牌栏目。可以看到，传统主流媒体正在以内容呈现方式和传播手段的创新，进一步提升媒体传播力、引导力、公信力，唱响时代主旋律，传唱时代最强音，抢占意识形态新阵地。随着媒体融合的纵深发展，传统媒体与新兴媒体正在从过去的产品融合、渠道融合，逐渐演变为平台融合、生态融合，迈向合而为一的一体化发展新阶段。

作为新时代党中央推进媒体融合向纵深发展的

一项重要举措，我国全面推进县级融媒体中心建设，为媒体融合发展，特别是地方县级媒体融合带来新机遇和新契机。2018 年 11 月 14 日，中央全面深化改革委员会第五次会议审议通过了《关于加强县级融媒体中心建设的意见》，指明了县级融媒体中心建设的总体要求和基本思路。2019 年 1 月 15 日，中宣部和国家广电总局联合发布了《县级融媒体中心建设规范》《县级融媒体中心省级技术平台规范要求》，为县级融媒体中心制定了操作指南和建设规范。目前，不少县域正在加快整合县级媒体资源，打造全媒体一体化传播矩阵，着力加强县级媒体中心建设，并已取得初步成效。这些县级媒体中心或服务于国家建设，或服务于地方宣传，部分融媒体中心已摆脱了对财政资金的依赖，积极探索多元化的经营模式，实现了社会效益和经济效益的双赢。以县级融媒体中心建设为立足点，媒体融合发展有了广阔的施展空间。

（三）人工智能技术应用场景日益深化

当前，出版业已成为人工智能技术应用的重要领域。人工智能技术越来越多地应用于内容的创作、审核、流量预测、运营、推荐、交互等诸多环节，应用程度无论从深度和广度来看都在不断拓展。

一方面，人工智能技术在优化出版流程方面将发挥更大作用。目前方正电子运用大数据和人工智能技术，正在打造智能编纂、智能审校、智能排版等相关产品，为出版业智能化生产提供解决方案。其中，智能审校系统由方正电子与北京印刷学院联合开发，并成立智能审校实验室，通过双方优势互补，为提升出版编审效率和编校质量提供智能化解决方案①。另一方面，人工智能技术在人机交互层面的应用不断深化。如人工智能可应用于为文学作品中的人物角色赋予虚拟形象和情感表达。2019 年初，微软（亚洲）互联网工程院与阅文集团旗下红袖读书达成战略合作，为该平台代表作品《全职高手》中叶修等五个主要人物构建虚拟人物。基于情感计算框架开发，通过对《全职高手》这部代表作品进行文本学习，对书中人物角色的外貌和性格以及语言风格进行模拟，构建出相匹配的虚拟人物，实现与读者进行情感对话交流，为书中人物角色赋予生命。目前，《全职高手》书中的五个角色的虚拟人物已经在《红袖读书》APP 上线，读者在阅读时，不仅可以与它们进行文字交流，还可以实现语音对话，在阅读体验方面获得极大的陪伴感和代入感②，同时也进一步提升了网络文学 IP 的影响力。未来，人工智能在提升 IP 价值方面将发挥更大作用。据悉，优酷已将 AI 技术应用于 IP 运营过程中，包括运用 AI 技术进行影视剧作品的选角、流量预测、宣传推广等，大大提高了 IP 运营效率。特别是在剧本改编环节，运用 AI 技术对内容价值点进行深挖，从而进行剧本的完善。此外，目前已有网络文学企业尝试将人工智能应用于作品的 IP 价值评估，通过建立量化的 IP 价值评估指标和分析体系，为 IP 价值评估过程提供数据支撑，削弱人为因素和主观色彩，为数字内容企业战略决策降低人为风险。

（四）5G 将为出版融合创新提供广阔空间

2019 年，工业和信息化部发放 5G 牌照，包括中国移动、中国联通、中国电信和中国广电等四家企业，标志着我国正式步入 5G 商用元年。我国 5G 实现商用，早于预期大约半年，充分体现我国借助 5G 在移动互联网实现弯道超车、构筑国际竞争力的信心和决心。5G 的运用，将极大提升信息的共享效率和传递能力，将为经济发展、社会服务、个人生活都带来深远影响，更将为出版传媒行业带来颠覆性变革，对出版业选题策划、生产传播、消费等各个环节都带来深远影响，为出版业融合创新开拓更加广阔的想象空间与实践路径。

一方面，5G 将为新技术、新媒体、新业态在出版领域的应用提供更加便利、顺畅的条件，万物互联将真正实现。大数据、云计算将成为出版传媒业的标配技术。特别是 5G 将为虚拟/增强现实技术在出版传媒领域的真正落地、更深层次的创新应用提供有力支撑，将构建起信息传播的全新场域，真正实现沉浸式体验，“3R”技术（VR、AR、MR）将成为游戏、新闻媒体、数字教育等领域的研究和投入的重点。目前已有游戏企业在着力开发云端化游戏等基于 5G 环境的产品。可以预见，在 VR、AR、物联网、智能传播领域将涌现出一批现象级产品。另一方面，5G 环境下富媒体特别是视频内容占比将大幅提升，除了三大运营商外，中国广电也获得了 5G 牌照，这将推动视频内容在移动互联网实现巨大增量。带宽的增加让可视化内容传递更快、画面更加清晰。

① 智能审校联合实验室［EB/OL］.［2019-06-28］. http://www.cuobiezi.net/t/show/58043.

② 红袖读书联手微软小冰 AI 再次拓展 IP 开发的边界［EB/OL］.［2019-07-03］. https://tech.sina.com.cn/n/k/2019-01-16/doc-ihqfskcn7716320.shtml.

在5G环境下，将激发更加多元的数字内容消费需求，由此也将催生更丰富多元的数字内容呈现、产品形态和服务模式。出版业创新融合在迎来空前的发展机遇的同时，也面临着重大挑战，推动融合纵深发展这一课题的紧迫性也日益提升，同时，对于出版单位精准把握用户需求，提供精准化服务、交互式体验提出了更高要求。如何借助5G东风，把握5G时代下的新需求提升资源整合能力，进行产品创新开发、业务布局和商业模式探索，为优质内容构建更加多样化的消费场景，提供更加多样化的服务，成为出版单位提升融合发展能力、打造竞争力的重中之重。

（五）知识付费将迎来发展拐点

2018年的最后一天，罗振宇的跨年演说像往年一样引发了热议。不同的是，这一次的演讲获得更多的是争议。受到争议的不仅是演讲内容本身，也是对近年来处于互联网风口的知识付费领域的一次程度空前的质疑。事实上，2018年人们对知识付费的态度已在悄然发生改变。尽管知识付费平台公布的销售数据仍然在逐年大幅攀升，但与此同时，对知识付费的批评质疑也不绝于耳。知识付费被诟病为是在贩卖身处信息“井喷”时代的人们心中的知识焦虑，还有的知识付费产品则被认为是在打着“知识”的旗号兜售“伪知识”。这与其说是热潮冷却，不如说是知识付费逐步迈向成熟的表现。当前知识付费正处于去粗取精、去伪存真的阶段。同时，业界和市场的质疑，倒逼知识付费平台从内容到模式上求新求变，要求平台在品控环节更加严格，追求内容的精品化、精致化和服务上人性化、个性化。当前对知识付费的批评与质疑，恰恰反映出新的市场需求，如何把握这些需求，将是知识付费未来发展的决胜关键。

未来，知识付费仍有很大的发展空间，但在内容和形式上都将面临新的变化。从内容上看，情感鸡汤类的热度将逐渐削弱，知识付费已逐渐成为人们利用碎片化时间补充专业知识的重要方式，因此专业化、实用性强的内容将成为市场主流，市场持续加剧细分。垂直领域内，标签清晰、受众目标和价值点明确、专业化程度高而讲授方式深入浅出的知识付费产品，将更容易获得用户认可，从而对平台在内容打造上提出更高的要求。从行业格局上来看，知识付费领域马太效应日益明显，二八分化现象持续，知识付费领域的独角兽平台在激烈的市场竞争后终将出现。从市场上来看，目前知识付费的用户群体高度集中在一、二线城市，而三、四线及以下城市的市场尚有较大开发空间，有望成为内容生态者和知识付费平台的下一个机遇。与此同时，富媒体的传播效应在知识付费产品形式上正在凸显。目前的知识付费产品以音频为主，配以文字和图片说明，但今后将向视频拓展，将满足更丰富的消费场景和多元的用户需求。如抖音在2018年就已先行布局知识付费市场，推出视频课程产品。知识付费产品整体互动性偏强，重视交互形式为用户带来的全新体验。用户除了为知识买单，还享受对创作者人设和气场以及对整体视听的综合体验。随着以AI、5G为代表的技术的发展，以及用户消费意愿的常态化，知识付费仍将存在新的发展空间和市场机会。

（六）数字内容产业将构建新的发展格局

近年来，数字内容产业不断发展壮大，成为数字经济的重要组成部分。与此同时，数字内容产业的发展格局也在悄然发生转变。在内容形态方面，音视频业务无疑将成为数字内容产业的发展重心。特别是短视频领域，随着4G高度普及、5G开启商用，短视频有望迎来新一轮的爆发式增长，并将与教育、新闻资讯、知识付费等多个领域实现更深入的融合。在网络直播领域，真人秀场直播的发展前景堪忧，未来网络直播更多的是与游戏、体育等领域的结合。在电商、教育等领域，网络直播的部分职能或逐步被短视频或其他新的可视化形态所取代。可以预见，网络直播将成为一种过渡性或是边缘性的产业形态。因为相对于网络直播而言，短视频虽然在用户参与感上有所欠缺，但无论在信息传播的密集度还是丰富性上都更具优势，表现形式也更加多元化，且在场景方面也不受时间约束，更加符合碎片化的用户体验习惯。同时，伴随5G的商用落地，人们对网络视频的消费需求仍将不断提升，且不再过分依赖Wi-Fi环境，将催生出新的、丰富度更高的可视化数字内容形态和模式。

在产业市场竞争格局方面，互联网龙头企业中，近年来百度在人工智能等技术研发应用上更为专注，成绩也更加突出。在内容上，百度以百家号为重点，以《百度》APP作为其网络文学、资讯、游戏等各类内容流量的总入口，同时也加快布局短视频领域，但明显在各个领域都未能进入第一梯队阵营。在移动互联网时代强者恒强的游戏规则下，只能期待百度在5G场景下在内容产业上有创新性突破。未来，腾讯和阿里巴巴仍将围绕IP在数字内容产业方面加大布局，持续丰盈各自的文娱生态闭环。《抖音》的所属公司字节跳动凭借着在抖音、西瓜视频、火山小视频三家平台在短视频领域的强势布局，以及其旗舰产品《今日头条》在移动资讯领域积累的行业领先优势，正在视频社交、游戏、在线教育等多个领域逐步构建数字内容产品体系，有望跻身与腾讯、阿里巴巴并列的数字内容产业矩阵的第一梯队。同时，在现有的产业细分领域中，马太效应将愈发凸显，第一梯队头部企业的“卡位”已基本完成，第二梯队虽然“排位赛”竞争激烈，但已基本形成了差异化发展格局。因此，留给小型企业和初创企业的空间已较为有限。在5G环境下，挖掘新的需求点，开拓新的消费场景，探索新的内容呈现方式和变现方式，将成为数字内容创业者的发展重点。

（七）跨品类跨场景融合加深，业态复合化趋势渐显

近年来，随着人工智能、大数据、物联网等技术的高速发展，消费升级不断催生新需求，不同领域之间的融合壁垒逐渐被打破，带来的不仅仅是产业链条的重塑，也为数字内容产业开拓了更为广阔的发展空间，业态复合化趋势逐渐明显。

一方面，互联网内容企业将把线下运营放在与线上运营同等重要的位置，加大线下场景的深耕，以实现品牌的全面覆盖和用户数据的多层次、多维度把握。在数据化、智能化的加持下，线下市场需求和场景的价值得到重估和升级。知识付费和在线教育等领域，都呈现从线上拓展至线下的趋势。如喜马拉雅打造了“大脑加油站”；得到开办了以线上学习结合线下讨论为模式的“得到大学”；知乎在线下也推出了“不知道诊所”“好奇冰屋”等体验活动；知名自媒体团队十点读书则于2018年底创办了其第一家线下实体书店，不仅有图书、咖啡、文创产品等书店的常见商品，还包括线下知识付费和文化活动等模式，实现了与其线上业务的链接。另一方面，数字内容企业的品牌跨界能力不断增强，为打造多层次立体化受众体验，跨品类的融合将成为企业品牌建设的重要途径。不仅仅包含网络文学、动漫、游戏、影视剧、短视频这种文化产业内部的跨界融合，而且拓展到跨行业、跨品类、跨场景的融合。如2018年，腾讯音乐娱乐与鲜花网上零售商“花点时间”合作，联合出品主题鲜花，让自身品牌触达注重高品质、精致生活的目标人群，实现了音乐与鲜花两种完全不同品类之间的“混搭”；腾讯音乐还联合梦想加共享办公空间，开展了“乐享Space”系列活动，为上班族打造释放工作压力的休闲娱乐空间。未来，类似这样不同领域、不同品类，连接线上、线下的融合将日益普遍。只要有相似的目标族群，就能找到不同领域、品类的契合点，就为融合创造了可能。通过不同的话题和元素，数字内容与其他不同领域实现品牌衔接，数字内容的呈现场景更加丰富、立体。

通过线上与线下场景的有机结合，跨行业、跨品类的品牌运营，数字内容企业实现的将不再仅仅是内容和品牌的传播，也是一种企业文化的传播，一种价值观的传递，从而获得受众对品牌更强的认知度和认同感。

（八）电子竞技将成为产业融合新节点

电子竞技业是近两年互联网发展最快的领域之一。中国电竞战队iG在全球电竞赛事中获得总冠军，不仅让更多国人了解和关注电子竞技这一领域，也让其得到了世界瞩目。电子竞技游戏作为游戏的重要分支之一，已经成为我国游戏行业新的收入增长点。据数据显示，2018年中国电子竞技游戏市场实际销售收入达834.4亿元，占到中国游戏市场整体收入比例的38.9%。电子竞技属于复合型业态，一方面与游戏行业密不可分——游戏收入是我国电子竞技收入的主要构成；另一方面，电子竞技也作为一项竞技项目被纳入正式体育项目。

电子竞技正在成为资本流向的新入口。腾讯、阿里等互联网龙头企业纷纷加大对电竞行业的布局，将其纳入大文娱生态。如2019年初，腾讯互娱和拳头游戏宣布共同成立“腾竞体育”，专注发力电子竞技领域；电子竞技也为体育直播带来新的发展机遇，虎牙和斗鱼等体育直播平台纷纷入局。北京、上海等多地都在积极推进电竞行业发展，电竞特色小镇、电竞产业园区、电竞馆在全国各地涌现，各种电竞赛事纷纷设立。我国电竞产业生态正在逐步构建，由上游游戏厂商为核心的内容版权方、电竞赛事和职业联盟为核心的衍生内容制作方以及下游赛事直播平台等环节构建的电竞产业链条已基本形成。一方面，电子竞技开拓了中国游戏行业发展的新空间，成为我国游戏行业发展的重要方向之一；另一方面也成为游戏、体育、媒体、娱乐等领域跨界融合的新节点。虽然目前电子竞技产业的收入很大程度上仍然依赖于游戏带来的收入，但随着产业的加速成熟，我国电竞行业的商业模式将日益多元，同时也将会出现更多专为电竞赛事打造的竞技类游戏。

5G时代的到来，VR、AR以及MR等技术在电竞业的加速应用，将进一步丰富移动电竞的内容与体验。同时，电竞将成为IP产业生态中的重要一环，带动其他文化领域的消费。以电竞为主题，配合赛事，与影视、网络综艺、动漫、文创产品、主题公园等线上、线下多元文化形态融合，将成为电竞产业发展的重要方向。电竞的受众边界也将随之不断扩大，触达非游戏玩家群体。如 2019 年腾讯视频联合王者荣耀推出职业电竞真人秀节目《终极高手》，实现了英雄联盟和王者荣耀两大 IP 在综艺节目领域的强强联合。

2018 年中国广播电视产业发展报告

国家广播电视总局广播影视发展研究中心

2018 年，全国广播电视内容创作持续繁荣，全国广播节目制作时间 801.76 万小时，比 2017 年（788.83 万小时）增加 12.93 万小时，同比增长 1.64%。全国公共电视节目播出时间 1 925.03 万小时，比 2017 年（1 881.02 万小时）增加 44.01 万小时，同比增长 2.34%。2018 年全国公共广播节目播出时间 1 526.74 万小时，比 2017 年（1 491.89 万小时）增加 34.85 万小时，同比增长 2.34%。

一、广播电视节目自主创新深入破题，原创优秀节目大量涌现

2018 年，总局大力倡导“小成本、大情怀、正能量”的自主创新方向，大力扶持公益、文化、原创节目，进一步完善政策引导、创作指导、扶持激励、宣传推广有机衔接的工作机制，推动形成广播电视节目创新创优热潮。各广播电视机构坚持以人民为中心的工作导向，紧密结合主题主线和时代热点，积极创新节目表现形式和表达方式，突出价值引领、效果引导，努力与时代同频共振。广播电视节目新风扑面，在多个领域取得了突破性进展，一批具有中国风格、中国气派的自主原创节目成为国内外关注的热点亮点。一是理论类节目热度持续提升，展示马克思主义创新理论思想的力量；二是文化类节目深耕传统文化，彰显文化自信；三是公益类节目回应群众关切，紧随时代前行；四是善用新媒体新技术，融合制播打开创新创优新局面。

二、国产纪录片记录时代发展，国内外影响力与日俱增

2018 年全国制作纪录片 7.59 万小时，比 2017 年小幅增长。电视纪录片播出时间 44.67 万小时，比 2017 年（35.10 万小时）增加 9.57 万小时，同比增长 27.26%。纪录片国内投资额 23.77 亿元，比 2017 年（17.42 亿元）增长 36.45%；纪录片国内销售额 11.62 亿元，比 2017 年（12.59 亿元）下降 7.70%。一是展示 40 年来改革发展成就，现实题材精品迭出；二是文化科技类纪录片内涵丰富，为受众开启智慧之窗；三是 4K 技术广泛应用，先进技术助力纪录片创新发展；四是播出渠道拓展优化，新媒体带来发展新空间；五是大力开展国际合作，外宣纪录片亮点突出。

三、国产电视动画片创作持续繁荣，产业转型升级稳步推进

2018 年，国产电视动画片进一步深化内涵、提升品质，涌现出一大批聚焦中国梦、社会主义核心价值观、中华优秀传统文化的优秀作品，为广大未成年人提供了丰富多样、健康向上的收视选择。与此同时，动画生产制作 IP 化趋势明显，产业衍生价值开发能力显著增强，国产动画在从规模数量增长为主转变为质量效益提升为主的产业升级之路上稳步前进。一是产量稳定，题材多样；二是优秀作品大量涌现，亮点突出异彩纷呈；三是技术手段丰富多样，融合传播成为潮流；四是 IP 化品牌运营日趋成熟，全产业链模式不断完善；五是国际交流合作深入推进，国际视野更加开阔。

2018 年，国产电视动画片创作紧紧围绕时代热点，更加注重文化价值挖掘和艺术表达。全年经总局备案公示的国产电视动画片共计 460 部、约 19.43 万分钟，比 2017 年备案数量增加 110 部；获得国产电视动画片发行许可证的动画片共计 241 部、约 8.63 万分钟，与 2017 年基本持平。童话、教育、科幻、现实题材成为中国动画片创作的主要题材，其中童话和教育题材动画片备案数量均比 2017 年有较大提升。从备案情况看，童话题材最多，制作备案数量达 227 部、97 601.7 分钟，比 2017 年增加 42 部；教育题材 76 部、32 662.6 分钟，比 2017 年增加 37 部；科幻题材 48 部、21 259 分钟；现实题材 37 部、18 127 分钟；历史题材 28 部、7 691 分钟；神话题材 22 部、11 375 分钟；其他题材 22 部、5 629 分钟（见图 1）。

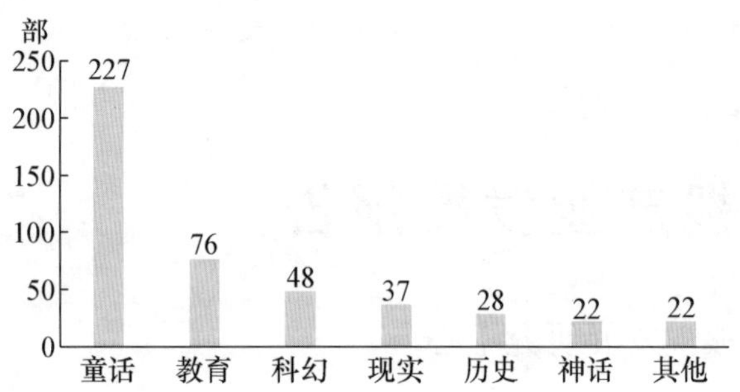

图 1 2018 年总局备案公示的国产电视动画片分类数量

资料来源：总局宣传司。

四、国产电视剧艺术品质明显提升，制作与投入进入调整期和转型期

2018 年，电视剧管理部门持续加强政策扶持、市场规范和评论推介，进一步营造良好的发展环境。电视剧创作保持活跃，艺术品质得到明显提升，现实题材主导地位得到巩固，国产电视剧稳步向精品化、规范化、专业化方向转变。电视剧市场进一步回归理性，电视剧制作与投入进入调整期和转型期。经过近年来政策的引导和推动，越来越多的一线制作机构参与到了现实题材创作中，提升品质成为行业共识。从播出上看，电视剧依然是视听媒体最看重的核心竞争资源，电视剧产业仍是文化领域最具活力的中坚产业。

一是电视剧创作热情依然高涨。2018 年，通过备案公示的剧目共 1 178 部、46 290 集，分别占申报总数的 71.31％和 71.93％，与 2017 年相比增加 3 部。其中，当代题材共 710 部、26 426 集，分别占公示剧目总数的 60.27％和 57.09％；现代题材共 63 部、2 312 集，分别占总数的 5.35％和 4.99％。现实题材仍是创作热点。

二是电视剧产量依然保持稳定。在近年来整体发展趋势保持平稳的前提下，2018 年电视剧发行数量首次有所回升，全年制作完成并获得发行许可的电视剧共 323 部、13 726 集，较 2017 年增加 9 部、256 集，电视剧的平均集数则延续上一年的趋势有所下降（见表 1）。获准发行的剧目中，现实题材共 204 部、8 270 集，分别占总发行部数、集数的 63.16％、60.25％，其数量和占比较 2017 年均有所增加，现实题材主流地位进一步巩固（见表 2）。

表 1 2011—2018 年获得发行许可的电视剧数量

年份	2011 年	2012 年	2013 年	2014 年	2015 年	2016 年	2017 年	2018 年
部数	469	506	441	429	394	334	314	323
集数	14 942	17 703	15 770	15 983	16 540	14 912	13 470	13 726
平均集数	32	35	36	37	42	45	43	42

资料来源：总局电视剧司。

注：平均集数＝集数/部数。

表 2 2018 年获得发行许可的电视剧题材比例

题材	当代题材	现代题材	近代题材	古代题材	重大题材	合计
部数	186	18	69	47	3	323
占比	57.59％	5.57％	21.36％	14.55％	0.93％	100％
集数	7 531	739	3 082	2 264	110	13 726
占比	54.87％	5.38％	22.45％	16.49％	0.80％	100％

资料来源：总局电视剧司。

三是浙京沪发行集中度依旧较高。2018 年，电视剧发行数量超过 10 部的地区共 7 个。其中，浙江、北京、上海发行电视剧数量为 154 部、6 861 集，占发行总量 47.68％和 49.99％，电视剧区域发行格局趋于固定（见表 3）。

表 3 部分地区电视剧发行数量

序号	地区	部数	集数
1	浙江	52	2 361
2	北京	51	2 315
3	上海	51	2 185
4	广东	23	954
5	江苏	12	533
6	陕西	10	412
7	湖南	10	406

续表

资料来源：总局电视剧司。

五、广播电视广告经营取得新成效

各级广播电视行政部门坚持广告规范管理与广

告高质量发展并举。各级电台电视台不断强化广告导向要求，进一步规范商业广告播出秩序，大力推进公益广告发展。同时持续加大广告经营创新力度，创收收入和广告收入结构呈现持续调整和不断优化的态势。

广告经营持续创新，收入平稳增长，结构持续向好。2018 年全国广播电视服务业总收入 6 952.14 亿元，比 2017 年（6 070.21 亿元）增加 881.93 亿元，同比增长 14.53%；实际创收收入 5 639.61 亿元，比 2017 年（4 841.76 亿元）增加 797.85 亿元，同比增长 16.48%。全年广告收入 1 864.49 亿元，比 2017 年同期（1 651.24 亿元）增加 213.25 亿元，同比增长 12.91%（见图 2）。以网络等新媒体广告为主的其他广告收入 765.26 亿元。

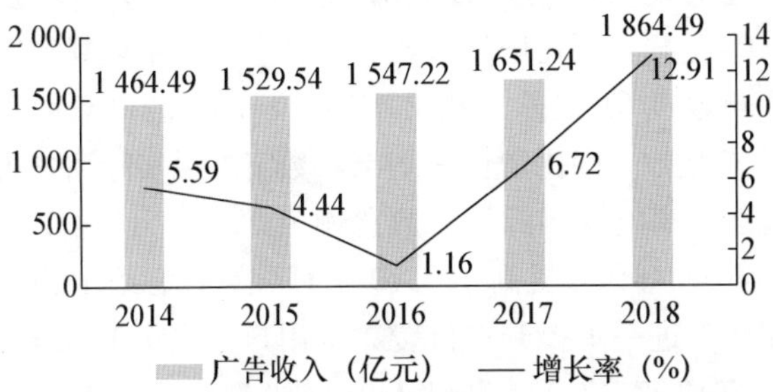

图 2　2014—2018 年全国广播电视行业广告收入情况

资料来源：总局财务司。

广播电视广告收入结构进一步优化。广播电视行业广告收入结构发生明显变化。传统媒体广告收入比重下滑，网络等新媒体广告收入比重增加，收入和占比迅速攀升。传统广播电视广告收入 1 099.23 亿元，比 2017 年（1 123.90 亿元）减少 24.67 亿元，下降 2.2%，这是近年来传统广播电视广告首次出现下滑。其中，广播广告收入 140.37 亿元，比 2017 年（155.56 亿元）减少 15.19 亿元，同比下降 9.76%（见图 3）；电视广告收入 958.86 亿元，比 2017 年（968.34 亿元）减少 9.48 亿元，同比下降 0.98%（见图 4）；网络媒体广告收入 491.88 亿元，比 2017 年（306.71 亿元）增加 185.17 亿元，同比增长 60.37%，占广告收入总额的比例从 2017 年的 18.57%提高到 26.38%，成为新的收入增长点。

广播电视行业广告收入居前 10 位的省份收入总额相对稳定，新疆维吾尔自治区广播电视行业广告

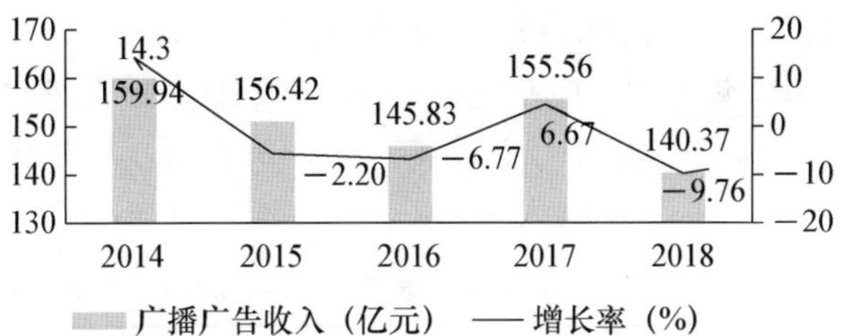

图 3　2014—2018 年全国广播广告收入情况

资料来源：总局财务司。

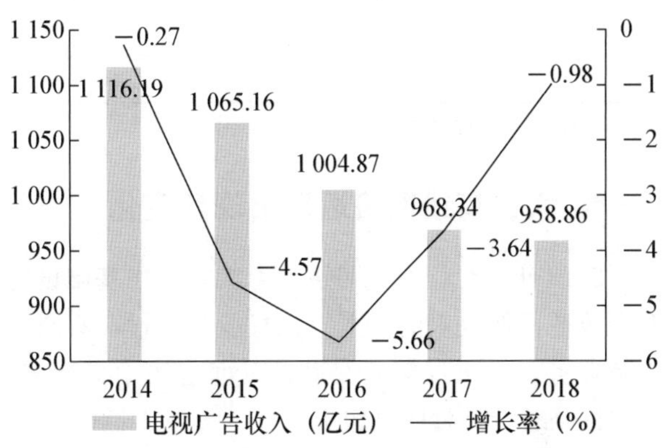

图 4　2014—2018 年全国电视广告收入情况

资料来源：总局财务司。

收入 22.18 亿元，超过四川省和贵州省跻身第 9 位。北京市、湖南省、广东省广播电视行业广告收入增长明显。北京市广播电视行业广告收入 568.62 亿元，比 2017 年同期（383.99 亿元）增加 184.63 亿元；特别是网络媒体广告收入达 314.60 亿元，居全国之首，同比（169.64 亿元）增加 144.96 亿元，增幅高达 85.45%。湖南省广播电视行业广告收入 140.36 亿元，比 2017 年同期（113.53 亿元）增长 23.63%；特别是电视广告收入 103.38 亿元，成为全国电视广告收入最高的省份，同比（89.89 亿元）增长 15.01%；网络媒体广告收入 25.54 亿元，同比（13.75 亿元）增长 85.75%。广东省广播电视行业广告收入 113.93 亿元，其中网络媒体广告收入 38.73 亿元，同比（6.80 亿元）增长 469.56%。广播电视行业广告收入居前 10 位的省份广告收入总和为 1 302.58 亿元，占全国广播电视行业广告收入的 69.86%，比 2018 年同期（67.40%）略有提升（见表 4）。

表 4　2018 年广播电视行业广告收入居前 10 名的省份及收入情况　　单位：亿元

省份	北京	湖南	上海	浙江	广东	江苏	山东	安徽	新疆	四川
收入	568.62	140.36	139.07	124.58	113.93	92.9	48.63	30.22	22.18	22.09

资料来源：总局财务司。

从广播电视广告收入分布情况来看，中央级广播电视行业广告收入 337.10 亿元（2017 年 297.74

亿元），占比 18.08%；省级收入 1 255.51 亿元（2017 年 1 099.10 亿元），占比 67.34%；地市级收入 197.86 亿元（2017 年 186.42 亿元），占比 10.61%；县级收入 74.02 亿元（2017 年 67.98 亿元），占比 3.97%（见表 5）。其中，中央级收入同比增幅达 13.22%，省级同比增幅达 14.23%。特别是省级广播电视机构立足本土，服务当地，不断创新开展多元化经营成效显现。

表 5　2014—2018 年广播电视行业广告收入分级占比情况（%）

地区	2013 年	2014 年	2015 年	2016 年	2017 年	2018 年
中央直属	24.26	21.78	19.08	18.92	18.03	18.08
省级	58.84	58.51	64.16	65.72	66.56	67.34
地市级	17.02	16.01	13.43	12.42	11.29	10.61
县级	3.88	3.70	3.33	2.94	4.12	3.97

资料来源：总局财务司。

六、有线网络运营出现新变化

2018 年，全国有线网络大力实施网络基础设施升级改造，加快双向化宽带化智能化建设，不断开拓新业务，寻求经营新突破。贯彻落实中央部署，有线网络整合进程明显加快。

2018 年全国有线广播电视覆盖用户数达 3.46 亿户，比 2017 年（3.36 亿户）增加 0.10 亿户。其中，数字电视覆盖用户数 3.23 亿户，双向电视覆盖用户数 2.08 亿户，比 2017 年（3.04 亿户和 1.86 亿户）分别增长 6.25%和 11.83%。2018 年全国有线广播电视实际用户数 2.18 亿户，比 2017 年增加 0.04 亿户，同比增长 1.87%。其中，数字电视实际用户数 2.01 亿户，比 2017 年（1.94 亿户）增加 0.07 亿户，同比增长 3.61%；数字电视实际用户占有线广播电视实际用户数比例为 92.27%，比 2017 年（90.48%）提高了 1.79 个百分点，有线电视数字化率进一步提升；付费数字用户 7 729.94 万户，比 2017 年（7 013.78 万户）增加 716.16 万户，增幅高达 10.21%（见图 5）。

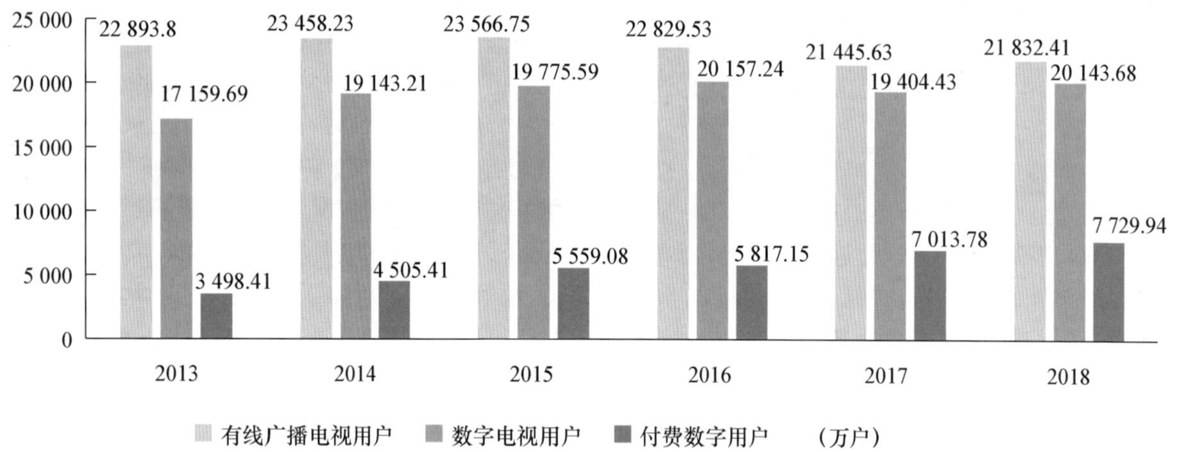

图 5　2013—2018 年全国有线广播电视用户、数字电视用户、付费数字用户情况

资料来源：总局财务司。

虽然近年有线广播电视用户持续负增长或增量较少，数字电视缴费用户流失，宽带用户增速放缓，但是有线电视网络高清化、智能化发展态势良好。2018 年全国高清有线电视用户 9 257 万户，比 2017 年（7 371 万户）增加 1 886 万户，同比增长 25.59%；有线电视智能终端用户 1 884 万户，比 2017 年（701 万户）增加 1 183 万户，同比增长 168.76%，智能终端普及提速；4K 终端用户达到 1 264.2 万户，用户加速增长。智能电视用户、4K 电视用户增长动力不减。

七、网络视听由高速发展转向高质量发展

2018 年，中国网络视听行业在用户规模、内容创作、产业发展、技术应用等方面继续保持较快发展，从量的增长转向质的提升，由高速发展转向高质量发展。

市场集中度进一步提升。截至 2018 年底，获准开办互联网视听节目服务的机构基本保持不变。

BAT所属的爱奇艺、优酷、腾讯视频在用户流量、原创内容上线数量和播放量、商业模式等方面优势明显，进一步与其他平台拉开差距。这三大平台用户占整体视频用户的九成，播放量占整体播放量的八成。与此同时，短视频、直播、音频、知识付费等网络视听新业态表现突出，特别是短视频发展迅猛，成为新媒体和移动互联网的制高点。

产业加速迈向成熟。2018年，网络视听行业市场规模达2 016.8亿元，同比增长39.1%，其中在线视频市场规模达1 249.5亿元，同比增长31.2%；短视频市场规模达到118亿元，同比增长106%，泛娱乐直播市场规模达649.2亿元，同比增长47.3%。网络视听营收模式正大幅由广告等后向收入转为付费等前向收入，付费收入逐年增长，发展质量提升。2018年全网共上线超3 134部网络视听节目，其中会员付费内容超过1 853部，占总内容的近60%，付费观看已成通行收看模式。2018年，爱奇艺会员服务收入已超过广告收入，达到106亿元，同比增长72%。

付费用户大幅增长。截至2018年12月，中国网络视频用户规模达6.12亿，同比增加3 309万，增幅为5.7%，占网民整体的73.9%，用户规模增幅放缓；视频观看移动化趋势更加明显，手机网络视频用户规模达5.9亿，同比增加4 101万，占手机网民的72.2%；网络短视频用户规模达6.48亿，用户使用率为78.2%；网络直播用户规模达3.97亿，同比减少2 533万，用户使用率为47.9%。2018年，中国在线视频付费会员规模超2.3亿，近三年复合增长率达119%，远高于中国网民规模近三年6.28%的复合增长率；网络视频付费用户比例达53%，同比增长23.8%。2018年，腾讯视频会员规模达8 900万人，同比增长58%；爱奇艺会员规模达8 740万人，同比增长72%。

2018 年中国电影产业发展报告

中国文联电影艺术中心

2018 年，国内外形势发生深刻复杂变化，电影产业面临着外部环境的重重挑战。从国内环境来看，国内经济由高速增长阶段转向高质量发展阶段，供给侧结构性改革深入推进，产业发展形势愈发复杂，金融风险加剧，中美经贸摩擦也引起国内经济环境一系列变化。从国际范围来看，世界经济复苏乏力，国际战略机遇不甚明朗，以大数据、云计算、人工智能、数字制造、工业机器人等为特征的新一轮科技革命和产业革命给各行各业带来颠覆性冲击。在转变发展方式、优化经济结构、转换增长动力的发展关键期、矛盾凸显期，社会思想意识更加纷繁复杂，使电影产业的发展危机与机遇并存。

2018 年，电影自改革开放以来在党的新闻宣传舆论阵地中的作用得到空前重视与强化。党中央加强对电影工作的领导，电影管理机构再次进行改革，电影行业积极适应我国发展新的历史方位。

2018 年，电影产业取得了来之不易的成绩。在以习近平同志为核心的党中央坚强领导下，经过十几年电影产业化改革的蓄力，在市场规模上，完成 600 亿元票房突破，全国总票房为 609.76 亿元，同比增长 9.06%。全国共生产故事电影 902 部，国产电影票房 378.97 亿元，占比 62.15%，较 2017 年略有提高。全年票房过亿影片 82 部，其中国产电影 44 部，国产过亿影片占总过亿影片的 53.66%。影院数量、银幕数量、观影人次等继续保持增长，其中全年观影人次达 17.16 亿，同比增长 5.93%。

2018 年，电影行业聚焦高质量发展。行业生产水平不断提高，努力推动产品结构优化升级。立足“高原”攀“高峰”，回归电影艺术规律，从艺术本体进行创新突破，精品佳作不断涌现，创作活力大大增强，作品品质明显提升，涌现了一大批杰作。2018 年，电影行业也经历着自身改革进入深水区的种种阵痛。多年高速发展的积弊，在脆弱的大众舆论环境和严谨的政策环境中暴露出来。代表性明星“人设崩塌”、天价片酬、“阴阳合同”和影视公司大规模撤离霍尔果斯等背后，是多年积累的行业投机乱象、浮躁之风，这已成为阻碍行业高质量发展的病灶。经由多部门联手治理，市场规范得以进一步加强，行业强化自律，行风进一步清朗。在产业结构上，产业链各环节淘汰冗余产能，挤去投机的游资泡沫，行业阵容变动急遽，电影生产制作发行放映机构经历大规模调整。

也要看到，与 2017 年相比，电影业所处的宏观环境运行稳中有变、变中有忧，股市不断下挫，消费降级有虞。影视股不断探底，大部分影视公司市值大幅缩水，市场流动性进一步紧缩，电影总票房和观影人次等的增速继续下降，影院上座率、单银幕票房产出都有明显下降。电影“走出去”方面仍待开拓，电影作为文化名片的作用仍待进一步发挥。

站在改革开放 40 周年的节点，回望中国电影发展进程，电影管理部门不断推动产业结构优化，电影产业化改革一路披荆斩棘，电影人一路风雨同舟，才迎来建成世界第二电影大国的成就，实现了电影在国际视域中从“追跑”向“并跑”再到“领跑”的转变。中国电影的发展，任重道远。

一、2018 年电影产业发展情况与发展环境

2018 年，中国电影迎来时隔 32 年的再一次机构改革，将更好地发挥在宣传思想和文化娱乐方面的特殊重要作用，提升发展质量，改善发展环境。

（一）机构改革，电影发展更受党中央重视

2018 年 2 月 28 日，党的十九届三中全会决定调整完善电影管理体制，由中央宣传部统一管理电影工作。这是加强党对电影工作全面领导的战略安排，是以习近平同志为核心的党中央对电影工作的高度重视和亲切关怀，有利于发展和繁荣电影事业。

3 月，中共中央印发《深化党和国家机构改革方案》。其中第十二条规定：“中央宣传部统一管理电影工作。为更好发挥电影在宣传思想和文化娱乐方面的特殊重要作用，发展和繁荣电影事业，将国家新闻出版广电总局的电影管理职责划入中央宣传部。中央宣传部对外加挂国家电影局牌子。”

4月16日，新组建的国家广播电视总局、国家新闻出版署（国家版权局）、国家电影局分别挂牌，原国家新闻出版广电总局一分为三。国家电影局搬至北京市宣武门原国家新闻出版总署旧址办公。原国家新闻出版广电总局下属的电影频道、中国电影股份有限公司、中国电影集团公司、中国电影科学技术研究所等事业单位和企业，也划转中央宣传部管理。

5月24日，国务院任命中央宣传部常务副部长王晓晖兼任国家电影局局长。

9月以来，全国各省（自治区、直辖市）原新闻出版广电局（厅）的机构改革陆续推进到位，省级行政管理部门的电影职能划转到省委宣传部。

电影管理职责的划转，标志着党管电影的手段更加有力，电影产业和电影事业发展的目标更加明确，更加有利于发挥电影在宣传思想方面的重要作用和作为文化产业排头兵的表率作用。

机构改革后，中央宣传部关于电影管理的主要职责有五方面：(1) 管理电影行政事务；(2) 指导监管电影制片、发行和放映工作；(3) 组织对电影内容进行审查；(4) 指导协调全国性重大电影活动；(5) 承担对外合作制片、输入输出影片的国际交流等。

机构改革以后，关于电影方面的文件，由中央宣传部或国家电影局发布。

此外，根据军队改革方案中关于军队非作战体系的改革要求，撤销军队各级专业文工团、体工队、出版社、电影制片厂和解放军艺术学院等文体机构。八一电影制片厂和总政歌舞团等组成解放军文化艺术中心，八一电影制片厂改革后更名为解放军文化艺术中心电影电视制作部，由副军编制降为正师编制，除部领导和机关保留少量军人外，其他全是军内文职人员。

（二）电影从高增长发展向高质量发展转变

经过改革开放40年的洗礼，尤其是自2003年正式启动的电影产业化改革，电影产业取得了较为明显的成就。经过一个时期的迅猛发展，有近20家影视制作企业上市，社会投资活跃，成为电影繁荣发展的重要力量。当前，中国电影产业已经站在了新的发展起点，最鲜明的特征就是走向高质量发展，这是适应经济发展新常态的必然选择，也是适应大国产业升级和社会进步的必然选择。新时代对电影行业提出了新要求，增强了推动电影产业高质量发展的使命感。受经济下行压力影响，电影行业发展模式需要继续深入转变。

从行业增速看，电影行业补偿式的高增长时代已基本结束，电影产业走向成熟，传统的铺摊子等策略已经很难奏效，市场发展进入平稳发展阶段。

从市场结构看，电影产业是文化产业中市场竞争较为充分的门类，高成本盲目扩张不仅无法带来竞争优势，甚至可能带来沉重的负担。

从价格水平看，尽管制作发行费用和影院建设成本不断上升，但在长期的市场化改革中，电影平均票价波动一直较为平稳、增幅不大，促使电影成为最为普遍而大众化的文化消费之一。

从服务水平来看，传统电影企业优化升级，对接国际标准，现代化服务水平不断提高。影视企业与文化创意、数字内容、主题娱乐融合发展，各类影视技术和作品成果IP应用于开发游戏、音像、书籍、休闲旅游、演艺等衍生产品，产业品牌价值、衍生价值提高。尤其是2018年电影创作生产质量的明显提高，是15年市场化改革的果实。

从竞争环境看，电影行业面临着越来越多跨界、跨领域的非传统竞争对手的挑战。由于电影是文化、科技与商业相结合的行业，技术飞速进步不断带来颠覆式的竞争模式和竞争对手，如近几年在制作领域出现的各种新技术新应用，在产品领域出现的网络大电影，在放映领域出现的点播院线与点播影院，都在倒逼电影行业传统发展模式的更新迭代。

（三）电影产业发展的政治经济社会科技环境

2018年，中国电影产业发展的宏观背景主要涉及如下方面：

宪法修订，全面深化改革取得突破。中国共产党第十九届中央委员会第二次全体会议于2018年1月18日至19日在北京举行，审议通过了《中共中央关于修改宪法部分内容的建议》。2018年3月11日，第十三届全国人大一次会议第三次全体会议经投票表决通过了《中华人民共和国宪法修正案》。《宪法修正案》中写进了习近平新时代中国特色社会主义思想。法治体系日益完善，全社会法治观念明显增强。经济增长下行带来发展压力和消费降级之虞。总的来看，我国经济已由高速增长阶段转向高质量发展阶段，正处在转变发展方式、优化经济结构、转换增长动力的攻关期，供给侧结构性改革深入推进、经济下行压力增大。中国经济由高速增长转向高质量发展，贯彻新发展理念。根据国家统计局2019年1月21日公布的数据，2018年GDP总量首次超过90万亿元，比上年增长6.6%，实现预期发展目标。按平均汇率折算，经济总量达到13.6万亿美元，稳居世界第二位。总的来看，2018 年国民经济继续运行在合理区间，实现了总体平稳。全国人均可支配收入实际增长 6.5%，略快于人均 GDP 6.1%的增速。其中，农村居民收入增长快于城镇居民增长。我国中等收入群体人口已经超过 4 亿人。2018 年全国居民人均消费支出实际增长 6.2%，增速比上年加快 0.8 个百分点，农村居民人均消费支出实际增长 8.4%，快于城镇居民。与此同时，消费结构继续升级，服务消费持续提升。2018 年全国居民恩格尔系数 28.4%，比上年下降 0.9 个百分点，达到了发达国家水平。

几年来涌入影视行业的热钱有所减退，有助于行业自身的健康发展。几年来，影视行业经历资本乱局，并购潮、重组案此起彼伏。2018 年 1 月，万达电影宣布重组方案不包括美国传奇影业，乐视网停止对乐视影业的重组，宣告了行业逐渐进入冷静期，逐渐聚焦产品本体。

中国城镇化率还有很大提升空间，客观上为电影产业继续储备观影人群。2018 年末中国总人口（不含港澳台）139 538 万人。从城乡结构看，城镇常住人口 83 137 万人，城镇化率达 59.58%，比上年末提高 1.06 个百分点。中国的城镇化进程逐渐进入相对成熟阶段，常住人口城镇化率提高幅度有所降低，不过仍然保持在较高的水平，我国仍处于城镇化率 30%～70%的快速发展区间。以城市群为主体，大中城市和小城镇协调发展的城镇格局，有利于延展电影人口红利。在振兴乡村经济的趋势下，小城镇居民享受电影文化服务的品质有望继续提升，电影市场的下沉还有不少空间。

新一轮技术革命带来电影产业链格局深刻变化。虚拟现实、云计算、大数据、人工智能、物联网、区块链等技术快速发展，短视频、微博、微信、客户端日益成为传播主渠道，5G 业务等一些新业务新应用不断出现。

两岸经济文化交流合作扩大。2018 年 2 月 28 日，国务院台湾事务办公室、国家发展和改革委员会发布《关于印发〈关于促进两岸经济文化交流合作的若干措施〉的通知》，明确提出“台湾人士参与大陆广播电视节目和电影、电视剧制作可不受数量限制。大陆电影发行机构、广播电视台、视听网站和有线电视网引进台湾生产的电影、电视剧不做数量限制。放宽两岸合拍电影、电视剧在主创人员比例、大陆元素、投资比例等方面的限制；取消收取两岸电影合拍立项申报费用；缩短两岸电视剧合拍立项阶段故事梗概的审批时限”等，有利于两岸经济文化共同发展。

二、把牢正确政治方向，强化价值引领：电影在宣传思想方面的重要作用全面加强

党的十九大以来，电影管理深入贯彻党的十九大精神，努力开创新时代中国电影新局面，进一步发挥优秀主旋律影片在思想引领和教育人民方面的重要作用。尤其是机构改革以来，电影内容管理进一步加强，坚持团结稳定鼓劲、正面宣传为主的宣传舆论指导方针与工作原则进一步贯彻，电影自觉承担起举旗帜、聚民心、育新人、兴文化、展形象的使命任务，在振奋民族精神、增强文化自信，夯实全国人民共同团结奋斗的思想基础，推进中国特色社会主义事业，提供强大精神力量方面，不断发挥重要作用。

（一）党对电影创作的要求进一步提高

与电影产业化改革以来的往年相比，2018 年，党中央对电影工作更加关心，对电影人的工作提出更严格的要求。

6 月 26 日，习近平写信勉励新近入党的电影表演艺术家牛犇，继续在从艺做人上做表率，带动更多文艺工作者做有信仰有情怀有担当的人。

4 月 13 日，中共中央政治局委员、中宣部部长黄坤明在北京主持召开电影创作调研座谈会，强调要深入学习贯彻习近平新时代中国特色社会主义思想特别是习近平有关文艺工作的重要讲话精神，聚焦坚持和发展中国特色社会主义、实现中华民族伟大复兴的中国梦这个时代主题，用当代中国的影像和故事表现崇高价值、美好情感，用时代发展的光影和色彩呈现恢宏画卷、万千气象，推动我国从电影大国向电影强国迈进。

4 月 16 日，黄坤明出席国家广播电视总局、国家新闻出版署（国家版权局）和国家电影局揭牌仪式并召开座谈会时，强调要坚持以习近平新时代中国特色社会主义思想为指导，切实把思想和行动统一到党中央决策部署上来，用机构改革的新成效，激发宣传思想文化工作的新能量新作为。尤其要求电影切实贯彻党的全面领导，推动中国电影走进新时代，迈上新台阶，开创新局面。

12 月 28 日，中国电影家协会第十次全国代表大会在北京召开。黄坤明出席开幕式并讲话，要求电影人“用镜头银幕礼赞伟大时代，用真心真情谱写光影华章，团结一心向着电影强国目标奋力迈进”。

（二）突出主题主线，加大主旋律电影放映力度

组织主旋律电影展映活动。国家电影局成立后，文件由中央宣传部办公厅代为发布。2018 年，国家电影局共发布四个文件（见表 1），其中的 1 号文件和 3 号文件分别于暑期档和岁末档期间发布，分别要求加大《李保国》和《黄大年》等主旋律影片的展映展播，旨在加强电影在弘扬主旋律、传播正能量方面的重要作用。这些政策紧扣改革开放 40 年纪念活动，加强重大主题宣传、重大活动宣传和重大典型宣传，体现了机构改革之后，电影在坚持正确政治方向、坚定文化自信方面的变化。

建设好主旋律电影展映空间。机构改革前的 2018 年 1 月 30 日，国家新闻出版广电总局电影局下发《关于申报人民院线影厅的通知》（影字[2018] 27 号），要求全国选出 5 000 个座位数不低于 100 座的影厅，组建"人民院线"，"专厅专用"，采取组织观看、优惠票价、政策资金扶持或奖励方式保证主旋律影片的放映阵地。在此基础上，国家电影局 4 号文件专门强调了加快发展"人民院线"，为国产优秀主旋律影片提供更大放映空间的精神。

强调弘扬传承优秀电影文化。2018 年 11 月，国家电影局下发关于《国产电影复映暂行规定》的 2 号文件，下发单位除各省（区、市）电影主管部门外，亦发至中央和国家机关有关部委、有关人民团体宣传部门和中央军委政治工作部宣传局，目的是"为进一步弘扬和传承优秀电影文化"等。

表 1　2018 年国家电影局发布文件一览

发文时间	文号	文件名	主要内容
6 月 27 日	国影发［2018］1 号	《国家电影局关于认真组织观看电影〈信仰者〉〈李保国〉的通知》	为庆祝中国共产党成立 97 周年，要求精心做好《信仰者》和《李保国》这两部电影的发行放映工作，认真组织广大党员干部观看这两部电影，并积极配合影片的发行放映做好推介。
11 月 8 日	国影发［2018］2 号	《国家电影局关于印发〈国产电影复映暂行规定〉的通知》	依据《中华人民共和国电影产业促进法》和相关法规，制定本规定规范和完善电影复映管理。要求首次公映结束超过两年的国产电影复映，需要严格保护各版权相关方合法权益，需按属地管理原则报属地电影主管部门重审，并将重审意见和放映安排报国家电影局。中央和国家机关有关部委、有关人民团队、军队所属电影单位为第一出品单位的影片直接报国家电影局重审。复映影片全部放映范围不超过 2 500 个影厅，每家影院放映单部复映影片的影厅不超过 1 个。
11 月 26 日	国影发［2018］3 号	《国家电影局关于开展庆祝改革开放 40 周年影片展映展播活动的通知》	为庆祝改革开放 40 周年，自 12 月 1 日起全国城市院线、全国各电影频道、全国农村、城市社区、校园开展"庆祝改革开放 40 周年优秀国产影片展映"活动，并部署相关安排。
12 月 11 日	国影发［2018］4 号	《国家电影局印发〈关于加快电影院建设促进电影市场繁荣发展的意见〉的通知》	为深入贯彻落实党的十九大精神，深化电影供给侧结构性改革，健全现代电影产业体系和市场体系，加强电影院建设的统筹规划和分类指导，加大政策支持力度，有效激发社会资本投资积极性，构建覆盖全面、分布合理、设施先进、惠及城乡的电影院建设发展格局，形成统一开放、管理科学、竞争有序、充满活力的电影市场，要求到 2020 年，全国加入城市电影院线的电影院银幕总数达到 8 万块以上；县级城市影院数量稳步增长，有条件的地区加入城市院线的乡镇电影院数量快速增长；深化院线制改革等。

（三）强化价值引领，严肃创作导向

2018 年，行业主管部门在内容管理上主要着力于如下两个方面：

加强电影内容不规范问题治理。3 月 16 日，原国家新闻出版广电总局办公厅出台《关于进一步规范网络视听节目传播秩序的通知》（新广电办发[2018] 21 号），坚决禁止非法抓取、剪拼改编视听节目的行为；加强网上片花、预告片等视听节目管理；加强对各类节目接受冠名、赞助的管理；严格落实属地管理责任。

加强电影在维护社会公共利益方面的管理。4 月 27 日，《中华人民共和国英雄烈士保护法》出台，7 月 5 日，国家广播电视总局下发《关于学习宣传贯彻〈中华人民共和国英雄烈士保护法〉的意见》。《中华人民共和国英雄烈士保护法》第十八条要求："文化、新闻出版、广播电视、电影、网信等部门应当鼓励和

支持以英雄烈士事迹为题材、弘扬英雄烈士精神的优秀文学艺术作品、广播电视节目以及出版物的创作生产和宣传推广。”第二十二条要求：“禁止歪曲、丑化、亵渎、否定英雄烈士事迹和精神。英雄烈士的姓名、肖像、名誉、荣誉受法律保护。任何组织和个人不得在公共场所、互联网或者利用广播电视、电影、出版物等，以侮辱、诽谤或者其他方式侵害英雄烈士的姓名、肖像、名誉、荣誉。任何组织和个人不得将英雄烈士的姓名、肖像用于或者变相用于商标、商业广告，损害英雄烈士的名誉、荣誉。公安、文化、新闻出版、广播电视、电影、网信、市场监督管理、负责英雄烈士保护工作的部门发现前款规定行为的，应当依法及时处理。”

（四）空前重视电影在青少年教育中的重要作用

2018 年 12 月，教育部和中央宣传部联合出台《关于加强中小学影视教育的指导意见》，显示了政府和党中央对影视教育的空前重视。这一意见的出台，具有如下方面的重要意义：

一是落实相关政策文件精神，深化影视教育工作。十八大以来，党中央和国务院对青少年影视教育工作空前重视。根据 2015 年 1 月中共中央办公厅、国务院办公厅下发的《关于加快构建现代公共文化服务体系的意见》，2016 年 12 月出台的《公共文化服务保障法》和 2017 年 3 月 1 日起施行的《中华人民共和国电影产业促进法》等相关法律和政策文件精神，国家鼓励和支持包括电影在内的公共文化服务与学校教育相结合，充分发挥其社会教育功能，提高青少年思想道德和科学文化素质，并明确要求相关部门开展向中小学生推荐优秀影片等工作，将为中小学生每学期提供两部爱国主义教育影片纳入公共文化基本服务项目。

二是有助于进一步发挥优秀影视作品在弘扬主旋律、传递正能量，尤其是培养青少年良好的思想道德素质和科学文化素质方面的独特作用。“青年的价值取向决定了未来整个社会的价值取向”，电影在帮助青少年确立正确价值观方面有重要作用。

三是有助于丰富学校育人方法，加强青少年美育教育。多个文化大国都很重视中小学影视教育。近年来，《国务院办公厅关于全面加强和改进学校美育工作的意见》《教育部关于加强和改进普通高中学生综合素质评价的意见》《中小学德育工作指南》等政策文件，对各地各校开展好影视教育提出了明确要求。2015 年、2017 年教育部与国家新闻出版广电总局先后举办了两届“全国中小学生电影周”活动。加强影视教育，对提高学生人文底蕴和综合素质，培养学生审美观念作用明显。

三、规范治理沉疴，促进行风清朗：2018 年中国电影市场发展相关政策分析

2018 年，针对影视产业发展过程中多年来积累的天价片酬、“阴阳合同”、偷逃税等乱象，中央层面有针对性地出台了严格措施进行治理。此外，也陆续出台了一些鼓励措施，推动电影市场继续扩大规模。

（一）重拳治理影视行业沉疴，遏制浮躁之风

电影产业积弊已久的浮躁之风，给行业发展带来了明显风险。针对影视行业天价片酬、“阴阳合同”、偷逃税等问题，党和政府强化治理手段，控制不合理片酬，推进依法纳税，促进影视业健康发展。经过整治，天价片酬问题得到遏制，影视行业税收秩序进一步规范，依法纳税者的合法权益得到保障，营造和维护了公平竞争的税收环境，有利于提升影视行业在薪酬、资本、核算等财务方面的管理水平，促进行业健康发展。

1. 政府强力规范，遏制影视行业天价片酬

影视行业片酬过高的问题已存在多年，早在 2012 年对此类问题的报道就曾见诸报端，近年这一现象更是愈演愈烈，演变成为影视明星天价片酬问题。这一现象助长了浮躁之风、降低了作品品质、败坏了行风行规，明星浮华奢侈的不良生活作风也对社会风尚造成了恶劣影响，成为人民群众意见较大、行业发展不堪重负的严重问题。

2018 年，党和政府规范引导、行业加强自律、各方协同综合治理，遏制明星片酬过高、影视制作浮躁之风取得明显效果。

一是政府强力规范引导，严格落实限制片酬比例为“70%”和“40%”。2017 年，中国广播电影电视社会组织联合会电视制片委员会等行业协会曾联合发布《关于电视剧网络剧制作成本配置比例的意见》（以下简称《意见》），其中提道：“各会员单位及影视制作机构要把演员片酬比例限定在合理的制作成本范围内，全部演员的总片酬不超过制作总成本的 40%，其中，主要演员不超过总片酬的 70%，其他演员不低于总片酬的 30%。”2018 年 6 月，中央宣传部、文化和旅游部、国家税务总局、国家广播电视总局、国家电影局联合印发《通知》治理影视行业天价片酬、“阴阳合同”、偷逃税等问题，由官方正式将这一《意见》的要求以“通知”的形式推及电影、电视剧、网络视听节目。五部委

《通知》强调，要制定出台影视节目片酬执行标准，明确演员和节目嘉宾最高片酬限额，现阶段严格落实已有规定，每部电影、电视剧、网络视听节目全部演员、嘉宾的总片酬不得超过制作总成本的40%，主要演员片酬不得超过总片酬的70%。影视行业主管部门要加强监管，对影视明星参与综艺娱乐节目、亲子类节目、真人秀节目等进行调控，严格执行网络视听节目审批制度，严格规范影视剧、网络视听节目片酬合同管理，加大对偷逃税行为的惩戒力度。电视台、影视制作机构、电影院线、互联网视听网站、民营影视发行放映公司，不得恶性竞争、哄抬价格购买播出影视节目，坚决纠正高价邀请明星、竞逐明星的不良现象。政府资金、免税的公益基金等不得参与投资娱乐性、商业性强的影视剧和网络视听节目、助长过高片酬。五部委《通知》要求，坚持把社会效益放在首位，坚决反对唯票房、唯收视率、唯点击率。要加强影视行业征信体系建设，强化行业协会组织管理能力，健全经纪公司、经纪人管理机制，加强对从业人员的教育监督。各级各类媒体要加强宣传引导和舆论监督，强化对娱乐新闻报道的总量控制，为影视业健康发展营造良好舆论氛围。

二是行业加强自律。五部委《通知》发布后，8月，中国电影导演协会发表《团结一致，自律自强，维护影视行业健康发展》声明，强调“支持从政府到民间显示出的对于影视产业的关心和维护产业发展的积极态度”，也指出“行业内某些问题的原因是多方面的”，比天价片酬、“偷税漏税”更重要的问题是“市场公平”，对于影视业内的薪酬和制作经费等问题应交由市场调节、政府监督，强调在法律的基础之上，政策指导、市场调节、行业自律并行，方可保障影视业正常发展。同时，首都广播电视节目制作业协会发表《关于加强行业自律　遏制行业不正之风的倡议》，横店影视产业协会发表《关于“加强行业自律、规范行业秩序、促进影视精品创作”的倡议》，倡议加强行业自律，规范行业秩序，营造良好的影视文化创作氛围。

三是各方协同综合治理。五部委《通知》发布后，8月，爱奇艺、优酷、腾讯视频、正午阳光、华策影视、柠萌影业、慈文传媒、耀客传媒、新丽传媒三家视频网站和六家影视制作公司发布《关于抑制不合理片酬，抵制行业不正之风的联合声明》，强调共同抵制艺人天价片酬现象，倡导成本用于制作、投入服务品质、演员戏比天大的行业风气。

2. 重点规范影视行业税收秩序

6月下发的五部委《通知》还有另一重要政策，主要针对“阴阳合同”和治理税收秩序问题。根据这一方针，10月2日，国家税务总局下发通知，部署开展规范影视行业税收秩序工作。从2018年10月10日起，各地税务机关通知本地区影视制作公司、经纪公司、演艺公司、明星工作室等影视行业企业和高收入影视从业人员，根据税收征管法及其实施细则相关规定，对2016年以来的申报纳税情况进行自查自纠。对自查自纠并到主管税务机关补缴税款的影视企业及相关从业人员，免予行政处罚，不予罚款。2019年1月至2月底，税务机关根据纳税人自查自纠等情况，有针对性地督促提醒相关纳税人进一步自我纠正。对经提醒自我纠正的纳税人，可依法从轻、减轻行政处罚；对违法情节轻微的，可免予行政处罚。2019年3月至6月底，税务机关结合自查自纠、督促纠正等情况，对个别拒不纠正的影视行业企业及从业人员开展重点检查，并依法严肃处理。2019年7月底前，对在规范影视行业税收秩序工作中发现的突出问题，要举一反三，建立健全规范影视行业税收管理长效机制。在规范影视行业税收秩序工作中，对发现税务机关和税务人员违法违纪问题，以及出现大范围偷逃税行为且未依法履职的，要依规依纪严肃查处。

影视行业税收秩序失范问题，是当前影视产业发展过程中必须正视和解决的矛盾，它已明显侵害影视产业肌体的健康，更是人民群众较为关注的问题。现行国家税收法律和地方优惠政策之间、既有政策和执行方式之间，存在着的局部的、具体的矛盾，理应通过明确统一的法律依据，公开、公平、公正的程序手段推动解决。

（二）着力加快影院院线建设，要求提升影院服务水平

2018年12月11日，国家电影局印发《关于加快电影院建设　促进电影市场繁荣发展的意见》的4号文件（以下简称国家电影局4号文）。其中将电影院的作用空前提高，专门提道：“只有加快建设电影院，大幅度提高银幕数量，才能适应新时代新要求，增强人们的文化获得感、幸福感，才能促进电影市场持续繁荣，为实现电影强国提供坚实支撑，才能落实城乡统筹发展要求，让中国电影发展成果更多惠及广大人民群众。”

关于今后一段时间内的影院院线建设，重点需要关注的内容如下：

1. 加快银幕建设，旨在让人民共享电影发展

成果

一是加快银幕建设速度。到2020年，全国加入城市电影院线的电影院银幕总数达到8万块以上。

二是要求大中城市电影院建设提质升级。除延续《电影产业促进法》等此前相关政策的原则性要求外，将鼓励政策落到实处，给予安装先进技术设备的影院每家不超过50万元的资助。

三是继续加快中西部地区县级城市影院建设。国家电影局4号文目标任务包括有条件的地区加入城市院线的乡镇电影院数量快速增长。通过国家电影事业发展专项资金资助中西部地区（含国务院规定全面比照享受西部开发政策的地区）县城（县级市）新建（改扩建）影院。

2. 加快院线制改革，提升行业集中度

国家电影局4号文鼓励发展电影院线公司，鼓励院线并购重组，并推行年检制度，完善奖惩机制和退出机制。按照这一政策，国内目前院线数量有望缩减，有助于提升院线核心竞争力、进一步规范院线市场，加快骨干院线的示范作用，也引导前几年雨后春笋般遍地开花的影投公司进行市场整合。此外，国家电影局4号文鼓励人民院线、艺术电影放映联盟和校园院线等特色院线发展。此举除有利于加大主旋律电影放映力度外，也有望助力多样化放映市场的成长成熟，有效应对市场分层和观众个性需求的电影消费趋势。

（三）规范播映秩序，加强市场规范

2018年，面对网络传播的多样快速发展，行业主管部门日趋重视，按照“同一标准、同一尺度”加强网上网下管理治理。

1. 将点播影院、点播院线纳入治理范围

点播影院和点播院线于2012年在市场上萌芽，并于2014年蔚然成风。基于点播影院和点播院线发展的成熟情况，国家新闻出版广电总局曾于2017年4月发布《关于规范点播影院、点播院线经营管理工作的通知》（新广电发［2017］81号），又于同年6月公布《点播影院、点播院线管理暂行规定（征求意见稿）》。在此基础上，2018年3月6日，《点播影院、点播院线管理规定》（国家新闻出版广电总局令第14号）正式出台，并于2018年3月30日起施行。机构改革后，前述国家电影局4号文也特别强调了规范发展点播影院和点播院线，要制定完善相关技术标准和业务规则，推动点播影院和点播院线规范发展，积极拓展电影放映创新业务。

《点播影院、点播院线管理规定》进一步体现了“放管服”精神，在推动简政放权、放管结合、优化服务改革方面进行了探索。例如，在业务许可（第二章第六条）、经营规范（第三章第十条）、监督管理（第四章第二十六条）等方面的相关规定，有利于促使市场在资源配置中进一步发挥作用、更好地发挥政府作用，降低制度性交易成本，优化营商环境，激发市场活力。

《点播影院、点播院线管理规定》在加强市场监管、建立全国点播影院经营管理信息系统和影片著作权授权信息公示查询系统、依法获得放映许可、防范偷漏瞒报票房等不规范现象、保证放映质量等方面，做出了相应规定，其中对著作权的保护尤为突出。这一规定体现了加强电影市场管理规范的宗旨，有利于进一步拓展电影市场、增加电影渠道供给、延长电影盈利周期、促进电影产业链各环节协调发展。

2. 推动简政放权和职能划转

机构改革后，国家广播电视总局继续推动电影方面的简政放权和职能划转，10月下发《关于取消部分规章和规范性文件设定的证明事项材料的决定》，对引进境外影视剧相关工作去繁就简。

3. 细化市场规范，加强行业自律

行业管理部门细化市场规范。2018年11月，国家电影局发布2号文，在肯定了旧片复映对丰富电影市场产品供给的意义外，也强调要规范和完善电影复映管理，复映复审、属地审查、结果报备、规模控制。

行业加强自律。2018年9月，中国电影发行放映协会下发《关于电影票“退改签”规定的通知》；10月，电影资金办下发《关于开展“云播控”试点实验项目的通知》，与2017年底行业主管部门提出的2018年“市场规范加强年”方针相呼应，通知规定有明显延续性，有利于行业沿着正轨发展。

此外，行业主管部门还发布了一些政策。在版权方面，2018年2月，国家新闻出版广电总局改革办公室发布《关于印发〈新闻出版广播影视企业版权资产管理工作指引（试行）〉的通知》，旨在推动落实版权资产管理工作。因国家版权局也划入中宣部，电影相关版权资产管理的工作如何展开，仍待进一步明确。

（四）财税政策继续支持行业发展

1. 规范专资管理

2018年6月16日，财政部发布《财政部关于调整国家电影事业发展专项资金使用范围的通知》和《财政部关于调整中央级国家电影事业发展专项资金使用范围和分配方式的通知》，明确中央电影专资使用范围、中央补助地方电影专资分配方式，及关于《深化党和国家机构改革方案》机构调整后省级财政部门会同电影主管部门的中央补助地方电影专资预算编制下达工作相关事宜，并将资助国产电影宣传推广和购买农村电影公益性放映版权纳入国家电影事业发展专项资金使用范围。

2. 推动财政政策支持

2018 年 10 月由财政部办公厅、中共中央宣传部办公厅和商务部办公厅联合发布的《关于申报 2019 年度文化产业发展专项资金（重大项目方面）的通知》以及 9 月由国家电影专项资金管委会办公室发布的《2018 年中央级专项资金资助国产电影发行（推广）工作申报指南》，都体现了中央财政在两个方面的着力：一是“文化自信”——以直接补助重点项目方式推动影视产业发展；二是“讲好中国故事”“文化走出去”——以事后奖励方式推动国产电影的海外推广。

2018 年 12 月 18 日，国务院办公厅发布《关于印发文化体制改革中经营性文化事业单位转制为企业和进一步支持文化企业发展两个规定的通知》，旨在进一步深化文化体制改革，继续推进国有经营性文化事业单位转企改制，多角度促进文化企业发展。

3. 推动税收政策支持

2018 年 12 月 18 日，国务院办公厅发布《关于印发文化体制改革中经营性文化事业单位转制为企业和进一步支持文化企业发展两个规定的通知》，执行期限为 2019 年 1 月 1 日至 2023 年 12 月 31 日。其中，在《进一步支持文化企业发展的规定》第一条第二款中特别提到，延续部分电影相关税收优惠，即对电影制片企业销售电影拷贝（含数字拷贝）、转让版权取得的收入，电影发行企业取得的电影发行收入，电影放映企业在农村的电影放映收入免征增值税。一般纳税人提供的城市电影放映服务，可以按现行政策规定，选择按照简易计税办法计算缴纳增值税。

上述政策是相关政策的到期延续。根据《财政部　海关总署　国家税务总局关于继续实施支持文化企业发展若干税收政策的通知》（财税［2014］85 号）、《财政部　国家发展改革委　国土资源部　住房和城乡建设部　中国人民银行　国家税务总局　新闻出版广电总局关于支持电影发展若干经济政策的通知》（财教［2014］56 号），2014 年 1 月 1 日至 2018 年 12 月 31 日，新闻出版广电行政主管部门（包括中央、省、地市及县级）按照各自职能权限批准从事电影制片、发行、放映的电影集团公司（含成员企业）、电影制片厂及其他电影企业取得的销售电影拷贝（含数字拷贝）收入、转让电影版权（包括转让和许可使用）收入、电影发行收入以及在农村取得的电影放映收入免征增值税。

（五）扩大和引导电影文化消费

2018 年 9 月 20 日，中共中央、国务院出台《关于完善促进消费体制机制　进一步激发居民消费潜力的若干意见》，强调完善现代文化市场体系和现代文化产业体系，构建更加成熟的消费细分市场，壮大消费新增长点，促进实物消费不断提档升级，推进服务消费持续提质扩容，推动农村居民消费梯次升级，逐步缩小城乡居民消费差距。鼓励和引导农村居民增加交通通信、文化娱乐、汽车等消费。

（六）电影科技环境与科技相关政策分析

2018 年，电影迎来更深层的科技进步，也获得更好的科技发展契机。电影的高质量科技供给，有助于构建电影产业体系新支柱。尤其是近年来，虚拟现实（含增强现实、混合现实，即 VR）融合应用了多媒体、传感器、新型显示、互联网和人工智能等多领域技术，能够拓展人类感知能力，改变产品形态和服务模式，给经济、科技、文化、军事、生活等领域带来深刻影响。全球虚拟现实产业正从起步培育期向快速发展期迈进，我国面临同步参与国际技术产业创新的难得机遇。虚拟现实在电影领域应用广泛且前景看好。2018 年 5 月 28 日，习近平在中国科学院第十九次院士大会、中国工程院第十四次院士大会上发表讲话，强调要充分认识创新是第一动力，提供高质量科技供给，着力支撑现代化经济体系建设。此外，在外交活动中，习近平也多次强调科技创新的重要性。

2018 年 12 月，工业和信息化部发布《关于加快推进虚拟现实产业发展的指导意见》，强调对虚拟现实发展的重视。针对当前虚拟现实存在关键技术和高端产品供给不足、内容与服务较为匮乏、创新支撑体系不健全、应用生态不完善等问题，该文件给出了一系列解决方案。提倡“VR＋文化”，即在文化等领域，丰富融合虚拟现实体验的内容供应，推动现有数字内容向虚拟现实内容的移植，满足人民群众文化消费升级需求。发展虚拟现实影视作品和直播内容。打造虚拟电影院等，提供多感官体验模式，提升用户体验。该文件的出台，有利于加快我国虚拟现实产业发展，推动虚拟现实应用创新，培育信息产业新增长点和新动能，更有利于电影科技的进一步发展。

2018 年出台的电影市场发展政策见表 2。

表 2　2018 年出台的电影市场发展政策一览

发文时间	文号	发文单位	文件名	主要内容
2 月 13 日		国家新闻出版广电总局改革办公室	《关于印发〈新闻出版广播影视企业版权资产管理工作指引（试行）〉的通知》	强调高度重视版权资产管理工作，积极推动落实版权资产管理工作，提出总结先进经验予以表扬及推广。
2 月 28 日		国务院台湾事务办公室、国家发展和改革委员会	《关于印发〈关于促进两岸经济文化交流合作的若干措施〉的通知》	台湾人士参与大陆广播电视节目和电影、电视剧制作可不受数量限制。大陆电影发行机构、广播电视台、视听网站和有线电视网引进台湾生产的电影、电视剧不做数量限制。放宽两岸合拍电影、电视剧在主创人员比例、大陆元素、投资比例等方面的限制；取消收取两岸电影合拍立项申报费用；缩短两岸电视剧合拍立项阶段故事梗概的审批时限。
3 月 1 日	新广电办发［2018］14 号	国家新闻出版广电总局办公厅	《关于印发〈国家新闻出版广电总局改革发展项目库项目评价指引（试行）〉的通知》	强调高度重视项目评价管理工作，积极推动开展项目评价管理工作，并总结推广先进经验。
3 月 6 日	国家新闻出版广电总局令第 14 号	国家新闻出版广电总局	《点播影院、点播院线管理规定》	明确规定点播影院、点播院线的相关业务许可、经营规范、监督管理及法律责任。
3 月 16 日	新广电办发［2018］21 号	国家新闻出版广电总局办公厅	《关于进一步规范网络视听节目传播秩序的通知》	坚决禁止非法抓取、剪拼改编视听节目的行为；加强网上片花、预告片等视听节目管理；加强对各类节目接受冠名、赞助的管理；严格落实属地管理责任。
4 月 27 日		全国人民代表大会常务委员会	《中华人民共和国英雄烈士保护法》	要求电影发挥传承和弘扬英雄烈士精神、爱国主义精神，培育和践行社会主义核心价值观，激发实现中华民族伟大复兴中国梦的强大精神力量方面的作用。鼓励和支持以英雄烈士事迹为题材、弘扬英雄烈士精神的优秀作品创作。禁止歪曲、丑化、亵渎、否定英雄烈士事迹和精神。
6 月 14 日	财文［2018］48 号	中华人民共和国财政部	《关于下达 2018 年补助地方国家电影事业发展专项资金预算的通知》	下达 2018 年补助地方国家电影事业发展专项资金 74 142 万元，支持电影事业发展。
6 月 16 日	财税［2018］67 号	中华人民共和国财政部	《财政部关于调整国家电影事业发展专项资金使用范围的通知》	将资助国产电影宣传推广和购买农村电影公益性放映版权纳入国家电影事业发展专项资金使用范围。
6 月 16 日	财文［2018］46 号	中华人民共和国财政部	《财政部关于调整中央级国家电影事业发展专项资金使用范围和分配方式的通知》	明确中央电影专资使用范围、中央补助地方电影专资分配方式，及关于《深化党和国家机构改革方案》机构调整后省级财政部门会同电影主管部门的中央补助地方电影专资预算编制下达工作相关事宜。
6 月 27 日		中央宣传部、文化和旅游部、国家税务总局、国家广播电视总局、国家电影局	《关于治理影视行业天价片酬“阴阳合同”偷逃税等问题的通知》	要求加强对影视行业天价片酬、“阴阳合同”、偷逃税等问题的治理，控制不合理片酬，推进依法纳税，促进影视业健康发展。

续表

发文时间	文号	发文单位	文件名	主要内容
7月5日	广电发［2018］23号	国家广播电视总局	《关于印发〈国家广播电视总局关于学习宣传贯彻《中华人民共和国英雄烈士保护法》的意见〉的通知》	
9月18日	影协字［2018］10号	中国电影发行放映协会	《关于电影票“退改签”规定的通知》	强调有关各方对所制定的“退改签”规定，均要优化流程、简化手续，充分体现公平合理、亲民便民的原则，履行对观众的告知义务，便于观众查阅和社会监督。
9月20日		中共中央、国务院	《关于完善促进消费体制　进一步激发居民消费潜力的若干意见》	鼓励和引导农村居民增加交通通信、文化娱乐、汽车等消费。
9月29日		国家电影专项资金管委会办公室	《2018年中央级专项资金资助国产电影发行（推广）工作申报指南》	对国产电影海外推广和发行具有文化特色、艺术创新的国产电影的工作给予资助。
10月12日	财办文［2018］56号	财政部办公厅、中共中央宣传部办公厅、商务部办公厅	《关于申报2019年度文化产业发展专项资金（重大项目方面）的通知》	一是推动影视产业发展（中央宣传部牵头负责），采取对重点影视项目直接补助方式，重点支持用于增强文化自信、保障国家文化安全的重大革命历史题材，反映改革开放和中国特色社会主义伟大实践取得重大成就和宏伟业绩题材的重点影视剧。 二是推动对外文化贸易发展（商务部牵头负责），采取对文化服务出口后奖励方式，鼓励和支持我国文化企业参与国际竞争，扩大文化服务出口，推动中华文化“走出去”。对列入《2017—2018年度国家文化出口重点企业目录》且在2018年1月1日至8月31日具有较好文化服务出口业绩的企业，根据其期间内文化服务出口额按比例予以奖励。
10月31日	国家广播电视总局令第2号	国家广播电视总局	《国家广播电视总局关于取消部分规章和规范性文件设定的证明事项材料的决定》	对现行有效的广播电视规章和规范性文件设定的证明事项材料进行了全面清理。 1. 取消《广电总局关于进一步加强和改进境外影视剧引进和播出管理的通知》（广发［2012］9号）第一条第二项以及第二条第二项规定的立项通过的境外影视剧或申报续约后再次引进的境外影视剧，应向总局报审并按规定提交的“供片机构资质证明”，此证明事项材料原为广播电视节目制作经营许可证复印件，现改由总局和省局通过内部政务系统数据信息共享核查替代。 2. 取消《国家新闻出版广电总局办公厅关于印发〈专门用于信息网络的境外影视剧引进计划申报办法〉等文件的通知》（新广电办发［2014］142号）中的《专门用于信息网络的境外影视剧内容审核实施办法》第三条第六项规定的“其他相关证明材料”。

续表

发文时间	文号	发文单位	文件名	主要内容
10月31日	广电发［2018］60号	国家广播电视总局	《国家广播电视总局关于进一步加强广播电视和网络视听文艺节目管理的通知》	为确保广播电视和网络视听文艺节目健康有序发展，需牢牢把握正确的政治方向，强化价值引领；坚持以人民为中心的创作导向，坚决遏制追星炒星、泛娱乐化等不良倾向；鼓励以优质内容取胜，不断创新节目形式，严格控制嘉宾片酬；加大电视剧网络剧（含网络电影）治理力度，促进行业良性发展；坚持同一标准、同一尺度，维护广播电视与网络视听节目的健康有序发展；加强收视率（点击率）调查数据使用管理，坚决打击收视率（点击率）造假行为；落实意识形态工作责任制，强化主管主办责任和属地管理责任。
10月		国家电影专项资金管委会办公室	《关于开展"云播控"试点实验项目的通知》	"云播控"系统可通过技术手段将售票系统、检票系统、放映系统、监播系统进行有效串联，将影院管理整体上移至"云端"，对放映场次和观影人次数据实施有效监控，强化对电影市场的监管。
12月18日	国办发［2018］124号	国务院办公厅	《国务院办公厅关于印发文化体制改革中经营性文化事业单位转制为企业和进一步支持文化企业发展两个规定的通知》	进一步深化文化体制改革，继续推进国有经营性文化事业单位转企改制，促进文化企业发展，延续增值税优惠政策。
12月21日	工信部电子［2018］276号	工业和信息化部	《关于加快推进虚拟现实产业发展的指导意见》	提出到2020年我国虚拟现实产业链条基本健全，到2025年我国虚拟现实产业整体实力进入全球前列，并提出6大重点任务，包括突破关键核心技术、丰富产品有效供给、推进重点行业应用、建设公共服务平台、构建标准规范体系和增强安全保障能力。
12月21日	教基［2018］24号	教育部、中共中央宣传部	《关于加强中小学影视教育的指导意见》	为深入学习贯彻习近平新时代中国特色社会主义思想和党的十九大精神，落实全国教育大会精神，充分发挥优秀影片在促进中小学生德智体美劳全面发展中的重要作用，要加强中小学影视教育。

四、2018年世界电影产业发展情况及中国的定位

（一）中国在全球电影产业发展中的定位

2018年，全球电影票房411亿美元。其中北美票房最高，全年总票房118.88亿美元[①]，超过全球电影总票房的四分之一。中国全年总票房合90亿美元，与北美相差约30亿美元，相比2017年的22.23亿美元，票房差距有所扩大。中国仍是全球票房增长最快的国家，增幅为9.06%。

亚洲地区，日本全年电影票房2 225.11亿日元，同比下降了2.65%。韩国电影票房2018年同比增长了8.10%，全年票房18 140亿韩元，增幅较为明显。2018年部分主要电影国家/地区的票房收入情况见表3。

① http://www.boxofficemojo.com.

表 3　2018 年部分主要电影国家/地区的票房收入情况

排序	国家/地区	票房（亿美元）	票房（本土货币）	票房同比增幅
1	北美	118.88	118.88 亿美元	7.40%
2	中国	90	609.76 亿元人民币	9.06%
3	日本	20.07	2 225.11 亿日元	−2.65%*
4	英国	17	13.28 亿英镑	−20.24%
5	韩国	16.15	18 140 亿韩元	8.10%
6	德国	10	8.99 亿欧元	−14.87%

资料来源：http：//www.boxofficemojo.com.
注：为避免汇率波动引起统计数值偏差，本表中“票房同比增幅”除中国、韩国和日本外暂时依据美元数据计算所得。
＊为依据本土票房计算所得。

2018 年，中国电影银幕数新增 9 303 块，银幕总数达到 60 079 块，同比增长 18.32%，幕均覆盖人口 2.31 万人。相较于 2017 年的 2.72 万人，幕均覆盖人口在逐渐减少。影院数量 11 031 家，同比增长 16.06%。3D 银幕数 53 470 块，同比增长 22.11%。从全球范围来看，美国的幕均覆盖人数仍是最少的，而日本幕均覆盖人数最多。中国的幕均覆盖人数接近美国幕均覆盖人数的三倍，银幕建设仍有一定空间。2018 年部分主要电影国家的银幕建设情况见表 4。

表 4　2018 年部分主要电影国家的银幕建设情况

排序	国别	银幕数（块）	幕均覆盖人口（万人）
1	中国	60 079	2.31
2	美国	40 837①	0.80
3	英国	4 264②	1.55
4	日本	3 561	3.56
5	德国	4 803	1.72
6	韩国	2 937	1.75

注：①数据来源：NATO，统计截至 2018 年 7 月，http://www.natoonline.org/data/us-movie-screens/。
②数据来源：statista，https://www.statista.com/statistics/297393/number-of-cinema-screens-in-the-uk/.

2018 年，中国电影观影人次 17.16 亿，同比增长 5.93%。相当于年人均观影 1.23 次，同比增长 5.13%。中国总观影人次于 2017 年超过美国，在全球范围内名列前茅。年均人观影次数与美国和韩国相比仍有较大差距，但与世界其他电影大国如日本、德国相比已不相伯仲。韩国观众观影习惯最为成熟，年均人观影次数最高，为 4.24 次。2018 年部分主要电影国家/地区的观影人次情况见表 5。

表 5　2018 年部分主要电影国家/地区的观影人次情况

排序	国家/地区	总人次数（亿人次）	总人口（亿人）	年均人观影次数（次）
1	中国	17.16	13.90	1.23
2	北美	13.05	4.30	3.03
3	日本	1.69	1.27	1.33
4	韩国	2.16	0.51	4.24
5	德国	0.84①	0.83	1.01

资料来源：国家统计局、美国人口调查局、世界银行、德国联邦统计局。
注：①数据来源：INSIDEKIN。

2018 年，中国电影平均票价 35.53 元人民币（约合 5.16 美元）。与其他国家相比处于中等偏低的水平。北美电影平均票价有小幅增长，日本、德国和韩国平均票价相对平稳。2018 年部分主要电影国家/地区的平均票价情况见表 6。

表 6　2018 年部分主要电影国家/地区的平均票价情况

排序	国家/地区	平均票价（美元）
1	中国	5.16
2	北美	9.11
3	日本	11.86
4	韩国	7.46
5	德国	10.39

（二）中国与全球电影产业的交流

近年来，中国电影不断加强对外交流，主要通过合拍片、电影节展等形式进行合作交流。

2018 年，中国继续加强“一带一路”沿线国家的电影合作。6 月，上海国际电影节设立全新板块“‘一带一路’电影周”。9 月，中国电影博物馆主办的首届“‘一带一路’国际电影交流活动”在俄罗斯莫斯科举办。10 月，中国电影家协会在白俄罗斯首都明斯克市举办“中国电影展”，与波兰莎士比亚剧院在格但斯克举办“中国电影周”等系列电影交流活动。

2018 年，中国继续积极推动金砖国家电影合作与交流。7 月，第三届金砖国家电影节在南非德班举办，并举办了“中国日”活动。继 2017 年的首部金砖电影《时间去哪儿了》之后，由金砖国家电影工作者合作制作的新版金砖电影《半边天》在“中国日”亮相。

2018 年，中国加强中非合作，携手打造文化共兴的中非命运共同体。7 月，华夏电影公司与南非铂丝沃德影业和南非国家电影基金会就合拍、发行放映、影院投建事宜签署了协议。

中国电影家协会持续组织举办规模化国际影展交流活动。10 月，在佛山举办的中国金鸡百花电影节上，来自法、英、俄、波等 21 个国家和地区的 40 余部影片进行了展映，111 位国际电影界人士应邀出席并进行了多方位合作交流。

（三）2018 年其他国家/地区电影产业发展基本情况

1. 北美电影产业：稳中有升

2018 年，北美电影迎来市场回暖，总票房为 118.88 亿美元，同比增长 7.4%，稳居世界第一。观影人次达到 13.05 亿，同比增长 5.4%。2018 年北美电影市场的基本情况见表 7。

北美电影市场回暖原因：一是 2018 年银幕上映影片更多样化；二是上映数量多，北美共有 868 部电影上映，达到有史以来最高，相比 2017 年的 724 部有明显增长；三是平均票价提高，达到 9.11 美元，已是历史新高。

尽管北美电影市场在 2018 年有所增长，但在资本市场看来，影院在以奈飞、亚马逊等为代表的流媒体平台的冲击下，仍旧很难扭转颓势。AMC、Cinemark、IMAX 等上市院线运营商的股价表现均不太理想。

表 7　2018 年北美电影市场的基本情况

分类	2018 年	2017 年	同比增长
票房（亿美元）	118.88	110.65	7.40%
人次（万人次）	13 005	12 336	5.40%
平均票价（美元）	9.11	8.97	1.89%
影片公映数（部）	868	724	19.89%

资料来源：http：//www.boxofficemojo.com.

2018 年，迪士尼出品的《黑豹》成为美国电影票房冠军影片。迪士尼出品的“复仇者联盟”系列第三部《复仇者联盟 3：无限战争》和皮克斯出品的《超人总动员 2》分列年度票房亚军和季军，三部影片的票房之和超 19 亿美元，占据年度总票房的六分之一，迪士尼成为年度最大赢家。迪士尼和华纳的票房争战，实际上也演变成了漫威和 DC 的票房之争。迪士尼收购了漫威，华纳长期合作 DC，两大漫画公司从漫画书市场打到了电影市场。漫威在 2018 年交出了《黑豹》《复仇者联盟 3：无限战争》《蚁人 2：黄蜂女现身》这三部重磅影片，《黑豹》是年度冠军，《复仇者联盟 3：无限战争》也拿到了暑期档的票房冠军。相比之下，DC 的《海王》2.9 亿美元的成绩似乎远不如《黑豹》那么耀眼。纵观 2018 年的北美票房年度前十，大部分是好莱坞盛产的科幻片、动作片等类型片，续集占到了 7 席之多。票房前十名的影片，占总票房的 33%（见表 8）。

表 8　2018 年北美票房前十影片情况

排序	片名	公映时间	票房（万美元）
1	黑豹	2 月 16 日	70 005.9
2	复仇者联盟 3：无限战争	4 月 27 日	67 881.5
3	超人总动员 2	6 月 15 日	60 858.1
4	侏罗纪世界 2：堕落王国	6 月 22 日	41 771.9
5	死侍 2：我爱我家	5 月 18 日	31 849.1
6	海王	12 月 21 日	29 291.5
7	绿毛怪格林奇	11 月 9 日	27 007.5
8	碟中谍 6：全面瓦解	7 月 27 日	22 015.9
9	蚁人 2：黄蜂女现身	7 月 6 日	21 664.8
10	游侠索罗：星球大战外传	5 月 25 日	21 376.7

资料来源：http://www.boxofficemojo.com.

2. 日本电影产业：小幅萎缩

2018年日本电影产业发展维持平稳，相较2017年，总票房和观影人次小幅下滑，票房下滑2.65%，观影人次下滑3.02%。共上映影片1 192部，同比增长了0.42%，其中本土影片613部，进口影片579部，银幕数缓慢增长了36块①（见表9）。

表9　2018年日本电影市场基本情况

分类	2018年	2017年	同比增长
票房（亿日元）	2 225.11	2 285.72	−2.65%
人次（万人次）	16 921	17 448	−3.02%
平均票价（日元）	1 315	1 310	0.38%
影片公映数（部）	1 192	1 187	0.42%
银幕数	3 561	3 525	1.02%

日本本土影片仍然保持过半份额，生产供应仍较为繁荣，共上映613部影片，较2017年有所增长。2018年日本本土电影与进口电影市场份额见表10。

表10　2018年日本本土电影与进口电影市场份额

分类		2018年	2017年	同比增长
票房（亿日元）	本土影片	1 220.29	1 254.83	−2.75%
	进口影片	1 004.82	1 030.89	−2.52%
票房占比	本土影片	54.80%	54.90%	—
	进口影片	45.20%	45.10%	—
公映数（部）	本土影片	613	594	3.20%
	进口影片	579	593	−2.36%

2018年，日本票房前十的热映大片有3部本土电影，7部外国电影。票房冠军是音乐传记片《波西米亚狂想曲》，票房104.6亿日元。本土续集剧场版电影《Code blue——急救直升机》《名侦探柯南之执行者》分列亚军和季军，票房分别为93.0亿日元和91.8亿日元（见表11）。纵观日本电影票房排行榜，整体呈纺锤形分布。缺乏极具票房号召力的大片引领，票房过百亿的仅有一部，而且低于2017年的票房冠军《美女与野兽》124亿日元的票房。值得重视的是，荣获第71届戛纳金棕榈奖的《小偷家族》6月于日本上映时获得45.5亿日元的票房成绩，在日本本土电影排行榜中列第四。低成本影片《摄影机不要停》票房31.2亿日元，在日本本土电影排行榜中位列第七。

表11　2018年日本票房前十影片情况

排序	片名	公映时间	国别	票房（亿日元）
1	波西米亚狂想曲	11月	美国、英国	104.6
2	Code blue——急救直升机	7月	日本	93.0
3	名侦探柯南之执行者	4月	日本	91.8
4	侏罗纪世界2：堕落王国	7月	美国	80.7
5	星球大战：最后的绝地武士	12月	美国	75.1
6	哆啦A梦：大雄的金银岛	3月	日本	53.7
7	最伟大的表演者	2月	美国	52.2
8	寻梦环游记	3月	美国	50.0
9	超人总动员2	8月	美国	49.0
10	碟中谍6：全面瓦解	8月	美国	47.2

① 数据来源：一般社团法人日本映画制作者联盟。

3. 韩国电影产业：持续增长

2018 年，韩国电影产业总票房 18 140 亿韩元，同比增长了 8.10%。共发行影片 1 646 部，较 2017 年的 1 621 部增长了 25 部。本土电影的生产能力保持增长，2018 年发行数量增长了 20.74%，进口电影发行数量减少了 4.26%。从观影人次上看，2018 年的本土电影观影人次小幅下降了 3.29%，总观影人次小幅下降了 1.58%。本土电影的票房仍保持过半份额，略微下降了 1.48 个百分点。2014—2018 年韩国电影市场份额情况见表 12。

表 12　2014—2018 年韩国电影市场份额情况

年度	本土电影			进口电影			总计	
	总发行数（部）	人次（万人次）	市场份额	总发行数（部）	人次（万人次）	市场份额	发行总数（部）	总人次（万人次）
2014	217	10 770	50.10%	878	10 737	49.90%	1 095	21 507
2015	257	11 294	52.00%	946	10 436	48.00%	1 203	21 730
2016	339	11 657	53.70%	1 234	10 045	46.30%	1 573	21 702
2017	376	11 390	51.80%	1 245	10 597	48.20%	1 621	21 987
2018	454	11 015	50.32%	1 192	10 624	49.68%	1 646	21 639

资料来源：2018 年韩国电影产业结算报告书（KOFIC）。

2018 年，《与神同行：因与缘》《与神同行：罪与罚》分列本土电影票房冠军和亚军。其中《与神同行：罪与罚》于 2017 年 12 月上映，2017 年报告期内观影人次 854 万人次，仅次于《出租车司机》，2018 年报告期内观影人次 587 万人次，观影人次总数达到 1 441 万人次。而在 2018 年 8 月上映的续集《与神同行：因与缘》观影人次也达到了 1 227 万人次（见表 13）。两部电影不仅在韩国本土票房成功，还分别在亚洲 10 个国家和地区以及南美 14 个国家上映，成为继《釜山行》之后，又一部正式进军全球电影市场的韩国电影。

表 13　2018 年韩国本土电影票房前十影片情况

排序	片名	公映时间	观影（万人次）
1	与神同行：因与缘	2018 年 8 月	1 227
2	与神同行：罪与罚	2017 年 12 月	587
3	安市城：浴血围城 88 天	2018 年 9 月	544
4	完美的他人	2018 年 10 月	529
5	1987	2017 年 12 月	529
6	毒战	2018 年 5 月	520
7	特工	2018 年 8 月	497
8	暗数杀人	2018 年 10 月	379
9	国家破产之日	2018 年 11 月	375
10	那就是我的世界	2018 年 1 月	324

2018 年韩国电影市场进口电影票房前十的影片大部分由美国引进，票房冠军为《复仇者联盟 3：无限战争》，亚军为《波西米亚狂想曲》（见表 14）。《波西米亚狂想曲》在亚洲地区的日本和韩国都获得了很好的票房成绩。

表 14　2018 年韩国进口电影票房前十影片情况

排序	片名	公映时间	国别	观影（万人次）
1	复仇者联盟 3：无限战争	4 月 25 日	美国	1 121
2	波西米亚狂想曲	10 月 31 日	美国、英国	922
3	碟中谍 6：全面瓦解	7 月 25 日	美国	658
4	侏罗纪世界 2：堕落王国	6 月 6 日	美国、西班牙	566
5	蚁人 2：黄蜂女现身	7 月 4 日	美国	545

续表

排序	片名	公映时间	国别	观影（万人次）
6	黑豹	2月14日	美国	540
7	毒液：致命守护者	10月3日	美国	389
8	死侍2：我爱我家	5月16日	美国	378
9	寻梦环游记	1月11日	美国	351
10	海王	12月29日	美国、澳大利亚	349

五、2019年中国电影业发展对策建议

2019年是中华人民共和国成立70周年的重大节点，电影业不但肩负着进一步发挥在宣传思想和文化娱乐方面特殊重要作用的重担，也面临着科技环境和国际竞争环境赋予的工业化转型这一重大挑战。

电影产业化改革以来的政策实施经验表明，在工业化初期和中期阶段，政策为电影产业发展实现赶超发挥了重要的保驾护航作用。经过多年快速增长，中国电影产业已取得较大积累，已步入工业化后期，迫切需要更快转向高质量发展阶段，迫切需要对现行产业结构政策进行调整。承继2018年行业内外的种种巨大变化，2019年，中国电影业的发展，须在如下四个方面着力。

（一）要尽快理顺各级电影管理体制机制，尤其是加快电影依法发展进程

电影管理职能划转过程中，不可避免地会出现一些衔接不畅现象。这是暂时的、局部的困难。要尽快理顺各级电影管理体制机制，确保全行业稳定生产，稳定销售。要通过宣传，更重要的是通过实际行动，向行业发出鼓舞人心的信号。

电影管理职能的划转，涉及电影相关政策法律规章制定出台的机构要做相应调整。电影管理部门要尽快推动《电影产业促进法》配套细化措施的制定出台，这对行业进一步平稳健康发展将有立竿见影之效。

（二）把握行业发展机遇，切实提升建设质量

国家电影局4号文件发布了一系列鼓励电影市场发展的政策，显示了机构改革以来党中央对电影行业的支持和发展的信心，更显示了让人民共享电影发展成果的决心。关于今后一段时间内的影院院线建设，要对更加激烈严峻的市场竞争有清醒认识，要思考如何引导社会资金有序健康地流向电影院升级改造，切忌盲目上马乡镇影院，要真正促进院线和影投公司市场结构优化。要谨防行业浮躁之风引发一些不利于团结的社会舆论，伤害行业肌体。

（三）要真正改善发展环境，提振行业信心

在电影产业发展告别幼稚期时，行业主管部门要尽可能协调相关部门，做好相关工作，提振行业信心，增强动力投入生产经营。

一是帮助行业建立清晰完善的税收规则，扶持起企业的投资意愿与创新动力。

二是要改善法制环境，坚持依法行政。

三是要根据电影行业发展的真实情况，进一步激发市场活力，营造宽松、公平的营商环境，推进产业组织结构调整，着力做优市场主体。

（四）要警惕经济增长下行带来发展压力

2019年开年第三周，国务院总理李克强三次召开会议谈经济形势。2019年，宏观经济下行压力加大，有可能出现较为宽松的货币政策和更加积极的财政政策，中国经济内部的负债率将日益高企。未来几年，中国经济增长可能面临持续的下行压力。这一环境将导致电影行业发展缺乏前几年的良好环境，多方面信心不足将影响电影市场预期。对此必须高度重视，做好应对困难挑战的充分准备。但也要看到，影视板块估值渐入底部，未来，行业格局的重整将有利于行业本身的健康发展。

2019年是中华人民共和国成立70周年，是决胜全面建成小康社会关键之年。影视业关系宣传思想工作和文化产业两方面，是中国的文化名片。对电影业来讲，既要充分认识到行业发生了重大的历史变化，行业发展将会震荡前行；也应该看到，行业面临的是局部的、暂时的困难与调整。不应目光短浅，盲目悲观。要从宏观大局的高度，从文化自信和民族崛起的高度，从人类命运共同体的高度，转变视角，紧扣我国社会主要矛盾的变化，登高望远、勇于创新、开拓进取，容许市场、相信市场，相信产业的自我纠错能力。全行业要在行业主管部门全力指导下，像前几年一样继续勠力同心，增强推动电影产业高质量发展的紧迫感和使命感，携手投身和见证中国电影的蜕变。

2018 年中国动漫产业发展报告

牛兴侦

2018 年是全面贯彻党的十九大精神的开局之年、改革开放 40 周年，也是按照高质量发展要求、全面深化改革、适应经济发展新常态、深入推进供给侧结构性改革，努力全面建成小康社会的重要年份。中国动漫产业在逐步优化的产业环境中，加快产业结构优化升级，进一步保质提量地发展，产品生产发行数量和产业规模效益等指标平稳增长（见表 1）。

表 1　2011—2018 年中国动漫产业发展主要指标

项目	2011 年	2012 年	2013 年	2014 年	2015 年	2016 年	2017 年	2018 年
动漫图书出版数量（种）	1 809	2 041	2 448	2 163	2 262	3 190	2 805	2 144
电视动画生产备案数量（部）	566	580	465	425	399	425	350	460
电视动画生产备案数量（分钟）	491 814	470 721	327 955	271 133	298 114	232 135	145 390	194 346
电视动画完成生产数量（分钟）	261 224	222 938	204 732	138 579	138 273	125 053	83 599	86 257
电视动画播出时长（小时）	280 254	304 877	293 140	304 839	309 060	328 864	362 825	374 500
动画电影生产备案数量（部）	80	70	84	134	148	194	158	131
动画电影完成生产数量（部）	24	33	29	40	51	49	32	51
动画电影票房收入（亿元）	16.35	14.24	16.18	30.31	44.10	70.56	47.50	40.64

一、中国动漫产业发展状况

（一）漫画加速从纸质媒介向移动媒介迁移

2018 年我国共出版动漫类图书 2 144 种，较 2017 年下降 23.57%，其中，漫画图书 1 525 种，动画图书 619 种。截止到 2018 年底，当当网在销动漫类图书共计 99 069 种，其中少儿类 46 176 种、非少儿类 52 893 种，占所有在销图书总量（27 372 954 种）的 0.36%。

随着信息化技术的发展，以漫画网站和漫画 APP 作为主要载体的网络漫画平台在中国漫画出版中扮演着重要角色。国内网络漫画平台普遍都推出了各自的 APP 应用，迎合了近年来持续移动互联网化的潮流趋势。从全年整体情况来看，活跃用户渗透率排名居前的 APP 仍然为《快看漫画》和《腾讯动漫》，《微博动漫》在 2018 年快速崛起，正在逼近千万活跃用户规模。《看漫画》《咪咕圈圈》《网易漫画》《动漫之家》《漫画台》《漫画岛》《咚漫》等第二阵营 APP 与前者相比，仍有较大差距（见表 2、图 1）。

表 2　2018 年 12 月国内漫画应用前 10 名

序号	应用名称	开发商名称	活跃用户（万人）	活跃用户领域渗透率
1	快看漫画	快看世界（北京）科技有限公司	2 261.37	43.62%
2	腾讯动漫	深圳市腾讯计算机系统有限公司	1 102.50	21.27%
3	微博动漫	北京炫果壳信息技术股份有限公司	926.39	17.87%
4	看漫画	成都二次元动漫有限公司	595.46	11.49%
5	咪咕圈圈	咪咕动漫有限公司	412.63	7.96%
6	网易漫画	杭州朗和科技有限公司	321.55	6.20%
7	动漫之家	尚科齐（北京）网络科技有限公司	254.87	4.92%
8	漫画台	成都二次元动漫有限公司	234.18	4.52%

续表

序号	应用名称	开发商名称	活跃用户（万人）	活跃用户领域渗透率
9	漫画岛	上海元聚网络科技有限公司	231.02	4.46%
10	咚漫		217.81	4.20%

资料来源：易观千帆（http://qianfan.analysys.cn）。

注：月活跃用户是指在所选取的时间范围内至少启动过1次的用户。通过对Android用户访问行为持续监测数据进行属性加权，并根据iOS/Android用户调研数据建模得出中国移动互联网用户规模以及相应的用户结构。

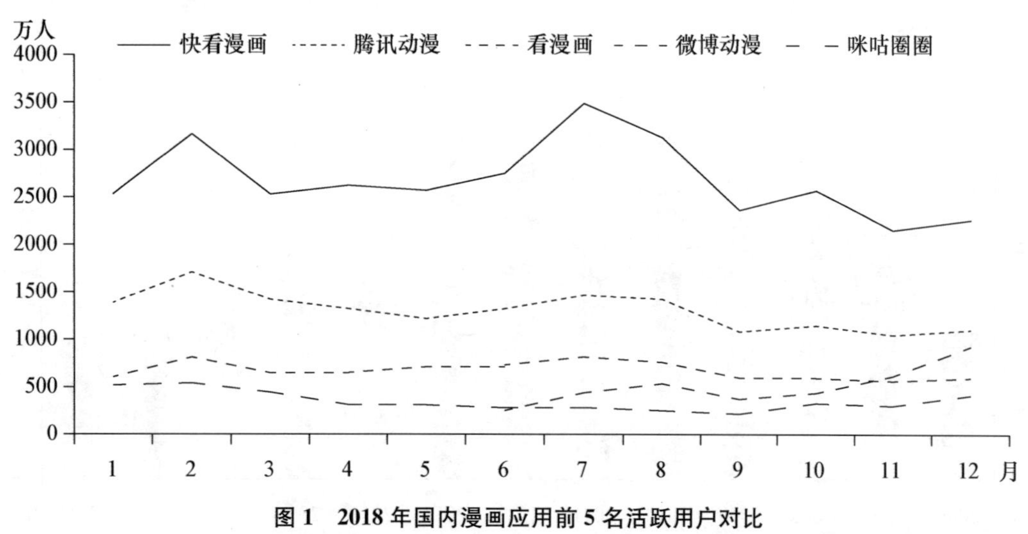

图1　2018年国内漫画应用前5名活跃用户对比

资料来源：易观千帆（http://qianfan.analysys.cn）。

（二）电视动画产量触底反弹，质量持续提升

在政策调控和市场杠杆的双重引导下，2018年中国电视动画行业总体上调控数量，提高质量，由数量增长转向质量提升的趋势更加明显。2018年备案公示的国产电视动画片剧目数量为460部194 346分钟（见图2），同比增长分别达到31%和34%。自2010年以来备案数量持续减少，在2017年触及14.54万分钟的底部后开始反弹，主要是由于参与电视动画片制作备案的生产机构开始恢复增多。2018年参与制作备案的生产机构达到264家，备案数量前十强中既有央视动画有限公司、浙江中南卡通股份有限公司、深圳市欢乐动漫股份有限公司、广东咏声动漫股份有限公司等老牌企业，也有深圳琦萌传媒有限公司、西安中南卡通文化创意有限公司、宁波熙盛文化传媒有限公司、七彩森林（北京）教育科技有限公司等新增机构。

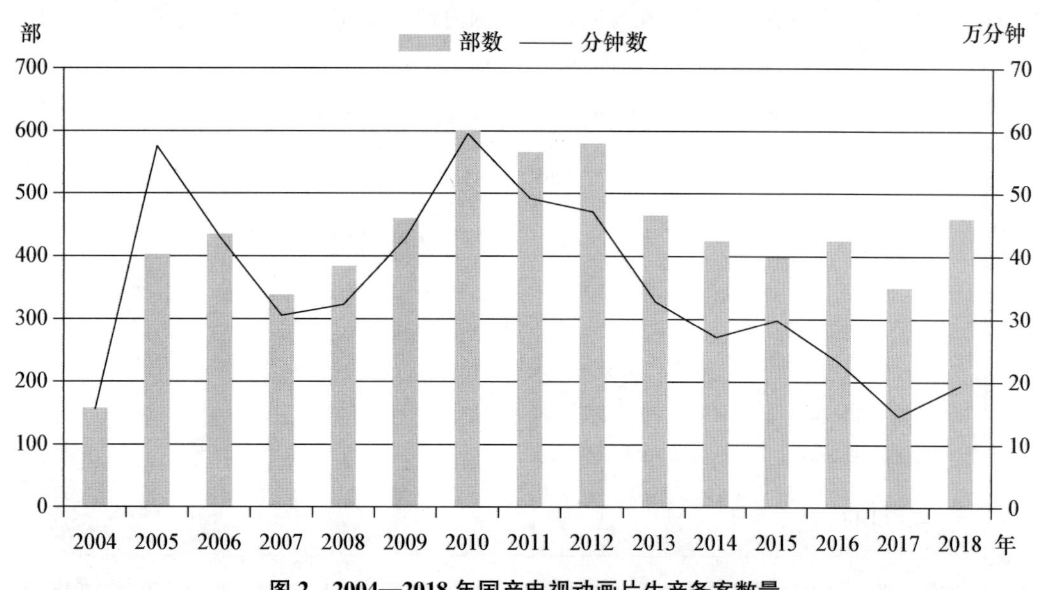

图2　2004—2018年国产电视动画片生产备案数量

资料来源：国家广播电视总局。

总体看来，国产动画产业继续保持产量平稳回升、质量不断突破的发展态势，全年制作发行电视动画片 241 部、8.63 万分钟（见图 3）。2018 年，《梦幻乐园奇遇记》、《新大头儿子和小头爸爸》（第 5 季）、《熊熊乐园 2》、《星星梦》（第 2 季）、《酷跑英雄》等 48 部优秀国产动画片获得原国家新闻出版广电总局推荐播出，合计 1 601 集 21 689 分钟，约占全年总产量（分钟）的 25%。综合 2005 年以来优秀动画片名单来看，浙江、江苏、广东、上海等省市和央视等机构制作生产优秀动画片数量较多。

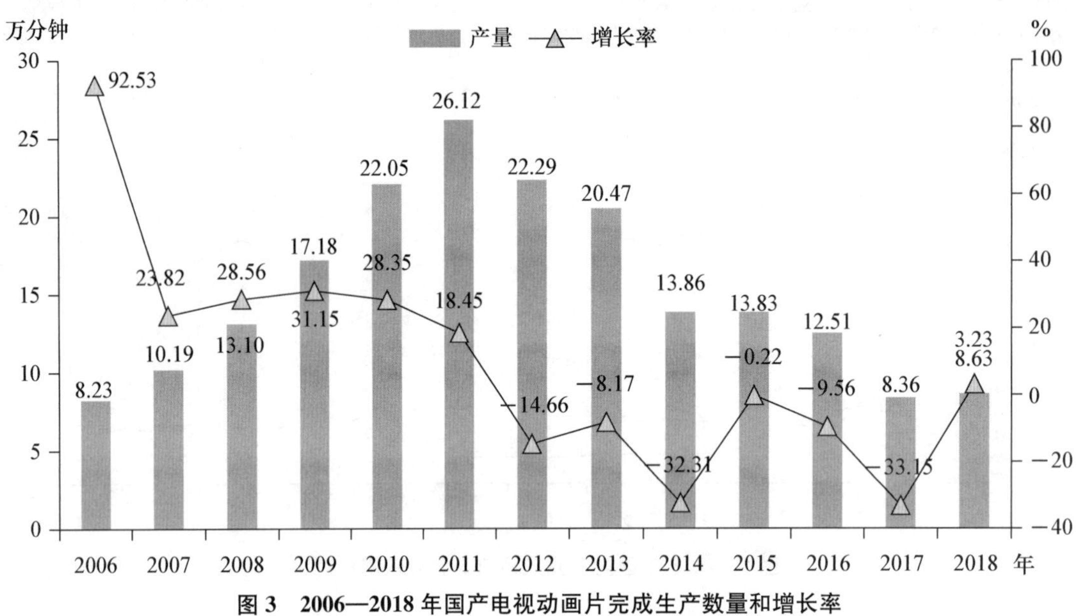

图 3　2006—2018 年国产电视动画片完成生产数量和增长率

资料来源：国家广播电视总局。

为促进国产电视动画片精品创作生产，进一步扩大优秀作品的影响力和覆盖面，充分发挥优秀作品的引领示范带动作用，国家广播电视总局设立国产动画发展专项资金，对优秀国产电视动画作品及制作机构等予以奖励。经过组织动画机构、专家和观众代表评议推荐，并向社会公示，最终确定 2018 年度优秀国产电视动画片 20 部、优秀制作机构 4 家（央视动画有限公司、江苏广电影视动漫传媒有限责任公司、杭州天雷动漫有限公司、华强方特（深圳）动漫有限公司）。

电视动画片制作投资额保持平稳，销售额实现较快增长。2018 年全国电视节目制作投资额达 427.24 亿元，与 2017 年基本持平；电视节目国内销售额 387.86 亿元，比 2017 年（360.37 亿元）增长 7.63%。其中，电视动画国内投资额 16.53 亿元，比 2017 年（14.43 亿元）增长 14.55%；电视动画国内销售额 15.69 亿元，比 2017 年（13.77 亿元）增长 13.94%（见图 4）。

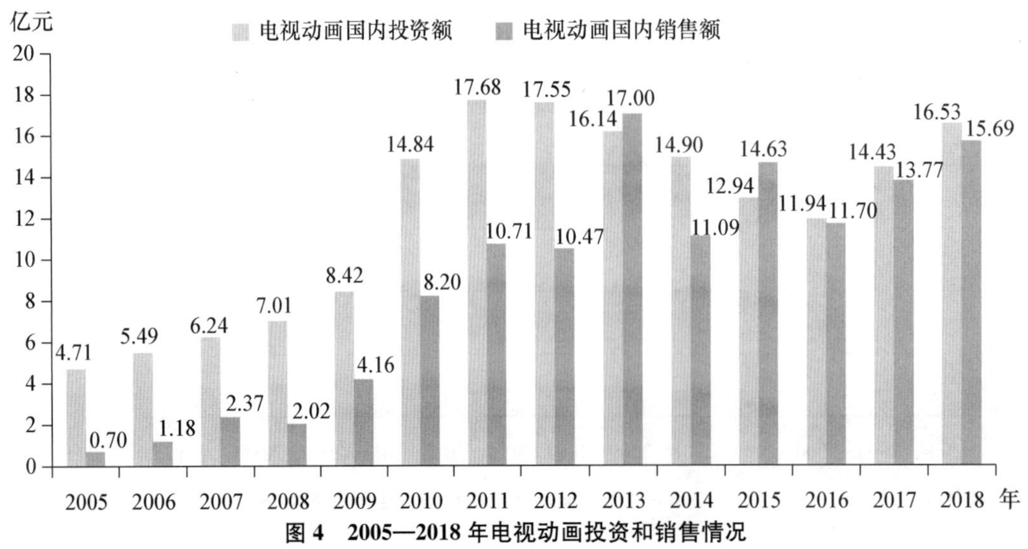

图 4　2005—2018 年电视动画投资和销售情况

资料来源：根据历年《中国统计年鉴》整理。

电视动画片播出时间持续增加，内容播出结构不断优化。目前，我国已形成了以6个少儿动画卫星频道和33个少儿地面频道为主体，各电视上星综合频道和各地各级电视频道动画栏目为补充的动画播映体系。除了动画专业频道、少儿频道之外，其他电视频道也是我国动画播出平台的重要组成部分。我国已经开播了6个少儿动画卫星频道，19个省、9个省会城市、4个计划单列市和1个地级市开播了少儿地面频道，以及3套付费数字电视动画频道。2017年，全国各级电视频道动画片播出数量为362 825小时，其中国产片351 345小时、进口片11 480小时，与2016年相比，增长率分别为10.33%、9.82%和28.34%，国产片和进口片所占比值为96.84∶3.16（见表3）。2018年全国电视动画片播出时间37.45万小时，比2017年（36.28万小时）增加1.17万小时，同比增长3.22%。

表3　2011—2017年全国电视动画播出数量

统计指标	2011年	2012年	2013年	2014年	2015年	2016年	2017年	平均值
全年动画电视播出时间（小时）	280 254	304 877	293 140	304 839	309 060	328 864	362 825	311 980
进口动画电视播出时间（小时）	14 822	12 063	14 015	15 883	9 655	8 945	11 480	12 409
国产动画电视播出时间（小时）	265 432	292 814	279 125	288 955	299 405	319 920	351 345	299 571
进口动画电视播出时间所占比例	5.29%	3.96%	4.78%	5.21%	3.12%	2.72%	3.16%	3.98%
国产动画电视播出时间所占比例	94.71%	96.04%	95.22%	94.79%	96.88%	97.28%	96.84%	96.02%

资料来源：根据历年《中国统计年鉴》整理。

中央电视台少儿频道是我国电视动画节目播出的主力军，是全国最具影响力的少儿频道，也是国产动画片首播量最大的电视频道。全年首播5万多分钟，每天首播国产动画片230分钟。根据酷云EYE Pro电视大数据平台，央视少儿频道2018年各季度观众关注度分别为0.22%、0.16%、0.19%和0.13%，市场占有率分别为3.03%、2.39%、2.74%和2.15%，远高于其他少儿动画类卫星频道（见图5）。收视数据显示，《熊出没之环球大冒险》《熊出没之探险日记》《汪汪队立大功》《熊出没》《大头儿子和小头爸爸》《新猫和老鼠》《棉花糖和云朵妈妈》《神兵小将》《新大头儿子和小头爸爸》《熊出没之年货》《大耳朵图图·美食狂想曲》《百变马丁》《猪猪侠》《熊熊乐园》等动画片取得了较高的观众关注度。

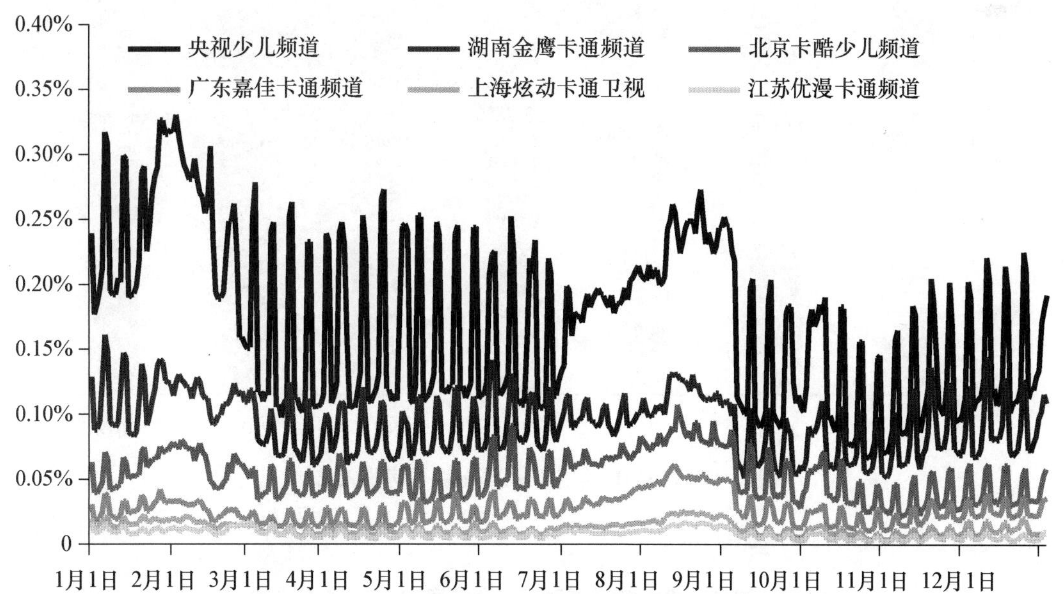

图5　2018年少儿动画类卫星频道观众关注度对比

资料来源：根据酷云EYE Pro电视大数据整理。

（三）中外动画电影表现分化，总体规模稳中有降

近年来，在国家大力发展动画产业和电影产业的有利政策支撑下，我国动画电影制作和票房市场持续升温，2016年动画电影票房收入达到前所未有的71.41亿元。2018年，国产动画电影制作备案

131 部，制作完成并取得公映许可证的影片有 51 部，备案数量相较前两年持续减少。全年动画电影票房收入为 41.73 亿元（见图 6），在总体电影票房中所占比例从 2016 年的 15.78%下降到 6.96%。其中，国产片 15.18 亿元，进口片 24.05 亿元，合拍片 2.50 亿元，分别占 36.38%、57.63%和 5.99%（见图 7）。2018 年动画电影票房较前两年大幅减少，主要系因缺少像《疯狂动物城》《功夫熊猫 3》《你的名字。》《愤怒的小鸟》等爆款进口大片，缺乏票房收入突破 10 亿元的影片。在 5 亿元以上的只有《熊出没・变形记》1 部，票房超过 1 亿元的有《超人总动员 2》《蜘蛛侠：平行宇宙》《无敌破坏王 2：大闹互联网》《精灵旅社 3：疯狂假期》《哆啦 A 梦：大雄的金银岛》《公牛历险记》《比得兔》《龙猫》《新大头儿子和小头爸爸 3：俄罗斯奇遇记》《名侦探柯南：零的执行人》《风语咒》《神秘世界历险记 4》等 12 部，过亿元票房的国产片有 4 部（见表 4）。

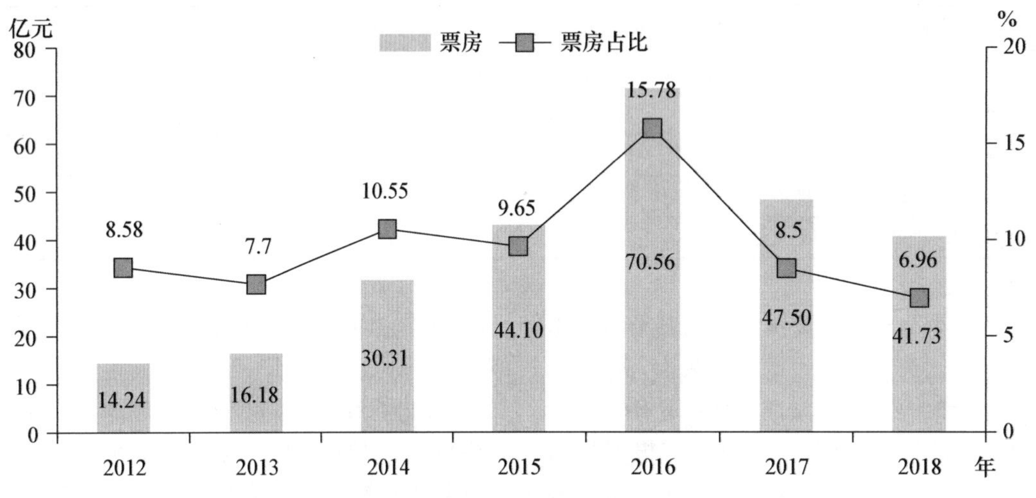

图 6　2012—2018 年全国动画电影票房收入和所占比例

资料来源：艺恩数据（http://www.cbooo.cn/）。

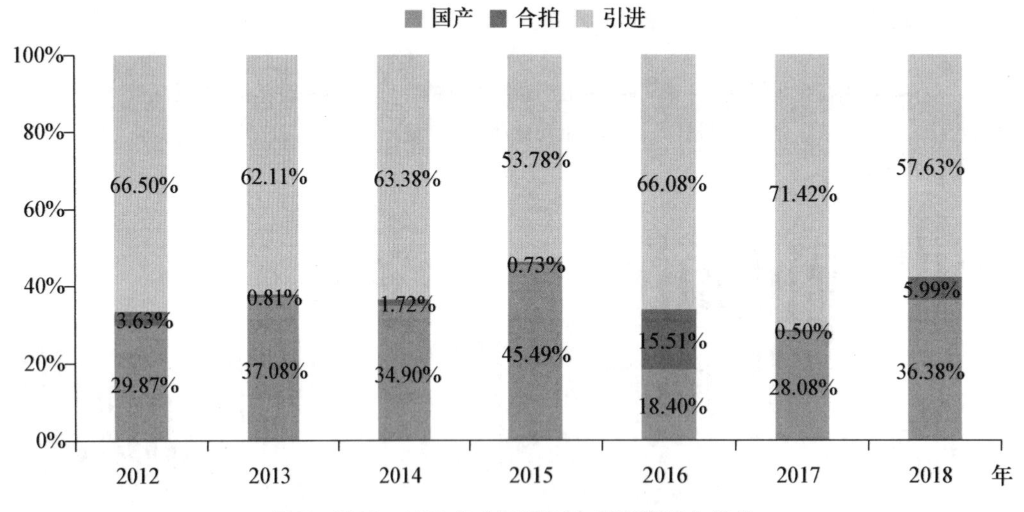

图 7　2012—2018 年全国动画电影票房收入结构

资料来源：艺恩数据（http://www.cbooo.cn/）。

表 4　2016—2018 年全国动画电影票房收入前 10 名影片　　单位：亿元

排名	2016 年		2017 年		2018 年	
	片名	票房	片名	票房	片名	票房
1	疯狂动物城	15.30	寻梦环游记	11.53	熊出没・变形记*	6.06
2	功夫熊猫 3**	10.02	神偷奶爸 3	10.38	超人总动员 2	3.54
3	你的名字。	5.66	熊出没之奇幻空间*	5.22	蜘蛛侠：平行宇宙	3.53

续表

排名	2016 年		2017 年		2018 年	
	片名	票房	片名	票房	片名	票房
4	大鱼海棠*	5.65	欢乐好声音	2.16	无敌破坏王 2：大闹互联网	2.71
5	愤怒的小鸟	5.14	蓝精灵：寻找神秘村	1.74	精灵旅社 3：疯狂假期	2.23
6	冰川时代 5：星际碰撞	4.47	哆啦 A 梦：大雄的南极冰冰凉大冒险	1.49	哆啦 A 梦：大雄的金银岛	2.09
7	爱宠大机密	3.89	赛车总动员 3：极速挑战	1.37	公牛历险记	1.72
8	熊出没之熊心归来*	2.88	十万个冷笑话 2*	1.34	比得兔	1.68
9	海底总动员 2：多莉去哪儿	2.54	大卫贝肯之倒霉特工熊*	1.26	龙猫	1.59
10	海洋奇缘	2.14	赛尔号大电影 6：圣者无敌*	1.03	新大头儿子和小头爸爸 3：俄罗斯奇遇记*	1.58

资料来源：艺恩数据（http://www.cbooo.cn/）。
注：标 * 者为国产片，标 ** 者为合拍片。

（四）网络动画内容数量和播放量稳步增长

根据艺恩视频智库对国内主流视频网站的统计，2018 年动画总播放量达到 2 761.28 亿次，较上年增长约 11.42%（见图 8）。海量内容是视频网站入局动画领域的首要策略，2018 年各视频平台播放动画内容数量达到 3 222 部，其中，2018 年新上线动画超过 600 部，暑期上线动画作品数量最多。目前，优质头部内容把持着动画平台的流量入口，具有强大的聚集流量的优势，依然是视频网站着力布局动画领域的焦点。亿级播放量以上的优质头部动画内容仍为稀缺资源，联播依然是头部动画作品播放主流，每月在播作品播放量第 1 名均为联播。从全年播放量来看，排名较高的日本动画作品包括《海贼王》《火影忍者》《名侦探柯南》等，美国动画作品包括《汪汪队立大功》《小巴林》《猫和老鼠》等（见表 5），国产动画作品包括《熊出没之探险日记》《斗罗大陆》《贝乐虎儿歌》等（见表 6）。从 2018 年视频网站播出动画类别流量分布来看，儿童动画占 66%，青少年动画占 10%，成年动画占 17%，全年龄动画占 7%。由此可见，经典国产儿童动画是头部内容主力，平台版权覆盖及内容深耕是联播领先的主因；腾讯视频、优酷、爱奇艺等成为自制成年动画的主要平台。

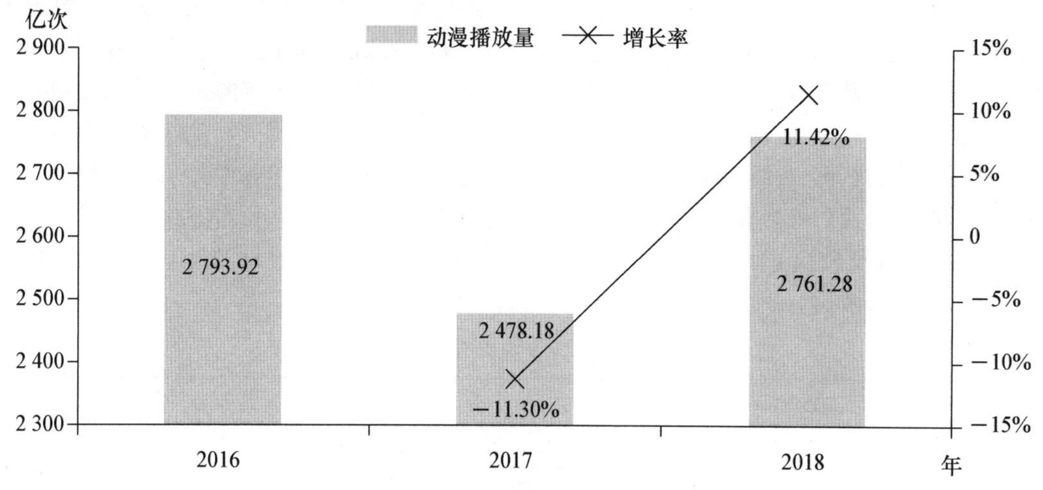

图 8　2016—2018 年视频网站动漫播放量

表 5　2018 年视频网站播放量前 10 名日本和美国动画作品

排名	日本动画作品	播放量（亿次）	美国动画作品	播放量（亿次）
1	海贼王	37.18	汪汪队立大功全集	97.64
2	火影忍者	28.53	汪汪队立大功第 1 季	44.96
3	名侦探柯南	26.77	汪汪队立大功第 2 季	42.43

续表

排名	日本动画作品	播放量（亿次）	美国动画作品	播放量（亿次）
4	蜡笔小新全集	25.86	汪汪队立大功第 4 季	33.61
5	蜡笔小新第 2 季	14.98	小巴林	24.12
6	博人传火影忍者新时代	10.36	猫和老鼠全集	20.41
7	蜡笔小新第 6 季	9.52	海绵宝宝	18.01
8	捷德奥特曼	8.51	巴塔木儿歌	11.73
9	龙珠超	8.03	汪汪队立大功第 5 季*	8.66
10	罗布奥特曼	7.84	睡衣小英雄*	7.04

资料来源：艺恩视频智库，统计周期：2018 年 1 月 1 日—12 月 31 日。
注：标*者为 2018 年新播剧目。

表 6　2018 年视频网站播放量前 10 名国产动画作品

排名	儿童动画作品	青少年动画作品	成年动画作品
1	熊出没之探险日记	斗破苍穹第 2 季*	斗罗大陆*
2	贝乐虎儿歌	一人之下第 2 季	魔道祖师*
3	萌鸡小队	喜羊羊与灰太狼之奇幻天空岛*	狐妖小红娘
4	宝宝巴士儿歌	峡谷重案组第 2 季*	武庚纪第 2 季
5	可可小爱	乌龙院之活宝传奇	画江湖之侠岚*
6	超级飞侠全集	巨神战击队之超救分队	超神学院之雄兵连
7	超级飞侠第 4 季*	兽王争锋第 2 季原石之力	妖神记第 1 季
8	熊熊乐园	妖神记之影妖篇*	我的逆天神器
9	宝宝巴士亲子游戏	雄兵连（下）乾坤篇*	斗罗大陆 2 绝世唐门*
10	帮帮龙出动之恐龙探险队	聪明的顺溜之雄鹰小子第 1 季	天行九歌

资料来源：艺恩视频智库，统计周期：2018 年 1 月 1 日—12 月 31 日。
注：标*者为 2018 年新播剧目。

根据对 2018 年百度搜索风云榜动漫榜单的统计，全年共有 205 部国产动漫上榜，搜索指数合计值为 1.06 亿人次（见表 7），关键词数量所占总体的比例为 31.20%，搜索指数合计值所占比例为 39.20%。在《斗破苍穹》《炮炮兵》《万古仙穹》《狐妖小红娘》《一人之下》《西游记》《京剧猫》《四海鲸骑》《灵契》《小鸡彩虹》等热门动画的助推下，国产动漫观众关注度较 2013 年的 20.69%几乎增长了一倍，而以《海贼王》《银魂》《流星花园》《火影忍者》《阴阳师》《一拳超人》《龙珠超》《名侦探柯南》《进击的巨人》《王者天下》等为代表的日本动漫的观众关注度持续下降，从 2013 年的 73.20%下降到 2018 年的 50.83%；此外，欧美动漫关注度也在《星球大战》《愤怒的小鸟》《铁血战士》《海绵宝宝》《猫和老鼠》《芭比之梦想豪宅》《汪汪队立大功》《小马宝莉》《爱探险的朵拉》《天线宝宝》等爆款作品的助攻下，达到了前所未有的 9.87%（见图 9）。

表 7　2013—2018 年百度搜索风云榜动漫榜单构成

类别	关键词数量（部）						搜索指数合计（亿次）					
	2013 年	2014 年	2015 年	2016 年	2017 年	2018 年	2013 年	2014 年	2015 年	2016 年	2017 年	2018 年
日本	192	278	313	350	365	360	3.60	3.55	2.98	2.64	1.57	1.38
国产	163	171	180	182	182	205	1.02	1.12	1.20	1.11	1.16	1.06
欧美	71	79	82	79	70	91	0.28	0.42	0.37	0.26	0.16	0.27
其他	2	2	2	2	2	1	0.02	0.02	0.02	0.01	0.00	0.00
合计	428	530	577	613	619	657	4.92	5.11	4.57	4.02	2.89	2.71

资料来源：根据百度搜索风云榜动漫榜单（http://top.baidu.com/category?c=5）每日提供的基础数据进行全年汇总，可能与官方实际数据略有出入。

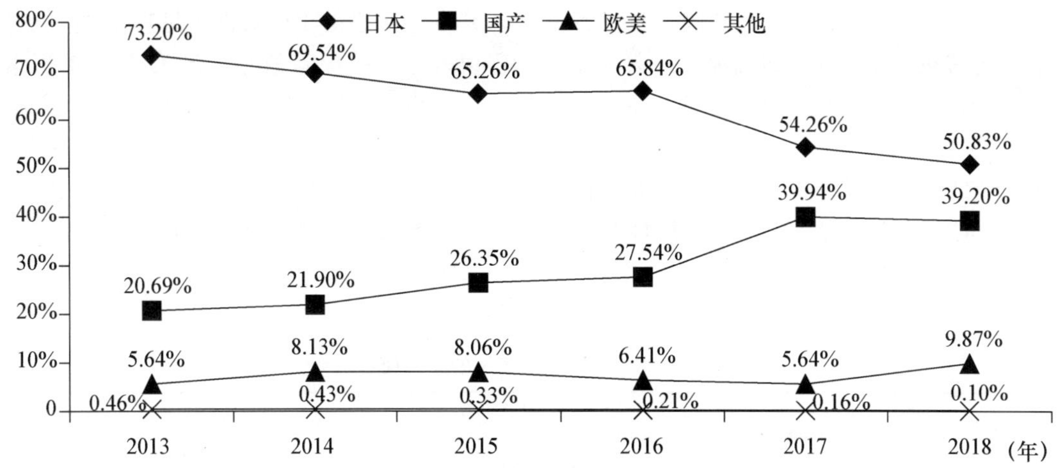

图 9　2013—2018 年百度搜索风云榜动漫榜单构成比例

注：图中数据核算基于原始数据。

二、中国动漫产业发展趋势

（一）头部机构规模实力持续攀升，行业集中度有所提高

自 2004 年《关于发展我国影视动画产业的若干意见》等一系列扶持政策实施以来，中国动画产业逐步形成了多种经济成分共同发展的产业格局，有力地推动了中国动画产业的发展进程。作为市场主体的动画企业在产业化潮流中快速成长，规模实力持续增强，一批有实力、有特色的动画企业脱颖而出。经过多年的积累发展，中国动漫逐步涌现出奥飞娱乐、腾讯互动娱乐、华强方特动漫、中南卡通、美盛文化、长城动漫等综合运营商，央视动画、炫动传播、原创动力、玄机科技、蓝弧文化、咏声动漫、宏梦卡通、追光动画等专业内容供应商，以及光线传媒、恒大文化、海尔文化等战略投资者。

作为中央电视台全额投资的国有独资企业，央视动画有限公司由原中央电视台青少节目中心动画部整建制转制而成，自 2007 年成立以来，先后打造了《美猴王》《新大头儿子和小头爸爸》《熊猫和小鼹鼠》等 48 部优秀动画片（其中自主生产 36 部、合拍 12 部）；其中，《新大头儿子和小头爸爸》作为一部充满温馨与正能量的优质动画，先后推出了 6 季 500 余集电视动画片和《新大头儿子和小头爸爸 1：秘密计划》《新大头儿子和小头爸爸 2：一日成才》《新大头儿子和小头爸爸 3：俄罗斯奇遇记》3 部动画电影，累计票房近 3 亿元；中捷合拍的《熊猫和小鼹鼠》以深受全世界孩子喜爱的中国国宝“熊猫”和捷克国家级动画形象“小鼹鼠”共同作为主角，讲述了鼹鼠在中国遇到熊猫，以及他们跟许多好朋友之间的一系列温馨、幽默、和谐的故事。浙江中南卡通股份有限公司、广东原创动力文化传播有限公司、上海炫动传播有限公司、杭州阿优文化创意有限公司、广东咏声动漫股份有限公司、华强方特（深圳）动漫有限公司等制作单位也推出了《天眼》《乐比悠悠》《喜羊羊与灰太狼》《京剧猫》《哈哈大冒险》《阿优》《猪猪侠》《虹猫蓝兔》《熊出没》等脍炙人口的国产动画精品。

（二）战略投资者以动画娱乐营销推动产业发展

在产业融合和跨业经营的商业潮流下，玩具、游戏、服装、文具、家电、食品等行业企业纷纷涉足动画领域，联手动画设计发行运营企业共同开发商业动漫形象，以全方位、立体化的动漫营销来推动自身产业的发展（见表 8）。奥飞、骅威、高乐、小白龙、可儿、星原文化等玩具企业，美盛文化、盛克鞋服、小猪班纳、卡西龙、小顽皮、大拇哥等鞋服企业均已经制作播出了各自主打品牌的动画片。天洋投资控股有限公司旗下梦东方集团有限公司（00593. HK），以及梦东方文化娱乐集团有限公司、梦东方电影有限公司等附属企业，聚焦旅游度假区、影视动画等领域，创造自有 IP 生态系统，计划用 13 年创作 520 集动画片《鹿精灵》，现已完成《鹿精灵》《鹿精灵之寻找兵马俑》两季 104 集动画片的制作，《鹿精灵之寻找兵马俑》于 2018 年 10 月 22 日在北京电视台卡酷少儿频道首播，并入选 2018 年第三季度优秀动画片。

2018 年，主打动画营销的《海尔兄弟宇宙大冒险》、《超级伊仔》和《奇幻牙仙堡》等动画项目在市场上备受瞩目。《海尔兄弟宇宙大冒险》是由青岛海尔文化产业发展有限公司、青岛海尔兄弟影业有限公司共同出品的系列科幻动画片。该片主要讲述海尔兄弟根据智慧老人留下的"智慧的足迹"，进行太空探险的故事。《超级伊仔》是由上海来伊份股份有限公司旗下伊奇乐文化传媒（浙江）有限公司制作发行运营的大型原创 3D 动画作品。该动画将故事背景延伸到宇宙空间，通过讲述一名来自银河系外 KOKAKA 星球上的美食精灵伊仔误入地球的探险故事，激发青少年探索世界、追逐梦想的勇气。《奇幻牙仙堡》由纳爱斯集团联手广东英扬传奇广告有限公司、广州游益网络科技有限公司共同打造，讲述了人类男孩皮皮误闯入牙仙精灵所居住的奇幻大陆，在其间学习各种魔法抵御黑暗女王入侵，维护现实世界与奇幻大陆安宁的故事。

表 8　部分主打娱乐营销的动画项目

投资者	所属行业	动画片名	作品题材	规格数量
香港衍丰集团（控股）有限公司	儿童健康	《草本家族》	童话/奇幻/冒险	13 分钟×52 集
可儿玩具有限公司	玩具（娃娃）	《东方可儿之摩登学园》	未来/喜剧/时尚	13 分钟×52 集
安徽三只松鼠电子商务有限公司	休闲食品（坚果）	《三只松鼠与坚果侠》	幽默/时尚/喜剧	13 分钟×52 集
浙江小王子食品股份有限公司	休闲食品（薯片）	《小王子与土豆仔》	童话/奇幻/冒险	13 分钟×52 集
上海来伊份股份有限公司	休闲食品（餐饮）	《超级伊仔》	科幻/喜剧/动作	10 分钟×52 集
单车侠动漫科技有限公司	单车	《单车侠》	动作/科幻	13 分钟×52 集
爹地宝贝股份有限公司	婴童	《爹地宝贝之神奇哈酷》	家庭/娱乐/科技	14 分钟×52 集
特步（中国）有限公司	鞋服	《X 梦想总动员》	梦幻/生活/科技	14 分钟×104 集
协丰（福建）卫生用品有限公司	婴童	《小熊优恩》	亲子/娱乐/动作	13 分钟×26 集
福建省童猫科技有限公司	电子商城	《小童猫之喵星来客》	环保/科技/搞笑	13 分钟×208 集
浙江贝贝依依服饰有限公司	童装	《超能小星探》	星际/科幻	13 分钟×52 集

资料来源：功夫动漫网站（http://www.kfdm.cn/）。

（三）"IP＋"战略推动优秀动漫品牌价值愈加彰显

近年来，包括文学、动漫、游戏、电影、电视剧等在内的文化形态加速跨界融通，形成了"泛娱乐"的生态体系。优质的 IP 资源成为整个文化娱乐产业维持用户黏性的纽带，以 IP 为核心的布局成为国内文化娱乐产业的发展趋势。

动漫企业对 IP 重视程度的持续攀升，直接推动了以 IP 为核心的"一源多用"的"IP＋"战略，作品创作呈现出系列化、品牌化、推陈出新、连续迭代的特点。《新大头儿子和小头爸爸》《秦时明月》《熊出没》《喜羊羊和灰太狼》《赛尔号》等经典品牌通过《新大头儿子和小头爸爸》第 5 季、《秦时明月之伍：君临天下》、《熊熊乐园》、《喜羊羊与灰太狼之智趣羊学堂》、《赛尔号》第 9 季等新系列实现品牌价值的持续开发和升级。

随着国家动漫精品工程的实施和动漫企业品牌意识的树立，我国动漫企业推出了一批优秀的动画精品和动画品牌。根据对 2018 年百度搜索风云榜动漫榜单的统计，《斗破苍穹》《炮炮兵》《万古仙穹》《狐妖小红娘》《一人之下》《西游记》《京剧猫》《四海鲸骑》《灵契》《小鸡彩虹》等国产动漫品牌在网络平台上具有较高关注度、知名度和影响力，跻身 2018 年百度搜索动漫风云榜中国动漫前 20 名（见表 9）。根据原生产品形态和首发媒体平台来看，既有根植于网络小说的《斗破苍穹》《万古仙穹》《四海鲸骑》《魔道祖师》《妖神记》《斗罗大陆 2 绝世唐门》等，又有改编自漫画的《狐妖小红娘》《一人之下》《灵契》《尸兄》《爱神巧克力》《中国惊奇先生》《武庚纪》等，还有原生 IP 动画《京剧猫》《熊出没》《天行九歌》等；既有生发于电视平台的《京剧猫》《小鸡彩虹》《熊出没》等，也有走红于网络平台的《斗破苍穹》《万古仙穹》《狐妖小红娘》《一人之下》《四海鲸骑》《灵契》《尸兄》《魔道祖师》《爱神巧克力》《中国惊奇先生》《天行九歌》《武庚纪》《妖神记》等，以及脱胎于网络社交表情的《炮炮兵》等。其中，《斗破苍穹》涵盖小说、漫画、动画、游戏、电影、电视剧等多种产品形态，由阅文集团、腾讯视频联合出品的动画系列已经播出了两季。

表 9　2018 年百度搜索动漫风云榜中国动漫前 20 名

序号	关键词	搜索指数合计	序号	关键词	搜索指数合计
1	斗破苍穹	14 492 698	11	尸兄	2 680 320
2	炮炮兵	9 553 502	12	魔道祖师	2 502 007
3	万古仙穹	8 219 366	13	爱神巧克力	2 043 868
4	狐妖小红娘	7 482 693	14	熊出没	1 698 510
5	一人之下	6 945 128	15	中国惊奇先生	1 668 037
6	西游记	6 384 476	16	红楼梦	1 470 978
7	京剧猫	4 191 342	17	天行九歌	1 277 627
8	四海鲸骑	4 037 095	18	武庚纪	1 164 231
9	灵契	3 823 108	19	妖神记	1 159 520
10	小鸡彩虹	3 113 648	20	斗罗大陆 2 绝世唐门	1 020 710

资料来源：根据百度搜索风云榜动漫榜单（http://top.baidu.com/category? c=5）每日提供的基础数据进行全年汇总，可能与官方实际数据略有出入。

（四）二次元助推动漫游戏加速协同发展

近年来国内二次元文化发展迅速，用户规模持续增加，对于二次元用户消费市场的发展也起到了促进作用。2018 年中国二次元用户中，核心用户规模达 1.0 亿人，非核心用户达 2.7 亿人。国内游戏市场发展已经相对成熟，各大企业开始在细分领域探索新机会，二次元用户偏好的游戏产品凭借内容丰富、用户忠诚度高获得企业青睐。2018 年中国二次元移动游戏市场实际销售收入达 190.9 亿元，同比增长 19.5%，占中国移动游戏市场 14.3%。2018 年收入前 20 的二次元移动游戏中，卡牌类游戏、动作角色扮演类游戏、回合制角色扮演类游戏收入占比分别为 52.7%、28.4%、15.6%。

动漫 IP 成为移动游戏市场的主要增量，加速了二次元用户群体的价值释放。随着用户红利消退、新增用户减少，移动游戏市场增长率出现下滑，二次元用户偏好的动漫 IP 改编游戏被视为重要的增长点。得益于动漫 IP 改编游戏模式的成熟，动漫 IP 改编新游占移动游戏市场新游比例正在快速增加，移动游戏市场对动漫 IP 改编游戏的迫切性也在增强。动漫 IP 能提高二次元的知名度，促使泛二次元用户和核心二次元用户不断相互转化，进一步增强用户黏度。凭借其用户优势以及剧情内容，动漫 IP 尤其是具有较高知名度的日本动漫 IP 改编的产品能够迅速打开市场，并获取较长的生命周期，如《火影忍者》《海贼王》。

深耕二次元消费群体的典型企业包括哔哩哔哩、网易游戏、米哈游、盛大游戏等。哔哩哔哩在国内拥有大量的二次元用户，经过多年的发展已经建立了成熟的社区生态体系，游戏产品是其社区流量变现的重要途径，其代表产品包括《命运—冠位指定》《碧蓝航线》等。网易游戏拥有丰富的专门针对二次元用户的 IP 资源，《阴阳师》《初音速》《魔法禁书目录》等产品的来源涵盖了游戏、动漫、小说等多个领域，运营模式的成熟有助于其 IP 实现价值最大化。“崩坏学园”系列产品是米哈游游戏业务的核心，米哈游游戏围绕“崩坏学园”推出了游戏、漫画、动画、轻小说、周边产品等多个形态的产品，为用户提供不同娱乐方式的产品体验，相互渗透的各类产品共同拓展了“崩坏学园”的 IP 商业价值。

2018 年中国软件产业发展概况

国家工业和信息化部信息化和软件服务业司

2018 年，全球新一轮科技革命和产业变革引发社会深刻变化，尽管世界经济整体保持增长，但经济危机造成的深层次影响仍未消除，经济增长新旧动能转换尚未完成。以美国为首的发达经济体货币政策转向带来的外溢效应以及美国贸易保护主义行为等各类风险叠加牵制着经济复苏进程。2018 年也是中国改革开放 40 周年，我们战胜各种风险挑战，推动经济高质量发展，加快新旧动能转换，保持经济运行在合理区间。2018 年全年国内生产总值 900 309 亿元，比上年增长 6.6%①。与此同时，经济运行稳中有变、变中有忧，国际政治经济环境更加严峻，中美经贸摩擦不确定性明显上升。在中国制造、中国创造、中国建造共同发力的背景下，我国软件和信息技术服务业运行态势良好，收入和效益保持较快增长，吸纳就业人数稳步增加；产业向高质量方向发展转变的步伐加快，结构持续调整优化，新的增长点不断涌现，服务和支撑两个强国建设能力显著增强，正在成为数字经济发展、智慧社会演进的重要驱动力量。

一、2018 年中国软件产业发展的宏观环境

软件是信息技术之魂、网络安全的支撑、经济转型的动力、数字社会的基石，是引领新一轮科技创新的原动力。软件定义正在全面融入经济社会各领域，驱动数字经济蓬勃发展，推动智慧社会加速演进。围绕制造强国、网络强国、数字经济等国家战略，软件和信息技术服务业在融合创新和转型升级中起到核心支撑作用，能够凝聚社会共识，推动产业高质量发展。当前我国经济已由高速增长阶段转向高质量发展阶段，作为引领科技创新的核心力量，做强做大软件和信息技术服务业，是我国构建竞争新优势、抢占新工业革命制高点的必然选择。

国家发布一系列利好政策，大力促进软件和信息技术服务业发展。党的十九大明确提出“加快建设制造强国，加快发展先进制造业，推动互联网、大数据、人工智能和实体经济深度融合”。《“十三五”国家信息化规划》《关于深化制造业与互联网融合发展的指导意见》《软件和信息技术服务业发展规划（2016—2020 年）》等政策为软件和信息技术服务业开拓了新的广阔发展空间，为产业发展提供了更多的创新突破口。在具体领域方面，《大数据产业发展规划（2016—2020 年）》全面部署“十三五”时期大数据产业发展工作，为实现制造强国和网络强国提供强大的产业支撑。《云计算发展三年行动计划》致力于进一步提升我国云计算发展与应用水平，为积极抢占信息技术发展的制高点提供政策保障。工业和信息化部结合产业特色发布了《促进新一代人工智能产业发展三年行动计划（2018—2020 年）》《工业控制系统信息安全行动计划（2018—2020 年）》《扩大和升级信息消费三年行动计划（2018—2020 年）》《推动企业上云实施指南（2018—2020 年）》等一系列指导政策文件。随着国家级规划文件的实施和落实，各地将结合自身优势出台促进大数据、云计算、人工智能等新兴信息技术发展的配套措施和支持政策，软件和信息技术服务业的政策环境将得到进一步优化，为软件和信息技术服务业突破式发展提供新机遇。

当前世界经济下行风险加大。美国实施保护主义和单边主义对世界经济产生的消极影响扩大，全球金融环境收紧，世界经济增速将放缓。我国经济增长稳中有缓，虽然外部环境复杂严峻，但我国发展仍处于并将长期处于重要战略机遇期。2018 年底召开的中央经济工作会议提出要坚持稳中求进工作总基调，坚持以供给侧结构性改革为主线不动摇，重点抓好推动制造业高质量发展、促进形成强大国内市场等领域的工作。软件产业创新的成果不断涌现，产业发展的环境也在持续优化。新时期，国家软件发展明确了新的战略思想，软件企业的所得税

① 中华人民共和国 2018 年国民经济和社会发展统计公报［EB/OL］.［2019－03－28］. http://www.stats.gov.cn/tjsj/zxfb/201902/t20190228_1651265.html.

两免三减半的优惠政策继续实施，知识产权的保护力度也在不断加强，国际交流合作广泛而深入。

二、2018 年中国软件产业发展基本情况①

2018 年，我国软件和信息技术服务业运行态势良好，收入和效益保持较快增长，吸纳就业人数稳步增加；产业向高质量发展转变的步伐加快，结构持续调整优化，新的增长点不断涌现，服务和支撑两个强国建设能力显著增强，正在成为数字经济发展、智慧社会演进的重要驱动力量。

（一）综合情况

软件业务收入保持较快增长。2018 年，全国累计完成软件业务收入 63 061 亿元，同比增长 14.4%，如图 1 所示。

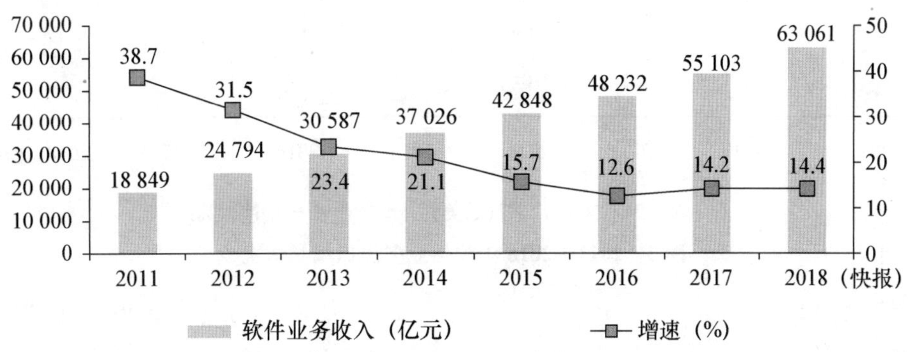

图 1　2011—2018 年软件业务收入增长情况

盈利能力稳步提升。经初步统计，2018 年软件和信息技术服务业实现利润总额 8 079 亿元，同比增长 9.7%；行业人均创造业务收入 98.06 万元，同比增长 9.9%，高质量发展成效初显。2011—2018 年软件业人均创收情况如图 2 所示。

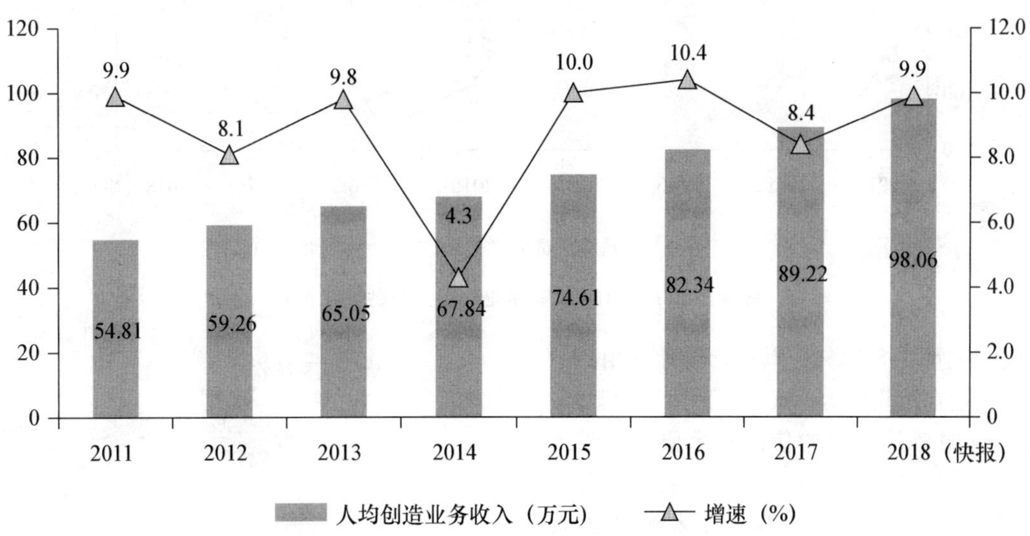

图 2　2011—2018 年软件业人均创收情况

软件出口形势低迷。2018 年，全国软件和信息技术服务业实现出口 554.5 亿美元，同比增长 2.5%，如图 3 所示。

从业人数稳步增加。2018 年，全国软件和信息技术服务业从业人数 643 万人，比上年增加 25 万人，同比增长 4.0%，如图 4 所示。

（二）分领域运行情况

软件产品收入实现较快增长。2018 年，全行业实现软件产品收入 19 353 亿元，同比增长 12.1%，占全行业比重为 30.7%。其中，信息安全和工业软件产品实现收入 1 698 亿元和 1 477 亿元，分别增长 14.8%和 14.2%，为支撑信息系统安全和工业领域发展发挥了重要作用。

信息技术服务加快云化发展。2018 年，全行业实现信息技术服务收入 34 756 亿元，同比增长 17.6%，增速高出全行业平均水平 3.2 个百分点，

① 2018 年软件和信息技术服务业统计公报［EB/OL］.［2019-03-29］. http://www.miit.gov.cn/n1146312/n1146904/n1648374/c6633883/content.html.

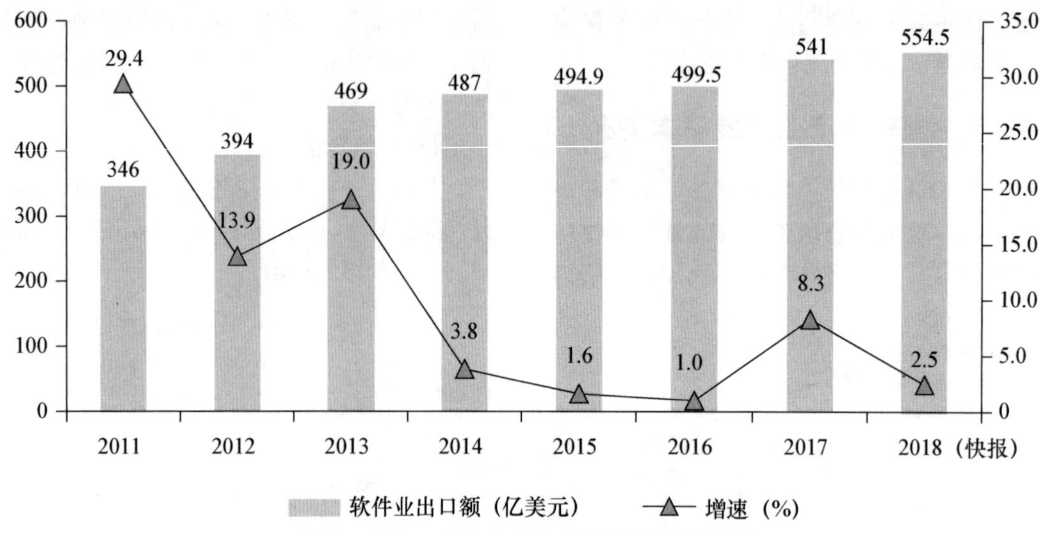

图 3　2011—2018 年软件业务出口增长情况

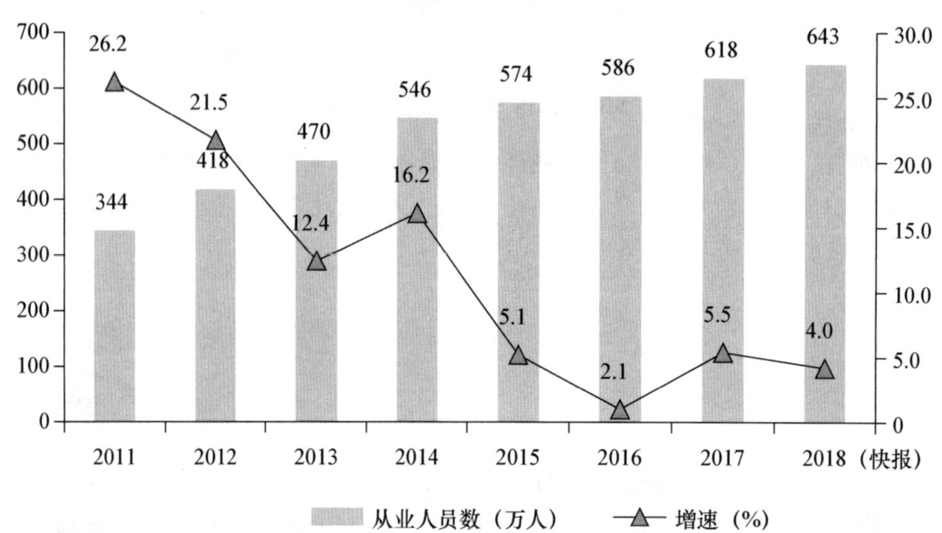

图 4　2011—2018 年软件业从业人员数变化情况

占全行业收入比重为 55.1%。其中，云计算相关的运营服务（包括在线软件运营服务、平台运营服务、基础设施运营服务等在内的信息技术服务）收入 10 419 亿元，同比增长 21.4%，占信息技术服务收入比重达 30.0%；电子商务平台技术服务收入 4 846 亿元，同比增长 21.9%。

嵌入式系统软件收入平稳增长。2018 年，全行业实现嵌入式系统软件收入 8 952 亿元，同比增长 6.8%，占全行业收入比重为 14.2%。嵌入式系统软件已成为产品和装备数字化改造、各领域智能化增值的关键性带动技术。2018 年软件产业分类收入占比如图 5 所示。

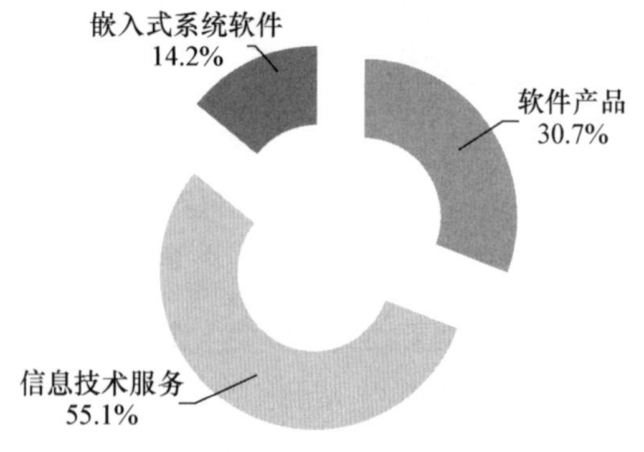

图 5　2018 年软件产业分类收入占比

（三）分地区运行情况

东部地区稳步发展，中西部地区软件业加快增长。2018 年，东部地区完成软件业务收入 49 795 亿元，同比增长 14.2%，占全国软件业的比重为 79.0%。中部和西部地区完成软件业务收入为 3 163 亿元和 7 189 亿元，分别增长 19.2%和 16.2%，高于全国增速 4.8 和 1.8 个百分点；占全国软件业的比重为 5.0%和 11.4%，同比均提高 0.2 个百分点。东北地区完成软件业务收入 2 914 亿元，同比下降 0.4 个百分点，占全国软件业的比重为 4.6%。2018 年软件业分区域增长情况如图 6 所示。

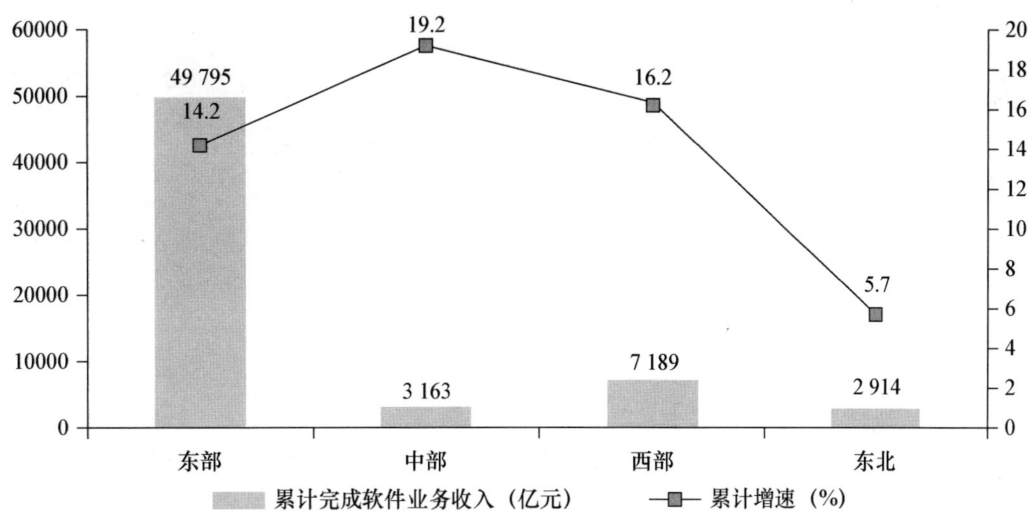

图 6　2018 年软件业分区域增长情况

主要软件大省保持稳中向好，海南及部分中西部省市快速增长。软件业务收入居前 5 名的广东（增长 12.2%）、江苏（增长 10.7%）、北京（增长 16.8%）、山东（增长 15.9%）、浙江（增长 21.1%）共完成软件业务收入 40 192 亿元，占全国软件业比重的 63.7%。软件业务收入增速高于全国平均水平的省市有 19 个，其中海南同比增长达 89.9%，西部的广西、青海、云南和贵州增长分别达 77.0%、50.3%、23.7%和 23.4%，中部的江西、安徽增长达 37.7%和 27.7%。2018 年软件业务收入前 10 位省市软件业务收入增长情况如图 7 所示。

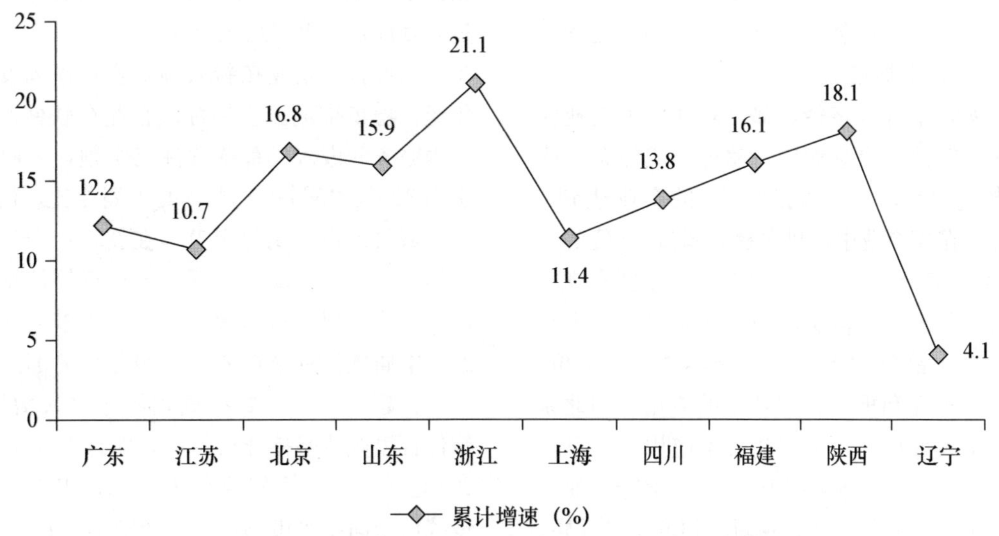

图 7　2018 年软件业务收入前 10 位省市软件业务收入增长情况

重点城市软件业保持集聚发展。2018 年，全国 4 个直辖市和 15 个副省级中心城市实现软件业务收入 51 237 亿元，同比增长 14.2%，占全国软件业的比重为 81.2%。其中，软件业务收入超过千亿元的城市包括 4 个直辖市和 11 个中心城市，合计软件业务收入占全国的比重达到 78.3%。2018 年软件业务收入前 10 位中心城市软件业务收入增长情况如图 8 所示。

（四）主要软件企业发展情况①

根据国家统计局批准、工业和信息化部统计的 2017 年全国软件和信息技术服务业年报数据，经各地工业和信息化主管部门初步审核、工业和信息化部最终核定，2018 年（第 17 届）中国软件业务收入前百家企业（以下简称软件百家企业）名单揭晓。

2018 年（第 17 届）软件百家企业入围门槛为软件业务年收入 16.2 亿元，比上届提高 1.7 亿元，

① 2018 年（第 17 届）中国软件业务收入前百家企业发展报告［EB/OL］.［2019-03-29］. http://www.miit.gov.cn/n1146285/n1146352/n3054355/n3057511/n3057518/c6472762/content.html.

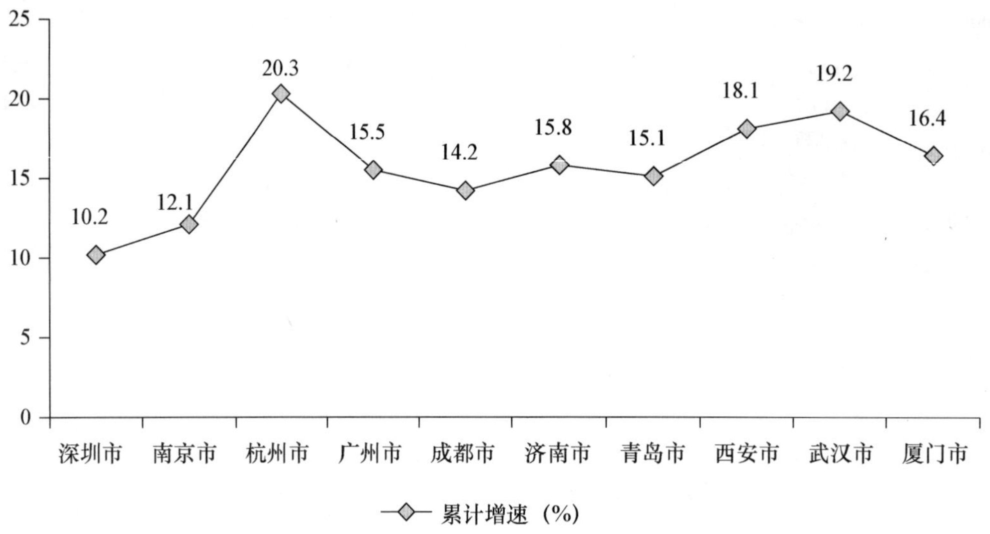

图 8　2018 年软件业务收入前 10 位中心城市软件业务收入增长情况

增长 11.7%。软件百家企业更新率明显下降，两年都在榜企业 93 家，有 7 家企业首次或重新进入名单，企业持续增长能力增强。软件百家企业整体规模继续扩大，共完成软件业务收入 7 712 亿元，比上届增长 16.5%，增速同比加快 6.3 个百分点，高于全行业收入增速 2.1 个百分点，占全行业收入比重达到 12.2%。其中，软件业务收入过 100 亿元的企业达 13 家，比上届增加 4 家。

加快探索转型升级路径，部分软件百家企业实现领先发展。软件百家企业中，超过三成的企业收入增长率超过 20%；增速超过 50%的企业达到 9 家；两年持续在榜企业中，排名提升超过 10 位的企业达到 15 家。部分企业依靠积极转型和创新实现突破，如北京华胜天成公司实施服务转型以及在云计算领域打造自主品牌“天成云”，排名提升 41 位；部分企业深入研究和推进新兴技术的应用，如北京易华录公司将大数据和人工智能技术应用于智慧城市和交通、安防领域，排名提升 29 位；部分企业将推动专业领域的高端化发展和在新兴领域布局并重，如江苏润和科技在聚焦金融信息化领域的同时，围绕物联网“芯片、平台、应用”的战略布局也初步成型，排名提升 20 位；部分企业如科大讯飞、大疆创新等在新兴领域积累独特核心技术，连续两年排名大幅提升，2018 年分别提升 18 位和 14 位；另有部分企业依托自有终端品牌优势，深耕产业链上下游，提供移动端解决方案，如广东维沃软件、小米移动、云中飞均实现 10 位以上排名提升。

软件百家企业研发投入保持增长，创新质量进一步提升。软件百家企业共投入研发经费 1 550 亿元，占全行业研发投入的 27.6%，远超其收入和利润在全行业的比重，是软件业研发投入的关键主体。企业平均研发强度（研发经费占主营业务收入比例）9.7%，高于全行业平均水平 2.1 个百分点；研发强度超过 15%的企业有 15 家，其中有 12 家连续两年研发强度超过 15%；参与研发的人员数接近 46 万人，占软件百家企业总从业人员数的 46%，与上届相比增长 17.9%。软件百家企业的著作权登记量超过 3 万件，比上届增长近 40%。

软件百家企业在新兴领域实现蓬勃发展，国际化经营稳步推进。软件百家企业在软件产品、信息技术服务和嵌入式系统软件三个领域的收入占比分别为 30%、45%和 25%，与上届相比，信息技术服务领域收入占比明显上升。在新兴产业领域，充分运用大数据、移动互联网、云计算等信息技术和手段，企业实现快速迭代，催生出更多的新兴服务业态，本届软件百家企业的云服务相关的运营服务收入增长超过 90%，数据处理服务收入增长一倍多。软件百家企业坚持开放发展，2017 年实现软件出口 257 亿美元，比上届增长 22.4%；出口主要市场由传统市场向新兴市场拓展，特别是随着“一带一路”基础设施的互联互通以及各类国际合作不断落地，对“一带一路”沿线国家和地区的软件出口明显上升。

三、2018 年中国软件正版化工作开展情况

中国一贯高度重视科学技术创新和知识产权保护，通过软件正版化加强软件知识产权保护，是鼓励和促进知识与技术创新的重要举措。2018 年，工业和信息化部继续落实《关于计算机预装正版操作系统软件有关问题的通知》和《关于政府部门购置计算机办公设备必须采购已预装正版操作系统软件产品的通知》等一系列指导文件精神，并联合多部

委开展软件正版化督查工作，维护计算机市场和软件市场秩序，营造良好的软件知识产权保护社会环境，推动软件产业创新。

（一）巩固计算机预装正版操作系统工作成果

2018年，根据计算机预装正版操作系统软件工作部署要求，工业和信息化部下发《关于报送2017年度计算机预装正版操作系统软件有关问题的通知》，继续要求国内主要品牌计算机生产商和操作系统软件提供商上报2017年度计算机销售数量、操作系统软件的预装数量。近年来，随着预装工作的稳步推进，在计算机生产企业和软件企业的共同努力下，我国新出厂计算机正版操作系统软件的装机数量和预装率逐年提高，对推进国家软件正版化，改善国内软件知识产权保护环境发挥了积极的作用。2007年预装率为87.75%，2008年预装率为93.52%，自2009年预装率达到98.02%以来，新出厂计算机预装正版操作系统比例连续9年稳定在98%以上，2017年预装率为98.62%，2018年预装率达100%。

（二）通过“剑网行动”落实版权保护工作①

2018年7月，国家版权局、国家互联网信息办公室、工业和信息化部、公安部四部委联合下发《关于开展打击网络侵权盗版“剑网2018”专项行动的通知》，对专项行动进行动员部署。“剑网2018”聚焦网络转载、短视频、动漫、知识分享、有声读物等重点领域，各级版权执法部门守正创新、真抓实干，查办了一批侵权盗版大要案件，为庆祝改革开放40周年营造了良好的网络文化环境。专项行动期间，各级版权执法监管部门删除侵权盗版链接185万条，收缴侵权盗版制品123万件，查处网络侵权盗版案件544件，其中查办刑事案件74件、涉案金额1.5亿元，专项行动取得显著成效。

（三）软件著作权登记高速增长

软件正版化工作的持续推进，提高了中国软件产业整体知识产权保护意识，间接推动了软件知识产权水平的提升和能力创建。

2018年，全国共完成计算机软件著作权登记1 104 839件，同比增长48.22%。从登记区域分布情况看，软件著作权登记区域主要分布在东部地区，登记量约80万件，占登记总量的72.78%；东北地区虽然登记量相对较少，但增长较快，高于全国整体增速约42个百分点，相比其他地区增长最快。从各地登记数量情况看，软件著作权登记量较多的省（市）依次为：广东、北京、上海、江苏、浙江、山东、四川、福建、湖北、河南。上述地区共登记软件约85万件，占登记总量的77.38%，其中，广东省登记软件约28万件，占登记总量的24.28%。从各类热点领域软件登记情况看，APP软件登记量增长较为明显，同比增长76.29%，是增长较快的热点领域软件类别之一。另外，人工智能软件登记数量同比增长104.02%，大数据软件登记数量同比增长64.27%，增速均高于软件登记整体增速，呈现出不同程度的快速发展态势。

根据中国版权保护中心著作权质权登记信息统计，2018年全国计算机软件著作权质权登记350件，同比增长50.21%；涉及合同数量350个，同比增长50.21%；涉及作品数量1 171件，同比增长18.64%；涉及主债务金额475 282.2万元，同比增长123.89%；涉及担保金额465 786万元，同比增长119.11%。

四、2018年中国软件产业发展特点

（一）产业规模效益持续快速增长，促进稳增长、稳就业

中国软件产业规模进一步扩大，有力拉动了经济增长。2018年，我国软件产业实现业务收入6.3万亿元，同比增长14.2%；实现利润总额8 079亿元，同比增长9.7%。中国软件产业已成为经济平稳较快增长的重要推动力量，软件产业盈利能力稳步提升，高质量发展成效初显，全行业正在形成具有实力的大企业和充满活力的小企业协同发展的良好局面。中国软件产业从业人数平稳增加，为稳定就业做出贡献。2018年末，我国软件和信息技术服务业从业人员同比增长4.2%，占我国城镇就业总人数的1.47%，比2017年末稍有提升；软件和信息技术服务业从业人员工资总额增长13.4%，人均工资增长8.8%②。从国家统计局2012年至2018年年度平均工资发展趋势来看，在我国，软件行业工资水平已超过金融业，成为薪资水平最高的行业。

（二）产业结构持续优化，软件定义深入发展③

产业结构持续优化。2018年，软件产品、信息

① 国家版权局通报“剑网2018”专项行动工作成果［EB/OL］.［2019-03-28］. http://www.cac.gov.cn/2019-02/28/c_1124171978.htm.

② 2018年软件和信息技术服务业统计公报解读［EB/OL］.［2019-03-28］. http://www.miit.gov.cn/n1146285/n1146352/n3054355/n3057511/n3057518/c6633639/content.html.

③ 同②.

技术服务和嵌入式系统软件收入比为 31∶55∶14，其中信息技术服务收入同比增长 17.6%，快于行业平均水平 3.2 个百分点。龙头骨干企业利润总额增长 19.6%，销售利润率为 9.2%，全行业正逐步形成大企业和中小企业融通发展的良好局面。

软件定义深入发展。软件定义全面融入经济社会各领域，软件创新引擎作用更加凸显，软件信息服务消费占比提升至 46.8%，全国开展网络化协同、服务型制造和个性化定制的企业比例分别达到 33.7%、24.7%和 7.6%；工业企业数字化研发设计工具普及率、关键工序数控化率分别增至 68.6%和 48.5%。

（三）新兴信息技术快速发展，培育新动能

新兴业态拉动软件业加快发展，已成为新的增长点。我国特有的人口基数庞大、互联网普及程度高、基础数据资源丰富等特点，有力促进了云计算、大数据以及人工智能技术的快速落地和应用发展。同时，云计算、大数据和人工智能技术也全面影响到传统软件开发领域，促使开发、交付和盈利等模式转型，引发计算平台重构并带来新的市场空间，使平台软件、APP 软件等快速兴起，软件产品实现收入增长 12.1%。

新兴信息技术与传统产业融合加深，为经济发展注入新动能。新一代信息技术在经济社会各领域开展广泛应用和模式创新，支撑制造业、农业、金融、能源、物流等传统产业优化升级，为传统产业"赋智赋能"，出现越来越多的典型应用案例，特别是在工业领域的应用加快，2018 年工业软件收入增长 14.2%，工业互联网正在成为新一轮工业革命和产业变革的焦点；支持智慧城市、智慧交通、智慧社区、智慧医疗等建设，帮助解决社会管理和民生问题的同时，创造出新的市场需求，对重点龙头软件企业的监测显示，交通、安防领域的信息技术需求增长明显。

（四）软件业科研创新活力进一步提升，创新体系不断完善

中国软件企业研发投入不断增强。软件和信息技术服务业研发呈现"龙头领先、中小微跟进"的趋势。对重点龙头软件企业的监测显示，2018 年企业研发投入增长达 20.4%，高于其业务收入增速 13.3 个百分点，研发强度达 10.4%①。应用拉动型的创新体系正在形成和完善。云计算、大数据技术逐渐成熟和落地，已成为大多数软件企业创新发展和业务应用的主流方向；人工智能、区块链等技术打开了新的创新路径，初步形成多种创新应用成果，在计算机视觉、语音识别等领域引领发展；开源社区改变传统开发模式，正在成为新的创新原动力；以应用拉动创新的体系，催生出大量新兴业态，吸引了来自不同行业和领域的投资和资源，不断向软件和信息技术服务业倾斜。

（五）软件业集聚发展效应进一步凸显，布局合理调整

中国软件业就地区而言，东部地区产业优势地位更为突出。中西部地区通过走特色发展之路，部分省市增势突出。中西部地区部分省市利用新业态迅速发展、产业转型升级、布局出现调整的机遇期，积极打造特色产业，推动软件业快速发展。全国重点城市在软件业发展中的作用突出，重点城市立足人才、创新、资源等方面优势，形成各自的软件产业发展特色，获得质量效益双提升，并辐射和带动周边地区发展。

（六）信息技术服务业开展创新与合作，提升服务能力

2018 年，我国信息技术服务业骨干企业通过创新，服务能力和水平均获得较大提升，以企业为主体、以核心技术为重点、以应用为导向的产业技术创新体系不断完善，技术创新和服务研发取得显著进展。在新兴领域，百度、阿里巴巴、腾讯等企业纷纷加快大数据、云计算、人工智能、物联网等领域布局，通过加大研发投入、引导业务模式创新、组建聚焦于新兴领域的研发团队来塑造企业在新兴领域的竞争能力。百度在人工智能领域率先发力，人工智能研究院正成为构筑企业全球市场竞争力的重要利器；阿里巴巴在云计算领域实现突破，成为全球第二大云计算服务提供商，正探索基于大数据的企业发展新路径；腾讯主要依托移动互联网的率先布局，不断深化基于移动互联网的应用创新。

（七）软件国际合作活跃，国际化经营稳步推进

在 G20 等多边框架下国际合作不断深化，智能制造、工业互联网等领域的政策交流和合作不断扩大。2018 年，中国软件业实现出口 554.5 亿美元，占全行业业务收入的 6%左右，其中软件外包服务出口增长 5.1%②。出口主要市场由传统市场向新兴

① 2018 年软件和信息技术服务业统计公报解读［EB/OL］.［2019-03-28］. http://www.miit.gov.cn/n1146285/n1146352/n3054355/n3057511/n3057518/c6633639/content.html.

② 同①.

市场拓展，特别是随着“一带一路”基础设施的互联互通以及各类国际合作不断落地，对“一带一路”沿线国家和地区的软件出口明显上升，虽整体规模不大，但增势突出。比如本届软件百家企业跨国经营活动深度和广度不断拓展，有四成以上企业持续开展跨国经营活动，有 20 家在境外设立了分公司或研发中心，有 18 家在境外设立分支机构，在海外的本地化经营稳步推进①。

综上，2018 年，我国软件和信息技术服务业总体保持平稳较快发展，产业规模进一步扩大，盈利能力稳步提升，行业就业形势保持稳定，产业服务化、平台化、融合发展态势更加明显，软件正版化工作稳步推进，在为制造强国和网络强国建设提供基础支撑、为经济高质量发展提供新动能等方面的作用进一步凸显。

① 2018 年（第 17 届）中国软件业务收入前百家企业发展报告［EB/OL］.［2019-03-29］. http://www.miit.gov.cn/n1146285/n1146352/n3054355/n3057511/n3057518/c6472762/content.html.

2018 年中国网络游戏产业发展报告

廖旭华

一、2018 年中国网络游戏产业发展背景

（一）中国网络游戏产业政策背景

1. 游戏监管进入调整升级阶段

2018 年 3 月，《深化党和国家机构改革方案》和《国务院机构改革方案》分别印发。根据该等方案，原属于国家新闻出版广电总局的出版管理职责划入中共中央宣传部。在机构改革进行的过程中，在出版管理职责范畴内的网络游戏出版运营的审批工作（即版号审批）于 2018 年 4 月至 11 月被暂停。

根据《出版管理条例》《网络出版服务管理规定》《关于移动游戏出版服务管理的通知》等规定，版号审批是网络游戏上线运营及商业化的必经流程。而此次的版号审批暂停，虽然在一定程度上影响了网络游戏市场的产品供应，但以中共中央宣传部为主的监管部门亦在此期间进行了深入的改革，优化了审批流程，强调了精品扶持，加强了发展引导。

随着以版号审批为主的游戏监管机制的调整和升级，国家将会不断加强对网络游戏产业的支持和引导，促进产业转型升级，以实现更加高质量的可持续发展。

2. 未成年人保护机制建设持续推进

在 2018 年 8 月由八部门联合印发的《综合防控儿童青少年近视实施方案》中，国家新闻出版署提出将“实施网络游戏总量调控，控制新增网络游戏上网运营数量，探索符合国情的适龄提示制度，采取措施限制未成年人使用时间”，这是未成年人网络游戏沉迷问题引起社会广泛关注之后，由监管部门正式提出的相关政策指引。

在此背景下，以腾讯游戏为代表的网络游戏企业开始积极参与到未成年人保护机制的探索和试验过程中来，联合相关协会及机构共同研究相关的适龄提示和行为保护机制，并向监管部门积极表达意见，为尽快出台专门针对未成年人沉迷网络游戏的规范性文件提供充分的支持。

未成年人行为保护机制的建设正在持续推进。虽然在使用时间、消费金额等方面的限制会在短期内对个别网络游戏企业的营业收入造成一定程度的影响，但是，未成年人行为保护是网络游戏产业实现社会价值和产业价值的全面统一的重要组成部分之一，将会成为网络游戏健康发展的重要基础。

（二）中国网络游戏产业经济环境背景

1. 互联网投融资保持整体增长

2017—2018 年我国互联网投融资整体情况见图 1。

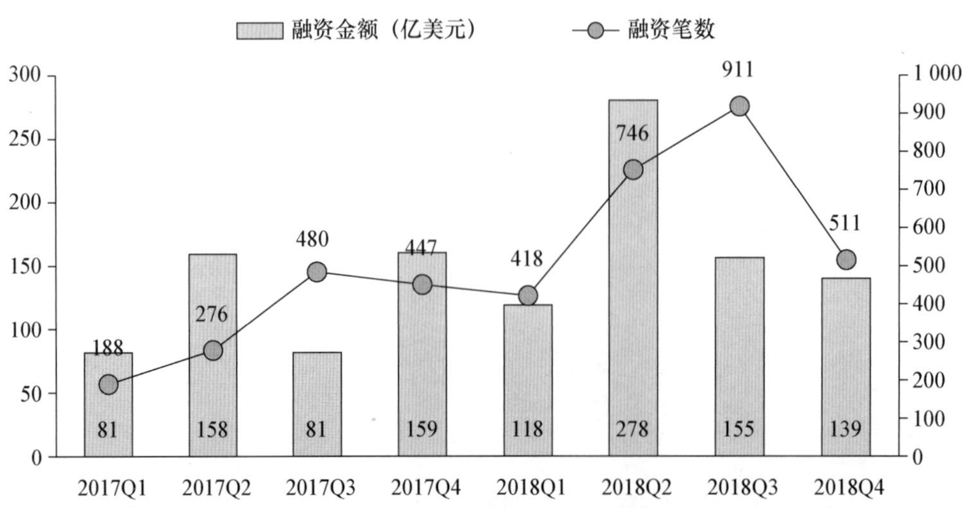

图 1 2017—2018 年我国互联网投融资整体情况

信通院数据显示，2018 年，中国互联网投融资披露总金额为 690 亿美元，相较于 2017 年的 479 亿美元，增长 44.1%。其中，各季度的同比增长率情况如表 1 所示。

表 1　2018 年各季度互联网融资同比增长率

季度	融资金额同比增长率	融资笔数同比增长率
2018Q1	45.7%	122.3%
2018Q2	75.9%	170.3%
2018Q3	91.4%	89.8%
2018Q4	12.6%	14.3%

数据表示，即使是在全球资本市场收紧和二级市场低迷的背景下，中国互联网的增长潜力和投资价值依然受到了投资者的肯定。这主要是由于中国互联网经济在经历了高速发展之后依然能够持续创新，在全球经济复苏的大背景下，拥有优于其他产业的投资价值，吸引了大量投资者的持续关注。同时，互联网投融资的整体增长，亦为作为互联网重要组成部分之一的中国网络游戏产业提供了良好的资本环境基础，为产业升级和创新创业提供了资本支持。

2. 居民文化娱乐消费支出持续增加

国家统计局数据显示，2016 年我国人均可支配收入达到 23 821 元人民币，2017 年我国人均可支配收入则达到了 25 974 元人民币，而 2018 年，全国居民人均可支配收入 28 228 元，比上年增长 8.7%。扣除价格因素，实际增长 6.5%。2016 至 2018 年的年均复合增长率（不扣除价格因素）为 8.9%。伴随着人均可支配收入的逐步增长，居民消费结构逐步发生变化，教育文化娱乐消费占比基本稳定，2018 年达到 11.2%，这表明居民的教育文化娱乐需求日益增长，教育文化娱乐支出亦持续增加，为网络游戏产业的发展提供了重要的消费环境基础。2016—2018 年全国居民人均消费支出及构成见图 2。

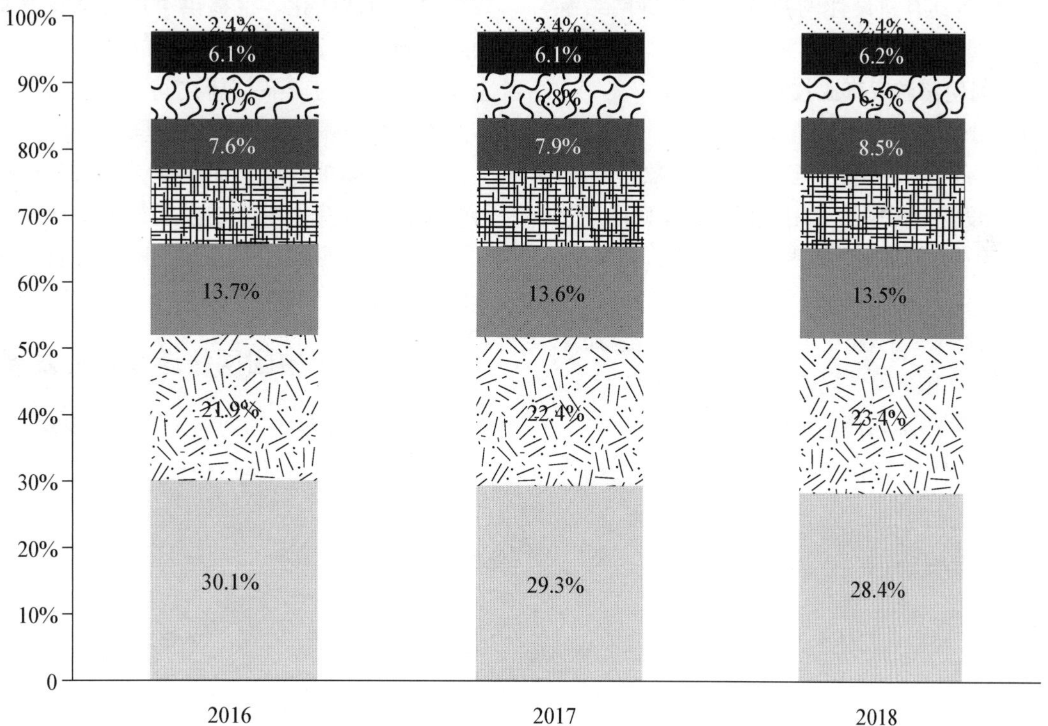

图 2　2016—2018 年全国居民人均消费支出及构成

（三）中国网络游戏产业社会环境背景

1. 公众对网络游戏产业的认知和理解不断加深

2018 年版号审批的暂停影响了网络游戏企业的产品上线计划，直接引起了游戏玩家和普通公众的广泛关注。在此契机下，更多的普通玩家和公众开始去了解网络游戏企业和网络游戏产品的发行、运营等流程，并关心游戏产品的研发及商业化状况，这不仅体现在各大社交网络平台上的广泛讨论之中，也体现在持续增多的媒体报道之中。例如，在社交和视频媒体平台也涌现了一大批以“游戏行业人士”身份向普通公众普及相关产业知识的自媒体。

这是在网络游戏被熟知的范围不断扩大的基础上，公众自发的大型产业科普活动。在此过程中，普通玩家不仅开始认识到网络游戏企业的发展情况，也对与版号审批息息相关的网络游戏商业化的相关问题有了更多的理解。而《人民日报》等主流媒体亦发表《疏堵结合，让孩子远离游戏瘾》等相关评论，引导公众正确和辩证地认识网络游戏的价值。

这体现了社会舆论环境对网络游戏产业的理性探讨和认知，为日后网络游戏产品的发行和运营提供了更加良好的舆论基础和更加理性的消费认知。

2. 媒体正在积极履行监督职能

虽然网络游戏产业取得了重大的产业成功，但过于粗放化的发展过程也给网络游戏产业带来了诸多问题，如粗制滥造、诱导消费、误导价值观等。2018 年，社会媒体环境开始对网络游戏产业的发展问题进行全面深入的关注和监督，使得众多发展问题持续见诸报端，引起广泛关注的同时也促进了产业自律和监管的升级。同时，主流媒体亦对网络游戏市场净化、产业转型升级、青少年保护等议题进行了诸多积极的探讨。

主流媒体积极履行监督职能，在指出相关网络游戏产业发展问题的同时，也为游戏产业的可持续发展提出了众多具有建设性的建议，是促进网络游戏产业发展的重要社会力量。

（四）中国网络游戏产业技术环境背景

1. 网络传输技术水平不断提升

中国通信标准化协会旗下宽带发展联盟数据显示，2018 年第四季度，全国平均可用宽带下载速率已经达到了 28.06Mbit/s，同比提升幅度高达 47.61%，其中，4G 网络平均下载速率为 22.05Mbit/s，同比提升幅度为 21.29%。此外，中国互联网普及率亦达到了 59.6%。同时，在国务院“提速降费”政策的领导下，三大运营商的移动互联网流量价格均下降超过 50%。

固定宽带和移动网络的传输技术水平的不断提升，不仅能够为网络游戏产业提供更加庞大的网民用户基础，也可以不断促进网络游戏用户体验的升级。尤其在移动游戏逐渐成长为网络游戏产业主要细分市场的基础上，游戏产品对网络传输水平和成本的要求正在不断提高，而不断优化的速率和费率的支撑，也减少了网络游戏企业在产品研发过程中的忧虑，使其能够更加专注地为用户打造更优质的游戏产品，吸引更多的用户。

2. 云计算及 5G 等技术将带来新的产业升级

在众多领先公司的共同努力下，云计算的技术和产品在 2018 年继续升级，不仅分发网络的建设更加成熟，应用于网络游戏研发、测试、运营等场景的解决方案也在持续专业化。对于长期存在网络服务困扰的中国网络游戏产业来说，云计算的不断成熟能够有效降低网络运营事故的风险，也可以通过分发优化等方式提升用户体验，从而减少运营方面的收益损失，获得更多用户的认可和支持。

5G 网络的商用化建设亦在 2018 年得到了全面的积极推进，5G 给网络游戏产业带来的不仅是传输效率的革命性变化，也提供了进行全新产业升级的网络基础。在 5G 的网络能力的基础上，网络游戏企业拥有更多的产品创新空间，可以为用户研发更多的创新和技术突破型产品。同时，在云计算、5G 等技术的保障下，以实时响应、无须客户端计算的云游戏将有望获得更大的发展机会，从而在游戏研发、发行、商业模式等方面给网络游戏产业带来全新的产业升级。

二、2018 年中国网络游戏产业发展现状

（一）2018 年中国网络游戏市场规模

图 3 为 2016—2021 年中国网络游戏市场规模及

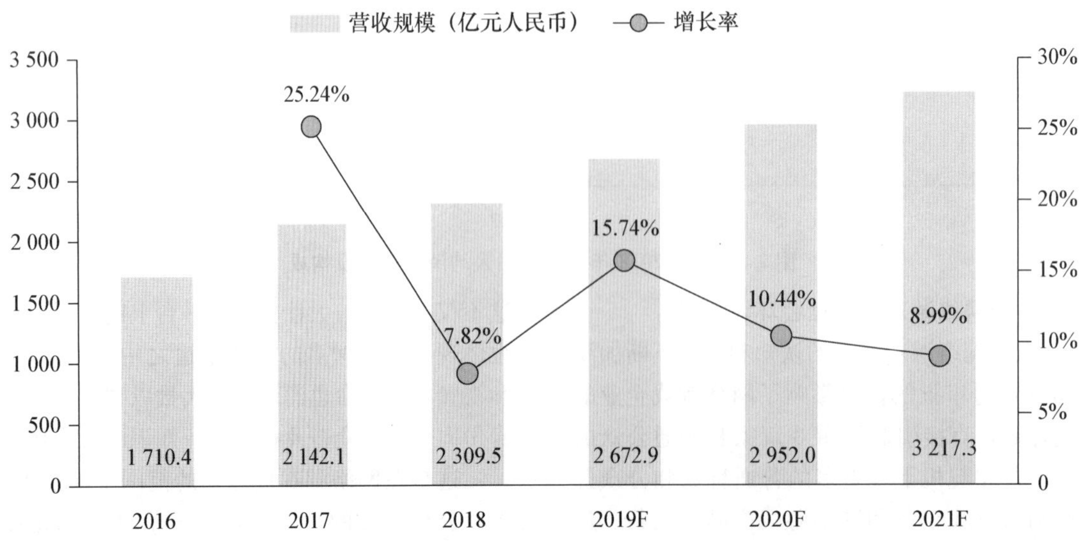

图 3　2016—2021 年中国网络游戏市场规模及预测

预测。网络游戏市场规模是指网络游戏（PC互联网游戏和移动互联网游戏，不包括主机游戏）在中国大陆境内所产生的全部收益规模，包括版权分成、自主研发及代理产品运营所产生的充值卡、虚拟道具付费、游戏内广告收入等线上收入在内的全部收益规模。

从我国网络游戏市场来看，2018年的增长情况略低于预期。2018年全国网络游戏市场规模达到了2 309.5亿元人民币，增长率为7.82%。预计在2021年整体的网络游戏市场规模将达3 217.3亿元人民币。2018年的增速下滑主要是由于版号审批的短期暂停影响了大部分网络游戏企业的新产品上线，从而将网络游戏用户增速下滑、产品能力不足、同质化问题严重等深层次因素的影响进一步催化，更多的网络游戏企业选择将产品发行至海外地区。2018年的网络游戏市场主要体现出两大特征：领先型产品对市场的影响力不断加大，主要是指由知名版权所改编而来的IP游戏和成本投入较大的精品游戏吸引了更多用户的支持；长线产品运营投入增长，主要是指游戏企业不断在已发行较长时间的游戏中投入大量的内容更新和活动运营成本。这都是在产业升级调整的过程中，网络游戏企业为了降低业务运营风险和保持业绩增长所做的主动选择。

2018年，战术竞技游戏的崛起吸引了大量的新进用户，从而促使中国网络游戏用户规模实现了优于预期的增长率，达到了6.90%，整体规模为6.20亿人（见图4）。虽然用户增速有所回升，但由于主要游戏商业化计划推迟和整体游戏质量水平不足等原因，用户的需求并没有得到充分的满足和挖掘，所以未能对市场规模产生有效的推动作用。随着整体渗透率趋于饱和，用户规模从增量时代进入存量时代已成定局，预计将继续保持较低的增长率。而较大的用户规模存量将为中国网络游戏产业提供充分的发展基础，在用户需求的持续升级和挖掘过程中进一步促进中国网络游戏产业的可持续发展。

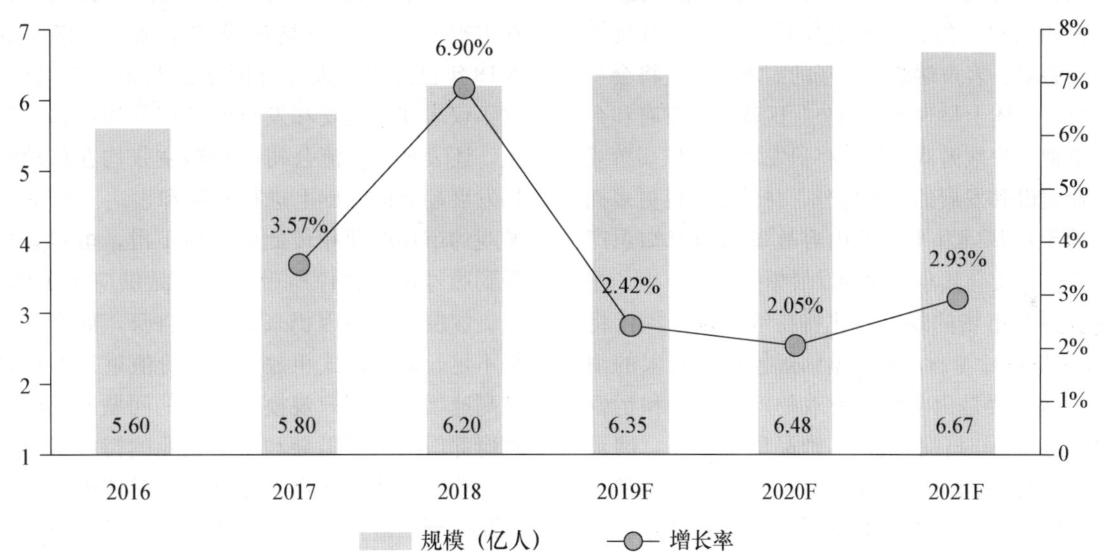

图4　2016—2021年中国网络游戏用户规模及预测

（二）2018年中国网络游戏细分市场结构

目前我国网络游戏市场主要存在三类游戏产品：通过客户端形式在个人电脑中下载、安装和运行的客户端游戏；通过网页形式在个人电脑中通过浏览器等工具直接打开和运行的网页游戏；在以手机为主、平板电脑为辅的移动个人设备中运行的移动游戏。

从市场规模占比来看，移动游戏已经成为目前的核心市场，2018年，移动游戏在整体网络游戏市场中的占比为62.8%，预计将于2021年突破70%（见图5）。

客户端游戏市场在2018年出现了一定的负增长，主要原因是持续的用户流失和产品供应的严重不足。2018年中国客户端游戏市场仍以拥有一定发展历史的产品为主，这主要是因为客户端游戏是研发成本更高、内容丰富程度更大、用户忠诚度更高的游戏，游戏企业更加注重已有产品的维护，并注重长远价值的实现，致力于将客户端游戏打造成具备市场影响力的知识产权，并通过改编成移动游戏、影视等娱乐产品扩大收益。作为中国网络游戏发展历史最长的市场之一，客户端游戏市场的发展为中国网络游戏市场培养了大量的团队和核心用户，其历史作用不可忽视。但是目前国内端游市场面临着难以解决的供应与需求矛盾。供应方面，虽然中国企业将会制作出更多影响小众乃至境外市场的端游产品，但在出版、成本和市场等多重因素的影响下，

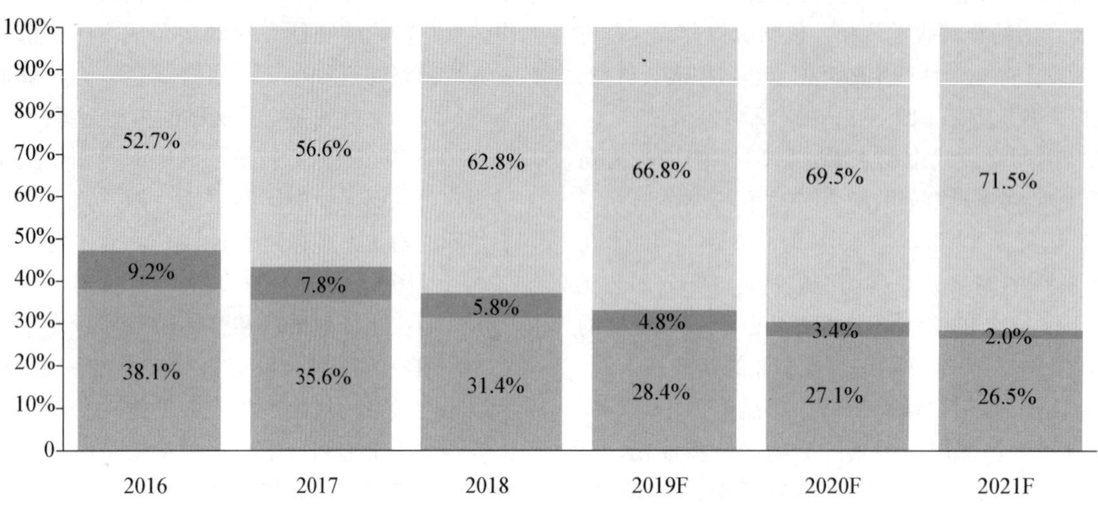

图 5　2016—2021 年中国网络游戏细分市场占比及预测

大部分游戏企业不断减少客户端游戏的研发投入，导致产品供应不足。但是，在需求方面，游戏经验日益丰富的用户必然将追求更加高质量和高可玩性的客户端游戏，客户端游戏市场的需求的发展将会与供应相反，整体上呈现增长趋势。这就要求政府和企业重新重视客户端游戏市场，将研发新的客户端游戏作为产业建设和发展的重要部分，并借此培育更多拥有庞大的受众基础和丰富的内容故事的国产知识产权，从而促进文化娱乐产业的发展繁荣。

网页游戏市场的规模占比将持续下降，预计将于 2021 年降至 2.0%，成为整体规模相对有限的细分市场。这主要是由于网页游戏的产品质量和运营模式已经落后于时代的发展。产品质量方面，网页游戏由于只能由网页浏览器运行，产品质量受到了严重的限制，整体的内容丰富程度、产品设计水平等都比较低，市场呈现出粗制滥造、同质化等特征，这与游戏用户持续追求更高质量游戏体验的发展趋势相悖；运营模式方面，网页游戏严重依赖广告投放这一用户获取方式，缺乏对游戏用户的吸引能力，同时研发商所能获得的收入分成比例也相对较小，运营模式亦在广告费用持续上升的宏观经济环境中受到了持续的挑战。在此基础上，网页游戏不仅市场规模逐渐进入成熟期，市场竞争格局亦将更加固化，大部分的市场收入将由有较为成熟的产品运营经验和稳定的自有渠道的主流企业掌控。而更多的网页游戏企业将继续推动其多元化布局，将更多的资金和人力等资源投入到移动游戏市场中，从而实现转型。

移动游戏是目前中国网络游戏市场规模占比最大的市场，亦是市场增长的主要动力。与客户端游戏和网页游戏不同，在移动互联网不断发展的过程中，移动游戏积累了大规模的用户，而用户规模的增长和需求的升级则不断驱动着移动游戏的发展。在占据 62.8%的市场规模的基础上，移动游戏在 2018 年已经成为大部分网络游戏企业布局的重点，这不仅表现为研发和发行的新产品均以移动游戏为主，还表现为主流公司的战略主张均在移动游戏市场发展趋势的基础上进行制定和表达。2018 年移动游戏的市场增速相较此前有所下滑，虽然客观上是受到版号审批暂停所带来的产品供应不足的影响，但更深层次的原因仍来自产业自身，如产品质量水平不足、运营模式粗放、社会价值重视不足等过去被高速增长的用户规模所掩盖的问题开始凸显。在政府部门的积极引导和主流企业的持续努力下，移动游戏的产业升级已开始加速，具体表现为：粗劣产品受到严格控制，精品产品成为研发和发行的重点；粗放化运营逐渐式微，渠道市场逐渐规范化，企业更加注重通过产品质量的提升来吸引用户；主流企业开始注重游戏产品的社会文化价值，并积极履行社会责任。

（三）2018 年中国网络游戏产品结构

根据国家广电总局公布的信息，2018 年全年共有 2 084 款国产网络游戏过审（见图 6），即获得游戏版号，相较于 2017 年的 9 356 款有较大幅度的下降，这主要是由于国务院机构改革的进行，导致 4 月至 11 月期间的版号审批工作的暂停和调整。在此期间，虽然没有新的产品供应，但由于市场上拥有较多的存量产品，并且主流企业更加注重现有产品的长线运营，因此并没有严重影响市场发展。从整体上看，移动游戏总共为 2 020 款，整体占比为 96.9%，依然在产品产出方面保持绝对的渗透率。

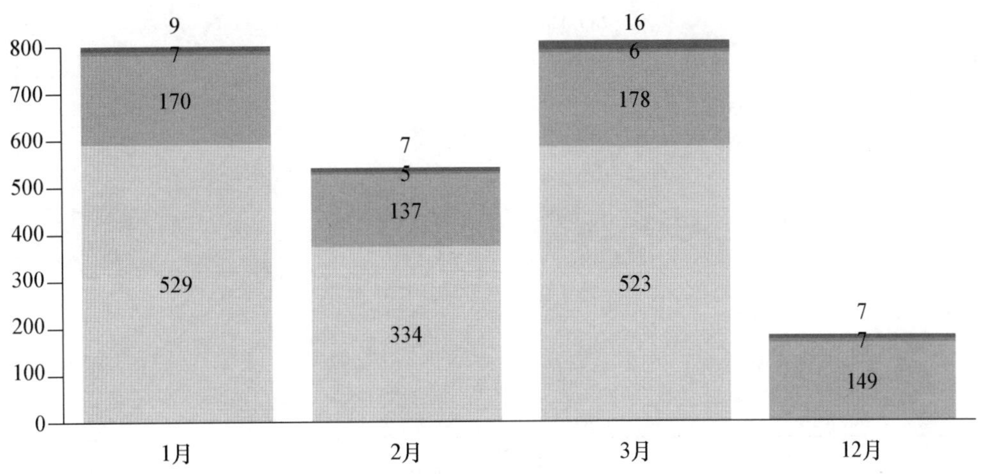

图 6　2018 年中国过审国产网络游戏统计

2018 年 12 月是版号审批工作调整过后的第一个月，相比较而言，过审产品总数有较大幅度的下滑。这主要是由于监管机构在总量控制的政策下通过审批工作推动和引导中国网络游戏产业的产品精品化。其中，此前长期占比高于 30%的归属于“休闲益智移动游戏”分类的棋牌游戏，由于产品的同质化问题较为严重，已不再是过审的主要产品。因此，虽然调整过后的过审产品总数有所下降，但更多的是受到扶持和肯定的精品产品，代表的是中国网络游戏产品质量水平的提升，数量减少并不会影响市场的增长和发展，相反，这将成为中国网络游戏产业全面升级的重要驱动因素之一。

（四）2018 年中国网络游戏用户省份分布

易观千帆数据显示，2018 年的中国网络游戏用户省份分布中，广东省占据 11.73%（见图 7），这主要是因为广东不仅拥有更多的人口和更高的互联网渗透率，还拥有以腾讯游戏、网易游戏为代表的网络游戏企业。

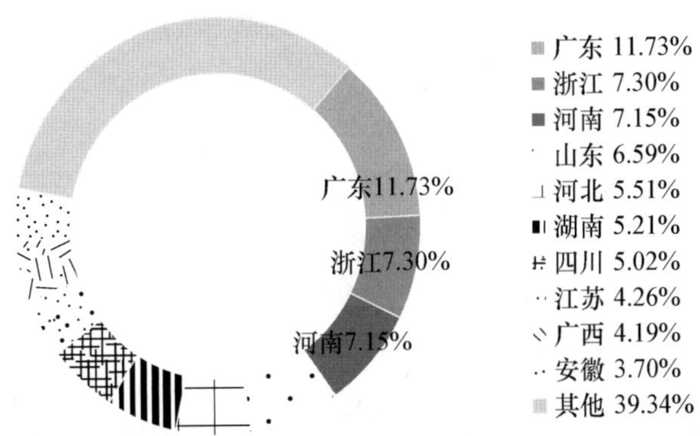

图 7　2018 年中国网络游戏用户省份分布

从整体上看，中国网络游戏市场的分布正在逐渐多元化，虽然从企业产值分布的角度看仍以广东为主，广东省的网络游戏企业营收在 2018 年占全国的 78%，但用户市场已经不再集中于一线城市，更多地向二、三线乃至更低线级的地域渗透。这既受宏观经济的影响，也受移动互联网发展的影响，还受网络游戏市场的影响。宏观经济方面，我们的城乡发展差距正在逐渐缩小，非一线城市的人民的收入水平不断提高，从而拥有了更好的文化消费能力和需求；移动互联网方面，通信基础设施的覆盖率不断提高，非一线城市的用户也拥有了充分的网络消费经验和基础；网络游戏市场方面，随着社交媒体和资讯平台的发展，网络游戏产品获得了更好的推广渠道和方式，从而能够为非一线城市用户提供更多的网络游戏产品资讯和触达机会。同时，市场渗透的多元化，也为网络游戏产业的发展提供了基础，能够为更多网络游戏经验相对有限的新进用户提供丰富的高质量产品，并实现市场规模的增长和产品结构的升级。

（五）2018 年中国网络游戏产业境外收入

2018 年，中国网络游戏境外收入达到了 118.7 亿美元，增长率为 28.60%，较 2017 年有较大幅度的提升（见图 8），这说明中国的网络游戏出口在 2018 年取得了优异的成绩。这不仅是因为境内市场的增速下滑驱动了更多的网络游戏企业向境外市场寻找新的增长空间，更是因为中国网络游戏公司已经具备参与国际竞争的实力。尤其在移动游戏的研发、发行和运营等方面，拥有领先于境外公司的发展经验和规模的中国网络游戏企业，能够在移动游戏方面制作出更加符合移动用户的游戏产品，亦能够有效地将通过广告、营销等方式扩大游戏用户规模。腾讯游戏、网易游戏等领先企业已经进入全球游戏企业进行移动游戏研发和发行的首选合作伙伴之列，开始从产品出口向能力出口升级。

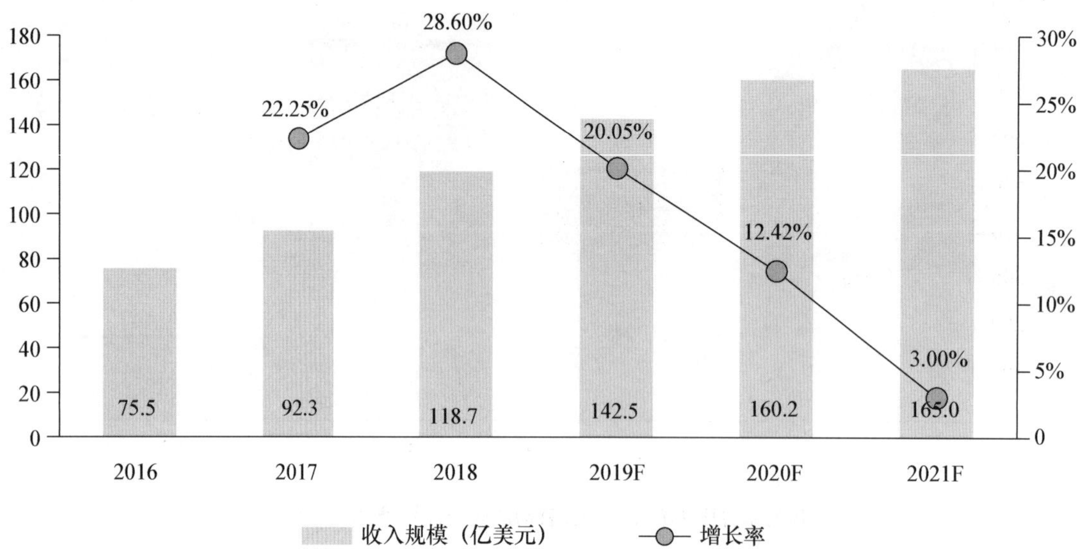

图 8　2016—2021 年中国网络游戏境外收入规模及预测

注：中国网络游戏境外收入是指由总部在中国大陆境内的网络游戏企业所研发或发行的网络游戏产品在境外（包括港澳台）地区所创造的充值和广告收入的总和，不包括中国网络游戏企业所收购或投资的总部在境外地区的网络游戏公司的收入。

除收入规模增长率提升外，2018 年的中国网络游戏出口主要体现出三大特点：市场持续扩张，开始全面走出以港澳台与东南亚为代表的传统市场，向更具挑战性的日韩、欧美以及中东等市场大举推进，并以多产品、多企业、高收入的姿态不断提升在各个区域市场所占据的市场份额；产品多维突破，产品数量持续突破，新进企业的增多给各个市场都带去了大量的优秀产品，同时产品品类也突破了固有僵局，将更多具备中华文化特色的网络游戏带到了各个境外市场；产业链成熟，在市场收入不断提升的过程中，提供推广、运营、云计算、支付等服务的企业也获得了持续成长，网络游戏出口产业链逐渐成熟。

作为内容丰富并且持续消费的文化产品，网络游戏将成为中华文化传播的重要载体，向海外用户传播中国传统文化，弘扬中国价值，提升中国文化的国际影响力。

三、2018 年中国网络游戏产业发展特点

（一）领先公司持续掌控市场

以中国移动游戏企业在中国市场内（不含港澳台）发行的移动游戏产品的充值流水计，2018 年，腾讯游戏占据 52.25%的市场份额，远高于其他游戏企业（见图 9）。腾讯游戏作为全国乃至全球营业收入最高的

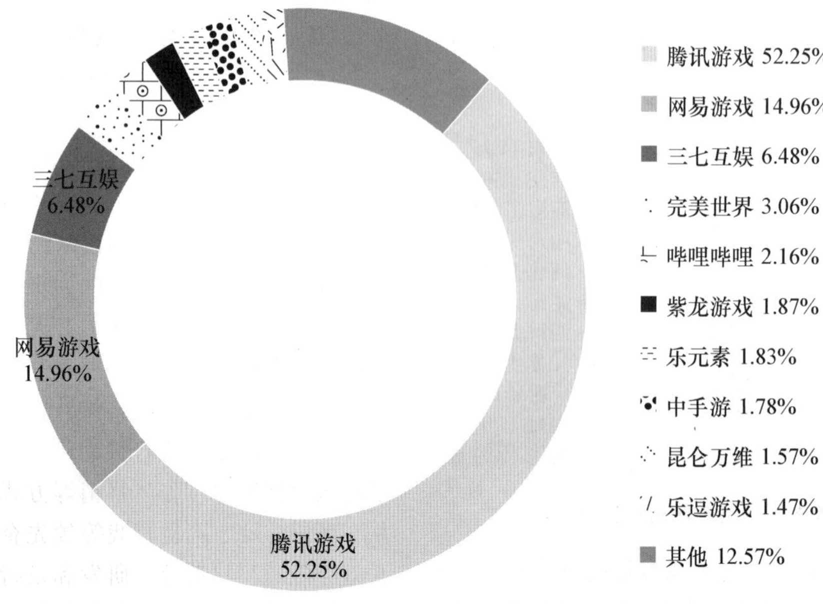

图 9　2018 年中国移动游戏发行竞争格局

网络游戏公司，拥有遥遥领先于其他网络游戏企业的产品研发能力和发行渠道资源，同时，依靠自身丰富的资源基础，腾讯亦获得了大量优秀网络游戏研发企业的支持，成为其重要的发行商，拥有众多精品产品的发行权，从而进一步扩大了自身的发行市场规模。而网易游戏则获得了14.96%的发行市场份额，这主要是由于网易游戏公司更多以自主研发的产品为主，发行业务较无优势，同时，网易游戏在2018年亦以境外发行业务为重点发展方向，在日本、韩国等市场拥有在当地领先的发行产品和收入。

除此之外，排名第三到第十的分别是三七互娱、完美世界、哔哩哔哩、紫龙游戏、乐元素、中手游、昆仑万维以及乐逗游戏。而其他企业所占市场份额仅为12.57%，这说明领先公司对市场的掌控依旧较为强势。

同时，各领先企业在2018年的业务更趋于多元化，新兴品类、海外等市场成为拓展布局重点。在存量市场中，包括三七互娱的“多元化”战略、中手游“全球化IP游戏运营商”的发展目标等，都显示了领先企业们对于市场拓展的积极态度。此外，领先企业亦拥有更为丰富的产品、资本等资源储备，这将使其在市场竞争中掌握更好的优势，能够在持续的布局和发展过程中促进其市场份额的提升，从而不断增强领先优势，这也对中小企业的能力提出了更加严苛的要求。

（二）创业风险和成本持续走高

一方面，根据公开信息，2018年中国网络游戏产业主要融资仅为96起，相较2017年的129起有一定的下降（见图10）。这不仅是因为网络游戏企业投资受到了国家相关政策的影响，更是因为网络游戏产业自身发展的问题。在2016年及以前，中国网络游戏产业由于市场增速过快，导致企业的业务能力出现分层，部分企业的产品研发和运营能力的不足被市场趋势所掩盖。而进入2018年后，企业自身不足的问题开始显现，从而导致了投资价值的下降，并影响了资本市场对于网络游戏产业的信心。其中的典型表现即为2018年网络游戏上市公司的大面积商誉减值，如天神娱乐、游久游戏、掌趣科技等均因收购标的企业业绩不达标而发生了高额的商誉减值，从而导致高额的亏损。商誉是收购价格与被收购企业净资产的差额，体现的是企业对被收购企业的盈利和发展能力的肯定和预测。正常情况下，商誉将在被收购企业逐年兑现业绩承诺的过程中被合理减值和补偿。而缺乏业绩兑现的高额商誉减值，则发生在被收购企业业绩严重不达预期的过程中，体现了企业在收购当时对于被收购企业未来盈利能力过于乐观的预测和不理性的收购估值。2018年的网络游戏上市公司大面积商誉减值，主要是由于2014、2015年行业环境过于乐观，出现了大量的激进收购案例，但这些被收购企业在2018年的业务情况和成绩不达标。

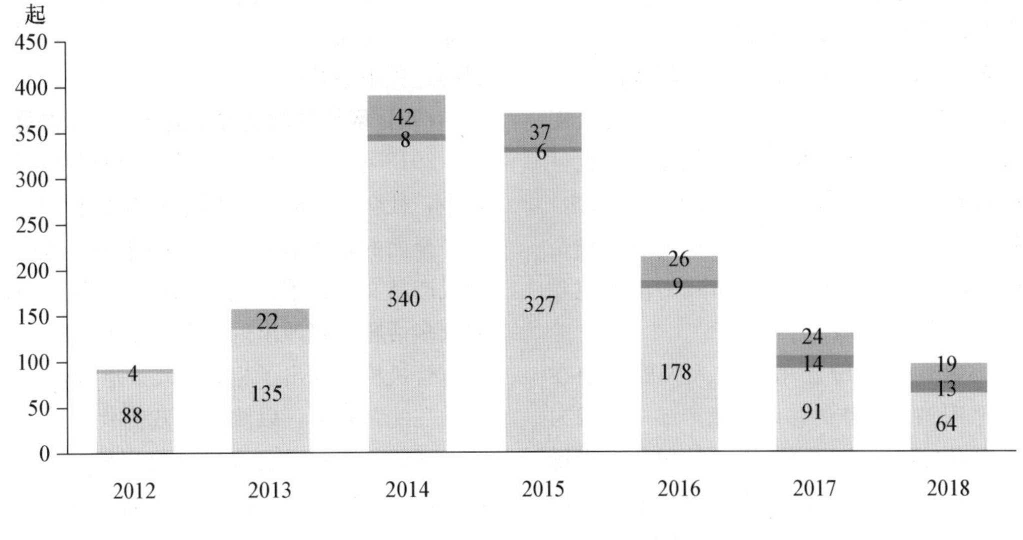

图10 2012—2018年中国网络游戏产业主要融资统计

注：图中数据仅统计了研发、发行及渠道，不包括其他非产业链核心角色的融资情况。

另一方面，战略投资的数量在2017年和2018年均有所提升，这说明资本市场对于拥有较为充足的资源储备、优秀的产品能力和成绩的大型企业的投资价值依旧保持较高的认可态度。但是，由于战略投资的被投企业一般都是规模较大的企业，也说明网络游戏产业的大型公司的领先优势有望持续加强，中小企业的发展空间进一步减小。

更为重要的是，由于融资数量的不断下降，在网络游戏企业研发和运营成本持续高涨和市场风险持续加剧的环境下，网络游戏创业的风险和成本将持续走高，创业者不仅难以寻找资本方的支持以分担创业风险和资金投入，还将面临领先企业竞争力不断加强的激烈的市场环境。

（三）IP 游戏持续崛起

2018 年，中国移动 IP 游戏收入规模达到了 972.4 亿元人民币，增长率为 29.36%，远高于整体市场增速（见图 11）。这说明，IP 游戏正在持续崛起，不仅市场收入持续增长，其所占的市场份额亦不断提升，正在成为最重要的细分市场之一。

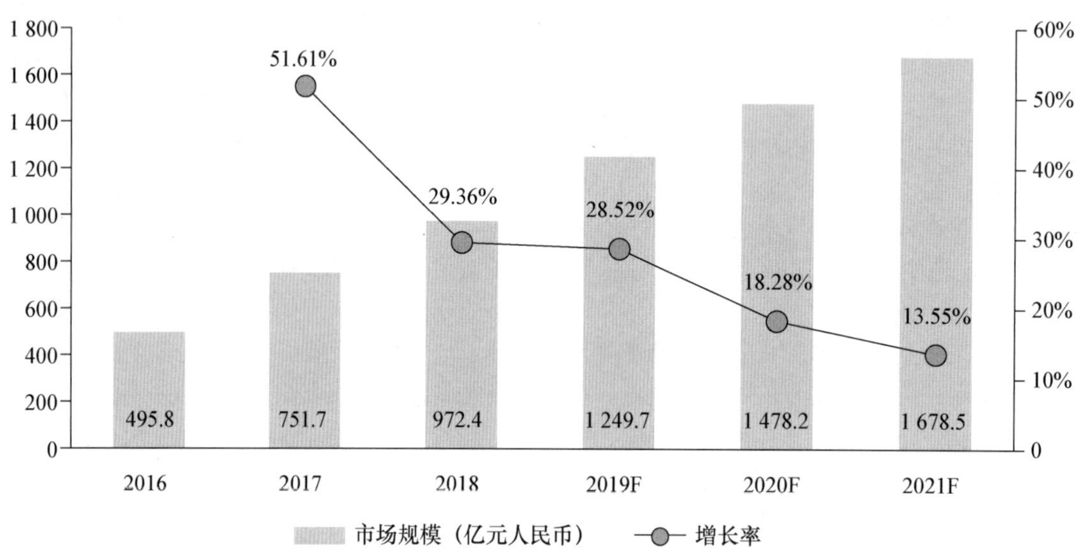

图 11　2016—2021 年中国移动 IP 游戏收入规模及预测

注：移动 IP 游戏是指获得了客户端游戏、电影、漫画、动画等其他文化娱乐产品的故事、美术、人物等知识产权的授权而制作发行的游戏。

一方面，与其他游戏相比，IP 游戏由于使用了其他文化娱乐产品的授权，因此在创作和研发过程中可以节省更多的支出，可直接引用原知识产权产品的元素，亦可以降低创作所带来的市场风险。另一方面，由于原知识产权产品已拥有一定的受众规模，因此 IP 游戏不仅拥有更明确的市场定位，也可以在发行的过程中节约更多的发行收入。换言之，选择研发和发行 IP 游戏，可以有效降低网络游戏企业的业务风险，也正因为如此，IP 游戏的市场重要性才会受到广泛的重视。

2018 年，中国移动 IP 游戏的收入主要集中在由客户端游戏 IP 改编制作的移动游戏产品中，因为客户端游戏拥有与移动游戏完全重合的用户，市场风险远低于其他 IP。同时，移动 IP 游戏的发展亦给大量的客户端游戏企业提供了充分的市场发展空间，从而避免因客户端游戏市场增长不足而陷入经营困难。

预计未来移动 IP 游戏的收入规模将持续增长，这不仅能促进网络游戏产业的发展，还可以促进其他文化娱乐产业的发展。网络游戏产品相对高效的营收能力，将为其他产业的创作者提供充足的商业化前景保障，提升其创作的信心和投入。网络游戏产业对于文化娱乐产业的推动，将在 IP 游戏持续崛起的过程中不断体现。

（四）网络游戏企业社会责任意识加强

2018 年，在中国网络游戏产业阶段性调整的过程中，社会、政府等对网络游戏企业的社会价值进行了全面的审视和评价。包括未成年人保护、网络游戏产品文化价值、网络游戏企业社会贡献等在内的众多话题频繁地出现在主流媒体、社交媒体之中，而监管机构亦提出了相关的政策指引和发展期待。

在此背景下，以腾讯游戏为代表的网络游戏企业亦开始不断提升自身的社会责任意识，积极履行社会责任，促进网络游戏产业的社会价值和产业价值的全面统一。

在战略主张上，腾讯游戏提出“新文创”战略，探索游戏的社会与产业二元价值；网易游戏提出“为热爱赋新”，探索网络游戏的新价值；盛趣游戏提出“精品化、全球化、新文化”，立足“科技赋能文化”；中手游提出“全球化 IP 游戏运营商”的发展目标，致力于促进文化娱乐产业发展壮大；完美世界坚持“精品化、多元化、全球化”，致力于持续推出融合传统文化精髓又结合时代发展特色的精品内容。总而言之，越来越多的领先网络游戏企业开始全新的战略升级，以强调自身的文化发展责任、使命和愿景。

在文化弘扬方面，腾讯游戏在2018年提出了“功能游戏”计划，投入大量的资源去研发和发行具有教育或公益价值的功能游戏；网易游戏发行了《绘真·妙笔千山》等以优秀传统文化为主要内容的网络游戏产品；盛趣游戏与国家文物局、南海博物馆等文化机构共同打造和发行相关的弘扬优秀传统文化的产品；三七互娱通过推动具有中国传统文化特色的产品的海外发行，助力中华文化的海外传播。网络游戏企业对其所研发和发行的产品的文化价值的重视正在日益提升，纷纷探索通过网络游戏这一新颖的形式弘扬优秀中华传统文化的方式和途径。

在公益贡献方面，三七互娱成立了“游心公益基金会”，开展教育精准扶贫工作，助力边远地区教育扶贫事业；掌趣科技发起“掌趣公益”计划，参与捐资助学、扶贫助困等活动；完美世界在2018年成立企业社会责任推进委员会，推动完美世界公益专项基金活动的丰富；中手游不仅开展了“中手游筑梦图书馆”计划，还积极组织员工参与慰问及志愿活动；游族网络以“游族公益基金会”为主，积极联合合作伙伴，开展儿童关爱、贫困救助等活动。网络游戏企业在履行作为企业的市场经营责任的同时，亦不断提升对社会公益的重视，通过积极的贡献来回馈社会。

除此之外，在未成年人保护、内容安全、数据安全、用户服务等方面，网络游戏企业的重视程度亦在不断提升，同时不断加强行业自律，自觉治理相关不当行为，积极探讨游戏产品的社会和产业价值的统一。

四、中国网络游戏产业发展趋势

（一）网络游戏市场将继续洗牌

虽然，中国网络游戏市场已经在2017年开始全面进入存量时代，并在2018年对主流市场开启了全面的企业洗牌，产品能力不足的企业正在持续退出市场，但是，在2018年的内外因素影响下，海外市场、小游戏等市场的快速崛起，仍为大量的游戏企业提供了可观的生存空间。进入2019年后，海外市场的竞争压力将急速增加，而细分市场又将在大厂的投入加码的推动下日益集中，只有以微信、手机QQ、抖音等各大媒体平台为依托的仍处于推广期和竞争期的小游戏是目前唯一存在增量红利的市场。可以预见的是，随着媒体平台对用户和产品争夺的结束，小游戏市场的增量红利将全面消亡，网络游戏市场将迎来进一步的大洗牌，不注重网络游戏产品内容质量和价值的粗放型流量思维彻底走向末路，最终市场将仅存三类企业：头部企业掌控市场、中等实力企业补全市场、长尾创新企业灵活生存。

其中，头部企业具备通过产品升级和深度运营提升收益，并依靠资源优化成本的能力，最终20家头部企业就可掌控90%的市场；而拥有各自核心优势的中等实力企业，将以专业和专注的姿态在创新游戏、小游戏、下沉市场、棋牌出海、女性互动等细分市场中找到生存空间，补全头部企业难以顾及的细分市场；最后，当产品品质无法升级以提升收益，而流量价格又持续走高时，大部分以流量为生的企业将走向末路。最终只会留下两类长尾企业：能够灵活运营的渠道创新团队与能够灵活试错的产品创新团队。

（二）网络游戏服务产业竞争将加剧

网络游戏作为数字文化创意产业，不仅拥有研发商、发行商和渠道商，在研发、发行和运营阶段，均拥有大量的产业服务企业，如提供研发支持的音乐、美术等物料供应商，提供云服务的云计算商，提供推广服务的广告服务商，提供运营和决策支持的数据服务商，等等。在庞大的市场规模和精品化的产品的基础上，网络游戏产业形成了完整且丰富的产业链。

然而，相较于研发商、发行商和渠道商，其他产业服务商的进入门槛和服务溢价均较低，各个环节都存在较多的参与企业，并且市场空间相对有限。随着网络游戏产业市场的逐渐升级，网络游戏企业对于专业服务的需求将愈加成熟，对服务商的专业能力要求更高，并且更加注重成本和收益效率。

因此，网络游戏服务产业的竞争将持续加剧，依靠价格优势进行市场拓张的企业将进入竞争力和运营状况的困境，而拥有更好的专业服务水平的企业将得到更多的网络游戏企业的认可。

具体而言：由于研发专业化趋势的增强，物料供应商市场仍将继续发展，但服务价格将趋于理性；由于大型企业市场竞争投入的增加，不具备综合能力和技术优势的中小云计算商将退出市场；由于广告市场的成熟，网络游戏企业独立进行广告投放的能力不断成长，缺乏资源优势的广告服务商的生存空间将持续压缩，网络游戏企业更倾向于自主程序化投放；由于发展前期价格竞争激烈，无数据资源和精细化算法技术积累的数据服务商将逐渐开启洗牌模式，部分牺牲利润争夺市场而忽略自身资源能力建设的中小数据服务商将退出市场。

（三）产品市场将进一步细分化和精品化

在市场增速下降的市场环境中，绝大部分网络游戏企业均将战略目光和资源投入聚焦在具有快速增长前景的细分市场，如女性游戏、二次元游戏、沙盒游戏、创新游戏等。在 2018 年，各大网络游戏企业对于细分市场的布局均已基本完成，随着产品研发和发行工作的逐渐推进，各个细分市场将迎来开发热潮。一方面，市场中将出现更多区别于传统品类的网络游戏产品；另一方面，细分市场的收入增长情况将得到进一步的推进。

同时，在监管机构的积极引导下，网络游戏市场将全面进入产品红利时代。与依靠持续进入的新增用户所带来的低用户获取成本发展的粗放的流量红利时代不同，产品红利时代发展的主要动力是现阶段所拥有的海量存量用户持续增加的对精品产品的需求。产品红利时代是精细化和精品化的，网络游戏企业之间的竞争不再是资源和市场投入的竞争，而是产品研发和创新能力的竞争。在此基础上，网络游戏产业将迎来更多制作标准、研发质量、内容创新、文化价值等各方面均处于较高水平的精品产品，从而促进中国网络游戏产业的高质量可持续发展。

版权

典型案件选编

DIAN XING AN JIAN XUAN BIAN

［编者按］　本栏目刊登四部分内容：1. 2019 年 4 月 17 日，最高人民法院发布了 2018 年中国法院 10 大知识产权案件和 50 件典型知识产权案例，本栏目选取其中 10 件著作权司法保护典型案件；2. 2019 年 4 月 26 日，国家版权局在 2019 年中国网络版权保护与发展大会上公布的 2018 年度全国打击侵权盗版十大案件；3. 2019 年“4·26”知识产权宣传周期间，部分省、自治区、直辖市高级人民法院公布了 2018 年度知识产权典型案件，本栏目选取其中的著作权典型案件；4. 部分省、自治区、直辖市公布或报送的 2018 年度著作权行政执法案件。

2018 年全国著作权司法保护典型案件

一、北京微播视界科技有限公司与百度在线网络技术（北京）有限公司、百度网讯科技有限公司侵害作品信息网络传播权纠纷案［广东省高级人民法院（2016）粤行终 492 号行政判决书］

【案情摘要】 北京微播视界科技有限公司（以下简称微播视界公司）是抖音平台的运营者。百度在线网络技术（北京）有限公司、百度网讯科技有限公司（合称百度公司）是伙拍平台的运营者。汶川特大地震十周年之际，2018 年 5 月 12 日，抖音平台的加 V 用户“黑脸 V”响应全国党媒信息公共平台（以下简称党媒平台）和人民网的倡议，使用给定素材，制作并在抖音平台上发布《5·12，我想对你说》短视频（以下简称《我想对你说》短视频）。经“黑脸 V”授权，微播视界公司对《我想对你说》短视频在全球范围内享有独家排他的信息网络传播权及独家维权的权利。《伙拍小视频》手机软件上传播了《我想对你说》短视频，该短视频播放页面上未显示有抖音和用户 ID 号水印。微播视界公司以《我想对你说》短视频构成以类似摄制电影的方法创作的作品（以下简称类电作品），百度公司上述传播和消除水印的行为侵犯了微播视界公司的信息网络传播权为由，提起诉讼。北京互联网法院一审认为，《我想对你说》短视频构成类电作品，百度公司作为提供信息存储空间的网络服务提供者，对于《伙拍小视频》手机软件用户提供被控侵权短视频的行为，不具有主观过错，在履行了“通知—删除”义务后，不构成侵权行为，不应承担相关责任，判决驳回微播视界公司的全部诉讼请求。

【典型意义】 本案为 2018 年度“中国十大传媒法事例”之一，引发了各界的广泛关注。本案涉及短视频节目能否得到著作权法保护、能得到何种程度保护等一系列新类型法律问题的解决，对人民法院如何在著作权司法实践中平衡好创作与传播、权利人与网络服务提供者以及社会公众的利益关系，提出了新的挑战。与传统类型的电影作品相比，短视频时间较短，是否具备著作权法对保护客体提出的“独创性”要求，是本案双方当事人争议的焦点。人民法院在本案中充分贯彻合理确定不同领域知识产权的保护范围和保护强度的司法政策，根据文学艺术类作品在作品特性、创作空间等方面的特点，充分考虑“互联网＋”背景下创新的需求和特点，合理确定了本案短视频节目独创性的尺度，正确划分了著作权范围与公共领域的界限，充分实现了保护知识产权与促进创新、推动产业发展的和谐统一。

二、深圳市快播科技有限公司与深圳市市场监督管理局、深圳市腾讯计算机系统有限公司著作权行政处罚纠纷案［北京互联网法院（2018）京 0491 民初 1 号民事判决书］

【案情摘要】 腾讯公司从权利人处获得涉案 24 部作品信息网络传播权的独家许可之后，又将其中 13 部作品的信息网络传播权以直接分销或版权等值置换等方式非独家许可第三方使用。腾讯公司提交的合同显示，该 13 部作品的分销或者置换价格总计人民币 8 671.6 万元。2014 年 3 月 18 日，腾讯公司向深圳市市场监督管理局（以下简称市场监管局）投诉称，快播公司侵害了其享有的涉案作品信息网络传播权，请求予以查处。市场监管局向深圳市盐田公证处申请证据保全公证。公证书显示，在手机上登录《快播》客户端搜索涉案 24 部影视作品，每一部影视作品首选链接均为“腾讯视频”，点击“腾讯视频”旁的下拉选项，均有其他链接（多数伪装成乐视网、优酷、电影网等知名视频网站）；点击其他链接播放具体集数，视频显示的播放地址均是一些不知名的、未依法办理备案登记的网站。2014 年 6 月 26 日，市场监管局做出深市监稽罚字〔2014〕123 号《行政处罚决定书》，决定：第一，责令立即停止侵权行为；第二，处以非法经营额 3 倍的罚款 26 014.8 万元人民币。快播公司申请行政复议，广东省版权局于 2014 年 9 月 11 日做出《行政复议决定书》，维持市场监管局的行政处罚决定。快播公司起诉至深圳市中级人民法院，请求判令撤销《行政处罚决定书》。深圳市中级人民法院驳回快播公司的诉讼请求，广东省高级人民法院维持一审判决。

【典型意义】 腾讯公司、快播公司均为互联网领域受众较多的企业，案件涉及的处罚金额亦高达 2.601 48 亿元，本案受到社会各界的高度关注。案件的法律适用不仅涉及知识产权民事、行政以及破产等多部门法的交织，程序及实体问题繁杂，还涉及著作权民事侵权行为是否同时损害公共利益、如何认定互联网企业存在非法获利以及非法经营额的计算等法律问题的适用。该案的判决起到了惩处侵权、净化版权市场的良好社会效果，对促进依法行政与加强知识产权保护、规范互联网市场的竞争秩序均有积极的导向作用。

三、葛怀圣与李子成侵害著作权纠纷案〔最高人民法院（2016）最高法民再 175 号民事判决书〕

【案情摘要】 2008 年 9 月，李子成与葛怀圣合作点校民国版《寿光县志》，根据查明的事实，涉案民国版《寿光县志》点校本至少有 85%的部分应由李子成、葛怀圣共同享有著作权，2011 年 4 月，葛怀圣将民国版《寿光县志》点校本正式出版，但未列明李子成为合作作者。李子成认为葛怀圣的行为侵害了其著作权，请求法院判令葛怀圣赔偿经济损失并赔礼道歉。

【判决结果】 涉案民国版《寿光县志》点校本构成著作权法意义上的作品。

第一，涉案民国版《寿光县志》点校本属于智力劳动成果。涉案点校本系对民国版《寿光县志》的首次点校，需要点校者具备一定的历史、人文、文学等素养，且需要投入人力物力进行调查研究，该点校过程属于智力劳动。

第二，涉案点校行为可被视为具有独创性思维的表达。一方面，对一部文学作品而言，通过对民国版《寿光县志》进行标点符号添加、段落层次划分，已加入了点校者的理解；另一方面，对点校者而言，在面对无标点无分段，甚至部分文字残损的原本时，尽管其目的是要探寻原意，但均是依照点校者的理解对原本含义进行推敲、句读、分段等，客观上形成了一种特殊形式的表达。

第三，涉案民国版《寿光县志》点校本的表达方式并非唯一或极为有限，点校者在对民国版《寿光县志》进行句读、分段的过程中存在一定的选择空间，存在形成不同表达的可能。

葛怀圣未经李子成许可，单独将其发表，构成侵害李子成著作权的行为。

【典型意义】 本案系涉及“古籍点校本”的新类型著作权侵权案件。通过对著作权法中作品独创性理论的准确分析，依法认定“古籍点校本”构成著作权法意义上的作品，应受著作权法的保护。本案的裁判，对我国古籍点校行业的健康发展、古籍作品的传播及传统文化的传承具有积极意义。

四、未来电视有限公司与银河互联网电视有限公司、河南大象融媒体集团有限公司、中国移动通信集团河南有限公司、浪潮软件集团有限公司侵害作品信息网络传播权纠纷案〔天津市滨海新区人民法院（2017）津 0116 民初 1592 号民事判决书〕

【案情摘要】 中央电视台作为涉案节目《综艺盛典：这箱有礼特别节目》的制作方，于 2009 年 4 月 20 日将其对该节目享有的著作权或者与著作权有关的权利授权央视国际网络有限公司在全世界范围内独占行使。原告未来电视有限公司（以下简称未来公司）经央视国际网络有限公司转授权，就涉案节目在互联网电视业务上享有相应独占专有使用等相应权利。

被告银河互联网电视有限公司（以下简称银河公司）成立于 2012 年 7 月，负责“中央银河”互联网电视集成平台和“央广 TV”、“江苏互联网电视”内容服务平台的运行管理和开发经营。

被告河南大象融媒体集团有限公司（以下简称大象公司）成立于 2014 年 10 月，是河南省新闻出版广电局下属单位，负责建设管理河南省 IPTV 集成播控分平台，系河南广电新媒体业务唯一出口和平台。

被告中国移动通信集团河南有限公司（以下简称河南移动公司）是中国移动通信集团公司下属单位。

涉案“魔百和”业务（高清电视业务办理）是指以移动“和家庭”宽带为承载网络，通过定制终端设备（如智能机顶盒），以电视机等大屏幕为显示终端，向家庭客户提供丰富的互联网电视视频资源的业务。“魔百和”必须以移动“和家庭”宽带为承载网络，其他固定网络不能承载。

2015 年 12 月 19 日，被告河南移动公司与大象公司签订《关于“魔百和”业务合作协议》，双方约定在河南省范围内开展“魔百和”业务合作，向用户提供电视服务及本地新闻、音视频聚合等服务，双方约定分成比例并依此进行结算。

2015 年 12 月 30 日，河南移动公司与银河公司签订《关于“魔百和”业务合作合同》。约定：乙方保证其自身拥有互联网电视内容服务平台，为互联网电视用户提供合法的丰富的点播等内容服务，甲方负责双方系统平台之间的业务基础网络相关的建设并负责向用户收取互联网电视内容服务费，按月与乙方结算，并有权按照本协议约定获得相应收益。

2016 年 2 月 16 日，央视国际网络有限公司代理人刘晓艳、李鑫在北京市信德公证处公证员俞鼎轩、张彤监督下，使用“Inspur 浪潮”高清网络电视机顶盒连接电视进行操作点播并对现场播放情况进行了录制，过程如下：

打开上述电视机及机顶盒，开机画面显示“中国移动”字样后进入相关页面，页面上方同时显示“中国移动互联网高清电视”“大象融媒”“GITV”字样。

操作机顶盒恢复出厂设置后，依次显示“中国移动”“中国移动网络电视伴侣”字样，进入“欢迎使用中国移动互联网电视”页面，该页面介绍：“中国移动互联网电视及多屏互动业务，依托运营商专用网络或者公共互联网，以电视机或者机顶盒为终端，传送包含视频、声音、图形、数据等富媒体信息……”

连接无线网络后点击下一步，进入相关页面，点击完成，进入主页面。页面上方同时显示“中国移动互联网高清电视”“大象融媒”“GITV”标识，点击屏幕右上角的设置图标，进入设置页面。

使用遥控器按“返回”键，进入相关主页面，点击页面左下方“电视台”，显示“大象融媒”后进入相关页面，按菜单“进入回看”页面，左侧列表自上而下为“收藏”“直播”“回看”。遥控器选择回看，进入“回看”，遥控器选择列表中“3 中央三套”，列表显示 2016 年 2 月 9—15 日的该频道节目，点击 2 月 11 日星期四“20：58 综艺盛典”，涉案作品《综艺盛典：这箱有礼特别节目》可进行正常播放，按动右翻键，显示时间进度条。经查，开庭时涉案节目已不存在。

另，互联网电视又称 OTT，是指以电视机为显示终端，以公共互联网为传输介质，通过经国家广电行政部门批准的集成服务平台，向绑定特定编号的电视一体机或者机顶盒提供经互联网电视内容平台审核的包括电影和电视剧等视频点播和增值服务在内的多种服务的业务。

IPTV 即交互式网络电视，是指以电视机为显示终端，中央和省两级 IPTV 集成播控平台引入内容并集成播控后，规范对接到电信运营商利用互联网架设专网的定向传输通道，向公众提供包括广播电视节目等视听节目及增值服务在内的多种交互式服务的业务。

原告未来电视有限公司认为四被告未经许可，分工合作，在被告银河公司、大象公司、河南移动公司联合运营的互联网电视平台上，通过被告浪潮软件集团有限公司（以下简称浪潮公司）生产制造的“Inspur 浪潮”设备向公众提供涉案作品，严重侵害了原告的合法权益并给原告造成了严重的经济损失，遂提起本案诉讼，请求判令四被告停止被控侵权行为，共同赔偿原告经济损失及合理费用 70 000 元。

被告银河公司辩称，涉案作品已不存在，原告请求停止侵权的诉讼请求不应得到支持；其在河南地区“魔百和”业务中，仅提供点播内容，并未提供电视节目直播、回看内容，并非本案适格被告；其在涉案内容的传播过程中不存在分工合作行为，不构成共同侵权；原告主张的赔偿数额没有依据。

被告大象公司辩称，原告主张的是电视节目的直播回看，但直播回看仅提供七天，涉案节目已不存在；原告被授权范围仅限于互联网电视而不包含 IPTV 业务，涉案“魔百和”业务属于 IPTV 业务，未落入原告之权利范围。

被告河南移动公司辩称，其是网络运营商，无法从后台监控银河公司、大象公司提供的节目内容，不应承担侵权责任；原告请求赔偿的经济损失数额过高，不应得到支持。

被告浪潮公司辩称，浪潮涉诉机顶盒中已没有相关作品；被告仅为机顶盒硬件制造商，不经营不参与也未提供任何涉案作品，不应承担侵权责任。

【判决结果】 第一，关于被诉侵权行为是否落入原告主张的权利范围的问题。

根据中央电视台及央视国际网络有限公司出具的相关授权书，原告未来电视公司对涉案节目享有互联网电视端的信息网络传播权。被告银河公司、大象公司、河南移动公司主张其提供的“直播＋回看”模式属于 IPTV 业务，不在原告授权范围内，法院认为三被告的该抗辩不能成立。

首先，根据国家相关政策，目前互联网电视集成平台暂不得开展广播电视节目直播类服务，但这是由于行政监管需要而非互联网电视无法实现直播功能，实际上互联网电视因违规提供广播电视节目直播类服务而被叫停及整顿的情况亦有发生。此外，符合规范的 IPTV 业务应当取得 IPTV 集成播控平台、IPTV 内容服务平台和 IPTV 传输服务三项许可，即三方均需取得相应许可后方可对接开展该项业务。

其次，涉案“魔百和”业务既能提供点播内容也能实现对电视节目的直播及回看，但对于该业务是否属于 IPTV，应结合相关政策法规及该业务的具体模式加以认定：

(1) 河南移动公司分别与银河公司、大象公司签订了合作协议，但其内容中均没有开展 IPTV 业务的意思表达和相关约定。

(2) 河南移动公司作为传输服务提供方，当时并未获得 IPTV 传输服务资质。银河公司本身即为互联网电视业务集成播控与内容服务的提供方，涉案节目播放平台的主页面上亦有银河公司的呼号“GITV”。本案现有证据并不足以证明大象公司在“魔百和”业务中所提供的涉案节目系中央集成播控平台引入并播出，各被告亦未提供相应证据加以证明。

(3) “魔百和”业务提供涉案节目的播放平台 EPG 首页同时显示有“中国移动”、“GITV”及“大象融媒”的标识，但该业务始终未显示 IPTV 的呼号。

综上，涉案“魔百和”业务虽然在其播放平台开设的“电视台”栏目中提供了相关视听节目的“直播”与“回看”服务，但不能据此认定其为 IPTV 业务，故被告提出被诉侵权行为所涉及的业务未落入原告的权利范围的主张，不能成立。

第二，关于涉案节目的性质。

涉案节目《综艺盛典：这箱有礼特别节目》系对舞台表演进行录制，导演、摄像对素材的选择、拍摄、编排等方面的个性化选择有限，该节目所体现的独创性，尚不足以达到著作权法所规定的以类似摄制电影的方法创作的作品的程度。根据《中华人民共和国著作权法实施条例》第五条第（三）项之规定，应认定为录像制品。录音录像制品是信息网络传播权保护的客体，原告享有涉案节目的信息网络传播权。

第三，关于被告是否构成共同侵权的问题。

首先，从各方签订的协议内容看，涉案作品的播放平台依托被告河南移动在河南省境内开展的“魔百和”业务，河南移动公司分别与掌握直播内容资源的大象公司、持有互联网电视内容服务和集成播控牌照的银河公司签订了合作协议。三被告虽未共同签订合同，各方在合同中约定的权利义务也不尽相同，但对于河南移动公司开展的“魔百和”业务所涉内容及业务性质，三方理应知晓并从中获益。同时，河南移动公司所负的义务显然并非其所主张的仅提供网络传输服务；银河公司在提供视频点播内容及服务之外亦负有对点播节目的集成播控及互联网电视业务 EPG 界面的设计、制作、管理、发布等义务。

其次，从涉案节目的播放平台及播放过程看，根据已查明案件事实，播放平台中相关页面的显示内容、涉案平台的 EPG 界面及栏目设计，直到涉案节目的获取阶段，均显示有与三被告相关的品牌标识或呼号。

由此可见，“魔百和”业务本身既包括直播内容也包括点播内容，该项业务作为整体不可分割，其对用户的吸引及利益获取亦源于此。同时，银河公司、大象公司与河南移动公司均参与了平台运营并从该业务中分享利益，可以认定，三被告不仅存在分工合作的主观意思，且在内容合作与审核、利益共享与分配等方面有着紧密的联系，通过分工合作，实现涉案作品的提供，构成共同侵权，故应依法承担连带责任。

被告浪潮公司是机顶盒生产方，原告没有证据证明浪潮公司参与了平台运营、获得利益分成，因此被告浪潮公司不承担责任。

第四，关于被告的责任承担问题。

经法院核实，被告提供的是涉案节目的回看，现涉案平台已无涉案节目的在线播放，故判令被告停止侵权已无必要。综合考虑涉案节目的知名度、影响力、侵权行为的持续时间以及过错程度等因素，酌情确定赔偿数额及合理支出。

【典型意义】 在国家“三网融合”政策广泛推行、相关技术不断发展、新兴经营模式相继涌现的背景下，司法实践中涉“三网融合”的著作权侵权案件也随之增加，如互联网电视侵犯著作权、IPTV 侵犯著作权、机顶盒侵犯著作权等。本案被控侵权的“魔百和”业务即是“三网融合”下由河南移动公司与银河公司、大象公司合作开展的一种新型传播技术与盈利模式。案件所涉未经许可提供回看服务的性质，互联网电视与 IP 电视的业务划分、政策要求及其对原告权利范围界定的影响，互联网电视业务各经营主体的责任承担等问题，均为该类案件审理中的新型疑难问题。生效裁判明确了回看服务受信息网络传播权调整，并从政策法规、经营模式、在案证据等多角度对涉案“魔百和”业务的性质进行了深入分析，在认定被控侵权行为落入原告权利范围的基础上，结合各方签订的协议内容、涉案节目的播放平台及播放过程等事实，最终认定涉案节目的提供并非由被告大象公司独立完成，而是由被告河南移动公司与银河公司、大象公司以分工合作的方式共同完成，应由各方承担合作共同侵权的法律责任。本案的审理，不仅充分考虑了相关政策法规和行业发展的现状，依法保护了权利人的合法权益，同时回应了司法实践的热点难点问题，为类似案件的审理提供了可资借鉴的思路和参考。

五、上海知豆电动车技术有限公司与达索系统股份有限公司侵害计算机软件著作权纠纷案［上海市高级人民法院（2018）沪民终429号民事判决书］

【案情摘要】 原告达索系统股份有限公司（以下简称达索公司）系涉案软件CATIA V5 R20的软件著作权人，被告上海知豆电动车技术有限公司（以下简称知豆公司）系一家从事电动车技术研发与服务的创新企业。原告曾因被告使用侵权软件于2017年2月向上海市文化市场行政执法总队投诉，行政执法过程中查获被告使用侵权软件8套，其间原被告双方达成和解，被告承诺不再非法使用原告软件，并与原告授权代理商签订了正版软件采购合同，上海市文化市场行政执法总队（以下简称上海文化执法总队）因此对被告依法减轻行政处罚，罚款65 404元，但被告并未按软件采购合同支付合同款。同年11月，原告向上海知识产权法院申请证据保全。保全过程中，法院经被告同意，采取随机抽查的方式对计算机中安装涉案软件的情况进行证据保全，同时明确告知被告抽查比例以及将根据所抽查计算机中安装CATIA软件的比例推算经营场所内所有计算机中安装涉案软件的数量。经清点，被告经营场所内共有计算机73台，保全结果为抽查的15台计算机中100%安装了涉案软件。原告遂向上海知识产权法院起诉，要求被告停止侵权，并赔偿原告经济损失及律师费共计1 800余万元。

被告认为，其曾系原山东新大洋电动车有限公司的下属部门，该公司曾于2015年向原告授权代理商购买了正版CATIA软件，亦即行政处罚时发现的8套软件。行政处罚后，被告系因内部管理不善导致未能及时付款。原告在本案中主张的涉案软件单价过高，被告经营场所内的计算机亦并非都安装了涉案软件，且被告不存在侵权的主观恶意，不应适用惩罚性赔偿。

【判决结果】 知豆公司未经达索公司许可，在其经营场所内的计算机上安装了涉案软件，侵害了达索公司对涉案软件享有的复制权，依法应当承担相应的民事责任。本案中，虽然达索公司的实际损失及知豆公司的违法所得均难以确定，但现有证据已经可以证明达索公司因侵权所受到的损失超过了著作权法规定的法定赔偿数额的上限50万元，故法院综合全案证据情况，同时考虑双方提交的销售合同软件单价、知豆公司的侵权期间、安装侵权软件的计算机数量，以及知豆公司在被行政机关查获使用侵权软件后仍扩大侵权规模的主观恶意等因素，在法定赔偿最高限额之上酌定赔偿数额，判决知豆公司赔偿达索公司经济损失及律师费共计900万元。

一审判决后，知豆公司不服，提起上诉。上海市高级人民法院认为，本案权利人的实际损失或者侵权人的违法所得均不能确定，法院应当根据侵权行为的情节，判决给予50万元以下的赔偿。但本案事实表明，达索公司和知豆公司已经就上海文化执法总队查获的知豆公司的侵权行为达成过和解协议。其后，知豆公司未履行和解协议，反而扩大侵权规模，经原审法院证据保全，在相同的经营场所又查获73台工作电脑安装了侵权软件。由此可见，知豆公司存在重复侵权行为，侵权主观恶意明显，且达索公司的实际损失已经明显超过法定赔偿50万元的最高限额，故应在法定赔偿最高限额之上酌情确定赔偿金额。原审法院根据知豆公司安装侵权软件的数量、侵权期间、主观恶意及权利人为维权所支出的合理开支等因素，酌定知豆公司赔偿达索公司经济损失及律师费900万元并无不当。判决驳回上诉，维持原判。

【典型意义】 如何积极探索加大赔偿力度的具体实现方式，合理确定侵权损害赔偿数额和制止侵权的合理开支，一直是知识产权审判中需要解决的难题。本案是法院依法加大赔偿力度的典型案例。本案中法院综合全案的证据情况，在法定赔偿最高限额之上酌情确定被告应赔偿原告的经济损失并支持了原告主张的合理开支，依法加大了对权利人的保护力度，也为类似案件的审理提供了一定的参考，体现了法院不断加强知识产权司法保护的态度和决心。同时，法院也通过本案判决倡导社会公众全面使用正版软件，尊重软件开发者的劳动和付出，推进企业软件正版化工作，形成尊重和保护知识产权、激励和发展创新的营商环境。

六、北京字节跳动科技有限公司与江苏现代快报传媒有限公司、江苏现代快报传媒有限公司无锡分公司及北京字节跳动网络技术有限公司侵害著作权纠纷案［江苏省高级人民法院（2018）苏民终588号民事判决书］

【案情摘要】 江苏现代快报传媒有限公司（以下简称现代快报公司）、江苏现代快报传媒有限公司无锡分公司（以下简称现代快报无锡分公司）发现《今日头条》手机新闻客户端未经许可使用其享有著作权的《出租屋爆燃　一家三口烧成重伤》等6篇新闻作品。另，头条网（https：//www.toutiao.com）的ICP备案显示备案号为京ICP备12023439号，主办单位为北京字节跳动科技有限公司（以下简称字节跳动科技公司）；苹果系统中《今日头条》APP下载页显示的开发者是字节跳动科技公司，安卓系统中《今日头条》客户端显示的开发者是北京字节跳动网络技术有限公司（以下简称字节跳动网络公司）。因此，现代快报公司、现代快报无锡分公司诉至一审法院，请求字节跳动科技公司、字节跳动网络公司赔偿损失20万元，支付合理费用1万元。

【判决结果】 第一，现代快报公司、现代快报无锡分公司对涉案文章《出租屋爆燃　一家三口烧成重伤》享有著作权，可以单独提起诉讼。

字节跳动科技公司上诉主张《出租屋爆燃　一家三口烧成重伤》系合作作品，未经合作作者唐奕同意，现代快报公司不享有该文章著作权。对此，二审法院认为，现代快报刊登的《出租屋爆燃　一家三口烧成重伤》，署名“现代快报记者　唐奕　朱鲸润”，现代快报公司、现代快报无锡分公司与朱鲸润签订了《职务作品创作合同》，朱鲸润在任职期间，为完成工作任务而创作的与工作性质相关的新闻作品属于职务作品，其著作权归现代快报公司、现代快报无锡分公司。二审查明，《出租屋爆燃　一家三口烧成重伤》一文系唐奕在现代快报公司工作期间，与朱鲸润共同采编撰写，唐奕也确认该文著作权属于现代快报公司。因此，现代快报公司、现代快报无锡分公司享有著作权，可单独提起诉讼。

第二，字节跳动网络公司在《今日头条》客户端提供涉案4篇文章构成侵权。

首先，现代快报公司、现代快报无锡分公司公证保全证据证明字节跳动科技公司未经许可，在其经营的《今日头条》客户端使用了涉案4篇作品，使公众可以在其个人选定的时间和地点获得涉案作品，侵害了现代快报公司、现代快报无锡分公司享有的信息网络传播权，应当对其侵权行为承担相应的法律责任。

其次，字节跳动科技公司称其与第三方网站签订了以链接方式进行作品传播的相关协议，且第三方网站存在涉案作品，但其并未提供证据证明用户阅读《今日头条》客户端中的涉案作品时存在跳转或链接到第三方网站的情形。另外，字节跳动科技公司在一审期间提交的9395号公证书中4篇文章的后台信息的URL地址并无与之对应的《今日头条》客户端页面显示信息予以佐证，且该公证保全时间为2016年7月15日，系在现代快报公司、现代快报无锡分公司起诉后取得的证据，不能证明现代快报公司、现代快报无锡分公司主张侵权事实发生时后台信息显示的相关情况。

最后，即使字节跳动科技公司仅对涉案4篇文章提供了链接服务，其亦构成侵权。字节跳动科技公司主张《为能多见见孙子……》《女子民政局……》2篇文章分别系从与其有授权许可协议的中国江苏网及东方网链接而来，但是字节跳动科技公司与中国江苏网及东方网签订的合作协议均明确约定其可设链转载的内容为该两家网站“自有版权内容”。字节跳动科技公司虽在协议中要求两家网站承担知识产权权利瑕疵担保责任，却未要求其提供任何关于其享有合法的信息网络传播权所涉权利人的清单列表。《为能多见见孙子……》一文左上角虽有“中国江苏网”字样，但文章首页首段后标明“现代快报记者　薛晟　通讯员　苟连静”，该文对于作者的明确记载足以引起字节跳动科技公司注意，而字节跳动科技公司却未尽到充分的审查义务，未通过设置关键词等方式对合作网站不享有信息网络传播权的作品进行筛选甄别，进而避免所链接的作品不是其合作网站自有版权作品情况的出现。因此，可以认定字节跳动科技公司主观上存在过错，其应当知道所链接的作品可能构成侵权。另外，字节跳动科技公司主张《仪仗队……》《煤气泄漏……》2篇文章系通过新浪网合法授权链接而来，但其与新浪网的合作协议有效期至2014年12月31日已终止，而《今日头条》客户端登载《仪仗队……》《煤气泄漏……》两文时间为2015年9月。字节跳动科技公司虽称其与新浪网的协议可续展执行，但并未提供证据证明，故其无权对新浪网内容设链转载。

第三，一审判决确定的赔偿数额并无不当。

一审期间，现代快报公司、现代快报无锡分公司未提供其因字节跳动科技公司侵权所受损失及字节跳动科技公司因侵权获利数额，主张法定赔偿。《今日头条》系业内具有相当影响力的媒体，经营规模大，涉案文章通过网络进行传播，受众多，影响范围广，字节跳动科技公司主观上具有一定的过错。综合考虑以上相关因素，一审法院酌情判决字节跳动科技公司赔偿现代快报公司、现代快报无锡分公司经济损失10万元及为维权支出的合理费用10 100元并无不当。

【典型意义】 本案涉及在现行著作权法框架下对《今日头条》作为新闻集合式新媒体未经许可转载他人作品行为性质的认定。法院根据查明事实，以及字节跳动科技公司的陈述，认为《今日头条》的算法技术完全可以支持对特定关键词的筛查检索，《今日头条》也已经注意到其设链行为存在侵害信息网络传播权的可能性。在此前提下，字节跳动科技公司仅在与第三方的合作协议中要求第三方网站承担权利瑕疵担保责任，而未要求其提供合法权利人清单列表，也未设置可能引发侵权的关键词进行筛查，在搜索所得内容显示的权属情况与来源网站不一致的情况下，未采取措施进行甄别，应当认定未尽到合理审查义务，其为涉案4篇文章设链的行为对相关作品的传播提供了便利，主观上为“应知”。关于赔偿数额的确定，法院综合考虑《今日头条》作为新闻集合式浏览媒体这一网络平台的特殊性，结合平台的受众范围、影响范围，侵权作品的传播速度和传播广度，以及其主观上具有过错等因素，确定赔偿金额10万元，并支持两原告为本案支出的律师费、公证费等合理费用。本案中，人民法院最终确定的裁决尺度，特别是结合个案情形判决较高的赔偿额，对于明晰不同媒体之间的竞争关系，规范网络转载，打击和遏制侵犯信息网络传播权的行为，具有积极的社会意义。

本案涉及《今日头条》，确定的赔偿额高，具有广泛的社会影响力。案件判决后，引起了媒体界的广泛关注，新浪网、搜狐网、网易订阅、新京报网等多家媒体进行了报道，中国报业协会亦对本案高度关注。在2018年举行的第七届中国国际版权博览会上，国家版权局有关负责人对媒体表示本案“对规范网络转载是一个很好的判例”。

七、李惠卿、陈文灿与福州大学著作权权属、侵权纠纷案［福建省厦门市中级人民法院（2018）闽02民终1515号民事判决书］

【案情摘要】 1986年，人民大会堂福建厅装修，有关部门确定由福建工艺美术学校承接该厅壁画创作，工艺美校组织吴景希、陈文灿等部分师生创作了1987年版《武夷之春》。工艺美校四十周年校庆作品集收录了该幅作品，作品署名：设计者吴景希、陈文灿、王明照；制作者吴景希、陈文灿、王明照、黄国强、林德耀等。1994年，福建厅重新装修，福建工艺美术学校再次承接厅内壁画的创作任务，该校组织部分师生在1987年版《武夷之春》的基础上创作了1994年版《武夷之春》。相比原画作，1994年版《武夷之春》的尺寸、细节均有所变化。工艺美校五十周年校庆作品集收录了该幅作品，作品署名：设计者吴景希、陈文灿；制作者吴嘉诠、陈文灿、黄国强、王明照。吴景希去世后，其母亲李惠卿以陈文灿将《武夷之春》登记在个人名下等行为侵犯吴景希的署名权、展览权诉至法院。审理过程中，合并了福建工艺美术学校的福州大学认为两幅作品系法人作品，主张享有全部著作权。

【判决结果】 关于讼争两幅作品究竟属于自然人作品、职务作品抑或法人作品的问题，1987年版《武夷之春》创作完成之时，我国现行的著作权法尚未颁布，其他法律法规也未对特定作品著作权的享有和行使的主体做出明确规定，而1994年版《武夷之春》系在1987年版《武夷之春》的基础上调整修改而来，故对两幅《武夷之春》作品著作权归属的确定，应兼顾历史与现实，将作品的创作置于当时的创作背景、社会历史环境等条件之下，并依照现行著作权法的相关规定来予以确定，既最大限度保护创作者的合法权益，褒扬创作者的艺术贡献，又依法维护法人的合法权益和社会公共利益。讼争作品系工艺美校承接人民大会堂福建厅翻新工程任务而创作，作品的规格尺寸分别达到4.3米×7.4米和4.2米×10米，对于传统的漆画作品而言实属罕见，远非某个人或数人短期内所能够独立完成。现有的证据可以证明，工艺美校为确保吴景希等主要创作人员顺利完成创作工作，协调安排吴景希等人前往武夷山采风，抽调部分师生参与到作品的创作之中，充分发挥了作品创作过程中所需的组织协调、后勤保障职能作用，有关部门和领导同样为作品创作的提出、立意、审核、组织保障等做了大量工作。创作如此巨幅的漆画作品，所需资金量大，上级有关部门专门下拨创作所需经费，涉案合同书中记载两幅《武夷之春》作品造价分别达到12万元和42万元，讼争作品从创作思路的提出，直至作品完成历时逾两年，耗费大量时间。因此，离开有关部门和领导、工艺美校等提供的组织保障及其为吴景希等人完成作品创作专门提供的资金、场地、人力等物资技术条件，仅凭个人的力量是难以完成作品的。同时，讼争作品创作之时，我国尚处于改革开放初期，与市场经济相伴的个人主义观念并未被人们普遍接受，个人利益寓于集体利益之中，舍小我顾大局、集体利益高于一切的观念为全社会广泛推崇，以创作者为核心的保护制度也尚未形成。吴景希等人作为工艺美校的工作人员完成单位交付的工作任务是其职责所在，履行工作职责所形成的成果归属于工作单位，符合当时人们的普遍认知。有理由相信，在当时特定历史背景下，吴景希等作者不会对讼争作品的全部著作权益提出主张。基于上述分析，李惠卿主张讼争作品的著作权完全由创作者个人享有，既不符合当时的客观实际，也难谓公平合理，且有损社会公共利益。李惠卿以工艺美校校庆作品集上的署名情况等为由，主张讼争两幅作品属于自然人作品，吴景希等人对作品享有全部的著作权益，缺乏事实和法律依据，不予支持。由于法人作品与职务作品的外延存在交叉，基于讼争作品的上述特征，便将其认定为法人作品，容易陷入任何为完成单位工作任务创作的职务作品均属于法人作品的误区，也无法在法人作品与职务作品尤其是特殊职务作品之间划清界限。并且，由于法人意志的抽象化，在法人意志的认定上如果不加以严格限制，法人在作品创作方面做出的任何指示都可以成为“法人意志”的话，会导致忽视创作者的创造性劳动才是推动作品形成的主要因素的问题产生。著作权法是保护文学、艺术和科学作品作者的著作权以及与著作权有关的权益的专门法，保护创作者能够获得直接或间接的利益回报，实现人格独立和自我发展，是著作权法立法的应有之义，没有创作者个人所付出的创造性劳动，就不会有文学、艺术和科学作品的诞生，保护著作权，首要在于保护创作者的权益，鼓励创作的积极性。因此，认识把握是否代表法人意志创作这一关键所在同时也是实践中最具争议的构成要件时，应限定于创作者个人自由思维的空间不大，不能充分发挥主观能动性，创作思想及表达方式完全或主要代表、体现法人的意志的情形。如果创作时仅仅遵循法人总体的思路或是确定的“调子”的，则不能认为作品体现了法人的意志。还需强调的是，将法人视为作者，确认作品的著作权完全归法人所有，系基于某些政策目标或更好地保护法人合法权益的考量，从这个角度而言，在不违背政策目标并能够充分有效保护法人合法权益的情况下，赋予法人以全部的著作权并非必需。具体到本案而言，与单位发布的工作总结、研究报告等典型的法人作品有所不同，讼争作品系美术作品，本质上属于高度个性化的创作行为，创作者在有关部门提出的创作主题和原则性要求下，仍可自由发挥主观能动性和个人创造力，在作品上充分注入个人的思想和情感。现有的证据表明，1987 年省机关事务管理局与工艺美校校办企业签订的合同书只约定漆画的创作主题，并未明确漆画的表达内容等要素，作品的立意、构图和色调等的确定均来自创作者，而 1994 年省机关事务管理局与工艺美校校办企业签订的合同书，在 1987 年版《武夷之春》的基础上，明确约定漆画的构成要素包括“大王峰”“玉女峰”，但并未涉及 1994 年版《武夷之春》新增的另一构成要素“鹰嘴岩”，该构成要素来自吴景希早年创作的作品《武夷鹰嘴岩》。在案证据也不能证明讼争作品的构图、色调等系由工艺美校的领导机构集体讨论后提出。从样稿图的审批过程来看，讼争作品的法人意志因素亦主要来自上级有关部门和领导而非工艺美校，不应认定作品贯彻了工艺美校的意志。李惠卿提交的证据还证明，在创作札记中吴景希对作品的写生过程、构图思路、绘画技法等做了详尽记载，其为绘制设计以供后续制作漆画之用的样稿图，反复修改，几易其稿。由于漆画创作的特殊性以及讼争作品罕见的规格尺寸，需要制作者在事先绘制好的样稿图的基础上进行再创作，这个过程同样需要制作者的创造性劳动，这也是两幅《武夷之春》作品上的署名既包括设计者又有制作者的原因。两幅《武夷之春》美术作品无论是在绘画技法、漆画材料等的选择和运用上，还是在构图布局、设计元素、色彩效果等方面，都体现了创作者个人的构思、选择和表达，充分彰显了创作者独特而鲜明的思想、情感和美学修养，体现了创作者独特的审美眼光和高超的绘画技法。因此，上级有关部门和领导对作品进行审核把关并提出原则性修改意见的事实，并不影响对讼争作品做出实质性贡献的仍然是吴景希等个人的事实。因此，讼争两幅《武夷之春》美术作品并非完全或者主要体现代表了法人的意志，并且不需要以法人的名义使用作品，不应认定为法人作品。赋予讼争作品的创作者以有限的著作人身权，也不必然损害福州大学的合法权益，或有违立法者设定的政策目标。故一审法院将讼争两幅作品定性为法人作品并将其中的署名权让渡吴景希等人享有显属不当，应予纠正，对陈文灿、福州大学提出的讼争作品属于法人作品的理由，不予采纳。考虑到讼争作品系工艺美校的工作人员为完成单位的工作任务、由有关部门提供物质技术条件并由有关部门承担责任的职务作品，讼争作品虽然不属于《著作权法》第十六条第二款第（一）项所列举的四种具有实用目的的作品之一，但考量立法的本意，可依照该条规定，确定本案讼争作品的著作权归属，即两幅《武夷之春》作品的署名权由吴景希、陈文灿等人享有，工艺美校享有除署名权之外的著作权，工艺美校并入福州大学作为内设教学机构之后，相应的著作权由福州大学承继。

【典型意义】《武夷之春》美术作品以武夷山大王峰、玉女峰、鹰嘴岩等主要景色为元素，反映了福建的秀丽风光，作品悬挂于人民大会堂福建厅，随着媒体对国家领导人重要外事活动的报道而广为人知，堪称“上镜率最高”的美术作品之一，在福建漆画艺术史上有着举足轻重的地位。但是，针对《武夷之春》的著作权归属，自2014年以来在几方当事人之间引发了诉讼争夺战。现行著作权法借鉴两大法系的立法例，同时规定“视法人为作者”的法人作品制度和自然人仅享有署名权、法人享有其他著作权的特殊职务作品制度，表面上两种作品类型无论在构成要件还是著作权归属方面都有很大差别，但实践中要划清界限绝非易事，可能出现某一作品既可归入法人作品，也可认定为特殊职务作品的情况。立法者将这两种作品类型界限模糊、功能重叠的制度引入著作权法中，作为独立的作品类型进行规定，引发了一定的混乱，导致著作权归属纠纷频发。《武夷之春》案件再次提出了两种作品类型的认定标准这一长期困扰中国法院的问题。为妥善解决本案纠纷，二审法院采取以下做法：一是对法人意志进行严格限定。法人意志应当是具体而非抽象的，在把握作品是否代表法人意志创作上，应限定于创作者自由思维的空间不大，创作思想及表达方式完全或主要体现法人意志的情形。如果创作时仅仅遵循法人总体的思路或原则，为创作者留有很大发挥空间的，则作品并不是代表法人的意志创作的。涉案作品系美术作品，本质上属于高度个性化的创作行为，创作者在有关部门提出的创作主题和原则性要求下，仍可自由发挥个人创造力，作品充分彰显了创作者独特而鲜明的思想、情感和美学修养，作品主要体现的是创作者而非法人的意志。二是扩张特殊职务作品的适用范围。对于美术作品能否适用特殊职务作品的规定来确定著作权的归属，确实存在争议，例如特殊职务作品的第一种情形是否仅限于所列举的四种作品。二审法院认为，根据《著作权法》第十六条第二款第二项规定，法院可依据特别法之规定或依照当事人的特别约定，将某一类型的职务作品认定为特殊职务作品，因此扩张特殊职务作品类型的做法并不违反立法者的本意。随着经济社会发展变化，新类型的作品将越来越多，适当地做开放性解释更加符合未来著作权发展趋势。据此，二审法院从著作权法的立法目的、鼓励创作的积极性和平衡当事人及社会公共利益的角度出发，对法人作品的认定采取严格、审慎的态度，依法将涉案作品认定为特殊职务作品，创作者享有署名权，其他著作财产权均归属法人，切实加强对自然人创作者权益的保护，激励创作热情，较好地实现创作者、法人和社会公共利益之间的利益平衡。

八、广州求知教育科技有限公司与北京新浪互联信息服务有限公司侵害计算机软件著作权纠纷案

［广州知识产权法院（2016）粤73民初1387号民事判决书］

【案情摘要】《考无忧全国专业技术人员计算机应用能力考试辅导软件》是广州求知教育科技有限公司（以下简称求知公司）开发并享有著作权的软件，该软件通过在求知公司官方网站 http：//www. k51. com. cn 下载客户端后购买各模块注册码的方式供用户使用。

新浪公司是新浪网（https://www. sina. com. cn）的主办单位，经营范围包括计算机互联网技术服务。

新浪博客用户“蓝魔之泪”2014年11月12日16：11：35在新浪博客平台 http://blog. sina. com. cn/576400832cbp 发布涉案博客文章，2016年7月1日显示的文章名称为《【考无忧】2016职称计算机软件破解版（亲测可用）》，博文网址 http://blog. sina. com. cn/s/blog_6626e1510102v77v. html，文章标签为“职称计算机”，分类为“酷软推荐”，内容为考无忧职称计算机模块考试软件及对破解版软件的介绍，包括电脑桌面文件夹内容，软件运行界面的截图及文字说明，被诉侵权软件的下载链接、安装步骤、破解方法、说明等内容。下载链接并按说明步骤运行操作的结果显示，软件经破解后显示的多界面内容与涉案软件正常运行时显示的内容相同，且无须通过注册码注册即可使用。

2015年6月9日，求知公司向新浪公司 vipfax@vip. sina. com 邮箱发出投诉邮件，内容为：“新浪博客管理员：贵用户发布的【考无忧】2015职称计算机软件破解版（亲测可用）网址 http://blog. sina. com. cn/s/blog_6626e1510102v77v. html 侵犯我司知识产权，请予以删除”，邮件底部留有求知公司名称、联系电话，并包含经办人彭某身份证和在职证明、公司营业执照、软件著作权、申请资料、公司组织机构代码证等六个附件，除申请资料外，其余附件均为 JPG 方式，可清晰显示内容。申请资料文档系求知公司依据新浪公司提供的格式文本填写的申请删帖文档。新浪公司回复邮件，内容包括“要求以快递或寄信的形式，将书面材料送至新浪网，否则为无效申请”。

2016 年 4 月 20 日，求知公司向新浪公司 vipfax@vip. sina. com 邮箱再次发出“新浪网删帖申请”邮件，内容大致如前。针对该邮件，新浪公司系统邮件自动回复，仍然要求以快递或寄信的形式将书面材料送至新浪网，否则申请无效。

2016 年 8 月 8 日，求知公司提起本案诉讼，认为新浪公司经求知公司两次邮件通知，作为网络服务提供者应知其用户的侵权行为，至起诉时仍拒绝删除涉案博客文章，该行为损害了求知公司的权益，请求判令新浪公司：（1）停止侵害求知公司涉案软件信息网络传播权的行为，从新浪公司网站上撤下侵权文章与链接；（2）在新浪公司网站上对求知公司赔礼道歉；（3）赔偿求知公司经济损失及维权费用共计 100 000 元。

2016 年 8 月 30 日 14：14，涉案博客文章被新浪管理员删除。

【判决结果】《考无忧全国专业技术人员计算机应用能力考试辅导软件》是求知公司开发并享有著作权的软件，该软件通过在求知公司官方网站 http://www. k51. com. cn 下载客户端后购买各模块注册码的方式供用户使用。计算机软件著作权人在授权用户使用涉案软件时要求用户接受“一个注册码注册一个模块”等内容的服务模式，是其行使著作权的方式。行为人采取故意避开或者破坏著作权人为保护计算机软件而采取的技术措施，属于侵害计算机软件著作权的行为；网络用户明知涉案软件系未经许可提供的破坏技术措施的侵权软件而予以信息网络传播，应当认定其构成侵害计算机软件著作权中的信息网络传播权的行为。

新浪博客用户“蓝魔之泪”在新浪博客平台上发布了附被诉侵权软件下载链接及破解方法、说明等内容的涉案博客文章；下载链接并按说明步骤运行操作的结果显示，软件经破解后显示的多界面内容与涉案软件正常运行时显示的内容相同，且无须通过注册码注册即可使用，该用户未经求知公司许可发布信息传播破坏技术措施软件的行为，侵害了求知公司对涉案软件享有的著作权，包括信息网络传播权。

新浪公司为涉案博客文章提供网络技术服务，符合法律规定的网络服务提供者的主体条件。

求知公司依照新浪公司公开的网络联系方式，两次发送邮件投诉涉案博客文章侵害其知识产权，要求新浪公司删除，并提供了其作为权利人的名称、公司地址、联系方式等主体资料，以及涉案软件的权利证书、要求删除文章的地址链接。求知公司的投诉内容客观、具体，投诉行为合法、有效。是否需要进一步提供纸质材料，不影响已有效抵达新浪公司的投诉通知的合法有效性，且提供纸质材料供审核为网络服务提供者新浪公司自行设定的规则，加重了求知公司的义务，投诉不当的抗辩意见，不予采纳。

涉案博客文章不仅在标题标示“破解版（亲测可用）”，还在文章正文贴图说明软件破解前后区别，进行软件功能对比，提供软件下载安装链接，标示破解方法。经求知公司两次邮件通知，新浪公司作为网络服务提供者应知网络用户通过信息网络侵害求知公司对涉案软件享有的信息网络传播权，其至起诉时仍未采取删除、屏蔽、断开链接的必要措施，应当认定其构成帮助侵权行为。因求知公司的权益被持续侵害，新浪公司应就帮助网络用户实施侵害信息网络传播权行为、因未及时采取必要措施导致求知公司进一步扩大的损失，承担法律责任。

鉴于涉案博客文章已删除，求知公司的第一项诉讼请求已实现，不再处理。因本案并非人身权益的侵权之诉，求知公司无证据支持其曾遭受精神上的损害，对求知公司要求新浪公司赔礼道歉的主张不予支持。在求知公司未对实际损失、侵权人的违法所得有效举证的情况下，考虑到涉案软件以模块为单位收取注册码费用、一个软件内包含多个模块、每个注册码优惠价 19 元/科等情况，酌定新浪公司赔偿求知公司包括合理维权费用在内的经济损失 50 000 元，超出该部分的赔偿数额不予支持。故判决：第一，新浪公司自本判决生效之日起十个工作日内赔偿求知公司经济损失及维权费用共计 50 000 元；第二，驳回求知公司的其他诉讼请求。案件受理费 2 300 元，由求知公司负担 575 元，新浪公司负担 1 725 元。

【典型意义】 互联网的蓬勃发展为学习提供了多种路径。教育类软件通过对相应领域知识素材的积累、结构体系的搭建、学习方法的展示、学习成果的检验，为广大网民提供了便利。本案系广州知识产权法院第一例因破解学习软件加密措施引发的计算机软件著作权侵权案。北京新浪互联信息服务有限公司自行设定的投诉规则阻碍了权利人正常、及时、有效的维权，应就帮助服务对象实施侵权的行为承担法律责任。

九、重庆市设计院与同方股份有限公司侵害著作权纠纷案［重庆市高级人民法院（2018）渝民终234号民事判决书］

【案情摘要】 2016年6月，原告同方公司与石柱建委签订《县城夜景灯饰建设项目设计合同》，合同约定同方公司为项目的设计单位，承担该项目设计任务，并对项目范围、设计内容、设计进度、设计费支付等进行了约定。其后，同方公司向石柱建委提交了设计图纸。2017年4月11日，项目方将同方公司的设计图纸发布于石柱县公共资源交易网，用于工程施工合同招投标。2017年4月19日，石柱建委向裕兴公司出具《委托支付函》，将前述项目业主明确为裕兴公司，并委托裕兴公司与同方公司进行设计任务的往来以及支付设计费用。2017年7月23日，石柱建委向同方公司发出《解除合同通知书》，称同方公司虽履行了部分设计服务，但未根据修改意见修改到位，通知解除双方签订的《县城夜景灯饰建设项目设计合同》。2017年8月3日，裕兴公司与被告重庆市设计院签订了《建设工程设计合同（一）》，将原建设项目委托重庆市设计院进行设计，并将同方公司的设计图交与重庆市设计院。其后，项目方对重庆市设计院设计的施工图进行项目施工招投标。将同方公司设计图与重庆市设计院设计图进行比较，二者实质性相同。同方公司向法院起诉，认为重庆市设计院侵犯其著作权，要求被告停止侵权并赔偿损失。

【判决结果】 一审法院认为重庆市设计院侵犯了同方公司的著作权，判决：（1）被告重庆市设计院于本判决生效之日起立即停止使用原告享有著作权的涉案作品《石柱县县城夜景灯饰建设项目设计方案》；（2）被告重庆市设计院于本判决生效之日起十日内赔偿原告经济损失及合理开支共计43.7万元；（3）驳回原告同方股份有限公司的其他诉讼请求。重庆市设计院不服一审判决，向二审法院提出上诉，其主要理由：（1）涉案图纸的著作权应归委托方享有，同方公司不享有著作权；（2）上诉人进行施工图设计是履行设计单位职责，系建设单位（委托人）在约定建设项目特定目的的范围内继续使用设计图纸的行为。二审法院认为，以合同约定方式决定著作权的归属要求合同的约定应当明确、具体，否则著作权应属于受托人，本案中涉案合同并未对设计作品的著作权明确约定；同时，从合同的主要内容及履行情况看，即使合同明确约定了设计成果的著作权归委托人所有，但在委托人未履行对待给付义务时，著作权仍应由受托人享有，故涉案图纸的著作权应归同方公司。针对重庆市设计院的行为是否应视为建设单位在约定工程项目范围内对图纸作品的继续使用的问题，二审法院认为：根据《最高人民法院关于审理著作权民事纠纷案件适用法律若干问题的解释》第十二条之规定“按照著作权法第十七条规定委托作品属于受托人的情形，委托人在约定的使用范围内享有使用作品的权利；双方没有约定使用作品范围的，委托人可以在委托创作的特定目的的范围内免费使用该作品”，不可否认，基于委托创作合同的性质和建设工程设计合同的目的，即使在涉案图纸著作权归同方公司所有的情况下，石柱建委作为委托人也可以在合同约定的工程项目上使用同方公司设计，如利用设计图进行施工、竣工验收，根据工程项目的变化对原有的设计图进行必要的修改等，但上诉人设计院剽窃前设计单位同方公司的设计成果显然不属于前述规定的情形。本案中，由于原委托人石柱建委认为同方公司的设计不符合合同约定并发函解除合同，裕兴公司作为委托人与上诉人设计院签订建设工程设计合同，由设计院负责施工图设计，设计院理应独立进行创作、设计，但其设计图纸却与同方公司的设计图纸构成了实质性相似。如果将设计院的行为视为石柱建委或裕兴公司在工程项目范围内的使用行为，既不符合前款司法解释的规定，与前述合同背景及合同约定相悖，也违反诚实信用原则。也正是如此，本案与上诉人设计院所称应参照适用的（2016）最高法民再336号案件，并不相似。（2016）最高法民再336号案件中，全部工程设计已完成且绝大部分工程已经竣工，在原设计单位不配合进行主体基础工程验收的情况下，发包人与新设计单位签订设计合同，新设计单位按照合同及发包人的要求，根据工程建设实际情况复制、修改施工设计图纸，并以设计单位名义出具设计图纸用于报审、验收。如前所述，本案系发包人认为原设计单位（同方公司）的设计不符合要求并发函解除合同，并由发包人与后设计单位（设计院）签订设计合同，由设计院进行施工图设计。两案中，发包人与后设计单位签订合同的背景，合同的目的、内容均不相同，不能参照适用。据此，二审法院判决驳回上诉，维持原判。

【典型意义】 根据《最高人民法院关于审理著作权民事纠纷案件适用法律若干问题的解释》第十二条，在委托作品著作权属于受托人的情形下，委托人可以在合同约定或委托创作的特定目的范围内使用作品，但在实践中，如何确定该使用范围却不无争议。尤其是在委托设计建设工程施工图的情况下，常常存在建设单位与原设计单位因履行合同产生争议并解除合同的情形，建设单位因招标、施工及验收等都离不开工程设计图，往往另行委托其他设计单位进行工程设计，而建设单位及后设计单位是否系在约定工程项目内使用原设计图纸的情形值得研究。如果后设计单位根据工程项目的变化对原有的设计图进行必要的修改，或者纯粹利用原设计图进行工程施工、竣工验收等，可以视为建设单位在约定工程项目范围内使用；如果原设计单位提交了设计图且没有证据证明其违约的情况下，建设单位另行与后设计单位签订工程设计合同，并将原设计图提供给后设计单位，后设计单位完成的设计图与原设计图实质相同时，不能视为建设单位在约定工程项目范围内对图纸作品的继续使用，其行为侵犯了原设计单位的著作权。

十、巨石在线（北京）科技有限公司、黄明侵犯著作权罪案［北京市海淀区人民法院（2018）京0108刑初1932号刑事判决书］

【案情摘要】 北京市海淀区人民检察院于2018年9月21日向北京市海淀区人民法院提起公诉，起诉指控：2016年至今，被告人黄明伙同他人，未经著作权人北京闲徕互娱网络科技有限公司（以下简称闲徕互娱公司）许可，通过其经营的被告单位巨石在线（北京）科技有限公司（以下简称巨石在线公司）运营与闲徕互娱公司享有著作权的《闲徕琼崖海南麻将》游戏源代码具有高度同一性的《巨石海南麻将》游戏，并通过代理人员销售用于启动游戏的虚拟货币的方式进行非法营利，非法经营数额为人民币162 912.9元。2017年12月16日，被告人黄明被抓获。公诉机关认为被告单位巨石在线公司、被告人黄明的行为触犯了《中华人民共和国刑法》第二百一十七条、第三十一条之规定，已构成侵犯著作权罪，提请北京市海淀区人民法院依法惩处。

被告单位巨石在线公司诉讼代表人李勇对起诉书指控的事实和罪名没有提出实质性异议。辩护人史玉梅发表辩护意见认为，巨石在线公司没有实际盈利，系初犯，愿意退交违法经营所得，且认罪、悔罪态度较好，提请法庭从宽处理。被告人黄明对起诉书指控的事实和罪名没有提出异议。辩护人姚华发表辩护意见认为黄明没有给被害单位造成实际损失，犯罪情节较轻；且系初犯，到案后如实供述自己的罪行，认罪、悔罪态度较好，提请法庭对其从宽处罚。

【判决结果】 被告单位巨石在线公司及其直接负责的主管人员被告人黄明以营利为目的，未经著作权人许可，复制发行他人享有著作权的计算机软件，情节严重，其行为已构成侵犯著作权罪，应予惩处。北京市海淀区人民检察院指控被告单位巨石在线公司、被告人黄明犯有侵犯著作权罪的事实清楚，证据确实充分，指控罪名成立。鉴于被告人黄明到案后及在庭审中能如实供认自己的基本罪行，被告单位及被告人认罪、悔罪态度较好，且被告单位积极退交违法所得，北京市海淀区人民法院对被告单位及被告人黄明依法从轻处罚。依照刑法有关规定，判决：（1）被告单位巨石在线公司犯侵犯著作权罪，判处罚金人民币20万元。（2）被告人黄明犯侵犯著作权罪，判处有期徒刑一年，罚金人民币10万元。

一审宣判后，被告单位和被告人没有提出上诉。

【典型意义】 随着互联网经济的快速发展，知识产权犯罪逐渐从现实生活蔓延到网络虚拟空间，特别是手机终端网络游戏（以下简称手游）领域。近年来，在侵犯计算机软件著作权犯罪案中，复制网络游戏作品，经营山寨版手机网络游戏非法牟利的案件明显增多。此类案件的盗版侵权数据大部分都储存在服务器或云端，采用违法获利途径与盗版网站经营公司账户分离的方式躲避侦查。本案被害单位闲徕互娱公司系集研发与运营于一体的知名棋牌类手游公司，涉案游戏亦为知名手游，受众广泛，嫌疑人的盗版行为造成了恶劣的社会影响；且本案在案发后，嫌疑人企图通过篡改和销毁数据、账目等方式逃避处罚或减轻自己罪责，使认定该公司经营游戏币的主要收入的电子数据受到破坏，一度给司法审判工作带来了较大挑战。本案审理主要采取对第三方代理公司为被告公司销售“星钻礼品”等用于启动游戏的虚拟货币的收入来认定被告单位的犯罪数额，充分运用新类型电子商务支付平台数据及手游营销模式的新特点，对此类新型犯罪的电子证据进行梳理和评判，确立了通过第三方平台数据印证涉案犯罪情节的规则，为打击此类故意躲避侦查的新类型犯罪树立了典范。

2018年度全国打击侵权盗版十大案件

一、北京环球天下教育科技有限公司传播盗版电子出版物案

2018年8月，根据权利人投诉，北京市文化市场行政执法总队对北京环球天下教育科技有限公司侵犯文字作品著作权案进行调查。经查，该公司于2017年6月至2018年8月期间，未经权利人剑桥大学出版社许可，通过网站向公众提供《剑桥雅思考试全真试题》等9种出版物的PDF格式下载阅读服务。2018年8月，北京市文化市场行政执法总队对该公司做出罚款22.5万元的行政处罚。

【点　评】 本案系侵犯出版发行机构著作权的典型案件。版权执法部门高度关注网络环境下的侵权盗版行为，对侵犯国外出版发行机构著作权的违法行为依法严厉查处，体现了中国政府履行国际承诺、严格保护知识产权的坚定立场和鲜明态度。

二、上海《3D播播VR》APP传播3D盗版影视作品案

2018年7月，根据权利人投诉，上海市文化市场行政执法总队对《3D播播VR》APP侵犯电影作品著作权案进行调查。经查，上海乐欢软件有限公司自2015年12月起经营《3D播播VR》APP，未经权利人许可，向公众提供《环太平洋2：雷霆再起》《黑豹》等25部电影作品的观看服务。2018年10月，上海市文化市场行政执法总队对该公司做出罚款25万元的行政处罚。

【点　评】 本案系VR新型行业侵犯著作权的典型案件。当事人系VR产业头部企业，但其著作权保护意识淡薄，通过信息网络传播3D类侵权影视作品。版权执法部门积极关注新兴产业版权保护，不断拓展执法领域，为查处新型案件做了有益探索。

三、江苏无锡“紫薯影院”微信公众号传播盗版影视作品案

2018年6月，根据权利人投诉，江苏省无锡市版权局对“紫薯影院”微信公众号侵犯电影作品著作权案进行调查。经查，无锡佳酷信息技术有限公司通过其运营的“紫薯影院”微信公众号及相关网站，向公众提供侵权影视作品在线播放服务吸引用户，并通过诱导购物，与第三方联合运营游戏、小说等多种经营模式获利。2018年7月，江苏省无锡市版权局对该公司做出罚款12万元的行政处罚。

【点　评】 本案系利用微信公众号传播侵权影视作品的典型案件。近年来，侵权盗版分子利用微信、微博等社交平台，淘宝、闲鱼等电商平台，以及网盘等存储平台传播盗版作品的现象多发，严重损害了权利人的合法权益，破坏了网络版权秩序。版权执法部门严厉打击通过各类平台从事侵权盗版的行为，对加强网络平台治理、促进产业健康发展具有积极意义。

四、天津百练教育科技集团有限公司销售盗版培训教材案

2018年6月，根据权利人投诉，天津市文化市场行政执法总队联合各区执法队对天津百练教育科技集团有限公司侵犯文字作品著作权案进行调查，检查该集团六个校区，现场查获《经济法》等大量涉嫌侵权的图书。经权利人认定，有31种169本图书系侵权盗版。2018年8月，天津市文化市场行政执法总队对该公司做出没收侵权图书、罚款10.36余万元的行政处罚。

【点　评】 本案系教育培训机构侵犯他人著作权的典型案件。近年来，部分教育培训机构缺乏基本著作权意识，肆意使用盗版教材教学，不仅严重损害权利人合法权益，也给教育培训行业带来不良影响。本案对各类教育培训机构树立版权意识、维护图书市场经营秩序具有示范意义。

五、北京“8·8”销售盗版少儿图书案

2016年4月，根据举报线索，北京市文化市场行政执法总队会同北京市公安局治安管理总队、西城公安分局和通州公安分局成立专案组，对赵某某等销售盗版少儿图书案进行调查，共查获盗版少儿图书360万余册，涉案码洋达9 100万元。2018年1月，北京市通州区人民法院以侵犯著作权罪，判处赵某某有期徒刑六年六个月，并处罚金150万元；判处赵树某有期徒刑四年，并处罚金30万元；判处其余被告人有期徒刑三年三个月至二年六个月不等，并处罚金。

【点　评】 本案系销售侵权盗版少儿图书的典型案件。本案是近年查办的数量最大、案值最高、涉及面最广、涉少儿图书种类最多、社会影响最恶劣的销售侵权盗版图书案，极大地震慑了不法分子，规范了出版物市场版权秩序。

六、广东龙某某等运营网络游戏私服案

2017 年 6 月，广东省广州市公安局黄埔区分局对龙某某等侵犯网络游戏著作权案进行调查。经查，龙某某等未经权利人许可，赴泰国利用电脑和远程控制软件架设、运营私服游戏《歪歪神武》。2017 年 9 月起，机械牛网络科技（苏州）有限公司明知该运营方运维私服游戏，仍通过“派爱支付”平台与私服网站进行连接，为其提供玩家充值通道和支付结算服务，共为其支付结算玩家充值金额 362.6 万余元，并按比例收取手续费。2018 年 12 月，广东省广州市黄埔区人民法院以侵犯著作权罪，判处龙某某和李某有期徒刑二年和一年六个月，并处罚金；以帮助信息网络犯罪活动罪，判处机械牛网络科技（苏州）有限公司罚金 3 万元，判处法人代表程某有期徒刑十个月，并处罚金 1 万元。

【点　评】 本案系跨国网络侵权犯罪案件，具有手法隐蔽、跨境作案、产业化经营等特点。办案部门充分利用技术手段，破解了跨境取证难题。同时，准确适用 2015 年 11 月实施的《刑法修正案（九）》有关为利用信息网络实施犯罪提供技术支持或帮助的、情节严重的予以刑事处罚的规定，对帮助信息网络犯罪行为进行惩戒，具有重要的示范意义。

七、江苏淮安“BT 天堂”网传播盗版影视作品案

2016 年 7 月，根据权利人报案，江苏省淮安市公安局、淮安市版权局和文化市场综合执法支队成立专案组，对“BT 天堂”网侵犯影视作品著作权案进行调查。经查，2015 年以来，袁某某以营利为目的，通过网络购得“BT 天堂”网站域名、服务器及虚拟主机后，未经权利人许可，将大量影视作品的种子文件链接发布在该网站上供网民点击下载以赚取广告收入。2015 年 5 月至 2016 年 7 月，网站发布影视作品资源 24 737 个，非法获利 140 万余元。2018 年 12 月，江苏省淮安市中级人民法院以侵犯著作权罪判处袁某某有期徒刑三年，并处罚金 80 万元。

【点　评】 本案系利用 P2P 技术提供非法链接传播侵权影视作品的典型案件。当事人主观故意明显，法制意识淡薄，大肆侵犯影视作品信息网络传播权，国内外影响广，涉案作品数量大，非法经营额高。本案的查办在网络影视传播领域产生了重要影响。

八、四川成都伍某某等制售盗版教辅案

2017 年 11 月，四川省成都市公安局天府新区分局对伍某某等制售盗版教辅案进行调查。经查，2015 年 8 月起，伍某某以营利为目的，伙同他人盗印《生物化学基础》等盗版教辅共计 1.6 万余册。2018 年 11 月，四川省成都市双流区人民法院以侵犯著作权罪，判处伍某某有期徒刑四年六个月，并处罚金 40 万元，禁止其四年内从事图书、期刊销售经营活动；判处高某某有期徒刑三年六个月，并处罚金 20 万元；判处蒋某某有期徒刑三年，并处罚金 5 万元；判处其他被告人有期徒刑缓刑，并处罚金。

【点　评】 本案系侵犯复制权、发行权构成侵犯著作权罪的典型案件。由于制售盗版图书数量、违法经营额较大，办案检察机关在向法院提出量刑建议的同时，建议对侵权人适用“从业禁止”，取得了良好的法律效果和社会效果。

九、浙江嘉兴段某某等制售盗版图书案

2017 年 3 月，根据举报线索，浙江省嘉兴市公安局、版权局会同海盐县公安局、版权局对段某某等制售盗版图书案进行调查。专案组赴北京、山东、河南等地，在当地公安、版权部门配合下，共出动警力 200 余人次，抓获以段某某等为首的生产销售盗版图书团伙 16 人，捣毁犯罪窝点 2 个、印刷厂 1 家，查扣各类盗版图书 50 余万册，涉案金额 200 余万元。2018 年 8 月，浙江省海盐县人民法院以侵犯著作权罪，判处段某某、孙某某有期徒刑三年，并处罚金 5 万元；判处其他 14 名被告人有期徒刑缓刑不等，并处罚金。

【点　评】 本案系打击盗版团伙的典型案件。该案涉及犯罪人数众多，涉及制作、印刷、销售等多个环节，侵权盗版图书数量巨大，性质恶劣。版权行政执法与公安部门加强跨区域执法协作，密切配合，对侵权盗版全链条进行有效打击，取得了积极成效，受到媒体广泛关注。

十、江西永新陈某某等销售盗版教辅案

2016 年 9 月，根据日常巡查线索，江西省永新县版权行政执法部门发现多个书店涉嫌销售盗版教辅资料且数量较大，即将本案移转公安部门立案查办。本案共抓获犯罪分子 9 人，捣毁销售窝点 6 个，捣毁生产窝点 1 个，缴获盗版图书 10 万余册，涉案盗版图书码洋 1 000 余万元，成功追缴涉案财物 200 余万元。2018 年 7 月，江西省永新县人民法院以侵犯著作权罪，判处陈某某有期徒刑五年，并处罚金 80.35 万元；判处赵某有期徒刑二年一个月，并处罚金 43.10 万元；判处五名被告人有期徒刑缓刑或拘役，并处罚金 50 万元至 7.8 万元不等；判处两名被告人罚金。

【点　评】 本案是加强打击侵权盗版两法衔接的典型案件。版权行政执法人员根据日常巡查发现的线索，及时将案件移转公安机关深挖彻查，最终成功破获该起跨地区、多省份的侵权盗版图书“窝案”，在版权执法加强两法衔接、强化区域执法协作方面积累了成功经验。

2018年地方著作权司法保护典型案件

北　京　市

一、"短视频"著作权侵权纠纷案［北京市海淀区人民法院（2017）京0108民初51249号］

【简要案情】《快手》APP用户于2015年4月在《快手》APP上传、发布了名为《这智商没谁了》的视频（以下简称涉案短视频）。北京快手科技有限公司（以下简称快手公司）认为，涉案短视频蕴含丰富艺术创造性，与二人转相似，通过对话和动作使视频内容诙谐幽默，属于具有独创性的作品。根据《快手网服务协议》《知识产权条款》等约定以及用户的授权，快手公司合法取得涉案短视频在全球范围内的独家信息网络传播权。2017年，广州华多网络科技有限公司（以下简称华多公司）在其运营的《补刀小视频》APP安卓端和iOS端中上传并发布了涉案短视频。快手公司认为，华多公司的上述行为侵害其对涉案短视频享有的著作权，故起诉要求华多公司赔偿经济损失1万元及相应合理开支。一审法院认为，涉案短视频虽仅持续18秒，但其在该时间段中所讲述的情景故事，融合了两名表演者的对话和动作等要素，且通过镜头切换展现了故事发生的场景，已构成具有独创性的完整表达。结合涉案短视频以数字化视频的形式发布在《快手》APP上的事实，涉案短视频系摄制在一定介质上，由一系列有伴音的画面组成，并通过网络传播的作品，属于以类似摄制电影的方法创作的作品。虽然时长短的确可能限制作者的表达空间，但表达空间受限并不等于表达形式非常有限而成为思想范畴的产物；相反，在10余秒的时间内亦可以创作出体现一定主题，且结合文字、场景、对话、动作等多种元素的内容表达。华多公司未经快手公司许可，在其运营的《补刀小视频》中发布涉案短视频，侵害了快手公司对涉案短视频依法享有的信息网络传播权，应当承担赔偿经济损失等侵权责任。据此，一审法院判决：华多公司赔偿快手公司经济损失1万元及相应合理开支。一审宣判后，双方当事人均未提起上诉。

【点　评】　近年来，短视频因其形式新颖、内容丰富、传播迅速等特点而成为最受欢迎的互联网产品之一，与短视频相关的著作权纠纷案件开始大量涌现。本案结合著作权法关于作品构成要件、作品类型等规定，对短视频是否能构成作品以及可以构成何种类型的作品等颇具争议的问题进行了充分论证，最终认定涉案短视频具有独创性，符合以类似摄制电影的方法创作的作品的构成要件。本案被媒体称为全国首例认定短视频构成作品的案件，其典型意义在于，首次以裁判形式认定短视频的可版权性以及其可构成以类似摄制电影的方法创作的作品。在短视频产业已渐成规模并亟待明晰相关主体行为边界的当下，及时回应了短视频行业加强知识产权保护及明晰规则的需求，对产业发展将起到司法保护应有的导向作用。

二、"音乐喷泉"作品著作权侵权纠纷案［北京市海淀区人民法院（2016）京0108民初15322号、北京知识产权法院（2017）京73民终1404号］

【简要案情】　北京中科水景科技有限公司（以下简称中科水景公司）主张其对所创作的青岛世界园艺博览会（以下简称青岛世园会）音乐喷泉《倾国倾城》《风居住的街道》乐曲的喷泉编辑享有著作权，认为杭州西湖风景名胜区湖滨管理处（以下简称西湖管理处）以考察名义从该公司获得包含涉案作品在内的视频、设计图等资料并交给北京中科恒业中自技术有限公司（以下简称中科恒业公司），中科恒业公司剽窃涉案音乐喷泉编曲并在西湖施工喷放，侵犯其著作权。为此，中科水景公司诉至法院，请求判令中科恒业公司、西湖管理处停止侵权、赔礼道歉，赔偿经济损失20万元及合理支出8万元。一审法院认为，音乐喷泉作品所要保护的对象是喷泉在特定音乐配合下形成的喷射表演效果。著作权法虽无音乐喷泉作品或音乐喷泉编曲作品的类别，但这种作品本身具有独创性，应受到著作权法的保护。考虑到中科恒业公司、西湖管理处曾接触过中科水景公司的相关喷泉视频、资料，西湖音乐喷泉相关曲目的喷射效果与中科水景公司享有著作权的喷泉音乐作品构成实质性相似，故中科恒业公司、西湖管理处构成侵犯著作权。据此，一审法院判决中科恒业公司、西湖管理处停止侵权、公开致歉、赔偿经济损失及合理支出共计9万元。中科恒业公司、西湖管理处不服，提起上诉。二审法院认为，涉案请求保护的权利载体可以称为涉案音乐喷泉喷射效果的呈现，由于涉案客体通过对喷泉水型、灯光及色彩的变化与音乐情感结合而进行的取舍、选择、安排，展现出的一种艺术美感表达，亦满足“可复制性”要求，符合作品的一般构成要件。由于涉案客体是由灯光、色彩、音乐、水型等多种要素共同构成的动态立体造型表达，其喷射效果的呈现具有审美意义，符合美术作品的构成要件。从价值解释角度出发，法律解释要顺应科技的发展、跟上时代的步伐。将涉案客体认定为美术作品的保护范畴，有利于鼓励对美的表达形式的创新，有助于喷泉相关作品的创作。在此基础上，二审法院对一审判决关于涉案作品著作权归属以及中科恒业公司、西湖管理处侵犯涉案作品的著作权及责任承担的认定，亦予以确认。据此，二审法院判决：驳回上诉，维持原判。

【点　评】　随着科技的发展，视觉美感的表达形式呈现多样化的趋势。对于富有美感、能为人们所感知，但不属于法律明确规定的作品类型的独创性表达，是否构成作品的判断，引发了作品认定与法定作品类型判断之间顺序关系的讨论。如何在符合法律逻辑的前提下，妥善处理尊重现行法律规定和维护智力创新成果的关系，正是本案的难点和典型意义所在。本案二审判决通过对《著作权法》第三条和《著作权法实施条例》第二条的合理解释和适用解决了上述问题。一方面，涉案音乐喷泉喷射效果的呈现是设计师借助声光电等科技因素精心设计所展现出的一种艺术美感表达，符合作品的一般构成要件。另一方面，二审判决通过运用文义解释、价值解释等解释方法对涉案相关条款进行了解释，认为涉案音乐喷泉喷射效果的呈现是一种由灯光、色彩、音乐、水型等多种要素共同构成的动态立体造型表达，这种喷射效果的呈现显然具有审美意义，符合美术作品的构成要件，属于美术作品的保护范畴。二审判决既体现了裁判者对立法者在法律规定中明确无误地表达意思的尊重，也充分展现了裁判者科学地解释法律、以理服人的专业技巧，受到了业界的普遍好评。

三、“销售盗版网络游戏”侵犯著作权罪案［北京市海淀区人民法院（2018）京0108刑初1932号］

【简要案情】　2016年至今，黄明伙同他人，未经著作权人北京闲徕互娱网络科技有限公司（以下简称闲徕互娱公司）许可，运营与闲徕互娱公司享有著作权的《闲徕琼崖海南麻将》游戏源代码具有高度同一性的《巨石海南麻将》游戏，并通过代理人员销售用于启动游戏的虚拟货币的方式进行非法营利，非法经营数额162 912.9元。2017年12月16日，黄明被抓获。公诉机关于2018年9月21日向一审法院提起公诉，认为巨石在线（北京）科技有限公司（以下简称巨石在线公司）、黄明的行为触犯了《刑法》第二百一十七条、第三十一条之规定，已构成侵犯著作权罪，提请依法惩处。巨石在线公司诉讼代表人李勇对起诉书指控的事实和罪名没有提出实质性异议。黄明对起诉书指控的事实和罪名没有提出异议。一审法院认为，巨石在线公司及其直接负责的主管人员黄明以营利为目的，未经著作权人许可，复制发行他人享有著作权的计算机软件，情节严重，其行为已构成侵犯著作权罪，应予惩处。公诉机关指控巨石在线公司、黄明犯有侵犯著作权罪的事实清楚，证据确实充分，指控罪名成立。鉴于黄明到案后及在庭审中能如实供认自己的基本罪行，巨石在线公司及黄明认罪、悔罪态度较好，且巨石在线公司积极退交违法所得，对巨石在线公司及黄明依法从轻处罚。依照《刑法》有关规定，判决：巨石在线公司犯侵犯著作权罪，判处罚金20万元；黄明犯侵犯著作权罪，判处有期徒刑1年，罚金10万元。一审宣判后，巨石在线公司和黄明均未提起上诉。

【点　评】　随着互联网经济的快速发展，知识产权犯罪逐渐从现实生活蔓延到网络虚拟空间，特别是手机终端网络游戏领域。近年来，在侵犯计算机软件著作权犯罪案中，复制网络游戏作品，经营山寨版手机网络游戏非法牟利的案件明显增多。此类案件的盗版侵权数据大部分都储存在服务器或云端，采用违法获利途径与盗版网站经营公司账户分离的方式躲避侦查。本案被害单位闲徕互娱公司系集研发与运营于一体的知名棋牌类手游公司，涉案游戏亦为知名手游，受众广泛，嫌疑人的盗版行为造成了恶劣的社会影响；且本案在案发后，嫌疑人企图通过篡改和销毁数据、账目等方式逃避处罚或减轻自己罪责，使认定该公司经营游戏币的主要收入的电子数据受到破坏，一度给司法审判工作带来了较大困难。本案主要采用第三方代理公司为被告公司销售“星钻礼品”等用于启动游戏的虚拟货币的收入认定被告单位的犯罪数额，充分运用新类型电子商务支付平台数据及手游营销模式的新特点，对此类新型犯罪的电子证据进行梳理和评判，确立了通过第三方平台数据印证涉案犯罪情节的规则，对打击此类故意躲避侦查的新类型犯罪具有示范意义。

河　北　省

桂林周氏顺发食品有限公司与北京北大方正电

子有限公司侵害其他著作财产权纠纷案［石家庄市中级人民法院（2017）冀民初 910 号、河北省高级人民法院 2018 冀民终 655 号］

【简要案情】 北京北大方正电子有限公司（以下简称北大方正公司）于 2000 年 7 月 7 日改编完成美术作品《方正倩体系列（细倩、中倩、粗倩）》，2000 年 8 月 31 日在北京首次发表，该公司以演绎作品身份依法享有著作权，登记日期为 2013 年 8 月 5 日。

2017 年 4 月 19 日，北大方正公司发现河北省石家庄市的一家超市售卖桂林周氏顺发食品有限公司（以下简称周氏顺发公司）包装显示为“五谷粗粮营养燕麦片”字样的食品，北大方正公司认为“五谷粗粮营养燕麦片”文字与方正粗倩简体字体相同，遂将周氏顺发公司诉至法院，要求：判令周氏顺发公司立即停止侵犯北大方正公司著作权的行为，停止使用、销售并销毁所有带有方正粗倩简体字库单字的产品包装、标示、产品名称、产品广告等，并赔偿经济损失 10 万元。

法院经审理认为，涉案《方正倩体系列（细倩、中倩、粗倩）》是在汉字的基本笔画之上，对基本笔画（横、竖、弯、勾等）施加了不同的粗细、长短、弧度及笔画之间富有特点的艺术衔接等形态加以改编，形成的一个与现有公有领域的文字笔画明显不同的完整字库体系，这些字体均是北大方正公司通过人工智慧并运用一定的技术手段获得的，属于《中华人民共和国著作权法》规定的美术作品的范畴，应当受到该法保护。涉案商品上“五谷粗粮营养燕麦片”九字的表达方式，使用了需要付费的倩体字又未经权利人授权，属于侵害北大方正公司其他著作财产权的行为，周氏顺发公司应当承担侵权责任。法院综合考量倩体字的类型、侵权销售行为的性质及后果、周氏顺发公司的悔过态度、北大方正公司请求赔偿的其他合理开支等诸多因素后，确定由周氏顺发公司赔偿北大方正电子公司经济损失及合理维权费用共计 5 万元。

【点　评】 电脑文字是人们生活及工作的必需品，电脑字体是否属于法律保护的客体，对其进行保护是否影响或限制了电脑字体的应用，这些问题在目前的社会中甚至于法律界中都存在一定的争议，本案即对这些问题进行了界定，以厘清人们的认识。另外需要说明，涉案字体不允许未经授权的经营使用，也就是说不能无偿地拿着别人的智力成果去赚你的钱，但这并不妨碍公众个人的使用行为，公众在自己使用的过程中应当把握好这个度，不能跨界。

黑龙江省

一、七田阳光公司诉阳光教育中心侵害著作权纠纷案［鸡西市中级人民法院（2018）黑 03 民初 4 号、黑龙江省高级人民法院（2018）黑民终 518 号］

【简要案情】 七田阳光公司对其编写的头脑能力合格训练册（5～6 岁）感知力训练、专注力训练、观察力训练、思维力训练、色彩记忆等多套作品进行了著作权登记，对上述作品享有著作权。阳光教育中心为从事教育咨询服务的个体工商户，该中心自北京博睿恩公司购进《博睿恩儿童早教训练册》30 套，以上述训练册为课程教材，为当地适龄儿童提供头脑能力训练课程培训，并以该培训课程对外经营。经比对，阳光教育中心自北京博睿恩公司购进的全脑训练册中，有数十页内容与七田阳光公司编写的头脑能力合格训练册内容完全相同。七田阳光公司以阳光教育中心使用的《博睿恩儿童早教训练册》大量内容系抄袭、复制其作品为由诉至法院，请求判令阳光教育中心停止销售、使用并销毁侵权训练册，赔偿其经济损失及合理维权费用 30 万元。

一审法院认为，根据《中华人民共和国著作权法》第二十二条第一款第（六）项规定，为学校课堂教学或者科学研究，翻译或者少量复制已经发表的作品，供教学或者科研人员使用的，属于“合理使用”。阳光教育中心购买博睿恩公司的教育训练册后，仅在课堂上作为教材使用，可不必支付著作权人报酬。但阳光教育中心将博睿恩公司的教育训练册向学生出售，则属不当使用行为，应停止不当行为。判决阳光教育中心立即停止对外销售博睿恩公司出版的全脑潜能训练册，驳回七田阳光公司的其他诉讼请求。

二审法院认为，著作权法上的合理使用要求使用作品的目的必须是出于非商业用途，如此才能在著作权人与社会公众之间实现利益的协调与平衡。阳光教育中心系个体工商户，以营利为目的开展经营，其使用被诉侵权作品的目的是为招收学生获取利益，虽然形式上也用于课堂教学，但在使用目的上与《中华人民共和国著作权法》第二十二条规定的“为学校课堂教学”使用作品有本质区别，不属于著作权法上的合理使用。阳光教育中心使用的教材系自博睿恩公司合法购买，该教育中心作为购买者和使用者，要求其审查所购买的作品是否存在抄袭等侵犯著作权的内容，确实超出其应尽的注意义务。故阳光教育中心合法来源抗辩成立，依法不应承担赔偿损失的侵权责任。一审判决虽然适用法律存在瑕疵，但判决结果正确，判决驳回上诉，维持原判。

【点　评】　本案典型意义在于对课堂教学合理使用的理解。根据《中华人民共和国著作权法》第二十二条第一款第（六）项的规定，为学校课堂教学或者科学研究，翻译或者少量复制已经发表的作品，供教学或者科研人员使用，但不得出版发行的，为合理使用。使用人可以不经著作权人许可，不向其支付报酬，但应当指明作者姓名、作品名称，并且不得侵犯著作权人依照该法享有的其他权利。结合“合理使用”的立法目的，该条中的“学校”，既包括全日制的普通学校，也包括各类业余学校，但不包括营利性的培训机构。该条中的“课堂教学”，专指面授教学，函授、广播或电视教学不在此列。该条中的使用方式限于少量复制与翻译，“少量”不仅是指所用部分占整个作品的比例，也包括复制的份数。本案中，阳光教育中心将被诉侵权产品用于课堂教学，形式上与合理使用具有相似之处，但该中心从事的是营利性培训，且教材大量抄袭他人享有著作权的作品，超出了“翻译或者少量复制”的范畴，不属于合理使用。

二、刘某诉陈某侵害著作权纠纷案［哈尔滨市中级人民法院（2018）黑01民初133号、黑龙江省高级人民法院（2018）黑民终528号］

【简要案情】《通河县交通志（1906—2014）》由通河县人民政府主办，通河县交通局承办，县政府地方志办公室组织具体编纂工作。该书编辑部主编为闫某，编辑为陈某等多人。2018年，刘某诉至法院，称《通河县交通志（1906—2014）》的编辑陈某以帮助刘某打字、协助刘某工作为名，将刘某多年来收集的资料据为己有，剽窃刘某作品，并将刘某作品收录进《通河县交通志（1906—2014）》，侵害了刘某的著作权。请求判令陈某立即停止使用刘某享有原始著作权的《通河县交通志（1906—2014）》中的历史记录、纪实部分，在通河县电视台公开赔礼道歉，并赔偿刘某经济损失8 000元。

法院经审理认为，《中华人民共和国著作权法》第十一条第三款规定，由法人或者其他组织主持，代表法人或者其他组织意志创作，并由法人或者其他组织承担责任的作品，法人或者其他组织视为作者。《通河县交通志（1906—2014）》由通河县人民政府主办，通河县交通局承办，县政府地方志办公室组织编纂工作，通河县交通志编纂委员会在该书封面署名，故《通河县交通志（1906—2014）》系代表法人或其他组织意志、由法人或其他组织承担责任的“法人作品”，其作者应为法人或其他组织。陈某作为《通河县交通志（1906—2014）》编辑之一，其编辑工作为职务行为，对《通河县交通志（1906—2014）》的相关内容是否构成著作权侵权不应承担侵权赔偿责任，刘某应向该书作者主张权利。判决驳回刘某诉讼请求。

【点　评】　本案明确了法人作品的认定问题。关于法人作品，应从由谁组织主持、代表谁的意志、由谁承担责任三个要件入手，准确认定法人作品。对于法人作品，法人或者其他组织视为作者，享有作品的著作权，同时也承担作品的相应责任。起诉法人作品侵害其权利的，应以创作法人作品的法人或者其他组织为被告，而非从事创作的自然人。

上　海　市

一、南品仁与复旦大学出版社有限公司、老古文化事业股份有限公司、上海老古文化教育有限公司侵害著作财产权纠纷案［上海市第一中级人民法院（2014）沪一中民五（知）初字第170号、上海市高级人民法院（2017）沪民终223号］

【案情摘要】 2001年1月31日，南怀瑾与郭姮妟签署委托书，记载“兹委托郭姮妟为本人的特别授权代理人，全权代理本人处理我所有的作品在大陆的全部著作权事项。代理权限：代为签订著作权许可使用合同及处理著作权许可使用的其他有关事务。代为处理其他一切有关本人所有作品在大陆的著作权之法律事务。代理人在代理权限内签署的一切文件，本委托人均予以认可。代理人有转委托权”。郭姮妟出具署名日期为2001年6月8日的许可使用证书，记载“1. 南先生作品在中国境内的许可使用权专属老古公司。老古公司得自行或许可第三人使用。2. 老古公司之专属使用权期与法令规定南先生之作品权利年限同。3. 老古公司应支付之版税权利金悉数留作筹设上海老古文化事业及其营运之用”。此后，南怀瑾作品在大陆地区曾分别由复旦大学出版社、东方出版社、上海人民出版社等出版，授权主体既有老古公司也有南怀瑾，版权使用费有的由南怀瑾本人收取，有的则由上海老古公司收取，对上述情况南怀瑾及郭姮妟均知悉。

2014年10月，南怀瑾之子南小舜提起本案诉讼，主张其继承南怀瑾大陆地区的著作财产权，因复旦大学出版社出版南怀瑾多部作品后未支付部分著作权使用费，故要求老古公司与复旦出版社连带赔偿经济损失 988 万余元、合理费用 35 万余元。老古公司提起反诉要求确认其对南怀瑾作品享有著作权。

【裁判结果】 一审法院认为，复旦大学出版社在 2012 年 7 月前出版南怀瑾作品及已经支付给上海老古公司的版权费，南怀瑾均知悉，故复旦大学出版社不构成侵权。对于南怀瑾去世后未支付的 136 万余元版权费，属于使用他人作品未支付费用，构成侵权，因复旦大学出版社对此并无主观过错，故无须承担维权费用。对老古公司的反诉予以驳回。一审判决后，老古公司、复旦大学出版社不服，提起上诉。二审法院认为，许可使用证书法律性质上不属于转委托，老古公司据此可授权复旦大学出版社出版南怀瑾作品。复旦大学出版社前期向南怀瑾、后期根据老古公司指令向上海老古公司支付著作权许可使用费，系正常履约行为，亦不与南怀瑾本人意愿相违，因此复旦大学出版社并不存在侵害著作权的行为。据此，二审法院维持驳回老古公司全部反诉请求的一审判决，并改判驳回南品仁（南小舜死亡后承继诉讼）的全部诉讼请求。

【典型意义】 本案涉及南怀瑾作品归属争议，受到社会各界甚至海内外华人的关注。本案事实错综，法律关系复杂。本案二审判决通过探求南怀瑾本人生前的真实意思表示，准确界定各方行为的法律意义，对涉案各方的相关权益进行了符合南怀瑾生前意愿的合理分配，取得了各方之间的利益平衡。二审宣判后，各方均服判息诉，判决结果也得到社会各界好评，取得了良好的法律效果和社会效果。

二、原告达索系统股份有限公司与被告上海知豆电动车技术有限公司侵害计算机软件著作权纠纷案［上海知识产权法院（2018）沪 73 民初 81 号、上海市高级人民法院（2018）沪民终 429 号］

【案情摘要】 原告系计算机软件 CATIA V5 R20 的著作权人。原告曾因被告使用侵权软件于 2017 年 2 月向文化执法总队投诉，行政执法过程中查获知豆公司使用侵权软件 8 套，其间双方达成和解，并签订了正版软件采购合同，文化执法总队因此对被告依法减轻行政处罚，但被告并未按约支付软件采购款。同年 11 月，原告向法院申请证据保全。保全过程中，经原告同意，法院采取确定抽查比例随机抽查的方式对计算机中安装涉案软件的情况进行证据保全，同时根据所抽查计算机中安装涉案软件的比例推算经营场所内所有计算机中安装涉案软件的数量。经清点，被告经营场所内共有计算机 73 台，其中抽查的 15 台计算机均安装了涉案软件。原告遂诉至法院，要求被告停止侵权，并赔偿经济损失及律师费共计 1 800 余万元。

【裁判结果】 一审法院审理后认为，被告未经原告许可，在其经营场所内的计算机上安装了涉案软件，侵害了原告对涉案软件享有的复制权。虽然原告的实际损失及被告的违法所得均难以确定，但现有证据可以证明原告损失超过了著作权法规定的法定赔偿数额的上限 50 万元，故法院综合全案证据情况，同时考虑双方提交的销售合同软件单价、侵权时间、安装侵权软件的计算机数量，以及被告在被行政机关查获使用侵权软件后仍扩大侵权规模的主观恶意等因素，在法定赔偿最高限额之上酌定赔偿数额，判决被告赔偿原告经济损失及律师费共计 900 万元。一审判决后，被告不服，提起上诉。二审法院认为，本案原、被告双方已经就文化执法总队查获的侵权行为达成过和解协议。其后，被告未履行和解协议，反而扩大侵权规模，存在重复侵权行为，侵权主观恶意明显，且原告的实际损失已经明显超过法定赔偿的最高限额，故应在法定赔偿最高限额之上酌情确定赔偿金额。遂判决驳回上诉、维持原判。

【典型意义】 本案是法院依法加大知识产权侵权赔偿力度的典型案例。法院综合全案证据情况，在法定赔偿最高限额之上酌情确定被告应赔偿原告的经济损失并全额支持了原告主张的合理开支，依法加大了对权利人的保护力度，也为类似案件的审理提供了一定的参考，体现了法院不断加强知识产权司法保护的态度和决心。同时，通过本案判决倡导社会公众全面使用正版软件，尊重软件开发者的劳动和付出，推进企业软件正版化工作，形成尊重和保护知识产权、激励和发展创新的营商环境。

江　苏　省

一、涉新闻集合式新媒体著作权侵权纠纷案［无锡市中级人民法院（2015）锡知民初字第 00219 号、江苏省高级人民法院（2018）苏民终 588 号］

【简要案情】 江苏现代快报传媒有限公司（以下简称现代快报公司）、江苏现代快报传媒有限公司无锡分公司（以下简称现代快报无锡分公司）发现《今日头条》手机新闻客户端未经许可使用其享有著作权的《出租屋爆燃　一家三口烧成重伤》等 6 篇新闻作品。头条网（https://www.toutiao.com）的 ICP 备案显示备案号为京 ICP 备 12023439 号，主办单位为北京字节跳动科技有限公司（以下简称字节跳动科技公司）；苹果系统中《今日头条》APP下载页显示的开发者是字节跳动科技公司，安卓系统中《今日头条》客户端显示的开发者是北京字节跳动网络技术有限公司（以下简称字节跳动网络公司）。因此，现代快报公司、现代快报无锡分公司诉至法院，请求字节跳动科技公司、字节跳动网络公司赔偿损失20万元，支付合理费用1万元。

（一）涉案6篇文章构成《著作权法》意义上的作品。涉案的6篇文章是由记者采访、撰写并经编辑后发表在《现代快报》的书面语言表达形式，无证据显示其内容与他人已有作品相同或实质性相似，亦无其他证据表明存在其他作者，故涉案6篇文章系从无到有的独立创作，符合作品的要件要求。涉案6篇文章虽是对客观事实的描述，但其文字表达中不仅包含单纯事实情况，还含有以文艺创作手法创作的新闻评论，该表达属于作者的独创性智力劳动，属于《著作权法》意义上的作品。（二）现代快报公司、现代快报无锡分公司为适格原告。涉案作品均有署名，在无相反证据的情况下，应认定在作品上署名的人为作者。涉案6篇文章作者薛晟、朱鲸润、陈泓江签订的《职务作品创作合同》中明确其作为现代快报公司聘用的记者，所创作的作品系完成工作任务的职务作品，著作权属于两原告，故两原告享有涉案文章的著作权，与本案有直接利害关系，具有原告主体资格。现代快报无锡分公司作为现代快报公司的依法设立并领取营业执照的分支机构，属于民事诉讼法规定的可作为原告的其他组织。虽然涉案的《出租屋爆燃……》的作者唐奕并未在《职务作品创作合同》上签字，但该文署名“现代快报记者　唐奕　朱鲸润”，属于合作作品，根据《著作权法实施条例》，合同作品不可分割使用的，著作权由各合作作者共同享有。现朱鲸润明确其作品著作权属于两原告，则两原告可据此对该文主张著作权。（三）《今日头条》客户端提供涉案6篇文章构成部分侵权。《打工妹……》及《9旬老太……》两篇文章显示于《今日头条》客户端时，左上角都标明了具体的上传用户的名称，结合字节跳动科技公司提供的公证书中成都商报和汉网注册该头条账号时所提交的相应证明文件的后台记录，能够证明涉案作品系第三方头条号上传，字节跳动科技公司提供的是信息存储空间服务。此外，本案中，没有证据证明字节跳动科技公司知道或有合理的理由应当知道涉案作品侵权，也没有证据证明其改变了涉案作品并从中获利，故在字节跳动科技公司及时删除上述两篇涉案文章的情况下，其不应对上述涉案作品的传播行为承担赔偿责任。

对于《为能多见见孙子……》等其余涉案的4篇文章，字节跳动科技公司未经许可，在其经营的《今日头条》客户端上使用了涉案作品，使公众可以在其个人选定的时间和地点获得涉案作品，侵害了两原告享有的信息网络传播权，应当对其侵权行为承担相应的法律责任。字节跳动科技公司主张其仅提供链接服务，但没有充足证据予以证明。首先，字节跳动科技公司提交的9395号公证书中虽然有该4篇文章的后台信息，但是该后台信息显示的URL地址并无与之对应的《今日头条》客户端页面显示信息予以佐证，也即9395号公证书中该4篇文章的后台信息仅为字节跳动科技公司的单方陈述内容，无相应证据予以证明；而字节跳动科技公司提交的20345号公证书并非针对涉案文章进行的公证，与本案无关。其次，字节跳动科技公司现有举证只能证明其与第三方网站存在以链接方式进行作品传播的协议，并不能进一步证明其对涉案4篇文章确实仅提供链接服务，而未将涉案文章复制至其服务器中。再次，本案缺乏证据证明用户阅读《今日头条》客户端中的涉案作品时存在跳转或链接到第三方网站的情形。最后，两原告否认就涉案作品授权江苏网、中青网、东方网等使用，也无证据证明两原告对涉案作品许可他人转授权使用。

退一步说，即使字节跳动科技公司确实仅提供链接服务，字节跳动科技公司只有在证明其不存在“明知或者应知”的情形下，才能免除赔偿责任。《为能多见见孙子……》及《女子民政局……》分别由中国江苏网及东方网提供，在字节跳动科技公司于这两家网站的授权许可协议中，均明确可设链转载的内容为两网站“自有版权”的内容。庭审中字节跳动科技公司及字节跳动网络公司均确认“自有版权”为“合法拥有”之意，也即字节跳动科技公司在签订协议时即认为中国江苏网及东方网应对可设链的内容拥有合法的信息网络传播权。但字节跳动科技公司并未要求该两家网站提供任何关于其拥有合法的信息网络传播权所涉权利人的清单列表，而仅在合同中要求网站承担知识产权权利瑕疵担保责任，尚不足以认定字节跳动科技公司尽到了审查义务。同时，在《为能多见见孙子……》一文中，左上角有“中国江苏网”字样，而文章首页首段后标明“现代快报记者薛晟　通讯员　荀连静”，基于《今日头条》的管理信息的能力，这种明显差异应引起字节跳动科技公司的注意从而通过诸如设置关键词等方式将此类作品进行筛选甄别，现字节跳动科技公司并无证据证明其进行相应操作，故应当认定其主观上存在过错，构成应知。另外，字节跳动科技公司主张《仪仗队……》《煤气泄漏……》2 篇文章系通过新浪网合法授权链接而来，但其与新浪网的合作协议有效期至 2014 年 12 月 31 日已终止，而《今日头条》客户端登载《仪仗队……》《煤气泄漏……》两文时间为 2015 年 9 月。字节跳动科技公司虽称其与新浪网的协议可续展执行，但并未提供证据证明，故其无权对新浪网内容设链转载。

关于赔偿主体，因头条网的 ICP 备案为字节跳动科技公司，且字节跳动科技公司在本案中明确其为头条网及《今日头条》客户端的经营者和运营者，其应承担侵权责任。虽然在安卓应用系统下的开发者信息为字节跳动网络公司，但并不能因此认定字节跳动网络公司属于法律意义上的网络服务提供者，故字节跳动网络公司无须承担侵权责任。

关于赔偿金额，法院认为，当前网络环境下，网络服务提供者是信息网络传播的中枢，是连接版权人和用户的桥梁和媒介，在网络传输中起着举足轻重的作用。这一新的经营主体和法律主体成为相关权利义务关系的连接点。网络服务提供者客观上为大量分散的用户的网络传播行为提供了便利条件，对其法律责任的考量应注意平衡各方利益、有效节约诉讼成本而又不阻碍技术的发展。但是，此种考量的前提依然是充分尊重著作权利人的合法权益，以促进创新、促进知识生产为核心。具体到本案而言，两原告主张法定赔偿，一审法院综合考虑《今日头条》系业内具有相当影响力的媒体，经营规模大，涉案文章通过网络进行传播，受众多，影响范围广，字节跳动科技公司主观上具有一定的过错等因素，支持本案赔偿金额 10 万元。两原告为本案支出律师费和公证费，系为制止侵权所支出的合理费用，应当予以支持。

据此，法院判决：字节跳动科技公司赔偿江苏现代快报公司、江苏现代快报传媒公司分公司经济损失 10 万元及为维权支出的合理费用 10 100 元。

【点　评】 本案涉及在现行著作权法框架下对《今日头条》这种新闻集合式新媒体未经许可转载他人作品行为性质的认定。法院根据查明事实，以及字节跳动科技公司的陈述，认为《今日头条》的算法技术完全可以支持对特定关键词的筛查检索，《今日头条》也已经注意到其设链行为存在侵害信息网络传播权的可能性。在此前提下，字节跳动科技公司仅在与第三方的合作协议中要求第三方网站承担权利瑕疵担保责任，而未要求其提供合法权利人清单列表，也未设置可能引发侵权的关键词进行筛查，在搜索所得内容显示的权属情况与来源网站不一致的情况下，未采取措施进行甄别，应当认定未尽到合理审查义务，其为涉案 4 篇文章设链的行为对相关作品的传播提供了便利，主观上为"应知"。关于赔偿数额的确定，法院综合考虑《今日头条》作为新闻集合式浏览媒体这一网络平台的特殊性，结合平台的受众范围、影响范围，侵权作品的传播速度和传播广度，以及其主观上具有过错等因素，确定赔偿金额 10 万元，并支持两原告为本案支出的律师费、公证费等合理费用。本案中，人民法院最终确定的裁决尺度，特别是结合个案情形判决较高的赔偿额，对于明晰不同媒体之间的竞争关系，规范网络转载，打击和遏制侵犯信息网络传播权的行为，具有积极意义。

本案涉及《今日头条》，确定的赔偿额高，具有广泛的社会影响力。案件判决后，引起了媒体界的广泛关注，新浪网、搜狐网、网易订阅、新京报网等多家媒体进行了报道，中国报业协会亦对本案高度关注。在 2018 年举行的第七届中国国际版权博览会上，国家版权局有关负责人对媒体表示本案"对规范网络转载是一个很好的判例"。

二、BT 天堂网站影视作品侵犯著作权罪案［淮安市中级人民法院（2018）苏 08 刑初 26 号］

【简要案情】 2015 年，被告人袁某某以营利为目的，通过网络购得 BT 天堂网站（http:www.bttiantang.com）域名、服务器及虚拟主机后，在均未取得相关影视作品著作权人许可的情况下，将大量影视作品的磁力链接、种子文件链接发布在其管理运行的 BT 天堂网站上供网民点击下载以赚取广告收入。2015 年 5 月至 2016 年 7 月，被告人袁某某通过此方式共获取广州星众信息科技有限公司投放在 BT 天堂网站上的广告费用 1 402 513 元。经远程勘验，BT 天堂网站共有影视作品资源 24 737 个，通过抽样下载，有效下载率达 43.956%，有效链接影视作品资源数达 10 873 个。2016 年 9 月 9 日，被告人袁某某被公安机关抓获，归案后如实供述相关犯罪事实，并主动退回违法所得人民币 30 万元。

被告人袁某某以营利为目的，未经相关影视作品著作权人许可，复制发行他人影视作品，违法所得数额巨大，情节特别严重，属于《刑法》第二百一十七条规定的"违法所得数额巨大"，其行为已构成侵犯著作权罪。被告人袁某某的非法经营数额应为 1 402 513 元，对辩护人提出的 1 402 513 元中只有43.956%属于违法犯罪所得的辩护意见，不予采纳。被告人袁某某归案后如实供述自己罪行，系坦白，可以从轻处罚，但因其犯罪情节特别严重，不宜适用缓刑。

据此，为维护社会主义市场经济秩序，保护著作权所有权人合法权益不受侵害，法院最终依法判决被告人袁某某犯侵犯著作权罪，判处有期徒刑三年，并处罚金人民币80万元。

【点　评】 本案系国家版权局挂牌督办案件。被告人袁某某以营利为目的，通过网络购得BT天堂网站（http://www.bttiantang.com）域名、服务器及虚拟主机后，在均未取得相关影视作品著作权人许可的情况下，将大量影视作品的磁力链接、种子文件链接发布在其管理运行的BT天堂网站上供网民点击下载以赚取广告收入，侵犯了著作权人的著作权，已构成侵犯著作权罪。

本案判决以后，被告人未上诉。案件登上微博热搜，引发网民热议，点击量过亿，跟帖评论数6 000余次。本案判决对于严厉打击侵权，引导创新主体诚信创业、公平竞争，具有积极的社会效应。

浙　江　省

一、王晓泉、王纪芳、王翔鹏与乐清市王十朋纪念馆、上海世纪出版股份有限公司古籍出版社侵害作品署名权、保护作品完整权、作品复制权、作品发行权纠纷案［乐清市人民法院（2016）浙0382民初7139号、温州市中级人民法院（2018）浙03民终1520号］

【案情介绍】 1994年1月，梅溪集重刊委员会经乐清市政协批复成立，其主编为王晓泉，副主编为王纪芳、王翔鹏。乐清市王十朋纪念馆（以下简称王十朋纪念馆）于2005年3月注册登记，业务范围为搜集、整理、研究、展览王十朋遗物和生平事迹。

1995年11月，梅溪集重刊委员会与上海世纪出版股份有限公司古籍出版社（以下简称古籍出版社）签订《关于出版〈王十朋全集〉的协议》，并于1998年6月签订了补充协议，对《王十朋全集》的出版事宜进行了约定。2011年7月，经王十朋纪念馆申请，乐清市政协出具一份给古籍出版社的函，表示同意增印《王十朋全集》。同年8月，王十朋纪念馆与古籍出版社签订《图书约稿出版合同》，并于2012年8月签订《补充协议书》，对《王十朋全集（修订本）》的出版事宜进行了约定。

《王十朋全集》由古籍出版社于1998年10月出版，注明“［宋］王十朋著、梅溪集重刊委员会编”，另在前言之前编入《政协乐清市委［1994］5号文件》作为版权页，载明“主编：王晓泉　副主编：王纪芳、王翔鹏”等。《王十朋全集（修订本）》由古籍出版社于2012年12月出版，注明“［宋］王十朋著、梅溪集重刊委员会编、王十朋纪念馆修订”，印数为5 600本。

王晓泉、王纪芳、王翔鹏以王十朋纪念馆和古籍出版社未经其许可复制、发行《王十朋全集（修订本）》，并恶意删除原书中刊登编者署名的版权页，侵害其著作权为由诉至法院，请求判令：王十朋纪念馆和古籍出版社立即停止侵害，刊登声明赔礼道歉以消除影响，并赔偿王晓泉、王纪芳、王翔鹏经济损失10万元、精神损害抚慰金2万元、合理费用10 276.60元（二审变更为赔偿合理费用2万元）。

【裁判结果】 乐清市人民法院经审理认为：《王十朋全集》在内容的选择或者编排上不具有独创性，不构成新的汇编作品。王晓泉、王纪芳、王翔鹏主张《王十朋全集》系汇编作品并享有著作权依据不足，不予支持。如王晓泉、王纪芳、王翔鹏主张《王十朋全集》系演绎作品或其对《王十朋全集》中部分内容享有单独的著作权，可另行主张。

综上，该院于2017年12月28日判决：驳回王晓泉、王纪芳、王翔鹏的全部诉讼请求。

王晓泉、王纪芳、王翔鹏不服，向温州市中级人民法院提起上诉。

温州市中级人民法院查明：王晓泉、王纪芳、王翔鹏在一审第二次庭审中主张《王十朋全集》除构成汇编作品外，还构成演绎作品。后一审法院要求其明确以演绎作品还是汇编作品作为请求权基础，逾期不明确的，以汇编作品作为权利基础进行判决。王晓泉、王纪芳、王翔鹏遂确定按汇编作品主张权利。

温州市中级人民法院经审理认为：《王十朋全集》中王十朋所著作品均已进入公有文化遗产的范围，可以被公众自由使用，故仅对王十朋作品的整理、点校并不必然达到最低程度独创性水平而受著作权法的保护。但是，评判古籍点校、整理的独创性不能仅从作品中的基本构成元素是否处于公共领域和具有复原古籍的意图进行抽象讨论，如果古籍点校、整理的整体成果与古籍本身之间存在显著改变，即使作者力求忠实历史原貌，也不能就此径直否认作品整体成果的独创性，而应从古籍点校、整理后的成果是否体现了作者的特有选择与安排，是否达到独创性标准等方面进行评述。基于上述认识，《王十朋全集》从编排体例、点校内容和成书的整体内容上均已具备独创性，应认定为著作权法意义上的作品。一审法院以确定作品类型作为审理的前提和权利基础，在王晓泉、王纪芳、王翔鹏按照法院释明确定作品类型后驳回其诉讼请求明显不当，应予纠正。本案中，《王十朋全集》既包含了对原有作品、佚诗佚文的选择、增减和编排，也包含了在考据和校勘基础上进行的酌校异同、添加注释和标点分隔，还包含重刊说明等原创作品，故从整体上看，将《王十朋全集》简单归类于汇编作品或演绎作品并不恰当，不可否认，《王十朋全集》属于具有独创性、能以文字形式表现的作品。王晓泉、王纪芳、王翔鹏作为《王十朋全集》的著作权人，其署名权、复制权、发行权及保护作品完整权应受法律保护。王十朋纪念馆未经许可，复制、发行与涉案作品内容基本一致的《王十朋全集（修订本）》，构成对《王十朋全集》复制权、发行权的侵害。古籍出版社作为《王十朋全集》的出版单位，未尽到合理注意义务，主观上与王十朋纪念馆存在共同过错，应与王十朋纪念馆对侵权后果承担连带责任。

综上，该院于 2018 年 11 月 8 日判决：撤销一审判决；王十朋纪念馆和古籍出版社立即停止侵害，连带赔偿王晓泉、王纪芳、王翔鹏维权合理开支 2 万元，并刊登声明，赔礼道歉、消除影响。

【入选理由】 王十朋是南宋著名政治家和诗人，在民间具有很高声望，至今仍有大量著作留存。本案系因对王十朋古籍作品进行整理出版而引发的著作权纠纷。司法实践中对于古籍整理的作品类型和可版权性存在较大争议，案件审理引起王氏后人及社会各界的关注。本案二审判决认为，应在现有法律框架下对古籍整理作品的类型和可版权性评定赋予更大的弹性，评判古籍点校、整理的独创性不能仅从作品中的基本构成元素是否处于公共领域和具有复原古籍的意图进行抽象讨论，而应从古籍点校、整理后的成果是否体现作者特有选择与安排的角度，判断是否符合作品的独创性标准，从而鼓励更多具备较高文史知识、丰富古籍整理和考据经验的劳动者投入到古籍作品的保护、传播事业中。

二、义乌市楚菲化妆品有限公司、张某假冒注册商标罪、侵犯著作权罪案［义乌市人民法院（2018）浙 0782 刑初 429 号］

【简要案情】 2016 年底以来，义乌市楚菲化妆品有限公司（以下简称楚菲公司）经法定代表人张某决定，未经注册商标所有人、著作权人许可，伙同他人（身份不详）生产假冒第 990446 号“Vaseline”、第 212780 号“MAYBELLINE”、第 834258 号“M.A.C”等商标的化妆品，生产销售带有“”美术作品图样的化妆品牟取非法利益，后被查获。经鉴定，被查扣的标有上述商标的假冒化妆品，价值人民币 401 099 元；被查扣的标有上述美术作品图样的假冒化妆品，价值人民币 393 023 元，数量为 187 472 个。

义乌市人民检察院指控楚菲公司、张某犯假冒注册商标罪、侵犯著作权罪，于 2018 年 2 月 9 日向义乌市人民法院提起公诉。

【裁判结果】 义乌市人民法院经审理认为：楚菲公司未经注册商标所有人许可，在同一种商品上使用与其注册商标相同的商标，情节特别严重，构成假冒注册商标罪。楚菲公司以营利为目的，未经著作权人许可，复制发行其作品，情节特别严重，构成侵犯著作权罪。张某系楚菲公司的法定代表人及该公司本案犯罪行为的直接责任人员，应当负刑事责任。楚菲公司、张某犯数罪，应数罪并罚，其归案后能如实供述自己的罪行，依法可以从轻处罚。

综上，该院于 2018 年 3 月 19 日判决：(1) 楚菲公司犯假冒注册商标罪，判处罚金 21 万元；犯侵犯著作权罪，判处罚金 20 万元。数罪并罚，决定执行罚金 41 万元。(2) 张某犯假冒注册商标罪，判处有期徒刑三年四个月，并处罚金 21 万元；犯侵犯著作权罪，判处有期徒刑三年八个月，并处罚金 20 万元。数罪并罚，决定执行有期徒刑五年六个月，并处罚金 41 万元。(3) 扣押在案的化妆品，予以没收。

一审宣判后，楚菲公司与张某均未提出上诉，检察院未提出抗诉，判决现已生效。

【入选理由】 本案的特殊性在于被查扣的部分假冒化妆品上使用的标识与他人注册商标相同，构成假冒注册商标罪，而部分假冒化妆品上使用的标识并未进行商标注册，该部分假冒行为不构成假冒注册商标罪。然而，该批假冒化妆品数量巨大，若流入市场将造成极其恶劣的后果。法院经审查认为，虽然相关图形标识未进行商标注册，但该图形已进行著作权登记，具有独创性，属于《刑法》第二百一十七条中“其他作品”。被告单位和被告人生产侵犯著作权的化妆品数量巨大，非法经营数额巨大，情节特别严重，构成侵犯著作权罪。被告单位和被告人同时犯假冒注册商标罪、侵犯著作权罪，应数罪并罚。本案中，法院对生产假冒商品的行为从商标权和著作权两个角度进行严格保护，依法打击了

知识产权犯罪行为，充分保护了权利人及消费者的合法权益。

安 徽 省

一、陶袁与阮正旺著作权侵权及名誉权纠纷案

2012年，阮正旺委托陶袁为阮氏家族续修族谱。陶袁书写前序后跋、收执字号议等文。后跋被部分修改后印入阮氏家族族谱，并标明有“请师陶隆然（陶袁笔名）”及尾部“陶隆然敬撰”等字样。收执字号议主要载明阮氏族谱刊印的数量、保管者姓名及要求保管者妥善保管的内容。阮氏族谱初印时收执字号议尾部有陶袁的署名，正式刊印时删去了陶袁的署名。阮正旺支付陶袁2 000元作为续修族谱的报酬。

陶袁起诉主张，其享有阮氏族谱跋的著作权。阮正旺未经其同意，擅自对跋进行修改，致使跋文义不通，侵害其对作品的修改权、保护作品完整权及名誉权。

安徽省高级人民法院认为，族谱是一种以表谱形式记载一个以血缘关系为主体的家族世系繁衍和重要人物事迹的特殊图书题材，其主要作用为尊祖、敬宗、睦族，承载一个家族的历史、记忆、血缘纽带和情感，具有特殊的历史、人文及情感意义。陶袁受阮正旺的聘请帮助阮氏家族续修族谱，并撰写跋、收执字号议，其内容和形式应当遵照阮氏家族的要求，体现阮氏家族的意愿，贴合阮氏家族的情感。基于族谱的特殊功能和作用，就陶袁为阮氏族谱撰写的跋、收执字号议，阮氏家族可以根据其意愿及相关事实进行合理修改。本案中阮氏族谱对陶袁撰写的跋中的相关内容的修改，系对作品的合理修改，不属于歪曲和篡改，不构成对陶袁的修改权及保护作品完整权的侵犯，亦不构成对陶袁名誉权的侵犯。

安徽省铜陵市中级人民法院一审判决驳回陶袁的诉讼请求。安徽省高级人民法院二审维持原判。

二、娱美德娱乐有限公司、株式会社传奇IP与三七互娱（上海）科技有限公司、安徽尚趣玩网络科技有限公司等著作权侵权及不正当竞争纠纷案

娱美德娱乐有限公司、株式会社传奇IP诉称其与案外人亚拓士软件有限公司为《热血传奇》游戏软件的共有著作权人。2018年6月，其发现三七互娱（上海）科技有限公司、安徽尚趣玩网络科技有限公司在“37手游”网站上推广和运营《屠龙破晓》游戏，江苏智铭网络技术有限公司在腾讯手游平台上推广《屠龙破晓》游戏，该游戏由绍兴上虞掌娱网络科技有限公司开发。经比对，《屠龙破晓》的人物角色、装备、道具、技能、怪物、NPC、地图、界面、特殊功能设计，角色与武器、服装、首饰、技能之间的特殊关联关系，以及在地图、怪物、NPC、玩法等的玩家特有习惯设计方面，均与其《热血传奇》完全相同或高度相似，且运营方在游戏推广过程中自认《屠龙破晓》抄袭自《热血传奇》，侵害了其《热血传奇》游戏的著作权改编权并构成不正当竞争，遂诉至法院。

安徽尚趣玩网络科技有限公司在答辩期内提出管辖权异议，认为本案不属于计算机软件民事纠纷，不属于合肥知识产权法庭在安徽省内跨辖区管辖的案件，请求根据《中华人民共和国民事诉讼法》第二十八条的规定，将本案移送至安徽省芜湖市中级人民法院审理。

安徽省合肥市中级人民法院民事裁定认为，网络游戏的人物角色、服装、道具、地图、场景、配乐、旁白等组成要素可以单独构成美术、音乐、文字等一般作品，不属于《计算机软件保护条例》所指的“程序”或“文档”，故本案不适用集中管辖的规定。

安徽省合肥市中级人民法院裁定：安徽尚趣玩网络科技有限公司对管辖权提出的异议成立，本案移送安徽省芜湖市中级人民法院审理。裁定书已发生法律效力。

三、科大讯飞股份有限公司与吉林省辰迅网络科技有限公司侵害商标权纠纷案；江山与孙晶、北京燕山出版社有限公司、合肥新腾图书有限公司侵害著作权纠纷案

科大讯飞股份有限公司（以下简称科大讯飞公司）是一家专门从事智能语音及语言技术、人工智能技术研究、电子政务系统集成及芯片等产品开发的软件企业，在行业内有较高的知名度，多次荣获国家级科技奖项。科大讯飞公司系第1959350号“科大讯飞 Iflytek”、第1967743号“科大讯飞 Iflytek”、第5440612号“讯飞”注册商标的权利人。2018年3月，科大讯飞公司在百度搜索“讯飞云”时，发现吉林辰迅公司擅自使用了与其注册商标相近似的文字作为产品名称，并在网站醒目位置使用“讯飞互联”等字样，该行为易使公众对吉林辰迅公司产品来源产生误认，侵犯了科大讯飞公司的商标权。安徽省合肥高新技术产业开发区人民法院受理该案后，为节约当事人诉讼成本，通过远程视频系统，组织双方当事人梳理案件事实，当场制作调解

协议，并传输给吉林辰迅公司，吉林辰迅公司即刻打印盖章回传，实现案件当庭调解。

江山于 2003 年 3 月开始翻译美国作家梭罗的《种子的信仰》，2004 年 9 月结束原始译稿，2005 年 6 月 24 日与上海六点文化传播有限公司签订合同。2006 年 7 月，江山查到数十家网站销售的燕山出版社 2005 年 12 月出版、孙晶编译的《种子的信念》推荐语存在侵权，认为孙晶翻译的《种子的信念》一书与其翻译的《种子的信仰》一书相比较存在大量精心修改、相同或类似文字，甚至沿袭其书稿中许多错误。江山于 2011 年 9 月曾委托律师向北京燕山出版社发出律师函，就《种子的信念》一书涉嫌抄袭向该社提出交涉，因未得到反馈遂提起诉讼。由于本案被告孙晶居住于瑞士联邦，为方便当事人诉讼，安徽省合肥高新技术产业开发区人民法院受理后，采用远程系统审理此案，实现中国和瑞士远程视频庭审，大大提高了审判效率，通过信息化手段切实为当事人减少诉累，节约了司法资源。

福　建　省

一、可适用特殊职务作品的规定来确定美术作品著作权的归属——李惠卿诉陈文灿、福州大学著作权权属、侵权纠纷案［厦门市思明区人民法院（2017）闽 0203 民初 3467 号、厦门市中级人民法院（2018）闽 02 民终 1515 号］

【简要案情】 1986 年，人民大会堂福建厅装修，有关部门确定由福建工艺美术学校承接该厅壁画创作，工艺美校组织吴景希、陈文灿等部分师生创作了 1987 年版《武夷之春》。工艺美校四十周年校庆作品集收录了该幅作品，作品署名：设计者吴景希、陈文灿、王明照；制作者吴景希、陈文灿、王明照、黄国强、林德耀等。1994 年，福建厅重新装修，福建工艺美术学校再次承接厅内壁画创作任务，该校组织部分师生在 1987 年版《武夷之春》基础上创作了 1994 年版《武夷之春》。相比原画作，1994 年版《武夷之春》的尺寸、细节均有所变化。工艺美校五十周年校庆作品集收录了该幅作品，作品署名：设计者吴景希、陈文灿；制作者吴嘉诠、陈文灿、黄国强、王明照。吴景希去世后，其母亲李惠卿以陈文灿将《武夷之春》登记在个人名下等行为侵犯吴景希署名权、展览权诉至法院。审理过程中，合并了福建工艺美术学校的福州大学认为两幅作品系法人作品，主张享有全部著作权。

思明区人民法院一审认为，两版《武夷之春》为法人作品，著作权人系福州大学，但工艺美校在其编撰的公开出版物上署有吴景希、陈文灿等相关人员姓名，可以视为其承认相关人员对作品的署名权。

厦门市中级人民法院二审认为，讼争作品系吴景希等人为完成单位交付的工作任务所创作的美术作品，作品的著作权不属于创作者个人。但作品创作本质上属于高度个性化的创作行为，充分彰显创作者独特而鲜明的思想、情感和美学修养，并非完全或者主要体现法人意志，并且不需要以法人名义使用作品，不应认定为法人作品。二审法院综合本案实际情况，并考量《著作权法》第十六条第二款第（一）项的立法本意，确定讼争作品署名权由吴景希、陈文灿等人享有，福州大学享有除署名权之外的著作权。

【点　评】 《武夷之春》美术作品以武夷山大王峰、玉女峰、鹰嘴岩等主要景色为元素，反映了福建秀丽风光，作品悬挂于人民大会堂福建厅，随着媒体对国家领导人重要外事活动的报道而广为人知，堪称“上镜率最高”的美术作品，在福建漆画艺术史上有着举足轻重的地位。但是，针对《武夷之春》的著作权归属，自 2014 年以来在几方当事人之间引发了诉讼。现行著作权法借鉴两大法系立法例，同时规定“视法人为作者”的法人作品制度和自然人仅享有署名权、法人享有其他著作权的特殊职务作品制度，表面上两种作品类型无论在构成要件还是著作权归属方面都有很大差别，但实践中要划清界限绝非易事，可能出现某一作品既可归入法人作品，也可认定为特殊职务作品的情况。立法者将这两种作品类型界限模糊、功能重叠的制度引入著作权法，作为独立作品类型进行规定，引发了一定混乱，导致著作权归属纠纷频发。《武夷之春》案件再次提出了两种作品类型认定标准这一长期困扰中国法院的问题。为妥善解决本案纠纷，二审法院采取以下做法：一是对法人意志进行严格限定。法人意志应当是具体而非抽象的，在把握作品是否代表法人意志创作上，应限定于创作者自由思维空间不大，创作思想及表达方式完全或主要体现法人意志的情形。如果创作时仅仅遵循法人总体思路或原则，为创作者留有很大发挥空间的，则作品并不是代表法人意志创作的。涉案作品系美术作品，本质上属于高度个性化创作行为，创作者在有关部门提出的创作主题和原则性要求下，仍可自由发挥个人创造力，作品充分彰显创作者独特而鲜明的思想、情感和美学修养，作品主要体现的是创作者而非法人的意志。二是扩张特殊职务作品的适用范围。对于美术作品能否适用特殊职务作品的规定来确定著作权归属，确实存在争议，例如特殊职务作品的第一种情形是否仅限于所列举的四种作品。二审法院认为，根据《著作权法》第十六条第二款第（二）项规定，法院可依据特别法之规定或依照当事人特别约定，将某一类型职务作品认定为特殊职务作品，因此扩张特殊职务作品类型的做法并不违反立法者本意。随着经济社会的发展变化，新类型作品将越来越多，适当地做开放性解释更加符合未来著作权发展趋势。据此，二审法院从著作权法立法目的、鼓励创作积极性和平衡当事人及社会公共利益角度出发，对法人作品认定采取严格、审慎态度，依法将涉案作品认定为特殊职务作品，创作者享有署名权，其他著作财产权均归属法人，切实加强对自然人创作者权益的保护，激励创作热情，较好地实现创作者、法人和社会公共利益之间的利益平衡。

二、欧某某与泉州市多祥工艺品发展有限公司侵害其他著作财产权纠纷案［泉州市中级人民法院（2018）闽05民初1050号］

【简要案情】 原告欧某某创作完成“树脂男孩摆件”和“树脂女孩摆件”系列美术作品，并于2018年7月25日向版权机构申请，取得该作品的著作权登记证书。审理过程中，被告提供“趣味女孩”“趣味男孩”系列美术作品的著作权登记证书，证书显示被告已于2018年4月8日向版权机构申请，并取得上述作品的著作权登记证书。泉州中院经审理认为，从原告欧某某及被告多祥公司提供的著作权登记证书来看，两者的图样、构思、设计元素及表现手法基本一致。从两份著作权登记证书上所体现的创作完成日期及登记日期看，被告多祥公司均早于原告欧某某，虽然原告欧某某提供了其电子邮箱中的部分证据，以证明其是涉案作品的创作人，但这些证据并不能体现其整个作品的创作过程，且原告欧某某自己声明的作品完成时间为2015年10月10日，后又主张其作品完成时间最迟为2013年11月5日，明显前后矛盾，且该时间也远晚于被告多祥公司声明完成创作的时间，故于本案中，原告在被告多祥公司有相反证据的情况下，并不能充分举证证明自己系涉案作品的著作权人，故对其诉讼主张，法院不予支持。

本案宣判后，双方当事人均未提起上诉。

【点　评】 我国实行著作权自愿登记制度，作品不论是否登记，作者或其他著作权人依法取得的著作权不受影响，对国内的作者，著作权自作品完成时起自动产生，对外国作者，著作权自首先在中国境内发表时起自动产生，并不需要办理著作权登记。根据《中华人民共和国著作权法》第十一条第四款规定：“如无相反证明，在作品上署名的公民、法人或者其他组织为作者。”本案中，在被告有相反证据的情况之下，原告未能进一步提供其创作底稿等相关证据，来证明其系该作品的著作权人，故其应承担不利的法律后果。因此，创作者应注意保存其创作过程中的底稿及相关资料，可通过公证或第三方电子存证平台等方式对前述材料进行固定，以便在维权过程中，最大限度地保护自身合法权益。

三、房某、李某侵犯著作权罪案［南安市人民法院（2018）闽0583刑初1483号］

【简要案情】 2013年8月30日，完美世界（北京）网络技术有限公司创作取得《诛仙3》网络游戏软件著作权。2013年12月份至2017年6月份期间，被告人房某未经完美世界（北京）网络技术有限公司许可，出资从被告人李某等人处租用服务器，架设网址，使用向QQ好友“梦坊”购买的登录器等私服服务器架设工具，私自架设《紫叶诛仙》和《帝王诛仙》等游戏服务器端程序在互联网上发布，通过支付宝和“维维点卡”支付平台收取玩家充值共计人民币141 663元，获利人民币84 787元。经福建中证司法鉴定中心鉴定，涉案IP所在服务器硬盘中的游戏服务端程序与完美世界（北京）网络技术有限公司《诛仙3》游戏服务端程序存在实质性相似。2014年6月至2017年6月，被告人李某在明知被告人房某开设《诛仙》系列网络游戏私服的情况下，除向被告人房某出租服务器提供互联网接入等服务外，还向被告人房某提供“维维点卡”支付平台用于游戏玩家使用人民币兑换《诛仙》系列网络游戏私服内的游戏元宝，提供代收费及费用结算服务，在此期间被告人房某非法收取游戏玩家充值人民币128 400元，获利人民币84 787元。

法院审理认为，被告人房某以非法占有为目的，未经授权复制发行他人计算机软件作品牟利，情节严重，其行为已构成侵犯著作权罪；被告人李某明知被告人房某未经授权复制发行他人计算机软件作品牟利，仍向被告人房某出租服务器提供互联网接入、代收费及费用结算等服务，情节严重，其行为亦已构成侵犯著作权罪。

【点　评】 本案是新型的著作权网络侵权案例。传统领域的侵犯著作权犯罪表现为盗版书籍、光碟等，随着网络服务的普及和电子商务的繁荣，传统有形载体的复制已经发展成为信息网络中的数字复制，在数字版权领域表现为为他人提供下载等服务的形式。本案中，房某私自架设的《紫叶诛仙》和《帝王诛仙》游戏服务端程序与《诛仙 3》游戏服务端程序存在实质性相似，即《紫叶诛仙》和《帝王诛仙》游戏服务端程序并不属于独立的智力创造成果，其本质是复制品。房某通过向游戏玩家提供游戏服务端程序的下载、安装及运行服务，客观在玩家的计算机终端产生了计算机软件的复制品。房某通过向玩家收取相应费用用于支付互联网接入服务以及游戏软件中实现某种游戏效果的游戏元宝的对价，客观上挤占了游戏软件著作权人完美世界（北京）网络技术有限公司的市场份额，不当地损害了软件著作权人的合法权益，该行为依然属于“复制发行”他人享有著作权作品的行为，房某利用上述游戏服务端程序牟利的行为应认定为对《诛仙 3》游戏服务端程序的“复制发行”。李某明知房某未经授权复制发行他人计算机软件作品牟利，仍向房某提供私服运行营利的关键环节的支持，共同完成发行、牟利，成立共同犯罪。

河　南　省

一、朱爱民与河南冰熊制冷设备有限公司、浙江华美电器制造有限公司侵犯著作权纠纷案［商丘市中级人民法院（2018）豫 14 民初 112 号、河南省高级人民法院（2018）豫民终 1547 号］

【简要案情】 朱爱民于 2016 年获得“卡通熊”作品登记证书，其发现河南冰熊制冷设备有限公司（以下简称冰熊公司）生产、浙江华美电器制造有限公司（以下简称华美公司）销售的“冰熊冰柜”使用了“卡通熊”图案，故诉至法院。一审法院判令冰熊公司、华美公司停止使用“卡通熊”图案。二审法院查明：虽然“冰熊冰柜”上使用的图案与朱爱民“卡通熊”作品构成高度近似，但冰熊公司提供了 2014 年 4 月 26 日中央电视台新闻联播视频、《2015 年度冰熊产品展销合同》等证据，证明冰熊公司、华美公司在朱爱民取得“卡通熊”作品登记证书之前已经在先使用了“卡通熊”图案。河南省高级人民法院二审改判驳回朱爱民的诉讼请求。

【点　评】 著作权登记应当遵循诚实信用原则。我国法律规定著作权取得方式是自动取得，即著作权自作品创作完成之日起产生，不以行政管理部门登记为要件。著作权登记采取“自愿登记，形式审查”原则，如果权利发生冲突，人民法院应当在实质审查后对著作权归属做出认定，不能仅以著作权登记证书作为判断依据。作品登记权人抢先将他人作品进行著作权登记，并向人民法院主张权利以谋取利益的恶意诉讼行为，违反了诚实信用原则，其相关权利主张不应得到法律支持。本案在规范公平竞争市场秩序、遏制恶意诉讼等方面具有典型意义。

二、辉县市新兴印刷有限公司、郭某某侵犯著作权罪案［洛阳市中级人民法院（2017）豫 03 刑初 20 号、河南省高级人民法院（2018）豫刑终 68 号］

【简要案情】 2016 年 5 月份，被告单位辉县市新兴印刷有限公司及被告人郭某某在未取得权利人授权的情况下，非法印刷中国时代经济出版社的《2016 审计专业技术资格考试辅导教材（上册）审计专业相关知识》10 080 册、《2016 审计专业技术资格考试辅导教材（下册）审计理论与务实》3 693 册、中国建筑工业出版社的《建筑工程与实务》3 000 册以及陕西人民教育出版社的《小学教材全解六年级语文（上）》17 540 册，共计 34 313 册。2016 年 5 月 15 日，辉县市文化局文化市场综合执法大队对辉县市新兴印刷有限公司进行查处，当场扣押了上述非法出版物，并依法将郭某某移交公安机关。经鉴定，上述出版物为侵犯他人著作权的非法出版物，涉案价值总计为 1 200 516 元。法院认定被告单位辉县市新兴印刷有限公司犯侵犯著作权罪，判处罚金人民币 70 万元；被告人郭某某犯侵犯著作权罪，判处有期徒刑三年，并处罚金人民币 60 万元。

【点　评】 教辅图书市场是著作权侵权的高发区，教辅图书盗版侵权行为阻碍了原创作品的出版发行，侵害了著作人和出版人利益，极大影响了创新的积极性，扰乱了图书市场健康有序发展，影响文化产业的发展。本案被告印制侵权出版物数量多，犯罪数额大，影响十分恶劣。人民法院通过对被告人处以刑罚，加大对被告人及被告单位在罚金刑方面的惩处力度，增强了法律威慑力，彰显了法院严厉打击知识产权犯罪行为的决心和力度。

三、杨某、胡某、秦某、任某侵犯著作权罪案［郑州市中级人民法院（2017）豫 01 刑初 180 号、河南省高级人民法院（2018）豫刑终 418 号］

【简要案情】 2016 年 6 月至 2017 年 5 月 6 日，被告人杨某以营利为目的，未经著作权人许可，非法印刷《经济法》《韩心怡讲民诉之金题卷：8》等五种图书，后将非法印刷的《2017 年注册会计师考试应试指导及全真模拟测试：税法（上册）》《经济法》图书交给被告人秦某、任某装订，再由被告人杨某进行销售。截至案发时被告人杨某、胡某共复制发行侵权出版物37 321册，被告人秦某、任某共复制侵权出版物29 702册。一审认定被告人杨某犯侵犯著作权罪，判处有期徒刑三年六个月，并处罚金人民币12万元；被告人胡某犯侵犯著作权罪，判处有期徒刑三年，没收违法所得人民币3万元，并处罚金人民币3万元；被告人秦某犯侵犯著作权罪，判处有期徒刑三年，没收违法所得人民币2万元，并处罚金人民币4万元；被告人任某犯侵犯著作权罪，判处有期徒刑三年，没收违法所得人民币2万元，并处罚金人民币4万元。被告人均不服，提起上诉，二审维持原判。

【点　评】　加大对侵害知识产权行为的惩罚力度，提高知识产权违法成本，是中央对知识产权保护的重大决策。本案被告人为实施侵犯知识产权犯罪分工合作，侵犯了著作权人的合法权益，危害了图书出版市场的正常秩序。法院判决认定各被告人行为均积极主动，均系主犯，彰显了对知识产权严格保护的原则，严厉打击了知识产权刑事犯罪行为。

湖　北　省

小黄鸭动漫美术作品复制权、表演权纠纷案［武汉市中级人民法院（2017）鄂01民初3996号］

2005年3月22日，香港居民许夏林以小黄鸭为创作对象，完成B. DUCK小黄鸭系列美术作品创作，并于2014年4月24日获得广东省版权局著作权登记。森科公司为该动漫美术作品的著作权人。

2017年1月4日，森科公司通过证据保全发现，零点公司在天猫电商平台销售的品牌为“可可哥”的咕噜鸭脖、无敌鸭掌、劲爆鸭翅、光溜鸭舌等四种规格的鸭产品，在外包装袋右下方装潢设计为镂空鸭形。同时，该网点还在短视频广告、音乐作品中使用了这一设计。

经比对，被诉的咕噜鸭脖、无敌鸭掌、劲爆鸭翅、光溜鸭舌产品外包装袋右下角的镂空鸭形图案，突出了小黄鸭嘴大、唇厚、脸胖、眼圆的动漫造型特征，与森科公司设计的站姿小黄鸭动漫造型一致；短视频促销广告中的鸭的动态造型特征与森科公司小黄鸭的造型设计特征一致。为此森科公司起诉要求零点公司停止侵犯著作权并赔偿经济损失。

武汉市中级人民法院审理认为：零点公司未经森科公司授权，将与涉案动漫美术作品相同的图案用于产品包装袋的行为构成复制；将涉案作品主角形象制作成短视频广告，构成动漫美术作品的表演。被诉行为侵犯了森科公司对涉案动漫美术作品依法享有的复制权、表演权，应当承担停止侵权、赔偿损失的民事责任。判决零点公司停止侵权行为，并赔偿森科公司经济损失38 000元，承担维权合理费用3 536元。

广　东　省

一、快播公司诉深圳市场监管局著作权行政处罚纠纷案［广东省高级人民法院（2016）粤行终492号］

【简要案情】　腾讯公司为涉案24部作品信息网络传播权的独占许可权利人。2014年3月18日，腾讯公司以快播公司侵害其涉案作品信息网络传播权为由投诉至深圳市场监管局，请求予以查处。在手机上登录《快播》客户端搜索涉案24部影视作品，首选链接均为“腾讯视频”，点击“腾讯视频”旁伪造成乐视网、优酷、电影网等知名视频网站的“其他链接”下拉选项，再点击进入播放具体集数，视频显示的播放地址却是一些不知名的、未依法办理备案登记的网站。

2014年6月26日，深圳市场监管局做出行政处罚决定，责令快播公司立即停止侵权行为并对其处以非法经营额3倍的罚款26 014.8万元。快播公司申请行政复议，广东省版权局做出维持的行政复议决定。

快播公司遂向法院起诉，请求判令撤销上述行政处罚决定。一审判决驳回快播公司诉讼请求。快播公司不服，上诉至广东高院。二审判决驳回上诉，维持原判。

【点　评】　本案系全国标的额最大的涉互联网行政处罚纠纷案件，社会关注度极高。宣判之后，主流媒体以及学者均给予了高度评价，《人民法院报》的评论员文章称本案的终审判决“具有极强的警示意义”。本案涉及知识产权民事、行政以及破产等多部门法的交织，程序及实体问题繁杂，为著作权民事侵权行为是否同时损害公共利益、如何认定互联网企业存在非法获利、互联网企业非法经营额的计算等疑难法律问题的处理提供了有借鉴意义的范本。案件的审理起到了惩处侵权、净化版权市场的良好社会效果，对于促进依法行政与加强知识产权保护、规范互联网市场的竞争秩序均有积极的导向作用。

二、求知公司与新浪公司侵害计算机软件著作权纠纷案［广州知识产权法院（2016）粤 73 民初 1387 号］

【简要案情】 求知公司是《考无忧全国专业技术人员计算机应用能力考试辅导软件》的著作权人，该软件通过官网 http：//www.k51.com.cn 发布，由用户下载客户端后购买各模块注册码进行使用。该公司在 2015 年发现新浪公司经营的新浪博客上，某博客用户在其个人博客主页发布介绍前述考试软件及破解版软件的文章，侵害了求知公司的著作权。求知公司依照博客平台投诉规则，两次向新浪公司发送投诉邮件，告知博客管理员相关用户发布的文章侵害其知识产权，要求予以删除，但新浪公司以求知公司未提供纸质投诉材料为由未予删除。求知公司以新浪公司经合理告知，知晓其博客网站用户的侵权行为，仍然拒绝删除涉案博客文章的行为严重损害了求知公司的计算机软件著作权，向法院提起诉讼。

法院认为，求知公司依照新浪公司公开的网络联系方式，两次发送邮件投诉涉案博客文章侵害其知识产权，要求新浪公司删除，并提供了其作为权利人的名称、公司地址、联系方式等主体资料，以及涉案软件的权利证书、要求删除文章的地址链接。求知公司的投诉内容客观、具体，投诉行为合法、有效。是否需要进一步提供纸质材料，不影响已有效抵达新浪公司的投诉通知的合法有效性，且提供纸质材料供审核为网络服务提供者新浪公司自行设定的规则，加重了求知公司的义务，投诉不当的抗辩意见，不予采纳。

【点　评】 本案系因破解学习软件加密措施引发的计算机软件著作权侵权案。经权利人以合理方式告知，网络服务提供者应知网络用户侵权行为的存在，而未采取删除、屏蔽、断开链接的必要措施的，构成帮助侵权。网络服务提供者应积极保护知识产权，不应自行设定阻碍权利人正常、及时、有效维权的投诉规则。

广西壮族自治区

南宁轨道交通集团有限责任公司与广西辣椒蒜米科技有限公司著作权侵权纠纷案［南宁市中级人民法院（2018）桂 01 民初 800 号］

【简要案情】 南宁轨道交通集团通过委托设计方式于 2011 年取得"NNRT"字母组合及"朱槿花"图案美术作品著作权，随后将之作为南宁轨道交通标识及企业标识使用。案外人未经轨道交通集团同意将上述作品申请注册了第 10064070 号商标，并将该商标最终转让给辣椒蒜米公司。轨道交通集团认为，上述商标注册行为侵害了轨道交通集团对涉案作品享有的著作权，故起诉请求判令停止侵权、赔偿经济损失及为制止侵权行为支付的合理开支 1 万元等。诉讼中经法院主持调解，双方当事人达成调解协议，辣椒蒜米公司同意将第 10064070 号注册商标转让给轨道交通集团。

【点　评】 本案主要涉及注册商标与在先著作权的冲突问题。在处理注册商标与其他权利冲突时，一般遵循保护在先权利、诚实信用等原则。注册商标的注册及使用不能侵害他人的在先权利，否则有可能构成侵权，并被禁止使用该注册商标。涉案注册商标的标识为"NNRT"字母组合及"朱槿花"图案，"NNRT"字母组合及"朱槿花"图案美术作品系南宁市轨道交通标志性 logo，本案的协商解决有效平衡了著作权人与商标权人之间的利益，有利于维护该标识的合理、正当使用，保障南宁轨道公司顺利健康运营，为首府南宁有序畅通的交通环境提供了有力的司法保障。

海　南　省

一、海南南海网传媒股份有限公司诉海口在现文化传媒有限公司侵害作品信息网络传播权纠纷案

2017 年 1 月 18 日 15 时 20 分，海南南海网传媒股份有限公司（以下简称南海网公司）在其开办的南海网网站发布标题为《海口大乐透 1 006 万得主现身　得知中奖 3 小时后抱走大奖》的新闻报道，载明作者为南海网记者孙令正。海口在现文化传媒有限公司（以下简称在现公司）在未经原告授权许可的情况下，在其主办经营的海口在线网站上转载使用该篇新闻报道及 1 张新闻图片。南海网公司认为在现公司的行为侵犯了其对上述新闻报道享有的信息网络传播权。

在现公司辩称，南海网公司的公证书以及劳动合同、版权说明记载的内容都不清晰，其主张在现公司侵权的文章，都不是南海网发布的，故其主张在现公司侵权无事实和法律依据。

海口中院认为，根据法律规定，孙令正为南海网公司的专职新闻记者，其在工作任务范围之内创作的新闻报道应属于职务作品，著作权人为南海网公司，故南海网公司享有该作品的信息网络传播权。在现公司未举证证实其在网络上转载并传播涉案新闻报道及图片经过南海网公司的同意，或支付了报酬，故应认定在现公司的行为侵犯了南海网公司的著作权，应承担相应的民事责任。

海口中院做出判决，限在现公司立即停止侵权并删除网站上的新闻报道及图片，并赔偿南海网公司经济损失及为制止侵权行为所支付的合理费用共计 1 500 元。

二、中国音像著作权集体管理协会诉海南涛东文化传媒有限公司、海口美兰海腾华超市侵害作品放映权纠纷案

2012 年 3 月 6 日，中国音像著作权集体管理协会（以下简称音集协）（甲方）与滚石公司（乙方）签订《音像著作权授权合同》。合同约定：乙方将其依法拥有的音像节目的放映权、复制权（前述二者仅限卡拉 OK 经营场所）、广播权信托甲方管理，以便上述权利在其存续期间及在合同有效期内完全由甲方行使。

音集协诉称，海南涛东公司、海口美兰海腾华超市未经音集协授权，亦未经权利人授权，以营利为目的，擅自在其 KTV 经营场所内的点唱机中收录，并以卡拉 OK 方式向公众放映音集协管理的上述 MTV 音乐电视作品，严重侵犯了音集协的合法权益，给音集协造成了较大的经济损失，请求停止侵权，立即从曲库中删除侵权作品，并赔偿音集协经济损失及合理费用共计 10 000 元。

海南涛东公司辩称，公司仅提供放映装置，未直接实施侵权行为。同时，音集协没有提供最先出版的涉案音像制品，依法不享有涉案音像制品的著作权。

海口中院认为，音集协要求海南涛东公司停止侵权、立即从曲库中删除侵权作品、赔偿经济损失及维权合理费用的诉讼请求，有事实和法律依据。海口美兰海腾华超市仅向客人出售茶饮，并没有证据证明其与海南涛东公司共同实施了放映涉案音乐作品的侵权行为，不应承担侵权责任。

海口中院依法做出判决，海南涛东公司停止使用并从其经营场所使用的歌曲点播系统中删除涉案的《BA BA BA》等 8 首音乐电视作品，并赔偿音集协经济损失及为制止侵权的合理费用共计 2 400 元。

陕 西 省

西安工业经济职业学校与陕西国际商贸学院侵犯著作权纠纷案［咸阳市中级人民法院（2017）陕 04 民初 194 号］

【案情简介】 陕西国际商贸学院（以下简称商贸学院）未经许可在《商贸学院招生简章》等招生宣传资料中使用了西安工业经济职业学校（以下简称工业学校）员工按照工作要求拍摄的 4 张属于职务作品的照片。工业学校以商贸学院侵犯其对上述照片的著作权为由诉至法院，请求判令立即停止侵权、赔偿损失 105 000 元（含合理费用）并承担诉讼费用。

【裁判要点】 咸阳市中级人民法院认为，《中华人民共和国著作权法》第十六条规定，公民为完成法人或者其他组织工作任务所创作的作品是职务作品。工业学校提交的有关证据可以证明涉案 4 张照片的著作权人为工业学校。工业学校有权以自己的名义提起诉讼，工业学校的著作权权利来源合法，诉讼主体适格。本案中商贸学院未经工业学校许可，以营利为目的，在其招生简章中使用工业学校享有著作权的作品，事实清楚。《中华人民共和国著作权法》第四十七条规定，有下列侵权行为的，应当根据情况，承担停止侵害、消除影响、赔礼道歉、赔偿损失等民事责任：……（七）使用他人作品，应当支付报酬而未支付的……。依据上述法律规定，商贸学院的行为已经侵犯工业学校对涉案作品的著作权。商贸学院辩称涉案招生简章为设计公司制作，其只存在把关不严的过失，及其在招生简章中所使用的照片属于从网络上所获取的普通照片，故其构成侵权的理由不能成立。根据查明的事实，商贸学院未经著作权人许可，使用涉案作品，应承担停止侵害、消除影响、赔礼道歉、赔偿损失等民事责任。一审判决，商贸学院立即停止侵权，赔偿经济损失 15 000 元（含合理费用）。宣判后，商贸学院、工业学校均未上诉，一审判决已发生法律效力。

【典型意义】 本案原、被告双方均为培养职业实用技术的大专院校，在专业设置上相同或类似，每年在招收新生中存在着生源竞争。被告未经许可在招生宣传资料中使用原告作品，侵犯了原告享有的著作权。涉案照片中有学生就业回访拍摄的照片，是吸引生源的重要因素，其行为具有一定欺骗性，违背了诚实守信的社会主义核心价值观。社会教育机构具有教书育人的职责，本应严格遵守国家法律法规，却在招生广告中违法使用他人享有著作权的作品，搞虚假宣传，侵犯他人合法权益。本案的审理，对于引导形成尊重他人著作权的良好氛围具有重要促进意义。一审法院通过辨法析理，使被告认识到行为的违法性，宣判后双方均未提出上诉，且执行完毕，取得了良好的法律效果和社会效果。

2018年地方著作权行政执法案件

天 津 市

天津百练教育科技集团有限公司非法销售盗版图书案

2018年6月26日，天津市文化市场行政执法总队（以下简称天津文化执法总队）接到中国财政经济出版社、经济科学出版社举报，反映天津百练教育科技集团有限公司销售使用盗版图书。6月27日，天津文化执法总队联合天津市河东区、河西区、南开区、河北区、红桥区、北辰区文化执法大队，分别对天津百练教育科技集团有限公司的六个校区进行了检查。现场发现《经济法》《企业会计岗位特训实战（一）基础入门篇》等586册图书疑为非法出版物，执法人员依法扣押。6月28日，天津文化执法总队联合红桥区文化执法大队对天津百练教育科技集团有限公司总部进行执法检查，发现《企业会计岗位特训实战（一）基础入门篇》《CPA就业通关营大型企业会计实战》等10种4 436册图书疑为非法出版物，执法人员依法扣押。天津百练教育科技集团有限公司涉嫌发行非法出版物，其行为涉嫌违反了《出版物市场管理规定》第二十条第（二）项的规定。天津文化执法总队依法对其予以立案调查。

6月29日，天津文化执法总队将扣押的署名百练会计教育公司的出版物13种，署名会计职业教育专业委员会APOIT研究组编著的出版物4种提交天津市出版物质量检测中心鉴定。经鉴定，上述出版物共计17种4 853册均为非法出版物。

7月10日，经中国财政经济出版社、经济科学出版社认定，天津文化执法总队扣押的署名为中国财政经济出版社的图书共计20种83册和署名为经济科学出版社的图书共计11种86册，均为侵犯了著作权和专有出版权的出版物。

天津百练教育科技集团有限公司采购署名为中国财政经济出版社、经济科学出版社的盗版图书并发给各分校使用的行为违反了《出版物市场管理规定》第二十条第（三）项和《著作权法》第四十八条第（一）项的规定，发行了侵犯他人著作权的出版物，构成了未经著作权人许可发行其作品，同时损害公共利益的违法行为，总码洋人民币8 769元认定为违法经营额，无违法所得；天津百练教育科技集团有限公司自行编写教材的行为违反了《出版管理条例》第九条第一款的规定，构成了擅自从事出版物的出版业务的违法行为，印刷费人民币12 727.5元应认定为违法经营额，无违法所得；天津百练教育科技集团有限公司处存留署名会计职业教育专业委员会APOIT研究组编著的出版物的行为违反了《出版物市场管理规定》第二十九条第一款规定，构成了储存非法出版物的违法行为，违法经营额难以计算，无违法所得。

天津文化执法总队于2018年9月4日对天津百练教育科技集团有限公司做出如下行政处罚：(1) 没收侵权复制品图书31种169册；(2) 没收非法出版物17种4 853册；(3) 罚款人民币103 637.5元（对天津百练教育科技集团有限公司未经著作权人许可，发行其作品，同时损害公共利益的行为，罚款人民币40 000元；对天津百练教育科技集团有限公司擅自从事出版物的出版业务的行为，罚款违法经营额的5倍，即人民币12 727.5元×5＝63 637.5元）。

（天津市版权局）

河 北 省

一、石家庄市张某某销售盗版光盘案

2017年2月17日，石家庄市公安局根据线索组织新华分局警力，依法对位于新华电子城的张某某光盘窝点进行了突击检查，现场查扣疑似盗版光盘161 576张。后经鉴定：其中95 611张共计1 299种为盗版光盘，1 243张为淫秽光盘。经审查，张某某自2005年以来租赁门市从事销售光盘生意，通过柜台现金结算、网络QQ、微信销售等方式非法批发零售盗版光盘。

2018年8月20日，石家庄市新华区人民法院依法做出刑事判决：(1) 被告人张某某犯侵犯著作权罪，判处有期徒刑一年六个月，并处罚金人民币59万元，犯贩卖淫秽物品牟利罪，判处有期徒刑三年，并处罚金人民币1万元，合并执行有期徒刑三年九个月，并处罚金人民币60万元。(2) 公安机关扣押的盗版光盘95 611张、淫秽光盘1 243张依法没收。张某某不服，提出上诉。2018年11月21日，石家庄市中级人民法院对该案做出驳回上诉、维持原判

的终审裁定。

二、保定市清苑区霍某某销售侵权复制品案

2017年12月25日，省、市两级版权执法人员根据举报，在保定市清苑区霍某某家的后院库房内发现存放标有“河北科学技术出版社”字样的“聚焦课堂”系列丛书35种，共计77 990册，码洋合计275.120 2万元。霍某某无法提供出版物经营许可证，经出版社工作人员现场认定，上述图书疑为盗版出版物。后经河北省出版物鉴定中心鉴定，涉案图书为非法出版物。

2018年12月26日，保定市清苑区人民法院依法做出刑事判决：被告人霍某某犯销售侵权复制品罪，判处有期徒刑一年六个月，并处罚金人民币20万元。

三、河北大德图书文化有限公司侵犯著作权案

2018年7月26日，石家庄市文化市场行政执法大队根据举报，对河北大德图书文化有限公司进行了检查。检查中发现，大德图书文化有限公司售卖的标注由中国言实出版社出版的《全国各类成人高考应试专用教材·政治》《全国各类成人高考应试专用教材·英语》等13种共758册出版物在用纸、工艺等方面与言实出版社出版的出版物不一致。经河北省出版物鉴定中心鉴定，涉案图书均系侵权盗版出版物。

2018年9月19日，石家庄市文化市场行政执法大队依据《中华人民共和国著作权法》《中华人民共和国著作权法实施条例》相关条款，给予河北大德图书文化有限公司没收涉案非法出版物758册，没收违法所得142元，罚款人民币1.3万元的行政处罚。

四、河北鼎达创意文化有限公司侵犯著作权案

2018年10月16日，石家庄市文化市场行政执法人员根据举报，对河北商贸学校使用的标注由高等教育出版社出版的教材教辅进行了检查。经检查，河北商贸学校从河北鼎达创意文化有限公司购进了540册由高等教育出版社出版的《心理健康（修订版）》图书，其中122册是河北鼎达创意文化有限公司从网上非正规渠道购进的，属于盗版出版物。

2018年12月6日，石家庄市文化市场行政执法大队依据《中华人民共和国著作权法》《中华人民共和国著作权法实施条例》相关条款，给予河北鼎达创意文化有限公司罚款人民币0.5万元的行政处罚。

五、保定市满城区乐播私人影院侵犯著作权案

2018年3月16日，保定市满城区文化综合行政执法队执法人员依法对乐播私人影院进行检查时，现场发现该场所包间内全部安装有投影设备和视频点播服务器。检查人员通过查看该影院前台电脑，发现主机内存有影片1 527部，包间内顾客可以点播上述影片消费观看。该影院现场负责人未能出具影片著作权人授权许可等相关证明，当事人李某承认未经著作权人许可，放映、复制、网络传播涉案影视作品供包间内的顾客消费观看。

2018年3月17日，保定市满城区文化广电新闻出版局依据《中华人民共和国著作权法》《中华人民共和国著作权法实施条例》相关条款，对乐播私人影院给予警告，责令其立即改正违法行为，并处罚款人民币1万元的行政处罚。

六、保定市满城区乐喵影咖侵犯著作权案

2018年6月11日，保定市满城区文化综合行政执法队检查乐喵影咖时发现，该场所12个包间内都安装有投影设备和视频点播服务器，包间内顾客可以点播该影院前台电脑主机内381部影片消费观看。该影院负责人未能出具影片著作权人授权许可等相关证明，当事人田某某承认未经著作权人许可，放映涉案影视作品供包间内的顾客消费观看。

2018年6月19日，保定市满城区文化广电新闻出版局依据《中华人民共和国著作权法》《中华人民共和国著作权法实施条例》相关条款，对乐喵影咖给予责令改正违法行为，补齐相关手续后才可营业，并处罚款人民币2万元的行政处罚。

七、邯郸科技信息工程学校私自盗印教辅图书案

2018年7月24日，邯郸市文化市场执法大队根据举报，对位于邯郸市丛台区的邯郸科技信息工程学校进行了执法检查。现场检查发现，该学校存放有私自印制的中等职业教育《语文（基础模块）》《语文练习册》等非法出版物共计810册，码洋金额合计1.493万元，经调查取证，邯郸科技信息工程学校在未经著作权人许可情况下私自盗印图书，并发放给学生使用，侵犯了著作权人的复制权、发行权。

2018年8月8日，邯郸市文化广电新闻出版局依据《中华人民共和国著作权法》《中华人民共和国著作权法实施条例》相关条款，对邯郸科技信息工程学校做出没收、销毁侵权复制品，并处罚款人民币3万元的行政处罚。

八、衡水市舒心书店销售盗版教材案

2018年10月，衡水市文化市场行政执法大队执法人员根据举报，对桃城区舒心书店进行检查，发现该书店销售的九年级课本《语文》、《数学》、《化学》、《世界历史》、《道德与法治》（以上图书均为下册），《物理》（全一册），《英语》（全一册）印刷字迹深浅不一，插图模糊不清晰，疑似盗版出版物，执法人员当场扣押疑似盗版出版物 280 册。后经对该书店负责人调查询问，该书店负责人承认销售的涉案图书是从非正规渠道购进的盗版出版物。

2018 年 11 月 2 日，衡水市文化广电新闻出版局依据《中华人民共和国著作权法》《著作权法实施条例》相关规定，对舒心书店做出没收、销毁侵权复制品 280 册，并处罚款人民币 0.2 万元的行政处罚。

（河北省版权局）

内蒙古自治区

一、ehshig 蒙古文音乐网侵权案

2018 年上旬，接到群众举报，ehshig 音乐网涉嫌通过信息网络传播未经授权音乐。执法人员对该网站开展取证工作，发现该网站上传了大量未经授权音乐作品，经核实有 168 首未经授权。

呼和浩特市文化旅游综合行政执法局经过立案调查，做出罚款 1 万元、关停整改一个月的行政处罚。

二、乌拉特在线电影网站侵权案

2018 年 3 月 12 日，巴彦淖尔市文化旅游综合行政执法局执法人员在网络巡查中发现“乌拉特论坛”微信公众号中链接乌拉特在线电影网站，提供 442 部电影影片在线观看。通过远程勘验取证，初步认定西大数码网络科技有限公司开办的乌拉特在线电影网站，其相关行为构成侵权。

巴彦淖尔市文化旅游综合行政执法局经过立案调查，于 9 月 12 日做出行政处罚决定：罚款 2.5 万元，并删除相关网站链接。

三、“包头同城 VIP”微信公众号侵权案

2018 年 5 月 16 日，包头市文化新闻出版广电局执法人员在网络巡查中发现“包头同城 VIP”微信公众号提供大量电影在线观看服务。经调查，其相关行为构成侵权。

包头市文化新闻出版广电局经过立案调查，做出对包头市昆都仑区百盟广告服务部罚款 8 000 元，对“包头同城 VIP”微信公众号经营者祁慧东罚款 2 000 元，并要求其对相关链接进行删除的行政处罚。

（内蒙古自治区版权局）

辽 宁 省

沈阳欢乐影城娱乐服务有限公司侵权放映影片案

2018 年 6 月初，沈阳市文化市场行政执法总队执法人员对沈阳欢乐影城娱乐服务有限公司现场检查时，发现当事电影院有涉嫌未经著作权人方爱奇艺影业公司许可，放映《熊出没》等多部作品，侵犯影片版权方利益，并扰乱电影放映市场秩序，损害公共利益的情节。当事方法定代表人王某某到沈阳市文化市场行政执法总队接受调查询问时，承认了电影院有未经著作权人许可，放映其作品的违法行为。

本案是对电影放映场所违反著作权法的行为进行行政处罚的典型案例，有着对相似案件进行处理的指导性意义，并且受处罚方是标准的电影放映场所，证照齐全，依托院线进行影片片源提供及放映，但依然存在违反著作权法的违法行为，这对加强电影放映场所管理也有一定的警示作用。

2018 年 7 月 10 日，沈阳市文化市场行政执法总队根据《中华人民共和国著作权法》第四十八条第（一）项、《中华人民共和国著作权法实施条例》第三十六条，给予沈阳欢乐影城娱乐服务有限公司以下行政处罚：（1）立即停止侵权行为；（2）没收违法所得 1 375 元；（3）行政罚款 20 000 元。

（辽宁省版权局）

吉 林 省

一、长春市拾光私影咖啡吧电影播放侵权案

2018 年 9 月 3 日，根据群众举报，吉林省版权局执法人员对位于长春市虎林路万达广场 4 栋的拾光私影咖啡吧涉嫌播放盗版电影行为进行现场调查。经查，该咖啡吧自 2017 年 4 月份运营以来，在经营场所内建立小型局域网，设置电影播放服务器、机顶盒及投影机等设备，根据顾客点播需要或由顾客直接通过机顶盒控制操作，点播后台电脑服务器存储的电影文件或链接到有关影视资源网站，通过投影机投影到各包房屏幕上，同时收取观影及包房服务费，并以“拾光私影影咖（红旗街店）”为名在美团上推广营销。调查过程中，执法人员发现该场所在营业场所的播放服务器电脑中，存储各类影片 1 686 部，其中 2018 年最新影片 79 部。服务器存储的影片一部分系从相关网站下载，另一部分高清影片则通过微信公众号付费分享下载，当事人无法提供

该批电影作品的合法授权证明。在播放服务器中存储的电影作品中，执法人员可以确认存在 10 部属于 2018 年国家版权局预警保护的电影作品，有 11 部经美国电影协会出具认证函认定为未经著作权人许可。据此可以认定，上述作品的著作权人没有对该单位做出相应的版权授权许可。

该咖啡吧的行为违反了《中华人民共和国著作权法》《信息网络传播权保护条例》的有关规定，2018 年 10 月 15 日，根据相关规定，吉林省版权局对长春市拾光私影咖啡吧做出罚款 2 万元人民币的行政处罚。

二、长春市易通书店侵犯著作权案

2018 年 10 月 10 日，长春市文化市场综合执法支队根据群众举报，对长春市高新园区易通书店涉嫌销售侵犯他人著作权图书的行为进行现场调查。经查，该书店经营场所内存放的《文学通论导论》等共计 5 种 134 册图书，无法提供合法有效的进货凭证和销售凭证，疑似侵权复制品，执法人员当场对该批图书进行先行证据登记保存，并出具了《现场检查笔录》、《调查询问通知书》、《证据先行登记保存通知书》及《物品清单》等执法文书，并在立案后进一步调查。2018 年 10 月，根据吉林大学出版社等出具的鉴定证明材料，执法机关认定上述图书为未经授权的侵权复制品。

2018 年 11 月 2 日，根据相关规定，长春市文化广电新闻出版局对长春市高新园区易通书店做出没收侵权复制品、罚款 3 万元人民币的行政处罚。

三、永吉县微易生活信息服务有限公司侵犯信息网络传播权案

2018 年 7 月 19 日，吉林市文化广电新闻出版局执法人员在日常网络巡查中发现微信公众号“永吉县微易生活信息服务有限公司”（微信号：yongji5987）涉嫌侵犯他人的信息网络传播权。立案后，经远程勘验和现场调查取证，当事人承认其未经权利人授权擅自存储下载涉案的电影、电视剧和动漫影视作品多部，当事人为了增加公众号的访问量，通过微信联系以 500 元的费用购得某非法网站的链接置入自己的微信公众号内，向其微信公众号用户免费提供播放服务。本案可以认定的违法经营额为 500 元，涉案侵权作品包括电影《我不是药神》、电视剧《扶摇》、动漫《我的狐仙女友》等 356 部作品。

2018 年 8 月 29 日，吉林市文化广电新闻出版局根据相关规定，给予永吉县微易生活信息服务有限公司罚款人民币 3.5 万元的行政处罚。

（吉林省版权局）

上海市

一、“CATIA”计算机软件侵权纠纷案

原告达索系统股份有限公司（以下简称达索公司）系计算机软件 CATIA V5 R20 的著作权人。达索公司曾因被告上海知豆电动车技术有限公司（以下简称知豆公司）使用侵权软件于 2017 年 2 月向相关行政机关投诉，行政执法过程中查获知豆公司使用侵权软件 8 套，其间，知豆公司与达索公司达成和解，并与达索公司的授权代理商签订了正版软件采购合同，行政机关因此对知豆公司依法减轻行政处罚，但知豆公司并未按约支付软件采购款。同年 11 月，达索公司向上海知识产权法院申请证据保全。保全过程中，法院经知豆公司同意，采取确定抽查比例随机抽查的方式对计算机中安装涉案软件的情况进行证据保全，同时根据所抽查计算机中安装涉案软件的比例推算经营场所内所有计算机中安装涉案软件的数量。经清点，知豆公司经营场所内共有计算机 73 台，其中抽查的 15 台计算机均安装了涉案软件。达索公司遂诉至法院，要求知豆公司停止侵权，并赔偿经济损失及律师费共计 1 800 余万元。

上海知识产权法院审理后认为，知豆公司未经达索公司许可，在其经营场所内的计算机上安装了涉案软件，侵害了达索公司对涉案软件享有的复制权，依法应当承担相应的民事责任。本案中，虽然达索公司的实际损失及知豆公司的违法所得均难以确定，但现有证据已经可以证明达索公司因侵权所受到的损失超过了著作权法规定的法定赔偿数额的上限 50 万元，故法院综合全案证据情况，同时考虑双方提交的销售合同软件单价、知豆公司的侵权期间、安装侵权软件的计算机数量，以及知豆公司在被行政机关查获使用侵权软件后仍扩大侵权规模的主观恶意等因素，在法定赔偿最高限额之上酌定赔偿数额，判决知豆公司赔偿达索公司经济损失及律师费共计 900 万元。一审判决后，知豆公司提起上诉，二审法院驳回上诉，维持原判。

CATIA 系列软件产品广泛应用于汽车、航空航天、电力与电子、消费品和通用机械制造等领域，具有较高的应用价值和市场认同度。在案件处理中，上海法院运用证据规则、经济分析方法等手段，在法定赔偿最高限额之上酌情确定被告应赔偿原告的经济损失并支持了原告主张的合理开支，努力实现侵权损害与知识产权市场价值的协调性和相称性，切实保障权利人获得充分赔偿，积极营造尊重和保护知识产权、激励和发展创新的营商环境。同时，人民法院也通过本案裁判倡导市场主体全面使用正版软件，推进市场主体软件正版化工作，尊重软件开发者的劳动和付出，提升知识产权权利人的安全感和获得感。

二、真彩公司破坏技术措施设置链接行为著作权侵权及不正当竞争纠纷案

腾讯公司系视频内容提供商，通过授权取得电视剧《北京爱情故事》的独占信息网络传播权，向网络用户提供视频播放服务，并通过设置片前广告、暂停广告以及会员制度等方式收取广告费。经鉴定，腾讯公司采取了针对其视频剧集播放地址的技术保护措施。真彩公司《千寻影视》播放器播放的《北京爱情故事》跳转链接至腾讯视频，但播放这些视频时没有片前、暂停广告。腾讯公司认为，真彩公司构成破坏技术措施、侵犯信息网络传播权及不正当竞争。请求判令真彩公司停止上述行为，消除影响并赔偿经济损失及合理费用共计 500 000 元。

杨浦区法院经审理认为，腾讯公司对涉案作品采取了技术保护措施。真彩公司在其《千寻影视》软件上播放了涉案电视剧，该视频链接于腾讯公司，但其无法向一审法院展示使用何技术手段绕开腾讯公司的加密措施直接通过该软件在线播放涉案电视剧，应当承担违反著作权法的责任。《反不正当竞争法》对于《著作权法》起到兜底和补充的作用。真彩公司的行为在专门法中已做穷尽性保护的，不能再在《反不正当竞争法》中寻求额外的保护。由于被诉行为已经停止，一审判决真彩公司赔偿腾讯公司经济损失 110 000 元（含合理费用 6 000 元）。

一审判决后，真彩公司不服，认为其仅仅提供单纯的信息检索和链接服务，不直接提供视频的播放，主观上没有过错，依法不构成信息网络传播侵权，故提起上诉。

上海知识产权法院认为，一审判决对真彩公司的行为是否侵犯腾讯公司的信息网络传播权未做评价。破坏技术措施的行为与侵犯信息网络传播权的行为是两类不同性质的侵权行为，即使上诉人通过破坏技术措施的方式设置链接，破坏技术措施行为的存在并不能够当然得出侵犯信息网络传播权的结论。在腾讯公司未实施将涉案作品置于对公众开放的服务器的行为的情况下，真彩公司虽然实施了破坏技术措施的行为，但仍不构成对涉案作品信息网络传播权的直接侵犯。腾讯公司系合法授权的网站，在腾讯公司不构成直接侵权的情况下，真彩公司提供链接的行为亦不可能构成共同侵权。因此，真彩公司的行为未侵犯腾讯公司的信息网络传播权，但其破坏权利人为涉案影片采取的技术措施，违反了著作权法的相关规定，客观上导致作品传播范围的扩大，且屏蔽了暂停广告、片前广告等内容，给被上诉人造成了经济损失，应当承担相应的赔偿责任。二审法院判决驳回上诉，维持原判。

虽然著作权法并未为权利人设置技术措施权，但其对于禁止破坏技术措施有着明确的规定，可以为权利人维权提供明确的法律依据。以往的司法实践中，对于以破坏技术措施的方式设置深层链接的行为，权利人通常主张该行为构成侵犯信息网络传播权或不正当竞争，较少单独以破坏技术措施的行为提起诉讼。本案的权利人在主张上述两项侵权行为的同时单独针对破坏技术措施的行为提出了诉讼主张。本案的一审判决明确了破坏技术措施行为的认定规则，破坏技术措施行为的认定可以从权利人设置了技术措施、侵权人实施了设置链接播放作品的行为、侵权人未对其采取何种方式避开技术措施提供反证等三方面进行考量。本案二审判决在一审判决的基础上进一步厘清了破坏技术措施行为与侵犯信息网络传播权的行为之间的关系，指出破坏技术措施的行为具有独立性，即使上诉人通过破坏技术措施的方式设置链接，破坏技术措施行为的存在并不能够当然得出侵犯信息网络传播权的结论。与认定信息网络传播侵权行为可能面临的实践争议以及主张构成不正当竞争行为的不确定性相比，本案二审判决适用有关技术措施的规定禁止深层链接行为，是对《著作权法》第四十八条第（六）项规定的准确适用，为权利人维权提供有效的救济，是加强知识产权司法保护的典型案例。

三、李某侵犯著作权案

《机动战士高达》系日本株式会社万代创作的作品，后株式会社万代又根据该作品制作、生产了立体的高达系列拼装玩具，并在市场上销售。2016 年至 2017 年 9 月间，被告人李某在未经日本株式会社万代许可的情况下，采用拆分株式会社万代销售的《雪崩能天使》《蓝异端》等高达玩具原作品及仿制模版、图纸的方式，在广东省汕头市金平区金陇中路海达玩具厂内生产、复制上述高达玩具，并冠以“龙桃子”品牌销售给林应达（另案处理）。被告人李某共生产《雪崩能天使》玩具 28 880 个（单价人民币 111.8 元）、《蓝异端》玩具 3 256 个（单价人民币 73 元）、《独角兽》玩具 2 000 个（单价人民币

165.2元），非法经营数额合计人民币379万余元。2017年9月28日，公安机关从被告人李某的上述玩具厂内扣押《蓝异端》玩具3 256个、生产模具3套。经中国版权保护中心版权鉴定委员会鉴定，被告人李某生产的上述玩具与株式会社万代的作品基本相同，构成复制关系。

2018年5月28日，上海市奉贤区人民检察院依法对李某侵犯著作权案提起公诉。2018年6月26日，上海市闵行区人民法院判处被告人李某有期徒刑三年六个月，并处罚金人民币190万元。被告人李某上诉，2018年10月10日，上海市第三中级人民法院二审裁定驳回上诉、维持原判。

本案涉及立体作品著作权的保护，专业性强。犯罪分子在其生产的玩具产品中夹杂一些自己设计的零部件来掩盖侵权事实，作案手段隐蔽。准确把握复制行为的本质是办理该案中的关键问题，也是能否准确打击刑事犯罪、保护被害人合法权益的关键问题。在本案中，司法机关重点论证了李某生产的"龙桃子"玩具未脱离《机动战士高达》系列拼装玩具作品躯干结构、整体造型的基本特征，虽然在武器、背包上存在细微差别，但并没有体现行为人创作的个性化特征，保留了原作品的基本表达，与原作品构成实质性相似，而内部零件及拼接方法并不影响体现在外部的立体艺术造型，属于侵犯著作权罪中的复制行为。本案对于准确把握复制行为、正确认定侵犯著作权犯罪、解决类似案件中的疑难问题具有重要意义。同时，查处结果也彰显了我国刑法对严重侵犯知识产权犯罪的惩治及对知识产权的保护力度。

此外，本案也是一起典型的涉外著作权保护案件，通过严格遵守《伯尔尼公约》等版权国际条约，实施平等保护，彰显了我国知识产权保护的良好国际形象以及上海建设亚太地区知识产权保护中心城市的信心与能力。

四、陈某等人系列侵犯著作权案

2017年6月初，上海市公安局经侦总队经基础工作发现，陈某等人未经著作权人授权，大肆生产印有《冰雪奇缘》卡通图案的箱包，通过"大途旗舰店""垄垒箱包专营店""大途箱包""垄垒箱包""大途箱包工厂""地平线箱包工厂店"等6家天猫、淘宝网店大肆对外销售。经查，2015年下半年起，被告人陈某为牟取非法利益，利用迪士尼3D动画电影《冰雪奇缘》较高的知名度和影响力，在未经《冰雪奇缘》著作权人授权的情况下，伙同被告人徐某、孙某生产并对外销售带有《冰雪奇缘》卡通图案的拉杆箱，共计2 891件。陈某等人合谋约定，由徐某负责提供带有《冰雪奇缘》图案的板材，孙某负责将板材压制成箱包，陈某负责租用位于上海市闵行区景洪路的某仓库进行仓储，并通过淘宝网店对外销售。

2018年6月20日，上海市第三中级人民法院判决陈某犯侵犯著作权罪，判处有期徒刑三年，缓刑五年，并处罚金人民币8万元。同日，上海市第三中级人民法院判决孙某犯侵犯著作权罪，判处有期徒刑三年，缓刑三年，并处罚金人民币6万元；徐某犯侵犯著作权罪，判处有期徒刑一年六个月，缓刑一年六个月，并处罚金人民币5 000元。

本案系一起利用迪士尼知名动漫作品实施著作权侵权的典型案件。本案被告正是利用了《冰雪奇缘》较高的知名度和影响力，成功实施侵权行为。本案成功查处为此类案件提供了有益思路与实践，即除了商标权等保护外，还应考虑从著作权角度加强保护。本案说明知识产权保护不仅要重拳出击，更应体现组合拳优势，要依法实现对知识产权保护的最有效、最有力、最合理的保护。

五、上海乐欢软件有限公司通过信息网络擅自向公众提供他人的电影作品案

当事人上海乐欢软件有限公司自2015年12月起经营客户端软件《3D播播VR》，未经权利人许可，供用户从当事人经营的"3D播播VR"网下载并安装后，利用当事人客户端软件搜索、浏览、观看《环太平洋2：雷霆再起》等25部电影作品。

当事人的该行为违反了《信息网络传播权保护条例》第二条的规定，构成了未经权利人许可，通过信息网络擅自向公众提供他人电影作品的侵权行为，同时损害了公共利益。因本案中侵权电影作品数量较多，依据《信息网络传播权保护条例》第十八条第（一）项的规定，对当事人未经权利人许可，通过信息网络擅自向公众提供他人电影作品的行为予以责令停止侵权行为，并做出罚款人民币25万元的行政处罚。当事人已履行将罚款人民币25万元交至银行代收机构的行政处罚。

本案是对VR头显的内置移动软件版权侵权依法进行查处的案件，属于对新兴行业的探索性执法，充分反映新技术背景下版权执法面临的挑战。在本案中，执法部门通过技术手段，突破固定证据、情节认定等难关，依法从重做出了行政处罚，显示了执法部门对打击盗版的决心与能力。同时，本案有效维护了新兴行业版权市场秩序，也为行业内其他企业的合法经营提出了要求、明确了标杆。

六、上海步升大风音乐文化传播有限公司、上海东华广播电视网络有限公司与东方有线网络有限公司侵害录音录像制作者权纠纷案

原告上海步升大风音乐文化传播有限公司（以下简称步升公司）系许巍《爱如少年》等涉案专辑的录音录像制作者。2013 年 5 月 29 日，原告步升公司在“EasyTV（天天看）影视资讯频道”网站（www. ttsee. cn），通过点击网页上设置的“迅雷下载”键下载涉案专辑。上述迅雷地址经过转换，均显示为以“211. 167. 105. 15”开头的 IP 地址。上海市通信管理局出具的查询结果单显示，该 IP 地址 2008 年 3 月 31 日至 2014 年 12 月 2 日的报备单位与分配对象均为东方有线公司，分配使用状况为自用。步升公司认为，东华公司和东方有线公司未经许可，通过“EasyTV（天天看）影视资讯频道”网站向公众传播涉案专辑，严重侵犯了其权益，故请求法院判令东华公司和东方有线公司承担停止侵权、赔偿损失的民事责任。

上海市浦东新区人民法院一审认为，因步升公司的现有证据无法证明系东方有线公司直接提供了涉案音乐专辑的内容，对步升公司主张东方有线公司侵害了步升公司作为录音录像制作者享有的信息网络传播权的诉请，不予支持；东华公司通过其“EasyTV（天天看）影视资讯频道”网站帮助了侵权内容的传播，构成帮助侵权，故判决东华公司应赔偿步升公司经济损失 71 300 元及步升公司为制止侵权行为而产生的合理开支 8 300 元，合计 79 600 元。一审判决后，步升公司和东华公司均提起上诉。

上海知识产权法院认为，“EasyTV（天天看）影视资讯频道”网站并非通过迅雷软件在互联网上根据关键词抓取并下载获得涉案侵权内容，而是利用链接技术及迅雷软件，有目的地将用户指向“211. 167. 105. 15”这一固定的 IP 地址获取侵权内容。“EasyTV（天天看）影视资讯频道”网站与“211. 167. 105. 15”服务器系以分工合作的方式共同向用户提供被诉侵权专辑。东华公司与东方有线公司应对“EasyTV（天天看）影视资讯频道”网站与 IP 地址为“211. 167. 105. 15”的服务器的合作提供行为共同承担责任，做出如下判决：（1）维持上海市浦东新区人民法院（2016）沪 0115 民初 14380 号民事判决第二项；（2）撤销上海市浦东新区人民法院（2016）沪 0115 民初 14380 号民事判决第一项；（3）东方有线网络有限公司、上海东华广播电视网络有限公司于本判决生效之日起十日内连带赔偿上海步升大风音乐文化传播有限公司经济损失 71 300 元及制止侵权行为而支出的合理开支 8 300 元，合计 79 600 元；（4）东方有线网络有限公司于本判决生效之日起十日内赔偿上海步升大风音乐文化传播有限公司为制止侵权行为而支出的合理开支 22 000 元。

本案涉及利用迅雷软件下载侵权内容的行为认定及网络服务器提供商侵权责任的认定问题。本案看似为东华公司提供搜索链接，东方有线公司提供网络接入服务，利用第三方迅雷软件进行下载，但通过对证据的深入分析，并利用一定的技术手段，可以认定所谓的搜索链接及第三方软件下载，只是实施侵权行为的工具和手段，不影响设置链接的网站及其所导向的服务器的侵权责任的认定。本案对于深入分析鉴别各类技术手段，准确把握网络接入服务商与网络公司合作向用户提供侵权内容的行为性质，提供了技术方面的解决方案和法律方面的裁判思路，体现了人民法院严格知识产权司法保护的司法导向。

七、葫芦娃游戏形象著作权侵权及不正当竞争纠纷案

原告美影厂系知名动画片《葫芦兄弟》的权利人，享有七个葫芦娃角色造型美术作品除署名权以外的其他著作权。被告中青宝公司委托被告跳跃公司开发涉案游戏《300 英雄》，约定游戏的软件著作权归中青宝公司享有，独家运营权由跳跃公司享有，后中青宝公司将涉案游戏软件著作权转让给跳跃公司。涉案游戏中的战士娃、猎人娃、牧师娃、骑士娃、术士娃、法师娃及盗贼娃七个角色形象以及战士娃皮肤与葫芦娃角色造型美术作品存在一定程度的相似之处。星游公司运营的电玩巴士网站对涉案游戏进行了宣传推广，或直接以葫芦七兄弟指代涉案游戏中的前述角色，或明示前述游戏角色即为葫芦七兄弟，并使用了动画片《葫芦兄弟》的部分情节。美影厂向法院起诉，要求判令中青宝公司、跳跃公司、星游公司刊登声明消除影响，并赔偿经济损失。

上海知识产权法院经审理认为，美影厂系涉案葫芦娃美术作品的著作权人，有权提起本案诉讼。因涉案战士娃系列角色形象与葫芦娃美术作品在具体构图设计上具有一定程度的相似性，可以认定系在葫芦娃美术作品基本表达基础上的再创作，但鉴于两者在具体设计上仍存在一定程度的差异，该差异亦体现了一定的独创性，使得战士娃系列角色形象相较于葫芦娃设计构成新的作品，故认定构成对葫芦娃作品改编权的侵犯。电玩巴士网站中的宣传内容已足以使相关公众认为涉案战士娃系列角色造型与美影厂葫芦娃角色形象具有一定的关联，游戏角色造型的制作使用已经美影厂许可或者游戏与美影厂存在一定关联，构成虚假宣传的不正当竞争行为。跳跃公司、中青宝公司在游戏的开发过程中对于战士娃系列角色形象、战士娃皮肤的设计使用侵犯了美影厂对葫芦娃角色形象享有的改编权；在涉案游戏的运营过程中，以及与星游公司在涉案游戏的宣传推广过程中对于涉案战士娃系列角色形象、战士娃皮肤的使用，侵犯了美影厂对葫芦娃角色形象享有的信息网络传播权；跳跃公司、中青宝公司、星游公司共同实施了前述宣传行为，共同构成不正当竞争行为。法院判决三被告刊登声明消除影响，中青宝公司、跳跃公司连带赔偿经济损失及合理费用52.6万元，星游公司对于其中的7.6万元承担连带赔偿责任。

本案系涉及知名美术作品葫芦娃的著作权侵权纠纷案，争议焦点和审理难点均在于涉案网络游戏中的战士娃系列角色形象是否侵犯葫芦娃美术作品的著作权，尤其涉及思想与表达的区分、复制权与改编权的边界认定问题。二审判决明确了，因涉案战士娃系列角色形象与葫芦娃美术作品在具体构图设计上具有一定程度的相似性，可以认定系在葫芦娃美术作品基本表达基础上的再创作，但鉴于两者在具体设计上仍存在一定程度的差异，该差异亦体现了一定的独创性，使得战士娃系列角色形象相较于葫芦娃设计构成新的作品，故认定构成对葫芦娃作品改编权的侵犯，并在此基础上对三被告各自应承担的责任进行了充分阐述。本案判决对于保护动画影片人物角色形象具有一定的借鉴意义。

八、浦睿公司、湖南音像出版社侵害著作权纠纷案

原告叶肇鑫从2008年10月开始构思创作以“细说昆曲”为主题的昆曲艺术讲解纪录片《昆曲百种　大师说戏》(以下简称《说戏》)，后原告又以纪录片为蓝本，将纪录片改编为以“说戏”为书名的五辑配套图书。2013年4月5日，原告叶肇鑫以自费独资的身份，与被告浦睿公司签订《出版协议》，由浦睿公司提供《说戏》的光盘、图书的生产、出版和发行等服务工作，被告浦睿公司将复制发行权转授予被告湖南音像出版社。被告湖南音像出版社未经原告授权许可，超出原限定发行数量，擅自再版、发行《说戏》产品，被告国家出版基金规划管理办公室为上述侵权作品提供资金支持，并在产品封面处印有“国家出版基金项目”标识。故原告诉至法院请求确认三被告侵害了原告涉案作品的复制权、发行权，并就侵犯著作权的行为向原告赔礼道歉。

普陀区法院经审理认为，被告湖南音像出版社作为一家专业出版机构，在明知被告浦睿公司仅为转授权人的情况下，并未对著作权人与转授权人之间的权利约定尽到审慎注意义务，超出合同授权权限，发行带有“国家出版基金”字样的图书，侵犯了原告的著作权。被告浦睿公司在转授权后，未对被告湖南音像出版社是否按约履行合同进行合理的、基本的提示和督促，不但主观上有过错，客观上也有侵权行为，与被告湖南音像出版社就涉案著作权侵权行为构成共同侵权。被告出版基金办依据被告湖南音像出版社提交的申报材料，进行立项，已尽到合理的审慎审查注意义务，不构成侵权。据此，法院判决认定被告浦睿公司、湖南电子音像出版社超出授权数量范围的出版行为侵害了原告就涉案作品《昆曲百种　大师说戏》享有的复制权、发行权，对原告叶肇鑫的其余诉讼请求不予支持。

本案系著作权人自费出版图书过程中，因出版机构超越著作权人约定发行数量，擅自出版图书引发的著作权侵权纠纷。本案中，法院在对涉案作品性质进行界定的基础上，从出版合同履约过程，包括预购发行模式、财务决算情况等因素予以综合判断，认定被告湖南音像出版社超越合同授权权限，发行带有“国家出版基金”字样的图书，侵犯了原告的著作权。被告浦睿公司在转授权后，未对被告湖南音像出版社是否按约履行合同进行合理的、基本的提示和督促，与被告湖南音像出版社就涉案著作权侵权行为构成共同侵权。被告出版基金办依据被告湖南音像出版社提交的申报材料，进行立项，已尽到合理的审慎审查义务，不构成侵权。

图书出版涉及著作权人、出版机构、文化传播公司等多类法律主体，亦包含了著作权许可、图书发售等多重法律关系。实践中，各方可对著作权许可使用费、发行成本分摊、图书销售盈利分配等予以灵活约定，这一方式具有高效性，但履约中的不规范、不严谨操作，容易引发著作权侵权风险。本案的判决对于明晰出版从业主体著作权保护注意义务的边界、提升行业规范运作意识具有一定的参考价值。

九、某泵业公司侵害某中德合资企业产品说明书著作权、不正当竞争纠纷案

某中德合资企业经授权，在中国境内享有涉案产品说明书除人身权外的著作权。某泵业公司在专利申请书及其公司网站中使用了涉案产品说明书中的内容。某中德合资企业向法院起诉，要求法院判令某泵业公司停止侵害著作权和不正当竞争行为，刊登声明、消除影响、赔礼道歉，赔偿经济损失及合理开支。徐汇区人民法院经审理认为，原告在本案中主张产品说明书中的文字、图形和照片构成著作权法保护的作品，即使产品涉及的技术是公知技术，也不妨碍对该项技术及其产品的说明表达得到著作权法的保护。某泵业公司在专利申请书中使用的文字和图形，以及在其网站上使用的图表与涉案说明书中相应内容构成实质性相似，而某泵业公司并未举证证明上述内容系其自主创作或经合法授权，构成著作权侵权。然而，某中德合资企业主张某泵业公司将其技术方案以自己的名义申请专利的行为构成侵权，法院不予认同，因某中德合资企业已就上述行为以专利申请权纠纷起诉，生效判决业已对此做出判定，无法再适用反不正当竞争法进行额外保护，某中德合资企业关于不正当竞争的诉讼主张不成立。法院判决：某泵业公司赔偿某中德合资企业经济损失及合理开支 66 000 元。一审判决后，某中德合资企业不服，提起上诉。二审判决驳回上诉，维持原判。

著作权法所称的作品是独创性的智力成果，即作品应由作者独立创作完成，并具有一定的智力创作性，但著作权法对于“创造性”并未设置明确的标准。涉案说明书中的文字内容虽然是对产品部件的阐述，但已满足著作权法对文字作品的形式要求，即使其中涉及的技术是公知技术，也不妨碍对该项技术及其产品的说明表达得到著作权法的保护，毕竟同一种技术和产品可以通过不同种方式进行表达，其中的独创性部分正是著作权法保护的核心。然而，产品说明书中承载的产品技术方案本身受专利法规制，在专利法已有明确规定的情况下，同一行为即使未得到专利法保护，也不能再依据反不正当竞争法第二条原则性条款得到额外保护。本案判决对明确产品说明书是否构成著作权法意义上的作品，以及对产品说明书的侵权行为应当以何法律关系予以规制进行了积极的探索，对于准确把握作品的独创性以及反不正当竞争法原则条款的适用具有积极意义。

十、上海海关查办侵犯足球世界杯相关著作权侵权系列案

2018 年 6 月，第 21 届世界杯足球赛在俄罗斯举办，针对赛事前后假冒盗版行为高发的情况，上海海关先后在海、空、邮等多个渠道查获出口南美洲、亚洲、欧洲、非洲等地，侵犯著作权的商品 6 批，共计 2.5 万余件，价值合计人民币 24 万余元：分别在邮递渠道成功查获发往俄罗斯的“大力神杯”侵权复制品，在海运、空运渠道连续查获与俄罗斯世界杯官方比赛用球“电视之星”同款的侵权足球等多起典型案件。上海海关先后对出口侵犯著作权货物的当事人做出了没收侵权货物并处罚金的行政处罚。

本系列案件中，上海海关通过专项行动有力保护了俄罗斯世界杯的相关著作权，积极推动实现了知识产权保护助力体育产业的蓬勃发展。知识产权海关保护的主动执法程序，是以知识产权完成海关备案为前提的。为提升打击成效，赛事举办之前上海海关主动联系国际足联以及世界杯相关赞助商，提供赛事期间开展海关保护的最佳方案，协助企业向海关总署申请完成世界杯比赛用球图案、世界杯会徽设计等多项著作权海关备案；同时针对著作权表现形式丰富，相比商标权较难查发的特点，联合权利人开展专项执法技能培训，进一步培塑现场关员对相关著作权的查缉意识，提升查缉能力和水平。此外，该系列案件积极应用大数据分析理念，实现精准打击。

（上海市版权局）

江　苏　省

一、南京金名城置业有限公司未经著作权人许可复制他人软件案

2017 年 12 月 11 日，欧特克公司（Autodesk, Inc.）委托上海凌云永然律师事务所向南京市文化市场综合执法总队投诉，称南京金名城置业有限公司未经欧特克公司许可，在办公经营场所的计算机内复制安装使用 AutoCAD 和 3DMax 计算机软件 200 余套，请求责令停止侵权行为并追究侵权责任。2018 年 1 月 23 日，经现场检查发现 4 台计算机中复制安装有 AutoCAD 软件。

2018 年 5 月，经调解，双方达成一致，双方签订软件销售合同，南京金名置业有限公司购买欧特克公司 Autodesk 软件 400 件，价值 200 多万元。2018 年 11 月 9 日，南京市版权局依法从轻做出行政处罚，责令南京金名置业有限公司停止侵权行为，并罚款人民币 400 元整。

二、无锡佳酷信息技术有限公司侵犯著作权案

根据江苏省版权局提供的案件线索，无锡市文化市场综合执法支队于 2018 年 5—6 月对无锡佳酷信息技术有限公司运营的多个网络载体进行远程勘验，发现该公司利用网站、微信公众号和微信群传播他人影视作品，诱导他人实施购物行为，从而获得经济利益。2018年6月6日，无锡市文化广电新闻出版局立案。经查，该公司2017年10月至2018年7月未经著作权人许可，利用其经营网站和微信公众号传播他人作品。同时，利用微信公众号及微信群充当淘宝客营销、微信公众号内运营手机游戏和小说等多种方式牟利，3个月获利10 031.82元；利用影视网站关联的微信公众号与北京豪腾嘉科科技有限公司联合运营游戏，5个月获利44 696.83元；利用影视网站关联的微信公众号与福州掌中云文化传媒有限公司联合运营网络小说，7个月获利34 769.43元。

2018年7月18日，无锡市版权局给予无锡佳酷信息技术有限公司责令停止侵权行为，并罚款12万元的行政处罚。

三、徐州李某等游戏私服侵犯著作权案

2015年5月至2017年8月间，李某、霍某、刘某明知未取得游艺春秋网络科技（北京）有限公司授权或许可，不具备网络游戏 *Silkroad Online*（中文名《丝路传说》《新丝路》）的代理权、经营权，仍通过互联网私自架设《火越丝路》服务器，以向玩家出售游戏币的方式牟利，非法经营数额共计22万余元。

2018年8月22日，徐州市中级人民法院判决李某犯侵犯著作权罪，判处有期徒刑二年，并处罚金人民币14万元；霍某犯侵犯著作权罪，判处有期徒刑一年十个月，并处罚金人民币13万元；刘某犯侵犯著作权罪，判处有期徒刑一年六个月，缓刑二年，并处罚金人民币12万元。

四、徐州徐某某游戏私服侵犯著作权案

2015年5月至2016年5月期间，犯罪嫌疑人徐某某未经北京畅游时代数码技术有限公司授权，明知其不具备《天龙八部》游戏经营权和代理权的情况下，通过互联网私自架设《武神天龙》私服，在"好天龙"网站上进行推广，通过向游戏玩家出售游戏币的方式非法牟利，非法经营数额共计人民币278万余元。

2018年5月9日，徐州市中级人民法院判决徐某某犯侵犯著作权罪，判处有期徒刑三年，缓刑四年，并处罚金人民币140万元，违法所得人民币30万元予以追缴，上缴国库。

五、常州孙某某游戏私服侵犯著作权案

2017年4月3日，常州市文广新局接到游艺春秋网络科技（北京）有限公司举报，称有人未经该公司授权私自开设《新破天一剑》网游，严重侵犯了该公司《中广联合破天一剑》的软件著作权。2017年4月20日，该案件移送常州市公安局钟楼分局。2017年5月25日，侦查人员在孙某某开设私服的作案现场将其抓获，当场缴获作案手机2部、作案电脑1台。案发后，犯罪嫌疑人孙某某赔偿游艺春秋网络科技（北京）有限公司人民币28万元，取得该公司谅解，并退出部分违法所得4.8万元。

2018年1月31日，常州市钟楼区人民法院判决被告人孙某某犯侵犯著作权罪，判处有期徒刑二年，缓刑二年，并处罚金人民币10万元。

六、张家港"4·28"侵犯著作权案

2018年4月，张家港市文化市场综合执法大队在日常巡查中发现杨舍镇长泾东路一场所涉嫌制售盗版音像制品，现场查封音乐光盘3 839张、刻录母盘91张、待发光盘包裹16个、办公主机4台和刻录机3台。经查，该场所负责人方某通过经营"香蕉数码旗舰店"淘宝网店，从事各类光盘刻录、定制、复制业务，内容包括音乐歌曲、婚庆视频、宣传片、学生作业等，售价为每盘8元或18元。2017年10月至2018年4月，当事人从事淘宝网店的交易记录1 400余条，刻录复制音乐作品均未经著作权人许可，涉及音乐作品47 816首，非法经营额2万余元。

2018年6月11日，张家港市文化广电新闻出版局对当事人方某做出了罚款10万元，并没收侵权复制品885张音乐CD和刻录使用的电脑、刻录机的行政处罚。

七、南通川姜镇知识产权管理办公室查处著作权侵权系列案

2018年，南通市通州区川姜镇知识产权管理办公室共计受理了美术作品侵权案投诉133件。办公室根据投诉人提供的相关信息，协调公安部门、村干部和上级版权部门到市场门市、库房、运输途中和印染企业进行调查取证，封样登记保存，并及时了解情况，组织调解等相关工作。

全年行政调解结案共计86件，行政调解为权利人挽回直接经济损失69万余元；移交法院案件47件，司法调解和判决为权利人挽回直接经济损失80多万元。

八、淮安"BT天堂"侵犯著作权案

2016年7月25日，深圳市腾讯计算机有限公司向淮安市公安局报案，称"BT天堂"网站涉嫌侵犯其影视作品著作权。随即淮安市公安局与市版权局、市文化市场综合执法支队沟通协调，决定成立专案组，并责成淮安区公安局办理。2016年8月12日，淮安区公安局立案并于2016年9月9日将袁某某在苏州抓获。经查，2015 年 5 月以来，袁某某以营利为目的，购买 BT 天堂网站（www.bttiantang.com），在未取得相关影视作品著作权人许可的情况下，将大量影视作品在 BT 天堂网站上发布以赚取广告收入，截至案发共获利 1 402 513 元。犯罪嫌疑人归案后如实供述相关犯罪事实，并主动退出违法所得人民币 30 万元。

2018 年 12 月 6 日，淮安市中级人民法院判处袁某某有期徒刑三年，并处罚金人民币 80 万元。

九、盐城“3·4”侵权盗版案

2016 年 3 月 4 日，盐都区公安局龙冈派出所在龙冈镇捣毁一个非法刻录盗版光盘的窝点，现场抓获张某成、张某两名犯罪嫌疑人，现场查获电脑、刻录机、刻录的未包装光碟 15 831 张、刻录的黑胶 HRDJ 音乐 CD 光碟 4 695 张、网上购买的光盘等累计 90 000 余张。

2018 年 3 月 27 日，盐城市中级人民法院判处张某林有期徒刑三年，缓刑四年，并处罚金人民币 28 000 元；判处张某成有期徒刑三年，缓刑三年六个月，并处罚金人民币 25 000 元；判处张某有期徒刑一年六个月，缓刑二年，并处罚金人民币 5 000 元。

十、扬州《天龙八部》私服侵犯著作权案

2017 年 9 月，扬州市江都区文新局接到北京畅游天下网络技术有限公司举报，有人架设私服游戏《王者天龙》侵犯了其网络游戏《天龙八部》著作权。2017 年 12 月 1 日，江都区公安局立案侦查。经查，2017 年 6 月至 2018 年 1 月，犯罪嫌疑人钟某某伙同史某某等人，未经授权利用互联网私自建立《王者天龙》服务器运营网络私服游戏，并采用租用直播厅直播的方式招揽玩家注册、充值购买游戏道具的方式向玩家收费，游戏注册人数达 3 000 余人，非法经营额 54 万余元。

2018 年 10 月 23 日，扬州市广陵区人民法院做出判决，判决钟某某犯侵犯著作权罪，判处有期徒刑三年，缓刑三年，并处罚金 9 万元；判决史某某犯侵犯著作权罪，判处有期徒刑三年，缓刑三年，并处罚金 7 万元。

（江苏省版权局）

安 徽 省

一、合肥众源电子科技有限公司侵犯著作权案

2018 年 4 月 17 日，安徽省版权局接到权利人美国微软（中国）公司投诉，合肥众源电子科技有限公司涉嫌未经其许可，复制发行微软操作系统软件，发行至蚌埠市五河县教体局及相关中小学。经蚌埠市五河县文化广电旅游新闻出版局立案调查，合肥众源电子科技有限公司在 2016 年 12 月 8 日中标的“五河县 2016 年改薄项目教师办公电脑采购与安装项目”中，其销售的电脑安装侵权的操作系统软件 400 套。

2018 年 12 月 21 日，蚌埠市五河县文化广电旅游新闻出版局对当事人做出行政处罚：罚款人民币 104 000 元。

二、梁某某等侵犯著作权案

2017 年 11 月 29 日，宿州市版权局接到举报，萧县某中学使用的部分教辅图书涉嫌侵权盗版。经宿州市文化市场综合执法支队、萧县文化市场综合执法大队调查，梁某某委托张某某的印刷企业翻印教辅图书 7 800 余本，同其购买的部分正版教辅图书，共 8 695 本销售给萧县某中学，总价款人民币 171 572 元。

2018 年 12 月 24 日，宿州市萧县人民法院依法判处梁某某有期徒刑三年，缓刑四年，并处罚金人民币 90 000 元，公安机关扣押的 3 794 本盗版书籍等依法予以没收。判处张某某有期徒刑三年，缓刑三年，并处罚金人民币 20 000 元，追缴张某某违法所得人民币 20 000 元。

（安徽省版权局）

江 西 省

一、永新“9·8”侵犯著作权案

2016 年 9 月，永新县文化市场综合执法大队执法人员在日常巡查时，发现多个书店涉嫌销售侵权盗版“英才教程”系列教辅资料且数额较大。

2018 年 3—8 月，永新县人民法院以侵犯著作权罪，先后判处陈某某等 7 人有期徒刑五年至拘役缓刑不等并处罚金，对贺某某等 2 人处罚金。该案被国家版权局、全国“扫黄打非”工作小组办公室列为 2018 年度全国打击侵权盗版十大案件之一。

二、南昌“6·4”侵犯著作权案

2016 年 5 月，南昌市文化市场综合执法支队根据举报线索，对南昌国云科技服务有限公司涉嫌侵犯著作权案进行调查。经查，该公司所经营“火课旗舰店”淘宝网店未经权利人授权，销售视频课件及《股市操练大全》等 68 本 PDF 版文字作品，供付费用户通过百度云链接下载。传播上述作品数量共计 12 199 件（部），营业收入 34 万余元。

2018年5月14日，南昌市青山湖区人民法院以侵犯著作权罪，判处公司法定代表人廖某某有期徒刑二年，并处罚金6万元。该案系全国“扫黄打非”工作小组办公室、国家版权局办公厅等五部门挂牌督办案件。

三、江西每日网络科技公司微信公众号侵犯著作权案

2017年4月，新余市文化市场综合执法支队根据案件线索，对江西每日网络科技有限公司利用“暴风电影院”“大宝剑影院”等微信公众号涉嫌侵权传播影视作品案进行立案调查。经查，江西每日网络科技有限公司共注册微信公众号43个、域名69个，确定侵权影视作品522部（集）。

2018年11月23日，新余市渝水区人民法院以侵犯著作权罪，判处当事人陈某拘役五个月，并处罚金人民币1万元，扣押的平板电脑、电脑主机等予以没收。该案系全国“扫黄打非”工作小组办公室、国家版权局办公厅等五部门挂牌督办案件。

四、江西宏扬技术服务有限公司侵犯著作权案

2017年7月，根据省版权局移转案件线索，南昌市文化广电新闻出版局执法人员对南昌市11所学校进行电脑软件检查，其中9所学校单位有复制的侵权Windows和Office软件程序。经调查，这些软件由江西宏扬技术服务有限公司提供，共安装复制447台次。根据微软（中国）有限公司出具的认定意见，江西宏扬技术服务有限公司未取得授权证书。

2018年5月18日，执法人员对江西宏扬技术服务有限公司做出没收侵权复制品Windows和Office软件母盘3张、罚款4.47万元的行政处罚。

五、景德镇未一花纸经销店侵犯著作权案

2017年11月，深圳国瓷永丰源股份有限公司向景德镇市文化广电新闻出版局举报景德镇市中国陶瓷城未一花纸经销店侵犯其公司“西湖牡丹”（“夫人瓷”）系列产品著作权。经过执法人员的走访、调查、取证和中国版权保护中心的鉴定，当事人孔某某对侵权事实供认不讳。

景德镇市文化市场综合执法支队责令未一花纸经销店停止侵权行为，没收其违法所得1万元，没收其侵权系列花纸300张、陶瓷餐具1套，并处罚款3万元。

六、新余渝天文化传媒发展有限公司侵犯著作权案

2018年7月，新余市文化市场综合执法支队对新余市渝天文化传媒发展有限公司进行例行检查，发现该公司运营的微信公众号“新余秀yt0790”，未经著作权人许可，向公众传播中央电视台CCTV-3、CCTV-5、CCTV-6、CCTV-8电视节目，并无法出示相关授权证明。

新余市文化市场综合执法支队责令当事人停止侵权行为，并做出罚款3万元的行政处罚。

七、鹰潭动力网络有限公司侵犯著作权案

2018年10月，鹰潭市文化广电新闻出版局执法人员对鹰潭市月湖区动力网络有限公司广场分公司进行例行检查，发现公司在营业场所电脑服务器中下载安装的名称为《动力影视VIP》的影视点播程序系“奇领6080影院”的客户端。经查“奇领6080影院”网站传播的影视节目未经著作权人的许可和授权。

执法人员给予当事人罚款人民币2万元的行政处罚。

八、武汉世纪方舟图书发行有限责任公司侵犯著作案

2018年8月，接群众举报，九江市文化市场综合执法支队执法人员对九江市起点书店门店及仓库进行查处，经分类抽样送检，有《幼儿手工制作》《数学练习册》《音乐·美术》等书籍系侵权出版物。经调查，这些书籍是从武汉世纪方舟图书发行有限责任公司采购的，涉案金额3 800元。

执法人员给予武汉世纪方舟图书发行有限责任公司法定代表人张某某销毁侵权复制品、罚款1.5万元的行政处罚。

九、吉安怪兽文化创意有限公司侵犯著作权案

2018年3月，吉安市文化市场综合执法支队执法人员对辖区的江西怪兽文化创意有限公司（慢游时光）进行日常检查，发现该营业场所包厢内正在播放当时影院的上映热片。经查，该店包厢内用于顾客点播的影视作品未取得著作权人授权许可。

2018年4月11日，吉安市文化市场综合执法支队对当事人做出罚款1万元的行政处罚。

十、于都龙门一号音乐会侵犯著作权案

2018年3月，赣州市于都县文化广电新闻出版局执法人员对于都县龙门一号音乐会所进行例行检查时，发现会所曲库内及包厢点歌台内含有《冰雨》《上海滩》等上千首未经著作人授权许可的曲目。

执法人员责令其停止侵权行为，并处罚款人民币1万元。

（江西省版权局）

山 东 省

一、滨州市阳信县“11·22”侵犯著作权案

2017年11月22日，滨州市文化市场综合执法局接到国家版权局移交的“拼多多”网络销售涉嫌盗版图书的案件线索后，立即派出执法人员赴阳信县进行核查。经查，发现一辆车牌号为鲁M·DJ665的“福田五星”三轮车，后车厢内装有一批包装好待寄递的涉嫌盗版的图书（《查理九世》系列）。随后检查其房间发现大量包装盒散放的《查理九世》系列（1～27册），部分涉嫌盗版的《阳光姐姐幽默派》，以及正在使用的打包机一台。执法人员立即对现场的书进行清点，涉嫌盗版的《查理九世》计437套，每套27册，共计11 799册，《阳光姐姐幽默派》计16套，每套10册，共计160册。总计涉嫌盗版图书11 959册，码洋总计179 545元。经鉴定，涉案图书均为盗版。

2018年1月，阳信县文化市场综合执法局与县公安局双方研究，成立“11·22”侵犯著作权专案组。阳信县公安局已将该案侦查完毕，并按法律规定移交县检察院。2018年，该案被列入国家版权局、全国“扫黄打非”领导小组办公室、公安部、最高人民检察院联合挂牌督办案件。

二、山东菏泽“3·12”制售盗版图书案

2017年11月，根据群众举报线索，菏泽市、定陶县两级版权行政执法部门会同公安部门对闫某某等制售盗版图书案进行调查。经查，自2016年起，闫某某未经权利人许可，委托菏泽市贸易公司印刷厂和菏泽信艺印刷厂印制图书，办理虚假出版物经营许可证，并通过淘宝、闲鱼、微信、QQ等平台销售大量侵权图书。执法部门共查获盗版图书15万多册，光盘1.5万多张，码洋总计1 500多万元，半成品图书（为裁剪装订）12吨，收缴非法所得近200万元。

6名犯罪嫌疑人已被批准逮捕，3名犯罪嫌疑人已被取保候审，案件正在进一步查办中。2018年，该案被列入国家版权局督办案件。

三、山东济宁“10·19”王某某涉嫌侵犯影视作品著作权案

2017年10月18日，济宁市文化市场综合执法局接到省版权局转办案件，济宁市任城区有利用网络平台注册“云播爱好者”公众号实施播放他人作品的侵权行为，主体证件号为370811198805172815，运营者为王某某。济宁市文化市场综合执法局高度重视，立即做出部署，安排执法人员进行远程勘验、暗访，发现举报情况属实，且盗版种类、数量较多。2017年10月19日，济宁市文化市场综合执法局协调市公安局启动快速反应联动预案，抽调精干办案力量，成立“10·19”王某某网络侵权盗版专案组，立即对其违法行为进行远程勘探。执法人员登录电脑微信客户端打开该公众号，按照该公众号的提示在文本框输入“电影”点击发送后，该公众号提供有电影、剧集、综艺、动漫的文章推送，点击“电影”后进入提供的页面，页面底部共有“电影”“剧集”“综艺”“动漫”四个栏目，逐个点击，都能正常、完整播放。经统计共有电影1 171部、剧集153部、综艺32部、动漫9部，合计1 365部。

依据《中华人民共和国著作权法》第四十八条、《信息网络传播权保护条例》第十八条的规定，2019年2月，济宁市文化市场综合执法局做出行政处罚：（1）警告；（2）没收违法所得2 354元；（3）罚款30 000元。2018年，该案被列入国家版权局、全国“扫黄打非”领导小组办公室、公安部、最高人民检察院联合挂牌督办案件。

四、山东青岛“8·1”侵犯软件著作权案

2017年7月28日，深圳巨龙科教网络有限公司到青岛市文化市场行政执法局投诉称：该公司在青岛市市北区行政服务大厅内参加“互联网＋”校园安全防控体系项目招标会时，发现苏州某电子科技有限公司生产的智慧校园安全防控体系系列产品使用的是深圳巨龙科教网络有限公司生产的学安“互联网＋”校园安全防控体系，其行为涉嫌侵犯其软件著作权及商业秘密，请求青岛市文化市场执法局立案查处。接到投诉后，青岛市文化市场执法局与青岛市市北区综合执法局、青岛市公安局市北公安分局经侦二大队在市北教育局招标会现场封存了苏州某电子科技有限公司参与竞标的样品，并对有关人员进行了调查询问，初步认定苏州某电子科技有限公司涉嫌侵犯软件著作权。之后，青岛市文化市场行政执法局联系中国版权保护中心及工业和信息化部软件与集成电路促进中心知识产权司法鉴定所，对样品的软件进行侵犯著作权及商业秘密鉴定。中国版权保护中心鉴定结论：深圳市巨龙科教网络有限公司的软件与苏州某电子有限公司的软件基本相同。中国工业和信息化部软件与集成电路促进中心知识产权司法鉴定所鉴定结论：深圳市巨龙科教网络有限公司所主张的产品，与苏州某电子有限公司产品的同一性为99.66%。初步查明深圳市巨龙科教网络有限公司被侵犯著作权所造成的经济损失已

达上亿元。

青岛市北区公安分局已经对此案侦查完毕，并按法律规定移交检察院。2018年，该案被列入国家版权局督办案件。

五、山东菏泽“11·7”侵犯著作权案

出版社维权人员举报反映，曹县境内有地下印刷厂及图书仓库从事非法经营活动。菏泽市领导高度重视，市公安局遂指派东明县公安局办理此案。由于案情重大，市文化市场综合执法局、东明县公安局成立专案组。2018年11月7日，文化、公安检查人员兵分两路，一路在曹县孙花园宏盛毛纺有限公司院内查处一无证印刷厂，查获图书成品《口算题卡》、半成品《金星教育中学教材全解》等图书一宗，当场将犯罪嫌疑人张某、王某某抓获；另一路在曹县兵马楼行政村查处图书仓库一处，查获《金星教育中学教材全解》、课本《数学》共计6万余册。据张某交代并指认，该窝点就是被查处无证印刷厂储存非法印刷的图书仓库。

经初步调查，张某、王某某系夫妻关系，于2018年9月在该处租用一生产车间设立印刷厂，开展非法印刷活动，直接销往菏泽周边地区个体书店、中心学校等。该案涉及人民教育出版社、中国环境出版社、山东画报出版社、山东科学技术出版社、山西人民出版社等多个出版社。菏泽市文化市场综合执法局分别向涉案出版社发出《鉴定函》，经出版社认证，涉案图书均为盗版，涉嫌侵犯其著作权。

2018年11月8日，犯罪嫌疑人张某、王某某、曹某某被刑事拘留，12月13日，被东明县人民检察院批准逮捕，12月14日，被执行逮捕。该案共行政拘留16人，其中逮捕3人，取保候审13人，并进入检察院起诉阶段。

六、山东潍坊昌邑立聚达纺织有限公司未经著作权人许可复制美术作品（纺织品花布）案

2018年5月15日，根据著作权人投诉线索，山东省潍坊市昌邑市文化市场综合执法局执法人员对昌邑立聚达纺织有限公司进行了调查。经查，该公司为追求经济利益，在未经权利人许可的情况下，擅自接受委托人的委托，印制权利人拥有作品登记证书（苏作登字2017-F-002257330、苏作登字2017-F-00229026）的两个纺织品花纹图案，涉案纺织品花布共14包10 093.30米，金额4.99万元。

该案违反了《中华人民共和国著作权法》第四十八条之规定，根据《中华人民共和国著作权法》第四十八条、《中华人民共和国著作权法实施条例》第三十六条的规定予以处罚：（1）没收侵权复制品（印花布）10 093.30米（货值4.99万元）；（2）罚款人民币2万元。

七、广东华丽金科技有限公司侵犯著作权案

山东省威海市文化市场综合执法局在查办一起侵犯著作权案件中，发现广东华丽金科技有限公司涉嫌明知他人实施侵犯著作权犯罪，而为其提供生产制造侵权产品的主要原材料，依法应以侵犯著作权罪的共犯论处。2018年1月4日，威海市文化市场综合执法局将案件线索移交给市公安局，当日成立公安与文化执法联合专案组。1月16日，联合专案组赴广东省广州市，将广东华丽金科技有限公司销售副总经理方某某和湛江华丽金音影碟有限公司副总经理陈某某抓获。2月13日，经威海经济技术开发区人民检察院批准，二人被威海市公安局直属分局逮捕。经依法审查查明：2014年5月至2016年8月，张某某、陈某某、刘某（三人已判决），未经著作权人许可，通过被告单位广东华丽金科技有限公司订购印刷有“哆咪音乐”字样的空白光盘30余万张，上述光盘通过湛江华丽金音影碟有限公司（已做相对不起诉处理）生产后，交付张某某、陈某某、刘某，用于刻录侵权盗版音乐光盘。至被查获时，刘某已通过淘宝网店将15万余张私自刻录好的“哆咪音乐”侵权光盘销售至全国27个省份，涉案金额26万余元，已确认侵权的音乐作品5 252首。

2018年11月，威海经济技术开发区人民检察院就本案向威海经济技术开发区人民法院提起公诉。

八、济南天岳包装有限公司侵犯著作权案

2016年7月至8月，济南天岳包装有限公司员工郄某某、王某某未经济南红霖联合实业有限公司许可，擅自使用红霖公司享有著作权的《九间棚杂粮》《蒙山蜂蜜》《盛世珍果》等作品绘制包装盒，销售给山东九间棚食品有限公司，共销售包装盒16 000个，销售额43 450元。2017年3月，经中国版权保护中心版权鉴定委员会鉴定，天岳公司销售给九间棚的《盛世珍果》《开心时嗑》共7 000个包装盒美术作品与红霖公司对应的美术作品相同。天岳公司销售给九间棚的《九间棚杂粮》《蒙山蜂蜜》共9 000个包装盒美术作品与红霖公司对应的美术作品相同。

针对上述事实，济南市长清区人民法院认为被告人郄某某、王某某以营利为目的，未经著作权人许可，复制其美术作品，情节特别严重，构成侵犯著作权罪。依照《中华人民共和国刑法》第二百一十七条、第二十五条等规定，判决如下：被告人郄某某犯侵犯著作权罪，判处有期徒刑二年，缓刑二年，并处罚金2.2万元；被告人王某某犯侵犯著作权罪，判处有期徒刑一年六个月，缓刑一年六个月，并处罚金 2.2 万元。

（山东省版权局）

湖 北 省

一、咸宁谢某某等制售盗版出版物案

2018 年 4 月，湖北省咸宁市嘉鱼县公安局接群众举报线索，对谢某某等涉嫌制售盗版出版物案进行调查。经查，2017 年以来，谢某某等在嘉鱼县渡普镇、赤壁市中伙铺镇等地开设工作室，在网上下载教材教辅、医疗保健类、名著类等畅销电子书籍，打印成册后在网上出售，累计印刷 5 万余册，有 3 万余人购买，非法获利 10 万余元。2 名犯罪嫌疑人已被公安机关依法刑事拘留，案件正在进一步查办中。

二、襄阳周某、黄某某、陈某、桂某、刘某、孙某某、郭某等 11 人侵犯网络游戏著作权案

2018 年 3 月 22 日，襄阳市公安局襄州区分局根据权利人投诉，经过连续三个月缜密侦查，成功侦破一起特大《绝地求生》游戏外挂案，先后在湖北、四川、河北、吉林、江西等地，成功抓获黄某某等犯罪嫌疑人 11 人，摧毁制售外挂工作室窝点两处，冻结涉案资金 1 200 余万元，扣押电脑、银行卡等大量作案工具。

2018 年 12 月 26 日，襄阳市襄州区人民法院依法对本案做出判决：被告人周某、黄某某、陈某、桂某、刘某、孙某某、郭某犯提供侵入、非法控制计算机信息系统程序、工具罪，分别判处有期徒刑三年至五年，并处罚金。

三、武汉晃游网络科技有限公司未经著作权人许可向公众传播影视作品案

2018 年 8 月，东湖新技术开发区教育文化体育局根据上级交办线索对位于武汉市东湖新技术开发区汤逊湖北路 33 号华工科技园 · 创新基地的武汉晃游网络科技有限公司进行了现场检查，发现当事人未经著作权人许可向公众传播影视作品，涉嫌侵犯权利人著作权并损害社会公共利益。东湖新技术开发区教育文化体育局根据《著作权法》第四十八条第（一）项的规定，对当事人做出责令停止侵权行为、罚款人民币 20 000 元的行政处罚。

四、湖北兴楚伟业科技有限公司未经著作权人许可通过信息网络向公众传播其影视作品案

2018 年 8 月，东湖新技术开发区教育文化体育局根据上级交办的线索对湖北兴楚伟业科技有限公司备案的网站（xingchu. net）进行了远程勘验，发现当事人未经著作权人许可，复制、发行、表演、放映、广播、汇编、通过信息网络向公众传播其作品，涉嫌侵犯著作权并损害社会公共利益。

2018 年 8 月 16 日，东湖新技术开发区教育文化体育局根据《著作权法》第四十八条第（一）项的规定，对当事人做出责令停止侵权行为、罚款人民币 9 000 元的行政处罚。

五、潜江“品源音乐会所”侵犯音像作品著作权案

2018 年 1 月 31 日，潜江市文化市场综合执法支队对潜江市品源音乐会所的投资人钱庆平出示行政执法证件后，对当事人营业场所进行检查。执法人员在 6002 包间内的歌曲点播系统中随机抽查了十首歌曲，当事人现场不能提供相关权利人的授权证明材料。当事人未经著作权人许可，在其经营的歌舞娱乐场所通过歌曲点播系统公开播送著作权人作品的表演的行为，侵犯了著作权人的表演权，同时损害了公共利益，违反了《著作权法》第十条第一款第（九）项的规定，损害了著作权人的权益。依照《中华人民共和国著作权法》第四十八条第（一）项和《中华人民共和国著作权法实施条例》第三十六条的规定，对当事人做出没收违法所得 8 366.4 元、罚款 50 000 元的行政处罚。

六、荆州“9553. com”网站侵犯软件著作权案

2018 年 1 月，洪湖市文化执法综合执法大队根据上级移转函，依法对崔某和廖某某进行了调查询问，廖某某承认 2017 年 9 月借用崔某身份证注册了 9553. com 网站，网站办公地址设在武汉市关山大道光谷创意大厦。经现场勘验调查取证，发现该网站擅自提供各类应用软件的下载使用，涉嫌侵犯著作权。依照《中华人民共和国著作权法》第四十八条和《中华人民共和国著作权法实施条例》，对当事人做出责令停止侵权行为、罚款人民币 1 万元的行政处罚。

七、潜江曹某侵权软件著作权案

2018 年 1 月，潜江市文化市场综合执法支队根据上级转办线索对域名为“uzzf. com”的网站进行了远程勘验，经查由当事人运营的网站——东坡下载（www. uzzf. com），提供明知或应知未经权利人许可被删除或者改变权利管理电子信息的作品。该网站未经权利人许可，通过信息网络向公众提供明知或应知未经权利人许可被删除或者改变权利管理电子信息的作品，上述行为违反了《信息网络传播权保护条例》第五条之规定，同时损害公共利益。

潜江市文化体育旅游新闻出版局对曹某做出了责令停止侵权行为、罚款1万元的行政处罚。

（湖北省版权局）

湖南省

一、“深度汽车音乐”网站侵犯音乐作品著作权案

根据国家版权局转交的国际唱片业协会的投诉函，新宁县文化市场综合执法大队对“深度汽车音乐”（www.shendumv.com）涉嫌侵权一案进行调查。经查，当事人邓某某未经录音制品制作者权利人许可且未支付报酬，通过开办深度汽车音乐网，擅自向公众提供他人享有著作权的400余首歌的录音制品供下载，违反了著作权法相关规定。

新宁县新闻出版文化广电局对邓某某处以没收违法所得人民币1 972元、罚款人民币5万元的行政处罚。

二、“网盘影视”网站侵犯影视作品著作权案

长沙市知识产权局根据国家版权局转交的国际唱片业协会的投诉函，发现“网盘影视”网站未经许可向公众提供他人享有著作权的电影在线播放服务，长沙市知识产权局执法人员进行了线上线下取证，确定了网站创办人为王某某。后经查实，王某某共提供了136部未经授权影片的免费供公众在线播放服务，侵犯了著作权人的信息网络传播权。

长沙市知识产权局责令王某某关闭网站，并处罚款人民币5 000元。

三、胡某某销售盗版图书案

娄底市文化市场综合执法支队根据群众举报，通过网络远程勘验发现，胡某某于2017年以来分别用李益新、柯小辉的身份证注册了“hexiaohui1735”“火影6003”两家淘宝店铺，2018年1月31日，支队通过杭州文化市场综合执法总队从淘宝公司调取了“hexiaohui1735”和“火影6003”两家店铺的后台交易数据。经统计：两家店铺合计销售盗版图书1 002册，非法获利2 700元，违法经营额41 551元。

娄底市局对当事人处以没收违法所得2 700元、罚款37 300元的行政处罚。

四、澧县创新计算机有限公司侵犯软件著作权案

常德市文化市场综合执法局根据群众举报，经执法人员现场检查发现，澧县创新计算机有限公司销售给澧县中医医院的电脑中装载的Windows 7旗舰版操作系统涉嫌盗版。执法人员按照立案、调查询问等步骤，最终查明了澧县创新计算机有限公司未经软件著作权人许可，故意避开或者破坏著作权人为保护其软件著作权而采取的技术措施，并且复制他人享有著作权的软件的违法事实。

常德市文化市场综合执法局遂责令其停止侵权行为，并处罚款人民币5 000元。

五、长沙市芙蓉区瑞某大酒店侵犯音乐作品著作权案

芙蓉区知识产权局根据福州大德文化传播有限公司的投诉，对瑞某大酒店涉嫌未经权利人许可，擅自复制并通过信息网络传播音乐作品的行为进行了检查，在点播系统中查到多部由投诉人管理的音乐作品。经查，当事人未经许可在KTV点播系统中使用著作权人的音乐作品，侵犯了权利人的复制、信息网络传播权。

芙蓉区知识产权局责令其停止侵权，罚款人民币15 000元。

六、李某侵犯文字作品著作权案

衡山县文化市场综合执法大队接举报电话后，对当事人李某涉嫌在衡山县岳云中学图书馆向学生发行盗版出版物的行为进行调查，发现李某不能提供合法的进货单据、手续，执法人员依据法律法规对3 062册（110件）图书进行证据保全，经广西师范大学等出版社鉴定并来函确认，被证据保全的图书中有378册属侵权出版物。后李某对擅自从盗版书商处进货向学生销售的行为供认不讳。

衡山县文体广电新闻出版局遂对其处以罚款24 000元。

七、博某数码专营店侵犯软件著作权案

岳阳市文化市场综合执法局根据举报发现岳阳市某贸易公司在淘宝天猫购物网站上注册的博某数码专营店未经著作权人授权许可，擅自拆分软件激活码向公众销售，此行为已构成未经著作权人许可，破坏其用于软件保护的技术措施，经查，该网店系岳阳市龙某贸易有限公司开办，共销售软件激活码及软件200余套。

岳阳市文化市场综合执法局遂对其处以没收违法所得3 760元人民币，责令下架其侵权商品，并罚款2万元人民币的行政处罚。

（湖南省版权局）

广东省

一、广州市龙某某、李某侵犯网络游戏著作权案

2017年6月始，龙某某、李某以营利为目的，

未经著作权人广州多益网络股份有限公司许可，在泰国利用电脑和远程控制软件架设、运营私服游戏《歪歪神武》，非法经营额达25万元以上。

2018年12月25日，广州市黄埔区人民法院做出刑事判决：龙某某犯侵犯著作权罪，判处有期徒刑二年，并处罚金人民币2万元；李某犯侵犯著作权罪，判处有期徒刑一年六个月，并处罚金人民币1万元。

二、广州市“MTV235在线手机电影天堂”网侵犯影视作品著作权案

2017年8月始，汤某某未经著作权人许可，在其建立、经营的“MTV235在线手机电影天堂”网站上，先后发布深圳市腾讯计算机系统有限公司、优酷网络技术（北京）有限公司等单位电影、电视作品584部11 324集供公众观看，并在该网站上投放广告，获利8 338.84元。

2018年4月18日，广州市白云区人民法院做出刑事判决：汤某某犯侵犯著作权罪，判处有期徒刑一年，并处罚金人民币4万元。后汤某某提出上诉。2018年6月26日，广州市中级人民法院做出终审判决：汤某某犯侵犯著作权罪，判处有期徒刑九个月，并处罚金人民币1万元。

三、广州市胡某某制售盗版图书案

2015年6月始，胡某某以营利为目的，纠集数人在广州市达林纸制品加工厂内大肆印制盗版图书。执法人员现场查获《约翰·汤普森简易钢琴教程1》等239种970 722册（张）出版物，经鉴定其中935 360册（张）为非法出版物。

2018年8月1日，广州市白云区人民法院做出刑事判决：胡某某犯侵犯著作权罪，判处有期徒刑三年，并处罚金人民币12万元。

四、深圳市胡某某销售盗版软件案

2017年3月始，胡某某以营利为目的，未经著作权人深圳市拓邦股份有限公司许可，擅自销售其软件，销售额11余万元。

2018年5月31日，深圳市南山区法院做出刑事判决：胡某某犯侵犯著作权罪，判处有期徒刑六个月，并处罚金人民币5万元。

五、深圳市西瓜影音科技有限公司侵犯影视作品著作权案

2018年9月，深圳市市场稽查局经调查，发现深圳市西瓜影音科技有限公司运营《电影天堂》APP，未经权利人许可，通过第三方网站提供的解析视频原代码方法，将“优酷视频”链接放入《电影天堂》APP，以此向手机用户提供相关影视作品在线播放及下载服务，并通过广告获利2 000元。

2018年12月10日，深圳市市场稽查局做出行政处罚：没收违法所得2 000元，罚款10 000元。

六、深圳市“好听轻音乐网”侵犯网络音乐作品著作权案

2017年11月1日，根据权利人国际唱片业协会投诉，深圳市市场稽查局调查发现，好听轻音乐网（www.htqyy.com）未经许可，通过网站向公众传播陈奕迅《十年》《好久不见》等音乐作品，违反了《信息网络传播权保护条例》相关规定。

2018年5月14日，深圳市市场稽查局做出行政处罚：罚款10 000元。

七、珠海市来魅力假日酒店侵犯影视作品著作权案

2018年6月22日，珠海市版权局执法人员在工作检查中发现，珠海市来魅力假日酒店未经授权，通过在客房电视上安装《盛阳智慧酒店服务平台》非法传播《红雀》等影视作品。

2018年11月15日，珠海市版权局做出行政处罚：责令停止侵权行为，罚款20 000元。

八、汕头市澄海区悦辉玩具厂侵犯美术作品著作权案

2018年5月18日，汕头市版权局会同汕头市文化市场综合执法大队在工作检查中发现，汕头市澄海区悦辉玩具厂未经著作权人许可擅自制售侵权玩具12 288只。

2018年7月6日，汕头市版权局做出行政处罚：没收侵权复制品12 288只和涉案电脑1台，罚款125 337.6元。

九、茂名市张某某等5人侵犯网络游戏著作权案

张某某、黄某某未经著作权人上海恺英科技有限公司授权，私自架设《全民奇迹》手机游戏私服。2018年1月份又陆续纠集刘某某、孙某、杨某某，组建“小苹果”团队，对外宣传推广《怀旧觉醒奇迹》，非法获利70余万元。

2018年12月11日，茂名市茂南区人民法院做出刑事判决：张某某犯侵犯著作权罪，判处有期徒刑三年，缓刑三年，并处罚金人民币65万元；黄某某犯侵犯著作权罪，判处有期徒刑一年六个月，并处罚金人民币65万元；孙某犯侵犯著作权罪，判处有期徒刑一年，缓刑一年六个月，并处罚金人民币20万元；刘某某犯侵犯著作权罪，判处有期徒刑九个月，并处罚金人民币15万元；杨某某犯侵犯著作权罪，判处有期徒刑八个月，缓刑一年，并处罚金人民币15万元。

十、茂名市“九头鸟书院”网侵犯网络文学作品著作权案

2015年始，柏某某运营“九头鸟书院”网（www.9wh.net），未经“起点中文网”授权，利用软件大量复制《世家名门》等作品，获利142 556.47元。

2018年2月6日，茂名市茂南区人民法院做出刑事判决：柏某某犯侵犯著作权罪，判处有期徒刑一年六个月，并处罚金人民币20万元。

（广东省委宣传部版权和印刷管理处）

四 川 省

一、成都“吹妖动漫”网侵犯著作权案

2016年10月，成都市文化市场综合执法总队依法对“吹妖动漫”网站开展远程勘验查实，该网站ICP备案号为“蜀ICP备14016877号-6”，主办单位为成都五二天科技有限公司，法定代表人孙某、技术总监朱某。该网站是开放的动漫作品网站，漫画作品共2万余部，以中、美、日、韩、欧等国和港台地区作品为主，大量动漫作品未经著作权人授权，无法提供著作权人授权证明，涉嫌违反《著作权法》及《刑法》有关规定。12月2日，成都市文化市场综合执法总队将此案移交公安机关，成都市公安局网安支队以涉嫌侵犯著作权罪对“吹妖动漫”网站经营者正式立案侦查。2017年5月12日，公安机关对孙某、朱某采取刑事拘留措施。6月16日，孙某被成都市人民检察院批准逮捕，朱某违法情节轻微被依法取保候审。8月3日，孙某被移送武侯区人民法院起诉，朱某不予起诉。

“吹妖动漫”网站经营者未经著作权人许可擅自使用其作品的行为违反了《刑法》第二百一十七条之规定。2018年9月25日，武侯区人民法院一审判决成都五二天科技有限公司犯侵犯著作权罪，判处罚金人民币18万元；孙某犯侵犯著作权罪，判处有期徒刑三年三个月，并处罚金人民币10万元；对成都五二天科技有限公司的违法所得187 414.5元继续予以追缴。

二、成都“11·18”涉嫌侵犯著作权案

2017年11月，成都市版权行政执法部门会同公安部门对成都天府新区某印刷厂进行检查，发现该印刷厂不能提供印刷经营许可证，其印刷品1.5万余册和相关PS版涉嫌侵权，并当场查获《同步练习册语文二年级下册》（藏文）、《天欣驾校机动车驾驶人科目一考试题库》、《实验班提优训练》（八年级语文·上）等印刷品，共计26个品种，15 160册。其中，藏文印刷品11个品种，共计1 538册。经鉴定，送检的7种图书均为非法出版物，涉嫌违反《刑法》第二百一十七条之规定。

2018年11月23日，成都市双流区人民法院依法对6名涉案人员以侵犯著作权罪做出判决：被告人伍某某犯侵犯著作权罪，判处有期徒刑四年六个月，并处罚金人民币40万元；被告人张某某犯侵犯著作权罪，判处有期徒刑三年六个月，并处罚金人民币20万元；被告人蒋某某犯侵犯著作权罪，判处有期徒刑三年，并处罚金人民币5万元；被告人顾某某犯侵犯著作权罪，判处有期徒刑三年，缓刑四年，并处罚金人民币5万元；被告人刘某某犯侵犯著作权罪，判处有期徒刑一年，缓刑一年，并处罚金人民币5 000元；被告人李某犯侵犯著作权罪，判处有期徒刑一年，缓刑一年，并处罚金人民币5 000元。

三、绵阳麦慕咖啡店侵犯电影作品著作权案

2018年1月10日，四川省绵阳市文化市场综合执法支队依法对位于绵阳市涪城区临园路的麦慕咖啡店进行检查，发现该经营场所共有22间放映室，1间储存影片的服务器机房，其点播影片《奇门遁甲》《羞羞的铁拳》等共计399部影片无法提供著作权人授权证明，疑似为侵权影片，涉嫌违反《著作权法》有关规定。执法人员现场责令麦慕咖啡店立即停止违法经营活动，开具《调查询问通知书》要求其法定代表人接受进一步调查询问。1月16日，绵阳市文化市场综合执法支队对麦慕咖啡店涉嫌违反《著作权法》行为正式立案调查。2018年1月12日、24日、31日，该公司法定代表人傅某和该场所负责人张某分别接受调查询问，承认违法事实。经查，该场所非法经营额124 650.86元。

麦慕咖啡店未经著作权人许可擅自放映其作品行为违反了《著作权法》的规定。2018年2月5日，绵阳市文化广电新闻出版局依据《著作权法》第四十八条第（一）项、《著作权法实施条例》第三十六条的规定，对当事人做出罚款人民币13万元的行政处罚。

四、刘某、邵某某涉嫌侵犯网络游戏著作权案

2018年4月25日，经成都市公安局新都区分局会同成都市公安局网安支队、成都市文化市场综合执法总队查实，2017年9月至2018年4月期间，刘某伙同邵某某通过非法途径获取北京畅游时代数码技术有限公司的网络游戏《天龙八部OL》源代码，私自架设《巨星天龙》网络游戏服务器，并通过郭某租用虎牙直播平台账号对该私服游戏进行宣传推广。邵某某负责技术支持，对北京畅游时代数码技

术有限公司的网络游戏《天龙八部 OL》游戏源代码进行修改，并帮助刘某租赁游戏服务器，从而在刘某处获得经济利益。该网络游戏上线运营以来，刘某等人共获利 90 余万元。

刘某等人行为违反《著作权法》及《刑法》的规定，涉嫌侵犯著作权罪。2018 年 6 月 22 日，成都市公安局新都区分局对 7 名涉案人员采取强制措施，其中刘某、邵某某、郭某等 3 人被执行逮捕，杨某某、雷某、郑某某等 3 人被执行拘留，杨某取保候审。该案件已由成都市新都区检察院向新都区法院提起刑事诉讼。

五、泸州"6·8"侵犯著作权案

2017 年 6 月 8 日，泸州市公安局根据权利人投诉，调查核实犯罪嫌疑人陈某在未经"精准脱贫"题材电影《大地赤子——史来贺》投资方河南前卫文化传媒有限公司、北京春迪梦源影视文化有限公司授权的情况下，聘用他人以中共中央国家机关工委办公室《关于组织党员干部观看电影〈大地赤子〉的通知》名义，骗取泸州市直机关工委、市教育局等部门联合发文，在泸州四县三区组织党员干部观看电影《大地赤子——史来贺》。泸州 200 余家单位组织观看，涉案金额 100 余万元。

陈某的行为违反了《著作权法》及《刑法》第二百一十七条的规定。2018 年 12 月 10 日，泸州市江阳区人民法院做出刑事判决：被告人陈某犯侵犯著作权罪，判处有期徒刑二年，缓刑三年，并处罚金人民币 15 万元，违法所得财物依法予以追缴。

六、四川博文网络科技有限责任公司侵犯著作权案

2018 年 5 月，经遂宁市射洪县文化广电新闻出版局查实，四川博文网络科技有限责任公司未经权利人许可，将权利人发表于《图书馆建设》期刊的文章，通过"学术之家"网站向公众提供自由浏览及下载服务。6 月 18 日，射洪县文化广电新闻出版局对该公司涉嫌侵犯权利人著作权行为正式立案调查。

经查实，四川博文网络科技有限责任公司"学术之家"网站上述行为，违反了《信息网络传播权保护条例》第二条之规定，同时损害公共利益。射洪县文化广电新闻出版局责令该公司停止侵权行为、消除影响，并做出罚款人民币 2 万元的行政处罚。

（四川省版权局）

陕 西 省

一、文汇书店未经著作权人许可发行其作品案

2018 年 11 月 1 日，西安市文化执法总队在西安市碑林区文汇书店进行执法检查中，抽检了《肖秀荣考研政治命题人考点预测》《肖秀荣考研政治命题人 1000 题》等 5 种出版物，该店负责人现场不能提供进货手续。执法人员依据《行政处罚法》第三十七条之规定，对以上出版物依法进行抽样取证。随后进一步查证《肖秀荣考研政治命题人考点预测》《肖秀荣考研政治命题人 1000 题》等 4 种出版物为侵犯专有出版权的非法出版物。2018 年 11 月 1 日、12 日，西安市碑林区文汇书店负责人到总队接受询问调查，承认该书店的违法事实，该经营行为违反了《著作权法》第四十八条第（一）项之规定。该单位被处以：(1) 没收侵权出版物 32 本；(2) 行政处罚 3 000 元人民币。

二、陕西省科技资源统筹中心未经著作权人许可发行其作品案

2018 年 9 月 7 日，西安市文化执法总队接到上级转办案件，对陕西省科技资源统筹中心在培训期间涉嫌未经著作权人许可发行其作品一案进行调查。同日，陕西省科技资源统筹中心授权委托人雷某接受调查。执法人员向授权委托人雷某出示执法证件，表明身份依法进行调查询问。调查中执法人员要求雷某提供涉案的《专业技术人员诚信建设培训教程》《专业技术人员常用法律知识培训教程》《中国传统文化概论》3 种出版物的进货发票及进货单位发行资质。授权委托人雷某只能提供进货发票，但不能提供进货单位的发行资质。执法人员依据《行政处罚法》第三十七条之规定，对以上 3 种出版物依法进行抽样取证。2018 年 9 月 10 日，经批准立案开展调查工作。经调查：陕西省科技资源统筹中心在从事培训过程中，所发行的《专业技术人员诚信建设培训教程》《专业技术人员常用法律知识培训教程》《中国传统文化概论》3 种出版物不能提供进货单位的发行资质。同时，经国家行政学院出版社、高等教育出版社有限公司鉴定，以上 3 种出版物为侵权出版物。2018 年 9 月 7 日、20 日，陕西省科技资源统筹中心授权委托人雷某到总队接受询问调查，承认该单位的违规经营事实，该经营行为违反了《著作权法》第四十八条第（一）项之规定。该单位被处以：(1) 没收侵权出版物 315 本；(2) 行政处罚 30 000 元人民币。

三、西邮书屋未经著作权人许可发行其作品案

2018年4月23日，西安市文化执法总队到西安市长安区西邮书屋检查。在检查中执法人员抽检了《中级财务管理》《中级会计实务》等10种出版物，法定代表人姚某某现场不能提供进货手续。执法人员依据《行政处罚法》第三十七条之规定，对以上10种出版物依法进行抽样取证。经调查：西安市长安区西邮书屋在从事图书经营过程中，所销售的《中级财务管理》《中级会计实务》等10种出版物无进货票据，是从非出版发行单位进货的。同时，经陕西省印刷产品质量检测中心鉴定，《中级财务管理》《中级会计实务》等10种出版物为侵权出版物。2018年5月3日、6月28日，西安市长安区西邮书屋法定代表人姚某某到总队接受询问调查，承认该书店的违规经营事实，该经营行为违反了《著作权法》第四十八条第（一）项之规定。该单位被处以：（1）没收侵权出版物12本；（2）行政处罚3 000元人民币。

四、智海书店未经著作权人许可发行其作品案

2018年4月26日，西安市文化执法总队到西安市长安区智海书店检查。执法人员向法定代表人吴某出示执法证件，表明来意后依法检查该场所。在检查中执法人员抽检了《经济法》《税法》等8种出版物，法定代表人吴某现场不能提供进货手续。执法人员依据《行政处罚法》第三十七条之规定，对以上8种出版物依法进行抽样取证。经调查：西安市长安区智海书店在从事图书经营过程中，所销售的《经济法》《税法》等8种出版物无进货票据，是从非出版发行单位进货的。同时，经陕西省印刷产品质量检测中心鉴定，《经济法》《税法》等8种出版物为侵权出版物。2018年5月3日、6月28日，西安市长安区智海书店法定代表人吴某到西安市文化执法总队接受询问调查，承认该书店的违规经营事实，该经营行为违反了《著作权法》第四十八条第（一）项之规定。该单位被处以：（1）没收侵权出版物10本；（2）行政处罚3 000元人民币。

五、睿智书店未经著作权人许可发行其作品案

2018年4月26日，西安市文化执法总队到西安市长安区睿智书店检查。执法人员向法定代表人李某某出示执法证件，表明来意后依法检查该场所。在检查中执法人员抽检了《税法》《中级会计实务》等7种出版物，法定代表人李某某现场不能提供进货手续。执法人员依据《行政处罚法》第三十七条之规定，对以上7种出版物依法进行抽样取证。经调查：西安市长安区睿智书店在从事图书经营过程中，所销售的《税法》《中级会计实务》等7种出版物无进货票据，是从非出版发行单位进货的。同时，经陕西省印刷产品质量检测中心鉴定，《税法》《中级会计实务》等7种出版物为侵权出版物。2018年5月3日、6月28日，西安市长安区睿智书店法定代表人李某某到西安市文化执法总队接受询问调查，承认该书店的违规经营事实，该经营行为违反了《著作权法》第四十八条第（一）项之规定。该单位被处以：（1）没收侵权出版物9本；（2）行政处罚3 000元人民币。

六、榆林市卓讯商贸有限公司、榆林市天和中智实业有限公司未经著作权人许可复制其作品系列案

2018年初，横山区文体广电局接陕西省版权局电话通知，有几家公司在榆林市横山区教育局城区学校教育教学设备设施采购项目中采购的电脑中提供盗版软件侵犯著作权，便立即召开会议并成立调查小组，随后约谈横山区教育局得知：榆林市横山区教育局委托陕西中财招标代理有限公司，经政府采购管理部门批准，按照政府采购程序，对榆林市横山区教育局城区学校教育教学设备设施采购项目（采购项目编号：SXZC2017－HW－007）进行公开招标、投标。榆林市横山区教育局提供的招标文件显示，在这次采购项目中有一家N6标段中标公司叫榆林市卓讯商贸有限公司，N6标段中标公司（榆林市卓讯商贸有限公司）在采购电脑中涉及的学校有横山区第七小学、横山区第二中学、横山区第六小学、横山区第八小学。N3标段中标公司（榆林市天和中智实业有限公司）在采购电脑中涉及的学校有横山区第三中学。教育局在招标文件中明确规定，要求采购的电脑中：教师电脑或管理电脑系统为正版Windows 7 64位Pro版操作系统，每台机身均需贴COA标贴，微软正版可查，安装正版WPS Office 2016教育版文档处理类办公软件（包括Word，Excel，PPT，金山词霸）并提供原厂商针对本项目的授权书原件和售后服务承诺函原件。原厂三年有限保修及上门，服务体系通过CCC认证。为确认是否侵权，在2018年5月31日11时20分至2018年5月31日12时28分，横山区文体广电局执法人员，赴横山区第七小学、横山区第二中学、横山区第八小学、横山区第六小学、横山区第三中学对共285台电脑依法进行现场检查。根据现场检查情况，两家公司未能提供授权许可、合同等相关手续，其行为违反了《中华人民共和国著作权法》第四十八条第（一）项的规定。执法人员当即责令其停止侵权行为，立即卸载侵权软件，随后调查取证并进行立案查处。经查，给予榆林市卓讯商贸有限公司以下处罚：(1) 罚款 23 400 元；(2) 立即卸载侵权软件。给予榆林市天和中智实业有限公司以下处罚：(1) 罚款 5 100 元；(2) 立即卸载侵权软件。

（陕西省版权局）

青海省

盛志营侵犯著作权案

2018 年 3 月 27 日，西宁市城中区文化市场综合执法大队与区公安分局联合执法检查，在西宁市城中区南川东路水磨村 9 号发现一涉嫌无证经营的非法印刷作坊。经查：该印刷作坊涉嫌非法盗印，现场查获《颂词汇编》、《现观论集》、《四部医典注释》(上)、《普贤上师言教》等书籍 14 792 册，非法经营额共计 387 788 元，经鉴定全部为非法、盗版出版物。

依据《中华人民共和国刑法》第二百一十七条第（一）项，第七十二条第一款、第三款，第七十三条第二款、第三款，第五十二条，第六十四条之规定，2019 年 1 月 31 日，西宁市城中区人民法院判决如下：被告人盛志营犯侵犯著作权罪，判处有期徒刑三年，缓刑三年，并处罚金人民币 30 000 元；被告人盛志营退缴的违法所得 20 000 元，依法没收，上缴国库；随案移送的扫描仪 1 台、电脑 1 台、手机 1 部及书籍等物品，留作证据保存。

（青海省版权局）

法律法规及规章文件

FA LYU FA GUI JI GUI ZHANG WEN JIAN

中华人民共和国电子商务法

（2018年8月31日第十三届全国人民代表大会常务委员会第五次会议通过）

第一章 总 则

第一条 为了保障电子商务各方主体的合法权益，规范电子商务行为，维护市场秩序，促进电子商务持续健康发展，制定本法。

第二条 中华人民共和国境内的电子商务活动，适用本法。

本法所称电子商务，是指通过互联网等信息网络销售商品或者提供服务的经营活动。

法律、行政法规对销售商品或者提供服务有规定的，适用其规定。金融类产品和服务，利用信息网络提供新闻信息、音视频节目、出版以及文化产品等内容方面的服务，不适用本法。

第三条 国家鼓励发展电子商务新业态，创新商业模式，促进电子商务技术研发和推广应用，推进电子商务诚信体系建设，营造有利于电子商务创新发展的市场环境，充分发挥电子商务在推动高质量发展、满足人民日益增长的美好生活需要、构建开放型经济方面的重要作用。

第四条 国家平等对待线上线下商务活动，促进线上线下融合发展，各级人民政府和有关部门不得采取歧视性的政策措施，不得滥用行政权力排除、限制市场竞争。

第五条 电子商务经营者从事经营活动，应当遵循自愿、平等、公平、诚信的原则，遵守法律和商业道德，公平参与市场竞争，履行消费者权益保护、环境保护、知识产权保护、网络安全与个人信息保护等方面的义务，承担产品和服务质量责任，接受政府和社会的监督。

第六条 国务院有关部门按照职责分工负责电子商务发展促进、监督管理等工作。县级以上地方各级人民政府可以根据本行政区域的实际情况，确定本行政区域内电子商务的部门职责划分。

第七条 国家建立符合电子商务特点的协同管理体系，推动形成有关部门、电子商务行业组织、电子商务经营者、消费者等共同参与的电子商务市场治理体系。

第八条 电子商务行业组织按照本组织章程开展行业自律，建立健全行业规范，推动行业诚信建设，监督、引导本行业经营者公平参与市场竞争。

第二章 电子商务经营者

第一节 一般规定

第九条 本法所称电子商务经营者，是指通过互联网等信息网络从事销售商品或者提供服务的经营活动的自然人、法人和非法人组织，包括电子商务平台经营者、平台内经营者以及通过自建网站、其他网络服务销售商品或者提供服务的电子商务经营者。

本法所称电子商务平台经营者，是指在电子商务中为交易双方或者多方提供网络经营场所、交易撮合、信息发布等服务，供交易双方或者多方独立开展交易活动的法人或者非法人组织。

本法所称平台内经营者，是指通过电子商务平台销售商品或者提供服务的电子商务经营者。

第十条 电子商务经营者应当依法办理市场主体登记。但是，个人销售自产农副产品、家庭手工业产品，个人利用自己的技能从事依法无须取得许可的便民劳务活动和零星小额交易活动，以及依照法律、行政法规不需要进行登记的除外。

第十一条 电子商务经营者应当依法履行纳税义务，并依法享受税收优惠。

依照前条规定不需要办理市场主体登记的电子商务经营者在首次纳税义务发生后，应当依照税收征收管理法律、行政法规的规定申请办理税务登记，并如实申报纳税。

第十二条 电子商务经营者从事经营活动，依法需要取得相关行政许可的，应当依法取得行政许可。

第十三条 电子商务经营者销售的商品或者提供的服务应当符合保障人身、财产安全的要求和环境保护要求，不得销售或者提供法律、行政法规禁止交易的商品或者服务。

第十四条 电子商务经营者销售商品或者提供服务应当依法出具纸质发票或者电子发票等购货凭

证或者服务单据。电子发票与纸质发票具有同等法律效力。

第十五条　电子商务经营者应当在其首页显著位置，持续公示营业执照信息、与其经营业务有关的行政许可信息、属于依照本法第十条规定的不需要办理市场主体登记情形等信息，或者上述信息的链接标识。

前款规定的信息发生变更的，电子商务经营者应当及时更新公示信息。

第十六条　电子商务经营者自行终止从事电子商务的，应当提前三十日在首页显著位置持续公示有关信息。

第十七条　电子商务经营者应当全面、真实、准确、及时地披露商品或者服务信息，保障消费者的知情权和选择权。电子商务经营者不得以虚构交易、编造用户评价等方式进行虚假或者引人误解的商业宣传，欺骗、误导消费者。

第十八条　电子商务经营者根据消费者的兴趣爱好、消费习惯等特征向其提供商品或者服务的搜索结果的，应当同时向该消费者提供不针对其个人特征的选项，尊重和平等保护消费者合法权益。

电子商务经营者向消费者发送广告的，应当遵守《中华人民共和国广告法》的有关规定。

第十九条　电子商务经营者搭售商品或者服务，应当以显著方式提请消费者注意，不得将搭售商品或者服务作为默认同意的选项。

第二十条　电子商务经营者应当按照承诺或者与消费者约定的方式、时限向消费者交付商品或者服务，并承担商品运输中的风险和责任。但是，消费者另行选择快递物流服务提供者的除外。

第二十一条　电子商务经营者按照约定向消费者收取押金的，应当明示押金退还的方式、程序，不得对押金退还设置不合理条件。消费者申请退还押金，符合押金退还条件的，电子商务经营者应当及时退还。

第二十二条　电子商务经营者因其技术优势、用户数量、对相关行业的控制能力以及其他经营者对该电子商务经营者在交易上的依赖程度等因素而具有市场支配地位的，不得滥用市场支配地位，排除、限制竞争。

第二十三条　电子商务经营者收集、使用其用户的个人信息，应当遵守法律、行政法规有关个人信息保护的规定。

第二十四条　电子商务经营者应当明示用户信息查询、更正、删除以及用户注销的方式、程序，不得对用户信息查询、更正、删除以及用户注销设置不合理条件。

电子商务经营者收到用户信息查询或者更正、删除的申请的，应当在核实身份后及时提供查询或者更正、删除用户信息。用户注销的，电子商务经营者应当立即删除该用户的信息；依照法律、行政法规的规定或者双方约定保存的，依照其规定。

第二十五条　有关主管部门依照法律、行政法规的规定要求电子商务经营者提供有关电子商务数据信息的，电子商务经营者应当提供。有关主管部门应当采取必要措施保护电子商务经营者提供的数据信息的安全，并对其中的个人信息、隐私和商业秘密严格保密，不得泄露、出售或者非法向他人提供。

第二十六条　电子商务经营者从事跨境电子商务，应当遵守进出口监督管理的法律、行政法规和国家有关规定。

第二节　电子商务平台经营者

第二十七条　电子商务平台经营者应当要求申请进入平台销售商品或者提供服务的经营者提交其身份、地址、联系方式、行政许可等真实信息，进行核验、登记，建立登记档案，并定期核验更新。

电子商务平台经营者为进入平台销售商品或者提供服务的非经营用户提供服务，应当遵守本节有关规定。

第二十八条　电子商务平台经营者应当按照规定向市场监督管理部门报送平台内经营者的身份信息，提示未办理市场主体登记的经营者依法办理登记，并配合市场监督管理部门，针对电子商务的特点，为应当办理市场主体登记的经营者办理登记提供便利。

电子商务平台经营者应当依照税收征收管理法律、行政法规的规定，向税务部门报送平台内经营者的身份信息和与纳税有关的信息，并应当提示依照本法第十条规定不需要办理市场主体登记的电子商务经营者依照本法第十一条第二款的规定办理税务登记。

第二十九条　电子商务平台经营者发现平台内的商品或者服务信息存在违反本法第十二条、第十三条规定情形的，应当依法采取必要的处置措施，并向有关主管部门报告。

第三十条　电子商务平台经营者应当采取技术措施和其他必要措施保证其网络安全、稳定运行，防范网络违法犯罪活动，有效应对网络安全事件，保障电子商务交易安全。

电子商务平台经营者应当制定网络安全事件应急预案，发生网络安全事件时，应当立即启动应急预案，采取相应的补救措施，并向有关主管部门报告。

第三十一条　电子商务平台经营者应当记录、保存平台上发布的商品和服务信息、交易信息，并确保信息的完整性、保密性、可用性。商品和服务信息、交易信息保存时间自交易完成之日起不少于三年；法律、行政法规另有规定的，依照其规定。

第三十二条　电子商务平台经营者应当遵循公开、公平、公正的原则，制定平台服务协议和交易规则，明确进入和退出平台、商品和服务质量保障、消费者权益保护、个人信息保护等方面的权利和义务。

第三十三条　电子商务平台经营者应当在其首页显著位置持续公示平台服务协议和交易规则信息或者上述信息的链接标识，并保证经营者和消费者能够便利、完整地阅览和下载。

第三十四条　电子商务平台经营者修改平台服务协议和交易规则，应当在其首页显著位置公开征求意见，采取合理措施确保有关各方能够及时充分表达意见。修改内容应当至少在实施前七日予以公示。

平台内经营者不接受修改内容，要求退出平台的，电子商务平台经营者不得阻止，并按照修改前的服务协议和交易规则承担相关责任。

第三十五条　电子商务平台经营者不得利用服务协议、交易规则以及技术等手段，对平台内经营者在平台内的交易、交易价格以及与其他经营者的交易等进行不合理限制或者附加不合理条件，或者向平台内经营者收取不合理费用。

第三十六条　电子商务平台经营者依据平台服务协议和交易规则对平台内经营者违反法律、法规的行为实施警示、暂停或者终止服务等措施的，应当及时公示。

第三十七条　电子商务平台经营者在其平台上开展自营业务的，应当以显著方式区分标记自营业务和平台内经营者开展的业务，不得误导消费者。

电子商务平台经营者对其标记为自营的业务依法承担商品销售者或者服务提供者的民事责任。

第三十八条　电子商务平台经营者知道或者应当知道平台内经营者销售的商品或者提供的服务不符合保障人身、财产安全的要求，或者有其他侵害消费者合法权益行为，未采取必要措施的，依法与该平台内经营者承担连带责任。

对关系消费者生命健康的商品或者服务，电子商务平台经营者对平台内经营者的资质资格未尽到审核义务，或者对消费者未尽到安全保障义务，造成消费者损害的，依法承担相应的责任。

第三十九条　电子商务平台经营者应当建立健全信用评价制度，公示信用评价规则，为消费者提供对平台内销售的商品或者提供的服务进行评价的途径。

电子商务平台经营者不得删除消费者对其平台内销售的商品或者提供的服务的评价。

第四十条　电子商务平台经营者应当根据商品或者服务的价格、销量、信用等以多种方式向消费者显示商品或者服务的搜索结果；对于竞价排名的商品或者服务，应当显著标明“广告”。

第四十一条　电子商务平台经营者应当建立知识产权保护规则，与知识产权权利人加强合作，依法保护知识产权。

第四十二条　知识产权权利人认为其知识产权受到侵害的，有权通知电子商务平台经营者采取删除、屏蔽、断开链接、终止交易和服务等必要措施。通知应当包括构成侵权的初步证据。

电子商务平台经营者接到通知后，应当及时采取必要措施，并将该通知转送平台内经营者；未及时采取必要措施的，对损害的扩大部分与平台内经营者承担连带责任。

因通知错误造成平台内经营者损害的，依法承担民事责任。恶意发出错误通知，造成平台内经营者损失的，加倍承担赔偿责任。

第四十三条　平台内经营者接到转送的通知后，可以向电子商务平台经营者提交不存在侵权行为的声明。声明应当包括不存在侵权行为的初步证据。

电子商务平台经营者接到声明后，应当将该声明转送发出通知的知识产权权利人，并告知其可以向有关主管部门投诉或者向人民法院起诉。电子商务平台经营者在转送声明到达知识产权权利人后十五日内，未收到权利人已经投诉或者起诉通知的，应当及时终止所采取的措施。

第四十四条　电子商务平台经营者应当及时公示收到的本法第四十二条、第四十三条规定的通知、声明及处理结果。

第四十五条　电子商务平台经营者知道或者应当知道平台内经营者侵犯知识产权的，应当采取删除、屏蔽、断开链接、终止交易和服务等必要措施；未采取必要措施的，与侵权人承担连带责任。

第四十六条　除本法第九条第二款规定的服务外，电子商务平台经营者可以按照平台服务协议和交易规则，为经营者之间的电子商务提供仓储、物流、支付结算、交收等服务。电子商务平台经营者为经营者之间的电子商务提供服务，应当遵守法律、行政法规和国家有关规定，不得采取集中竞价、做市商等集中交易方式进行交易，不得进行标准化合约交易。

第三章　电子商务合同的订立与履行

第四十七条　电子商务当事人订立和履行合同，适用本章和《中华人民共和国民法总则》《中华人民共和国合同法》《中华人民共和国电子签名法》等法律的规定。

第四十八条　电子商务当事人使用自动信息系统订立或者履行合同的行为对使用该系统的当事人具有法律效力。

在电子商务中推定当事人具有相应的民事行为能力。但是，有相反证据足以推翻的除外。

第四十九条　电子商务经营者发布的商品或者服务信息符合要约条件的，用户选择该商品或者服务并提交订单成功，合同成立。当事人另有约定的，从其约定。

电子商务经营者不得以格式条款等方式约定消费者支付价款后合同不成立；格式条款等含有该内容的，其内容无效。

第五十条　电子商务经营者应当清晰、全面、明确地告知用户订立合同的步骤、注意事项、下载方法等事项，并保证用户能够便利、完整地阅览和下载。

电子商务经营者应当保证用户在提交订单前可以更正输入错误。

第五十一条　合同标的为交付商品并采用快递物流方式交付的，收货人签收时间为交付时间。合同标的为提供服务的，生成的电子凭证或者实物凭证中载明的时间为交付时间；前述凭证没有载明时间或者载明时间与实际提供服务时间不一致的，实际提供服务的时间为交付时间。

合同标的为采用在线传输方式交付的，合同标的进入对方当事人指定的特定系统并且能够检索识别的时间为交付时间。

合同当事人对交付方式、交付时间另有约定的，从其约定。

第五十二条　电子商务当事人可以约定采用快递物流方式交付商品。

快递物流服务提供者为电子商务提供快递物流服务，应当遵守法律、行政法规，并应当符合承诺的服务规范和时限。快递物流服务提供者在交付商品时，应当提示收货人当面查验；交由他人代收的，应当经收货人同意。

快递物流服务提供者应当按照规定使用环保包装材料，实现包装材料的减量化和再利用。

快递物流服务提供者在提供快递物流服务的同时，可以接受电子商务经营者的委托提供代收货款服务。

第五十三条　电子商务当事人可以约定采用电子支付方式支付价款。

电子支付服务提供者为电子商务提供电子支付服务，应当遵守国家规定，告知用户电子支付服务的功能、使用方法、注意事项、相关风险和收费标准等事项，不得附加不合理交易条件。电子支付服务提供者应当确保电子支付指令的完整性、一致性、可跟踪稽核和不可篡改。

电子支付服务提供者应当向用户免费提供对账服务以及最近三年的交易记录。

第五十四条　电子支付服务提供者提供电子支付服务不符合国家有关支付安全管理要求，造成用户损失的，应当承担赔偿责任。

第五十五条　用户在发出支付指令前，应当核对支付指令所包含的金额、收款人等完整信息。

支付指令发生错误的，电子支付服务提供者应当及时查找原因，并采取相关措施予以纠正。造成用户损失的，电子支付服务提供者应当承担赔偿责任，但能够证明支付错误非自身原因造成的除外。

第五十六条　电子支付服务提供者完成电子支付后，应当及时准确地向用户提供符合约定方式的确认支付的信息。

第五十七条　用户应当妥善保管交易密码、电子签名数据等安全工具。用户发现安全工具遗失、被盗用或者未经授权的支付的，应当及时通知电子支付服务提供者。

未经授权的支付造成的损失，由电子支付服务提供者承担；电子支付服务提供者能够证明未经授权的支付是因用户的过错造成的，不承担责任。

电子支付服务提供者发现支付指令未经授权，或者收到用户支付指令未经授权的通知时，应当立即采取措施防止损失扩大。电子支付服务提供者未及时采取措施导致损失扩大的，对损失扩大部分承担责任。

第四章　电子商务争议解决

第五十八条　国家鼓励电子商务平台经营者建

立有利于电子商务发展和消费者权益保护的商品、服务质量担保机制。

电子商务平台经营者与平台内经营者协议设立消费者权益保证金的，双方应当就消费者权益保证金的提取数额、管理、使用和退还办法等作出明确约定。

消费者要求电子商务平台经营者承担先行赔偿责任以及电子商务平台经营者赔偿后向平台内经营者的追偿，适用《中华人民共和国消费者权益保护法》的有关规定。

第五十九条　电子商务经营者应当建立便捷、有效的投诉、举报机制，公开投诉、举报方式等信息，及时受理并处理投诉、举报。

第六十条　电子商务争议可以通过协商和解，请求消费者组织、行业协会或者其他依法成立的调解组织调解，向有关部门投诉，提请仲裁，或者提起诉讼等方式解决。

第六十一条　消费者在电子商务平台购买商品或者接受服务，与平台内经营者发生争议时，电子商务平台经营者应当积极协助消费者维护合法权益。

第六十二条　在电子商务争议处理中，电子商务经营者应当提供原始合同和交易记录。因电子商务经营者丢失、伪造、篡改、销毁、隐匿或者拒绝提供前述资料，致使人民法院、仲裁机构或者有关机关无法查明事实的，电子商务经营者应当承担相应的法律责任。

第六十三条　电子商务平台经营者可以建立争议在线解决机制，制定并公示争议解决规则，根据自愿原则，公平、公正地解决当事人的争议。

第五章　电子商务促进

第六十四条　国务院和省、自治区、直辖市人民政府应当将电子商务发展纳入国民经济和社会发展规划，制定科学合理的产业政策，促进电子商务创新发展。

第六十五条　国务院和县级以上地方人民政府及其有关部门应当采取措施，支持、推动绿色包装、仓储、运输，促进电子商务绿色发展。

第六十六条　国家推动电子商务基础设施和物流网络建设，完善电子商务统计制度，加强电子商务标准体系建设。

第六十七条　国家推动电子商务在国民经济各个领域的应用，支持电子商务与各产业融合发展。

第六十八条　国家促进农业生产、加工、流通等环节的互联网技术应用，鼓励各类社会资源加强合作，促进农村电子商务发展，发挥电子商务在精准扶贫中的作用。

第六十九条　国家维护电子商务交易安全，保护电子商务用户信息，鼓励电子商务数据开发应用，保障电子商务数据依法有序自由流动。

国家采取措施推动建立公共数据共享机制，促进电子商务经营者依法利用公共数据。

第七十条　国家支持依法设立的信用评价机构开展电子商务信用评价，向社会提供电子商务信用评价服务。

第七十一条　国家促进跨境电子商务发展，建立健全适应跨境电子商务特点的海关、税收、进出境检验检疫、支付结算等管理制度，提高跨境电子商务各环节便利化水平，支持跨境电子商务平台经营者等为跨境电子商务提供仓储物流、报关、报检等服务。

国家支持小型微型企业从事跨境电子商务。

第七十二条　国家进出口管理部门应当推进跨境电子商务海关申报、纳税、检验检疫等环节的综合服务和监管体系建设，优化监管流程，推动实现信息共享、监管互认、执法互助，提高跨境电子商务服务和监管效率。跨境电子商务经营者可以凭电子单证向国家进出口管理部门办理有关手续。

第七十三条　国家推动建立与不同国家、地区之间跨境电子商务的交流合作，参与电子商务国际规则的制定，促进电子签名、电子身份等国际互认。

国家推动建立与不同国家、地区之间的跨境电子商务争议解决机制。

第六章　法律责任

第七十四条　电子商务经营者销售商品或者提供服务，不履行合同义务或者履行合同义务不符合约定，或者造成他人损害的，依法承担民事责任。

第七十五条　电子商务经营者违反本法第十二条、第十三条规定，未取得相关行政许可从事经营活动，或者销售、提供法律、行政法规禁止交易的商品、服务，或者不履行本法第二十五条规定的信息提供义务，电子商务平台经营者违反本法第四十六条规定，采取集中交易方式进行交易，或者进行标准化合约交易的，依照有关法律、行政法规的规定处罚。

第七十六条　电子商务经营者违反本法规定，有下列行为之一的，由市场监督管理部门责令限期改正，可以处一万元以下的罚款，对其中的电子商务平台经营者，依照本法第八十一条第一款的规定处罚：

（一）未在首页显著位置公示营业执照信息、行政许可信息、属于不需要办理市场主体登记情形等信息，或者上述信息的链接标识的；

（二）未在首页显著位置持续公示终止电子商务的有关信息的；

（三）未明示用户信息查询、更正、删除以及用户注销的方式、程序，或者对用户信息查询、更正、删除以及用户注销设置不合理条件的。

电子商务平台经营者对违反前款规定的平台内经营者未采取必要措施的，由市场监督管理部门责令限期改正，可以处二万元以上十万元以下的罚款。

第七十七条　电子商务经营者违反本法第十八条第一款规定提供搜索结果，或者违反本法第十九条规定搭售商品、服务的，由市场监督管理部门责令限期改正，没收违法所得，可以并处五万元以上二十万元以下的罚款；情节严重的，并处二十万元以上五十万元以下的罚款。

第七十八条　电子商务经营者违反本法第二十一条规定，未向消费者明示押金退还的方式、程序，对押金退还设置不合理条件，或者不及时退还押金的，由有关主管部门责令限期改正，可以处五万元以上二十万元以下的罚款；情节严重的，处二十万元以上五十万元以下的罚款。

第七十九条　电子商务经营者违反法律、行政法规有关个人信息保护的规定，或者不履行本法第三十条和有关法律、行政法规规定的网络安全保障义务的，依照《中华人民共和国网络安全法》等法律、行政法规的规定处罚。

第八十条　电子商务平台经营者有下列行为之一的，由有关主管部门责令限期改正；逾期不改正的，处二万元以上十万元以下的罚款；情节严重的，责令停业整顿，并处十万元以上五十万元以下的罚款：

（一）不履行本法第二十七条规定的核验、登记义务的；

（二）不按照本法第二十八条规定向市场监督管理部门、税务部门报送有关信息的；

（三）不按照本法第二十九条规定对违法情形采取必要的处置措施，或者未向有关主管部门报告的；

（四）不履行本法第三十一条规定的商品和服务信息、交易信息保存义务的。

法律、行政法规对前款规定的违法行为的处罚另有规定的，依照其规定。

第八十一条　电子商务平台经营者违反本法规定，有下列行为之一的，由市场监督管理部门责令限期改正，可以处二万元以上十万元以下的罚款；情节严重的，处十万元以上五十万元以下的罚款：

（一）未在首页显著位置持续公示平台服务协议、交易规则信息或者上述信息的链接标识的；

（二）修改交易规则未在首页显著位置公开征求意见，未按照规定的时间提前公示修改内容，或者阻止平台内经营者退出的；

（三）未以显著方式区分标记自营业务和平台内经营者开展的业务的；

（四）未为消费者提供对平台内销售的商品或者提供的服务进行评价的途径，或者擅自删除消费者的评价的。

电子商务平台经营者违反本法第四十条规定，对竞价排名的商品或者服务未显著标明“广告”的，依照《中华人民共和国广告法》的规定处罚。

第八十二条　电子商务平台经营者违反本法第三十五条规定，对平台内经营者在平台内的交易、交易价格或者与其他经营者的交易等进行不合理限制或者附加不合理条件，或者向平台内经营者收取不合理费用的，由市场监督管理部门责令限期改正，可以处五万元以上五十万元以下的罚款；情节严重的，处五十万元以上二百万元以下的罚款。

第八十三条　电子商务平台经营者违反本法第三十八条规定，对平台内经营者侵害消费者合法权益行为未采取必要措施，或者对平台内经营者未尽到资质资格审核义务，或者对消费者未尽到安全保障义务的，由市场监督管理部门责令限期改正，可以处五万元以上五十万元以下的罚款；情节严重的，责令停业整顿，并处五十万元以上二百万元以下的罚款。

第八十四条　电子商务平台经营者违反本法第四十二条、第四十五条规定，对平台内经营者实施侵犯知识产权行为未依法采取必要措施的，由有关知识产权行政部门责令限期改正；逾期不改正的，处五万元以上五十万元以下的罚款；情节严重的，处五十万元以上二百万元以下的罚款。

第八十五条　电子商务经营者违反本法规定，销售的商品或者提供的服务不符合保障人身、财产安全的要求，实施虚假或者引人误解的商业宣传等不正当竞争行为，滥用市场支配地位，或者实施侵犯知识产权、侵害消费者权益等行为的，依照有关法律的规定处罚。

第八十六条　电子商务经营者有本法规定的违法行为的，依照有关法律、行政法规的规定记入信用档案，并予以公示。

第八十七条　依法负有电子商务监督管理职责

的部门的工作人员，玩忽职守、滥用职权、徇私舞弊，或者泄露、出售或者非法向他人提供在履行职责中所知悉的个人信息、隐私和商业秘密的，依法追究法律责任。

第八十八条 违反本法规定，构成违反治安管理行为的，依法给予治安管理处罚；构成犯罪的，依法追究刑事责任。

第七章 附 则

第八十九条 本法自2019年1月1日起施行。

关于印发《2017 年推进使用正版软件工作总结》和《2018 年推进使用正版软件工作计划》的通知

国版函［2018］4 号

各省、自治区、直辖市人民政府，推进使用正版软件工作部际联席会议各成员单位：

《2017 年推进使用正版软件工作总结》和《2018 年推进使用正版软件工作计划》已经推进使用正版软件工作部际联席会议第七次全体会议审议通过，现予印发，请认真贯彻执行。请各省（区、市）制定本省（区、市）2018 年推进使用正版软件工作计划，并于 2018 年 4 月 30 日前报送至部际联席会议办公室。

推进使用正版软件工作部际联席会议
国家版权局 代章
2018 年 3 月 23 日

2017 年推进使用正版软件工作总结

2017 年，推进使用正版软件工作部际联席会议（以下简称“部际联席会议”）认真贯彻落实党的十九大精神和党中央、国务院的决策部署，加强统筹协调、服务指导和督促检查，推进使用正版软件工作取得了新的成效。

一、取得的成效

2017 年，部际联席会议各成员单位各司其职，密切协作，坚持制度与技术并重，加强政策指导和督促检查，进一步巩固扩大了软件正版化工作成果。

（一）软件正版化工作取得了新的进展。2017 年，各级党政机关共采购操作系统、办公和杀毒软件 127.7 万套，采购金额 6.12 亿元，采购国产办公软件的套数和金额同比分别增长 73.97%和 65.58%；中央企业和金融机构共采购操作系统、办公和杀毒软件 245.11 万套，采购金额 21.45 亿元，采购国产办公软件的套数和金额同比分别增长 59.98%和 48.09%；全国累计推进 37 667 家企业实现软件正版化。2017 年，部际联席会议共督查单位 389 家、检查计算机 26 989 台。党政机关和大中型企业带头使用正版软件，起到了很好的示范引领作用，激发了软件企业的研发动力，促进了软件创新能力不断增强，带动了全社会软件版权保护水平不断提高，软件著作权登记量大幅增长。2017 年，软件著作权登记量达到 74.54 万件（同比增长 82.79%），软件和信息技术服务业收入达到 5.5 万亿元（同比增长 13.9%）。

（二）党政机关软件正版化不断规范。各级党政机关认真贯彻落实国务院办公厅印发的《政府机关使用正版软件管理办法》等相关政策措施，按照部际联席会议编制的《正版软件管理工作指南》，不断健全软件正版化工作机制，加强制度建设，规范软件采购，建立软件台账，严格使用管理。各级党政机关软件正版化工作年度报告制度落到实处，129 家中央和国家机关、31 个省（区、市）政府按期向国家版权局报送了 2017 年软件正版化工作年度报告。各省（区、市）进一步完善了党政机关计算机软硬件采购源头管理相关规定。30 个省（区、市）出台了党政机关软件正版化工作考核办法，并开展了软件正版化考评工作。各级党政机关基本建立了软件正版化工作责任制度，明确了责任部门和责任人。辽宁、吉林、黑龙江、宁夏等省（区、市）政府主要负责同志率先垂范，带头签署使用正版软件承诺书。一些省（区、市）采用场地授权方式为党政机关集中统一采购国产办公软件，不仅有效从源头上防止了盗版办公软件流入党政机关，还有效提高了财政资金的使用效益。

（三）企事业单位软件正版化全面铺开。在巩固中央企业和大中型金融机构软件正版化工作基础上，推进小型金融机构和地方企事业单位软件正版化工作取得积极进展。中央企业、大中型金融机构、大中型新闻出版广电企事业单位基本实现软件正版化。2017 年，各省（区、市）制定了推进企事业单位软件正版化工作规划和实施方案，全面部署推进地方企事业单位软件正版化工作，共推进 6 135 家企业实现软件正版化；北京、天津、河北、内蒙古、上海、江苏、浙江、安徽、福建、山东、湖北、广西、重庆、云南、陕西等 15 个省（区、市）成效明显，共推进5 210家企业实现软件正版化，共采购操作系统、办公和杀毒软件6.45亿元。北京、江苏、宁夏启动了医疗卫生系统软件正版化工作；重庆启动了文化教育卫生系统软件正版化工作。

（四）软件版权保护环境持续改善。部际联席会议加强软件市场监管，积极推进使用正版软件，促进了软件版权保护环境持续改善，为软件产业发展提供了良好的市场环境。国家版权局会同有关部门开展的“剑网2017”专项行动，严厉打击软件侵权盗版行为，查处了一批软件侵权盗版案件。工业和信息化部持续开展的新出厂计算机预装正版操作系统软件监管工作，推动新出厂计算机预装正版操作系统软件比例稳步提高。国家工商总局依法稳步推进涉嫌垄断案件的调查，加大对软件行业等重点领域的竞争执法力度，维护了软件市场公平竞争秩序。银监会指导银行业金融机构妥善解决与软件企业的合同纠纷，促成一些银行机构与境外软件企业达成和解，维护了银行机构的合法权益。

二、主要措施

（一）部门密切协作，加强工作部署。为贯彻落实国务院领导同志重要批示指示和全国打击侵权假冒工作领导小组会议精神，部际联席会议召开了第六次全体会议，对2017年推进使用正版软件工作进行了部署。部际联席会议各成员单位根据职责分工，各司其职，狠抓工作落实。国务院国资委、银监会、证监会、保监会、全国工商联根据部际联席会议工作部署，组织召开了专题会议并印发通知，进一步细化工作要求，全面部署中央企业、银行业金融机构、证券期货业经营机构、保险企业、民营企业软件正版化工作。部际联席会议围绕源头监管、使用管理、考核评议等关键环节，推进各地各部门补齐制度短板，完善长效机制，巩固工作成果。

（二）完善资产管理，规范软硬件采购制度。财政部将中央和国家机关正版软件采购经费纳入了2017年度财政预算；联合有关部门完善软件资产管理制度；指导有关集中采购机构持续做好正版软件政府采购工作。国管局进一步完善资产管理绩效考评指标体系，连续五年将软件资产正版化率作为重要考评指标，并增加了软件国产化率的考核；研究修订中央国家机关软件资产管理办法和配置标准；建立了各类软件的采购技术指标和服务标准。中直管理局进一步调整完善软件采购平台，丰富软件产品种类；推进软件正版化工作与信息化建设有机结合，推动中直机关巩固软件正版化工作成果。

（三）强化督促检查，推进责任落实。部际联席会议办公室组织了11个督查组，对辽宁、吉林、黑龙江、浙江、湖北、宁夏6个省（区）的全部省级政府机关进行了全覆盖督查，对北京、河北、山西、内蒙古、福建、海南、四川、西藏、青海、新疆10个省（区、市）进行了抽查，重点抽查了省级机关和省（区、市）国资委监管企业。国务院国资委推动中央企业开展了软件正版化工作全面自查，加强企业软件资产管理。国管局对中央国家机关本级通用办公软件正版化、软件资产管理情况进行了专项检查。银监会共抽查了573家银行业金融机构软件正版化工作。证监会对各交易所、各证监会下属单位进行了全覆盖督查，对证券、期货和基金经营机构进行了抽查。保监会对6家保险企业进行了现场检查。全国工商联推动省级工商联组织联合督查组对民营企业软件正版化工作进行了督查，并指导省级工商联结合重点工作推进民营企业软件正版化工作。

（四）聚焦产业发展，正版化信息化同步推进。工业和信息化部通过推动软件企业享受税收优惠政策、开展中国软件名城提升行动、利用“核高基”等专项支持软件关键核心技术研发、组织举办中国国际软件博览会等多种方式指导软件产业发展。国务院国资委要求中央企业积极稳妥推进核心信息系统软硬件安全可控，积极推进使用国产软件。银监会共通报12期基础软硬件缺陷信息，妥善处置信息安全风险事件；组织银行业金融机构开展终端设备国产操作系统软件的开发和应用推广，引导银行业使用国产软件。证监会积极推进软件正版化工作与网络安全工作相结合。保监会积极推进部署信息化项目建设时，同步推进软件正版化工作。部际联席会议办公室会同有关部门，与泰国商务部知识产权厅共同举办中泰软件版权合作论坛，推动金山、中望、一铭等软件企业在“一带一路”沿线国家发展，与泰国、印度、波兰等30余国的企业签署投资、合作、销售协议；在宁夏盐池县、西吉县，贵州黔西县，山西平顺县，湖北云梦县开展了国产软件应用试点工作。

（五）加强宣传培训，营造良好氛围。部际联席会议办公室会同有关部门，授予22家企业“全国版权示范单位（软件正版化）”荣誉称号，充分发挥先进典型的示范引领作用；编制了《软件正版化在中国（2017）》和《软件正版化在中国（英文版）》，系统全面展示软件正版化工作成果。商务部通过多双边交流机制、知识产权海外交流活动，加强对外宣传软件正版化工作成果，及时回应外方关切。部际联席会议各成员单位共举办软件正版化工作培训班12期，指导各地共举办培训班 2 622 期，累计培训人员 26 万余人。部际联席会议各成员单位通过会议、简报、网站、微博、微信等方式，及时发布软件正版化工作成果。

（六）加强工作指导，推广典型经验做法。部际联席会议积极指导各地抓好源头监管和考核评议，推广各地可复制、可推广的经验做法。源头监管方面，黑龙江要求纳入政府采购序列的各级党政机关和事业单位在采购计算机办公设备时必须落实办公软件采购经费，不一并采购办公软件的要经版权部门审核同意；云南以全省场地授权方式，集中采购国产办公软件；浙江采用场地授权方式，为省级预算单位集中采购国产办公软件；山东采用场地授权方式，为部分省级机关 2017 年度新采购计算机统一配装国产办公软件。考核评议方面，内蒙古将软件正版化工作纳入了盟市党政领导班子考核指标体系；浙江将软件正版化工作纳入了“平安市县”和建设法治政府的考核指标；湖北将软件正版化工作纳入了党政机关年度工作绩效考核和新闻出版广电（版权）行业年度工作责任考核；江苏将软件正版化纳入省级行政事业单位国有资产管理绩效考核；安徽将软件正版化纳入诚信示范企业评选指标。

三、存在的问题

（一）工作进展不平衡。一些地区仍存在思想认识不到位、工作机制不健全、推进措施不扎实等问题，工作进展滞后。一些单位软件正版化工作相关制度可操作性不强，职责分工不明确、要求不具体。一些单位源头监管把关不严，采购预装了不适用的正版操作系统软件的计算机现象比较普遍。

（二）一些党政机关使用盗版软件出现反弹。一些单位软件使用管理不规范，日常监管不严，没有做到常态化、规范化，采购的正版软件没有“真装真用”。一些单位为迎接检查突击安装正版软件现象非常明显。有的单位使用盗版软件反弹情况比较严重。

（三）部分地区企业软件正版化进展较慢。一些地区对推进企业软件正版化工作重视程度不够，推进力度不大。一些企业使用正版软件意识不强，落实主体责任不到位。有的企业使用盗版软件情况比较严重。

（四）正版化与信息化结合不紧密。一些单位信息系统完全基于特定软件建设，兼容性差，只能依赖特定软件实现正版化，软件采购选择性小、成本高，增加了软件采购成本，不利于形成公平竞争的市场环境，阻碍了软件正版化推进工作。

推进使用正版软件是贯彻新发展理念、强化知识产权保护、加快建设创新型国家的重要举措，对倡导创新文化、增强经济创新力和竞争力、保障信息安全具有重要意义。2018 年，部际联席会议要全面深入贯彻落实党的十九大精神，以习近平新时代中国特色社会主义思想为指导，强化知识产权创造、保护和运用，进一步健全长效机制、加强源头监管、强化督促检查，坚持制度与技术并重，正版化与信息化同步推进，持续深入推进使用正版软件工作，巩固扩大工作成果，开创新时代推进使用正版软件工作新局面。

2018 年推进使用正版软件工作计划

2018 年是全面深入贯彻落实党的十九大精神的开局之年，是改革开放四十周年，是决胜全面建成小康社会、实施“十三五”规划承上启下的关键一年。推进使用正版软件工作部际联席会议要以习近平新时代中国特色社会主义思想为指导，强化软件知识产权创造、保护和运用，进一步加强制度建设，强化督促检查，完善长效机制，坚持制度与技术并重，正版化与信息化同步推进，巩固扩大工作成果，努力开创新时代推进使用正版软件工作新局面，为加快建设创新型国家做出新贡献。

一、健全长效机制，规范软件使用管理

（一）加强统筹协调和服务指导。推进中央和国家机关及各地各部门进一步完善长效机制，抓好计算机软硬件采购源头监管、督促检查和考核评议等关键环节，确保软件正版化工作政策措施落地生效。（国家版权局牵头，部际联席会议各成员单位按职责分工负责）

（二）完善软件资产管理制度。修订完善中央和国家机关通用办公软件配置标准，从制度层面规范软件资产管理工作。（财政部、国管局、中直管理局按职责分工负责）

（三）加强软件资产管理绩效考评。继续做好中央国家机关软件资产配置计划管理和绩效考评工作。严格审核中央国家机关通用办公软件资产配置计划，与采购管理相结合，定期核实采购数据。（国管局牵头）

（四）推广正版软件管理工作指南。指导中央和国家机关及各地各部门以落实部际联席会议印发的《正版软件管理工作指南》为抓手，坚持制度与技术

并重，建立健全正版软件管理制度和正版软件管理台账。（国家版权局牵头，部际联席会议各成员单位按职责分工负责）

二、加强源头监管，规范计算机软硬件采购

（五）规范计算机软硬件采购流程。推进中央和国家机关及各地各部门新采购计算机时，采购预装适用的正版操作系统软件的计算机，严格审核需要购置的办公软件和杀毒软件的购置计划，从源头上防止盗版软件流入党政机关。（财政部、国管局、中直管理局按职责分工负责）

（六）优化党政机关软件采购服务。做好 2018 年中央和国家机关软件采购服务，指导各地改进采购工作。进一步丰富协议供货软件产品种类，根据实际需要扩大软件联合采购范围。（财政部、国管局、中直管理局按职责分工负责）

（七）继续推进中央企业软件集中采购。发挥集中采购优势，帮助中央企业降低正版软件采购价格，节约信息化建设成本。（国资委牵头）

（八）研究探索金融机构软件集中采购模式。做好金融机构软件采购服务指导，研究行业集中采购方式方法，帮助行业机构降低正版软件采购价格，节约信息化建设成本。（银监会、证监会、保监会按职责分工负责）

三、密切协调配合，巩固扩大企业软件正版化成果

（九）巩固中央企业软件正版化成果。制定并印发中央企业软件正版化年度工作通知，重点要求中央企业健全长效机制，巩固现有成果，防止反弹。（国资委牵头）

（十）持续推进金融机构软件正版化。进一步完善监管制度，推进金融机构软件正版化工作规范化。加大推进中小金融机构软件正版化工作力度，补齐金融机构软件正版化工作短板。（银监会、证监会、保监会按职责分工负责）

（十一）加快推进地方国有企业、民营企业软件正版化。推动各省（区、市）企事业单位软件正版化工作规划落到实处。指导省级工商联结合“四好”商会建设等重点工作，加快推进民营企业软件正版化工作。（国家版权局、国资委、全国工商联按职责分工负责）

（十二）积极推进行业软件正版化。加强与相关主管部门协调配合，推进上市企业、出口企业，以及教育、卫生、铁路、邮政、烟草、旅游、勘察设计等行业软件正版化工作。（国家版权局牵头，部际联席会议各成员单位按职责分工负责）

四、强化督促检查，推进落实主体责任

（十三）开展中央和国家机关软件正版化工作督促检查。随机抽查 30 家中央和国家机关软件正版化工作开展情况。（国家版权局牵头）

（十四）开展地方政府软件正版化工作督促检查。对 10 个省（区、市）软件正版化工作进行抽查，重点抽查省级机关和省（区、市）国资委监管企业。对 6～9 个省（区、市）省级政府机关软件正版化工作进行全覆盖督查。对 2017 年督查发现问题较多的地区和单位开展“回头看”。指导各省（区、市）督查本省（区、市）党政机关和企业软件正版化工作。（国家版权局牵头）

（十五）开展企业软件正版化工作督促检查。开展中央企业，银行业、证券期货业、保险业，民营企业软件正版化工作督查，督促企业落实软件正版化工作主体责任。（国资委、银监会、证监会、保监会、全国工商联分别牵头，部际联席会议办公室做好服务和配合工作）

（十六）继续优化督查方式方法。发挥第三方专业机构和技术手段优势，扩大督查深度和广度。推广使用软件检查工具，通过技术手段提高督查效率。（部际联席会议各成员单位按职责分工负责）

五、软件正版化与信息化同步推进，保障信息安全

（十七）软件正版化与信息化结合。推动中央和国家机关及各地各部门信息化建设与软件正版化同步进行，信息系统兼容国产操作系统软件、国产办公软件等国产软件，采购的计算机软硬件兼容国内外主流操作系统软件。倡导使用国产软件，助推信息系统自主安全可控。（国家版权局牵头，部际联席会议各成员单位按职责分工负责）

（十八）软件正版化与信息安全结合。推进中央和国家机关及各地各部门软件正版化与信息安全融合发展，相互支撑，相互促进，防范信息系统和基础设施建设信息安全风险。（国家版权局牵头，部际联席会议各成员单位按职责分工负责）

（十九）开展知识产权风险防范研究。开展信息系统知识产权风险防范研究，重点研究开源操作系统软件知识产权风险防范。（工业和信息化部牵头）

（二十）开展国产软件应用试点。巩固国产软件应用试点工作成果，适度扩大国产软件应用试点工作范围。指导具备条件的地区开展国产软件应用试点工作。研究探讨软件正版化工作中推动民族软件产业发展措施。（国家版权局牵头，部际联席会议各成员单位按职责分工负责）

六、加强市场监管，维护软件市场公平竞争秩序

（二十一）严厉打击软件侵权盗版行为。将打击软件侵权盗版行为纳入 2018 年打击侵权假冒工作和打击网络侵权盗版“剑网 2018”专项行动。（国家版权局牵头）

（二十二）依法查处软件行业垄断和不正当竞争行为。继续加大对软件行业等重点领域的竞争执法力度，严厉查处垄断和不正当竞争行为，维护软件市场公平竞争市场秩序和消费者合法权益。（国家工商总局牵头）

（二十三）持续做好年度预装正版操作系统软件监管和统计工作。加强对新出厂前正版操作系统软件预装的监督管理，继续扩大报送企业范围，不断提高预装率。（工业和信息化部牵头）

七、做好宣传培训，营造良好氛围

（二十四）积极做好宣传培训。加强软件正版化工作责任人培训。及时发布软件正版化工作成果。推广典型经验做法。（部际联席会议各成员单位分别牵头）

（二十五）加强国际交流合作。充分利用现有多双边知识产权磋商和交流机制，加大推进使用正版软件工作对外宣传力度，进一步做好国际应对工作。指导国内软件企业在“一带一路”沿线国家发展。（商务部、国家版权局按职责分工负责）

国家版权局关于奖励 2017 年度查处侵权盗版重大案件的决定

国版函［2018］36 号

各省、自治区、直辖市版权局，北京市、天津市、上海市、重庆市、西藏自治区文化市场行政执法总队，工业和信息化部、公安部、文化和旅游部、海关总署、国家市场监督管理总局办公厅，国家互联网信息办公室秘书局，最高人民法院、最高人民检察院办公厅，全国打击侵犯知识产权和制售假冒伪劣商品工作领导小组办公室，各相关协会、新闻媒体：

为进一步发挥版权相关执法部门查处侵权盗版案件的积极性和主动性，充分彰显查处侵权盗版案件先进典型的引导和示范作用，根据《国家版权局举报、查处侵权盗版行为奖励暂行办法》及实施细则的规定，国家版权局决定对各地推荐的 2017 年度查处侵权盗版重大案件给予奖励。其中，在查处侵权盗版案件工作中做出突出贡献的有功单位 212 家，有功个人 249 名。

各级版权相关执法部门及广大执法人员要向查处侵权盗版案件有功单位和有功个人学习，进一步加强版权执法监管工作，严厉查处各类侵权盗版行为，有效维护权利人合法权益，积极推动版权相关产业健康发展，为提升我国版权保护水平做出更大贡献。

国家版权局

2018 年 11 月 20 日

2017 年度查处侵权盗版案件有功单位及有功个人名单

有功单位一等奖

1. 公安部治安管理局一处

2. 公安部经济犯罪侦查局知识产权处

3. 最高人民检察院侦查监督厅立案监督处（保护知识产权处）

4. 北京市文化市场行政执法总队执法五队

5. 北京“5·8”制售侵权盗版图书案专案组（北京市文化市场行政执法总队执法一队、北京市公安局海淀分局青龙桥派出所）

6. 天津“吉吉影院”网侵犯影视作品著作权案专案组（天津市文化市场行政执法总队执法二队、天津市公安局经济犯罪侦查总队四支队、天津市南开区人民检察院公诉科、天津市南开区人民法院刑事审判庭）

7. 河北石家庄“8·12”销售盗版光盘案专案组（河北省石家庄市“扫黄打非”领导小组办公室、河北省石家庄市公安局治安警察支队治安行动大队、河北省石家庄市版权局版权管理处、河北省石家庄市新华区人民检察院公诉科、河北省石家庄市新华

区人民法院）

8. 吉林省版权局版权管理处

9. 上海市版权局版权管理执法（版权产业促进）处

10. 上海市文化市场行政执法总队稽查五处

11. 上海郑某某等侵犯著作权案专案组（上海市徐汇区人民检察院金融检察科、上海市徐汇区人民法院民三庭、上海市公安局徐汇分局）

12. 江苏省新闻出版广电局（版权局）版权管理处

13. 江苏省公安厅网络安全保卫总队

14. 江苏镇江“10·26”淘宝店制售盗版图书案专案组（江苏省镇江市版权局、江苏省镇江市公安局网络安全保卫支队）

15. 江苏徐州“3·11”侵犯著作权案专案组（江苏省徐州市版权局、江苏省徐州市公安局治安支队、江苏省徐州市文化市场综合执法支队）

16. 江苏扬州“私服村”系列侵犯著作权案专案组（江苏省扬州市版权局、江苏省扬州市文化市场综合执法支队、江苏省宿迁市文化行政综合执法支队、山东省东营市文化市场综合执法局）

17. 江苏常州吴某侵犯网络游戏著作权案专案组（江苏省常州市文化行政综合执法支队、江苏省常州市钟楼区人民法院）

18. 江西省新闻出版广电局（版权局）版权管理处

19. 江西省南昌市文化市场综合执法支队

20. 山东省版权局版权管理处

21. 山东省济南市贺某某侵犯著作权案专案组（山东省济南市文化市场综合行政执法局、山东省济南市公安局市中区分局）

22. 山东威海刘某制售盗版光盘案专案组（山东省威海市文化市场综合执法局、山东省威海市公安局、山东省威海市经济技术开发区人民检察院、山东省威海市经济技术开发区人民法院）

23. 河南尉氏“12·15”侵犯著作权案专案组（河南省开封市“扫黄打非”办公室、河南省开封市尉氏县文化市场综合执法大队、河南省开封市尉氏县公安局治安大队）

24. 河南郑州“11·14”郑某某侵犯著作权案专案组（河南省郑州市文化广电新闻出版局、河南省郑州市中级人民法院知识产权法庭、河南省郑州市公安局经济技术开发区分局）

25. 河南新郑“3·4”胡某某侵犯著作权案专案组（河南省新郑市文化市场综合执法大队、河南省新郑市公安局治安管理警察大队）

26. 湖北省黄冈市罗田县公安局公共信息网络安全监察大队

27. 湖北省武汉市江岸区人民法院知识产权审判庭

28. 湖北武汉戴某某侵犯著作权案专案组（湖北省武汉市硚口区文化体育局、湖北省武汉市硚口区公安分局汉中街派出所、湖北省武汉市硚口区人民检察院）

29. 湖北恩施赵某某等侵犯著作权案专案组（湖北省恩施市文化市场综合执法大队、湖北省恩施市人民检察院）

30. 湖北省荆门市公安局东宝区分局经侦大队

31. 湖北省黄冈市罗田县公安局经济犯罪侦查大队

32. 湖南省株洲市攸县公安局网络安全保卫大队

33. 广东省版权局版权管理处

34. 广东省茂名市茂南区人民检察院侦查监督科

35. 重庆市两江新区知识产权法庭

36. 重庆市公安局两江新区分局鸳鸯派出所

37. 四川成都“爱漫画”网侵犯著作权案专案组（四川省成都市文化市场综合执法总队、四川省成都市人民检察院公诉二处、四川省成都市温江区人民检察院、四川省成都市温江区人民法院）

有功单位二等奖

1. 公安部网络安全保卫局十二处

2. 工业和信息化部信息通信管理局互联网处

3. 国家互联网信息办公室网络综合协调管理和执法督查局综合协调处

4. 全国打击侵权假冒工作领导小组办公室法规信息组

5. 最高人民检察院公诉厅起诉四处

6. 最高人民法院民事审判第三庭第五合议庭

7. 北京市版权局版权管理处

8. 山西省版权局版权管理处

9. 内蒙古自治区版权局版权管理处

10. 内蒙古自治区巴彦淖尔市文化旅游综合行政执法局

11. 辽宁省大连市金州区人民检察院

12. 吉林省长春市文化市场综合执法支队

13. 吉林省通化市辉南县文化市场综合执法大队

14. 吉林省公主岭市文化市场综合执法大队

15. 上海市文化市场行政执法总队稽查三处

16. 上海市通信管理局互联网管理处

17. 上海市公安局松江分局

18. 上海市徐汇区人民法院民三庭

19. 江苏省通信管理局网络安全管理处

20. 江苏省无锡市新吴区人民检察院

21. 江苏徐州卢某某等侵犯网络文学著作权案专案组（江苏省徐州市“扫黄打非”办公室、江苏省徐州市公安局云龙分局、江苏省徐州市中级人民法院民三庭、江苏省徐州市公安局网安支队）

22. 浙江省版权局版权处

23. 浙江省义乌市市场监督管理局

24. 浙江省嵊州市公安局治安大队

25. 安徽省版权局版权管理处

26. 安徽马鞍山游某某侵犯著作权案专案组（安徽省马鞍山市“扫黄打非”办公室、安徽省马鞍山市文化旅游市场综合执法支队、安徽省马鞍山市公安局治安支队直属大队、安徽省马鞍山市人民检察院侦查监督处、安徽省马鞍山市雨山区人民法院刑事审判庭）

27. 福建省版权局版权管理处

28. 福建省福州市鼓楼区人民法院知识产权庭

29. 江西省上饶市文化市场综合执法支队

30. 山东省青岛市文化市场行政执法局

31. 山东省潍坊市文化市场综合执法局

32. 山东省泰安市文化市场综合执法支队

33. 河南省版权局版权管理处

34. 河南省打击侵权盗版专案组（河南省“扫黄打非”办公室、河南省公安厅治安总队二支队、河南省检察院侦查监督处、河南省通信管理局信息通信管理处）

35. 河南郑州“10・20”朱某某侵犯著作权案专案组（河南省郑州市文化市场综合执法支队、河南省郑州高新区文化旅游局、河南省郑州市公安局高新区分局经侦大队）

36. 河南中牟魏某某侵犯著作权案专案组（河南省郑州市中牟县文化广电旅游局、河南省郑州市中牟县公安局治安大队）

37. 湖北省版权局版权管理处

38. 湖北黄冈“9・13”侵犯著作权案专案组（湖北省黄冈市红安县公安局经侦大队、湖北省黄冈市红安县公安局网监大队）

39. 湖北黄石亿通建筑书店侵犯著作权案专案组（湖北省黄石市文化市场综合执法支队、湖北省黄石市黄石港区公安分局）

40. 湖北省十堰市郧阳区安监和综合执法局

41. 湖北省鄂州市公安局西山分局刑警大队

42. 湖南省新闻出版广电局版权处

43. 湖南省永州市道县文化市场综合执法大队

44. 广东省广州市文化市场综合行政执法总队执法五处

45. 广东省深圳市南山区人民法院知识产权审判庭

46. 广西壮族自治区版权局版权管理处

47. 广西“皮皮小说网”侵犯著作权案专案组（广西壮族自治区南宁市文化新闻出版广电局、广西壮族自治区南宁市公安局治安警察支队七大队、广西壮族自治区南宁市西乡塘区人民法院刑事审判庭、广西壮族自治区南宁市西乡塘区人民检察院刑事检察部）

48. 重庆市版权局版权管理处

49. 重庆韩某等侵犯网络游戏著作权案专案组（重庆市南岸区人民法院、重庆市南岸区文化市场行政执法大队、重庆市南岸区公安分局网安支队、重庆市南岸区公安分局广阳派出所）

50. 四川省版权局版权管理处

51. 四川省成都市双流区人民检察院

52. 新疆维吾尔自治区版权局版权管理处

53. 新华社中央新闻采访中心政文采访室

54. 人民网采访中心

55.《中国新闻出版广电报》出版周刊中心

56. 河南开封晟华印务有限公司盗印图书案协办组（外语教学与研究出版社有限责任公司、中国人力资源和社会保障出版集团营销中心打击盗版办公室、商务印书馆有限公司营销中心）

57. 中国建筑工业出版社法律事务部

有功单位三等奖

1. 国家互联网信息办公室网络评论工作局网评管理处

2. 国家市场监督管理总局执法稽查局执法协调处

3. 海关总署政法司知识产权处

4. 国家计算机网络应急技术处理协调中心互联网行业服务二处

5. 首都版权产业联盟

6. 天津市河西区文化市场行政执法大队

7. 河北省版权局版权管理处

8. 河北省通信管理局网络安全管理处

9. 河北省石家庄市栾城区文化行政执法队

10. 河北省衡水市文化市场行政执法大队

11. 河北省邯郸市文化市场行政执法大队

12. 内蒙古自治区通辽市文化市场综合执法局

13. 辽宁省人民检察院侦查监督处

14. 辽宁沈阳“1·9”侵犯影视作品著作权案专案组（辽宁省沈阳市文化市场行政执法总队直属执法二大队、辽宁省通信管理局信息通信管理处）

15. 辽宁省沈阳市文化市场行政执法总队直属执法一大队

16. 辽宁省沈阳市文化市场行政执法总队直属执法四大队

17. 吉林省长春市二道区文化市场综合执法大队

18. 吉林省吉林市文化市场综合执法支队

19. 吉林省延边州珲春市文化市场综合执法大队

20. 吉林省延边州敦化市文化市场综合执法大队

21. 吉林省四平市文化市场综合执法支队

22. 吉林省通化市文化市场综合执法支队

23. 吉林省辽源市东辽县文化市场综合执法大队

24. 吉林省白山市文化市场综合执法支队

25. 吉林省梅河口市文化市场综合执法大队

26. 河南卓邮软件科技有限公司、冷某某等侵犯著作权案专案组（上海市虹口区人民检察院航运（金融）科、上海市杨浦区人民法院知识产权审判庭、上海市公安局虹口分局网安支队）

27. 上海市互联网信息办公室网络管理处

28. 上海市人民检察院金融检察处

29. 上海海关法规处

30. 江苏省互联网信息办公室网络信息管理和执法督查处

31. 江苏省南京市文化广电新闻出版局

32. 江苏南京杨某某侵犯软件著作权案专案组（江苏省南京市文化市场综合执法总队、江苏省南京知识产权法庭）

33. 江苏省南京市江宁区文化市场综合执法大队

34. 江苏省苏州市张家港市文化广电新闻出版局

35. 江苏省南通市文化广电新闻出版局

36. 江苏省南通市文化行政综合执法支队

37. 江苏省南通市如皋市文体旅游综合执法大队

38. 江苏省南通市通州区川姜镇知识产权管理办公室

39. 江苏省连云港市文化市场综合执法支队

40. 浙江宁波“8·1”侵犯软件著作权案专案组（浙江省宁波市版权局、浙江省宁波市文化市场行政执法总队）

41. 浙江省宁波市海曙区文化广电新闻出版局

42. 浙江省杭州市余杭区文化市场行政执法大队

43. 浙江丽水徐某侵犯著作权案专案组（浙江省丽水市文化广电新闻出版局、浙江省丽水市莲都区文化广电新闻出版局）

44. 浙江省嘉兴市文化广电新闻出版局

45. 浙江省嵊州市文化市场行政执法大队

46. 浙江省丽水市公安局经济开发区分局治安大队

47. 浙江省台州市公安局治安支队

48. 安徽省“扫黄打非”领导小组办公室

49. 福建省通信管理局网络安全管理处

50. 福建福州“1·27”庞某某销售盗版光盘案专案组（福建省福州市文化市场综合执法支队、福州市鼓楼区人民检察院公诉科）

51. 厦门海关法规处知识产权科

52. 福建省福州市台江区人民检察院侦查监督科

53. 福建省泉州市文化市场综合执法支队

54. 福建省厦门市文化市场综合执法支队

55. 福建省平潭综合实验区市场监督管理局知识产权处

56. 江西省新闻出版广电稽查总队

57. 江西省赣州市文化市场稽查支队

58. 江西省赣州市安远县文化市场管理办公室

59. 江西省赣州市兴国县文化广电新闻出版局

60. 江西省赣州市于都县文化广电新闻出版局

61. 江西省萍乡市文化市场综合执法支队

62. 江西省上饶市万年县文化广电新闻出版局

63. 江西省宜春市文化广电新闻出版综合执法支队

64. 江西省鹰潭市文化市场综合执法支队

65. 江西省上饶市鄱阳县文化广电新闻出版局

66. 江西省九江市彭泽县文化市场综合执法大队

67. 江西省九江市湖口县文化执法大队

68. 山东省青岛市平度市文化市场行政执法局

69. 山东省东营市广饶县文化广电新闻出版局

70. 山东省烟台市文化市场执法支队

71. 山东省潍坊市安丘市文化市场综合执法局

72. 山东省潍坊市寿光市文化市场综合执法局

73. 山东省潍坊市诸城市文化市场综合执法局

74. 山东省潍坊市寒亭区文化市场综合执法局

75. 山东省潍坊市临朐县文化市场综合执法局

76. 山东省泰安市宁阳县文化广电新闻出版局

77. 湖北省互联网信息办公室网络管理处

78. 湖北省通信管理局网络安全管理处

79. 湖北省武汉市文化市场综合执法支队

80. 湖北武汉李某某侵犯著作权案专案组（湖北省武汉市江汉区文化局、湖北省武汉市江汉区公安分局水塔街派出所）

81. 湖北省荆州市监利县文化旅游市场综合执法大队

82. 湖北省潜江市文化市场综合执法支队

83. 湖南省株洲市文化市场综合执法局

84. 湖南省益阳市文化市场综合执法局

85. 湖南省湘西土家族苗族自治州凤凰县文化市场综合执法局

86. 湖南省衡阳市文化市场综合执法局

87. 湖南省永州市文化市场综合执法局

88. 湖南省岳阳市文化市场综合执法局版权大队

89. 湖南省永州市宁远县文化市场综合执法大队

90. 广东省委网信办网络舆情和应急指挥协调处

91. 黄埔海关法规处

92. 广东省深圳市市场稽查局市场稽查处

93. 广东省汕头市澄海区人民法院刑事审判第二庭

94. 广东省揭阳市文化市场综合执法大队一中队

95. 广西壮族自治区桂林市文化市场综合执法支队

96. 重庆市奉节县文化市场行政执法大队

97. 四川省德阳市文化市场综合行政执法支队

98. 四川崇州“5·18”杨某侵犯著作权罪专案组（四川省崇州市文化体育旅游局、四川省崇州市公安局）

99. 四川成都李某某侵犯著作权罪专案组（四川省成都市金牛区文化旅游体育广电新闻出版局、四川省成都市公安局金牛区分局黄忠派出所）

100. 四川南充“9·20”侵犯著作权案专案组（四川省南充市南部县文化广播影视体育局、四川省南充市南部县文化市场综合执法大队）

101. 云南省新闻出版广电局版权管理处

102. 云南省昭通市新闻出版广电局

103. 西藏自治区文化市场综合执法总队

104. 陕西省版权局版权管理处

105. 陕西省西安市文化市场行政执法总队

106. 陕西西安贾某某侵犯著作权案专案组（陕西省西安市长安区文化体育广播电视局、陕西省西安市公安局长安分局）

107. 宁夏回族自治区版权局版权管理处

108. 宁夏回族自治区银川市版权局

109. 新疆维吾尔自治区出版物市场稽查队

110. 新疆维吾尔自治区阿克苏地区新闻出版局新闻出版文化市场管理科

111. 新疆维吾尔自治区阿克苏地区温宿县文化体育广播影视局

112. 新疆维吾尔自治区石河子市文化体育新闻出版局文化市场综合行政执法支队

113. 新疆维吾尔自治区伊犁州文化市场稽查支队

114. 新疆和田孜丽塔西音像店销售盗版音像制品案专案组（新疆维吾尔自治区和田地区文化市场稽查支队、新疆维吾尔自治区和田市文化市场稽查大队）

115. 中国国际广播电台新闻中心国内部

116. 中国知识产权报社版权周刊

117. 科技日报社新闻中心

118.《中国版权》杂志社编辑部

有功个人一等奖

1. 罗强，最高人民检察院侦查监督厅立案监督处（保护知识产权处）

2. 王文利，最高人民检察院公诉厅起诉四处

3. 张牙，工业和信息化部信息通信管理局

4. 冯艳，国家互联网信息办公室网络综合协调管理和执法督查局

5. 孙晓慧，公安部治安管理局一处

6. 孙勇，全国打击侵权假冒工作领导小组办公室督察联络组

7. 北京优阅盈创科技有限公司侵犯著作权案专案组（刘铁京，北京市文化市场行政执法总队；熊伟、孙琦健，北京市文化市场行政执法总队执法五队）

8. 北京“5·8”制售盗版图书案专案组（邵大明、英薇薇，北京市文化市场行政执法总队执法一队；王凯、王凤桐，北京市公安局海淀分局青龙桥

派出所）

9. 北京“2·27”制售盗版图书案专案组（张权、杜鹏，北京市文化市场行政执法总队执法一队；张春晖，北京市文化市场行政执法总队法制监督处；李福龙、刘潇潇，北京市公安局海淀分局曙光派出所）

10. 天津“吉吉影院”网侵犯影视作品著作权案专案组（李和，天津市文化市场行政执法总队执法二队；王浩，天津市公安局经济犯罪侦查总队四支队；李铁，天津市南开区人民检察院公诉科；张磊，天津市南开区人民法院刑事审判庭）

11. 河北廊坊“5·19”制售图书案专案组（宋慧杰，河北省廊坊市文化广电新闻出版局反非法和违禁出版物科；赵兴华、安松波，河北省廊坊市文化市场行政执法大队；李莹，河北省廊坊市三河市人民法院刑事审判庭）

12. 吉林长春星座影咖微影院等侵犯著作权系列案专案组（李东鹏、王春和，吉林省版权局版权管理处）

13. 张静，黑龙江省大庆市龙凤区人民法院刑事审判庭

14. 薛彬，上海市版权局版权管理执法（版权产业促进）处

15. 上海智器投资咨询有限公司侵犯著作权案专案组（毛新炜、万赟，上海市文化市场行政执法总队稽查五处）

16. 万进萍，江苏省新闻出版广电局（版权局）版权管理处

17. 何森，江苏省镇江市公安局网络安全保卫支队

18. 江苏徐州“3·11”印制盗版图书案专案组（艾新建、解硕群，江苏省徐州市版权局；于湃，江苏省徐州市公安局治安支队；王晓东，江苏省徐州市公安局鼓楼分局铜沛派出所）

19. 杨剑，安徽省版权局版权管理处

20. 福建福州张某某侵犯著作权案专案组（郑军，福建省福州市鼓楼区人民检察院公诉科；张黎明，福建省福州市鼓楼区人民法院知识产权庭；方松峰，福建省福州市文化市场综合执法支队）

21. 杨旭，江西省新闻出版广电局（版权局）版权管理处

22. 江西南昌“摇头网”侵犯网络音乐著作权案专案组（饶兴奇、邹爱强、罗盛磊，江西省南昌市文化市场综合执法支队）

23. 张晓生，山东省版权局版权管理处

24. 张继河，山东省公安厅治安总队

25. 山东济南贺某某侵犯著作权案专案组（贺广文，山东省新闻出版广电局反非法和违禁出版物处；刘建峰、宋涛、刘琳，山东省济南市文化市场综合行政执法局；冯明华，山东省济南市公安局市中区分局刑警四中队）

26. 山东威海刘某等制售盗版光盘案专案组（张海舰、韩兵，山东省威海市文化市场综合执法局；杨玉平、梁虎，山东省威海市公安局治安警察支队；于丽君，山东省威海经济技术开发区人民检察院）

27. 李峰，河南省版权局版权管理处

28. 河南开封“12·15”侵犯著作权案专案组（王伟，河南省开封市文化广电新闻出版局；王建坤，河南省开封市“扫黄打非”办公室；王炜，河南省开封市尉氏县文化广电新闻出版局；李民立，河南省开封市尉氏县文化市场综合执法大队；王永峰，河南省开封市尉氏县公安局）

29. 河南新郑“5·15”伽某某侵犯著作权案专案组（李世英、贾武军、李冬冬，河南省新郑市文化市场综合执法大队；王玉林，河南省郑州市文化广电新闻出版局；张彪，河南省新郑市公安局郭店派出所）

30. 河南郑州“12·15”制售盗版图书案专案组（赵彩霞，河南省郑州市新密市文化广电旅游局；郭晓勇，河南省郑州市新密市公安局；王书彬，河南省郑州市新密市文化市场综合执法大队；苏晓霞，河南省郑州市文化广电新闻出版局）

31. 河南郑州“11·14”郑某某侵犯著作权案专案组（宋志伟，河南省郑州市文化市场综合执法支队；钱红军，河南省郑州市中级人民法院；楚栋锋、杨正泰，河南省郑州市公安局经济技术开发区分局）

32. 张威，湖北省版权局版权管理处

33. 湖北黄冈摄某某等侵犯著作权案专案组（张津，湖北省黄冈市罗田县公安局公共信息网络安全监察大队；李航，湖北省黄冈市公安局网络安全保卫支队）

34. 陈饰，湖北省恩施市人民检察院刑事检察科

35. 朱相东，湖北省荆门市公安局东宝区分局经侦大队

36. 梁斯洛，广东省广州市文化市场综合行政执法总队执法五处

37. 广东广州胡某某等侵犯著作权案专案组

（吴雪梅，广东省广州市人民检察院；平文林，广东省广州市中级人民法院刑二庭）

38. 广东茂名李某某等侵犯著作权案专案组（杨观耀、余伟玲、苏国佳，广东省茂名市公安局茂南分局公共信息网络安全监察大队）

39. 四川成都“爱漫画”网侵犯著作权案专案组（夏应添、田晋宝、杜林，四川省成都市文化市场综合执法总队；郑睿，四川省成都市人民检察院公诉二处；石凌云，四川省成都市温江区人民法院）

40. 史竟男，新华社国内部

41. 曾文甫，中央电视台社会新闻部

42. 张红兵，法制日报社经济新闻部

43. 赖名芳，《中国新闻出版广电报》出版周刊中心

44. 成琪，中国经济网文化产业资讯部

45. 河南新密“12·15”制售盗版图书案协办组（侯俊英、宁建群，外语教学与研究出版社；张志良、李松，中国人力资源和社会保障出版集团）

有功个人二等奖

1. 王海镔，公安部治安管理局一处

2. 秦元明，最高人民法院民事审判第三庭

3. 北京橙子维阿科技有限公司侵犯著作权案专案组（刘立新、史曙亮，北京市文化市场行政执法总队执法五队）

4. 李振忠，河北省版权局版权管理处

5. 杨志云，山西省版权局版权管理处

6. 李钧，内蒙古自治区版权局版权管理处

7. 内蒙古鄂尔多斯王某某等销售盗版音像制品案专案组（陈宇红，内蒙古自治区鄂尔多斯市文化新闻出版广电局；郭栋、石瑞，内蒙古自治区鄂尔多斯市文化市场综合执法局；那日苏，内蒙古自治区鄂尔多斯市公安局经侦支队；张恒源，内蒙古自治区鄂尔多斯市杭锦旗公安局呼和木独派出所）

8. 辽宁沈阳全民阅读文化传媒有限公司销售盗版图书案专案组（任东晖、刘曙光、汤景海，辽宁省沈阳市文化市场行政执法总队四大队；张洋，辽宁省沈阳市文化市场行政执法总队办公室）

9. 陈萍，上海市文化市场行政执法总队稽查三处

10. 上海郑某某等侵犯著作权案专案组（张晨昊，上海市公安局徐汇分局治安支队治安管理（行动）中队；谢丁，上海市公安局徐汇分局网安支队）

11. 许磊，上海市徐汇区人民检察院公诉科

12. 上海卿某侵犯著作权案专案组（刘慧，上海市松江区人民检察院金融检察科；张国华，上海市公安局松江分局治安支队食品药品犯罪侦查大队）

13. 江苏扬州“私服村”系列侵犯著作权案专案组（季培均，江苏省扬州市版权局；刘光明、唐海宁，江苏省扬州市文化市场综合执法支队；陈亚力，江苏省宿迁市文化行政综合执法支队；常光兴，山东省东营市文化市场综合执法局）

14. 江苏常州王某侵犯著作权案专案组（姜海，江苏省常州市文化行政综合执法支队；樊力纲，江苏省常州市公安局经济开发区分局网安大队）

15. 江苏常州林某某等侵犯著作权案专案组（孙飞，江苏省常州市钟楼公安分局网络安全保卫大队；王海岸，江苏省常州市钟楼区人民法院知识产权案件综合审判庭）

16. 江苏扬州学苑书店发行盗版图书案专案组（刘文献、顾明，江苏省扬州市文化市场综合执法支队；杨高华、韦俊，安徽省黄山市版权局）

17. 杨春虎，浙江省温州市平阳县文化市场综合执法大队

18. 郭林，浙江省公安厅治安监督管理总队

19. 安徽游某某侵犯著作权案专案组（刘俊，安徽省人民检察院侦查监督一处；王兰兰，安徽省马鞍山市文化旅游市场综合执法支队；吕生强，安徽省马鞍山市委宣传部；潘盛，安徽省马鞍山市公安局治安支队）

20. 安徽合肥戴某某发行侵权复制品案专案组（张辉、朱正胜，安徽省合肥市文化市场综合执法支队）

21. 庄刚，江西省赣州市兴国县文化广电新闻出版局

22. 谢志宏，山东省青岛市文化市场行政执法局

23. 孙章，山东省青岛市文化市场行政执法局

24. 山东威海三鹰印务有限公司侵犯著作权案专案组（刘培臻、谷祖喜，山东省威海市文化市场综合执法局；姜文涛，山东省威海市环翠区文化市场综合执法局）

25. 山东威海崇善堂生物科技有限公司复制盗版图书案专案组（辛进波、徐水平，山东省威海市文化市场综合执法局；王海生，山东省威海市公安局治安警察支队；鞠成科，山东省威海市公安局环翠分局治安管理大队）

26. 山东淄博“8·9”侵犯著作权案专案组（毕雪峰，山东省淄博市文化市场执法局；王长永，山东省淄博市文化市场执法支队；张洪强、张钧法，山东省淄博市公安局直属分局；王翠玉，山东省淄

博市人民检察院）

27. 牛兆星，山东省潍坊市文化市场综合执法局

28. 胡维钊，山东省潍坊市文化市场综合执法局

29. 山东济宁“6·2”销售侵权教辅案专案组（颜廷爱、张连成，山东省济宁市文化市场综合执法局）

30. 王新民，山东省泰安市文化广电新闻出版局

31. 张安军，山东省泰安市文化广电新闻出版局

32. 山东聊城“11·2”销售侵权复制品案专案组（龙清达，山东省聊城市文化市场综合执法局；王殿宝，山东省聊城市公安局东昌府分局）

33. 山东新世纪印刷有限公司侵犯著作权案专案组（訾士勇、冯修国，山东省聊城市阳谷县文化广电新闻出版局；于俊海，山东省聊城市阳谷县公安局；孙代贤，山东省聊城市阳谷县人民法院；孟庆存，山东省聊城市阳谷县人民检察院）

34. 河南新郑“7·28”郭某某侵犯著作权案专案组（刘永强、史超、郭治强，河南省新郑市文化市场综合执法大队；王宏亮，河南省新郑市公安局龙湖派出所）

35. 河南新郑“6·8”郝某某等侵犯著作权案专案组（罗忠良、王龙彬、杨帅兵，河南省新郑市文化市场综合执法大队；王晓辉、任大乾，河南省新郑市公安局）

36. 河南郑州“12·15”张某某销售侵权复制品案专案组（王成立、王献民、乔冬梅，河南省郑州市中牟县文化广电旅游局；李大杰，河南省郑州市中牟县公安局治安大队；魏海洲，河南省郑州市中牟县公安局郑庵派出所）

37. 河南郑州“10·20”朱某某侵犯著作权案专案组（孙建理、付志坚，河南省郑州市文化广电新闻出版局；孔锋，河南省郑州市公安局高新分局经侦大队）

38. 河南省打击侵权盗版专案组（翟邵午，河南省新闻出版广电局反非处；李波，河南省新闻出版广电局网络视听节目管理处；李雅萍，河南省公安厅治安总队；张光亮，河南省检察院侦查监督处；陈光辉，河南省通信管理局）

39. 河南开封“6·9”侵犯著作权案专案组（姚春贵、李现峰，河南省开封市文化广电新闻出版局；张超峰，河南省开封市尉氏县文化市场综合执法大队）

40. 上海有趣岛文化传播有限公司侵犯著作权案专案组（黄斌、陈霄、张成，湖北省鄂州市公安局网安支队）

41. 湖南左某某侵犯软件著作权案专案组（马军，广东省佛山市禅城区文化体育局；朱黎，广东省佛山市禅城区文化市场综合执法局；谭琪琳，湖南省娄底市文化市场综合执法大队；王德阳，湖南省娄底市双峰县文体广电新闻出版局）

42. 陆斌，广东省广州市文化市场综合行政执法总队执法五处

43. 黎辉涵，广东省佛山市南海区文体局

44. 林婷，广东省深圳市南山区人民检察院

45. 赵明明，广西壮族自治区版权局版权管理处

46. 广西“皮皮小说网”侵犯著作权案专案组（罗峰，广西壮族自治区南宁市公安局治安警察支队法制大队；李密，广西壮族自治区南宁市西乡塘区人民法院刑事审判庭；卢文霆，广西壮族自治区南宁市西乡塘区人民检察院）

47. 杨一，四川省版权局版权管理处

48. 四川“轻之国度”“轻之文库”网侵权案专案组（肖梅、李巍、张林，四川省成都市文化市场综合执法总队三支队；曾祥璐，四川省成都市人民检察院公诉二处）

49. 何源，中央人民广播电台中国之声时政采访部

50. 王座桥，中国互联网新闻中心科创频道专题部

51. 王运平，《中国出版》杂志社

52. 王志艳，新华网股份有限公司新闻中心

53. 河南郑州张某某侵犯著作权案协办组（胡永旭、王军钧，中国建筑工业出版社）

有功个人三等奖

1. 黄韵铮，国家互联网信息办公室网络新闻信息传播局

2. 臧睿，公安部网络安全保卫局

3. 蔡斐屹，国家市场监督管理总局价格监督检查和反不正当竞争局法制和监督处

4. 蒽晶文，文化和旅游部文化市场综合执法监督局执法督导处

5. 王丽婷，海关总署政法司知识产权处

6. 曹伟，中国互联网协会

7. 北京小蚁互动网络科技有限公司侵犯著作权案专案组（千旭、刘文昌，北京市文化市场行政执

法总队执法四队）

8. 北京“1·17”侵犯著作权案专案组（张清、王宝忠，北京市文化市场行政执法总队执法五队；张少帅，北京市文化市场行政执法总队法制监督处）

9. 幻维世界（北京）网络科技有限公司侵犯著作权案专案组（王玉军、梁放，北京市文化市场行政执法总队执法五队；陈宜，北京市文化市场行政执法总队法制监督处）

10. 河北保定周某某侵犯著作权案专案组（韩长勇、王文升，河北省保定市文化市场行政执法大队）

11. 河北保定龙潭宾馆侵犯著作权案专案组（崔坤灿、金喆，河北省保定市文化市场行政执法大队）

12. 谢方正，辽宁省人民检察院侦查监督处

13. 吉林关东图书文化发展有限公司侵犯著作权案专案组（朱爽、付伟峰，吉林省长春市文化市场综合执法支队）

14. 吉林长春奇想职业培训学校等侵犯著作权系列案专案组（路野、张文胜，吉林省长春市文化市场综合执法支队）

15. 吉林长春九台百书汇等侵犯著作权系列案专案组（孟德富、徐凯峰，吉林省长春市九台区文化市场综合执法大队）

16. 费泽忠，吉林省延边州敦化市文化市场综合执法大队

17. 刘洋，吉林省通化市辉南县文化市场综合执法大队

18. 何方岩，吉林省辽源市东辽县文化市场综合执法大队

19. 马刚，吉林省辽源市东辽县文化广电新闻出版局

20. 吉林松原百花印业有限公司印制盗版教辅案专案组（姜英华、高谡，吉林省松原市文化市场综合执法支队）

21. 靳立伟，吉林省公主岭市文化市场综合执法大队

22. 周湘宇，吉林省梅河口市文化市场综合执法大队

23. 黑龙江齐齐哈尔齐网网络科技有限公司侵犯著作权案专案组（戴云峰、刘国强，黑龙江省齐齐哈尔市文化广电新闻出版局；郭虹、张巍，黑龙江省齐齐哈尔市文化市场综合执法支队）

24. 步屹军，上海市文化市场行政执法总队稽查三处

25. 上海乐欢软件有限公司侵犯著作权案专案组（王浩、陈启光，上海市文化市场行政执法总队稽查五处）

26. 李斌，上海市互联网信息办公室网络管理处

27. 朱薇，上海市通信管理局互联网管理处

28. 刘燕萍，上海市杨浦区人民法院知识产权审判庭

29. 韩敏，上海市黄浦区人民法院民三庭

30. 上海海关打击侵犯著作权行为专项整治系列案专案组（徐浩，上海海关隶属洋山海关；殷啸锋，上海海关隶属外高桥港区海关；徐敏，上海海关现场业务二处）

31. 滕美丽，上海市浦东新区知识产权局

32. 魏志东，江苏省淮安市文化行政综合执法支队

33. 周俊，江苏省常州市文化行政综合执法支队

34. 江苏常州私人影院系列侵权案专案组（沈屹峰、周晓龙，江苏省常州市文化行政综合执法支队）

35. 江苏扬州美特网络科技有限公司侵犯著作权案专案组（施文兵、王丁祥，江苏省扬州市文化市场综合执法支队）

36. 江苏昆山某汽车装备制造有限公司软件纠纷调解案专案组（王斌，江苏省昆山市版权局；宗琮、胡钰湘，江苏省昆山市文化市场综合执法大队）

37. 江苏徐州杨某侵犯著作权案专案组（郭静，江苏省徐州市公安局网安支队；曾志强，江苏省徐州市云龙区公安分局）

38. 江苏徐州“12·25”侵犯著作权案专案组（朱启川，江苏省徐州市版权局；刘连浩，江苏省徐州市文化市场综合执法支队；孙斌，江苏省徐州市鼓楼区公安分局）

39. 江苏南京仁晶信息科技有限公司侵犯软件著作权案专案组（蔡健、汪庆平，江苏省南京市文化广电新闻出版局；曹岚、任越群，江苏省南京市文化市场综合执法总队）

40. 王蔚敏，江苏省南通市通州区川姜镇知识产权管理办公室

41. 施颖，江苏省南通市海门市三星镇版权管理办公室

42. 浙江宁波小满影咖侵权案专案组（潘剑武、柳伟，浙江省宁波市海曙区文化市场行政执法大队）

43. 浙江宁波小喵影院侵权案专案组（郭振、

宫卫波，浙江省宁波市海曙区文化市场行政执法大队）

44. 周晓江，浙江省永康市文化市场行政执法大队

45. 余术威，浙江省金华市金东区东孝街道东关派出所

46. 王林霞，安徽省通信管理局网络安全管理处

47. 安徽黄山陈某销售盗版图书等系列案专案组（韦俊、杨高华，安徽省黄山市版权局）

48. 安徽滁州冯某某发行侵权复制品案专案组（韦荣、郭俊杰，安徽省滁州市文化广电新闻出版局；徐芳芳，安徽省滁州市“扫黄打非”工作小组办公室；张莉、王超，安徽省滁州市文化市场综合执法支队）

49. 安徽工业大学印刷厂印制盗版图书案专案组（李敏、杨冲，安徽省马鞍山市文化旅游市场综合执法支队；董惠玲，安徽省马鞍山市文化和旅游委员会）

50. 福建泉州“速8影院”网侵犯著作权案专案组（林俊杰，福建省“扫黄打非”领导小组办公室；石恒，福建省泉州市版权局版权科；吴艺敏，福建省晋江市文化市场综合执法大队；邱益民、颜希宇，福建省泉州市文化市场综合执法支队二大队）

51. 福建福州依强珠宝首饰有限公司侵犯著作权案专案组（卓雄英、林晓艺，福建省福州市文化广电新闻出版局版权管理处；刘超，福建省福州市文化市场综合执法支队）

52. 福建麦迪驰杰（厦门）模具科技有限公司侵犯软件著作权案专案组（蔡云斌，福建省厦门市文化市场综合执法二大队；洪露，福建省厦门市文化市场综合执法支队执法监督科；刘德芬，福建省厦门市思明区人民法院审判委员会；李缘缘，福建省厦门市思明区人民法院民三庭）

53. 福建厦门欣欢乐唱娱乐有限公司侵犯音乐作品著作权等系列案专案组（林翔莺，福建省厦门市文化市场综合执法支队二大队；刘前程，福建省厦门市文化市场综合执法支队三大队；胡新、林珽璟，福建省厦门市文化广电新闻出版局版权处）

54. 江西抚州“佳佳影院”网侵犯著作权案专案组（胡光斌、付峻峰，江西省抚州市文化综合执法支队）

55. 董显祥，江西省赣州市文化广电新闻出版局

56. 杨雨露，江西省赣州市兴国县文化广电新闻出版局

57. 谢芸华，江西省赣州市于都县文化广电新闻出版局

58. 彭小芸，江西省赣州市于都县文化市场综合执法大队

59. 谭春森，江西省赣州市于都县文化市场综合执法大队

60. 尧飞武，江西省赣州市安远县文化市场管理办公室

61. 程麟峰，江西省景德镇市文化市场综合执法支队

62. 徐涵，江西省景德镇市文化市场综合执法支队

63. 汪志勇，江西省九江市彭泽县文化市场综合执法大队

64. 李跃，江西省九江市湖口县文化市场综合执法大队

65. 江西壹陆伍科技开发有限公司侵犯著作权案专案组（周明、赵扬超，江西省南昌市文化市场综合执法支队）

66. 江西萍乡爱沫咖啡店侵犯著作权案专案组（彭全环、谢国良，江西省萍乡市安源区文化市场综合执法大队）

67. 谢鹏，江西省赣州市瑞金市文化稽查大队

68. 朱海泉，江西省赣州市瑞金市文化稽查大队

69. 杨振华，江西省赣州市瑞金市文化稽查大队

70. 邹志深，江西省上饶市广丰区文化市场综合执法大队

71. 麻卫清，江西省上饶市余干县文化市场综合执法大队

72. 李曰威，江西省新余市分宜县文化广电新闻出版局

73. 江西新余朋克炫音工作室侵犯网络音乐著作权案专案组（蓝波、张小安，江西省新余市文化市场综合执法支队；张志平、黄有利，江西省新余市渝水区文化执法大队）

74. 江西鹰潭阳光地带娱乐有限公司侵犯著作权案专案组（周四军、孙剑，江西省鹰潭市文化市场综合执法支队）

75. 山东济南程某某侵犯著作权案专案组（赵骑韬，山东省济南市文化市场综合行政执法局；张文安、王家军，山东省济南市文化市场综合行政执法支队；李萌，山东省济南市公安局天桥区分局黄

台派出所）

76. 杜荣华，山东省青岛市文化市场行政执法局

77. 傅德宝，山东省青岛市文化市场行政执法局

78. 孙晨光，山东省青岛市文化市场行政执法局

79. 山东青岛杰雅教育服务有限公司侵犯著作权案专案组（邹少卫、王松涛，山东省青岛市平度市文化市场行政执法局）

80. 山东青岛冯某某侵犯著作权案专案组（马宗讯、宫海波，山东省青岛市李沧区文化市场行政执法局；徐涛、朱滨，山东省青岛市公安局李沧分局治安管理警察大队）

81. 山东东营“7·27”侵犯著作权案专案组（周民旺、王磊，山东省东营市文化市场综合执法局；刘洪起、成红波，山东省东营市广饶县文化广电新闻出版局）

82. 于利，山东省潍坊市文化市场综合执法局

83. 王兆剑，山东省潍坊市临朐县文化市场综合执法局

84. 云增建，山东省潍坊市安丘市文化市场综合执法局

85. 山东安丘徐某某侵犯著作权案专案组（王维山、胡旭东，山东省潍坊市文化市场综合执法局；王金柱、解宝，山东省安丘市文化市场综合执法局）

86. 江尔玉，山东省潍坊市昌乐县文化市场综合行政执法局

87. 山东潍坊闫某某发行盗版出版物案专案组（王希坤、姜婷婷，山东省潍坊市文化市场综合执法局；孙庆国、李乔，山东省潍坊市奎文区文化市场综合执法局）

88. 山东济宁爱尚电影放映中心侵犯电影作品著作权案专案组（孟杰、张浩，山东省济宁市任城区文化市场综合执法局）

89. 山东济宁万张街道中学印制盗版图书案专案组（周可义、王守俊，山东省济宁市嘉祥县文化市场综合执法局）

90. 吕宗峰，山东省泰安市文化市场综合执法支队

91. 山东泰安自由时光咖啡厅侵犯著作权案专案组（赵永磊、杨红雨，山东省泰安市文化市场综合执法支队）

92. 石玉奎，山东省泰安市宁阳县文化广电新闻出版局

93. 山东滨州大学时光影城有限公司侵犯著作权案专案组（刘建忠、冯天翔，山东省滨州市文化市场综合执法局）

94. 山东滨州黄河书业侵犯著作权案专案组（任敬民、王文静，山东省滨州市文化市场综合执法局）

95. 山东烟台华彩图文有限公司侵犯著作权案专案组（林乐进、曲景舜，山东省烟台市文化市场执法支队）

96. 河南南阳跃动文化传媒公司侵犯著作权案专案组（葛松峰、张乐，河南省南阳市文化市场综合执法支队）

97. 河南南阳“3·16”侵犯著作权系列案专案组（栗山、杨欣军，河南省南阳市文化市场综合执法支队）

98. 王丽杰，河南省濮阳市文化市场综合执法支队

99. 河南周口中瑞网络科技公司侵犯著作权案专案组（轩昆鹏，河南省周口市文化广电新闻出版局；魏小均、王磊，河南省周口市文化市场综合执法支队）

100. 河南周口马某某侵犯著作权案专案组（李锋，河南省周口市文化广电旅游局；于河川、李西海，河南省周口市项城市文化广电新闻出版局；张高强、闫明，河南省周口市项城市文化市场综合执法大队）

101. 河南驻马店系列教辅侵权案专案组（肖宏伟、张宏图，河南省驻马店市文化市场综合执法支队）

102. 河南商丘天才书店销售盗版图书案专案组（卢学锋、叶超，河南省商丘市柘城县文化市场综合执法大队）

103. 河南驻马店天智等书店系列侵权案件专案组（殷小喜、王伟松，河南省驻马店市文化市场综合执法支队）

104. 河南商丘“DY电影网”侵犯著作权案专案组（董健、周清华，河南省商丘市文化广电新闻出版局；闫勇，河南省商丘市睢县文化广电新闻出版局；刘华，河南省商丘市睢县文化市场综合执法大队）

105. 刘雯，湖北省公安厅治安总队治安管理支队

106. 何浏，湖北省打击侵权假冒工作领导小组办公室

107. 王品明，湖北省通信管理局网络安全管

理处

108. 周来来，湖北省互联网信息办公室网络管理处

109. 许星，湖北省襄阳市文化市场综合执法支队

110. 徐勇，湖北省黄石市公安局黄石港分局经侦大队

111. 吴小安，湖北省潜江市文化市场综合执法支队

112. 湖南湘西向某侵犯音乐作品著作权案专案组（王宴、张希，湖南省湘西土家族苗族自治州凤凰县文化市场综合执法局）

113. 湖南衡阳谢某某侵犯著作权案专案组（刘意福、尹忠国，湖南省衡阳市文化市场综合执法局）

114. 沈蓓，湖南省衡阳市文化市场综合执法局

115. 陈超，湖南省衡阳市文化市场综合执法局

116. 陈炜，湖南省衡阳市文化市场综合执法局

117. 王松林，湖南省衡阳市文化市场综合执法局

118. 钟淙，湖南省衡阳市文化市场综合执法局

119. 胡文艺，湖南省衡阳市文化市场综合执法局

120. 湖南衡阳唐某某侵犯影视作品著作权案专案组（商章勤、万燕萍，湖南省衡阳市文化市场综合执法局）

121. 王用权，湖南省常德市文化市场综合执法局

122. 乌翔宇，湖南省永州市道县文化市场综合执法大队

123. 深圳茶颜悦色饮品有限公司长沙店侵犯美术作品著作权案专案组（尹承丽、张宇，湖南省长沙市知识产权局）

124. 李军，湖南省岳阳市文化市场综合执法局版权大队

125. 刘伟，湖南省岳阳市文化市场综合执法局版权大队

126. 王拙，广东省珠海市文化市场综合执法支队

127. 邓少元，广东省深圳市市场稽查局市场稽查处

128. 张启敏，广西壮族自治区南宁市文化市场综合执法支队

129. 彭云，四川省通信管理局网络安全管理处

130. 四川博文网络科技有限责任公司侵犯著作权案专案组（张路，四川省遂宁市“扫黄打非”工作小组办公室；晏刚，四川省遂宁市射洪县文化广电新闻出版局；罗毅，四川省遂宁市文化市场综合执法支队；刘明华、何春松，四川省遂宁市射洪县文化广电新闻出版局综合执法大队）

131. 四川南充“8·13”侵犯著作权案专案组（朱成平、王海，四川省南充市文化广电新闻出版局；鲜明，四川省南充市公安局嘉陵区分局经侦大队；李杨，四川省南充市嘉陵区人民检察院；樊志兵，四川省南充市嘉陵区文化市场综合执法大队）

132. 张信，云南省昭通市永善县文化市场综合执法大队

133. 陕西西安侵犯电影作品著作权系列案专案组（樊军艳、张云，陕西省西安市文化市场行政执法总队）

134. 陕西西安文汇书店著作权侵权案专案组（张宗立、楚源，陕西省西安市文化市场行政执法总队）

135. 王新民，陕西省版权局版权管理处

136. 王建存，陕西省网信办网络管理处

137. 甘肃白银继学书业有限公司等侵犯著作权案专案组（王玉梁、李振宇，甘肃省白银市文化市场综合执法支队）

138. 袁国儒，甘肃省张掖市文化广播影视新闻出版局

139. 宁夏银川“8·15”侵犯软件著作权案专案组（张宁学，宁夏回族自治区版权局；李银海，宁夏回族自治区银川市版权局；买玉龙，宁夏回族自治区银川市文化市场综合执法队）

140. 宁夏银川博学苑书店侵犯著作权案专案组（徐地方，宁夏回族自治区银川市文化市场综合执法队；丁伟，宁夏回族自治区银川市公安局侵犯知识产权犯罪侦查支队）

141. 杨建新，新疆维吾尔自治区版权局版权管理处

142. 艾克然木·尼扎木，新疆维吾尔自治区阿克苏地区库车县文化市场稽查队

143. 汪晓方，新疆维吾尔自治区伊犁州霍城县文化体育广播影视局文化市场稽查队

144. 余刚，新疆维吾尔自治区博州精河县文化市场稽查大队

145. 新疆和田爱丽库依音像店销售盗版音像制品案专案组（陈丽萍、孟庆和，新疆维吾尔自治区和田地区文化市场稽查支队；色比拉提·赛吾丁、王疆宏，新疆维吾尔自治区和田市文化市场稽查大队）

146. 刘志军，新疆维吾尔自治区石河子市文体新局文化市场综合行政执法支队

147. 李苑，光明日报社评论部

148. 倪伟，新京报社时政新闻部

149. 郭虹，中国出版传媒商报社党委办公室

150. 马李文博，中国艺术报社理论副刊部

151. 苏墨，工人日报社社会文化新闻部

国家版权局办公厅关于 2017 年全国著作权登记情况的通报

国版办发［2018］3 号

各省、自治区、直辖市版权局，新疆生产建设兵团版权局，中国版权保护中心：

2017 年，各地版权行政管理部门和著作权登记机构高度重视著作权登记工作，全面贯彻落实国家版权局相关文件精神，采取有效措施，积极宣传、重点拓展、改善服务，各类作品和软件的创造、创新能力极大提升，登记数量持续增长，全国著作权登记工作取得新进展新突破。现将 2017 年全国著作权登记情况通报如下：

一、总体情况

2017 年，全国著作权登记总量达 2 747 652 件，其中，作品登记 2 001 966 件、计算机软件著作权登记 745 387 件、著作权质权登记 299 件，相比 2016 年的 2 007 698 件，同比增长 36.86%。

二、作品登记有关情况

根据对全国 31 个省、自治区、直辖市和中国版权保护中心的作品登记信息统计，2017 年，全国共完成作品登记 2 001 966 件，相比 2016 年（1 599 597 件）作品登记量提升了 402 369 件，增长率为 25.15%。

全国作品登记量总体呈现稳步增长趋势。其中登记总量增长较快的分别是北京市 809 586 件，占登记总量的 40.44%；江苏省 286 596 件，占登记总量的 14.32%；上海市 234 658 件，占登记总量的 11.72%；中国版权保护中心 159 189 件，占登记总量的 7.95%；四川省 140 271 件，占登记总量的 7.01%；山东省 83 722 件，占登记总量的 4.18%。以上登记量约占 2017 年全国登记数量总量的 85.62%。相较于 2016 年，北京市、江苏省作品登记量的增长突破了 100 000 件；河北省、云南省、安徽省、宁夏回族自治区、广西壮族自治区作品登记量增长率均超过了 100%；四川省、陕西省、江西省、河南省、贵州省和广东省的作品登记量增长率均达 50%以上。

从作品类型来看，登记量最多的是摄影作品 734 998 件，占登记总量的 36.71%；其次是美术作品 653 820 件，占登记总量的 32.66%；第三是文字作品 480 640 件，占登记总量的 24.01%；影视作品 45 171 件，占登记总量的 2.26%。以上类型的作品登记量占全国登记总量的 95.64%。录像制品 38 045 件，占登记总量的 1.90%；音乐作品 11 619 件，占登记总量的 0.58%；图形作品 8 007 件，占登记总量的 0.40%；录音制品 4 714 件，占登记总量的 0.23%。模型、戏剧、曲艺、建筑等共计 24 952 件，共占登记总量的 1.25%。

三、计算机软件著作权登记有关情况

根据中国版权保护中心计算机软件著作权登记信息统计，2017 年，全国共完成计算机软件著作权登记 745 387 件，同比增长 82.79%，登记数量继 2016 年达到 40 万件后，连续跨过 50 万件和 60 万件整数关口，一举突破了 70 万件。

从计算机软件著作权登记的地区分布情况来看，2017 年东部地区登记软件 569 781 件，约占全国登记总量的 76.44%；中部地区登记软件 78 872 件，约占全国登记总量的 10.58%；西部地区登记软件 76 331 件，约占全国登记总量的 10.24%；东北部地区共登记软件 19 867 件，约占全国软件登记总量的 2.67%。从上述地区登记量增长情况来看，东部地区以 85.20%的增速处于全国的领跑位置，超过了中部地区 82.77%、西部地区 69.02%以及东北部地区 75.26%的登记增速。

从地区登记量情况来看，2017 年全国登记量较多的省市依次为：广东省、北京市、上海市、江苏

省、浙江省、福建省、四川省、山东省、湖北省和安徽省。上述地区共登记软件 607 035 件，约占全国登记总量的 81.44%。其中，广东省登记软件 219 860 件，约占全国总量的 29.50%。

从热点类别软件登记情况来看，2017 年，游戏软件、金融软件、APP、教育软件、医疗软件、物联网软件、地理信息软件、云计算软件和信息安全软件登记数量均较上一年度有不同程度提升。其中，APP 登记 154 977 件，约占全国软件登记总量的 20.79%，相比其他类别软件登记数量最高；金融软件登记 38 248 件，同比增长 133.95%，是增长最快的类别之一。另外，地理信息软件登记 17 780 件，同比增长 75.78%，增速较上一年度提升约 50 个百分点，呈现出高速增长的发展态势。

四、著作权质权登记有关情况

根据中国版权保护中心著作权质权登记信息统计，2017 年，全国共完成著作权质权登记 299 件，同比下降 5.38%；涉及合同数量 269 个，同比下降 6.27%；涉及作品数量 1 053 件，同比下降 1.03%；涉及主债务金额 297 448 万元，同比下降 6.45%；涉及担保金额 300 798.2 万元，同比下降 7.51%。

计算机软件著作权质权登记 233 件，同比下降 10.73%；涉及合同数量 233 个，同比下降 10.73%；涉及作品数量 987 件，同比下降 2.18%；涉及主债务金额 212 279.5 万元，同比下降 24.76%；涉及担保金额 212 578.7 万元，同比下降 26.79%。

作品（除计算机软件之外）著作权质权登记 66 件，同比增长 20.00%；涉及合同数量 36 个，同比增长 38.46%；涉及作品数量 66 件，同比增长 20.00%；涉及主债务金额 85 168.5 万元，同比增长 137.83%；涉及担保金额 88 219.5 万元，同比增长 152.91%。

希望各地版权行政管理部门和著作权登记机构在进一步贯彻落实《关于进一步规范作品登记程序等有关工作的通知》《关于规范作品登记证书的通知》《关于规范电子版作品登记证书的通知》的基础上，结合本地区、本部门实际，关注著作权登记工作的发展趋势和增长点，充分利用国家版权监管平台，不断提升著作权登记工作规范化、标准化、信息化水平，加强著作权登记工作队伍建设，妥善解决作品登记工作中存在的普遍性问题，全面提升著作权登记工作的效能，使著作权登记工作再上新台阶。

国家版权局办公厅

2018 年 2 月 13 日

关于做好 2018 年全国知识产权宣传周版权宣传活动的通知

国版办发［2018］4 号

各省、自治区、直辖市版权局，新疆生产建设兵团版权局；中国版权保护中心，中国版权协会，各著作权集体管理组织：

为贯彻落实党的十九大精神，加强版权宣传普及，庆祝第 18 个“4·26 世界知识产权日”，做好 2018 年“全国知识产权宣传周”（简称“宣传周”）的相关工作，国家版权局拟自 4 月初起集中开展版权宣传活动，并以 2018 年 4 月 20 日至 4 月 26 日为重点宣传时段。现将有关事项通知如下：

一、国家版权局将围绕 2018 年世界知识产权组织发布的“世界知识产权日”主题“变革的动力：女性参与创新创造”，全国知识产权宣传周组委会确定的 2018 年全国知识产权宣传周主题“倡导创新文化，尊重知识产权”，我局确定的主题“保护创作，推进运用”，以网络环境下的版权保护和产业发展为主要内容，制作版权宣传片、海报并开展系列主题宣传活动，相关素材将于 4 月上旬陆续上传到国家版权局官方网站（www. ncac. gov. cn）的宣传周专区。各地版权局要配合这一宣传方向，着重利用国家版权局提供的素材开展宣传，积极联系本地区平面媒体、网络媒体等媒体资源和学校单位、公交地铁、写字楼等公共资源播出和投放，做到与国家版权局上下联动、形成合力，扩大版权宣传周的社会影响力。

二、国家版权局将以鼓励查办网络侵权盗版案件为重点，在宣传周期间发布“2017 年度打击侵权盗版十大案件”，树立先进典型，发挥典型案例的震慑教育作用。各地版权局要着重梳理本地区查处侵权盗版案件情况，挖掘宣传报道重点和亮点，以案说法，并配合国家版权局对重点案件相关方的采访工作，积极开展版权执法工作宣传。

三、国家版权局将于 4 月 26 日“世界知识产权日”当天召开“第三届中国网络版权保护大会”，聚焦网络版权年度热点，发布国家版权局年度重要版权保护事件，促进版权保护助推产业发展。各地版权局、各相关单位要积极关注大会进展和相关发布报道，并利用本地媒体配合开展宣传；并可结合本地、本单位工作实际，开展相关版权专业研讨和宣传工作。

四、国家版权局将在宣传周期间开展中日韩三国版权主管部门联合宣传活动，通过采用中国孙悟空、日本柯南和韩国啵乐乐等国际熟知、深受公众喜爱且与版权保护主题契合度较高的动漫形象，共同设计制作版权宣传片和海报，向各自国家公众宣传推广。届时将通过国家版权局中英文网站、官方微博微信、报纸、电视、网站等渠道推广。请各地版权局、各相关单位密切关注宣传活动的发布和推广渠道，及时利用本地区、本单位的媒体资源播放宣传片及海报，提高我国版权保护工作的国际认可度。

五、国家版权局在宣传周期间将通过国家版权局官方网站“www.ncac.gov.cn”、新浪微博“@国家版权局”、腾讯微信“国家版权”、今日头条公众号、百度百家号等网络平台全面跟踪报道宣传周期间举办的各项活动。请各地版权局、各相关单位密切关注以上宣传渠道，及时利用本地区、本单位的资源转载相关信息，参与互动活动，扩大宣传周活动在全国的影响。

六、各地版权局、各相关单位要根据本地区、本单位的实际情况，认真做好宣传周活动计划和安排。积极筹划，充分准备，采用网络媒体、平面媒体和电视媒体全方位结合的多种形式，多角度、多渠道地做好宣传工作，扩大宣传影响，引导正面舆论氛围，提高全社会的版权保护意识。

七、各地版权局、各相关单位要及时将本辖区相关部门或本单位制作的宣传周宣传素材和举办宣传活动的现场视频、照片（配说明）、新闻报道等资料的电子版或链接报送至我局联系人邮箱，以便在国家版权局官网宣传周专区进行同步宣传，形成宣传周全国联动的态势。

八、举办宣传周各项活动要落实中央八项规定，厉行勤俭节约，严格遵守各项财务管理制度，杜绝形式主义，注重活动内容，务求宣传实效。

九、宣传周活动结束后，请各地版权局、各相关单位于 5 月 8 日前将宣传周活动情况以书面和电子版形式上报国家版权局。

国家版权局办公厅

2018 年 3 月 22 日

国家版权局等关于开展打击网络侵权盗版“剑网 2018”专项行动的通知

国版发电［2018］1 号

各省、自治区、直辖市版权局、通信管理局、公安厅（局）、网信办，北京市、天津市、上海市、重庆市、西藏自治区文化市场行政执法总队：

为深入贯彻习近平新时代中国特色社会主义思想和党的十九大精神，根据党中央、国务院关于建设网络强国、加强产权保护的决策部署，国家版权局、工业和信息化部、公安部、国家互联网信息办公室（以下简称“国家版权局等四部门”）定于 2018 年 7 月至 11 月联合开展第 14 次打击网络侵权盗版专项治理“剑网行动”（以下简称“剑网 2018”专项行动）。现将有关事项通知如下。

一、工作目标

以网络侵权多发领域为重点目标，以查办案件为重要抓手，通过集中整治和引导规范，有效运用分类监管、约谈整改、行政处罚、刑事打击等多种措施，集中整治网络转载、短视频、动漫等领域侵权盗版多发态势，重点规范网络直播、知识分享、有声读物等平台版权传播秩序，深入巩固网络影视、网络音乐、电子商务平台、应用商店、网络云存储空间等领域专项整治成果，维护清朗的网络空间秩序，营造良好的网络版权环境。

二、工作重点

一是开展网络转载版权专项整治。以网站、应用程序、自媒体、新闻聚合类平台为重点，严厉打击未经授权转载新闻作品的侵权行为；严厉打击未经授权摘编整合、歪曲篡改新闻作品的侵权行为；坚决整治自媒体通过“洗稿”方式抄袭剽窃、篡改删减原创作品的侵权行为；着力规范搜索引擎、浏览器、应用商店、微博、微信等涉及的网络转载行为。集中查处一批违法转载案件，依法取缔、关闭一批非法新闻网站（网站频道）及微博账号、微信公众号、头条号、百家号等互联网用户公众账号。

二是开展短视频版权专项整治。严厉打击短视频平台和短视频作品上传者未经授权复制、表演、通过网络传播他人影视、音乐、摄影、文字等作品的侵权行为；坚决整治短视频作品上传者以合理使用为名对他人作品删减改编并通过网络传播的侵权行为；坚决整治短视频平台以用户上传为名滥用“避风港”规则的侵权行为，并要求平台企业注明作品来源。将抖音短视频、快手、西瓜视频、火山小视频、快视频、美拍、秒拍、微视、梨视频、小影、56视频、火萤、哔哩哔哩等短视频应用程序列为本次行动重点监管对象，着力强化对短视频平台企业的版权监管。

三是开展重点领域版权专项整治。严厉打击未经授权通过网站、应用程序、互联网用户公众账号、视频字幕组传播动漫的侵权行为，严厉打击未经授权使用他人动漫形象制作传播游戏、玩具、文具、服装等动漫衍生品的侵权行为；着力整治网络直播、知识分享、有声读物等平台未经授权复制、表演、通过网络传播他人文字、音乐、口述等作品的行为；进一步加强对网络影视、网络音乐、电子商务平台、应用商店、网络云存储空间等领域的版权监管，突出打击通过网络销售教材教辅、少儿出版物、音乐和影视移动存储介质以及使用聚合链接、设置境外服务器等手段的侵权行为。

三、工作措施

（一）大力查办案件。坚持线上线下相结合，畅通投诉举报渠道，强化案件线索核查，加强网上巡查，及时固定证据。版权行政执法监管部门要发挥优势，强化运用约谈、预警等工作手段，加大对网络侵权盗版案件的行政处罚工作力度；对人民群众意见强烈、社会危害大的侵权盗版分子，要一律依法从严查处，依法吊销其备案资格或相关行政许可资质；要加大刑事打击工作力度，对涉嫌构成犯罪的，根据“两法衔接”机制及时移交公安机关立案查处。

（二）强化主体责任。版权行政执法监管部门要建立健全与辖区内互联网企业的指导协调工作机制，督促企业履行违法犯罪线索报告责任，督促电子商务平台企业和电信运营商强化版权监管义务，督促网络服务提供商履行“通知—删除”等法定处置责任。要求网站、应用商店在显著位置设立举报投诉窗口，明确专人负责举报受理和快速处理，对群众举报、版权行政执法监管部门通报的侵权盗版信息应迅速核查删除。对为侵权盗版行为提供帮助的网络服务提供商，依法追究其相关行政、刑事责任。

（三）加强社会共治。积极发挥权利人、社会团体、广大群众的“信息员”作用，强化打击侵权盗版社会共治。加大对大案要案和典型案件的宣传力度，坚决曝光具有恶劣情节的违法犯罪分子，坚决曝光不履行主体责任的互联网企业。充分发挥中国新闻媒体版权保护联盟等版权自律组织的作用，进一步引导传统媒体与商业网站开展版权合作，完善网络转载版权许可付酬机制。积极运用电信运营商、版权监测机构的技术优势，提高对网络侵权盗版信息的发现、研判、处置效率。

四、工作要求

（一）加强组织领导。各级版权、通信、公安、网信部门要进一步加强配合，因地制宜制定工作计划，明确任务和责任分工。版权行政执法监管部门负责专项行动的牵头工作，具体负责组织梳理网上侵权信息，搜集案件线索，查处违法行为，移送涉嫌犯罪案件，提请通信主管部门予以暂时停止网络接入直至关闭网站；开展版权监管工作，组织专项行动的宣传工作。通信主管部门协助开展网络侵权盗版案件调查取证工作，协助提供查处网络侵权盗版案件涉及网站的备案信息；对经版权行政执法监管部门、公安机关查处且侵权盗版情节严重的网站、应用程序依法吊销电信业务经营许可证或者注销ICP备案，并通知相关接入服务商停止为其提供网站接入服务；组织开展行业自律活动。公安机关要加大对涉嫌侵犯著作权犯罪案件的立案查处工作，及时受理版权执法监管部门移送的涉嫌犯罪案件，进一步加大对网络侵权盗版犯罪案件的刑事打击力度。互联网信息内容主管部门负责指导、协调、督促有关部门加强网络内容管理，有效利用各种手段加强对网络内容的监管。

（二）开展督导检查。国家版权局等四部门将围绕重点整治任务对各地开展督导检查，重点检查移转的案件材料的办理情况，并将督查情况特别是发现的问题进行通报。各地版权行政执法监管部门也要联合相关部门组成督查组，对本辖区专项行动开展情况进行督导检查，重点督查案件查办的情况，并对督查中发现的问题及时通报、限期整改。

（三）及时报送材料。各省、自治区、直辖市版权局，北京市、天津市、上海市、重庆市、西藏自治区文化市场行政执法总队要汇总本地办案信息，填写工作统计表，按月报送国家版权局，并于本通知下发后 15 日内报送本地区“剑网 2018”专项行动工作通知，12 月 10 日前报送专项行动工作总结，遇重要情况、重大案件和阶段性进展随时报送。

国家版权局

工业和信息化部

公安部

国家互联网信息办公室

2018 年 7 月 20 日

中国乡村建设百年图录

该书由著名“三农”问题专家温铁军和重庆大学人文社会科学高等研究院文学与文化中心主任、博士生导师潘家恩联合主编，为“十三五”国家重点图书规划项目。该书以乡村建设的“实践—研究者”为独特视野，以“百年”为单位重新梳理乡村建设的内外环境与基本脉络，通过打破历史与当代实践在时空和叙述上的割裂,从数千幅照片中遴选出自清末实业家张謇到新世纪乡村建设的珍贵照片近千幅,辅以专文导读与详细注释,以图片的形式系统展现了不同历史时期各种形式的乡村建设整体面貌,以全新视角探寻了乡村振兴的历史先声与鲜活经验。

董俊山 | Dong Junshan
第四届中国出版政府奖优秀出版人物

董俊山自2010年10月以来担任学习出版社社长，领导完成了出版社转企改制任务，致力于加强出版社制度体系改革、业务流程改造、主营业务拓展、发行渠道开辟、数字出版平台建设、人才队伍改善和领导班子建设，使学习出版社作为宣传思想文化战线的最前沿阵地的地位进一步巩固和增强。

近10年来，董俊山守初心、担使命，团结带领全社干部职工，始终坚持正确的出版导向，把社会效益放在首位；始终坚持服务党和国家工作大局、服务宣传思想文化工作全局、服务中宣部重点工作布局的根本宗旨；始终清醒认识肩负着引领主流意识形态的政治使命与社会责任，坚守宣传思想文化工作的重要阵地；始终坚持导向正、高品质、有特色、优而强的办社方针。无论是图书还是音像制品，从未出现过政治性问题、导向性问题、内容性问题，同时，他始终秉持一丝不苟的态度，使学习出版社出版物质量和品质不断提高。在中央宣传主管部门的领导、指导下，顺利完成了《习近平总书记系列重要讲话读本》（2014年版、2016年版）、《习近平新时代中国特色社会主义思想三十讲》、《习近平新时代中国特色社会主义思想学习纲要》和“理论热点面对面”系列图书的出版发行工作任务；组织撰稿并制作了《百年潮•中国梦》《劳动铸就中国梦》《中国之路》《大抗战》《信仰的力量》等电视政论片，实现了学习出版社的跨越式发展。

董俊山带领学习出版社，紧跟新媒体新技术的发展步伐，创立创办了学习云公司和学习时代网，开发搭建了时事政治在线学习和融媒体出版等平台，通过微信公众号、微信小程序、H5等，先后推出了《全民经典朗读范本》《新时代面对面》《习近平新时代中国特色社会主义思想三十讲》《习近平新时代中国特色社会主义思想学习纲要》《新中国发展面对面》等融媒体出版物，受到广泛好评。

董俊山率先垂范，以身作则，严格遵守和执行各项规章制度，廉洁自律。出版专著《冲突与抉择》《科技普及与精神文明建设》，发表《放歌改革大业•聚焦改革热点》《弘扬主旋律•传递正能量•唱响正气歌》等文章10余篇。2012年荣立个人三等功，2017年被评为第四届中国出版政府奖优秀出版人物。

学习出版社
第四届中国出版政府奖
优秀出版人物奖
国家新闻出版广电总局
2018 · 北京
中华人民共和国
国家新闻出版广电总局
第四届中国出版政府奖
图书奖
国家新闻出版广电总局
2018 · 北京

《习近平新时代中国特色社会主义思想学习纲要》　《习近平新时代中国特色社会主义思想三十讲》

《习近平总书记系列重要讲话读本》（2016版）

学习出版社由中央宣传主管部门主管主办。自1993年成立以来，坚持服务党和国家工作大局、服务宣传思想工作全局、服务中宣部重点工作布局的根本宗旨，秉持“专注传播先进文化、致力弘扬主流价值”的核心理念，严把正确的政治方向、出版导向和价值取向，推出了“中国特色社会主义理论读本”系列、“理论热点面对面”系列、“社会主义核心价值观”系列、“错误思潮辨析”系列、“学习理论文库”系列、“时代楷模”系列等一大批精品出版物，形成了具有社会影响力和市场号召力的品牌。被评为首届中国出版政府奖先进出版单位、全国百佳图书出版单位、全国文化体制改革工作先进单位；出版物多次荣获中国出版政府奖、提名奖，中华优秀出版物奖图书奖、音像电子游戏出版物奖；多种图书和音像制品入选年度主题出版重点出版物选题。

学习出版社出版的宣传贯彻习近平新时代中国特色社会主义思想重要辅助读物，其中《习近平新时代中国特色社会主义思想三十讲》单品发行量超3 500万册，被《人民日报》、新华网、中央广播电视总台、《光明日报》等媒体报道，有声读物在“学习强国”平台推出，社会反响热烈。作为干部群众、青年学生进行理论学习和开展形势政策教育的重要辅导读物，《新时代面对面——理论热点面对面•2018》图书销售突破600万册，《新中国发展面对面——理论热点面对面•2019》于2019年7月出版发行，受到广泛好评。

专业传播先进文化　致力弘扬主流价值

王斌 | Wang Bin

2018年度“中国版权事业卓越成就者”

王斌，中信出版集团股份有限公司党委书记、董事长。曾经入选“中国书业改革开放30年30人”，2010年被新闻出版主管部门授予“中国百名优秀出版企业家”荣誉称号，2015年被中国出版协会评为2015年度“中国十大出版人物”，2018年被中国版权协会授予“中国版权事业卓越成就者”称号，并当选“2018中国文化产业十大年度人物”。

王斌投身出版行业30余年，曾一手创建“华章图书”品牌。自2001年担任中信出版社社长以来，他高举“激情出版”的旗帜，保持了突出的专注力、热情和创意，不断改革创新，建立了中信出版独特的运作方式和精准的流程，打造了一本本诸如《谁动了我的奶酪》《杰克•韦尔奇自传》《从优秀到卓越》《激荡三十年》《黑天鹅》《史蒂夫•乔布斯传》《从0到1》《人类简史》《未来简史》《原则》等深受读者喜爱的畅销书，也开创了“奶酪”“黑天鹅”“长尾理论”“基业长青”“魔鬼经济学”“人类简史”“灰犀牛”等口碑概念。

王斌始终以“改革、创新、求变”的精神带领企业发展，一直坚持“裂变、延展”的业务发展逻辑。对做得风生水起的出版业务，他不为成规所囿，2014年力推“举手制”，鼓励有想法、有能力的年轻人“举手”成立工作室或分社，依托平台的品牌价值和管理优势去创造新的价值。目前，图书出版业务已经由2014年的7个分社裂变成为30余个独立出版人，超过10个子品牌码洋过亿元。

在王斌的带领下，中信出版在近20年里以独特的业务模式和自我进化的方式不断裂变扩张，以其管理理念、组织变革方式以及进化理念重塑了出版机构的商业逻辑，成为出版行业改革发展的标杆企业。中信出版2018年全年出版新书1 300余种，出版码洋超26亿元，动销品种6 800种。根据开卷信息的统计数据，2018年公司在整体图书零售市场的码洋占有率为2.47%，为单体出版社排名第二，其中经管类图书市场占有率排名继续保持领先，学术文化排名第二，科普类排名第三，生活类排名第五。中信出版已成为国内出版市场颇具影响力的综合出版集团。

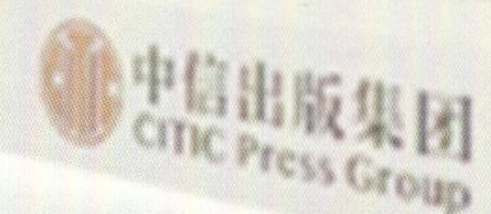

中信出版社成立于1988年，隶属于中国中信集团有限公司，2008年改制为中信出版股份有限公司，2013年发展成为中信出版集团，具有国家新闻出版主管部门颁发的出版、发行、零售全牌照。2019年7月，中信出版集团成功登陆A股市场，正式在深圳证券交易所挂牌交易。

中信出版集团秉承“我们提供知识，以应对变化的世界”的理念，为转型中的中国社会提供思想和知识服务，引领和满足大众读者多样化的知识与文化需求。随着公司业务的不断发展，中信出版集团的版权储备领先优势逐渐形成，已先后与超过11 000位国际、国内的优秀作者建立了合作关系。

中信出版集团高度重视版权输出工作，在“讲好中国故事，让世界看懂中国”的理念引领下，布局“聚焦欧美、润泽亚洲、撒播丝路”多元化战略，助力出版“走出去”。在过去十多年间与全球近200家知名出版商建立了深度合作关系，成功向美国、英国、法国、德国、意大利、罗马尼亚、西班牙、瑞典、波兰、俄罗斯、新加坡、日本、韩国等国家以及我国台湾、香港地区输出图书版权近1 000种。

其中，从2014年开始策划的“投资中国”系列顺利售出英语、法语、俄语、日语、韩语、阿拉伯语、希伯来语等多个语种，海外市场表现出色。

2016年策划的“中国主题”系列是一套面向法国读者全面介绍中国经济、社会、文化等的丛书，由《读懂中国改革》、《制度改变中国》、《必要的改革》、《甲子》（1~3）、《中国人的自觉》等10余本代表性图书组成。法语版由法国纽维斯出版社出版上市，并在法国亚马逊、Fnac、Decitre等主流书店热销。

2018年，中信出版集团成功向美国、英国、日本、韩国、俄罗斯、土耳其、阿尔巴尼亚等17个国家及地区输出图书版权近400种。此外，中信出版携手日本茑屋书店的母公司CCC集团合资成立了中信出版日本株式会社，以内容运营为主，致力于打造中日文化交流的新平台，已成功推出《蚂蚁金服》《中国新零售》等44种图书。

除积极推广自有图书资源，中信出版集团也通过挖掘外部优秀原创内容，将更多好作品推广至海外市场，推动出版“走出去”。目前，中信出版已代理《腾讯传》《藏地密码》等10余种优质图书的海外版权，并成功将《腾讯传》输出至韩国、日本、以色列、越南以及我国台湾地区。

未来，中信出版集团将继续加大投入力度，基于在版权引进领域的经验和客户资源，与国际市场接轨，将出版“走出去”作为一项长期的工作目标来执行。

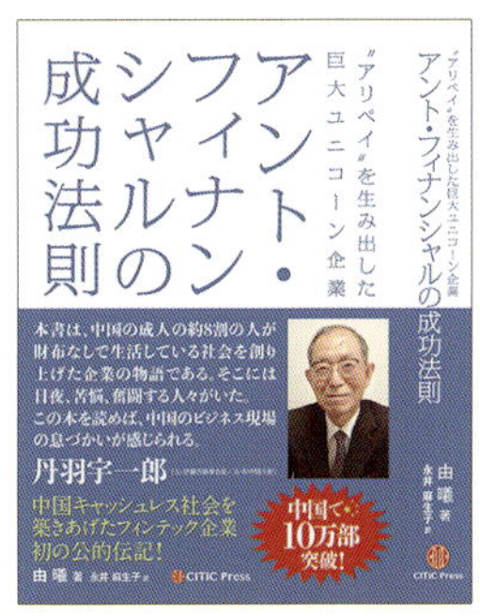

刘东杰 | Liu Dongjie
2018年度“中国十大出版人物”

刘东杰，1963年3月生，山东教育出版社社长，编审，中国版协教育图书工作委员会副主任、中国教育学会教育出版研究专业委员会副理事长。

1985年参加工作，1987年开始从事出版工作，历任山东科技出版社编辑、副总编辑，山东美术出版社副社长，山东教育出版社总编辑，2011年3月始担任山东教育出版社社长。

1994年获首届全省优秀中青年编辑奖；1998年被评为“山东省出版系统十佳人才”；2012年被选拔为山东省第二批齐鲁文化英才；2014年获第二届山东省新闻出版奖优秀人物奖；2017年入选“2016年度全国新闻出版行业领军人才”，获第四届中国出版政府奖优秀出版人物奖；2018年被评选为2018年度“中国十大出版人物”。

矢志不渝从事出版工作三十多年，始终把出版作为实现人文情怀和理想抱负的终生志业；秉持着对出版理想的坚守和对社会责任的担当，依托着丰厚的出版经验和敏锐的行业洞察力，在出版领域勤恳耕耘，开拓进取，做出了突出的出版业绩。

一、坚守出版使命，勇于开拓创新，取得突出社会效益

刘东杰策划、编辑的图书获国家图书奖、“五个一工程”奖等国家大奖多项，其本人荣获“全国新闻出版行业领军人才”、中国出版政府奖优秀出版人物奖等多项国家级大奖。自2011年担任山东教育出版社社长以来，带领该社荣获中国出版政府奖图书奖等国家级奖项30余个，18个项目入选“十二五”“十三五”国家重点出版规划，4个项目入选国家新闻出版改革发展项目库，16个项目获得国家出版基金资助，13个项目入选总局“经典中国国际出版工程”、“丝路书香工程”和“中国图书对外推广计划”等资助项目。该社先后获得山东省新闻出版奖优秀集体奖、山东省第三批重点文化企业、山东省首批传统出版数字化转型示范单位、山东省全民阅读示范单位、全国版权示范单位等荣誉称号。

二、科学谋划布局，善于经营管理，实现较好经济收益

刘东杰为山东教育出版社确定了以服务教育教学为主线，全力做好教材教辅研发，深度挖掘精品力作，重点培育数字出版，努力打造一个具有全媒质出版功能的一流教育出版企业的发展战略。一是以基础教育出版为中心，建设基础教育出版基地、阅读与写作基地，形成了在国标教材、地方教材和教辅产品等领域出版研发的专业优势。二是注重精品力作的品牌建设，培育出教育学、学科史、名家文集、原创儿童文学等特色板块，在凸显品牌影响力的同时，使市场化转型取得突出成效。三是坚持内容为本，科技引领，一体化融合创新发展，搭建起全媒体一体化教育出版服务体系。四是运用融合理念不断开拓新的市场空间，构建起线上线下立体化的市场营销网络。在刘东杰的带领下，山东教育出版社利润总额从2010年的2 300多万元增长到2018年的6 300多万元，增长了173%。

山东教育出版社
Shandong Education Press

山东教育出版社成立于1982年，是全国优秀出版社、全国版权示范单位。以“出书育人、服务社会、传播科学、繁荣文化”的文化情怀和责任担当，紧跟时代发展脉搏，围绕服务教育教学专业出版方向，在教材教辅研发、精品力作出版、数字出版开发方面，形成了自身的专业优势和品牌特色，走出了一条专业化、市场化、数字化、多元化、国际化的创新发展之路。

成立山东基础教育出版基地，聘请一流教育专家组建教育出版智库，研发出版有17个学科的国标教材、6个学科的地方课程教材和八大系列教辅品种，国标教材品种数量位居全国前列。

注重精品力作品牌建设，培育出教育学、人文社科、自然科学、传统文化、原创儿童文学、高端绘本等特色板块，推出了一大批具有高水平影响力和传承价值的精品力作，有36种出版物荣获国家图书三大奖，其中8种图书连续四届荣获中国出版政府奖，8种出版物连续六届荣获中华优秀出版物奖，在凸显品牌影响力的同时，市场化转型取得突出成效。

以“内容为本，科技引领，一体化融合创新发展”理念为引领，将网络技术、数字技术广泛应用到教育产品开发上，积极研发推送个性化新型教育产品，由纸质图书向电子书、有声书、视频书、纸电纸网融合书和智能化教育产品研发迈进，全力打造具有全媒质出版功能的现代教育出版企业。

围绕国家“走出去”战略，先后有150余种图书版权输出到20多个国家，其中13个项目获“经典中国国际出版工程”、“丝路书香工程”和“中国图书对外推广计划”资助。2017年与澳大利亚教育管理集团合作在墨尔本注册成立澳山国际教育出版公司，2018年与罗马尼亚欧洲思想出版社共同设立中国主题图书编辑部。建立海外出版发行平台，联合国际著名机构一体化运作，是立足当前、谋划长远的重大战略决策。

面向未来，山东教育出版社以创新驱动发展、用质量铸就品牌、靠人才成就未来，努力打造一个满足教育现代化需求具有全媒质出版功能和高市场影响力的一流教育出版企业。

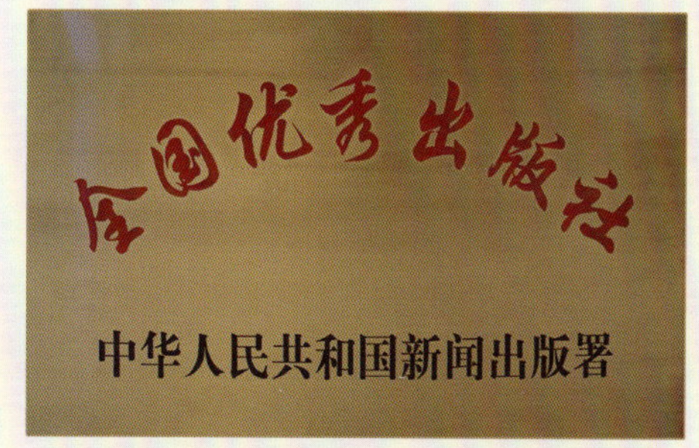

全国优秀出版社

全国版权示范单位

奖牌

惠西平 | Hui Xiping
2018年度“中国十大出版人物”

惠西平，1958年10月生，陕西甘泉人，本科学历，编审职称，现任陕西新华出版传媒集团有限责任公司党委委员、董事，陕西人民出版社有限责任公司社长。

1976年11月参加工作，1989年加入中国共产党，历任华岳文艺出版社编辑部主任，太白文艺出版社副社长、副总编辑，陕西科学技术出版社社长，陕西人民出版社副社长兼副总编辑（主持工作）、社长。多年出任陕西省出版专业高级职称任职资格评审委员会学科组组长、评委会主任。并担任中国出版协会常务理事、中国武侠文学会副会长、陕西文化交流协会常务理事、陕西省教育学会副会长等。

先后获评新中国60年“百名有突出贡献的新闻出版专业技术人员”、享受国务院特殊津贴专家、“全国百佳出版工作者”、“全国新闻出版行业领军人才”、第十二届韬奋出版奖、第四届中国出版政府奖优秀出版人物奖、2018年度“中国十大出版人物”、陕西省“四个一批”经营管理人才、陕西省“三五人才”第二层次人选、陕西省重点领域顶尖人才、第二届“陕西最具文化影响力十大产业领军人物”、陕西出版集团“优秀经营管理者”和先进个人等奖项和荣誉称号。

独立编辑和参与策划编辑图书逾千种，复审、终审书稿数百种，所责编的数十种图书获省部级以上奖励。其中，《蓝天下的永恒——最美女孩熊宁》入选“第二届百种优秀青春读物”；《鼎立南极》获第十二届全国“五个一工程”奖；《梦跟颜色一样轻》获第二届中国出版政府奖装帧设计奖；《中国少数民族法史通览》《日本味儿》分别获得第四届中国出版政府图书提名奖和装帧设计提名奖；《法门寺》获第三届中华优秀出版物（音像出版物）奖；《陕北民歌集萃》获第四届中华优秀出版物奖；《中国动力》获“中国好书”提名奖。主持策划的《四部文明》被誉为“为中华文明聚原典，为子孙后代存信史”之集大成之作，在海内外产生了广泛影响。2018年，策划出版的纪实文学《梁家河》引起了社会的广泛关注，深受读者喜爱，在全国各地掀起学习的热潮，荣获2018年度非虚构类畅销书奖。

惠西平政治站位高，改革和创新意识强，懂经营、善管理，熟悉出版行业编、印、发各个环节。他勇于创新，锐意进取，使出版社各项事业取得了巨大进步。2007年，陕西人民出版社在全国综合实力排名第36位，社科类出版实力排名第12位。2008年，在“最受读者欢迎的出版社”评选中排名全国出版单位第6位。被授予“全国良好出版社”荣誉称号；多次被陕西省委、省政府评为省级精神文明建设最佳单位。2018年，被评为“2018中国版权年度最具影响力企业”、西安市文化创意产业“十佳企业”、“十佳陕版图书”出版单位、陕西省“三秦书月”全民阅读活动先进单位等。

惠西平从事出版工作37年，在工作上业绩卓著，屡获殊荣，为陕西出版事业的发展做出了突出的贡献。

陕西人民出版社有限责任公司

SHAANXI PEOPLE'S PUBLISHING HOUSE CO., LTD.

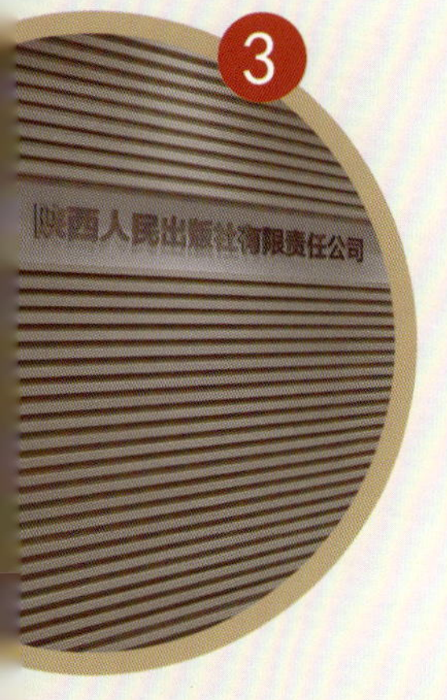

陕西人民出版社（1954年10月前称西北人民出版社）成立于1951年1月，2010年11月改制转企，更名为陕西人民出版社有限责任公司。目前已发展成为以出版社科图书为主，具有图书、报纸、杂志、音像制品、电子出版物等多种出版能力，以及经营中小学教材等的功能齐全、具有一定规模和影响力的综合性出版社，主办有陕西电子音像出版社、阳光报社、文化艺术报社、时代人物杂志社等；与人民教育出版社联合组建了陕西西北人教玉成文化传媒有限公司；与中国延安精神研究会、中共延安市委共同组建成立了延安书局。

60多年来，陕西人民出版社共出版各类图书4万多种，发行40多亿册，数百种图书输出到日本、法国、澳大利亚等国家以及我国台湾、香港地区，数千种图书获得省部级以上奖励，多种图书荣获“五个一工程”奖、中国出版政府奖、中华优秀出版物奖等国家级奖项。

全社现有职工180余人，具有高级职称专业技术人员50余人，其中有韬奋出版奖、中国出版政府奖优秀出版人物获得者，新中国60年“百名有突出贡献的新闻出版专业技术人员”，享受国务院特殊津贴专家，新闻出版总署突出贡献专家，“全国新闻出版行业领军人才”，全国宣传文化系统“四个一批”人才，全国新闻出版系统劳动模范，全国中青年优秀编辑，陕西省有突出贡献专家，陕西省宣传文化系统首批经营管理人才，陕西省重点领域顶尖人才等。

先后被相关主管部门授予“全国良好出版社”、“精神文明建设单位”、“2018中国版权年度最具影响力企业”、西安市文化创意产业“十佳企业”、陕西省“三秦书月”全民阅读活动先进单位等荣誉称号。

1. 办公大楼 2. 陕西人民出版社展厅 3. 公司铭牌 4. 陕西人民出版社办公区

覃超 | Qin Chao
2018年度“中国十大出版人物”

自任职广西出版传媒集团党委书记、董事长以来，覃超带领广西出版传媒集团奋力打造广西标杆文化企业，坚持社会效益与经济效益相统一，推动偏居一隅的广西出版走出广西、走向东盟。2018年，覃超荣获2018年度“中国十大出版人物”称号。

覃超带领广西出版传媒集团，主要完成以下工作：

一是加强党的建设，推动企业管理水平提升。坚定党建引领的企业治理，试行党代表任期联系制，完善“三重一大”决策制度，开创性构建纪检监察、法律事务、审计督查一体的风险管控组织架构。顺利推进与新华书店集团的融合发展。聚焦主业，关、停、并、转不良企业40余家。

二是实施精品战略，推动社会效益提升。从数量规模增长向质量效益提高转变。举办2018中国出版创新年会暨集团出版规划研讨会，承办中国编辑学会第十九届年会和理事会，提升集团精品出版意识，出版“我们的广西”丛书等一批“双效”俱佳的优秀出版物。多种出版物入选国家主题出版目录；7个项目获年度国家出版基金扶持。

三是创新出版“走出去”，推动集团国际传播能力提升。在越南河内建成运行集团首家海外阅读体验店——“彤•阅读体验中心”，得到中央领导充分肯定和业界高度关注。《中国—东盟博览》杂志在东盟多国设立分社。建设东盟网络文学平台等数字交流平台。

四是深化出版业供给侧结构性改革，推动集团高质量发展。提高出版质量，狠抓内容建设；探索首席编辑工作室、项目负责制、职业经理人等制度；推进实体书店文化改造，探索连锁经营模式，加大优秀出版物的市场供给和营销力度；开源节流降本增效。

五是实施数字融合战略，推进出版转型升级。实施一批重大出版融合项目，接力出版社获“十佳出版新技术应用企业”；落户“党员小书包”平台，融合传统出版资源与互联网技术，实现传统出版的增值服务。集团被列入第一批ISLI应用标准主要起草单位。

六是倡领阅读风尚，全民阅读工作成效显著。创建广西读书节，举办2018中国全民阅读年会、2018广西书展。联合各行各业合作建立37个彤书屋•全民阅读基地，建成使用5家校园书店，建设网红书店——漓江书院三祺广场24小时店、南宁三街两巷店。

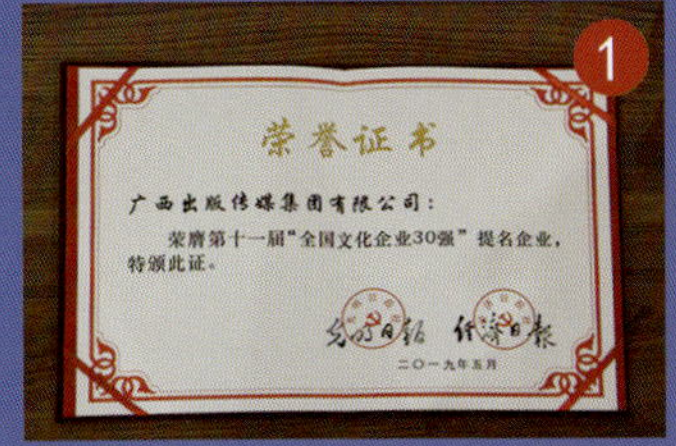

1. 广西出版传媒集团有限公司荣膺第十一届“全国文化企业30强”提名企业
2. 能干事、会干事、干实事，让地处祖国西南边陲的广西出版传媒集团，始终在我国出版业板块中占有一席之地
3. 广西出版传媒集团主办2018中国出版创新年会
4. 广西出版传媒集团主办2018中国全民阅读年会

广西出版传媒集团有限公司

2009年12月，广西出版传媒集团有限公司成立。拥有接力出版社、漓江出版社等24家全资、控股子公司，业务涵盖图书、期刊、音像、电子、网络等出版、印刷（复制）、发行等主业经营。集团立足广西特色，提升广西出版品牌影响力，获得国际卓越奖、中华优秀出版物奖、“五个一工程”奖、中国出版政府奖、“世界最美的书”、“中国最美的书”等奖项20余项，获第十一届“全国文化企业30强”提名企业。2018年集团资产总额77.32亿元，营业收入34.58亿元，实现利润3.25亿元，创历史最好业绩。

社会效益稳步提升。2018年，集团出版图书4 535种、1.8亿册，持续实施精品战略，出版了“我们的广西”丛书、《万物简史（少儿彩绘版）》、《中国道路的文化基因》等一批“双效”俱佳的优秀出版物，主办2018中国出版创新年会暨集团出版规划研讨会，承办中国编辑学会第十九届年会，社会影响力显著提升。

国际传播能力不断增强。集团在越南良好运营“彤•阅读体验中心”，得到中央宣传主管部门充分肯定和业界高度关注；接力出版社埃及分社出版发行26种阿语版图书，获得埃及“最佳儿童图书翻译奖”；广西美术出版社日本编辑部出版销售9种图书；“中国—东盟国际合作出版计划”出版《实用越汉•汉越词典》等面向东盟国家的精品出版物；2018年对外图书版权输出229 种（不含港澳台），创历史新高。

全民阅读工作成效显著。集团在北京9所高校承办“庆祝改革开放40周年、广西壮族自治区成立60周年”——广西好书推介及读书分享会，取得热烈反响。举办2018中国全民阅读年会，创建“广西读书节”，开展“春节，带一本好书回家”公益活动，与机构合作建立了37家彤书屋•全民阅读基地，建成8家国企书院、5家校园书店。

5. 2018年，广西出版传媒集团“我们的广西”丛书出版，献礼改革开放40周年、广西壮族自治区成立60周年
6. 漓江书院三祺广场24小时书店成为网红书店
7. 8. 2017年11月，广西出版传媒集团首家海外阅读体验空间——“彤•阅读体验中心”建成使用

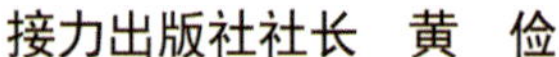

接力出版社社长　黄　俭

接力出版社总编辑　白　冰

接力出版社于1990年建社，29年来，曾连续八届荣获中央宣传主管部门“五个一工程”奖，三次荣获中国出版政府奖先进出版单位奖。2016年，在由伦敦书展和英国出版协会共同主办的国际卓越奖评选中，接力出版社荣获“国际儿童及青少年出版商奖”，成为中国出版行业率先获得此奖项的出版单位。

多年来，接力出版社始终坚持“以社会效益为先，两个效益统一”的原则。截至2018年10月，接力出版社共有62种图书获得中外奖项、入选重点推荐书单。《乌龟一家去看海》荣获国际儿童读物联盟颁发的2018年国际儿童读物联盟（IBBY）荣誉作品奖。《小饼干和围裙妈妈：第一次分开睡》荣获埃及文化部国家翻译中心颁发的2017儿童文学翻译奖，也是中国图书首次在阿拉伯国家获此奖项。《本草纲目（少儿彩绘版）》《萤火虫女孩》《时间之城》入选国家新闻出版主管部门2018年向全国青少年推荐的百种优秀出版物。其中，《萤火虫女孩》还入选2017年度“大众喜爱的50种图书”、《中华读书报》2017年十佳童书。《中国汉字听写大会•我的趣味汉字世界（儿童彩绘版）》入选第二届向全国推荐中华优秀传统文化普及图书。《资本论（少儿彩绘版）》被《中国新闻出版广电报》评为2018年上半年优秀少儿图书。《山海经（少儿彩绘版）》入选十八大以来30本桂版好书、《中华读书报》2017年度百佳图书。《一只特立独行的猪》被评为2018年深圳读书月“年度十大童书 ”。《鄂温克的驼鹿》入选《父母必读》2018 年优秀童书排行榜 Top 10。

接力出版社荣获第四届中国出版政府奖先进出版单位奖

首届接力杯金波幼儿文学奖、首届接力杯曹文轩儿童小说奖颁奖典礼

接力出版社首届婴幼儿图画书创作研习营

证 书

接力出版社有限公司：

荣获第四届中国出版政府奖先进出版单位奖。

特颁此证

国家新闻出版广电总局

二〇一八年

接力出版社荣获第四届中国出版政府奖先进出版单位奖

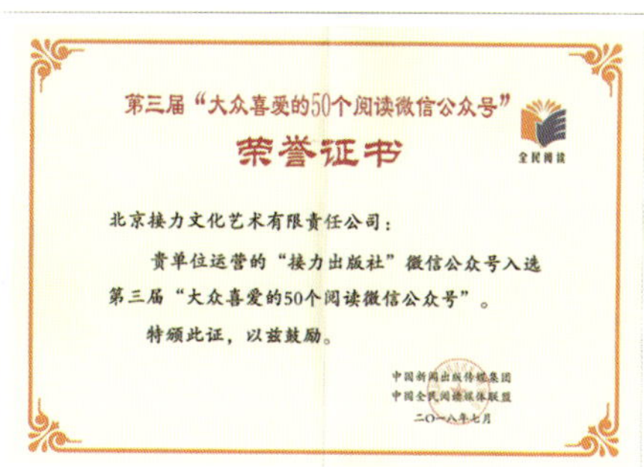

第三届“大众喜爱的50个阅读微信公众号”

荣誉证书

北京接力文化艺术有限责任公司：

贵单位运营的“接力出版社”微信公众号入选第三届“大众喜爱的50个阅读微信公众号”。

特颁此证，以兹鼓励。

中国新闻出版传媒集团

中国全民阅读媒体联盟

二〇一八年七月

“接力出版社”微信公众号入选第三届“大众喜爱的50个阅读微信公众号”

2018年1月，首届接力杯金波幼儿文学奖、首届接力杯曹文轩儿童小说奖揭晓，16部作品分获金、银、铜奖。接力出版社精心策划出版、深度营销推广，扩大获奖作品的中外影响力，发现更多新人作家及作品。

接力出版社长期与国内外众多优秀作家有着良好的合作，包括金波、曹文轩、秦文君、郑春华、彭懿、黑鹤、贝尔•格里尔斯等，并推出了“大王书”系列、“小鸟公主”系列、“黑鹤动物文学精品系列”、“小饼干和围裙妈妈”系列、“少儿万有经典文库”系列、“中国梦之歌校园朗诵诗”系列、“巴巴爸爸”系列、“蓝精灵”系列、“荒野求生少年生存小说系列”等一大批“双效”显著的优秀图书。

接力出版社始终坚持“让世界读者感受中国精彩，让中国读者与世界同步阅读”的出版理念，截至2018年10月，接力出版社图书版权输出108种，版权输出到法国、俄罗斯、加拿大、埃及、伊朗、韩国、斯里兰卡、越南、泰国等国家和地区。接力出版社埃及分社于2016年10月注册并正式运营，目前，分社已有26种阿语版图书出版发行。

2018年，中国首次担任博洛尼亚国际童书展与阿尔及尔国际童书展的主宾国。接力出版社承办了“中外童书出版合作新趋势”和“阿中童书出版合作机遇与前景”产业论坛，旨在加强中外童书出版界的沟通和理解，促进中外童书出版合作的创新和探索。接力出版社积极与国外出版社共同策划，即将出版曹文轩与俄罗斯插画家欧尼可夫合作的图画书《无法停止的奔跑》，与韩国插画家Suzy Lee合作的图画书《雨露麻》。

2018年，接力出版社携手俄罗斯莫斯科州立综合图书馆合办“比安基国际文学奖”，通过与国际机构合作设奖，推动原创自然文学作家及作品“走出去”，引进自然文学优秀作品，为原创提供借鉴。

2019年4月，接力出版社携手中国出版协会、法国驻华大使馆举办首届中法童书出版高研班，吸引了众多从业者，更有全国各地的学员不远万里赴京，一睹行业大咖风采，汲取童书出版前沿讯息及知识，与业内专业人士交流互动。

接力出版社在博洛尼亚书展

“比安基国际文学奖暨童书交换”仪式现场

2019年首届中法童书出版高研班

人民出版社

人民出版社
“不忘初心、牢记使命”
主题图书

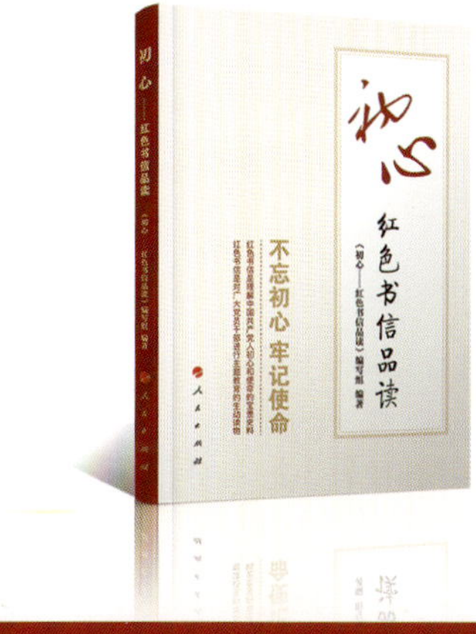

《初心——红色书信品读》编写组 编著
定价：39.00 元

邵维正 刘晓宝 著
定价：48.00元

北京市纪委市监委机关
北京市委宣传部 编著
定价：59.00元

本书编写组 编
定价：46.00元

文丰安 著
定价：46.00元

崔耀中 编著
定价：58.00元

《初心和使命（图解版）》
编写组 编著
定价：39.80元

学习时报编辑部 编
定价：15.00元

南湖革命纪念馆 编
定价：65.00元

社址：北京市东城区隆福寺街99号金隆基大厦 邮编：100706 网址：http://www.ccpph.com.cn/

发行电话：010-84095046 010-84095121 邮购地址：100706 北京市朝内大街166号 人民东方图书销售中心 邮购电话：010-65250042

致敬伟大新时代

献礼共和国华诞 定心精品出版
坚持高质量发展 推进“三型集团”建设

中国出版集团是适应出版业改革发展的需要，经中共中央、国务院批准于2002年成立的中央级出版机构。2004年，国务院授权中国出版集团公司对所属成员单位行使出资人权利。2011年，集团所属出版及有关业务板块完成股份制改革，组建中国出版传媒股份有限公司，并于2017年8月21日在上海证券交易所公开发行股票。2019年，集团本级完成公司制改革，更名为中国出版集团有限公司。

中国出版集团是中国较大的大众出版和专业出版集团，旗下有商务印书馆、中华书局、生活•读书•新知三联书店、人民文学出版社等38家著名出版和文化机构，拥有各级子公司、控股公司等法人企业98家，拥有海外出版社、连锁书店和办事机构29家。目前，集团年出版图书2万余种，出版期刊报纸58种，实现版权贸易1 000多种，经营进出口各类出版物70多万种。

集团自2008年以来连续11年入选“全国文化企业30强”，连续入选 “全球出版业营业收入50强”，正在进一步向主流出版型、融合发展型、国际传播型“三型集团”迈进。

主题出版唱主角，用精品力作飨广大读者

近年来集团党组明确提出“做响主题出版”的基本理念，在国家宣传主管部门指导下，集团在主题出版上取得了明显成绩，逐渐形成了具有中版特色的主题出版体系，推出了《抗日战争》《中华文明的核心价值》《重读抗战家书》《红星照耀中国》《天开海岳：走近港珠澳大桥》《走近卡尔•马克思》等一批颇具影响的重点图书，在出版界起到了示范作用。

2019年以来，集团主题出版工作也可圈可点，推出了《如何讲好中国故事》《香港政制发展历程》《敢为天下先：中国航展二十年》《走进古田会议》《支部音乐课：用歌声宣誓》等重点新书，《国家相册：改革开放四十年的家国记忆》作为集团代表性主题出版物入选“中国好书”2018年度图书，“新中国70年70部长篇小说典藏”、“中华人物故事汇”系列丛书（第一辑）、《中国儿童太空百科全书•中国航天》、《中国多党合作制度七十年（1949—2019）》等4种选题入选国家宣传主管部门2019年主题出版重点出版物选题目录。为庆祝新中国成立70周年，集团各出版单位全年计划推出近120种主题图书，其中60种已经出版，包括荣宝斋出版社《老一辈革命家书法艺术精选》，商务印书馆《精神的力量——改革开放中的邓小平》《不凡的历程——陈云与改革开放》，三联书店《迈向新赛道——华为系列故事》，研究出版社《中共中央在延安：一个马克思主义政党的崛起》《人类减贫史上的中国奇迹——中国扶贫改革40周年论文集》等一大批思想知识含量厚重的学术图书和学术普及图书。还有中国大百科全书出版社《中国儿童太空百科全书•中国航天》，天天出版社《犇向绿心》《正阳门下》等儿童图书。

——主题图书——

新中国70年70部长篇小说典藏

我和我的祖国

人民就是江山·庆祝中华人民共和国成立70周年连环画集

精神的力量——改革开放中的邓小平

人类减贫史上的中国奇迹
——中国扶贫改革40周年论文集

中国儿童太空百科全书·中国航天

光荣与道路：
中国大时代的精英记忆

国家相册：改革开放四十年的家国记忆

逄先知文丛（4种）

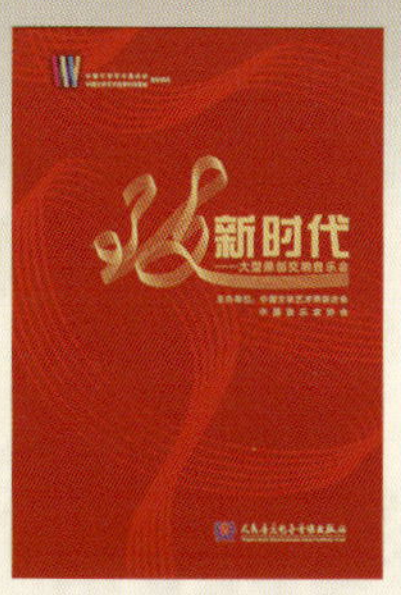

致新时代

走进古田会议

集团举办“讲述扶贫故事，中国出版在行动”主题活动

引领出版扶贫　展现“国家队”担当

中版集团自2015年起定点帮扶青海省泽库县，派出精兵强将，积极参与脱贫攻坚实践。集团2019年进一步加大力度，以12项措施加大对青海省泽库县的帮扶力度，直接投资加引进帮扶资金、购买农牧产品等，总投资超千万元，还通过文化产业开发合作、人才干部培训、特色文化宣传、党建结对帮扶等方式提升扶贫的智力基础，让精准扶贫、稳定脱贫落到实处、取得实效。2019年北京国际图书博览会（BIBF）期间，集团举办主题为“讲述扶贫故事，中国出版在行动”的活动集中展示、发布全国扶贫书单、“中国扶贫书系”，引起广泛关注。

融合发展重积淀，立足内容推动知识服务

近年来，集团在融合发展方面以文化资源为主导，以内容数据为中心，以平台开发为龙头，以投入产出为主线。通过内容数字化向内容数据化的转变，实现软资产的有效聚集，逐步形成集团内容动能较强的软实力和核心竞争力。

2012年，集团召开第一次数字化战略推进会，明确了以内容资源建设为基础，以重大项目为突破口的基本定位和发展思路，通过“（1+6）×4”的重大平台发展架构，重点解决的是集团数字化做什么的问题。2016年，集团召开第二次数字化战略推进会，确立了集团“十三五”时期融合发展的战略目标，提出了“六强三抓”的战略重点和关键举措，重点解决的是怎么做的问题。2019年，集团召开第三次数字化战略推进会，确定了集团融合发展以重大项目为主要带动方式，重点解决了融合发展重大项目机制改革问题。

商务印书馆《新华字典》APP

中华经典古籍库

《中国大百科全书》第一、二版合照，第三版网络版即将推出

国际舞台展形象，以书会友搭虹桥传扬先进文化

2019年北京国际图书博览会期间，集团各出版单位签约多语种版权输出534项目，再次领先业界。

人民文学出版社茅盾文学奖作品《牵风记》和《应物兄》，版权输出黎巴嫩、土耳其、英国。中华书局“中华先贤人物故事汇”“中华传奇人物故事汇”签约多语种输出。

中图公司承办的北京国际图书博览会进一步巩固全球第二国际书展地位。版权贸易数量增长5.6%，达到5 995项。出色完成第13届“中华图书特殊贡献奖”颁奖仪式、2019北京出版高峰会议、“中马出版合作新计划”启动仪式等重要活动的承办工作，率先亮相的中图•联通5G新阅读展区备受关注。

茅盾文学奖作品《牵风记》
和《应物兄》版权推介会

集团主办2019国际出版企业高层论坛

中国教育出版传媒集团有限公司

CHINA EDUCATION PUBLISHING & MEDIA GROUP LTD.

中国教育出版传媒集团有限公司（以下简称"中教集团"）成立于2010年12月18日，控股企业包括中国教育出版传媒股份有限公司、人民教育出版社、高等教育出版社、语文出版社、中教华影电影院线股份有限公司、畅想投资集团有限公司、中国教学仪器设备有限公司、中国教育图书进出口有限公司等单位，以图书、期刊、电子音像产品、数字出版物出版和销售为主业，兼营电影院线、影视节目投资制作，以及图书、期刊、教学仪器设备进出口等业务。

中教集团为了贯彻落实中央关于提高出版"走出去"水平的要求，更好地服务国家"一带一路"建设，大力对外推介、输出本土优秀图书作品。2018年，集团公司在输出品种、产品形态、合作伙伴开拓等方面均有新的突破，全年共向美国、英国、俄罗斯、巴基斯坦、印度、印度尼西亚、阿联酋、南非、新加坡、日本、韩国等国以及我国香港、台湾等地区的出版机构输出版权515项。集团公司所属人民教育出版社、高等教育出版社、中国教育图书进出口有限公司均被评为"2017—2018年度国家文化出口重点企业"。

2018年，人民教育出版社"澳门特区《品德与公民》教材合作出版"项目被评为"2017—2018年度国家文化出口重点项目"，并凭借2018年优秀的版权输出和合作出版业绩，被列入2019年度文化产业发展专项资金"推动对外文化贸易发展"中央本级拟支持项目。

高等教育出版社当代科技前沿专著系列、*Frontiers in China*系列英文学术期刊和体验汉语泰国中小学系列教材三个出版物海外推广项目被评为"2017—2018年度国家文化出口重点项目"。《自治和非自治不连续微分方程中的分岔》（英文版）、《Hodge理论和 L^2分析》（英文版）、《中国审美文化简史》（韩文版）3种图书获评"第十七届输出版优秀图书"；《中国地理》《中国文学概论》2种图书获评"海峡两岸出版交流30周年优秀版权图书"。在"2018年中国图书海外馆藏影响力英文图书排行榜"中，高教社以63种英文图书位列第三名。同时，高教社还被评为"首都新闻出版广电'走出去'示范企业"。

2018年，中国教育图书进出口有限公司版权输出的语种和国家数量再创历史新高。签约作品包括刘慈欣《三体》三部曲、《球状闪电》、《超新星纪元》，周浩晖《暗黑者》，宝树《三体X•观想之宙》，以及马伯庸《欧罗巴英雄记》等，合作出

版社均为版权输出所在国知名出版社，2018年出版的作品均在海外产生了良好的社会影响。如《暗黑者》英文版出版发行之际，先后得到《纽约时报》、《华尔街日报》、《星期日泰晤士报》、《海峡时报》、《中国日报》、新华网英文版等大篇幅热情报道，成为我国类型文学“走出去”新名片。

2019年，中教集团将继续借势国家“一带一路”倡议，维护巩固欧美和东南亚已有市场，大力开拓新市场，不断加强与国际著名教育、出版、发行机构的合作，形成长效工作机制，建立战略合作伙伴关系，建设以美国、英国、德国、新加坡等国际出版制高点和“一带一路”沿线国家及区域为重点的市场营销网络，借势提升中教集团品牌的国际影响力，形成海外业务新格局。

图片注释

1. 中国教育出版传媒集团有限公司自成立以来连续九年荣获“全国文化企业30强”
2. 2018年北京国际图书博览会上，黄坤明视察中国教育出版传媒集团展位
3. 人民教育出版社“澳门特区《品德与公民》教材合作出版”项目被评为“2017—2018年度国家文化出口重点项目”
4. 伦敦书展期间，人民教育出版社与外商签订《快乐汉语》等版权转让协议
5. 高等教育出版社参加《中国学术出版“走出去”上海共识》发布仪式
6. 高等教育出版社获得世界知识产权组织（WIPO）创意金奖——单位奖
7. 中国教育图书进出口有限公司与刘慈欣签署《三体》三部曲独家版权合作协议

PEOPLE'S EDUCATION PRESS 人民教育出版社

在新的历史时期，人民教育出版社继续弘扬工匠精神，追求精益求精，实施“以中小学教材为核心的品牌拓展战略”，着力打造有分量、有影响的精品纸质出版物、配套电子音像出版物、数字出版物及期刊，产品立体化建设卓有成效。2018年在时间紧、任务重、要求高的情况下，全社团结协作、奋力拼搏，圆满完成了语文、历史、道德与法治三科统编教材编写、编辑、出版发行、试教试用、培训回访等工作，在教材中充分体现国家意志，坚持社会主义意识形态，弘扬社会主义核心价值观，得到了国家教育主管部门和中央宣传主管部门的充分肯定。

人教社积极落实以内容建设为基础的融合发展战略，加强数字产品体系建设。持续开发全学科全学段成体系的优质数字资源，推进资源库建设与应用管理。2018年完成义务教育数字教材（统编三科）、高中阶段数字教材、中小学优质数字教学资源库等10余项数字资源的开发工作，建设优质少数民族双语教育教学资源，持续优化数字教材服务平台及人教智慧教学平台，全面开展移动学习产品的研发及运营。

人教社在全国出版界率先将“以版权运营为重点的合作共赢战略”列入“十三五”规划。将版权资源作为战略性资源，加强保护和开发，开展多领域、多区域、多形式的合作。

作为人教版教科书的版权人，人教社通过版权管理、经营，实现了教科书的版权价值。一方面，以重签教材代理协议为基础，完善中小学教材代理工作管理办法，加强市场工作的目标管理和新通过审定学科的市场工作力度，确保教材市场占有率稳定增长；另一方面，修订了《公告目录教辅材料授权管理办法》和《非公告目录教辅材料授权管理办法》，根据新的管理办法有序开展教辅授权工作，通过授权使人教版教科书的配套教辅市场得到治理和规范，为师生提供合法出版的、有质量保证的教辅产品。全年中小学教材著作权收入稳中有增，教辅著作权使用费保持平稳。

作为人教版教科书的版权人，人教社还积极进行版权维护。2018年，人教社继续担任京版十五社反盗版联盟理事长单位，针对统编三科教材、“中日交流标准日本语”、“快乐读书吧•名著阅读课程化丛书”和“名著阅读课程化丛书”等图书的侵权行为开展重点维权工作，并积极应对处理诉人教社相关产品责任纠纷案和侵权案。完成《红星照耀中国》授权出版事宜。

人教社代表京版十五社反盗版联盟与拼多多达成知识产权保护合作

《红星照耀中国》授权协议签字

北京图书博览会业务洽谈

古巴哈瓦那书展中国主宾国活动

人教社积极开展版权贸易，加强对外合作交流。2018年，与英国、巴基斯坦、印度、俄罗斯、印度尼西亚、日本以及我国香港、澳门、台湾地区等12家境外出版机构，就《中国古代100位科学家故事》（英文版）、《跟我学汉语》（第二版）（俄语版）、《跟着桐桐学数学》（阿拉伯语版）、《BCT标准教程》（印尼语版）、《义务教育教科书•历史与社会》（日语版）等145个项目达成版权输出协议。并凭借2018年出色的版权输出和合作出版业绩，被列入2019年度文化产业发展专项资金“推动对外文化贸易发展”中央本级拟支持项目。

在义务教育教科书和国家规划教科书编写过程中，人教社严格执行《著作权法》和《教科书法定许可使用作品支付报酬办法》的相关规定，严格按照国家法律法规规定的标准和方式向作者或著作权集体管理组织支付著作权使用费，并已将其作为日常工作进行管理。人教社以自身的实际行动，树立了尊重版权的良好形象，为全国出版业做出了表率。

圣智学习出版集团访问人教社

组织京版十五社反盗版联盟成员单位与淘宝网召开网络维权座谈会

清華大學出版社
TSINGHUA UNIVERSITY PRESS

作者：
马翼翔
定价：99.60元

率先创立中国静态作文教学、十几年探索经验倾囊相授——马翼翔老师给孩子的15堂课——培养写作思维闭环，让孩子轻松学会、轻松写出言之有物、有真情实感的好作文。

作者：
钟思嘉　王　宏
李　飞　雨　露
定价：55.00元

《儿童时间管理训练手册——30天让孩子的学习更高效》（升级版）根据孩子的心理特点，针对4～18岁孩子提出30天儿童时间管理训练方案。该方案分为四个步骤，简称“一立三高”，分别是建立时间观念、提高做事速度（快）、提高做事准确度（准）、提高做事效率（快而准）。按照“一立三高”的训练流程，帮助孩子制定“三表一录”（时间表、星星表、礼物表、美言录），其核心是把家长的期望转化为孩子的目标，为家长提供儿童时间管理训练的抓手和杠杆，帮助孩子快快乐乐地完成任务，达到家长的期望——搞定一切还能玩！

作者：
故园风雨前
定价：55.00元

以为活着是为了收悉美。某公笑叹，什么是美？即“不知生活艰辛”。我点头，但转头还得给他补半句，“或佯作不知生活艰辛”。

作者：
小甲鱼
定价：89.00元

本书提倡理解为主，应用为王。因此，只要有可能，小甲鱼都会通过生动的实例来让大家理解概念。虽然这是一本入门书，但本书的“野心”并不止于“初级水平”的教学。本书前半部分首先讲解基础的Python 3语法知识，包括列表、元组、字符串、字典以及各种语句；之后循序渐进地介绍一些相对高级的主题，包括抽象、异常、魔法方法以及属性迭代器。后半部分则围绕着Python 3在爬虫、界面开发和游戏开发上的应用，通过实例引导读者进行深入学习和探究，既富有乐趣，又锻炼读者的动手能力。

作者：
[美]克雷格•莱特
(Craig Wright)
定价：128.00元

本书是一部不可多得的音乐欣赏指南，可帮助读者理解任何时代及文化中的音乐，发展和提高聆听技巧。通过阅读，你将会发现前所未有的、快乐的、自信的聆听感受。本书配有在线音乐，读者可以边学习、边欣赏、边练习，深入了解音乐的方方面面。本书适合对音乐特别是对西方音乐感兴趣的读者阅读，亦可以作为高校音乐普及类教材，提升读者在音乐方面的基本素养。

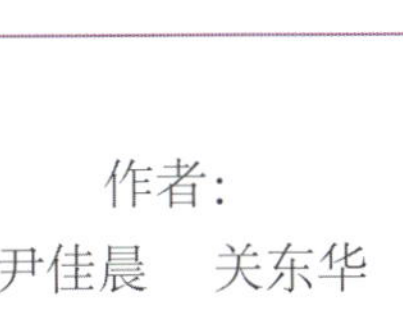

作者：

尹佳晨　关东华

郑　彤

定价：59.00元

自2017年以来，中小微企业创业环境全面恶化，营销缺少渠道与流量，招商缺少团队与经验，融资缺少模式与优势，很多创业者面临模式不会说话，产品不会说话，人更不会说话的困境。如何在这个时代，用自己的方式发声，借时代风口起飞？阿里巴巴总参谋长曾鸣提出："S2B将是未来五年取代电商的全新模式。"因此，本书将对S2B商业模式进行详细的解析与案例分析。

作者：

像玉的石头

定价：69.00元

《秘书工作手记2：怎样写出好公文》是手记系列的第二本，主题聚焦公文写作。它将用切实可行的方法、真诚而毫无保留的态度、生动传神的语言、丰富真实的案例教给读者，老笔杆到底是怎样写出领导满意、群众称赞的公文的。

作者：

眠　眠

定价：72.00元

《人类学+：科学的B面》是一本从科普的角度，讲述关于人类学的一些冷门故事和罕见历史的书。它重点关注人类学和其他相关学科，比如考古学、生物学、医学、社会学等学科的交叉。简单地说，人类学就是研究人类本身的一个学科，正如人类拥有多样的特性一样，人类学也同时研究人类的生物性和社会性，此外，还关心人类之所以形成各种特性的原因，以及其演变过程。

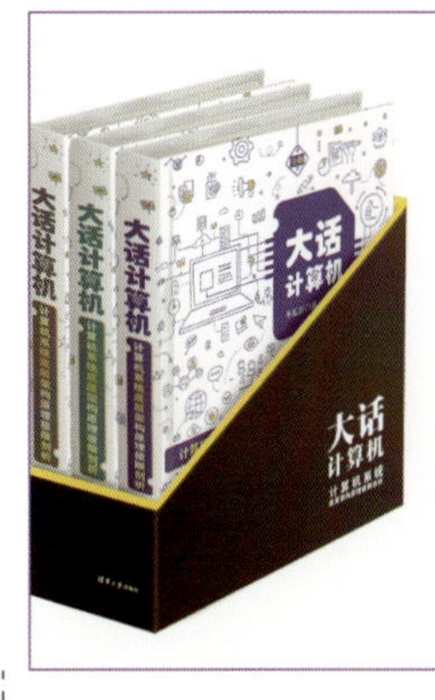

作者：

冬瓜哥

定价：598.00元

现代计算机系统的软硬件架构十分复杂，是所有IT相关技术的根源。书中尝试从原始的零认知状态开始，逐步从基础的数字电路一直介绍到计算机操作系统以及人工智能。全书脉络清晰，带领读者重走作者的认知之路。

作者：

网易新闻学院

定价：49.00元

网易《了不起的中国制造》栏目将近年来的超级工程、大国重器，通过专业人士的文笔通俗易懂地介绍给读者，可以说是做了件极有价值的事。在这本书里，我们不仅可以看到有关中国高铁、中国核电等核心技术的关键突破和最新进展，还可以看到来自权威人士的专业解读。这样的内容深入浅出又不失权威性，具有很高的阅读价值。

清華大學出版社

TSINGHUA UNIVERSITY PRESS

作者：

孙会峰　朱恒源 等

定价：49.00元

本书通过对中国制造产业跃迁的内在逻辑、演进方向、驱动要素、创新生态和发展路线图等的分析，为读者展现中国制造未来十年的重塑发展理念、重构竞争优势的创新之路。

作者：

[芬]马库•维莱纽斯

(Markku Wilenius)

定价：59.00元

本书使用康德拉季耶夫周期理论（康波理论）来解读我们眼前的世界。席卷全球的第六次浪潮将挑战我们当前的价值观、体制以及商业模式。

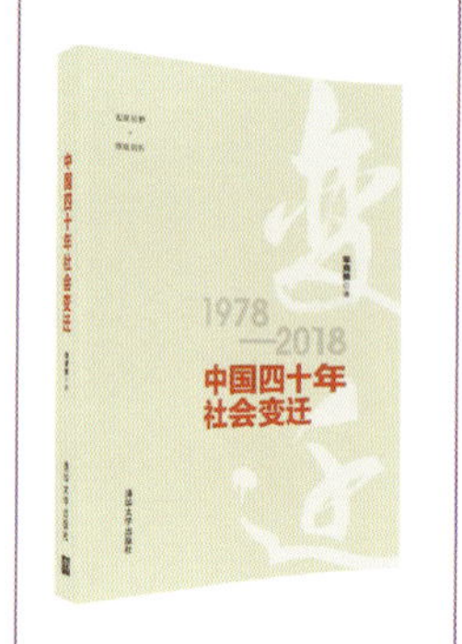

作者：

毕竞悦

定价：49.00元

中国改革开放四十年来，社会生活发生了巨大变化，实现了从乡土中国向城镇中国、从农业社会向工商社会的转型。家庭联产承包责任制解放和发展了农村生产力，这是中国城市化进程的动力之源。随着中国由计划经济模式转向市场经济模式，多元化的市场主体出现，带来了商品的极大丰富。随着改革开放的推进，中国加入了世界全球化和现代化进程，成为开放社会和信息社会。

作者：

汪　波

定价：79.00元

《时间之问》是一部少有的打通学科边界，融合科技与人文内涵的通识之作。作品以大学师生的问答对谈开始，选取“时间”作为跨学科讨论的媒介，联结起数学、天文、信息技术、音乐、生物、物理等不同学科。一来一往的对话中不仅隐含了作者精心设置的问题，而且还配有精心制作的插图和经过严谨考证的学术资料。

作者：

吴家喜

定价：59.00元

未来30年，人类将迎来创新黄金时代，创新秩序将成为世界秩序新主线。中国必将实现创新崛起，阔步迈向世界创新舞台中央，与各国共享全球创新红利。

地址：清华大学学研大厦A座　邮编：100084　网址：http://www.tup.tsinghua.edu.cn/index.html
发行电话：010-62770175转3525　邮购地址：北京市海淀区清华大学出版社邮购组收　邮购电话：010-62786544

作者：
段云峰
定价：49.00元

《晓肚知肠：肠菌的小心思》获评2018“中国好书”。作者结合当前最新的人体微生物组研究成果，介绍了肠道微生物影响人体健康的基本原理，将不起眼的微生物与人们日常生活习惯和身心健康联系起来，为认识微生物与健康的关系提供了生动有趣的知识科普。

作者：
杨　斌　李东红
汤玲玲
定价：69.00元

本书的研究成果主要基于2017年中国—中东欧国家关系研究基金委托研究项目“中国与中东欧国家的产业合作共赢研究——基于产业政策、产业竞争力分析”。全书共分4章，分别讨论“16+1”合作共赢的基础与进展、“16+1”合作共赢关键影响因素分析、“16+1”合作共赢建议和“16+1”合作共赢典型案例。本书除力求阐明合作共赢概念和“16+1”合作共赢主要影响因素外，也注意从中东欧国家视角出发，提出合理、科学、可行且务实的合作分析与对策建议。

作者：
范　红　胡　钰
定价：88.00元

《国家形象：“一带一路”与品牌中国》汇集了政府、学界和业界的领导们和专家们最新的研究和实践成果。作为清华大学国家形象传播研究中心的最新成果，聚焦“一带一路”和品牌战略，将国家形象的研究向更加系统化、更加国际化、更具实操性的方向纵深推进，以期为中国的国际战略规划和国家软实力建构献策。本书在“一带一路”和“国家形象”之外，率先引入了“品牌”的概念，并且纳入了国外领先的研究成果，同时呈现大量案例和数据，对政府、企事业单位的宣传部门和品牌管理部门具有启发意义。

作者：
魏　杰
定价：58.00元

2018年是中国改革开放40周年，我们不能以纪念的心态来进行回顾，而应该以欢庆的心态来庆贺改革开放的进一步深化。改革开放没有终止日，只有进行时，因而不能讲纪念改革开放40周年，而应该讲庆贺改革开放进行了40年，还要继续改革开放。正是基于此认识，作者根据自己在改革开放这40年中的亲身经历，对改革开放的一些问题做了梳理，既涉及经验，也涉及教训，当然更多的是通过总结40年中国改革开放的进程，提出自己的一些设想与建议，试图能对中国改革开放起到推动作用。

作者：
萧　璇　杨宇菲
杨　静　雷建军
定价：49.00元

本书将笔触触及与现代音乐人苏阳有过交集的四位中国传统音乐（花儿、陕北说书、秦腔、皮影）民间音乐艺人，关注他们在社会变革背景下的手艺、音乐技能和人物命运；除此之外，本书还追随四位黄河边的艺人，寻迹传统音乐之河流经21世纪的艺术生态，溯源其源头活水和新的支脉。

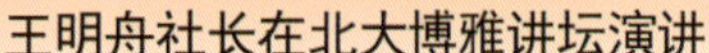
王明舟社长在北大博雅讲坛演讲

“走出去”图书成果展示

北京大学出版社把发展版权贸易作为走向世界、融入国际社会、参与国际竞争的重要途径，在版权贸易工作中一直坚持“输出引进并举”的工作思路，建立了让版权贸易健康发展的长效机制。目前，北京大学出版社已同几十个国家、地区的上百家出版社建立了业务往来。

北京大学出版社在引进版权图书上坚持“为我所需”和“双效并重”方针，坚持社会效益与经济效益并重，引进各种版权3 000余种。北京大学出版社组织翻译的一系列高质量的优秀外版图书，如《全球通史》《科学的旅程》《经济学原理》等，受到读者的广泛欢迎，并多次获得各级图书奖。

近年来北京大学出版社积极响应党中央、国务院的中国文化“走出去”战略，立足于版权输出，整合全社资源，结合本社的发展规划，大力推进本社图书“走出去”工作。北京大学出版社根据自身

《中国历史十五讲》阿拉伯文版新书发布

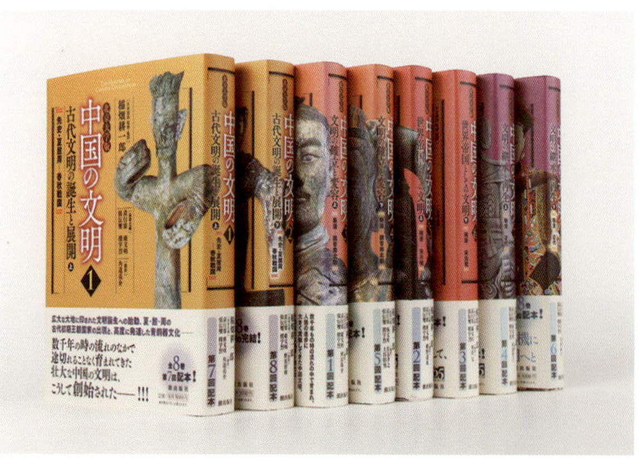

《中华文明史》日文版

参加北京国际图书博览会

与香港中和出版有限公司签署合作协议

的出版特点和优势，将对外汉语教材和人文社科类图书作为版权输出的重点领域，与剑桥大学出版社、荷兰博睿出版社、施普林格出版社等一批国际知名出版社展开深入广泛的合作，共向海外输出版权1 800余种，涉及英语、德语、法语、俄语、日语、韩语、泰语、越南语等十几个语种。其中《中华文明史》成功输出了英文版、日文版、韩文版、塞尔维亚文版、匈牙利文版和印地文版，《解读中国经济》成功输出了英文版、日文版、韩文版、德文版、阿拉伯文版、泰文版、吉尔吉斯文版等，出版后在国际市场上产生了良好反响。北京大学出版社共获得“经典中国国际出版工程”、“中国图书对外推广计划”、“中华文化著作翻译出版工程”、“丝路书香工程”重点翻译资助项目、“外国人写作中国计划”、“中华学术外译项目”等“走出去”项目立项170余项。

北京大学出版社是全国“新闻出版‘走出去’先进单位”、“中国版权最具影响力企业”以及“中国图书对外推广计划”工作小组成员单位之一，并被商务主管部门、文化主管部门、国家广电主管部门、新闻出版主管部门联合认定为2007—2008年度、2009—2010年度、2011—2012年度、2013—2014年度、2015—2016年度、2017—2018年度、2019—2020年度“国家重点文化出口企业”。

北大社图书亮相阿尔及尔国际书展1

北大社图书亮相阿尔及尔国际书展2

华东师范大学出版社

华东师范大学出版社创建于1957年6月，秉承大夏大学（华东师大前身）的人文精神，依托华东师范大学深厚的学术底蕴，形成了以大教育为出版宗旨的综合性出版特色。华东师范大学出版社在出版业向市场经济转型、经营性新闻出版单位转企改制等历次出版改革中，始终走在前列，既坚持大学出版社的出版方向、以教材和学术著作为主的出版结构，又持续在体制和机制上进行改革创新，实现了超常规的发展。2018年，共出版图书5 378种，其中初版与重版图书1 430 种、重印图书3 948种；回款码洋12.42亿元，销售收入4.87亿元。华东师范大学出版社始终坚持为教育和学术服务，注重出版物的高质量，荣获了许多奖项：获第四届中国出版政府奖先进单位奖，获“全国良好出版社”“全国百佳图书出版单位”“数字出版转型示范单位”“全国版权示范单位”“先进高校出版社”“上海文化企业十强”称号。

如今，华东师范大学出版社正按照本社“十三五”规划目标，以大教育为出版宗旨，在引领中国教育出版、建设国内一流国际知名出版社的道路上继续前行。

1. 在古巴哈瓦那国际书展中国主宾国活动“中古出版合作签约仪式”上，董事长、社长王焰女士与古巴南方出版社总编辑阿莱克斯·保西德斯先生签署版权输出协议
2. 在博洛尼亚国际儿童书展中国主宾国活动区举办《新说山海经》系列新书发布暨“传统文化下的童书创作”主题分享会
3. 在吉尔吉斯作家艾特玛托夫逝世10周年诞辰90周年之际举办“艾特玛托夫作品在中国的译介传播——‘一带一路’视域下的民族文学暨《一日长于百年》新书研讨会”
4. 在北京国际图书博览会上举办华东师范大学出版社与瑞士兰培德国际学术出版集团教育类图书战略合作签约仪式
5. 在北京国际图书博览会上举办《WSPC—ECNU中国书系》赠书仪式
6. 在北京国际图书博览会上举办“数学基础教育的海外传播——以《华东师大版一课一练·数学》‘走出去’为例”研讨活动
7. 接待古巴图书委员会主席胡安·罗德里格斯先生、驻沪总领事托雷斯先生等来访
8. 接待上海国际童书展国际出版人访问团（SHVIP）

扎根中国教育出版，讲好中国教育故事

中国人民大学出版社

中国人民大学出版社成立于 1955 年，是中华人民共和国成立后的第一家大学出版社。1982 年被教育部确定为全国高等学校文科教材出版中心，2007 年获首届中国出版政府奖先进出版单位奖，2009 年获首届全国百佳图书出版单位荣誉称号，2017 年再度获中国出版政府奖先进出版单位奖，是中国最重要的高校教材和学术著作出版基地之一。

人大出版社始终秉承“出教材学术精品，育人文社科英才”的出版理念，实施精品战略，以优秀的出版物传播先进文化，建社 60 多年来已累计出书四万余种，出版了一大批具有文明传播、文化累积价值的优秀教材和学术著作。作为涵括图书、音像、电子、网络和数字出版物等形式的跨媒体经营大型综合性出版社，人大出版社已成为我国哲学社会科学出版的重镇和旗舰。

新中国的大学出版事业，从这里开始

2019 年 4 月 23 日，由“一带一路”共建国家出版合作体、中国人民大学、伊朗政治与国际问题研究院（IPIS）主办，中国人民大学出版社承办的“‘一带一路’与民心相通”论坛在伊朗首都德黑兰成功举办。此次论坛是第 32 届德黑兰国际书展中国主宾国重大活动之一，也作为“一带一路”共建国家出版合作体的重要活动之一列入了第二届“一带一路”国际合作高峰论坛成果清单

“十三五”国家重点出版物出版规划项目

“治国理政新理念新思想新战略”研究丛书

为了更全面、更深刻、更细致地学习和领会习近平治国理政思想，中国人民大学组织全校的著名专家学者，研讨、撰写、出版“治国理政新理念新思想新战略”研究丛书。靳诺书记、刘伟校长担任丛书主编，丛书作者均为中国人民大学各学科带头人。该丛书分为十卷——理论卷、经济卷、政治卷、法治卷、社会卷、历史文化卷、科技教育卷、生态文明卷、治党卷、外交卷，从多个领域深入领会、梳理与呈现习近平治国理政思想。该丛书出版了中文版、英文版，并同时在国内外发行，以便更广地促进对习近平治国理政思想的学习与传播。这十卷著作将会对人们学好用好习近平治国理政思想带来帮助。

靳诺 刘伟 主编

中文版 / 英文版

书名	作者
中国特色社会主义新论	秦宣
马克思主义政治经济学在当代中国的新发展	邱海平
建设更加成熟更加定型的制度	杨光斌 王衡 林雪霏
全面依法治国新征程	冯玉军
社会治理新蓝图	冯仕政
民族复兴的历史根基与文化底蕴	刘后滨
建设世界科技教育强国	王伯鲁 等
开创社会主义生态文明新时代	张云飞 李娜
全面从严治党新阶段	杨凤城 赵淑梅 张世飞
构建人类命运共同体	陈岳 蒲傅

“认识中国 · 了解中国”书系

书名	作者
中国道路能为世界贡献什么	韩庆祥 黄相怀
我眼中的中韩关系	［韩］金胜一
中国治理：东方大国的复兴之道	燕继荣 等
社会主义核心价值观与中国文化国际传播	韩震
时代大潮和中国共产党	李君如
中国声音：国际热点问题透视	中国国际问题研究院
中国智慧：十八大以来中国外交	金灿荣 等
中国道路的世界贡献	韩庆祥 黄相怀 等
全球治理的中国担当	靳诺 等
当代中国社会：基本制度和日常生活	李路路 石磊 等

书名	作者
当代中国教育	顾明远
当代中国农村	孔祥智 钟真 李宾等
当代中国人权保障	常健
中国大视野2：国际热点问题透视	中国国际问题研究院
国际关注 · 中国声音	本书编写组
中国大视野：国际热点问题透视	中国国际问题研究院
中国经济发展的轨迹	贺耀敏
中国之路	程天权
中国人的价值观	宇文利
中国共产党就是这样成功的	杨凤城

为了更好地向国际社会介绍新时代中国的发展理念、发展道路、发展方向、政策主张，宣介习近平新时代中国特色社会主义思想，阐释中国治国理政丰富实践为全球治理提供的中国智慧、中国方案，中国人民大学出版社组织策划了“认识中国 · 了解中国”书系。书系精心编撰而成，注重通俗性和感染力，努力讲好中国故事，体现新时代中国学者和出版企业的责任与担当。目前，该系列图书已经推出40多本。绝大多数图书都成为中宣部、国新办外宣重点出版物，并被翻译成多种语言文字，多次在各大国际书展和中外文化交流活动中予以重点宣介和陈列，为中国图书“走出去”和中国文化国际传播做出了一定的贡献。

对话中国

作者：《对话中国》编写组

本书邀请中外知名学者就中国政治、经济、文化、社会、教育等领域的热点问题进行深入探讨和交流，从不同视角向国内外读者介绍新时代中国的发展理念、发展方向、发展道路、政策主张，系统回应国际社会对中国各方面发展的关切，客观阐述中国在一系列重大问题上的立场和观点，充分展示新中国成立70年来的辉煌成就。本书兼具学术性、理论性与可读性，是一本适合国内外读者认识中国、了解中国的简明读物。

5G时代

——什么是5G，它将如何改变世界

作者：项立刚

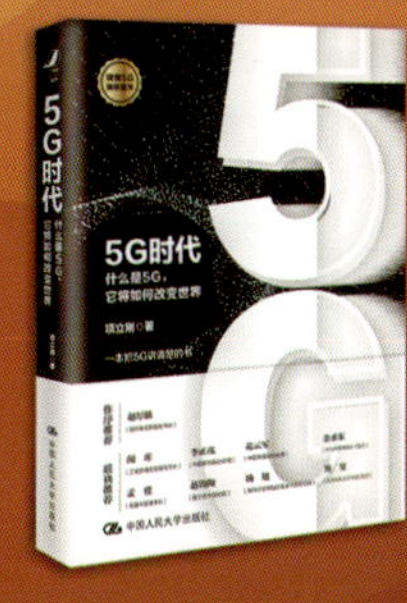

《5G时代》指出，第七次信息革命是智能互联网，5G是第七次信息革命的基础。本书对5G的三大场景、六大特点、核心技术、全球格局等做了清晰的介绍，回答了“什么是真正的5G”。本书还对5G赋能传统产业做了深入阐释，为读者勾勒了交通、医疗、工业、农业等因5G而将产生的深刻变革。最后，对于后5G时代人类社会面临的机遇与挑战，作者进行了大胆的设想。对于想全面了解5G的读者，本书提供了重要参考，是一本必备好书。

新教育实验

——中国教育改革的民间样本

（当代中国教育改革与创新书系）

作者：朱永新

2000年，朱永新教授发起了“新教育实验”，至今全国各地5 200余所学校、570余万名师生投身其中，其理论和实践让诸多身处应试教育压力下疲于应付的教师找到了努力的方向，改变了许多区域的整体教育生态。近20年来，新教育实验因其强调教育者自身的行动反思，以及新教育共同体对社会公益的关注而备受瞩目，成为中国教育改革的一个民间样本。2018年，新教育实验被评为基础教育国家级教学成果一等奖。本书梳理了新教育实验的发展历程，列举了新教育的“专业阅读＋专业写作＋专业交往”的教师专业发展模式，以及“晨诵、午读、暮省”“新生命教育”等特色课程，全面总结了新教育实验的理论与实践，是一本全面介绍新教育实验的重要著作。

2018年，商务印书馆继续与英、美、德、日等20余个国家的一流出版机构，如英国牛津大学出版社、英国剑桥大学出版社、英国泰勒和弗朗西斯集团、德国德古意特出版社、德国施普林格出版社、荷兰威科集团等国际知名的出版机构保持着密切的业务往来，持续深化与战略合作伙伴的关系，加强双向出版合作；积极实施中国品牌辞书海外传播项目，就英、格、俄、葡等4个语种的《新华字典》及《现代汉语词典》汉外双语项目实现签约，分别与英国牛津大学出版社（中国）、格鲁吉亚金羊毛出版社成立国际编辑部；向德国、英国、韩国、日本、印尼等国家输出主题出版、语言、社科、管理、文学、对外汉语教学等类别的图书版权，全年输出版权58项。《改革大道行思录》《奇迹是如何创造的》《"一带一路"——引领包容性全球化》《世界是通的》《吃货辞典》《现代汉语》等优秀图书顺利实现"走出去"。其中，《奇迹是如何创造的》积极配合改革开放40周年宣传，中英文版于当年同时推出，实现学术图书"走出去"的新突破。3月，商务印书馆授权英国卢德里奇出版社出版的《法治秩序的建构》英文版面世，标志着双方的合作再结新成果。全年引进版权328项，引进图书品种涉及外语工具书和教材、人文社科学术著作和大众文化类图书等。获得多项荣誉：《新华字典》在国家版权主管部门与世界知识产权组织联合举办的2018年"中国版权金奖"评选活动中，荣获"中国版权金奖•作品奖"。《中国古代化学》荣获"第十

2018年8月20日，商务印书馆与牛津大学出版社（中国）参加中国出版集团国际编辑部年会，在会上举行了牛津—商务国际编辑部签约仪式

2018年8月22日，商务印书馆与牛津大学出版社在北京国际图书博览会（BIBF）展场举行了《牛津高阶英汉双解词典》（第9版）和《牛津学术英语词典》新书发布会暨牛津—商务国际编辑部揭牌仪式

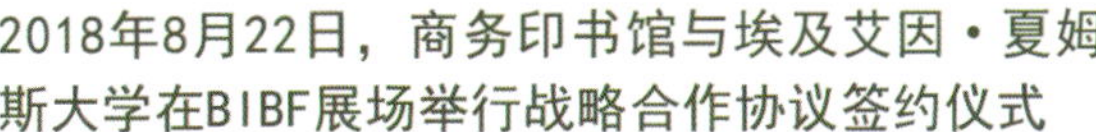

2018年8月22日，商务印书馆与埃及艾因·夏姆斯大学在BIBF展场举行战略合作协议签约仪式

2018年8月23日，商务印书馆与格鲁吉亚金羊毛出版社在BIBF展场举行国际编辑部揭牌仪式暨《新华字典》汉语—格鲁吉亚语翻译出版协议签约仪式

七届（2017年度）输出版优秀图书奖”，郭朝凤被评为“第十七届（2017年度）优秀版权经理人”。《农民的鼎革》（英文版）、《中欧智慧城市比较研究报告（2014年）》等12种“走出去”图书荣获国家新闻出版广电主管部门“图书版权输出奖励计划”的普遍奖励。《汉语与文化交际》（韩文版）被选为2018韩国文化体育部的世宗图书，即优秀学术图书。

2018年，商务印书馆参加了第25届北京国际图书博览会、第70届法兰克福国际书展，以及英国伦敦国际书展、美国纽约书展等各种大型的版权贸易和文化交流活动。全年共接待英国牛津大学出版社、英国剑桥大学出版社、德国施普林格出版社等合作伙伴代表来访100余人次。各项展览和会谈活动推动了商务印书馆的版权贸易工作，扩大了商务印书馆的品牌影响力。2018年，商务印书馆跻身2018年度海外馆藏出版社百强排行榜，位居第十。

2018年8月23日，商务印书馆与匈牙利罗兰大学在BIBF展场举行“商务印书馆—罗兰大学中东欧十六国汉语教材合作协议签约仪式”

2018年8月24日，商务印书馆于殿利总经理赴英国大使官邸参加英国国际贸易大臣利亚姆·福克斯（Liam Fox）及英国驻华贸易公使彭雅贤（Richard Burn）见证的中英贸易签约仪式，与牛津大学出版社（中国）总经理丁锐共同签署牛津—商务国际编辑部协议

江苏凤凰出版传媒股份有限公司

JIANGSU PHOENIX PUBLISHING & MEDIA CORPORATION LIMITED

凤凰出版传媒股份有限公司（以下简称“凤凰传媒”）是全国较有影响力和规模较大的出版发行公司之一，兼有内容生产和渠道优势。公司统筹内容、渠道、平台、团队和翻译，优化海外传播布局，版权输出和国际合作取得明显成效。

“十三五”以来，凤凰传媒输出非华语版权1 150种，超“十二五”时期总和；《青铜葵花》实现16国版权输出，荣获美国“弗里曼图书奖”等多项重要国际奖项，英语、意大利语版销量超过2万册，受到当地主流媒体高度评价；获“中国图书对外推广计划”“丝路书香工程”“经典中国国际出版工程”等外向型资助230余种，在地方出版集团中位居前列；凤凰传媒被评为“2018中国版权年度最具影响力企业”。母公司凤凰集团在“中国图书对外推广计划”年度综合排名中，在集团社中位居前列，荣获“2017—2018年度图书‘走出去’优秀奖”。

地址：南京市湖南路1号　　电话：025-83658992　　网址：http://www.ppm.cn（中文）；http://en.ppm.cn（英文）

1. 2018年5月28日，凤凰传媒在南京举办“凤凰国际出版研讨会”
2. 2018年8月1日，凤凰集团与省侨办、省文化厅、省新闻出版广电主管部门联合举办“华文大赛”颁奖典礼
3. 2018年8月23日下午，黄坤明视察第25届北京国际图书博览会，来到凤凰传媒展台
4. 2018年12月7日，凤凰传媒在南京举办“2018年度国际文化交流合作杰出使者”授证仪式

南京大学出版社

NANJING UNIVERSITY PRESS

南京大学出版社是南京大学主办的综合性大学出版社，是南京大学的直属业务单位，坐落于虎踞龙盘的历史文化名城南京。南京大学出版社自1984年成立之日起，就浸润于深厚的历史文化底蕴之中。一直以来，南大社坚持“学术立社，品牌兴社”的出版理念，坚持“昌明国粹，融化新知”的出版宗旨，坚持以精品出版为“魂”、学术出版为“本”的经营思路，注重社会效益和经济效益的有机结合，并始终如一贯彻“社会效益优先”的原则，不忘初心，牢记使命，形成了自身在高品位学术专著、高校精品教材、传统思想文化出版、国外学术名著译介等方面的出版特色，是中国传统思想文化出版高地、中华民国史出版重镇、国外学术前沿重要译介平台。

时代出版传媒股份有限公司

时代出版传媒股份有限公司成立于2008年，由安徽出版集团以其所持有的出版、印刷等文化传媒类资产在全国率先以出版业务整体上市，目前拥有全资或控股子公司23家，其中有9家出版社。公司成立以来，高度重视版权推广运用，把版权作为提高出版竞争力、抢占竞争制高点、提升文化影响力的重要战略资源。近年来，公司不断创新发展模式，加快版权资源产业化进程，推动“走出去”由单一版权贸易向新媒体、新业态、多元合作模式转型。

2018年，按照国家文化“走出去”发展新要求和省委文化发展战略新部署，时代出版在版权输出、文化服务贸易、国际交流等领域取得系列合作成果。

一是坚持精品战略，版权输出由高数量增长向高质量发展转变。全年共输出版权500多项，分别输出到俄罗斯、波兰、黎巴嫩、塞尔维亚等18个国家和地区。与“一带一路”沿线20余家出版机构建立了深度合作，共同策划开发选题，推动皖版图书“本土化”运作。

二是积极推进“走出去”重大项目建设。积极申报国家重大外宣出版工程项目。与全球版权与许可交易平台IPR公司签订合作协议，利用该平台在线展示皖版图书。

三是“走出去”工作屡获殊荣。入选2018年度国家外宣项目任务类重点选题1项、回购类重点选题3项，2018“经典中国国际出版工程”2项，“中国图书对外推广计划”翻译资助项目6项，“丝路书香工程”重点翻译资助项目1项；9种图书入选“年度输出版优秀图书”，1人入选“年度优秀版权经理人”；5种图书入选“BIBF遇见的50本好书”，入选数位居前列。此外，“推动对外文化贸易发展”转移支付项目获2018年度国家文化产业发展专项资金支持。

1. 董事长王民率工作团与保加利亚潘索夫特出版公司就版权贸易、联合出版、数字出版等领域达成一系列合作意向
2. “深化‘一带一路’出版合作　纪念改革开放40周年——2018时代出版国际合作签约仪式”在第25届BIBF展会上成功举办
3. 安徽出版集团向波兰哥白尼大学赠送1 000余册介绍中华文化的优秀图书

中南出版传媒集团
CHINA SOUTH
PUBLISHING & MEDIA GROUP

中南出版传媒集团股份有限公司

中南出版传媒集团股份有限公司（以下简称“中南传媒”）成立于2008年12月，2010年10月在上海证券交易所上市（股票代码:601098），成为中国全产业链整体上市的出版传媒龙头股。集团经营业务涵盖图书、报纸、期刊、音像、电子、网络、动漫、电视、手机媒体、框架媒体等多种媒介，集编辑、印刷、发行各环节于一体，是典型的多介质、全流程、综合性出版传媒集团，形成了出版、印刷、发行、报刊、新媒体、金融六大产业格局，下辖29家子（分）公司。2018年实现营业收入95.76亿元、净利润13.71亿元，市值和利润均居中国出版传媒上市公司前列，连续十一年入选“中国文化企业三十强”，多次被评为“国家文化出口重点企业”，荣获“中国版权最具影响力企业”奖、“版权输出先进奖”、“中国图书对外推广计划特别贡献奖”等多个国家奖项。

中南传媒执行援南苏丹教育项目，
为南苏丹培训教师并编制小学教材

中南传媒与法兰克福书展集团
联合开发IPR在线版权交易平台

中南传媒图书多次入选国家“走出去”项目

中国图书进出口（集团）总公司

CHINA NATIONAL PUBLICATIONS IMPORT & EXPORT (GROUP) CORPORATION

中国图书进出口（集团）总公司（以下简称“中图公司”）是一家与共和国同龄的大型国有文化企业，已成为中国出版业规模较大、实力较强的进出口企业和国际性书展服务机构。

构建立体化“走出去”服务体系。公司提供国际出版、版权贸易、翻译审校、国际品牌推广、业务培训、国际渠道建设等服务，目前海外联系出版社500多家、译者人才库成员300多名，版权输出1 000 多种、授权语种近30种。

积极推动数据化转型。由公司自主研发的数字资源交易与服务平台“易阅通”（https://www.cnpereading.com），已聚合丰富数字资源，成为引领行业、技术先进的国际数字出版物进出口旗舰中盘。移动阅读产品“主题书柜”，甄选党建时政、传统文化、商业财富、亲子教育等领域精品电子书，以主旋律、正能量为价值导向，打造精准的“5G新阅读”。

地址：北京市朝阳区工体东路16号　　邮编：100020
总机：010-65066688　　传真：010-65063101　　网址：http://www.cnpiec.com.cn

1. “易阅通”平台已聚合200多万种中外优质电子书刊、1 000万篇全文数据，服务34个国家和地区的客户
2. “主题书柜”系列产品之“习近平的书柜”
3. 第25届北京国际图书博览会在中国国际展览中心举办，达成中外版权贸易协议5 000多项。该展会由中图公司创办并承办，已成功跃居世界第二大书展
4. 第25届北京国际图书博览会期间，中图公司举办“故事沟通世界——余华对话30国汉学家”等多场活动，推动中国优秀作品“走出去”

长风破浪 外研社 40周年 1979-2019 FLTRP 40th Anniversary 致敬新时代

外语教学与研究出版社（以下简称“外研社”）由北京外国语大学于1979年创办并主管，是一家以外语教育出版为特色，国内领先、国际知名的综合性教育出版机构。外研社以“记载人类文明，沟通世界文化”为使命，依托北京外国语大学的学术优势，每年以80多种语言出版万余种图书期刊，并积极探索教育服务转型与数字化融合创新，有力推动国际化布局与中外文化交流，取得显著社会效益与经济效益，在国内外享有优质品牌与广泛影响。

外研社先后荣获“全国优秀出版社”、“先进高校出版社”、“新闻出版‘走出去’先进单位”、“国家文化出口重点企业”、“讲信誉、重服务”出版单位、“全国教材先进管理单位”、“全国文化企业30强”提名单位、“首都文化企业30强”等荣誉称号，被评为国家一级出版社。外研社出版的众多图书获得了中国出版政府奖、中华优秀出版物奖等重要奖项。

目前，外研社与700多家国际出版机构及300多位海外作者建立了出版合作并积极践行“走出去”战略。外研社已在全球11个国家创立海外机构，在英国牛津设立孔子学院，发起成立“中国—中东欧国家出版联盟”。2017年被国家新闻出版广电主管部门授予“中国图书对外推广计划特别贡献奖”，2018年度版权输出数量超过200种，为中外文化融通与文明互鉴搭建了交流与合作平台。

人民邮电出版社成立于1953年10月，是工业和信息化部主管的大型专业出版社，隶属于中国工信出版传媒集团。

人民邮电出版社是全国优秀出版社、全国百佳图书出版单位，近年来连续三届荣获中国出版政府奖先进出版单位奖，以及“全国文明单位”、“中央国家机关文明单位标兵”和“首都文明单位标兵”等重要荣誉。

人民邮电出版社先后有数百种图书、期刊、音像电子及网络出版物荣获中国出版政府奖、中华优秀出版物奖、文津图书奖等国家和行业重大荣誉或入选“三个一百”原创出版工程、向全国青少年推荐百种优秀出版物、“百强报刊”、“十二五”“十三五”国家重点出版规划及国家出版基金等重要项目，具有广泛的行业和社会影响。

地址：北京市丰台区成寿寺路11号邮电出版大厦　邮编：100164
电话：010-81055137（总经理办公室）
010-81055315（出版业务管理部）
010-81055059（发行部）
传真：010-67656995　网址：http://www.ptpress.com.cn
电子邮箱：315@ptpress.com.cn

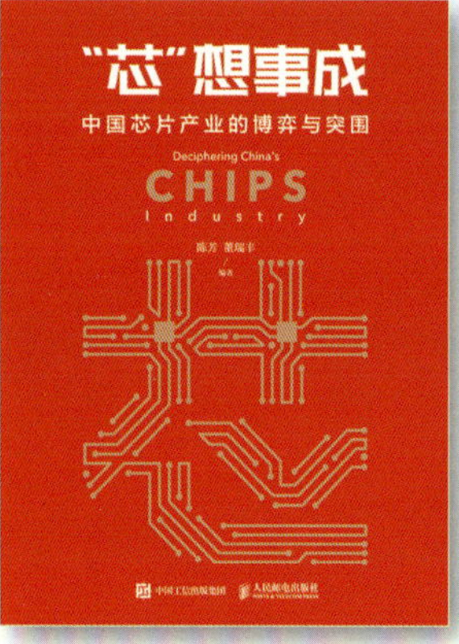

★ 2018年度中国30本好书

★ 2018年全国优秀科普作品
★ 原创动漫作品版权开发优秀项目内容开发类铜奖
★ 第十四届文津图书奖推荐图书
★ 2018年度全国文化遗产十佳图书

★ 第五届中国科普作家协会优秀科普作品奖金奖

★ 2019年上半年优秀少儿图书

★ 第十四届文津图书奖推荐图书

陕西师範大學出版总社

SHAANXI NORMAL UNIVERSITY GENERAL PUBLISHING HOUSE

陕西师范大学出版总社是集图书、期刊、电子音像、数字出版、教育文化服务于一体的综合出版传媒机构。出版的图书荣获“中国图书奖”“国家图书奖”“中华优秀出版物奖”“茅盾文学奖”“鲁迅文学奖”“中国好书”“最美的书”等奖项，先后被陕西省版权主管部门、国家版权主管部门授予“陕西省版权示范单位”“全国版权示范单位”称号，被中国版权协会评为“中国版权最具影响力企业”。

陕西师范大学出版总社在大项目带动的精品战略指引下，自主研发创新能力显著增强，精品图书不断涌现。与此同时，高度重视版权管理与开发工作，在制度建设、软件正版化、尊重作者著作权、拓展合作平台、加快“走出去”步伐等方面取得可喜成绩。与俄罗斯、美国、英国、韩国等国出版机构建立合作关系，成立俄语、英语、小语种三个翻译出版基地，拓展版权贸易，一大批图书入选国家对外出版项目、“丝路书香工程”、“经典中国国际出版工程”等。

陕西师范大学出版总社正在高质量发展的道路上阔步前进。

2018年8月，总社与俄罗斯科学出版社举行俄语版《中国通史——从远古时期到二十一世纪初》授权签约仪式

2019年5月，总社举行“感恩出版•致敬作者”2018年度优秀作者表彰会，贾平凹、阿来、王子今等10位作者受到表彰

荣获海峡两岸出版交流30周年优秀版权奖图书

入选中央宣传主管部门对外出版项目

入选国家“丝路书香工程”项目

入选“经典中国国际出版工程”图书

入选2018年“中国图书对外推广计划”项目

总社部分精品图书

上海人民出版社成立于1951年，1999年2月成为上海世纪出版集团成员单位。自2016年9月起，上海世纪出版集团全面启动上海人民出版社综合改革试点工作，将上海人民出版社、学林出版社、上海远东出版社、上海书店出版社、格致出版社和北京世纪文景文化传播有限公司、上海《理财周刊》社等七家单位实施整合重组。上海人民出版社是中国知名的社科类综合性出版机构，主要出版政治、历史、文化、哲学、法律、经济等方面的学术著作和普及读物，多年来始终坚持以专业学术打造品牌，以社会责任引领阅读，努力将国家文化“走出去”重大战略与专业出版战略紧密结合，已输出图书200余种，涉及10多个语种，其中仅张维为的“中国三部曲”丛书（《中国震撼》《中国触动》《中国超越》）就已分别成功输出8个国家及地区。此外，“东方编译所译丛”“当代国际政治丛书”“当代经济学系列”等品牌图书在全社会和广大读者中拥有广泛知晓度和重大影响力。自2017年以来，上海人民出版社先后荣获“上海市版权示范单位”、“全国版权示范单位”和“中国版权最具影响力企业”称号。

所获荣誉（从左至右）：“第六届国家图书奖（特别奖）”“全国版权示范单位” “2018年度中国版权最具影响力企业”

张维为“中国三部曲”成功输出8个国家及地区

引进版图书形成系列品牌

上海人民出版社

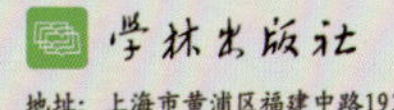
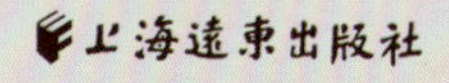

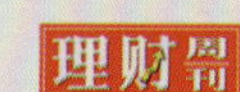

地址：上海市黄浦区福建中路193号 邮编：200001 电话：021-53594508 传真：021-63914796 邮箱：spph@sina.com 微信订阅号：spph_spph

明天出版社

明天出版社成立于1984年，是山东省一家以少年儿童为服务对象的专业少儿图书出版社，是国家一级出版社、全国百佳图书出版单位。自建社以来，明天出版社上下团结一心，砥砺前行，经营规模不断扩大，市场影响力不断提升，在全国同行业处于领先地位。2018年，明天出版社销售码洋超过10亿元，在全国583家出版社中，明天出版社在全国整体零售图书市场综合排名居第29位。明天出版社先后被人力资源和社会保障主管部门、新闻出版主管部门评为“全国新闻出版系统先进集体”，被山东省委宣传主管部门、省新闻出版主管部门、省人力资源和社会保障主管部门、省财政主管部门授予“山东省新闻出版奖优秀集体奖”，被中国版权协会授予“中国版权最具影响力企业”称号。

文学类

《属猫的人》

《雪山上的达娃》

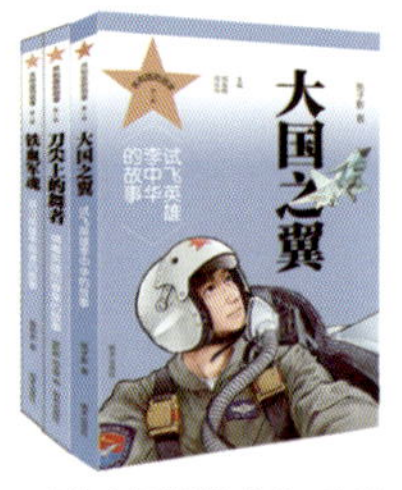

“共和国的勋章”系列

“童年在中国”系列

《隐形巨人》

《我是一个透明人》

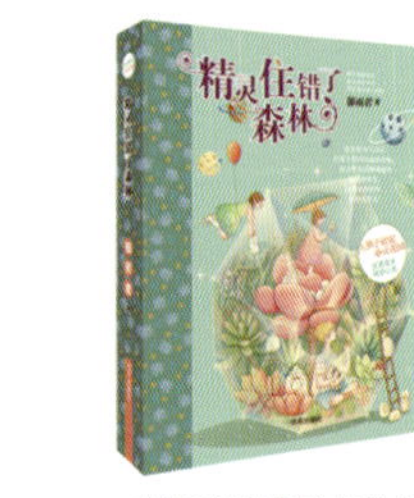

《我的呆萌新朋友》

《精灵住错了森林》

《花豹母女》

低幼类

“李如青人文绘本”系列

《幼儿园有个怪》

《阿泥》

《乡下路》

《小老鼠的家》

知识类

“少年健康成长必读书系”

“阳光姐姐小书房成长智慧书”系列

“马小跳发现之旅”系列

“阳光姐姐科普小书房”系列

“沈石溪动物探索营”系列

联系地址：山东省济南市市中区万寿路19号
联系电话：0531-82098622
欢迎关注明天出版社官方微信公众号

2018中国版权年度最具影响力企业

希望出版社
HOPE PUBLISHING HOUSE

希望出版社成立于1985年，是一家专业少儿出版社。出版范围以少儿类图书为主，涉及教育、文学、科普、低幼、文史、艺术等多个板块。多年来，希望出版社始终坚持正确的出版方向，突出社会效益，努力实现社会效益与经济效益的统一，取得了一系列突破性的成绩。

希望出版社一直在展示中华文化、国际合作方面做着不懈努力，并取得了一定的成果。2018年被评为“中国版权最具影响力企业”。截至当前，已经有50余种图书实现版权输出。值得一提的是，“中国风•儿童文学名作绘本书系”输出至英国、法国等欧洲主流国家，入选“经典中国国际出版工程”；2015年，“中国风•儿童文学名作绘本书系”中9册图书版权又被成功输出至“一带一路”沿线国家——约旦，并获得了国家新闻出版主管部门“丝路书香工程”的资助。

希望出版社将牢牢秉承开放的出版理念，讲好中国故事，让更多精品童书“走出去”，让世界倾听中国童书的声音。

已输出图书——“中国风・儿童文学名作绘本书系”等

2019年版权输出至英国的图书

2019年版权输出至俄罗斯、乌克兰、白俄罗斯的图书——“中国精神・我们的故事”丛书

版权

年度发布

NIAN DU FA BU

2018 年中国网络版权保护年度报告

国家版权局委托中国信息通信研究院撰写

2018 年是全面贯彻党的十九大精神的开局之年，也是改革开放四十周年。四十年来，我国版权事业从无到有、从小到大，社会公众版权保护意识大幅提升，版权法律制度体系逐步完善，版权行政执法监管力度不断加强，版权司法保护的强度不断提高，版权保护推动版权产业快速发展，版权保护和社会服务体系初具规模，版权国际交流合作不断深入。版权制度已成为新时代激发内容创新、促进文化繁荣的基础规则和重要保障。2018 年，我国网络版权行政保护和司法保护力度进一步加强，网络版权社会共治机制进一步完善，重点领域网络版权专项整治成效显著，网络版权秩序进一步规范，网络版权生态持续好转，网络版权产业规模不断扩大。

2018 年，中国网络版权产业各领域积极融合发展，产业上下游多业态、线上与线下融合联动，培育了更加繁荣的网络版权原创市场。与此同时，网络内容产品的移动化、社交化、碎片化，也带来了更复杂的侵权盗版和利益分配问题，需要政府引导各方协力构建良好的网络版权运营和保护机制，共同探索净化网络版权环境、构建良性商业模式的新途径。

本报告从网络版权的行政保护、司法保护和社会保护等多个层面，展示 2018 年我国网络版权保护情况，阐明网络版权保护对净化版权环境、促进版权产业发展、提高民族创新创造活力的重要作用。

一、2018 年中国网络版权保护的发展机遇

（一）党中央、国务院高度重视知识产权工作为版权保护指明了前进方向

2018 年，习近平总书记先后在博鳌亚洲论坛 2018 年年会、全国网信工作会议、首届中国国际进口博览会上发表重要讲话，强调加强知识产权保护是完善产权保护制度最重要的内容，也是提高中国经济竞争力最大的激励，从理论和实践层面深刻阐述了知识产权保护在完善产权保护制度、提高中国经济竞争力方面的重大意义，为加强版权保护提供了根本遵循。在 8 月 21—22 日召开的全国宣传思想工作会议上，习近平总书记强调要推动文化产业高质量发展，以高质量文化供给增强人们的文化获得感、幸福感。版权是推动文化创新发展的重要保障，这为版权保护和产业发展指明了目标任务和努力方向。2018 年 2 月，中共中央办公厅、国务院办公厅印发了《关于加强知识产权审判领域改革创新若干问题的意见》，这是党中央出台的第一个专门面向知识产权审判的里程碑式的纲领性文件，它将“树立保护知识产权就是保护创新的理念”作为指导思想的重要内容，这将进一步激发全社会创新热情，推动大众创业和万众创新，不断增强我国经济的创新力和竞争力。

（二）改革开放四十年取得巨大成就为版权保护奠定了坚实基础

中国知识产权事业与改革开放同步而行。40 年知识产权规模高速增长的历史，也是我国版权法律制度不断完善、保护力度不断加强、版权对外交流不断深化的历史。版权法律制度方面，我国先后颁布了 1 部法律、6 部条例以及 9 个部门规章和 44 个规范性文件，已基本形成以《著作权法》为统领和核心、由多层次法律规范构成的中国特色社会主义著作权法律体系。《著作权法》于 2001 年、2010 年进行了两次修订，2012 年启动了第三次修订。版权监管保护方面，各级版权行政管理部门坚持日常监管与专项行动相结合，严厉打击各类侵权盗版行为。据不完全统计，2000—2018 年，全国版权行政执法部门共办理行政处罚案件近 14 万件，移送司法机关案件 5 600 余件，收缴各类侵权盗版制品超过 8 亿件。特别是连续 14 年开展“剑网行动”，共查处网络侵权盗版案件 6 573 件，关闭侵权网站 6 266 个，删除侵权盗版链接 256 万条，移送司法机关追究刑事责任 609 件，相继查处了天线视频网侵权案、思路网高清视频侵权案等一批侵权盗版大案要案。版权对外交流方面，中国相继签署、加入和批准了 8

部著作权国际条约。2012年6月，中国成功承办世界知识产权组织保护音像表演外交会议，缔结《视听表演北京条约》，不断增强在国际版权领域的话语权和影响力。近十年来，中国版权产业的行业增加值增加两倍①，占全国GDP的比重从6.51%增长到7.35%，版权生态环境进一步优化，版权事业更加繁荣发展。

（三）深化党和国家机构改革为版权保护强化了组织保障

党的十九大以来，建设社会主义文化强国已成为党和政府的工作重点之一，作为知识产权体系和现代文化产业体系的集合点，版权在我国经济社会发展中的地位不断上升。根据2018年3月中共中央印发的《深化党和国家机构改革方案》，将国家新闻出版广电总局的新闻出版管理职责划入中央宣传部。中央宣传部对外加挂国家新闻出版署（国家版权局）牌子，贯彻落实党的宣传工作方针，拟订新闻出版业的管理政策并督促落实，管理新闻出版行政事务，统筹规划和指导协调新闻出版事业、产业发展，监督管理出版物内容和质量，监督管理印刷业，管理著作权，管理出版物进口等。深化党和国家机构改革，有利于加强党对新闻舆论工作的集中统一领导，有利于加强对出版、版权活动的管理，有利于发展和繁荣中国特色社会主义出版、版权事业，对推进版权领域治理体系和治理能力现代化具有重要意义。

（四）网络版权产业规模持续扩大为推动版权经济高质量发展提供了强劲动力

近年来，我国版权产业呈持续增长态势，已经成为国民经济新的增长点和经济发展中的支柱产业。最新数据显示，我国版权产业的行业增加值已达60 810.92亿元，占全国GDP比重为7.35%；其中，核心版权产业行业增加值为38 155.90亿元，占全国GDP比重为4.61%，比上年提高0.03个百分点②。网络版权产业用户规模不断扩大，网络版权产业增长较快。截至2018年12月，网络新闻、网络视频、网络音乐、网络游戏和网络文学的用户规模分别为6.75亿、6.12亿、5.76亿、4.84亿和4.32亿，使用率均超50%，其中网络新闻网民使用比例超过80%，网络版权产业市场规模高达7 400亿元③。网络版权产业已成为推动版权经济高质量发展的重要引擎，为网络版权保护工作带来新气象。

二、2018年中国网络版权保护的重要进展

（一）行政保护方面，专项整治与重点监管相结合，引导短视频等热点领域规范发展

1. 专项行动成果斐然，严厉查处大案要案

“剑网2018”专项行动期间，各级版权执法监管部门删除侵权盗版链接185万条，收缴侵权盗版制品123万件，查处网络侵权盗版案件544件，其中查办刑事案件74件、涉案金额1.5亿元，专项行动取得显著成效。

“剑网2018”针对重点领域，结合重点作品预警名单，主动出击，查办了一批侵权盗版大案要案，为庆祝改革开放四十周年营造了良好的网络文化环境。为打击传播盗版影视作品，江苏淮安查处“BT天堂”影视侵权案，判处袁某某有期徒刑3年并处罚金80万元；为打击盗版手游，江苏徐州查处《天天街机捕鱼》手机游戏侵权案，抓获犯罪嫌疑人4人，扣押涉案金额1 000余万元；为保护动漫行业的发展，四川成都查处吹妖动漫网动漫侵权案，判处孙某有期徒刑3年3个月并处罚金10万元；此外，针对有声读物领域，安徽滁州查处懒人听书网侵权案，涉案的有声小说等录音作品共12 398部。

2. 热点领域专项整治，规范网络版权秩序

针对互联网版权治理的热点难点，版权执法监管部门实施分类管理，聚焦网络转载、短视频、动漫、知识分享、有声读物、微信公众号等重点领域进行专项整治，取得了较好的法律效果和社会效果。

针对新兴的短视频、网络转载领域中的版权问题，版权监管部门通过约谈重点企业、行政处罚、推动行业自律等方式，进一步规范行业秩序，取得了良好的法律效果和社会效果。根据整改要求，抖音短视频等15家短视频平台加强版权保护，积极履行企业主体责任，共下架删除各类涉嫌侵权盗版短视频作品57万部，短视频版权秩序得到显著改善；13家网络服务商不断完善版权转载机制，为权利人提供便捷多样的维权渠道，积极为本平台用户的原创内容提供版权保护服务，签约各类版权合作单位累计超过4 300家。

针对社会关注的动漫、知识分享及有声读物平台的版权问题，各级版权执法部门相继查办了福建

① 从2008年的1.9万亿元增长到2017年突破6万亿元，数据源自中国新闻出版研究院2018年12月25日发布的“2017年中国版权产业的经济贡献”的调研结果。

② 数据来源同上。

③ 数据源自腾讯研究院。

嘀哩嘀哩网案、四川吹妖动漫网案、上海侵权万代玩具案、常州43423在线漫画网案、北京听伴有声读物案、江苏昆山99听书网案、安徽滁州懒人听书网案等一批涉及动漫、知识分享、有声读物的侵权案件，督促相关平台企业落实主体责任。

3. 深化版权重点监管，构建产业良性生态

针对网络新技术和商业新模式，版权执法监管部门不断创新工作理念和工作方法，强化网站版权重点监管，采取监管新措施，进一步扩大专项行动的覆盖面和影响力。目前，各地版权部门实施重点监管的网站达到了3 000多家，其中，国家版权局直接进行重点监管的大型视频、音乐、文学网站58家。

2018年，国家版权局按照“双随机一公开”要求，抽查了16家重点网站的2 389部作品版权授权文件，下架无授权作品1 091部；公布七批72部重点作品版权保护预警名单，对春晚节目、世界杯赛事节目、《舌尖上的中国》（第三季）及《红海行动》等院线电影进行重点预警保护，要求相关网络服务商对重点作品采取预警保护措施；推动阿里巴巴集团、拼多多平台分别与京版十五社反盗版联盟、少儿出版反盗版联盟签订图书版权保护合作协议，对重点图书的线上盗版销售进行主动防控，共同保护权利人的合法权益。

自2015年国家版权局开展网络音乐版权专项整治行动以来，我国的网络音乐版权环境不断净化，网络音乐侵权案件占比从2015年的44%骤降至2018年的1.6%，版权秩序明显改善。2018年，国家版权局巩固工作成果，推动网络音乐版权规范授权，推动腾讯音乐与网易云音乐达成音乐作品转授权合作，将各自独家音乐作品数量的99%以上向对方开放转授权，得到社会舆论的积极评价。

各级版权行政管理部门立足于“从被动等待转变为及时主动介入，从打击个案转变为重点遏制类案”的理念，针对不同地区、不同行业、不同作品的特点和版权保护的不同需求，提高重点监管的针对性和精准性。国家版权局深入推进国家版权监管平台二期建设，进一步提升版权执法监管工作的信息化水平。北京市版权局以微信、微博、各类公众号为突破口，对未经授权盗播高清电影的“三无网站”进行技术分析和全面检测。上海市版权局利用互联网大数据监控技术，通过互联网版权监测平台，围绕“剑网2018”重点领域以及上海地区热播影视剧作品、重点新闻作品等进行主动监测。广东省广州文化执法总队成立中科实数联合取证实验室，结合版权司法鉴定量身定做远程调查取证软件。贵州省版权局利用“版权云”新技术手段，对该省新闻、视听、出版、微博、微信等领域进行版权监测。

（二）司法保护方面，版权审判规则日趋完善，审理模式不断创新

1. 各级法院出台相关司法规定，版权审判规则日趋完善

2018年，各级法院不断完善审判规则，推进网络版权审判工作更加完备、全面、科学。2018年4月20日，北京市高级人民法院发布《北京市高级人民法院侵害著作权案件审理指南》，从提供信息存储空间服务、提供链接服务、“避风港”条款、技术措施等多个方面完善了侵害信息网络传播权的认定规则，有效提升了网络版权案件的审理质量和效率。2018年12月12日，最高人民法院发布了《最高人民法院关于审查知识产权纠纷行为保全案件适用法律若干问题的规定》，将“时效性较强的热播节目正在或者即将受到侵害”列为“情况紧急”情形之一，确保了热播节目的信息网络传播权受到侵害时能获得及时救济，防止网络侵权行为造成难以弥补的损害。

2. 增设互联网法院，互联网案件审理模式不断创新

近年来，侵害信息网络传播权等涉互联网案件数量与日俱增，新类型案件不断涌现，对传统审理机制提出了新要求。为探索互联网空间司法治理，回应涉网案件的司法需求，2018年8月9日，最高人民法院印发《关于增设北京互联网法院、广州互联网法院的方案》，加上2017年挂牌运行的杭州互联网法院，我国互联网法院试点已达三家。为统一规范互联网法院的线上诉讼活动，2018年9月6日，最高人民法院印发《最高人民法院关于互联网法院审理案件若干问题的规定》，对互联网法院的管辖范围、上诉机制和诉讼平台建设以及在线诉讼的身份认证、立案、应诉、举证、庭审、送达、签名、归档等诉讼规则，做出了一系列明确规范。互联网法院采用“网上案件网上审理”方式，优化诉讼程序，高效便捷实现在线诉讼。杭州互联网法院审理的涉网案件开庭平均用时28分钟，平均审理期限38天，比传统审理模式分别节约时间60%和50%，有效降低了诉讼成本。

互联网法院管辖互联网著作权权属和侵权纠纷等涉网案件，将在网络版权案件审理方面发挥重大作用。截至2018年11月9日，北京互联网法院共收到立案申请6 580件，其中，著作权权属、侵权

纠纷 3 502 件，占比高达 53%。2018 年 12 月 26 日，北京互联网法院公开宣判了第一起案件——“抖音短视频”诉“伙拍小视频”侵害作品信息网络传播权纠纷一案，对短视频是否构成类电作品，短视频浮水印的法律属性，以及“通知—删除”规则的适用原则等确立了裁判标准，是短视频保护的里程碑事件。

3. 网络版权案件数量爆发式增长，审判效率逐渐提高

人民法院通过案件审理有效解决各类版权纠纷，不断提高司法救济的及时性和有效性。通过检索查询[①]，2018 年案由为“侵害作品信息网络传播权纠纷”的民事、刑事判决书共 4 785 份。网络版权侵权案件增长率连续两年超过 80%，呈爆发式增长态势；网络版权案件平均审理期限 120 天；98%的案件赔偿请求获得了法院支持。

从侵权作品类型看，2018 年，图片作品案件数量占比最高，其次为文字作品案件和视频作品案件，音乐作品案件和游戏作品案件占比很低。图片作品案件数量剧增，比 2017 年增长两倍，占比高达 44%，案件起诉主体集中程度较高，个人诉讼占比仅为 10%，主要是“商业化”维权。视频作品案件增长迅猛，比 2017 年增长 1.5 倍，案件数量占比为 25%；在视频作品案件中，长视频、短视频占比分别为 84%、16%。音乐作品案件数量骤减，下降幅度高达 66%，占比不足 2%，网络音乐领域版权保护环境已有非常明显改善。

从侵权案件传播途径来看，2018 年，通过网站侵权的案件数量最多，占比 47%；通过微信侵权的案件数量增长明显，占比 27%，其中四成为文字侵权，公众号抄袭、非法转载现象严重。

从审理法院地域分布看，2018 年案件数量排名前七的省份分别是北京市、广东省、湖南省、天津市、浙江省、湖北省和上海市，这些省份集中了全国 90%的网络侵权案件，其中，北京市 2018 年判决案件数量占比高达 50%，比 2017 年增长 1 倍以上，区域集中态势非常明显。知识产权法院在网络版权案件审理中起到重要作用，审判案件数量占案件审理总量的 17%。

刑事司法是网络版权保护的重要手段，在网络版权保护中发挥着不可或缺的作用，侵犯网络版权的刑事案件数量在整个著作权刑事案件中占比达到 44%。在网络版权侵权刑事案件中，游戏作品领域仍然是侵权重灾区，占比高达 59%。从平均刑期看，侵犯网络版权刑事判决的平均刑期为有期徒刑 1.42 年。从案件罚金来看，大部分案件罚金较低，三分之二的案件罚金小于等于 10 万元。

（三）社会保护方面，各主体积极维护版权，推动社会共治

1. 著作权集体管理组织改进管理方法，开展多维度合作

中国音乐著作权协会（下称“音著协”）不断扩大会员规模，2018 年发展新会员 506 个，较 2017 年增长 25%，截至 2018 年底，会员总数达 9 413 个[②]（含出版公司和自然人会员）。音著协不断改进管理方法，推出网上著作权许可系统；加强维权力度，为会员权利人办理维权案件共 244 件，其中网络侵权 76 件，包括中国移动咪咕音乐、小米音乐和北京快手科技有限公司侵权案等；此外，音著协还积极与抖音、好看、秒拍等平台企业开展版权合作，加强内容版权管理。

2018 年，中国文字著作权协会（下称“文著协”）新增个人、集体会员 656 个，截至 2018 年底，会员数达到 9 917 个[③]。文著协通过设立剽窃者“曝光台”回应会员关切和其他著作权人的投诉，追究侵权者法律责任；代表协会会员汪曾祺起诉中国知网侵权、支持李迪等 6 位作家起诉出版社维权均获胜诉；2018 年文著协为文字作者收取版权费首破 1 000 万元。

中国摄影著作权协会在 2018 年的全国“两会”期间，联合近 50 位著名艺术家委员为《著作权法》修订建言献策。

权利人通过音著协、文著协等集体管理组织“抱团”维权。凸凹等 6 位作家就江苏凤凰教育出版社有限公司对《人生之痛》《凡俗与高雅》等 10 余篇作品的著作权侵权行为向南京市鼓楼区人民法院提起诉讼，维护了自己的合法权益。

2. 行业协会开展行业自律，联合企业联盟发布自律公约

行业协会、社团联盟持续深入开展行业自律行动。针对近年侵权现象高发的短视频领域，中国网

① 从最高人民法院主办的中国裁判文书网以及知产宝数据库、北大法宝数据库中对相关民事、刑事裁判文书进行检索查询，查询案件检索时间截至 2019 年 2 月 28 日，选取案件的结案时间为 2018 年 1 月 1 日到 2018 年 12 月 31 日。

② 数据源自中国音乐著作权协会 2018 年会讯，总第 35 期。

③ 数据源自中国文字著作权协会 2018 年年报。

络版权产业联盟发布《中国网络短视频版权自律公约》，中国网络视听节目服务协会发布《网络短视频平台管理规范》，通过自律公约规范短视频行业发展和传播秩序，促进短视频内容质量不断提升。

3. 互联网企业完善内部版权管理制度，利用区块链等新技术保护版权

网络服务商针对侵权盗版内容和侵权盗版账号开展自查整改。搜狐新闻、今日头条、一点资讯、百度百家号完善自媒体入驻协议，发布版权警示公告，封禁侵权自媒体账号 124 436 个，对 19 882 个违规自媒体账号进行降级等处理；建立账号信用分制度或黑名单制度。抖音短视频、快手等 15 家重点短视频平台共下架删除各类涉嫌侵权盗版短视频作品 57 万部；微信公众平台发布《微信公众平台“洗稿”投诉合议规则》等文件，共同保护权利人的合法权益。互联网企业为抵制网络转载乱象，保护媒体自身版权，通过区块链、公钥加密和可信时间戳等技术，为新闻原创作品提供权属认证、取证服务，主动防控版权侵权行为。

三、2018 年中国网络版权保护的基本特点

（一）前沿科技赋能业态融合，技术创新助力版权保护

2018 年，我国 5G 发展进入快车道，大数据、AR/VR、人工智能等新一代信息通信技术快速发展。新技术与内容产业深度融合，突破文化资源传播形态与空间的边界，促使文化消费向虚拟式、碎片式、沉浸式发展，新业态不断涌现。

2018 年短视频应用迅速崛起，用户规模达 6.48 亿人，网民使用率高达 78.2%[①]，市场规模达到 140.1 亿元，同比增长率达 520.7%[②]，成为各大内容平台竞相布局的战略高地，与音乐、新闻等领域的跨界融合进一步加深。

人工智能、大数据、区块链等新兴技术的应用，为网络环境下版权保护提供了新方法和新模式，为网络版权环境的治理提供了新思路。2018 年，北京互联网法院实行案件审理“全程在线”，发布“天平链”电子证据平台；杭州互联网法院首次确认区块链技术存证的电子数据的法律效力，创新采用“异步审理模式”，突破时间、空间限制，为当事人诉讼提供便利的同时提高庭审效率，体现了司法机关在技术新态势下的有益探索和制度创新，降低了权利人维权成本。各大互联网企业也在积极探索和实践用技术手段对版权内容的保护方案，在大数据、区块链等技术的支撑下，主动防控盗版侵权行为，开发智能化、专业化的版权管理系统，加强对侵权行为的在线识别、实时监测、源头追溯，对侵权盗版行为实行永久封禁、注销账号等更为严厉的处理措施。

（二）严格保护倒逼内容升级，正版付费推动产业发展

近年来，版权产业政策体系进一步完善，行业监管愈加有力严格，为塑造风清气朗、保护原创的网络版权环境提供了有力保障，提升了用户的付费意愿。2018 年，多个互联网产业的付费比例都在显著增加，其中网络视频付费用户比例高达 53.1%[③]，音乐、游戏等各个细分领域的在线版权销售额远超实体部分，内容产业正在由线下模式转变为线上模式。用户对付费产品的理性选择，加快了内容产业的优胜劣汰。在严格监管与市场遴选的双重推动下，优质内容成为各平台的核心竞争力，并走出国门，开拓海外版权市场，成为中外文化交流的纽带。《我就是演员》原创节目与美国 IOI 公司签署模式销售协议，开国产综艺向欧美输出的先河；热播剧《延禧攻略》版权输出到 90 个国家和地区，海外版权收益和广告收益创新高；中国自主研发的网络游戏实现海外销售收入 46.3 亿美元[④]。内容产业在海外的布局与推广，对于推动中国文化走出去、增强文化自信具有重要的意义。

数字内容产业的规范发展使得商业模式进一步升级，产业生态进一步改善。在网络音乐领域，国家版权局推动主要网络音乐服务商达成版权合作，99%以上独家音乐作品开放授权，企业在资源趋同的情况下，对市场进行精细化运作，围绕“音乐IP—艺人话题—音乐影视—线上线下演唱会”拓展音乐 IP 内容，打造多模式、立体化粉丝经济形式，行业发展释放巨大潜力[⑤]。在网络游戏领域，在人口红利不断减弱的背景下，网络游戏电竞行业异军突起，围绕其诞生的明星选手、游戏主播、赛事活动等新生业态逐渐成熟，进入爆发期。在网络视频

① 数据源自中国互联网络信息中心发布的第 43 次《中国互联网络发展状况统计报告》。

② 数据源自艾瑞咨询发布的《2018 年中国短视频营销市场研究报告》。

③ 数据源自中国网络视听节目服务协会发布的《2018 中国网络视听发展研究报告》。

④ 数据源自中国音数协游戏工委发布的《2018 年 1—6 月中国游戏产业报告》。

⑤ 《全球版税报告 2018》显示，中国音著协已成为亚太地区收费第四高的协会，数字收入增长超过 433%。

领域，视频企业与线下影视企业合作，打通产业链实现优质内容同步；视频内容分发的跨屏化发展推动广告精准营销。在短视频领域，各短视频平台纷纷加强与优质 MCN（多频道网络）机构、达人合作，打造优质 PGC（专业生产内容）并带动 UGC（用户生产内容），共同生产更优质的内容。

（三）社交平台海量传播作品，平台治理重塑行业生态

依托开放共享的技术架构，社交平台不仅汇聚了互联网上的信息，也为信息的供给方和需求者搭建了连接渠道。随着融媒体时代内容分发的碎片化、社区化，社交平台成为传播作品的重要载体，也成为滋生侵权的新型传播方式，侵权者借助朋友圈、微博、小程序等社交渠道，以免费之名吸引大量人关注或者加入盗版内容群。这种通过小程序等社交平台传播盗版内容的方式，给创作者带来了巨大的经济损失，影响了整个内容行业的原创生产。

2018 年，在国家版权局的支持推动下，各大互联网平台依托技术优势和资源整合能力，承担社会责任，积极探索网络版权保护新路径，在网络版权治理体系中发挥重要作用。在完善平台规则方面，各大网络平台均建立了较为完善的侵权投诉流程，微信“洗稿”投诉合议小组评判首例“洗稿”案，有效保障了权利人的合法权益与用户的良好体验。在保护手段方面，通过技术优势优化平台网络版权保护新模式，利用大数据、人工智能等技术手段检测和防御盗版行为；各类游戏防沉迷系统相继投入使用，利用人脸识别、强制公安实名校验、未成年人游戏消费提醒等技术手段对未成年用户的游戏时长和付费行为进行管理。在维权合作方面，阿里巴巴集团、拼多多等主要电商平台与出版社积极开展版权合作，通过事前预防、主动防控等方式合力遏制通过电商平台销售盗版图书等侵权行为，共同保护权利人的合法权益。平台主动参与包括版权保护在内的平台治理，体现出的“主动合规”“高效合规”的能力成为平台企业的重要能力与核心竞争力之一。

四、2018 年中国网络版权保护的诸多挑战

（一）现行著作权法律制度不能适应产业发展新需求

《著作权法》第三次修订工作自 2012 年 3 月启动以来备受社会关注，但修法进程十分缓慢。由于制定时间较早，现行的著作权法律制度无法跟上数字时代产业发展的步伐。一些新兴的文化消费热点（如“洗稿”、人工智能作品、体育赛事等）中的权利认定和传播行为的可版权性在实践中引起广泛争议。立法滞后和已有规则缺陷的长期存在，使得法院和行政执法机关不得不通过大量司法解释和自由裁量权来应对，造成法律适用的混乱。此外，侵权赔偿数额远低于实际损失，抑制了行业维权的积极性；对著作权刑事案件的判罚尺度不一，“同案不同判”也凸显了著作权法律制定震慑力的不足。

（二）侵权盗版方式“去中心化”增加版权保护难度

近年来，随着版权严格保护政策深入实施和行业正版化的推进，较大规模的盗版网站受到了行政执法和企业诉讼的持续打击，大型网站盗版率不断下降。与此同时，侵权盗版方式随技术发展不断变异，网络侵权盗版逐渐形成以资源型网站为源头的地下黑色产业链形态，通过“资源型网站—小网站—微博、微信公众号”的途径向公众非法传播侵权盗版作品。一方面，中小型侵权盗版网站朝隐蔽化“地下化”境外化发展，据统计[①]，目前常见的 5 576 个疑似侵权视频网站共有 6 630 个网站服务器 IP 地址，来自境外的服务器占比高达 82.05%，权利人跨国维权困难重重，执法部门打击难度显著上升。另一方面，侵权方式从以往利用单一的网络平台公然传播盗版内容，逐渐转为利用网盘、社交平台、二手交易平台等多平台相互关联、快速传播，侵权行为呈现“去中心化”的特征。由于侵权人发布侵权信息的平台并不固定，侵权链接、关键词不断变异，确定侵权人比较困难，这使得打击盗链的难度大大增加。

（三）内容产业“重产轻质”创新能力不足

数字内容产业具有高创新性特征，但在商业利益和流量的驱动下，目前市场上充斥着大量同质化的叙事重复、观点雷同的低质内容产品。内容缺乏创新、优质内容稀缺是行业发展面临的核心挑战。以网络文学为例，尽管网络文学作品的绝对数量不断增长[②]，但整体内容质量不高，优质、精品的原创文学作品偏少，质量参差不齐的问题依然突出。此外，内容产业“急功近利”的现象依然突出，部分自媒体用户为了导流获利，抄袭剽窃、盗稿、篡

① 数据源自中国版权协会版权监测中心。

② 据统计，截至 2017 年底，45 家主要文学网站的原创作品总量超过 1 646 万种，年新增作品超过 233 万部。

改删减原创作品，自媒体内“洗稿”行为屡见不鲜，内容创作沦为“流水线生产”。2018 年，自媒体人六神磊磊指控周冲“洗稿”案引发业内热议。“洗稿”不仅可以规避平台的原创保护机制，甚至可以利用法律界定上的模糊性绕开侵权风险，直接打击了权利人创作和创新的积极性，不利于我国数字内容产业的健康发展。

（四）版权国际应对面临更多挑战

目前，知识产权背后的高新技术主导权已成为国际竞争的新焦点，在 2018 年的中美经济贸易摩擦中，中国的知识产权保护成为双方争议的焦点之一，我国的网络盗版、知识产权法律框架和行政执法水平被美国“301 调查”报告诟病。面对当前国际贸易合作形势以及我国“一带一路”等扩大对外开放的政策导向，版权保护工作涉外事务繁多，双边、多边和区域问题复杂，对我国《著作权法》修订和执法水平提出了新要求。随着我国国际地位的提升和国际竞争的加剧，版权涉外应对形势愈加复杂，任务更加繁重。

五、建议与展望

（一）加快推进《著作权法》修订进程，完善版权制度体系

版权保护，立法先行。在知识产权体系中，《专利法》已完成三次修订，《商标法》第三次修订亦已完成。相对于这两者，《著作权法》的修订进展缓慢，需加快进程。在制度设计上，《著作权法》应基于我国版权产业在创新驱动发展战略中的现状，从作品复制环节的控制转向传播环节的控制，理顺信息网络传播与传统广播的关系，厘清网络条件下作为私权的著作权与公共利益的界限，指明信息存储空间或搜索、链接服务的网络服务提供商在侵权行为中的责任界限，并对网络环境下的侵权赔偿等问题进行重新思考和相应调整，真正实现具有中国特色的著作权法制度创新。在立法目的上，可借鉴美国、日本、欧洲等主要国家和地区版权法修改的最新趋势，适应第四次产业革命浪潮，在严格保护的同时，提高作品许可与传播效率，降低创新风险和成本。在与国际规则的对接上，从被动适应国际规则转变到主动参与、推动国际规则制定，与国际标准接轨，不断提升我国在版权领域的国际话语权和影响力。

（二）鼓励创新激发原创动力，推动优秀作品创作生产

创作是版权保护的目的，也是文化产业繁荣发展的“活水”。在文化产业高质量发展的战略指导下，营造创新氛围，激发原创动力是赋能产业升级的重要手段。政府应尽快完善鼓励和扶持优秀原创的政策，建立与网络版权产业发展相适应的管理体制和扶持机制，对重点企业和优秀原创作品积极鼓励，培植一批具有国际影响力和创新能力的数字内容企业和精品 IP。企业平台一方面应创新规则，激励原创优秀作品，优化内容生态；另一方面要加强协作，打通跨平台的侵权投诉渠道，建立保护原创的长效机制。著作权集体管理组织应当建立更有效的机制，更好地发挥其专业维权的作用。

（三）创新版权治理模式，建立协同治理联动机制

传统的版权治理模式过度关注权利人，因版权持有分散，版权管理分而治之，由于治理规则、利益分配、保护手段的差异，不同主体之间、不同平台之间的版权治理工作存在障碍，耗费了大量的对接、沟通与合作成本。在数字技术和网络平台的语境下，应当考虑引入新治理模式，在保障合作各方版权利益的前提下，建立有效、可持续的合作机制，提高网络环境下版权保护的效率。比如，对于打击“三无网站”盗版侵权，需要国家有关部门、网络运营商、网络平台、广告联盟等多方主体建立联动机制，加强信息共享，建立一体化的监管治理平台，切断非法网站的传播源头和资金源头，共同维护网络健康生态。

（四）推动版权信息共享，促进交易平台透明化

在版权付费阶段，信息不对称、版权授权机制不通畅导致的作品使用与确权、收益不匹配，成为影响版权运用与流转效率的主要因素。权利人不得不采用“商业化”维权的方式，这在某种程度上不利于版权市场的有序发展。著作权集体管理部门和企业一方面应通过创新技术手段和管理运营模式，完善授权交易保障机制和信用机制，疏通网络版权交易渠道，明晰授权规则，提高许可效率，鼓励原创 IP 的多元化开发，以实现版权增值；另一方面可以尝试共建版权内容数据库，推动建立统一、透明的版权确权和交易平台，在政府、权利持有人和集体管理协会之间进行信息共享。

2018 年“中国版权金奖”获奖名单

［编者按］ 2018 年 10 月 19 日，“中国版权金奖”颁奖典礼在苏州举行。“中国版权金奖”是中国国家版权局与世界知识产权组织（WIPO）开展的合作项目，每两年评选一次，是中国版权领域评选的唯一国际性奖项，也是国内版权领域的最高奖项。2018 年“中国版权金奖”设有作品奖、推广运用奖、保护奖和管理奖四个奖项，共有 6 件作品和 14 家机构获奖。

一、作品奖

1.《新华字典》（文字作品，著作权人：商务印书馆）

2.《平凡的世界》（类电作品，制作者：华视娱乐投资集团股份有限公司）

3.《朱鹮》（舞蹈作品，著作权人：上海歌舞团）

4.《红海行动》（类电作品，制作者：北京博纳影业集团有限公司）

5.《活着》（文字作品，作者：余华）

6.《鸡毛飞上天》（类电作品，制作者：杭州佳平影业有限公司）

二、推广运用奖

1. 北京华录百纳影视股份有限公司
2. 中国图书进出口（集团）总公司
3. 雅昌文化集团
4. 中国人民大学出版社有限公司
5. 江苏国泰新点软件有限公司

三、保护奖

1. 湖北省武汉市江岸区人民法院知识产权审判庭
2. 中国轻纺城花样版权登记管理保护办公室
3. 上海市公安局治安总队
4. 广州市文化市场综合行政执法总队
5. 北京联合信任技术服务有限公司

四、管理奖

1. 苏州市版权局
2. 中国音乐著作权协会
3. 中央电视台办公室版权和法律事务室
4. 西安电视剧版权交易中心有限公司

2018 年度查处侵权盗版案件有功单位及个人

［编者按］ 2019 年 11 月 28 日，国家版权局印发《关于奖励 2018 年度查处侵权盗版重大案件的决定》（国版发［2019］5 号），对在 2018 年度查处侵权盗版案件工作中做出突出贡献的 182 家有功单位及 240 名有功个人给予奖励。

【有功单位一等奖】

1. 公安部治安管理局一处

2. 最高人民检察院第四检察厅第一办案组

3. 北京市文化市场行政执法总队执法五队

4. 北京“8·8”销售盗版儿童绘本案专案组（北京市文化市场行政执法总队执法一队、北京市人民检察院第四检察部、北京市通州区人民检察院第二检察部、北京市公安局通州分局治安支队、北京市公安局治安管理总队五支队）

5. 天津市文化市场行政执法总队执法二队

6. 河北省保定市文化市场行政执法大队

7. 吉林省版权局版权处

8. 上海市版权局版权管理处

9. 上海李某某侵犯著作权案专案组（上海市奉贤区人民检察院第三检察部、上海市人民检察院第三分院第六检察部、上海市公安局奉贤分局）

10. 江苏省委宣传部版权管理处

11. 江苏无锡“紫薯影院”微信公众号侵犯著作权案专案组（江苏省无锡市文化市场综合执法支队、江苏省无锡市江阴市市场监管执法大队文旅中队、江苏省无锡市江阴市公安局网络安全保卫大队）

12. 江苏徐州徐某某侵犯著作权案专案组（江苏省徐州市版权局、江苏省徐州市人民检察院知识产权案件办案组、江苏省徐州市公安局网安支队）

13. 江苏淮安“BT 天堂”网传播盗版影视作品案专案组（江苏省淮安市版权局、江苏省淮安市文化市场综合执法支队、江苏省淮安市公安局网络安全保卫支队、江苏省淮安市公安局淮安分局、江苏省淮安市中级人民法院）

14. 浙江省版权局版权处

15. 浙江嘉兴段某某等制售盗版图书案专案组（浙江省嘉兴市文化广电旅游局、浙江省嘉兴市公安局、浙江省嘉兴市海盐县文化和广电旅游体育局、浙江省嘉兴市海盐县公安局）

16. 安徽省委宣传部版权管理处

17. 安徽肥西谢某侵犯著作权案专案组（安徽省公安厅治安总队、安徽省合肥市公安局治安支队一大队、安徽省合肥市肥西县公安局、北京市公安局通州分局治安支队、安徽省合肥市文化市场综合执法支队）

18. 福建省委宣传部版权管理处

19. 江西省委宣传部版权管理处

20. 江西永新“9·8”侵犯著作权案专案组（江西省吉安市永新县文化广电新闻出版旅游局、江西省吉安市永新县文化市场综合执法大队、江西省吉安市永新县公安局、江西省吉安市永新县人民法院、江西省吉安市永新县人民检察院）

21. 江西省南昌市文化市场综合执法支队

22. 山东省委宣传部版权管理处

23. 河南荥阳“8·5”侯某某侵犯著作权案专案组（河南省荥阳市文化广电和旅游局、河南省高级人民法院民三庭）

24. 河南省郑州市荥阳市公安局经侦大队

25. 河南西平“7·17”任某某侵犯著作权案专案组（河南省驻马店市西平县文化市场综合执法大队、河南省郑州市中级人民法院知识产权综合审判庭）

26. 广东省委宣传部版权和印刷管理处

27. 广东省汕头市澄海区人民检察院侦查监督科

28. 四川成都“11·18”侵犯著作权案专案组（四川省成都市公安局天府新区分局刑侦支队二大队、四川省成都市文化市场综合执法总队）

29. 四川成都“吹妖动漫”网侵犯著作权案专案组（四川省成都市版权局、四川省成都市武侯区人民法院）

【有功单位二等奖】

1. 公安部网络安全保卫局十二处

2. 最高人民法院民事审判第三庭（知识产权审判庭）第五调研组

3. 中央网信办网络综合协调管理和执法督查局搜索引擎管理处

4. 北京市通信管理局网络安全管理处

5. 河北省委宣传部版权管理处

6. 河北石家庄张某某侵犯著作权案专案组（河北省石家庄市版权局、河北省石家庄市“扫黄打非”办公室、河北省石家庄市公安局新华分局、河北省石家庄市新华区人民法院、河北省石家庄市新华区人民检察院公诉科）

7. 山西省委宣传部版权管理处

8. 内蒙古自治区党委宣传部版权管理处

9. 辽宁省大连市西岗区人民法院知识产权审判团队

10. 吉林省长春市文化市场综合执法支队

11. 上海市文化市场行政执法总队稽查三处

12. 上海金某某等侵犯著作权案专案组（上海市杨浦区人民法院知识产权审判庭、上海市虹口区人民检察院第七检察部）

13. 上海市徐汇区人民法院知识产权审判庭

14. 上海市公安局经侦总队陈某某侵犯著作权案专案组

15. 上海市通信管理局互联网管理处

16. 上海市委网络安全和信息化委员会网络管理处

17. 江苏省通信管理局网络安全管理处

18. 江苏徐州“看戏网”侵犯影视作品著作权案专案组（江苏省徐州市“扫黄打非”办公室、江苏省徐州市文化市场综合执法支队）

19. 江苏张家港“4·28”侵犯著作权案专案组（江苏省苏州市张家港市文体广电和旅游局、江苏省苏州市张家港市文化市场综合执法大队）

20. 江苏盐城“3·4”侵犯著作权案专案组（江苏省盐城市版权局、江苏省盐城市盐都区公安局龙冈派出所、江苏省盐城市文化市场综合执法支队）

21. 江苏扬州《天龙八部》私服侵犯著作权案专案组（江苏省扬州市版权局、江苏省扬州市江都区委宣传部、江苏省扬州市江都区公安局网络安全保卫大队、江苏省扬州市江都区文化行政综合执法大队、江苏省扬州市江都区人民检察院）

22. 浙江省义乌市市场监督管理局

23. 安徽合肥众源电子科技有限公司侵犯软件著作权案专案组（安徽省“扫黄打非”领导小组办公室、安徽省蚌埠市文化旅游市场管理局、安徽省蚌埠市五河县文化市场综合执法大队、安徽省蚌埠市固镇县文化市场综合执法大队、安徽省蚌埠市怀远县文化市场综合执法大队）

24. 福建泉州“7·13”网络游戏私服侵犯著作权案专案组（福建省泉州市版权局、福建省泉州市文化市场综合执法支队、福建省泉州市人民检察院金融与知识产权犯罪检察部、福建省南安市公安局）

25. 福建省通信管理局网络安全管理处

26. 江西省新余市文化广电新闻出版旅游局

27. 山东省潍坊市临朐县文化市场综合执法大队

28. 山东潍坊寒亭区盛世娱乐广场侵犯著作权案专案组（山东省潍坊市文化市场综合执法支队、山东省潍坊市文化市场综合执法支队寒亭大队）

29. 河南省版权局版权和印刷发行处

30. 河南省打击侵权盗版专案组（河南省“扫黄打非”办公室、河南省公安厅治安管理总队二支队、河南省人民检察院第四检察部）

31. 湖北省委宣传部版权管理处

32. 湖北省版权保护中心

33. 湖北省荆门市公安局高新区掇刀区分局网络安全保卫大队

34. 湖北省咸宁市通山县公安局网络安全保卫大队

35. 重庆唐某某等人侵犯著作权案专案组（重庆市北碚区文化和旅游委员会、重庆市北碚区公安分局、重庆市公安局打假总队、重庆市人民检察院知识产权刑事检察专业团队）

36. 重庆宋某等侵犯著作权案专案组（重庆市北碚区文化市场行政执法大队、重庆市北碚区公安分局、重庆市公安局打假总队、重庆市人民检察院知识产权刑事检察专业团队）

37. 四川省委宣传部版权管理处

38. 四川省绵阳市文化市场综合执法支队

39. 宁夏回族自治区党委宣传部版权管理处

40. 人民出版社办公室

41. 外语教学与研究出版社有限责任公司

42. 中国建筑工业出版社法律事务部

43. 新华社中央新闻采访中心政文采访室

44.《中国新闻出版广电报》出版周刊中心

45. 上海冠勇信息科技有限公司

【有功单位三等奖】

1. 海关总署口岸监管司监管一处

2. 中国信息通信研究院泰尔终端实验室

3. 天津市滨海新区文化市场行政执法大队

4. 天津市南开区文化市场行政执法大队

5. 河北省石家庄市正定县文化市场行政执法队

6. 河北省保定市满城区文化综合行政执法队

7. 河北省衡水市文化市场综合行政执法局

8. 山西省忻州市文化市场综合行政执法队

9. 山西省朔州市文化市场综合行政执法队

10. 山西省临汾市文化市场综合行政执法队

11. 内蒙古自治区巴彦淖尔市文化旅游综合行政执法局

12. 辽宁省沈阳市文化市场综合执法总队直属二大队

13. 辽宁省大连市文化旅游综合执法服务中心

14. 吉林省吉林市文化市场综合执法支队

15. 吉林省四平市文化市场综合执法支队

16. 吉林省延边州珲春市文化市场综合执法大队

17. 黑龙江省委网络安全和信息化委员会办公室网络管理处

18. 上海谈某等侵犯著作权案专案组（上海市普陀区人民法院知识产权庭、上海市普陀区人民检察院第三检察部）

19. 上海市长宁区人民检察院第三检察部

20. 江苏省南京市文化市场综合执法总队

21. 江苏省南京市溧水区文化市场综合执法大队

22. 江苏省无锡市版权局

23. 江苏常州孙某某侵犯著作权案专案组（江苏省常州市文化市场综合行政执法支队、江苏省常州市钟楼区人民法院知识产权案件综合审判庭）

24. 江苏省苏州市知识产权保护中心

25. 江苏省苏州市常熟市文化市场综合执法大队

26. 江苏省南通市文化市场综合执法支队

27. 江苏省南通市通州区川姜镇知识产权管理办公室

28. 江苏省连云港市文化市场综合执法支队

29. 江苏镇江谷某某等非法运营网页游戏侵犯著作权案专案组（江苏省镇江市版权局、江苏省镇江市公安局京口分局网安大队）

30. 浙江宁波“9·10”侵犯软件著作权案专案组（浙江省宁波市文化市场行政执法总队、浙江省宁波市宁海县文化和广电旅游体育局）

31. 浙江省杭州市余杭区文化市场行政执法大队

32. 浙江省金华市永康市公安局

33. 浙江省台州市公安局治安支队

34. 安徽帕特森进出口有限公司侵犯网络文学著作权案专案组（安徽省人民检察院第四检察部、安徽省合肥市文化市场综合执法支队）

35. 安徽省滁州市广播电视新闻出版局

36. 福建福州雷某某侵犯著作权案专案组（福建省福州市文化市场综合执法支队、福建省福州市鼓楼区人民检察院公诉科、福建省福州市鼓楼区人民法院知识产权庭）

37. 福建省厦门市文化市场综合执法支队

38. 福建省莆田市文化市场综合执法支队

39. 福建省宁德市文化市场综合执法支队

40. 厦门海关综合业务处知识产权科

41. 江西省新余市文化市场综合执法支队

42. 江西省吉安市文化市场综合执法支队

43. 江西省南昌市文化市场综合执法支队三大队

44. 江西省九江市文化市场综合执法支队

45. 江西省九江市文化广电新闻出版旅游局

46. 江西省赣州市安远县文化市场管理办公室

47. 江西省赣州市于都县文化广电新闻出版旅游局

48. 江西省萍乡市文化市场综合执法支队

49. 江西省宜春市文化市场综合执法支队

50. 江西省鹰潭市文化市场综合执法支队

51. 江西省新余市渝水区文化广电新闻出版旅游局

52. 山东济南郄某某、王某某侵犯著作权案专案组（山东省济南市文化市场综合行政执法支队、山东省济南市公安局长清区分局）

53. 山东省青岛市文化市场行政执法局

54. 山东省淄博市临淄区文化旅游综合执法大队

55. 山东省淄博市周村区文化市场综合执法大队

56. 山东省潍坊市昌邑市文化市场综合执法大队

57. 山东省潍坊市青州市文化市场综合执法大队

58. 山东省潍坊市文化市场综合执法支队奎文大队

59. 山东省寿光市文化市场综合执法大队

60. 山东省济宁市文化市场综合执法局

61. 湖北省黄冈市文化市场综合执法支队

62. 湖北省通信管理局网络安全管理处

63. 湖北省委网信办网络管理处

64. 湖北武汉范某某等侵犯著作权案专案组（湖北省武汉市江岸区人民检察院、湖北省武汉市江岸区人民法院知识产权审判庭）

65. 湖北省武汉市武汉东湖新技术开发区教育文化体育局

66. 湖北省潜江市文化市场综合执法支队

67. 湖北省襄阳市谷城县文化市场综合执法大队

68. 湖北省襄阳市宜城市文化旅游综合执法大队

69. 湖北省荆州市洪湖市文化市场综合执法大队

70. 湖南省衡阳市衡东县文化市场综合执法大队

71. 湖南省衡阳市祁东县文化市场综合执法大队

72. 湖南省株洲市文化市场综合执法局

73. 湖南省邵阳市新宁县文化市场综合执法大队

74. 湖南省岳阳市文化市场综合执法局版权大队

75. 湖南省常德市桃源县文化市场综合执法大队

76. 湖南省永州市道县文化市场综合执法大队

77. 湖南省永州市文化市场综合执法局

78. 湖南省怀化市文化市场综合执法局版权网络执法科

79. 湖南湘西自治州凤凰县文化市场综合执法局

80. 广东省深圳市南山区人民检察院知识产权检察部

81. 广东省惠州市惠阳区文化广电旅游体育局

82. 广东省揭阳市揭西县文化广电旅游体育局

83. 广东省深圳市市场稽查局知识产权稽查处

84. 广东省珠海市文化广电旅游体育局综合执法一支队

85. 深圳海关隶属蛇口海关法规科

86. 广西贵港江南中学使用盗版教辅材料案专案组（广西壮族自治区贵港市新闻出版局、广西壮族自治区贵港市文化市场综合执法支队、广西壮族自治区贵港市公安局治安警察支队五大队、广西壮族自治区贵港市港南区人民检察院、广西壮族自治区贵港市港南区人民法院）

87. 重庆市委宣传部版权管理处

88. 重庆市渝中区文化市场行政执法大队

89. 四川泸州陈某侵犯著作权案专案组（四川省出版物市场稽查总队、四川省泸州市文化市场综合执法支队、四川省泸州市公安局治安管理支队、四川省泸州市江阳区人民检察院）

90. 四川省遂宁市射洪县文化市场综合执法大队

91. 贵州省版权局版权管理处

92. 贵州省贵阳市文化市场综合行政执法支队

93. 云南省委宣传部版权管理处

94. 云南省文化市场综合行政执法总队

95. 陕西省版权局版权管理处

96. 陕西省人民检察院第四检察部

97. 青海省版权局版权管理处

98. 宁夏固原亿阳计算机销售有限公司侵犯软件著作权案专案组（宁夏回族自治区固原市新闻出版局、宁夏回族自治区固原市文化市场综合执法支队）

99. 新疆维吾尔自治区党委宣传部版权管理处

100. 新疆维吾尔自治区乌鲁木齐市文化市场稽查支队

101. 新疆维吾尔自治区阿克苏地区文化体育广播电视和旅游局

102. 中国知识产权报《版权周刊》

103. 中国国际广播电台

104. 经济日报社综合采访部

105. 科技日报社新闻部

106. 南方都市报社

107. 北京联合信任技术服务有限公司

【有功个人一等奖】

1. 王海镔，公安部治安管理局一处

2. 张建忠，最高人民检察院第四检察厅第一办案组

3. 秦琳，中央网信办网络综合协调管理和执法督察局网络生态治理处

4. 吴韶鸿，工业和信息化部信息通信管理局互联网处

5. 曹祎宇，全国打击侵犯知识产权和制售假冒伪劣商品工作领导小组办公室

6. 北京环球天下教育科技有限公司传播盗版电子出版物案专案组（刘铁京，北京市文化市场行政执法总队；王晓花、梁放，北京市文化市场行政执

法总队执法五队）

7. 北京“12·6”侵犯著作权案专案组（杜鹏，北京市文化市场行政执法总队执法一队；于洋，北京市文化市场行政执法总队综合协调处；樊宏宇，北京市公安局治安管理总队；高振强，北京市公安局西城分局治安支队；邱飞，北京市公安局西城分局牛街派出所）

8. 北京“8·8”销售盗版儿童绘本案专案组（彭燕芬，北京市通州区人民检察院第二检察部；赵程宇，北京市通州区人民法院刑事审判庭）

9. 刘丽娜，北京市人民检察院第四检察部

10. 王红奎，北京市西城区人民法院刑事审判庭

11. 天津百练教育科技集团有限公司销售盗版培训教材案专案组（王哲、任钊，天津市文化市场行政执法总队；徐洪涛，天津市和平区文化市场行政执法大队；顾建波，天津市北辰区文化市场行政执法大队）

12. 尹志军，河北省委宣传部版权管理处

13. 河北保定霍某某销售侵权复制品案专案组（王维山，河北省保定市委宣传部文艺处；金喆、崔坤灿，河北省保定市文化市场行政执法大队；卜海滨，河北省保定市清苑区人民检察院；陈汉斌，河北省保定市公安局经济犯罪侦查支队）

14. 王骞，上海市版权局版权管理处

15. 上海乐欢软件有限公司侵犯著作权案专案组（陈启光、王浩，上海市文化市场行政执法总队稽查五处）

16. 周少鹏，上海市奉贤区人民检察院

17. 宋晓春，江苏省委宣传部版权管理处

18. 江苏淮安“BT天堂”网传播盗版影视作品案专案组（陈冬梅，江苏省淮安市版权局；罗时学，江苏省淮安市文化市场综合执法支队；郑杨，江苏省淮安市公安局网络安全保卫支队；顾杏如，江苏省淮安市公安局淮安分局；孙晓明，江苏省淮安市中级人民法院）

19. 肖斌，浙江省版权局版权处

20. 浙江嘉兴段某某等制售盗版图书案专案组（陆冰，浙江省嘉兴市文化广电旅游局；丁啸，浙江省嘉兴市海盐县文化和广电旅游体育局；颜建荣，浙江省嘉兴市海盐县公安局）

21. 安徽肥西谢某侵犯著作权案专案组（刘志平，安徽省公安厅治安总队；马海林，安徽省合肥市肥西县公安局治安大队；谢叶青，安徽省合肥市肥西县公安局城关派出所；张青云，安徽省合肥市肥西县公安局紫蓬山派出所；汪闻敏，安徽省文明办创建协调处）

22. 阙米秋，江西省委宣传部版权管理处

23. 江西永新“9·8”侵犯著作权案专案组（周建忠，江西省吉安市永新县文化广电新闻出版旅游局；旷胜军、刘丹丹，江西省吉安市永新县文化市场综合执法大队；唐灵龙、王小云，江西省吉安市永新县公安局）

24. 江西南昌“6·4”火课旗舰店侵犯著作权案专案组（邹爱强、罗盛磊，江西省南昌市文化市场综合执法支队；涂晓斌，江西省南昌市公安局直属分局）

25. 河南新乡李某某等侵犯著作权案专案组（张海涛，河南省新乡市文化市场综合执法支队；胡玉波，河南省新乡市公安局平原分局）

26. 王平钦，湖北省荆州市公安县公安局经济犯罪侦查大队

27. 广东佛山“6·27”销售盗版图书案专案组（劳燕贞，广东省佛山市版权局；朱黎，广东省佛山市文化广电旅游体育局；罗运成，广东省佛山市南海区文化广电旅游体育局；崔标文，广东省佛山市公安局南海分局经侦大队；魏国粦，广东省佛山市南海区公安分局平洲派出所刑警中队）

28. 许滢，广东省广州市白云区人民法院刑事审判庭

29. 周园，广东省广州市黄埔区人民检察院派驻夏港检察室

30. 四川成都“11·18”侵犯著作权案专案组（郭晓东，四川省成都市公安局天府新区分局刑事犯罪侦查支队；熊成高，中共成都市委宣传部反非法与违禁出版物处；陈志强、龚秉贵，四川省成都市文化市场综合执法总队）

31. 史竞男，新华社国内部

32. 赖名芳，《中国新闻出版广电报》出版周刊中心

33. 曾文甫，中央广播电视总台

34. 成琪，中国经济网

【有功个人二等奖】

1. 方鹏，公安部治安管理局十三处

2. 马秀荣，最高人民法院民事审判第三庭（知识产权审判庭）第五调研组

3. 陈逸舟，中国互联网协会数据部

4. 北京新浪互联信息服务有限公司侵犯文字作品著作权案专案组（孙琦健、史曙亮，北京市文化

市场行政执法总队执法五队）

5. 北京百度网讯科技有限公司侵犯著作权案专案组（熊伟，北京市文化市场行政执法总队执法五队；于鹏，北京市文化市场行政执法总队法制监督处）

6. 北京陈某某等侵犯软件著作权案专案组（董立波，北京市公安局海淀分局警务支援大队；林辛建，北京市第一中级人民法院刑二庭）

7. 覃波，北京市海淀区人民法院

8. 蒋为杰，北京市通州区人民法院刑事审判庭

9. 任晓英，河北省石家庄市委宣传部

10. 郝子谋，山西省委宣传部版权管理处

11. 辽宁大连王某某等侵犯著作权案专案组（董刚、李杰，辽宁省大连市公安局食药侦支队综合大队；李胜瑾、魏春生，辽宁省大连市文化旅游综合执法服务中心）

12. 吉林长春私人影院侵犯著作权系列案件专案组（杜宇震、田庆权，吉林省版权局版权处）

13. 杨育成，上海市公安局经侦总队食品药品环境犯罪侦查支队

14. 张胤，上海市通信管理局互联网管理处

15. 周雯娟，上海市委网络安全和信息化委员会网络管理处

16. 扎西生格，江苏省公安厅治安总队

17. 江苏无锡“紫薯影院”微信公众号侵犯著作权案专案组（程峰、陈黄春，江苏省无锡市文化市场综合执法支队；曹健、毛伊卉，江苏省无锡市江阴市市场监管执法大队文旅中队；朱宏伟，江苏省无锡市江阴市公安局网络安全保卫大队）

18. 江苏徐州李某某等侵犯著作权案专案组（艾新建、李南，江苏省徐州市版权局；孙林强，江苏省徐州市公安局网安支队；赵冉，江苏省徐州市人民检察院）

19. 江苏张家港“4·28”侵犯著作权案专案组（孙建忠、孙天华，江苏省苏州市张家港市文体广电和旅游局；蔡平、朱群军，江苏省苏州市张家港市文化市场综合执法大队）

20. 江苏盐城“3·4”侵犯著作权案专案组（陈连锋、李翔，江苏省盐城市盐都区公安局龙冈派出所）

21. 方浩，浙江省公安厅治安监督管理总队

22. 何孝武，安徽省委宣传部版权管理处

23. 安徽萧县梁某某侵犯著作权案专案组（侯敬利，安徽省宿州市萧县“扫黄打非”办公室；杨同站，安徽省宿州市萧县文化和旅游局；刘龙、谢冰燃，安徽省宿州市萧县文化市场综合执法大队；杨端习，安徽省宿州市萧县公安局治安大队）

24. 谢雯，福建省委宣传部版权管理处

25. 福建泉州“7·13”网络游戏私服侵犯著作权案专案组（石恒，福建省泉州市版权局；陈能贤、张良才，福建省泉州市文化市场综合执法支队；林俊峰，福建省南安市公安局；黄海波，福建省南安市人民检察院）

26. 江西新余“6·15”侵犯影视作品著作权案专案组（蓝波，江西省新余市“扫黄打非”办公室；刘刚、张小安，江西省新余市文化市场综合执法支队；宋海峰，江西省新余市公安局治安支队第四大队）

27. 董显祥，江西省赣州市文化广电新闻出版旅游局

28. 张灵，江西省上饶市文化广电新闻出版旅游局

29. 山东潍坊大华印务有限公司复制侵权盗版出版物案专案组（蒋金坤，山东省委宣传部版权管理处；牛兆星，山东省潍坊市文化市场综合执法支队；付志杰，山东省潍坊市昌邑市文化市场综合执法大队）

30. 山东青岛爱你宝贝商贸有限公司侵犯著作权案专案组（时桂琴、柴寿宁，山东省青岛西海岸新区综合行政执法局）

31. 山东潍坊三泉书店销售盗版图书案专案组（刘亚鹏，山东省委宣传部反非法反违禁处；由庆，山东省潍坊市文化市场综合执法支队）

32. 李峰，河南省委宣传部新闻发布办公室

33. 卢文俊，湖北省委宣传部版权管理处

34. 王玮，湖北省咸宁市公安局网安支队

35. 廖建新，湖南省衡阳市衡山县文化市场综合执法大队

36. 刘书进，广东省委宣传部版权和印刷管理处

37. 广东中博汽车零部件有限公司计算机软件侵权案专案组（黄俊禧，广东省广州市文化广电旅游局；何琪，广东省广州市番禺区文化广电旅游体育局）

38. 广东茂名张某某等侵犯手机游戏著作权案专案组（邹光伟、陈彩燕，广东省茂名市公安局茂南分局公共信息网络安全监察大队）

39. 广东茂名“九头鸟书院”网侵犯网络文学著作权案专案组（杨贤、陈森友，广东省茂名市公安局茂南分局公共信息网络安全监察大队）

40. 郑彬杰，广东省汕头市版权局

41. 赵海群，广西壮族自治区党委宣传部版权管理处

42. 重庆宋某等侵犯著作权案专案组（秦东，重庆市北碚区文化市场行政执法大队；姜华，重庆市北碚区公安分局网络安全保卫支队；王旭，重庆市北碚区公安分局经济犯罪侦查支队；王志刚，重庆市北碚区人民检察院）

43. 重庆唐某某等侵犯网络游戏著作权案专案组（黄舸，重庆市北碚区文化市场行政执法大队；丁健，重庆市公安局打假总队；胡卫平、唐鹏，重庆市北碚区公安分局经济犯罪侦查支队；薛飞，重庆市北碚区人民检察院）

44. 云南“6·11”侵犯著作权案专案组（王成，云南省委宣传部版权管理处；张益品，云南省文化市场综合行政执法总队；邹云扬，云南省文山州文化市场综合行政执法支队；刘建呈，云南省玉溪市高新技术产业开发区管理委员会综合行政执法局）

45. 孙涛，陕西省委宣传部版权管理处

46. 郝辉，宁夏回族自治区党委宣传部版权管理处

47. 京版十五社反盗版协办工作组（何永禄，北京师范大学出版社（集团）有限公司；马德祥，高等教育出版社有限公司；王芳、夏有利，外语教学与研究出版社有限责任公司）

48. 张红兵，法制日报社

49. 王志艳，新华网股份有限公司

【有功个人三等奖】

1. 戚梦媛，公安部网络安全保卫局

2. 吕晓菲，中央网信办网络社会工作局网络社会组织处

3. 辛群，国家市场监督管理总局价监竞争局反不正当竞争处

4. 高平，文化和旅游部文化市场综合执法监督局

5. 李丹，海关总署综合业务司知识产权处

6. 北京“喵喵折”网文案作品侵犯著作权案专案组（刘春旺，北京市文化市场行政执法总队执法五队；王辉，北京市文化市场行政执法总队法制监督处）

7. 晨致国际教育科技（北京）有限公司侵犯影视作品著作权案专案组（张清，北京市文化市场行政执法总队执法五队；张少帅，北京市文化市场行政执法总队法制监督处）

8. 北京王某某侵犯著作权案专案组（高坤、朱郑，北京市文化市场行政执法总队执法四队；王云光、张曼缇，北京市海淀区人民检察院第二检察部）

9. 李文卫，天津市委宣传部版权管理处

10. 天津爱迪自动化科技有限公司侵犯软件著作权案专案组（李和、高旋，天津市文化市场行政执法总队）

11. 袁伟，天津海关

12. 河北保定乐喵影咖侵犯著作权案专案组（李满义、张树辉，河北省保定市满城区文化综合行政执法队）

13. 河北保定贾某某侵犯著作权案专案组（王涛、金彦青，河北省保定市莲池区文化和旅游局）

14. 马达，内蒙古自治区党委宣传部版权管理处

15. 吴二柱，内蒙古自治区包头市委宣传部

16. 李冉，内蒙古自治区赤峰市文化市场综合执法局

17. 辽宁沈阳欢乐影城娱乐服务有限公司侵犯著作权案专案组（马洪峰、李来春，辽宁省沈阳市文化市场综合执法总队）

18. 辽宁大连孙某某侵犯著作权案专案组（罗志勇、王吉庆，辽宁省大连市文化旅游综合执法服务中心）

19. 吉林长春新理想等书店销售盗版图书案专案组（张雷、潘万路，吉林省长春市文化市场综合执法支队）

20. 吉林启思课外培训学校销售盗版教辅案专案组（李少阁、赵一明，吉林省吉林市文化市场综合执法支队）

21. 高俊涛，吉林省延边朝鲜族自治州珲春市文化市场综合执法大队

22. 孟宪勇，吉林省四平市文化市场综合执法支队

23. 张宇，吉林省白城市镇赉县文化市场综合执法大队

24. 何方岩，吉林省辽源市东辽县文化市场综合执法大队

25. 王琳，吉林省白山市江源区文化市场综合执法大队

26. 缪赟，上海市文化市场行政执法总队稽查三处

27. 谷申安，上海市文化市场行政执法总队稽查三处

28. 江春明，上海市文化市场行政执法总队稽查三处

29. 严佳颖，上海市长宁区人民检察院

30. 上海海关查办侵犯足球世界杯相关著作权系列案专案组（王钰、薛军、张宇财、瞿元、樊上华）

31. 陈立俊，江苏省委宣传部反非法和反违禁处

32. 黄光明，江苏省互联网信息办公室

33. 江苏南京大全电气研究院有限公司侵犯软件著作权案专案组（杨丽，江苏省南京市江宁区文化市场综合执法大队；何进，江苏省南京市江宁区文化市场综合执法大队）

34. 江苏无锡朱某某侵权案专案组（牟峰、朱轩枫，江苏省无锡市文化市场综合执法支队）

35. 江苏徐州彭某某侵犯著作权案专案组（陈伟、朱启川，江苏省徐州市版权局；张蕾，江苏省徐州市人民法院民三庭；苏牧，江苏省徐州市文化市场综合执法支队）

36. 江苏常州孙某某侵犯著作权案专案组（谢春林，江苏省常州市委宣传部；沈鑫伟，江苏省常州市文化市场综合行政执法支队）

37. 江苏常州微讯信息科技有限公司侵犯影视作品著作权案专案组（徐晖、相薇，江苏省常州市文化市场综合行政执法支队）

38. 江苏常州李某某通过信息网络擅自向公众提供他人作品并牟利案专案组（张杰源、张晗，江苏省常州市文化市场综合行政执法支队）

39. 周俊，江苏省常州市文化市场综合行政执法支队

40. 江苏常州王某通过信息网络擅自向公众提供他人作品并牟利案专案组（徐静、陶沙，江苏省常州市文化市场综合行政执法支队）

41. 顾人英，江苏省苏州市张家港市文化市场综合执法大队

42. 钱欢，江苏省苏州市张家港市文化市场综合执法大队

43. 董建芳，江苏省苏州市张家港市文化市场综合执法大队

44. 沈正刚，江苏省苏州市常熟市文化市场综合行政执法大队

45. 邵爱军，江苏省南通市通州区川姜镇政府川姜镇知识产权管理办公室

46. 施颖，江苏省南通市海门市三星镇版权管理办公室

47. 沈欣，江苏省连云港市文化市场综合执法支队

48. 唐海宁，江苏省扬州市文化市场综合执法支队

49. 单继震，江苏省宿迁市沭阳县文化行政综合执法大队

50. 廖忠文，江苏省宿迁市沭阳县文化行政综合执法大队

51. 安徽黄山市民网络有限公司侵犯著作权案专案组（孙德勇，安徽省公安厅治安总队；胡荣孙，安徽省黄山市文化和旅游局；韦俊，安徽省黄山市文化市场综合执法支队）

52. 章余胜，安徽省宣城市文化市场综合执法支队二大队

53. 安徽合肥张某某侵犯著作权案专案组（汝梦芸、汤明，安徽省合肥市文化市场综合执法支队）

54. 安徽分秀科技有限公司侵犯著作权案专案组（林光莹、杜仙林，安徽省合肥市文化市场综合执法支队）

55. 何祥，安徽省蚌埠市文化旅游市场管理局文化市场管理科

56. 崔艺竞，福建省通信管理局网络安全管理处

57. 福建泉州轻工工艺进出口（集团）公司侵犯著作权案专案组（郑川，厦门海沧海关查验一科；朱斯琦，厦门海关综合业务处综合科）

58. 福建泉州市美影网络科技有限公司侵犯影视作品著作权案专案组（邱益民、颜希宇，福建省泉州市文化市场综合执法支队）

59. 福建厦门威迪思汽车设计服务有限公司侵犯软件著作权案专案组（王卫强，福建省厦门市文化市场综合执法二大队；李缘缘，福建省厦门市思明区人民法院民三庭）

60. 福建厦门音像影视作品侵权系列案专案组（王栋，福建省厦门市文化市场综合执法支队二大队；魏帆，福建省厦门市文化市场综合执法支队三大队；林珽璟，福建省厦门市版权局版权管理处）

61. 福建厦门“诉调对接”化解著作权纠纷系列案专案组（雷荣通，福建省厦门市文化市场综合执法支队；黄国平，福建省厦门市文化市场综合执法支队二大队；潘伟生，福建省厦门市思明区人民法院）

62. 福建三明音像制品侵权系列案专案组（谢志毅，福建省三明市版权局新闻出版科；潘梦婷，福建省三明市文化市场综合执法支队综合科）

63. 福建南平出版物侵权系列案专案组（兰林凯，福建省南平市版权局新闻出版版权科；曹瑞岗、林汉钦，福建省南平市文化市场综合执法支队）

64. 冯骏，江西省景德镇市文化市场综合执法支队

65. 刘秋华，江西省吉安市文化市场综合执法支队

66. 傅慧强，江西省吉安市文化市场综合执法支队

67. 江西南昌洪流书店侵犯著作权案专案组（饶兴奇、刘凯，江西省南昌市文化市场综合执法支队）

68. 江西南昌昌大书店侵犯著作权案专案组（朱军、万建明，江西省南昌市文化市场综合执法支队）

69. 江西宏扬技术服务有限公司侵犯著作权案专案组（万魁东、万绍鹏，江西省南昌市文化市场综合执法支队）

70. 江西新余好拍档商贸有限公司侵权案专案组（张志平、黄有利，江西省新余市渝水区文化市场综合执法大队；罗强、胡清云，江西省新余市文化市场综合执法支队）

71. 尧飞武，江西省赣州市安远县文化市场稽查大队

72. 黄婧，江西省赣州市安远县文化市场稽查大队

73. 尧沐淋，江西省赣州市安远县文化市场稽查大队

74. 谢芸华，江西省赣州市于都县文化广电新闻出版旅游局

75. 张县春，江西省赣州市于都县文化广电新闻出版旅游局

76. 谭春森，江西省赣州市于都县文化市场综合执法大队

77. 易长军，江西省赣州市于都县文化市场综合执法大队

78. 张玉华，江西省九江市文化广电新闻出版旅游局

79. 武汉世纪方舟图书发行有限责任公司侵犯著作权案办案组（朱斌、丁峰，江西省九江市文化市场综合执法支队）

80. 江西九江漫时光视界咖啡吧侵犯著作权案专案组（万来仪、姜睿，江西省九江市文化市场综合执法支队）

81. 江西九江海慧教育咨询有限公司侵犯著作权案专案组（杨军、张磊，江西省九江市文化市场综合执法支队）

82. 江西九江剑飞文化传媒有限公司侵权案专案组（沈师、张宸淞，江西省九江市文化市场综合执法支队）

83. 刘东明，江西省九江市彭泽县文化市场综合执法大队

84. 罗华英，江西省瑞金市文化市场稽查大队

85. 邹立强，江西省瑞金市文化广电新闻出版旅游局

86. 谢鹏，江西省瑞金市文化市场稽查大队

87. 张琳，江西省瑞金市文化市场稽查大队

88. 麻卫清，江西省上饶市余干县文化市场综合执法大队

89. 江西鹰潭好电影网侵犯著作权案专案组（周四军、徐志勇，江西省鹰潭市文化市场综合执法支队）

90. 山东烟台炳森图文设计有限公司侵犯著作权案专案组（种道洋、曲景舜，山东省烟台市文化市场综合执法支队）

91. 谢志宏，山东省青岛市文化市场行政执法局

92. 山东淄博海天教育培训学校侵犯著作权案专案组（张洋、王桂清，山东省淄博市周村区文化市场综合执法大队）

93. 曹晨光，山东省潍坊市安丘市文化市场综合执法局

94. 韩申军，山东省潍坊市文化市场综合执法支队寒亭大队

95. 山东潍坊私人影院侵犯著作权案专案组（马寿果、王晓荣，山东省潍坊市文化市场综合执法支队；成爱军、闫海涛，山东省潍坊市青州市文化市场综合执法大队）

96. 山东嘉祥房某某侵犯著作权案专案组（王守俊、陆连臣，山东省济宁市嘉祥县文化市场综合执法局）

97. 山东济宁联邦印务有限公司盗印他人出版物案专案组（孟杰、田阳，山东省济宁市任城区文化市场综合执法局）

98. 山东济宁“10·19”王某某侵犯著作权案专案组（王天湖、颜廷爱，山东省济宁市文化市场综合执法局；李寅，山东省曲阜市文化市场综合执法局；宗恩锋，山东省济宁市公安局治安警察支队；满明，山东省济宁市公安局济东分局治安管理大队）

99. 杨宝雨，山东省德州市文化市场综合执法支队

100. 河南省打击侵权盗版专案组（陈国军，河南省“扫黄打非”办公室；邹伟，河南省公安厅治安管理总队；丁萌伟，河南省公安厅网安总队；张光亮，河南省人民检察院第一检察部）

101. 张海涛，河南省新乡市文化市场综合执法支队

102. 河南南阳唐风华韵店铺侵犯著作权案专案组（董全生、栗山，河南省南阳市文化市场综合执法支队）

103. 李靖，湖北省委网信办网络管理处

104. 向安贵，湖北省通信管理局网络安全管理处

105. 湖北武汉晃游网络科技有限公司侵犯著作权案专案组（舒洪波、姚红波，湖北省武汉市武汉东湖新技术开发区教育文化体育局

106. 吴小安，湖北省潜江市文化市场综合执法支队

107. 刘伟，湖北省黄冈市文化市场综合执法支队

108. 湖南衡阳瀚博文化传播有限公司侵犯著作权案专案组（曾剑鸣、邓洺，湖南省衡阳市文化市场综合执法局）

109. 刘意福，湖南省衡阳市文化市场综合执法局

110. 湖南常宁航空科技教育培训中心侵犯著作权案专案组（唐能平、尹忠国，湖南省衡阳市文化市场综合执法局）

111. 湖南衡阳杨某某侵犯著作权案专案组（王友良、沈蓓，湖南省衡阳市文化市场综合执法局）

112. 陈炜，湖南省衡阳市文化市场综合执法局

113. 钟淙，湖南省衡阳市文化市场综合执法局

114. 商章勤，湖南省衡阳市文化市场综合执法局

115. 湖南衡阳吴某侵犯影视作品著作权案专案组（谢建军、陈超，湖南省衡阳市文化市场综合执法局）

116. 湖南衡阳乐汀影视文化传媒有限公司侵犯影视作品著作权案专案组（刘小平、胡文艺，湖南省衡阳市文化市场综合执法局）

117. 湖南衡阳密汇咖啡休闲会所侵犯影视作品著作权案专案组（沈登成、万燕萍，湖南省衡阳市文化市场综合执法局）

118. 湖南衡东兴东中学侵犯著作权案专案组（左朝霞，湖南省衡阳市衡东县文化市场综合执法局；肖珍珠，湖南省衡阳市衡东县文化旅游广电体育局）

119. 赵新林，湖南省衡阳市衡山县文化市场综合执法大队

120. 李振球，湖南省衡阳市祁东县文化市场综合执法大队

121. 李安民，湖南省衡阳市祁东县文化市场综合执法大队

122. 湖南耒阳煌宫会娱乐有限公司侵犯音乐作品著作权案专案组（欧阳昭苏、刘超，湖南省衡阳市耒阳市综合行政执法局）

123. 湖南达嘉智能包装设备有限公司侵犯软件著作权案专案组（谭励军、周淼，湖南省株洲市文化市场综合执法局）

124. 刘伟，湖南省岳阳市文化市场综合执法局版权大队

125. 李军，湖南省岳阳市文化市场综合执法局版权大队

126. 曾利宏，湖南省岳阳市文化市场综合执法局版权大队

127. 蒋德忠，湖南省永州市宁远县文化市场综合执法大队执法二室

128. 湖南永州刘某某侵犯著作权案专案组（文晖、张德文，湖南省永州市文化市场综合执法局）

129. 湖南娄底袁某某等侵犯著作权案专案组（谭琪琳、胡清，湖南省娄底市文化市场综合执法支队；杨黎军、陈超，湖南省娄底市新化县文化市场综合执法大队）

130. 湖南凤凰美丽人生娱乐城侵犯音乐作品著作权案专案组（王宴、张希，湖南省湘西土家族苗族自治州凤凰县文化市场综合执法局）

131. 广东广州“MTV235 网”侵犯影视作品著作权案专案组（温上京，广东省广州市文化广电旅游局；卢昱成，广东省广州市公安局治安管理支队六大队）

132. 张思勇，广东省惠州市文化广电新闻出版局

133. 钟岭林，广东省汕头市文化广电旅游体育局

134. 邓少元，广东省深圳市市场稽查局知识产权稽查处

135. 珠海咖影文化传播中心侵犯著作权案专案组（刘建平、张旭，广东省珠海市文化广电旅游体育局）

136. 广西贵港江南中学使用盗版教辅材料案专

案组（韦家会，广西壮族自治区贵港市新闻出版局印刷发行和版权管理科；李燃，广西壮族自治区贵港市公安局治安警察支队五大队；潘丽安，广西壮族自治区贵港市文化市场综合执法支队综合执法科）

137. 唐闰来，广西壮族自治区河池市文化市场综合执法支队

138. 刘震坤，重庆市文化市场行政总队三处

139. 黄俊，重庆市江津区文化市场行政执法大队

140. 邓智勇，贵州省贵阳市文化市场综合执法支队

141. 云南“6·19”侵犯著作权案专案组（杨茂森，云南省保山市委宣传部；周成东，云南省保山市文化和旅游市场综合执法支队）

142. 刘志强，云南省文化市场综合行政执法总队

143. 陕西西安杨某等侵犯著作权案专案组（李军、赵宇，陕西省西安市文化市场行政执法总队）

144. 陕西科技资源统筹中心侵犯著作权案专案组（程原力、何勇刚，陕西省西安市文化市场行政执法总队）

145. 甘肃博雅职业培训学校侵犯著作权案专案组（芦世宏、冯斌，甘肃省兰州市文化市场综合行政执法队）

146. 青海新华百货商业有限公司大通店销售盗版图书案专案组（张成贵、韩学梅，青海省西宁市大通县文化市场综合执法大队）

147. 宁夏奥康尼工贸有限公司等侵犯软件著作权系列案专案组（杨建忠、余钧彦，宁夏回族自治区吴忠市文化市场综合执法队）

148. 徐地方，宁夏回族自治区银川市文化市场综合执法队

149. 加娜尔，新疆维吾尔自治区党委宣传部版权管理处

150. 艾克拜·牙生，新疆维吾尔自治区乌鲁木齐市文化市场稽查支队

151. 潘晨，高等教育出版社法律事务与版权管理部

152. 唐玮，中国建筑工业出版社

153. 付长超，人民网

154. 倪伟，新京报社

155. 马李文博，中国艺术报社

156. 穆宏志，中国出版传媒商报社

157. 张晓瑜，中国教育电视台

2018 年中国版权十件大事

［编者按］ 2019 年 3 月 15 日，国家版权局在官网发布了国家版权局评选出的“2018 年中国版权十件大事”。

一、中宣部统一管理全国版权工作

2018 年 3 月，中共中央印发《深化党和国家机构改革方案》，中央宣传部对外加挂国家新闻出版署（国家版权局）牌子，著作权管理工作由中央宣传部负责。4 月 16 日，国家新闻出版署（国家版权局）揭牌仪式在京举行。党中央决定中宣部统一管理版权工作，充分体现了以习近平同志为核心的党中央对宣传思想和知识产权工作的高度重视，版权工作迎来重要发展新契机。

二、网络音乐版权生态持续好转

2018 年，国家版权局继续推动网络音乐版权秩序不断规范，先后约谈大中型唱片公司和网络音乐服务商，推动腾讯音乐、网易云音乐、阿里音乐等主要网络音乐服务商达成版权合作，各方将 99%以上独家音乐作品开放授权，引起社会广泛关注和好评，国家版权局相关微博阅读量达 4 174 万次。国家版权局指导各方完善授权模式，协调各方合作共赢，推动构建健康有序的网络音乐版权生态，取得进一步积极成效。

三、“剑网 2018”专项行动重点整治短视频版权秩序

2018 年 7 月至 12 月，国家版权局、国家互联网信息办公室、工业和信息化部、公安部开展“剑网 2018”专项行动，针对新兴短视频领域的版权问题多措并举、重拳出击，重点整治短视频领域各类侵权盗版行为。按照“剑网 2018”专项行动要求，抖音短视频等 15 家短视频平台切实加强版权保护，积极履行企业主体责任，共下架删除各类涉嫌侵权盗版短视频作品 57 万部，短视频版权秩序得到显著改善。

四、中国财经媒体版权保护联盟成立

为推动媒体融合发展、加强媒体版权保护，2018 年，有关媒体行业协会在完善授权交易机制、加强行业版权自律、开展行业版权合作等方面开展了许多探索，推动版权保护、媒体融合向纵深发展。12 月 15 日，30 多家主流财经媒体发起成立“中国财经媒体版权保护联盟”，共同抵制未经授权擅自转载新闻作品的行为，提高对作品转载的议价能力，推动实现常态化监控和维权、市场化交易等。

五、电商平台与反盗版联盟合力遏制网上销售盗版行为

2018 年 10 月 21 日，阿里巴巴集团与京版十五社反盗版联盟在第七届中国国际版权博览会期间，就图书版权保护计划签订合作协议；11 月 9 日，拼多多平台与京版十五社反盗版联盟及少儿出版反盗版联盟在中国国际进口博览会期间，就图书版权保护签订合作协议。各方共同推动版权社会共治，切实履行企业主体责任，加强电商平台与权利人版权合作，构建从源头遏制各类侵权盗版行为的新模式。

六、多地查处盗版案件保护金庸作品版权

2018 年 10 月 30 日，著名作家金庸先生逝世，引发社会各界怀念热潮，盗版金庸作品图书乘机牟利。北京、天津、浙江、河南、河北、广东等地版权执法部门集中查处了多起销售盗版金庸作品图书案件并移送公安机关立案侦查，有效保护金庸作品版权。其中，北京顺义查获盗版金庸作品图书 18 万余册，天津静海查获盗版金庸作品图书 11 万余册，浙江杭州查获盗版金庸作品图书 2.7 万余册，广东广州查获盗版金庸作品图书近 2 万册，河南郑州查获盗版金庸作品图书 1 万多册。

七、北京互联网法院审理首起著作权案件

2018 年 9 月 9 日，北京互联网法院挂牌成立。“抖音短视频”案成为其受理的第一起案件，也是我国首个短视频平台帮助用户维权的案件。该案中，北京互联网法院认定涉案短视频符合《著作权法》的独创性要求，构成类电作品，该案对于短视频著作权纠纷类案件具有一定的借鉴意义。该案也凸显了在网络案件中，著作权案件占有较突出的比重。

八、2018 年“中国版权金奖”颁发

2018 年 10 月 19 日，中国国家版权局与世界知识产权组织在苏州举办 2018 年“中国版权金奖”颁奖仪式。《新华字典》等 6 部作品获作品奖；北京华录百纳影视股份有限公司等 5 家单位获推广运用奖；北京联合信任技术服务有限公司等 5 家单位获保护奖；苏州市版权局等 4 家单位获管理奖。“中国版权金奖”作为我国版权领域最高奖项，用以鼓励和表彰在版权创作、运用、保护和管理中做出突出贡献的单位或个人，引起国内外广泛关注，收到良好社会反响。

九、我国版权产业增加值突破 6 万亿元

2018 年 12 月 25 日，中国新闻出版研究院发布了 2017 年中国版权产业的经济贡献调研结果：2017 年我国版权产业的行业增加值为 6.08 万亿元人民币，占全国 GDP 的 7.35%。其中核心版权产业行业增加值为 3.81 万亿元人民币，占我国 GDP 的 4.61%。2017 年中国网络版权产业的市场规模达 6 365 亿元人民币，同比增长 27.2%。调研结果显示，近年来我国版权产业呈持续增长态势，网络版权产业增长较快，版权产业对促进经济社会发展的重要作用日益凸显。

十、版权司法审判规则不断完善

2018 年 4 月，北京市高级人民法院颁布《北京市高级人民法院侵害著作权案件审理指南》，涉及基本规定、权利客体、权利归属、侵权认定、抗辩事由等 11 个方面的问题。12 月，最高人民法院发布《最高人民法院关于审查知识产权纠纷行为保全案件适用法律若干问题的规定》，包括程序性规则、实体性规则、行为保全申请错误认定与处理、行为保全措施的解除等 4 个方面内容。国家和地方一系列司法相关规则的出台，对于提升包括版权在内的知识产权案件的审判质量具有重要意义。

2018 年（第十届）全国大学生版权征文获奖名单

［编者按］ 2018 年 10 月 21 日，由国家版权局主办、中国人民大学国家版权贸易基地和中国人民大学创意产业技术研究院承办的第十届全国大学生版权征文活动颁奖仪式在江苏苏州举行。本届征文活动共收到参赛论文 1 496 篇，其中本科生组 1 168 篇，研究生组 328 篇。经专家评审，最终评选出特等奖论文 3 篇，本科生组和研究生组一等奖论文各 10 篇、二等奖论文各 20 篇、三等奖论文各 30 篇，优秀指导老师奖 20 名，优秀组织奖 16 名。

优秀论文奖

一、特等奖

奖项	姓名	学校	论文题目
特等奖	臧佳兴	同济大学	论非演绎类同人作品所涉“借鉴元素”的侵权问题
	虞婷婷	武汉大学	论网络服务商承担著作权审查义务的正当性
	徐瑛晗	中南财经政法大学	论“聚合盗链行为”的定性与法律规制

二、研究生组优秀论文奖

奖项	姓名	学校	论文题目
一等奖	尹　庆	中南大学	作品深层链接行为的著作权法规制
	刘　乐	中山大学	网游直播中著作权合理使用问题探析——以美国合理使用制度为视角
	齐立文	浙江工商大学	人工智能生成物的可版权性研究
	陆莹莹	华东政法大学	文学角色著作权侵权初探
	夏梦妍	中南财经政法大学	人工智能生成物著作权归属问题研究
	李昕玥	南京大学	网络游戏界面著作权保护
	李小雪	南京理工大学	论网络环境下的著作权默示许可制度
	何　佳	华东政法大学	二次提供理论与深度链接行为的定性——与张金平博士商榷
	付贤会	华东政法大学	从《绝地求生》“抄袭”案浅谈游戏的可版权性及侵权判定
	于先诚	内蒙古大学	人工智能创作物可版权性之否定
二等奖	蔡　睿	华东政法大学	音乐作品实质性相似判断标准——以美国案例为参考
	李　漭	华东政法大学	公共数据开放的版权许可研究——以知识共享许可为视角
	刘　星	中南大学	浅谈网络游戏抄袭的侵权认定
	李　安	中南财经政法大学	电子游戏直播版权问题之管见——兼评“梦幻西游 2”案
	周子威	华东政法大学	论“模仿讽刺”与侵犯保护作品完整权的界限
	陆　慧	山东科技大学	论人工智能创作物的版权性质与归属
	潘柏华	中国政法大学	加框链接间接侵权中“传播行为”之界定——基于梳理欧盟相关案例的趋势与启示
	金　宁	华东政法大学	论保护作品完整权的侵权判断标准
	曾祥瑞	中南财经政法大学	日本著作权集体管理组织一揽子许可的反垄断认定——以“JASRAC 排除型私人垄断案”为研究对象

续表

奖项	姓名	学校	论文题目
二等奖	李逸竹	中国人民大学	古琴琴曲“打谱”著作权问题试析
	周宣辰	南京理工大学	戏仿短视频作品的“转换性使用”认定——以谷阿莫为例
	刘　桢	西安交通大学	由文字作品与书法作品的比较分析看跨类型作品的认定
	方　芳	清华大学	保护作品完整权侵权行为方式的符号学分析
	赵韵琳	中国科学院大学	三网融合下广播组织权的重构
	衡敬之	西南医科大学	《著作权法修订草案（送审稿）》合理使用制度之评述——以学术研究性合理使用为例
	姚　辰	华东政法大学	数字经济时代版权保护的路径转换——以区块链+数字版权保护为视角
	陈鸿权	南京师范大学	论信息网络传播权授权中的“端”限制——基于权利概念的分析
	张奕婕	中国政法大学	“表演者权”，狄厄尼索斯还是赫尔墨斯？
	葛亚妍	南京师范大学	真人秀节目模板的著作权保护
	李思敏	南京师范大学	思想与表达二分法的司法适用
三等奖	顾晨昊	中南财经政法大学	禁止规避技术措施例外制度完善研究
	周　朗	华中师范大学	网络游戏改编中的侵权认定之类型化分析
	刘丛革	河北经贸大学	教辅材料著作权保护问题研究
	刘　乾	北京外国语大学	浅析角色扮演行为的著作权侵权问题
	金　锐	山东科技大学	智能合约技术在数字音乐版权中的应用——以 Ujo Music 为例
	沈浩蓝	西南政法大学	数字时代电子出版变革与版权对策
	彭亚媛	复旦大学	论知识产权的公共领域哲学原理及其发展困境
	符炎红	中山大学	人工智能生成物的著作权归属浅析
	陶芷松	华东政法大学	从损害理论角度论我国合理使用制度的重构
	王舒婷	中南财经政法大学	自媒体时代下网络转载法定许可制度探析
	李京霈	华东政法大学	电子游戏著作权法保护方式的思考
	王榕榕	同济大学	区块链证据在著作权案件中的作用
	赵林翔	华东政法大学	电子游戏数值策划的著作权保护探析
	曹　磊	清华大学	加框链接行为之中的侵权认定标准的新探讨
	郭雨笛	中南财经政法大学	独创性判断中“创作高度”概念批判——以“新浪诉凤凰案”为切入点
	蒋启蒙	重庆理工大学	人工智能生成物著作权保护问题的研究综述
	唐益亮	西南政法大学	合理使用“三步检验法”的转变与调整
	初　萌	北京大学	论网络接入服务商版权侵权屏蔽义务
	朱静漪	中国传媒大学	电影故事评述类短视频合理使用的认定
	田小楚	西安交通大学	虚拟现实三维数字模型著作权问题初探
	陈　薇	中山大学	人工智能生成物的可作品性研究
	杨尹佩	中南大学	广播组织权制度向网络环境延伸的相关问题探讨——兼论 WIPO 版权与相关权常设委员会最新发展动向
	冯铁拴	武汉大学	复制抑或创作：AI 技术下画作风格迁移的法律定性
	李贤森	中国人民大学	强化我国版权保护的商事仲裁路径
	宋　景	西北政法大学	GDPR 对于数据库版权的权利限制
	于旭晖	同济大学	电视直播中电影作品的固定性要求
	余佩诗	华南理工大学	网络环境中保护作品完整权界限研究——基于对谷阿莫系列短视频作品的探讨
	贾润田	河北经贸大学	人工智能发展对著作权挑战的初探
	杨笑宇	南京师范大学	同人作品“借用”行为与“转换性”使用
	张阳珂	重庆理工大学	我国著作权集体管理模式再审视

三、本科生组优秀论文奖

奖项	姓名	学校	论文题目
一等奖	邵稚权	中国政法大学	博弈论视角下中国发展版权保险的必要性分析
	陈越飞	湘潭大学	实质性相似判断标准的客观化——以洗稿为例
	林锦晖	中南财经政法大学	作品概念的科学构建与属性划分
	易书农	华东政法大学	论云盘服务商网络分享服务著作权间接侵权的认定
	郑子璐	集美大学	数字音乐独家版权模式问题及对策研究
	钟　玲	集美大学	美国网络服务商保护的司法判例及对我国的启示
	李嘉宁	北京理工大学	同人文学作品著作权侵权问题分析
	林子未	华东政法大学	私人复制中补偿金制度研究
	孙　文	华东政法大学	网络环境下转载摘编法定许可适用性分析
	关　爱	西北政法大学	我国著作权裁量性赔偿适用的反思及完善
二等奖	张珈玮	澳门科技大学	论避风港原则适用的三阶层构造
	许　静	华东政法大学	摄制权内涵及修改趋势探析
	赵慧慧	湖南师范大学	论人工智能创作物的权利归属
	黄知远	西南科技大学	电子游戏设计及规则的著作权保护问题研究
	张凯丽	江苏师范大学	游戏整体画面著作权法律保护的实证探究
	王莫菲	中南民族大学	从西湖音乐喷泉案看作品类型化的困境与立法完善
	王盈盈	华东政法大学	论人工智能生成内容之不可版权性及法律保护问题
	何　苗	重庆理工大学	人工智能创作物获得版权保护的合理性研究
	邵泽豪	中国政法大学	网络混剪视频侵权问题研究
	杨紫茹	华东政法大学	论短视频平台侵权责任的认定——限于热门影视、综艺、体育赛事等内容
	周梓忻	杭州师范大学	综艺节目模式的著作权保护问题研究
	阮芳芳	广州医科大学	KTV 歌曲版权许可纠纷实证研究
	贺顺琪	华东政法大学	游戏直播的著作权定性与权利归属
	张东晖	华东政法大学	论游戏规则在著作权法中的保护问题
	钱怡婷	华东政法大学	论著作权中的“实质性相似”判断
	唐兴蓉	山东科技大学	人工智能创造物的可版权性及归属之探析
	舒　颖	华东政法大学	3D 打印著作权保护问题研究——基于中德对比分析
	郑少嵘	重庆理工大学	浅析我国体育赛事转播权的保护
	陈　慧	集美大学	非人摄制照片的法律保护
	吴锴豪	华东政法大学	介绍类短视频合理使用问题研究
三等奖	欧文杰	华东政法大学	架空类同人小说的著作权侵权问题研究
	梁恺为	湖南大学	试论人工智能创作物是否适用著作权法
	张　翔	中南民族大学	自媒体“洗稿”行为的反不正当竞争法规制初探
	陈　曦	广西师范学院	浅谈保护作品完整权中的种种问题——以网络小说作者诉改编电影侵权案为例
	郭捧捧	河南科技大学	音乐喷泉作品认定——以西湖音乐喷泉案为例
	唐梓博	烟台大学	非演绎类同人小说的著作权问题分析
	赵光正	中南财经政法大学	浅析美术作品的判定标准
	张　蓓	湖北警官学院	反思版权起源于特权
	熊予晴	华中师范大学	知识产权的地域性突破与域外效力
	王雅薇	江苏师范大学	对我国著作权侵权裁量性赔偿制度的思考与展望
	李炫圻	华中科技大学	浅析同人小说的版权问题

续表

奖项	姓名	学校	论文题目
三等奖	刘　静	山东大学	人工智能创作物的版权保护问题
	周　爽	中南民族大学	论实用艺术作品的著作权保护
	颜柯丞	重庆理工大学	从 cosplay 的角度简析著作权与商品化形象权的关系
	王浩宇	中山大学	论在著作权侵权案件中引入公益诉讼的合理性
	王依劼	华中科技大学	“用户创造内容”的合理使用分析
	彭小洪	重庆理工大学	云环境下我国著作权“临时复制”法律问题研究
	洪丹萍	华南师范大学	我国动漫角色商品化权保护的探索与发展研究
	汪诗桐	中南民族大学	流媒体翻录技术对著作权侵权认定的冲击与应对
	张　婕	中南财经政法大学	论我国版权登记制度的现状与完善
	李　佳	陆军勤务学院	初探高校大学生优秀毕业论文被侵权应对策略
	李心怡	湖南师范大学	对同人作品适用合理使用制度的法律思考
	蒋明宇	中南财经政法大学	论短视频著作权侵权与保护要点
	杜媛媛	西南科技大学	试论编曲之著作权保护
	侯淑涵	杭州师范大学	视频分享网站中音乐作品私人复制侵权问题研究
	薛　芮	华东政法大学	中美关系下的著作权问题研究
	于　一	华东政法大学	戏仿作品合理性的判定
	张逸文	南京理工大学	论人工智能创作物的著作权保护问题
	赵启萌	华东政法大学	对著作人身权、财产权二分法合理性的质疑
	李林凡	中国海洋大学	网络音乐传播中的侵权问题及改进建议

优秀指导老师奖

吴汉东　中南财经政法大学
郭　禾　中国人民大学
冯晓青　中国政法大学
黄武双　华东政法大学
何炼红　中南大学
肖志远　中南财经政法大学
陈绍玲　华东政法大学
贺　炯　华东政法大学
张春艳　江苏师范大学
苏　平　重庆理工大学
马晓燕　南京师范大学
黄玉烨　中南财经政法大学
刘　华　华中师范大学
刘春霖　河北经贸大学
张怀印　同济大学
罗施福　集美大学
王　鑫　西南科技大学
袁杏桃　杭州师范大学
侍孝祥　华东政法大学
黄　军　中南民族大学

优秀组织奖

华东政法大学
中南财经政法大学
中国政法大学
中国人民大学
同济大学
中国传媒大学
南京理工大学
华南理工大学
重庆理工大学
南京师范大学
湖南师范大学
河南科技大学
江西农业大学
西南科技大学
太原师范学院
青岛大学

2018 CPCC 十大中国著作权人

［编者按］　2019 年 3 月 28 日，在中国版权保护中心（CPCC）主办的 2019 CPCC 中国版权服务年会上，“2018 CPCC 十大中国著作权人”年度评选结果揭晓。

2018 十大中国著作权人

沈阳新松机器人自动化股份有限公司
太极计算机股份有限公司
掌阅科技股份有限公司
海尔集团公司
中国软件与技术服务股份有限公司
中国教育电视台
新华影轩（北京）影视文化有限公司
北京泡泡玛特文化创意股份有限公司
北京十二栋文化传播有限公司
新华网股份有限公司

专家特别提名奖

深圳华侨城文化集团有限公司
光橙（上海）信息科技有限公司
九派（武汉）全媒体股份有限公司
梦东方电影有限公司
北京锦熹文化传媒有限公司
厦门阅趣信息科技有限公司
北京大米未来科技有限公司

2018 年中国版权年会年度评选获奖名单

［编者按］ 2018 年 12 月 1 日，由中国版权协会主办的 2018 年中国版权年会暨首届远集坊论坛在武汉举行，年会主题为“新时代助力文化发展”。大会评选出中国版权事业终生成就者 2 名、2018 中国版权事业卓越成就者 9 名、2018 中国版权最具影响力企业 44 家、2018 中国版权新锐企业 27 家。

中国版权事业终生成就者

柳斌杰

阎崇年

2018 中国版权事业卓越成就者

白京兆　福建省版权协会理事长

毕飞宇　当代知名作家

江　波　腾讯集团法务副总裁

刘　恒　《北京文学》主编、中国作家协会副主席、北京市作家协会主席、全国政协常委

刘　昕　咪咕文化科技有限公司董事长

王　斌　中信出版集团股份有限公司党委书记、董事长

王亚民　全国政协委员、故宫博物院研究员、故宫出版社社长、故宫博物院原常务副院长

张良成　湖北省新闻出版广电局（版权局）局长、党组书记

赵东亮　全国政协委员，江西省出版集团公司、中文天地出版传媒股份有限公司党委书记、董事长

2018 中国版权最具影响力企业

二十一世纪出版社集团有限公司

上海人民出版社有限责任公司

上海交通大学出版社有限公司

上海译文出版社有限公司

上海阅文信息技术有限公司

上海瑛麒动漫科技有限公司

山东天成书业有限公司

天津人民出版社有限公司

中文在线数字出版集团股份有限公司

中国水利水电出版社

中国农业出版社

中南出版传媒集团股份有限公司

长春出版社

世纪天鸿教育科技股份有限公司

北京四达时代传媒有限公司

北京曲一线图书策划有限公司

北京语言大学出版社有限公司

北京数码大方科技股份有限公司

江西凯天动漫有限公司

江苏凤凰出版传媒股份有限公司

江苏锐丰智能科技股份有限公司

安徽五星东方影视投资有限公司

安徽少年儿童出版社

苏州科达科技股份有限公司

希望出版社

沈阳治图文化传媒有限公司

武汉大学出版社有限责任公司

武汉深之度科技有限公司

青岛出版社有限公司

杭州凡闻科技有限公司

杭州日报报业集团

河北教育出版社有限责任公司

陕西人民出版社有限责任公司

陕西文化产业（影视）投资有限公司

南京大学出版社有限公司

哈尔滨日报报业集团

重庆猪八戒知识产权服务有限公司

教育科学出版社

深圳广播电影电视集团
雅昌文化集团
景德镇陶邑文化发展有限公司
湖南广播电视台
福建省佳美集团公司
潍坊北大青鸟华光照排有限公司

2018 中国版权新锐企业

三昧动漫设计有限公司
上海映脉文化传播有限公司
天津电子出版社有限公司
天津画国人动漫创意有限公司
中国中医药出版社
北京鼎阅文学信息技术有限公司
吉林禹硕影视传媒股份有限公司
成都锐拓传媒广告有限公司
华声在线新闻网站
华强方特（芜湖）文化科技有限公司
江苏风云科技服务有限公司
江苏金太阳纺织科技股份有限公司
江苏宝缦家纺科技有限公司
张家港幸运金属工艺品有限公司
武汉博润通文化科技股份有限公司
杭州刀豆网络科技有限公司
河北乐聪网络科技股份有限公司
河北精英动漫文化传播股份有限公司
陕西广电影视文化产业发展有限公司
南宁峰值文化传播有限公司
泉州阳光创艺陶瓷股份有限公司
恐龙园文化旅游集团股份有限公司
鄂尔多斯蒙古源流文化产业发展有限公司
斯达高瓷艺发展（深圳）有限公司
愉悦家纺有限公司
福建省德化县成艺陶瓷有限公司
横琴国际知识产权交易中心有限公司

版权理论研究

LI LUN YAN JIU

2018 年中国著作权法研究综述

向　波[*]　史若琪[**]

一、关于著作权法基础理论问题的研究

（一）独创性

有学者在探讨短视频著作权保护时梳理了国内外独创性的概念和标准，认为总体而言，因为奠定其版权理论基础的主要是劳动财产论和功利主义经济理论，版权体系更注重作品的经济价值，对作品独创性的判断也多是从作品而非作者的角度出发，对作者的保护程度较低①。还有学者提出作品可看作由多个独立的意思表达单元“元素”组成的集合，其独创性等于该集合中元素排列组合数与各元素的表达方式连续相乘的积（$M!\ C_n^m \prod X_i$）。不同类型的作品，独创性的外在表现不同，本质上是因为不同作品中各元素的变化特点不同。裁判者在判断是否构成侵犯著作权时，只需计算在先作品和在后作品中相同部分的相对独创性数值，如该数值较高，则构成侵权②。

（二）排他性

有学者认为著作权随着历史的发展排他性逐渐增强，体现在权利内容的扩展、权利期限的长久性以及权利程序要件的取消上。如今，人们依旧利用不合时宜的正当性理论不当扩大著作权的排他性，致使著作权失去了原本之义。目前普遍存在的在权利人作品之上的二次创作，更是对著作权排他性的正当发展提出急切要求。二次创作的著作权侵权问题其实是两个平等基本自由的价值选择问题，无法在立法中对二者进行价值比较，著作权的排他性应在权利人的财产权和使用者的表达自由权的平衡中健康发展③。

（三）思想表达二分法

有学者在探究艺术/实用二分法的先天适用局限时，指出其与思想表达二分法存在相同的问题，这种分立方法事实上无法提供统一普适的裁判标准，并且认为二分法的本质属性是演绎的起点而非归纳的终点④。还有学者研究了思想表达二分法在文学作品相似侵权判定中的适用，认为思想表达二分法在文学作品侵权判定中的适用需要先适用独创性的标准，并排除思想表达混同等因素后，继而运用整体比对法与部分比对法相结合的方法进行实质性相似的判定⑤。另外，有学者认为实用艺术作品的认定遵循分离规则，即艺术成分可以区分于实用功能并独立存在。而这种分离规则是由思想表达二分法中的合并理论衍生而来的，实用艺术作品的实用功能可以归入“思想”范畴，艺术元素可以归入“表达”范畴，那么分离规则实质的含义即艺术表达不得与功能思想发生合并⑥。

（四）其他问题

有学者通过梳理本土制度变革历史，揭示了实现中国著作权法制度创新的关键，即管制规则和自治规则如何在价值定位上协调和互补，以及如何解决继受规则的制度理念与本土规则的运作传统的协同配合⑦。还有学者对知识产权法定原则进行了深入探讨，认为权利法定原则中的“权利”仅为绝对权，法官依据自由裁量权在个案中保护的，是未上升为权利的法益，并不存在权利推定，只有未上升为权利的法益的推定创设⑧。

---

* 向波，法学博士，南开大学法学院副教授，从事知识产权法学研究。

** 史若琪，南开大学法学院法学硕士研究生。

① 孙飞，张静. 短视频著作权保护问题研究 [J]. 电子知识产权，2018 (5).

② 杨敏锋. 论作品独创性的数学计算模型 [J]. 知识产权，2018 (8).

③ 陈倩荣. 论著作权的排他性 [J]. 传播与版权，2018 (8).

④ 谢晴川. 论实用艺术作品的“美”和“艺术性”要件：以适用路径的反思与重构为中心 [J]. 法律科学（西北政法大学学报），2018 (3).

⑤ 钟娟，王月璇. “思想表达二分法”在文学作品相似侵权判定中的适用 [J]. 合肥工业大学学报（社会科学版），2018 (5).

⑥ 宋戈. 实用艺术作品分离规则的适用：以合并原则为视角 [J]. 电子知识产权，2018 (2).

⑦ 熊琦. 中国著作权立法中的制度创新 [J]. 中国社会科学，2018 (7).

⑧ 孙山. 重释知识产权法定原则 [J]. 当代法学，2018 (6).

二、人工智能与著作权保护问题的研究

（一）人工智能生成内容的保护模式

关于这个问题，存在“（狭义）著作权说”和“邻接权说”两种观点。持“（狭义）著作权说”的学者大多认为人工智能生成内容可纳入作品的范围，通过（狭义）著作权来加以保护。如有学者认为随着人工神经网络和类脑计算等技术的进步，人工智能创作物已经可以满足现行著作权法对于“作品”的认定标准，可以被纳入保护的范围①。还有学者认为根据康德“主客体统一认识论”和“人是目的”的哲学视点，无论人工智能发展到何种阶段，都只能将其作为人利用的客体和工具处理，而不能将其拟制为与人享有平等地位的法律主体。以此为前提，人工智能生成物应当作为人利用人工智能创作的作品并按照现行著作权法关于作品的构成要件判断其独创性②。也有学者提出，“思想”“人格”是否属于作品的隐藏构成要件目前还存在较大争议，但通过还原相关概念的规范目的不难发现，独创性判断的对象只能是已经生成的表达本身，智力成果的结论只能根据已经生成的表达结果进行推定，在具备生成一定数量不重复内容可能性的情况下推定为智力成果，“思想”“人格”不具有实质上的规范意义。因此，人工智能生成内容符合作品的构成要件③。当然，也有学者指出人工智能创作物虽然在满足一定条件后可在客观上获得“独创性”，但是因其既非人的“智力成果”，也非“工具主义”下人“手”的延伸，因此无法被解释进当前著作权的范围④。

持“邻接权说”的学者则主张应通过邻接权来保护人工智能生成内容。有学者认为，人工智能生成内容是人工智能程序在人类参与度极低的情况下基于数据和算法通过自主学习和建模所自动生成的内容，并非人类以人工智能为工具进行的个性化表达。鉴于人工智能生成内容的保护价值与邻接权制度的价值相契合，可将人工智能生成内容作为广义上的邻接权之客体⑤。还有学者认为，人工智能创作物因投资人的“非创作性投入”而产生，投资人的利益应当成为相关法律制度的保护重心。由此，将人工智能创作物纳入邻接权制度保护范围进行保护更具合理性⑥。也有学者认为，在区分强保护模式（著作权）与弱保护模式（邻接权）的基础上，基于制度成本的考量，应通过邻接权这一产权模式来保护人工智能生成内容⑦。

（二）人工智能生成内容的权利归属

在认可人工智能生成物属于著作权法保护的对象后，有学者对人工智能生成物的权利归属展开探讨，认为对人工智能生成物的权利分配，应平衡操作者、设计者、雇主、委托人及相关公众等主体之间的利益。人工智能作为创作辅助工具，在一般场合，人工智能生成物的著作权归属于创作者所有。鉴于人工智能生成物的创作具备高风险、高投资的特征，在雇主与委托人等投资人参与的特殊场合，其著作权归属于人工智能投资者是最为经济的一种处理方式⑧。也有学者认为人工智能不具有法律人格，因此其本身不能成为人工智能作品的权利主体。人工智能作品的创作由人工智能的创造者或所有者主导；将该类作品的著作权归属于人工智能的创造者或所有者，能够激励其创作新作品和改进人工智能，且能促进作品流通进而增加公共利益⑨。还有学者认为智能机器人因创作、劳动等民事活动而享有的财产权由其所有者代为享有，人类代替智能机器人所享有的财产权在智能机器人侵权情况下将自动成为特定机器人的责任财产，但宜认定保险责任财产先于获利予以赔付⑩。

三、关于著作权对象问题的研究

（一）网络游戏相关问题

关于网络游戏直播画面的作品属性，有学者认为界定游戏直播画面的作品属性应以游戏画面与直播画面的三种不同关系进行类型化分析。游戏画面具有独立的作品属性，直播画面的作品属性应根据实际的独创性判断。游戏画面与类电影作品的差异远大于共性，不宜归入类电影作品，直播画面可以

---

① 马治国，刘桢. 人工智能创作物的著作权定性及制度安排［J］. 科技与出版，2018（10）.

② 李扬，李晓宇. 康德哲学视点下人工智能生成物的著作权问题探讨［J］. 法学杂志，2018（9）.

③ 孙山. 人工智能生成内容著作权法保护的困境与出路［J］. 知识产权，2018（11）.

④ 秦涛，张旭东. 论人工智能创作物著作权法保护的逻辑与路径［J］. 华东理工大学学报（社会科学版），2018（6）.

⑤ 陶乾. 论著作权法对人工智能生成成果的保护：作为邻接权的数据处理者权之证立［J］. 法学，2018（4）.

⑥ 许明月，谭玲. 论人工智能创作物的邻接权保护：理论证成与制度安排［J］. 比较法研究，2018（6）.

⑦ 向波. 人工智能生成内容的著作权保护：正当性评价与模式选择［J］. 中国版权，2018（5）.

⑧ 李晓宇. 人工智能生成物的可版权性与权利分配刍议［J］. 电子知识产权，2018（6）.

⑨ 尹卫民. 论人工智能作品的权利主体：兼评人工智能的法律人格［J］. 科技与出版，2018（10）.

⑩ 石冠彬. 论智能机器人创作物的著作权保护：以智能机器人的主体资格为视角［J］. 东方法学，2018（3）.

根据独创性和投资情况构成类电影作品或录像制品①。还有学者对竞技类游戏网络直播是否侵犯开发商著作权问题展开了分析，指出由于竞技类游戏注重玩家亲身操作体验的特点，该类游戏直播并未侵占到原有游戏著作权人的盈利模式。同时，游戏网络直播的目的在于展示主播对游戏的理解和操作，与游戏画面本身所展示的游戏剧情、思想感情等相距甚远，符合合理使用制度的构成要件。因此，竞技类游戏网络直播并未侵犯游戏开发商著作权②。

对游戏操作画面的作品属性，有学者认为判定游戏操作画面的作品属性时，应将其特性和作品的定义进行结合，分析其是否具有独创性和可复制性。在判定游戏操作画面是否构成电影或类电影作品时，不应对摄制的技术方式进行限制，而应考察其本质特征。若其符合电影或类电影作品本质特征，能够形成连续的活动画面，则可将其视为电影或类电影作品进行保护③。还有学者认为网络游戏画面具有艺术审美价值性，饱含游戏制作者的智力创造性以及可固定、可复制性，其符合著作权法意义的作品构成要件，具有可著作权性。网络游戏画面是一个集合概念，涉及不同方式形成的画面，故其具体可作为何种作品类型进行保护需要具体分析，不可做“一刀切”规定④。另有学者指出，网络游戏作品通常归属于计算机作品，网络游戏画面涵盖的作品有美术作品、文字作品、音乐作品等。网络游戏直播画面和电影作品具有相似的制作方法和表现形式，可以纳入类电影作品的范畴。游戏玩家未经许可对游戏画面进行直播，属于《著作权法》中合理使用的范畴⑤。

（二）体育赛事节目

有学者对体育赛事本身和体育赛事的转播画面的属性进行了探讨，认为花样滑冰、艺术体操等项目作为作品，能够满足可以复制、表达情感、具有独创性三项条件，是适当的著作权客体。同时，其认为体育赛事转播画面制作过程所体现的独创性是一个事实问题，即便有争议，空间也相当有限。真正决定转播画面是否构成作品的因素是我们的价值判断⑥。关于体育赛事节目的法律性质，有学者认为体育赛事节目是指对正在发生的体育比赛进行现场摄制并直播的电视节目，具有现场性和实时性的特征。确定体育赛事节目的独创性应以客体的类型化为前提，“故事型”体育赛事节目应作为电影作品受到保护，“记录型”体育赛事节目则属于录像制品的范畴⑦。也有学者主张借鉴《保护文学和艺术作品伯尔尼公约》与美国《版权法》的解释方法，认为通过直播传输体育赛事画面时，录制与传播在同时进行，体育赛事画面被固定，且符合“摄制在一定介质上”的要求，因而符合固定要求，从而构成电影作品⑧。

关于盗播体育赛事节目的救济途径，有学者认为体育赛事节目实时转播侵权救济困境只是诸多法律盲点之一，但却折射出我国著作权法专有权利内容应对互联网传播技术带来的新型法律现象时所暴露的滞后和被动反应——“定时播放视频行为既不符合信息网络传播权的交互性特征，又不符合广播权以有线传播或者转播的方式向公众传播广播的作品的特征”的法律现状业已得到共识⑨。还有学者认为面对信息网络传播权与广播权都难以对体育赛事节目盗播现象进行规制的困境，只能通过适用“其他权利”兜底条款予以解决。立法者应明确体育赛事节目的作品地位，通过重新定义信息网络传播权或广播权适应技术发展，并辅以反不正当竞争法进行补充保护等⑩。也有学者认为，司法中的困境不仅仅体现于对该类节目的不同定性上，而且还体现在立法方面的不足上，因为不管该类节目被认定为作品，还是录像制品，包括从信号角度保护，现行著作权法的广播权、网络信息传播权、其他权利以及广播组织权等都无法对网络实时转播行为进行很好规范。因此，在技术中立原则基础上，创设“向公众传播权”与扩展“广播组织权”，成为有效

① 焦和平. 网络游戏在线直播画面的作品属性再研究［J］. 当代法学，2018（5）.

② 蒋雨达. 竞技类游戏网络直播是否侵犯开发商著作权简析［J］. 东南大学学报（哲学社会科学版），2018（S1）.

③ 吴雷. 论游戏操作画面的作品属性及其类型［J］. 企业科技与发展，2018（5）.

④ 郭壬癸，周航. 著作权视域下网络游戏画面的作品定性与思辨［J］. 中国石油大学学报（社会科学版），2018（2）.

⑤ 孔思冰. 论网络游戏直播的著作权［J］. 河南工程学院学报（社会科学版），2018（4）.

⑥ 王磊.“网络转播体育赛事”的法律保护路径探讨［J］. 电子知识产权，2018（10）.

⑦ 张耕，孙正樑. 论体育赛事节目的独创性［J］. 电子知识产权，2018（10）.

⑧ 万勇. 功能主义解释论视野下的“电影作品”：兼评凤凰网案二审判决［J］. 现代法学，2018（5）.

⑨ 张鹏.“互联网＋”视域下体育赛事节目的可版权性研究［J］. 新媒体研究，2018（23）.

⑩ 刘宁，林嗣杰. 体育赛事节目网络实时转播著作权保护研究［J］. 电视研究，2018（10）.

保护网络实时转播的现实选择①。另有学者主张从立法论角度出发，立足体育赛事节目的特征，应肯定体育赛事节目的独创性，在现有著作权客体类型中将其确定为以类似摄制电影的方法创作的作品有利于实现各方利益最大化②。

（三）民间文艺作品

有学者提出构建民间文艺作品的立法保护机制，主要包括四个方面：一是明确民间文艺作品著作权的主体；二是在确定民间文艺作品保护范围时可以采用“列举＋兜底规定”的形式予以固定；三是确定民间文艺作品的保护期限；四是探索建立健全民间文艺作品的信息公示公开制度，细化利益分配的具体程序规则③。还有学者从不同角度对我国民间文学艺术知识产权保护提出建议。首先是制定的知识产权保护法律法规等需要有国际法、国家立法和地方立法三个层次。其次是建立民间文学艺术知识产权登记和注册制度。最后是成立统一的机构，对外参与民间文学艺术保护国际规则的制定，维护国家现实或潜在的利益，对内负责起草、制定、实施相关的法律法规和政策措施④。

（四）其他问题

针对近几年兴起的有声读物、短视频、综艺节目、媒体融合下的新闻作品等等，学者们对其法律属性进行了分析。有学者认为严格对照文字作品原文朗读形成的有声读物，无论其是否添加了背景音乐、音效，都没有改变文字作品的独创性表达，因而不构成改编作品。有声读物作为一种录音制品，是文字作品的复制件⑤。还有学者指出非作者独立创作的网络短视频、通过机械劳动产生而不具备创造内涵的网络短视频、仅存在于作者脑海中并未付诸实现的想法，以及抄袭他人发表的网络短视频均不能称为著作权法上的作品⑥。《著作权法》并未明确综艺节目模板的性质，有学者认为综艺节目模板是具有独创性“思想”的固定“表达”。具有独创性“思想”只是用于修饰固定“表达”这个主语的定语而已。综艺节目模板的法律属性应该为作品⑦。由于媒体融合，涉及传统媒体的条款已不能与现今的新闻作品相适应，所以有学者认为针对新闻作品独创性低的特性，应当在制度上删除《著作权法》中“时事新闻”不受该法保护的条款，在实践中对新闻作品与其他作品的独创性要求适用同一标准，为新闻作品提供最大范围的保护；针对新闻作品时效性的特性，完善《著作权法》中的法定许可制度；针对新闻作品公益性的特性，完善《著作权法》中的合理使用制度⑧。

另外，有学者对电影作品⑨、云服务提供商提供的软件⑩、动漫卡通形象⑪、沙画表演⑫、雷同辩护词⑬、实用艺术作品⑭、短时艺术品⑮、混编创作⑯、文学作品虚拟角色形象⑰等是否属于著作权保护的对象以及保护的方式展开讨论，还有学者论述了作品类型化的意义⑱。

四、关于著作权内容的研究

（一）著作人身权

有学者探讨了著作人身权和人格权的关系，认为将著作人身权一般规定以权利客体列举形式安置在人格权编中，为著作人身权的知识产权人格条款找到人格权编的制度归宿，是我国民法典的特色，最终著作人身权和人格权编相互呼应也展示出我国民法典所具有的人文关怀⑲。还有学者在著作人身

① 赵双阁，艾岚．体育赛事网络实时转播法律保护困境及其对策研究［J］．法律科学（西北政法大学学报），2018（4）．
② 马秋芬，郑友德．体育赛事节目著作权保护比较法证成［J］．华中科技大学学报（社会科学版），2018（6）．
③ 刘立甲．著作权保护视阈下的民间文艺作品［J］．理论月刊，2018（11）．
④ 蒋涵．民间文学艺术保护与传承发展的知识产权制度回应［J］．知识产权，2018（9）．
⑤ 张书青．“有声读物”涉著作权若干问题浅析［J］．法律适用（司法案例），2018（22）．
⑥ 孙铭锴，刘宇轩，李世研．网络短视频版权问题研究［J］．传播与版权，2018（10）．
⑦ 黄昊．综艺节目模板保护的现状、困境及可行性分析［J］．湖南科技学院学报，2018（9）．
⑧ 孙昊亮．媒体融合下新闻作品的著作权保护［J］．法学评论，2018（5）．
⑨ 郑悦迪．中英电影作品著作权立法比较研究：兼评《著作权法（修订草案送审稿）》相关规定［J］．传播与版权，2018（5）．
⑩ 郭鹏．云计算 SaaS 模式下的著作权侵权分析［J］．知识产权，2018（11）．
⑪ 衣硕朋，王瑞．动漫卡通形象的著作权保护［J］．人民司法（案例），2018（20）．
⑫ 张科．浅议沙画表演著作权保护［J］．传播与版权，2018（12）．
⑬ 朱泽阳．雷同辩护词引著作权之争［J］．检察风云，2018（10）．
⑭ 杨慧．实用艺术作品著作权保护的现实困境及其消解［J］．财经法学，2018（4）．
⑮ 崔立红．短时艺术品著作权保护的实证研究［J］．山东大学学报（哲学社会科学版），2018（6）．
⑯ 黄云平．论混编创作行为的实质与规制［J］．浙江大学学报（人文社会科学版），2018（5）．
⑰ 牛强．文学作品虚拟角色形象的固定及版权保护［J］．中国出版，2018（19）．
⑱ 李琛．论作品类型化的法律意义［J］．知识产权，2018（8）．
⑲ 罗祥，张国安．著作人身权和人格权的关系探究：兼议著作人身权在人格权编配置［J］．科技与法律，2018（4）．

权妨碍著作财产权交易问题的讨论中提出著作人身权虽与主体之间具有一定的可分离性，但这与著作财产权的可完全分离性有着本质上的不同；著作人身权进入商业流转有悖设权初衷，等于变相取消了著作人身权。建议我国著作权立法在规定著作人身权不可以转让但允许适当放弃的同时，对著作人身权做出必要的限制，以利于著作财产权交易，促进文化产业发展①。

近年来IP改编影视剧成为热潮，但对于这种作品而言，存在着改编权与保护作品完整权的冲突。有学者分析了导致这种法律冲突存在的主要原因，主张采取积极措施协调改编权与保护作品完整权之间的关系，如：合理限制保护作品完整权的应用，避免权利的滥用；允许精神权利的有限转让、放弃；统一侵权的判定标准等②。还有学者认为面对改编行为范围及界限约定不明确、侵权评定没有具体的客观标准，以及权利适用细则规定不完善的问题，需要在坚持诚实信用原则的同时，适当限制保护作品完整权的行使，并完善著作权法实施条例的适用细则③。

（二）追续权

有学者介绍了保加利亚的追续权制度，受追续权保护的原创艺术作品是指平面或立体艺术品，如图画、拼贴画、油画、素描、雕刻、版画、平版画、雕塑、挂毯、陶瓷制品、玻璃器皿和照片，应由作者亲自制作。经作者授权编写序号的一定数量的复制品也可视为原创艺术作品。该项权利不可转让，不能放弃，但可以继承，保护期限与著作权同④。还有学者对我国《著作权法（修订草案送审稿）》中关于追续权规定的现状进行了梳理，并对该制度的科学性、操作性进行了探讨，指出虽然追续权实行后，对艺术品市场及社会的影响还需实践来检验，但是追续权制度的创建应该能够使国内艺术家缺少著作权保护方面的情况有所改变，矫正销售商和艺术家间的利益关系，提高艺术家的创造热情和积极性⑤。

（三）其他权利

有学者分析了邻接权客体的判断标准，指出邻接权客体的判断标准包括“无独创性”标准、“与作品或作品相近信息相关”标准、“传播功能”标准和“非创作性投入”标准。“无独创性”标准是邻接权制度的逻辑前提，“无独创性”标准优于“独创性较低”标准。“传播功能”是邻接权客体的核心功能，传播功能的彰显能够促进邻接权制度的发展。应当以“非创作性投入”的重要性和成熟度作为新型邻接权客体判定的考量因素⑥。还有学者认为在3D打印背景下，复制权也应被赋予新的含义。鉴于3D打印技术给私人复制及相关利益主体造成的影响，应当对3D打印下的合理使用进行适当限制。上述应对措施在短期内可通过法律解释及技术手段加以实现；而从长远来看，从制度设计层面和立法层面对技术革新予以回应方为治本之策⑦。

另外，有学者研究探讨了广播权⑧、信息网络传播权⑨、广播组织权⑩、网络时代的版权保护边界⑪、数字版权的发展与应用⑫、数字音乐专辑的版权转化⑬、团体标准版权⑭、国际条约中的提供权⑮、著作权的产权配置⑯等问题。

五、关于著作权限制问题的研究

（一）合理使用

有学者提出在互联网背景下，为了解决现有的合理使用认定标准已不合时宜的问题，除了现有的规则外，应再添加两项原则性规定，即：当事人的

① 吴小评．著作人身权问题探疑：为促进著作财产权交易［J］．重庆理工大学学报（社会科学），2018（4）．

② 胡海涛，曾莉．论改编权与保护作品完整权的冲突与协调：以IP改编影视作品为背景［J］．安徽电子信息职业技术学院学报，2018（6）．

③ 徐晰．论文化创意产业中保护作品完整权和改编权的问题［J］．科技广场，2018（3）．

④ 李菊丹．“一带一路”倡议下保加利亚知识产权保护制度研究［J］．法学杂志，2018（12）．

⑤ 刘大成．欧盟追续权制度在我国《著作权法》中的适用探讨［J］．科技与出版，2018（4）．

⑥ 王国柱．邻接权客体判断标准论［J］．法律科学（西北政法大学学报），2018（5）．

⑦ 范瑞．3D打印视域下复制权理论的冲击与对策［J］．中财法律评论，2018（0）．

⑧ 刘银良．制度演进视角下我国广播权的范畴［J］．法学，2018（12）．

⑨ 黄卉．司法审查对于侵犯信息网络传播权的认定［J］．法律适用（司法案例），2018（16）．

⑩ 王超政．论广播组织权客体的界定：兼评“广播信号说”之谬误［J］．北方法学，2018（6）．

⑪ 米竞．对网络时代版权过度保护的制度性反思：以DRM技术为例［J］．河南工业大学学报（社会科学版），2018（5）．

⑫ 臧晓然．数字版权的管理与应用［J］．传媒论坛，2018（17）．

⑬ 崔恒勇，王哲．数字音乐专辑的版权转化研究［J］．中国出版，2018（10）．

⑭ 朱翔华．从著作权法看团体标准版权及团体标准版权制度设计［J］．标准科学，2018（8）．

⑮ 相靖．国际条约中提供权的发展及其在著作权法中的实践［J］．知识产权，2018（8）．

⑯ 苏力．昔日“琼花”，今日“秋菊”：关于芭蕾舞剧《红色娘子军》产权争议的一个法理分析［J］．学术月刊，2018（7）．

使用行为是否会对原作品权利人的应有权益造成直接的消极影响，当事人在使用原作品时主观上是否具有故意情节或出于恶意。这样可以使得判断标准更加清晰完整，也可以在个案中发挥法官的自由裁量权①。还有学者认为在互联网环境下，可以从著作权法立法目的、使用目的的正当性、作品来源的正当性和使用是否导致了显而易见的不良后果四个要素去判断互联网环境下的使用行为是否构成合理使用②。另有学者认为著作权合理使用制度是著作权人、使用人和公众利益的平衡器，我国封闭式的合理使用立法模式不能充分实现其利益平衡器的功能。司法实践中，法院采取类推适用法定列举，并借用国际条约中的“三步检验法”和美国的“四要素”、“转换性使用”等方法扩张适用合理使用③。

有学者提出合理使用规则的功能设计有赖于规则本身的明确统一和灵活调节。我国应当遵循这样一种演进的路径——从立法和司法两个方面同步进行合理使用规则的完善。立法层面，将概括式的概括条款与现行法中的列举规则相结合，构建合理使用规则的完整的成文化法律规范；司法层面，则通过案例指导制度的框架设计实现合理使用规则在实践中适用的灵活性和动态性④。也有学者结合近年来日益受到追捧的二次创作，探讨了著作权与表达自由的界限——“合理使用的界定”，指出在修订完善合理使用制度的时候，必须高度重视对著作权和基于表达自由的二次创作行为加以平衡保护⑤。

还有学者对人工智能⑥、微信平台⑦、大数据环境下个人信息⑧、网页快照⑨、个人下载⑩中的合理使用制度进行分析。

（二）转换性使用

“转换性使用”是由美国判例法发展出来的，可作为裁判是否构成合理使用的标准。有学者指出目前司法实践对“转换性使用”的应用存在认定不全面、在合理使用判定中的作用不明显等问题。在认定标准方面，认为“转换性使用”的认定应当包含两个方面：内容转换和目的转换。这比较符合“转换性使用”概念提出时的原本含义⑪。也有学者介绍了“转换性使用”范式兴起的过程，指出合理使用制度最有活力之处在于它实现了版权法的最终目标——促进文化创新，法官应当着重考虑版权法的功利目的，避免因版权保护的过度扩张而限制创新，进而损害二次创新⑫。还有学者指出我国著作权法可采用合理使用制度解决新作品使用行为而不必移植“转换性使用”这一法律概念，但美国“转换性使用”规则所体现的重视公共利益、强调版权合理使用制度灵活性的立法理念仍值得我国著作权法借鉴⑬。

（三）首次销售原则

有学者认为首次销售原则实质上是对发行权的行使做出的必要补充，不能扩张用于数字环境中。数字作品转售行为在性质上属于网络传输行为，而非发行行为，无法适用首次销售原则。基于维护著作权人和消费者之间利益平衡以及促进数字作品产业发展的考量，应当根据数字技术的性质特征创设信息网络传播权有限用尽原则，在附条件和附期限的情况下允许消费者转售数字作品，以适应数字作品二手市场的发展需求⑭。也有学者指出在传统的著作权法理论中，基于首次销售原则，合法的作品复制件通过合法的方式首次发行以后，著作权人即丧失了对该复制件再次流转的控制权。而对于电子书，下载者是否仍然可以不经过版权人许可而以网络传输的方式将作品复制件加以转让还存在争议。网络传播的特性决定了首次销售原则不能完全适用

① 刘岩. 从互联网时代看著作权的合理使用［J］. 东南大学学报（哲学社会科学版），2018（S2）.

② 焦蕾. 论互联网环境下合理使用的判断标准：以微信公众号文章添加音乐行为为例［J］. 广东开放大学学报，2018（4）.

③ 刘宇晖. 论著作权合理使用扩张适用的路径选择［J］. 知识产权，2018（10）.

④ 孙阳. 演进中的合理使用规则及其启示［J］. 知识产权，2018（10）.

⑤ 董天策，邵铄岚. 关于平衡保护二次创作和著作权的思考：从电影解说短视频博主谷阿莫被告侵权案谈起［J］. 出版发行研究，2018（10）.

⑥ 孙阳. 人工智能的合理使用之辩［J］. 海峡法学，2018（3）.

⑦ 周贺微. 微信平台上的著作权合理使用问题研究［J］. 武汉科技大学学报（社会科学版），2018（3）.

⑧ 江波，张亚男. 大数据语境下的个人信息合理使用原则［J］. 交大法学，2018（3）.

⑨ 张薇子. 网页快照适用“合理使用”的问题研究［J］. 南京理工大学学报（社会科学版），2018（6）.

⑩ 虞婷婷. 个人下载的合法性边界：兼评《著作权法》（修订草案送审稿）第43条［J］. 福建法学，2018（3）.

⑪ 杨莹. 合理使用裁判中“转换性使用”标准适用［J］. 中国出版，2018（18）.

⑫ 罗娇，严之. 著作权合理使用的转换性使用理论研究［J］. 人民法治，2018（9）.

⑬ 李国庆. 版权法转换性使用规则研究：从《80后的独立宣言》海报侵权案说起［J］. 科技与出版，2018（9）.

⑭ 黄玉烨，何蓉. 数字环境下首次销售原则的适用困境与出路［J］. 浙江大学学报（人文社会科学版），2018（6）.

于电子书的转售①。

六、关于著作权行使问题的研究

（一）孤儿作品

有学者指出，网络不可对作品进行特有署名的特点导致越来越多的孤儿作品产生。针对这种情况，应该从以下三点着手对孤儿作品进行管理：一是我国著作权法相关领域对孤儿作品的认定与管理应该充分结合大数据时代的优势，实现在对作品的全面收录过程中准确识别孤儿作品的真正身份。二是建立公共管理机构进行系统管理。三是应考虑我国孤儿作品产生的特殊历史背景与当今大数据发展的国情，量体裁衣地制定适合我国整体法律体系的孤儿作品公共管理机制②。也有学者在分析目前我国立法情况以及世界通行的三种版权保护模式（扩展性集体授权模式、强制许可模式、责任限制模式）的基础上，提出我国应借鉴扩展性集体授权模式和非自愿性许可模式，并明确非营利性机构利用的例外③。还有学者指出虽然我国第三次《著作权法》修订也增加了孤儿作品方案，但采取的中央授权许可模式并不适合数字图书馆大规模利用作品的现实需求。建议增加延伸性集体管理模式，在保证孤儿作品利用法律确定性的同时降低授权成本，实现数字图书馆的长远发展④。

（二）著作权许可

针对数字网络背景下的音乐著作权许可模式，有学者指出，我国音乐著作权许可模式的路径选择，存在着“左右为难”的现实挑战：直接许可制度和集中许可制度都难以开展。该学者认为重塑我国数字音乐著作权许可模式的应然走向是既需要充分尊重音乐产业自身的商业模式，也需要有效转变“家长式管理”的行政指导理念，以及运用好相应的法律规制手段⑤。也有学者指出，美国长期以来占据全球音乐产业首席地位，流媒体音乐在美国更是发展迅猛，了解美国的流媒体音乐商业模式创新与竞争，以及它们与音乐、录音作品相关权利人之间的法律关系，对于我国音乐产业的发展具有重要的启示意义⑥。还有学者认为，对音乐版权方与网络音乐服务商之间达成的各具体独家交易类型进行违法性甄别和分析，清晰可见当前网络音乐市场困境的成因并非独家交易模式本身。合理运用与有效规制网络音乐版权独家交易模式，可以实现激发网络音乐市场竞争活力与维护市场竞争秩序的双重目标⑦。

有学者认为数字音乐版权独家授权模式不仅存在数字音乐版权人与网络音乐平台之间、网络音乐平台相互之间的利益冲突，而且存在个体利益与公共利益间的冲突，这导致理论界和实务界对该种授权模式质疑较多。但鉴于数字音乐版权独家授权模式具有诸如打击盗版行为、刺激作品生产等积极效应，不宜直接否定此种授权模式，而应将关注重点放在减缓利益冲突和减少消极后果上⑧。还有学者认为在现阶段，音乐独家版权模式在降低交易成本、打击盗版侵权、促进音乐市场发展等方面发挥了积极的作用；同时，也可能迅速推高行业集中度，挤压中小网络音乐服务商的生存空间，对市场竞争产生一定影响。未来，在发挥音乐独家版权模式积极作用的同时，应引导音乐产业许可方式多元化，并加大对网络数字音乐产业有关市场界定、竞争评估等问题的研究⑨。

（三）著作权集体管理

有学者指出目前我国著作权集体管理制度存在多方面问题，尤其是在有关主体的权利与义务上尚不能平衡配置的问题，包括在集体管理组织内部及其与著作权人、第三人之间⑩。还有学者分析了著作权集体管理组织垄断的合理性，指出长期以来，我国著作权集体管理制度一直采取垄断模式中的单一管理模式，已经引发一连串的问题，并引来引入竞争模式的强烈要求。但基于当前竞争模式与垄断模式均无取代对方的绝对优势、集体管理对数字时代更强的适应性以及法律制度的延续性，继续保持现有管理模式仍是最佳选择。但同时应通过反垄断法对集体管理组织的行为予以规制⑪。也有学者对

① 郑万青，高金强．数字出版中电子书版权保护难题辨析［J］．中国出版，2018（17）．

② 龙杨．对我国孤儿作品保护的探讨［J］．北京政法职业学院学报，2018（2）．

③ 张晓燕．孤儿作品版权利用模式探讨及适用综述［J］．图书馆研究与工作，2018（3）．

④ 邵燕．数字图书馆建设中的孤儿作品利用模式研究［J］．重庆工商大学学报（社会科学版），2018（6）．

⑤ 孙松．我国数字音乐著作权许可模式的动因、路径与展望［J］．编辑之友，2018（7）．

⑥ 金海军．流媒体音乐的著作权许可与付费问题：美国的最新发展与借鉴［J］．电子知识产权，2018（8）．

⑦ 宁立志，王宇．叫停网络音乐市场版权独家交易的竞争法思考［J］．法学，2018（8）．

⑧ 叶明，张洁．利益平衡视角下的数字音乐版权独家授权模式研究［J］．电子知识产权，2018（11）．

⑨ 钱晓强．网络时代下数字音乐市场独家版权模式探析［J］．电子知识产权，2018（8）．

⑩ 段海风．权利与义务的平衡配置：我国著作权集体管理制度的完善方向［J］．科技与出版，2018（11）．

⑪ 王辉．数字时代著作权集体管理组织垄断合理性分析［J］．传播与版权，2018（5）．

著作权集体管理组织的市场功能、角色安排与定价问题进行了分析，认为著作权集体管理组织具有降低交易成本、“润滑”交易的市场功能，但其对于著作权人、使用者的价值并不完全一致。我国集体管理组织获得了制度上的垄断地位，但由于私人授权与作品资源问题，它们尚未拥有事实上的市场垄断地位，而延伸性管理规则的引入则可以使集体管理组织获得制度垄断与市场垄断的双重优势①。还有学者认为目前我国著作权集体管理组织代表性不强，面对实际运作中的困局，应拓宽作品的授权渠道，在使用量大的作品类别领域逐步建立适度竞争的集体管理组织；借鉴俄罗斯和英国立法例，对集体管理组织予以国家授权使之获得延伸性集体管理的资格；著作权人自己难以有效行使的权利，皆可延伸性集体管理，以提高著作权集体管理组织的代表性②。针对数字化的绝版作品，有学者提出利用著作权集体管理组织进行延伸性集体管理，建议完善我国《著作权法（修订草案送审稿）》第 63 条的规定，引入著作权延伸性集体管理作为公共文化机构数字化利用绝版作品的一种可行路径③。还有学者认为引入著作权延伸性集体管理制度符合我国国情，但需谨慎移植，建议删除《著作权法（修订草案送审稿）》第 63 条“其他方式”的表述，增加集体管理组织的通知义务；在第 74 条中增加，在非会员权利人起诉使用人侵权，法院判决使用人支付赔偿时，集体管理组织应向使用人退还所收取的使用费④。

也有学者提出可以借鉴国外相关制度规制我国的数字化绝版作品。欧盟数字单一市场版权改革方案和法国采取的推定集体管理制度力图为解决绝版作品利用问题建立合适的许可制度，能为我国解决绝版作品版权问题提供一条可供借鉴的路径⑤。另外，有学者分析了著作权集体管理组织对数字环境下的音乐版权⑥和数字图书馆⑦的管理方式。

（四）著作权登记

有学者针对著作权登记制度存在的问题，提出完善的对策：首先，从确权、维权、用权的角度去深度调整产业结构；其次，建立一套著作权登记的核心数据标准，利用大数据、区块链等先进技术对著作权登记的数据进行统一的规划、梳理和存储；再次，打造一个收费型公益性社会服务机构，或允许第三方机构执行这项公益性社会服务；最后，实现可视化、可交互的知识图谱展示方式⑧。

七、关于著作权法律保护问题的研究

（一）民事保护

（1）保护作品完整权侵权认定。有学者指出，目前国内著作权司法实践中，在保护作品完整权方面，在采用侵权主观标准还是客观标准上未能统一。对于保护作品完整权的侵权认定采用过高标准势必会影响我国文化产业的发展，束缚文化创造力，建议《著作权法》第三次修订应该明确规定：保护作品完整权，即禁止他人歪曲、篡改或以其他方式改变作品，损害作者声誉的权利⑨。也有学者认为保护作品完整权侵权认定采取客观标准不失为平衡改编者与原作者利益及可操作性强的合理选择。此外，也应当考虑影视改编作品具有双重著作权属性特点，确定原作者在改编作品中改编权的保护范围，通过该保护范围的确定来明确判定侵权的前提，即通过影视改编作品中原作品的保护作品完整权的保护范围，最终认定影视改编是否侵犯保护作品完整权⑩。还有学者认为根据我国《著作权法》的现行规定，保护作品完整权是指保护作品不受歪曲、篡改的权利。由于立法没有明确“歪曲”“篡改”的确切含义，造成了侵权认定上的不确定性。因此，应当通过修改《著作权法》有关规定的方式，将“是否损害作者声誉”作为判断是否侵犯保护作品完整权的侵权认定的判断标准，从而明确保护作品完整权的权利界限⑪。

（2）间接侵权。有学者认为在我国日趋完善的民事共同侵权制度之下，著作权间接侵权并无共存的必要和平台，应当构建著作权共同侵权规则以化

① 向波．著作权集体管理组织：市场功能、角色安排与定价问题［J］．知识产权，2018（7）．

② 杜伟．我国著作权集体管理组织代表性审视［J］．知识产权，2018（12）．

③ 何炼红，郑宏飞．公共文化机构数字化利用绝版作品的著作权授权机制探讨［J］．中南大学学报（社会科学版），2018（4）．

④ 孙新强，姜荣．著作权延伸性集体管理制度的中国化构建：以比较法为视角［J］．法学杂志，2018（2）．

⑤ 华劼．绝版作品数字化版权问题研究：以欧盟和法国的版权制度调整为视角［J］．电子知识产权，2018（9）．

⑥ 谷鑫娜．数字环境下对音乐版权保护的思考：引入延伸集体管理制度之构想［J］．柳州职业技术学院学报，2018（4）．

⑦ 何蓉．面向数字图书馆的延伸性著作权集体管理制度研究［J］．图书馆建设，2018（5）．

⑧ 王悦彤．新时期著作权登记存在的问题与思考［J］．出版发行研究，2018（8）．

⑨ 祁净玉．论保护作品完整权采用侵权客观判断标准的必要性：兼评陈世清诉北京快乐共享文化发展有限公司等侵害保护作品完整权案二审判决［J］．出版发行研究，2018（6）．

⑩ 张俊发．论影视改编侵犯网络文学作品完整权行为的认定规则［J］．科技与法律，2018（5）．

⑪ 方月悦．论保护作品完整权侵权判定标准：以“九层妖塔”案为切入点［J］．传播与版权，2018（7）．

解间接侵权之难题。著作权共同侵权应采客观化认定标准，帮助型共同侵权和教唆型共同侵权应做适当扩大解释，以涵盖辅助侵权、引诱侵权及扩大侵权损害后果的行为①。还有学者探讨了视频分享网站著作权间接侵权的过错认定问题，认为在兼顾技术的自然属性和社会属性的“技术价值论”视野下，视频分享网站在著作权间接侵权中的过错可分为“故意”和“过失”两种形态。作为过失认定的客观标准，注意义务在性质上系安全保障义务在网络空间的自然延伸，应以侵权结果预见义务为视频分享网站注意义务的主要内容，并应强调依据不同行为对象设置不同程度的注意义务②。

(3) 著作权纠纷解决机制。有学者对网络著作权侵权纠纷在线调解机制进行了研究，提出发展多元纠纷解决机制是应对繁杂的网络著作权侵权案例的当务之急。由于网络技术发展能够达到要求，审判人员和当事人意愿上均可行，并且调解人员具备一定的专业素质，这使得在线调解机制有发展的可行性③。也有学者研究了互联网法院纠纷处理机制，指出互联网法院的问题和改良方向。首先是互联网法院的“异步审理”模式是对司法亲历性的挑战。其次是“强制性调解”会对司法效率和当事人选择权产生减损，因此互联网法院可以考虑将前置性调解的适用情况做出更为精细化的区分④。

(4) 损害赔偿。有学者指出著作权侵权惩罚性赔偿金通常认为归属于受害人，但惩罚性赔偿金过高时容易使得受害人获得不当得利，而惩罚性赔偿金过低时无法使惩罚性赔偿制度发挥惩罚侵权人的目的。要解决两者之间的矛盾，应当将惩罚性赔偿金中的一部分分配给受害人，使受害人通过补偿性赔偿没有获得足额赔偿的那部分损失和维权成本未获得法院支持的部分得到足额补偿，剩下的惩罚性赔偿金分配给著作权维权基金⑤。还有学者指出节目模式等新的知识经济时代下的产物，给著作权法的保护模式带来了更大的冲击，法定赔偿的最高限额已经无法弥补价值巨大的作品所遭受的损失，应进一步提高法定赔偿的限额⑥。还有学者认为相比于以实际损失为内容的侵权损害赔偿，著作权侵权获利赔偿责任的适用需要特殊的要件：侵权人的获利以及实际损失难以确定。前者是指侵权人获得了财产收益；“实际损失难以确定”的认定应当由权利人提出损害难以确定的证据或者权利人提出损害的初步证据，由法官来裁量是否属于实际损失难以确定⑦。

(5) 同人作品。有学者认为非演绎性同人作品理应享有与原作品同等的著作权地位，并受到著作权法的保护；并且认为单纯角色元素不能等于作品表达形式本身，非演绎性同人作品虽有对原作品中角色元素的使用，但并没有沿用原作品的独创性表达，读者很难从作品本身的表达形式中寻找到原作的痕迹，是全新的创作，不构成对原作著作权的侵权⑧。也有学者认为同人作品借鉴在先作品中的人物名称或形象进行二次创作，若具备独创性，理应受到著作权法的保护，但其与原作品的著作财产权存在冲突的风险。将虚拟角色商品化权纳入著作权法制度框架来规制同人作品的使用不失为一种可行性考量，商业性使用借用他人知名虚拟角色创作的同人作品应向原著作权人支付相应的报酬⑨。还有学者提出对同人作品的保护方法，同人作品可分为演绎类和非演绎类，演绎类同人作品大体与演绎作品相似，可以按照演绎作品相关法律制度对其进行管理和保护。但非演绎类同人作品与演绎作品并不相似，无法将非演绎类同人作品划分到“改编作品”这一类别中。这就需要我们对著作权法进行合理修订，通过扩大相关范围和制定相关法律条款的方式，将非演绎类同人作品纳入保护范围⑩。另外，有学者认为部分同人作品应在法律层面获得足够的发展空间，但如果同人作品违反诚实信用原则，则应以著作权法和反不正当竞争法加以规制，以期实现二次创作作品著作权人与原作品著作权人之间的利益平衡⑪。

(6) 与微博、微信有关的著作权保护问题。有学者提出公益性微信公众号著作权保护艰难，主要

① 刘平. 著作权“间接侵权”理论之检讨与展望 [J]. 知识产权，2018 (1).

② 马一德. 视频分享网站著作权间接侵权的过错认定 [J]. 现代法学，2018 (1).

③ 周仪娟. 我国网络著作权侵权纠纷在线调解机制研究 [J]. 河北工业大学学报（社会科学版），2018 (10).

④ 秦汉. 互联网法院纠纷处理机制研究：以网络著作权纠纷为例 [J]. 电子知识产权，2018 (10).

⑤ 袁杏桃. 从制度功能谈著作权侵权惩罚性赔偿金的归属 [J]. 杭州师范大学学报（社会科学版），2018 (4).

⑥ 刘承韪. 侵害信息网络传播权的司法救济与赔偿标准：《中国好声音》信息网络传播权案的启示 [J]. 科技与法律，2018 (4).

⑦ 黄芬. 著作权侵权获利赔偿责任的特殊构成要件研究 [J]. 中国出版，2018 (7).

⑧ 胡婧. 论非演绎性同人作品与原作品的知识产权“对碰”[J]. 政法学刊，2018 (1).

⑨ 陈秋英. 同人作品著作权侵权风险评析：以虚拟角色商品化权为视角的考量 [J]. 浙江万里学院学报，2018 (1).

⑩ 庞萌苗. 同人作品著作权探究 [J]. 出版广角，2018 (17).

⑪ 马瑞洁. 再论同人作品的法律规制：基于著作权法和反不正当竞争法的框架 [J]. 出版广角，2018 (15).

原因是原创力不足、原作品作者维权难。解决的方案一方面，首先要形成对文化表达的自身理解，其次要找准自身运营的定位，最后应确定微信平台的运营模式。另一方面，要提高注册门槛，确定侵权主体，简化投诉审核的流程①。对微博转发的著作权侵权行为，有学者认为应当区分两种情况：第一，转发原创性微博时，被转微博的发布者作为著作权人行使信息网络传播权，并许可其他用户通过转发扩大该微博的影响，转发行为不构成侵权。第二，当被转发的微博本身侵犯他人著作权时，无论是发布者还是转发者的行为都脱离著作权人对其作品享有的信息网络传播权之控制。不同之处在于转发者只可能因存在主观过错而构成间接侵权②。也有学者认为微媒体给著作权保护带来的挑战，应从选择较优监管、明确监管对象、完善监管体系、加强立法、界定运营商法律责任及重视数字媒介素养教育等方面加以改进③。

（7）网络文学作品改编。目前，著作权侵权问题的存在影响了网络文学和IP产业的良性发展。有学者认为可以从以下三个角度思考完善的方法：第一，构筑多元救济格局；第二，营造合法改编氛围；第三，建立健全包括版权所有者、版权范围和版权期限等在内的科学测量指标体系。当IP改编作品发生版权纠纷时，可依据这些量化指标进行测量④。也有学者结合案例分析了网络文学版权保护的侵权形态与司法认定。对于网络小说搜索链接、存储以及改编，学者阐释了司法判决中出现的如下几个问题：原告没有提起间接侵权诉讼，法官要不要行使释明权？提供改编服务是不是可以被列为对网络小说改编的情形？应知状态的确立超越“红旗标准”是常态还是例外⑤？还有学者认为《著作权法》中有关作品改编的规定是基于传统的纸质作品，而随着网络文学作品IP改编而来的二次创作作品版权问题、网络文学IP作品侵权界定问题等均很难援引。为了解决上述问题，可以考虑通过在《著作权法》中引入“两分法”标准、“许可费推定”的损害赔偿计算方法等完善《著作权法》⑥。

（8）“洗稿”著作权保护问题。通过“洗稿”方式抄袭剽窃、篡改删减原创作品的侵权行为日益增多，这种高级抄袭行为令人难以甄别是否侵犯著作权。有学者认为，为了鼓励和保护作品创新，有必要通过法律、法规或规章明确“洗稿”的违法性及其法律责任，并规定“洗稿”的防治措施⑦。还有学者探讨了司法实践中侵权的认定标准，指出司法实践中通过抽象观察法和整体观察法来鉴别被诉侵权作品与权利作品是否构成实质性相似，并在分析案例的基础上抽象出了认定实质性相似的一般法律标准。排除法定的合理使用情形，明确“接触＋实质性相似－合理使用”是司法实践中认定侵权的标准⑧。

另外，还有学者对网络深层链接行为⑨、深度链接服务提供者侵权⑩、加框链接直接侵权的判定标准⑪、视频聚合盗链行为⑫、非法演绎作品后续利用行为⑬、大数据知识产权立法保护⑭、未经许可创作的演绎作品的保护⑮、电子书著作权侵权⑯、剧照侵权⑰、视频分享网站侵权责任认定⑱、云盘分享侵权⑲、3D打印侵权⑳、滥用技术措施行为的规制㉑等

---

① 郝翌彤．公益性微信公众号的版权保护研究［J］．当代经济，2018（16）．

② 陈奕．微博转发行为的著作权侵权问题研究［J］．广东开放大学学报，2018（2）．

③ 岳宇君，张耀珍．微媒体著作权保护面临的际遇及其路径选择［J］．行政与法，2018（3）．

④ 杨萌芽，余沐芩．网络文学IP改编中的版权问题探讨［J］．中国编辑，2018（12）．

⑤ 彭桂兵．网络文学版权保护：侵权形态与司法认定：兼评近期的几个案例［J］．出版科学，2018（4）．

⑥ 高婷．网络文学作品IP改编存在的版权问题及对策思考［J］．中国出版，2018（7）．

⑦ 胡志斌．“洗稿”的违法性解析与法律规制［J］．出版发行研究，2018（11）．

⑧ 官正艳．论司法实践中洗稿侵犯著作权的认定标准［J］．电子知识产权，2018（11）．

⑨ 万勇．网络深层链接的著作权法规制［J］．法商研究，2018（6）．

⑩ 张玲玲．深度链接服务提供者侵犯著作权的司法实践与思考［J］．苏州大学学报（法学版），2018（3）．

⑪ 范长军．加框链接直接侵权判定的“新公众标准”［J］．法学，2018（2）．

⑫ 孙那．视频聚合盗链行为法律性质的再探讨［J］．法学论坛，2018（5）．

⑬ 张书青．非法演绎作品后续利用行为的侵权定性［J］．电子知识产权，2018（3）．

⑭ 何隽．大数据知识产权保护与立法：挑战与应对［J］．中国发明与专利，2018（3）．

⑮ 杜牧真，李仁玉．未经许可创作的演绎作品著作权保护探析［J］．知识产权，2018（12）．

⑯ 甄森森．电子书著作权侵权行为及保护措施［J］．经济研究导刊，2018（36）．

⑰ 洪舟．影视剧照的“娘家”：论剧照著作权侵权［J］．河南科技，2018（24）．

⑱ 雷凯悦．视频分享网站著作权侵权责任认定的探析［J］．佳木斯职业学院学报，2018（8）．

⑲ 万浩，高伟．基于云盘之作品资源分享的侵权研究［J］．科技与法律，2018（2）．

⑳ 冷怀华．3D打印中的侵权责任研究［J］．科技与法律，2018（1）．

㉑ 王迁．论版权法对滥用技术措施行为的规制［J］．现代法学，2018（4）．

问题进行了深入的探讨和分析。

（二）刑事保护

（1）以营利为目的。有学者认为侵犯著作权罪和销售侵权复制品罪都要求以营利为目的，那么虽无营利目的，但故意以著作权为侵害目标的侵犯著作权行为就不可能构成犯罪。但前述行为既侵害了著作权人的私权，又妨碍了国家对著作权的管理秩序，金钱只能作为定罪情节的一种，所以从法益上来说，将以营利为目的作为著作权犯罪的入罪门槛是不必要的①。也有学者认为目前我国刑法侵犯著作权罪既遂标准设定不合理，我国《刑法》第二百一十三条到二百一十九条规定了必须具备“以营利为目的”、“情节严重”或者“特别严重”、“违法所得数额较大”或者“巨大”等情形才构成犯罪，给予刑事处罚。然而，这样的规定在司法实践中凸显出诸多的不合理性，设定的入罪门槛不利于惩治与预防侵犯著作权犯罪行为②。还有学者认为，为弥补我国前置法与刑法之间的立法代沟，需要对侵犯著作权罪的“发行”要件做扩大解释，使之包含“信息网络传播”。为防止民事归责与刑事归责之间的标准倒挂，需要以实质呈现标准取代服务器标准与社会危害性标准，将其作为认定信息网络传播行为的标准③。

（2）入罪门槛。通过和域外国家相关制度比较，有学者指出从总体上看，德、法、英、美等域外法对于知识产权犯罪较多采用行为犯标准，而我国主要采用金额、数额犯标准，入罪门槛明显更高。在犯罪构成的主观方面，明示或暗含要求行为人必须存在主观故意，而部分域外国家或地区将有些主观过失下的侵害行为也纳入刑法规制的范围，相比较，我国知识产权犯罪的入罪门槛较高④。还有学者认为在网络版权犯罪高发的背景下，中国版权犯罪的门槛确实较高，应当适时调整。具体到路径上，中国版权犯罪的数额门槛应当变通微调，同时需要扩充直接侵犯版权犯罪的行为类型，建立规制妨害版权犯罪的刑事责任体系以及预留兜底条款来合理降低版权犯罪的门槛⑤。

（3）其他问题。有学者提出《著作权法》与《刑法》的条文规定在著作权保护领域存在实体性衔接缺失，需要通过扩展著作权犯罪的客体、扩充著作权犯罪的行为对象、拓展著作权犯罪规制的行为类型、取消主观方面的“营利目的”等方面来构建实体性衔接⑥。也有学者通过整理分析我国近十年247件著作权犯罪案例，发现著作权犯罪刑法规制存在保护范围局限、规制手段滞后、刑罚适用混乱、“运动式”司法痕迹明显等问题⑦。另外，还有学者研究了单位侵犯著作权犯罪从业禁止。对单位侵犯著作权犯罪适用从业禁止应坚持目的的侧重性、内容的针对性等基本原则，必要时可以结合对适用单位的社会调查进行。从业禁止的宣告应当和刑事判决同时进行，从业禁止的执行主体应当为我国各级新闻出版广电管理机关，同时，还应当赋予被适用单位救济权利⑧。

八、结语

从2018年发表的相关论文来看，学者们对于著作权制度基础理论问题的探究仍然较为有限。而在著作权具体制度问题的研究方面，如人工智能生成内容的著作权保护、网络游戏与体育赛事节目的著作权保护、著作人身权的保护、合理使用、著作权许可以及著作权的集体管理等问题都属于学界讨论的热点问题。当然，学者们在对种种具体问题展开多角度的深入研究时，也愈来愈多地触及对著作权制度的基础理论问题及相关基本概念的批判与分析，从而为著作权制度的基础研究积累了较为丰富的素材。总的来说，由于著作权制度的诸多规则并不能妥当地解决新技术条件下所出现的法律保护问题，学者们较为关注从立法论的视角对著作权制度的完善提出建议与意见。不过，相较于其他民法制度，包括著作权制度在内的知识产权制度对于技术进步与社会变迁的反应要更敏感一些。从这个角度来说，包括著作权制度在内的知识产权制度是否能够达致和维持较为稳定的规范结构，本身就是一个值得探讨的法律问题。

① 陈骁. 论我国知识产权犯罪刑事立法保护范围［J］. 广西政法管理干部学院学报，2018（3）.

② 崔汪卫. 我国侵犯著作权罪的立法瓶颈与域外立法启示［J］. 嘉应学院学报（哲学社会科学），2018（9）.

③ 欧阳本祺. 论网络环境下著作权侵权的刑事归责：以网络服务提供者的刑事责任为中心［J］. 法学家，2018（3）.

④ 刘军华，丁文联，张本勇，等. 我国知识产权刑事保护的反思与完善［J］. 电子知识产权，2018（5）.

⑤ 张燕龙. 中美比较视野下调整我国版权犯罪门槛的思考［J］. 西安交通大学学报（社会科学版），2018（3）.

⑥ 谷永超. 论我国著作权犯罪实体性行刑衔接制度之建构［J］. 中国出版，2018（19）.

⑦ 程莹，孟文玲. 网络文化背景下著作权刑法保护的困境与出路：基于近10年著作权犯罪相关案件的实证分析［J］. 理论导刊，2018（11）.

⑧ 陈庆安. 单位侵犯著作权犯罪从业禁止适用研究［J］. 中国出版，2018（13）.

2018年版权热点问题研究

论版权法对滥用技术措施行为的规制

王　迁

引言

在数字环境中，“技术措施”成为版权人阻止他人未经许可利用受版权法保护的客体（以下统称“作品”），维护其自身利益的重要手段。有些技术措施的功能在于：阻止他人未经许可实施受复制权、信息网络传播权等专有权利控制的行为，也就是预防他人侵害作品的版权，从而实现保护版权的效果。这些技术措施被称为“版权保护措施”。有些技术措施并不直接阻止他人未经许可复制、传播作品，而是阻止他人在未经许可（多为未向权利人付费）的情况下阅读、欣赏作品（也就是“接触”作品内容），因此被称为“接触控制措施”。

所谓“道高一尺，魔高一丈”，再先进的技术措施都有可能被破解（即被“规避”）。失去了技术措施的保护，作品就容易被未经许可地复制、传播或被无偿使用。鉴于技术措施在保护权利人利益方面的巨大作用以及规避技术措施可能造成的严重后果，《世界知识产权组织版权条约》和《世界知识产权组织表演和录音制品条约》要求缔约方保护技术措施，制止规避技术措施的行为①。我国《著作权法》和《计算机软件保护条例》均规定了“故意避开或者破坏”技术措施的法律责任②。《信息网络传播权保护条例》则对技术措施的保护做出了较为详细的规定，不仅禁止出于自己使用作品的目的而避开、破坏技术措施的行为，即“直接规避行为”；还禁止向他人提供用于避开、破坏规避技术措施的装置、部件或向他人提供规避服务，也就是“提供规避手段”③。

版权法对技术措施的保护，对于权利人预先防止他人未经许可复制、传播作品，或者在未付费的情况下以阅读等方式“接触”作品内容起到了积极的作用。然而，某些技术措施，特别是某些“接触控制措施”的主要功能并不是防止版权侵权或不付费使用作品，而是通过阻止对作品的使用，实现捆绑销售和划分销售区域等与版权法保护利益无关的商业模式，如一些电信运营商将苹果手机与其电信服务相绑定的技术措施。还有一些技术措施虽然也能在一定程度上保护作品，但兼具维护权利人商业模式的功能。如后文将讨论的索尼 PlayStation 游戏机中的“控制码”就兼备防止用户运行盗版游戏和对游戏机及游戏光盘划分销售区域的作用。这就给版权法对技术措施的保护带来了复杂的问题。一方面，如果不保护此类技术措施，表面上与版权法保护技术措施的规定不符；另一方面，如果对此类技术措施提供保护，又可能影响消费者的利益、技术发展和正常的市场竞争秩序。

此类技术措施已经在不少国家引发了诉讼。法院对于是否应根据版权法保护此类技术措施存在不同观点。同时，澳大利亚和新西兰等国家和地区的版权法还针对此类技术措施做出了专门规定。遗憾的是，此类技术措施虽然已在我国被使用，而且权利人还对规避行为实施者提起过诉讼，但《著作权法》、《计算机软件保护条例》和《信息网络传播权保护条例》等为技术措施提供保护的立法对此均未做出规定。

一、版权法保护技术措施的正当性与对滥用技术措施的界定

无论中外，版权法对技术措施提供保护的历史都很短。如英国第一部版权法迄今已有 300 余年的历史，但直至 1988 年，英国才在修改后的《版权法》中对用于计算机程序的技术措施提供保护。这种强烈的反差说明，对技术措施的保护，并不是版权法保护权利人利益的传统方法。长期以来，版权法的核心是复制权、发行权和表演权等专有权利。

---

① 参见《世界知识产权组织版权条约》（WCT，1996）第十一条，以及《世界知识产权组织表演和录音制品条约》（1996，WPPT）第十八条。

② 参见《著作权法》（2010）第四十八条第（七）项和《计算机软件保护条例》（2013）第二十四条第（三）项。

③ 参见《信息网络传播权保护条例》（2013）第四条。

"专有权利"亦称"排他权利"，其作用是控制特定行为，也就是使权利人排斥、阻止他人未经许可实施复制、发行和表演等利用作品的行为。技术措施本身并不属于专有权利，但"版权保护措施"是用于保护专有权利的，它可以自动阻止他人未经许可复制、传播作品。权利人无须在版权侵权行为实际发生后再诉诸法律手段维护自身利益，实现了防患于未然的保护效果。因此，版权法对"版权保护措施"的保护，实际上就是对专有权利的间接保护，其正当性是非常充分的。

"接触控制措施"则并不直接保护专有权利并防止版权侵权。这是因为中外版权法中均无所谓"接触权"，也就是阻止他人未经许可以阅读、收听或收看等方式"接触"作品的专有权利。假设某人贪图便宜，购买了一本盗版书阅读，此人的行为并不构成版权侵权，因为他并未实施复制、发行或表演等任何一种受专有权利控制的行为。其"未经许可阅读"的行为，并不侵害任何一项专有权利。因此版权法保护"接触控制措施"的正当性与保护"版权控制措施"不同，并不在于保护专有权利和防止版权侵权。

为什么版权法要保护不能直接防止版权侵权的"接触控制措施"呢？笔者认为：版权法保护"接触控制措施"的正当性，源于"接触控制措施"所保护利益的正当性。权利人在版权法中的正当利益，在于从他人对作品的使用中获得合理收益。版权法规定的专有权利是保护这种正当利益最为重要的途径，但并非唯一途径。对于许多未经许可对作品价值的利用行为，包括对盗版作品的阅读、收听、收看等欣赏行为（即"接触"行为），版权法并不设置专有权利（如"接触权"）进行控制，因为它可能造成对消费者私人生活的干涉（此类行为多为消费者在私人空间进行的）、过高的法律实施成本和严重的利益失衡。但这仅意味着实施此类行为不构成版权侵权，并不意味着权利人不可以采用某种技术手段加以阻止，以促使他人为利用作品而向自己支付合理的报酬。这正如读者在书店翻阅纸质书时，并不会因"未经许可阅读作品"而侵害版权，但权利人和书店可以用透明的塑料纸将纸质书密封起来，以防止因过多翻阅影响销售[①]。正是由于"接触控制措施"能用于保护权利人在版权法中的正当利益——从他人对作品的使用中获得收益，版权法才对其提供保护，这种保护也才具有正当性[②]。

既然版权法保护技术措施的正当性在于维护权利人在版权法中的正当利益——从他人对作品的使用中获得合理收益，不用于保护权利人在版权法中正当利益的技术措施就不应被纳入版权法的保护范围。否则，版权法对技术措施的保护将偏离其立法目的，丧失正当性。如果权利人设置的技术措施用于阻止他人对作品进行不损害其在版权法中正当利益的使用，就违背了版权法保护技术措施的目的，属于对技术措施的滥用。当他人对该技术措施实施直接规避或提供规避手段后，权利人以此人违反了版权法中保护技术措施的规定为由，要求其停止相关行为或追究其法律责任，则属于对版权法保护技术措施条款的滥用。总结现实中权利人设置技术措施的情况和已经发生的中外案例，可以发现，目前利用技术措施实现与权利人在版权法中正当利益无关的情形主要有两类，分别为"借技术措施实现捆绑销售"，以及"借技术措施进行划分销售区域"。

二、借技术措施实现捆绑销售和划分销售区域

一些权利人设置的技术措施，表面上也控制着对相关作品的利用，特别是对计算机程序的"接触"，但其实质作用在于将作品与其他产品或服务进行捆绑销售，以垄断产品的配件市场、服务市场，或者对产品的销售区域进行划分，以便在不同区域以不同的价格销售设备或软件，从而实现"价格歧视"。

（一）技术措施与捆绑销售及对销售区域的划分

用于进行捆绑销售的技术措施往往针对工业产品中的计算机程序。随着工业产品越来越智能化，大多安装了智能控制模板，其中的芯片自然含有计算机程序。用户对产品的操作以及产品功能的实现，都离不开对计算机程序的调用，即对计算机程序的"接触"。因此，计算机程序权利人设置的任何限制调用计算机程序的技术措施，形式上都属于受版权法保护的"接触控制措施"。但这种"接触控制措施"可被用于实现产品与相关配件或服务的捆绑销售。例如，美国苹果公司在推出iPhone手机后，与美国AT&T公司签订协议，在两年的协议期内iPhone只能使用AT&T的无线通信网络。为此，苹果公司在iPhone中设置了技术措施，导致用户在合法购买的iPhone中插入其他无线通信公司的通信卡

① 当然，这种做法也可以用保护纸质书本的物权加以解释。但即使不从物权角度，权利人仍然有权以塑封的方式阻止他人对书本内容的翻阅。

② 对版权法保护"接触控制措施"正当性的进一步讨论，参见王迁《版权法保护技术措施的正当性》，载《法学研究》2011年第4期。

后，无法使用 iPhone 拨打电话。这一技术措施属于“接触控制措施”，因为手机的通信功能是通过运行内置的系统程序（操作系统）实现的，只有使用 AT&T 的通信卡才能正常地调用手机中的系统程序（即“接触”计算机程序）拨打电话。如果有用户对该技术措施实施了直接规避（也就是常说的“刷机”），并在 iPhone 中插入其他公司的通信卡，使用其他公司的通信服务，AT&T 就有可能以规避技术措施为由对其提起诉讼。

苹果公司的 iPhone、平板电脑（iPad）和一些品牌的智能电视中还设有另一种技术措施。如果用户正在进行安装或运行的相关应用程序不是下载自“苹果应用程序商店”（App Store）或其他官方来源，该“接触控制措施”将拒绝调用已在硬件设备中固化的系统程序，导致用户无法安装和运行这些第三方应用程序。此类技术措施也属于“接触控制措施”，因为要在智能设备中安装和运行应用程序，必须先调用（“接触”）系统程序。该技术措施阻止了用户对系统程序的“接触”，用户如果希望安装和运行第三方应用程序，就必须规避该技术措施，也就是进行所谓的“越狱”。该行为在表面上违反了禁止直接规避技术措施的规定。

如果说用于进行捆绑销售的技术措施通常针对的是工业产品中的计算机程序，而不是针对作为销售主要标的的工业产品本身，用于划分销售区域的技术措施则往往针对作为销售主要标的的作品。例如，日本索尼公司在其与 PlayStation 游戏机配套的游戏光盘中采用了被称为“控制码”的技术措施，其主要功能之一就是在全世界划分销售区域，它使消费者无法在日本销售的索尼 PlayStation 游戏机上运行在美国销售的正版游戏。美国电影协会各大会员公司出品的电影 DVD 中也均含有用于进行区域划分的“区域码”技术措施，全世界被划分为 8 个区域，在中国内地（第 6 区）的 DVD 播放机上是无法正常播放在我国香港特别行政区（第 3 区）销售的电影 DVD 的。同时，在不同区域销售的设备或相关软件的价格也有区别，这就是经济学中所说的“价格歧视”。划分销售区域和与之相关的价格歧视是跨国公司常见的营销策略，本身并不一定违法。但是，此类技术措施会导致在一个区域合法获取的作品无法在另一区域购买的设备（如 DVD 播放机或游戏机）上被正常读取（即“接触”），因此它属于“接触控制措施”。如果设备的购买者希望使用在另一区域购买的正版作品，必须规避该技术措施，表面上该行为也违反了禁止直接规避技术措施的规定。

（二）各国司法判例中的观点之辩

对于规避用于实现捆绑销售和划分销售区域的技术措施的行为，在一些国家已经引发了诉讼。在现有的案例中，法院对于用于实现捆绑销售的技术措施采取了否定的态度，即认为不应将其纳入版权法的保护范围。但对于用于划分销售区域的技术措施，则出现了截然相反的观点，实须进行考察与分析。

在涉及用于实现捆绑销售的技术措施的案例中，最为著名的是美国的“Chamberlain 诉 Skylink 案”（以下简称“车库门案”）和“利盟诉 Static Control Components 案”（以下简称“利盟打印机案”）。审理两案的法院均认定被告规避技术措施的行为并不违反版权法有关保护技术措施的规定，从而达到了规制滥用技术措施的效果。

在“车库门案”中，原告 Chamberlain 公司开发了一套“安全型车库大门开启系统”，该系统由一个遥控器和一个装在车库大门上的开启装置组成。遥控器和开启装置中均包含一套被称为“滚动代码”的计算机程序，它可以不断改变开启车库大门所需的遥控信号。这样就可以防止窃车贼用记录装置录下遥控信号，并利用该遥控信号开启车库大门。Skylink 公司随后开发出了与该系统相兼容的“39 型遥控器”。该遥控器并不使用 Chamberlain 公司的“滚动代码”程序，却能发出可被车库大门开启装置接收和认可的遥控信号，从而起到了与“安全型车库大门开启系统”相兼容的作用，可以替代 Chamberlain 公司的遥控器。Chamberlain 公司认为：“安全型车库大门开启系统”中的遥控器和开启装置中均含有计算机程序，而“滚动代码”程序是一种控制“调用”（access）这些程序的“接触控制措施”。即只有当“滚动代码”程序验证了遥控器发出的信号之后，才会启动其他计算机程序开启车库大门。Skylin 公司的“39 型遥控器”主要是为了规避该“接触控制措施”而设计和制造的，属于规避手段。Skylink 公司销售“39 型遥控器”的行为违反了美国《千禧年数字版权法》（即 1998 年美国《版权法》的修改法案）中有关禁止针对技术措施提供规避手段的规定①。

在“利盟打印机案”中，原告利盟公司生产激光打印机，其为了防止消费者在硒鼓中的墨粉用尽

① The Chamberlain Group v. Skylink Technologies，381 F. 3d 1178，1183－1185 (Fed. Cir. 2004).

后不购买原装硒鼓，就在其生产的激光打印机和硒鼓中使用了一种验证技术。其硒鼓的芯片含有一段“墨粉调入程序”，用以向激光打印机中的“打印引擎程序”输出正确的验证数据。如果用户使用了非原装硒鼓，或者向利盟公司的旧硒鼓中充填墨粉，则“墨粉调入程序”输出的验证数据就是错误的，“打印引擎程序”就会拒绝指挥打印机正常工作。被告Static公司破解了利盟公司的这种“验证技术”，生产了一种被称为“SMARTEK”的芯片。它可以向利盟打印机输出正确的验证数据，使装有这种芯片的兼容硒鼓能在利盟打印机中正常使用，而且允许硒鼓在充填墨粉后反复使用。利盟公司认为自己使用的“墨粉调入程序”是一种对“打印引擎程序”的调用加以控制的“接触控制措施”，而Static公司出售的“SMARTEK”芯片属于规避手段，因此销售该芯片的行为违法①。

显然，无论是“车库门案”中的“滚动代码”程序，还是“利盟打印机案”中的“墨粉调入程序”，虽然表面上属于“接触控制措施”，但与保护软件权利人在版权法中的正当利益毫无关系。一方面，该“接触控制措施”并不用于防止消费者或竞争对手未经许可复制或传播内置在车库开启系统或打印机中的计算机程序。另一方面，它也不是为了保证从消费者对这些内置程序的利用中获得合理回报，因为需要更换遥控器或硒鼓的消费者都已付费购买了车库开启系统或打印机，也就是为调用其中的内置程序支付了费用。两案中的原告起诉被告提供用于规避其技术措施的手段，用意只在于利用版权法对技术措施的保护垄断遥控器和硒鼓配件市场，打击兼容遥控器和硒鼓的生产商，迫使消费者只能购买原装遥控器和硒鼓。该行为构成典型的滥用技术措施的行为。

对此，审理两案的法院均依据版权法保护技术措施的立法目的和精神做出了正确的判决，拒绝支持原告的诉讼请求。两案法院均认为，消费者一旦购买了原告的产品，就不仅获得了硬件的所有权，还获得了调用（即“接触”）该产品中计算机程序的法定权利，至少也获得了默示许可。他们使用兼容配件调用程序的行为，虽然表面上绕过了“接触控制措施”，但本质上属于行使消费者权利的行为，因此不能被认定为未经许可规避技术措施。两案被告的行为也不能被认定为属于非法提供规避手段②。

更为重要的是，审理两案的法院均指出了原告利用“接触控制措施”实现捆绑销售的实质目的。审理“车库门案”的联邦巡回上诉法院认为：

根据Chamberlain公司的解释，任何产品的制造商只要在其产品中增加一句受版权保护的句子或软件片段，并用简单的加密机制加以包装，就可以限制消费者将其产品与其竞争对手的产品配套使用的权利。……（这）将允许任何公司尝试将其销售行为转换成售后市场的垄断。而这种垄断通常是反垄断法和版权滥用原则所共同禁止的③。

审理“利盟打印机案”的联邦第六巡回上诉法院也认为：如果我们采纳利盟公司对《千禧年数字版权法》的解释，产品制造商就有可能使用与涉案“打印引擎程序”相似，但多一点独创性的控制代码以垄断配件市场。例如，汽车制造商可以通过在其汽车中装入控制芯片来控制对其汽车的全部配件市场。国会不会允许《千禧年数字版权法》以这种侵害他人权利的方式被利用。……如果利盟公司希望利用《千禧年数字版权法》保护其版权作品，就不能用该作品去阻止在其打印机中使用与其原装硒鼓相竞争的硒鼓④。

欧盟《版权指令》虽然并没有明确将那些单纯用于实现将作品与其他产品捆绑销售的技术措施排除出保护范围，但欧盟委员会向欧洲理事会和欧洲议会呈交的报告完全赞同美国“车库门案”与“利盟打印机案”的判决结果，并明确指出：当技术措施被用于控制硬件的零部件销售时，《版权指令》并不对其提供保护⑤。

与法院拒绝用版权法保护用于实现捆绑销售的技术措施的态度相比，对于借技术措施划分销售区域的行为，各国法院的观点并不统一，这突出反映在由“直读芯片”——专门用于规避索尼公司的PlayStation游戏机和游戏光盘中技术措施的计算机

① Lexmark International v. Static Control Components，387 F. 3d 522，529-531 (6th Cir. 2005).

② The Chamberlain Group v. Skylink Technologies，381 F. 3d 1178，1201-1202 (Fed. Cir. 2004)；Lexmark International v. Static Control Components，387 F. 3d 522，563-564 (6th Cir. 2005).

③ The Chamberlain Group v. Skylink Technologies，381 F. 3d 1178，1201 (Fed. Cir. 2004).

④ Lexmark International v. Static Control Components，387 F. 3d 522，552 (6th Cir. 2005).

⑤ Commission of the European Communities. Report to the Council，the European Parliament and the Economic and Social Committee on the application of Directive 2001/29/EC on the harmonisation of certain aspects of copyright and related rights in the information society [R]，Brussels，2007，para. 7-8.

芯片引起的系列诉讼中。索尼公司在PlayStation游戏机和与之相配套的游戏软件光盘中均设有相互匹配的“控制码”，且在不同国家销售的游戏机和光盘中所使用的“控制码”是不同的。如果有人企图运行盗版游戏光盘或将在一个区域购买的正版游戏光盘插入在另一个区域购买的游戏机运行，都会因为游戏机无法从光盘中读出与之相匹配的“控制码”而无法运行游戏。一些计算机高手则制作了用于破解“控制码”的特定芯片，即“直读芯片”。用户将该芯片安装到索尼公司的游戏机上之后，无论放入的游戏光盘是否含有正确的“控制码”，游戏机都会误认为游戏光盘含有正确的“控制码”，从而使游戏可以正常运行[①]。

在澳大利亚发生的“索尼诉史蒂文斯案”中，索尼公司指称史蒂文斯销售“直读芯片”的行为违反了澳大利亚《版权法》禁止对技术措施提供规避手段的规定[②]。澳大利亚高等法院拒绝保护“控制码”这一技术措施，其理由之一在于：“控制码”具有进行划分销售区域的功能。法院认为：进行区域限制的用意明显是降低全球市场的竞争，约束澳大利亚财产（指正版游戏光盘）所有者通常应获得的依其视为合适的方式，对其财产进行使用和为其利益加以改装的权利。而这与版权侵权行为毫无关系[③]。法院指出：

索尼公司的观点将……允许其实现有别于版权法通常保护的利益之外的、一种额外的经济目的。……索尼公司对版权法的解释将允许其通过技术措施，有效地实现其所希望的对全球市场的划分。它将导致在这些不同的市场中采用，或至少是可能采用不同的定价。简言之，这会给予索尼公司在其自行分割的市场中对其产品制定价格的广泛权力，这超越了澳大利亚《版权法》通常允许的范围[④]。

然而，在事实背景与“索尼诉史蒂文斯案”几乎完全相同的“索尼诉欧文案”和“索尼诉保尔案”中，英国高等法院做出了与澳大利亚高等法院完全不同的判决。这两起诉讼涉及的同样是索尼公司的PlayStation游戏机和游戏光盘，被告欧文和保尔同样销售用于规避游戏机中“控制码”的“直读芯片”（该芯片在两案中分别被称为Messiah和Messiah2芯片）。索尼公司起诉欧文和保尔违反英国《版权法》中关于禁止提供规避手段的规定[⑤]。

在这两个案件中，索尼公司在日本出售的PlayStation游戏光盘上面印有“仅限于在日本使用”。因此法院认为索尼公司并未许可在日本以外的地方使用该游戏光盘。法院还认为：版权在本质上是有地域性的，消费者如果需要在几个地域使用受版权法保护的作品，应当在每一个地域都获得许可，否则就是侵权[⑥]。法院据此判决被告败诉[⑦]。这实际上是认为“区域码”起到了防止用户侵权（即在英国运行在外国销售的正版游戏）的作用。

英国高等法院对“索尼诉欧文案”与“索尼诉保尔案”的判决，反映了一些对用于划分销售区域的“控制码”与权利人在版权法中正当利益之间关系的不当认识。在面对几乎完全相同的案情时，英国高等法院与澳大利亚高等法院做出不同判决的原因之一可能在于，澳大利亚《版权法》允许平行进口，而英国《版权法》并不允许平行进口。但是，英国高等法院对与平行进口有关的“地域性”的解释是缺乏说服力的。因为根据英国《版权法》的规定，只有未经许可将作品复制件“进口”至英国的行为才可能构成侵权[⑧]。仅仅利用该复制件中的作品，本身并不是侵权行为。许多用户仅是在英国购买了从国外进口的游戏光盘和“直读芯片”，并没有直接实施“进口”行为，谈何“侵权”呢？同时，即使该用户是自己在国外购买了游戏光盘且带入英国，也就是实施了“进口”行为，根据英国《版权法》的规定，只要是“为其私人和家庭的使用”，该行为也不构成侵权[⑨]。因此这些用户的行为也不会因禁止平行进口的规定而构成侵权。至于以用户违反“仅限于在日本使用”的协议而认为用户侵权或无权运行正版游戏的观点，就更无法成立了。

更为重要的是，诸如“区域码”的“接触控制

① Sony v Owen，[2002] EWHC45，para. 5-6；Sony v Ball，[2004] All ER (D) 334 (Jul)，para. 7.

② 澳大利亚当时的《版权法》保护技术措施的条款（现已被替换）禁止针对技术措施（“版权保护措施”和能起到间接保护版权作用的“接触控制措施”）提供规避手段，但并不禁止实施直接规避行为。Australia Copyright Act (2001)，Section 116 (A).

③ Stevens v Kabushiki Kaisha Sony Computer Entertainment and Others，[2005] HCA 58：175.

④ 同③214.

⑤ 同①.

⑥ Sony v Owen，[2002] EWHC45，para. 19.

⑦ Sony v Ball，[2004] All ER (D) 334 (Jul)，para. 32-33.

⑧ Copyright，Designs and Patents Act 1988，Section 22.

⑨ 同⑧.

措施”是权利人保障其商业营销策略得以有效实施的手段。但正如在“RealNetworks 诉 DVD 复制控制联盟案”中美国法院所指出的那样：“版权法的目的，……并不是保护任何特定的商业模式。”[①] 前文已经指出：权利人在版权法上的正当利益应是其从对作品的利用中获得的收益，只有那些能够保障这种正当利益的技术措施才应当受到版权法的保护。单纯用于划分销售区域的“区域码”保护的仅仅是权利人的商业模式，而非其在版权法中的正当利益。欧盟委员会在向欧洲理事会和欧洲议会提交的报告中，也不赞成用《版权指令》保护那些用于实现划分销售区域的技术措施[②]。对于此类“接触控制措施”，版权法对其进行保护无正当性可言。

（三）对具有双重功能的技术措施的法律定性

为什么对于用以划分销售区域的技术措施，各国法院的态度大相径庭，但对于用于捆绑销售的技术措施，则没有出现太大的意见分歧呢？笔者认为，这可能是因为用于进行捆绑销售的技术措施通常并不针对作为销售主要标的的工业产品本身，而是针对工业产品中的计算机程序。同时对该程序的调用又是为正常使用产品所必需的，极少有人会脱离产品单独利用该程序。因此此类技术措施除了用于进行捆绑销售之外，很少兼具保护计算机程序的版权或防止未付费者使用该程序的功能。换言之，此类技术措施保护的只是权利人在版权法之外的利益，并不保护权利人在版权法中的利益。与之形成对比的是，“控制码”和“区域码”等可用于实现划分销售区域的技术措施，往往还兼具防止他人未经许可复制、传播作品或在未付费的情况下使用作品的功能。如 PlayStation 游戏机和游戏光盘中的“控制码”不仅能够进行“区域控制”，还能防止消费者运行盗版游戏。换言之，此类技术措施同时保护了权利人在版权法之中的利益和在版权法之外的利益。那么此类技术措施能否受到版权法的保护呢？

有一种观点认为：能够同时实现上述两种功能的技术措施仍然应当受到版权法的保护。欧盟委员会在向欧洲理事会和欧洲议会提交的报告中，尽管并不赞成用《版权指令》保护那些用于划分销售区域的技术措施，却为英国的“索尼诉保尔案”辩护。欧盟委员会一方面提出：“那些单纯用于实现区域划分的技术措施，如‘区域码’，只有在其能够阻止对复制权、提供权（相当于我国《著作权法》中的‘信息网络传播权’）和发行权的侵害时，才能受到保护”[③]。另一方面却认为：“在‘索尼诉保尔案’中，法院认定即使该案中涉及的技术措施能够使索尼公司将全球划分为 3 个区域并阻止平行进口，其也能同时阻止复制受版权保护的作品，因此该技术措施针对的是版权侵权行为。”[④] 显然，欧盟委员会认为，即使一种技术措施具有实现区域划分的功能，但只要其也能同时阻止版权侵权，就仍然能够受到版权法的保护。

这一观点是不能成立的，它等同于鼓励版权人将旨在划分销售区域的技术措施和旨在防止使用盗版的技术措施合为一体，以便使前者也能受到版权法的保护。权利人在知悉立法者和法院的这一观点后，不会愚蠢到只在数字化内容中加入一种“单纯用于划分销售区域”而不能“用于阻止版权侵权或未付费而接触作品”的技术措施。这样一来，一切主要用于划分销售区域的技术措施就会因此而受到保护。欧盟委员会所称的“单纯用于实现区域划分的技术措施在其不能制止版权侵权时不受保护”的观点也将被架空。笔者认为：如果权利人使用的技术措施既具有捆绑销售、划分销售区域的功能，也能够通过防止版权侵权或“接触控制”起到维护权利人在版权法中正当利益的作用，那么这种技术措施能否受到版权法的保护应当取决于这两种功能能否分离。换言之，如果该技术措施所具有的上述两种功能在技术上独立存在，且规避技术措施中实现捆绑销售、划分销售区域的那部分技术，不会影响技术措施发挥保护权利人在版权法中正当利益的功能，则两种功能可以分离，否则就无法分离。在可以分离的情况下，该技术措施才能受到版权法的保护，但规避技术措施中实现捆绑销售、划分销售区域的那部分技术不应被认定为违法行为。如果两种功能无法分离，则该技术措施作为一个整体不能受

① RealNetworks v DVD Copy Control Association，641 F. Supp. 2d 913，943 (N. D. Cal. 2009).

② Commission of the European Communities. Report to the Council，the European Parliament and the Economic and Social Committee on the application of Directive 2001/29/EC on the harmonisation of certain aspects of copyright and related rights in the information society [R]，Brussels，2007：8.

③ 同②.

④ 同②. 需要说明的是，英国《版权法》承认在计算机程序运行过程中临时调入计算机内存的“临时复制”属于复制行为（Copyright，Designs and Patents Act 1988，Section 17），因此在“索尼诉保尔案”中，英国高等法院认为用户利用“直读芯片”在索尼游戏机上运行盗版索尼游戏的行为构成对复制权的侵害（Sony v Ball，[2004] All ER (D) 334 (Jul)，para. 329－330）。

到版权法的保护。否则势必导致技术措施所具有的实现捆绑销售和划分销售区域功能也可以受到版权法的保护。这样一来，版权法就会沦为权利人垄断配件市场、划分市场及实现价格歧视的工具。此时，牺牲版权法对技术措施的保护是必需的。

三、不同立法对策的选择

对用于实现捆绑销售和划分销售区域的技术措施，在权利人就他人实施的直接规避行为或提供规避手段的行为提起诉讼时，法院当然可以根据版权法保护技术措施的目的和精神，将其排除出受保护的范围。然而，不同法院对于立法目的和精神的理解难免存在差异，在缺乏法律明确规定的情况下，就可能出现判决结果的差异。因此，通过立法明确将用于实现捆绑销售和划分销售区域的技术措施排除在保护范围之外，是更加可取的选择。但是，在具体模式上，各国又出现了两种做法：一是以澳大利亚为代表，直接在版权立法中做出规定；二是美国的做法，在定期颁布并更新的例外情形中做出规定。

（一）在立法中规定不予保护的技术措施

澳大利亚 2000 年通过《数字议程法案》、修改《版权法》时，对于不能间接防止版权侵权的“接触控制措施”并不提供保护①。对于能间接防止版权侵权的“接触控制措施”，也只禁止提供规避手段，并不禁止实施直接规避行为②。因此对于实现捆绑销售的技术措施，无论其是否同时具有间接防止版权侵权的作用，对其实施直接规避的行为都不违法。但是，美国于 2004 年与澳大利亚签订的《美澳自由贸易协定》要求澳大利亚立法禁止直接规避“接触控制措施”，即使该技术措施不能直接或间接防止版权侵权，而仅是防止对作品未经许可的“接触”③。在澳大利亚为实施该协定而修改《版权法》的过程中，许多人和立法者都充分认识到：权利人有可能利用版权法对“接触控制措施”的保护，借助技术措施进行捆绑销售和划分销售区域，从而抑制公平竞争，损害跨境消费者的利益。因此，2006 年澳大利亚修改《版权法》时，将那些用于实现捆绑销售和划分销售区域的“接触控制措施”明确排除出了保护范围。修改后的澳大利亚《版权法》在界定“接触控制措施”时规定：

> ……（接触控制措施）不包括一种设备、产品、技术或组件，如果：
>
> …………
>
> (c)（受接触控制措施保护的）作品或其他客体是电影或计算机程序（包括计算机游戏），（该设备、产品、技术或组件）阻止在澳大利亚播放（运行）从澳大利亚之外获得的作品或其他客体的非侵权复制件，从而实现了对地理市场划分的控制。
>
> (d)（受接触控制措施保护的）作品是机器或设备之中的计算机程序，（该设备、产品、技术或组件）限制了与该机器或设备相关的商品或服务的使用④。

该规定意味着，如果一种技术措施限制对正版作品的跨区域使用（即“划分销售区域”），或者起到了将机器或设备与其他产品或服务加以绑定（即“捆绑销售”）的作用，则该技术措施不属于澳大利亚现行《版权法》所保护的“接触控制措施”。据此，前文提及的苹果公司在 iPhone 中设置的“接触控制措施”就不能受到保护。因为其作用正是“限制了与该机器或设备（iPhone）相关的商口或服务（AT&T 之外的其他公司提供的无线通信服务）的使用”，从而实现了 iPhone 与 AT&T 无线通信服务之间的绑定。同样，如果一种技术措施的作用是划分销售区域，即阻止在澳大利亚播放从国外获得的正版电影，或者阻止在澳大利亚运行从国外获得的正版计算机程序，包括正版计算机游戏，则这种技术措施也不属于受保护的“接触控制措施”。这样一来，澳大利亚就通过修改立法实现了对滥用技术措施行为的规制。

新西兰 2008 年《版权法》在定义“技术措施”时也有类似规定：为避免疑义，（技术措施）不包括任何方法、处理过程、机制、设备或系统，其在正常运行过程中仅控制为非侵权目的而接触作品的行为（例如，不包括一种方法、处理过程、机制、设备或系统，其在正常运行过程中，通过阻止在新西兰播放作品的非侵权复制件而控制对市场地域的划分）⑤。

由此可见，新西兰《版权法》只保护能直接防止版权侵权的“版权保护措施”和能起到间接防止

① Australia Copyright Act (2001), Section 10, “technological protection measure”.

② Australia Copyright Act (2001), Section 10, “technological protection measure”.

③ The U. S. -Australia Free Trade Agreement (FTA), Article 17. 4.

④ Australia Copyright Act (2007), Section 10 (1), “access control technological protection measure”.

⑤ New Zealand Copyright Act, Section 226.

版权侵权作用的“接触控制措施”，并不保护不能起到间接防止版权侵权作用的“接触控制措施”。这就意味着用于实现捆绑销售的技术措施并不能受到保护，因此在上文所述的各案例中，用户使用兼容设备调用（“接触”）产品中的计算机程序都不可能是出于侵害该程序版权的目的，而且由于用户已经购买了产品，也就是为调用其中的计算机程序支付了报酬，该行为也不属于“未经许可”使用程序。因此此类技术措施“仅控制为非侵权目的而接触作品的行为”。同时，新西兰《版权法》还明确将用于划分销售区域的技术措施排除出了保护范围。

我国香港特别行政区则在2007年修订后的《版权条例》中明确规定：如果技术措施包含了“区域码”或其他任何为了以地域为基础实现市场划分，而具有防止或限制接触作品作用的技术、设备、部件或方法，则只要作品的复制件并非侵权复制件，仅为了破除该技术措施中的“区域码”、技术、设备、部件或方法的行为就无须承担责任①。虽然新加坡与澳大利亚一样，与美国签订了《美新自由贸易协定》，并根据协定的要求对其《版权法》进行了修改，提高了对技术措施的保护水平，但新加坡政府以“附函”（side letter）的形式向美国政府澄清：“对于唯一作用在于控制电影合法复制件的市场区域划分的技术措施，如果一种设备能使该技术措施失效，本协定并未要求新加坡限制对这种设备的进口或其在国内的销售”②。美国政府代表则回复确认“美国政府认同该解释，且其构成《美新自由贸易协定》的内在组成部分”③。换言之，新加坡是以对法律进行解释的方法，澄清了用于划分销售区域的技术措施并不受《版权法》的保护。我国香港特别行政区和新加坡将用于划分销售区域的技术措施排除出版权法的保护范围，值得赞许。但遗憾的是香港特别行政区的《版权条例》没有提及用于实现捆绑销售的技术措施，因此在规制滥用技术措施的范围上不及澳大利亚和新西兰《版权法》。

（二）定期颁布禁止规避技术措施的例外情形

美国则采取了另一种立法策略。作为最早对技术措施提供全面保护的立法，美国的《千禧年数字版权法》中并没有与上述澳大利亚和新西兰《版权法》类似的一般性规定。但是，立法者考虑到了禁止“接触控制措施”可能造成的负面后果，因此在该法中设置了一个“安全保障机制”，即在该法通过后2年之内，以及以后每3年，美国版权局局长应在征询相关部门的意见后，就“特定类别的作品”的使用者是否可能因版权法禁止规避“接触控制措施”的规定而受到不利影响的情况，发布报告和评论，并向美国国会图书馆提出颁布例外情形的建议④。美国国会图书馆馆长应当根据该建议，颁布有效期为3年的例外情形。指明那些因禁止规避技术措施的规定而导致其使用者利益受到不利影响的作品类别，并规定禁止规避技术措施的条款不适用于这些类别作品使用者的例外情形⑤。在随后的2000年至2015年的15年时间里，美国国会图书馆根据美国版权局的建议，已先后6次公布了针对禁止规避技术措施的例外情形。

由于国会图书馆颁布的例外情形必须针对“特定类别的作品”（a class of works），因此它没有像澳大利亚《版权法》那样，一般性地将任何用于捆绑销售和划分销售区分的“接触控制措施”都排除出受保护的技术措施范围。即使如此，国会图书馆也多次在美国版权局的建议下，将用于捆绑销售的几种“接触控制措施”排除在禁止实施规避行为的范围之外。具体而言，美国国会图书馆在2006年、2010年、2012年和2015年颁布的例外情形均允许在特定条件下“刷机”，也就是允许手机或其他移动设备的用户规避将设备与特定运营商加以绑定的“接触控制措施”，以使用户转换运营商⑥。在此过程中，还发生了颇具戏剧性的事件。在2010年之

① Copyright Ordinance (CAP. 58)，Section 273D (7).

② 新加坡贸易与工业部部长（Minister for Trade and Industry Singapore）杨荣文（George Yeo）致美国贸易代表（United States Trade Representative）佐利克（Robert B. Zoellick）的函。Letter from George Yeo to Robert B. Zoellick：4 [EB/OL].（2003-05-06）[2010-03-18]. http://www. worldtradelaw. net/fta/agreements/USSing_SL_IP(OpticalDisks). pdf.

③ 美国贸易代表（United States Trade Representative）佐利克（Robert B. Zoellick）致新加坡贸易与工业部部长（Minister for Trade and Industry Singapore）杨荣文（George Yeo）的复函。Letter from Robert B. Zoellick to George Yeo：4 [EB/OL].（2003-05-06）[2010-03-18]. http://www. worldtradelaw. net/fta/agreements/USSing_SL_IP(OpticalDisks). pdf.

④ 美国国会图书馆隶属于美国国会，有颁布行政规章的法定权力。美国版权局作为作品登记机关，隶属于美国国会图书馆。

⑤ 17 USC 1201 (a) (1) (D).

⑥ Library of Congress. Exemption to Prohibition on Circumvention of Copyright Protection Systems for Access Control Technologies [S]，2006：71 FR 68472-01：68476；Library of Congress. Exemption to Prohibition on Circumvention of Copyright Protection Systems for Access Control Technologies [S]，2010：75 FR 43825：43830；Library of Congress. Exemption to Prohibition on Circumvention of Copyright Protection Systems for Access Control Technologies [S]，2015：80 FR 65944：65952；37 CFR part 201 § 201.40 (b) (3).

后，苹果手机的销售策略发生了变化。此前，市场上只有绑定了运营商的合约手机出售，而2010年之后也有所谓“裸机”，也就是不绑定运营商的手机出售。同时，运营商自己也开始提供有条件的“解锁”服务。在这种情况下，美国版权局认为，如果市场上存在着可供消费者选择的多种方案，以使他们获得“解锁版”的手机，就没有必要对新手机再适用“刷机”例外了①。因此，在2012年颁布的例外中，国会图书馆将允许“刷机”的条件设定得更为严格，规定只有对该次例外颁布之前以及颁布之后90天内购买的手机才可进行“刷机”②。这意味着在该例外颁布90天后任何“刷机”行为都将违反《千禧年数字版权法》有关禁止规避“接触控制措施”的规定，这引起了消费者的普遍不满。2013年1月，一名消费者在白宫网站上发起了要求使“刷机”合法的请愿，希望“白宫要求国会图书馆撤销此项决定，如果未能撤销，则应支持一项使解锁永久合法的法案”③。该请愿征集到了超过11万个签名。对此，白宫做出了积极的回应，赞同请愿者的观点④。

在各方的呼吁下，美国国会于2014年8月1日通过了《释放消费者的选择权及无线（设备）竞争法案》，该法案废止了国会图书馆2012年颁布的手机“刷机”例外，要求国会图书馆今后颁布例外时，不仅应针对手机，还应考虑“任何其他类别的无线设备”，这实际上是要求扩大例外情形的适用范围，将平板电脑（如iPad）等无线设备也纳入其中⑤。同时，被允许实施直接规避行为的主体也由无线设备的所有者拓展到经所有者请求的其他人，包括商业性移动服务或数据的提供者⑥。也就是允许其他无线通信服务商为用户提供“刷机”服务。随后，国会图书馆根据该法案修改了之前颁布的“刷机”例外，针对“能够使已使用的无线手提电话连接到无线电话通信网络的计算机程序”，允许程序复制件的所有者为了合法连接到无线通信网络，规避用于限制无线电话连接到无线通信网络的技术措施。换言之，2012年颁布的例外中，90天等限制条件不再适用。同时，修改后的例外还允许无线电话或其他设备的所有者、经所有者请求的其他人，包括商业性移动服务或数据的提供者，为使所有者或其家庭成员连接无线通信网络而规避技术措施⑦。换言之，此项例外的适用范围拓展到了手机之外的其他无线设备，被允许实施规避行为的主体也增加了。

据此，2015年国会图书馆颁布的“刷机”例外在范围上得到了拓展，它针对的是能使下列类型的无线设备连接到无线通信网络的计算机程序：（1）无线手提电话；（2）通用平板电脑；（3）便携式移动连接设备，如移动热点、可拆卸宽带路由器和类似的设备；（4）可穿戴的无线设备，如智能手表或健康设备。当规避仅是为了连接到无线通信网络，以及该连接经过该网络运营商授权时，该规避就可以进行。条件是该设备之前已经被合法获取且已在某一运营商的无线通信网络中被激活⑧，这样可以防止从对由运营商补贴资费的全新手机（从未连接到无线通信网络）的交易中牟利⑨。

同时，美国国会图书馆在2010年、2012年和2015年颁布的例外情形还允许在特定条件下“越狱”⑩，也就是允许规避限定手机或其他通用移动计算设备安装和运行特定来源的应用程序的“接触控制措施”，以“使合法获得的应用程序与智能手机或上述设备中的该程序相兼容，或从该智能手机或该

① Library of Congress. Exemption to Prohibition on Circumvention of Copyright Protection Systems for Access Control Technologies [S]，2012：77 FR 65260-1：65265.

② Library of Congress. Exemption to Prohibition on Circumvention of Copyright Protection Systems for Access Control Technologies [S]，2006：71 FR 68472-01：68476；Library of Congress. Exemption to Prohibition on Circumvention of Copyright Protection Systems for Access Control Technologies [S]，2010：75 FR 43825：43830.

③ 消费者白宫请愿 [EB/OL]. [2014-07-04]. https://petitions.whitehouse.gov/petition/make-unlocking-cell-phones-legal/1g9KhZG7.

④ 白宫回复 [EB/OL]. [2014-07-04]. https://petitions.whitehouse.gov/petition/make-unlocking-cell-phones-legal.

⑤ The Unlocking Consumer Choice and Wireless Competition Act，Public Law 113-144，128 Stat. 1751，2014：Section 2 (a).

⑥ 同⑤Section 2 (a)，2 (c).

⑦ 37 CFR part 201 § 201.40 (b) (3)，(c).

⑧ Library of Congress. Exemption to Prohibition on Circumvention of Copyright Protection Systems for Access Control Technologies [S]，2015：80 FR 65944：65952；37 CFR part 201 § 201.40 (b) (3).

⑨ 同⑧.

⑩ Library of Congress. Exemption to Prohibition on Circumvention of Copyright Protection Systems for Access Control Technologies [S]，2010：75 FR 43825：43828；Library of Congress. Exemption to Prohibition on Circumvention of Copyright Protection Systems for Access Control Technologies [S]，2012：77 FR 65260-1：65264.

设备中移除软件”[①]。2015年颁布的例外还允许对智能电视进行“越狱”，也就是为了在智能电视中安装合法获取的第三方应用程序，可以规避只允许智能电视安装和运行特定来源的应用程序的“接触控制措施”[②]。这实际上也是针对将作品（系统软件或其他计算机程序）与特定产品（应用程序）进行捆绑的“接触控制措施”提供的法律对策。

与澳大利亚《版权法》规制滥用技术措施的规定相比，美国定期颁布例外的做法效果十分有限。澳大利亚《版权法》将用于实现捆绑销售和划分销售区域的技术措施排除出受保护的范围，这就意味着无论是对该技术措施实施直接规避行为，还是提供规避手段，都不会违反《版权法》。与之相比，美国国会图书馆颁布的是“例外”。换言之，符合条件的“刷机”和“越狱”（对用于捆绑销售的“接触控制措施”的直接规避行为）不再受禁止，从而使行为人被豁免了法律责任。但例外并不能使此类技术措施被排除出美国《版权法》的保护范围。多数情况下对此类技术措施提供规避手段仍然属于违法行为。同时，例外只针对极为有限的特定情形，它考虑的只是与技术措施有关的特定类型作品（如设备中以固件形式存在的计算机程序），而不是相关技术措施保护的利益是否为权利人在版权法中的正当利益。因此，在国会图书馆颁布的历次例外中，并不存在允许规避用于划分销售区域的技术措施的例外。对于用于实现捆绑销售的技术措施，也只涉及手机等具备无线通信功能的设备及需要安装程序的智能电视等设备，且每次颁布的例外仅有3年的有效期。这就意味着，如果再发生前文提及的“车库门案”和“利盟打印机案”，法院无法在国会图书馆颁布的例外中找到使被控侵权人免责的依据，仍然只能根据《版权法》保护技术措施的立法目的和精神进行判决。由此可见，在规避滥用技术措施方面，美国定期颁布例外情形的做法不及澳大利亚《版权法》那样明确、清晰和具有包容性。

四、我国应采取的规制滥用技术措施的方式

我国现行版权立法中并无规制滥用技术措施的规定，但现实中已经出现了利用技术措施实现捆绑销售的行为和相关诉讼。对此，正在修订的《著作权法》应当有所回应。相较之下，澳大利亚在《版权法》中将实现捆绑销售和划分销售区域的技术措施排除出保护范围，较美国定期颁布例外的做法更值得我国借鉴。当然，随着技术的发展和商业模式的创新，今后滥用技术措施的表现可能并不止于借助技术措施实现捆绑销售和划分销售区域。为此，我国《著作权法》不仅应当借鉴澳大利亚《版权法》，明确将实现捆绑销售和划分销售区域的技术措施排除出保护范围，还应当用具有包容性的用语，将任何与实现权利人在版权法中正当利益无关的技术措施排除出保护范围。这样才能使立法具有前瞻性和充分的弹性，实现版权法保护技术措施的目的。

（本文原发表于《现代法学》2018年第4期，
系2015年国家社会科学基金重大项目
“互联网领域知识产权重大立法问题研究”
（项目批准号：14ZDC020）的阶段性成果。
发文时内容有删减。
作者单位：华东政法大学）

中国著作权立法中的制度创新

熊　琦

中国著作权立法从经验借鉴转向主动调整，制度安排应以回应中国问题为目标。然而如何从著作权理论和实践中准确提炼中国本土问题，却因比较法和本土法的价值设定差异而存在分歧。我国现今更多采取的著作权立法取向，是直接以法定化的权利分配来取代需要经历市场博弈达致的意定安排，而权利人和使用者又从各自立场出发，期待法律赋予符合自身利益的自治空间，最终导致在立法选择和司法审判上缺乏基本共识而陷入困境。通过梳理本土制度变革历史可以发现，实现中国著作权法制度创新的关键，是管制规则和自治规则如何在价值定位上协调和互补，以及如何使继受规则的制度理念与本土规则的运作传统协同配合。解决该问题的方法，是在中国社会、产业与文化背景下划定著作权领域私人自治与政府管制的边界，一方面允许本土版权产业主体根据自身的市场和社会环境创制著作权市场交易规则，另一方面在存在市场失灵之处优化政府干预。

一、问题的提出

随着我国知识产权战略的深入推进，全社会已

① Library of Congress. Exemption to Prohibition on Circumvention of Copyright Protection Systems for Access Control Technologies [S], 2015: 80 FR 65944; 65953; 37 CFR part 201 § 201.40 (b) (4).

② 同①80 FR 65944; 65953; 37 CFR part 201 § 201.40 (b) (5).

形成了尊重和保护知识产权的共识，加快建设知识产权强国也已先后写入《国家创新驱动发展战略纲要》、国家“十三五”规划纲要和政府工作报告等重要文件。在此背景下，我国技术密集型产业和文化产业得以迅速发展壮大，正逐步成为推动世界知识产权增长的主要力量，知识产权立法也从回应国际社会转为满足本土需求。《著作权法》、《专利法》和《商标法》在第三次修订进程中，产业界都前所未有地提出了自己的诉求①。然而，在《专利法》和《商标法》先后顺利完成第三次修订，甚至《专利法》第四次修改草案已经开始征求意见之时，2011年即已启动的《著作权法》第三次修改却停滞不前②。回顾《著作权法》第二次修订还会发现，所谓第二次修订其实仅涉及两个条文，当时看来已经较为急迫的权利类型衔接漏洞、权利归属公平和网络环境下侵权认定规则等诸多问题并未解决③。问题应对的迟延，从微观上看，是因为利益各方用相同的话语体系表达对立的立法诉求，权利人提高保护标准的目标和使用者强调获取自由的立场对立，却都自认为符合促进文化发展的目标，造成立法选择上难以去伪存真；从宏观上看，则是如何在创新驱动发展时代创造性地构建著作权法的包容性，在保障各产业模式协调发展的基础上，通过法定的权利配置安排来划分不同主体利益的价值位阶的问题。

上述立法争议和解释困境的出现，是因为我国以往继受的部分著作权规则已无法回应新时代的制度创新需求，同时本土著作权法又尚未在理论积累上形成稳定成熟的法价值基础，这使得制度设计上难以拿出令各方信服的解释，继受规则与本土创新之间尚难形成一个从理论到制度都能逻辑自洽的体系。随着近年来我国互联网产业所涉疆域的扩大，本土版权产业在尚缺乏对抗能力的情况下已被互联网产业彻底“改造”，形成了互联网产业借传播渠道优势主导版权产业的局面。两大产业迥异的商业模式和利益诉求，也对我国著作权立法提出了新要求④。然而，我国著作权法在早期存在对国际一般规则的大量借鉴，如今的本土创新，需要在继受法本体上纳入中国特色的新内容，如何协调新老制度，还需要进一步的理论探索和实践积累。

针对我国著作权法修订和适用中的疑难，首先应该从立法史的角度回溯我国著作权法在继受之初即已存在的不足，探寻现今著作权法中国问题出现的历史原因；其次应该梳理我国当今版权产业制度需求中的矛盾争议，通过比较制度基础和产业需求之间的差异来定位中国著作权法制度创新进程中的法价值预设；最后则以重新设定和校准的著作权法价值基础为基点，围绕私法的基本原理解决我国著作权法制度设计中因历史前见和继受错误而出现的问题。

二、著作权法继受中的原理与表达

著作权法律继受的历史意义，很大程度上是借助外来规则来改革本土传统。我国著作权法是在20世纪70年代末改革开放政策驱动下进入立法规划的，进行著作权立法为了达到当时发达国家的要求，我国不得已只能在既无产业基础也无制度积累的情况下仓促借鉴《伯尔尼公约》等相关国际公约。因此，这时的著作权法同时还肩负着借助外来制度纠正本国公众作品使用习惯的任务。在此前提下，著作权法律继受的最大问题，在于被继受的对象乃是以不情愿的方式和片面实用主义的态度完成继受的，这一过程不但缺少历史法学派所看重的民族精神基础，也无法获得比较法上系统研究的时间。因为在缺乏本土产业基础和需求的历史阶段，著作权立法主要是为了满足当时国家发展战略的需要，即使存在质疑也需要让位于开放和入世这两个先后出现的国家基本战略目标⑤。由于改革开放和入世都有不容拖延的时间表，迫于时间的紧迫性，著作权立法也就只能采取制度继受为主的策略，难以及时兼顾制度背后的体系要求和理论积淀。但在本土版权产业发展壮大且特色凸显的今天，在产业主体急需明晰的法律体系和科学的解释规则来应对具体问题的

① 从“被动性调整”到“主动性安排”是各方对我国著作权法第三次修改背景的共识。吴汉东.《著作权法》第三次修改的背景、体例和重点［J］. 法商研究，2012（4）；刘春田.《著作权法》第三次修改是国情巨变的要求［J］. 知识产权，2012（5）.

② 2017年8月28日，全国人大常委会副委员长王晨在第十二届全国人民代表大会常务委员会第二十九次会议上做了全国人民代表大会常务委员会执法检查组关于检查《中华人民共和国著作权法》实施情况的报告，其中即明确提出“积极推进著作权法修改工作，尽快形成较为完善的法律草案提请全国人大常委会审议”。

③ 虽然当时改革开放的基本国策需要我国尽快加入《伯尔尼公约》和《世界版权公约》等知识产权相关国际公约，达到国际社会知识产权保护的最低标准，但《著作权法》其实是新中国三部知识产权法中最晚出台的，起草历时11年，在全国人大常委会三次讨论才得以于1990年通过。相比之下，《专利法》和《商标法》从起草到颁布则顺利得多。当时的历史情况介绍参见郑成思《中国知识产权法：特点、优点与缺点》，载沈仁干主编的《郑成思版权文集》（第2卷），中国人民大学出版社2008年版第401页。

④ 熊琦. 互联网产业驱动下的著作权规则变革［J］. 中国法学，2013（6）.

⑤ 沈仁干. 改革开放中的著作权立法［J］. 中国出版，2008（10）.

时候，著作权法缺乏稳定价值基础和自洽制度体系的缺陷就显露无遗。

首先，从继受法层面看，我国著作权法主要以《伯尔尼公约》为制度继受和解释蓝本，造成相关条款在引入后缺乏稳定的法价值基础和解释学支持。在脱离价值基础的情况下照搬法律文本，肯定无法实现对被继受制度的准确适用。制度继受成功的关键，一方面在于对被继受文本价值基础和解释规则的全面理解，另一方面在于对各自适用环境和社会背景的全面深入比较。

《伯尔尼公约》作为协调各国著作权保护传统和水平的国际公约，其文本乃是兼顾作者权和版权两大法系传统的产物，目的旨在为缔约各国的著作权立法提供一个可参照的最低保护标准。这导致公约条文仅能涉及原则性规定且表述繁复，更多内容允许各成员国自行设定或保留，缺乏直接适用的可能性①。相比而言，真正能够适用的法律，需要植根于本土社会和文化之中，回应特定社会中特定时间和地点所出现的特定需求②。以他国法为参照的法律继受，优势就在于继受对象生成于具体的本土社会环境和历史中，不但拥有明晰的立法价值基础和法律解释经验，有助于制度继受国全面理解继受对象的法律适用方法，而且对他国制度的历史研究能反映其真实的实施绩效，使得制度继受国在适用时能够在具体的案例分析上有来自比较法的鲜活经验可供借鉴。

我国在改革开放之初由于急需建立包括著作权法在内的知识产权法律体系，并规划在短期内加入相关国际公约，著作权法中的诸多概念和制度直接选择了借鉴《伯尔尼公约》和《世界版权公约》③。在当时缺乏版权产业环境和社会认知基础的情况下，私权意义上的著作权法本来就没有适用的空间，因而暂时不需要融通立法价值和把握解释规则，也避免了在当时语境下以某一国著作权法为继受对象可能导致的“姓资姓社”争议，只需统一以“国际惯例”作为正当性基础来取得支持即可。换言之，我国第一部著作权法更多的是一部“宣言书”，而尚未成为合理规范社会版权产业和市场的裁判规则，所以直接以缺乏适用基础的《伯尔尼公约》为继受对象在当时并无不妥。然而，与继受特定域外国家的著作权法相比，将公约作为继受对象的最大缺陷在于，缺乏可供借鉴的通过适用法律获得的解释经验，著作权法难以通过具体的案例比较来矫正立法者和裁判者理解继受法时的偏差。随着我国文化产品在国内和国际市场上的经济价值迅速提升，产业主体开始在法律适用层面要求稳定精确的著作权法律解释，在立法层面要求回应本土版权产业争议甚至加入各自利益考量。自此第一部著作权法在继受对象选择上的缺陷就逐步显现，在之后的修订过程中，这一问题也未能完全得到解决。

其次，从本土法层面看，我国相关主管部门在著作权认知和管理上的路径依赖，与著作权法的基本立法价值观存在差异，导致著作权法在本土化进程中难以实现制度体系上的自洽。著作权法之所以在三部主要知识产权法律中是最晚出台的，原因之一即在于主管部门尚未扭转对传统管理路径的依赖。长期以来，我国涉及作品传播的相关法律关系更多发生在事业单位之间，这导致行政主管部门更多采取行政管理的方式来调整著作权人与使用者之间的法律争议。

在权利配置上，我国著作权多头管理的体制导致政府干预过多。在现今主管著作权工作的国家版权局设立之前，著作权立法主要由当时的文化部和广播电视部主导。其中涉及书籍保护的立法归属文化部出版局，录音录像制品保护的立法归属广播电视部④。在此分头管理体制下，作品许可和转让并没有被视作一种市场行为，在立法上普遍表现为对稿酬标准的严格控制和对作品使用性质的非商业化认定⑤。在私权体系下本由权利人和使用者协商认定的版税，被法律设定了最高标准⑥。由于报社和广播组织在当时不被认为是营利性法人，所以报刊

① Silke von Lewinski. International Copyright Law and Policy [M]. Oxford: Oxford University Press, 2008: 100-101.

② 梅利曼. 大陆法系：第2版 [M]. 顾培东，禄正平，译. 北京：法律出版社，2004: 10.

③ 郑成思. 版权法与国际法 [J]. 著作权，1992 (4).

④ 著作权法出台以前，文化部出版局先后颁布了《关于书籍稿酬的暂行规定》(1980)、《书籍稿酬试行规定》(1984)、《美术出版物稿酬标准》(1984) 以及《图书、期刊版权保护试行条例》(1984) 等；当时的广播电视部则颁布了《录音录像制品管理暂行规定》(1982) 和《录音录像出版物版权保护暂行条例》(1986)。

⑤ 相关文件对版税制的批评，可参见文化部、中国作家协会《关于废除版税制、彻底改革稿酬制度的请示报告》，载周林、李明山主编的《中国版权史研究文献》，中国方正出版社1999年版第321页。

⑥ 例如《书籍稿酬试行规定》(1984) 分别针对著作稿、翻译稿、古籍稿和词书稿设定了详尽的基本稿酬和印数稿酬标准，这种做法甚至在2009年《广播电台电视台播放录音制品支付报酬暂行办法》中被继续沿用，该暂行办法中有大量条文被用来限定版税标准的范围，只是条文属性由强制性条款变为任意性条款，当事人可以通过约定加以排除，但指导定价的功能仍然明显。

转载和广播组织播放作品的行为可以既不经过许可也不支付报酬①。这种强制性规范使得著作权变动的对价无法体现交易双方的真实意思，作品供求关系不能以版税的方式体现，从而难以真正激励作者根据市场需求进行创作。允许自由使用的例外范围过大，也导致作品的后续衍生产品开发缺乏经济诱因。

在纠纷解决机制上，事业单位对作品的控制决定了涉及作品传播的纠纷基本通过上级主管部门协调解决。比如在著作权法颁布之前，广播电视领域未经许可播放他人作品的纠纷一般发生在广播组织之间，而且广播组织之间处理纠纷的方式，都是选择由上级主管部门出面协调②。对于主管机关而言，针对被管理的下级部门在作品传播中产生的纠纷，不会如司法机关那样完全从实践中的权利界定和保护出发，或者围绕法律关系来考虑责任和损害赔偿的认定，而是加入了诸如地区利益分配、行业利益保护等法律之外的考量因素。很多调整行为由于并未落实在法规或文件中，所以显得缺乏稳定性和可预期性，这使当事人在作品创作和传播中无法依赖事前规则来判定行为的后果。

三、著作权法本土化中的理论基础调适

虽然《伯尔尼公约》和《世界版权公约》缺少直接适用的法解释学经验积累，但作为现代著作权制度的“国际版本”，其以私权为基础的体系架构仍具有不可替代的意义。著作权作为私权，其核心价值当然是私人自治，著作权法的制度设计亦当然围绕私人自治的实现来安排。在前两次《著作权法》修改中，无论是权利类型的扩张，还是出版管制条款的修改，都体现了“使市场在资源配置中起决定性作用”这一中央文件精神在著作权领域的落实③。然而，我国著作权法虽然已基本体现以私权为核心的立法价值，但适用时却仍延续著作权法颁布以前的管制理念，倾向于以法律或政策直接介入著作权市场的方式来回应争议，这种继受价值与本土价值之间的理念冲突，造成各方对著作权法中国问题的认定截然相反，也导致《著作权法》第三次修改相关条文和相关司法审判结果之间的争议难以调和。

（一）继受著作权立法价值设定及其渊源

作为继受法的著作权法，其本源既是以私人自治为价值内核的特别私法，也是产业主体在不同传播技术条件下不断博弈和妥协的产物。私人自治在著作权法史上的积极作用，主要表现在两个方面：

第一，作为著作权制度现代化的标志，著作权在从特权到私权的转换过程中通过“产权化”所注入的私人自治基因，旨在对抗国家强制力对私人行为的干预和控制，使得版权产业主体首次成为行使和运用著作财产权的核心，最终形成了今天经济发展与文化繁荣的双赢局面④。

著作权从特权到私权的产权化进程，让基于作品享有的权利首次由创作者和传播者掌控，作品创作和传播行为也开始积极回应市场供求关系的变化，版权产业自此成为繁荣文化的主要推手⑤。被视为世界首部现代著作权法的《安妮法令》（Statute of Anne，1710），其全称为《为鼓励知识创作而授予作者及购买者就其已印刷成册的图书在一定时期内之权利的法》（An Act for the Encouragement of Learning，by Vesting the Copies of Printed Books in the Authors or Purchasers of Such Copies，During the Times Therein Mentioned），其保护对象除创作作品的“作者”之外，还有继受取得著作权的“购买者”。这种制度安排的目的，一方面是向实际创作作品的主体赋权，使其能够独立于贵族或其他资助者的控制，从而实现面向公众创作；另一方面则旨在允许著作权人自由处分权利，掌握印刷技术和设备的出版者得以取得作品著作权，并在当时的传播技术条件下发挥作品的最大效用。著作权私权化在客观上开启了著作权人自由处分作品的先例，保证了著作权的得丧变更完全由著作权人自行决定。自此以后，作品就不再是特定阶层或少数权贵的定制物，而成为被大众消费的商品，著作权市场正是在私权

① 参见《图书、期刊版权保护试行条例》（1984）第十六条第二款，1990 年的著作权法仍然延续了这一权利安排，直到我国为加入世贸组织第一次修改《著作权法》时才被调整为法定许可。

② 郑成思. 论我国的全面版权立法 [J]. 法学研究，1986（6）.

③ “使市场在资源配置中起决定性作用”是在党的十八届三中全会审议通过的《中共中央关于全面深化改革若干重大问题的决定》中提出的重大理论观点，该观点延续和深化了从 1978 年十一届三中全会到 2013 年十八届三中全会对市场和政府关系的界定，并在 2017 年十九大报告中得到再次确认，已经成为我国包括著作权法在内的私法领域立法、司法和执法的最高纲领。

④ 根据 Goldstein 教授的经典表述，著作权法的意义在于让作者得以摆脱贵族赞助的控制，而使作品达致更为广泛的受众。（Paul Goldstein. Copyright，Law & Contemp. Probs.（1992），p. 79.）而私人自治有助于大规模著作权市场形成的观点可参见 Robert P. Merges 的“Autonomy and Independence：The Normative Face of Transaction Costs”，53 Ariz. L. Rev. 145，（2011），p. 147。

⑤ 产权化与著作权法关系的表述在美国学者的研究中长期存在，代表性文献可参见 Shubha Gosh 的“Deprivatizing Copyright”，54 Case W. Res. L. Rev. 387，（2003），pp. 387-390。

提供的经济诱因下迅速繁荣，版权产业分工也随之逐步完善和专业化，最终通过经济激励的方式实现了文化和知识的最大化传播①。

第二，现代著作权法中的私人自治，旨在使产业主体得以在新兴传播技术和商业模式下及时根据特定市场情势完成有效率的权利配置②。

在私权属性已成为著作权最为基本的特征被确认后，私人自治并未结束其历史使命，其仍在著作权法应对历次传播技术变革时发挥积极作用。回顾著作权制度变革的历史可以发现，著作权类型和范畴会随着传播技术的发展和新兴市场的出现而变化。对于大部分作为作者的初始著作权人而言，其创作动机并非自用，而是通过向使用者许可或转让作品来获得收益。因此如何在权利类型增加的情况下保障许可效率不受影响，始终是著作权制度变革中的难点问题。排他性著作财产权作为绝对权，其意义在于借助绝对权的排他性为作品在新的使用方式上划定了一个明晰的边界，最大程度实现作品成本和收益的内部化，著作权人能够在此基础上基于成本收益的事前判断来合理决定如何使用作品③。相比之下，以法定许可为代表的报酬请求权设定则是以弱化权利排他性的方式降低交易成本，直接以立法预设交易条件来提高许可效率。法定许可将作品许可的版税标准改由法律或国家主管机关设定，使符合法定条件的使用者皆可跳过协商环节直接使用作品，著作权人不再有自主决定作品使用条件的权利④。为保证私人自治在著作权法中的贯彻，法定许可在历史上从来都是作为排他性权利设定的补充⑤。美国国会自2005年至今所提出的多项著作权修法草案中，调整排他性权利范畴和回归由私人决定的授权许可机制始终是修法重点。美国版权部门负责人一再重申，保障著作权人控制自己作品并从中获利乃是修法的基本出发点⑥。

（二）本土著作权立法价值设定及其演变

本土著作权法在产生之初虽然已建立起了以私权为基础的法律框架，但我国既有的管制法传统显然不会随着继受相关国际公约自行消失，而是通过赋予继受概念以新的含义和替换继受制度的价值内核来间接延续原有的管制理念。

管制理念在我国私法体系中的确立，是特定历史条件下中国整个私法理念的体现。1986年民法通则中的诸多条款，就曾明显体现出国家介入私人生活的政府干预色彩。同理，在著作权立法价值中注入过多管制理念，是当时我国从计划经济向市场经济转型初期整个私法体系立法价值取向的缩影，同时也有源于著作权领域的特殊之处。然而，在民法已随市场经济发展而逐步落实私人自治的同时，著作权法却没有同步调整。我国著作权法的起草者亦承认该法乃是计划经济下的产物，立法上倾向于维护“国营文化事业单位”的利益⑦。集中体现在版税标准由著作权主管机关决定，部分事业单位使用作品可以不经许可不付报酬⑧。即使经过2001年唯一的一次大规模修法，上述立法理念也仍未得到调整。随着版权产业的不断发展，既有著作权法这种表里不一的状况，不但在司法实践中引发了诸多争议，也导致修法进程陷入僵局。具体来看，管制理念在著作权领域的延续，主要表现于四个方面。

第一，权利归属上的介入。该领域的管制主要体现在电影作品二次获酬权和职务作品立法上。我国电影作品与职务作品著作权归属上允许将创作者以外的投资人视为作者，是借鉴版权法体系实用主义立法的结果。电影作品在创作过程中和表现形态上包含了音乐、文字等多种作品类型，著作权法直

① Robert P. Merges. Justifying Intellectual Property [M]. Cambridge：Harvard University Press，2011：199-200.

② 私人自治在著作权法中的表现方式，是以创作者享有初始著作权为权利配置原则的制度安排。这种安排使得权利主体得以根据传播技术和商业模式的变化来随时通过许可机制调整权利配置，以实现作品效用的最大化。类似观点可参见 Robert P. Merges 的“To Waive and Waive Not：Property and Flexibility in the Digital Era”，34 Colum. J. L. & Arts 113（2011），p. 118。

③ Henry E. Smith. Institutions and Indirectness in Intellectual Property. 157 U. Pa. L. Rev. 2083（2009），p. 2092.

④ Register of Copyrights，Copyright Law Revision：Report of the Register of Copyrights on the General Revisions of U. S. Copyright Law. 87th Cong.，1st Sess.（1961），p. 33.

⑤ 主张国家介入的代表性学术观点可参见 William Patry 的 *How to Fix Copyright*，Oxford：Oxford University Press，2012：177-178；180。主张限缩和取消法定许可的修法论证可参见 U. S. Copyright Office，Satellite Television and Localism Act，§ 302 Report，2011。

⑥ Maria A. Pallante. The Next Great Copyright Act. 36 Colum. J. L. & Arts 315（2013），p. 323. 作者系美国版权事务办公室负责人，美国版权法在21世纪修订的主要发起者和参与者。

⑦ 沈仁干. 论我国著作权法的修改 [J]. 知识产权，2001（6）. 作者当时系国家版权局副局长，曾长期参与著作权法起草和修订工作。

⑧ 例如《著作权法》（1991）第四十三条曾规定广播电台、电视台非营业性播放已经出版的录音制品，可以不经著作权人、表演者、录音制作者许可，不向其支付报酬。

接将电影作品的著作权集中赋予制片者，电影作品中包含的独立作品由各自著作权人单独行使，且允许电影作品中包含的独立作品著作权人与制片人通过合同议定报酬，兼顾了投资人和创作者对各自作品的处分权。将投资人与创作者之间的法律关系以合同确定，不但避免了因权利分散导致的高额交易成本，而且保障了私人自治原则的充分发挥。但在《著作权法》第三次修订草案送审稿中，立法者曾增设一项法定"分享收益的权利"[①]，意味着无论有无合同约定，"导演、编剧以及专门为视听作品创作的音乐作品的作者等"，甚至相关权中的表演者皆有权向制片者请求支付报酬，由此引发了我国著作权法是否增设二次获酬权的广泛讨论。

以法定权利代替约定安排，本意是保障视听作品市场中部分弱势创作者从视听作品传播中获取收益的权利，却因强制介入权利配置引发了新问题[②]。从主体上看，究竟哪些主体有权二次获酬，修订送审稿并无明确规定，如此将出现所有参与电影作品摄制的主体皆能请求报酬的情况。从请求事由上看，二次获酬的二次究竟指哪个环节，条文并无准确界定。从付酬标准上看，法定二次获酬意味着无须合同约定，但合同除设立债权之外还有确定版税标准的功能，而鉴于市场情势的变化，法定收益请求权的版税标准不可能通过立法在事前确定，可能在后期落入主管机关职能范畴，司法上的争议也会因此而起。同理，在职务作品著作权归属的修法中，修订草案也将"法人或者其他组织可以给予作者奖励"改为"单位应当根据创作作品的数量和质量对职工予以相应的奖励"[③]。从"可以"变为"应当"，条款属性究竟是倡导性规范提升为强制性规范，还是倡导性规范的不同表述，未来在法律适用过程中必然产生争议。

第二，权利许可上的介入。此类管制主要体现在集体管理组织市场支配地位的强制安排上。从制度源起上观察，集体管理制度是著作权人为降低大规模许可交易成本所自发创制的，其本质乃权利人、集体管理组织和使用者三方合同规则[④]。只有当集体管理组织利用许可渠道及带来的市场支配力歧视权利人或使用者时，政府才以反垄断诉讼的方式事后介入[⑤]。相比之下，我国集体管理组织和制度的形成乃政府主导的产物，其中没有产业主体通过博弈推动的利益分配协调过程，这种产生机理使得我国集体管理制度的价值基础与继受对象正好相反，集体管理组织并非大规模许可机构，而更多的是协助主管部门的交易管制机关，不但其设立须主管机关审批后方能生效，而且集体管理组织之外的主体皆无权实施任何意义上的大规模许可[⑥]。在版税标准的确定上，我国亦存在一系列限定作品定价的法律规章[⑦]，成为阻碍当事人自由协商的"最高限价"。即使上述条例明确将上述指导性定价作为允许当事人排除的任意性条款，但无论协商结果高于或低于条例规定，任何一方都能以"协商不成"为借口恢复适用法定标准，事实上剥夺了权利人协商的可能性。

与此同时，为了解决现有集体管理组织"代表性不足"的问题，立法者在《著作权法》第三次修订过程中不是放松管制，允许私人创设新的大规模许可组织，而是加强管制，试图以延伸性集体管理破解使用者无法以合理成本获得海量作品授权的困境[⑧]。立法者将制度失灵原因归结为"我国权利人、使用者、社会公众著作权集体管理意识淡薄，著作权集体管理组织面对的社会外部环境较差"，因此其试图在修法中借助延伸性集体管理来增强集体管理组织的控制力，以解决"集体管理组织缺乏广泛代表性"的问题[⑨]。

第三，权利限制上的介入。该领域的管制主要体现为法定许可使用范围的举棋不定。追溯历史上的法定许可制度，可以发现其立法价值定位既非公共利益，亦非鼓励传播，而是调和新兴传播技术介

① 参见《著作权法（修订草案送审稿）》（2014）第十九、三十七条。

② 有观点认为，这种修改将导致享有法定报酬请求权的主体不承担风险却享受利益。徐炎. 著作权法第三次修改草案第二稿评析［J］. 知识产权，2013（7）.

③ 参见《著作权法》（2010）第十六条，《著作权法（修订草案送审稿）》（2014）第二十条。

④ 熊琦. 著作权集体管理制度本土价值重塑［J］. 法制与社会发展，2016（3）.

⑤ ASCAP v. MobiTV. Incorporation. 681 F. 3d 76，78（2d Cir. 2012），p. 79.

⑥ 我国《著作权集体管理条例》（2005）在集体管理组织的设立程序上要求采取行政许可主义，即集体管理组织须由版权局和民政局两个国家主管机关先后批准后方可设立，而且设立条件除条例已有的规定外，还有须经过上述机关的考察和认可。

⑦ 具体参见《使用文字作品支付报酬办法》（2014）、《使用音乐作品进行表演的著作权许可使用费标准》（2011）、《广播电台电视台播放录音制品支付报酬暂行办法》（2011）、《电影作品著作权集体管理使用费收取标准》（2010）。

⑧ 参见国家版权局《关于〈中华人民共和国著作权法〉（修改草案）的简要说明》（2012 年 10 月）。

⑨ 汤兆志. 中国著作权集体管理法律制度的理论与实践［J］. 中国出版，2014（3）.

入著作权产业后的新旧产业主体利益分配。因此立法并未基于鼓励公众获取的目的大幅简化许可程序，而是人为要求增加严格的申报和付费要件，以鼓励产业主体之间通过自由协商达成许可协议。鉴于制度功能的补充性和临时性，在发达国家，法定许可从未获得过广泛适用，甚至被视为著作权许可制度适应网络商业模式的阻碍而在网络环境下被限制适用①。虽然历史上每次出现因传播技术变革而导致在利益分配上僵持不下的情形时，法定许可都成为被优先考虑的立法政策，但其狭窄的适用范围和严格的适用条件，在某种程度上也成功塑造了发达国家在各个历史传播技术阶段都极为高效的版权产业。

在著作权市场出现争议的情况下，我国立法者更多选择法定许可，而非留足时间和空间由市场主体通过博弈形成②。最高人民法院曾在2001年的司法解释中把报刊转载摘编法定许可扩大到网络环境下③，但最终未能进入2006年的《信息网络传播权保护条例》，该司法解释随后也被废止。但在互联网内容聚合平台迅速兴起的情况下，网络海量授权的效率问题成为焦点，网络服务提供者再次呼吁增加网络转载摘编法定许可④。作为市场主体，网络服务提供者扩大法定许可适用范围的建议显然不是出于形成著作权市场竞争，而是试图借用法定许可特有的限制性定价和过于简化的程序安排来直接获取海量作品，因此问题出在我国法定许可制度本身的简略和低效使得市场主体觉得有机可乘，并非市场主体接受这种非自治性的制度选择。

第四，权利效力上的介入。该领域的管制主要体现在司法解释中对著作权排他性的不当限定，近年来集中体现于对信息网络传播权"提供行为"要件的认定上。随着移动互联网时代聚合平台商业模式的普及，"深层链接"或"加框链接"已成为实现信息网络传播的重要途径，然而不同区域和不同层级的法院在审理相关案件时，对"深层链接"是否构成信息网络传播权中"提供行为"的解释，在法律适用上已出现同案不同判的情况。

然而，信息网络传播权所具备的排他性，决定了将"服务器标准"视为唯一认定方法的司法解释片面地以侵害行为的技术手段限制了法律上的权利安排。信息网络传播权作为一项排他性私权，其排他效力需要在两个方面来实现，其一为权利人对"提供行为"的控制，其二为权利人对公众范围的控制。保障这种排他性，乃著作权人自主行使信息网络传播权的关键。反之，如果权利人提供作品的方式和渠道能够被任意替代，信息网络传播的排他性效力则无从实现，著作权人自由行使权利的安排亦无从说起。

综上，虽然表面上本土著作权法困境表现为权利人无法通过行使权利获得利益，或者说继受的制度无法在本土环境下实现其功能，但放在两种立法价值的语境下分析却发现，中国著作权立法问题的本质，事实上出自著作权法价值内涵和文本表达的不协调，即在"自治法"体系内增加了"管制法"内涵，著作权人行使权利和维护权利的方式由此遭遇种种限制，造成了著作权法在诸多领域难以实现其功能。

四、著作权法创新中的制度体系融通

自治法表达与管制法内核的矛盾，使得著作权法在我国版权产业勃兴的今天难以实现其应有功能，实质性修法亦因此无法真正展开。针对自治法和管制法的对立关系，并非简单选择回归自治或坚持管制，而是需要在分析著作权制度失灵原因的基础上，发掘真正阻碍著作权法在我国发挥作用的根源。同时，作为继受对象的发达国家，正在进行的著作权法改革也同样存在尖锐矛盾，面对互联网传播技术的颠覆式冲击，其著作权法也在本国遭遇从正当性基础到制度安排的全面质疑⑤。卸下历史包袱从而另起炉灶制定一部互联网时代著作权法的呼声也获得了越来越多的支持⑥。

我国虽然已基本完成社会主体法律体系的构建，但在日趋深入的全球化进程中，仍有必要在相当一段时期内继续学习发达国家的著作权理论和立法经

① 熊琦. 著作权法定许可制度溯源与移植反思［J］. 法学，2015（5）.

② 虽然"网络转载"法定许可未能入法，但法定许可一直是立法者更为倾向的著作权市场构建手段。王维. 著作权法进行第三次修订，补全信息网络法制短板［N］. 21世纪经济报道，2014-09-26（2）.

③ 参见最高人民法院《关于审理涉及计算机网络著作权纠纷案件适用法律若干问题的解释》（2000）第三条，该解释在《信息网络传播权保护条例》（2006）通过后即被替代。

④ 陶鑫良. 互联网及新媒体传播的著作权授权许可制度改革探讨［J］. 中国知识产权，2014（91）.

⑤ Jessica Litman. The Copyright Revision Act of 2026. 13 Marquette Intel. Prop. L. Rev. 250，2009，pp. 252-257.

⑥ 相关论述可参见美国版权办公室负责人在国会听证会上的发言。The Register's Call for Updates to U. S. Copyright Law，Statement of Maria A. Pallante，Register of Copyrights of the United States Subcommittee on Courts，Intellectual Property and the Internet Committee on the Judiciary，U. S. House of Representatives 113th Congress，1st Session (Mar. 20，2013).

验，但这种借鉴将不再是以往那种缺乏本土问题意识和现实目的指向的“综述式引介”，而是以我国著作权领域现阶段的国家需求、产业追求和社会诉求为导向，不再局限于相关概念或条文的具体表达，致力于在制度内涵和功能上寻找突破。如何掌握本土传统改造和本土特征保留的限度，是首先需要回应的问题。在此情况下，为避免不顾已有的成熟经验而追求理论特色的盲目本土化，以及不顾产业和社会现状差异的盲目制度嫁接，必须从理论基础和调整手段两个方面解决著作权法的自治法表达与管制法内涵的对立问题，为具体修法中的问题讨论提供基础。

（一）立论基础调整：主体自治能力反思

我国立法者和主管机关之所以提倡管制规则，根本原因在于：一方面认为我国著作权人“无维权意识”“无维权能力”，另一方面又将著作权人的维权行为视为“滥用司法资源”。前者是管制规则介入的合法性基础，后者则是排斥自治性立法的正当性理由[①]。根据立法者的逻辑，既然著作权人“无维权意识”“无维权能力”，那么为了保证著作权人的权利得以合法行使，以及获得行使权利所获收益，著作权法应该替代缺乏相关能力的主体实现权利的流转，也因此有了修法建议稿中二次获酬权、职务作品、追续权和延伸性集体管理等管制型制度设计。上述制度设计在强调立法介入权利配置之外，还体现出两个特点。一是权利配置上以实际创作者为优先。职务作品中的职工，视听作品中的导演和编剧等，在不同程度上针对著作权人享有法定的报酬请求权，或在没有约定的情况下优先于投资者独立享有著作权[②]。二是权利行使上以法定安排取代私人协商。追续权和延伸性集体管理制度分别对著作财产权的权利变动做了看似有利于原著作权人的安排，追续权旨在帮助美术、摄影作品的作者及其继承人在手稿原件转让后对该原件或者手稿所获得增值部分享有报酬请求权，延伸性集体管理则旨在让集体管理组织代表包括非会员在内的著作权人行使权利，以“被代表”的方式达到为权利人维权的目的，解决一般权利人无法控制权利行使的问题[③]。

然而，上述权利配置和权利行使上的管制规则立论基础，不但无法保护所谓处于弱势地位的主体，反而会破坏真实反映著作权市场供求关系的交易机制，造成各方收益皆处于扭曲状态。著作权人代表在评述上述修法时，显然没有接受立法者的“好意”，反而异口同声地反对管制，并形象地认为该修法方式将会把版权产业打回“统购统销的供销社时代”[④]。立法者将特定著作权主体预设为权利行使和保护上的弱者，并将主管机关预设为知晓著作权市场供求关系的全能者。但需要注意的是，与直接参与市场行为的著作权人相比，政府在权利变动的相关决策信息获取上也存在处于弱势的情形，这直接导致基于立法者预设所制定的管制规则产生了无效率的调整结果，反而因市场主体加入规避行为徒增交易成本，造成作品在交易过程中的价值减损。换言之，立法者无法真正获取和整理出正确反映著作权市场真实情况的信息，因为市场情势本身在不断变化，相关信息是以分散的状态存在于市场之中，任何主体皆无法将其完全集中或整合[⑤]。

从主体地位看，无论是参与视听作品创作的导演和编剧，还是直接参与职务作品创作的职工，其在真实著作权市场中的主体地位并非整体如立法者所预设的那样低下。有很多创作者基于其创作质量和口碑，在与视听作品和职务作品的投资者缔约中具有相当优势，并能通过合同约定获得比上述法定安排更好的收益。相比之下，如果按照实际创作者为弱者的立论思维，在职务作品中优先将著作权归属于职工，在视听作品中强制赋予参与创作的诸多主体享有二次获酬权，必然造成作品在后续使用过程中因权利归属高度分散而造成价值减损。上述作品的创作往往需要多人参与，其中哪些是真正的创作者，哪些仅为创作行为的辅助人，实践中本就难以区分和证明，因而在请求权主体范围的认定上就会出现分歧。即使请求权主体得以确定，二次获酬权也并不能够保护真正的弱势创作者。在参与创作之初的缔约过程中，制片者将可能以实际创作者还有二次获酬的机会为由降低首次付酬标准，而二次

① “无维权意识”“无维权能力”的表述来自国家版权局《关于〈中华人民共和国著作权法〉（修订草案送审稿）的说明》（2014 年 6 月）。

② 参见《著作权法（修订草案送审稿）》（2014）第十九、二十条。

③ 胡建辉. 著作权不仅仅是私权：国家版权局法制司司长王自强就著作权法修改草案热点答记者问 [N]. 法制日报，2012-05-03（6）.

④ 施建. 著作权法“大修”争议：被代表的私权 [N]. 21 世纪经济报道，2012-04-06（20）.

⑤ 早有学者明确指出，在我们过度关注的市场失灵之外，政府同样存在管制失灵（regulatory failure）的问题，政府管制的运行成本和决策错误甚至更甚于市场调节手段的成本和错误。因此，无论是著作权法还是其他知识产权法，其功能应限于设定信息上的财产权，而不应过分介入权利的具体配置。Frank H. Easterbrook. Copyright and Contract. 42 Hous. L. Rev. 953，2005，p. 959.

获酬权又可能因为作品本身在市场中没有盈利而无法行使，结果导致创作者的实际收益反而因二次获酬权的存在而下降。由此可见，任何人其实都无法直接在著作权法中设定著作权主体的真实地位，应该回归主体平等的一般法理，让相关主体根据自身掌握的市场信息选择权利配置方式。对确实存在的缔约地位差异，合同法中显失公平等制度早有具体救济措施可供选择，劳动合同法也已从保护劳动者的角度提供了诸多合同内容上的限制，无须在著作权法中另行安排。

从缔约能力看，“无维权意识”和“无维权能力”与“滥用司法资源”的认识影响了著作权人自行行使权利的便利性。基于立法者的认知，著作权人普遍缺乏维权能力，导致“著作权人明明知道自己的作品被众多的市场主体经营性使用，自己又不清楚谁在具体使用，也控制不了他人使用自己的作品，而且不能从这些使用中获得正当的报酬”①。因此无论是既有法律对集体管理组织“全国性”和“唯一性”的安排，还是《著作权法》第三次修改送审稿中的延伸性集体管理，目的都是使著作权人得以在集体管理组织的帮助下行使权利并获取收益。上述立法的合理性，建立在著作权人始终愿意向多数使用者授权的基础上。但是，同时还应重视以下两个问题：第一，基于作品类型差异和商业模式需要，著作权人在特定情况下不希望作品大规模传播或使用，或者不希望通过集体管理组织来大规模传播，而试图通过专有许可从特定权利人那里获得更大收益，所以上述保障著作权得以有效行使的预设反而禁锢了权利人对传播渠道的自由选择。第二，鉴于集体管理组织如今缺乏广泛代表性且许可效率不高的实际情形，那些希望实现大规模许可的著作权人可能更愿意选择其他渠道，例如通过版权代理公司，或者直接通过网络以数字形式传播，但由于立法对主体自治能力的错误预设，前者被法院直接认定为非法集体管理，后者也因其事实上的市场支配地位引发了是否构成垄断的讨论。由此可见，著作权人在市场中的真实状态，并非一成不变地缺乏缔约能力，而是在很多情况下存在不愿意授权，或者不愿意以集体管理方式授权的意图。上述权利人的真实意思和拒绝许可的自由，无论是在立法上还是在司法上，显然都应该受到尊重和保护。

现行立法对主体地位和缔约能力的预设，主要建立在认为创作者和权利人能力缺位的基础上，忽略了市场环境下直接参与创作和传播行为的著作权人事实上比政府和立法者更能了解产业现状。在主体地位和缔约能力的具体判断和权利配置安排上，市场手段往往有着政府干预无法比拟的优势。只有将如何利用客体的决定权赋予那些掌握具体信息的当事人，才能发挥作品的最大效用。质言之，权利变动方式的私人创制，实质上是新激励机制的生成途径；允许私人通过合同主导权利配置，则是使依赖分散知识的经济行为能够符合市场规律的必要条件。事实上，立法者也理解私人自治的重要性，曾公开认为“只有当利益主体之间没有协商或协商不成情况下，才根据不同利益主体在创作或传播作品过程中所作的贡献做出合理的规定”②，但这一论断却没有追问著作权人在协商不成的情况下是否有不缔约的意图，而是想当然地按照促进权利变动发生的结果来代替权利人做出安排。从某种程度上看，拒绝缔约或不允许他人使用作品，本来就是排他性权利赋予权利人的竞争手段，只有司法严格尊重和保护权利人的这种意图时，权利才能真正以权利主体期待的方式实现③。

（二）法律适用调整：自治与管制的价值整合

立论基础的不稳定，意味着立法者无法预设著作权主体在社会或市场中的具体地位，因而既有的法律调整手段也应随之改变。管制法的内核既然无法解决著作权法本土化后的制度失灵问题，就有必要重新审视和设定自治法的立法价值基础，使立法表达与制度内涵相匹配。需要注意的是，回归自治法的应对路径并非如某些学者所担心的那样，将导致中国著作权法除了等待制度上与国际知识产权制度接轨之外就无他事可做④。相反，回归自治法既可以为本土著作权规则的形成创造条件，也是发掘真正符合中国特色著作权规则的合理途径。鉴于我国版权产业因历史和现实原因已经走上了不同于发达国家的道路，因此尤其需要基于自治法设定来构建符合本土产业特点的著作权规则。另外，如今发达国家以“后工业经济时代”著作权理论为代表的学说，是建立在私权保护充分、并已形成一批具备市场支配地位的版权产业主体之基础上的，旨在抑制上述主体因维护既得利益而

① 胡建辉. 著作权不仅仅是私权：国家版权局法制司司长王自强就著作权法修改草案热点答记者问［N］. 法制日报，2012-05-03（6）.

② 王自强. 著作权法第三次修订有关问题解读［J］. 中国国情国力，2015（10）.

③ 研究著作权作为财产权所具有的优势可参见 Richard A. Epstein 的“Liberty Versus Property? Cracks in the Foundations of Copyright Law”，42 San Diego L. Rev. 1，2005，p. 4.

④ 李琛. 论知识产权法的体系化［M］. 北京：北京大学出版社，2005：103.

阻碍新传播技术的普及和作品传播。从我国目前的保护水平和产业状况来看，引入上述学说来指导立法显然为时过早。

基于各国产业发展的历史经验，立法者和政府作为各领域产业发展方向的预测者和主导者，其行为都曾出现大量无效率的结果①。相比之下，产业主体则更能利用分散于市场的信息和知识来实现创新。回顾著作权制度变革历史也可以发现，每次面对传播技术的发展，新兴著作权市场中有效率的权利配置往往由著作权人自行实现。例如历史中的集体管理制度，就随市场情势变化经历了从早期的单一维权诉讼机构到大规模许可中介组织的蜕变。20世纪初期正值音乐产业商业模式首次发生重大变革的时期，音乐作品不再局限于在剧院中以戏剧表演的方式呈现，而是在餐厅和酒吧等诸多场所被广泛演奏，表演行为的经济价值由此凸显②。针对当时部分使用者拒绝支付版税的情况，著作权人首次以集体诉讼的方式应对极为分散的表演者，最终通过判例法认定了餐厅里演奏音乐作品的行为侵犯著作权③。在获得司法上的肯定后，集体管理组织随后根据大规模许可的需要在集体诉讼的基础上构建了权利许可机制，以致力于解决确权后面临的交易成本问题。进入网络时代以来，数字化作品许可的交易成本大幅降低，诸多手握大量作品的著作权人已有能力自行实施许可。美国主要的两家集体管理组织再次调整策略，允许著作权人自行许可涉及网络环境下使用作品的权利，使著作权人得以利用新技术优势自由设置更为丰富的许可类型④。而上述许可模式调整策略所依赖的信息，显然只可能由直接参与市场交易行为的主体及时获取，不但立法者无能力及时整合，法律自身的稳定性特点也要求其不得频繁根据市场情势变化来调整。由此可见，集体管理制度最初并非来自立法者的预先设计，而是版权产业主体私人创制的产物，其早期功能在于帮助权利人通过维权来保障营利，大规模许可的功能乃是在确权实现后才逐步具备的，体现出自治规则在保障集体管理制度及时回应市场变化方面的优势。

与此同时，对于著作权法难以类型化的主体法律关系，留待权利人自行决定权利配置，并在其他部门法的帮助下解决也是重要的调整手段。在二次获酬权存废的立法讨论中，支持入法的观点同样缺乏对著作权市场信息获取成本的考量，前期也并无对他国相关领域立法经验的深入研究。事实上，发达国家在视听作品创作者和表演者在后续作品使用的报酬请求权的设定上，极少直接设定法定二次获酬权，而是更多由相关主体借助行业协会和集体合同的方式设定⑤。即使是在肯定创作者有权获取报酬的国家，也只能在个案中认定哪些是享有请求权的主体，而无法在立法中事前规定⑥。上述立法经验说明，对视听作品这类主体众多且流程复杂的作品来说，各个主体在不同商业模式中的地位千差万别，因而难以在创作者身份的认定上一概而论。既然获酬主体的范围都无法确定，保护创作者利益、鼓励创作优秀作品等目的也就都无从谈起。相反，这种法定获酬权的存在，不但在作品创作阶段即埋下了利益分配的矛盾之因，而且极大地增加了作品后续使用和衍生开发的交易成本。在实践中，究竟是视听作品的首次摄制行为还是后续使用行为更能为实际创作者提供收益，是不可能在事前预期的。这种强制预设两类行为皆能获利，然后将类似劳动合同法条款的保障规则纳入著作权法的思路，其实是把主体之间的市场博弈行为看作“市场失序”或“市场乱象”⑦，并将再正常不过的讨价还价看成需要干预的市场失灵，使得排他性权利所赋予当事人的不缔约的自由被剥夺⑧。因此，在保护实际创作

① Randy T. Simmons. Pathological Politics：The Anatomy of Government Failure. Society，vol. 32，no. 6，(1995)，pp. 32-33；张维迎. 市场的逻辑［M］. 上海：上海人民出版社，2010：22-24.

② Bernard Korman，I. Fred Koenigsberg. Performing Rights in Music Performing Rights Societies. 33 J. Copyright Soc'y. U. S. A. 332 (1986)，p. 334.

③ Herbert v. Shanley Co.，242 U. S. 591 (1917)，pp. 594-595.

④ United States v. Broad. Music，Inc.，207 F. Supp. 3d 374 (S. D. N. Y. 2016).

⑤ 美国即通过行业协会之间的集体协议明确二次获酬问题，属于纯粹约定式的债权报酬请求权。宋海燕. 论中国版权法修改稿中涉及视听作品的二次获酬权［J］. 中国专利与商标，2012 (4).

⑥ M. 雷炳德. 著作权法［M］. 张恩民，译. 北京：法律出版社，2004：197.

⑦ 胡建辉. 著作权不仅仅是私权：国家版权局法制司司长王自强就著作权法修改草案热点答记者问［N］. 法制日报，2012-05-03 (6).

⑧ 从某种程度上说，无论是对于新增长还是新制度，创新本身即伴随着旧体制或模式的毁灭，这也是发展经济学中所鼓励的“创造性破坏”(creative destruction) 之精髓。R. Caballero & M. Hammour. On the Timing and Efficiency of Creative Destruction. 111 Quart. J. Econ. 805 (1996).

者的制度安排上，我们更需要做的不是介入权利配置，而是鼓励相关主体自行创制集体组织或类似中介机构来保护自己的利益。

相比较而言，互联网环境下商业模式的变革和更替更快，使得该领域内的管制规则尚未及时跟上，权利人与使用者之间得以形成了一些行之有效的"私立规则"。代表着互联网开放平台和社交网络的新兴商业模式，已不再将作品许可效率的最大化作为权利配置的唯一目标，反而更强调作品的传播效率，即通过免费提供和自由传播作品的方式提高用户数量和使用黏性，然后借助用户规模优势向第三方获取收益。所以网络服务提供者通过用户许可协议一方面要求作品提供者放弃部分法定著作财产权，以促进作品的自由传播，另一方面仍借助许可协议和技术措施禁止用户在本网络平台以外使用作品，以保障用户使用黏性。这种通过许可合同实现的权利再分配，打破了法定权利范畴及其配置方式，完全基于互联网商业模式来增设和放弃权利，既可避免因烦琐权利变动而降低许可效率，也可通过新兴商业模式获取经济收益。例如我国数字音乐服务平台纷纷选择从著作权人处获取专有许可的权利配置安排，就完全有别于通过集体管理获得的非专有许可。上述禁止跨平台获取作品的互联网"行业惯例"，是相关著作权主体在私法"法不禁止即自由"的原则下根据市场情势自由选择的结果。因此只要合同内容不违反法律强制性规定或公序良俗，就不存在干涉当事人自由缔约的合法性基础。如果强制性地将数字作品授权设定为非专有许可，不但会弱化各平台之间的竞争，更会因传播渠道的单一化而损害著作权人的利益。从著作权人的角度看，既然任何平台都有权取得授权，那么就无人为优质和稀缺的内容支付更高的版税，而高标准的使用费，恰恰是专有许可带给著作权人的积极收益。从网络服务提供者的角度看，非专有许可带来的内容同质化，将使网络服务提供者丧失发掘上游优质内容的动力，最终影响优秀作品传播。由此可见，如果通过扩大法定许可的范围来介入社交网络环境下的作品传播，上述权利配置和依赖私人权利配置所形成的商业模式皆无法存在了。

当然，正如任何权利皆有限制一般，私人自治也需要著作权法中的强制性规范来调节程序上和实质上的不公平，以及避免因私人过度自由而损害公共利益。除了上文所列借助民法和反垄断法的配合之外，管制法特色应同步在法定许可和孤儿作品两个问题上加以坚持和完善。法定许可中"以教育为目的使用"的主要适用对象为实施九年义务教育的学校，在"慕课"等网络远程教学模式迅速普及和常态化的今天，法定许可版税标准、网络环境下的作品使用范围等问题的解决，难以通过著作权人的主动参与实现。同理，社交网络时代作品数字化程度的显著提高，使得孤儿作品带来的潜在侵权风险问题已成为信息传播效率的阻碍力量，而著作权人身份不明意味着权利人在解决该问题上只能缺席。针对这两个问题，政府的高效介入就显得尤为重要。无论是法定许可版税移转机构的设计，还是孤儿作品申请和提存职能的实现，都必然对我国互联网时代文化传播和公众信息获取自由具有重要意义，著作权法中显然应强化上述政府管制的角色和功能，用政府公共服务弥补市场的不足。

五、结论

从被动继受到主动立法的转型，意味着我国市场经济早期确立的"缺什么补什么"和拿来主义的立法模式已经无法解决今天本土社会和产业面临的问题。这一方面是由于在制度继受历史上缺乏对所援引制度的价值基础进行深层论证，只是直接在制度设计层面将问题和解决方案进行了嫁接；另一方面则是延续本土管制法传统，并试图在自治法的表达上加入价值基础迥异的制度设计。因此，著作权制度失灵，并非制度本身失灵，而是制度价值设定上的失误。著作权法律继受必须首先理解继受对象的立法价值目标与制度设计逻辑，才能为本土化继受或创新提供评判标准。回归自治法传统，并非亦步亦趋地重复发达国家的老路，而是允许本土产业主体在明晰的著作权体系下自主形成最有利于自身发展的法律关系，打破著作权立法僵局。

（本文原发表于《中国社会科学》2018年第7期。发文时内容有删减。
作者单位：华中科技大学）

著作权集体管理组织：市场功能、角色安排与定价问题

向　波

通常认为，著作权集体管理制度及著作权集体管理组织具有降低交易成本、"润滑"著作权许可交易的市场功能。"著作权集体管理制度一直被视为解决大规模授权与降低授权成本并扩大著作权作品许

可范围的最佳规则。"[①] 不过，在既定的市场环境下，作为著作权许可交易市场的一方参与者，著作权集体管理组织的角色扮演与功能发挥要受到其他主体如著作权人、作品使用人、行政主管部门、法院以及消费者等行为策略的影响与制约。换句话说，并非著作权集体管理组织一成立，便自动实现了降低交易成本、"润滑"市场交易的功能。在关于著作权集体管理制度的研究中，学者们更多关注著作权集体管理组织的垄断性与竞争性、延伸性集体管理等法律问题。本文将结合我国立法现状与司法实践，从著作权许可交易的角度对著作权集体管理组织的相关法律问题展开分析，并对我国著作权集体管理制度的完善提出合理建议。

一、著作权集体管理组织的市场功能

基于作品的非物质性与可再现性，作品一旦以某种方式发表、传播，就意味着著作权人很难监督与控制已发表作品的后续传播与利用，或者说需要花费极高的成本才能获取传播与利用作品的相关信息。从著作权许可使用交易的进程来看，著作权人一般可对作品的首次传播与利用加以有效控制，即可与使用者就著作权的许可使用交易条件进行谈判协商。而在作品首次传播公开以后，往往由潜在使用者主动向著作权人发出交易的要约邀请或要约，著作权人则处于较为被动的谈判地位。对于需要经常使用大量作品的使用者而言，如果要与众多著作权人就每个作品的许可使用进行谈判，并一一确定每个作品的使用费率，基于高昂的搜寻成本、谈判成本与个别授权使用费，使用者宁愿冒着承担法律责任的风险而径行使用他人作品。换句话说，高昂的交易成本与授权费用在一定程度上首先堵塞了这部分使用者就作品许可使用问题向著作权人发起交易协商的渠道。对于那些市场需求较大且缺乏弹性的作品类型，如音乐作品、文字作品、电影作品等，其利用与传播行为的发生数量极为庞大，著作权人难以完整地获取此类信息，并从中得到合理报酬。即使著作权人花费高昂成本获取了传播与利用作品行为的信息，基于诉讼成本与收益的考量，著作权人也只能选择性地针对部分侵权行为主张权利。

就此而言，著作权集体管理制度的目的在于弥补著作权人在获取信息与维权能力方面的不足，同时降低使用者的交易成本、法律风险与许可费用，从而促进著作权许可交易的顺利进行。在著作权集体管理制度中，需要设立专门的著作权集体管理组织以专业化和规模化经营的方式来克服交易成本与使用费率高昂的问题。而著作权集体管理组织的出现也改变了原先直接发生于著作权人与使用者之间的许可交易模式。一方面，著作权集体管理组织首先需要获得著作权人的授权，才能依法以自己的名义从事著作权许可交易及相关的其他活动。著作权集体管理组织在取得授权的过程中，同样会产生搜寻成本、谈判成本等交易成本。对于个体分散、能力有限的著作权人来说，更重要的是存在一个专门的机构可以代替自己去搜集作品传播与利用的相关信息，同时由著作权集体管理组织以协商、诉讼或仲裁的方式收取作品的使用费，并在扣除适当的管理费后将收益合理分配给著作权人。从这个角度来说，著作权集体管理组织专业化和规模化的经营方式更侧重于降低著作权人一方的信息成本与维权成本。另一方面，在获得著作权人授权后，著作权集体管理组织就可以直接与使用者展开谈判，以自己的名义与使用者签订著作权许可使用合同，并以著作权许可使用费标准为基准收取许可使用费。对于作品使用者而言，著作权集体管理组织的存在极大地降低了原有许可交易模式中的搜寻成本、谈判成本等交易成本，著作权许可使用费标准的存在也使得使用者需要支付的许可费用降低到较为合理的水平，同时消除了使用者在经营过程中与作品使用相关的法律风险。

从上述内容来看，虽然可以在笼统的意义上认为著作权集体管理组织具有降低交易成本、"润滑"著作权许可交易的市场功能，但实际上著作权集体管理组织对于著作权人、使用者的价值并非完全一致。当然，在著作权集体管理情形下发生的许可交易同样存在着管理成本、信息成本、谈判成本等交易成本。尽管如此，相较于著作权人与使用人之间的直接交易模式，尤其是在涉及海量作品的使用时，以著作权集体管理组织为媒介的许可交易模式更有效率，即具有更低的交易成本，可以增加著作权许可交易的范围与数量，从而增进社会福利[②]。"著作权集体管理区别于其他制度的本质特征，是将集中许可建立在私人自治的基础上，一方面通过自由协

① 陈可欣，林秀芹. 英国引入延伸性集体管理的论争及其启示［J]. 东南学术，2016 (6).

② 有学者认为，著作权集体管理组织可以将基于使用者的搭便车使用作品而产生的负外部性予以内部化，著作权集体管理组织也是降低搜寻成本、谈判成本、执行成本与促进许可交易的最佳途径。Zijian Zhang. Rationale of Collective Management Organizations: An Economic Perspective. 10 Masaryk U. J. L. & Tech. 73 (2016).

商从权利人处获得许可，另一方面根据权利人代表的意思决定集中许可方式与费率。”[①] 总之，著作权集体管理制度及著作权集体管理组织存在的合法性正在于人们预期其所发挥的市场功能。如果在相关主体的博弈结构和各种现实条件的约束下，著作权集体管理制度及著作权集体管理组织没能发挥出预期的市场功能，则其存在的合法性难免受到质疑。

二、著作权集体管理组织的角色安排

关于著作权集体管理组织，《著作权法》（2010）第八条第二款规定强调了它的非营利性特征，而《著作权集体管理条例》（2013）第三条第一款则进一步明确了著作权集体管理组织的法律性质。从“非营利性”与“为权利人的利益依法设立”这样的立法表述来看，立法者实际上限定了著作权集体管理组织在著作权许可交易市场中的角色立场，即著作权集体管理组织所实施的相关行为与活动都要以著作权人（包括邻接权人）合法利益的实现为首要目标。我国《著作权法》（2010）与《著作权集体管理条例》（2013）也对著作权集体管理组织的行为方式与活动范围做出了明确的规定，由于著作权集体管理组织在获得著作权人的授权后要以自己的名义与作品使用者从事交易，它在事实上已经成为著作权许可交易的一方当事人，而非如消费者协会这样仅提供公益性社会服务的社会团体[②]。尽管我国现行《著作权法》为了缓解或者消除著作权集体管理组织与著作权人之间潜在的利益冲突，特别强调了著作权集体管理组织的非营利性特征——暂且不论非营利性对于著作权集体管理组织实施相关行为、活动的激励效果，但这也并非意味着赋予著作权集体管理组织公共管理的职能。

考察《著作权集体管理条例》（2013）的相关规定，其中对著作权集体管理组织的设立主体、设立条件、章程内容、审核登记等方面均做了明确规定。尤其是《著作权集体管理条例》（2013）第九条规定，明显体现了立法者对于著作权集体管理组织采用了行政许可主义的设立原则。在《著作权集体管理条例》（2013）第七条第二款有关设立条件的规定中，第二项要求设立的著作权集体管理组织不与已经依法登记的著作权集体管理组织的业务范围交叉、重合，第四十四条规定又禁止擅自设立著作权集体管理组织或者擅自从事著作权集体管理活动。由此，上述规则相互衔接形成闭合，从制度上排除了同一行业内著作权集体管理业务方面的潜在竞争，使得我国著作权集体管理组织事实上获得了一种制度上的垄断地位。但是，这种依托制度而获得的垄断地位显然与通过市场竞争而形成的自然垄断有所不同。更重要的是，著作权集体管理组织的运营资源——作品——必须来源于著作权人的私人授权[③]。也就是说，尽管我国著作权集体管理组织获得了制度上的垄断地位，但如果缺乏足够的作品作为运营资源，著作权集体管理组织仍然不能依托其制度上的垄断地位获得交易市场上的垄断地位。而想要获得某一行业大多数著作权人的私人授权从而拥有市场垄断地位，著作权集体管理组织仍然要与著作权人进行协商以获得授权。不过，《著作权集体管理条例》（2013）第二十条的规定却突显了著作权人与著作权集体管理组织之间的潜在利益冲突，在一定程度上挤压了著作权人与著作权集体管理组织之间的谈判空间，实际上不利于授权行为的发生。当然，立法者之所以做出如此规定，其目的是排除来自著作权人一方的市场竞争，进一步维护我国著作权集体管理组织的制度垄断地位，以便于作品的广泛使用。当“立法者更多地从促进利用的角度出发，强调使作品以更便捷的方式为更多主体所获取”，“过于注重减少导致交易成本的协商环节，主张以法定条件取代协商中的私人自治”，著作权集体管理制度便会丧失其制度优势与合法基础[④]。所以，我国现行著作权集体管理制度的上述规则之间并没有融洽衔接，这也在一定程度上造成了我国著作权集体管理组织实际运行中的困境。

在我国，著作权人基于制度环境与自利动机不能充分信任著作权集体管理组织，著作权集体管理组织往往只能获得部分著作权人的授权，只能就较少比例的作品展开著作权集中许可交易业务及其他活动。同时，部分著作权人选择自主行使权利，或者交由其他商业机构代为行使权利，这些现象的出现都在一定程度上侵蚀了著作权集体管理组织的市场基础。虽然著作权集体管理组织在著作权许可交易市场中拥有制度上的垄断地位，实践中行政机关或法院也会阻止所谓非法著作权集体管理业务的开

---

① 熊琦. 论著作权集体管理中的私人自治：兼评我国集体管理制度立法的谬误［J］. 法律科学（西北政法大学学报），2013（1）.

② 有学者认为，只有正确地将著作权集体管理组织定位为市场交易主体而不是行政管理主体，才能够更好地对其性质和运作做出符合市场经济发展的规制。卢海君. 论市场导向的著作权集体管理［J］. 电子知识产权，2007（3）.

③ 关于著作权人与著作权集体管理组织的法律关系，学者多倾向于将其理解为信托关系。

④ 同①.

展，但基于著作权人的缺乏信任与自利动机，我国著作权集体管理组织仍然无法获得充分的私人授权与作品资源。从近几年公布的著作权法修订草案相关内容来看，我国准备在著作权集体管理制度中引入延伸性集体管理规则①。按照《关于〈中华人民共和国著作权法〉（修改草案）的简要说明》中的意见，著作权延伸性集体管理主要解决使用者使用作品的困境。不过，除了学者们强调的多项积极功能以外②，延伸性集体管理规则的引入显然可以极大缓解我国著作权集体管理组织面临的私人授权和作品资源问题，从而实现制度垄断与市场垄断的双重优势。延伸性集体管理规则的引入激起了部分著作权人的强烈反对，以至于起草机关部分修订了修改草案中的相关内容。从《著作权法（修订草案送审稿）》的相关规定来看，一方面在一定程度上限定了延伸性集体管理的适用范围，另一方面也允许著作权人通过书面声明排除集体管理。在我国现行著作权集体管理制度框架下，笔者赞成限制性地引入延伸性集体管理。同时认为，立法者需要关注著作权集体管理组织通过延伸性集体管理获得的双重优势——制度垄断与市场垄断——对于相关主体之间的博弈状态和博弈结果的潜在影响，在立法上进一步完善著作权集体管理制度，以平衡相关主体之间的利益态势③。

三、著作权集体管理许可标准：制定程序与法律性质

著作权集体管理组织在与使用者就著作权的许可交易展开谈判时，核心是要解决著作权的许可交易费用即许可交易的价格问题。如果著作权集体管理组织仍然要通过一一协商的方式来确定许可交易的价格问题，其谈判成本十分高昂。在实践中，著作权集体管理组织往往会首先提出著作权集体管理的许可标准，主要内容即是确定许可交易价格的系列条款。著作权集体管理组织依据许可标准与使用者展开协商，无疑会极大地降低谈判成本。由于著作权集体管理许可标准确定的许可费用同时关涉著作权人与使用者双方的重大利益，在著作权集体管理许可标准制订程序中需要著作权人、使用者的深度参与，或者在制度上提供相关主体就许可标准引发争议的解决机制④。如在 2014 年 2 月通过的《欧盟关于版权及相关权利的集体管理与在内部市场多国领土在线使用音乐作品授权的指令》中，强调著作权集体管理组织与使用者需要在一个诚信原则和客观标准下通过一个费率进行协商，这个费率要反映权利和服务的经济交易价值⑤。在美国，集体管理组织所遵守的规则，皆来自与司法部在一系列反垄断诉讼后达成的和解协议。其中要求集体管理组织提供的版税标准和分配方式必须公平合理，如果使用者对此存在异议，将交由法院裁决版税标准⑥。而依据我国台湾地区于 2010 年新修订的“著作权集体管理团体条例”，在订立使用报酬率时，都是以集体管理组织与利用人协议订立为原则，必要时才由著作权主管机关介入。利用人对于著作权集体管理团体订立的使用报酬率有异议时，允许利用人提出异议，申请著作权主管机关介入审议⑦。

我国《著作权集体管理条例》(2013) 第十三条规定，著作权集体管理组织应当根据使用作品的时间、方式和地域范围以及权利的种类等因素制定使用费收取标准。而依据《著作权集体管理条例》(2013) 第四十六条规定，著作权集体管理组织应

---

① 关于我国是否引入著作权延伸性集体管理的问题，学者们观点不一。有学者认为延伸性集体管理适合我国国情，但需谨慎或有选择性地引入。陈可欣，林秀芹．英国引入延伸性集体管理的论争及其启示 [J]．东南学术，2016 (6)．当然，也有学者持保留态度。卢海君，洪毓吟．著作权延伸性集体管理制度的质疑 [J]．知识产权，2013 (2)．

② 有学者指出，基于应对作品海量使用需求、管理非会员作品的实践需要、降低交易成本，我国有必要引入著作权延伸性集体管理制度。孙新强，姜荣．著作权延伸性集体管理制度的中国化构建：以比较法为视角 [J]．法学杂志，2018 (2)．

③ 有学者提出，关于著作权延伸性集体管理，应保证著作权集体管理组织在特定领域的代表性和运行成熟良好，明确著作权集体管理组织延伸管理的管理范围及权能限制范围，完善使用费的协商机制和司法最终裁决权机制，明确规定著作权集体管理组织实施延伸管理的义务，完善对作品交易情况的监督机制，防止集体管理组织滥用市场优势。李玉香．延伸性著作权集体管理研究：写在我国《著作权法》第三次修订之际 [J]．法学杂志，2013 (3)．

④ 有学者归纳了解决著作权集体管理许可标准争议的三种模式，即由普通民事法庭解决争议、由专门设立的特殊法庭或仲裁机构处理争议、由行政主管机关裁定使用费标准。曹世华．著作权集体管理组织版权使用费标准争议解决机制探讨 [J]．电子知识产权，2009 (1)．

⑤ 关于《欧盟关于版权及相关权利的集体管理与在内部市场多国领土在线使用音乐作品授权的指令》的详细评介，可参见 Silke von Lewinski 的 “EU Challenges and Solutions in the Field of Collective Management of Copyright and Related Rights”, 1 Soc. Persp. *J. Legal Theory & Prac*，104 (2014)。也可参见赵师权《文化产业发展下欧盟著作权集体管理制度的一体化》，载《西安电子科技大学学报（社会科学版）》，2015 年第 2 期。

⑥ 熊琦．著作权集体管理中的集中许可强制规则 [J]．比较法研究，2016 (4)．

⑦ 倪静．我国著作权集体管理组织许可使用费决定机制检讨与改革 [J]．河南财经政法大学学报，2012 (2)．

当将其章程、使用费收取标准、使用费转付办法等材料报国务院著作权管理部门审核。从实践状况来看，国务院著作权管理部门在收到相关材料后，会通过官方网站、召开座谈会等方式征求社会公众、著作权人、使用者的意见，定稿后即向社会公告，并由著作权集体管理组织予以施行。关于著作权人、使用者参与著作权集体管理许可标准制订程序的问题，我国现行《著作权法》《著作权集体管理条例》没有做出规定，同时也没有就实施中的许可标准争议的解决机制做出规定。这就意味着著作权人、使用者就著作权集体管理许可标准的意见表达没有得到制度上的支持，而最终形成的著作权集体管理许可标准也很难充分反映著作权人、使用者等相关主体的意愿。

关于著作权集体管理许可标准的性质，我国《著作权法》《著作权集体管理条例》并未明确规定，笔者只能从有关规则加以推测。在著作权集体管理许可标准审核公告后，著作权集体管理组织即可依此展开相关业务活动。具体来说，一方面，依据《著作权集体管理条例》（2013）第二十五条规定，除法定许可情形外，集体管理组织应当根据国务院著作权管理部门公告的使用费收取标准，与使用者约定收取使用费的具体数额。而《著作权集体管理条例》（2013）第二十三条则规定，当使用者以合理的条件与著作权集体管理组织协商时，著作权集体管理组织不得拒绝订立许可使用合同。另一方面，依据《著作权集体管理条例》（2013）第三十四条、第三十九条规定，当著作权集体管理组织未根据公告的使用费收取标准约定收取使用费的具体数额时，使用者可向国务院著作权管理部门检举，由国务院著作权管理部门责令限期改正。总体说来，上述规则既要求集体管理组织必须依据许可标准约定收取许可使用费的具体数额，同时又允许使用者以合理的条件与著作权集体管理组织订立合同。这些规则的确切意义与操作尺度，实难把握。国家版权局 2010 年公告的《电影作品著作权集体管理使用费收取标准》明确说明：“本使用费收取标准为基准价。在实施过程中根据实际情况可作适当浮动”。结合著作权集体管理许可标准的制订程序及相关规则，笔者倾向于将著作权集体管理许可标准理解为：由著作权集体管理组织单方拟定、用以确定许可交易价格、非强制性的格式条款。显然，之所以得出这样的结论，主要理由是在我国现行著作权集体管理制度框架下，公告的许可标准更多反映了著作权集体管理组织一方的意思。如果著作权集体管理许可标准是在多方参与、充分讨论、相互妥协的基础上形成的，则它可以被视为行业规范或者许可交易合同的部分内容。

四、著作权集体管理许可标准的有效性：实施效果与定价模式

关于著作权集体管理许可标准的有效性问题，实际上是要考察许可标准在实践中被著作权人、使用者、法院等相关主体接受、认可、施行的程度与状态。在著作权集体管理许可标准审核公告后，著作权集体管理组织就要以此标准展开相关业务活动。而在我国现有制度框架下制订出的著作权集体管理许可标准，在实施中难免会受到著作权人、使用者不同程度上的拒绝与抵制。著作权人一方如果不认可依据著作权集体管理许可标准确定的交易价格、往往会一开始就选择自主行使权利，或者选择退出集体管理组织而自行主张权利。对于使用者而言，当其不认可许可标准时，双方就会陷入谈判僵局。在美国，“如果双方在法定期间内未能确定版税标准或无法与缔约者达成合意，都可以请求法院裁定版税标准。使用者在版税标准未定期间内，即可按法院裁定的临时价格标准支付版税并使用作品”①。在我国台湾地区，当著作权主管机关介入审议后，利用人可以就其利用情形按照原订或原约定的使用报酬率或者主管机关核定的数额，先支付暂付款，由此可以免除侵害著作权的民事及刑事责任，等待审议决定后，再依据审议结果调整使用报酬②。下文将结合我国司法实践，就著作权集体管理许可标准的有效性问题展开分析。

首先，著作权人独立主张权利时，往往会提出高于依据著作权集体管理许可标准计算的使用费用，在司法实践中，这样的主张往往也会得到法院的支持。如在杨川林诉成都好乐迪音乐娱乐有限责任公司等著作权侵权纠纷案中，一审、二审法院根据该案的具体情况，综合考虑被告的经营规模、作品的类型及数量、侵权行为的方式、影响范围、持续时间、地域和主观过错等因素，酌情确定被告的赔偿金额为 6 890 元，再加上原告为制止侵权行为而支付的各种合理费用共计 26 139 元，合计 3 万多元③。

① 熊琦. 著作权集体管理中的集中许可强制规则［J］. 比较法研究，2016（4）.

② 倪静. 我国著作权集体管理组织许可使用费决定机制检讨与改革［J］. 河南财经政法大学学报，2012（2）.

③ 四川省成都市中级人民法院（2006）成民初字第 664 号民事判决书；四川省高级人民法院（2007）川民终字第 286 号民事判决书。

就此案判决确定的赔偿费用来看，在扣除原告为制止侵权行为而支付的各种合理开支后，赔偿金额也远远超出了依据著作权集体管理许可标准可获得的许可费用（一首歌曲每年平均为 10 元人民币）。在这样的情形下，个体著作权人受到此类较高判决数额的激励，会独立于著作权集体管理组织而自行维权，直接通过诉讼向作品使用者收取更高的著作权使用费①。而在中国音像著作权集体管理协会诉上海水田商务信息咨询有限公司等著作权侵权纠纷案中，中国音像著作权集体管理协会未经授权而对该案著作权人的作品实施了集体管理，以明示的方式向嘉乐迪公司发放了非会员作品的使用许可，由此被著作权人诉至法院，最终法院判令音集协停止使用作品，并承担损害赔偿责任②。上述两个案例典型地反映了我国著作权人、著作权集体管理组织之间微妙的博弈状态，而类似案例的发生实际上会进一步侵蚀著作权集体管理组织的市场基础，当然也会影响到著作权集体管理许可标准的实施效果。

其次，由于没有深度参与作品著作权集体管理许可标准的制定过程，同时制度上也没有提供有关著作权集体管理许可费用标准争议的解决机制，作品使用者在实践中并不完全认同著作权集体管理许可费用标准，他们要求与著作权集体管理组织就许可费用问题展开协商，但这样的谈判容易陷入僵局③。在这样的情形下，著作权集体管理组织只能通过诉讼的途径来收取已授权作品的著作权许可使用费，交易成本显然十分高昂。当然，在司法实践中，作品使用者也会做出策略性的选择，当依据著作权集体管理许可费用标准可支付更低的许可费用时，使用者会主张按照著作权集体管理许可标准计算许可使用费④。另外，基于著作权集体管理组织在制度上的垄断地位，使用者也可能质疑著作权集体管理组织依据集体管理许可标准收取许可费用的行为，认为著作权集体管理组织是在“滥用市场支配地位”，其行为属于“以不公平的高价销售商品”的价格垄断行为⑤。

最后，考察司法实践，关于著作权集体管理许可标准的效力，我国地方法院存在两种截然不同的态度：一方面，部分法院在确定法定赔偿数额时并不考虑著作权集体管理许可费用标准的因素。如在中国音乐著作权协会诉北京伟地电子出版社等侵犯著作权纠纷案中，原告主张要求被告按照国家版权局审定的《使用音乐作品制作数字化制品著作权许可使用费标准》向其支付侵权赔偿金，而法院则认为原告就赔偿数额未能提供充分的证据加以证明，因此法院依据被告实施的侵权行为的性质、数字化录音制品支付使用费的相关规定、合理费用支出的合法依据等予以判定⑥。又如在吴昌海等与中国音像著作权集体管理协会侵害著作财产权纠纷上诉案中，一审法院认为，关于赔偿数额的确定，因 KTV 经营行业尚未形成双方共同认可的著作权许可使用费给付标准作为赔偿数额的参照，诉讼期间，音集协也未提供证据证明其因侵权所遭受的实际损失或者被告因侵权所获利益，准许适用法定赔偿。该案一审、二审法院在综合考虑涉案作品的数量、作品知名度、发行时间、制作费用，侵权行为的性质、主观过错程度、侵权持续时间及侵权后果，被控 KTV 经营的模式和规模、经营地点、本地社会经济发展状况等因素的基础上，确定了赔偿数额⑦。另一方面，也有部分法院在确定法定赔偿数额时明确将著作权集体管理许可费用标准作为参考因素之一。如在哈尔滨市南岗区好声音音乐娱乐中心与中国音像著作权集体管理协会侵害著作权纠纷上诉案中，一审、二审法院均赞同参照国家版权局、黑龙江省版权局、黑龙江省文化厅确定的许可使用费标准，综合考量被告的经营地点、侵权时间及为制止侵权行为进行调查、取证所支付的合理开支，酌情确定赔偿数额⑧。而在中国音乐著作权协会诉上海福乐思特房地产发展有限公司著作权侵权纠纷案中，法院认为中国音乐著作权协会提供的《使用音乐作品进行表演的著作权许可使用费标准》，系其与不同类别的音乐作品使用者之间协商使用音乐作品时适用

① 刘平. 著作权集体管理组织与权利人个体维权诉讼的区别及其解决途径 [J]. 知识产权，2016 (9).

② 浙江省高级人民法院（2012）浙知终字第 165 号民事判决书。

③ 吴亚东. 音集协收费合法性遭质疑 [N]. 法制日报，2009-12-17 (5).

④ 广东省深圳市中级人民法院（2014）深中法知民终字第 511 号民事判决书。

⑤ 倪静. 论著作权集体管理组织反垄断规制的新思路：兼论《著作权集体管理条例》的完善 [J]. 西南民族大学学报（人文社会科学版），2013 (6).

⑥ 北京市第二中级人民法院（2003）二中民初字第 174 号民事判决书。

⑦ 江苏省高级人民法院（2017）苏民终 1845 号民事判决书。

⑧ 黑龙江省高级人民法院（2017）黑民终 311 号民事判决书。

的标准，可以作为赔偿参考因素之一①。

总体来看，在我国著作权许可交易市场中，实际上主要存在三种定价模式：第一，由著作权人自行与使用者协商确定许可交易价格，可称为自主定价模式；第二，著作权集体管理组织依据许可标准或者以许可标准为谈判基础来确定交易价格，可称为集体管理定价模式②；第三，我国法院在具体的案例纠纷中依据《著作权法》第四十九条规定确定赔偿费用，它可以被理解为法院通过责任规则所确定的隐性价格，此种模式可称为诉讼定价模式。在这三种定价模式中，著作权集体管理许可标准仅在集体管理定价模式中发挥实质性作用，而自主定价模式基本上排斥了著作权集体管理许可标准的适用，著作权集体管理许可标准也几乎对诉讼定价模式不发生影响，或者仅具有微弱的影响。就此而言，著作权集体管理许可标准的实施效果并不理想，在著作权许可交易市场中并没有得到著作权人、使用者等相关主体的广泛认同。因此，笔者并不赞同在著作权许可交易市场中强制性地推广集体管理定价模式，以替代著作权人主导的自主定价模式。毕竟，著作权集体管理制度及著作权集体管理组织设立的目的首先在于维护著作权人的正当利益，而非与著作权人争抢交易机会。另外，当著作权人或著作权集体管理组织以使用者侵犯著作权为由提起诉讼时，法院所要裁判的案件属于侵权纠纷，而非合同纠纷。如此，要求法院在裁判此类案件时过多提高著作权集体管理许可标准在确定赔偿数额时的影响因子，也未必合理③。

五、结语

从博弈论的角度来说，由不同位阶的法律规则所构成的制度框架是相关主体进行博弈时需要遵守的主要博弈规则，同时相关主体也会在既有的制度框架下做出策略性选择，以寻求或形成有利于自己的交易规则。从前述内容可以看出，原本被赋予积极市场功能的著作权集体管理组织，在我国的实际运行中并未完全实现其预期的市场功能。行政权力的过分干预与制度上的垄断地位虽然可以在一定程度上提升著作权集体管理组织的谈判地位与谈判能力，但也正因为如此，著作权人、使用者等主体往往就会采取相对的策略行为，以消减拥有制度优势的著作权集体管理组织所带来的不利影响。在我国现有的著作权集体管理制度框架下，著作权人与著作权集体管理组织之间存在着微妙且显著的利益冲突，著作权人、著作权集体管理组织、使用者等主体之间也未达成合意的均衡状态，这在一定程度上反映出现有著作权集体管理制度的效率缺乏与不合理。立法者在修订与完善著作权集体管理制度时，首先需要尊重著作权人的自主意志与正当利益，并减少行政干预的范围与力度，认清、摆正相关主体的角色位置。

（本文原发表于《知识产权》2018年第7期，系2017年中央高校基本科研业务费资助项目的阶段性成果，获南开大学亚洲研究中心资助。发文时内容有删减。作者单位：南开大学）

论著作权法对人工智能生成成果的保护

——作为邻接权的数据处理者权之证立

陶　乾

随着机器学习和神经网络等各类技术的发展，人工智能程序能够生成小说、诗歌、美术、编曲等内容，其所生成的内容效果甚至与人类创作的内容难以区分。包括欧盟议会法律事务委员会和日本知识产权战略总部在内的政府机构已开始着手研究对高级自动化程序在未受人类干涉时的智能生成成果给予保护的必要性和可行性、人工智能的“独立智力创造”之界定标准和成果权属，以及人工智能生成成果对已有著作权法体系的影响等问题④。对此，中外知识产权学界亦进行了积极研究并展开了激烈讨论，并形成以下观点：首先，关于人工智能生成成果是否是作品，有“反对说”“支持说”“中立说”三种态度。“支持说”“中立说”建议现在或将来在

① 上海市普陀区人民法院（2016）沪0107民初22949号民事判决书。

② 美国学者C. Scott Hemphill认为，著作权集体管理组织还可以采用另外两种定价方式：一是根据每个版权人提出的价格来收取费用；二是著作权集体管理组织提出一套模拟个人定价的定价方案。C. Scott Hemphill. Competition and the Collective Management of Copyright. 34 Colum. J. L. & Arts 645 (2011).

③ 广东省深圳市中级人民法院（2014）深中法知民终字第511号民事判决书。

④ 2017年2月16日，欧盟议会通过了法律事务委员会提交的决议，将就机器人和人工智能提出立法提案。法律事务委员会建议对于计算机或者机器人创作的可版权作品，需要制定可以用来界定人工智能的“独立智力创造”的标准，以便明确版权归属。European Parliament：Robots and Artificial Intelligence：MEPs Call for EU-wide Liability Rules [EB/OL]. [2017-12-11]. http://www.europarl.europa.eu/news/en/news-room/20170210IPR61808/robots-and-artificial-intelligence-meps-call-for-eu-wide-liability-rules.

法律上明确人工智能创造物为知识产权的新客体。其次，对于人工智能生成成果的权属问题能否在传统著作权法的理论框架下予以解决，“工具说”将人工智能视为使用者的工具，使用人是作者；“意志说”将人工智能的生成过程视为按照使用者或程序编写者的意志所产生的表达；“创制说”或“程序编写者说”认为对人工智能生成成果的保护可参照雇佣作品或职务作品制度；“公共领域说”将人工智能生成成果视为没有作者的作品，任何人均可加以利用；“邻接权说”认为以邻接权保护人工智能生成成果，可以缓解人工智能创作物保护与著作权原理的冲突。最后，认为传统版权理论无法解决此问题的学者提出了“虚拟人类作者说”，“孳息说”则从民法上的孳息制度寻求支撑。本文认为，对此问题的讨论应跳出可版权性的窠臼，首先应讨论对人工智能生成成果予以专有权保护的价值考量是否与著作权法的制度价值契合；在此基础上，再思考人工智能生成成果应如何在著作权法的制度框架下获得保护。

一、在著作权法框架下对人工智能生成成果提供保护的必要性

（一）人工智能生成成果的商业化

随着越来越多种类的人工智能生成成果的出现，人工智能生成成果被不断地商业化，具有经济价值的人工智能生成成果已成为事实上可交易的财产权客体。这种商业化是符合社会公共利益的。如果权利的归属处于不确定的状态，会带来时间和成本的浪费①。没有被精确界定的财产权会增加法律的不确定性，进而增加交易成本，最终将阻碍创新②。所以，人工智能生成成果这项具有财产价值的客体，法律应当认可并做出规定，进而明确其权利归属，这不仅关乎权利保护与权利行使，而且还关乎当人工智能生成成果涉嫌侵权时责任主体的确定。

（二）人工智能生成成果与著作权法的价值

为了鼓励对有价值的思想的外在表达，促进作品的利用和传播，著作权法给予著作权人和邻接权人一定范围的专有性权利，使其能够从作品的利用和传播中获得利益。这从根本上说，是利用作者的才智和包括传播者在内的相关人的劳动促进科学和文学艺术的发展。因此，可以说著作权法的终极目标在于整个社会福利的最大化。而从实用主义角度，对于是否应给人工智能生成成果以著作权法保护，需要考虑的核心问题就是，如对其给予知识产权保护，将对公众福祉具有哪些方面的促进效用。具体而言，应具有以下方面的促进效用：

第一，只有肯定人工智能生成成果的价值，人们才会愿意购买此类人工智能程序软件或人工智能设备硬件的使用权或所有权。而只有人工智能产品有市场，才会有人愿意投资此类程序的开发或此类产品的研发，对于人工智能的开发者来说，其才会有动力去继续优化人工智能的技术能力和开发新的产品，激励其在计算机（人工智能设备）的功能设计上进行更多的投入③。从根本上而言，这必然有助于科技的进步。

第二，著作权法上的独创性所要求的智力投入标准较低，所以著作权法的政策导向并不是鼓励有较高创造性的智力付出，而在于鼓励更多的新的和有潜在价值的成果的出现④。人工智能生成成果的形成是一个正循环链条，生成的新成果越多，可供人工智能学习的数据量也就越多，相应地，后续生成的成果也会越来越好。所以，对人工智能生成成果加以保护，符合著作权法鼓励新成果的这一政策导向。

第三，成果只有通过传播，才能使社会受益。人工智能的使用者对于人工智能生成成果的公开具有决定性作用。对人工智能生成成果加以财产权保护，才能促使占有人工智能生成成果的人为实现其经济利益而将其公开。否则，他可以谎称成果是自己创作的，进而对其行使著作权，而不是如实披露成果生成主体的人工智能身份，这显然不是立法者所期望看到的。

第四，人工智能生成成果的生成过程是对人类已有文化艺术科学成果的利用过程，所以人工智能提高了已有成果的效用，挖掘了其价值，使得包括公有领域的作品、孤儿作品、已退出流通市场的作品等在内的已发表作品的价值得到进一步的重新发挥。对人工智能生成成果的保护，能够促进对人类已有成果的再利用。

综上，对人工智能生成成果进行保护的价值与

① Jani McCutcheon. The Vanishing Author in Computer-generated Works: A Critical Analysis of Recent Australian Case Law. 36 U. Melb. L. Rev. 915 (2013), p. 956.

② Michael Heller. The Gridlock Economy: How Too Much Ownership Wrecks Markets, Stops Innovation, and Costs Lives [M]. New York: Basic Books. 2008: 22.

③ Karl F. Milde, Can a Computer Be an "Author" or an "Inventor". 51 J. PAT. OFF. Soc'Y 378 (1969), p. 390.

④ 同①36 U. Melb. L. Rev. 915-969, 956 (2013), p. 957.

著作权法的价值契合。不给予人工智能生成成果法律保护，无助于鼓励技术的应用，也无助于促进人工智能生成成果产品的交易。长远来看，也无助于激励人工智能技术本身的开发。

二、人工智能生成成果成为著作权客体的根本障碍

（一）人工智能生成成果的独创性

虽然对独创性并无一个明确的判断标准，但可以达成共识的是，独创性并不是一个非常高的标准。假设同一成果是由人类创作的，能够被认定为具有独创性，那么，当同一成果是由人工智能生成的时，在不考虑成果所源自的主体身份这一前提下，该成果的独创性亦应被认可。

人工智能生成成果以已有数据为基础，已有数据是由数字化的受著作权保护的作品、公有领域的作品以及不构成作品的信息构成。在作品类型中，与人工智能生成成果最接近的是汇编作品和演绎作品。汇编若干作品、作品的片段或者不构成作品的数据或者其他材料，对其内容的选择或者编排体现出独创性的作品为汇编作品。在已有作品基础上经过作者创造性的劳动而派生出来的作品为演绎作品。但与汇编作品和演绎作品不同的是，人工智能生成成果不是对某些作品的复制编排或者对某个作品的演绎，而是运用算法从已有数据中提炼出相关规律和要素，所生成的内容与数据中的任何作品的全部或部分内容均不构成实质性相似，也不是实质性地以某个作品为基础所进行的再创作。

存在的一种情形是，人工智能提取某一位特定作者的所有作品，通过数据处理掌握该作者的作品风格，从而能够“模仿”这一风格生成“作品”，使得公众难以区分其是否为该作者所创作①。有学者指出，此种人工智能生成成果属于对原作者作品的演绎作品，应适用强制许可对作者做出经济补偿②。但是基于思想表达二分法，作品风格应属于思想的范畴，不属于著作权法保护的对象。所以，此类人工智能生成成果不属于演绎作品。

（二）人工智能的非工具性

如果人工智能仅仅是辅助人类创作的工具，如同照相机、文本编辑软件、制图软件等，那么其产生的成果即是人类的独创性表达。若是如此，则讨论人工智能生成成果的著作权问题没有意义。问题在于，人工智能在其成果生成过程中所扮演的并非仅仅是工具的角色。

在摄影作品中，作品的独创性体现在摄影者对光线、角度等的选择上，照相机是摄影者的工具，摄影者是独创性的实质贡献者。与此类似，打字机、复印机、扫描仪、文字编辑软件等，均是将使用者的表达予以固定下来的工具。但是，人工智能生成成果主要是依赖大数据和信息技术本身，在人工智能成果的生成过程中，没有人类的个性化表达。美国国会曾经成立的“关于新技术条件下享有版权作品使用的委员会”（the Commission on New Technological Uses of Copyrighted Works，CONTU）在1978年的一份报告中认为，没有合理的理由给予计算机作者身份，计算机相当于一台相机或者打字机，直接或间接地由人启动，仅能按照人所要求的方式做人要求其做的事情，所以仅仅是一个“惰性的”工具③。1986年，美国国会技术评估办公室（Office of Technology Assessment，OTA）在一份报告中评估了当时交互计算技术发展背景之下的知识产权政策，针对的内容包括交互式故事叙述、计算机辅助设计、数字音乐采样和编辑、交互式计算机图形和图像编辑等。OTA认为，CONTU将计算机看成惰性工具的看法具有误导性。文字处理程序与内容自动生成程序不同，对于后者，创造性活动融汇于机器的智能中④。在其后的三十多年里，与智能相关的机器学习、深度学习、认知分析等技术出现了突破性的发展。

人工智能生成成果源自人工智能，人工智能并非仅仅是工具。人类的贡献在于创造人工智能，而对于人工智能所生成的内容，人类的参与可能仅仅是对生成内容的细微修改和整理，甚至在有些情况下，仅仅是点击“生成”按钮。综上，人工智能生成成果不是人类以人工智能为辅助工具使得人的独创性思想被表达出来的成果。

① Scott French 开发的程序 Hal 成功生成了一部与已故作者 Jacqueline Susann 的文体风格类似的小说 *Just This One*。Scott Turner 开发的 Minstrel 系统可以生成有关亚瑟王和他的圆桌骑士的文本故事。Stephan Thaler 开发了基于神经网络技术自动作曲的程序。

② Tal Vigderson. Hamlet II: The Sequel? The Rights of Authors vs. Computer-Generated “Read-Alike” Works. 28 Loy. L. A. L. Rev. 444，401 (1994)，p. 430.

③ Final Report of the National Commission on New Technological Uses of Copyrighted Works，U. S. Government Printing office，Washington，D. C.，July 31，1978，pp. 44-45.

④ U. S. Congress，Office of Technology Assessment. Intellectual Property Rights in an Age of Electronics and Information，OTA-CIT-302. U. S. Government Printing office，Washington，D. C.，April 1986，p. 72.

（三）人工智能生成成果的非智力性

人工智能生成成果的基础是人工智能程序被技术人员赋予的一种能力。现有的人工智能技术使得人工智能装置或者程序本身具备一定程度的与人类智力相似的“智能”。然而，智能不等于智力。即便人工智能每一次运行所生成的内容不具有重复性和可预测性，但人工智能生成成果终究不是对人类思想的表达。人工智能生成成果是在对已有的人类创作作品以及不构成作品的数据和信息等进行整理和学习之后，按照人类的表达规则而对信息要素进行的排列组合。虽然人类创作所产生的内容也需要遵守一定的表达规则，以便能够产生在一定群体范围内进行沟通和传播的效果，但人类是将思想、观点等融入创作过程从而形成个性化的表达，而机器并无思想、创意和情感。因此，人工智能、机器智能所产生的内容不属于著作权法上的智力成果。

综上，人工智能生成成果虽然可以成为具有独创性的客体，但是该成果不是人类的创作，也不是人类在机器辅助下所进行的表达，而是人工智能程序或设备在人类参与度极小的情况下所自动生成的成果。人工智能生成成果的诸多特性导致其不同于著作权法上现有的所有保护客体。在大陆法系著作权法理论中，作品是作者人格的延伸。因此，作品只能是人类的创作成果。虽然基于人工智能的机器属性以及人对作品独创性的低参与度两方面的原因，人工智能的生成成果无法根据传统著作权法理论成为著作权法上的作品，然而，如前所述，在著作权法框架下对其予以保护确有必要性。既然将人工智能生成成果认定为作品存在根本障碍，同时还会造成传统著作权法理论的“动荡”，那么，将人工智能生成成果纳入邻接权制度的调整范围是否可行殊值探讨。

三、人工智能生成成果作为邻接权客体的可行性

（一）人工智能生成成果作为邻接权客体与该制度目的与价值的契合

诚然，人工智能技术的出现为法律规则的解释和适用带来了一些疑惑。当出现新事物时，最佳的解决路径不是动摇和改变著作权法有关“作者”与“作品”的传统规则，而是应在原有的理论体系中以灵活的解释和适用应对新问题。事实上，在著作权法的历史演进过程中，其不断对技术进步做着积极回应[①]。邻接权制度自其产生之始即与技术为伴。录音录像技术和广播技术扩大了作品的传播方式和途径，一件版权产品的商业价值不仅包括作者独创性表达的价值，而且包括传播者为版权产品的生产、发行投入的努力，正是由于这些传播者的存在，作品才会有其商业化市场。为此，以作者权体系为基础的国家和地区，均在其著作权法体系中增设了邻接权制度用于鼓励对作品的传播。因此，著作权法上的权利主体不仅包括著作权人，也包括出版者、广播组织者、录音录像制作者这一类对作品传播有所贡献的人。

随着邻接权制度的发展，“邻接权就是作品传播者权的观念正在被打破”[②]。对于现代邻接权而言，一些邻接权的客体与作品并无联系，比如未使用他人作品制作的录像制品、广播电台或电视台未使用他人作品制作的载有声音或图像的广播电视节目、对与作品无关的声音的录制品。还有一些国家对数据库、科学版本、戏剧布景、报刊出版者提供的邻接权保护亦属此类。在许多国家，邻接权制度逐渐发展成为对不具有独创性、无法成为作品但又与著作权相关的利益进行保护的兜底性制度[③]。因此，可以将邻接权进行广义与狭义的区分。狭义的邻接权是与作品传播有关的权利，广义的邻接权是指“一切传播作品的媒介所享有的专有权，或对那些与作者创作的作品尚有一定区别的产品、制品或其他既含有‘思想的表达形式’，又不能称为‘作品’的内容所享有的权利”[④]。有学者主张，应当“以开放的眼光来认识邻接权制度”[⑤]，在“保护投资者”的理论认识下，邻接权制度理应接纳因科技发展而产生的新内容[⑥]。

著作权法体系中的邻接权制度应当包括对不构成作品但依然有财产价值的一些客体进行保护之内容，这为将人工智能生成成果纳入邻接权客体提供了空间。进一步分析，对人工智能生成成果提供保护能够与邻接权制度的设置目的和价值相吻合。具体而言，首先，保护人工智能生成成果能够鼓励投资。其投资不仅包括对生成内容的人工智能程序的

① Lyman Ray Patterson. Copyright in Historical Perspective [M]. Nashville, TN: Vanderbilt University Press, 1968: 61-69.

② 王迁. 知识产权法教程 [M]. 北京：中国人民大学出版社，2014：198.

③ 刘洁. 邻接权归宿论 [M]. 北京：知识产权出版社，2013：24.

④ 郑成思. 版权法 [M]. 北京：中国人民大学出版社，2009：61.

⑤ 韦之. 欧盟数据库指令评介 [J]. 著作权，2000 (2).

⑥ 王超政. 科技推动下的邻接权制度体系构建 [J]. 中国版权，2013 (2).

人力、物力和财力的投入，而且包括对人工智能生成成果的商业化投资。这从根本上不仅有助于科技进步，而且也有助于促进人工智能生成成果的传播和利用，使更多的人获益。其次，对于人工智能生成成果，人工智能程序的操作者对于具体内容本身没有实质性贡献，但其控制着内容的生成和传播。这种对内容的贡献度以及对内容生成与传播的控制力，与广播组织者、录音录像制作者对广播节目、录音录像制品的贡献度和控制力是类似的。所以，给人工智能生成成果以邻接权保护，是为了激励更多的人工智能生成成果的生成、传播和商业化利用。最后，人工智能生成成果既包括满足独创性标准的内容，也包括不具有独创性的内容。对人工智能生成成果统一予以邻接权保护，是基于其是否有财产价值，而非基于其是否有独创性。用邻接权保护人工智能生成成果，也避免了上文所述的当人类对人工智能生成成果做出修改时，人工智能生成成果与人类表达之间的界限难以区分而为独创性判断带来难度的问题。

不可否认的是，人工智能生成成果具有低成本、高效率的特点，将会削弱一般的人类作者在版权市场的定价能力，人类作者将会承受过大的竞争压力①，因此，对人工智能生成成果予以财产权保护会严重挫败人类发挥创造性的积极性。基于此种考量，对人工智能生成成果的保护应弱于对人类创作作品的保护。因此，将人工智能生成成果作为邻接权客体更为合适，因为著作权法在进行制度设计时，在保护期限和权利内容等方面对邻接权客体的保护水平显著低于对著作权客体的保护水平。

（二）作为邻接权的数据处理者权之设立

人工智能生成成果本质上是一项数据成果。在如今大数据时代，对数据的收集、开发和利用成为常态，人工智能生成成果只是运用数据和技术而衍生生成的诸多类数据成果的一种。数据成果是对数据资料进行处理所产生的具有独创性的成果或不具有独创性但有经济价值的成果。前者如人工智能法律机器人出具的法律意见书，人工智能生成的曲谱、图片、诗歌和小说；后者如经过大数据处理的数据统计报告。对于数据成果，因数据的来源、特性以及数据与个人信息之间的杂糅性等因素的制约，既要对其予以财产权保护也要对其进行适当的权利限制，因此，将其放在知识产权法的框架下予以保护较为合适，因为知识产权是一定时期内有法定限制情形的垄断权，而不是一项永久的、排他的、不受限制的财产权。在此范畴内，遵循上文的论证逻辑，将其纳入著作权法框架并通过邻接权制度予以保护较为适合。本文将数据成果所对应的邻接权称为数据处理者权，指的是数据成果处理者对其以数据为基础通过技术获得的数据成果享有的财产权。数据处理者权是与录音录像制作者权、广播组织者权平行的邻接权。

数据成果不能被数据库概念所涵盖。数据库是数据资料的集合，虽然数据成果的生成有赖于数据库或者大数据，但其本身不是数据库。我国著作权法对数据库提供的保护仅是针对其所具有的“独创性的选择或编排”的表达，而非针对它所选择或编排的内容。本文提出的数据处理者权与我国著作权法上作为汇编作品的数据库之著作权并不相同。当然，在特定情况下，二者会存在关联。第一种情况是，数据处理者权所处理的对象可能是构成汇编作品的数据库，也可能是不构成作品的数据集。第二种情况是，数据成果处理者基于其对若干人工智能生成成果的独创性编排或整理，除可享有数据处理者权之外，还可享有著作权。正如北京湛庐文化传播有限公司可基于《著作权法》第十四条对其出版的诗集《阳光失了玻璃窗》享有汇编作品著作权。

数据处理者权亦不同于欧盟国家立法上确定的独立于著作权的数据库“特殊权利”（sui generis），后者保护的是制作者对于其付出了实质性投资的数据库内容的质和/或量上的全部或实质性部分的提取权和再利用权②，是“对特定对象在并没有满足可版权性要件的情况下所提供的类似于版权的保护”③，而前者保护的是对大量数据信息进行处理所生成的结果。虽然同样是基于保护权利人“投资”的考虑，前者是对数据信息的处理和挖掘的投资，后者是对数据信息的收集、编排和整理的投资；前者更多是基于海量的大数据，而后者是基于特定的某类数据。

综上，就本文构建的数据处理者权而言，人工智能生成成果作为一项数据成果是该权利的客体之

---

① 曹源．比较法和产权视角中的人工智能创作物［J］．中国版权，2017（4）．

② Directive 96/9/EC of the European Parliament and of the Council of 11 March 1996 on the Legal Protection of Databases，Chapter III“Sui Generis Right”，Article 7“Object of protection”；Database Investment and Intellectual Property Antipiracy Act of 1996，H. R. 3531，104th Cong.

③ 卢海君．版权客体论［M］．2版．北京：知识产权出版社，2014：217．

一。数据处理者权能够合理有效地应对目前理论界和实务界对于数据权利的争议，该项构建在大数据时代尤其具有重要意义。在著作权法的制度框架下，将数据库汇编作品著作权与数据处理者邻接权并列，则可以有效解决有关数据的收集、整理、加工、处理、挖掘等一系列行为所生成的各阶段成果的权利界定问题。

四、数据处理者权架构下人工智能生成成果的权利内容及行使

（一）人工智能生成成果的权利主体

在现有法律体系下，人工智能程序或设备不能成为权利主体的根本原因在于人工智能没有人格。如果给予没有人格的人工智能权利，显然有悖于法理，这会在理论上造成不可调和的矛盾，并带来实务操作中的困惑，比如人工智能如何提起侵权诉讼，人工智能如何转让或许可其权利。从著作权法的角度看，著作权法的目的是通过给予作者在某一有限期间内一定的垄断性权利控制其作品的复制和传播，进而激励其创作出更多的作品，从而促进更多创造的产生和促进人类文明的进步。如果赋予创作了某项小说作品的人工智能程序著作权人资格，却并不会对它产生任何激励作用①。因为从目前的技术来看，无论多么复杂和智能化的机器或程序，都没有自主意识。人工智能不具有是否生成内容的决策能力。当然，正如一些科学家所预言的，如果人工智能未来发展到一定程度并拥有直觉、感觉和情绪②，其能够自主决定是否进行创作，届时也许人工智能的作者身份会获得确认。但这一天的到来并非是始于版权法意义上作者身份的要求，而应是在生命科学和法律上对其人格予以确认之后，版权法顺势给予其作者身份的结果③。

人工智能生成成果涉及多方主体。人工智能程序开发者或配置有人工智能程序或设备的制造者和所有者，以及这一程序或设备的使用者均是与生成内容有密切关系的人，这些主体身份之间存在交叉。当人工智能程序开发者与程序或设备的使用者不是同一主体时，对于人工智能生成成果的权属，应采用的规则是“合同约定说”“使用权人说”，即：人工智能程序开发者与使用者在协议中明确人工智能生成成果权属的，从其约定；没有约定时，人工智能生成成果的权利人为人工智能程序的使用权人，因为其是人工智能生成成果诞生的促成者，是对人工智能生成成果的生成负有责任的人，是人工智能生成成果的实际支配者，而且也是人工智能生成成果能够传播的决定者，同时，当人工智能生成成果构成侵权时，其亦是责任主体。具体分析如下。

作为人工智能程序开发者，其对该程序拥有著作权，有权控制该程序的发表、复制、发行和传播。其可以自己使用程序生成人工智能生成成果，然后通过行使邻接权获得经济利益。此时，程序开发者同时又是程序使用者。其也可以选择许可他人使用该程序，转让程序的著作财产权，租售配置有人工智能程序的智能设备。程序开发者与相对方通常会在协议中明确人工智能生成成果的权属，在没有约定的情况下，基于下列几个方面的原因，将人工智能生成成果的权利归属于人工智能程序的被许可人或受让人、智能设备的受让人或承租人更为公平。

第一，对于程序开发者而言，赋予其对程序的著作权法保护已经足够对其产生激励作用，没有必要再使其对程序生成内容主张权利。第二，程序开发者并不是客观上使人工智能生成成果得以生成的人，也不是将人工智能生成成果固定的人。第三，若赋予使用者人工智能生成成果的邻接权，则能够激励其购买程序或通过付费方式取得许可以使用该程序，进而使得程序开发者获得编写更多程序的激励。第四，人工智能程序或设备的使用者多是对人工智能程序或设备进行投资的人，赋予其权利与将影视作品的权利归属于制片人的政策考量类似，也与一些国家著作权法规定数据库创建者④权利的政策考量一致，使得使用权人对于其所使用的程序或设备的实质性投资能够获得回报。这样的权属安排才能鼓励投资，从而有助于人工智能产业的发展。第五，程序的使用者包括文化艺术领域的从业者，相比于程序开发者来说，他们更懂得如何对人工智

① Timothy L. Butler. Can a Computer Be an Author Copyright Aspects of Artificial Intelligence. 4 Comm/Ent L. S. 707 (1982), p. 738.

② Ray Kurzweil. How to Create a Mind: The Secret of Human Thought Revealed [M]. London: Penguin Books, 2013: 28; Marvin Minsky. The Emotion Machine: Commonsense Thinking, Artificial Intelligence, and the Future of the Human Mind [M]. New York: Simon & Schuster, 2006: 96-101.

③ James Grimmelmann. There's No Such Thing as a Computer-Authored Work—And It's a Good Thing, Too. 39 Colum. J. L. & Arts, p. 403.

④ 比如，《意大利著作权法》第一百零二条第二附条规定，数据库创建者指的是为数据库的创建、核对或者引荐做出重大投资，即为前述目的投入金钱、时间或者劳动的主体。

能生成成果进行加工、整理，以及甄别挑选其中有价值的部分。

（二）人工智能生成成果的权利行使与权利限制

对于人工智能生成成果，一方面鉴于其对社会福祉的有益性，其具有保护的价值；另一方面基于社会公共利益的考量，其权利范围不宜过大，而且需要予以必要的限制。权利限制应体现在以下三个方面：第一，在权利内容上，数据处理者权的权利内容应少于著作权的权利内容，不能像作品那样享有著作人格权和更广泛的诸如表演权、广播权等其他的著作财产权保护。数据处理者对其数据成果的权利内容可以参照录音录像制作者对其制作的录音录像制品的权利内容，即人工智能程序或设备的使用权人对其人工智能生成成果应享有许可他人复制、发行、通过信息网络向公众传播并获得报酬的权利。权利人可以将其权利转让、许可他人使用或放弃。第二，就权利的保护期而言，数据成果的保护期应短于著作财产权的保护期和一般邻接权的保护期。原因在于，数据成果与产生成果的程序密不可分，而程序本身具有获得著作权或专利权保护的可能性，对于数据成果的独立保护水平不宜过高。而且，数据成果的生命期通常很短，很容易随着产生它的程序的更新而获得同步更新或重生。因此，适宜为其设定一个较短的保护期，在其内容发生实质性变化时，应认为产生了新的成果，其保护期重新起算。可以参照版式设计权的保护期，将数据成果享有的邻接权保护期设定为十年，截止于该成果首次发表后第十年的12月31日。第三，围绕权利的行使，鉴于人工智能生成成果本身来源于其程序对已发表的作品和信息的深度学习，不应限制其他主体运用技术对人工智能生成成果进行再次提取和利用。一方面，这样能够避免不当地限制其他主体对信息的接触；另一方面，也更符合著作权法律制度所追求的文化多样性和激励更多文化产品产生的价值取向。但是，此处所述的再次提取和利用行为不同于权利范围中的"复制"，而是指人工智能生成成果在被发表之后，与其他已发表的作品或已公开的信息一样，成为其他的人工智能设备或程序生成内容的数据资料源。

五、结语

人工智能生成成果的产生过程包括感知、机器学习、建立模型、人类输入指令、关联要素、产生内容等几个步骤。在整个过程中起关键作用的是可归类为深度神经网络的算法，并且新内容的生成强烈依赖由已有作品和不构成作品的数字化信息等构成的数据。即便有些人工智能生成成果具备独创性，但因其不是人类的智力成果，不能作为作品获得著作权保护。然而，许多人工智能生成成果具有财产价值，对这些人工智能生成成果的传播和利用有利于社会福祉，对人工智能生成成果在我国《著作权法》的制度框架下予以一定程度的保护具有合理性和必要性。鉴于人工智能生成成果的保护价值与作为邻接权客体的录音录像制品、广播电视节目的保护价值类似，因此建议将人工智能生成成果作为一项数据成果，归入广义的邻接权的客体。同时，建议在著作权法上的邻接权制度中创建数据处理者权，即数据成果处理者对其以数据为基础通过技术处理获得的具有独创性的成果或不具有独创性但有经济价值的成果所享有的财产权，具体包括许可他人复制、发行、通过信息网络向公众传播并获得报酬的权利。当人工智能程序开发者与程序或设备的使用者不是同一主体时，对于人工智能生成成果的权属，应采用的规则是"合同约定说"和"使用权人说"。另外，对其权利内容、保护期限及权利行使应予以一定限制。

（本文原发表于《法学》2018年第4期，
获国家社会科学基金重大项目
"创新驱动发展战略下知识产权公共领域问题研究"
（项目批准号：17ZDA139）资助。
作者单位：中国政法大学）

功能主义解释论视野下的"电影作品"

——兼评凤凰网案二审判决

万　勇

2018年3月，北京知识产权法院就北京新浪互联信息服务有限公司诉北京天盈九州网络技术有限公司（该公司系凤凰网所有权人及运营商）案（以下简称凤凰网案），做出二审判决[①]。该判决撤销了北京市朝阳区人民法院的一审判决，认为：体育赛事直播画面不属于电影作品和以类似摄制电影的方法创作的作品。此外，由于法院在《著作权法》第三条规定的法定作品类型之外，无权设定其他作品类型，因此，赛事直播画面也不属于"其他作品"。该判决在法学理论界、实务界引起了高度关注。本

① 北京知识产权法院（2015）京知民终字第1818号民事判决书。

文拟从解释论的视角，重点考察“电影作品和以类似摄制电影的方法创作的作品”（以下简称电影作品）的含义，并结合北京知识产权法院判决涉及的几个争议焦点展开讨论。

就技术发展引起的法律问题进行的解释论大致可以分为两类，即功能主义解释论与形式主义解释论。功能主义解释论关注的是技术引起了什么后果，而不是技术如何运作，强调技术对现实世界的影响，而不纠缠于细节。形式主义解释论关注的则是技术的错综复杂之处，强调技术的精准架构①。具体到电影作品，形式主义解释论强调只有制作方法与电影作品类似，才可视为电影作品；功能主义解释论则关注制作效果。本文认为，在技术发展日新月异，而修法和立法进程相当缓慢的当下，盲目地固守形式主义，不仅将阻碍产业发展与创新社会的建立，也会影响人们对法治社会的功能性期待。当然，在进行功能主义解释时，必须建立在对法律文本的法解释学基础上，不能突破基本的著作权法原理。

一、法院可否创设新的作品类型

北京知识产权法院在得出法院“无权设定其他作品类型”这一结论时，在注释中援引了《保护文学和艺术作品伯尔尼公约》（以下简称《伯尔尼公约》）第二条，认为：“使用‘诸如’二字只是给各国立法者提供若干指导，但世界上作品的主要各类全部都列举出来了。”那么，《伯尔尼公约》列举若干作品类型，究竟有何用意？

（一）《伯尔尼公约》对作品类型的列举及其作用

《伯尔尼公约》第二条第一款采取了以下结构：首先对“文学和艺术作品”概念的要点做出规定，然后对这些作品进行了非穷尽性列举（其使用了“诸如”一词明确表明列举的非穷尽性）②。

可能还有未被列举的其他作品，它们仍有资格受到《伯尔尼公约》的保护。尽管如此，某一类作品是否被第二条第一款列举出来仍然极为重要，因为只有这样，《伯尔尼公约》第二条第六款（“本条所提到的作品在本联盟所有成员国内受到保护”）才能使公约对这类作品的保护确定无疑③。那些未被列举出来的客体是否属于一类文学和艺术作品，则是对《伯尔尼公约》第二条第一款的解释问题，因而可能产生各成员国之间不同解释的情形。如果在解释上发生了争议，只有一种可能的解决方法，就是提交给国际法院④。然而，这在《伯尔尼公约》的历史中并不是一种可行的机制。正因为如此，《伯尔尼公约》的历次修订会议一般倾向于在各方达成充分一致的条件下，通过在非穷尽性列举中不断增加新种类的成果，来解决可能产生的关于它们是否应受保护的疑问⑤。但这绝不意味着未被明确列举的作品类型不属于《伯尔尼公约》意义下的作品。

（二）我国《著作权法》中“法律、行政法规规定的其他作品”的含义

之所以使用“法律、行政法规规定的其他作品”这一用语，是立法者为适应未来发展需要所采取的技术措施，以便于随着科技的发展增加新的作品种类；但是，作品种类的增加，不能是随意性的，需要由法律、行政法规规定⑥。

然而，需要注意的是，由于第三条开始的措辞是：“本法所称的作品，包括以下列形式创作的……作品”，其中“包括”一词既可以做穷尽性列举的解释，也可以做非穷尽性列举的解释（包括但不限于）。如果采用后一种解释，则第三条的意思是指：如果法律（尤其是著作权法以外的其他法律）、行政法规规定了其他种类的作品，则它们自然也是《著作权法》意义下的作品，而无须由法院来判断；至于法律、行政法规没有规定的客体是否属于作品，则需要法院来判断。申言之，作品有以下三类：《著作权法》第三条第（一）～（八）项明确列举的具名作品、第三条第（九）项规定的“法律、行政法规规定的其他作品”以及不属于前两类由法院确定符合作品构成要件的其他作品。不过，不管对作品类型做何种解释，并不影响本文的结论，因为本文认为赛事公用信号所承载的连续画面可以归入“以类似摄制电影的方法创作的作品”。

二、电影作品的含义

我国《著作权法》所使用的“电影作品和以类似摄制电影的方法创作的作品”这一用语来自《伯

① Copyright Act of 1976-Transmit Clause-ABC，Inc. v. Aereo，Inc.，128 Harv. L. Rev. 371，377 (2014).

② 世界知识产权组织. 世界知识产权组织管理的版权及相关权条约指南以及版权及相关权术语汇编. 2004：17.

③ 山姆·里基森，简·金斯伯格. 国际版权与邻接权：伯尔尼公约及公约以外的新发展［M］. 郭寿康，等译. 北京：中国人民大学出版社，2016：352.

④ 参见《伯尔尼公约》第三十三条。

⑤ 同②19.

⑥ 李明山，常青，等. 中国当代版权史［M］. 北京：知识产权出版社，2007：214.

尔尼公约》①，因此，要准确理解该用语在我国著作权法语境下的含义，考察《伯尔尼公约》的缔约历史及相关术语的含义非常有必要。

（一）《伯尔尼公约》语境下的解释

1. 1908年柏林文本

《伯尔尼公约》1908年文本第二条与1971年文本的第二条的结构类似，都是先对文学和艺术作品进行一般定义，再对基本定义所涵盖的客体类型进行示例②。不过，1908年文本第二条的作品示例中并未提及电影作品。第十四条倒是对电影做了规定，但它使用的用语是“电影制品”（cinematographic production）：“电影制品应得到与文学或艺术作品同等的保护，只要由于作者通过对演出形式的编排或对表现情节的组合而赋予作品以个性和独创性特征。”③

1908年，当时电影工业尚处于起步阶段，而柏林外交会议就通过了上述规定来管理电影作品，这令不少人都大感困惑。其原因可能是电影作品的特殊性。因为通常而言，制作一部电影耗资巨大，因此要很好地保护制片商的权利，在国际公约中做出相应的规定，似乎是最好的方式④。

2. 1928年罗马文本

《伯尔尼公约》1908年柏林文本第十四条的规定并不能使有关的利益方感到满意。国际文学艺术协会、国际电影制片人协会一直提议对该条款进行修改，它们建议：应当删除《伯尔尼公约》第十四条第二款定义独创性电影作品时所做的限制⑤。也就是说，应当使电影作品享有不受限制的保护：即使电影作品不能满足第十四条第二款规定的独创性要求，也应获得保护⑥。

在1928年召开罗马外交会议时，法国代表团也提出了上述建议⑦。但是意大利代表团和伯尔尼国际局对此表示反对，他们认为这种规定太超前了，并且建议：只应当删除第十四条第二款中的“个性”一词，因为加入这一词语以后，会使得人们认为对于电影作品的独创性要求要高于一般的文学或艺术作品。此外，他们还建议《伯尔尼公约》应明确规定：如果电影不具有独创性，则其只能享有摄影作品所能享有的保护水平。最终，第十四条第二款做了修改，修改后的文本如下：“在作者赋予电影制品以独创性特征的情况下，该作品应得到与文学或艺术作品同等的保护。如果电影制品缺少这一特征，则其享有与摄影作品同等的保护。”

3. 1948年布鲁塞尔文本

1948年布鲁塞尔文本将电影作品纳入第二条第一款列举的作品名单中，原因是在罗马会议之后，各方基本上达成了一致意见。此外，布鲁塞尔外交会议还增加了“以类似摄制电影的方法制作的作品”这一用语。这一用语来源于柏林文本第十四条第四款：“上述规定适用于以类似摄制电影的其他方法产生的复制品或制品。”做出这一规定的原因是柏林外交会议认为，鉴于电影产业不断发展的特点，各种新方法都有可能发明出来，应该规定将这些新事物纳入公约⑧。

此后，由于电视的大规模发展，各方对“以类似摄制电影的方法制作的作品”是否可以涵盖“电视作品”产生了一定的疑问。原因是电视作品可能以未固定的形式存在，即使固定，也是以并非类似摄影电影的方法固定的——就是说，尽管制作的效果类似，但制作的方法并不类似。

4. 1967年斯德哥尔摩文本

为了解决上述问题，20世纪50年代和60年代，电影专家委员会进行了详细考察和认真研究。最后，各方普遍一致的意见是：电视作品应被视为电影作品。但在如何视同的问题上以及固定的问题上，仍然存在意见分歧⑨。为了解决后一问题，1967年文本在第二条中单独增加一款：允许成员国国内立法规定所有作品或特定种类的作品如果未以某种物质形式固定下来便不受保护。为了解决前一问题，

---

① 刘春田. 知识产权法［M］. 5版. 北京：中国人民大学出版社，2014：62.

② 山姆·里基森，简·金斯伯格. 国际版权与邻接权：伯尔尼公约及公约以外的新发展［M］. 郭寿康，等译. 北京：中国人民大学出版社，2016：352.

③ 参见《伯尔尼公约》1908年柏林文本第十四条第二款。

④ Stephen P. Ladas. The International Protection of Literary and Artistic Property ［M］. New York：The Macmillan Company，1938：446.

⑤ 同④。

⑥ Sam Ricketson，Jane C. Ginsburg. Appendices to International Copyright and Neighboring Rights：The Berne Convention and Beyond ［EB/OL］. ［2018-04-07］. htpp://www.oup.com/uk/booksites/content/9780198259466.

⑦ 同⑥。

⑧ 同②373.

⑨ 同②374.

1967年文本将“制作”一词改为“表现”，原因之一是因为制作一词可理解为事先录制，而表现则表示其效果是在电影作品放映中产生的。这样，该规定就可适用于电视直播，即无事先录制的情形①。另一个原因是修改以后行文更为精确，因为它指制作效果的类似而不是制作方法的类似②。

因此，从《伯尔尼公约》缔约历史来看，“电影作品和以类似摄制电影的方法表现的作品”的表述十分宽泛，足以涵盖视听作品。这一术语今天一般用来涵盖由“一系列相关画面”构成、借助机器或设备观看的电影和类似作品。也就是说，如果过去一度曾因受保护种类的“方法”要素而对需要通过不同固定形式来制作的视听作品能否受保护提出过怀疑的话，如今鉴于电影摄制使用的诸多不同介质和方法，“电影作品”“以类似摄制电影的方法表现的作品”与一般视听作品之间的区别看起来也就不具有什么重要意义了③。

综上所述，在《伯尔尼公约》的框架下，以类似摄制电影的方法表现的作品可以涵盖所谓未固定的电视直播。当然，《伯尔尼公约》允许成员国对于固定做出特别要求。

（二）我国著作权法语境下的解释

尽管我国《著作权法》中“以类似摄制电影的方法创作的作品”的用语来源于《伯尔尼公约》，不过二者还是略有不同，因为其中“创作”一词，《伯尔尼公约》使用的是“表现”。正是由于这一文字上的不同，导致中国的学者和法院在进行解释时，尤其是涉及动画片或者使用计算机制作的视频是否可以归入这一类作品时，产生了分歧④。本文认为，我国《著作权法》所使用的“以类似摄制电影的方法创作的作品”可以解释为与《伯尔尼公约》所使用的“以类似摄制电影的方法表现的作品”同义。

1. 文义解释

法律解释必先由文义解释入手。文义解释，指按照法律条文用语的自然和通常意义，阐释法律之意义内容⑤。根据《现代汉语大词典》的解释，“创作”的含义是：(1) 塑造艺术形象的创作过程；(2) 文学艺术作品⑥。就第一种含义而言，实际上没有任何实质性意义，它只是表明创作可以作动词使用。因此，从文义解释来看，“以类似摄制电影的方法创作的作品”可以涵盖的范围相当广泛。

2. 体系解释

一般而言，除非有其他明确规定，同一法律使用同一概念时，应当做相同解释。我国《著作权法》第三条在具体列举作品类型之前，有一段概述性的内容：“本法所称的作品，包括以下列形式创作的文学、艺术和自然科学、社会科学、工程技术等作品”。其中也使用了“创作”这一用语。此外，我国《著作权法实施条例》对著作权法中的“创作”一词做了进一步解释：“著作权法所称创作，是指直接产生文学、艺术和科学作品的智力活动。”⑦

从以上分析来看，“以类似摄制电影的方法创作的作品”除了表示“以类似摄制电影的方法”产生出具有独创性的作品之外，没有任何进一步的实质意义。因为要构成作品，其必须是“以下列形式创作”，此处已经用“下列形式”对作品进行了限制。

3. 目的解释

《著作权法实施条例》对电影作品进行了如下定义：“摄制在一定介质上，由一系列有伴音或者无伴音的画面组成，并且借助适当装置放映或者以其他方式传播的作品”⑧。著作权法的立法目的是保护创作者、传播者权益，促进作品的创作和传播。从上述立法目的来看，没有理由将电影作品限制在传统的“摄制”方式制作的范围内，也没有必要要求作品一定被“摄制在一定介质上”。因此，《著作权法实施条例》的定义可能背离了《著作权法》的立法本意⑨。事实上，《著作权法（修订草案送审稿）》采用了“视听作品”的概念，删除了“摄制在一定介质上”的要求。

4. 历史解释

我国1991年《著作权法》并没有使用“电影作

① 德利娅·利普希克. 著作权法与邻接权［M］. 联合国教科文组织，译. 北京：中国对外翻译出版公司，2000：512.

② 山姆·里基森，简·金斯伯格. 国际版权与邻接权：伯尔尼公约及公约以外的新发展［M］. 郭寿康，等译. 北京：中国人民大学出版社，2016：375.

③ 同②376.

④ 何怀文. 中国著作权法：判例综述与规范解释［M］. 北京：北京大学出版社，2016：119.

⑤ 梁慧星. 民法解释学［M］. 北京：中国政法大学出版社，1995：214.

⑥ 阮智富，郭忠新. 现代汉语大词典［M］. 上海：上海辞书出版社，2009：286.

⑦ 参见《著作权法实施条例》(2013) 第三条。

⑧ 参见《著作权法实施条例》(2013) 第四条第（十一）项。

⑨ 崔国斌. 著作权法：原理与案例［M］. 北京：北京大学出版社，2014：154.

品和以类似摄制电影的方法创作的作品”这一表达，而是使用“电影、电视、录像作品”①。1991年《著作权法实施条例》对后者的定义是：“摄制在一定物质上，由一系列有伴音或者无伴音的画面组成，并且借助适当装置放映、播放的作品”②。将该定义与2002年《著作权法实施条例》对“电影作品和以类似摄制电影的方法创作的作品”的定义相比，发现除了个别文字上略有改动，二者几乎是完全一样的。

2001年《著作权法》将“电影、电视、录像作品”修改为“电影作品和以类似摄制电影的方法创作的作品”，主要是因为前者只涉及了电影、电视、录像三种媒体形式，涵盖不了1991年《著作权法》颁布后又出现的新媒体形式。因此，2001年《著作权法》按照国际上通行的做法进行了修改③。

综合上述各种解释方法，本文认为“以类似摄制电影的方法创作的作品”是一个涵盖范围非常广泛的用语，其并不限于类似拍摄传统电影那样由诸多作者共同创作并以拍摄电影的步骤制成的作品，而是可以涵盖所有视听作品，只要其符合相关作品构成要件。

三、“固定”与“独创性”的含义

北京知识产权法院认为，要构成电影作品，至少应符合“固定”及“独创性”两个要件④。

（一）“固定”的含义

一般来说，作者权体系的国家不将“固定”作为保护作品的条件，这也符合作者权体系所依循的自然法哲学的思想，因为按照自然法哲学，一旦作品被创作出来，无论其以何种形式表达，作品上的权利即自动产生⑤。相比较而言，版权体系的国家通常都会要求固定。一般来说，只有当一国具有明确的公共政策目标，并且通过固定的要求才能最好地实现该政策目标时，才应当考虑规定这样的要求⑥。

历史上，《伯尔尼公约》曾对舞蹈作品和哑剧有过固定要求，原因是避免取证困难。在布鲁塞尔修订会议上，完全删除固定要求的提案遭到了否决，理由是：作为证据的一种形式，固定仍然十分重要。在斯德哥尔摩外交会议上，一个类似的提案也遭到了反对，这导致各方达成了以下妥协方案，即：一方面删除对舞蹈作品和哑剧的强制性固定要求，另一方面允许国内法对所有类型作品规定固定要求。结果是，任何缔约方此后都可以要求外国作品被固定后才能获得保护。从某种意义上可以认为这是公约要求给予的保护水平的倒退，不过却提高了美国加入《伯尔尼公约》的可能性⑦。需要指出的是，世界知识产权组织编写的指南强调，即使对于那些国内立法包含有固定要求的国家而言，这一要求可以——而且通常也是在——合理地适用。例如，可以认为对现场表演进行同步固定即足以符合这一要求⑧。

美国1976年《版权法》第一百零二条（a）款规定：受版权保护的作品必须“固定在有形的表达媒介上”。因此，在美国版权法中，“固定”是作品获得版权保护的条件之一。第一百零一条的定义首先对“固定”进行了一般性规定，“将作品固定在有形的表达媒介上是指作者本人或经作者授权，使作品被包含在复制品或录制品中，其持久性、稳定性足以使作品在不仅仅是短暂的时间内可以被感知、复制或以其他方式传播”。

“固定”定义首句的一般性规定给直播传输带来了问题：以广播信号为载体的歌曲或电视节目是否足够稳定到保持多于“短暂的时间”，从而符合版权法保护的条件？为了解决这一问题，同时在版权法中保留固定的要求，美国国会选择了一种与“固定”定义首句宽泛的、技术中立的方法截然相反的狭窄的、视具体情况而定的解决方案，规定：“为了本法的目的，被播送的由声音、图像或两者相结合组成的作品，如果是在播送的同时进行同步录制，即为固定作品。”这一规定解决了面向公众的包括体育直播等没有固定形式的边录制、边直播的现场转播行为的地位认定问题。美国众议院报告特别强调：如果直播的内容可以按照电影作品或录音作品的方式进行版权保护，则该直播的内容应该被认定为固定的。如果其录制与传播同时进行，则该作品应获得

① 参见《著作权法》(1991) 第三条第（五）项。
② 参见《著作权法实施条例》(1991) 第四条第（九）项。
③ 郭寿康. 知识产权法［M］. 北京：中共中央党校出版社，2002：43.
④ 北京知识产权法院（2015）京知民终字第1818号民事判决书。
⑤ 西尔克·冯·莱温斯基. 国际版权法律与政策［M］. 万勇，译. 北京：知识产权出版社，2017：40.
⑥ UNCTAD. Resource Book on TRIPs and Development［M］. Cambridge：Cambridge University Press. 2005：148.
⑦ 同⑤112-113.
⑧ 世界知识产权组织. 世界知识产权组织管理的版权及相关权条约指南以及版权及相关权术语汇编. 2004：21.

法定保护①。

在我国著作权法语境下，并没有一般性地将作品被固定作为获得著作权保护的前提条件。根据《著作权法实施条例》的规定，作品是指“文学、艺术和科学领域内具有独创性并能以某种有形形式复制的智力成果”②。其中“以某种有形形式复制”（可复制性）中的“复制”应当做何种解释，存在不同观点。有的法院将之解释为重复③。有的法院将之解释为：“非仅存在于人脑/构思中”④。也有的法院将之解释为“固定”⑤。一般认为，第三种观点是可取的⑥。事实上，《著作权法（修订草案送审稿）》也采取了此种观点，对作品的定义进行了修改：“本法所称的作品，是指文学、艺术和科学领域内具有独创性并能以某种形式固定的智力表达。”⑦

需要指出的是，即使认为作品定义中的复制是固定的意思，构成作品的要件“可复制性”也只是要求“可固定性”，并不以实际固定为条件。事实上，《著作权法》第三条第（二）项规定的“口述作品”显然就是尚未固定，但仍然构成作品。当然，以上论述只是针对一般情况，并不排除著作权法对某些特殊类型的作品施加固定要求。

《著作权法实施条例》在对电影作品进行定义时，要求“摄制在一定介质上”。虽然上文指出，这一定义可能背离了《著作权法》的立法本意，但在其被修改之前，还是应当从解释论的角度进行阐释。本文认为，对于直播传输节目，即使特别强调固定要求的美国《版权法》也承认其符合固定的要求，显然，我国著作权法不应采取高于美国法对固定的要求，也可采取类似的解释路径：录制与传播同时进行，从而构成固定，符合“摄制在一定介质上”的要求。

（二）独创性

一般来说，作者权体系的国家对获得版权保护所要求的独创性程度比版权体系的国家要高⑧。之所以如此，主要是两个法律体系所采用的哲学基础不同。作者权体系主要受自然法理论、人格理论的影响⑨。因此，作者的创作物自然就属于他所有，作品是作者人格的外化，作品是人类智力的创作成果，因而要求具有某种主观上的新颖性或创作性的要素⑩。版权体系采取的则是功利主义进路，认为之所以提供版权保护，原因在于鼓励创作从而提高社会的整体福利是必要的。

虽然大陆法系和英美法系对独创性的理解存在一些差异，不过这种差异有一种逐渐淡化和趋同的趋势。单纯的“辛勤劳动”不足以使成果构成作品，它还必须是一种智力创作；但是，超出单纯的智力创作条件而要求某种更高水平的创作性，或要求在某种程度上体现作者个性，则是不合情理的⑪。也就是说，尽管《伯尔尼公约》将独创性的确切特征留给成员国国内法自行确定，但它还是暗示了对成员国自由划定这些界限的某些限制：对于公约所明确列举的作品类型，各成员国不可以将独创性标准提高到实际上完全排除对这类作品的保护的程度⑫。

那么，我国《著作权法》究竟属于作者权体系还是版权体系，其要求的独创性标准为何？从法律结构与具体条文中所使用的术语——著作权和邻接权，采用的权利体系——人身权和财产权，规定的例外与限制——封闭式的立法模式等方面来看，我国《著作权法》似乎属于作者权体系⑬。然而，从正当性基础来看，我国《著作权法》似乎采用的是功利主义进路，而非自然法哲学⑭。因为《著作权

① 朱莉·E. 科恩，等. 全球信息经济下的美国版权法［M］. 王迁，等译. 北京：商务印书馆，2016：82.

② 参见《著作权法实施条例》（2013）第二条。

③ 上海市中级人民法院（2013）沪一中民五（知）终字第59号民事判决书。

④ 浙江省杭州市中级人民法院（2011）浙杭知终字第54号民事判决书。

⑤ 陕西省西安市中级人民法院（2008）西民四初字第119号民事判决书。

⑥ 何怀文. 中国著作权法：判例综述与规范解释［M］. 北京：北京大学出版社，2016：24.

⑦ 参见《著作权法（修订草案送审稿）》（2014）第五条第一款。

⑧ 西尔克·冯·莱温斯基. 国际版权法律与政策［M］. 万勇，译. 北京：知识产权出版社，2017：41.

⑨ 同⑧34.

⑩ 同⑧.

⑪ 世界知识产权组织. 世界知识产权组织管理的版权及相关权条约指南以及版权及相关权术语汇编. 2004：17.

⑫ 山姆·里基森，简·金斯伯格. 国际版权与邻接权：伯尔尼公约及公约以外的新发展［M］. 郭寿康，等译. 北京：中国人民大学出版社，2016：349.

⑬ 有关作者权体系与版权体系的区别，参见西尔克·冯·莱温斯基《国际版权法律与政策》，万勇译，知识产权出版社2017年版第30-58页。

⑭ 崔国斌. 知识产权法官造法批判［J］. 中国法学，2006（1）.

法》第一条规定："为保护文学、艺术和科学作品作者的著作权，以及与著作权有关的权益，鼓励有益于社会主义精神文明、物质文明建设的作品的创作和传播，促进社会主义文化和科学事业的发展与繁荣，根据宪法制定本法。"

立法目的与具体法律条文之间存在的紧张关系，导致我国法院在确定独创性的标准时观点各异。有的法院认为：创作性只要求一定水准的智力创作高度①——这一标准与版权体系标准类似。有的法院认为：应表现作者独特个性②——这一标准基本上与作者权体系标准类似。也有的法院认为：处于一定创作高度与作者个性之间③——这一标准则兼采作者权体系与版权体系。

本文认为，既然我国《著作权法》明确规定其立法目的是鼓励作品的创作和传播，而且我国历史上也并不存在植根于自然法哲学的个人本位的传统财产法观念，相反，我国社会传统更强调公共利益，社会本位的财产观更契合中国④。因此，我国《著作权法》采取的独创性标准应当更接近于版权体系，而非作者权体系。

就凤凰网案而言，尽管公用信号制作手册对于拍摄提供了一定的指导和建议，但不能就此认为拍摄不具有独创性。该手册从某种意义上讲就相当于摄影师在学习摄影课程时的教科书或教师讲授的拍摄技巧，例如对于人物、山水、花草，都各有拍摄重点与技巧，不能因为摄影师学习过相关内容，就否认其拍摄作品的独创性。如果按照判决的逻辑，则摄影师学习拍摄课程或资料越多，学得越好，摄影师受到的限制也就越多（类似作家中的考据派，句句有出处）⑤，拍摄作品具有的独创性也就越低，这显然不合理。因此，本文认为，根据公用信号制作手册的指导拍摄，不能当然否认拍摄出来的画面无独创性。进一步而言，对于涉案体育赛事画面，由于存在多个机位拍摄，每个机位拍摄的画面有多种选择（摄影师对于拍摄重点、景别和构图的选择），导演在收到各个机位拍摄的画面后，也存在选择和编排。因此，即使在没有添加解说、慢动作和集锦的情况下，赛事画面也具有独创性。

四、结语

北京知识产权法院在否认涉案赛事直播公用信号承载的连续画面构成电影作品和以类似摄制电影的方法创作的作品之后，又讨论了网络直播行为的性质。令人感到困惑的是，其认为被诉网络直播行为是对广播权中第一种广播行为——"无线广播"——的信号的网络直播行为，"属于广播权调整的第二种行为，即'以有线传播或者转播的方式向公众传播广播的作品'的行为"。然而，需要指出的是，广播权中第一种广播行为针对的客体是作品，第二种广播行为针对的客体是"广播的作品"，无论哪一种行为，要适用广播权，前提都是首先需要存在作品。如果按照二审法院对于广播权的上述解释，则其已经承认了涉案赛事节目是作品，而这与其之前的认定是矛盾的。

事实上，关于网络直播行为的性质，尽管此前曾有过争议，但后来各方基本达成了共识，认为：其属于《著作权法》第十条第一款第（十七）项"应当由著作权人享有的其他权利"的规制范围⑥。

综上所述，本文认为，通过法律解释的方法，可以将"以类似摄制电影的方法创作的作品"解释为《伯尔尼公约》中的"以类似摄制电影的方法表现的作品"，从而将判断的重点由制作方法，转为制作效果：是否由投射到银幕或屏幕上的连续视觉画面构成。此外，世界知识产权组织出版的公约指南明确指出：《伯尔尼公约》中"电影作品和以类似摄制电影的方法表现的作品"与"视听作品"的概念相当⑦。由于赛事直播画面符合独创性要求，录制与传播同时进行，因而符合固定要求，从而构成电影作品。

（本文原发表于《现代法学》2018年第5期，获上海市教育发展基金会和上海市教育委员会"曙光计划"（项目批准号：13SG15）、中国人民大学科学研究基金（中央高校基本科研业务费专项资金）（项目批准号：17XNA002）资助。
作者单位：中国人民大学）

① 上海市第一中级人民法院（2013）沪一中民五（知）终字第170号民事判决书。
② 北京市高级人民法院（2010）高民终字第772号民事判决书。
③ 北京市朝阳区人民法院（2011）朝民初字第31507号民事判决书。
④ 崔国斌. 知识产权法官造法批判［J］. 中国法学，2006（1）.
⑤ 需要指出的是，即使是作家中的考据派，也并不妨碍其创作的成果具有独创性而构成作品，因为选择和编排可体现独创性。
⑥ 参见《北京市高级人民法院关于涉及网络知识产权案件的审理指南》第十五条。
⑦ 世界知识产权组织. 世界知识产权组织管理的版权及相关权条约指南以及版权及相关权术语汇编. 2004：218.

论著作权合理使用扩张适用的路径选择

刘宇晖

随着科学技术的发展，公众对作品的利用更加便捷多样，与作品著作权范围多有交织。如插花消费者购买插花后拍照并在朋友圈展示，插花设计师主张自己对其独创的插花享有著作权，插花消费者在朋友圈展示该插花作品的行为属于未经许可的展览，构成著作权侵权。再如明星在他的胳膊上进行了文身，当该明星为某款游戏角色提供形象时，胳膊上的文身也显露在游戏中，文身设计师主张对该明星胳膊上的文身享有著作权，在电子游戏中展示该文身构成著作权侵权。上述两种情况都存在受著作权法保护的作品，插花和文身都可因独创性而属于著作权法保护的作品，都存在他人对作品的利用，属于著作权的权利范围，插花在朋友圈的公开展示、文身在游戏中的展示可属于著作权之展览权、信息网络传播权的范围，两种行为人只有通过合理使用的抗辩才可能摆脱著作权人侵权的指控。但是我国著作权法合理使用的规范，即《著作权法》第二十二条的规定过于僵化，仅仅穷尽式地列举出了 12 种合理使用的具体情形，远远不能适应新技术时代作品利用的复杂性。我国司法实践中早有对具体情形列举的突破，有利用《伯尔尼公约》的“三步检验法”，也有直接在裁判文书中引入美国合理使用判断的四要素，更有紧随美国合理使用判定的新发展，在我国合理使用的司法判断中考虑“转换性使用”。有学者推崇我国法院在司法实践中借鉴美国合理使用判断因素向转换性使用的转变，也有学者质疑我国法院的这一做法。无可置疑的是，著作权合理使用的判定不能局限于穷尽式的列举，合理使用的扩张适用无可避免，是借鉴《伯尔尼公约》的“三步检验法”还是引进美国合理使用的四要素、“转换性使用”、“市场中心”等判断标准，抑或另辟蹊径，下文将逐一讨论，并对我国《著作权法》合理使用条款的修订提供浅见。

一、著作权合理使用的理论基础

大陆法系和英美法系对著作权法律性质的认识存在差异，大陆法系国家，也被称为作者权体系，多以康德、黑格尔等哲学家的作品观为基础，认为作品是作者人格的外化，作者对作品的控制是基于一种自然权利，以自然权利的观点构建著作权权利体系，保护作者的人格权和财产权。英美法系国家，也被称为版权体系，自《安妮法令》始就认为著作权是财产性权利，该法全称《为鼓励知识创作而授予作者及购买者就其已印刷成册的图书在一定时期内之权利的法》，书商是该法案的主要推动者，意图通过对作者复制权的保护延续其对图书的垄断控制。只要书商能够说服作者将其权利转让给他们，上述规定的效果就是给书商提供了一个机会以收回他们以往在图书交易上所行使的某些控制权[①]。边沁的功利主义对英美法系著作权的影响巨大，英美法系功利地将著作权法的立法目的界定为促进社会文化的最大化发展，并以此构建著作权法的权利体系和著作权的合理使用。

自然权利和功利主义的著作权理论基础导致两大法系著作权合理使用制度的性质不同。作者权体系认为合理使用是著作权的例外，而版权体系则认为合理使用属于公众的权利。对合理使用性质的不同认识影响了各国合理使用的制度构造。作者权体系合理使用的规范采用严格的封闭式，立法者创制著作权例外类型，司法机关只能基于法定类型进行法律解释，防止合理使用在司法适用时不当扩张，侵害作者的自然权利。《伯尔尼公约》允许各国通过立法限制著作权的范围，但必须满足“三步检验法”，即在特定且特殊情形下，不得影响作品的正常使用，不得不合理地损害著作权人的合法利益。唯有符合“三步检验法”方判定为合理使用。版权体系合理使用的适用采取宽松的开放式，法官在司法实践中依据一般标准考量使用行为的多个方面，特别是使用行为对著作权人作品市场的影响，综合评价合理使用适用的市场效果，裁量是否适用合理使用。法官在司法实践中不断创造出合理使用的考量因素。

我国《著作权法》的立法既受作者权体系的影响，也有版权体系的身影。在立法目的上，兼顾作者的著作权、邻接权的保护和社会公共利益的促进。在法律内容上，规定了作者除享有财产权之外还享有不可让渡的人格权，规定自然人作品的同时也承认法人作品。这种兼容的立法模式缺乏认识论上的统一性、严谨性，但具有更多的灵活性，在合理使用的模式选择上有更多的空间，并非必然要选择作者权体系或版权体系的模式。

① 布拉德·谢尔曼，莱昂内尔·本特利. 现代知识产权法的演进：英国的历程（1760—1911）[M]. 金海军，译，北京：北京大学出版社，2006：12.

二、作者权体系合理使用的判定模式与补充

（一）“著作权例外”模式

作者权体系著作权法合理使用的判定模式被称为“著作权例外”模式。该模式表现为：立法中明确穷尽式列举合理使用适用的具体情形，司法实践中严格比对是否与具体条款规定的要件一致，以判定能否适用合理使用，不允许法官自由增加合理使用的适用情况，属于封闭式的合理使用判定。“著作权例外”模式的理论基础在于作者权体系国家认为著作权是作者的自然权利，著作权人对权利的享有是原则，合理使用对著作权的限制属于例外。这种例外源于著作权人、公众、使用者三方的利益平衡，体现为对权利的非正常限制，这种非正常的例外应受到严格的限制，不能由法院在司法实践中自由地裁量判定构成合理使用，否则就是损害著作权人的自然权利。

“著作权例外”模式的优点显而易见，法官和公众明确地知悉何种情况属于合理使用，何种情况的使用需要许可。但它的弊端同样明显，“著作权例外”模式的封闭性不可能包含社会多样化的对作品合理使用的情况，更不可能预见技术进步引发的新的合理使用的情况。“著作权例外”模式固守着立法的穷尽式列举，维持着法律制定时著作权人与公众、使用者的利益平衡，殊不知社会的进步使得利益处于不断的变动中，合理使用这一利益平衡器亦需要不断地变化。

（二）补充

面对“著作权例外”模式的弊端，作者权体系的国家有着自己的应对方式。在德国，著作权侵权判定的要件之一是需要对作品进行“实质性利用”。“实质性利用”包含了对作品利用的质和量的判断，法官对此具有自由裁量的权力。一旦认定不构成“实质性利用”就不构成侵权，与合理使用具有同样的效果。如在电影作品中使用他人的音乐作品时长7秒，就属于非“实质性利用”，不构成侵权。而我国著作权法不存在“实质性利用”，法官只能认定构成合理使用，才不构成侵权。德国著作权法还通过“自由利用”的概念，弥补封闭式合理使用的不足。该国《著作权法》第二十四条规定：对他人作品进行与著作权无关的利用而创作的独立作品，可不经被利用的作品的著作权人许可，予以发表或使用。在很多国家被认为是合理使用的效仿，在德国被认为是“自由利用”[①]。此外，德国法院还可以援引著作权法以外的法律认定不构成著作权侵权。德国联邦宪法法院曾经根据宪法上的艺术自由，认定一位戏剧家的引用行为合法[②]。

作者权体系国家合理使用判定的“著作权例外”模式从权利逻辑上符合著作权属于自然权利的初始预设，但权利不仅源于自然理性，还根植于以生产力为基础的人与人之间的关系，严谨的数学逻辑思维并不能适应社会的多样性和进步性。利用合理使用之外的规范对“著作权例外”的封闭性模式予以补充，虽维系了合理使用的权利逻辑，但增加了法律准确适用的难度、公众全面准确理解法律的成本，并不值得推崇。我国《著作权法》片面采用“著作权例外”模式，缺少“实质性利用”、“自由利用”及宪法原则的支持，未能形成全面的合理使用规范体系。未来我国《著作权法》的修订也不宜再增加“实质性利用”“自由利用”等概念或直接援引宪法原则判定他人对作品的使用构成合理使用。

三、从“潜在市场分析”到“转换性使用”——美国合理使用判定标准的发展

（一）以“潜在市场分析”为重点的合理使用判定

1841年，约瑟夫·斯托里法官在Folsom v. Marsh一案[③]中首次使用的合理使用的四要素检验法，后被写入美国《版权法》。该法第一百零七条规定，检验合理使用的四个要素包括：（1）使用的目的和性质，即该使用是商业性还是为教育目的的非营利性使用；（2）受版权保护作品的性质；（3）使用受版权保护作品的数量和比重；（4）该使用对版权作品潜在市场和价值的影响[④]。该四要素的检验非常灵活，各要素所占权重没有固定的比例，不像数学公式那样通过严谨的推论得到绝对的结果。法院需要综合考量四要素来评价未经许可的使用是否促进了社会文化的最大化发展。四要素的综合判断导致合理使用判定的极端不确定。有学者认为这四个判断标准具有很强的可塑性，仅通过这些标准做出合理使用判决近乎神话[⑤]。

美国合理使用判定四要素中第四个要素，即

① 李琛. 论我国著作权法修订中“合理使用”的立法技术［J］. 知识产权，2013（1）.

② 同①.

③ Folsom v. Marsh，9. F. Cas. 342，美国合理使用第一案。

④ Section 107 of the US Copyright Law.

⑤ David Nimmer. —Fairest of Them All‖ and Other Fairy Tales of Fair Use，66 Law & Contemp. Probs. 263，287（2003）.

对版权作品潜在市场和价值的影响在合理使用判定中具有重要的意义。假使使用作品的目的是商业性的而非非营利性的，受保护作品的性质是虚拟的而非纪实的，使用作品的数量较多而不是少量，也不必然会认定不构成合理使用，如商业性的滑稽模仿，即使较多地使用了虚拟作品，只要未不当损害作品的潜在市场和价值，就认为构成合理使用。正如有学者明确指出，第四个要素是合理使用各要素中最重要也是最核心的要素①。Gordon 教授认为合理使用是市场失灵的对策，在市场交易成本过高的情况下，市场失灵，就只得允许公众自由使用作品。Gordon 教授据此提出了界定合理使用的新标准：首先，认定是否存在市场失灵；其次，判断使用者的使用行为所带来的社会福利是否大于该使用行为对版权人造成的损害；最后，考量假如认定使用者构成合理使用是否会对版权人的激励造成实质损害②。根据该理论，在市场失灵的情况下，作品使用者的使用不会损害版权人的潜在市场价值，就存在合理使用的适用。1985 年美国联邦最高法院在审理"Harper 案"时指出：合理使用的第四个要素是被告能够主张合理使用最重要的依据③。

（二）"转换性使用"——合理使用判定标准的转向

合理使用的四要素分析法需要在个案中具体分析，各要素抽象性强，且各要素的个体判断难以形成合理使用能否适用的必然结果，导致司法实践中各法院的判决依赖直觉而难以预测且时有分歧。Lavel 法官反思自己的审判实践，认为合理使用的四要素缺乏指导性理论学说与价值准则，力图挖掘"一个植根于版权法目标的切实可行的指导原则"④。其在 1990 年《哈佛法学评论》上发表了《合理使用标准》（"Toward a Fair Use Standard"）一文，首次提出了"转换性使用"理论。所谓"转换性"，是指在前一作品的基础上增加了新的表达、含义或信息。Lavel 法官认为：第一百零七条中的第一个判断标准，也即"使用的目的和性质"标准，事关合理使用的正当性问题，被告的抗辩应当首先回答受指控的行为是否以及在何种程度上具有"转换性"。如果被引用的文献仅被作为原始材料，转换就存在于创造新的信息、新的美感、新的视角与见解的行为之中，而合理使用保护这种行为是为了社会进步⑤。

1994 年发生的"Campbell 案"中，联邦最高法院首次采用了"转换性使用"理论。对潜在市场的分析不再是合理使用判定的最重要的依据，法院开始更加关注考察合理使用四要素中的第一个要素：使用的目的和性质。但对第一个要素的考量不再局限于"商业性还是非商业性"的二分，而是考量对作品的使用是否属于或者在多大程度上属于"转换性使用"。法院认为被告对原告作品的滑稽模仿，并非简单地改写或者包装原作，而是以类似书评的方式说明了原作，具有高度的"转换性"，因而构成合理使用⑥。该案在美国版权法合理使用发展史上具有里程碑的意义，此后众多案例将其视为先例，适用"转换性使用"理论判断是否构成合理使用。Netanel 教授实证研究了 1995—2010 年间美国联邦法院系统所有的合理使用案例，指出 2005 年之前的美国合理使用判例处于"市场中心"范式之下，自 2005 年起，"转换性使用"范式在美国合理使用判例中兴起，合理使用判定的首要、决定性因素转变为被告的行为是否具有"转换性"⑦。

开放式的合理使用的判定方式极大地赋予了法官依据个案自由裁量是否构成合理使用的权力，在适应社会多样性和进步性上具有天然的优势。然而，不管是"合理使用四要素"还是"转换性使用"都过于抽象，缺少足够的预见性，对法院自由裁量的指导和限制也非常少，并不适合我国现有的司法状态。

四、我国合理使用扩张适用中的各自为政

（一）"三步检验法"——我国合理使用扩张适用的立法倾向

我国合理使用的判定一直采用"著作权例外"的封闭模式，体现为《著作权法》第二十二条。该条穷尽式地列举了合理使用的具体情况，没有"其

① MELVILLE B. NIMMER，NIMMER ON COPYRIGHT § 13.05 [A]，13-76 (1984).

② Wendy J. Gordon. Fair Use as Market Failure：A Structural and Economic Analysis of the " Betamax " Case and Its Predecessors，82Colum. L. Rev . 1600，1614 (1982).

③ Harper & Row Publishers，Inc. v. Nation Enters.，471 U. S. 539，566 (1985).

④ Pierre N. Leval. Toward a Fair Use Standard，103 Harv. L. Rev. 1105，(1990)，p. 1105.

⑤ 同④1111.

⑥ Campbell v. Acuff-Rose Music，510 U. S. 569，579 (1994).

⑦ Neil Weinstock Netanel. Making Sense of Fair Use，15 Lewis & Clark L. Rev (2011). p. 736.

他情况”的兜底性规定，也没有抽象的一般条款。《著作权法实施条例》第二十一条规定：依照著作权法有关规定，使用可以不经著作权人许可的已经发表的作品的，不得影响该作品的正常使用，也不得不合理地损害著作权人的合法利益。该条存在两种解读：一种认为这是我国合理使用的一般条款；另一种解读认为这条是对《著作权法》第二十二条适用的限定，即使在符合《著作权法》第二十二条明确规定的情况下，也应不得影响该作品的正常使用，不得不合理地损害著作权人的合法利益。后一种解释更符合法律规范的效力解释，《著作权法实施条例》仅是对《著作权法》的解释，而不能突破《著作权法》的规定创设新的规范。

《著作权法》合理使用的封闭式规范很早就受到学者的批判，他们主张应制定合理使用的一般条款。《著作权法》修订草案的送审稿中第四十三条规定了著作权合理使用的适用情况，在延续现行《著作权法》的具体列举之外增加了“其他情形”，并吸收《著作权法实施条例》的规定，各列举的使用作品的情形包括其他情形都不得影响作品的正常使用，也不得不合理地损害著作权人的合法利益。“其他情形”的增加体现了我国著作权合理使用立法的趋势——增加合理使用适用的广泛性，不再局限于具体列举的情形。这一变化是有益的，是立法对社会多样性和技术进步的回应。但是借鉴《伯尔尼公约》的“三步检验法”对合理使用的适用进行限制，过于抽象，不利于司法实践的运用。

（二）开放式合理使用判定——我国合理使用扩张适用的司法偏爱

尽管我国法律并未赋予法官创设法律的权力，但在合理使用的司法实践里，法官在不断地突破合理使用的法定情况，在阐述合理使用的扩张适用时展现出不同的思路，包括类推适用、“三步检验法”、“合理使用四要素”及“转换性使用”。

北影录音录像公司诉北京电影学院一案类推适用了我国《著作权法》第二十二条第一款第（六）项。法院认为北京电影学院组织学生改编、拍摄他人作品的行为是为学生完成毕业作业及锻炼学生的实践能力，在校内放映该片是为了教学观摩及评定，均为课堂教学必要的组成部分，属于合理使用①。这一类推适用的依据是使用行为目的的一致性，都为了课堂教学的需要。

中国音乐著作权协会诉福建周末电视有限公司等侵犯著作权纠纷案借鉴了《伯尔尼公约》中的“三步检验法”。法院认为被告在其电视剧《命运的承诺》中仅使用《一无所有》这一音乐作品中的一句演唱，时长7秒，不构成侵权。理由是“被告的使用行为对该作品的正常使用不产生任何实质不利影响，也未实质损害该作品的权利人的合法权益”②。覃绍殷诉北京荣宝拍卖有限公司侵犯著作权纠纷案同样借鉴了《伯尔尼公约》中的“三步检验法”。法院认为：被告作为拍卖公司，其复制国画《通途劈上彩云间》并向特定客户发行，以及在拍卖过程中以幻灯的方式放映该画的行为，不属于侵权行为。理由是“上述使用行为系出于其他目的，没有影响作品的正常使用，也没有不合理地损害原告的合法权益”③。

在谷歌公司与王莘侵害著作权纠纷案中法院则引用了美国合理使用的四要素。北京市高级人民法院认为：谷歌公司在其搜索结果中显示涉案作品的概述、作品片段、常用术语和短语、作品版权信息等内容构成合理使用。理由是：“判断是否构成合理使用，一般应当考虑使用作品的目的和性质、受著作权保护的作品的性质、所使用部分的质量及其在整个作品中的比例和使用行为对作品现实和潜在市场及价值的影响等因素”④。

在上海美术电影制片厂与浙江新影年代文化传播有限公司侵权案中，上海知识产权法院则引用了美国“转换性使用”理论。法院认为新影年代公司未经许可在其制作的海报上引用“葫芦娃”“黑猫警长”美术作品，不是单纯地展现原作品的艺术美感和功能，而是反映“80后”一代曾经经历“葫芦娃”“黑猫警长”动画片盛播的时代年龄特征，属于“转换性使用”，并不影响涉案作品的正常使用，也没有不合理地损害著作权人的合法利益，故构成合理使用⑤。

我国合理使用的司法实践已然超出了法院依法享有的自由裁量的权力范围，越来越向美国的开放式合理使用模式靠拢。有学者推崇法院这种对法律的创造性适用，也有学者质疑这种做法。

① 北京市第一中级人民法院（1995）一中知终字第19号民事判决书。
② 北京市第一中级人民法院（2003）一中民初字第11687号民事判决书。
③ 北京市第一中级人民法院（2003）一中民初字第12064号民事判决书。
④ 北京市高级人民法院（2013）高民终字第1221号民事判决书。
⑤ 上海知识产权法院（2015）沪知民终字第730号民事判决书。

（三）各执一词——我国合理使用扩张适用的理论现状

在我国《著作权法》修订的过程中，学者基本都赞同修改我国著作权合理使用的封闭式立法模式，允许法官在法定列举之外适用合理使用，但在对合理使用扩张适用的规范设计上，还存在较多的争鸣。

有学者主张未来我国著作权合理使用修法的正确选择是改造“三步检验法”，删除破坏“特定且特殊情形”要件的兜底条款——“其他情形”，转而在法定列举上加以调整，以此限定“三步检验法”中的“特定且特殊情形”，在法定类型限度内再适用“不得影响作品的正常使用”和“不得不合理地损害著作权人的合法利益”①。该学者认为：我国法院以美国版权法上的“合理使用四要素”作为替代解释，以及将法定列举和一般条款综合考虑的做法，都是违背“三步检验法”解释规则的错误选择。有学者反对我国《著作权法（修订草案送审稿）》中借鉴“三步检验法”的做法，认为“三步检验法”过于抽象，并不能给予法官和公众有价值的预测，美国的“合理使用四要素”标准能更明确地指导法官形成裁判，我国著作权法立法应引入美国的四要素标准②。有学者认为我国应增加合理使用的一般性条款，并借鉴美国“转换性使用”理论③。也有学者认为可以继续沿用“三步检验法”的表述，但不赞同在“三步检验法”的判定中嫁接美国“转换性使用”理论，认为合理使用的判定应回归市场中心主义，以市场因素来衡量作品的使用行为是否对原著作权人潜在市场造成实质上的负面影响，导致原著作权人严重丧失创作动力④。

学者对我国著作权法合理使用扩张适用的分歧可以分为两个层级：第一层级是制定一般性条款还是类推适用合理使用的法定列举，以缓解封闭式立法的弊端。第二层级为扩张适用的判定标准是“三步检验法”、“合理使用四要素”、“转换性使用”还是“以市场为中心”，各个不同的标准都试图找到合理使用的本质，为合理使用的判定提供有效的标准。

五、我国著作权法合理使用扩张适用的立法建议

笔者不赞同以类推适用法定列举加“三步检验法”限定的方式实现司法对合理使用的扩张适用。这种立法路径虽然能更好地限定合理使用的范围，更明晰地指导司法实践，更多地增加公众对合理使用与否的可预测性，但就解决作品利用方式多样化与法定列举片面化的矛盾来说，实属杯水车薪，无法达成技术进步后著作权人、使用人、公众间的利益平衡。此外，此种立法路径的前提之一是将现有法定列举抽象化，放宽法定列举的条件限制，为类推适用留下空间。但这种做法有违背“三步检验法”精神的嫌疑。“三步检验法”的第一步“特定且特殊情形”要求合理使用仅适用于具体的特殊的情形，过于抽象化、没有具体指向的列举是不符合这一要求的，容易导致合理使用的滥用，危害著作权人的正当利益。

制定合理使用的一般条款更符合社会生活的复杂性和技术进步导致的作品利用方式的多样化对合理使用制度的需要。封闭式的法定列举或者具体列举的类推适用都无法涵盖日益增多的可能的合理利用作品的方式，正如本文开头所提到的微信朋友圈展示自己购买的插花、网络游戏中出现的原型人物的文身。在立法中引入一般条款才能为司法实践中法院的自由裁量留有空间。我国司法实践中屡屡突破法定列举的范围判定构成合理使用的做法，严格说来属于超法现象，实不可取，亦属无奈。在《著作权法》修订之际，在法定列举之外制定合理使用的一般条款，方能回应司法实践的真实需要，并将法院对合理使用的自由裁量纳入法律规范之内。

在合理使用一般条款的表述上，简单借鉴“三步检验法”的弊端已被多方阐述：过于抽象的语句无法指引合理使用的自由裁量，也无法约束合理使用的判定。直接转向美国的“合理使用四要素”、“潜在市场分析”、“转换性使用”或“市场中心”都不符合我国的立法惯例和司法环境，但也为形成我国自己的合理使用扩张适用的判断标准提供了方向。我国合理使用扩张适用的判断标准不宜缺乏具体内容，也不宜仅有考量因素，借鉴“三步检验法”，细化“特定且特殊情形”，以著作权法立法目的限定合理使用的扩张适用更符合我国国情。“特定且特殊情形”可细化为使用作品的目的、方式或范围不同于著作权人使用作品的目的、方式或范围，使用的后果应促进文学艺术的发展。即我国合理使用的一般条款可表述为：他人利用作品的目的、方式或范围

① 熊琦. 著作权合理使用司法认定标准释疑［J］. 法学，2018（1）.
② 李琛. 论我国著作权法修订中“合理使用”的立法技术［J］. 知识产权，2013（1）.
③ 袁锋. 论新技术环境下“转换性使用”理论的发展［J］. 知识产权，2017（8）.
④ 谢琳. 论著作权合理使用的扩展适用：回归以市场为中心的判定路径［J］. 中山大学学报（社会科学版），2017（4）.

不同于著作权人使用作品的目的、方式或范围，促进文学艺术发展的，不构成侵权。上文在网络游戏中因原型人物形象附带使用文身师文身作品的情形应属合理使用，游戏作者对文身的利用目的为真实展示人物原型的形象，不同于文身师正常的利用目的；戏仿对作品的利用方式不同于著作权人对作品的再现和演绎；在微信朋友圈展示插花作品与插花师展示作品的范围存在不同。目的、方式或范围不同，又可促进文学艺术的发展，这类对作品的利用应予鼓励而非禁止。

六、结语

我国的立法、司法传统与现状使得我国不宜照搬“三步检验法”或美国的开放式立法模式，但不妨碍我们借鉴他国解决问题的思路。著作权合理使用的封闭式立法只能淘汰，在法定列举之外补充一般条款，符合社会发展的需要，也是立法技术的趋势。一般条款抽象但不可无迹可循，否则无法适用。以著作权法的立法目的为总体限定，具体考察作品利用的目的、方式和范围，能够较好地区分作品著作权人的权利范围和合理利用他人作品的范围。

（本文原发表于《知识产权》2018年第10期。
作者单位：华北电力大学）

制度演进视角下我国广播权的范畴

刘银良

在著作权法领域，广播权是作者的一项重要经济权利。我国《著作权法》于1990年制定伊始就为作者规定了控制其作品“播放”的权利，而且2001年《著作权法》（第一次修正案）中明确规定了“广播权”。然而在我国著作权法学界和司法界，关于如何理解广播权的范畴却有持续争议，相关的案件判决亦引起广泛争论。这反映了我国广播权制度的实际境地：虽然在理论上它是一项重要的传播权，但其保护却并未取得良好效果。我国著作权法学界对于广播权的研究亦难称深入，这从研究论文或专著的不足就能够看出，甚至广播权制度的一些基础问题尚未得到全面研究，如本文将要探讨的广播权范畴问题。鉴于我国著作权法关于广播权的法律规定及其适用皆存在不足，本文拟运用历史分析和比较研究等方法，从国际广播权制度演化角度分析我国广播权的立法和司法问题，借以审视我国广播权制度的缺陷及其完善路径，并就此厘定广播权的范畴。本文将首先回归至《伯尔尼公约》《世界知识产权组织版权条约》（WCT）等国际法文本，从历史演化视角分析广播权发展，然后再结合我国著作权法的相关规定，比较其他国家立法，探究我国广播权制度的立法与司法问题。除非明确说明，本文中的“广播权”仅指作者的广播权。

一、《伯尔尼公约》下的传统广播权

在国际公约视野内，广播权源于20世纪20年代后期。在《伯尔尼公约》《罗马公约》等著作权或邻接权公约框架下，“广播”仅指通过“无线方式”实施的广播或播放行为。21世纪初以来，随着流媒体技术的应用，广播已从传统的无线广播和有线广播（播放）扩展至包括网络广播（播放）或称网播。随着电信网、广播电视网和互联网的融合，广播和信息网络传播在信号和传输路径等方面趋于一致，无线广播、有线广播和网络广播产生交叉与融合，综合广播时代到来。此时再坚持区分各类广播行为已不再具有技术上的意义。当然从《伯尔尼公约》规定的广播权限制角度看，界定传统的无线广播和有线广播或网播仍可能有著作权法上的意义①。

广播权于1928年被纳入《伯尔尼公约》罗马文本，其所规范的仅是无线广播行为②。这是国际公约关于广播权的最初文本，标志着电子环境下作者远程传播权的国际源起。随着有线传播技术的应用，针对广播节目的再传播行为亦须规范。1948年《伯尔尼公约》布鲁塞尔文本扩增了广播权内容，使其所规制的行为从无线广播扩展至包括针对无线广播信号的有线或无线转播以及利用扩音器等设备的再传播行为（实质为机械表演行为）。涵盖无线广播以及对由此产生的广播信号的转播和再传播行为的传统广播权基本定型。其后《伯尔尼公约》的斯德哥尔摩文本（1967年）和巴黎文本（1971年）均未对广播权进行实质修改，只是优化了其英文版文本③。这意味着《伯尔尼公约》关于广播权的现行规定基本由布鲁塞尔文本固定于1948年。

《伯尔尼公约》巴黎文本第十一条之二第（1）

① Jörg Reinbothe，Silke von Lewinski. The WIPO Treaties on Copyright：A Commentary on the WCT，the WPPT，and the BTAP [M]. 2nd ed. Oxford：Oxford University Press，2015：para. 7. 8. 44.

② Berne Convention (Rome Act，1928)，Article 11bis (1).

③ WIPO. Guide to the Berne Convention for the Protection of Literary and Artistic Works (Paris Act，1971) [M]. WIPO Publication No. 615 (E)，1978：para. 11bis. 1.

款规定了广播权的内容（实质为布鲁塞尔文本）①。根据《伯尔尼公约指南》的解释，《伯尔尼公约》规定的广播权包括三种权利，它们分别覆盖三类与（无线）广播相关的广播、转播或传播行为②。值得注意的是，在《伯尔尼公约》各官方语言的文本中会有一些表达上的差异。为求全面理解其规定，本文将以英文文本为主，并视需要比较其中文、法文和西班牙文文本的规定。

第一类是（无线）广播或无线传播行为。

这类行为是广播权所规范的基础行为。它又包括两种行为。其一是无线广播行为。该行为的主体是向公众发射广播信号的广播电台或电视台。该广播行为可称为作品的“初始广播”，相应的广播组织可称为“初始广播组织”，由此形成的广播信号可称为“初始广播信号”。其二是通过任何其他无线方式向公众传播作品的行为。该行为的主体可以是任何从事其他无线传播行为的主体，该行为的客体也是作者的作品，其中《伯尔尼公约》英文文本的概念是“thereof”即被广播的作品，中文文本使用的概念是“其作品”即作者的作品，法文文本与西班牙文文本皆使用“这些作品”。应该注意的是，该无线传播行为的客体与公约广播权条款所列第二类及第三类针对初始广播信号的转播或传播行为（它们分别由《伯尔尼公约》第十一条之二第（1）款第（ii）和（iii）目所规定）的客体即“作品的广播”明显不同（该概念的中文、法文和西班牙文文本皆称为“广播的作品”）。

这表明由《伯尔尼公约》第十一条之二第（1）款第（i）目所定义的“其他无线传播行为”并非转播或传播由该款所定义的第一种行为即由初始广播组织广播作品所产生的初始无线广播信号，而是行为主体独自实施的无线传播行为。WIPO 版权立法示范条款专家委员会在《著作权示范法草案》中明确说明，在《伯尔尼公约》下，广播仅是一种向公众传播作品的无线传输手段（尽管是最典型的无线传播手段），也存在向公众传播作品的“其他无线方式”③。《伯尔尼公约》关于“其他无线传播行为”并无更多限定条件，它因而具有开放性，即“任何”通过非广播之无线形式向公众实施的作品传播行为都可归属于该行为范畴，如通过无线网络或无线电信网络向公众传播作品的行为，也可以或应当被理解为属于广播权范畴。

第二类是通过有线传播或无线方式转播初始广播信号的行为。

这类行为的主体是转播初始广播信号的其他广播组织，客体是初始广播信号即“作品的广播”——虽然本概念的中文、法文和西班牙文文本皆为“广播的作品”，但被转播的显然是作品的广播信号。在该类行为界定中，英文文本与中文文本皆将其表述为通过“有线传播或转播”方式向公众传播。依据《罗马公约》，“转播”意指某广播组织对于其他广播组织广播节目的“同步广播”，仅指无线转播④。但该款英文文本与中文文本的用语即“有线传播或转播”使公众乃至研究者可能产生误解，认为仅包括有线转播⑤。然而规定此类行为的法文文本（soit par fil，soit sans fil）或西班牙文文本（por hilo o sin hilo）均明确了“有线或无线”的条件，因而不易引起误解⑥。

进一步而言，此处所称“有线”或“无线”并无其他技术上的限定，因此只要属于电子传播技术即可⑦。例如，通过有线或无线网络对初始无线广播信号实施的实时的（或稍有延迟的）转播，就属于转播初始广播信号的行为，可落入由广播权覆盖的第二类行为范畴。从《伯尔尼公约》或 WCT 等国际公约的解释角度看，人们对此应无异议。欧盟版权法专家认为，WCT 第八条后半段规定的向公众提供权强调公众成员可在其个人选定的时间和地点获得作品，有助于排除网络电台或电视台的网络直播或实时转播等情形⑧。这意味着，在欧盟版权法专家的视野内，网播组织实施的实时网络转播初始

---

① Berne Convention (1979)，Article 11bis (1).

② WIPO. Guide to the Berne Convention for the Protection of Literary and Artistic Works (Paris Act，1971) [M]. WIPO Publication No. 615 (E)，1978：para. 11 bis. 2-11bis. 5.

③ 同②paras. 94.

④ Rome Convention (1961)，Articles 3 (f)，3 (g).

⑤ 王迁. 论我国《著作权法》中的“转播”：兼评近期案例和《著作权法修改草案》[J]. 法学家，2014 (5).

⑥ Convention de Berne pour la protection des oeuvres littéraires et artistiques，Article 11bis (1) (2°)；Convenio de Berna para la Protección de las Obras Literarias y Artísticas，Artículo 11bis (1) (ii).

⑦ 同②11bis. 4.

⑧ Jörg Reinbothe，Silke von Lewinski. The WIPO Treaties on Copyright：A Commentary on the WCT，the WPPT，and the BTAP [M]. 2nd ed. Oxford：Oxford University Press，2015：para. 7. 8. 33.

无线广播节目的行为亦属广播权范畴。

第三类是利用设备向公众传播初始广播信号的行为。

这类行为是通过扩音器、电视屏幕等机械设备把接收到的初始无线广播信号再向公众传播的行为，其实质为机械表演。从著作权法角度看，此种行为已非广播，而是关于广播信号（以及它所承载的作品）的机械表演，可被称为“附随性”传播或表演行为，其实质在于判断行为人是否将其接收的广播信号再向公众传播或表演。

覆盖上述三类行为的广播权并非互相排斥，而是可累积或叠加的①。而且，在同属于广义的向公众传播范畴的广播与表演之间并无必然界限。在《伯尔尼公约》框架下，一方面，作者的作品可被现场表演，而现场表演又可以通过有线方式被远程传播而构成机械表演，实质上这已经属于有线广播范畴，只是因为《伯尔尼公约》所界定的广播权局限才被纳入机械表演范畴②。另一方面，被广播的作品又可以被扩音器或电视屏幕等设备接收并向公众再传播而构成作品的机械表演。这意味着在广播权与表演权各自覆盖的行为之间有一定交叉。

概言之，根据《伯尔尼公约》规定，广播权是作者授权他人广播其作品（或通过其他无线方式传播其作品）并将该作品的广播信号再通过有线或无线方式向公众转播或传播的权利。从初始广播信号的性质看，由《伯尔尼公约》规定的广播权体系基本包括无线广播权，它所规范的广播信号仅为“初始无线广播信号”，广播权的范畴基本覆盖“无线广播”以及针对“初始无线广播信号”的有线或无线转播、利用扩音器等设备的再传播或表演行为。这可称为由《伯尔尼公约》规定的“传统广播权体系”，与之对应的则是传统广播权制度。

二、WCT 下的综合广播权

鉴于《伯尔尼公约》规定的广播权范畴已基本固定，难以再扩展，为保证作者在电子空间（包括互联网）享有广泛的传播权益，WCT 第八条前半段规定了内容广泛的向公众传播权，其中包括对《伯尔尼公约》下的传统广播权的补充。根据其规定，作者可授权他人将其作品以有线或无线方式向公众做任何形式的传播，其中的“任何”“向公众”“传播”等要素意味着它所界定的向公众传播权覆盖了所有通过有线或无线方式的远程电子传播行为，传播介质可包括空间电磁波或互联网等，作品承载信号包括模拟信号和数字信号③。由此可知，在不损害《伯尔尼公约》规定的广播权及其限制等情形下，由 WCT 第八条规定的向公众传播权包括各种广播或传播行为，其中包括初始有线广播和利用互联网实施的实时广播或转播，它们属于对《伯尔尼公约》规定的传统广播权的全面补充④。

具体而言，以《伯尔尼公约》为基础，在 WCT 规定的综合广播权下，初始广播行为可以是无线广播或有线广播，承载作品的广播信号可以是数字信号或模拟信号，而广播信号的载体（传播介质）可以是空间电磁波、电缆或光纤等。这几种因素的组合可支持综合的广播行为，使之成为 WCT 规定的综合广播权所覆盖的行为类型。在当今电子传播技术支持下，按照初始广播行为的技术特征，可把它们分为三种情形。

第一种是初始无线广播行为。此类行为属于《伯尔尼公约》界定的传统广播权范畴，包括初始无线广播行为以及对由此产生的初始无线广播信号（模拟信号或数字信号）的有线或无线转播或利用扩音器等设备的传播行为。第二种是初始有线广播行为（cablecasting）。此类行为包括广播组织等通过有线（电缆或光纤等）方式以模拟信号或数字信号直接发送有线广播节目的初始广播行为，以及针对由此产生的初始有线广播信号的有线或无线转播和利用扩音器等设备的传播。初始有线广播行为已不属于《伯尔尼公约》规定的传统广播权范畴，而属于 WCT 规定的综合广播权范畴。第三种是初始网络广播（播放）行为即网播行为。此类行为包括网播组织直接通过信息网络以有线或无线方式发送数字信号的初始网播行为，以及针对由此形成的初始网播信号的有线或无线转播和利用扩音器、电视机屏幕或计算机终端等设备的传播。从流媒体技术和信号可及性角度分析，在实时网络直播或转播情形下，承载作品的数据流只在互联网或视听终端存留极短时间就被其后的数据所覆盖，公众虽然是通过互联

① WIPO. Guide to the Berne Convention for the Protection of Literary and Artistic Works (Paris Act, 1971) [M]. WIPO Publication No. 615 (E), 1978: para. 11bis. 14.

② 同①paras. 11. 5, 11bis. 9, 11bis. 10.

③ WCT, Article 8.

④ Jörg Reinbothe, Silke von Lewinski. The WIPO Treaties on Copyright: A Commentary on the WCT, the WPPT, and the BTAP [M]. 2nd ed. Oxford: Oxford University Press, 2015: paras. 7. 8. 10-7. 8. 21.

网获得网播信号，但是和面对传统的无线或有线广播信号一样只能被动接收，因此它仍属广播行为①。

从《伯尔尼公约》和 WCT 分别规定的广播权角度看，如果网播组织是通过无线网络实施初始网播行为，其行为可归为上述第一类初始无线广播行为，从而落入《伯尔尼公约》规定的传统广播权范畴。如果网播组织是通过有线网络实施初始网播行为，它可被归为上述第二类初始有线广播行为，从而不属于《伯尔尼公约》规定的传统广播权，而落入 WCT 规定的综合广播权范畴。这意味着在 WCT 规定的综合广播权体系下，无论网播组织实施的初始网播行为是利用无线网络或有线网络直接播放数字节目的网络广播行为，还是针对其他广播组织或网播组织的无线或有线广播信号或网播信号实施的实时转播行为，皆无特别之处，从而可分别归为无线广播和有线广播行为，分别受《伯尔尼公约》规定的传统广播权和 WCT 规定的综合广播权规范。换言之，在《伯尔尼公约》和 WCT 规定的广播权视角下，网播未必需要单独成为一类初始广播行为。

概言之，以《伯尔尼公约》为基础，由 WCT 第八条规定的综合广播权所能够规范的广播行为包括：(1) 由广播组织或网播组织实施的无线或有线广播或网播行为；(2) 由广播组织或网播组织实施的实时或稍有延迟的无线或有线转播行为；(3) 由任何人通过扩音器、电视屏幕或计算机终端等实施的对无线或有线广播或网播信号的公开传播行为。此即 WCT 规定的综合广播权体系。这三种行为已经足可概括所有利用空间电磁波或互联网等传播介质实施的广播、转播或传播广播信号或网播信号的行为，从而可维护作者的广播权益。它可以和作者享有的向公众提供权或信息网络传播权形成互补，全面保护作者在电子环境下的向公众传播权。

综上可知，《伯尔尼公约》规定了传统广播权制度，WCT 对其提供了全面补充，将广播权的范畴从无线广播扩展到包括有线广播和网络广播，促进了综合广播权体系的形成。从初始广播信号看，广播权所覆盖的初始广播行为从无线广播扩展至包括有线广播和网络广播，从而使广播权制度能够顺应有线广播时代和互联网传播时代。与《伯尔尼公约》规定的传统广播权相比，WCT 规定的综合广播权体系更为全面与合理。历史地看，在国际公约层面，广播权制度包括《伯尔尼公约》规定的传统广播权和 WCT 规定的综合广播权两阶段，它们构成国际广播权制度的演进历程。在 WCT 生效后，至少在其缔约方境内，广播权制度就应当从《伯尔尼公约》规定的传统广播权时代发展到 WCT 规定的综合广播权时代。

三、我国广播权制度的法律文本：立法考察

我国《著作权法》于 1990 年为作者规定了控制其作品“播放”的权利②。其后，我国于 1992 年 7 月加入《伯尔尼公约》。2001 年的《著作权法》(第一次修正案) 赋予了作者专门的“广播权”③。该条款整体借鉴《伯尔尼公约》第十一条之二第 (1) 款。立法参与者强调，《著作权法》对于广播权的规定“是为了执行伯尔尼公约，与公约保持一致”④。

基于 WCT 的规定，可知电子环境下的向公众传播权主要包括广播权和信息网络传播权两种基本平行的权利。比较可知，在我国现行著作权法下，这两种权利的法律文本分别源自不同历史时期：广播权条款几乎整体源于 1948 年的《伯尔尼公约》布鲁塞尔文本；信息网络传播权条款则直接译自 1996 年通过的 WCT 第八条后半段⑤。相差几乎半个世纪的两个国际条约传播权文本，竟然于 21 世纪初在我国《著作权法》(第一次修正案) 中被汇集在一起，分别规范作品的广播和信息网络传播行为，我国著作权法关于电子环境下向公众传播权立法的不协调以及相应的法律适用困境或可由此推知。人们可能存在的疑惑是：我国著作权法既然已经全面接受 WCT 对向公众提供权 (信息网络传播权) 的规定，为何不同时引入 WCT 规定的综合广播权，而仅满足于引入《伯尔尼公约》规定的传统广播权？

或许有人主张 2001 年时我国尚未决定加入 WCT，从而没有必要提供综合广播权保护而只需保护《伯尔尼公约》规定的传统广播权，但该理由却难以成立。第一，与包括初始有线广播在内的综合广播权制度相比，无论如何，规范信息网络环境下的向公众提供权或信息网络传播权都对应着更新的互联网传播时代。第二，当时我国虽然尚未加入

① Jörg Reinbothe, Silke von Lewinski. The WIPO Treaties on Copyright: A Commentary on the WCT, the WPPT, and the BTAP [M]. 2nd ed. Oxford: Oxford University Press, 2015: para. 7. 8. 33.

② 参见《著作权法》(1990) 第十条第 (五) 项。

③ 参见《著作权法》(2001) 第十条第一款第 (十一) 项。

④ 胡康生. 中华人民共和国著作权法释义 [M]. 北京：法律出版社，2002：54.

⑤ 参见《著作权法》(2001) 第十条第一款第 (十一) 项、第 (十二) 项；Berne Convention, Article 11bis (1); WCT, Article 8.

WCT，但互联网时代的到来显然是不可逆转的历史趋势，我国加入该数字版权条约也仅是时间问题，事实上我国在2007年3月就选择加入了WCT。第三，仅属于WCT第八条前半段规定的向公众传播权范畴的广播权，即综合广播权与传统广播权之差，基本是对初始有线广播或网播的保护，正如立法参与者所说，“作者直接以有线的方式传播作品，并不包括在（传统）广播权之中”①。然而在21世纪初有线电视系统等早已在我国得到普及，因此从社会实践需求角度看，已极有必要借此扩充我国著作权法下的广播权范畴。

换个角度看，2001年我国《著作权法》（第一次修正案）规定的广播权直接源于1948年的《伯尔尼公约》布鲁塞尔文本，当时距离该广播权文本产生已逾半个世纪，然而我国立法者却几乎没有改变地把它转换为我国著作权法下的广播权文本，并持续使用至今。从广播权立法的社会需求看，即使《著作权法》（第一次修正案）于2001年引入对初始有线广播及其转播的保护，都已属落后于时代的立法。但遗憾的是，《著作权法》（第一次修正案）依然采用半个世纪前“经典的”广播权文本，从而再次选择落后于时代。

我国著作权法关于广播权的立法路径的确令人感到意外：它似乎没有明确的立法目标，或者说立法路径与目标基本脱离。无论如何，我国《著作权法》（第一次修正案）选择《伯尔尼公约》规定的传统广播权而无视WCT规定的综合广播权，的确属于无视时代的落后立法，以至于该广播权法律文本在被引入我国著作权法之初就落后于时代。在世界多国的广播权立法中，似乎再难找到如此落后于时代的法律文本。从法律文本和制度演化角度看，直到当前，我国现行著作权法规定的广播权制度仍属经典文本阶段，而未充分进入WCT规定的综合广播权阶段，因为至少初始有线广播行为尚未被明确规定在广播权范畴内，而当今距离传统广播权文本被固定于《伯尔尼公约》布鲁塞尔文本已有70年。

历史地看，我国著作权法关于电子环境下向公众传播权的两大权利即广播权和信息网络传播权的规定竟然如此不协调，相差几乎半个世纪的两个国际法文本被生硬地罗列在一起，其结果是由《伯尔尼公约》第十一条之二第（1）款规定的传统广播权基本能够得到我国著作权法规定的广播权保护，然而由WCT第八条前半段规定的有线广播（包括网播）权等隶属于综合广播权范畴的权利却难以得到广播权的明确保护。这或许意味着我国著作权法立法者或研究者对于《伯尔尼公约》规定的传统广播权和WCT规定的综合广播权及其演化并无清楚认识。在落后的广播权文本指引下，无论是在理论上还是在司法实践中，对于“有线广播行为”的法律性质该如何界定，在我国研究者和司法裁判者中，都存在广泛争议。

四、我国广播权的法律适用：司法解释的路径

一方面，基于我国广播权立法的传统文本，在此前十几年间的司法实践中，关于广播权的认知混淆及法律适用乱象难以避免。但另一方面，即使我国著作权法的广播权为《伯尔尼公约》下的传统广播权文本，如果研究者或裁判者能够秉持开放的法律解释规则，该文本亦可有宽泛的适用范围，从而可涵盖现代电子传播技术支持的如下多种广播行为：第一，初始无线广播行为。这是通过无线电技术实施的传统广播行为，其属于广播权范畴自不待言。第二，其他无线传播行为，如利用无线互联网或电信网等技术实施的传播行为。立法参与者也认为，广播一般是指作品通过电台、电视台广播，“但不限于电台、电视台的广播，还包括其他形式的播放”，广播权的“第一层意思”是“通过电台、电视台广播和其他无线方式传播”②。第三，对于初始无线广播节目实时的或稍有延迟的有线或无线转播行为，包括利用有线或无线网络实施的网络转播行为。第四，利用扩音器、电视屏幕、计算机终端等设备把接收到的初始无线广播信号再向公众传播的行为。在当今电子传播技术下，以上四类行为应该属于《伯尔尼公约》或我国著作权法所规定的传统广播权的正当范畴。

自2007年6月9日WCT在中国生效以后，我国广播权制度就应该发展至WCT规定的综合广播权时代，应当对超出《伯尔尼公约》规定的传统广播权之外的其他广播行为（如初始有线广播及其转播与传播等）予以规范。然而遗憾的是，在此之后，不仅我国著作权法关于广播权的法律文本没有任何改变，而且在司法实践中法院也未能依据WCT等规定，对我国著作权法下的广播权文本做出合理的扩大解释，借此弥补广播权立法的缺陷。相应地，我国广播权制度的漏洞和相关争议在此后的十几年

① 胡康生. 中华人民共和国著作权法释义［M］. 北京：法律出版社，2002：54.

② 同①.

间仍持续存在。应该认识到，我国广播权法律适用困境固然源于有缺陷的立法文本，但机械的法律解释也是重要原因。在广播权法律文本明显落后于时代的情形下，合理扩张的法律解释能够在较大程度上维护广播权制度的正当运行。与之相反，机械的法律解释与陈旧的立法文本的双重消极效应叠加，从而使我国广播权法律适用困境被固定，以至于在研究者或裁判者中形成关于广播权的思维定式，广播权的制度目标和功能难以实现。

如上所述，与《伯尔尼公约》规定的传统广播权相比，WCT 规定的综合广播权还可覆盖下列行为：第一，初始有线广播或网播行为。第二，对于初始有线广播或网播信号的有线或无线转播行为，包括网络转播。第三，利用扩音器、电视屏幕、计算机终端等设备把接收的初始有线广播或网播信号向公众传播的行为。相应地，在我国成为 WCT 成员国后，关于广播权范畴的解释就转换为如何在我国著作权法规定的传统广播权文本下，将初始有线广播（或网播）行为与由此产生的初始有线广播（或网播）信号的有线或无线转播行为以及利用扩音器等设备的传播行为解释为受我国著作权法保护的行为。其中的关键问题是对初始有线广播行为的界定。

根据《伯尔尼公约》、WCT 和我国著作权法规定，将初始有线广播行为解释为受著作权法规制依次可有广播权、表演权和其他权利三种路径。与表演权和其他权利两条路径相比，诉诸广播权路径更为合理。首先，在 WCT 第八条规定的综合广播权体系下，该行为本来就是广播权所覆盖的一种广播行为，即初始有线广播行为，因此该解释路径具有国际条约上的合理性，而无国际法的障碍。相反地，在广播权的国际法渊源中并无其他权利的概念与空间，把此类行为所归属的权利解释为其他权利并无国际法上的对应权利，其合理性大为降低。其次，从基本的文义解释规则出发，亦可通过合理延伸现行广播权法律文本含义的方法解决该问题。如果结合目的解释等法律解释方法，则将著作权法规定的广播权延伸至包括初始有线广播（或网播）更具合理性。

概言之，把初始有线广播行为纳入我国著作权法下的广播权范畴既无法律解释上的障碍，又有 WCT 等国际条约所赋予的国际法责任，也有行为与结果皆相似乃至相同的无线广播行为作为指引。与之相反，在《伯尔尼公约》和 WCT 等国际条约视野中，将初始有线广播行为等归入其他权利范畴并无合理性与必要性。归根到底，这涉及法律解释的封闭性与开放性路径选择。遗憾的是，在此前十几年间，我国著作权法学界和司法界多倾向于选择封闭的法律解释，诉诸兜底的“其他权利”路径，从而使广播权制度被肢解，其制度目标因而难以实现。

综上，我国著作权法下的广播权制度建设与适用之所以问题重重，原因包括滞后于时代的立法文本和机械的法律解释。我国著作权法下的广播权文本自《著作权法》（第一次修正案）出台就落后于时代，相应的法律解释也未能对该文本可以覆盖的广播权范畴做出合理界定，我国著作权法关于广播权的理论分歧与法律适用混乱现象持续存在，制度困境遂成定势。从更深层次理解，我国广播权制度之所以未能得到良好建设，其实质源于广播权法律规范的设定与实施皆未能有效规制社会现实中的多种广播行为，相应的法律关系和利益平衡亦难以得到有效调整。《著作权法》第三次修正案拟将“广播权”修改为“播放权”，这表明我国广播权制度将从《伯尔尼公约》规定的传统广播权演化为 WCT 规定的综合广播权。此前近二十年间我国广播权制度严重滞后于时代的立法与司法教训，或可成为立法者、裁判者和研究者的历史镜鉴。无论是立法环节对法律文本的确立还是在法律适用中对法律文本的解释，只有对广播行为的法律性质以及广播权法律规范等进行系统分析，才可能全面理解和构建广播权制度，相应的广播权法律文本才可能科学与全面，其法律解释与适用也才可能合理。

（本文原发表于《法学》2018 年第 12 期，
发文时内容有删减。
作者单位：北京大学）

论网络环境下著作权侵权的刑事归责

——以网络服务提供者的刑事责任为中心

欧阳本祺

网络环境下我国著作权侵权的刑事归责问题的复杂和困难主要表现在三个方面：第一，从立法来看，前置法与刑法之间存在“法律代沟”。《著作权法》已明确了信息网络传播权及其侵权责任，但《刑法》并未及时回应。第二，从司法来看，我国存在民事归责与刑事归责之间的“标准倒挂”，即民事审判的主流观点认为，深度链接不能单独构成对著作权的直接侵权；刑事审判的主流观点则认为，深度链接可以单独构成侵犯著作权罪的正犯。第三，从刑法理论来看，网络环境下著作权侵权的刑事归责涉及正犯与共犯的区分、中立帮助行为的处罚范围、不作为的义务来源等复杂问题。上述三个问题又是围绕网络内容服务提供者、网络技术服务提供者这两大主体的刑事责任展开的。就网络内容服务提供者而言，问题集中体现在，深度链接行为是否构成信息网络传播行为，从而成立侵犯著作权罪的正犯。就网络技术服务提供者而言，问题集中体现在作为犯归责和不作为犯归责两个层面。从作为犯层面来看，技术服务提供者明知他人实施侵犯著作权罪而提供技术服务的，是属于无责的中立帮助行为还是成立侵犯著作权罪的帮助犯？从不作为犯层面来看，技术服务提供者拒不删除侵权作品或拒不断开链接的行为能否成立不作为的帮助犯？

一、网络环境下著作权侵权刑事归责的前提

网络环境下对著作权的最大侵害主要来自信息网络传播行为。但我国现行《刑法》并未对此行为进行有效规制。判断信息网络传播行为是否符合侵犯著作权罪的构成要件是网络环境下著作权侵权刑事归责的前提且影响犯罪的成立与正犯、共犯归责。对此，我国存在肯定说与否定说两种完全相反的立场：司法实践明确持肯定说，刑法理论界多倾向于否定说。

除了司法实践，我国有少数学者也持肯定说①。肯定说认为，虽然我国《刑法》第二百一十七条没有规定信息网络传播行为，但是可以对“发行”概念做扩大解释使之包含“信息网络传播”。我国历次司法解释都采取这种立场，肯定信息网络传播行为的刑事可罚性②。但是，持本说的司法解释和学者观点的共同不足在于说理不充分，甚至说理有误。有学者以利用互联网传播淫秽物品构成传播淫秽物品罪、利用互联网传播虚假信息构成故意传播虚假信息罪为例，认为未经许可利用互联网传播他人作品的行为当然构成侵犯著作权罪③。显然在这里存在“传播”的概念混淆问题，实际上“信息网络传播”与“传播”是两个完全不同的概念：前者是受“信息网络传播权”控制的类型化行为，后者外延宽广，并未类型化；前者与“展览”“表演”“放映”“广播”等受其他专有著作权控制的行为处于并列关系，后者没有特定内涵，可以包含“展览”“表演”“放映”“广播”等行为。

否定说认为，在作为前置法的《著作权法》明确将“信息网络传播”与“发行”并列规定的情况下，《刑法》只规定对“发行”进行处罚而不涉及“信息网络传播”，这意味着不能对信息网络传播行为进行刑事归责。其理由主要有：第一，“信息网络传播”与“发行”两种独立行为互不包容。信息网络传播的对象是作品的电子载体，发行的对象是作品的有形载体④。两者有质的区别⑤。第二，对“发行”做扩大解释违背了法秩序的统一性原则。否定说论者认为刑法中的“发行”应同著作权法中的概念内涵保持一致，否则就会导致民事刑事概念不一，也导致（广义上的）附属刑法与刑事司法解释的概念矛盾⑥。第三，将“信息网络传播”解释为“发行”“不符合网络传播权国际刑事保护的通行做法”⑦。除美国外，多数国家立法都是对“发行”与“信息网络传播”分别进行刑法规制的。

本文认为，虽然我国《著作权法》明确区分了“发行”与“信息网络传播”，但《刑法》第二百一十七条侵犯著作权罪只规定了“发行”，因此在适用《刑法》时，可以且应当对“发行”做扩大解释，使之包含“信息网络传播”。我国司法实践的做法并不存在违反法秩序统一性原则的嫌疑。原因如下：

1. 我国《著作权法》的立法模式为“发行”的扩张解释留有余地

对于数字作品的流通能否涵摄于既有的“发行”概念的问题，世界上主要存在两种不同的立法例：欧盟模式与美国模式。

欧盟模式在保持发行权概念不变的情况下，新设公共传播权。在这种模式下，立法明确指出发行权的客体仅限于作品的有形载体。例如，《欧盟版权指令》规定，“发行权控制以有形物承载的作品复制

① 孙万怀. 慎始如终的民刑推演：网络服务提供行为的传播性质［J］. 政法论坛，2015（1）.

② 参见2004年《最高人民法院、最高人民检察院关于办理侵犯知识产权刑事案件具体应用法律若干问题的解释》第十一条；2008年《最高人民检察院、公安部关于公安机关管辖的刑事案件立案追诉标准的规定（一）》第二十六条；2011年《最高人民法院、最高人民检察院、公安部关于办理侵犯知识产权刑事案件适用法律若干问题的意见》第十二条。

③ 同①.

④ 王迁. 网络版权法［M］. 北京：中国人民大学出版社，2008：62.

⑤ 于志刚，于冲. 网络犯罪的裁判经验与学理思辨［M］. 北京：中国法制出版社，2013：205.

⑥ 林清红，周舟. 深度链接行为入罪应保持克制［J］. 法学，2013（9）.

⑦ 刘杨东，侯婉颖. 论信息网络传播权的刑事保护路径［J］. 法学，2013（7）.

件的传播"[①]；《德国著作权法》第十五条也明确规定，发行权是"以有形的方式利用其作品的排他性权利"，公共传播权是"以无形的方式公开再现其作品的排他性权利"[②]。学界也认为，"不能把发行这一概念理解为对作品内容的再现，而只能把它理解为对有形的作品附着物进行的传播"[③]。

美国模式则采用扩张既有发行权的适用范围的方法，把信息网络传播行为纳入发行权的规制范围内。美国《版权法》第一百零六条列举了版权人的专有权，其中包括发行权而缺乏信息网络传播权，发行权的内容是"以销售或其他转让所有权的方式，或者以出租、租赁或出借的方式向公众发行版权作品的复制品或录音制品"[④]。该规定并没有明确指出发行权的客体仅限于有形载体，而是通过制定一些具有很强弹性和前瞻性的条款从而为包容新的传播技术提供一定空间，也因此可以利用既有的复制权、发行权、表演权和展览权来涵摄新出现的概念[⑤]。因此，"美国法院和学术界普遍接受了通过网络公开传播作品构成'发行'的观点"[⑥]。

我国的著作权立法既不同于欧盟模式，也不同于美国模式。一方面，我国并没有明确规定发行权的客体仅限于"作品的有形载体"；另一方面，我国也同时另行规定了"信息网络传播权"。我国的立法模式为司法裁判与法律解释提供了较大余地。实际上，根据我国《著作权法》第十条的规定，"发行"包括两个要素：一是行为对象要素，即提供"作品的原件或者复制件"；二是行为方式要素，即"以出售或者赠与方式"向公众提供。在网络环境下，这两个要素都有必要扩张解释。作为发行对象的原件或复制件，不限于作品的有形载体，也包括作品的电子载体；发行的方式也不限于"出售或者赠与"，应包括出租、展销、网络传播等[⑦]。

2. 将"信息网络传播"解释为"发行"并不违反法秩序的统一性原则

"法秩序的统一性，是指在由宪法、刑法、行政法、民法等多个法域所构成的整体法秩序中不存在矛盾，法域之间也不应做出相互矛盾、冲突的解释"[⑧]。但是，一律要求对同一词语在不同法律部门做同一解释，形式上似乎符合法秩序统一性原则，实质却存在违背可能。

"整体法秩序的一致性，不是'形式上'的一致性，而是'实质上、评价上'的一致"[⑨]。对于同一用语，适用《刑法》时既可做扩大解释，使该用语在《刑法》中的外延大于前置法，也可做限制解释，使该用语在《刑法》中的外延小于前置法。这从我国《刑法》第一百二十九条丢失枪支不报罪同《枪支管理法》第二十五条对"丢失"与"被盗、被抢"的不同解释中可见一斑。当然，为了维护法秩序的统一性，不管是违法一元论还是违法多元论都不可能将前置法中的合法行为解释为犯罪。未经许可通过信息网络传播他人作品与未经许可发行他人作品一样是侵犯著作权的行为，因此将"信息网络传播"解释为"发行"并不违反法秩序的统一性要求。

综上所述，在适用《刑法》第二百一十七条时完全可以也应当对"发行"做扩大解释使之包含"信息网络传播"。在肯定"信息网络传播"可以涵摄于侵犯著作权罪的"发行"要件之后，需要研究信息网络传播行为及其网络技术服务行为在侵犯著作权罪中的归责问题。其中的难点在于，网络环境下何种行为可以构成侵犯著作权罪的正犯，何种行为可以构成侵犯著作权罪的共犯。

二、网络环境下著作权侵权的正犯归责

网络环境下侵犯著作权罪的正犯归责问题主要是围绕深度链接的定性展开的。深度链接同普通链接相对。普通链接只链接到他人网站的主页，当用户点击链接时即转跳到他人网站的主页，属于提供传输通道的技术服务，不可能成立侵犯著作权罪的正犯。深度链接则绕过他人网站的主页链接到次级网页或者媒体格式文件，当用户点击链接时直接在

① Copyright Directive（2001/29/EC）Article 4. Recitals para. 28.

② M. 雷炳德. 著作权法［M］. 张恩民，译. 北京：法律出版社，2005：714.

③ 同②228.

④ 十二国著作权法［M］.《十二国著作权法》翻译组，译. 北京：清华大学出版社，2011：729.

⑤ 李明德. 美国知识产权法［M］. 北京：法律出版社，2014：415-416.

⑥ 王迁. 网络版权法［M］. 北京：中国人民大学出版社，2008：54.

⑦ 我国1991年的《著作权法实施条例》明确规定"发行"包括"出租"，但2001年的《著作权法》将"出租"独立规定为一种与"发行"并列的专有权，2010年的《著作权法》沿用了2001年的规定。因此，有的学者认为我国《刑法》第二百一十七条中的"发行"不再包括"出租"。但是，刑法的解释不应完全依附于前置法，而应该具有一定的独立性。详细论述参见张绍谦《试论行政犯中行政法规与刑事法规的关系》，载《政治与法律》，2011年第8期。

⑧ 王昭武. 法秩序统一性视野下违法判断的相对性［J］. 中外法学，2015（1）.

⑨ 王骏. 违法性判断必须一元吗？［J］. 法学家，2013（5）.

设链网站浏览或者下载。实践中常见的加框链接、视频聚合平台属于典型的深度链接。对于深度链接的行为性质，理论与实务中的分歧极大。共犯正犯化说认为，深度链接难以成立侵犯著作权罪的帮助犯，可以依据共犯行为正犯化解释的原理将其认定为侵犯著作权罪的正犯。社会危害性正犯化说则认为，深度链接具有严重的社会危害性，应定性为信息网络传播行为，成立侵犯著作权罪的正犯。本文虽然也认为深度链接成立侵犯著作权罪的正犯，但理由不是上述两种观点，而是实质呈现正犯化说。

（一）共犯正犯化说的批判

共犯正犯化说的理由有如下三点：第一，深度链接是信息网络传播的帮助行为。深度链接本质上只提供了信息传输通道，当被链网站删除作品或者关闭服务器时，链接即告失效，因此深度链接并非提供作品内容的信息网络传播行为①，而是帮助作品得到更广泛的传播，同时帮助用户获取，因此其实质只能是信息网络传播行为的帮助行为②。

第二，深度链接难以构成侵犯著作权罪的帮助犯。一方面，帮助犯的帮助行为不可能发生在实行行为结束之后。深度链接形成于作品上传完成之后，其对直接侵权行为并无助益。另一方面，根据共犯从属性说，帮助犯以正犯成立为前提，实践中很多被链接的小网站侵犯著作权的行为并没有达到构成犯罪的数额或情节要件。

第三，深度链接可以根据共犯行为正犯化解释的原理而被认定为侵犯著作权罪的正犯。持共犯正犯化说的学者认为，民事上的帮助侵权上升为犯罪时，不一定只能对应刑法共同犯罪中的帮助犯，也可以直接认定为侵犯著作权罪的正犯③。

本文认为，共犯正犯化说的理由值得商榷。如果认为深度链接行为属于信息网络传播的帮助行为，就不应该将其认定为侵犯著作权罪的正犯；如果想把深度链接行为认定为侵犯著作权罪的正犯，就不能认为其只是信息网络传播行为的帮助行为。

1. 共犯正犯化是刑事立法方法，而不是刑法解释方法

首先，共犯的正犯化包括教唆犯的正犯化与帮助犯的正犯化，上述共犯正犯化说即为帮助犯的正犯化。在缺乏立法的情况下，这种处置一方面架空了《刑法》总则中关于帮助犯的规定，违背了共犯从属性原则；另一方面虚化了《刑法》分则对正犯的类型化规定，实属以解释之名行立法之实。

其次，我国司法实践并未采纳共犯正犯化解释。我国有司法解释规定，网站的建立者或管理者明知他人传播的是淫秽电子信息而“允许或者放任他人在自己所有、管理的网站或者网页上发布”的，或者网络服务提供者明知是淫秽网站而“为其提供互联网接入、服务器托管、网络存储空间、通讯传输通道”的，直接以传播淫秽物品罪的正犯（而不是帮助犯）定罪处罚。司法解释的理由并非依据共犯正犯化解释，而是把这些行为理解为不履行《全国人民代表大会常务委员会关于维护互联网安全的决定》与其他相关法规规定的义务的不作为正犯④。因此，“不能把不作为的正犯理解为共犯，然后通过解释才实现所谓的正犯化”⑤。

2. 认定信息网络传播行为不应采取服务器标准

前述共犯正犯化说之所以认为深度链接不构成信息网络传播行为，是因为其采取了服务器标准。服务器标准主张以网络服务提供者的服务器是否存储有侵权作品作为判断信息网络传播行为的标准。按照服务器标准，深度链接虽然能够使公众获得作品，但并未在服务器中存储作品，没有提供作品，因此不是信息网络传播行为。服务器标准是我国著作权侵权实务的主流观点。学界也有较多学者明确支持服务器标准⑥。

本文认为，在判断深度链接是否构成信息网络传播行为时不应采取服务器标准。根据我国《著作权法》第十条的规定，信息网络传播行为包括三个要素：提供作品的原因要素、展示作品的结果要素、连接原因与结果的控制要素。服务器标准只关注提供作品的原因要素，而忽视结果要素与控制要素，从而缩小了著作权侵权责任的范围。

首先，提供作品的原因要素不是信息网络传播行为的本质。在互联网环境下，即使作品被上传至向公众开放的服务器，但如果没有网页代码、搜索链接等控制要素，“上传于服务器的信息通常是谁也

① 李逸竹．深层链接行为入罪须谨慎［M］//蒋惠岭．网络刑事司法热点问题研究．北京：人民法院出版社，2016：269.

② 林清红，周舟．深度链接行为入罪应保持克制［J］．法学，2013（9）.

③ 蒋惠岭．网络司法典型案例：刑事卷［M］．北京：人民法院出版社，2016：206-207.

④ 李少平．解读最高人民法院司法解释、指导性案例：刑事卷［M］．北京：人民法院出版社，2016：907-908.

⑤ 陈兴良．快播案一审判决的刑法教义学评判［J］．中外法学，2017（1）.

⑥ 王迁．网络环境中的著作权保护研究［M］．北京：法律出版社，2011：339；刘家瑞．为何历史选择了服务器标准［J］．知识产权，2017（2）；陈绍玲．论网络中设链行为的法律定性［J］．知识产权，2015（12）.

找不到的海底针"[①]，或者是浩瀚的互联网大海中的一滴水，谁也注意不到[②]。因此，"上传到网络服务器"等作品提供要素不是信息网络传播行为的本质，使存储于某服务器的文件"能够被公众以有线或无线方式访问"才是其本质[③]。

其次，信息网络传播行为的结构随着技术的发展而变化。在互联网传播的早期，信息网络传播行为的三个要素合而为一，著作权人只要控制了提供作品的原因行为也就控制了公众获得作品的结果，所以传统的理论与实践都采纳服务器标准。但是，诸如加框链接和视频聚合平台的出现打破了原有三者合一的局面。对此，作品提供行为当然仍然是信息网络传播行为，但除此之外，在技术控制下的作品展示行为也应当认定为信息网络传播行为。

最后，服务器标准不利于维护作为著作权法领域中基本原则的利益平衡原则。按照服务器标准，只有把作品置于服务器才构成信息网络传播行为，这实际不利于当下对著作权的保护，并导致版权业的巨大损失。"随着最近技术的发展，目前已进入网络视频盗版的 3.0 时代，盗版模式日益隐蔽化。……2015 年，因为网络视频盗版而导致的行业潜在广告展示和版权付费损失超过 150 亿元"[④]。

（二）社会危害性正犯化说的不足

社会危害性正犯化说直接根据深度链接的社会危害性将其认定为信息网络传播行为，从而肯定其成立侵犯著作权罪的正犯。社会危害性正犯化说是我国司法实务的主流[⑤]。刑法学者的论述更是明确表达了应以社会危害性标准来判断深度链接行为性质的立场[⑥]。

本文认为，直接以社会危害性作为判断信息网络传播行为的标准值得商榷。首先，社会危害性标准完全脱离了我国《著作权法》的规范限制。根据《著作权法》第十条的规定，一个行为必须同时具备著作权法规定的提供作品的行为方式和展示作品的危害结果，才能构成信息网络传播行为。与服务器标准仅仅重视提供作品的行为方式相反，社会危害性标准则完全忽视提供作品的行为方式，而仅仅倚重展示作品的危害结果，从而导致对著作权的间接侵犯与直接侵犯被混为一谈，侵犯著作权罪的共犯与正犯将难以区分。

其次，社会危害性标准过度扩张了《刑法》的适用范围。将信息网络传播行为解释为"发行"已属对"发行"概念的扩大解释，如果再把提供网络技术服务行为也认定为"发行"，则距离"发行"的核心含义越发遥远。这实际上已不再属于解释，而是直接依据社会危害性来定罪的类推适用。

最后，社会危害性标准也不利于维护利益平衡原则。社会危害性标准倾向于把所有侵犯著作权的网络服务行为都作为正犯来处理，据此，普通链接与深度链接一样都构成侵犯著作权罪的正犯。这明显偏袒了著作权保护，而不利于网络服务业的发展。

（三）实质呈现正犯化说的提倡

共犯正犯化说与社会危害性正犯化说各执原因要素和结果要素一端，本文无法赞同。本文提倡实质呈现正犯化说，重视连接原因与结果的控制要素，认为当深度链接实质性地控制和改变了作品的呈现方式，把他人作品当作自己网页或者客户端的一部分时，成立信息网络传播行为，构成侵犯著作权罪的正犯。

首先，实质呈现标准有利于区分深度链接与普通链接的侵权责任。深度链接和普通链接在作品的呈现方式上完全不同，对通过网络传播作品的控制管理能力完全不同，并导致承担的责任、义务不同[⑦]。因此，按照实质呈现标准，深度链接应该构成侵犯著作权罪的正犯，而普通链接本身难以成立侵犯著作权罪。

其次，实质呈现标准有利于消除著作权侵权民事刑事归责"标准倒挂"的现象。如前所述，对于深度链接行为，我国民事审判实践多采取服务器标准，否定其成立信息网络传播行为；而我国刑事审判实践多采取社会危害性标准，肯定其成立信息网络传播行为。于是就会出现文首所提到的"标准倒

① 刘文杰. 信息网络传播行为的认定［J］. 法学研究，2016（3）.

② 杨勇. 从控制角度看信息网络传播权定义的是与非［J］. 知识产权，2017（2）.

③ 同①.

④ 王开广. 网络视频盗版致行业年损失超百亿［N］. 法制日报，2016-04-25.

⑤ 参见江苏省徐州市中级人民法院（2015）徐知刑初字第13号刑事判决书、上海市普陀区人民法院（2013）普刑（知）初字第11号刑事判决书、安徽省全椒县人民法院（2014）全刑初字第00094号刑事判决书、江苏省徐州市中级人民法院（2014）徐知刑初字第31号刑事判决书、广东省汕头市中级人民法院（2016）粤05刑终203号刑事判决书。

⑥ 于志刚. 传统犯罪的网络异化研究［M］. 北京：中国检察出版社，2010：269；徐松林. 视频搜索网站深度链接行为的刑法规制［J］. 知识产权，2014（11）.

⑦ 同②.

挂”问题。实质呈现标准处罚范围适中，理应被我国刑事、民事理论与实践采纳，以消除“标准倒挂”的不合理现象。

三、网络环境下著作权侵权的共犯归责

网络环境下侵犯著作权的行为主要有两种表现：一是直接侵犯著作权的信息网络传播行为；二是间接侵犯著作权的为信息网络传播提供帮助的技术服务行为。深度链接属于信息网络传播行为，可以成立侵犯著作权罪的单独正犯。而普通链接不是直接侵犯著作权的信息网络传播行为，不能成立侵犯著作权罪的正犯；同时，普通链接属于事后的帮助行为，也难以成立侵犯著作权罪的帮助犯。但普通链接的设链者在接到著作权人的通知以后拒不断开链接的行为是否成立不作为的正犯或共犯？另外，网络服务商明知他人实施侵犯著作权罪而为其提供互联网接入、服务器托管、网络存储、通信传输等技术服务行为，能否成立侵犯著作权罪的帮助犯？以下从作为与不作为两个方面探讨网络环境下侵犯著作权罪的共犯归责。

（一）明知侵权而提供网络技术服务能否归责

关于明知他人实施侵犯著作权罪而为其提供网络技术服务的行为性质，刑法学界一般在“中立帮助行为”范畴内讨论其归责性。对此，我国学界主要存在客观说与折中说的对立。

客观说认为，对于中立帮助行为的归责性，应该以客观构成要件符合性或者客观违法性为依据进行判断。客观说内部分为原则否定说与比例考察说两种具体观点。原则否定说认为，除非专门用于实施信息网络犯罪，否则，原则上应将技术支持的行为排除在刑罚处罚的范围之外①，进而否定中立行为成立帮助犯。比例考察说则以网络技术服务的人中是否“超过半数”实施犯罪为标准，判定网络技术服务行为是否构成帮助犯②。

折中说认为，关于中立帮助行为是否可罚，“应当通过综合考虑正犯行为的紧迫性，行为人（帮助者）对法益的保护义务，行为对法益侵害所起的作用大小以及行为人对正犯行为与结果的确实性的认识等要素，得出妥当结论”③。罗克辛教授认为，帮助犯的界定标准不仅要看帮助行为与正犯行为是否具有关联性④，而且也在于帮助行为人能否明确认识到这种关联性⑤。根据折中说，如果网络技术服务提供者已经清楚知道用户的犯罪行为，并且所提供的网络技术服务行为与用户的犯罪行为间具有关联性，则成立帮助犯；如果无法证明网络技术服务提供者明知用户的犯罪行为，即落入怀疑可能的情形而适用信赖原则⑥。我国司法实践采用的也是折中说⑦。

本文赞同折中说，认为如果网络服务提供者明知他人实施侵犯著作权罪的信息网络传播行为而为其提供技术服务行为，则构成侵犯著作权罪的帮助犯。

第一，离开主观要素难以确定帮助行为的行为性质。中立帮助行为的定性难题根源于普通人的“一般认知”与帮助行为人的“特别认知”之间的冲突：一般人可能只认知到帮助行为的日常性、职业性等中立性，而帮助行为人可能特别认知到帮助行为对法益的危险性。客观说否定了“特别认知”的意义，而仅以“一般认知”来判断行为的性质，“完全否定特别认知具有刑法意义的观点，存在问题”⑧。“知道的更多因此就意味着更多的行为可能性和更多的自由，这必然也会带来更多的答责性”⑨。

因此，当“一般认知”与“特别认知”发生冲突时，应该以“特别认知”作为判断行为性质的依据。就网络技术服务行为而言，“如果剥离这种明知，网络行业相关业务经营者、技术提供者的行为性质将失去评判依据”⑩。所以，当网络服务提供者明知他人实施侵犯著作权罪而为其提供技术帮助时，其提供的帮助就不再是无责的“中立帮助行为”，而

---

① 陈洪兵. 论中立帮助行为的处罚边界［J］. 中国法学，2017（1）.

② 刘宪权. 网络犯罪的刑法应对新理念［J］. 政治与法律，2016（9）.

③ 张明楷. 刑法学［M］. 5版. 北京：法律出版社，2016：425.

④ 关联性意味着正犯获得帮助的唯一目的就是去实施犯罪，假如正犯购买螺丝刀的唯一目的就是入室盗窃，则出售螺丝刀与入室盗窃之间具有犯罪关联性。但是面包店老板为正犯提供面包使之有力气去犯罪，不是针对以犯罪为唯一目的的行为提供帮助，不能说吃饭的唯一目的就是犯罪，所以提供面包的行为与正犯行为之间不具有关联性。

⑤ 罗克辛. 德国刑法学总论：第2卷［M］. 王世洲，主译. 北京：法律出版社，2013：156-162.

⑥ 蔡蕙芳. P2P网站经营者之作为帮助犯责任与中性业务行为理论之适用［M］. 东吴法律学报，2006（1）.

⑦ 参见《最高人民法院、最高人民检察院、公安部关于办理侵犯知识产权刑事案件适用法律若干问题的意见》第十五条。

⑧ 欧阳本祺. 论特别认知的刑法意义［J］. 法律科学（西北政法大学学报），2016（6）.

⑨ 何庆仁. 特别认知者的刑法归责［J］. 中外法学，2015（4）.

⑩ 陈兴良. 快播案一审判决的刑法教义学评判［J］. 中外法学，2017（1）.

应构成帮助犯。

第二，客观说中的原则否定说论理过于绝对，结论难以贯彻。持原则否定说的论者认为，“网络接入服务商的行为本来就属于正常的业务行为，客观上具有不可归责性，即便有网络监督者介入，也仍然可以得出帮助者无罪的结论”①。但这一论断过于绝对。“没有理由认为，具有一定职业的人可以为犯罪提供帮助。”② 实际上，原则否定说论者的立场前后矛盾，结论也难以贯彻。例如，上述学者一方面认为网络服务行为“属于正常的业务行为，客观上具有不可归责性”，另一方面又认为“提供播放器会作为违法犯罪的工具，行为人对此有认识，在此基础上再继续提供播放器的，不能否定其行为的不法性”③。可见，在具体判断网络技术服务行为是否成立侵犯著作权罪的帮助犯时，应当考虑行为人的主观认知。

第三，客观说中的比例考察说可能会桎梏网络技术的创新和发展。许多高科技产品或服务在投入市场之初，可能被大量用于实施侵权，但随着配套技术或产品服务的成熟，非侵权用途开始占据优势。如果一开始就以产品或服务多被用于侵权而追究其侵权责任，不仅会严重挫伤人们研发高科技产品的积极性，也会使产品或服务丧失在日后被用于合法用途的机会。

（二）经通知而不停止网络服务

1. 网络服务提供者是否具有删除作品或断开链接的作为义务

从形式上看，不作为犯的作为义务来源于法律、契约等；从实质上来看，不作为犯的作为义务包括保护特定法益的保护保证人义务和监督特定危险使之不侵害他人法益的监督保证人义务。首先，不能认为网络技术服务提供者具有删除侵权作品或者断开链接的法定义务。尽管美国《版权法》第五百一十二条，《德国电信媒体法》（TMG）第九、十条，我国《信息网络传播权保护条例》第二十二、二十三条都规定：网络技术服务提供者在接到著作权人的通知以后，及时删除侵权作品或者断开链接的，不承担责任。但不能据此认为法律赋予了网络服务提供者法定的作为义务。因为，诸如TMG的法律法规仅仅具有责任限制的功能，而没有责任确立的功能④。其次，应当否定网络技术服务提供者具有保护著作权的保护保证人义务。很明显，网络技术服务提供者与著作权人并不具有人身关系，网络技术服务提供者也并未接受对著作权的保护⑤。

接下来，需要研究网络技术服务提供者是否具有监督特定危险使之不侵害著作权的监督保证人义务。监督保证人义务包括对自己先前行为产生的危险的消除义务、监督危险物的义务、监督他人危险行为的义务⑥。争议的焦点在于，先前的网络技术服务行为能否成为不作为犯义务来源的先前行为。对此，否定说具有较大影响。

否定说认为，提供网络技术服务的行为不是危险的先前行为。理由有二：第一，先前行为必须是违反客观义务的行为，而非合法行为。而网络技术服务行为正是一种合法的业务行为，不能产生保证人义务⑦。第二，先前行为必须是蕴含并最终实现危险的行为。如果前行为人只是制造了某种危险或条件，后行为人利用该危险或条件而实施的犯罪应该由后行为人负责。因此，就侵犯著作权罪而言，“实际上从事资料散布的人是自我应负责的行为人，网络服务业者的保证人义务，便不存在”⑧。

否定论者一般认为，既然网络技术服务行为不是产生作为义务的先前行为，那么网络技术服务提供者事后不删除侵权作品或者不断开对侵权作品链接的不作为，就无须承担正犯或共犯的刑事责任⑨。少数否定论者认为，虽然网络技术服务提供者不具有基于先前行为的作为义务，但具有监督危险物的作为义务。

本文不赞同否定说，认为网络技术服务提供者有义务删除侵权作品或断开与侵权作品的链接，这

① 周光权. 刑法总论［M］. 3版. 北京：中国人民大学出版社，2016：353.

② 张明楷. 刑法学［M］. 5版. 北京：法律出版社，2016：424.

③ 周光权. 犯罪支配还是义务违反：快播案定罪理由之探究［J］. 中外法学，2017（1）.

④ 乌尔里希·齐白. 网络服务提供者的刑法责任［J］. 王华伟，译. 刑法论丛，2016（4）.

⑤ 同④；相同观点参见蔡蕙芳《用户著作权侵权之网路服务业者责任》，载《科技法学评论》，2004年第2期。

⑥ 耶赛克，魏根特. 德国刑法教科书［M］. 徐久生，译. 北京：中国法制出版社，2017：841；同②153.

⑦ 同②.

⑧ 蔡蕙芳. 用户著作权侵权之网路服务业者责任［J］. 科技法学评论，2004（2）.

⑨ 同⑧；卢映洁. 由危险概念论网路服务提供者或网站管理人成立刑事责任之可能性［J］. 中正大学法学集刊，2002（6）；黄惠婷. 帮助犯之帮助行为：兼探讨网路服务提供者之刑责［J］. 中原财经法学，2000（5）.

种作为义务来源于危险的先前行为。换言之，应当将提供网络技术服务的行为理解为产生作为义务的先前行为。

第一，成立先前行为不以违反义务为前提。当先前行为成为作为义务的来源，进而肯定不作为构成犯罪时，并不是将先前行为作为处罚根据①。换言之，制造风险者，必须始终控制风险；行为人如果违背控制风险的义务，即构成不作为犯罪②。

第二，先前行为必须是制造危险的行为，但无须同时是实现危险的行为。直接侵权人的责任并不否定网络技术服务提供者的责任。先前行为人如果制造了危险，就不仅有义务阻止自己实现该危险，也有义务阻止他人实现该危险，还有义务阻止该危险自我实现。他人实现该危险并承担责任，并不能否定先前行为人的不作为犯责任。

第三，认为网络技术服务提供者的作为义务不是来源于先前行为而是来源于对危险物的监督的观点，也值得商榷。危险物中的危险是危险物本身与生俱来的，而先前行为的危险是由行为制造出来的。在现有的条件下，通过过滤技术等手段，完全可以净化存储空间和信息通信平台，所以不能认为存储空间或信息通信平台本身就是一种“危险物”。因此，应该直接承认提供网络技术服务的行为构成不作为义务来源的先前行为。

2. 不作为犯的认定

在肯定网络技术服务提供者具有基于先前行为所产生的作为义务以后，需要讨论的问题是网络技术服务提供者明知存在侵权作品而不删除、不断开的不作为如何定性。

（1）不作为的共犯性。

有的学者认为，网络技术服务提供者明知存在侵权作品而不删除、不断开的不作为属于事后帮助行为，只能构成侵犯著作权罪的不作为单独正犯③。但是，这种观点值得商榷，本文认为网络技术服务提供者的不作为只能成立侵犯著作权罪的共犯而不是正犯。

第一，侵犯著作权罪的正犯只能是网络内容服务提供行为（信息网络传播行为），而不能是网络技术服务提供行为。网络技术服务提供者不删除作品、不断开链接只是为侵权作品的继续传播提供了技术帮助，但其本身并非信息网络传播行为，不能构成侵犯著作权罪的正犯。不删除、不断开的不作为行为虽然可以构成传播淫秽物品（牟利）罪的“传播”④，但不能构成侵犯著作权罪的“信息网络传播”。

第二，对网络技术服务提供者的不作为以正犯论并不合理。按照正犯论的观点，当网络服务提供者与直接侵权人有事前通谋时成立侵犯著作权罪的帮助犯（作为犯），而当网络服务提供者与直接侵权人没有事前通谋时反而成立侵犯著作权罪的正犯（不作为犯）。这一结论明显不合理。

第三，网络技术服务提供者的不作为属于承继的帮助犯。侵犯著作权罪属于继续犯，从直接侵权人上传侵权作品起到该作品被删除或被断开链接时为止，侵权行为与不法状态一直继续存在。因此，网络技术服务提供者在明知侵权事实后，放任侵权继续发生的不作为，具有帮助的片面故意与帮助的不作为行为，完全符合侵犯著作权罪承继帮助犯的构成要件。因此，“处于支配性地位的学说认为，应将不阻止‘作为的正犯行为’的不作为的参与认定为帮助犯”⑤。

（2）不作为共犯的罪数。

首先，如果网络技术服务提供者明知他人实施侵犯著作权的信息网络传播行为而为其提供技术支持，并在接到著作权人的通知以后拒不删除侵权作品或不断开链接的，只能把整个过程理解为一个以作为方式实施的侵犯著作权罪的帮助犯，而不是分阶段认定为作为犯与不作为犯。否则“无异于承认任何作为犯皆可同时成立一个不纯正不作为犯”⑥。

其次，侵犯著作权罪的不作为帮助犯与拒不履行信息网络安全管理义务罪之间不存在想象竞合的关系。拒不履行信息网络安全管理义务罪属于纯正不作为犯。侵犯著作权罪之不作为帮助犯属于不纯

① 张明楷. 不作为犯中的先前行为［J］. 法学研究，2011（6）.

② 萧宏宜. P2P业者的刑事责任问题［J］. 法令月刊，2008（9）.

③ 凌宗亮. 网络服务提供行为侵犯著作权刑事责任探析［J］. 中国版权，2014（4）.

④ 正如陈兴良教授所言，快播公司的不作为构成传播淫秽物品牟利罪（正犯）与传播淫秽物品罪（帮助犯）的想象竞合。陈兴良. 快播案一审判决的刑法教义学评判［J］. 中外法学，2017（1）. 这是因为传播淫秽物品（牟利）罪中的“传播”不具有定型性，同一个不作为，既可以构成传播淫秽物品牟利罪的“正犯行为”，也可以构成传播淫秽物品罪的“帮助行为”。但这一判断思路不能适用于侵犯著作权罪，因为侵犯著作权罪中的“信息网络传播行为”具有定型性。

⑤ 西田典之. 不作为的共犯［J］. 王昭武，译. 江海学刊，2006（3）.

⑥ 许玉秀. 当代刑法思潮［M］. 北京：中国民主法治出版社，2005：676.

正的不作为犯，其作为义务来源于先前行为，而不是法律法规。两者的义务来源各异，违反义务的行为也不存在交叉或重合，所以两者不能成立想象竞合犯。

最后，需要研究侵犯著作权罪之不作为帮助犯与帮助信息网络犯罪活动罪之间的关系。如果认为帮助信息网络犯罪活动罪中的网络技术服务行为只能是非法行为①，而作为先前行为的网络技术服务行为既包括非法行为也包括正当职业行为，那么两者可以构成交叉关系的想象竞合。即当先前行为是非法行为时，不作为才同时构成帮助信息网络犯罪活动罪与侵犯著作权罪帮助犯的竞合；当先前行为是合法行为时，只构成侵犯著作权罪的帮助犯。如果认为帮助信息网络犯罪活动罪中的网络技术服务行为既可以是非法行为也可以是合法行为，同时作为先前行为的网络技术服务行为也可以是非法行为或合法行为，那么两者是包含关系的想象竞合。即所有侵犯著作权罪之不作为帮助犯都同时构成帮助信息网络犯罪活动罪。

本文赞同这种包含关系的想象竞合说，认为当网络技术服务提供者的不作为同时构成侵犯著作权罪的帮助犯与帮助信息网络犯罪活动罪时，应该从一重处。具体来说，当侵犯著作权罪的正犯违法所得数额较大或者有其他严重情节时，侵犯著作权罪的第一档法定刑与帮助信息网络犯罪活动罪的法定刑完全相同，但由于帮助犯的处罚轻于正犯，所以应该以帮助信息网络犯罪活动罪论处。当侵犯著作权罪的正犯违法所得数额巨大或者有其他特别严重情节时，由于侵犯著作权罪的第二档法定刑重于帮助信息网络犯罪活动罪的法定刑，此时应该以侵犯著作权罪的帮助犯论处。

（本文原发表于《法学家》2018 年第 3 期，系国家社科基金项目“互联网法治化治理问题研究”（项目批准号：16BFX031）的阶段性成果。发文时内容有删减。作者单位：东南大学）

视频分享网站著作权间接侵权的过错认定

马一德

一、问题

视频分享网站是指提供信息内容存储和发布平台，供用户上传、在线观赏或下载热门影视作品和体育比赛录像等（即进行分享）的网站②。用户未经视频文件的著作权人许可而将视频上传至视频分享网站，供不特定第三人在其选择的时间和地点欣赏和下载，其行为构成对视频文件著作权人信息网络传播权的直接侵权。而为用户提供上传和分享服务的视频分享网站，为直接侵权的发生提供了工具。间接侵权在客观行为要件方面得到了满足，对视频分享网站主观过错的认定，便成了认定其是否承担间接侵权责任的关键，关乎用户、视频传播平台和社会大众三方的利益，亦事关网络空间秩序的维护、网络技术的发展。

《侵权责任法》第三十六条第三款规定，“网络服务提供者知道网络用户利用其网络服务侵害他人民事权益，未采取必要措施的，与该网络用户承担连带责任”。可见“知道”是判定网络服务提供者承担侵权责任的关键，但对于“知道”的具体内容，则无进一步规定③。《最高人民法院关于审理侵害信息网络传播权民事纠纷案件适用法律若干问题的规定》（以下简称法释［2012］20 号）规定，网络服务提供者的过错包括对于网络用户侵害信息网络传播权行为的“明知”或者“应知”。其废止了《最高人民法院关于审理涉及计算机网络著作权纠纷案件适用法律若干问题的解释》（法释［2006］11 号）中仅将“知道”限于“明知”的规定④。2013 年《信息网络传播权保护条例》第二十三条亦明确规定，网络服务提供者为服务对象提供搜索或者链接服务，明知或者应知所链接的作品、表演、录音录像制品侵权的，应当承担共同侵权责任。可见，我国现有法制体系已逐步承认“应知”为网络服务提供商的过错形式之一。

对于“知道”是否包含“应知”，学界观点亦愈

---

① 周光权教授持这种观点。周光权. 刑法总论［M］. 3 版. 北京：中国人民大学出版社，2016：353.

② 王迁. 视频分享网站著作权侵权问题研究［J］. 法商研究，2008（4）.

③ 从立法资料来看，《侵权责任法》草案第一稿和第二稿均使用“明知”，第三稿改为“知道”，第四稿改为“知道或应当知道”，而最终改为“知道”。这似乎表明，要么“知道”应当广于“明知”而不包括“应当知道”，要么是立法者故意回避“明知”和“应知”的选择问题而采用“知道”，从而为法律的解释留下空间。冯术杰. 论网络服务提供者间接侵权责任的过错形态［J］. 中国法学，2016（4）.

④ 《最高人民法院关于审理涉及计算机网络著作权纠纷案件适用法律若干问题的解释》第四条规定：“提供内容服务的网络服务提供者，明知网络用户通过网络实施侵犯他人著作权的行为，或者经著作权人提出确有证据的警告，但仍不采取移除侵权内容等措施以消除侵权后果的，人民法院应当根据民法通则第一百三十条的规定，追究其与该网络用户的共同侵权责任。”

倾向于肯定。反对观点集中于，若将“知道”解释为包含“应知”情形，则意味着网络服务提供者须承担事先审查义务，这样对其不公平、不合理①，亦会对互联网的发展和言论自由造成不当限制②。此类观点受到了诸多质疑，主要认为该论点无法得到事实的验证③。赞成者的观点则主要体现为，不能一概地免除网络服务提供者的注意义务，否则有失公平④；只有网络服务提供者承担一定的注意义务，才可充分预防和阻止侵权行为的发生，进而保护民事权益⑤。第三种为折中观点，折中观点虽在原则上否定了“知道”包括“应知”，但其主要顾虑在于“通知—删除”规则的适用空间问题⑥，且不排除特殊情况下包括“应知”的情形。在司法实践中，自《信息网络传播权保护条例》颁布之后，各级法院逐渐放宽对网络服务提供者过错的认定，“知道”包含“应知”得到了认可⑦。如2009年浙江省高级人民法院出台的《浙江省高级人民法院关于审理网络著作权侵权纠纷案件的若干解答意见》第二十九条⑧，明确了以“应知”认定网络服务提供者主观过错的观点。

然而，以“应知”认定视频分享网站的“知道”，虽在立法和司法领域已经达成共识，在学界亦有达成共识的倾向，但实质的问题并未得到解决，即以“应知”作为视频分享网站的主观要求，与视频分享网站对用户上传的视频内容不负审查义务的共识相冲突⑨。该冲突产生的根本原因在于，现有研究对“应知”具体内容的认识存在分歧，亦对所免除的审查义务与认定过失的注意义务之间的关系认识不清。因此，本文试图通过梳理“应知”所包含的过错形式背后的理论，对相关观点进行检视并予以纠正，对“应知”是否包括过失进行论证，希冀完善视频分享网站著作权间接侵权中的过错认定体系，并进一步理清视频分享网站对用户所上传的视频文件承担义务之体系，为立法、司法以及学界已经或正在达成的共识扫清逻辑的障碍，同时避免由于网络技术的发展而混淆了著作权法本身的意义，将问题的解决回归到著作权法的基本原则与精神上来。

二、“应知”认定思维的转变

《侵权责任法》第六条是以过错为侵权责任的归责原则的，而过错包含故意和过失两种形态。然而“应知”的认定应回归到与其相对应的主观过错状态，方可将其纳入侵权责任的构成要件。为解决视频分享网站的过错与其不负担审查义务的逻辑冲突，应先对“应知”在侵权责任过错形态上的含义进行梳理，即将其定位究竟为“故意”还是“过失”加以厘定。而该问题的模糊不清，直接造成法官对《侵权责任法》和《著作权法》等规范体系的错误理解，导致司法裁判标准高度不一。

（一）技术中立论：仅将“应知”理解为故意

在技术中立论理论指引下，当视频分享网站对用户侵权事实不知道时，强行课以其侵权责任是不可接受的。若赋予视频分享网站事前审查义务，便能为其在不知道侵权事实情况下承担侵权责任提供正当性基础。但在视频分享网站不负一般审查义务已达成共识的情况下，欲避免“应知”与不负审查义务间的逻辑冲突，有观点认为，可改变视频分享网站“应知”要求所赖以存在的基础——视频分享

---

① 杨立新教授认为“网络发表作品、信息，并非有编辑或者审查的过程，任何网络用户都可以上载文章，而网络服务提供者仅仅是提供平台支持，如果让其承担与新闻媒体的编辑出版者同样的责任，对作品进行事先审查，是不公平的，也不合理”。杨立新．侵权责任法［M］．上海：复旦大学出版社，2010：369.

② 王竹．侵权责任法疑难问题专题研究［M］．北京：中国人民大学出版社，2012：44-45.

③ 冯术杰．论网络服务提供者间接侵权责任的过错形态［J］．中国法学，2016（4）.

④ 同③.

⑤ 程啸．侵权责任法教程［M］．2版．北京：中国人民大学出版社，2014：176.

⑥ 若网上出现的侵权信息只要在一定期限内未被删除，就认为是“知道”，构成间接侵权，则“通知—删除”规则的存在就没有意义。王利明，周友军，高圣平．侵权责任法疑难问题研究［M］．北京：中国法制出版社，2012：332-333. 此类问题可以通过对“通知—删除”规则的具体适用条件进行调整而得到妥善解决。

⑦ 例如，在慈文影视公司诉海南网通公司案中，最高人民法院认为，虽然原告未向被告发送过侵权通知，且被告在收到起诉后立即删除了侵权作品，但被告提供深度链接“此种行为与仅提供指向第三方网站的普通链接不同，海南网通公司对该频道上的内容亦有一定程度的审核义务”。（(2009) 民提字第17号）

⑧ 《浙江省高级人民法院关于审理网络著作权侵权纠纷案件的若干解答意见》第二十九条规定：“判断是否应知，应以被告是否尽到合理的注意义务为标准。一般而言，网络服务提供者不具有审查提供的信息是否侵权的能力，也不负有事先对其提供的所有信息是否侵权进行主动审查、监控的义务，但网络服务提供者应当对其提供信息的合法性承担一定的注意义务。负有注意义务的网络服务提供者，在采取合理、有效的技术措施对侵权信息进行过滤和监控后，仍难以发现侵权信息的，不应认定其未尽到注意义务。”

⑨ 《最高人民法院关于审理侵害信息网络传播权民事纠纷案件适用法律若干问题的规定》第八条第二款规定：“网络服务提供者未对网络用户侵害信息网络传播权的行为主动进行审查的，人民法院不应据此认定其具有过错。”

网站客观事实上不知道侵权内容存在[①]。而围绕视频分享网站客观上是否知道侵权内容的论证，该观点否定了“应知”可理解为过失，将“应知”同“有理由知道”等同起来，而所谓“有理由知道”，是指“基于特定的事实或环境而获得的认知和推理”[②]，即根据与侵权行为相关的事实推定出视频分享网站在法律意义上知道侵权客观事实。

根据《最高人民法院关于民事诉讼证据的若干规定》第九条之规定，根据法律规定或者已知事实和日常生活经验法则，能推定出的另一事实，当事人无须举证证明。根据诉讼法上的证据理论，推定规则旨在解决案件客观事实无法查明的问题，在已知事实的基础上，结合法律规定或经验法则，推定出未知的且不易查明的事实。由推定规则所得出的结果须与客观事实间具有高度的盖然性或一致性，推定的效果在于由可证明的基础事实来推出推定事实的真实性[③]。通过推定规则得出视频分享网站知道侵权事实与“明知”一样均含有故意的主观状态，而不同的是，“明知”在证明标准上排除了一切合理怀疑，在证明逻辑上不存在断裂，而推定知道则在证明标准上只寻求高度的盖然性即可，并没有排除合理怀疑，只是在没有相反证据推翻之前维持推定结果。在无证据证明视频分享网站明显知道侵权事实的情况下，用户上传的视频文件的内容、知名度、制作成本等因素以及网站窗口的榜单设置等间接证据均可成为推定知道的事实基础。

将“应知”理解为“推定知道”，理解为过错中的“故意”而非“过失”，在我国现有著作权法体系中有迹可循。法释［2012］20 号第九条[④]对可以认定网络服务提供者“应知”的考虑因素进行了列举，其是以能够证明网络服务提供者对侵权事实“很可能知道”为目的的，其适用推定规则推定网络服务提供者知道，此条款中的“应知”应理解为故意。该解释第十条规定，网络服务提供者在提供网络服务时，对热播影视作品等以设置榜单、目录、索引、描述性段落、内容简介等方式进行推荐，且公众可以在其页面上直接以下载、浏览或者其他方式获得的，人民法院可以认定其应知侵权事实。第十二条规定，将热播影视作品等置于首页或者其他主要页面等位置，对热播影视作品等的主题、内容主动进行选择、编辑、整理、推荐，或者为其设立专门的排行榜的，可以认定提供信息存储空间服务的网络服务提供者应知侵权事实。上述两则条文列出了推定网络服务提供者知道的间接证据，据此可以保证推定的结果与客观事实高度的一致性。

可见，在“知道”是否包含“应知”的问题上持肯定观点者，并未全部将“应知”作过失予以理解，通过推定规则推定视频分享网站很可能知道侵权事实的，构成故意的主观状态，如此便可成功避免对网络服务提供者是否负担一般审查义务的争论。陈锦川院长认为“应知”或者“有合理理由知道”的前提是侵权事实非常明显，即当存在着明显侵权行为的事实或者情况，网络服务提供者从中应当能够意识到侵权行为的存在时，就可以认定其有过错[⑤]。将“应知”解释为推定知道，视频分享网站对用户上传的视频文件的审查义务便不再成为其是否承担侵权责任的影响因素。将“应知”认定为属于故意的范畴，是以视频分享网站知道用户直接侵权事实为前提的，而此种知道包含了事实上的知道和法律上的知道两种状态。将“应知”当作《侵权责任法》中的故意进行理解，与《侵权责任法》中规定的网络服务提供者侵权责任的规范目的一致，即限缩了网络服务提供者的责任承担，有利于当下我国网络技术的发展。但否定视频分享网站不知道侵权事实的条件，并非冲突解决方案的全部，“应知”在一般语境下还属于过失的范畴，论证以过失为归责原则的解决路径仍有必要。

（二）思维的转变：从技术中立论到技术价值论

将“应知”理解为构成故意之形态，而不具有过失的形态，是在技术中立论基础上的认知。然而，对于技术中立命题的假设，是否符合技术本身无价

---

① 徐伟. 网络服务提供者“知道”认定新诠：兼驳网络服务提供者“应知”论［J］. 法律科学（西北政法大学学报），2014（2）.

② 杨明.《侵权责任法》第 36 条释义及其展开［J］. 华东政法大学学报，2010（3）.

③ 江伟. 民事证据法学［M］. 北京：中国人民大学出版社，2011：137.

④《最高人民法院关于审理侵害信息网络传播权民事纠纷案件适用法律若干问题的规定》第九条规定：“人民法院应当根据网络用户侵害信息网络传播权的具体事实是否明显，综合考虑以下因素，认定网络服务提供者是否构成应知：（一）基于网络服务提供者提供服务的性质、方式及其引发侵权的可能性大小，应当具备的管理信息的能力；（二）传播的作品、表演、录音录像制品的类型、知名度及侵权信息的明显程度；（三）网络服务提供者是否主动对作品、表演、录音录像制品进行了选择、编辑、修改、推荐等；（四）网络服务提供者是否积极采取了预防侵权的合理措施；（五）网络服务提供者是否设置便捷程序接收侵权通知并及时对通知作出合理的反应；（六）网络服务提供者是否针对同一网络用户的重复侵权行为采取了相应的合理措施；（七）其他相关因素。”

⑤ 陈锦川. 网络服务提供者过错认定研究［J］. 人民司法，2010（17）.

值负荷的客观事实，仍有待进一步论证。支持技术中立的观点认为，网络仅为一种纯粹的信息传播工具，不承载任何价值判断，强令网络服务提供者承担事先审查义务，将违反互联网的客观规律，且不符合客观实际①。世界各国普遍对网络服务提供者采取技术中立的态度，为这方面的最好佐证②。对技术是否承载价值的判断，是将视频分享网站“应知”理解为“过失”还是“故意”的关键。实际上，技术中立命题真伪性的论证，应回归到命题本身，这也是现有研究的薄弱之处。

持技术中立论者以“科技价值中立说”为理论支撑。该学说认为，科学本身在伦理上不存在善恶对错之分，在价值上是中立的。科学关乎事实，与价值无涉，此为科学的自然属性。作为科学的运用形式，技术可被用于多种目的，而技术在主体使用过程中仅体现为一种工具，为主体的目的服务，与其他社会因素等无关，对于使用之后果则直接归责于该使用人。而作为技术研究的主体，其在从事技术研究时，往往遵循着科学的规律，此种规律运行于科学技术本身，研究的动机源于技术问题的解决，研究过程免于其他政治因素、道德因素等的干扰，所得成果为技术问题的解决方案，其更不具有价值色彩，因而可认定技术本身是价值中立的。网络技术作为最典型的现代技术，受科学价值中立的影响，网络技术价值中立便自然而然被推导出来。“技术中立”命题是基于技术的自然属性而得出的，但因为研发主体因素与技术所处的政治、文化环境，技术不仅表现出其自然属性的一面，其社会属性更不容忽视。

技术的社会属性体现为其本身所承载的认知价值。技术研究源于某种应然价值，此种应然价值多出于对社会的整体认知。而在技术研发过程中，研发主体并不能完全按照技术中立者所设想的，排除其他因素的干扰，研发设想、研究路径的选择等都不可能排除研发者的价值倾向，研发主体的心态及意念往往在其技术作品中得以呈现。技术所承载的价值与社会的文化环境紧密联系，技术是社会文化的产物，其可动态反映出社会价值取向，而技术的价值取向可对社会整体的价值取向起到重构的作用③。因此，技术中立是忽视技术社会属性的判断，具有片面性。技术价值论更契合技术价值负载的实际。网络技术作为现代技术的重要类型，其亦同时表现出自然属性和社会属性。其自然属性表现为网络技术运作过程中信息与信息交换的方式，但网络毕竟为社会中的人所创造，其必然服务于人类的需求。而满足人类需求的活动是一个社会过程，因而网络技术呈现出一定的社会性。具体而言，视频分享网站作为一种信息传播媒介，将信息由一个用户上传至网络平台，再传递给另一用户，其过程并不是无价值的，视频分享网站的内在物质结构和符号结构在塑造何种信息被编码、传输和如何被编码、传输以及在如何被编码的过程中扮演着解释和塑造性的角色。视频分享平台的结构决定了信息的本质，视频分享平台的物质和符号特征为其带来了价值上的偏倚或倾向④。而网络技术的价值取向还受到所处的社会环境的影响，社会整体的价值取向对技术的研发、使用均会产生影响，同时网络技术又会成为社会文化的一部分，并且不断影响着社会文化的发展和价值取向的重构。故而，在网络技术自然属性和社会属性基础之上得出的技术具备价值取向的结论证明了技术中立命题是站不住脚的。

（三）技术价值论：将“应知”认定为过失之必要

不能否认的是，对“应知”的理解除了“推定的知道”之外，较为通常的理解是“因过失而不知”，即存在应当知道的义务，却违反义务而归责于行为人。由上文所述可知，持技术中立论者认为，仅可将“应知”理解为“推定的知道”，其并不以应当知道的义务为前提。而由技术中立论转变为技术价值论后，网络被赋予了设计者或经营者的意识因素，可被视为其人格的自然延伸。这已然突破了网站的纯粹工具性质，使网站经营者承担民法上的义务成为可能。在如此背景下，将“应知”理解为“因过失而不知”乃是其题中之义。而具备承担某种应当知道义务的资格，并不意味着其必然承担该义务。课以视频分享网站对用户所上传的视频文件是否侵犯他人著作权应知义务的最大障碍在于，现行法规定网络服务提供者对用户是否侵犯他人信息网络传播权的行为不负有事前审查义务。免于承担事前审查义务涉及网络多方利益的权衡，减轻了网络

① 杨立新.《侵权责任法》规定的网络侵权责任的理解与解释［J］. 国家检察官学院学报，2010（2）.

② 杨明.《侵权责任法》第36条释义及其展开［J］. 华东政法大学学报，2010（3）.

③ 燕道成，李抟南. 网络价值的非中立性［J］. 中国传媒，2014（6）.

④ 同③.

服务提供者的负担，有利于网络技术的发展，且符合世界各国的普遍做法。然而，上述论据并不具备客观事实的可验证性，导致其本身对网站不承担应知义务的论证较为薄弱。若欲论证视频分享网站承担应知义务，则须对已达成的利益权衡进行再次评价，对视频分享网站承担应知义务做必要性论证。

在《侵权责任法》第三十六条出台之时，对于“知道”是否包括过失的“应知”学界多数人持反对意见，且集中出现于该法实施之后，诸如“强令网络服务提供者负有事先审查义务，会违反互联网的客观规律性，不符合客观实际”①，“网络服务提供者不等同于传统出版者的地位，也不可能承担普遍的审查义务”②。这些反对观点具有一定的合理性，网络用户虽在当时还处于被动接受阶段，但网络服务提供者的控制能力也处于相对较低阶段，不以过失为认定标准能够平衡双方的利益，且能够促进网络的健康发展。《侵权责任法》第三十六条的立法者使用了具有解释空间的立法用语“知道”，以应对网络侵权的快速发展引发的规范滞后问题。当互联网环境发生变化时，对“知道”的解读应更符合现实情形的发展。当下网络环境发生了深刻的变化，网络用户从信息接收者逐渐演变为信息创造者，其地位也由被动转为主动。有观点认为，网络服务提供者与网络用户的地位发生了巨大变化，网络服务提供者对网络用户的行为难以如之前那样实施有效监控，其对用户行为的控制能力和预期能力不断下降③。但此观点是以静态眼光看待网络服务提供者的控制能力，网络技术的提高同样使得网络服务平台监控能力提升④，其对用户上传的视频文件是否违法侵权已有能力判断，否则网络服务提供者与网络用户之间的力量失衡，网络空间的秩序也会随之陷入混乱。在视频分享网站监控能力得以提升，以及网络用户上传视频文件侵害著作权的现象较为普遍的情形下，课以视频分享网站应知的义务具有必要性。

是否课以视频分享网站对用户上传的视频文件予以注意的义务，还要考虑其是否符合《侵权责任法》的一般理论。危险是注意义务产生的根源，危险的制造者或管控者应承担损害预见义务和损害防止义务⑤。网络服务提供者在为用户提供便利服务时，也为用户侵犯他人作品著作权提供了可利用的工具，甚至诱发直接侵害著作权案件的发生，同时网络平台也从其提供的服务中获取了直接的经济利益。故而，作为信息传播的工具，网络平台应对所服务范围内的风险进行管控，此种风险源于网络服务平台系风险的制造者，不课以其对风险的注意义务，便会产生所有的风险最终由网络用户承担的后果，从而造成不公平、不合理的结果。此外，课以视频分享网站应知的注意义务，亦符合经济学上的成本收益规律。对视频分享平台承担义务所产生的成本与效益进行衡量，可避免因社会政策的实质内容空虚而导致前述不公平、不合理的结果出现。应知义务所产生的直接成本是对不确定用户所上传的大量文件给予注意所产生的时间成本，以及构建可供参照比对的受著作权法保护的视频文件数据库所消耗的金钱成本，其中，时间成本是总成本的主要构成部分，而该部分成本可通过研发信息过滤技术得以解决⑥。而因课以视频分享网站注意义务所产生的收益则是，因充分履行义务，间接侵权情形的认定减少。课以视频分享网站对用户上传视频文件的注意义务所产生的收益远远大于履行义务的成本，在视频分享网站个体利益得以最大化时，也保障了社会总福利的增加，故从经济学的角度而言，课以视频分享网站应知的注意义务具有必要性。

此外，我国现有著作权法体系对于网络服务提供者一般事前审查义务的免除，并不意味着网络服务提供者不承担任何注意义务。根据法释［2012］20号第八条第二款之规定，网络服务提供者未对网络用户侵害信息网络传播权的行为主动进行审查的，法院不应据此认定其具有过错。该条款仅仅是把未履行主动审查义务作为一种事实因素，判定网络服务提供者是否存在过错，其并未否定以过失为归责

① 杨立新.《侵权责任法》规定的网络侵权责任的理解与解释［J］. 国家检察官学院学报，2010（2）.

② 张新宝，任鸿雁. 互联网上的侵权责任：《侵权责任法》第三十六条解读［J］. 中国人民大学学报，2010（4）.

③ 梅夏英，刘明. 网络侵权归责的现实制约及价值考量［J］. 法律科学（西北政法大学学报），2013（2）.

④ 由于数字水印和指纹技术的发展，权利人可以在数字化作品中嵌入无法用肉眼识别的标识，以说明作品的状况、权利归属、授权状态，并追踪作品的使用和传播情况。而视频分享网站可以利用先进的过滤技术，将用户上传的视频与数据库中存储的视频作品进行对比，进而识别出那些未经许可而被上传的视频。王迁. 视频分享网站著作权侵权问题研究［J］. 法商研究，2008（4）.

⑤ 吴伟光. 网络服务提供者对其用户侵权行为的责任承担：不变的看门人制度与变化的合理注意义务标准［J］. 网络法律评论，2011（1）.

⑥ 崔国斌. 论网络服务商版权内容过滤义务［J］. 中国法学，2017（2）.

原则，即未否定网络服务提供者其他注意义务的存在①。根据2015年《互联网视听节目服务管理规定》第十六条之规定②，互联网视听节目服务单位提供的、网络运营单位接入的视听节目应当符合法律、行政法规、部门规章的规定，并不得具有扰乱社会秩序、破坏社会稳定、侮辱或者诽谤他人、侵害公民个人隐私等非法内容。因而对于上述内容，视频分享网站作为视听节目的运营单位负有事前审查义务，若将法释［2012］20号第八条第二款之规定理解为对于网络服务提供者所有注意义务的免除，则上述两个有效规范之间便产生了冲突。此外，须注意的是对于视频分享网站注意义务的认定，网络服务提供者所承担的法定义务体系并不局限于著作权法规范，除对网络服务提供者的服务性质、营销方式、盈利模式进行判断之外，还应遵循民法中规定的诚实信用原则，并履行由诚实信用原则产生的法定义务③。在对经营网络服务获取收益且具有能力监控和制止侵权行为的网络服务商与著作权人之间的利益进行权衡后，将对网络传输内容进行一定的审查监控义务赋予网络服务提供者，显然更为公平④。可见，视频分享网站的注意义务并未被完全免除，有争议的仅仅是注意义务的范围和程度问题。

三、注意义务的范围与程度

根据上文所述，视频分享网站在著作权间接侵权情形中承担过失责任具有必要性，而对于过失的认定，是以注意义务为客观标准的。注意义务包含了注意义务的设定和注意义务的违反两方面的内容，而注意义务的设定是核心内容。注意义务的设定既要考虑到对社会共同生活基本秩序的维护，确定社会成员对他人行为注意程度的合理预期，又要考虑到注意义务的合理限定，避免过高的义务要求影响社会主体的行为积极性⑤。通过审视现有侵权法和著作权法体系对网络服务提供者义务的设定，即视频分享网站仅在权利人通知侵权事实之后才承担制止侵权的义务，可看出该做法难以对网络侵权起到遏制的作用，亦不符合社会成员对视频分享网站的合理预期。以过失为视频分享网站间接侵权的归责原则具有必要性，且以过失论重置注意义务的范围和程度亦是必然。如何具体规划注意义务的设定，既必须考虑到不因注意义务的过重而影响视频分享网站的积极性，也须考虑到法官的自由裁量对注意义务设定的影响。

（一）注意义务的性质：与安全保障义务的关系

在对注意义务的程度和范围进行探讨之前，须对视频分享网站相关注意义务的性质进行明确。根据《侵权责任法》第三十七条之规定，宾馆、商场、车站、娱乐场所等公共场所的管理人或者群众性活动的组织者，未尽到安全保障义务，造成他人损害的，应当承担侵权责任。社会性场所的安全保障义务具有普遍性，是一项基础性任务。在当今网络技术对社会公众生活方式影响不断扩大的背景下，视频分享网站变得更加开放化和社会化，其体现出与现实社会公共场所无差别的特征，所以视频分享网站的经营者扮演着与社会性场所管理者相同的角色。鉴于此，在认定视频分享网站所承担的注意义务的性质时，须对其与侵权法上的安全保障义务的关系做出准确判断，注意义务究竟是安全保障义务在视频分享网站领域的体现，还是与安全保障义务分属不同的义务类型？若为不同的义务类型，则应如何对二者加以区分？

关于视频分享网站承担的注意义务与侵权法上的安全保障义务的关系，有观点认为，二者具有同质性，社会空间的安全保障义务应自然延伸到网络空间——“开启或加入交往空间者对其中的他人负有安全保障义务，应在合理限度内照顾他人权益”，所以在共同的法理基础之上，网络服务提供者所承担的注意义务为此种安全保障义务⑥。还有观点从义务设定的价值理性出发，论证网络服务提供者承担安全保障义务能够平衡各方利益，以及能比较公

---

① 冯术杰. 论网络服务提供者间接侵权责任的过错形态［J］. 中国法学，2016（4）.

② 《互联网视听节目服务管理规定》第十六条规定：“互联网视听节目服务单位提供的、网络运营单位接入的视听节目应当符合法律、行政法规、部门规章的规定。已播出的视听节目应至少完整保留60日。视听节目不得含有以下内容：（一）反对宪法确定的基本原则的；（二）危害国家统一、主权和领土完整的；（三）泄露国家秘密、危害国家安全或者损害国家荣誉和利益的；（四）煽动民族仇恨、民族歧视，破坏民族团结，或者侵害民族风俗、习惯的；（五）宣扬邪教、迷信的；（六）扰乱社会秩序，破坏社会稳定的；（七）诱导未成年人违法犯罪和渲染暴力、色情、赌博、恐怖活动的；（八）侮辱或者诽谤他人，侵害公民个人隐私等他人合法权益的；（九）危害社会公德，损害民族优秀文化传统的；（十）有关法律、行政法规和国家规定禁止的其他内容。”

③ 殷少平. 论互联网环境下著作权保护的基本理念［J］. 法律适用，2009（12）.

④ 同③.

⑤ 晏宗武. 论民法上的注意义务［J］. 法学杂志，2006（4）.

⑥ 刘文杰. 网络服务提供者的安全保障义务［J］. 中外法学，2012（2）.

平地分担社会总成本①。而持相反观点者认为，网络平台同物理性的社会场所存在差别，因网络平台不是危险的制造者，仅是有能力对制造危险的行为实现管控，且未从侵害他人的行为中直接获益，网络服务提供者的注意义务保护的是网络用户之外的第三人，并非处于管控范围内的主体②。上述观点体现出了学界对现实社会公共场所与社会化的网络空间的不同认知，支持安全保障义务适用于网络空间者以其与现实社会公共场所无实质性差别为由，而反对者则以其不同之处为出发点进行反驳。

笔者认为，开放性的网络平台与现实社会公共场所并无本质区别，尤其是交互式的网络平台更具有社会化的特征，由于该类网站的经营者通过设计网络平台的交往规则，实现对所有参与到平台的网络用户行为的管控，安全保障义务的适用对象自然应从现实社会公共场所延伸到该类网络平台。《侵权责任法》第三十六条与第三十七条的分别规定，并不能成为安全保障义务不适用于网络空间的理由，因第三十七条关于公共场所的规定属于开放而非闭合的规定，为将其他公共场所纳入其中提供了路径。在网络用户侵犯第三人著作权的情形中，以网络平台并非危险的制造者为由，否定注意义务与安全保障义务同质性的观点并不成立。因网络平台的交往规则是由其经营者设计并执行的，所以网络平台在其用户侵犯第三人作品信息网络传播权的情形中难以被免责，因为比照有形场合，在社会公共场所的管理者充分履行了安全保障义务时，亦可认定其为危险的管控者而非危险的制造者。而根据安全保障义务所保护的对象须是处于社会公共场所可控范围内的主体的观点，网络平台在间接侵权中所保护的是网络用户之外的第三人的合法权益，所以应否定其承担的注意义务为安全保障义务。但是作为开放性的空间场所，网络用户将他人的作品上传至网络平台，即意味着所侵犯的第三人的作品被置于网络空间的控制范围内，而不能仅以作品的所有人非注册用户来否定对其的保护。

（二）注意义务的范围：强化侵权结果预见义务

如上所述，视频分享网站所承担的注意义务的性质可认定为安全保障义务，而侵权法对于安全保障义务的规定较为粗略，据此认定注意义务的范围存在困难。根据注意义务的一般理论，注意义务包括侵权结果预见义务和侵权结果回避义务。所谓预见义务，就是指行为人根据案件发生时的具体情况，所负有的应当预见自己的行为可能引发危害结果的义务；而回避义务则是指，行为人所负有的避免因自己的行为引发危害结果的义务③。关于视频分享网站对于侵权结果的回避义务，在《侵权责任法》第三十六条第二款和法释［2012］20号第八条第三款涉及的“通知—删除”规则中均有体现：对于网络用户上传的视频文件如果涉及对他人的信息网络传播权的侵害，则须采取删除、屏蔽、断开链接等必要手段制止侵权结果的出现。因此，侵权结果的回避义务是指视频分享网站在视频作品的著作权人通知其侵权事实之后采取的被动措施，若网站经营者明知侵权事实存在而不采取措施避免侵害结果的出现，则可以认定其主观存在故意。而对于视频分享网站的侵权结果预见义务，根据《侵权责任法》之规定可看出，预防侵权行为是与制裁侵权行为并列的立法目标④，而预防义务的设定能够发挥行为人预防侵权发生的主观能动性。

现有侵权法和著作权法规范体系并未对有关视频分享网站的预见义务做出直接规定。但根据法释［2012］20号第八条第三款的规定，网络服务提供者能够证明已采取合理、有效的技术措施，仍难以发现网络用户侵害信息网络传播权行为的，法院应认定其不具有过错。从该条款可以看出，视频分享网站应采取有效的措施，积极预见和避免用户侵害他人信息网络传播权行为的发生，此种预见并不以侵权事实是否明显为前提。然而，对用户是否侵害他人信息网络传播权的判定并不是一件简单的事情，故把握视频分享网站采取技术措施后其预见义务的履行情况绝非易事。至于侵权结果预见义务中的预见内容，是否要求视频分享网站能够预见其用户侵犯他人信息网络传播权的具体社会危害性，则充满争议。学者们关于结果预见义务中的预见内容存在具体结果说和抽象结果说的分歧：具体结果说认为，行为的危害结果只能在法律规定的范围内理解，而抽象结果说则认为只需预见到侵权行为的一般结果

① 魏小雨. 论侵权法中网络服务提供者的安全保障义务［J］. 国家行政学院学报，2013（1）.

② 冯术杰. 论网络服务提供者间接侵权责任的过错形态［J］. 中国法学，2016（4）.

③ 周光权. 注意义务研究［M］. 北京：中国政法大学出版社，1998：8-9.

④ 《侵权责任法》第一条规定：“为保护民事主体的合法权益，明确侵权责任，预防并制裁侵权行为，促进社会和谐稳定，制定本法。”

即可[①]。而在视频分享网站间接侵权的侵权结果预见义务中，本文认为，基于视频分享网站的专业能力和预见能力，以及网络著作权侵权的复杂性和损害结果难以控制的特点，对用户侵害他人信息网络传播权结果的预见，只要求其对一般结果能够预见即可。

视频分享网站在履行侵权结果的预见义务时，并不要求其事前对用户上传的视频文件进行一一审查，即事前审查义务并不是侵权结果预见义务所包含的内容。审查义务意味着网络服务提供者必须积极采取措施对用户上传的视频文件主动逐个审视，并查验上传者是否有合法、完整的授权文件[②]。若对视频分享网站中用户上传的视频文件逐个审查，所消耗的可预期成本较大，进而会同侵权法设定预防义务所须符合的效益原则相悖。《互联网视听节目服务管理规定》第十六条对视听节目服务的提供者不得提供的视听节目做出了列举式的规定，其中就包括对反动、暴力、色情等文件的绝对禁止，此外包括针对个人权益进行保护的“侮辱或者诽谤他人，侵害公民个人隐私等他人合法权益”的禁止性规定。通过观察其列举的禁止项可以看出，该条款对于视频文件中具有危害社会公共利益和公民人格权的内容要求了审查义务，而对于一般财产权的保护则没有包含于其中，即意味着视听节目服务提供者对用户上传的视频文件不负担审查义务。视频分享网站在著作权间接侵权中承担的侵权结果预见义务，并未达到审查义务所要求的高度，其义务的设定和履行应取决于服务性质、职业要求、同行业中理性人在相同情况下应当达到的注意程度等一系列因素。此外，不能将审查义务视为侵权结果的预见义务，但也不能否定审查义务对该类注意义务的影响，因为在对视频文件进行合法性审查时，视频分享网站往往有能力同时发现用户上传的视频文件是否构成对他人信息网络传播权的侵害[③]。

（三）注意义务的程度：区分义务的设定

注意义务的程度问题关系到视频分享网站承担的义务成本问题，是注意义务设定的重要考虑因素。如上所述，视频分享网站负担的注意义务在性质上同安全保障义务并无本质区别，可认定为安全保障义务的适用对象从现实世界延伸至网络空间的体现。安全保障义务为一种基础性的义务，但这并不意味着视频分享网站负担无限的安全保障义务，其负担的注意义务需要根据认知能力进行有层次的划分，如此才符合义务设定的公平性与合理性要求。根据侵权法基本理论，视频分享网站应该承担善良管理人的注意义务，即行为人应具有特定职业或特定社会活动的参加者通常所具有的与其专业思维、认知能力相匹配的注意义务[④]。而对于网络侵权而言，善良管理人的标准难以确定，这与视频分享网站的规模大小、控制能力、技术水平等因素密切相关。以网络服务提供者的预见能力和预见范围为基础，注意义务的程度应取决于被保护的权利类型、网络服务的性质、网络服务提供者应具备的风险管控能力等因素[⑤]。视频分享网站通常会实施单纯的网络服务之外的其他行为，正是这些行为为视频分享网站负担不同层次的注意义务提供了合理性基础。

根据注意义务的一般理论，注意义务可以分为一般注意义务和较高注意义务。较高注意义务是从事较高技术含量职业者所应负担的义务类型，因从事该类职业的人员对技术安全性能和产品运行状态最为了解[⑥]。视频分享网站作为网络技术性较强的义务承担者，更有理由让人信赖其技能和服务可以保障用户和第三人的合法权益。与其他网络服务提供者相同的是，对于经常发生侵权或侵权损害较为严重的特定网络空间，网络服务提供者应负有与其能力相匹配的较高注意义务。另外，较多视频分享网站专门设置了与“原创栏目”并列的“影视频道”，供其用户上传视频文件，设置这种频道的视频分享网站应承担更高的注意义务。该义务的设定并不意味着视频分享网站对用户上传的侵权文件在事实上是知道的。此部分较高义务的设置源自视频分享网站的经营模式，因不收费的流行影视剧对大众具有较强的吸引力，其可从吸引用户下载的过程中直接获得较大的经济利益。故视频分享网站在设立

① 周光权. 注意义务研究［M］. 北京：中国政法大学出版社，1998：76-80.

② 王迁. 视频分享网站著作权侵权问题再研究［J］. 法商研究，2010（1）.

③ 在新传在线诉全土豆案中，法院认为，根据网站公布的流程，其对视频的上传施行的是事前审查机制，用户提供的视频由审片组的工作人员进行合法性审查，如果符合标准，则在12个小时后才能发布给公众。尽管网站辩称，其只是对视频中色情、反动等不合法内容进行审查，但由于涉案作品在当时是热播的影片，审片组在审查的过程中应当会意识到该影片属于未经许可的侵权作品，却对其采取放任的态度，主观上具有纵容和帮助他人实施侵犯信息网络传播权行为的过错。（参见（2008）沪高民三（知）终字第62号。）

④ 王泽鉴. 民法研究系列：侵权行为［M］. 北京：北京大学出版社，2009：242.

⑤ 殷少平. 论互联网环境下著作权保护的基本理念［J］. 法律适用，2009（12）.

⑥ 同①134.

“影视频道”时，有义务预见到用户上传未经授权影视作品的可能性。视频分享网站应能够预见到设立了“影视频道”可能产生的侵权风险，其有义务采取与之相对应的防范措施以避免侵权行为的发生。若视频分享网站未能对“影视频道”的内容进行持续监控，或者未能根据影视网站从业人员应有的专业知识发现未经许可上传的电视剧正片，则可认定其未尽到较高的注意义务①。

与较高注意义务相对应的是一般性的注意义务，此类注意义务并不是基于承担者所从事的职业而产生的，而是普通行为中的注意义务，如由先行行为产生的注意义务②。此类型义务的注意程度高于生活中最基本的注意义务，而低于上述的较高注意义务。在视频分享网站著作权间接侵权案件中，该类义务并不需要视频分享网站对用户上传的视频文件进行监控。透过过滤技术发现明显侵权的行为，以及在发现侵权事实之后及时采取措施避免侵权结果的出现，乃是一般性注意义务的基本内容。从信息过滤技术的角度考虑，当今基于代理和网关两大内容的系列过滤技术，包括名单过滤技术、关键词过滤技术、图像过滤技术、模板过滤技术和智能过滤技术等，都已经比较成熟③。视频分享网站负担该类义务并不需要承担较大的成本。一般性的注意义务所针对的侵权行为在客观上并非难以判断，对于明显侵权行为，视频分享网站有能力亦有义务对通过其平台侵害他人信息网络传播权的行为进行遏制，防止侵害结果的出现。由此可以发现，该一般性的注意义务同安全保障义务具有同质性，再次印证了视频分享网站负担的此类注意义务与其职业特点、盈利能力等无关，仅是对其可控范围内发生危险的可能性加以控制。

四、过错责任形式

由上文所述可知，在视频分享网站著作权间接侵权情形中，其负担的注意义务的性质系侵权法上的安全保障义务。而根据《侵权责任法》第三十七条第二款之规定：因第三人的行为造成他人损害的，由第三人承担侵权责任；管理人或组织者未尽到安全保障义务的，承担相应的补充责任。关于补充责任，参与《侵权责任法》制定的立法者解释认为，第三人的侵权责任和安全保障义务的补充责任有先后顺序，在无法找到第三人或者第三人没有能力承担全部赔偿责任时，才由安全保障义务人承担侵权责任，且所承担的部分是在其未尽到安全保障义务的范围内实际承担；如果第三人已经承担全部侵权责任，则安全保障义务人不再承担侵权责任④。可见，补充责任是一种特殊的连带责任⑤。在网络侵权中，部分学者和《侵权责任法》的立法者亦认为，网络服务提供者与网络用户应就其共同造成的损害结果承担连带责任⑥。从而可以推导出，在视频分享网站著作权间接侵权的案件中，视频分享网站所承担的责任形式应是连带责任，但此种推导是否符合网络著作权侵权的司法实践，仍有待进一步探讨。

（一）连带责任的实践困境：追偿成本过高

由视频分享网站与网络用户就侵害他人信息网络传播权造成的损害承担连带赔偿责任，基于网络侵权的特点，在司法实践中不具有可操作性。社会公众在注册申请成为视频分享网站的用户时，并不被要求提供真实的身份信息，这就让视频分享网站在承担损害赔偿责任之后，由于无法锁定用户的真实身份，对其追偿往往难以实现。即使确定了网络用户的真实身份，视频分享网站仍然面临难以获得追偿的困境。据中国互联网络信息中心 2017 年 8 月发布的第 40 次《中国互联网络发展状况统计报告》所提供的数据，截至 2017 年 6 月，我国网民仍以 10～39 岁群体为主，占整体的 72.1%：其中 20～29 岁年龄段的网民占比最高，达 29.7%；10～19 岁、30～39 岁群体占比分别为 19.4%、23.0%。我国网民仍然以中等学历群体为主，初中、高中学历的网民占比分别为 37.9%、25.5%。我国网民中学生群体占比仍然最高，为 24.8%；其次为个体户/自由职业者，比例为 20.9%。网民中月收入在 2 001～3 000 元及 3 001～5 000 元的群体占比较高，分别为 15.8%和 22.9%⑦。由此可看出，我国网络用户呈现出年轻化、学生为主、学历不高、工作收入低等特点。因此，视频分享网站在赔偿了著作权人的全

① 王迁. 视频分享网站著作权侵权问题再研究［J］. 法商研究，2010（1）.

② 周光权. 注意义务研究［M］. 北京：中国政法大学出版社，1998：134.

③ 李士林. 论网络服务提供者注意义务的设定［J］. 电子知识产权，2016（5）.

④ 王胜明. 中华人民共和国侵权责任法解读［M］. 北京：中国法制出版社，2010：194.

⑤ 隋彭生. 补充责任与连带责任的区别［EB/OL］.［2017-10-05］. http://blog.sina.com.cn/s/blog_6926eb870102e0la.html.

⑥ 同④187；吴汉东. 论网络服务提供者的著作权侵权责任［J］. 中国法学，2011（2）.

⑦ 中国互联网络信息中心. 第 40 次中国互联网络发展状况统计报告［EB/OL］.［2017-10-05］. cac.gov.cn/2017-08/04/c_1121427728.htm.

部损害后，由于网络用户经济赔偿能力低，不具备大额财产支付能力，视频分享网站往往难以获得追偿。

“如果期待私人以法为武器保护自身权利并与邪恶作斗争，法必须在便宜性、实效性、经济性上对私人具有实践的魅力”①。视频分享网站在承担了全部损害赔偿之后，由于网络用户真实身份难以查明，以及查明之后仍难以获得追偿等困境的存在，必然面对追偿的成本过高，而获得的收益极为有限的现实。此外，被追偿之后的网络用户极有可能选择不再接受视频分享网站提供的服务，而转投其他网站上传视频文件，直接导致该视频分享网站的信息流量和经营收入的减少，甚至出现亏损②。如此，追偿的高成本、低收益极有可能使得视频分享网站放弃追偿。依据连带责任的基本理论，设置连带赔偿责任的目的在于实现对权利人受损合法权益的充分救济，以及惩罚行为人的侵权行为。由于追偿制度的存在，连带赔偿责任并不会加重任何侵权人的赔偿数额，而只是将赔偿不能的风险在义务责任人之间进行分配。若由于实践中追偿困难发生的概率较高，且对困难产生可预期，那么赔偿不能便不再是一种风险，而是使得连带责任在实质上异化为加重的自己责任。故可以认定，在视频分享网站著作权间接侵权案件中，连带赔偿责任并不是一种公平的责任分担形式。

（二）按份责任的证立：以原因力为要素

《侵权责任法》对于安全保障义务设置的责任形式是补充责任，但对于这一责任形式，在学界和实务界并非不存在争议。反对补充责任形式的观点认为，安全保障义务人“由于没有尽到合理限度范围的安全保障义务就表明了他具有过错，此种过错行为与受害人的损害之间也存在相当因果关系，因此该义务人本身就应当承担一定的赔偿责任，而不能将其本身应当承担的赔偿责任转嫁给第三人”③。基于该安全保障义务的侵权违背了自己责任的原理，责任人具有一般的可归责性，应当对自己的过错承担最终的责任份额，而不是由他人来代受④。在司法实务中，针对学校内部发生的未成年人侵权案件，学校未尽到安全保障义务的，学校也并非承担补充责任。否定补充责任形式的做法，是以自己责任为违反安全保障义务的责任形式，并根据其过错和原因力确定其理应承担的损害赔偿责任。可见，补充责任并不是违反安全保障义务所须承担的唯一责任形式，其他责任形式在具体情况中仍有适用的余地。

当第三人侵犯他人合法权益时，如果安全保障义务人与直接侵害人在相同的责任层次上，即具有大致相同的过错情形，安全保障义务人的责任与直接侵权人的责任不应有明显的顺位关系，在此情况下，补充责任的责任形式并不适用⑤。本文认为，在视频分享网站侵害著作权的间接侵权案件中，视频分享网站负有在性质上属于安全保障义务的注意义务，其所承担的违反该注意义务的侵权责任形式应以自己责任为原则，排除补充责任的适用，确立按份责任的责任形式。一方面，如上所述，在违反安全保障义务的责任形式范围内，以自己责任为基础的按份责任存在适用的空间，其并不会与注意义务性质产生矛盾。另一方面，按份责任免除了连带责任形式中由视频分享网站对直接侵权人的追偿成本，以其侵权行为与著作权人损害之间的原因力为判断原则，由其承担由自己过错所造成的损害，体现出基于公平的要求，不能仅为了使受害人获得充分的赔偿，而课以视频分享网站自己过错之外的责任。且视频分享网站在追偿过程中，承担着与受害人向直接侵权人要求赔偿的相同风险，如此将赔偿不能的风险强加于视频分享网站，有违公平原理。可见，视频分享网站承担补充责任存在着理论上的弱点，让其承担按份责任更为科学。

五、结论

关于视频分享网站著作权间接侵权过错的认定，问题聚焦于《侵权责任法》第三十六条第三款中“知道”是否包含“应知”的争论，鉴于学界与司法实践对该问题存在认知方面的混乱，本文另辟蹊径，从视频分享网站过错认定背后的技术原理出发，尝试得出了如下结论：

第一，技术中立论的认识仅是从技术自然属性的角度出发，而忽略了技术的社会属性，兼顾技术的自然属性和社会属性，技术中立论应转变为技术价值论。视频分享网站的内在物质结构和符号结构在决定何种信息被编码、传输和如何被编码、传输

① 田中英夫，竹内昭夫. 私人在法实现中的作用［M］. 李薇，译. 北京：法律出版社，2006：前言2.

② 徐伟. 网络服务提供者连带责任之质疑［J］. 法学，2012（5）.

③ 王利明. 中国民法典学者建议稿及立法理由：侵权行为编［M］. 北京：法律出版社，2005：71.

④ 刘海安. 侵权补充责任类型的反思与重定［J］. 政治与法律，2012（2）.

⑤ 李中原. 论违反安全保障义务的补充责任制度［J］. 中外法学，2014（3）.

方面以及在如何被编码的过程中扮演着解释和塑造性的角色，所以视频分享网站体现了设计者和经营者的价值倾向。在技术价值论的基础上，对于视频分享网站在著作权间接侵权中“应知”的认定，应包含“过失”的过错形态。

第二，以“过失”为视频分享网站间接侵权归责原则具有必要性，而对过失的认定则须以注意义务为客观标准。视频分享网站所承担的注意义务，系安全保障义务从现实社会公共场所向网络空间的自然延伸。对于视频分享网站注意义务范围的设定，应以侵权结果预见义务为主，强化《侵权责任法》的侵权预防功能；对于视频分享网站注意义务程度的考量，应根据具体情况区分设置一般注意义务和较高注意义务，如此可做到不因注意义务的设置过重而影响视频分享网站经营的积极性。

第三，关于视频分享网站承担的过错责任形式，应根据其所负担的注意义务的性质予以认定。依据《侵权责任法》的规定，违反安全保障义务应承担补充责任，但补充责任本身存在理论支撑方面的弱点，且将其适用于网络侵权领域，在实践操作中存在追偿成本过高的困境。回归自己责任的理论原点，以按份责任为视频分享网站在著作权间接侵权中的责任形式，可以减轻因承担赔偿不能风险所增加的负担，且符合社会公平的要求。

（本文原发表于《现代法学》2018 年第 1 期，
系中央马克思主义理论研究和建设工程
重大项目兼国家社科基金重大项目
“知识产权保护与创新发展研究”
（项目批准号：2016MZD022）的阶段性成果。
作者单位：中南财经政法大学知识产权研究中心）

2018年著作权相关图书简介

《作家维权实用指南》，中国作家协会作家权益保障委员会办公室编，北京：作家出版社，2018年9月。

该书是中国作家协会作家权益保障委员会办公室编写的作家权益保障指南。中国作家协会作家权益保障委员会办公室负责中国作家协会作家权益保障委员会的日常工作，无偿为中国作家协会会员提供著作权保护服务，通过调解等方式解决相关著作权问题。他们将多年来在为作家维护权益过程中积累的实用经验，按系统汇编，出版成书，以期更多作家能够从中受益，更好地保障自己的权益。

《泛娱乐与著作权的那些事儿》，袁博著，北京：知识产权出版社，2018年9月。

该书从著作权法的角度出发，针对当代与娱乐活动相关的著作权前沿问题进行了探讨和分析，涵盖影视作品、动漫作品、体育比赛、艺术品、流行文学等领域，同时也对互联网环境下产生的一些著作权纠纷经典案例进行了解读，可供娱乐行业相关从业人员参考。

《著作权法》（第二版），张今著，北京：北京大学出版社，2018年8月。

该书立足于我国著作权法律制度，对我国著作权法律制度的基本概念、原理、知识和相关理论做了全面系统的介绍、分析和研究。同时，为了让大家更好地理解著作权法，该书重点章节引用了大量的真实案例，做到了真正的理论与实践相结合。该书作者拥有数十年一线教学经验，这些经验在书中得到了很好的体现，因此该书是极适合教学使用的教材。

本次改版主要根据我国近年来的司法制度的变化进行了修正、补充，使该书更加适合教学使用。

《著作权法一本通：中华人民共和国著作权法总成》，王迁主编，北京：法律出版社，2018年6月。

该书以《中华人民共和国著作权法》为轴心，将散见于不同法律法规之中但反映的是同一个法律问题的若干关联规定予以整理、集合，使读者能方便地一次性查找到与问题直接相关的常用法条，而不必辗转于不同法规文件。创新——突破传统模式，在结构与体例上做出不同于传统的法律汇编工具书的全新尝试。专业——编著者皆为法学专业研究和教学人员，全面收录相关法律法规，用专业、权威的眼光做出取舍、编辑。实用——对重点法条点评和解释；每页留出边栏，适于读者做笔记；并制作关键词索引，利于查找。

《数字网络时代著作权保护模式研究》，姚鹤徽著，北京：中国人民大学出版社，2018年5月。

该书以数字网络时代的著作权保护模式为研究对象。首先，分析数字网络环境下著作权保护的困境与传统著作权保护模式的失灵。其次，对“法律路径”、“技术路径”、“共享路径”和“补偿路径”这四种著作权保护模式进行研究与定位。最后，探寻数字网络时代著作权保护模式建构的理论依据，借鉴四种著作权保护模式的合理之处，完善著作权自愿许可制度和非自愿许可制度，构建适应网络环境的、能够有效促进作品创作和传播的新型著作权保护模式。

《文化产业发展视野下著作权集体管理组织的职能研究》，郑鲁英著，厦门：厦门大学出版社，2018年5月。

面对著作权集体管理组织（CMOs）新出路的探索以及我国推进“文化产业大发展”战略之情势，我国CMOs应调整自身以顺应文化产业的发展。基于此，该书试图通过分析CMOs职能对文化产业的应对，运用CMOs职能的合法性以及相关评价体系的研究，提出完善我国著作权集体管理制度的建议。

《文艺作品侵权判定的司法标准：琼瑶诉于正案的审理思路》，宋鱼水、冯刚、张玲玲著，北京：北京大学出版社，2018年5月。

近年来，文字作品被改编为影视作品的现象越来越多，在此潮流之下，未经授权的违法演绎、改编影视作品的情形日渐增多，对于以非法演绎方式侵犯文字作品著作权权利的相关法律问题的探讨及梳理成为著作权法律理论及司法实践需要研究的重要课题。该书对“琼瑶诉于正案”的实体及程序问题进行了全面分析，并通过该案梳理了文字作品中著作权保护的表达的确认问题，著作权侵权纠纷中被告与原告作品要素发生接触认定问题，共同侵权认定问题，赔礼道歉的适用问题，损害赔偿数额问题，侵权作品停止复制、发行、传播问题等诸多著作权法核心、前沿问题。

《数字公共图书馆著作权限制研究》，赵力著，北京：知识产权出版社，2018年2月。

著作权限制制度的逻辑在于，通过限制权利人排他权利，实现权利人利益与公共利益的平衡。广义的著作权限制制度包括保护客体范围限制、思想表达二分法、版权保护的独创性条件、版权保护期限限制、版权权利穷竭等。公共图书馆承担着传播文化信息、实现公民终身教育、促进文化和科技繁荣的功能。数字时代，公共图书馆缩小数字鸿沟、保障信息公平、促进社会正义的功能更为凸显。该书以著作权限制制度中的合理使用制度和法定使用制度为主线，研究适用于数字公共图书馆的著作权限制制度，探寻数字时代权利人利益与公共利益合理边界的构建。

《中国法院2018年度案例·知识产权纠纷》，国家法官学院案例开发研究中心编，北京：中国法制出版社，2018年1月。

该书是“中国法院2018年度案例”系列（全23册）的一个分册，内容包含专利纠纷、商标纠纷、著作权纠纷、侵害信息网络传播权纠纷、不正当竞争纠纷等案件。所选案例均是国家法官学院从各地2017年上报的典型案例中挑选出来的精品案例，全面涵盖该领域常见纠纷内容。案情凝练，并由主审法官精心撰写裁判要旨与法官后语，可读性、适用性强，能帮助读者节约查找和阅读案例的时间，获得真正有用的信息，为法官、检察官、执法人员、律师、法律顾问办理相关案件以及案件当事人处理纠纷必备参考书。

《著作权诉讼典型案例指引》，刘华俊著，北京：知识产权出版社，2018年1月。

著作权纠纷案件占知识产权案件比重相对较大，作者通过对大量著作权案例的阅览及研究，精心挑选出了多个典型的著作权纠纷案例进行专业评析。

该书中的案件事实基本涵盖了现实中经常发生的著作权案件类型，作者对每个案件的案情进行了概括，点出了案例中涉及的核心法律原理，并结合案例的争议焦点对每个案例进行全局性法律分析，并提出案件启示及建议。

该书通过对典型案例的评析，让读者深刻有效地掌握著作权的相关知识，同时让读者在学习理论知识时，接触到著作权诉讼的实务技巧，以律师的思维对案例进行综合性分析与思考，为推动我国知识产权教育贡献力量。

《著作权法解读与应用》，袁博著，北京：知识产权出版社，2018年1月。

该书对我国《著作权法》的条款进行了详细的解读，与同类书籍不同，该书融入了作者多年的司法实践经验和学理上的创新思考，在实践指导和理论分析之间找到了合理的平衡。同时，该书还向读者诚恳地展示了知识产权专业法官的认知逻辑和思维路径，诠释了“法官是如何思考的”。该书兼具理论性和可操作性，适合相关专业的法务人员和高校师生阅读参考。

《知识产权新型疑难案件法官裁判思维》，深圳市福田区人民法院编，陈新哲主编，北京：法律出版社，2018年1月。

该书上篇收录了深圳市福田区人民法院历年审理的具有代表性的、疑难及新型知识产权案例，案件类型覆盖著作权、商标权、不正当竞争等民事案件以及知识产权刑事、行政案件，在精准介绍每个案例案情的基础上，详细还原了审理思路，亦阐明了某类知识产权案件的裁判标准和裁判方法，旨在使读者了解目前知识产权案件的全新审判思路，并对每个案例裁判中的关键点及思路要点予以提取，提请读者特别注意。下篇针对审判中存在的新型或疑难问题，从理论与实践相结合的角度进行了详尽剖析。

该书内容精炼严谨、要旨明晰，对从事知识产权审判的法官、律师及法学研究者均具有重要的借鉴和启发意义。

《版权产业经济贡献调研指南（2015年修订版）》，世界知识产权组织著，中国版权保护中心译，北京：人民出版社，2018年9月。

2006年，世界知识产权组织出版了一本《版权产业的经济贡献调研指南》（以下简称《指南》）。该出版物试图总结现有经验，提出一个包括指导版权产业政策研究在内的通用分析框架，并提出一个测算版权产业规模和在本国内及国家之间对版权产业与其他产业进行比较的方法。《指南》中所包含的方法已经通过测试，被广泛应用于各个国家对创意领域的调研活动。到2014年底，它已在40多个不同发展水平的国家得到应用，并被公认为是评估版权在增加值、就业和贸易方面对国民经济具有贡献的一种可靠的国际性方法，已成为发展中国家和发达国家的参考范式。以世界知识产权组织的方法为基础，通过调研活动而收集来的数据，已成为量化版权在经济和社会发展中的作用的一个重要信息来源。

《中美数字内容产业版权政策与法律制度比较》，孙那著，北京：知识产权出版社，2018年12月。

该书选取中美两国的数字内容产业为研究对象，对比两国数字内容产业的行业发展情况、产业政策及以版权法为核心的法律制度。通过分析近三年来两国数字内容产业的发展情况，对比两国产业发展的特征，总结出各产业之间的发展现状及未来发展趋势，并从两国数字内容产业的政策维度进行分析，将两国不同时期的产业政策以相应的时间节点为依据进行切割，划分为不同的发展时期。由于美国的数字内容产业起步较早，产业发展较为成熟，形成了一批以好莱坞、迪士尼等为代表的全球内容产业发展的领军企业。我国的数字内容产业在发展初期有着较强的行政管制色彩，随着市场机制的不断健全，我国的数字内容产业发展在国家的政策引领下逐渐走向规范，迎来了历史发展的黄金期。在法律制度层面，分别从立法、司法和行政执法三个角度比较分析了两国的不同特点。

《中国版权集体管理制度研究》，芦世玲著，北京：中国财政经济出版社，2018年11月。

该书对中国版权集体管理制度进行了深入研究。中国版权集体管理制度在实践中备受争议，考察西方版权集体管理的经验，发现中西方版权制度背后的文化基础存在差异。中国版权集体管理制度是外力推动下对西方版权制度的移植。制度移植的被动性导致版权制度的正式规则与非正式规则缺乏相容的基础。因此，中国版权集体管理制度的完善，首先要面对的并不是关于该制度的争议，而是更深层次版权文化的建构。

《著作权法体系化研究》，王坤、王展著，北京：中国政法大学出版社，2018年8月。

该书主要针对著作权法学理论的缺陷，综合运用符号学、信息学和系统论，从建构科学的作品概念出发，同时基于民法基本原理，针对著作权法上几个方面的重要问题进行专题研究。通过科学化和民法化双轮驱动，以此来建构著作权法理论和制度体系，实现著作权法的体系化。

《版权法对技术措施的保护与规制研究》，王迁著，北京：中国人民大学出版社，2018年9月。

该书探讨了版权法保护与规制技术措施的诸问题。包括版权法中技术措施的概念、分类，及其与纯技术意义上的技术措施及权利管理信息、数字权利管理系统的关系；技术措施受版权法保护的条件，特别是"有效性"要件；版权法保护技术措施的范围，以及保护"版权保护措施"与"接触控制措施"的正当性；版权法对技术措施的保护手段，也就是只禁止提供规避手段，还是同时禁止实施直接规避行为；规避技术措施的法律责任及诉讼中举证责任的分配；技术措施保护与合理使用的冲突及各种法律解决方案，以及滥用技术措施的法律对策。该书还对完善我国保护与规制技术措施的版权立法提出了相关建议。

《全媒体时代数字图书馆版权授权模式研究》，朱娜娜著，北京：电子工业出版社，2018年8月。

全媒体时代数字图书馆建设方兴未艾，但版权纠纷层出不穷。利用高效的版权授权模式取得权利人的授权，是数字图书馆解决版权问题的根本途径。该书分析了全媒体时代数字图书馆所具有的社会价值，及其具有的特殊的法律性质和法律地位，对数字图书馆信息资源开发与利用过程的各环节涉及的不同的版权问题及其产生的根源进行了深入细致的剖析，并利用比较法对现行和尚处于探索中的各种授权模式进行了综合比较分析，在此基础上，提出全媒体时代数字图书馆版权授权模式整合的新思路。为方便读者阅读，该书附录部分收录了相关领域制定的法律法规及部分图书馆版权纠纷经典案例。

《变革中的版权制度研究》，梁志文著，北京：法律出版社，2018年5月。

在新技术条件下，制定一部伟大的版权法是人们的共识。但版权法改革的观点并不相同，不同国家的修法方案也各有侧重。该书从版权人游说、版权理论变迁与技术中立原则出发，以宏观反思整个版权制度为视角，构建版权制度变革的理论基础，研究新技术时代版权制度面临的具体挑战与应对策略。该书分别从保护客体、著作人格权、著作财产权、权利限制和责任承担规则等方面选择了具有代表性的制度展开研究，强调在解决新问题时既要回归版权法的本质或传统，也要回应新技术对版权制度的挑战。

《版权制度异化研究》，王洪友著，北京：知识产权出版社，2018 年 4 月。

版权制度异化论是马克思主义异化思想在知识产权制度研究领域的创造性延伸。版权制度异化是指版权制度的设计与运行逐渐偏离版权制度的根本价值、走向自己对立面的现象，它是一个过程，具有相对性，其结果是对版权制度内部协调性的破坏。该书不仅从异化角度探讨了版权制度的前生今世，还就我国版权制度的完善问题提出了诸多具体建议，全书论证深刻、说理透彻，具有很强的可操作性以及理论与实践双重参考价值。

《版权贸易经略》，姜汉忠著，北京：知识产权出版社，2018 年 1 月。

该书体现了作者从事版权贸易工作的丰富经验，也提出了与版权贸易工作有关的独到有用的理念，而这种经验与理念通过大量案例与信息的呈现得到了充分的提炼与阐释。该书有两个特点：一是该书来自版权贸易实践，对版权贸易实践有很强的指导作用；二是该书不仅涉及版权贸易本身，也对决定着版权买卖效果的选题策划与市场营销提出了符合实际的见解。该书不仅适合广大版权经理、版权编辑、版权代理人以及高校相关专业师生阅读、参考，也是出版社编辑从事图书选题策划与市场营销的百宝箱。

《版权的起源》，［美］马克·罗斯著，杨明译，北京：商务印书馆，2018 年 1 月。

该书围绕一系列著名的版权侵权案件展开，借以阐述版权制度的起源。作者认为，现代意义上的作者显著的特征就是与所有权有关，文学作品被视作特殊的商品流转于作者、书商、所有者等人之间，而版权制度正是依靠成为商品的文学作品来寻求市场垄断的，它与印刷机的产生、中世纪晚期至文艺复兴早期作者身份的个体化，以及 17、18 世纪商业社会的高度发展有着密切的关系。

《知识产权疑难案件律师代理思路与裁判精析》，陈浩主编，北京：法律出版社，2018 年 10 月。

该书系德衡律师集团知识产权团队律师根据现行的专利、商标、版权等知识产权类法律法规，汇聚多年处理知识产权争议的实践经验编撰而成。全书从专利权、商标权、著作权及不正当竞争角度出发，汇总近年来各律师亲自办理的或在知识产权领域具有较高影响力的典型案例，介绍案件概况，指出焦点问题并依据法律规定进行案件评析。

《最高人民法院知识产权审判案例指导（第 10 辑）》，最高人民法院知识产权审判庭编，北京：中国法制出版社，2018 年 7 月。

该书收录了最高人民法院每年发布的知识产权年度报告全文和该报告所涉及的所有裁判文书。该报告已经成为最高人民法院指导知识产权审判工作的重要载体和社会公众了解最高人民法院知识产权审判发展动态的重要渠道。本年度报告从最高人民法院 2017 年审结的知识产权和竞争案件中精选了 33 件（案件事实和法律问题基本相同的关联案件计为 1 件）典型案件。该书从中归纳出 42 个具有一定指导意义的法律适用问题，反映了最高人民法院在知识产权和竞争领域处理新型、疑难、复杂案件的审理思路和裁判方法。

《知识产权：技术颠覆背后的法律智慧》，中伦研究院编，北京：法律出版社，2018 年 4 月。

该书包括案例评析和法律评论文章两大类文章。其中案例评析主要是对 2016、2017 年两年新判决的知识产权诉讼案件和完成的知识产权非诉讼案件的分析和点评；法律评论文章囊括了知识产权的各个领域，涵盖了互联网与云服务、医药研发、网络安全、贸易等热点问题。

《中国知识产权理论体系研究》，吴汉东主编，北京：商务印刷馆，2018 年 10 月。

该书是在知识产权问题上对“中国道路”的理论概括，它是法学理论体系中的“知识版”、知识产权“知识体系”的“综合版”、发展中国家知识产权主张的“示范版”、国际知识产权话语体系中的“中国版”。

该书从整体化、本土化、科学化的学术规范和实践要求出发，探讨了中国特色知识产权理论体系的主要内容，包括本体论、价值论、制度论、政策论、运行论、文化论、发展论等。以社会主义法治观、发展观为理论基石，针对知识产权的“中国问题”，总结知识产权事业建设的“中国经验”，推出一大批思想自立和理论自信的成果，包括知识产权的基础理论、制度创新理论、法律本土化理论、保护模式理论、司法改革理论、强国建设理论、产业发展理论、国际战略理论、利益平衡理论、文化建设理论等，以实现知识产权理论的体系化和中国化。

《知识产权诉前禁令制度研究》，刘知函著，北京：中国政法大学出版社，2018年11月。

该书从对英美法系与大陆法系中诉前禁令制度的梳理入手，逐渐提炼出知识产权诉前禁令为实体法请求权的本质特征；然后以此为逻辑起点，从请求权的角度研究知识产权诉前禁令的类型、内容、构成要件以及权利边界；接着从实体法请求权的角度研究知识产权诉前禁令的程序制度，并以此为基础进行知识产权诉前禁令程序制度的构建；在全面研究梳理清楚知识产权诉前禁令的实体法本质和程序法基础之后，该书对我国最高院于2015年2月26日公布的《最高人民法院关于审查知识产权与竞争纠纷行为保全案件适用法律若干问题的解释（征求意见稿）》进行了详细的评析，在此基础之上，该书给出了自己关于该司法解释的学术建议稿。

《知识产权民事审判证据实务研究——以智慧的方式善待智慧》，秦善奎著，北京：知识产权出版社，2018年4月。

该书系作者在承办了1 000多件案件的实践经验基础上，吸收最高人民法院和各地法院最新案例裁判要旨，完成的国内第一部系统论述知识产权民事审判证据规则的专著。作者探索了知识产权举证责任的分配，以及知识产权实务中要件事实的构成、证明标准和常见证据，对证据的收集、证据交换、证据认定进行了系统梳理和实务研究。该书体现了知识产权民事证据规则研究的最新成果，内容翔实、结构新颖、实务性强，为知识产权理论和实务研究提供了重要参考，也为知识产权实务工作者提供了证据操作指南。

《知识产权法学基础理论导论》，李玉香著，北京：中国政法大学出版社，2018年3月。

该书从知识产权、知识产权法的基本概念入手，对知识产权的私权性与保护的正当性和现实合理性、知识产权的法律特征进行了探讨，对知识产权法律体系的构建进行了研究，并对世界范围内知识产权法律制度的发展趋势进行了分析和展望。该书还从知识产权的主体制度、客体制度、权利内容、权利限制制度、权利利用与资本化、权利的管理与保护等方面对知识产权的基本理论进行了全面探讨和研究，以求能够抛砖引玉，为尽快构建较为完善的知识产权法学基础理论体系做一初步建设工作。

《中国知识产权指导案例评注（第9辑）》，最高人民法院知识产权审判庭编，北京：中国法制出版社，2018年8月。

该书是最高人民法院在各高级人民法院推荐的基础上，向社会公布中国法院知识产权司法保护10大案件和50件典型案例。该书内容包括2016年中国法院知识产权司法保护案件和典型案例，以及相关解读评析，含专利侵权、著作权侵权、商标侵权、不正当竞争、商标授权确权、商标行政处罚、知识产权刑事案件等案件，几乎涉及知识产权领域的所有典型疑难问题。

《知识产权刑法保护的理论与实践》，李兰英、高扬捷等著，北京：法律出版社，2018年10月。

该书总共九章内容，既阐述了知识产权刑事法保护的现状困境、立场限度、发展构想、“两法衔接”、财产执行等基本问题，又分析了涉及各个具体知识产权犯罪的典型疑难问题；既对传统的侵犯商标权犯罪、侵犯专利权犯罪、侵犯著作权犯罪、侵犯商业秘密犯罪有较为深入的理论研究，又结合现实的新型知识产权犯罪具体形态，如互联网领域的知识产权犯罪进行前瞻性的思考。该书援引的案例主要以“品牌之都”泉州市发生的真实典型案例为代表，基本涵盖了知识产权犯罪各种典型的疑难问题，对于知识产权犯罪的实务探讨和理论研究都有相当的参考价值。

《知识产权法辞典》，吕淑琴、陈一痕编著，上海：上海辞书出版社，2018年6月。

该辞典为知识产权法律方面的专科类工具书。正文按分类编排，分知识产权概论、著作权、专利权、商标权、其他知识产权、国际组织与国际公约等类，有术语、短语、组织、法律文件共计900条。该辞典在收词方面，以我国最新的《著作权法》、《专利法》、《商标法》及相关的《计算机软件保护条例》、《植物新品种保护条例》、《集成电路布图设计保护条例》、《特殊标志管理条例》、《奥林匹克标志保护条例》等为依据，收入了常见的、实用的名词术语、短语（句）。

《知识产权侵权损害赔偿救济制度研究》，朱冬著，北京：知识产权出版社，2018 年 7 月。

该书是对知识产权侵权损害赔偿救济制度的系统研究。结合比较法和中国实践，从政策目标到制度框架再到规则适用，全面地对知识产权各领域侵权损害赔偿救济进行研究。通过对实践中存在的问题进行具体分析，并对现行加大赔偿力度、回归市场价值的司法政策进行学理上的解读，以期为知识产权侵权损害赔偿救济理论研究的深化和实践中相关难题的解决提供思路。该书适合知识产权领域的工作者及相关研究者阅读。

《知识产权典型案例分析》，李永波主编，北京：法律出版社，2018 年 5 月。

该书由北京市集佳律师事务所多年来代理的诸多有巨大影响力的专利、商标、不正当竞争及其他典型案例结集而成。其中不乏在业界广为流传的口碑案例，例如腾讯公司诉奇虎公司不正当竞争纠纷案、百度公司与搜狗公司发明专利权无效宣告案、“微信”商标异议复审行政案、腾讯诉上海祥游公司等商标侵权纠纷案、温瑞安武侠小说改编权及不正当竞争纠纷案等。该书作者对这些亲身参与的典型案例进行了深入和精辟的分析，可为知识产权领域从业者及知识产权律师等提供参考和借鉴。

《知识产权侵权责任理论研究》，何培育著，北京：法律出版社，2018 年 8 月。

该书以传统的侵权责任理论为基础，以知识产权侵权责任认定的裁判逻辑为线索，分别探讨了知识产权侵权责任的一般原理、归责原则、构成要件、促成性事由、免责事由、责任承担方式及其法律适用，以及多数人侵权行为与责任等问题，旨在通过对知识产权侵权责任领域的共同规则与特有规则系统化的发掘、分析和整理，厘清概念、规则、原则三元结构体系，进而描绘出知识产权侵权责任制度的体系化图景，为法律实践中知识产权侵权责任的认定提供合理标尺，为从事知识产权研究的专业人士提供参考与借鉴。

《知识产权融资风险规制研究：以专利权为中心》，彭飞荣著，北京：法律出版社，2018 年 6 月。

知识产权融资作为一项系统工程，不仅与国家政策的变迁密切相关，还涉及质押、许可、转让、投资、信托、证券化、典当、拍卖、担保、交易等各个环节。该书从风险社会理论出发，分析了知识产权融资风险的概念、特征及类型。在此基础上，借助风险规制理论与法政策学理论，进一步研究了知识产权融资风险规制方式。这包括两个层面：一是以知识产权信托融资风险为例，从宏观层面分析了风险中国语境下知识产权信托融资的困境与出路；另一是以专利权质押融资为例，从微观层面指出专利权质押融资风险规制须从风险的内部规制与风险的外部规制两方面入手。前者主要针对专利权质押融资中专利价值评估、交易、处置等重点环节采取降低风险的预防规制策略；后者则着眼于专利品质提升与风险分散或者转移，分别采取专利审查规制策略和专利保险规制策略，以实现降低知识产权融资风险的目的。

《中国知识产权蓝皮书（2016—2017）》，吴汉东主编，北京：知识产权出版社，2018 年 4 月。

该书除延续历年的风格，更新报告内容外，创新性地增加了知识产权法官对各类型案件的总结，并梳理了全国知识产权主题的重要会议，力争准确全面地展示过去一年内我国知识产权事业取得的辉煌成绩，表现知识产权界为完善知识产权制度贡献的才智，展示知识产权从业者为运用和保护知识产权所做的努力。

该书秉承“民间视野、学者观点”的编写方针，对热点问题进行分析，记录和总结 2016—2017 年中国知识产权事业发展情况。全书分为特稿、年度研究报告、专题研究报告等部分，依托理论，注重实证，力求精深，兼顾广博，旨在汇集中国知识产权界的智力资源，展示中国知识产权事业的发展成果。

《知识产权的国民待遇》，何隽著，北京：清华大学出版社，2018 年 6 月。

该书基于历史考察和文本分析，系统阐释国民待遇原则在主要知识产权公约中的内涵和适用性，揭示可能导致隐蔽性例外的原因及对策。通过深入分析司法实践和法理问题，对全球化背景下国民待遇的影响进行批判性思考，探究如何在一国司法自治内对国民待遇进行解释，以实现拓展国内政策空间与履行国际义务间的平衡。

《知识产权调查引致的贸易壁垒：形成机理、效应及预警机制研究》，代中强著，北京：知识产权出版社，2018 年 8 月。

该书从经济学、法学和国际政治学等多维视角出发，在对美国发起的知识产权调查的历史数据进行详细分析的基础上，研究影响知识产权启动及案例判决的主要因素，系统分析知识产权调查产生的贸易限制效应，并在此基础上提出我国跨越知识产权壁垒的预警及应对机制。具体来说，要达到以下四个目标：其一，利用美国国际贸易委员会的知识产权调查案件资料，采用面板 Tobit 回归模型实证研究影响知识产权调查频数的关键因素，以判断美国发起知识产权调查的真实动机；其二，根据已经结案的样本资料，利用实证模型考察影响案件判决的关键因素；其三，以反事实模拟分析为工具，详细探讨知识产权调查产生的贸易抑制效用；其四，提出我国跨越知识产权壁垒的预警及应对机制。

《网络知识产权诉讼中的证据问题研究》，李慧著，北京：知识产权出版社，2018年11月。

该书主要介绍网络知识产权诉讼中的证据问题，主要涉及网络知识产权诉讼中的证据收集、证据筛选、证据运用、证据审查和认定等证据调查问题。网络技术的迅猛发展拓展了知识产权载体的范围，形成网络化的知识产权，使之与传统的知识产权相比在复制、合理使用等方面都出现了不小的差异；同时，网络技术的广泛渗透改变了侵犯知识产权的行为方式。这使得在网络知识产权诉讼中既有与其他知识产权案件共同面临的证据问题，也出现了一些异于传统知识产权诉讼的证据问题。该书对这些共同的和变异的证据问题进行了综合研究，进而论及如何更好地应对网络技术对知识产权诉讼证明提出的挑战，并提出了网络知识产权诉讼证据制度未来的发展路径。

《知识产权出资风险的法律规制研究》，王娟著，上海：上海人民出版社，2018年8月。

该书以知识产权出资风险为研究内容，通过对实践中知识产权出资纠纷判例的研究，将知识产权出资给受资公司带来的风险进行归纳分类，总结出五大风险，即知识产权评估不实、隐性知识产权出资、出资知识产权缺乏实益性、知识产权出资交付中的风险以及出资知识产权价值非正常贬损的风险。通过对相关司法案例的分析，结合公司法、知识产权法、合同法及民事侵权理论，深入探讨了如何对上述知识产权出资风险予以法律防范和规制。

《知识产权默示许可制度比较与司法实践》，袁真富著，北京：知识产权出版社，2018年10月。

该书全面探讨了专利、版权和商标领域的知识产权默示许可，并努力归纳各种可能的默示许可情形，提出知识产权默示许可适用的构成要件和判断方法。对于知识产权默示许可，我国知识产权法上并无明文规定，司法实践也无成熟的审判经验，而学界的专门探讨也才刚刚开启。该研究通过调查研究、文献分析、案例剖析和比较分析，得出了一系列重要的观点。

《中国知识产权保护对技术创新影响的研究》，张源媛著，北京：中国财政经济出版社，2018年6月。

该书分析了开放条件下知识产权保护和技术创新的影响。第一，梳理了国内外知识产权保护对技术创新影响的文献。第二，基于开放条件下不同的技术获取方式，从理论的角度对知识产权保护如何影响技术创新进行了机制分析。第三，介绍了中国的知识产权保护和技术创新的现状及水平。第四，采用宏观、中观和微观的数据，从实证角度分析了知识产权保护和技术创新的关系。第五，在前面研究的基础上提出了中国加强知识产权保护及进行技术创新的对策。

《知识产权法院论丛（第二辑）》，宿迟主编，北京知识产权法院编著，北京：法律出版社，2018年1月。

该书为《知识产权法院论丛》的第二辑。站在知识产权司法保护的角度，该书第一部分从知识产权法院自身特殊状况出发探讨法院司法改革的路径；第二部分为审判研究，聚焦知识产权审判领域部分前沿问题，有对法理的解读，有对法律适用的钻研，有对案例的评析，具有理论和实践意义。

《知识产权论丛（第3卷）》，苏平主编，北京：法律出版社，2018年11月。

该书聚集了一批学者围绕知识产权的热点、焦点和难点开展探讨，尤其是围绕实行严格的知识产权保护、促进我国的创新发展和科技进步，从而促进产业发展的命题开展研究。该书既有知识产权与产业发展论坛的专家精彩发言，又有学者关于知识产权立法、司法保护方面的话题，内容丰富，观点独到，充分展示了专家、学者知识产权研究的水平。

《中国知识产权名家讲坛（第一辑）》，李雨峰主编，北京：知识产权出版社，2018年10月。

该书中的各篇文章都是对知识产权热点问题的探讨和思考，理论联系实际，具有一定的指导意义。

该书每一辑计划选取 10～12 篇文章，以年份和文章主题相关性为选取标准，经过各发言人同意和确认后，将其发言内容进行记录、整理后结集成书。该书可作为读者了解 2014—2017 年知识产权研究的争议焦点及各专家学者观点的资料性文件，供学术研究和实务指导使用。

《知识产权文献与案例综述研究（2017）》，唐春、李文红主编，北京：知识产权出版社，2018 年 6 月。

该书适合知识产权研究者阅读学习。华东政法大学与集佳律师事务所共办“集佳杯”专利商标法律问题文献与案例综述竞赛，该书为前两届竞赛的优秀作品的汇编，是针对现实存在的专利与商标法律问题进行的文献综述和研究综述。竞赛的主旨在于提高学生综合学术研究能力，包括：以判例综述为引导，培养分析实际问题、研究司法实践的能力；以文献综述为引导，培养掌握学术文献、把握学术脉络的学术基本功。该书汇集了很多实务中比较前沿、重要的问题。

《侵犯知识产权行为的非罪化研究》，曹博著，北京：中国社会科学出版社，2018 年 7 月。

该书从知识产权侵权行为的非罪化这一论题出发，看似逆潮流而动，但绝非哗众取宠，其根本取向在于通过对知识产权根本特性的深入探究，经由刑法上的犯罪化理论检讨已然形成的知识产权刑事保护规则，进而实现对知识产权救济规则体系的全面梳理乃至重新构造。

除引言外，全书共五章。第一章是对既有知识产权救济规则体系的全面审视，试图廓清知识产权民事保护、行政保护及刑事保护的适用条件与基本特点，以期呈现出知识产权法律救济的规则体系。第二章将视野扩展到全球范围，通过美国法及国际条约的演进对知识产权刑事保护的历史进行回溯与分析，得出知识产权刑事保护的正当性前提值得进一步推敲的结论。第三章通过对刑法上犯罪化理论的整理和归纳，检讨知识产权侵权行为的刑事保护是否正当，批判知识产权侵权行为犯罪化在理论方面存在的诸多问题。第四章通过对自由刑与知识产权侵权行为不对称性、罚金刑的可替代性进行论证，证成知识产权侵权行为非罪化的命题。第五章在重新认识知识产权制度功能、深度解析知识产权救济的基础上，探讨知识产权侵权行为的非罪化带来的制度影响，重构知识产权的救济规则体系。

《体育数字知识产权保护策略和方法研究》，谭秀湖著，北京：中国广播影视出版社，2018 年 9 月。

该书采用文献资料法、比较调查法和案例分析法，以我国体育知识产权数字传播版权作为分析研究的基本对象，结合体育信息数字传播特有规律，分析了我国体育知识产权数字传播版权保护现状和存在的问题，并对现行制度进行了能效分析。在此基础上，寻求体育数字知识产权保护机制上的一种突破与创新，构建适合我国体育实际的体育数字知识产权保护体系、策略和方法。

《法官智典·知识产权卷》，钱海玲主编，北京：人民法院出版社，2018 年 12 月。

该书针对目前知识产权审判中的几类主要案件——著作权、专利权、商标权、不正当竞争纠纷案件中的前沿问题、热点问题与难点问题进行了梳理和研究，书中讨论的问题大部分来源于司法审判实践。

《中国海关知识产权保护状况年鉴（2018）》，《中国海关知识产权保护状况年鉴》编委会编著，北京：中国海关出版社，2018 年 12 月。

该书以大量文字、图表、照片再现海关知识产权保护工作的各个方面，内容翔实、宣传面广、实用性强、权威性高，是一部集史料、查询、指引、宣传等功能于一体的大型工具书。其主要内容包括：综述、海关知识产权工作概况、文献法规、备案企业及代理人（机构）汇编、媒体报道、案例分析、工作指南、重大活动、大事记等。

《中国知识产权指数报告 2018》，王正志著，北京：中国财政经济出版社，2018 年 11 月。

该书第一章为中国知识产权指数报告 2018 总体排名、研究发现与深度解析。第二章为中国区域知识产权分项指数 2018 排名与分析。第三章为知识产权产出水平各项指标排名与分析。第四章、第五章、第六章分别为从流动水平、综合绩效、创造潜力等方面进行的分析。

《中国知识产权统计年报 2017》，国家知识产权局主编，北京：知识产权出版社，2018 年 11 月。

该年报由国家知识产权局主办，汇集了我国知识产权领域的年度统计数据，全面反映了我国知识产权领域每年的发展状况。该年报涵盖专利、商标、版权、集成电路布图设计、农业植物新品种、林业植物新品种、海关知识产权保护、知识产权司法保护等方面的内容。该书可供广大知识产权界业内人士、各级领导干部、企事业单位管理人员、科研人员、高等院校师生等参考阅读。

《守正创新的知识产权研究之路》，管育鹰著，北京：社会科学文献出版社，2018年10月。

这本汇编学科初创以来若干有代表性的集体和个人研究成果的文集，顺着娓娓道来的导论回顾学科的发展史，重温那些影响中国知识产权事业的经典篇章，审视新近以来学者们对国家知识产权战略实施中若干具体问题的思索，让读者感受到中国社科院知识产权学科的魅力。

该书题名的“守正”意指坚守学术研究正道，也指法学所“正直精邃”所训的“正”，当然也顺带指郑成思教授的“郑”；“创新”意指知识产权研究要服务于创新型国家建设，要面向新时代、迎接新挑战、解决新问题。

《创新与竞争：网络时代的知识产权》，中国社会科学院知识产权中心、中国知识产权培训中心编，北京：知识产权出版社，2018年10月。

2017年10月27—28日，“2017知识产权上地论坛”召开，论坛以“创新与竞争：网络时代的知识产权”为主题展开，旨在对网络时代知识产权和反不正当竞争法发展中的新问题进行研究讨论，进而从法律层面寻求知识产权发展和制度创新、实现市场主体公平竞争的现实途径。该书精选本届论坛收到的部分论文结集成册，内容涉及网络时代的知识产权研究、著作权法相关问题研究、专利与竞争相关问题研究、商标法相关问题研究、反不正当竞争法相关问题研究，可为相关领域研究者提供借鉴与参考。

《知识产权高额赔偿36计：知识产权诉讼必备秘笈》，岳利浩著，北京：知识产权出版社，2018年10月。

针对我国知识产权诉讼长期存在的侵权损害“赔偿难”问题，作者以自己长期在广东省高级人民法院从事知识产权司法审判的经验为基础，结合相关法律、司法政策、司法解释以及全国各法院的成熟做法，以各法院的真实案例为例证，结集成册，以期帮助相关企业和律师提高证据意识，增强举证能力，为破解知识产权诉讼的“赔偿难”问题提出中肯建议。

《知识产权法原理与案例》，沈世娟、杨伟红著，北京：中国政法大学出版社，2018年10月。

该书所讲的知识产权原理部分限于传统的、重要的著作权、专利权、商标权三部分，案例部分与疑难部分在原理部分的基础上进行论述。

该书的特点是：原理部分重点突出；案例与疑难问题相关联，以便考查理论部分学习之后分析问题、解决问题的实际操作能力，并结合实例，以进一步提升理论研究能力。

《知识产权——文化传统与民族创新（英文版）》（***Intellectual Property Rights: The Cultural Tradition and National Innovation***），田德新著，西安：西北工业大学出版社，2018年9月。

该书基于国内外有关知识产权保护和民族创新的理论、作者以往和新近的实践及研究成果，对中美两国知识产权保护与创新关系的文化根源，特别是两国在版权纠纷方面的解决方案，进行了质化实证研究。

该书的研究重点是中美版权法的异同、国人对知识产权的保护特别是对盗版问题的认知、美国在知识产权保护方面对中国所施加的霸权压力、中国针对其压力所进行的智慧博弈，以及政府在数字信息化时代所应扮演的角色。该研究的理论指导框架由知识产权保护与创新、霸权与应对策略、理性行为与文化变迁，以及社会、国家与市场和政府角色等理论组成。主要研究方法包括田野调查、深度访谈和文本阐释。其中田野调查的主要内容为中美知识产权争议的现实和传统市场与网络盗版现象；深度访谈包括两个时间段，接受访谈的136位人士来自全国各地的各行各业；一手文本资料包括美国贸易代表办公室发布的29份年度《特别301报告》和美国知识产权界针对政府制定网络知识产权保护和创新政策的150份建议报告。

通过对中美版权法的比较，对136人访谈记录的主题分析，以及对29份年度《特别301报告》和150份政策建议报告的文本分析，该研究发现，首先，中美版权法的共同点是既保护版权持有人的权利，又保障社会所保护的版权持有人的权利不能超过集体和国家的利益。其次，美国版权持有人的道德权利，除视觉作品外，不在版权法保护之列，而中国版权持有人的道德权利，即声誉和公众利益往往大于其经济利益。最后，司法是美国解决版权纠纷的途径，而在中国除了法律途径外，还有行政与协商两种渠道。依据创新理论和研究发现，作者认为，要解决中美版权争议最好采用阶段式策略，而非美方强加的“一刀切”模式，且事实证明阶段式策略已经初见成效。

《最高人民法院知识产权案例指导与参考》(套装上下册)，最高人民法院案例指导与参考丛书编选组编，北京：人民法院出版社，2018 年 8 月。

该书为最高人民法院案例指导丛书之一，全书从知识产权案件办理司法实践中反映的各种疑难问题着手，以案由为分类依据，整合近五年来最高人民法院指导性案例、最高人民法院公报案例、审判指导与参考中的知识产权纠纷案例资源，通过同类指导性案例梳理与比较，为司法工作者提供知识产权法律适用的具体指导，为广大人民群众提供同种纠纷的司法处理结果预见。

《河南省知识产权服务业发展研究》，赵传海、方润生等著，北京：中国经济出版社，2018 年 7 月。

该书在全面阐述国内外知识产权服务研究和知识产权服务业发展特征的基础上，梳理和分析了河南省知识产权服务业的发展现状。按照河南省知识产权强省试点省建设的实施方案，围绕实施方案确定的 2020 年河南省专利、商标、版权等主要知识产权发展目标，阐述和分析了河南需要培育和发展的相关知识产权服务业，并根据这些产业目前的发展现状，分析和阐述了河南省知识产权服务业的特征、存在的问题及其发展趋势，提出适应河南省知识产权服务业健康发展的路径选择，以及保障河南省知识产权服务业有效实现知识产权强省战略目标的主要运行模式。

《知识产权法概论》，刘宇光、吴雪莲、姜文明、宋世勇、葛凤华编著，北京：中国社会出版社，2018 年 7 月。

该书依据“知识产权法教学基本要求”的规定编写，包括总论、著作权法、专利法、商标法、反不正当竞争法和与知识产权有关的国际公约六部分内容。根据本专业教师多年的教学实践和对相关知识体系的理解，反不正当竞争法已包含在经济法的课程内容之中，而与知识产权有关的国际公约部分在相应的制度体系中也多有涉及，故该书对上述两部分未另设专章阐述。在实践拓展篇，该书根据齐鲁工业大学法律系的课程设置、专业特色和发展方向，结合相关教师的研究成果，另设商业秘密法和企业知识产权战略两部分内容，以辅助读者在形成体系化的理论思维之上，在实践运用中更多地进行思考。

《知识产权裁判观点选粹和文书推介》，杜华英、王俊河主编，北京：知识产权出版社，2018 年 7 月。

该书第一部分精选 2008—2017 年最高人民法院知识产权案件年度报告及编者收集保存的最高人民法院在 2008 年以前公布的部分案例和裁判观点，按照相近主题进行编排。第二部分推介编者承办的 20 件案件的裁判文书，按照案件类型和承办年份选择和排列。所选内容具有代表性，可为司法实务工作者提供借鉴。该书适合知识产权司法实务工作者及相关学习者、研究者阅读。

《中国知识产权审判年度典型案例评析 (2018 年卷)》，《中国知识产权审判年度典型案例评析》编委会编，北京：中国法制出版社，2018 年 4 月。

该书汇集全国法院新知识产权典型案例，聚焦知识产权热点疑难问题，涵括专利、商标、著作权、不正当竞争、植物新品种等案件，由主审法官撰写法官评析，展现审判思路，剖析法律依据，剔除无效信息，高度提炼案情和裁判要旨，突出争议焦点。

《著作权应用与维权知识手册》，北京市文学艺术界联合会，北京大学法学院、知识产权学院编著，北京：北京大学出版社，2018 年 3 月。

该书采用知识介绍与案例分析相结合的方式，就相关著作权重点问题设计问答 120 个，采编典型案例 36 个，将理论与实践完美结合，旨在向作家、编剧、舞蹈家、摄影家以及文艺团体、协会等组织中从事文艺创作和管理工作但不具备相关法学背景的人员普及著作权法知识。通过知识介绍与案例分析相结合的方式，采用通俗易懂的语言，就文艺创作和开发过程中与著作权权利保护相关的一系列重点问题进行了讲解。

版权

统计资料

TONG JI ZI LIAO

2018年中国版权统计资料

2018年全国作品自愿登记情况统计（按作品类别）

单位：件

	合计	文字	口述	音乐	戏剧	曲艺	舞蹈	杂技	美术	摄影	建筑	影视	图形	模型	录音	录像	其他
全国合计	**2 351 952**	**278 170**	**307**	**34 802**	**332**	**286**	**174**	**47**	**992 513**	**917 045**	**197**	**53 224**	**11 724**	**1 470**	**8 369**	**13 406**	**39 886**
北　京	919 543	82 059	0	15 548	2	0	0	0	199 443	615 756	0	593	543	80	346	2 454	2 719
天　津	410	99	0	19	5	0	0	0	253	0	0	5	11	12	0	0	6
河　北	11 871	7 001	0	37	13	214	26	0	3 394	925	0	96	37	64	0	19	45
山　西	277	133	0	23	0	0	0	0	55	0	0	11	55	0	0	0	0
内蒙古	335	37	0	28	1	0	0	0	204	0	4	20	2	0	1	2	36
辽　宁	10 224	3 037	0	624	0	0	0	2	1 639	348	0	3 621	11	0	47	895	
吉　林	2 146	565	0	64	67	0	0	0	631	0	0	102	12	11	0	20	674
黑龙江	585	374	0	119	0	0	0	0	88	0	0	4	0	0	0	0	0
上　海	261 642	49 657	0	209	20	0	1	1	111 640	57 347	6	21 890	122	13	4 667	8 207	7 862
江　苏	302 175	48 996	202	607	22	18	55	12	170 040	66 867	7	13 214	997	3	1 098	34	3
浙　江	21 326	781	1	84	0	0	0	0	17 914	1 577	0	47	3	0	0	57	862
安　徽	20 225	774	2	117	8	4	0	0	4 318	14 324	1	168	402	55	0	18	34
福　建	96 181	2 158	4	11 264	13	6	1	0	77 819	1 475	79	2 125	408	24	512	74	219
江　西	12 672	5 364	1	73	2	0	0	0	2 871	2 297	0	1 375	43	2	162	480	2
山　东	84 506	3 265	21	282	3	1	1	0	10 384	69 489	4	626	303	59	0	0	68
河　南	1 063	511	0	39	2	0	3	1	376	0	0	121	3	0	0	0	7
湖　北	30 998	5 949	0	48	4	0	0	0	23 925	468	0	299	48	0	22	232	3
湖　南	3 928	826	0	42	1	0	0	0	1 848	161	0	429	45	7	14	514	41
广　东	53 126	4 491	30	887	21	1	2	21	35 546	5 755	3	1 081	1 480	11	690	250	2 857
广　西	842	170	0	63	8	0	0	0	275	96	41	10	121	18	0	26	14
海　南	169	54	0	12	0	0	0	0	54	0	0	12	25	0	0	0	12
重　庆	91 786	4 768	0	638	0	0	6	0	60 538	5 137	17	2 598	283	14	76	96	17 615
四　川	170 133	40 030	16	998	6	40	51	8	48 218	73 906	32	128	5 593	1 085	12	0	10
贵　州	1 144	84	0	57	5	0	9	0	531	102	0	44	299	2	0	0	11
云　南	322	102	0	73	0	0	0	0	142	0	0	2	3	0	0	0	0
西　藏	0	0	0	0	0	0	0	0	0	0	0	0	0	0	0	0	0
陕　西	8 037	837	0	106	3	0	0	0	6 510	291	0	275	0	0	0	5	10
甘　肃	158	49	2	9	0	0	2	0	86	0	0	6	0	0	0	0	4
青　海	75	16	0	1	0	0	0	0	35	0	0	0	0	6	0	17	0
宁　夏	502	91	13	184	0	0	0	0	162	0	0	28	24	0	0	0	0
新　疆	1 401	114	10	84	0	0	2	0	1 129	36	0	4	22	0	0	0	0
中国版权保护中心	244 150	15 778	5	2 463	126	2	15	2	212 445	688	3	4 290	829	4	722	6	6 772

注：中国版权保护中心登记356 433件，含作品登记200 662件/系列，涉及作品244 150件，数字作品版权登记112 283件。

2018 年全国版权合同登记情况统计

单位：份

	合计	图书	期刊	音像制品	电子出版物	软件	电影	电视节目	其他
合　计	**20 339**	**16 600**	**85**	**1 877**	**420**	**1 045**			**312**
中国版权保护中心	1 915			1 823		92			
北　京	9 300	9 102	84		111	3			
天　津	484	447			37				
河　北	252	248			4				
山　西	53	53							
内蒙古	2								2
辽　宁	409	409							
吉　林	62	62							
黑龙江	202	202							
上　海	1 155	1 024		54	77				
江　苏	1 211	394			92	725			
浙　江	804	591				213			
安　徽	87	87							
福　建	102	98				4			
江　西	406	406							
山　东	249	249							
河　南	163	163							
湖　北	369	369							
湖　南	406	405	1						
广　东	528	120			99				309
广　西	368	368							
海　南	168	168							
重　庆	294	294							
四　川	725	719				6			
贵　州	2	2							
云　南	245	245							
西　藏									
陕　西	235	232				2			1
甘　肃	99	99							
青　海									
宁　夏	44	44							
新　疆									

2018 年全国版权执法情况统计

案件查处情况				收缴盗版品情况			
项目	上年度数量	本年度数量	同比增减(%)	项 目	上年度数量	本年度数量	同比增减(%)
行政处罚数量（件）	3 552	3 033	－14.61%	合计	9 709 248	7 440 122	－23.37%
案件移送数量（件）	442	203	－54.07%	书刊	5 468 163	4 937 904	－9.70%
检查经营单位数量（个）	636 864	522 135	－18.01%	软件	365 423	240 968	－34.06%
取缔违法经营单位数量（个）	4 102	2 361	－42.44%	音像制品	1 393 489	1 195 203	－14.23%
查获地下窝点数量（个）	155	203	30.97%	电子出版物	169 552	197 044	16.21%
其中：地下光盘生产线（条）	4	2	－50.00%	其他	2 312 621	869 003	－62.42%
违法经营网站服务器（个）	244	737	202.05%	未分类项			
罚款金额（人民币元）	10 024 793	16 155 654	61.16%				

2018 年全国版权引进地汇总表

单位：册、盒、张、件、部、集

原版权所在国家或地区	合计	图书	录音制品	录像制品	电子出版物	软件	电影	电视节目	其他
引进版权总数（项）	**16 829**	**16 071**	**125**	**192**	**214**	**114**	**15**	**98**	
美　　国	5 047	4 833	27	104	42	22	3	16	
英　　国	3 496	3 317	26	11	99	11	1	31	
德　　国	881	844	9	15	2	4	2	5	
法　　国	1 024	970	5	9	21	7		12	
俄 罗 斯	83	78	0			3		2	
加 拿 大	127	117				7		3	
新 加 坡	228	222	1	2		1		2	
日　　本	2 075	1 993	13	17	19	19	6	8	
韩　　国	124	120			1	3			
香港地区	266	236	23	6				1	
澳门地区	1	1							
台湾地区	824	798	12	1	5	6		2	
其　　他	2 653	2 542	9	27	25	31	3	16	

2018 年全国版权输出地汇总表

单位：册、盒、张、件、部、集

版权输出的国家或地区	合计	图书	录音制品	录像制品	电子出版物	软件	电影	电视节目	其他
输出版权总数（项）	**12 778**	**10 873**	**214**		**743**	**19**	**1**	**928**	
美　国	1 228	912			273			43	
英　国	533	476			16			41	
德　国	507	435	29		2			41	
法　国	286	244					1	41	
俄 罗 斯	477	452	25						
加 拿 大	226	103						123	
新 加 坡	430	334			26			70	
日　本	424	408	12		4				
韩　国	587	512	2		73				
香港地区	805	535	115		45	1		109	
澳门地区	67	25				1		41	
台湾地区	1 552	1 449			59	1		43	
其　他	5 656	4 988	31		245	16		376	

2018年中国新闻出版产业统计资料

2018年全国各地区图书出版总量

	图书总计											
	种数（种）			总印数（万册、张）			总印张（千印张）			定价总金额（万元）		
	合计	新版	租型	合计	新版	租型	合计	新版	租型	合计	新版	租型
全国总计	**519 250**	**247 108**	**11 194**	**1 000 974**	**251 713**	**171 820**	**88 252 795**	**25 948 117**	**12 432 207**	**20 029 054**	**8 271 683**	**1 320 025**
中　央	**206 873**	**99 936**	**177**	**269 952**	**91 963**	**368**	**30 322 318**	**11 301 655**	**28 277**	**7 492 402**	**3 575 952**	**7 049**
地　方	**312 377**	**147 172**	**11 017**	**731 022**	**159 750**	**171 452**	**57 930 477**	**14 646 462**	**12 403 930**	**12 536 652**	**4 695 731**	**1 312 976**
北　京	13 759	7 075		26 742	8 547		2 391 999	860 910		720 604	308 463	
天　津	7 897	4 974	178	9 536	4 004	965	842 016	385 976	67 567	287 588	148 106	7 108
河　北	10 434	2 805	377	31 674	4 620	8 439	2 423 875	350 423	651 697	486 144	111 545	66 134
山　西	3 304	1 888	253	10 174	3 053	3 556	989 822	442 720	271 553	151 111	76 497	25 687
内蒙古	3 719	1 668	353	5 974	602	3 112	484 610	59 007	258 000	75 423	20 632	26 440
辽　宁	11 487	5 421	329	19 080	4 951	3 072	1 625 065	475 129	236 186	396 072	168 700	27 006
吉　林	27 824	14 187	638	23 733	6 819	3 834	2 017 384	632 645	329 641	486 176	185 610	33 329
黑龙江	8 709	5 832	326	8 204	2 410	2 836	689 443	207 071	216 903	148 603	60 906	22 319
上　海	30 005	14 227	16	48 030	19 465	181	4 488 805	1 857 673	12 134	1 345 445	714 375	1 440
江　苏	30 892	11 990	427	68 474	14 912	8 696	5 071 157	1 232 566	609 522	1 076 287	390 663	66 228
浙　江	15 231	6 835	420	41 810	10 433	8 079	3 049 827	809 700	555 442	722 847	287 991	62 172
安　徽	10 040	4 248	615	32 077	5 369	9 398	2 365 273	421 924	693 952	476 537	137 287	79 035
福　建	4 359	2 372	209	11 461	2 359	3 677	927 633	217 501	267 531	180 039	66 958	26 867
江　西	8 242	4 949	236	24 587	6 500	6 826	1 770 494	606 451	542 877	370 355	171 991	50 717
山　东	18 312	6 196	699	59 987	10 006	15 048	3 890 677	654 924	861 196	737 044	191 593	101 686
河　南	8 868	4 506	274	31 068	4 087	12 069	2 381 192	339 786	946 814	361 560	99 992	86 982
湖　北	13 419	6 852	414	26 835	6 831	6 503	2 099 493	649 529	493 057	467 268	206 190	56 270
湖　南	9 805	3 797	460	45 340	7 596	12 002	3 944 388	889 889	784 472	752 411	246 106	91 090
广　东	11 033	5 795	155	35 257	5 736	8 292	2 635 074	503 096	620 355	464 063	159 880	61 149
广　西	6 855	2 705	501	29 877	3 660	8 180	2 219 227	314 458	610 509	390 610	108 143	61 283
海　南	4 240	1 843	269	5 959	856	1 588	415 658	81 879	99 367	87 643	29 134	11 064
重　庆	5 568	1 773	315	15 271	1 899	3 748	1 021 998	158 921	255 092	205 166	52 162	30 604
四　川	14 456	8 746	460	32 520	8 009	8 181	2 548 592	644 669	606 891	527 179	228 638	62 294
贵　州	1 001	674	603	9 754	433	8 076	708 363	58 325	585 586	96 585	17 262	65 763
云　南	7 056	3 995	334	16 044	3 180	6 417	1 364 795	356 875	503 571	234 480	93 272	48 178
西　藏	716	320	219	1 315	111	654	102 309	21 091	47 787	15 915	5 008	5 957
陕　西	11 923	5 566	547	21 651	3 984	6 018	1 944 680	447 504	446 607	460 379	139 523	44 663
甘　肃	3 611	1 838	251	8 384	1 513	3 053	589 412	136 065	223 564	113 848	41 971	21 436
青　海	520	286	225	1 020	56	767	83 448	9 072	56 725	11 185	3 424	6 295
宁　夏	3 303	1 544	192	8 070	3 355	832	928 039	382 484	62 894	252 794	106 219	7 820
新　疆	5 423	1 921	722	20 979	4 303	7 353	1 897 589	426 604	486 438	429 474	113 424	55 960
兵　团	366	344		135	91		18 140	11 595		5 817	4 066	

2018 年全国各级

	合　计					中央及省、自治区、直辖市级				
	种数（种）	平均期印数（万份）	总印数（万份）	总印张（千印张）	总金额（万元）	种数（种）	平均期印数（万份）	总印数（万份）	总印张（千印张）	总金额（万元）
全国总计	**1 871**	**17 584.84**	**3 372 583**	**92 789 511**	**3 934 465**	**977**	**13 561.95**	**2 302 851**	**62 555 555**	**2 764 304**
中　央	**213**	**2 928.13**	**782 607**	**21 895 213**	**922 840**	**213**	**2 928.13**	**782 607**	**21 895 213**	**922 840**
地　方	**1 658**	**14 656.72**	**2 589 976**	**70 894 298**	**3 011 625**	**764**	**10 633.82**	**1 520 244**	**40 660 343**	**1 841 464**
北　京	34	192.25	48 511	2 097 535	52 600	34	192.25	48 511	2 097 535	52 600
天　津	19	119.74	31 574	879 494	38 365	19	119.74	31 574	879 494	38 365
河　北	63	447.65	108 930	2 033 802	115 197	26	305.44	70 908	1 033 730	74 533
山　西	60	2 397.35	198 105	1 859 784	231 208	38	2 327.36	177 277	1 428 860	207 961
内蒙古	58	112.08	26 603	598 430	27 446	23	59.43	12 376	310 629	13 016
辽　宁	66	481.31	73 111	1 873 463	73 709	18	319.81	30 476	548 342	35 809
吉　林	51	887.01	69 801	1 454 380	100 861	24	777.45	53 625	1 049 212	82 366
黑龙江	68	288.34	49 910	876 289	58 501	27	113.26	24 170	419 633	23 064
上　海	70	374.86	81 297	3 488 909	98 398	70	374.86	81 297	3 488 909	98 398
江　苏	81	1 108.66	214 171	5 349 585	229 826	30	700.41	111 901	2 229 969	112 827
浙　江	66	773.29	211 181	6 481 101	216 683	19	300.88	74 367	1 638 763	82 563
安　徽	51	298.78	67 725	1 392 803	63 506	19	159.32	33 396	629 687	31 539
福　建	43	407.38	78 555	2 732 361	92 724	20	286.53	37 958	1 343 237	43 532
江　西	40	1 111.51	88 317	1 204 146	97 212	18	1 028.46	63 661	753 140	72 326
山　东	86	754.32	218 016	9 583 350	209 794	28	385.43	117 714	6 327 615	110 062
河　南	77	1 332.40	167 259	3 877 432	226 148	32	1 105.95	109 754	2 336 838	154 934
湖　北	73	379.03	89 408	2 401 662	107 727	27	140.71	34 681	1 114 973	43 815
湖　南	48	476.21	84 801	2 064 110	94 354	22	351.83	50 400	1 327 659	64 198
广　东	99	804.87	221 184	9 991 560	366 040	32	411.66	104 227	5 512 650	201169
广　西	49	190.67	54 325	1 254 842	53 856	20	102.56	25 997	702 337	25 822
海　南	14	67.77	19 044	563 943	25 056	10	51.24	14 681	457 179	18 976
重　庆	27	133.85	26 398	622 848	30 549	24	125.80	24 125	564 692	28 406
四　川	84	519.91	132 695	3 270 895	163 288	37	306.15	67 559	1 764 949	87 810
贵　州	27	88.88	26 604	647 070	32 411	11	40.78	11 560	336 353	15 667
云　南	42	134.47	33 269	629 822	37 010	17	85.64	19 300	378 140	24 496
西　藏	27	50.52	10 876	216 376	8 407	11	26.57	5 658	100 994	3 430
陕　西	43	225.66	52 265	1 389 544	58 518	27	145.03	32 020	911 524	36 009
甘　肃	50	220.25	42 841	752 067	37 720	23	153.07	21 688	308 229	24 163
青　海	26	35.89	8 873	290 844	7 895	13	19.55	4 382	114 884	5 101
宁　夏	14	46.57	10 284	251 673	14 069	10	41.33	8 921	231 093	12 422
新　疆	82	161.92	37 168	653 923	34 767	32	58.02	11 656	234 238	10 898
兵　团	20	33.33	6 875	110 253	7 781	3	17.32	4 425	84 856	5 187

报纸出版数量

地、市级					县　级				
种数（种）	平均期印数（万份）	总印数（万份）	总印张（千印张）	总金额（万元）	种数（种）	平均期印数（万份）	总印数（万份）	总印张（千印张）	总金额（万元）
875	**3 987.69**	**1 059 436**	**30 060 088**	**1 161 043**	**19**	**35.21**	**10 296**	**173 868**	**9 118**
875	**3 987.69**	**1 059 436**	**30 060 088**	**1 161 043**	**19**	**35.21**	**10 296**	**173 868**	**9 118**
36	140.93	37 715	993 928	40 308	1	1.28	307	6 144	356
21	69.68	20 799	430 636	23 194	1	0.30	29	288	53
32	51.36	14 028	285 914	14 262	3	1.30	198	1 888	167
45	159.69	42 327	1 323 578	37 604	3	1.80	309	1 543	296
27	109.57	16 176	405 168	18 495					
41	175.08	25 739	456 656	35 437					
51	408.24	102 269	3 119 616	116 999					
44	451.70	129 400	4 700 268	127 670	3	20.71	7 414	142 069	6 449
32	139.46	34 329	763 116	31 967					
23	120.86	40 597	1 389 124	49 192					
20	79.75	24 161	446 047	24 279	2	3.30	496	4 959	608
58	368.89	100 301	3 255 736	99 732					
45	226.45	57 505	1 540 594	71 214					
43	233.34	53 369	1 273 109	62 885	3	4.97	1 358	13 580	1 028
26	124.38	34 401	736 451	30 156					
67	393.21	116 958	4 478 911	164 872					
29	88.11	28 328	552 505	28 034					
4	16.53	4 363	106 764	6 079					
3	8.05	2 273	58 157	2 143					
47	213.76	65 136	1 505 946	75 478					
16	48.10	15 044	310 717	16 743					
25	48.83	13 969	251 682	12 514					
16	23.95	5 218	115 383	4 977					
16	80.63	20 246	478 020	22 509					
27	67.18	21 153	443 838	13 557					
11	14.94	4 322	172 645	2 648	2	1.39	169	3 315	146
4	5.24	1 363	20 580	1 647					
49	103.73	25 495	419 603	23 855	1	0.17	17	83	15
17	16.01	2 451	25 396	2 594					

2018 年全国各地区各类期刊出版的种数、印数、总印张、总金额（1）

	合计					综合					哲学、社会科学				
	种数（种）	平均期印数（万册）	总印数（万册）	总印张（千印张）	总金额（万元）	种数（种）	平均期印数（万册）	总印数（万册）	总印张（千印张）	总金额（万元）	种数（种）	平均期印数（万册）	总印数（万册）	总印张（千印张）	总金额（万元）
全国总计	**10 139**	**12 330.82**	**229 205**	**12 674 692**	**2 179 213**	**362**	**695.73**	**14 951**	**809 351**	**119 247**	**2 678**	**6 609.48**	**114 607**	**5 896 301**	**1 028 833**
中　央	**3 070**	**5 141.30**	**78 578**	**5 325 134**	**946 758**	**65**	**91.31**	**2 046**	**144 327**	**27 000**	**933**	**3 714.04**	**56 760**	**3 074 260**	**580 238**
地　方	**7 069**	**7 189.52**	**150 627**	**7 349 557**	**1 232 455**	**297**	**604.42**	**12 905**	**665 024**	**92 247**	**1 745**	**2 895.44**	**57 847**	**2 822 041**	**448 595**
北　京	174	157.86	2 751	183 990	33 020	2	0.15	0.40	79	32	51	71.43	1 311	76 131	13 360
天　津	256	165.75	2 665	132 942	27 925	3	1.80	21	1 238	206	49	50.71	936	43 109	7 195
河　北	227	192.15	4 214	195 948	32 612	10	2.35	28	1 625	553	58	91.82	1 727	79 909	11 732
山　西	202	115.61	2 259	137 382	24 100	3	1.09	33	2 490	813	53	50.84	823	45 319	8 377
内蒙古	152	70.65	1 309	70 137	9 005	3	1.15	12	876	212	51	46.94	793	37 241	4 831
辽　宁	322	392.78	7 159	312 987	50 140	6	2.91	46	2 688	458	73	234.38	4 785	203 544	29 876
吉　林	240	186.09	5 688	269 765	42 535	3	1.72	35	2 442	558	62	49.15	1 317	62 323	8 623
黑龙江	315	173.03	3 484	189 235	29 064	8	1.89	17	1 450	294	75	89.06	1 593	80 783	12 251
上　海	639	528.50	8 505	446 329	85 123	14	5.86	56	4 310	1 051	145	172.28	3 306	167 638	30 961
江　苏	472	350.29	11 272	493 171	105 807	17	2.86	25	2 517	682	104	137.54	4 283	190 063	40 223
浙　江	231	505.86	7 366	313 925	55 589	21	3.40	23	1 556	358	49	117.48	1 895	100 222	17 570
安　徽	186	232.91	4 321	197 419	38 587	25	2.83	19	1 551	360	35	68.43	1 205	55 939	10 089
福　建	176	155.16	2 481	126 396	24 120	8	4.92	56	2 362	664	55	101.67	1 677	76 206	15 101
江　西	166	270.45	7 435	233 604	46 409	6	2.62	63	4 274	1 025	48	79.43	1 795	69 897	12 594

续表

	合计					综合					哲学、社会科学				
	种数（种）	平均期印数（万册）	总印数（万册）	总印张（千印张）	总金额（万元）	种数（种）	平均期印数（万册）	总印数（万册）	总印张（千印张）	总金额（万元）	种数（种）	平均期印数（万册）	总印数（万册）	总印张（千印张）	总金额（万元）
山东	276	381.33	8 260	355 202	53 312	18	10.35	259	11 987	2 275	78	200.58	2 976	176 416	22 608
河南	248	316.71	8 351	399 511	54 995	21	2.55	15	1 410	250	68	155.38	3 657	189 185	23 674
湖北	430	513.34	11 872	599 399	92 205	21	195.74	4 244	178 878	28 457	105	150.33	3 842	170 046	27 190
湖南	259	409.38	8 768	432 563	64 342	13	1.98	13	1 060	205	53	126.19	2 362	113 466	15 752
广东	387	508.05	10 753	562 385	91 673	27	21.87	353	22 234	4 474	99	227.40	4 924	249 667	35 023
广西	181	168.19	3 772	164 638	29 522	12	5.36	118	6 550	1 199	48	73.78	1 334	63 801	9 547
海南	42	32.17	593	39 867	6 542	2	8.20	96	9 653	1 792	13	8.63	124	6 541	957
重庆	140	193.80	4 455	239 224	44 329	4	1.08	20	2 036	630	33	121.56	2 095	100 226	18 340
四川	362	278.08	4 997	283 520	56 652	14	21.36	639	17 510	4 840	75	127.44	2 249	128 081	21 918
贵州	93	69.04	1 722	100 543	16 155	6	2.13	29	1 770	529	29	43.10	1 173	77 991	11 631
云南	129	145.99	2 493	115 985	18 641	6	1.37	23	1 862	530	40	84.46	1 142	50 036	7 024
西藏	39	21.17	244	14 791	2 360	1	0.30	1	104	6	12	10.86	96	4 350	694
陕西	287	152.47	3 119	180 332	31 588	6	4.25	81	4 751	721	56	65.88	1 558	79 290	13 301
甘肃	131	364.64	8 093	437 510	48 831	7	271.17	6 332	359 868	38 749	33	67.03	1 349	51 796	6 558
青海	54	16.34	269	15 458	2 146						19	8.01	145	5 745	870
宁夏	37	22.73	516	36 782	6 038	1	0.35	4	522	153	14	15.95	422	28 079	3 932
新疆	199	88.11	1 313	62 839	7 715	8	20.80	244	15 361	172	56	43.53	869	35 086	6 009
兵团	17	10.88	130	5 778	1 372	1	0.03	0.10	9	0.40	6	4.18	84	3 915	787

注：含高校学报、公报、政报、年鉴1 620种，平均期印数317万册，总印数4 058万册，总印张737 553千印张。

2018 年全国各地区各类期刊出版的种数、印数、总印张、总金额（2）

	自然科学、技术					文化、教育					文学、艺术				
	种数（种）	平均期印数（万册）	总印数（万册）	总印张（千印张）	总金额（万元）	种数（种）	平均期印数（万册）	总印数（万册）	总印张（千印张）	总金额（万元）	种数（种）	平均期印数（万册）	总印数（万册）	总印张（千印张）	总金额（万元）
全国总计	**5 037**	**2 047.30**	**29 821**	**2 487 022**	**415 221**	**1 399**	**2 260.17**	**53 311**	**2 582 696**	**453 419**	**663**	**718.14**	**16 516**	**899 321**	**162 493**
中　央	**1 571**	**776.20**	**9 768**	**1 304 057**	**196 117**	**358**	**429.15**	**7 619**	**639 198**	**106 454**	**143**	**130.60**	**2 384**	**163 292**	**36 950**
地　方	**3 466**	**1 271.10**	**20 053**	**1 182 965**	**219 105**	**1 041**	**1 831.02**	**45 691**	**1 943 498**	**346 965**	**520**	**587.54**	**14 131**	**736 029**	**125 543**
北　京	76	26.02	339	26 628	5 718	33	50.94	971	67 176	11 804	12	9.32	129	13 975	2 106
天　津	148	57.07	720	40 678	9 689	33	22.24	437	18 475	4 242	23	33.93	551	29 441	6 593
河　北	109	45.49	710	49 520	9 886	36	44.07	1 590	54 714	9 058	14	8.42	159	10 181	1 384
山　西	92	26.15	293	22 503	3 732	34	24.75	887	54 568	8 785	20	12.78	224	12 502	2 394
内蒙古	51	11.85	318	21 209	2 364	24	5.82	138	7 494	1 087	23	4.90	47	3 317	511
辽　宁	180	70.71	855	50 995	10 265	45	79.12	1 389	50 314	8 469	18	5.66	82	5 446	1 074
吉　林	104	19.72	298	27 654	4 595	45	34.78	933	36 765	7 495	26	80.72	3 104	140 580	21 264
黑龙江	162	39.60	800	40 246	6 013	52	27.48	775	47 566	8 100	18	14.99	299	19 190	2 406
上　海	361	131.25	1 560	107 765	22 715	79	97.80	1 379	73 576	14 562	40	121.32	2 204	93 040	15 834
江　苏	262	99.26	1 954	87 940	18 073	61	79.70	4 158	175 515	37 091	28	30.93	852	37 136	9 739
浙　江	113	40.59	410	24 399	4 741	31	327.96	4 711	171 360	29 115	17	16.44	327	16 387	3 805
安　徽	88	42.20	688	40 722	5 218	26	102.30	2 114	77 729	14 515	12	17.15	297	21 478	8 406
福　建	72	23.68	220	20 877	3 760	30	17.30	414	20 386	3 489	11	7.60	114	6 565	1 107
江　西	70	17.58	240	12 475	2 194	32	163.22	5 134	138 491	28 945	10	7.60	203	8 467	1 651
山　东	134	46.06	817	38 748	6 639	30	102.93	3 494	107 973	17 485	16	21.42	715	20 077	4 305
河　南	115	37.96	922	42 212	8 124	24	93.10	2 893	127 284	15 435	20	27.72	863	39 420	7 512

续表

	自然科学、技术					文化、教育					文学、艺术				
	种数（种）	平均期印数（万册）	总印数（万册）	总印张（千印张）	总金额（万元）	种数（种）	平均期印数（万册）	总印数（万册）	总印张（千印张）	总金额（万元）	种数（种）	平均期印数（万册）	总印数（万册）	总印张（千印张）	总金额（万元）
湖 北	211	61.38	784	60 595	12 040	63	46.02	1 037	52 690	8 531	30	59.87	1 965	137 190	15 987
湖 南	133	78.33	996	54 481	9 067	45	178.91	4 744	225 896	34 406	15	23.96	654	37 660	4 912
广 东	181	181.29	3 966	197 998	32 914	48	59.36	1 252	71 441	15 522	32	18.13	259	21 045	3 740
广 西	76	33.90	558	27 661	5 212	29	50.97	1 730	64 278	13 172	16	4.18	32	2 347	393
海 南	14	4.51	111	6 750	952	10	9.58	251	15 984	2 691	3	1.25	10	939	150
重 庆	81	22.89	432	32 695	6 779	19	47.38	1 901	103 882	18 522	3	0.89	7	385	57
四 川	210	54.29	695	58 749	11 327	45	67.63	1 300	70 067	17 024	18	7.35	113	9 114	1 542
贵 州	35	6.81	65	4 885	1 077	16	14.25	401	10 677	2 084	7	2.76	55	5 221	834
云 南	51	16.32	283	15 188	2 851	20	17.63	449	22 310	3 410	12	26.22	596	26 589	4 828
西 藏	8	1.79	7	400	57	13	7.38	136	9 681	1 571	5	0.85	4	257	32
陕 西	174	45.42	767	51 574	10 028	37	29.57	552	34 829	5 767	14	7.35	160	9 888	1 770
甘 肃	65	10.96	96	8 449	1 625	20	14.41	309	16 789	1 825	6	1.07	8	608	74
青 海	18	2.09	11	695	106	9	4.13	87	6 794	872	8	2.11	26	2 223	298
宁 夏	11	2.74	29	2 483	467	7	2.50	48	4 337	1 366	4	1.20	13	1 360	120
新 疆	55	11.36	92	4 925	739	44	7.74	75	4 440	524	36	4.68	33	3 027	270
兵 团	6	1.83	16	863	139	1	0.06	0.36	19	2	3	4.79	29	972	445

注：含高校学报、公报、政报、年鉴 1 620 种，平均期印数 317 万册，总印数 4 058 万册，总印张 737 553 千印张。

2018 年全国各地区电子出版物出版品种、数量及发行数量（按载体形式分类）

单位：种、万张

	电子出版物合计					只读光盘（CD-ROM）				高密度只读光盘（DVD-ROM）				交互式光盘（CD-I）				其他载体			
	合计		其中：新版		发行数量	合计		其中：新版		合计		其中：新版		合计		其中：新版		合计		其中：新版	
	种数	数量	种数	数量		种数	数量	种数	数量	种数	数量	种数	数量	种数	数量	种数	数量	种数	数量	种数	数量
全国总计	**8 403**	**25 884.21**	**3 514**	**6 577.50**	**24 561.34**	**5 309**	**22 491.49**	**1 755**	**5 058.84**	**2 647**	**3 169.25**	**1 349**	**1 342.77**	**1**	**0.25**	**1**	**0.25**	**446**	**223.22**	**409**	**175.64**
中　央	**4 983**	**19 621.93**	**1 692**	**4 952.79**	**18 474.99**	**3 120**	**17 149.28**	**724**	**3 770.56**	**1 611**	**2 269.60**	**735**	**1 025.06**	**1**	**0.25**	**1**	**0.25**	**251**	**202.80**	**232**	**156.92**
地　方	**3 420**	**6 262.28**	**1 822**	**1 624.70**	**6 086.34**	**2 189**	**5 342.21**	**1 031**	**1 288.28**	**1 036**	**899.65**	**614**	**317.71**					**195**	**20.42**	**177**	**18.72**
北　京	141	44.65	138	19.65	43.92	45	43.64	42	18.64	96	1.01	96	1.01								
天　津	54	24.66	53	24.26	24.36	13	10.31	13	10.31	32	13.30	31	12.90					9	1.05	9	1.05
河　北	104	151.57	18	51.22	163.41	87	143.41	17	51.12	17	8.16	1	0.10								
山　西	48	2.62	48	2.62	2.68	8	0.38	8	0.38	38	2.23	38	2.23					2	0.01	2	0.01
内蒙古	38	14.55	28	4.93	14.49	35	10.48	28	4.93	3	4.07										
辽　宁	193	176.51	124	29.26	176.53	169	173.45	106	26.93	22	2.99	17	2.28					2	0.07	1	0.05
吉　林	35	17.37	35	17.37	17.22	19	16.32	19	16.32	11	0.55	11	0.55					5	0.50	5	0.50
黑龙江	5	0.37	5	0.37	0.37					4	0.32	4	0.32					1	0.05	1	0.05
上　海	558	1 305.97	84	102.73	1 081.99	387	1 015.18	38	36.32	131	284.86	20	61.07					40	5.93	26	5.35
江　苏	478	1 843.46	121	583.85	1 846.65	243	1 730.29	36	563.05	201	109.78	51	17.41					34	3.39	34	3.39
浙　江	287	942.89	150	83.46	943.09	170	754.07	80	16.76	114	188.41	67	66.30					3	0.40	3	0.40
安　徽	5	1.21	5	1.21	1.11	1	0.10	1	0.10	3	1.01	3	1.01					1	0.10	1	0.10
福　建	30	10.15	25	9.65	10.15	15	0.99	10	0.49	14	9.05	14	9.05					1	0.11	1	0.11
江　西	46	11.93	42	10.76	11.51	29	9.36	25	8.20	16	2.54	16	2.54					1	0.02	1	0.02
山　东	281	155.35	249	45.39	214.55	192	43.16	168	14.52	75	111.35	67	30.03					14	0.84	14	0.84
河　南	145	302.51	145	302.51	302.23	52	299.13	52	299.13	50	2.97	50	2.97					43	0.41	43	0.41

续表

	电子出版物合计					只读光盘（CD-ROM）				高密度只读光盘（DVD-ROM）				交互式光盘（CD-I）				其他载体			
	合计		其中：新版		发行数量	合计		其中：新版		合计		其中：新版		合计		其中：新版		合计		其中：新版	
	种数	数量	种数	数量		种数	数量	种数	数量	种数	数量	种数	数量	种数	数量	种数	数量	种数	数量	种数	数量
湖　北	108	87.50	78	68.61	87.34	83	21.80	61	4.93	23	65.65	15	63.64					2	0.04	2	0.04
湖　南	94	266.64	39	132.72	239.04	76	258.39	23	124.68	17	8.15	15	7.94					1	0.10	1	0.10
广　东	270	588.49	75	18.58	584.58	212	573.48	44	8.58	45	9.57	19	5.07					13	5.44	12	4.93
广　西	8	0.82	8	0.82	0.66	4	0.56	4	0.56	3	0.20	3	0.20					1	0.06	1	0.06
海　南	5	1.51	5	1.51	1.51					5	1.51	5	1.51								
重　庆	133	58.24	46	9.44	63.50	48	20.33	2	0.40	84	37.71	43	8.84					1	0.20	1	0.20
四　川	228	101.56	200	18.18	104.98	218	99.38	190	16.00	2	2.10	2	2.10					8	0.08	8	0.08
贵　州	5	0.30	5	0.30	0.30													5	0.30	5	0.30
云　南	44	102.16	33	77.27	102.01	24	70.58	17	59.21	20	31.57	16	18.06								
西　藏	13	3.70	13	3.70	3.44	11	3.30	11	3.30									2	0.40	2	0.40
陕　西	62	45.38	48	4.14	44.50	48	44.11	36	3.46	9	0.55	9	0.55					5	0.73	3	0.13
甘　肃																					
青　海																					
宁　夏	2	0.23	2	0.23	0.23					1	0.03	1	0.03					1	0.20	1	0.20
新　疆																					
兵　团																					

2018 年全国各地区录音制品出版品种、数量及发行数量（按载体形式分类）

单位：种、万盒（张）

	录音制品合计					录音带（AT）				激光唱盘（CD）				高密度激光唱盘（DVD-A）				其他载体			
	合计		其中：新版		发行数量	合计		其中：新版		合计		其中：新版		合计		其中：新版		合计		其中：新版	
	种数	数量	种数	数量		种数	数量	种数	数量	种数	数量	种数	数量	种数	数量	种数	数量	种数	数量	种数	数量
全国总计	**6 391**	**17 756.61**	**2 410**	**1 830.47**	**16 590.38**	**1 032**	**6 669.19**	**138**	**166.12**	**4 867**	**10 939.19**	**1 890**	**1 574.72**	**159**	**101.30**	**107**	**52.41**	**333**	**46.94**	**275**	**37.23**
中　央	**2 719**	**12 669.16**	**862**	**995.80**	**11 539.22**	**569**	**5 299.60**	**37**	**146.99**	**1 959**	**7 332.00**	**659**	**819.99**	**42**	**18.35**	**40**	**17.75**	**149**	**19.20**	**126**	**11.07**
地　方	**3 672**	**5 087.46**	**1 548**	**834.68**	**5 051.16**	**463**	**1 369.58**	**101**	**19.13**	**2 908**	**3 607.19**	**1 231**	**754.72**	**117**	**82.95**	**67**	**34.66**	**184**	**27.73**	**149**	**26.16**
北　京	229	104.27	204	80.24	98.92	15	1.50	15	1.50	196	90.15	171	66.12	1	0.10	1	0.10	17	12.52	17	12.52
天　津	22	20.99	17	18.37	23.91	2	1.87			20	19.12	17	18.37								
河　北	51	258.23	2	21.21	250.66	35	10.00	1	0.04	16	248.23	1	21.17								
山　西	67	80.31	67	80.31	80.31					67	80.31	67	80.31								
内蒙古	23	3.48	23	3.48	3.48					23	3.48	23	3.48								
辽　宁	136	104.62	40	29.55	98.34					135	104.22	40	29.55	1	0.40						
吉　林	123	173.14	22	3.40	170.52	59	86.84	9	0.90	64	86.30	13	2.50								
黑龙江	3	0.15	3	0.15	0.05					3	0.15	3	0.15								
上　海	1 364	1 191.22	212	134.96	1 196.55	78	96.04			1 184	1 027.39	170	106.66	59	65.47	18	26.63	43	2.32	24	1.67
江　苏	209	1 116.70	76	9.13	1 116.73	67	1 020.59	8	0.56	120	84.76	51	5.47	22	11.35	17	3.10				
浙　江	115	290.67	75	16.90	290.57	20	45.50	4	1.11	62	240.05	41	11.46	33	5.13	30	4.33				
安　徽	15	4.28	12	3.76	3.47	6	1.08	3	0.56	9	3.20	9	3.20								
福　建	26	27.18	15	20.59	28.37	8	4.16			18	23.02	15	20.59								
江　西	57	29.55	17	4.90	29.55	15	4.50	15	4.50	42	25.05	2	0.40								
山　东	100	11.87	86	8.17	11.52	19	1.90	19	1.90	78	9.67	64	5.97					3	0.30	3	0.30
河　南	6	1.40	6	1.40	1.40					6	1.40	6	1.40								

续表

	录音制品合计					录音带（AT）				激光唱盘（CD）				高密度激光唱盘（DVD-A）				其他载体			
	合计		其中：新版		发行数量	合计		其中：新版		合计		其中：新版		合计		其中：新版		合计		其中：新版	
	种数	数量	种数	数量		种数	数量	种数	数量	种数	数量	种数	数量	种数	数量	种数	数量	种数	数量	种数	数量
湖　北	38	6.40	19	1.12	6.40					38	6.40	19	1.12								
湖　南	117	335.87	29	81.04	331.24	12	9.35	8	4.58	104	326.02	20	75.96	1	0.50	1	0.50				
广　东	688	1 201.33	473	270.60	1 185.66	99	82.08	1	0.49	469	1 108.25	368	260.05					120	10.99	104	10.07
广　西	107	53.80	51	20.54	53.07					107	53.80	51	20.54								
海　南	18	2.98	18	2.98	2.45	14	2.73	14	2.73	4	0.25	4	0.25								
重　庆	37	11.98	14	3.38	12.02	7	0.68			30	11.29	14	3.38								
四　川	11	3.20	9	2.80	3.20					10	1.60	8	1.20					1	1.60	1	1.60
贵　州																					
云　南	27	5.65	24	5.17	5.37	7	0.75	4	0.27	20	4.90	20	4.90								
西　藏																					
陕　西	72	42.51	25	5.46	41.86					72	42.51	25	5.46								
甘　肃	6	0.90	6	0.90	0.88					6	0.90	6	0.90								
青　海																					
宁　夏	1	0.05	1	0.05	0.05					1	0.05	1	0.05								
新　疆	4	4.71	2	4.10	4.61					4	4.71	2	4.10								
兵　团																					

2018 年全国各地区录像制品出版品种、数量及发行数量（按载体形式分类）

单位：种、万盒（张）

	录像制品合计					录像带（VT）				数码激光视盘（VCD）				高密度激光视盘（DVD-V）				其他载体			
	合计		其中：新版		发行数量	合计		其中：新版		合计		其中：新版		合计		其中：新版		合计		其中：新版	
	种数	数量	种数	数量		种数	数量	种数	数量	种数	数量	种数	数量	种数	数量	种数	数量	种数	数量	种数	数量
全国总计	**4 672**	**6 367.48**	**3 335**	**3 254.36**	**6 027.03**					**485**	**1 174.00**	**127**	**310.61**	**4 022**	**5 163.85**	**3 049**	**2 914.57**	**165**	**29.63**	**159**	**29.18**
中　央	**2 269**	**3 485.64**	**1 451**	**965.85**	**3 197.08**					**255**	**1 084.19**	**16**	**271.72**	**1 895**	**2 381.35**	**1 318**	**674.43**	**119**	**20.10**	**117**	**19.70**
地　方	**2 403**	**2 881.84**	**1 884**	**2 288.51**	**2 829.96**					**230**	**89.82**	**111**	**38.89**	**2 127**	**2 782.50**	**1 731**	**2 240.14**	**46**	**9.52**	**42**	**9.48**
北　京	185	50.35	173	47.16	24.11					6	0.65	5	0.25	177	49.68	166	46.89	2	0.02	2	0.02
天　津	17	12.08	17	12.08	12.08									13	8.08	13	8.08	4	4.00	4	4.00
河　北	11	4.17	11	4.17	3.55									11	4.17	11	4.17				
山　西	28	1.67	28	1.67	10.00									28	1.67	28	1.67				
内蒙古	7	1.83	7	1.83	1.83									7	1.83	7	1.83				
辽　宁	51	30.36	49	30.10	27.80									51	30.36	49	30.10				
吉　林	99	9.15	96	8.75	8.64									99	9.15	96	8.75				
黑龙江	4	0.29	4	0.29	0.22					1	0.02	1	0.02	3	0.27	3	0.27				
上　海	534	2 140.00	317	1 736.55	2 134.05					120	41.92	69	19.60	410	2 098.04	248	1 716.95	4	0.04		
江　苏	66	16.56	43	8.41	13.86									65	16.41	42	8.26	1	0.15	1	0.15
浙　江	111	66.91	70	52.61	83.26					16	8.46	6	0.60	95	58.44	64	52.01				
安　徽	23	7.38	23	7.38	9.00									22	7.28	22	7.28	1	0.10	1	0.10
福　建	48	17.78	40	17.04	19.24									48	17.78	40	17.04				
江　西	80	35.67	52	19.20	35.67					30	16.50	17	8.50	50	19.17	35	10.70				
山　东	61	24.78	61	24.78	22.26									61	24.78	61	24.78				
河　南	35	3.41	35	3.41	2.79									25	3.16	25	3.16	10	0.25	10	0.25

续表

	录像制品合计					录像带（VT）				数码激光视盘（VCD）				高密度激光视盘（DVD-V）				其他载体			
	合计		其中：新版		发行数量	合计		其中：新版		合计		其中：新版		合计		其中：新版		合计		其中：新版	
	种数	数量	种数	数量		种数	数量	种数	数量	种数	数量	种数	数量	种数	数量	种数	数量	种数	数量	种数	数量
湖　北	65	21.48	16	3.41	20.43					22	3.14			42	18.29	15	3.35	1	0.06	1	0.06
湖　南	145	113.17	73	44.97	113.25					17	9.81	11	8.42	128	103.36	62	36.55				
广　东	291	68.51	272	44.36	50.80					4	1.82			270	62.49	255	40.16	17	4.20	17	4.20
广　西	23	9.94	22	4.24	4.84									19	9.54	18	3.84	4	0.40	4	0.40
海　南	7	1.70	7	1.70	1.70									7	1.70	7	1.70				
重　庆	31	14.15	24	10.25	21.18					2	3.34			29	10.81	24	10.25				
四　川	91	54.23	91	54.23	52.49									91	54.23	91	54.23				
贵　州	1	0.20	1	0.20	0.20													1	0.20	1	0.20
云　南	85	26.83	85	26.83	23.68					1	1.00	1	1.00	84	25.83	84	25.83				
西　藏	53	23.80	53	23.80	21.19									53	23.80	53	23.80				
陕　西	115	32.51	100	28.85	29.93					11	3.15	1	0.50	104	29.36	99	28.35				
甘　肃	15	2.95	15	2.95	2.94									14	2.85	14	2.85	1	0.10	1	0.10
青　海	10	2.90	10	2.90	0.60									10	2.90	10	2.90				
宁　夏	6	2.05	6	2.05	2.01									6	2.05	6	2.05				
新　疆	105	85.05	83	62.36	76.37									105	85.05	83	62.36				
兵　团																					

2018 年全国新华书店系统、出版社自办发行单位出版物发行进、销、存情况

单位：万册（张、份、盒）、万元

	购进		销售		库存	
	数量	金额	数量	金额	数量	金额
全国总计	**2 236 118**	**33 605 735**	**2 170 763**	**32 133 713**	**690 612**	**13 754 029**
中　央	**268 564**	**7 648 644**	**248 204**	**6 991 082**	**149 692**	**5 223 432**
地　方	**1 967 554**	**25 957 091**	**1 922 559**	**25 142 631**	**540 920**	**8 530 597**
北　京	22 315	659 322	23 027	644 081	14 778	497 723
天　津	11 825	233 553	11 342	225 969	5 298	120 979
河　北	98 397	1179 945	97 686	1 157 275	45 286	208 455
山　西	40 669	508 899	39 005	493 883	15 056	184 685
内蒙古	15 057	295 050	15 073	292 208	3 270	42 030
辽　宁	28 545	404 845	28 104	409 731	9 808	210 196
吉　林	19 565	355 002	20 242	362 544	5 707	133 224
黑龙江	13 437	210 272	13 592	214 425	4 870	87 809
上　海	46 547	1248 728	43 853	1 163 980	26 205	854 220
江　苏	223 068	2 531 473	207 906	2 407 555	79 393	1 070 428
浙　江	146 335	2 302 203	140 838	2 198 518	51 395	1 047 714
安　徽	119 752	1 460 595	117 513	1 415 747	22 018	355 958
福　建	43 942	514 152	44 668	499 737	10 257	144 140
江　西	92 279	1 276 034	90 546	1 247 435	14 697	244 524
山　东	165 074	2 007 940	165 670	1 960 710	54 772	590 375
河　南	172 638	1 423 339	170 365	1 409 289	18 391	229 149
湖　北	72 454	961 985	69 552	933 608	12 113	226 098
湖　南	112 171	1 599 528	102 136	1 468 679	43 712	589 306
广　东	81 893	1 057 600	82 207	1 003 830	35 306	486 099
广　西	71 777	693 173	70 517	673 799	5 401	123 604
海　南	15 471	179 533	15 254	178 458	1 217	24 100
重　庆	32 921	497 676	32 814	482 876	5 869	92 442
四　川	77 880	1 264 797	76 015	1 222 392	13 854	387 947
贵　州	39 049	384 788	38 768	384 976	3 433	29 975
云　南	53 590	734 256	53 996	742 055	6 342	119 950
西　藏	2 997	31 174	3 051	30 727	933	8 365
陕　西	70 453	849 421	71 159	837 211	18 245	224 484
甘　肃	29 108	328 666	28 488	326 031	4 159	44 923
青　海	2 223	34 114	2 134	33 287	1 353	12 226
宁　夏	7 033	101 730	6 648	101 428	1 086	19 342
新　疆	39 087	627 299	40 387	620 187	6 695	120 127

2018 年全国图书、期刊、报纸进出口情况

类别		出口		进口	
		数量（万册、万份）	金额（万美元）	数量（万册、万份）	金额（万美元）
总计		**1 478.09**	**5 723.00**	**4 088.02**	**36 202.19**
图书	合计	1 067.17	5 084.06	2 995.39	21 577.06
	哲学、社会科学	94.45	1 010.38	195.19	2 947.44
	文化、教育	124.37	828.90	777.00	5 390.23
	文学、艺术	140.85	920.46	400.54	3 218.94
	自然、科学技术	50.25	364.62	84.00	2 712.10
	少儿读物	481.36	846.47	981.84	3 089.47
	综合性图书	175.89	1 113.23	556.82	4 218.88
期刊		325.23	595.54	305.84	13 526.85
报纸		85.69	43.40	786.79	1 098.28

注：以上数据为全国有出版物进口经营许可证的出版物进出口经营单位数据。

2018 年全国音像制品、电子出版物、数字出版物进出口情况

类别		出口		进口	
		数量（盒、张）	金额（万美元）	数量（盒、张）	金额（万美元）
总计		**12 354**	**212.20**	**88 444**	**38 019.93**
录音	合计	10 795	34.39	82 248	87.75
	录音带（AT）	0	0.00	0	0.00
	激光唱盘（CD）	3 297	10.52	82 248	87.75
	高密度激光唱盘（DVD-A）	7 498	23.87	0	0.00
录像	合计	1 559	1.76	6 196	9.98
	录像带（VT）	0	0.00	0	0.00
	高密度激光视盘（DVD-V）	1 559	1.76	6 196	9.98
	数码激光视盘（VCD）	0	0.00	0	0.00
电子出版物		0	0.00	0	0.00
数字出版物			176.05		37 922.20

注：以上数据为全国有出版物进口经营许可证的出版物进出口经营单位数据。

2018年中国广播影视产业统计资料*

2018 年全国广播电视发展主要指标一览表（一）

	宣传情况				覆盖情况				有线广播电视发展情况				
	广播节目播出时间（万小时）	电视节目播出时间（万小时）	广播节目制作时间（万小时）	电视节目制作时间（万小时）	广播综合人口覆盖率（%）	电视综合人口覆盖率（%）	无线广播综合人口覆盖率（%）	无线电视综合人口覆盖率（%）	有线广播电视实际用户（万户）	数字电视实际用户（万户）	付费数字电视实际用户（万户）	有线广播电视用户占本地区总户数比重（%）	有线广播电视网络传输干线总长（不含县级前端以下）（万公里）
全国合计	**1 526.74**	**1 925.03**	**801.76**	**357.74**	**98.94**	**99.25**	**97.85**	**97.46**	**21 832.41**	**20 143.68**	**7 729.94**	**49.01**	**225.27**
中央直属	17.98	24.15	31.39	20.00	—	—	—	—	—	—	—	—	4.00
北京市	18.11	13.71	12.94	15.75	100.00	100.00	100.00	99.81	594.55	571.46	116.52	109.48	20.72
天津市	15.18	16.19	9.82	2.05	100.00	100.00	100.00	100.00	352.89	347.99	121.6	91.62	0.39
河北省	80.05	86.05	40.17	17.63	99.36	99.29	98.43	97.72	734.62	653.17	187.33	30.40	8.01
山西省	50.63	64.04	24.71	11.24	98.80	99.57	98.58	99.36	382.01	311.81	65.86	29.34	6.97
内蒙古自治区	66.39	64.90	31.21	7.83	99.24	99.22	99.02	97.32	228.40	216.09	150.66	23.34	2.72
辽宁省	68.89	77.54	39.25	16.44	99.09	99.17	99.00	98.13	732.84	666.43	165.94	47.91	3.12
吉林省	55.08	52.40	28.24	12.01	99.01	99.10	98.71	96.42	453.53	440.73	230.57	43.99	1.09
黑龙江省	58.80	59.34	24.52	10.51	99.04	99.07	99.04	99.07	591.64	568.79	202.63	38.56	7.58
上海市	15.06	17.92	9.01	7.59	100.00	100.00	100.00	100.00	484.03	451.50	194.34	88.56	4.78
江苏省	77.81	75.78	56.58	20.90	100.00	100.00	100.00	100.00	1 640.55	1 566.71	668.88	66.43	4.35
浙江省	77.08	74.44	52.98	19.49	99.73	99.80	99.71	99.74	1 434.67	1 405.62	550.45	85.81	7.85
安徽省	55.86	64.62	18.74	7.89	99.84	99.83	99.82	99.68	796.01	589.68	136.13	37.06	3.09

* 广播影视产业主要数据由国家广播电视总局财务司依据 2017 年 11 月国家统计局批准的最新《广播影视行业统计报表制度》调查统计得出。

续表

	宣传情况				覆盖情况				有线广播电视发展情况				
	广播节目播出时间（万小时）	电视节目播出时间（万小时）	广播节目制作时间（万小时）	电视节目制作时间（万小时）	广播综合人口覆盖率（%）	电视综合人口覆盖率（%）	无线广播综合人口覆盖率（%）	无线电视综合人口覆盖率（%）	有线广播电视实际用户（万户）	数字电视实际用户（万户）	付费数字电视实际用户（万户）	有线广播电视用户占本地区总户数比重（%）	有线广播电视网络传输干线总长（不含县级前端以下）（万公里）
福建省	52.88	39.54	26.63	6.23	99.04	99.19	98.05	96.76	716.23	716.23	411.3	65.22	19.21
江西省	37.12	66.51	16.25	9.24	98.54	99.09	98.24	98.84	618.23	576.74	224.06	48.06	9.97
山东省	96.96	141.81	55.91	24.38	99.01	99.09	98.73	98.58	1 684.23	1 567.69	612.70	52.99	44.06
河南省	69.35	95.89	30.40	14.99	99.05	99.04	99.01	98.99	974.89	811.71	44.76	29.86	4.96
湖北省	53.53	72.04	24.30	10.37	99.68	99.58	99.41	99.30	1 082.77	1 060.83	554.41	51.61	2.82
湖南省	47.14	75.66	22.69	12.33	99.02	99.64	97.92	98.52	1 014.58	874.84	234.43	47.89	11.36
广东省	80.84	84.85	60.35	25.70	99.98	99.98	98.92	97.93	1 844.82	1 760.68	747.08	71. 09	32.60
广西壮族自治区	42.64	60.46	23.52	9.30	97.56	98.78	95.90	97.15	689.31	605.68	280.10	43.48	1.15
海南省	14.20	10.13	7.36	2.10	99.06	99.08	99.06	99.08	226.66	151.97	29.02	85.66	0.23
重庆市	17.49	30.87	8.58	6.42	99.04	99.27	93.04	92.35	736.80	557.00	130.69	58.43	5.76
四川省	71.08	115.78	30.39	16.54	97.84	98.79	96.22	96.94	1 181.63	1 123.83	528.03	36.50	2.75
贵州省	25.65	45.15	14.61	4.65	93.92	96.76	83.95	74.90	702.92	702.92	412.17	53.19	0.91
云南省	38.01	89.44	20.02	13.72	98.69	98.90	96.61	96.77	460.34	434.60	303.29	32.95	2.88
西藏自治区	15.25	30.67	3.74	2.04	97.14	98.21	95.81	96.35	24.15	21.52	1.41	30.60	0.47
陕西省	46.71	61.16	24.48	12.19	98.84	99.34	97.97	98.26	730.75	730.75	176.09	56.20	3.74
甘肃省	37.93	55.26	14.87	7.26	98.45	98.81	94.79	95.20	191.62	144.49	83.01	22.69	1.67
青海省	21.14	29.59	5.46	1.67	98.62	98.65	98.55	98.31	95.85	94.74	36.72	53.90	0.74
宁夏回族自治区	14.00	17.02	5.39	2.53	98.98	99.79	98.91	96.40	105.70	104.58	52.17	48.42	0.51
新疆维吾尔自治区	87.87	112.10	27.27	8.74	97.83	98.07	97.67	97.81	285.80	282.35	77.60	43.15	3.49
新疆生产建设兵团	—	—	—	—	—	—	—	—	39.29	30.57	—	—	1.31

2018 年全国广播电视发展主要指标一览表（二）

	从业人员（万人）	总收入（亿元）	实际创收收入（亿元）	广告收入（亿元）	广播广告收入（亿元）	电视广告收入（亿元）	网络媒体广告收入（亿元）	网络收入（亿元）	有线电视收视维护费收入（亿元）	付费数字电视频道收入（亿元）	三网融合业务收入（亿元）	新媒体业务收入（亿元）	网络视听节目服务收入（亿元）	资产总额（亿元）
全国合计	**97.90**	**6 952.14**	**5 639.61**	**1 864.49**	**140.37**	**958.86**	**491.88**	**779.48**	**368.38**	**56.85**	**111.41**	**467.76**	**223.94**	**18 617.92**
中央直属	5.48	750.40	636.92	337.10	8.72	319.43	7.71	5.03	0.48	0.28	0.31	54.57	0.97	2 321.14
北京市	8.91	1 785.99	1 473.61	568.62	8.60	73.38	314.60	26.21	10.37	1.14	6.24	201.53	183.55	3 530.84
天津市	0.85	55.36	37.89	8.26	3.48	4.48	0.00	10.42	4.02	1.07	2.07	3.03	—	173.60
河北省	3.88	93.10	65.90	16.95	5.39	9.83	0.27	20.54	11.06	0.43	3.74	4.46	0.00	251.84
山西省	2.71	68.49	38.67	9.12	3.24	5.30	0.15	8.47	6.04	0.20	0.32	1.13	0.00	157.13
内蒙古自治区	1.78	49.46	19.08	3.92	1.27	2.57	0.00	13.98	7.82	1.52	—	0.79	—	128.43
辽宁省	2.74	69.93	45.73	15.84	5.52	9.65	0.08	22.80	17.38	0.48	1.67	1.16	0.09	240.24
吉林省	2.01	57.01	33.54	9.57	2.68	6.83	0.00	19.50	10.70	3.46	1.19	1.51	—	330.63
黑龙江省	2.75	59.78	38.04	13.08	4.47	8.21	0.01	18.02	13.04	1.07	2.07	0.56	0.01	198.05
上海市	2.66	572.00	478.00	139.07	6.48	50.19	78.01	37.30	13.47	4.39	8.12	27.59	0.22	1 382.31
江苏省	5.96	373.72	352.69	92.90	11.87	61.69	2.15	78.84	34.44	4.75	8.47	16.63	1.20	1 561.37
浙江省	5.86	531.35	488.47	124.58	12.74	94.94	4.17	77.24	29.50	6.28	13.96	21.13	8.61	2 211.01
安徽省	3.21	97.18	69.35	30.22	3.70	21.94	2.15	14.20	8.01	0.95	0.63	1.97	0.14	184.51
福建省	2.84	140.18	116.25	21.12	3.26	8.11	6.78	32.50	9.61	2.95	4.54	9.64	0.19	273.34
江西省	1.88	52.25	37.25	13.81	1.85	11.07	0.28	15.12	9.09	1.04	0.92	0.81	—	124.01
山东省	5.26	170.28	131.89	48.63	8.65	32.93	3.80	45.13	23.09	2.77	4.63	6.84	0.01	475.90
河南省	4.9	76.55	51.43	19.35	4.88	11.32	0.03	14.70	10.26	0.79	1.16	3.01	—	246.97

续表

	从业人员	总收入	实际创收收入	广告收入	广播广告收入	电视广告收入	网络媒体广告收入	网络收入	有线电视收视维护费收入	付费数字电视频道收入	三网融合业务收入	新媒体业务收入	网络视听节目服务收入	资产总额
	（万人）	（亿元）	（亿元）	（亿元）	（亿元）	（亿元）	（亿元）	（亿元）	（亿元）	（亿元）	（亿元）	（亿元）	（亿元）	（亿元）
湖北省	3.73	139.64	105.20	19.62	4.78	13.22	0.58	40.21	19.05	2.76	7.16	25.17	0.25	432.49
湖南省	4.42	295.48	270.56	140.36	5.65	103.38	25.54	26.92	14.52	2.05	3.47	24.26	9.17	660.01
广东省	7.11	452.21	384.24	113.93	10.41	47.78	38.73	80.92	43.34	4.17	15.30	31.15	7.98	1 009.32
广西壮族自治区	1.72	73.29	39.88	6.64	1.60	4.61	0.08	24.08	8.63	0.84	3.09	2.25	—	194.70
海南省	0.61	17.66	11.81	3.23	0.20	2.53	0.50	4.37	2.41	0.21	0.29	0.34	0.04	45.71
重庆市	1.38	72.49	55.12	10.98	1.62	8.17	0.41	21.78	8.84	1.83	5.08	2.36	0.11	148.81
四川省	4.70	210.55	113.38	22.09	5.22	11.65	1.45	38.49	15.23	2.67	7.89	6.92	0.81	531.08
贵州省	1.88	105.51	93.59	20.33	3.33	11.54	0.00	28.75	9.05	3.06	2.92	1.69	—	248.83
云南省	1.90	67.04	41.60	14.99	3.49	10.87	0.16	15.49	8.19	1.27	1.65	1.23	0.00	229.93
西藏自治区	0.44	13.16	0.85	0.38	0.02	0.36	0.00	0.43	0.38	0.01	—	—	—	20.21
陕西省	1.93	86.84	66.14	10.25	3.59	5.86	0.44	19.95	11.25	1.79	3.49	2.23	0.09	281.43
甘肃省	1.56	35.75	13.87	3.60	1.08	2.36	0.02	6.05	3.28	0.37	0.55	0.72	—	168.25
青海省	0.42	14.26	4.01	1.16	0.34	0.81	0.00	2.13	0.86	0.32	—	—	—	30.63
宁夏回族自治区	0.47	13.96	6.21	2.12	0.27	1.50	0.01	2.38	1.13	0.60	0.21	0.23	—	58.14
新疆维吾尔自治区	1.93	347.28	316.51	22.18	1.97	1.88	3.78	7.03	3.31	1.31	0.25	12.82	10.50	767.03
新疆生产建设兵团	—	4.01	1.92	0.46	—	0.46	—			—	—	0.01	—	—

2018年中国软件产业统计资料

2018年分省市软件和信息技术服务业业务收入表

单位：万元

地区	企业个数	软件业务收入				
		总收入	（一）软件产品收入	（二）信息技术服务收入	（三）信息安全收入	（四）嵌入式系统软件收入
全国合计	**36 331**	**619 087 338**	**173 785 598**	**375 630 760**	**11 629 203**	**58 041 777**
北　京	3 384	97 289 178	30 650 174	62 800 499	3 516 788	321 717
天　津	369	16 405 911	3 740 463	12 355 652	27 755	282 042
河　北	218	2 641 619	392 005	2 176 541	5 597	67 475
山　西	99	286 992	140 868	120 871	2 323	22 930
内蒙古	44	116 699	36 651	70 501	311	9 237
辽　宁	1 633	15 096 287	6 998 526	6 439 155	1 497 153	161 453
吉　林	941	6 671 132	2 022 633	3 411 101	129 853	1 107 545
黑龙江	111	482 541	190 838	161 818	73 604	56 280
上　海	1 677	48 368 600	12 126 226	36 106 661	133 610	2 104
江　苏	5 956	88 331 851	21 732 300	53 442 385	1 178 135	11 979 031
浙　江	1 600	52 006 148	12 039 185	36 900 871	433 666	2 632 426
安　徽	336	4 560 507	1 925 038	1 816 223	147 560	671 686
福　建	2 825	28 900 454	9 752 277	15 170 855	476 183	3 501 140
江　西	149	1 529 391	821 975	670 849	27 768	8 798
山　东	4 124	49 493 473	16 897 184	21 152 555	1 485 105	9 958 629
河　南	177	3 364 309	897 031	2 338 232	46 230	82 817
湖　北	2 447	17 914 892	8 005 682	9 063 547	791 595	54 068
湖　南	569	4 925 764	1 797 990	1 917 028	22 059	1 188 686
广　东	4 584	106 873 738	22 820 425	62 255 566	374 447	21 423 301
广　西	141	1 524 850	121 029	1 341 663	17 866	44 292
海　南	237	2 532 701	531 235	1 997 567	3 441	458
重　庆	1 495	13 929 501	3 222 232	8 783 399	293 896	1 629 975
四　川	1 818	31 726 385	11 402 522	17 728 544	825 449	1 769 870
贵　州	240	1 767 339	299 588	1 439 490	8 656	19 605
云　南	176	911 126	216 782	668 010	22 063	4 271
西　藏						
陕　西	654	19 948 948	4 660 556	14 208 275	45 505	1 034 612
甘　肃	128	522 835	192 557	320 829	7 748	1 701
青　海	13	14 106	3 456	9 684		966
宁　夏	57	185 752	63 158	118 836	950	2 808
新　疆	129	764 310	85 013	643 553	33 888	1 857

注：西藏暂无规模以上统计数据。

2018 年全国软件和信息技术服务业主要经济指标表

指标名称	单位	2018 年统计数据
企业个数	个	36 331
软件业务收入	亿元	61 908.7
其中：1. 软件产品收入	亿元	17 378.6
2. 信息技术服务收入	亿元	37 563.1
3. 信息安全收入	亿元	1 162.9
4. 嵌入式系统软件收入	亿元	5 804.2
软件业务出口	亿美元	510.7
利润总额	亿元	8 961.6
研发经费	亿元	6 267.3
从业人员平均人数	万人	644.5

资料来源：工业和信息化部运行监测协调局。

注：1. 软件和信息技术服务业统计范围为：

①在我国境内注册（港澳台地区除外），主要从事软件和信息技术服务业务，且主营业务年收入 500 万元以上，具有独立法人资格的软件企业；

②在我国境内注册，主营业务年收入在 1 000 万元以上，有软件和信息技术服务收入，且该收入占本企业主营业务收入 30%以上的独立法人单位；

③在我国境内注册，主要从事集成电路设计的企业或其集成电路设计和测试的收入占本企业主营业务收入 60%以上，且主营业务年收入 500 万元以上的独立法人单位。

2. 本表中数据为年度核定数据，与快报数据存在一定差异，主要有以下原因：一是年报数据对嵌入式系统软件的计算方法进行了较大调整；二是部分省市根据企业业务变化、收入规模等实际情况，对规模以上入统企业的数量进行了调整；三是部分企业根据年度审计后数据对快报数据进行了调整。

版权名录

MING LU

版权行政管理部门

国家版权局
分管副部长：梁言顺
地　址：北京市西城区宣武门外大街40号
邮　编：100052
电　话：010-83138740
传　真：010-83138737
邮　箱：guojiabanquan@163.com
网　址：www.ncac.gov.cn

北京市版权局
局　长：王野霏
地　址：北京市通州区运河东大街56号院1号楼
邮　编：100743
电　话：010-55569229

天津市版权局
局　长：石　刚
地　址：天津市河西区宾水道9号环渤海发展中心A座
邮　编：300000
电　话：022-28368166
传　真：022-28139740

河北省版权局
局　长：宋文新
地　址：石家庄市建华南大街100号
邮　编：050031
电　话：0311-87117085
传　真：0311-87117085

山西省版权局
局　长：夏　祯
地　址：太原市迎泽大街318号
邮　编：030001
电　话：0351-8301523
传　真：0351-8301523

内蒙古自治区版权局
分管副部长：乌恩奇
地　址：呼和浩特市如意开发区敕勒川大街1号
邮　编：010020
电　话：0471-4825647
传　真：0471-4825647
邮　箱：nmgbqjbqc@163.com

辽宁省版权局
分管副部长：邵玉英
地　址：沈阳市和平南大街45号
邮　编：110006
电　话：024-23128820
传　真：024-23128820
邮　箱：lnsbqj@163.com

吉林省版权局
局　长：姚玉和
地　址：长春市卫星路2066号广电大厦
邮　编：130033
电　话：0431-85816273
传　真：0431-85816273

黑龙江省版权局
局　长：朱德宝
地　址：哈尔滨市南岗区汉水路333号
邮　编：150010
电　话：0451-88622761
传　真：0451-88622760

上海市版权局
局　长：徐　炯
地　址：上海市绍兴路5号
邮　编：200020
电　话：021-64339268
传　真：021-64339268

江苏省版权局
局　长：焦建俊
地　址：南京市鼓楼区北京西路 70 号
邮　编：210013
电　话：025-88802956
传　真：025-88802954

浙江省版权局
分管副部长：李　杲
地　址：杭州市省府路 8 号
邮　编：310025
电　话：0571-81050763
传　真：0571-81050763

安徽省版权局
局　长：洪永平
地　址：合肥市中山路 1 号
邮　编：230091
电　话：0551-62609343
传　真：0551-62609343
邮　箱：anhuibanquan@126. com

福建省版权局：
局　长：陈立华
地　址：福州市东水路 76 号
邮　编：350001
电　话：0591-87532711
传　真：0591-87532711

江西省版权局
分管副部长：杨六华
地　址：南昌市红谷滩新区卧龙路 999 号
邮　编：330000
电　话：0791-88912724
传　真：0791-88912724

山东省版权局
分管副部长：魏长民
地　址：济南市纬一路 482 号
电　话：0531-51775308
传　真：0531-51775308
邮　箱：sdbq8606@126. com

河南省版权局：
分管副部长：谭福森
地　址：郑州市金水区金水路 17 号
邮　编：450002
电　话：0371-65905451
传　真：0371-65905450

湖北省版权局
分管副部长：陈树林
地　址：武汉市武昌区黄鹂路 39 号
邮　编：430077
电　话：027-68892427
传　真：027-68892427

湖南省版权局
局　长：蒋祖烜
地　址：长沙市韶山北路 1 号
邮　编：410000
电　话：0731-82219520
传　真：0731-82219520
邮　箱：hncopyright@126. com

广东省版权局
局　长：王桂科
地　址：广州市越秀区合群三马路省委大院 4 号楼
邮　编：510000
电　话：020-87197985
传　真：020-87197985

广西壮族自治区版权局
局　长：吕　洁
地　址：南宁市民族大道 112 号广西新闻中心 7 楼
邮　编：530028
电　话：0771-2092981
传　真：0771-2093005

海南省版权局
局　长：陈　莹
地　址：海口市国兴大道 69 号
邮　编：570203
电　话：0898-65396384
传　真：0898-65336134
邮　箱：wtt. tuyin@hainan. gov. cn

重庆市版权局
分管副部长：吴玉荣
地　址：重庆市江北区鸿恩路 25 号

邮 编：400020
电 话：023-67502723
传 真：023-67502723

四川省版权局
局 长：周 青
地 址：成都市红星路二段 119 号
邮 编：610072
电 话：028-86697076
传 真：028-86697076

贵州省版权局
局 长：谢 念
地 址：贵阳市延安中路 5-9 号
邮 编：550001
电 话：0851-85813428
传 真：0851-85813428

云南省版权局
局 长：蔡祥荣
地 址：昆明市环城西路 609 号新闻出版大楼
邮 编：650034
电 话：0871-64192869
传 真：0871-64192869

西藏自治区版权局
局 长：刘立强
地 址：拉萨市城关区江苏路 1 号
邮 编：850000
电 话：0891-6329729
传 真：0891-6329729

陕西省版权局
局 长：程宁博
地 址：西安市雁塔路南段 10 号
邮 编：710054
电 话：029-85223196
传 真：029-85223196
邮 箱：sxbqc@163. com

甘肃省版权局
局 长：王成勇
地 址：兰州市南昌路 1468 号
邮 编：730030
电 话：0931-8928809
传 真：0931-8414715

青海省版权局
局 长：董杰人
地 址：西宁市城中区七一路 346 号
邮 编：810000
电 话：0971-8484165
传 真：0971-8482518
邮 箱：qhsbqc@163. com

宁夏回族自治区版权局
局 长：马英俊
地 址：银川市金凤区康平路 1 号
邮 编：750002
电 话：0951-6669704
传 真：0951-6669704

新疆维吾尔自治区版权局
分管副部长：周旭勇
地 址：乌鲁木齐市北京南路 591 号
邮 编：830011
电 话：0991-3637543
传 真：0991-3637542

版权公共服务机构

中国版权保护中心
主 任：段桂鉴
地 址：北京市西城区天桥南大街 1 号天桥艺术大厦 A 座 3 层
邮 编：100050
电 话：010-68003887
网 址：www. ccopyright. com

北京版权保护中心
主 任：薛 峰

地　址：北京市东城区朝阳门内大街 55 号新闻出版大厦
邮　编：100010
电　话：010-64081206

北京计算机软件登记中心
主　任：崔玉军
地　址：北京市东城区朝阳门内大街 55 号新闻出版大厦
邮　编：100010
电　话：010-64081391

河北省版权保护中心
主　任：刘　浏
地　址：石家庄市和平西路新文里 8 号
邮　编：050071
电　话：0311-67561197
传　真：0311-67561091

浙江省版权服务中心
主　任：张蓓君
地　址：杭州市上城区庆春路 219 号 6 楼
邮　编：310006
电　话：0571-85062879
传　真：0571-85062879
网　址：home. zjbanquan. org

江西省版权保护中心
主　任：赖政兵
地　址：南昌市红谷滩区翠林路 339 号
邮　编：330038
电　话：0791-86895220
传　真：0791-86894610
邮　箱：jxcopyright@163. com
网　址：www. jxbq. gov. cn

湖北省版权保护中心
主　任：郑凌辉
地　址：武汉市武昌区公正路 9 号
邮　编：430077
电　话：027-87329148
传　真：027-87329148
网　址：www. ccct. net. cn

重庆市版权保护中心
副主任：马雪吟
地　址：重庆市渝中区人民路 248 号盛迪亚商务大厦 29 楼
邮　编：400015
电　话：023-67708231
传　真：023-67708231
邮　箱：cpc1604@yahoo. com. cn
网　址：www. cqca. com. cn

山西省版权保护中心
主　任：康瑞波
地　址：太原市并州北路 31 号
邮　编：030001
电　话：0351-4088107
传　真：0351-4113046
邮　箱：sxbanquan@163. com

版权协会

中国版权协会
理事长：阎晓宏
秘书长：孙　悦
地　址：北京市朝阳区化工路甲 18 号中国北京出版创意产业基地先导区 3 层
邮　编：100023
电　话：010-68003910
传　真：010-68004450
邮　箱：csc@csccn. org. cn
网　址：www. csccn. org. cn

首都版权协会
秘书长：韩志宇
地　址：北京市东城区朝内大街 55 号新闻出版大厦二期 209 室
邮　编：100010

电　话：010-64081992
邮　箱：bjcopyright@sdbq. org
网　址：www. sdbq. org

天津市版权协会
会　长：刘锦泉
秘书长：宋庆伟
地　址：天津市南开区长实道 19 号
邮　编：300191
电　话：022-23678898
传　真：022-23678898
邮　箱：TJBQXH@126. com

河北省版权协会
会　长：陈建英
秘书长：刘　浏
地　址：石家庄市和平西路新文里 8 号
邮　编：050071
电　话：0311-67561176
传　真：0311-67561112
邮　箱：hebeibanquan@126. com
网　址：www. hebeibanquan. com. cn

山西省版权协会
会　长：张金柱
秘书长：王　琦
地　址：太原市建设南路 21 号希望出版社
邮　编：030012
电　话：0351-4922243
传　真：0351-4922249
邮　箱：3523482@163. com

辽宁省版权保护协会
负责人：许科甲
地　址：沈阳市和平区十一纬路 25 号
邮　编：110003
电　话：024-23284110

吉林省版权保护协会
秘书长：李长江
地　址：长春市卫星路 2066 号广电大厦 18A-13
邮　编：130021
电　话：0431-85816271
传　真：0431-85816275

黑龙江省版权保护协会
会　长：丁一平
秘书长：赵傲莉
地　址：哈尔滨市道里区田地街 106 号
邮　编：150010
电　话：0451-84691240
邮　箱：65340255@qq. com

上海市版权协会
会　长：张　宏
秘书长：游闽键
地　址：上海市张江路 69 号 612
邮　编：200020
电　话：021-50278103
传　真：021-50278103

江苏省版权协会
会　长：傅杰三
秘书长：曹　阳
地　址：南京市鼓楼区高云岭 56 号
邮　编：210009
电　话：025-83207838
传　真：025-83207838
邮　箱：jssbqxh@163. com

浙江省版权协会
会　长：单　烈
秘书长：吾晓红
地　址：杭州市上城区庆春路 219 号
邮　编：310006
电　话：0571-88137853
传　真：0571-88137853

安徽省版权保护协会
主　席：李金华
联系人：李慧珺
地　址：合肥市桐城南路 355 号 A 座 1705 室
邮　编：230022
电　话：0551-62609342
传　真：0551-62609342
邮　箱：ahsbqbhxh@163. com

福建省版权协会
会　长：白京兆
秘书长：谢振芳

地　址：福州市东水路 76 号
邮　编：350001
电　话：0591-87535956
传　真：0591-87535956
邮　箱：fjsbqxh@163. com

山东省版权协会
地　址：济南市纬一路 482 号
邮　编：250062
电　话：0531-51775308
传　真：0531-51775308
邮　箱：sdbq8606@126. com

湖北省版权保护协会
会　长：陈　锋
秘书长：赵文福
地　址：武汉市武昌区黄鹂路 39 号
邮　编：430061
电　话：027-68892562
传　真：027-68892562

湖南省版权保护协会（湖南省反盗版联盟）
会　长：郑年田
秘书长：刘傅红
地　址：长沙市营盘东路 3 号
邮　编：410005
电　话：0731-82231655
传　真：0731-82231655

广东省版权保护联合会（广东省版权事务所）
副会长：陈冬云
秘书长：梁守坚
地　址：广州市环市东水荫路 44 号 4 楼
邮　编：510075
电　话：020-37667333，37638239
传　真：020-37638192
邮　箱：gdcopyright@gdpg. com. cn

广西壮族自治区版权保护协会
会　长：齐爱民
秘书长：陈　星
地　址：南宁市望园 13 号
邮　编：530023
电　话：0771-5346956
传　真：0771-5346956
邮　箱：gxbq123@163. com

海南省版权协会
会　长：王　琦
秘书长：唐　俐
地　址：海口市海南大学社科联楼 708 房
邮　编：570100
电　话：0898-66259079
传　真：0898-66259079
邮　箱：18907526181@189. cn

四川省版权保护协会
理事长：黄立新
地　址：成都市大石西路 36 号 9 幢 3 单元 4 楼 5 号
邮　编：610072
电　话：028-81700337
传　真：028-81700337

云南省著作权保护协会
会　长：艾罕炳
秘书长：马云虹
地　址：昆明市环城西路 609 号新闻出版大楼
邮　编：650034
电　话：0871-64110371
传　真：0871-64110371

陕西省版权协会
会　长：曹先觉
秘书长：党　雷
地　址：西安市碑林区建国五巷社团大厦三楼
邮　编：710054
电　话：029-89131693

新疆维吾尔自治区版权协会
地　址：乌鲁木齐市北京南路 591 号
邮　编：830011
电　话：0991-3637542
传　真：0991-3637542

深圳市版权协会
会　长：司　晓
秘书长：陈　彦
地　址：深圳市南山区沙河西路深圳湾科技生态园 6 栋 6 楼
邮　编：518057

电　话：0755-86185519
邮　箱：szcopyright@163. com
网　址：www. scs. org. cn

宁波市版权协会
会　长：陆开江
地　址：宁波市江东区兴宁路53号
邮　编：315000
电　话：0574-89187806
传　真：0574-89187806
邮　箱：1807614413@qq. com

苏州市版权协会
会　长：张　梅
秘书长：冯　坚
地　址：苏州市干将路178号苏州大学北校区科技园309（中）
邮　编：215004
电　话：0512-65156801
传　真：0512-65156801

青岛市版权保护协会
会　长：张　焱
秘书长：封红雨
地　址：青岛市市北区郑州路43号A栋125室
邮　编：266045
电　话：0532-67773267
邮　箱：gy1@rubbervalley. com
网　址：bqbh. org

大连市版权保护协会
会　长：李毅男
秘书长：吕启广
地　址：大连市西安路107号
邮　编：116021
电　话：0411-84522067
传　真：0411-84522067
邮　箱：wgj _ dcpa@dl. gov. cn
网　址：www. dlcopyright. org. cn

南京市版权保护协会
会　长：江　飞
副会长：陈　锷
秘书长：陈　锷
地　址：南京市中山东路532-1号中山坊科技文创园A座103室
邮　编：210016
电　话：025-84645491
邮　箱：1148694563@qq. com
网　址：www. njbq. org. cn

郑州市版权协会
理事长：倪天礼
地　址：郑州市西太康路19号郑州购书中心820室
邮　编：450018
电　话：0371-66280990
网　址：www. zzbq. org

厦门市版权协会
秘书长：詹朝晖
地　址：厦门市软件园二期望海路6号303
邮　编：361008
电　话：0592-5914419

著作权集体管理组织

中国音乐著作权协会
主　席：赵季平
总干事：屈景明
地　址：北京市东城区东单三条33号京纺大厦五层
邮　编：100005
电　话：010-65232656
传　真：010-65232657
网　址：www. mcsc. com. cn

中国音像著作权集体管理协会
理事长：周建潮
代理总干事：周亚平
地　址：北京市朝阳区呼家楼京广中心商务楼401室
邮　编：100020
电　话：010-66086468
传　真：010-66086475

邮　箱：cavca@cavca. org
网　址：www. cavca. org

中国文字著作权协会
会　长：陈建功
总干事：张洪波
地　址：北京市西城区珠市口西大街太丰惠中大厦 1027-1036 室
邮　编：100050
电　话：010-65978905
传　真：010-65978926
邮　箱：wenzhuxie@126. com
网　址：www. prccopyright. org. cn

中国电影著作权协会
理事长：任仲伦
秘书长：史文霞
地　址：北京市西城区北展北街 5 号楼 F 座 5 层
邮　编：100044
电　话：010-62364640
传　真：010-62369799
邮　箱：cfcac2009@163. com
网　址：www. cfca-c. org

中国摄影著作权协会
总干事：林　涛
地　址：北京市东城区东四十二条 48 号
邮　编：100007
电　话：010-65978100
传　真：010-65595720
邮　箱：hyb@icschina. net
网　址：www. icsc1839. org

版权相关行业协会

中国互联网协会网络版权工作委员会
主　任：高卢麟
秘书长：石现升
地　址：北京市海淀区板井路曙光花园智业园 B 座 6E 室
邮　编：100097
电　话：010-88466861-815
传　真：010-88546086
网　址：www. iscu. cn

中国音像与数字出版协会
理事长：孙寿山
常务副理事长兼秘书长：王　炬
地　址：北京市西城区莲花池东路 102 号天莲大厦 17 层
邮　编：100055
电　话：010-65122882
传　真：010-65127030
邮　箱：cava2008@163. com
网　址：www. cadpa. org. cn

版权代理公司

中华版权代理总公司
总经理：贺传军
地　址：北京市西城区天桥南大街一号天桥艺术大厦 A 座 4 层
邮　编：100050
电　话：010-68003887，84195154
网　址：www. cpcccac. com

中国图书进出口（集团）总公司版权部
主　任：雷建华
地　址：北京市朝阳区工体东路 16 号
邮　编：100020
电　话：010-65069500
邮　箱：publishing@cnpiec. com. cn
网　址：www. cnpiec. com. cn

中国出版对外贸易总公司
负责人：宋 旭
地 址：北京市朝阳区安定门外安华里 504 号
邮 编：100011
电 话：010-64210403
传 真：010-64214540
网 址：www.cnpitc.com.cn

中国国际电视总公司
地 址：北京市海淀区羊坊店路 9 号京门大厦
邮 编：100038
电 话：010-63950016
传 真：010-63955916
邮 箱：office@citvc.com

九洲音像出版公司版权贸易部
负责人：张小康
地 址：北京市西城区广安大厦 12 层
邮 编：100032
电 话：010-85286515

北京版权代理有限责任公司
负责人：张 巍
地 址：北京市海淀区知春路 23 号量子银座 1403
邮 编：100191
电 话：010-82915383

湖南省版权代理公司
负责人：张树清
地 址：长沙市营盘东路 3 号
邮 编：410005
电 话：0731-82231655

重庆市版权代理有限公司
负责人：马雪吟
地 址：重庆市渝中区人民路 248 号盛迪亚商务大厦 29 楼
邮 编：400015
电 话：023-67708231
传 真：023-67708231

国家级版权交易机构

中国人民大学国家版权贸易基地
主 任：白连永
地 址：北京市海淀区中关村大街甲 59 号文化大厦
邮 编：100872
电 话：010-62514334
传 真：010-62516959
邮 箱：copyrightyb@126.com

北京国际版权交易中心
董事长：李 蘅
地 址：北京市朝阳区团结湖公园南门内西侧独栋
邮 编：100020
电 话：010-65974890（总机）
传 真：010-65978017
邮 箱：kf@e-bq.com
网 址：www.e-bq.com

东方雍和国际版权交易中心
董事长：殷秩松
地 址：北京市东城区安定门东大街 28 号雍和大厦 E 座 208
邮 编：100007
电 话：010-64097700
传 真：010-84195406
网 址：www.cbice.com

华中国家版权交易中心
董事长：赵建潮
总经理：随晓英
地 址：武汉市武昌区公正路 9 号
邮 编：430077
电 话：027-87329679
传 真：027-87329612
网 址：www.ccct.net

成都国际版权交易中心
执行主任：杨　蛟
地　址：成都市高新区世纪城南路 599 号 2 栋 1 层
邮　编：610213
电　话：028-61375595
邮　箱：cdbqdj@cdice. com. cn
网　址：www. cdice. com. cn

国家版权贸易基地（上海）
负责人：任义彪
地　址：中国（上海）自由贸易试验区马吉路 2 号 33 层
邮　编：200131
电　话：021-58697777
传　真：021-58698366

广州市越秀区国家版权贸易基地
董事长：黎伟成
地　址：广州市越秀区文德北路 68 号
邮　编：510030
电　话：020-83349123
邮　箱：123@banquanmaoyi. com
网　址：www. banquanmaoyi. com

台儿庄国家版权贸易基地
管理办公室主任：李　伟
地　址：枣庄市台儿庄区大衙门街西首台儿庄古城
邮　编：277400
邮　箱：tezgczgb@163. com

青岛国际版权交易中心
总经理：安　波
地　址：青岛市市南区瞿塘峡路 47 号
邮　编：266000
电　话：0532-68607777
传　真：0532-68851222
邮　箱：Edward@qicec. net
网　址：www. qicec. net

国家海峡版权交易中心
总经理：王　斌
地　址：厦门市软件园二期望海路 6 号 2 层
邮　编：361008
电　话：0592-5953686
传　真：0592-5953687
邮　箱：contact@hxnce. net

西部国家版权交易中心
董事长：党　雷
地　址：西安市雁塔区雁塔南路陕西文化大厦 B 座 6 楼
邮　编：710061
电　话：029-89131653
传　真：029-89131698
邮　箱：ctvtc@ctvtc. cn
网　址：www. xtce. cn

横琴国际版权交易中心
负责人：陈钦禄
地　址：珠海市香洲区海洲路 8 号九昌大厦 6C
邮　编：519015
电　话：0756-3211668
传　真：0756-3210567

江苏国家版权贸易基地
秘书长：郑礼贵
地　址：南京市秦淮区水西门大街 2 号锦创广场 3 楼
邮　编：210004
电　话：025-87769375
传　真：025-87769375
邮　箱：13801584525@139. com

保利国家艺术品版权贸易基地
负责人：何　辉
地　址：北京市东城区朝阳门北大街 1 号新保利大厦 25A
邮　编：100010
电　话：010-65513130
传　真：010-65513130
邮　箱：hehui@polycc. cn

知识产权教学与研究机构

中国人民大学知识产权学院
地　址：北京市海淀区中关村大街59号中国人民大学明德法学楼612室
邮　编：100872
电　话：010-82500369
传　真：010-62514365
邮　箱：law612@126.com
网　址：www.law.ruc.edu.cn

北京大学知识产权学院
地　址：北京市北京大学凯原楼309室
邮　编：100871
电　话：010-62751268
邮　箱：zscq@pku.edu.cn
网　址：www.iplaw.pku.edu.cn

中国社会科学院知识产权中心
地　址：北京市东城区沙滩北街15号
邮　编：100720
电　话：010-64054144
邮　箱：ipstudies@163.com
网　址：www.iolaw.org.cn

中国政法大学民商经济法学院知识产权法研究所
地　址：北京市昌平区府学路27号
邮　编：102249
电　话：010-58909336
网　址：msjjfxy.cupl.edu.cn

中南财经政法大学知识产权研究中心
地　址：湖北省武汉市东湖高新技术开发区南湖大道182号
邮　编：430073
电　话：027-88386157
邮　箱：Justice_Appraise@iprcn.com
网　址：www.iprcn.com

上海大学知识产权学院
地　址：上海市宝山区上大路99号
邮　编：200444
电　话：021-66132597
传　真：021-66133938
网　址：www.ips.shu.edu.cn

华中科技大学法学院科技法与知识产权系
地　址：湖北省武汉市洪山区珞瑜路1037号东四楼
邮　编：430074
电　话：027-87545438
传　真：027-87542228
邮　箱：fxyxwzx@hust.edu.cn
网　址：law.hust.edu.cn

复旦大学知识产权研究中心
地　址：上海市淞沪路2005号法学楼410室
邮　编：200438
电　话：021-51630042
传　真：021-51630112
邮　箱：zhangng@fudan.edu.cn
网　址：www.ipcenter.fudan.edu.cn

华东政法大学知识产权学院
地　址：上海市松江区龙源路555号
邮　编：201620
电　话：021-57090083
邮　箱：zsb@ecupl.edu.cn
网　址：www.ipschool.ecupl.edu.cn

暨南大学知识产权学院
地　址：广东省广州市黄埔大道西601号
邮　编：510632
电　话：020-85228561
网　址：law.jnu.edu.cn

上海国际知识产权学院
地　址：上海市四平路1239号同济大学综合楼10楼
邮　编：200092
电　话：021-65983113
邮　箱：sicip@tongji.edu.cn
网　址：sicip.tongji.edu.cn

武汉大学知识产权高级研究中心
地　址：湖北省武汉市武昌区珞珈山街16号

邮　编：430072
电　话：027-68752135
邮　箱：cfchen@whu. edu. cn
网　址：www. whu. edu. cn

西安交通大学知识产权研究中心
地　址：陕西省西安市咸宁西路 28 号
邮　编：710049
电　话：029-82668972
邮　箱：xjtuiprc@126. com
网　址：ip. xjtu. edu. cn

中国科学技术大学知识产权研究中心
地　址：安徽省合肥市包河区金寨路 96 号
邮　编：230026
电　话：0551-63492241
邮　箱：songlan@ustc. edu. cn
网　址：pas. ustc. edu. cn

西北大学知识产权学院
地　址：陕西省西安市长安学府大道 1 号
邮　编：710127
电　话：029-88308080
传　真：029-88308079
邮　箱：lawdep@nwu. edu. cn
网　址：fxy. nwu. edu. cn

华南理工大学知识产权学院
地　址：广东省广州市广州大学城华南理工大学 B9
邮　编：510006
电　话：020-39380308
传　真：020-39380308
邮　箱：scutg06@scut. edu. cn
网　址：www2. scut. edu. cn/law

南京理工大学知识产权学院
地　址：江苏省南京市孝陵卫 200 号
邮　编：210094
电　话：025-84303386
传　真：025-84303386
网　址：ip. njust. edu. cn

中山大学知识产权学院
地　址：广东省广州市新港西路 135 号
邮　编：510275
电　话：020-84113148
网　址：law. sysu. edu. cn

重庆知识产权学院（重庆理工大学知识产权学院）
地　址：重庆市巴南区李家沱红光大道 69 号重庆理工大学花溪校区
邮　编：400054
电　话：023-62563375
传　真：023-62563375
邮　箱：cgzs@cqut. edu. cn
网　址：ipschool. cqut. edu. cn

湘潭大学知识产权学院
地　址：湖南省湘潭市雨湖区湘潭大学法学院知识产权学院
邮　编：411105
电　话：0731-58292281
邮　箱：zscqxy@xtu. edu. cn
网　址：ipf. xtu. edu. cn

厦门大学知识产权研究院
地　址：福建省厦门市思明南路 422 号厦门大学知识产权研究院
邮　编：361005
电　话：0592-2182729
传　真：0592-2182729
网　址：www. iprixmu. com

西南政法大学知识产权学院（民商法学院）
地　址：重庆市渝北区宝圣大道 301 号
邮　编：401120
电　话：023-67258430
邮　箱：xsczsb@supsl. cn
网　址：ccls. swupl. edu. cn

深圳大学知识产权学院
地　址：广东省深圳市南山区南海大道 3688 号
邮　编：518060
电　话：0755-26534171
传　真：0755-26535115
网　址：law. szu. edu. cn

中南大学知识产权研究院
地　址：湖南省长沙市麓山南路中南大学法学院

邮 编：410083
电 话：0731-88660219
传 真：0731-88660219
邮 箱：csuips@csu. edu. cn
网 址：law. csu. edu. cn/zscq

山东师范大学法学院（知识产权学院）
地 址：山东省济南市长清区长清大学科技园大学路 1 号
邮 编：250358
电 话：0531-89611070
网 址：www. law. sdnu. edu. cn

南京三江学院法律与知识产权学院
地 址：江苏省南京市雨花台区龙西路 10 号
邮 编：210012
电 话：025-52354934
网 址：www. sju. edu. cn/flyzs

青岛大学法学院
地 址：青岛市崂山区香港东路 7 号
邮 编：266071
电 话：0532-85955950
网 址：law. qdu. edu. cn

杭州师范大学沈钧儒法学院
地 址：浙江省杭州市余杭区仓前街道余杭塘路 2318 号
邮 编：311121
电 话：0571-28865484
传 真：0571-28865484
网 址：fxy. hznu. edu. cn

中国计量大学法学院（知识产权学院）
地 址：浙江省杭州市下沙高教园区学源街
邮 编：310018
电 话：0571-86835791
邮 箱：cjlufxy@cjlu. edu. cn
网 址：fxy. cjlu. edu. cn

浙江工商大学法学院（知识产权学院）
地 址：浙江省杭州市江干区学正街 18 号
邮 编：310018
电 话：0571-28008182
邮 箱：law@mail. zjgsu. edu. cn
网 址：law. zjgsu. edu. cn

重庆邮电大学网络空间安全与信息法学院
地 址：重庆市南岸区崇文路 2 号
邮 编：400065
电 话：023-62461824
传 真：023-62471932
网 址：sl. cqupt. edu. cn

温州知识产权学院（浙江工贸职业技术学院）
地 址：浙江省温州市鹿城区府东路 717 号
邮 编：325002
电 话：0577-88325601，88111397
传 真：0577-88325601，88111397
邮 箱：zscq@mail. zjitc. net
网 址：www. wzipb. com

中原工学院法学院（知识产权学院）
地 址：河南省新郑市双湖经济开发区龙湖镇淮河路 1 号
邮 编：451191
电 话：0371-69975763
网 址：fxy. zut. edu. cn

四川轻化工大学法学院（知识产权学院）
地 址：四川省自贡市汇兴路学苑街 180 号
邮 编：643000
电 话：0813-5364828
网 址：fxy. suse. edu. cn

北京知识产权学院（北京工业大学）
地 址：北京市朝阳区平乐园 100 号
邮 编：100124
网 址：bjip. bjut. edu. cn

郑州大学法学院（知识产权学院）
地 址：郑州市科学大道 100 号
邮 编：450001
网 址：www5. zzu. edu. cn/newlaw

辽宁大学法学院
地 址：辽宁省沈阳市沈北新区道义南大街 58 号
邮 编：110136
电 话：024-62602408
网 址：law. lnu. edu. cn

桂林电子科技大学法学院（知识产权学院）

地　址：广西桂林市灵川县桂林电子科技大学花江校区第一教学楼 1318 室
邮　编：541004
电　话：0773-2290081
网　址：www. gliet. edu. cn/dept9

中国科学院大学知识产权学院

地　址：北京市石景山区玉泉路 19 号（甲）
邮　编：100049
网　址：www. ucas. ac. cn

大连理工大学人文与社会科学学部法律系

地　址：辽宁省大连市高新区凌工路 2 号
邮　编：116024
电　话：0411-84706471
网　址：fhss. dlut. edu. cn

附录：国际版权动态

FU LU：GUO JI BAN QUAN DONG TAI

综述

信息时代的著作权制度为市场发展保驾护航

——2018年国际著作权法制发展回顾

郭 禾 白志晖

著作权法是应市场经济之需求而产生的。随着商品的出现、市场交换行为的出现、交易习惯的形成，当信息传播采取了作品的形态，传播技术发展到一定水平时，著作权法律制度也就应运而生[①]。著作权制度自诞生伊始，就为著作权市场保驾护航，推动着文化产业和经济稳步增长。国际知识产权联盟（International Intellectual Property Alliance，IIPA）在2018年12月发布的研究报告显示，在过去的一年，美国核心版权产业为国家经济增长贡献了1.3万亿美元，雇用了近570万名美国工人；而如果将与版权相关的附属产业（如生产获取版权作品的设备）也计算在内的话，版权产业的贡献值将达到惊人的2.2万亿美元，占美国经济总量的11.6%[②]。由此观之，著作权制度对于著作权市场可谓至关重要。

近年来，全球著作权市场日益庞大。2018年11月8日，国际作者和作曲者协会联合会[③]（International Confederation of Societies of Authors and Composers，CISAC）发布了《2018全球版税报告》。该报告显示，在过去一年里，全球创作者的版税收入增长6.2%，达到96亿欧元。这是全球创作者版税收入连续第五年增长，也是所有门类的作品（音乐、视听、视觉艺术、戏剧和文学）首次实现全部增长。其中来自数字渠道的版税突破10亿欧元，增幅达到24%，在过去五年中几乎增长了两倍。从中不难看出，全球著作权产业方兴未艾，国际著作权市场呈现出欣欣向荣、蓬勃发展的态势。这也向各国的著作权制度提出了挑战，能否妥善处理著作权市场运营中各类主体的利益诉求，能否保障著作权市场的公平有序，能否积极应对信息时代带来的新问题，将成为世界各国在相当长一段时间内所面临的主要课题。

2018年国际著作权制度的发展，主要体现为两大趋势：一是市场的蓬勃发展带来了著作权制度的积极回应，各国纷纷进行著作权法律制度的变革，保障著作权相关市场机制的顺利运行，强化对著作权的保护；二是数字版权市场已成星火燎原之势，网络环境下的著作权问题进一步凸显，关于网络环境下的专有权利、侵权认定以及著作权限制等问题，均引发了立法和司法层面的一系列讨论。

一、著作权制度发展积极回应市场变化

回顾2018年国际著作权制度发展，著作权制度对著作权市场变化积极回应，产生了正面的效果，具体从以下三个方面展开阐述：

（一）规范市场运行机制

著作权制度变革，规范市场运行机制，旨在更好地适应市场需求，最终对市场的发展产生积极的影响。以美国音乐产业和相关行业为例，各种流媒体服务商跟随传播技术的进步而快速发展，但音乐相关的法律法规却没有跟上近年来技术进步带来的消费方式的快速变化，传统产业链和创作者的个人权益均受到了巨大冲击。联邦和各州在音乐版权保护领域结构混乱，导致众多权利人求助无门。规范流媒体市场运行机制、保障音乐创作者在流媒体革命中的权益成为十分现实的需求[④]。

最终在2018年10月11日通过的《音乐现代化法案》将多部法案合并，统一了原本混乱的相关法

---

① 郭禾. 知识产权法选论［M］. 北京：人民交通出版社，2001：2.

② https://pmcdeadline2. files. wordpress. com/2018/12/copyright-industry-report-wm. pdf.

③ 国际作者和作曲者协会联合会成立于1926年，总部位于法国，是一家非政府、非营利组织，也是全球最大的创作者协会联合组织（集体管理组织），其宗旨为保护世界各地创作者的权利和利益。

④ https://eu. tennessean. com/story/money/2018/09/18/music-modernization-act-2018-clears-senate/1349368002/.

律法规，确立了一个新的集体管理机构，统一管理数字音乐作品的版权授权事宜，管理对象包括 Apple Music、Spotify、Amazon Music 等所有流媒体的内容服务。这一法案是对美国《版权法》第 115 条的重大改革。该机构的领导层由出版商和音乐创作者的代表组成，有权向数字服务商发布全面的录制许可，向其收取版税并支付给权利人。该机构还负责以专门的法律程序统一收取无人认领的版税，而此前，这些“无主”版税都被服务商所持有。对于音乐人来说，这意味着可以更简单地获得使用费；对于流媒体服务商而言，则能有效避免因未能识别正确的权利人而被诉侵权的情况，法律风险将大大降低①。《音乐现代化法案》更新了与流媒体相关的许可规范和版税标准，简化了音乐版权授权流程，便利了权利人从在线音乐播放中获得报酬，对市场需求做出了积极有效的回应。

日本在《著作权法》的修改上也充分体现了对市场变化的呼应。以物联网、大数据和人工智能为代表的第四次产业革命已经到来，然而日本的著作权保护仍然极为严苛。一些日本学者提出“日本现行著作权法不仅不能促进产业发展，反而妨碍了新技术、新服务诞生”②。2018 年 2 月 23 日，日本在内阁会议上通过了新的《著作权法》修正案，并于 2019 年 1 月 1 日正式实施。新《著作权法》旨在扩大网上使用作品的范围，规范作品使用的市场机制，接轨国际标准。以日本互联网企业为例，其对于他人作品的使用从“正面清单制度”转向了“负面清单制度”，互联网企业的自由度将大大提高。日本互联网企业过去对作品的使用，原则上必须征得著作权人的同意，法律以正面清单的方式规定哪些情况可以获得豁免；而在法律修改后，对作品的使用原则上无须著作权人同意，只有明显损害权利人相关权益的恶性行为才会受到处罚。一些日本媒体报道称“日本修正版权保护制度，只因时代所迫”。但日本政府则表示，新的《著作权法》对一些使用作品行为的允许，并不意味着知识产权制度的倒退，而是将著作权运行机制贴近市场需求，有助于创造新产业，为内容产业带来更大的附加值③。

（二）加强对权利人利益的维护

尽管著作权法的最终目的是通过赋予作者有限的垄断权，保障其从作品中获得合理的收益，以激励更多的人投身于创作活动，促使更多高质量的作品产生与传播，促进国家文化版权事业的进步，并非仅仅对创作者加以奖励或使权利人对作品的使用、传播进行绝对的垄断；但是保障著作权人所享有的专有权利是著作权制度实现的起点，也是达成著作权法最终目的的必要手段。2018 年，面对日益庞大的著作权市场，加强对权利人利益的维护成为各个国家的一致选择。

澳大利亚政府在 2018 年采取了一系列严厉措施打击网络盗版行为。早在 2015 年，澳大利亚官方就出台了《版权条例修订（网络侵权）草案》，根据此法，版权人可以向联邦法院提出申请，要求互联网服务提供商阻止对侵权网站的访问，以封锁大量的在线盗版网站。在此之后，尽管已有相当数量的盗版网站被关停，但仍然有不少盗版网站活跃着。这些网站为躲避打击，频繁地更换域名，致使将其完全封锁变得十分困难。为了加强对权利人利益的维护，一劳永逸地制止网络盗版行为，澳大利亚政府于 2018 年 10 月 18 日向议会提出新的立法法案。根据此法案，版权人可以向法院寻求禁令，要求搜索引擎删除或降级对盗版网站的搜索结果，如此一来盗版网站的镜像网站也更容易被屏蔽。此外，法院还允许像 Telstra 这样的互联网服务提供商过滤、屏蔽和限制有关盗版网站的搜索结果。Foxtel 的一位发言人表示：“Foxtel 欢迎政府新提出的版权修正法案，该法案维护合法权益、打击网络盗版，将促进创意产业和市场的发展完善。”④

无独有偶，西班牙议会在 2018 年 11 月通过了对《知识产权法》的新修正案。该法案允许权利人要求西班牙版权委员会（行政机构）对曾经有过侵权行为的网站运营商或信息服务提供商直接采取行动，以阻止正在发生的侵犯著作权的行为。在《知识产权法》的新修正案出台之前，版权委员会只有在得到法院批准的情况下，才有权采取必要措施制止侵权行为以达到保护著作权的目的，如施加罚款、下令采取限制性行动等；但根据修改后的法律，版权委员会可以在没有法院干预的情况下采取任何必要措施以阻止涉嫌在线重复侵犯著作权的行为，如

① https://themusicnetwork.com/us-music-modernisation-act-becomes-law-finally-updates-copyright-rules-and-payment/.

② http://www.xinhuanet.com/globe/2018-04/06/c_137084661.htm.

③ http://www.guancha.cn/Neighbors/2018_02_01_445500.shtml.

④ https://www.theguardian.com/australia-news/2018/oct/18/australia-to-target-google-and-yahoo-under-internet-piracy-crackdown.

要求删除内容，甚至关闭网站等①。据此，权利人的利益得到了十分完备的保障。

对权利人利益的维护不仅体现于制止侵权行为的层面，还体现在著作权保护范围的扩张。在一起发生在日本的案例中，舞蹈家 Kapu Alquiza 大约从 1984 年就开始指导九州夏威夷协会成员舞蹈。到 2014 年 10 月双方协议终止后，她要求九州夏威夷协会不得再继续使用她曾教授过的舞蹈编排。然而该协会没有理会其诉求并在草裙舞课堂和相关活动中继续使用相关舞蹈编排。该协会辩称，草裙舞的编舞缺少独创性，选择单一，仅仅是现有动作的排列组合。日本大阪地区法院在 2018 年 9 月的判决中指出："草裙舞是一系列由体现编舞者个性与不体现编舞者个性的两个部分所组成的有节奏的动作"，"从完整的一系列节奏动作中来认定编舞的著作权是合理的，能体现编舞者个性的部分在一定程度上会在其中显现"②。从中不难看出，在认定某种智力成果是否具备独创性、是否能够成为著作权法所保护的客体时，法院充分考虑了权利人为此所付出的努力与著作权市场的规律，对权利人的利益进行了积极的维护。

（三）协调各市场主体间的利益

牛顿曾说："如果说我看得比别人更远，是因为我站在巨人的肩膀上。"在科学领域，没有人能够撇开他人的知识与经验，构建一套只属于自己的理论体系。文学领域同样如此，任何作品都是在继承前人智慧和文化遗产的基础上，注入作者的智力创作完成的③。这些前人智慧和文化遗产属于社会的公共领域，为社会公众所共有，因而著作权人对其作品的控制与利用不是绝对的、无限制的。著作权制度应当能协调著作权人和其他市场主体间的利益，缓和权利独占与公共领域之间的关系。2018 年，国际著作权制度在维持著作权人利益与其他相关利益平衡的命题上，做出了不少有益的探索。

一方面，对著作权权利客体的扩张，应当持较为谨慎的态度。2018 年 11 月，欧盟法院（CJEU）裁定气味不受著作权法的保护。这是欧盟法院第一次直接阐述什么样的对象才能构成著作权法意义上的作品。该案件可以简单概括为：荷兰奶酪生产商 Levola Hengelo 声称其竞争对手 Smilde 抄袭了自己公司特制的"Heksnkaas"（奶酪酱）的味道，并认为这是侵犯著作权的行为。奶酪生产商 Levola Hengelo 公司在其主张被荷兰一审法院驳回后提起上诉，荷兰上诉法院向欧盟法院就食物的味道是否受著作权保护提出关于初审判决的咨询。该案件引起了广泛关注，在荷兰上诉法院向欧盟法院进行相关咨询的同时，法国和英国也就此案件向欧盟法院阐明了自己的看法。欧盟法院最终的裁判简洁明了，其认为著作权法下的作品应该"具有足够精确性和客观性"。食品的气味取决于变幻的味觉感受和个人的主观体验，无法通过科技的手段被客观地识别。其主观性导致法律上的定性不确定，缺乏相应的客观性，因此，"Heksnkaas"（奶酪酱）的味道不是受著作权法保护的作品。可以看到欧盟法院采取了十分谨慎的态度，为了保持著作权保护范围对公众的可预期性，没有将气味认定为著作权法保护的客体，将其留在了公共领域，很好地协调了市场主体间的利益关系④。

另一方面，即使是著作权的正常行使，也不应当对公共领域原有的秩序造成破坏，导致不同主体之间的利益失衡。2018 年下半年，迪士尼动画《狮子王》真人版翻拍引起了广泛关注，迪士尼电影中的经典台词"Hakuna Matata"成了焦点著作权问题。早在 1994 年迪士尼就已将"Hakuna Matata"一词用作自身的"文化资产"，主要用于商品推销。但"Hakuna Matata"一词事实上是斯瓦希里语，几乎每天都在东非部分地区使用。它同时也是 1982 年斯瓦希里语歌曲 *Jambo Bwana* 中的抒情诗，由 Kenyan 乐队的 Them Mushrooms 创作。瑞典流行乐团 Boney M 也是 20 世纪 80 年代录制了该版本歌曲的众多乐队之一，直到今天这首歌曲仍经常由乐队在东非的酒店演出⑤。那么著作权人与其他社会主体之间的利益应当如何协调呢？该事件的发展和结果还有待于进一步的持续关注。但我们至少可以说即便在法律规定的范围内行使权利，著作权人的利益也不是绝对的，需要和其他主体保持利益平衡。

二、网络环境下的著作权问题进一步凸显

前文提到的《2018 全球版税报告》指出：受流媒体热潮的推动，加之消费者对网络视频的热衷，过去一年来自数字渠道的版税首次突破 10 亿欧元，

① https://parlinfo.aph.gov.au/parlInfo/search/display/display.w3p; query=Id:%22legislation/ems/r6209_ems_b5e338b6-e85c-4cf7-8037-35f13166ebd4%22.

② http://japanip.blogspot.com/2018/10/japanese-court-finds-copyright.html? m=1.

③ 刘春田. 知识产权法［M］. 5 版. 北京：中国人民大学出版社，2014：119.

④ http://copyrightblog.kluweriplaw.com/2018/06/26/heksnkaas-cjeu-end-cheese-war-beginning-new-copyright-era/.

⑤ https://america.cgtn.com/2018/12/17/disneys-trademark-of-swahili-phrase-hakuna-matata-sparks-debate-on-cultural-copyright.

增幅达到24%，并在过去五年中实现了近两倍的增长。尽管传统版权市场仍然占有绝对比重，但整体来看数字版权市场的发展已成燎原之势。回顾2018年国际著作权制度发展，网络环境下的各类著作权问题进一步凸显，新技术的利用对著作权制度形成了不小的冲击，关于专有权利、侵权认定以及著作权限制等问题，均引发了业界的广泛关注。

（一）网络环境中的著作权的专有权利

有学者说，“著作权法，就是一部作品传播技术的发展史”。确实，著作权制度可以说是随着传播技术的发展而丰富起来的，技术对于传播作品是有益的，直接影响着著作权法律制度的发展；但同时技术也是复杂的，司法实践中法院需要应对许多涉及技术的法律问题。这就对司法机关提出了比较高的要求，即要能准确界定专有权利在网络环境中的适用范围。

以复制权为例，印刷、复印、录音、录像等著作权法下的典型复制行为，普遍离不开有形物质载体。往往是在有形载体上相对稳定地固定了作品的行为，才能构成对作品的复制。在ABS娱乐公司诉CBS公司的案件中，美国联邦第九巡回上诉法院就对网络环境中的复制权进行了阐明。在本案中，ABS娱乐公司专门聘请录音师将其拥有的1972年前录制的几首经典歌曲的模拟录音通过标准技术手段重新录制成数字形式。CBS公司未经ABS娱乐公司许可，通过地面无线电广播和网络流媒体播放了上述重新录制的歌曲。对于通过地面电台播放的内容，CBS公司没有支付任何许可费，原告ABS娱乐公司基于此向加利福尼亚州地区法院提起了诉讼，之后又上诉到联邦第九巡回上诉法院。本案争议焦点在于录音师在保留原作品词曲的前提下，改变作品音色、声音平衡和音量大小且包含个人主观情感和艺术思想的重录行为是构成版权法下的创作行为，还是仅仅构成对原作品的复制。联邦第九巡回上诉法院在判决中指出：数字形式的唱片并没有增加或删去乐曲的乐音，也没有改变乐音排列顺序或是进行重混，其本质上是对原曲的复制，因此不符合版权法对作品的要求。第九巡回上诉法院还进一步指出，本案中重录行为的目的和效果类似于技术改进，其并没有改变录音制品的基本特征，尽管与传统的复制行为表现上有所不同，但仅仅是改变了媒体形态，仍然属于复制，不能满足版权法的独创性要求①。

再如向公众传播权，由于网络环境下利用与传播作品的手段日渐丰富，特定行为能否纳入专有权利的范围进行规制，往往需要法院在个案中进行决断。2018年8月7日，欧盟法院在判决中重新对向公众传播权进行了阐释。在该案中，原告摄影师德克·仁可霍夫（Dirk Renckhoff）通过一家旅游门户网站公开发布了一张自己的摄影作品，所有人都可以通过该网站免费获取。一名来自德国的小学生从这家旅游网站上下载了此照片，随后该照片作为该学生作业的一部分被公布在了学校网站上。原告称其仅仅将照片使用权授予旅游网站，该学校在未经其许可的情况下发布该照片的行为侵犯了他的著作权。本案争议的焦点即为被告行为是否构成“向公众传播”。欧盟法院的认定分为两个步骤：首先采取广义解释对“传播行为”进行判断，不做过多技术形式的限定；其次对“公众”进行判断，传播行为必须产生了著作权人在授权作品传播时所指向的公众范围之外的受众群体，即“新公众”（new public）。据此，欧盟法院指出：一个在网络上合法发布的作品即使没有采取任何技术措施，可以被公众自由获取，在未经作者许可的情形下，其他网站仍然不得将该作品呈现在自己的页面，否则将侵犯作者享有的向公众传播权②。源自《世界知识产权组织版权条约》第8条的向公众传播权与我国《著作权法》中的信息网络传播权颇有渊源，前者规制的是以一切技术手段向公众传播作品的行为，后者则主要针对以交互式的手段向公众传播作品的行为，范围较之前者更窄。故而当向公众传播权面临是否要规制特定行为的选择难题时，“信息网络传播权”也难免陷入相同的困境。上述判决的思考路径对我国的司法实践也有一定的借鉴意义。

（二）网络环境中的侵犯著作权行为

在判断是否构成侵犯著作权行为时，要看该行为是否落入著作权人专有权利所控制的范围，如复制权控制复制作品的行为，向公众传播权控制将作品通过非复制件方式进行传播的行为等。但在实践中，有一些行为人虽未直接实施受专有权利控制的行为，但其行为与他人侵犯著作权的行为之间存在着特定的联系，如构成帮助关系等。但我国《著作权法》并没有对该类行为进行直接规定。在现实审判中，我国法院多援引《侵权责任法》第九条的规定，即教唆、帮助他人实施侵权行为的，应当与行为人承担连带责任。在英美等国家，出于保护著作权人

① https://www.natlawreview.com/article/abs-entertainment-inc-v-cbs-corporation-no-new-copyright-digital-remasters.

② https://www.out-law.com/en/articles/2018/august/copyright-ruling-internet-posting-photos/.

利益的需要，在某些特定行为不构成对著作权的“直接侵犯”时，则将其认定为“间接侵犯著作权”的行为。较之非网络空间，“间接侵犯著作权”在网络环境中有着极为特殊的地位。从技术角度来看，任何在网络环境中发生的“直接侵犯著作权”的行为都不可能离开网络服务提供商[①]的硬件设施和软件系统[②]。因此对于网络服务提供商“间接侵犯著作权”的行为能否规制、如何规制，很大程度决定着著作权人的利益在网络环境中能否得到维护。2018年，涉及网络服务提供商责任义务的立法、司法争议频发。

2018年关于网络服务商行为义务的立法，影响最大的当属2018年9月12日由欧盟委员会提出、欧洲议会以438∶226的票数通过的《数字化单一市场版权指令》。这一投票结果意味着欧洲议会、欧盟委员会和欧洲理事会之间的三方谈判将很快举行，他们将在2019年一起决定《数字化单一市场版权指令》的最终命运。《数字化单一市场版权指令》旨在更新互联网时代的版权法，却在欧洲掀起了一片反对浪潮。其中备受争议的条款主要是被称为“上传过滤器”的第13条。该条款要求网络服务平台，如YouTube和Facebook等网络服务商停止用户共享未经授权的受版权保护的内容。反对者指出，第13条实质是要求平台主动与著作权所有者合作，以阻止用户上传受著作权保护的内容。要达到这一目的，唯一的办法是监控上传到YouTube和Facebook等网站的所有数据。这将给欧洲的小型互联网平台带来极为沉重的负担。此外，立法者很有可能利用《数字化单一市场版权指令》对互联网内容进行广泛的审查，删除图像、视频和其他被认为具有攻击性的内容[③]。YouTube的首席执行官沃西基（Wojcicki）号召人们行动起来反对欧盟的这项互联网法规，他表示，“《版权指令》的第13条将危及成千上万个工作岗位，也将迫使YouTube等平台只接受那些精挑细选后的内容。对于平台来说，承载来自个体原创者的内容太冒险了，因为平台现在将直接对相关的内容承担责任”[④]。

而在欧洲议会投票通过《数字化单一市场版权指令》仅仅一日后，德国联邦最高法院就下达裁决，将YouTube因用户上传侵权内容而被诉侵权的《真爱永恒——冬之歌》一案呈交至欧洲法院（ECJ），并就“向公众传播”与“避风港”条款等法律概念提请欧洲法院解释。网络服务商有没有、在多大程度上对于第三方侵权行为负有监督义务，成为过去一年里各方争论的焦点问题。事实上，这也是一个需要谨慎对待的命题，一旦对网络服务者施加的义务负担过重，将极大地增加其运行成本，不仅影响网络服务行业本身的发展，而且还会对信息的自由流动造成极大的妨碍。这显然违背了互联网建立之初的基本价值观。

面临困境的不只是像YouTube和Facebook这样的网络储存服务提供商，还有像谷歌（Google）这样的网络搜索服务提供商。澳大利亚在2018年10月份提出的《2018年版权法修正案》（在线侵权法案）中，将针对盗版网站拦截的适用范围从互联网内容服务商扩展到网络搜索服务提供商。澳大利亚的网站拦截制度于2015年首次实施，该制度载于《2015年版权法》第115a条，该条规定了版权所有者可以向联邦法院申请禁止令，要求互联网服务提供商采取合理的措施阻止用户访问海外盗版网站。按照此次修改的内容，网站拦截制度的适用范围扩展到网络搜索服务提供商（如Google）。要求网络搜索服务提供商采取合理的步骤，不提供关于被阻止网站的搜索结果，但仅在澳大利亚范围内。在授予禁止令的情况下，相关的网络搜索服务提供商可以与版权所有者达成协议，将禁止令的应用扩展到域名、URL和IP地址[⑤]。Google公司随后发布了一份意见书对该法案表示强烈反对，指出该法案将取消联邦法院封锁哪些网站的控制权，而将其给予商业实体。此外也有不少担忧的意见称，该法案可能会被不适当地扩张甚至被滥用，澳大利亚应当慎重思考这一条文的法律效果[⑥]。

在对待网络服务提供商“间接侵犯著作权”的构成标准，即网络服务提供商在面对网络侵权行为时负有何种义务这一问题上，各国的观点不尽相同。

---

① 网络服务大致包括三种：网络接入服务，如中国电信、中国网通等提供的接入互联网的服务；网络储存服务，如微博、博客等允许用户上传信息储存并供他人浏览的服务；网络搜索服务，如谷歌和百度等提供的关键词搜索服务。

② 王迁．知识产权法教程［M］．5版．北京：中国人民大学出版社，2016：251.

③ https://www.theverge.com/2018/9/12/17849868/eu-internet-copyright-reform-article-11-13-approved.

④ https://www.rt.com/news/441971-youtube-article-13-memes-eu/.

⑤ http://www.mondaq.com/australia/x/758484/Copyright/New+Australian+law+to+provide+further+protections+for+copyright+owners+to+block+offshore+pirate+websites.

⑥ https://www.techdirt.com/articles/20181127/13425541113/australian-parliament-moves-copyright-amendment-out-committee-into-law.shtml.

比如美国在1998年通过的《千禧年数字版权法》(Digital Millennium Copyright Act，DMCA)中就曾明确规定：网络服务提供商没有监视网络、寻找侵权活动的义务。在网络服务商行为义务的探索中，欧美国家一直是先行者，但随着我国在第四次产业革命中迎头赶上，中国也必将面临许多关于网络环境下侵犯著作权、网络服务提供商义务确定等法律问题。欧美国家的立法、司法经验在一定程度上能为我国提供有益的思路。

（三）网络环境中对著作权的限制

在著作权权利限制制度的设计之初，网络技术尚不存在，权利限制的规定就是为了平衡创作者和作品使用者之间的利益。但随着网络技术的诞生和不断进步，作品的创作、利用以及传播方式都得到了极大的丰富和发展，不少在传统环境下产生了积极法律效果和社会效果的制度，在网络环境下表现出了严重的“水土不服”。以“个人复制”行为为例，该制度在传统环境下产生了十分积极的效果，避免了个人仅仅为了学习、研究、非商业性使用相应的作品而陷入侵犯著作权的桎梏。但在网络环境中“个人复制”这一条款却充满了“挑衅”意味，信息技术的发展几乎消除了复制品与作品原件之间的区别，不少作品直接依靠网络平台传播，大量的个体欣赏者或使用者可以轻松地在线获取作品信息，复制或者下载作品，而这些作品的复制、传播或使用行为都是以个人行为的方式存在的。著作权人的利益在这一过程中受到了极大的侵害。因此各国纷纷进行法律制度变革，严格限定“个人复制”条款的适用范围。以日本为例，即使是出于个人使用目的，对于明知是非法上传的电影和音乐进行下载的行为也是违法的。在2018年底，为了规制如“漫画村”网站等引起的盗版网站问题，日本政府更进一步决定将非法下载的范围扩大至包括漫画、杂志的静态画面在内的所有作品，并将此纳入著作权法的修正案中。该立法建议一经公布，就引起了不小的争议。反对意见称“该草案忽视了国民信息收集自由的重要性，过度限缩了网络资料收集、创作、研究活动等的范围”①。

但面对网络时代知识产品使用和传播的特点，国际上一些组织号召扩张现有的权利限制制度。在世界知识产权组织版权及相关权常设委员会(SCCR)2018年5月举行的第36届会议上，图书馆电子信息联盟就指出：“各国的版权法虽在不断发展，却并没有为图书馆及其广大用户提供能够广泛使用的新技术。在合法获取知识的途径上，这种不平等日益加剧。这将促使人们转向未经授权的知识来源。”美国档案协会则表示：“版权法的局限性给协会的研究人员带来了重大挑战。档案管理员要为全球读者服务，他们需要保存信息以便用户访问，因此有权利限制和例外是必要的。档案信息必须能够合法地在国内和跨国界共享，并在不需承担法律责任的情况下使用新的技术手段。”② 在国家层面，日本内阁在2018年2月23日通过了《著作权法》新修正案，其中一项亮点就是放宽了数字教科书的使用条件。修正案规定：学校出于教学目的，在使用作品制作电子教材或向学生在线分发作品的情形下，获得权利人许可不再是必要条件③。这也再一次反映了网络技术对著作权法律制度的影响。

三、小结

国际著作权法制的发展总是在积极回应著作权市场的变化，力求使相对稳定的法律制度能够在不断变化的市场中发挥有效的引导作用。但即便如此，仍存在着诸多理论上和实践上的困惑。以网络技术、人工智能为代表的新一轮产业革命，给著作权制度带来了前所未有的冲击与挑战，立法、司法各个领域的新问题层出不穷。世界各国、WIPO等国际组织均积极作为，通过宣传号召、修订法律、做出判例等手段，对新问题做出回应，以求定分止争、化解矛盾，最终保障著作权产业的持续发展。回首2018年国际著作权法制的发展，一方面，国际著作权市场欣欣向荣，著作权制度对著作权市场变化积极回应，在规范市场运行机制、加强对权利人利益的维护、协调各市场主体间的利益三个层面，发挥了十分高效的作用；另一方面，信息时代的到来使数字版权市场的发展已势不可挡，网络环境下的各类著作权问题进一步凸显，新技术的利用对著作权制度形成了不小的冲击，在网络环境中的著作权专有权利、侵犯著作权行为、对著作权的限制等三个层面均有不少让我们无法回避、必须进一步深入研究的问题。

（作者单位：中国人民大学知识产权学院）

① https://keisenassociates.com/japan-agency-for-cultural-affairs-alleged-unfair-report-downloading-copyright-policy/.

② http://www.ip-watch.org/2018/05/31/civil-society-issues-call-action-draft-wipo-copyright-exceptions/.

③ https://www.japantimes.co.jp/news/2018/02/24/national/social-issues/abe-administration-promotes-bill-allow-schools-use-digital-textbooks/#.WtJvbVWWbIU.

2018年国际版权动态

◆ 立法与行政

【欧盟理事会正式批准《马拉喀什条约》】

2018年2月15日，欧盟理事会做出决定，同意缔结《马拉喀什条约》。

《马拉喀什条约》(全称为《关于为盲人、视力障碍者或其他印刷品阅读障碍者获得已出版作品提供便利的马拉喀什条约》)于2013年6月27日在摩洛哥马拉喀什通过，并于2016年9月30日生效。作为世界知识产权组织所设立的版权条约之一，它为视力障碍者规定了一系列著作权的例外与限制措施，以便于制作、发行、进出口无障碍格式版作品，并允许经过授权的非营利性组织或政府组织进行这类作品的跨境交易。

欧盟早在2014年4月就签署了该条约，但直至理事会正式批准，其间经过了一系列程序，并非一帆风顺。最初，英国、法国、芬兰、意大利等八个成员国否认欧盟委员会拥有缔结该条约的专有权限，这一法律问题于2015年8月被提交至欧洲法院。欧洲法院于2017年2月给出肯定意见，确认委员会对于影响欧盟共同规则的协议享有缔结权限。同年3月，欧洲议会对委员会提交的相关指令草案进行投票。在随后的9月，理事会正式通过立法。根据条约的要求，新的强制性著作权例外规定被引入欧盟法律，允许受益人和相关组织以无障碍格式复制作品，并在整个欧盟和作为条约缔约方的第三国范围内传播作品。

在此次理事会授权缔结的决定后，欧盟才最终能够交存条约的批准文书。

目前，视力障碍者在获取可阅读的书籍和其他印刷材料方面仍然面临许多阻碍。推广无障碍格式的作品极为必要，如盲文书、有声读物和大字体读物等。国际上对此已形成普遍共识。保加利亚文化部部长博伊尔·巴诺夫(Boil Banov)称，“这个决定对于欧盟来说意义非常，因为该条约将帮助我们克服视力障碍群体接触文化资源的歧视性壁垒”。

在大西洋的另一侧，《马拉喀什条约》的影响也正在扩大。2018年3月15日，查克·格拉斯利(Chuck Grassley)等七名美国参议员向国会提交了《马拉喀什条约实施法案》(Marrakesh Treaty Implementation Act, S.2559)。这一提案能否变为现实，同样值得关注。

(信息搜集、编译：杨迪菲。

资料来源：http://www.consilium.europa.eu/en/press/press-releases/2018/02/15/marrakesh-treaty-on-access-to-published-works-for-blind-and-visually-impaired-persons-council-authorises-ratification/; http://www.consilium.europa.eu/en/press/press-releases/2017/05/10/marrakesh-treaty/; https://www.eff.org/deeplinks/2018/03/blind-users-celebrate-marrakesh-treaty-implementation-bill-drops)

【日本大尺度修改《著作权法》】

随着物联网、大数据、人工智能时代的到来，第四次产业革命也已经到来，著作权领域出现了很多新课题，对全球著作权格局提出了创新性挑战。众所周知，日本的著作权保护极为严苛，有些日本学者(如城所教授)认为“日本现行著作权法不仅不能促进产业发展，反而妨碍了新技术、新服务诞生”。在面对如此挑战时，日本已经开始行动，出台新《著作权法》。在日本政府看来，新法律并不意味着日本知识产权制度的倒退，反而将有助于创造新产业，并给内容产业带来更大的附加值。

2018年2月23日，日本在内阁会议上通过了旨在扩大网上使用作品范围的《著作权法》修正案，新法拟于2019年1月1日实施。新《著作权法》出台，意味着日本政府准备进行改革，接轨国际标准，迎接新时代的降临。对日本来说，这是一个非常大尺度的修正案。其主要内容的变动体现在如下几个方面：

(1)将书籍进行电子数据化，即使未获著作权人许可的服务也能实现，如在网上搜索含特定词语的文章、书籍。而此前，由于日本严苛的著作权保护制度，即使在网上输入关键词，也不会出现含有关键词的书籍、文献列表，很多海外的网络搜索服务商干脆放弃了日本这块市场。这些措施，将让有需要的日本民众不用再一次次前往图书馆和书店，节约了大量人力物力。

(2)基于教学使用目的，将书籍电子化、向学生传输电子书籍和照片，只要向管理机构统一支付了补偿金，便不需要获得著作权人的许可。

（3）关于软件，为了找出网络攻击方面的弱点而进行复制的行为也将合法化。

（4）日本著作权使用从“正面清单制度”转向了“负面清单制度”，日本互联网企业对著作权使用的自由度将大大提高。日本过去对著作权的使用，原则上必须征得著作权人的同意，以开列正面清单的方式规定哪些情况可以获得豁免。而在修改后，对著作权的使用变为原则上无须著作权人同意，只惩罚明显损害所有者权益的恶性行为。

1887 年，日本出台第一部版权相关的条例《版权条令》，1893 年，又形成了日本第一部版权法律《版权法》。1899 年，日本加入了《保护文学和艺术作品伯尔尼公约》。一百多年来，日本著作权保护的程度不断提升，达到了近乎严苛的地步。即使是学校的各种试题，如果出现作家的作品，也必须获得该作家的同意。哪怕是一道菜肴，在日本同样具有著作权，如果没有经过餐厅的同意随意拍摄，上传菜肴照片也构成对著作权的侵犯。因此，日本人在生活中对于可能涉及著作权的行为格外小心，很少因为贪图低价使用各种“山寨版”，最后让自己身陷囹圄。

在日本，对于侵犯著作权的行为，除了罚款，甚至还会有刑事处罚。按照日本相关法律规定，侵犯著作权可以被判处 10 年以下有期徒刑或 1 000 万日元以下罚款。而在实际执行中，日本法院倾向于严惩，一般都会对侵犯著作权者判处徒刑。中国在日公民也不乏因侵犯著作权而被逮捕的。例如中国驻日本大使馆 2018 年 2 月 1 日发布消息称：近日，几名在日中国公民因涉嫌违反《著作权法》被捕。中国驻日本大使馆提醒在日中国公民，未获得原作者或著作权方授权擅自翻译、发布、传播作品，即使不以营利为目的，也可能违反日本《著作权法》。

凡事过犹不及。事实上，早在 1994 年，日本就已研制出首个搜索引擎，在时间上几乎和美国同步，但为了避免著作权受到侵害，日本当时要求搜索引擎在收纳网站时必须征得著作权人同意，这导致日本本土搜索引擎发展滞后。这保护了著作权人的权益，使日本漫画等内容产业持续繁荣。但与此同时，由于对著作权的保护过于烦琐、细致，本土互联网创新受到严重遏制。最终，日本互联网市场被美国公司占领，从视频共享网站 YouTube，到个人社交网站 Facebook、Twitter 等，日本互联网产业几乎被外国公司独霸天下。

有分析人士认为，自由使用作品，在互联网时代至关重要。人工智能深度学习是一项热门的新技术。深度学习需要人工智能识别、分析大量信息。如果研发者在使用作品时需要取得所有者同意，那么研发效率、研发热情无疑将受到很大影响。

面对互联网大潮的冲击，日本的版权保护制度似乎有些跟不上时代。比如，日本学者开展研究和撰写论文时，查找与收集资料极为不便。他们不仅要一次次奔波于各个图书馆及书店，获得海外最新研究成果也要慢很多。所以，有日本学者调侃称，当我们还在苦苦等待海外相关资料寄送过来时，有些国家的同行就已经将成果应用于自己的最新论文了。甚至有日本学者认为，近年来日本学术水平提升滞后，与此有很大的关系。

毋庸置疑，严格的版权保护，曾经让日本涌现出了大量优秀的文化作品，繁荣了文化事业。但是，或许顺应时代不断调整，多有一些互联网共享精神，日本的版权保护才能走得更远。

（信息搜集、编译：宗倩倩。

资料来源：http://www.xinhuanet.com/globe/2018-04/06/c_137084661.htm；http://news.sina.com.cn/w/2018-02-28/doc-ifyrztfz5345119.shtml；http://www.guancha.cn/Neighbors/2018_02_01_445500.shtml）

【日本新法助力教育信息化改革：电子教材使用无须权利人许可】

2018 年 2 月 23 日，日本内阁通过了《著作权法》修正案，其中一项修订重点是放宽数字教科书的使用条件。修正案规定，学校出于教学目的，在使用作品制作电子教材或向学生在线分发作品的情形下，获得权利人许可不再是必要条件。

日本现行《著作权法》规定，除私人用途的复制之外，不允许使用数字设备进行非法复制。在线发放电子教材必须得到所涉作品权利人的许可，而对于传统的纸质教材则没有这一要求。面对互联网大潮的冲击，这一几近严苛的著作权保护制度似乎难以适应社会发展，也为正常的教研活动带来了种种不便。例如，即使是学校所出的试题，如果出现相关作品，也必须获得该作者的同意。针对这类现实问题，修正案提出，如果学校向文化事务部门指定的组织支付相应补偿金，那么网上分发电子教材将无须再得到权利人的同意。这一规定类似中国的“法定许可”制度。

该修订也被视为与日本接下来的教育信息化改革相衔接。就在同一天，内阁会议也通过了《学校教育法》修正案，将电子教材定为官方教科书。在小学、初中、高中教学中，作为课程的一部分，数字教科书可以与普通纸质教科书结合使用。尤其是对于存在视力、智力等障碍的学生来说，使用普通纸质教科书有较大难度，因此推动教学信息化的举措，将对这一学习群体大有裨益。

日本文部科学省于2018年2月20日发布了“2016年度学校教育状况调查”。其结果显示，数字教科书在小学、初中的使用率分别为52.1%和58.2%；在义务教育阶段之外的高中，数字教科书的使用率为12.5%；特殊教育学校的数字教科书普及率则为12.8%。文部科学省计划在2020年全面推出传统教科书的数字化版本，届时“主动性、互动性、深度学习”的新型课程指导方针将得到充分推广，电子教科书将逐步取代以往的传统教科书。

政府希望国会能于2018年批准这项法案。如果顺利通过，新法将于2019年1月正式生效实施。受益于新规定，教育科研领域将有望取得划时代的进步。

（信息搜集、编译：杨迪菲。

资料来源：https://www.japantimes.co.jp/news/2018/02/24/national/social-issues/abe-administration-promotes-bill-allow-schools-use-digital-textbooks/#.WtJvbVWWbIU；https://mainichi.jp/articles/20180224/ddm/012/010/037000c；https://resemom.jp/article/2018/02/23/43097.html）

【欧盟版权规则或将不再适用于脱欧后的英国】

2018年3月28日，欧盟委员会就脱欧问题中的版权制度安排，对利益相关者发布公告。公告中称，“除非脱欧协议中包含其他过渡安排，在脱欧之后，欧盟在版权领域的规则将不再适用于英国”。

公告首先指出，英国和欧盟同为“众多主要版权条约”的缔约方，在英国脱离欧盟之后，两者在版权方面的关系将主要有赖于国际条约的调整。但值得注意的是，欧盟同时还以“国际条约中绝无仅有”的方式为权利人的利益提供某些跨境保护。因此，脱欧将使英国在版权规则适用上产生一些具体更迭。公告主要对以下几个方面进行了说明：

（1）英国的广播组织将不再受益于欧盟指令中关于成员国之间跨境广播服务的优惠措施。例如，广播组织仅须在卫星信号发出国获得相关作者的版权许可即可。脱欧之后，英国的广播组织将必须在所有信号抵达国也获得相应的版权许可。

（2）对于作者无法确定或无法联系的孤儿作品，根据欧盟法律的规定，一旦某一作品在一个成员国被确认为孤儿作品，它将对所有成员国的公众开放。脱欧之后，英国承认的孤儿作品将不会在欧盟得到承认，反之亦然。

（3）脱欧后的英国将不会受益于欧盟2017/1564号指令，该指令允许视障人士获得受保护作品的副本。这意味着，英国的相关群体将无法从欧盟的授权组织获得作品副本，反之亦然。

（4）跨境的在线内容服务将受到限制。欧盟2017/1128号规则允许使用内容流媒体服务的用户从另一成员国访问这一服务，而不论所访问内容在该国合法与否。此规定不再适用后，英国用户在欧盟其他国家将不可访问前述服务，同时英国的在线内容服务商必须遵守服务所在国的版权以及其他法律制度。

其中，最后一项引发了尤为激烈的讨论。一些报纸称欧盟委员会想在英国脱欧后“阻止”英国公民获取在线服务。但英国政府在接受BBC采访时表示，目前对此尚未形成定论，“政府致力于为英国消费者争取最佳利益，关于跨境访问服务的问题仍然有待进一步的谈判”。

就在这一公告面世前不久，欧盟和英国政府共同发布了一项协议草案，以确认在脱欧过渡期间，即2020年12月31日之后，欧盟商标、外观设计专利、植物品种权和数据库权利的所有者在英国的权利仍然受到保护。根据该协议草案，脱欧不会影响这些既有权利的稳定状态，且无须经过任何形式的复审。

（信息搜集、编译：杨迪菲。

资料来源：http://www.bbc.com/news/technology-43581894；https://ec.europa.eu/digital-single-market/en/news/notice-stakeholders-withdrawal-united-kingdom-and-eu-rules-field-copyright；https://www.worldipreview.com/news/eu-copyright-rules-will-not-apply-post-brexit-15708）

【断开链接以保护漫画的著作权，政府的紧急对策涉嫌违宪而遭到反对】

2018年4月13日，日本政府针对在盗版网站可免费阅读漫画及杂志的网络服务提供者采取了紧急措施，促使其断开盗版网站的链接。但是，此举缺乏法律依据，有可能与宪法第二十一条中规定的禁止侵犯通信秘密相抵触，遭到网络服务提供者的反对。

同日，知识产权战略本部·犯罪对策内阁会议讨论决定：针对“漫画村”等三个主要的盗版网站采取紧急立法措施，因该三个网站具有相同性质，因此断开链接属于适当之举。

此次事件的背景包含了著作权侵权的严重化。根据业内团体的调查，该三个网站在截至 2018 年 2 月的半年时间内所导致的损害赔偿额预计达到约 4 000 亿日元。公益社团法人日本漫画家协会起诉称，“盗版网站没有付出任何创作努力而贪得利益。日本文化可能要泯灭了”。

但是，断开链接的前提是网络服务提供者了解网络使用者的全部通信情况，而这可能违背通信秘密保护。日本政府解释说，在此次危急情况下，不得已采取的应对方式适用刑法中的“紧急避难”，不构成违宪。

自 2011 年 4 月开始，日本国内断开了登载儿童淫秽作品的网站的链接。因为严重的性虐待事件一旦扩散开来，造成的损害将无法弥补。网络服务提供者或专业人士在讨论会上达成一致意见，为避免更多的受害者，“特殊事件不能草率解决”。

日本内阁府称，欧盟各国等 42 个国家都实行了断开与著作权侵权相关的链接的措施。许多国家实施了不侵害通信秘密的与著作权及其他知识产权保护相关的立法规定。日本网络服务提供者协会 2018 年 4 月 12 日提出要求优先考虑其他手段，声称“著作权可以通过禁令或损害赔偿实现侵权救济”。

（信息搜集、编译：兰鉴。

资料来源：https://mainichi.jp/articles/20180414/ddm/012/010/084000c）

【《广播组织保护条约》制定进行时】

2018 年 5 月以来，世界知识产权组织在积极推进制定世界性的《广播组织保护条约》。在 5 月的会议上，代表们就某些话题达成一致，制定《广播组织保护条约》这一事项已经获得广泛的支持。在随后的数次会议中，世界知识产权组织著作权委员会却因各方激烈的讨论而暂缓制定该条约的具体计划，但会议上已经形成一份完整的建议稿，准备提交世界知识产权组织大会讨论表决。在 9 月底举行的世界知识产权组织成员国大会上，成员们对这一条约的制定进行了更集中具体的讨论，主要关注“信号保护”这一话题，会议决定将相关建议稿提交讨论。

美国华盛顿法律学院信息公正和知识产权项目的负责人 Sean Flynn 撰文称，世界知识产权组织在会上重点关注了《广播组织保护条约》建议稿中的权利限制和豁免条款，但大会的精神是对其实施更多限制。条约建议稿要求各国政府保障广播组织对信号传输节目的内容享有更多专属保护，以减少信号被盗版的现象。建议稿提出了三种保护方案，分别为 50 年著作权保护期、20 年著作权保护期和无限期的保护。如果著作权保护期长于信号本身的寿命，那么他人能否合理使用该信号的问题则变得至关重要。例如，教师需要在教学中使用广播内容，电影制作者、记者等其他内容制作者也可能需要在作品中使用这些受保护的广播内容进行讨论、阐述、评价等。如果条约中没有对这些著作权豁免的情况进行规定，那么他人的言论自由、受教育权等可能因此受到侵害。

Sean Flynn 认为，经过长达 20 年的讨论，《广播组织保护条约》应当适应现代社会的发展。版权豁免与专属保护一样，对于促进创新、保护公共利益都具有重要作用。为了激励新作品的创作，同时保障作品的交叉使用，我们需要在著作权限制和保护之间寻找平衡。对于著作权豁免的范围，条约应当在《世界知识产权组织版权条约》框架性的规定之下，对数据时代的新版权豁免做出定义，而不是对原有的权利进行限制。

世界各地的广播组织对《广播组织保护条约》表示支持，希望可以借此扩大对盗版信号的打击。但也有人表示担忧，创设一个新的权利可能会让大型互联网公司（如脸书、谷歌、奈飞等）有机可乘，反而阻碍广播电视公司享受新的条约的保护，而且保护的范围和时限也受到了限制。

欧盟广播联盟知识产权法项目的负责人 Heijo Ruijsenaars 指出，现有国际法对于广播组织的保护并不够。除了 1961 年《保护表演者、音像制品制作者和广播组织罗马公约》（下称《罗马公约》）以外，广播组织希望获得更多的权利保护，例如，保护其对节目制作和传播的投资。现有公约对于广播技术的保护实际是不足的，如果观众想要随时随地获取广播内容，在现代社会中意味着广播组织要通过不同方式向用户提供，而不仅限于传统广播方式。技术的升级也导致了盗版，信号被盗版已然成为全球性的现象。但是，如果对新条约的讨论仅仅限于信号盗版，广播组织的许多活动可能会被忽略。广播组织先制作节目，然后将它通过信号传输，这才是完整的广播行为。广播是一种工具，节目制作者们通过广播这一方式向公众提供内容，产生信号只是其中的一环罢了。因此，广播行为中最重要的元素是相对于观众的独立性。观众人数多少并不会影响这一行为所受到的法律保护。并且，广播行为和内容、传输等也是相互独立的，不仅广播行为受到保护，节目内容和传输信号也应受到著作权的保护。

互联网与社会研究中心（the Center for Internet and Society，CIS）的成员 Anubha Sinha 认为，受到信号盗版影响最严重的是体育广播，但世界知识产权组织所讨论的新条约并不足以减少体育广播组织受到的损害。新条约的受益者似乎只有广播组织，但如今人们很难区分计算机网络、有线或无线方式的广播。我们应该考虑到新创设的权利被大型互联网公司滥用的风险。1961 年《罗马公约》规定的范围比较狭窄，导致广播组织面临以互联网为基础的广播服务的冲击。这类服务所需权利少，但能为公众提供所需的东西，因而更受欢迎。这对传统广播组织而言是个挑战。为了规避此类风险，有组织建议新条约增加以下内容或领域的版权豁免权：时事新闻、公共事务、纪录片、教育、文献引用。

其他组织也表示，新条约建议的“50 年保护期”不恰当。如果将这些信号保存 50 年，很可能没有技术可以继续解读它们。保护期应当限于几分钟，慷慨的立法者也可能允许达到 24 小时。在体育广播领域，对于信号的保护一般为数小时。如果将信号保护权的期限设置过长，对于公共领域也会有不良后果，妨碍文化多样性和民主发展。例如，人们可能难以获取历史信息，这种对内容的垄断无疑是有危害的。

其他从业者认为，现在的建议稿如果通过，可能会带来一系列负面影响。世界瞬息万变，创造规则已经不仅仅是本行业的权利，“每个人都是著作权人”，而建议稿并没有把公众作为著作权人纳入考虑范围。在过去，互联网行业曾面临下下策，而这一建议稿也未必是个好选择。立法者可能有牺牲整个行业生态而支持某一领域发展的嫌疑。并且，建议稿中的新设权利可能限制了不受著作权法保护的信息的传播，如即时新闻、官员演讲等，这可能牺牲了公众利益。

（信息搜集、编译：梁锐。

资料来源：http://www.ip-watch.org/2018/05/31/draft-broadcast-treaty-takes-restrictive-approach-limitations-exceptions/；http://www.ip-watch.org/2018/06/04/wipo-edges-toward-high-level-meeting-finish-treaty-ip-rights-broadcasters/；http://www.ip-watch.org/2018/09/28/protection-broadcast-signal-theft-steps-forward-wipo-general-assembly/；http://www.ip-watch.org/2018/05/31/broadcasting-treaty-moving-wipo-copyright-exceptions-libraries-not/；http://www.ip-watch.org/2018/10/09/broadcasters-eager-global-signal-protection-others-warn-major-players-sneaking/）

【韩国扩大表演权范围】

韩国《著作权法》第二十九条第二款规定，如果表演已经商业性发表的录音制品（如唱片）、视听作品，该表演未向公众收取费用，也未向表演者支付报酬时，可以不经著作权人许可。但根据 2017 年 8 月 22 日修订、2018 年 8 月 23 日实施的《韩国著作权法实行令》第十一条中涉及的关于著作权限制的规定，如果在咖啡店、饮料店、扎啤酒店、健身房、传统市场以外的大型购物街这些场所播放商业性唱片或视听作品的话，著作权人的表演权将不被限制。

一般来说，音乐和电影等创造性作品的作者可以享有著作权，所以如果将其作品对公众播放或公开广播的话，必须经过著作权人的许可。但是，按照韩国《著作权法》第二十九条第二款（此条接近于中国《著作权法》第二十二条第一款第（九）项），如果“免费表演”已经商业性发表的唱片、视听作品的话，那么著作权人的表演权将被限制。但如今，在《韩国著作权法实行令》第十一条规定的地方（KTV 等酒店、大型超市、百货商店等），著作权人的权利将不再被限制，换言之，播放音乐或电影的店铺老板必须获得著作权人的许可。

在韩国人经常光顾的咖啡店、饮料店、扎啤酒店、健身房、大型购物街等地点，总是能听到各种各样的音乐，人们也时常疑惑这些音乐是否都可以免费使用。按照过去的《著作权法》，对于在咖啡店等播放的音乐来说，其著作权人的表演权被限制，咖啡店等场所的经营者并不用获得权利人的许可或支付使用费给音乐的创作者、歌手、演奏者等人。

该限制性规定被人们诟病已久，因为比起外国立法例，这些规定过度地限制了韩国著作权人的表演权。因此，2018 年 8 月开始实施的新法令扩大了表演权的范围，那些音乐使用率高的、音乐对于营业重要性大的场所经营者需要获得著作权人的许可并支付使用费，这些场所具体包括咖啡店、饮料店、扎啤酒店、健身房、传统市场以外的大型购物街等。

但同时，为了减少经营者的负担，韩国政府免除了面积在 50 平方米以下的店铺的著作权许可费用；而且对于面积超过 50 平方米的店铺，规定每个月的许可费为定额 4 000 韩币（约人民币 24 元）。实践中，权利人团体要求每个月支付 2 万韩币（约人民币 120 元）的许可费，而店铺业主坚持支付 3 000 韩币（约人民币 18 元）。此外，为了减少店铺业主的烦恼和不便，韩国政府将几个权利人团体的收费途径一体化。

将韩国这次《著作权法》修改带来的影响整理如下：那些音乐使用率高的、营业中音乐的重要性大的店铺，例如咖啡店等，都需要为播放音乐支付许可费了；但对于那些面积在 50 平方米以下的店铺来说，播放音乐仍然是免费的。对于《韩国著作权法实行令》第十一条没有涉及的其他行业场所（例如服装店、美容院、食堂、便利店、书店、电器店等），其经营者无须承担著作权人表演权扩展带来的影响，仍然不用支付许可费。但相关的司法解释需要引起我们的关注，如果音乐是“非法地获得”的，那么对其进行播放必然会构成侵犯著作权的行为，因为“商业性唱片”限定于合法地购买的销售用唱片（光盘、MP3 文件等）。

在韩国著作权保护院（Korea Copyright Protection Agency）的一个判例中，一家电器店利用在线流媒体服务播放音乐被认定为侵犯著作权，应当支付使用费。商业性唱片即销售用唱片，不包括“数字流媒体音源”，所以用在线流媒体服务播放音乐应该支付表演的使用费。所以，第二十九条涉及的著作权例外应当限于通常的唱片。

（信息搜集、编译：魏泰焕。

资料来源：https://kcopastory.blog.me/221177938134；https://www.kcopa.or.kr/lay1/bbs/S1T233C234/F/39/view.do?mode=view&article_seq=308&cpage=1&rows=9&condition=&keyword=）

【韩国《著作权法》修改中的争议：是否承认出版者的版式设计权】

随着平板电脑用户增加以及图书扫描服务等数字复制方式盛行，越来越多的出版社选择关门大吉，甚至连韩国排名第二的出版社也在 2017 年初倒闭了。为此，出版者们为保护自己的权益，开始主张他们需要能独立行使的权利。2018 年，韩国国会议员提出一份《著作权法》修改草案，其中涉及给予出版者“版式设计权”，保护期限自出版之日起 25 年。

版式设计权旨在保护出版者与精神劳动、艰苦努力相关的权益，权利人基于对图书、期刊的字体设计、格式编排和版面布局等依法享有专有权，未经权利人许可他人不得使用。在韩国，版式设计权是一种和邻接权相似的权利，但是版式设计权相对于著作权独立性很强，因为是否拥有著作权并不影响版式设计权的享有。版式设计权最早被规定在 1956 年的《英国著作权法》中，之后英联邦国家（新西兰、南非、新加坡、牙买加等）及德国、中国、中国香港、中国台湾、印度尼西亚、爱尔兰等十多个国家和地区都规定了类似的权利。美国、法国、韩国的著作权法中虽然没有规定版式设计权，但是规定出版者享有出版权（复制作品后向公众提供）和排他性的发行权（复制作品后向公众传播），另外，日本《著作权法》规定出版权涵盖电子出版行为。

通过版式设计权，出版者（出版公司）得以控制大学附近的非法复制和图书扫描服务。现行的韩国《著作权法》规定在学校教育目的下进行复制只需要给著作权人一定补偿金，但是一旦规定了版式设计权，出版者也能收到类似的补偿金。

关于是否应该制定版式设计权，韩国国内争论如下：

（一）赞成的意见

（1）针对非法复制行为，出版者理应获得相应的救济。

一旦《著作权法》中规定了版式设计权，对于非法复制的书籍，非法复制者将同时侵犯版式设计权。出版者对版式进行了较大的投资与劳动，所以理应获得适当的保护。现已存在的出版权（复制作品后向公众提供）和排他性发行权（复制作品后向公众传播）的权利期间仅为 3 年左右，并且在针对以学校教育为目的的复制行为时被限制行使权利。

（2）图书市场得到激活。

出版者将更努力地制作好看的版式提高图书的可读性，好的作品也会越来越多，图书市场将得到激活。

（3）需要对出版公司进行实际补偿。

在出版图书的过程中出版者通过编辑、勘校、设计等工作非常辛苦地创造版式，提高作品价值，并向公众提供作品，所以出版者这种提高作品的价值和进行文化普及的努力应得到实际上的补偿。

（二）反对的意见

（1）制定新权利将增加使用者负担，造成社会混乱。

规定版式设计权将导致使用者的经济负担增加，现在出版者能享有出版权和排他性发行权，并且在满足条件的情况下可以用民法上的债权人代位权或不正当竞争法上的权利来主张诉求。

（2）立法背景上的差距不容忽视。

英国的立法背景是保护期满后的出版者的版式设计和印刷技术仍被视为非常重要的成果的时代，德国的立法背景是著作权人死后古书出版非常流行的时代。如今，大部分的版式设计都可以用电脑软件迅速处理，其费用和劳动都减少了，法律产生的背景条件有了很大不同。

（3）数字出版环境下缺乏创造性。

近年来电子出版流行，电子书籍增加，纸质书籍越来越少。在这种情况下，我们应该反思电子出版版式设计权存在的必要性。电子书籍一般使用EPUB等自动编辑软件的格式，所以缺乏满足版式设计权的条件。尤其是电子书籍通过各种各样的软件可以操作字体的大小、类型等，很容易变换本来的版式，所以缺乏传统意义上的版式设计权。此外，从用户的角度来讲，使用各种各样的电子读书器和平板电脑并不一定能维持原本的版式和格式。

（信息搜集、编译：魏泰焕。

资料来源：http://www.copyright.or.kr/information-materials/discussCopyrightIssues/view.do?brdctsno=41947&pageIndex=1&portalcode04=¬iceYn=&nationcode=&brdno=125&etc1=&searchkeyword=&portalcode=04&brdclasscode=&searchText=&searchTarget=ALL&servicecode=06&brdctsstatecode=；https://blog.naver.com/with_wraenoh/220932154376）

【USMCA 对著作权执法标准的新规定】

美国贸易代表办公室（USTR）称，墨西哥、美国、加拿大就推动《北美自由贸易协定》进入 21 世纪，使其成为现代化的高标准协议达成共识，形成了《美国—墨西哥—加拿大协议》（USMCA），并就提高知识产权执法标准达成初步协议。具体就著作权而言，该协议主要强化了对网络服务提供商在两方面的要求，一是防止侵犯版权，二是延长著作权保护期。

根据 USTR 发布的情况说明书，三国在该协议内提出了一系列执法标准，包括在某些情况下将盗版，假冒，摄录，窃取卫星、有线信号和商业秘密认定为刑事犯罪，同时将知识产权保护措施适用于电子环境和对邻接权的侵权行为。这可以给知识产权提供强有力的有效保护和执行，对于推动创新、创造经济增长和促进美国就业十分关键。整体而言，该协议就提高著作权执法标准呈现出三大亮点：

亮点一：最全面执行条款。

协议首次要求了以下全部条款：执法人员必须禁止涉嫌盗版或假冒的货物在任何协议国入境、出境和过境，对具有商业规模的假冒和盗版行为进行打击，对电影摄录（网上盗版电影的重要来源）适用有意义的刑事程序和罚则，对窃取卫星和有线信号的行为适用民事和刑事处罚，为防范窃取商业秘密提供广泛保护。

亮点二：加大对创作者的保护。

协议要求对版权及邻接权提供全面的国民待遇，使美国创作者在国外市场不被剥夺作为国内创作者所享有的权利。将歌曲表演等作品的最短版权保护期延长至 75 年，并确保通过技术保护措施和权利管理信息等现有技术保护数字音乐、电影和书籍等作品。

根据美国法律，为网络服务提供商（ISP）建立适宜的“避风港”“通知—移除”规则，为权利人提供知识产权保护的同时，也为不直接受益于侵权的合法技术企业提供可预测性。

亮点三：增强对数字贸易的保护。

关于数字贸易涉及的惩罚，该协议的规定严于任何国际协议。这为美国扩大其具有竞争优势的创新产品和服务的贸易和投资奠定了坚实基础。具体如下：禁止将关税和其他歧视性措施应用于以电子方式分发的数字产品（如电子书、视频、音乐、软件和游戏等）；确保数据可以跨境传输，并最大限度地减少数据存储和处理的限制，从而增强和保护全球数字生态系统；确保供应商不受限制地使用电子认证或电子签名，从而促进数字交易；实行强制性消费者保护，包括隐私和未经请求的通信，来适用于数字市场；限制政府要求披露专有计算机源代码和算法的能力，以更好地保护数字供应商的竞争力；促进合作应对网络安全挑战，寻求促进行业最佳实践，以确保网络和服务的安全；促进对政府生成的公共数据的开放访问，以加强商业应用和服务的创新使用；在知识产权执法领域之外，限制网络平台对其承载或处理的第三方内容的民事责任，从而提高依赖于用户交互和用户内容的增长引擎的经济活力。

（信息搜集、编译：方兴萍。

资料来源：http://www.ip-watch.org/2018/08/27/ustr-mexico-agrees-raise-ip-enforcement-standards-us/；https://ustr.gov/about-us/policy-offices/press-office/fact-sheets/2018/october/united-states%E2%80%93mexico%E2%80%93canada-trade-fa-1）

【欧洲议会批准通过颇具争议的《数字化单一市场版权指令》】

2018 年 9 月 12 日，欧盟委员会提出的《数字化单一市场版权指令》（以下简称《版权指令》）法律草案以 438∶226 的票数获得欧洲议会的通过。基本上，这一投票结果意味着欧洲议会、欧盟委员会和欧洲理事会之间的三方谈判将很快举行，他们将一起决定《版权指令》的最终命运。该指令本身仍面临 2019 年 1 月的最后投票。

有关引入新闻出版商决定他们新闻内容的数字使用之专有权利的建议，在被提议指令的批准版本中保持原封不动。但这一旨在更新互联网时代版权法的法案从始至终就充满争议，其最初在 7 月份被欧洲议会成员否决。支持者认为它是对内容创造者的保护，但批评者却指责该法案将是“一场灾难”。而受到主要批评的两项关键条款是被称为“互联网链接税”的第十一条以及被称为“上传过滤器”的第十三条。第十一条旨在为出版商和报纸提供一种获利的方式，使他们有权在诸如谷歌这样的公司链接到他们的报道时，向这些公司收取许可费。第十三条要求某些网络服务提供平台，如 YouTube 和 Facebook 等网站停止用户共享未经授权的受版权保护的内容。

针对第十一条的规定，反对者指出，向诸如 Google News 这样的平台收取共享文章“税”的尝试屡屡失败，而且这个系统可以轻易地被“版权蟑螂”滥用。而第十三条的规定在反对者看来甚至更糟。其要求平台主动与版权享有者合作，以阻止用户上传受版权保护的内容。要达到这一目的，唯一的办法是监控上传到 YouTube 和 Facebook 等网站的所有数据，这将给小型的互联网平台带来沉重的负担。批评者还认为，立法者很有可能利用《版权指令》对互联网内容进行广泛审查，关闭图像、视频和其他被认为具有攻击性的内容。这听起来似乎是完全虚构的场景。然而，这种情况目前已然在俄罗斯发生。更进一步，这一指令还会给整个欧洲数字经济带来阻碍。因此也就不难理解为何维基百科创始人吉米·威尔士（Jimmy Wales）和万维网创建人蒂姆·伯纳斯-李（Tim Berners-Lee）等人会如此强烈地反对这项指令。

而针对上述反对意见，支持者表示，这不过是美国大型科技公司在危言耸听，因为这些公司渴望保持对网络最大平台的控制。支持者认为现行法律和指令的修正案中的规定能有效避免上述滥用行为的出现。具体包括第十三条对于 GitHub 和维基百科这类网站的豁免，以及将单纯共享超链接和用“个别单词”对文章进行描述等行为排除在“链接税”的规制之外。

以上情况引发了众多围绕市场参与者在这一系列变化面前可能出现的反应的争论与研究。尤其令人瞩目的是，第十一条增加了措辞模糊的第 4a 款，其中规定“会员国应确保当信息社会服务提供者（即网站）为了对新闻出版物进行数字化使用而支付给新闻出版者额外报酬时，作者可以从中获得公平且适当的报酬”。这种再分配机制如何发挥作用，以及其在新闻产业中意味着什么，将会成为进一步考察的焦点。虽然争议此起彼伏，但是毫无疑问，如果《版权指令》在 2019 年 1 月最终获得欧洲议会的通过，它将会对欧盟甚至全世界的互联网生态产生巨大的影响。尽管具体如何解释这项立法将由各个国家自行决定，但权利平衡的转变是显而易见的：互联网中最大的技术公司正在失去其对互联网的控制。

（信息搜集、编译：林文静。

资料来源：https://www.theverge.com/2018/9/12/17849868/eu-internet-copyright-reform-article-11-13-approved；http://cmds.ceu.edu/article/2018-09-21/what-new-copyright-directive-will-mean-press-publishers-and-journalists；https://www.digitalmusicnews.com/2018/09/12/european-union-copyright-directive-approval/；http://www.techuk.org/insights/news/item/13915-copyright-directive-is-a-setback-for-the-european-digital-economy）

【美国《音乐现代化法案》深入改革音乐许可制度】

《音乐现代化法案》（Orrin G. Hatch-Bob Goodlatte Music Modernization Act），这部美国两党全票通过的法案意味着众多政策制定者、相关利益者和美国版权局多年的努力得以实现。该法案旨在改革音乐许可的相关规定以更好地促进数字音乐的法律许可，预期将使音乐市场中提供各种服务的诸多利益相关者受益，包括词曲作家、出版商、艺术家、唱片公司、数字服务提供商、图书馆和大众群体。

在该法案立法前，国会举行了一系列听证会，这也是国会对美国版权法进行全面评估的一部分内容。为了协助这一工作，美国版权局针对音乐许可的法律框架以及 21 世纪的音乐创作者和投资人的新需求进行了全面的调查研究，得到了一份《版权与音乐市场》报告。在此之前，美国版权局曾推出

《对1972年之前录音制品的联邦版权保护》政策报告，这份报告指出将1972年2月15日之前固定的录音制品置于联邦司法管辖内的需求和相应方法。

《音乐现代化法案》将是几十年来最重要的著作权法案之一。这部法案彰显了美国国会改变现行《版权法》难以适应音乐领域内变化的消费者喜好和科技发展的现状的决心。该法案由三部分组成：第一编是“音乐许可的现代化”（Music Licensing Modernization），第二编是“CLASSICS保护与利用”（CLASSICS Protection and Access，CLASSICS即Compensating Legacy Artists for their Songs，Service and Important Contributions to Society，作品对社会有重要贡献的艺术家遗产补偿），第三编是“音乐制作人分配”（Allocation for Music Producers）。

《音乐现代化法案》修改了现行《版权法》第一百一十五条关于录音作品复制和发行的机械许可的规定，新规定将为实施特定行为（比如永久下载、有限下载和交互式流媒体）的数字音乐提供商建立一个新的总许可。物质载体（比如CD、黑胶唱片）的许可依旧在单作品许可的基础上进行。第一编还建立了一个以市场为导向的“自愿买卖”的费率标准，该标准将适用于第一百一十五条规定的机械许可下的所有音乐作品授权行为。依据第一百一十五条（d）（3）条款，著作权的注册将由一个新建立的机构——机械许可协会——负责总许可的管理以及将收取的版税分发给词曲作者和音乐出版商的工作。机械许可协会以发展和维护一个涵盖音乐作品和录音制品的数据库为任务，这个数据库将对公众开放并且可能是音乐产业中最全面的数据库。在实施新的总许可之前将有一个过渡阶段，该阶段允许数字音乐提供商限制自身的著作权侵权责任，只要他们在鉴定音乐作品版权拥有者上做出了善意且具备商业合理性的努力。此外，第一编修改了选择联邦地区法院法官以裁决面临司法部同意判决书的表演版权组织（比如ASCAP和BMI）提起的市场化费率争议的过程。

“CLASSICS保护与利用”编通过延长对1972年2月15日之前形成的录音作品拥有者的著作权侵权保护，将1972年之前的录音作品部分地置于联邦著作权体系内。针对1972年之前录音作品的未授权使用行为的联邦救济有效期将是作品首次出版后的95年，以最后一年的12月31日为最后一日，此外还有一定的附加期。依据录音作品首次出版的时间规定了不同的附加期：

1923年之前首次出版的作品，额外保护期在2021年12月31日结束。

1923—1946年创作的作品，在通常的95年保护期上延长5年保护期。

1947—1956年创作的作品，在通常的95年保护期上延长15年保护期。

1957—1972年2月15日首次出版的作品，额外保护期在2067年2月15日结束。

第二编采用与1972年之后录音作品相似的法定许可制度，例如非交互式数字流媒体服务的法定许可（包括网络广播、卫星广播和有线电视音乐服务），还建立了未被商业化利用的1972年之前录音制品的合法非商业化使用过程。此外第二编采用了一些现有的关于专有权利的限制以及1972年之前录音作品的使用责任限制的规定，例如第一百零七条（合理使用）、第一百零八条（图书馆和档案馆的复制）、第一百零九条（首次销售）、第一百一十条（特定的公共表演免除责任）、第一百一十二条第（f）款（暂时复制）、第五百一十二条（在线服务提供商的安全港条款）。

“音乐制作人分配”编将音乐制作人与作曲家和艺术家放在同等地位保护，允许他们从依据第一百一十四条规定的法定许可使用音乐作品而支付的版税中获得补偿。收集和分配版权的机构（目前是Sound Exchange）将负责分配版税给制作人的工作。

该法案从2018年10月11日起生效，但其中的部分内容将在美国版权局和利益相关者采取必要的措施后才能应用。

（信息搜集、编译：倪思雨。

资料来源：https://www.copyright.gov/news-net/2018/728.html；https://www.copyright.gov/music-modernization/）

【美国颁布《马拉喀什条约实施法案》】

《马拉喀什条约》于2013年6月27日由世界知识产权组织成员国通过，旨在方便盲人、视障人士或其他印刷障碍人士阅读出版的作品。促使它被采纳的原因是人们普遍认识到一个被称为“书籍饥荒”的问题，即很少有书籍以盲人和视障人士可以阅读的形式出版。这项条约的目标是增加这些人获得印刷材料的机会。

2013年10月2日，美国以缔约国身份签署了《马拉喀什条约》，但在成为该条约成员国之前，美国需要采取更多措施修改本国法律。现行美国《版权法》中已经有一个特殊的例外——《版权法》第

121 条（有时也被称为“Chafee 修正案”），标题是“专有权的限制：盲人或其他残疾人的再生产”。这一法案主要适用于美国国会图书馆为盲人和残障人士提供的国家图书馆服务（NLS）。NLS 成立于 1931 年，目前为暂时性或永久性弱视、失明或身体残疾而无法阅读或持有印刷品的人提供免费的布莱叶盲文和有声读物。通过全国合作图书馆网络，NLS 以布莱叶盲文或音频格式免费邮寄或下载的方式发送材料以达到传播图书和杂志的目的。根据第 121 条，以及经过该条款未涵盖的作品的作者和出版商的许可，国家图书馆可以选择以布莱叶盲文、电子盲文和数字音频格式出版全文书籍和杂志。除了 NLS 外，美国还有其他组织和公司提供这种服务。

2016 年，美国参议院司法委员会和对外关系委员会的工作人员鼓励全国盲人联合会、图书馆版权联盟和美国出版商协会进行谈判以得到所有利益相关方、版权团体、公共利益团体、美国专利商标局和美国版权局的支持。第 2559 号法令第 17 条的修正案旨在履行美国在《马拉喀什条约》下的义务。

第 121 条没有明确授权进口或出口《马拉喀什条约》允许的无障碍格式副本的活动，于是增加了新的第 121A 条以解决这些问题。在《马拉喀什条约实施法案》颁布之前，第 121 条已经允许“授权实体”以“专门为盲人或其他残疾人使用的专门格式”复制或分发以前出版的“非戏剧性文学作品”的副本。但是，为了使第 121 条的某些条款和规定符合《马拉喀什条约》的用语，对第 121 条做了几项修正，使之前后一致：

首先，其中一项修正案将“盲人或其他残疾人”一词及其在上一节 121（d）（2）中的定义改为“符合条件的人”，用来描述那些可能成为可访问格式副本的受益人和用户的个人。为了明确一致地在两个部分中描述这些主体，NLS 将不能根据第 121A 条出口材料，因为《马拉喀什条约》没有类似的规定来确定这些个人是否“符合或可能符合”按照“特定国内法”作为受益人的资格。具体来看，该部分将“符合条件的人”定义为：（A）是盲人；（B）视力障碍或感知或阅读障碍，且无法使其视觉功能改善到与没有此类损伤或残疾的人的视觉功能基本相同，因此对印刷品的阅读程度将无法与没有这种缺陷或残疾的人大致相同的人；（C）由于身体残疾，不能拿或操纵一本书，不能集中或移动眼睛，使其达到通常可接受的阅读程度的人。

该修正案同样将第 121（d）（2）节中的“专门格式”一词及其定义改为“可访问格式”及其定义，并按照《马拉喀什条约》做出定义。所谓“可访问格式”，表示一种可选择的方式或形式，当符合条件的人使用可访问格式的副本或语音记录时，他就可以访问该作品，并被允许像没有这种残疾的人一样方便地访问该作品。

其次，虽然《马拉喀什条约》适用于文本或符号形式的受版权保护的作品，但它规定受保护作品的可访问格式副本应包括“相关插图”。根据该条约，国会的意图是，根据第 121 条和第 121A 条制作的可访问格式副本应当包括插图，这些插图与文本或符号合并成可访问格式。例如，如果教科书包括图表、地图或信息表，教科书的可访问格式版本应当以尽可能可访问的方式包含该信息的表示；如果一本书包括照片或插图附随文本，可访问的格式副本可包括对照片和插图的适当描述。如第 121 条及 121A 条所载文本主题内的插图、图形、地图、表格或照片属于独立的版权作品，则这些作品须受第 121 条及第 121A 条的限制，其程度与受版权保护的作品相同。

此外，授权实体可在受版权保护的作品中引入必要的变更，以使作品以另一种形式可访问，同时考虑到有关人员的可访问性需求。这些变化包括但不限于格式或表现的差异。尽管如此，这些改变不应改变文本的含义或内容。因此，新的第 121A 条中使用的术语，特别是“授权实体”和“合格人员”，旨在适用于域外。

最后，为了根据第 121A 条出口或进口无障碍格式副本，第 121A（c）条要求授权实体“建立并遵循其自身惯例”，以广泛确保其无障碍格式副本的创建、获取和分发服务于符合条件的人。每个被授权实体可以建立第 121A（c）条要求的做法，以适合授权实体自身特定情况的任何方式满足该条款规定的目标，包括但不限于第 121A 条活动的列举。因此，第 121A（c）条的“惯例”除其预期目标外没有统一的规定，第 121A 条既没有制定新的诉讼理由，也没有任何联邦机构就此类授权活动进行监管的依据。与此同时，在设立第 121A 条时，国会没有对标题进行全面分析，以确定在第 121 条或任何其他版权例外或限制下是否可能允许相同或类似的活动。最后，建立符合第 121A 条要求的实践的组织没有义务将这些实践应用于组织与版权作品相关的其他活动。

《马拉喀什条约实施法案》是美国总统特朗普于 2018 年 10 月 10 日签署的。美国现在将着手向世界知识产权组织递交正式加入该条约的文件。在美国正式向世界知识产权组织交存其条约文书之后，美国根据《马拉喀什条约》承担的义务将于 90 天后生效。

（信息搜集、编译：义娟花。

资料来源：https://www.copyright.gov/legislation/CRPT115srpt261.pdf；https://www.copyright.gov/legislation/2018_marrakesh_amendments.pdf；https://www.copyright.gov/legislation/CDOC-114tdoc6.pdf）

【澳大利亚议会通过《2018 年版权法修正案》】

在过去相当长的一段时间里，澳大利亚一直在考虑将其版权法由利用司法监督进行网站拦截修改为不利用司法监督的网站拦截、镜像拦截和搜索结果拦截，并且扩大拦截网站的类型范围。这一系列变化引起了政府部门和科技公司的广泛关注。

澳大利亚政府于 2018 年 10 月份提出了新的立法草案，建议将盗版网站拦截的范围从互联网服务提供商扩展到在线搜索引擎提供商。该法案还涉及更快地封锁镜像站点，减少证明站点在澳大利亚境外托管的负担，不仅将立法扩展到具有“主要目的”的网站，还扩展到具有侵犯版权的“主要效果”的网站。尽管对于《2018 年版权法修正案》（在线侵权法案）一直存在着较大的争议，但澳大利亚议会已正式通过该法案，联邦政府也表示这会使权利人能够更好地打击侵犯版权的行为。

（一）现行的网站拦截制度

网站拦截制度于 2015 年首次实施，该制度载于《2015 年版权法》第 115a 条，该条规定了版权所有者可以向联邦法院申请禁止令，要求互联网服务提供商采取合理的措施阻止用户访问海外盗版网站。因为难以调查在澳大利亚有没有存在侵权者，所以阻止此类网站被视为对版权所有者的有效补救措施。根据该法案第 115a 条，具备以下全部条件，可给予版权所有者禁止令救济：

（1）互联网服务提供商提供了对在澳大利亚境外运营的网站的访问权限；

（2）该网站必须侵犯或帮助侵犯版权；

（3）网站的主要目的必须是侵犯或帮助侵犯版权。

联邦法院在判断是否授予禁止令时需要考虑一些因素，包括网站运营商的行为是否必然发生、网站运营商是否表现出对版权的漠视以及根据比例原则判断是否封锁该网站。

（二）修改原因

首次在法案中引入网络拦截制度时，澳大利亚政府承诺将会在未来的 18 个月内审查其运作效果。该审查一直被推迟到 2018 年初，以便政府有更多的时间收集资料和分析该制度的有效性。

2018 年 2 月，通信和艺术部发布了一份咨询文件，主要就该制度应进行哪些修改以改善其运作向利益相关者寻求意见。该部门表示，利益相关者认为第 115a 条是有效的，自 2015 年以来，澳大利亚的版权侵权程度已经有所降低。但与此同时，利益相关者对该部门审查的反馈也表明，该法案第 115a 条仍然存在一些空白，这限制了该制度发挥作用。因此，政府决定修改该法案，以解决在这次审查中所提出的一些问题。

（三）修改内容

新的修正案规定，如果网站具有侵犯或帮助侵犯版权的“主要效果”，版权所有人将被允许获得禁止令。换句话说，法院判断是否授予禁止令不再需要确定网站的主要目的是实现侵犯版权或帮助侵犯版权，只要侵权或促进侵权效果达到即可。这意味着网站运营者的意图不再是必要的元素，相反，联邦法院可能只是简单地看一下证明侵权结果的证据。修正案的通过也使得搜索引擎提供商具有更多的义务去检查网站是否侵权。

该修正案将盗版网站拦截法律从互联网服务提供商扩展到在线搜索引擎提供商（如谷歌）。针对搜索引擎提供商获得的禁令要求提供商采取联邦法院认为合理的步骤，不提供涉及被阻止网站的搜索结果（仅在澳大利亚范围内，不针对全球）。由于担心在线搜索可能会提供有关访问被阻止网站的替代方法的信息，该法案做出了上述更改。该法案还规定在授予禁止令的情况下，相关的互联网服务提供商或在线搜索引擎提供商可以与版权所有者达成协议，将禁止令的应用扩展到域名、URL 和 IP 地址。

（四）修改争议

澳大利亚通信和艺术部部长米奇·费菲尔德（Mitch Fifield）指出，“在线海盗”未来绕过澳大利亚现有措施的“空间”将大大“减少”。“政府对网络盗版零容忍。这是因为盗窃，会对我们的创意经济和国内创作者造成损害。我们致力于保护澳大利亚的创意产业和我们每年生产的世界级内容。”米奇·费菲尔德部长说，“今天我们的法案通过也向‘在线海盗’传达了一个强烈的信息，即澳大利亚不容忍在线盗窃”。

然而，在一些社会评论中，澳大利亚绿党认为

“网站拦截不是阻止盗版的最有效手段”。绿党指出，“我们承认，虽然该法案旨在解决目前计划中的差距，但扩大网站拦截行为的意外后果是我们所关注的问题，并希望进一步探索以确保言论自由和公众话语不会受到不适当的影响”。

包括 Facebook 和 Twitter 在内的一些公司向委员会表明，通过的版权法修正案“将网站拦截制度扩展到远远超出合理范围”。谷歌也发表意见书强烈反对该法案，因为它将取消联邦法院封锁哪些网站的控制权，而将其交给商业实体。

昆士兰科技大学法学院知识产权与创新法教授马修·里默（Matthew Rimmer）在之前提交给参议院环境与通信常设委员会的提案中，严厉批评了现有的网站拦截制度以及修正案的扩展。该教授指出，澳大利亚的版权制度与美国版权制度密切相关，其中类似的网站拦截立法工作此前已被否定。“鉴于美国国会拒绝了有争议的停止在线盗版法案的网站拦截立法，澳大利亚议会应该同样拒绝修正案中的网站拦截制度。”根据该教授的说法，没有足够的证据表明目前的拦截措施是有效的。他说，可用的证据来自娱乐业，但这好像是新版权法的薄弱区域。里默教授建议废除原有的拦截制度，而不是扩展它。

但是，澳大利亚政府已经考虑了这些担忧，其声称已制定了一般性“保障措施”以防止滥用。新的版权修正案已经通过，此制度是否会被滥用，是否对版权侵权有很大的改善，只能通过澳大利亚政府在今后两年的审查来看，并期望其到时会做出合适的修改。

（信息搜集、编译：陈冉。

资料来源：http://www. mondaq. com/australia/x/758484/Copyright/New＋Australian＋law＋to＋provide＋further＋protections＋for＋copyright＋owners＋to＋block＋offshore＋pirate＋websites；https://torrentfreak. com/australian-parliament-passes-tough-new-anti-piracy-law-181128/；https://www.techdirt. com/articles/20181127/13425541113/australian-parliament-moves-copyright-amendment-out-committee-into-law. shtml；https://torrentfreak. com/copyright-law-professor-urges-australia-to-repeal-site-blocking-laws-181126/；https://torrentfreak. com/aussie-senate-dismisses-concerns-approves-new-tough-anti-piracy-law-181127/）

【西班牙议会通过新的《知识产权法》修正案】

2018 年 11 月，西班牙议会通过了新的《知识产权法》修正案。

新法案允许权利人要求西班牙版权委员会（行政机构）对曾经有过侵权行为的网站运营商或信息服务提供商直接采取行动，以阻止正在发生的侵犯著作权的行为。根据以前的法律，版权委员会有权采取任何必要措施制止侵权行为以达到保护知识产权的目的，这包括施加罚款和下令采取限制性行动的权力。但是，版权委员会的这些措施仅在得到法院批准的情况下适用。

修订后的法律将允许版权委员会在没有法院干预的情况下采取任何必要措施（例如请求删除内容，甚至关闭网站）以阻止涉嫌在线重复侵犯著作权的行为。在英国，知识产权局（IPO）表示正在研究建立“管理性网站拦截”（administrative site blocking），以阻止网络侵权事件的发生。

此外，修法还解决了一系列其他问题，例如，新修正案首次设定了对于图像和图像作品的转售权。同时，法案也明确了有关集体权利管理组织的规则，包括其成员权利、标准关税和津贴分配等。其他的制度变化还体现在对书目参考和新闻评论、版权委员会改革、与欧盟主管部门信息交流制度的规定上。

（信息搜集、编译：蒋海楠。

资料来源：https://www. pexels. com/search/spanish/；https://parlinfo. aph. gov. au/parlInfo/search/display/display. w3pquery＝Id：%22legislation/ems/r6209_ems_b5e338b6-e85c-4cf7-8037-35f13166ebd4%22）

【欧洲掀起《数字化单一市场版权指令》草案的反对浪潮】

超过 400 万的欧盟选民参与签署了反对新《数字化单一市场版权指令》草案的请愿书。根据组织者说，这是在 change. org 网站上发起的最大的一次请愿活动。在 2018 年 12 月 10 日，签署国代表团正式向在法国斯特拉斯堡举行的“三方会谈”（欧洲议会、欧盟成员国和欧洲委员会）的谈判代表提交了要求修改《数字化单一市场版权指令》的请愿名单。名单中的反对者包括“互联网之父”文特·瑟夫（Vint Cerf）、互联网创始人蒂姆·伯纳斯-李以及 70 多位互联网顶尖技术专家，同时也包括了欧洲最大的体育联盟和电影工作室。

《数字化单一市场版权指令》中饱受争议的条款主要是被称为“互联网链接税”的第十一条以及被称为“上传过滤器”的第十三条。第十一条旨在为出版商和报纸提供一种获利的方式，使得他们有权在诸如谷歌这样的公司链接到他们的报道时，向这些公司收取许可费。第十三条要求某些网络服务提供平台，如 YouTube 和 Facebook 等网站停止用户共享未经授权的受版权保护的内容。反对的声音认为，“三方会谈”的谈判者是时候认识到第十一条和第十三条是如此不可行、荒谬和受到普遍憎恶，以至于没有任何挽救的希望。他们应当采取措施将指令（以及欧洲和互联网）从可怕的条款中拯救出来。

《数字化单一市场版权指令》的第十一条授予了出版商权利，使得它们可以从互联网平台对它们出版物的小片段摘录中获得许可费。这一规定的有效性尚存疑问，在德国和西班牙，类似的条款并没有成为出版商的新收入来源。更多的争议则集中在指令的第十三条，该条要求网络平台必须避免受版权保护内容的发布和再发布。人们反对这一条款主要出于两个理由：一是这必将带来版权算法过滤器的创建，而这只有美国的大技术公司才可能负担得起，因而必然会对欧洲的许多互联网公司带来毁灭性打击；二是由于允许用户上传侵犯版权的内容会带来僵化的惩罚，而监控合法材料却没有后果，对于过滤器的使用将无法避免地出现算法的错误甚至滥用。正如 Tumblr 公司最近在过滤成人内容的尝试中所表明的，算法根本不能很好地确定用户何时违反了规则，更不用说像版权这样技术性和事实复杂型的规则了。

在与委员会和议会谈判人员进行最后讨论的文件中，成员国理事会考虑了一些选项，这些选项可以防止权利拥有者简单地阻止对受版权保护材料的使用，从而使向用户发放许可证成为交易的一部分。支持“拯救互联网”活动的 400 万个签名似乎太多了，因而难以被忽视。但欧洲企业观察站（the Corporate European Observatory，CEO）的一项专题研究显示，大量的数据很可能只是被大型游说组织操纵而得的，而非商业性的声音并未受到关注。

2018 年 12 月 13 日，在法国斯特拉斯堡举行的 2018 年最后一次会议上，由于前文提到的备受争议的第十一条和第十三条，欧盟谈判者没能拟定《数字化单一市场版权指令》的最终版本。而“三方会谈”也将在 2019 年上半年继续开展。目前，游说活动在不断进行。一些世界上较大的娱乐和互联网公司将在欧盟四处施压以寻找一种“妥协”，这种“妥协”不仅不会让任何人满意，而且会排斥互联网个体用户和欧洲创新者的需要和权利。

（信息搜集、编译：林文静。

资料来源：https://www. eff. org/deeplinks/2018/12/four-million-europeans-signatures-opposing-article-13-have-been-delivered-european; http://www. ip-watch. org/2018/12/13/four-million-eu-voters-sign-call-upload-filters-protection-snippets/; https://www. eff. org/deeplinks/2018/12/facing-criticism-all-sides-eus-terrible-copyright-amendments-stumble-new-year）

◆ 司法判例

【H&M 身陷街头涂鸦侵权争议】

2018 年 1 月，洛杉矶著名街头艺术家杰森·威廉姆斯（Jason Williams）向 H&M 发出警告信，称这一来自瑞典的快消时尚巨头未经允许，将其原创涂鸦包含在 H&M 产品的广告宣传中。

这一事件的起因，是 H&M 在官网上发布的旗下新品“New Routine”运动服的宣传片中出现了包含街头涂鸦的镜头。该短片摄于纽约市布鲁克林区威廉斯堡的一家手球场，而模特身后的背景正是手球场墙上威廉姆斯创作的涂鸦。威廉姆斯要求 H&M 立即停止使用包含涂鸦图像的广告宣传活动。

作为回应，H&M 向布鲁克林联邦地方法院提起诉讼，称威廉姆斯的涂鸦不在版权保护的范围内，因为它是非法制作的，涉及对纽约市公共财产的非法妨碍和破坏，请求法官判决允许其免费使用该涂鸦。H&M 称其聘请的制作公司在拍摄期间曾向纽约市的公园管理部门征询过是否需要为该涂鸦支付使用费的问题，该部门工作人员当天在回复中表示，涂鸦本不应当出现在墙上，她并不清楚是何人所为。正如美国时装设计师杰瑞米·斯科特（Jeremy Scott）及其时尚品牌 Moschino 在 2016 年的另一起涂鸦侵权案中所辩称的那样，H&M 在本案中也认为，当街头艺术属于妨碍或破坏行为的产物时，就不应当受版权保护。

在现行版权法案中，并无明文规定将非法作品排除于版权保护之外。但不乏学者认为，非法作品不能促进科学和实用艺术的发展，有违美国宪法赋予版权保护的首要目的，因而无法享有版权。值得注意的是，目前几乎所有关于涂鸦侵权的案件，要么达成庭外和解，要么以创作者败诉告终。在司法实践中，涂鸦真正能获得版权的可能性很低。

即使是威廉姆斯的代理律师杰夫·格鲁克（Jeff Gluck）也承认，这一诉讼将冒险进入悬而未决的法律领域。虽然他反对 H&M 方面的观点，但法院的确尚未定论未经许可的涂鸦是否落入版权法的保护范围。

然而，这一版权争议同样止步于和解。2018 年 3 月 15 日，备受舆论压力的 H&M 通过推特宣布撤销对威廉姆斯的诉讼，称“本应采取不同的方式处理这一纠纷”，并强调无意通过此事开创先例，也不愿激化关于街头艺术合法性的争论。

（信息搜集、编译：杨迪菲。

资料来源：http://www.thefashionlaw.com/home/hm-calls-foul-on-vandal-graffiti-artists-threat-of-lawsuit；https://www.nytimes.com/2018/03/15/nyregion/brooklyn-graffiti-hm-lawsuit.html；https://www.highsnobiety.com/p/hm-graffiti-coyright-lawsuit/）

【韩国：将未参与创作的人标注为作者需要承担刑事责任】

韩国几位国立大学的教授没参与撰述，却在真正的作者的同意下将自己列为共同作者——对于他们冒充作者的行为，韩国检察院以“非法出版发行罪”为由对他们提起公诉。《韩国著作权法》第一百三十七条第一款规定的“非法出版发行罪”如下：以他人的真名或假名冒充为作者，公开发表作品，承担刑事责任。本案例的核心问题是真正作者的“同意”是否影响犯罪成立，以及“公开发表”的具体意思。

首先，在作者的同意下将未创作的人标注为作者的行为是否构成“非法出版发行罪”跟犯罪条款设置的目的有关系。大法院判例表明，该规定的目的不仅在于保护真正的作者的人格权，也在于保护社会中一般公众的信赖。所以，即使获得真正作者的同意，将未创作的人标注为作者，也构成犯罪。

其次，该犯罪条款规定：“以他人的真名或假名冒充为作者，公开发表作品，承担刑事责任。”《韩国著作权法》第二条规定了“发表”包括“发行作品”的行为，“发行”是指将作品“复制·发行”。因此，“发表”意味着“复制·发行”。这里的问题在于，“复制·发行”的具体的意思是“复制作品及（and）向公众提供作品”还是“复制或者（or）向公众提供作品”。大法院表明，应该从文义解释、法律修订历史、罪刑法定主义的角度严格考虑“复制·发行”的具体意思：

（1）从文义解释的角度，词典表明“发表”是指“公之于众的行为”，所以，只复制的行为不能单独成为“发表”。“发表”是指将作品“复制·发行”，中圆点（·）一般是表示“还有、及”意思的符号。因此，“复制·发行”的具体的意思是“复制作品及（and）向公众提供作品”。

（2）从法律修订的历史来看，旧著作权法定义了“发行”是指“复制作品及（and）向公众提供作品”，现行著作权法规定为“复制·发行”仅仅是为了简洁，并未有意思上的改变。

（3）从罪刑法定主义的角度来看，对刑法法规不应进行扩大解释或类推解释。因此，考虑将“复制·发行”的意思进行严格解释，如果被告人复制作品及向公众提供作品，则应当认为他们进行了“发表”行为，但是被告人的复制行为不应单独被认定为“发表”行为。

本案中还有一个很有意思的地方，检察院过早地扣押了仓库里的复制书籍并防止其公布，因而阻止了该犯罪完成，法院宣告了被告“无罪”。也许检察院误会了“发表”的含义，发表应当是指复制作品及（and）向公众提供作品，而并非复制或者（or）向公众提供作品。

（信息搜集、编译：魏泰焕。

资料来源：http://glaw.scourt.go.kr/wsjo/panre/sjo100.do?contId＝2246460；https://www.lawtimes.co.kr/Legal-Opinion/Legal-Opinion-View?serial＝141106）

【“不爽猫”赢得 454 万元版权违约金】

据英国《卫报》2018 年 1 月 25 日报道，一只因忧郁表情在网上走红的猫在版权争议案件中获赔 71 万美元（约 454 万元人民币）。

这只原名叫“Tardar Sauce”的“不爽猫”因其一直郁郁寡欢的表情迅速走红，出现这种表情，是猫科动物侏儒症和下牙包含上牙共同导致的。这只猫的受欢迎程度催生了一部圣诞电影、多个电视节目及包括绒布玩具和衣服在内的一系列商品。

在加州联邦法院审理的这起案件中，“不爽猫”有限公司起诉美国咖啡企业 Grenade 违反了使用暴脾气喵星人形象的有关协议条款。

2013 年，咖啡公司 Grenade 的持有人签署了价值 15 万美元（约 96 万元人民币）的合同，合同约定出售印有这只猫的猫脸的冰咖啡饮料。然而，在向法院提交的文件中，“不爽猫”公司的负责人称，Grenade 咖啡公司在销售烘焙咖啡和印有猫脸的 T 恤时公然侵犯了他们的版权和商标权。

Grenade 咖啡连锁店的老板反驳说，“不爽猫”公司并未遵守约定在社交媒体上推广印有猫脸的咖啡直到合同结束。咖啡店还表示，他们得到通知说这只猫将和威尔·法瑞尔（Will Ferrell）及杰克·布莱克（Jack Black）一起出演电影，但实际上这件事从未发生。

法官最终支持了这只“不爽猫”，并下令咖啡公司支付赔偿金以及违约费。

（资料来源：国家知识产权局网站；作者：新华社。

http://www.ncac.gov.cn/chinacopyright/contents/519/358244.html）

【美国法院：深层链接不能规避版权侵权】

深层链接是否构成版权法中专有权利控制的行为在司法实践中长期存在争议。美国法院的一则判例对此给出了肯定的回答，明确深层链接不能使行为人规避版权侵权的责任。2018年2月15日，纽约南部地区法院在贾斯汀·戈德曼（Justin Goldman）诉布赖特巴特（Breitbart）公司等新闻出版商案（以下简称“推特图片案”）中做出认定，通过内嵌式链接使推特（美国社交网络平台Twitter）上发布的帖子（Tweets）显示于自己的网站上，侵犯美国版权法中的展览权（display right），而涉案内容存储于无关第三方的服务器这一事实不能使其规避侵权结果。

2016年7月2日，原告在东汉普顿的街道上抓拍了体育明星汤姆·布雷迪（Tom Brady）与丹尼·安吉（Danny Ainge）的照片。他最初将该照片发布于色拉布（美国社交网络平台Snapchat）上，该照片很快在各社交网络平台上大量传播，一些用户将该照片上传至推特。一些新闻出版商的网站通过内嵌式链接使该照片显示于其报道的文章之中，该文章内容是关于波士顿凯尔特人队是否会成功聘用NBA球星凯文·杜兰特（Kevin Durant），以及汤姆·布雷迪是否会促成此事。于是，原告将这些新闻出版商诉至法院，并声称其对于该照片的版权受到了侵犯。被告在2017年10月5日提交了即决判决的动议，主张提供链接不属于版权法中专有权利控制的行为，因此其不存在版权侵权。地区法院在2018年1月16日听审了双方的口头答辩。凯瑟琳·福里斯特（Katherine Forrest）法官驳回了被告提出的动议并做出了支持原告的简易判决。

福里斯特法官首先强调，版权法的发展应当适应技术的重要变化。美国1976年版权法中对于展览权采取了开放的定义，并没有将其限制于特定的展示设备或方式。专有权利控制的传播行为，既可以是现有技术中所知晓的方式，也可以是将来技术所发展出的方式。立法历史可以对此予以印证。1976年版权法修正案的国会报告指出，技术的进步为版权作品的复制和传播带来了新的方式，立法者不希望将版权的保护范围限制于现有的技术水平。展览权控制的行为包括以任何方式传播图像的行为。版权局在立法听证中也指出，展览权的定义被用于涵盖任何传送、再传送或其他传播的行为。

在“推特图片案”中，虽然被告没有控制或占有涉案照片的来源，但其在文章内粘贴了包含推特HTML指令的一段代码，该主动提供嵌入式链接的行为使涉案照片客观地显示于其网站上，这种传播行为符合美国版权法对于展览权的定义。从版权法的条文和目的来看，物理上占有图像的来源并非侵犯展览权的构成要件。

为了支持深层链接构成侵权的观点，福里斯特法官引用了美国最高法院在2014年判决的美国广播公司诉Aereo公司案（以下简称“Aereo案”）。在该案中，被告采用特殊的技术手段使用户可以通过互联网同时观看电视广播节目，该技术手段使被告并不控制或占有电视广播信号的来源。而美国最高法院仍然认定被告实施的传播行为侵犯版权，其判决意见的核心在于，单纯技术上的区别不能使行为人免于版权侵权的责任。该案的技术手段与嵌入式深层链接存在一定的区别，前者侵犯的是美国版权法中的表演权（performing right），后者侵犯的是展览权，而两者均属于公开传播权的范畴。虽然“Aereo案”和“推特图片案”存在一定的不同，但美国最高法院在“Aereo案”中明确，版权侵权责任不能取决于观众无法感受到的隐形技术手段，从这点来看，提供嵌入式深层链接也应当属于公开传播权所控制的行为。

认定深层链接构成侵权的一个主要障碍是美国司法实践中的服务器标准（server test）。福里斯特法官对该标准自身的正确性予以否定，认为其不符合版权法的条文及其原意。服务器标准来源于联邦第九巡回上诉法院在2007年判决的Perfect 10公司诉亚马逊公司案（以下简称“Perfect 10案”）。在该案中，谷歌的图片搜索功能采取的正是嵌入式链接的技术，使来自第三方服务器的图片以原始尺寸显示于谷歌的网站上，美国法院以服务器标准为由使这种行为免于被认定为展览权所控制的行为。然而，在联邦第九巡回上诉法院的法域范围之外，服务器标准并未受到广泛的认可。在其他的巡回上诉法院中，只有联邦第七巡回上诉法院在2012年判决的Flava公司诉Gunter案中判定深层链接不构成版权侵权，而该案的问题在于被告是否构成帮助侵权，并未涉及被告是否构成直接侵权的问题。不过，该案的地区法院曾明确否定过服务器标准。

纽约南部地区法院曾在四个案件中提到“Perfect 10 案”的服务器标准，但均未予以采纳。三个案件中的深层链接均关于发行权（distribution right，美国版权法中发行权可以适用于网络环境），其分别是 2016 年判决的 Live Face on Web 公司诉 Biblio 公司案、2012 年判决的 My Play City 公司诉 Conduit 公司案和 2013 年判决的 Pearson 教育公司诉 Ishayev 案。关于展览权的案子是 2013 年判决的 Capitol 唱片公司诉 ReDigi 公司案。仅少数的地区法院曾考虑采取服务器标准，如科罗拉多州地区法院在 2016 年的 Grady 诉 Iacullo 案中遵循“Perfect 10 案”，允许证据开示来调查被告是否在其计算机中存储了侵权内容。而得克萨斯州北部地区法院在 2017 年判决的 The Leader's Institute 公司诉 Jackson 案中明确否定了“Perfect 10 案”的服务器标准。

福里斯特法官退一步认为，即使“Perfect 10 案”正确，服务器标准也不能适用于“推特图片案”，并对两个案件予以了区分。在“Perfect 10 案”中，用户主动选择点击缩略图而使图片呈现，谷歌搜索引擎提供的服务仅是在协助用户实施该行为，用户在该过程中具有主要的地位。而“推特图片案”中无论用户是否希望看到照片，被告网站上都完整呈现了照片，这与“Perfect 10 案”存在明显不同。

另外，“推特图片案”的被告提出，原告的主张会严重损害链接技术以及网络的发展。对此，福里斯特法官指出，深层链接构成展览权控制的行为并不必然导致被告承担侵权责任，该案仍存在许多抗辩成立的可能性，如合理使用、“避风港”规则和无辜侵权所导致的损害赔偿限制。原告在其色拉布账号上传涉案图片的行为可能表明其主动放弃版权而使之落入公有领域，不过默示许可规则的适用仍可能存在有待明确的事实问题。

（资料来源：《中国知识产权报》；作者：阮开欣。http://www.nipso.cn/onews.asp?id=40515）

【因法院裁决　免费电子书网站“Project Gutenberg”不接受德国访问】

基于美国网站的免费电子书平台“谷登堡计划”（Project Gutenberg）近期阻止了德国访问者的所有访问。该网站上发布的一份声明表示，这是因在德国提起的一项针对“谷登堡计划”的裁决而做出的。

在德国法院的诉讼中，“谷登堡计划”托管的 18 本书的德国著作权人认为，虽然该网站在美国托管，但因为它可以在德国访问，德国居民也可以下载书籍，所以它仍属于德国法院的管辖范围。并且该网站的部分内容以德语编写，说明其旨在针对德国公民，这进一步确认此案属于德国管辖范围。

对此被告辩称这些作品在美国已不再受版权保护，并且“谷登堡计划”是为美国公民服务的非营利性美国组织，因此该诉讼应该属于美国管辖的范围。

2018 年 2 月 9 日，德国法院支持原告并发布了裁决：规定“谷登堡计划”必须阻止访问这 18 部作品，提供下载这些作品的用户名单，并支付部分原告的法律费用。

“谷登堡计划”不仅阻止访问这 18 部作品，并且决定阻止所有来自德国的访问，这样做是为了防止德国其他版权所有者可能提起的诉讼。对于此次阻止访问，“谷登堡计划”发布了一个疑问解释页面，其中包含有关该诉讼的信息以及为什么德国访问者将被阻止。

“谷登堡计划”首席执行官格雷戈里·纽比（Gregory Newby）博士告诉 Bleeping Computer，尽管显然有人希望只有 18 本书被封锁，但还有其他德国居民支持他们的停止所有德国访问的决定。格雷戈里·纽比还表示，他们将响应这一裁决，并感谢得到的支持。“PGLAF 非常感谢社区群众的参与和支持，这说明来自美国和其他地方的许多人都很重视‘谷登堡计划’的收藏。”对于那些希望能支持“谷登堡计划”上诉的群众，“谷登堡计划”将通过网站接受捐赠。

网站所有者从这场诉讼中得出的结论是：以其他语言代替原语言提供网站内容可能会导致其落入其他国家的管辖范围。虽然“谷登堡计划”提供其他语言是为了非美国访客的便利，但德国法院的裁决清楚地表明，其认为使用德语翻译表示该网站是以德国公民为特别受众的。

随着可以自动将网站翻译成另一种语言的脚本的出现，许多网站所有者利用其为访问者提供便利。虽然这些翻译经常令人感到困惑，并且可能不准确，但网站所有者认为它们仍然可以使其他国家的访问变得便捷。

但因为这样的裁决，网站所有者可能会开始思考如何以其他语言提供网站，以免被其他国家的法律制度束缚。

（信息搜集、编译：赵玲。

资料来源：https://www.bleepingcomputer.

com/news/legal/free-ebook-site-project-gutenberg-blocks-german-visitors-over-court-ruling/）

【甲骨文公司在与谷歌的版权之战中胜出】

甲骨文公司与谷歌公司长达八年的法律斗争仍未停止。从2010年开始，甲骨文针对Java的版权问题向谷歌提出了侵权诉讼。在最近一次可能对软件业产生深远影响的决定中，美国联邦巡回上诉法院做出判决，裁定谷歌在安卓系统中使用Java代码构成了对甲骨文公司版权的侵犯。2018年3月27日，上诉法院推翻了2016年加利福尼亚北部地区法院支持谷歌公司的陪审团裁决和随后的法院判决。联邦巡回上诉法院的三人审判庭已将该案发回地方法院重审以确定赔偿数额，但谷歌仍可以上诉到最高法院。上诉法院的这一裁决意味着谷歌需要为至少十年间它在手机操作系统中使用甲骨文的代码而向甲骨文公司支付数十亿美元。甲骨文已经向谷歌索赔超过八十亿美元的赔偿金，而由于当下安卓系统的使用范围比起2010年甲骨文首次提出诉讼时要广泛得多，所以实际的赔偿金还会更高昂。

本案围绕着应用程序编程接口（以下简称APIs）展开。简而言之，APIs就是不同软件交互的方式。软件公司长期借用现有产品的APIs来确保产品之间的兼容性或使得程序员更易掌握新技术。谷歌使用了部分的Java APIs使得Java的程序员可以在不用学习全新编程语言的情况下设计安卓的APP。现在，采取类似方法的大公司和小公司都会面临大量的版权诉讼。尽管这一裁决不会终止谷歌强大的安卓系统，但是它会迫使许多软件公司重新编写他们的产品，即便他们没有使用Java或者甲骨文的其他软件。这不仅仅会带来昂贵的费用问题，还会使得不同公司的应用程序和服务兼容性变差。换言之，如果上诉法院的判决未能被推翻，就会出现更多技术上的难题和更高的软件费用。

本案中甲骨文和谷歌的争议包含了37项Java API包，甲骨文声称这些API包受到著作权和专利权的保护，而谷歌将它们使用在安卓系统时则没有首先获得甲骨文的许可。谷歌对于使用Java API包的事实并无争议，但是声称这种使用构成合理使用。虽然甲骨文公司声称谷歌逐字抄袭了其受版权保护的内容，但谷歌坚持认为其使用API包是纯功能性的，而且对于编写Java中的程序十分重要。这种使用在实质上是符合美国版权法规定的合理使用和转换性使用的。在本案的一审中，地区法院对谷歌的行为是否构成合理使用没能达成一致。随后地区法院认定由于APIs本质上是功能性的，因而不具有可版权性，并据此判决谷歌胜诉。联邦巡回上诉法院则做出了有利于甲骨文的判决，认为某些Java APIs的声明代码与结构、序列以及组织能够受到版权的保护。谷歌此前曾试图提请美国联邦最高法院审查此案的核心争议，但迄今为止，联邦最高法院还未接受这一要求。

电子前沿基金会的法律主管科瑞尼·麦克谢里（Corynne McSherry）说："这一裁决将会大大刺激律师和'版权蟑螂'提出诉讼。"而甲骨文公司则不这样认为，该公司总法律顾问多里安·戴利（Dorian Daley）称："明确判决谷歌违反法律是对版权法基本原则的维护，这一裁决保护了创造者和消费者免受对他们权利的不法侵害。"

（信息搜集、编译：林文静。

资料来源：https://www.wired.com/story/the-case-that-never-ends-oracle-wins-latest-round-vs-google/；http://www.eweek.com/mobile/google-java-api-use-violates-oracle-copyright-appeals-court-rules）

【盗版网站"漫画村"运营者信息被公布】

2018年4月，一名东京漫画家向东京地方法院请求披露盗版网站"漫画村"的运营商信息，因为他的作品未经许可被公开而遭到版权侵权。这位漫画家的代理人中岛博之律师明确表示，在日本盗版网站"漫画村"的信息披露诉讼中，该网站的服务器提供商Cloudflare公司向原告方漫画家披露了几乎所有的通信记录（通信日志）。在此基础上，"漫画村"实际运营商的身份于2018年10月27日被确认。

中岛博之律师称，根据原告的诉求，Cloudflare在2018年8月披露了通信记录（通信日志），对此分析得出的结果可以确定原本未知的"漫画村"实际运营商。

政府专家委员会已考虑采取措施打击盗版网站，但对于引入强制中断浏览的"断开链接"还存在强烈争议，因此相关的会议被无限期推迟。熟知知识产权管理的专利律师上条由纪子女士说："这是日本第一起Cloudflare被起诉的案件。其中，Cloudflare在披露可以识别运营商的信息方面具有重要意义。这将对打击盗版网站产生一定的影响。"

（信息搜集、编译：钟翘骏。

资料来源：https://www.nikkei.com/article/DGXMZO37021530X21C18A0CC1000/；https://ranq-media.com/articles/3420）

【美国 ABS 娱乐公司诉 CBS 公司：以数字形式重录唱片不产生新的版权】

歌曲的词和曲都受到美国《版权法》保护，但在很长一段时间里，录音制品却不在《版权法》保护范围内。许多州在意识到这一保护漏洞后，纷纷制定了保护录音制品的法律。1971 年《版权法》修订后，录音制品也被纳入其保护范围，但保护对象限于 1972 年及 1972 年以后制作的录音制品。这就使得 1972 年前的录音制品仍然由各州自行立法进行保护。

美国联邦第九巡回上诉法院驳回了加利福尼亚州中区联邦法院所做的支持被告的简易判决，并认定以数字形式重录 1972 年前的唱片无法享有新的版权而获得联邦法律的保护。

本案中，ABS 公司专门聘请录音师将其拥有的 1972 年前录制的几首经典歌曲的模拟录音通过标准技术手段重新录制成数字形式，以完成对模拟录音的精确复制。CBS 公司未经 ABS 公司许可，通过地面无线电广播和网络流媒体播放了上述重新录制的歌曲。对于所广播的内容，CBS 公司均向基础音乐作品的作者支付了版税；对于在网络流媒体上播放的内容，CBS 也依据《录音制品法案》向非营利演出版权组织 Sound Exchange 支付了强制许可费；而对于通过地面电台播放的内容，CBS 没有支付任何许可费。

原告 ABS 公司基于此向加利福尼亚州中区联邦法院提起了集体诉讼，诉称 CBS 公司公开播放其拥有的 1972 年前录制的唱片违反了加利福尼亚州法律。CBS 公司辩称以数字形式重新录制的唱片是合法的具有独创性的衍生作品，仅受《版权法》保护，而不受州法律保护。本案争议焦点在于录音师在保留原作品词曲的前提下，改变作品音色、声音平衡和音量大小且包含个人主观情感和艺术思想的重录行为是否受到《版权法》的保护。CBS 公司的专家证人称此种重录行为具有独创性和审美判断，而 ABS 公司的专家证人则称重新录制的唱片内容与模拟唱片中的相同。地区法院采纳了 CBS 公司的证言，认为重新录制的录音制品是受《版权法》保护的合法衍生作品，并做出了简易判决。ABS 公司不服并提起了上诉。

联邦第九巡回上诉法院指出地区法院未能正确适用可版权性的判断标准，其认为衍生作品获得版权必须符合 Durham Indus. v. Tomy 案中确立的两个标准：第一，衍生作品由作者独创且与原作相比有非常微小的差异；第二，衍生作品作者不得妨碍原作品作者对其作品行使权利。经过分析联邦第十巡回上诉法院和第二巡回上诉法院的判例以及版权局的指南，联邦第九巡回上诉法院做出决定："重新录制的录音制品无法作为衍生作品获得独立的版权保护，除非其具有脱离原著作品的显著特点，从而达到了独立录音制品的标准。"

联邦第九巡回上诉法院指出数字形式唱片并没有增加或删去原曲的音乐，也没有改变音乐排列顺序或是进行重混，其本质上是对原曲的复制，因此不符合《版权法》对作品的要求。上诉法院还指出本案重录行为的目的和效果类似于技术改进，而没有改变录音制品的基本特征，仅仅改变媒体形式无法达到版权保护所要求的最低独创性标准。

（信息搜集、编译：刘慧。

资料来源：https://www. natlawreview. com/article/abs-entertainment-inc-v-cbs-corporation-no-new-copyright-digital-remasters）

【欧盟法院新判决再解"向公众传播"】

2018 年 8 月 7 日，欧盟法院发布的一项判决表明，一个在网络上合法发布的作品，即使没有采取任何技术措施，可以被任何人自由获取，在未经作者许可的情形下，其他网站仍然不得将该作品呈现在自己的页面，否则将侵犯作者享有的向公众传播权。但是，法院承认了在此情形下采用链接传播作品的合法性。

在本案中，原告摄影师德克·仁可霍夫通过一家旅游门户网站公开发布了一张自己的摄影作品，所有人都可以通过该网站免费获取。一名来自德国的小学生从这家旅游网站上下载了此照片，随后该照片作为学生学习作业的一部分被公布在了学校网站上。原告称其仅仅将照片使用权授予旅游网站，该学校在未经其许可的情况下发布该照片的行为侵犯了他的著作权。

欧盟法院的判决重点是被告行为是否构成"向公众传播"（communication to the public）。对此，判例建立的认定规则分为两个步骤，先后对"传播行为"（act of communication）和"公众"（public）进行判断。在判断是否构成"传播"时，通常采取广义解释，不做过多技术形式的限定；在判断向"公众"传播时，则必须产生了著作权人在授权作品传播时所指向的公众范围之外的受众群体，即"新公众"（new public）。

欧盟法院表示，之前的判决已经确定，著作权人有权"干预其作品的潜在用户向其他公众传播的行为”。如果法院认可网站在未经许可的情况下发布在其他网站上经授权发布的版权作品，那么这就“相当于让‘向公共传播权’适用权利用尽原则”，这直接违反欧盟著作权指令的规定，并且将“剥夺权利人因他人使用其作品而获得适当补偿的机会”。

欧盟法院认为，本案中学校的行为“必须被视为向新的公众提供了作品”。“在这种情况下，著作权人最初授权某网站传播其作品时考虑在内的公众仅限于该网站的用户，而不包括其后未经许可发布该作品的网站的用户或者其他互联网用户。”

品诚梅森律所的知识产权专家伊恩·康纳（Iain Connor）表示：“对于著作权人来说，这个案件至关重要，因为它证实了权利人有权控制他人访问其作品，并向使用者收取费用。如果该案件的判决不是这样的，那就意味着网站上第一次发布的图片可以由其他人在未经许可的情况下挪用，从而导致作品的版权价值遭到破坏。”

（信息搜集、编译：杨迪菲。

资料来源：https://www. out-law. com/en/articles/2018/august/copyright-ruling-internet-posting-photos/）

【德国联邦最高法院提请欧洲法院裁定 YouTube 著作权纠纷】

2018 年 9 月 12 日，欧洲议会投票通过新修改的《数字化单一市场版权指令》。仅仅一日后，德国联邦最高法院下达裁决，将 YouTube 因用户上传侵权内容而被诉侵权一案呈交至欧洲法院，并就“向公众传播”与“避风港”条款等法律概念提请欧洲法院解释。

在此时点，这一案件有着特殊的意义。首先，刚获初步通过的《版权指令》第十三条对“在线分享内容服务提供商”施以著作权审查义务，YouTube 首当其冲，这使得其责任承担成为一个亟待厘清的问题。其次，本案与欧盟法院依据现行著作权法确立的典型判例“The Pirate Bay”“Filmspeler ”等密切相关。德国音乐产业协会的董事会主席弗洛里安·德鲁克（Florian Druecke）表示：“该决定反映了我们长期以来要求解决的问题的法律复杂性。”在此背景下，欧洲法院的裁决十分值得关注。

本案中，原告的身份是一名音乐制作人，享有歌手莎拉·布莱曼（Sarah Brightman）的音乐专辑《真爱永恒——冬之歌》（*A Winter Symphony*）的著作权。2008 年 11 月初，使用假名的用户未经原告同意将专辑中的歌曲以及演唱会录音上传至 YouTube。毫无疑问，用户的这一上传行为构成对著作权的侵犯。在用户身份无法确定的情况下，原告向 YouTube 发出侵权通知。作为回应，YouTube 屏蔽了部分视频，但随后这些视频很快又重新出现。最终，原告将 YouTube 诉至法院，并寻求禁令救济，要求其披露用户信息并支付损害赔偿。

初审的德国汉堡地方法院批准了原告关于三个视频的禁令救济请求。在上诉过程中，汉堡地方高级法院还准许对另外四个视频授予禁令。同时，原告要求披露上传者信息的主张也获得认可。但在其他方面，尤其是损害赔偿责任方面，原告的主张均被驳回。法院认为 YouTube 并未实施任何侵犯著作权的行为。

与此同时，德国联邦最高法院决定暂停诉讼程序，将本案中涉及新法解释的几个重要问题提请欧洲法院解答，如“向公众传播”以及《电子商务指令》（E-Commerce Directive 2000/31/EC）第十四条规定的对网络托管服务商责任豁免的理解。欧洲法院须回答的具体问题如下：

（1）用户未经权利人许可将现有版权作品发布在网络视频平台上，而平台对违法内容不知情，或在意识到侵权后迅速删除侵权内容或断开其访问，那么该平台是否实施了《信息社会指令》（InfoSoc Directive 2001/29/EC）第三条中的向公众传播行为？回答这个问题时，需要考虑到以下情形：

1）该平台从广告中获益，且侵权内容的上传未经平台任何管控或审查程序；

2）在视频上线期间，平台根据服务条款获得该视频在全球范围内非排他性的免费许可；

3）在服务条款和用户上传过程中，平台已提醒用户禁止上传侵犯第三方著作权的内容；

4）平台为权利人提供了删除侵权内容的机制；

5）平台将视频按照分类向用户展示，并依据观看记录向其推荐更多相关视频。

（2）《电子商务指令》第十四（1）条对网络托管服务商设置的责任豁免是否适用于本案中的视频平台，以及条文中的“对违法行为或信息知情”和“意识到显然存在违法活动或信息的事实或情况”，是否必须指向具体的违法活动或信息？

（3）如果只有在发出明确侵权的警告后再次发生侵权行为时，权利人才能获得禁令，该情况是否符合《信息社会指令》第八（3）条的规定？

（4）如果前三个问题的答案是否定的，根据欧盟《执法指令》（Enforcement Directive 2004/48/

EC）第十一（1）和十三条，该视频平台是否须承担侵权损害赔偿？

值得一提的是，德国联邦最高法院也表明了对本案的倾向性意见，即 YouTube 不存在独立的著作权侵权行为，平台应当受欧盟《电子商务指令》中“避风港”条款的保护。

（信息搜集、编译：杨迪菲。

资料来源：https://www.jdsupra.com/legal-news/german-federal-court-of-justice-submits-78547/；http://www.chinaipr.gov.cn/article/internationalupdates/201809/1926630.html）

【草裙舞的著作权获日本法院认可】

在日本，尽管著作权法将“舞蹈作品”作为作品的例证，但就舞蹈编排所产生的著作权纠纷并不多。2018 年 9 月 20 日，在一位居住于夏威夷的草裙舞（Kumu Hula）编舞导师 Kapu Alquiza 对九州夏威夷协会提起的著作权（表演权）侵权案中，大阪地区法院对以下五首歌曲关于使用原告舞蹈的编排发出禁令，并判决被告方承担约 43 万日元（约 28 000 元人民币）的损害赔偿金。

五首歌曲分别是：*E Pili Mai*；*Lei Ho'ohen*；*Ua Lanipili I Ka Nani O Papakōlea*；*Blossom Nani Ho'i e*；*Mauna leo*。

通过案情可知，Kapu Alquiza 大约从 1984 年开始指导该协会成员舞蹈。直至 2014 年 10 月，协议终止后，她要求协会不得再继续使用她曾教授过的舞蹈编排。然而，协会没有理会其诉求并在草裙舞课堂和相关活动中继续使用相关舞蹈编排。该协会在法庭上辩称，草裙舞的编舞缺少独创性，因为其选择单一，仅仅是现有动作的排列组合。

草裙舞的编舞包含了能传达歌词含义的手部动作以及舞步，法院认为“草裙舞是一系列由体现编舞者个性与不体现编舞者个性的两个部分所组成的有节奏的动作（a series of flows）”，“从完整的一系列节奏动作中来认定编舞的著作权是合理的，能体现编舞者个性的部分在一定程度上会在其中显现”。法院同时指出，当一个表演中的节奏动作不仅包括体现编舞者个性的部分，而且还包括不体现个性的部分时，同样会产生侵犯著作权的问题。

本案中，九州夏威夷协会本应该更加小心，因为它已经得知草裙舞导师不希望她的编舞教学在协议终止后继续被使用。

由于编舞的著作权侵权认定并不容易，所以对于编舞者而言，无论是否发布自己的舞蹈编排，都应该将它记录下来以便于证明创作日期，防止将来卷入著作权纠纷中。

此外，在此前的交谊舞编舞（使用于电影 *Shall We Dance？* 的编舞）著作权的侵权案件中，法院以缺乏显著性和独创性为由，认定该编舞不享有著作权。

（信息搜集、编译：钟翘骏。

资料来源：http://japanip.blogspot.com/；http://japanip.blogspot.com/2018/10/japanese-court-finds-copyright.html？m=1）

【欧洲法院裁定澄清非法文件共享的举证责任】

2018 年 10 月 18 日，欧洲法院针对此前德国法院的一项争议裁决做出裁定。根据此裁定，如果被认定为非法文件共享的当事人想要避免承担侵犯版权的责任，他就必须证明与其有互联网连接（internet connection）的另一个用户应该承担责任。当该涉嫌侵权者寻找证明自己清白的证据时，不能仅仅提供访问其互联网的用户姓名，还应当提供诸如“与使用这种互联网连接的时间和性质有关的”细节。

裁定所针对的争议系一部有声读物（audio book）被非法共享而引起的版权争议，侵权者通过点对点互联网交换机供“无限量用户”下载该有声读物的副本。经追溯，迈克尔·斯特罗泽（Michael Strotzer）的互联网连接的 IP 地址被确定为非法文件共享的来源，因此，权利人 Bastei Lübbe 起诉斯特罗泽侵犯版权，但斯特罗泽声称他不对侵权行为负责，而且他的互联网连接非常安全。斯特罗泽确认他的父母是他的互联网连接的其他潜在用户，但他父母的计算机上并没有该文件，也并不知晓该文件的存在。

欧洲法院在此裁定中审查了德国判例法及其与欧盟版权法的兼容性。根据德国判例法的规定，如果互联网连接被确定为涉嫌侵犯版权的来源，则该互联网连接的所有者将被推定为对被指控的行为负责，除非他们的互联网连接不安全或被其他人故意使用。涉嫌侵权的互联网连接所有者可以举证证明另一个人能够独立访问其互联网连接，从而实施版权侵权行为，且举证不要求提供拥有此类访问权限的家庭成员的姓名以外的更多信息和细节。然而，欧洲法院在此裁定中表示：欧盟版权法，包括有关知识产权执法的规则，要求互联网连接所有者提供有关家庭成员使用其连接的更多信息；根据欧盟的版权制度，只要求提供家庭成员姓名的国家法律“被排除”。

“欧洲法院的此项将非法文件共享的举证责任转

移给网络连接所有者的裁定似乎是一项具有突破性的决定，但仍然可能被视为符合德国判例法。”慕尼黑法律专家伊戈尔·巴拉巴什（Igor Barabash）如是评价。

（信息搜集、编译：谭博迈。

资料来源：https://www.out-law.com/en/articles/2018/october/eu-ruling-burden-of-proof-illegal-file-sharing/?articleId=45589；http://curia.europa.eu/juris/document/document.jsf?docid=206891&text=&dir=&doclang=EN&part=1&occ=first&mode=DOC&pageIndex=0&cid=2777517）

【Spotify 与 Wixen 达成和解终结巨额诉讼】

Spotify（声田，是一家瑞典的流媒体音乐服务公司，也是当前全球最大的流媒体音乐服务商，提供包括环球音乐集团、索尼音乐娱乐、华纳音乐集团全球三大唱片公司及众多独立唱片公司所授权、由数字版权管理保护的音乐）与 Wixen 之间的巨额版权侵权诉讼尘埃落定。2018 年 12 月 20 日，Spotify 公司在声明中表示，和解的达成标志着双方更广泛的合作伙伴关系的确立，这一方面公平合理地解决了在受版权保护作品许可方面既有的法律争议，另一方面也建立了长远的双赢局面。Wixen 的总裁兰德尔·维克森（Randall Wixen）也在新闻稿中向 Spotify 公司表示感谢，并表明希望通过 Spotify 这个重要平台为公众带来更多音乐作品，让音乐创作者和发行商受益。

事情最早可以追溯到 2017 年底，总部位于美国洛杉矶的音乐发行商 Wixen，在加利福尼亚州向 Spotify 的 CEO——丹尼尔·艾克（Daniel Ek）提起诉讼，声称其未经任何许可，在 Spotify 平台上非法使用前者的过万首歌曲，并将部分作品外包给第三方，其中包括热门歌手汤姆·佩蒂（Tom Petty）、尼尔·杨（Neil Young）和大门乐队（Doors）的作品。Wixen 以每首歌曲 15 万美元的“故意侵犯版权补偿费”，提出至少 16 亿美元赔偿的诉求。

这场官司在《音乐现代化法案》的议案公开后不久即被提起，Wixen 公司一方有自己的考虑。尽管 Wixen 称赞了美国国家音乐出版商协会（NMPA）帮助立法的工作，但该公司反对新的许可机制和版权集体管理条款。因为一旦该法案成为法律，将会使得出版商起诉 Spotify 等流媒体平台侵权变得困难。Wixen 早在 2018 年 1 月的一份声明中就表示：“非常遗憾，这项法案剥夺了我们起诉流媒体未经许可非法使用我们歌曲的权利。除非我们能在 2018 年 1 月 1 日之前提起诉讼，否则以前的这些非法行为，将会获得法律的免费通行证。”

这并非 Spotify 首次卷入版权争议，但之前的数次争议也多以和解告终。2015 年，由音乐人戴维·洛厄里（David Lowery）和梅利莎·费里克（Melissa Ferrick）牵头，Spotify 在一宗集体诉讼中被控告侵害歌手利益，其被要求赔偿 1.5 亿美元。巧合的是，Wixen 也是当时的共同原告之一。2018 年 5 月，Spotify 以总值 1.125 亿美元的和解金平息了事件，其中 4 350 万美元会即时发放，其余的会作为授权费用和其他费用来支付。

有着大量用户的音乐流媒体已经成为音乐产业的重要部分。版权争议缠身的 Spotify 公司仍于 2018 年 4 月顺利挂牌在纽交所上市。与借力投行的一般上市路径不同，Spotify 选择跳过认购环节，直接进入股权拍卖环节。如此“大胆”的背后力量是其全球 7 000 万付费用户。传统发行商们向 Spotify 等流媒体的妥协，其实也是向更广阔市场的妥协。

虽然双方和解的金额不得而知，但最终金额不太可能达到最初 Wixen 所追讨的 16 亿美元，否则现在已经上市的 Spotify 负有对股东的披露义务。

（信息搜集、编译：杨迪菲。

资料来源：https://www.musicbusinessworldwide.com/spotify-sued-for-1-6bn-by-wixen-in-huge-copyright-infringement-lawsuit/；https://www.musicbusinessworldwide.com/spotify-settles-with-wixen-bringing-1-6bn-lawsuit-to-an-end/；https://www.cnet.com/news/spotify-reportedly-ends-1-6-billion-copyright-lawsuit-with-wixen/）

【欧盟法院做出裁定：食物的气味不受著作权法保护】

2018 年 11 月 14 日，欧盟法院裁定气味不受著作权法的保护。这份裁定需要引起我们的重视，因为这是欧盟法院第一次直接阐述什么样的对象才能构成著作权法意义上的作品。因此可以预见，欧盟法院在该案件中的相关表述将会在未来有关著作权保护对象的案件中被广泛引用。

该案件可以简单概括为：荷兰奶酪生产商 Levola Hengelo 声称其竞争对手 Smilde 抄袭了自己公司特制的“Heksnkaas”（奶酪酱）的味道，并认为这是侵犯著作权的行为。奶酪生产商 Levola Hengelo 公司在其主张被荷兰一审法院驳回后提起上诉，荷兰二审法院（Arnhem-Leeuwarden Court of Appeal）向欧盟法院就食物的味道是否受著作权保护提出关于初审判决的咨询。

在该案件中，Levola Hengelo 公司认为“Heksnkaas”（奶酪酱）的气味就是作者具有独创性的表达，且在欧盟法院没有把气味排除在著作权法保护对象之外的前提下，这种不具有视听性的成果应该构成作品。关于对气味的个人主观性，Levola Hengelo 公司认为每件艺术品都是主观的。用康德的话来说，即“真理存在，但我们无法知道”，缺乏准确定义气味或味道的能力不是拒绝根据欧盟法律保护气味的客观理由。被告 Smilde 公司认为气味不适用于著作权制度。这是因为气味本身是不稳定的，在不同的生产日期下、不同的温度下，不同的人群会产生不同的感知体验，法官无法对气味进行客观的判断。考虑到这种个人体验的不确定，Smilde 公司认为给予气味保护对整个社会来说是不可取的。一方面，这会导致权利被滥用的垄断，从而损害小企业的利益；另一方面，它会遏制创新，与知识产权法的立法精神相违背。

在荷兰法院向欧盟法院进行相关咨询的同时，法国和英国也就此案件向欧盟法院阐明了自己的看法。法国在承认《伯尔尼公约》中对于有关作品类型的条款是一种描述性说明而非封闭式列举的同时，认为气味因不具有独创性而不受到著作权法保护。主要理据是，欧盟法院曾在有关裁判中表明，著作权的对象应该能够以客观和明确的方式描述，而气味是无法被客观、明确地描述的。英国的观点有些不同，其认为《伯尔尼公约》第二条第六款是对作品类型的穷尽列举。如果欧盟法院认为该条款并非穷尽列举，那么也只适用于可见或可听作品。参考思想表达二分法，对作品的保护不应该延及思想，那么对配方的保护不该延及气味。如果授予气味著作权法的保护，那么也会带来如何客观地比较两种气味，如何认定侵权行为等一系列的问题。

欧盟法院最终的裁定简洁明了。法院认为的著作权法下的作品应该“具有足够精确性和客观性”。食品的气味取决于变幻的味觉感受和个人的主观体验，这种气味在如今还无法通过科技的手段客观地识别。气味的主观性导致法律上的不确定性，也就缺乏相应的客观性，因此，“Heksnkaas”（奶酪酱）的味道不是受著作权法保护的作品。

（信息搜集、编译：蒋海楠。

资料来源：https://www.jdsupra.com/legalnews/cjeu-pokes-holes-in-copyright-50150/；http://copyrightblog.kluweriplaw.com/2018/06/26/heksnkaas-cjeu-end-cheese-war-beginning-new-copyright-era/；https://www.out-law.com/en/articles/2018/november/taste-of-food-copyright-ruling/；https://europeanlawblog.eu/tag/information-society-directive-directive-200129ec/）

◆ 业界动态

【日本卡通形象熊本熊版权新规正式实施】

2018 年 1 月 8 日，风靡全球的日本卡通形象熊本熊（酷 MA 萌）版权新规正式实施。新规中，首次允许日本境外企业独立参与熊本熊形象的授权申请。申请成功后，企业支出 5%～7%的版权费即可使用。版权授权是熊本熊提高自身形象知名度和影响力的有力策略，在面对海外广阔市场时，熊本熊再一次秀出了“高情商”。借由版权新规，构建熊本熊形象与品牌产品的紧密联系，正是让熊本熊走向世界的推动力，也是使品牌和形象双赢的有力保证。

熊本熊原是 2010 年日本的熊本县为庆祝该地接入九州新干线而推出的吉祥物。为推广该地旅游业，它还被任命为熊本县营业部部长兼幸福部部长。其形象的构成，仅靠外观形象的设计和一系列营销事件，并不像传统卡通形象有漫画、电影、动画甚至故事书等文化产品实体作为承载。然而短短几年时间，熊本熊是如何风靡日本全国甚至走出国门火遍全球，成为使熊本县闻名于世界的第一推动者的？除了外形的呆萌和最初为塑造形象而进行的事件营销外，非常重要的一点是熊本熊形象所使用的特殊版权策略。

熊本县在推出熊本熊这一形象时，为了扩大宣传，对于熊本熊在日本境内的一切商业授权，均采取免费政策。只要获得县政府的许可，就可以免费获得熊本熊的商用权限。熊本县在日本国内以高质量的农副产品著称，这一策略让熊本县大量农副产品企业纷纷将熊本熊印在产品外包装上，呆萌憨实的小熊在促进了销量的同时，也渐渐建立起了自身的知名度，首先在日本本土获得了成功。代表熊本县的熊本熊和熊本县的农产品之间天然的联系，让二者的关系更加紧密，熊本熊成为熊本县产品的最好代言人。熊本熊“无私帮助”本土品牌，也实现了自身影响力的提升，可谓双赢。

但熊本熊的“高情商”并不限于本土影响，随着熊本熊的影响力逐渐扩大，带有熊本熊设计的产品，从刚开始的农产品逐渐变得更高端、更国际范。在包括德国宝马 MINI Cooper、日本本田摩托、德国泰迪熊等在内的产品上，都能看到熊本熊的身影。

申请授权的商品从 2011 年的 3 600 件上升至如今的 20 000 件，在为熊本县带来了可观经济收益的同时，也加快了熊本熊成为“世界知名熊”的步伐。熊本县也曾表示，此次开放海外产品授权，是为了扩大海外影响力，相应收入也将用于品牌维护。更为重要的是，其独辟蹊径，正一步步实现让熊本县知名于世界的初衷。

（资料来源：《中国知识产权报》；作者：昱知。）

【欧盟委员会发布打击在线非法内容的建议】

2018 年 3 月 1 日，欧盟委员会通过了一份有关有效监测在线非法内容的措施的建议。发布这项建议的主要目的与规范托管服务提供商的服务有关。众所周知，托管服务提供商在在线实施包括版权在内的权利中扮演着重要的角色。根据 3 月 1 日的建议，欧盟委员会加强了各种倡议框架内的相关措施。

该建议设定了一项基本原则，即线下非法的内容线上也是非法的，因此如果不符合欧盟及其成员国法律的任何信息在现实世界中是非法的，那么其在数字世界中也是非法的。

该建议使欧盟委员会在打击在线非法内容方面向前迈进一步，因为它正式地界定了企业和成员国应采取的可行性措施，即通过响应或者主动的措施（例如使用自动检测非法内容的工具）来侦测和删除非法内容。具体而言，该建议重申了《电子商务指令》（第 2000/31/EC 号指令）中的规定，即成员国对托管服务提供商所储存的非法内容具有注意义务。在采取“有效、适当且相称”的措施来阻止——并在可能的情况下防止——在线观看非法内容时，应考虑到所有的基本权利，特别是《欧盟基本权利宪章》所保障的所有基本权利，包括知识产权，并考虑目前技术发展的现状。

根据欧盟法院的判例，欧盟委员会重申道，托管服务提供商应从所涉主题中（以不同的方式）注意非法内容，就报告而言，应根据每个案件的具体特点对报告的准确性进行分析。这意味着，在侵犯知识产权的情况下，提供商收到的信息可能与所需的信息大不相同。为了确保托管服务提供商活动的透明度，它们应定期发布有关其删除非法内容或者其阻止访问含非法内容的网站等活动的报告，并向欧盟委员会提交具体的有关其监测活动的报告。欧盟委员会希望全面打击在线非法内容，因为此类内容通常从一个托管服务提供商转移到另一个托管服务提供商，执法人员应分享经验和技术解决方案。

最后，相当重要的是，欧盟委员会发布此建议的目的还在于影响所有托管服务提供商的活动，无论它们是在欧盟还是在第三国建立的，只要它们的活动是针对在欧盟境内居住的消费者。

（资料来源：http://ipr.mofcom.gov.cn/article/gjxw/gbhj/om/oum/201804/1919787.html）

【CPTPP 协定里的知识产权条款仍具有积极意义】

美国战略与国际研究中心（CSIS）称，尽管美国退出《跨太平洋伙伴关系协定》（TPP）之后，该协定进行了一些修正（知识产权章节有所缩减），但是《跨太平洋伙伴关系全面进步协定》（CPTPP）的知识产权章节所提供的标准仍是目前贸易协定中最详尽且最先进的。

2018 年 3 月 8 日，CSIS 针对 CPTPP 公布了一系列“批判性问题”。详情请参见以下链接：https://www.csis.org/analysis/tpp-cptpp。

CSIS 指出，“TPP 里的 22 项条款被搁置或修改，根据原来的协商，美国需要优先考虑却未得到其他 TPP 成员国支持的事情被搁置一旁。”

CSIS 称，根据修正后的知识产权章节的规定，“创新药物的专利保护期以及版权材料的版权保护期均被缩短，对技术和信息的保护范围缩小”。修正后的协定还对投资者—国家争端解决条款的覆盖范围提出了怀疑。

CSIS 认为这些修正不利于美国企业的发展或与美国的法律不一致：“与 TPP 相比，被搁置的条款在一定程度上缩小了 CPTPP 的范围和影响。尤其是在知识产权章节，美国在技术保护措施（TPM）、权利管理信息、加密卫星和电缆信号以及针对互联网服务提供商（ISP）的安全港规则方面的苛刻要求已被移除。”

CSIS 补充道：“缩短创新药物的专利保护期对于美国的制药公司而言是一种打击。较短的版权保护期目前已经偏离了美国的标准。在投资章节，与投资协定和投资授权相关的条款搁置的决定意味着此类投资将不会涵盖在投资者—国家争端解决条款中，因此这对于外国投资者来说比较危险。”

然而，CSIS 称：“尽管这些条款被搁置，但修正后的知识产权章节所提供的标准仍是目前贸易协定中最详尽且最先进的。它将为在国外运营的企业提供实质性的帮助，以防止其创新被剽窃。”

CPTPP 正在由 11 个亚太经济体磋商：澳大利亚、文莱、加拿大、智利、日本、马来西亚、墨西哥、新西兰、秘鲁、新加坡和越南。美国在 2017 年退出 TPP。

CSIS 称，TPP 的多数内容仍然原封不动，在 CPTPP 的 30 个章节中，2/3 的章节仍与 TPP 的条款保持一致。

CSIS 指出了两个积极的方面：第一，根据电子商务章节的规定，通过数字贸易创造的数据会受到广泛的保护，跨境信息的自由流动也会受到保护。第二，政府采购章节向国外投标人开放政府合同。

（资料来源：http://ipr.mofcom.gov.cn/article/gjxw/jlhz/bqjlhz/201803/1918326.html）

【埃及为改善知识产权保护与执法创建数据取证试验室】

2018 年 3 月 14 日，埃及政府宣布建立一个专门的知识产权数据取证试验室，以此打击软件盗版。

该试验室是中东和北非地区的首个此类试验室，主要用于分析企业软件与互联网盗版案件。试验室从数字设备中真实地获取数据，发现新的诈骗技术。

此项最新措施旨在提高调查能力，使数据证据的获取、分析与通报更加容易。

试验室的前沿技术为法官、检察官和律师设计了路线图，用于指导他们区分正品与假冒产品以及成功处理手头的知识产权和数字盗版问题。

埃及信息技术产业发展机构（ITIDA）是埃及信息通信技术部实施与软件产品和数据库相关的知识产权的执行机构。上述试验室由该机构托管。

ITIDA 知识产权负责人穆罕默德·赫加齐（Mohamed Hegazy）表示："在过去两年中，ITIDA 的知识产权办公室与所有利益相关方一起采取了促进知识产权执法的各种行动，法官与检察官、警察以及版权权利人都参与其中。"

为了培养必要的技能，知识产权办公室在 2017 年为 900 多名警察、来自国家广播机构的 97 名记者、来自不同软件企业的 125 名员工以及来自经济法院的 473 名法官与检察官提供了专门的法律、技术和实践培训。

赫加齐说："我们旨在维护在打击知识产权侵权与发展知识产权方面取得的成果。实现此类目标，试验室将助我们一臂之力。仅在 2017 年，我们就向经济法院递交了 96 起案件的专门技术报告，注册了 203 份计算机软件并首次颁发了 267 项许可。"

根据商业软件联盟委托市场调查公司 IDC 制作的《2016 年全球软件盗版研究报告》，埃及盗版率为 61%，低于大部分的竞争国，摩洛哥为 65%，菲律宾为 67%，越南为 78%。

埃及国家媒体报道称，埃及内阁正在准备数据保护与隐私法草案，并且已经就网络犯罪法达成一致，现正等待议会审批。

埃及的各大领域正在经历前所未有的发展，合理的政策、货币改革以及全球合作功不可没。

埃及技术创新与初创企业生态系统均保持良好发展势头，信息通信技术部已于 2016 年开始实施自由开放的软件战略。

新通过的软件许可政策是一项重大的知识产权规则调整，埃及在为软件制作与创新构建健康生态系统的同时制定了新的软件许可模式。

（资料来源：http://ipr.mofcom.gov.cn/article/gjxw/zfxd/fzzfxd/201803/1918300.html）

【国际作者和作曲者协会联合会：著作权"避风港"规则扰乱创作市场】

著作权保护领域中确立的"避风港"规则，旨在保障网络服务提供者免于承担内容侵权责任，从而促进互联网信息的自由传播。但是，2018 年 3 月 22 日国际作者和作曲者协会联合会（The International Confederation of Societies of Authors and Composers，CISAC）发布的《"避风港"规则的经济学分析报告》却指出，"避风港"规则"扰乱了数据市场，让技术巨头谋取巨大利益，而著作权人却难以获得应有的版权收入"。

该报告经 CISAC 委托，由来自得克萨斯州立大学的斯坦·利博维茨（Stan Liebowitz）教授主导撰写。报告评估了著作权法中的"避风港"规则如何损害了著作权人的合法利益。"避风港"规则在 25 年前诞生，其目的是促进早期网络商业的发展。

CISAC 总干事加迪·奥龙（Gadi Oron）称，"这个研究说明了著作权'避风港'规则是为 20 世纪的互联网所立下的规定，它并不能适应 21 世纪互联网的发展，亟须重新修正。设立'避风港'规则的原本目的是为了保护提供储存服务的互联网公司，而如今的'避风港'规则实际上在为技术巨头不付作者版权费提供合法借口。这个问题仅靠行业本身是无法解决的，这更是政府文化和创新部门的责任。21 世纪的法律应该保障创作者们获得合理报酬的权利，而不是让他们的创作价值被环球技术公司全部攫取。技术变革已经发生，法律也应当随之改革"。

根据《"避风港"规则的经济学分析报告》，利博维茨教授等人的研究成果包括：

（1）基于"避风港"规则，提供用户上传内容服务的网站（如 YouTube 等）在用户内容版权许可费的谈判桌上有着“不对称且不公平的优势”。

（2）因此，这些提供上传内容服务的网站或无须支付版权许可费，或支付的费用低于市场价格。

（3）其他网络服务商（如提供订阅服务的Spotify和Apple Music）在面对内容上传网站平台时，则处于竞争劣势。由于“避风港”规则的不利影响，这些服务商的营业额比内容上传网站低，用户基础也更薄弱。

（4）最终的后果是，“避风港”规则在整个创作市场上导致的连锁不良影响使得著作权人从内容上传网站和订阅服务网站获得的版权费用都在减少，而且是“大规模”的减少。

（信息搜集、编译：梁锐。

资料来源：https://www.ip-watch.org/2018/02/28/authors-group-study-copyright-safe-harbour-provisions-distort-market/；http://www.cisac.org/Newsroom/News-Releases/Gadi-Oron-Appointed-Director-General-of-CISAC）

【日本：产品销售中使用公共领域作品可能侵犯作者人格利益】

2018年8月，日本市场上出现了一种猴面包树幼苗的产品，该产品的包装上标有“小王子”的字样，同时印刷着《小王子》的原版插画与猴面包树的小故事。

包装上的小故事把猴面包树隐喻为恐惧的象征，这种负面的情绪可能会摧毁小王子故乡所在的恒星。而《小王子》一书中的猴面包树代表什么，这是见仁见智的问题。中国古语有云：“勿以恶小而为之，勿以善小而不为。”大概最能体现小王子与猴面包树的故事。《小王子》出版于1943年，伴随一代又一代人成长，70多年来经久不衰。好的作品就是有这样的魅力，一千个读者眼中有一千个哈姆雷特，每个人都可以读出自己的感悟。因此，猴面包树幼苗产品的市场营销人员也非常尊重《小王子》日本忠实粉丝的意见，该产品在售卖两天后停止销售。

《小王子》的书迷不接受这样一部艺术作品用作商业活动，因此该产品一经公开就遭到粉丝们的猛烈抨击。与此同时，此种营销手段也受到著作权的非难。尽管《小王子》的著作权保护期限早已届满，但此种营销手段存在侵犯插画作品的著作权和作者人格权的风险。

该产品停止销售的原因可能与日本《著作权法》中的作者人格权规定有关。主要观点有以下两点：

（1）《小王子》的作品和插图在日本的著作权保护期已届满。

《小王子》的插画是作者圣·埃克苏佩里（Saint Exupery）本人画的。因此插画的著作权在作者1944年去世50年后即告失效。此外，因为圣·埃克苏佩里是《伯尔尼公约》成员国国民，所以《小王子》的著作权保护期限在第二次世界大战期间延长了9年。

因此，我们认为《小王子》的日本著作权保护在2004年左右到期。然而，与圣·埃克苏佩里有关的协会拥有相关的注册商标，例如日本的“Le Petit Prince/星の王子さま”，如果要在某些商品或服务上使用“Le Petit Prince”或“星の王子さま”商标，必须首先获得许可。商标使用许可须视使用标志的特定商品或服务而定。

（2）日本《著作权法》除了为作者提供著作权保护外，还为作者的人格权提供了保护（而美国版权法没有保护这项权利）。

作者的精神权利是作者所独有的，原则上，作者死后便不享有该权利。但日本《著作权法》第六十条对作者死亡后的精神利益给予了保护，该条禁止个人以损害作者生前的精神权利的方式提供或呈现作者的作品。在日本，尽管有著名小说家夏目漱石（Natsume Soseki，1867—1916）的家属提起关于作者人格权的诉讼，但还尚未有法院做出在作品的著作权保护期满后使用作品会侵犯作者人格权的裁决。

上述事件表明，在没有有效许可的情况下，随意地使用公共领域的作品在日本是有风险的。即使作品本身不受著作权法或其他法律的限制，也存在作者人格权利的强大障碍。如果在商业中使用公共领域内的某个作品时没有得到该作品绝大部分受众的支持，该使用者可能会因此遭受舆论的巨大压力而无法继续使用作品。

（信息搜集、编译：邱雯黛。

资料来源：https://www.worldipreview.com/contributed-article/japan-jurisdiction-report-moral-rights-and-stories）

【无协议脱欧将导致英国公民境外使用Netflix和Spotify账号受阻】

在无协议脱欧背景下，英国的游客前往欧盟国家旅游时使用Netflix和Spotify账户会受到限制。如果不能达成退出协议，根据英国政府在2018年10月12日发布的文件，在线体育、电子游戏和电子书服务也可能无法使用。相关人士指出，如果欧盟法案在 2019 年 3 月不再适用，某些网站和服务的接入服务，譬如基于 27 国集团的云存储服务，会受到阻碍或者在英国境内使用受限。

根据 2017 年通过的欧盟范围内“可携性条例”，在欧盟成员国内，一国国民可以在前往其他成员国时访问原已注册的娱乐账户，而且法规将覆盖“电影、体育赛事、电子书、视频游戏及音乐服务”。营运公司通过使用各种数据分析用户的来源国，就能让英国公民在境外继续使用 Netflix 和 Spotify 等热门应用的账户。而欧洲大陆的公民在假日休闲或者商务出行期间，也可以享受 French Canal Play 和 MYTF1 等的服务。这使得英国游客在境外可以及时接收到来自 Netflix 的“奇闻轶事”等频道的实时信息，还能欣赏喜爱的音乐。

但是有关版权方面的文章指出，相关规则将伴随英国无协议脱欧而失效，“可携性条例”在英国公民进入欧盟成员国后会停止适用。这意味着在欧盟法规下，在线服务的提供商将不被要求、也不能够对英国的消费者提供跨境访问服务。英国消费者临时访欧可能会受到使用限制。

另有文章指出，英国无协议脱欧会排除适用 2017 年 12 月生效的欧盟有关“禁止地域屏蔽”的新规。这部法律涉及诸如在线商品和电子服务（如网络托管或云存储）等服务，旨在禁止贸易商基于消费者的国籍或住所地，在商品购买和在线服务方面给予消费者区别对待。

（信息搜集、编译：张皓月。

资料来源：https://www. dailymail. co. uk/wires/pa/article-6270089/Britons-face-block-Netflix-Spotify-accounts-abroad-no-deal-Brexit. html）

【日本提高海外电影的音乐版税】

根据国际作者和作曲者协会联合会 2018 年 11 月发布的《2018 全球版税报告》，2017 年，音乐、视听、视觉艺术、戏剧和文学创作者的全球版税收入跃升至 96 亿欧元，较上年增长 6.2%。主要受流媒体热潮的推动，加之消费者对网络视频的热衷，2017 年来自数字渠道的版税猛增 24%，首次突破 10 亿欧元大关，并在过去五年实现了近两倍（166%）的增长。

其中音乐版税增长 6.0%，攀升至 83 亿欧元，数字音乐的版税也首次超过 10 亿欧元大关。数字音乐版税越来越成为权利人收入的重要来源。日本最大的音乐著作权管理协会 JASRAC（Japanese Society for Rights of Authors，Composers and Publishers）宣布与院线集团达成协议，对 2021 年 3 月之前上映的海外电影，JASRAC 将以 6 级音乐版税标准并根据屏幕的数量收取 15 万日元到 30 万日元的版税。

依据此协议来计算，JASRAC 收入将增加 15% 到 20%。JASRAC 对日本电影是按照屏幕的数量来收取每一首音乐的版税的，即使双方达成此版税协议，日本电影和海外电影在费用的计算方式上仍有所不同。JASRAC 将继续与院线协商，让海外电影使用与日本电影相同的计算方式。

已经有不少业内人士质疑 JASRAC 征收版税的行为（例如曾经报道的对音乐课收取版税）以及对所征收的版税分配不确定或不公平。当然，日本目前的版税处理制度似乎是复杂而不清晰的。因此，日本政府应当着力完善能让艺术家获得合理份额的制度。具体来说，版权制度应当强化网络服务商的责任，保护艺术家的各类权益，从而维护版权市场的良性发展。

（信息搜集、编译：钟翘骏。

资料来源：http://japanip. blogspot. com/2018/09/japan-raises-music-royalty-for-foreign. html? m=1）

【多名艺人要求特朗普停止在集会上使用自己的音乐作品】

2018 年 12 月初，蕾哈娜（Rihanna）的歌曲在特朗普在田纳西州查塔努加举行的集会上被播放，蕾哈娜本人对此强硬回应：“不会再这样了，我和我的追随者都绝对不会出现在任何一个这样的悲剧的集会周围。”但是如果她想要保证她的歌曲不会被扩音器广播得到处都是，她该如何主张她的法律权利？

根据《时代周刊》（*Time*）对音乐版权律师斯潘格勒（Spangler）的采访可知，如果特朗普总统没有取得相应的许可，他对蕾哈娜的歌曲的使用可能会违反版权法。这也可能会损害蕾哈娜的商业标记权和公开权（个人，尤其是公众人物或知名人士，对自己的姓名、肖像及其他类似物的商业性利用行为实施控制或制止他人不公平盗用的权利）。

在大部分情况下，作品的作者声明反对就足够了，并不需要走法律程序。比如有艺术家反对政治人物使用他们的音乐时，一旦作者表明立场反对作品的使用，政治人物通常就会自觉地停止使用乐曲。音乐版权律师奥斯特罗（Ostrow）表示，一般来说，竞选人在政治活动上使用某个艺术家的歌曲时会事先进行法律上的许可付费，尤其是通过付费取得公共传播许可。许可证一般由 ASCAP（美国作曲家、作家与出版者协会）或者 BMI（广播音乐联合会）之类的版权集体管理组织来颁发。它们作为中介，在想要获取音乐的一方和制作音乐的一方中间授权许可使用和收取许可使用费。一般来说，大多数场所都会从版权集体管理组织那里取得一揽子许可，但这种许可通常会排除会议和集会的使用许可。如果集会的组织者没有仔细检查这些条款，他们可能会侵犯版权。

目前来说我们尚不清楚集会所在地田纳西大学的麦坚时竞技场与版权集体管理组织的协议条款如何，但蕾哈娜的主张也要受到她与BMI在2007年就 *Don't Stop the Music* 这首热歌所达成的合同限制，这取决于BMI有没有给总统特朗普颁发公共传播许可证或者他们是否愿意按照蕾哈娜的要求去主张特朗普总统停止使用歌曲。当然，蕾哈娜也可以选择召回她在BMI的全部曲目，但这是一个极端的措施，因为这也会影响到蕾哈娜未来歌曲的潜在收入，包括来自音乐广播、视频流播放以及公共传播的许可使用等途径的收入。

蕾哈娜不是第一个提出此类抗议的人。2018年10月29日，创作人法瑞尔·威廉姆斯（Pharrel Williams）就曾通过律师要求特朗普总统停止在政治集会上使用他的歌曲 *Happy*。*Happy* 这首歌由法瑞尔创作，是电影《神偷奶爸2》的主题曲，曲风欢快活泼，歌词唱道："只因我快乐，请跟我一起拍手，如果你也情不自禁地想拍手……"2018年10月27日，极端的民粹主义者在匹兹堡的犹太教堂实施枪击案造成11人死亡后的几个小时，总统特朗普在印第安纳州的政治集会上使用了法瑞尔的 *Happy* 一歌，两天之后，法瑞尔的律师向总统特朗普发出了停止使用歌曲的律师函，函中提及"周六发生的这起悲剧对我们国家而言没有任何'快乐'可言，你也无法从我这里获得在集会上使用这首歌曲的许可"。法瑞尔的律师说，未经许可使用法瑞尔的歌曲构成版权侵权，"法瑞尔现在不会，以后也不会允许你公开表演或者广播、传播他的任何一首歌"。

除此之外，很多艺术家都曾拒绝特朗普总统在他的集会上使用他们的音乐。2018年8月，空中铁匠乐队的主唱史蒂芬·泰勒（Steven Victor Tallarico）在特朗普总统未经许可在西弗吉尼亚州的活动集会上使用了他的歌曲 *Livin' on the Edge* 后，向白宫递交了勒令停止使用的律师函，要求特朗普总统停止使用乐队的歌曲 *Livin' on the Edge*，他的律师说道："歌曲的使用错误地使人认为我的委托人支持他的活动以及他的任职。"此外，泰勒早在2015年就两次要求特朗普停止在他的总统竞选活动上使用乐队的歌曲 *Dream On*。阿黛尔（Adele）、滚石乐队、皇后乐队也曾要求总统特朗普停止在他的集会上使用他们的音乐。但是正如滚石乐队的米克·贾格尔（Mick Jagger）所说，艺术家能做的有时候很有限，这要归因于许可证贸易，"如果你在麦迪逊广场花园或者影院的公共场所，你可以放任何你想放的音乐，而且没人能禁止你这么做"。他抱怨道，两年前，当特朗普使用他的音乐作为竞选活动的主题曲时，尽管他进行了反对，但他们还是可以播放任何他们想放的音乐。

（信息搜集、编译：李弘毅。

资料来源：https://www.dailymail.co.uk/news/article-6354719/Rihanna-tells-President-Trump-stop-playing-songs-rallies-endorses-Andrew-Gillum.html；https://www.cnn.com/2018/11/05/entertainment/rihanna-trump-music/index.html；https://www.tennessean.com/story/entertainment/music/2018/11/05/rihanna-donald-trump-song-copyright-dont-stop-music/1891727002/）

【"骄傲男孩"的创始人因侵犯版权遭YouTube封杀】

2018年12月，YouTube公司声明称，另类右翼（Alt-right）评论员、"骄傲男孩"（Proud Boys）的创始人加文·麦金尼斯（Gavin McInnes）因"多项第三方侵权指控"而被YouTube封杀。禁令颁布时，麦金尼斯拥有20多万订阅账户。1994年在参与众多民族主义事业之前，麦金尼斯与人联合创办了Vice Media。目前尚不清楚是哪个频道的视频导致禁令，但YouTube证实，该频道已经超过了版权警示的门槛，导致"重复违规者"禁令。

2018年11月，美国联邦调查局（FBI）将"骄傲男孩"列为一个极端组织。尽管一名特工后来澄清，这个标签是误解的结果，但FBI仍认为这些"骄傲男孩"与白人的民族主义有关，并认为一些成员可能带来潜在的暴力和犯罪威胁，可能危害国家安全。在FBI最初的分类之后，麦金尼斯已经开始与该组织保持距离，一定程度上是因为麦金尼斯在2018年10月在纽约市举行的活动中涉及与"骄傲男孩"成员的暴力争吵。

在Facebook、Twitter、PayPal和Instagram过去三个月里都删除了麦金尼斯的账户后，YouTube成为麦金尼斯最后一个获准与粉丝交流的主要平台。据右翼媒体公司Blaze media发布的推文称，麦金尼斯被驱逐出了该公司，麦金尼斯已与该公司断绝关系。麦金尼斯也向各大媒体表示，他已经脱离了平台，当“人们编造谎言或断章取义时”，他无法再做出回应。

YouTube 在一份声明中向科技博客 The Verge 解释了这一禁令。YouTube 发言人表示：“当版权所有人通知我们有一段侵犯其版权的视频时，我们会按照法律要求迅速删除内容。对于重复违反规则的用户，我们则会强制注销他的账户。”虽然麦金尼斯有机会回应这些侵犯版权的指控，但他似乎没有解决这些问题，这最终导致了禁令的颁发。

（信息搜集、编译：傅玮琳。

资料来源：https://www.theverge.com/2018/12/10/18134863/gavin-mcinnes-proud-boys-alt-right-youtube-ban-copyright-infringement；https://www.engadget.com/2018/12/10/youtube-bans-proud-boys-gavin-mcinnes/）

【《美国经济中的版权产业：2018 年报告》发布】

2018 年 12 月，国际知识产权联盟（International Intellectual Property Alliance）发布的研究报告显示：2017 年，美国的核心版权产业为国家经济增长贡献了 1.3 万亿美元，雇用了近 570 万名美国工人，占美国全体劳动力的 3.85%，占所有私营工作部门的 4.54%。

研究报告还指出，核心版权产业的增长速度快于其他经济产业——2014 至 2017 年间的年均增长率为 5.23%，而同期整个美国经济的年均增长率为 2.21%。该报告称：“核心版权产业的增长速度超过了美国经济的其他部分 137%。”核心版权产业工人的平均年薪（98 336 美元）也大大高于美国的平均年薪（70 498 美元），并比美国的平均年薪高出 39%。

该研究将核心版权产业界定为主要参与制作和传播版权内容的行业，如电影、电视和无线电广播、音乐、书籍、视频游戏、计算机软件、报纸和期刊等行业。但是，当附属产业也包括在版权内容的生产和销售中时，全部版权产业的产出就更加令人印象深刻。根据这项研究，全部版权产业在 2017 年对美国国内生产总值的增加值贡献超过 2.2 万亿美元，几乎占美国经济的 11.6%。全部版权产业不仅包括核心版权产业，还包括部分版权产业、非专用支持产业和相互依存的版权产业。

这些行业包括生产、制造和销售设备的行业，这些设备的功能主要是促进版权作品的创造、生产或使用，例如电视机、个人计算机和其他设备的制造商、批发商和零售商，生产诸如空白记录材料和某些类别的纸张等产品的公司，以及所创造的产品只有某些方面或部分具有版权保护资格的行业，包括玩具和游戏、织物、珠宝和家具。根据这份报告，全部版权产业在 2017 年雇用了超过 1 160 万名工人，占美国所有就业人口的 7.87%，占美国所有私人就业人口的 9.28%。他们的年平均工资（86 308 美元）比美国工人的平均工资高出 22%。

版权产业对国外销售和出口的贡献也很大，其表现优于美国许多主要产业部门。根据这项研究，2017 年美国部分版权产品在海外市场的销售额达到 1 912 亿美元，比前几年增长显著。

（信息搜集、编译：周坤。

资料来源：https://pmcdeadline2.files.wordpress.com/2018/12/copyright-industry-report-wm.pdf；https://deadline.com/2018/12/core-copyright-industries-added-1-3-trillion-to-u-s-economy-in-2017-employ-5-7m-americans-1202516240/）

索 引

0～9

2017 年北京版权产业增加值比上年上涨 9.2% 193a
2017 年全球版税收入达 96 亿欧元 中国市场潜力大 191b
2017 年中国版权产业的经济贡献 203
2017 年中国出版业版权输出同比增长 24.1% 168b
《2017 年重庆区县知识产权发展状况报告》发布 136a
2017 中国文化产业系列指数发布 171a
2018—2019 年中国数字出版产业年度报告 251
2018 CPCC 十大中国著作权人 428
2018 版权相关热点问题媒体研修班在京举办 146a
2018 北京国际文创产品交易会开幕 186b
2018 年版权公共服务机构与社会服务组织工作（版权工作概览） 77
2018 年版权热点问题研究 444
2018 年地方版权工作（版权工作概览） 22
2018 年地方著作权司法保护典型案件（典型案件选编） 334
2018 年地方著作权行政执法案件（典型案件选编） 350
2018 年（第十届）全国大学生版权征文获奖名单 424
2018 年度查处侵权盗版案件有功单位及个人 411
2018 年度全国打击侵权盗版十大案件（典型案件选编） 331
2018 年度中国版权行业十大热点案件公布 139b
2018 年分省市软件和信息技术服务业业务收入表 546
2018 年国际版权动态 573
2018 年国际版权贸易培训班在京举办 130b
2018 年京沪知识产权诉讼报告发布 138a
2018 年内地与香港特区、澳门特区知识产权研讨会在敦煌召开 146a
2018 年全国版权工作（版权工作概览） 15
2018 年全国版权合同登记情况统计 524
2018 年全国版权输出地汇总表 526
2018 年全国版权司法保护工作（版权工作概览） 19
2018 年全国版权行政管理工作（版权工作概览） 15
2018 年全国版权引进地汇总表 525
2018 年全国版权执法情况统计 525
2018 年全国各地区电子出版物出版品种、数量及发行数量（按载体形式分类） 534
2018 年全国各地区各类期刊出版的种数、印数、总印张、总金额（1） 530
2018 年全国各地区各类期刊出版的种数、印数、总印张、总金额（2） 532
2018 年全国各地区录像制品出版品种、数量及发行数量（按载体形式分类） 538
2018 年全国各地区录音制品出版品种、数量及发行数量（按载体形式分类） 536
2018 年全国各地区图书出版总量 527
2018 年全国各级报纸出版数量 528
2018 年全国广播电视发展主要指标一览表（二） 544
2018 年全国广播电视发展主要指标一览表（一） 542
2018 年全国软件和信息技术服务业主要经济指标表 547
2018 年全国图书、期刊、报纸进出口情况 541
2018 年全国新华书店系统、出版社自办发行单位出版物发行进、销、存情况 540
2018 年全国音像制品、电子出版物、数字出版物进出口情况 541
2018 年全国知识产权宣传周活动启动 132a
2018 年全国著作权司法保护典型案件（典型案件选编） 319
2018 年全国作品自愿登记情况统计（按作品类别） 523
《2018 年深入实施国家知识产权战略 加快建设知识产权强国推进计划》印发 129b
2018 年新闻出版产业分析报告 227
2018 年粤港两地中学生版权知识和版权保护交流活动在珠海举行 131a
2018 年“中国版权金奖”获奖名单 410
2018 年中国版权年会年度评选获奖名单 429

2018 年中国版权十件大事 422
2018 年中国版权统计资料 523
2018 年中国电影产业发展报告 272
2018 年中国动漫产业发展报告 288
2018 年中国广播电视产业发展报告 267
2018 年中国广播影视产业统计资料 542
2018 年中国软件产业发展概况 298
2018 年中国软件产业统计资料 546
2018 年中国网络版权保护年度报告 403
《2018 年中国网络视听发展研究报告》发布 192b
2018 年中国网络游戏产业发展报告 306
2018 年中国新闻出版产业统计资料 527
2018 年中国著作权法研究综述 433
2018 年著作权相关图书简介 511
《2018 全球音乐产业报告》发布 177a
2018 中国版权年会在武汉召开 150a
2018 中国网络版权保护大会在京召开 142a
2018 中国文化 IP 发展高峰论坛在京成功召开 146b
2018 中国知识产权保护高层论坛在京举办 142a
2019 年深入实施国家知识产权战略　加快建设知识产权强国推进计划 6
360 搜索上线原创图片版权认证平台 155a
4 篇新闻报道获赔 10 万元　给网络“新闻搬运工”敲响警钟 112b
78 个原创动漫项目获扶持 193b

A

阿里大鱼号合作法国希帕图片社　为创作者提供世界杯高清版权图片 181a
埃及为改善知识产权保护与执法创建数据取证试验室 596a
爱奇艺收购天象互娱 183a
安徽出版集团文创产品走进“一带一路” 186a
安徽省（版权工作概览） 46b
安徽省版权局开展电影院线版权专项治理工作 119a
安徽省（典型案件选编） 343a
安徽省（典型案件选编） 360a
安徽省动员部署软件正版化工作 121b
澳大利亚议会通过《2018 年版权法修正案》 583a
“澳门国际知识产权研讨会 2018”在澳门举办 196a
澳门知识产权研究中心揭牌 195a
AIPPI 中国分会版权热点论坛举行 150b

B

百度等承诺落实版权监管主体责任 159a
百度首个基于区块链技术的原创图片服务平台“图腾”上线 183a
版权代理公司（名录） 558
版权服务走进首届中国游戏节 153b
版权公共服务机构（名录） 553
版权工作概览 13
版权界动态 99
版权扫描 97
版权相关产业与版权贸易 201
版权相关行业协会（名录） 558
版权协会（名录） 554
版权行政管理部门（名录） 551
北方国家版权交易中心落户大连 153a
北京成动漫游戏研发和出口中心 185a
北京出版代表团亮相 2018 美国书展 165b
北京电视台因擅自使用油画作品一审被判侵权 108b
北京高院发布《侵害著作权案件审理指南》 104b
北京国际网络版权监测研讨会召开 141a
北京互联网法院首案开庭审理 113a
北京互联网著作权纠纷有了“全程在线”法院 112a
北京市（版权工作概览） 22a
北京市版权局组织召开网络盗版侵权案件推进协调会 121a
北京市（典型案件选编） 334a
北京市举行市属国企软件正版化工作培训 137a
北京市启动“剑网 2018”专项行动 126a
北京市为区级国家机关进行软件正版化培训 135b
北京首届互联网影视著作权高峰论坛召开 147a
北京新闻出版广播影视企业海外服务基地在伦敦挂牌 165a
博洛尼亚童书展：中国达成 800 多项版权输出意向及协议 162b
“不爽猫”赢得 454 万元版权违约金 586b

C

草裙舞的著作权获日本法院认可 592a
产业发展 171a
长春成立首批 4 家版权服务工作站 157b
长春市首批版权示范园区（基地）揭牌 151b
唱片公司为著作权法修法建言 99b
CNNIC：我国 74.1%的网民使用短视频应用 185b
CPTPP 协定里的知识产权条款仍具有积极意义 595b

D

盗版网站“漫画村”运营者信息被公布 589b

德国联邦最高法院提请欧洲法院裁定 YouTube 著作权纠纷 591a
第 25 届图博会达成中外版权贸易协议 5 678 项 168b
第二届中国 IP 30 人论坛在京举行 148a
第九届首都互联网知识产权保护论坛聚焦视听作品知识产权保护 141b
第十三届北京文博会重点项目签约 68 亿元 190a
第十三届中国文交会建立动漫版权交易平台 153b
第十四届海图会在台北举行 196b
典型案件选编 317
“电影的经济及文化价值与版权保护高端论坛”在上海举行 167a
《电子商务法》表决通过 着重强调知识产权保护 100a
抖音宣布加入 Apple Music 合作伙伴计划 187a
短视频版权与竞争问题研讨会举办 144b
短视频作品创作与版权保护研讨会在京举办 149b
断开链接以保护漫画的著作权，政府的紧急对策涉嫌违宪而遭到反对 575b
多名艺人要求特朗普停止在集会上使用自己的音乐作品 598b

F

法律法规及规章文件 371
方正电子与 10 家企业签订字体授权协议 179a
方正发布新品赋能出版融合 187a
福建德化多部门联合推广版权保护 135a
福建省（版权工作概览） 48b
福建省（典型案件选编） 344a
福建省局办 2018 年全省版权执法骨干培训班 135a
福建省召开推进使用正版软件工作厅际联席会议第五次全体会议 120b
附录：国际版权动态 565

G

甘肃省（版权工作概览） 71b
甘肃省级政府机关操作软件 97.98%为正版 125a
港澳台版权信息 195
功能主义解释论视野下的“电影作品” 475b
关于加强知识产权审判领域改革创新若干问题的意见 3
《关于加强知识产权审判领域改革创新若干问题的意见》印发 100b
关于印发《2017 年推进使用正版软件工作总结》和《2018 年推进使用正版软件工作计划》的通知（国版函［2018］4 号） 380
关于做好 2018 年全国知识产权宣传周版权宣传活动的通知（国版办发［2018］4 号） 397
《广播组织保护条约》制定进行时 576a
广东启动“剑网 2018”专项行动重点监管《抖音》《快手》等短视频 APP 126b
广东省（版权工作概览） 59b
广东省版权局召开促进软件著作权创造、保护和运用专家座谈会 140b
广东省（典型案件选编） 347b
广东省（典型案件选编） 365b
广东省工作组对茂名市版权工作进行考评 118a
广东召开版权登记工作座谈会 128a
广深港高铁列车播放音乐获音著协许可 157a
广西部署 2018 年全区自治区级机关使用正版软件工作 123b
广西书展在台北开幕 197b
广西壮族自治区（版权工作概览） 60b
广西壮族自治区版权局开展“版权四进”系列宣传活动 133b
广西壮族自治区（典型案件选编） 348a
贵州省版权登记中心揭牌 155b
贵州省（版权工作概览） 65b
国际交流与合作 161b
《国际影视版权授权协议范本》发布 154b
国际作者和作曲者协会联合会：著作权“避风港”规则扰乱创作市场 596b
国家版权局办公厅关于 2017 年全国著作权登记情况的通报（国版办发［2018］3 号） 396
国家版权局等关于开展打击网络侵权盗版“剑网 2018”专项行动的通知（国版发电［2018］1 号） 398
国家版权局：短视频平台版权整改取得阶段性成效 129a
国家版权局对网络转载等重点领域开展版权专项整治 125a
国家版权局关于奖励 2017 年度查处侵权盗版重大案件的决定（国版函［2018］36 号） 384
国家版权局引导版权社会共治 130a
国家版权局与中国版权协会、中国移动签署备忘录 152a
国家版权局约谈 13 家网络服务商 要求规范网络转载 128b
国家版权局约谈“抖音”等 15 家短视频企业 严打侵权盗版 128a
国家级版权交易机构（名录） 559

国新办举行 2017 年中国知识产权发展状况新闻发布会 133a

H

海南省（版权工作概览） 61b
海南省（典型案件选编） 348b
韩国：将未参与创作的人标注为作者需要承担刑事责任 586a
韩国扩大表演权范围 577b
韩国《著作权法》修改中的争议：是否承认出版者的版式设计权 578a
杭州法院宣判全国首例涉“小猪佩奇”著作权侵权纠纷判决案 110a
杭州互联网法院首次确立区块链电子存证的法律审查方式 107b
河北版权登记时限从 30 个工作日变一周 153a
河北廊坊：督导全国版权示范城市创建工作 124a
河北省版权保护中心在廊坊设立版权服务站 156a
河北省（版权工作概览） 26a
河北省版权信息数据库平台正式上线 152b
河北省（典型案件选编） 335b
河北省（典型案件选编） 350b
河北省：鼓励创作版权精品　满足人民精神文化需求 127a
河北省软件正版化工作考核组到衡水市督导考核 117b
河南省（版权工作概览） 54b
河南省（典型案件选编） 346a
黑龙江省（版权工作概览） 37b
黑龙江省（典型案件选编） 336b
横琴联手港澳打造大湾区知识产权保护新高地 160b
湖北利用网络直播讲版权保护 130b
湖北省（版权工作概览） 56a
湖北省版权局举办 2018 年版权行政执法工作培训班 134b
湖北省（典型案件选编） 347a
湖北省（典型案件选编） 364a
湖北省软件正版化工作督查小组到黄冈检查 118a
湖北省召开使用正版软件工作领导小组成员单位联席会议 123a
湖南省（版权工作概览） 58a
湖南省（典型案件选编） 365a
互联网内容平台的版权保护研讨会在京举行 143b
互联网企业发起短视频版权自律公约 160b
黄坤明出席国家广播电视总局、国家新闻出版署（国家版权局）和国家电影局揭牌仪式并召开座谈会 121b
“混搭”销售教辅出版物书商因违法获刑 109a
H&M 身陷街头涂鸦侵权争议 585b

J

吉林省（版权工作概览） 35b
吉林省版权局：完善版权资产管理制度　提高版权保护能力 122a
吉林省（典型案件选编） 352b
暨南大学发布基于区块链技术的版权链运行平台 145b
甲骨文公司在与谷歌的版权之战中胜出 589a
剪辑影视作品发到短视频平台被判侵权 112a
“剑网”专项行动启动　8 家沪上知名媒体签署自律公约 127a
江苏：国家版权贸易基地秘书处落户秦淮区 155a
江苏省（版权工作概览） 41a
江苏省版权局督查组对宿迁市侵权盗版案件查处情况进行督查 121a
江苏省（典型案件选编） 338b
江苏省（典型案件选编） 358b
江苏省开展 2018 年第一期网络侵权盗版案件集中打击行动 120b
江苏省医疗卫生机构软件正版化工作培训班在南京举行 136b
江苏省政府机关软件正版化培训班在常州举行 137a
江苏知识产权仲裁调解中心成立 153b
“江西版权保护宣讲会”走进革命老区 135b
江西省（版权工作概览） 50a
江西省（典型案件选编） 360b
交流研讨 140a
“骄傲男孩”的创始人因侵犯版权遭 YouTube 封杀 599b
今日头条开展版权保护专项行动 184a
今日头条为《一郭汇》维权获胜 110b
京蒙发行集团共谋文化产业发展 187b
《九层妖塔》字体侵权 105b
巨人网络进军虚拟偶像市场　首位虚拟主播即将推出 189a
聚焦互联网与新媒体环境下体育赛事直播权利保护研讨会在京召开 143a

K

康佳与南方新媒体达成战略合作 186a

酷狗苏州音乐产业孵化基地落成 177b
快手诉华多侵权一审获赔两万元 112b

L

李克强会见世界知识产权组织总干事高锐 169a
理论研究 431
立法 99a
立法与行政 573a
辽宁出版集团与咪咕数媒开展战略合作 176a
辽宁省（版权工作概览） 32b
辽宁省（典型案件选编） 352b
论版权法对滥用技术措施行为的规制 444a
论网络环境下著作权侵权的刑事归责 492b
论著作权法对人工智能生成成果的保护 469b
论著作权合理使用扩张适用的路径选择 482a

M

美国 ABS 娱乐公司诉 CBS 公司：以数字形式重录唱片不产生新的版权 590a
美国颁布《马拉喀什条约实施法案》 581b
美国法院：深层链接不能规避版权侵权 587a
《美国经济中的版权产业：2018 年报告》发布 600a
美国《音乐现代化法案》深入改革音乐许可制度 580b
咪咕联手微博布局体娱产业 187b
《芈月传》著作权引纠纷案 法院判决认为不构成侵权 101a
“面包新语”侵权案二审被判赔偿 119 万余元 109a
名录 549
磨铁动漫在杭打造“超级漫画家计划” 177b

N

内蒙古出版集团携手联通共推“互联网＋出版” 192a
内蒙古开展 2022 年北京冬奥会会徽版权保护工作 118b
内蒙古自治区（版权工作概览） 31a
内蒙古自治区版权局举办 2018 年区直机关单位软件正版化工作培训班 135a
内蒙古自治区（典型案件选编） 352a
内蒙古自治区国资委举办出资监管企业软件正版化业务培训 136b
年度发布 401
宁夏回族自治区（版权工作概览） 74a

O

欧盟版权规则或将不再适用于脱欧后的英国 575a
欧盟法院新判决再解“向公众传播” 590b
欧盟法院做出裁定：食物的气味不受著作权法保护 593b
欧盟理事会正式批准《马拉喀什条约》 573a
欧盟委员会发布打击在线非法内容的建议 595a
欧洲法院裁定澄清非法文件共享的举证责任 592b
欧洲掀起《数字化单一市场版权指令》草案的反对浪潮 584b
欧洲议会批准通过颇具争议的《数字化单一市场版权指令》 580a

P

赔 1800 万！网络点播公司因盗播热剧被重判 111b
PP 体育与法甲联盟达成为期 3 年的新媒体独家版权合作 183b

Q

青岛市召开软件正版化工作培训会暨首批版权保护重点镇街培训会 131b
青海省（版权工作概览） 73a
青海省（典型案件选编） 370a
青海省直机关软件正版化工作会议召开 123a
蜻蜓 FM 与纵横文学达成战略合作 184b
趣头条：向“下沉市场”挖掘内容版权价值 193a
全国版权执法监管工作会议在京召开 124b
全国法院 2017 年审理版权案件大幅增长 104b
全国首次青年版权征文大赛结果在上海揭晓 137b
全国首个省级电视 4K 超高清频道开播 188b
“全省高校版权知识巡回宣讲”活动走进赣州高校 134a

R

人民出版社与越南真理国家政治出版社签署版权合作协议 168a
日本：产品销售中使用公共领域作品可能侵犯作者人格利益 597a
日本大尺度修改《著作权法》 573b
日本卡通形象熊本熊版权新规正式实施 594b
日本提高海外电影的音乐版税 598a
日本新法助力教育信息化改革：电子教材使用无须权利人许可 574b

S

山东省（版权工作概览） 51b
山东省“版权进乡村”行动在潍坊启动 134b
山东省版权局召开版权工作座谈会 118a
山东省（典型案件选编） 362a
山东省举办“版权进校园”系列活动 134a
山西高院出台指导意见规范卡拉 OK 著作权纠纷赔偿标准 104a
山西省（版权工作概览） 29a
陕西省（版权工作概览） 71a
陕西省版权局调研铜川版权公共服务工作 120a
陕西省（典型案件选编） 349a
陕西省（典型案件选编） 368b
上海发布《2017 上海游戏出版产业数据调查报告》 多措并举保障游戏产业健康发展 181b
上海市（版权工作概览） 38b
上海市（典型案件选编） 337b
上海市（典型案件选编） 353b
上海知识产权法院判令盗版软件侵权者赔偿 1 505 万元 108a
“上镜率最高”的《武夷之春》引发的著作权争夺 106a
少儿数字出版维权联盟成立 155b
社会管理与服务 151a
摄影界为《著作权法》修改稿献言献策 99a
使用“葛优躺” 基金公司被判侵权 100b
世界杯赛事节目纳入重点作品版权保护预警名单 123b
世界知识产权组织副总干事福尔班一行视察冠勇科技 167a
视频分享网站著作权间接侵权的过错认定 500b
手游《花千骨》被判侵权 103a
首个互联网企业版权资产管理应用示范成果花落京企 158a
首届“国家音乐产业优秀项目奖励计划”入选项目公布 193b
首届粤港澳大湾区知识产权拍卖成交额逾 600 万元 199a
首届中国剧本推优与版权保护论坛举办 147b
首例 VR 著作权案 被告判赔 46 万元 103b
“数字时代下的著作权法修改”研讨会召开 141a
司法 100b
司法判例 585b
四川版权工作站正式揭牌 157b
四川省（版权工作概览） 64b
四川省版权局督导绵阳创建国家版权示范城市工作 117b
四川省（典型案件选编） 367a
搜狐视频在一著作权许可使用合同纠纷案中胜诉 115a
苏宁与咪咕联合运营体育内容 182a
苏浙沪皖签署一体化合作协议 携手打造长三角出版高地 127b
苏州市挂牌成立知识产权检察室 106a
苏州市召开图片版权保护座谈会 142b
苏州推出“映光计划”应对原创音乐版权危机 155a
索尼收购百代音乐出版公司 178b
Spotify 与 Wixen 达成和解终结巨额诉讼 593a

T

特载 1
腾讯内容开放平台对企鹅号版权保护系统整体升级 179a
腾讯设 1 亿元基金保护原创 178b
腾讯音乐娱乐 TMC 为国产音乐与国际交流架起桥梁 181a
腾讯音乐与网易云音乐就网络音乐版权事宜达成合作 174b
天合集团收费资格被音集协终止 158b
天津市（版权工作概览） 25a
天津市（典型案件选编） 350a
天津市召开 2018 年政府机关使用正版软件工作培训会 136a
“同人作品内地第一案”宣判 109b
统计资料 521
推进使用正版软件工作部际联席会议第七次全体会议召开 119a

U

USMCA 对著作权执法标准的新规定 579a

V

VR 非法提供作品 热波公司一审判赔 35 万元 117a

W

外研社·法国“中国主题编辑部”成立 165b
外研社“中国主题编辑部”落户匈牙利 164a
网络大电影市场正向院线电影看齐 180a
网络文学为阅文创造 41 亿元年收入 175a

网络游戏产业法律问题研讨会举行 140a
网易云音乐和阿里音乐达成版权互授合作 174b
网易云音乐与索尼音乐达成深度合作 176b
微博携手中国版权保护中心为原创内容开通版权认证 151a
"文创西藏"以版权交易为核心　提升文旅创意设计水平 139b
文著协诉中国知网一审有果 116b
我国网络版权产值突破 6 000 亿元 176b
无协议脱欧将导致英国公民境外使用 Netflix 和 Spotify 账号受阻 597b
武汉开展大学生版权辩论赛 132a
《雾都之恋》引纠纷　豆丁公司被判侵权 102b

X

西班牙议会通过新的《知识产权法》修正案 584a
西藏自治区（版权工作概览） 68a
习近平向 2018 年"一带一路"知识产权高级别会议致贺信 169a
香港"知识产权贸易及管理的人力统计调查"公布主要结果 199b
小霸王公司宣布重新回归游戏机市场 175b
小伙因非法获取课件被判拘役两个月 102a
"小咖秀"违法使用歌曲被判赔偿 101a
小米音乐与太合音乐达成版权合作 175a
新华网启动视频化战略 194a
新疆维吾尔自治区（版权工作概览） 75a
新中国成立以来最大盗版少儿图书案二审宣判 105a
信息时代的著作权制度为市场发展保驾护航 567
行政管理 117b
宣传教育 130b

Y

业界动态 594b
一份许可合同引发多起版权诉讼 113b
《一封家书》被改编　作者获单首作品高额赔偿 114b
一批直播和短视频网站开展自查自纠 178a
因法院裁决　免费电子书网站"Project Gutenberg"不接受德国访问 588a
音集协版权收费将采取新模式 160a
音著协向进博会发放音乐著作权许可 158b
优秀原创动漫作品版权开发奖励计划启动 151b
游戏产业发展中的法律问题研讨会聚焦游戏版权保护 144a
有道乐读推出"万书计划" 187a
"远集坊"："童话大王"郑渊洁讲述创作维权 143a
阅文集团举办 IP 生态大会 179b
阅文集团战略投资韩国网文企业文笔雅 189b
粤澳保护知识产权合作协议在广州签署 195a
粤港澳大湾区电影产业中心项目启动 175b
粤港澳大湾区知识产权法律联盟正式成立 198a
"粤港澳大湾区知识产权合作及机遇"分论坛在香港举行 199a
粤港版权产业企业交流活动在香港举行 195b
粤港保护知识产权合作专责小组第十七次会议在广州举行 197a
粤港知识产权与中小企业发展（佛山）研讨会在佛山举行 196a
云南省（版权工作概览） 67a
云南省版权行政执法骨干培训班举办 137a
云南省推进使用正版软件工作联席会议办公室召开 2018 年第一次联络员会议 122b

Z

掌阅文学：精品化策略让 40 余位作者年收入过百万 174b
浙江出版传媒股份有限公司成立 188a
浙江建立淘宝电子版权登记"快车道" 156a
浙江省（版权工作概览） 44a
浙江省（典型案件选编） 341a
知识产权保护促进视听产业发展论坛在京举办 143b
知识产权教学与研究机构（名录） 561
制度演进视角下我国广播权的范畴 487a
中版版权产业基金在沪发起筹备 159b
中超版权费大幅"缩水" 174a
中国版权保护中心（版权工作概览） 77a
中国版权保护中心与北京文投集团签约合作 159a
中国版权产业占 GDP 比重达 7.33% 177a
中国版权协会（版权工作概览） 79b
中国财经媒体版权保护联盟成立 160a
中国出版代表团亮相第 25 届匈牙利布达佩斯国际图书节 164a
中国出版企业亮相伊朗书展 165a
中国代表团参加都灵图书沙龙 165a
中国电影著作权协会（版权工作概览） 93b
中国国际出版中心在伦敦正式成立 163a
中国国际漫博会聚焦版权交易和产业融合 149a
中国国际数码互动娱乐展览会首办电竞大会 184b
《中国好声音（第三季）》信息网络传播权纠纷二审审结 101b

《中国互联网络发展状况统计报告》解读内容产业发展 173a
中国九大原创节目登陆戛纳电视节 163a
“中国喷泉著作权纠纷第一案”二审维持原判 107a
中国摄影著作权协会（版权工作概览） 92b
“中国书架”亮相德语区最大连锁书店 170a
中国图书亮相日内瓦国际书展 164b
中国图书亮相突尼斯国际书展 162b
“中国图书展”亮相第 20 届科伦坡国际书展 169b
“中国图书展”首次亮相马尼拉国际书展 169b
中国网络版权产业发展报告（2019） 209
中国网络作家村正式上链杭州互联网法院司法区块链 116a
中国文化 IP 100 发展联盟在京成立 156b
中国文联与首都版权产业联盟签约 152a
中国文字著作权协会（版权工作概览） 88b
中国音乐著作权协会（版权工作概览） 83b
中国音像著作权集体管理协会（版权工作概览） 86b
中国音像著作权集体管理协会召开第七次会员大会 154a
《中国知识产权指数报告》第十次发布 138b
中国主宾国活动在阿尔及尔国际书展掀起“中国热” 170a
中国著作权立法中的制度创新 453b
中华人民共和国电子商务法 373
中美法律专家纵论知识产权保护与创新 166b
中墨正式建立版权双边合作框架 163b
中欧数字环境下版权保护与许可研讨会在广州举行 170b
中日韩联合版权宣传活动启动 132b
中日聚焦网络音乐版权保护应对方案 162a
中日网络影视作品著作权保护研讨会在京召开 170b
中图公司与三单位共推数字阅读人工智能应用 185b
中央广播电视总台首个区域总部成立 188a
中英版权圆桌会议聚焦数字环境下版权执法面临的问题及挑战 167b
中影股份与甘肃文化机构开展战略合作 178b
《中影剧场》登陆美国城市电视台 191a
重庆市（版权工作概览） 63a
重庆市检察院和市文化委建立保护版权协作机制 122b
重庆首家区县级版权登记工作站启动 152b
周慧琳会见新加坡知识产权局局长邓鸿森一行 161b
著作权集体管理组织（名录） 557
著作权集体管理组织：市场功能、角色安排与定价问题 463b
庄荣文在京会见世界知识产权组织副总干事王彬颖一行 166a
字节跳动与 NBA 达成短视频版权合作 192a
综述 567